Text, Cases and Materials
on Medical Law

PEARSON

At Pearson, we take learning personally. Our courses and resources are available as books, online and via multi-lingual packages, helping people learn whatever, wherever and however they choose.

We work with leading authors to develop the strongest learning experiences, bringing cutting-edge thinking and best learning practice to a global market. We craft our print and digital resources to do more to help learners not only understand their content, but to see it in action and apply what they learn, whether studying or at work.

Pearson is the world's leading learning company. Our portfolio includes Penguin, Dorling Kindersley, the Financial Times and our educational business, Pearson International. We are also a leading provider of electronic learning programmes and of test development, processing and scoring services to educational institutions, corporations and professional bodies around the world.

Every day our work helps learning flourish, and wherever learning flourishes, so do people.

To learn more please visit us at: www.pearson.com/uk

Text, Cases and Materials on Medical Law

Lisa Cherkassky

PEARSON

Harlow, England • London • New York • Boston • San Francisco • Toronto • Sydney
Auckland • Singapore • Hong Kong • Tokyo • Seoul • Taipei • New Delhi
Cape Town • São Paulo • Mexico City • Madrid • Amsterdam • Munich • Paris • Milan

PEARSON EDUCATION LIMITED
Edinburgh Gate
Harlow CM20 2JE
United Kingdom
Tel: +44 (0)1279 623623
Web: www.pearson.com/uk

First published 2015 (print and electronic)

ISBN: 978-1-4479-0120-4 (print)
     978-1-4479-0123-5 (PDF)
     978-1-292-01691-7 (eText)

British Library Cataloguing-in-Publication Data
A catalogue record for the print edition is available from the British Library

Library of Congress Cataloging-in-Publication Data
Cherkassky, Lisa, author.
  Text, cases and materials on medical law / Lisa Cherkassky.
    p. cm.
  Includes bibliographical references and index.
  ISBN 978-1-4479-0120-4 (pbk.)
  1. Medical laws and legislation--Great Britain.   I. Title.
  KD3395.C44 2014
  344.4104'1--dc23
                        2014019774
10 9 8 7 6 5 4 3 2 1
18 17 16 15 14

Cover image © Getty Images

Print edition typeset in Charter ITC Std 9.5/12pt by 35
Print edition printed and bound by Ashford Colour Press, Gosport

NOTE THAT ANY PAGE CROSS-REFERENCES REFER TO THE PRINT EDITION

Brief contents

Contents

Guided tour

Chapter objectives located at the start of each chapter explain what topics are covered to help you focus your learning.

> **Chapter objectives**
>
> At the end of this chapter, you should have:
>
> - An understanding of the difference between medical ethics and bioethics.
> - An appreciation of human rights law and how it plays an important part in medical decisions regarding treatment, respect and autonomy.
> - A good knowledge of religious bioethics and secular bioethics and how they help doctors and lawyers reach difficult decisions about medical treatment.
> - An understanding of other medical ethics/bioethics that guide decisions in medicine, including utilitarianism, virtue ethics, principalism, casuistry, feminism, slippery slope and sanctity of life.

Setting the scene sections at the start of each chapter detail scenarios which reflect concepts to be discussed, helping you see how the law works in real life.

> **SETTING THE SCENE**
>
> Jenna is aged 56 and has been diagnosed with stomach cancer. It is quite advanced and even though she is having chemotherapy, she is not showing signs of improvement. Her daughter researches the condition on the internet, and finds evidence of a new drug being piloted in France called KL09. Jenna visits her oncologist straight away and asks for the drug. Her oncologist says that the drug is not licensed in the United Kingdom, so her NHS trust will not fund it for her unless she is an 'exceptional' case. She consults you, a medical lawyer, to ask about a judicial review into the NHS trust policy and asks you what the courts are likely to tell her. She argues that she is an exceptional case because she is not responding well to the chemotherapy. How do you, as a medical lawyer, deal with this kind of plea?

Thinking points provide an opportunity for deeper consideration and to explore your thoughts on the law.

> **THINKING POINT**
>
> The removal of a 'need for a father' in the HFEA 1990/2008 created considerable controversy. Should we turn away single women from fertility treatment services? If so, are single women who seek fertility treatment any different to the single women who raise children alone as a result of becoming pregnant after a one-night stand? Give reasons for your answer.

Key definitions clearly and concisely explain the meaning of important terms.

> **KEY DEFINITION**   **Macro decisions**: made by the big bodies at the top.
> **Micro decisions**: made by the little people at the bottom.

Extracts and **case extracts** explain and illustrate legal principles through real world cases showing how and why judgements were made.

> **EXTRACT**
>
> Margot Brazier, 'Exploitation and Enrichment: The Paradox of Medical Experimentation' (2008) 34 *Journal of Medical Ethics* 180–83
>
> Edward Jenner, injected an eight-year-old boy, James Phipps, with cowpox. Months later, he injected the boy with smallpox. The vaccination 'took' and the boy survived. Jenner's experiment has saved millions of lives and led to the virtual eradication of smallpox. [. . .] It has often been said no modern ethics committee would have sanctioned such an experiment. Consider the case – the experiment used a child subject, who was too young to consent for himself, in non-therapeutic research where there was a high risk of death or disfigurement. The 'exploitation' of James Phipps undoubtedly saved the lives of some of us reading this.

Activities allow you to use the knowledge you have acquired to develop and cement your topic understanding.

ACTIVITY

Dr Wells is a cardiovascular scientist and is running a large NHS research project. She wishes to research a new heart drug for older patients with angina. She does not know what the risks will be because the new drug has not been tested on elderly men before, and she does not know what the benefits will be, for the same reason.

Dr Valkerie is a biological scientist and is also running a large NHS research project into a common strain of winter flu. He wishes to research the effects of a recently rejected drug for flu sufferers. He knows what the risks will be because it was tested last year, and he anticipates that the benefits will be barely noticeable in the general population.

According to the Declaration of Helsinki in regards to the balancing of risks against benefits, who is proposing to perform unethical research on human subjects and why?

Chapter summaries located at the end of each chapter suggest areas of assessment and assignments for which this chapter provides useful insight.

Chapter summary

- The National Health Service (NHS) was born in 1948 as a result of the National Health Service Act 1946, right at the end of the Second World War.
- The National Institute for Health and Care Excellence (NICE) underpins a lot of the decisions by the NHS. The new drugs and treatments on the market are appraised by NICE in terms of their cost effectiveness. The NHS will make the new drug or treatment available within a reasonable amount of time.
- A judicial review can be sought if the patient is unhappy with a decision not to fund a certain treatment, but the grounds for judicial review must be as follows:
  - the decision to deprive was unlawful;
  - the decision to deprive was outside of the statutory powers of the health authority;

Chapter essay questions allow you to hone your essay writing skills while asking you to reflect on and consider what you have learned from the chapter.

 **Chapter essay**

'Critically analyse the current professional guidelines provided to general practitioners to help them decide whether to disclose the personal information of a patient in the public interest.'

Chapter case studies give you the opportunity to further apply what you have learned to realistic scenarios.

Chapter case study

Mike and David have been dating for thirteen years. They entered into a civil partnership two years ago, and their whole family joined the ceremony, wishing them well. They were a very well-suited couple, but they desperately want a child to make their family complete. Stephanie, David's sister, offered to carry a baby for them, but said it could only be using Mike's sperm, otherwise she would effectively be having her brother's child. Mike and David were not happy with this, because David was the younger and healthier partner and they both agreed some years ago if they ever had a child, that it would be using David's sperm. They therefore seek a surrogate through an agency, which they find, and they meet up with her. She is happy to give them a child for expenses of approximately £10,000, but she will not seek IVF treatment in a clinic because it is too invasive – she wants David to socially impregnate her instead. Describe the main differences between partial surrogacy (proposed by S) and full surrogacy (proposed by Mike and David), including the transferral of parental responsibility.

Suggestions for **further reading** at the end of each chapter encourage you delve deeper into the topic and read those articles which help you to gain higher marks in both exams and assessments.

Further reading

Bartlett, P. (2003) 'The Test of Compulsion in Mental Health Law: Capacity, Therapeutic Benefit and Dangerous as Possible Criteria', 11 *Medical Law Review* 326; (2006) 'Psychiatric Treatment in the Absence of Law?', 14 *Medical Law Review* 124–31; (2007) 'A Matter of Necessity? Enforced Treatment Under the Mental Health Act', 15 *Medical Law Review* 86.

Laing, J. (2000) 'Rights versus Risk? Reform of the Mental Health Act 1983', 8 *Medical Law Review* 210.

Large, M. (2008) 'The Danger of Dangerousness: Why We Must Remove the Dangerousness Criterion from our Mental Health Acts', 34 *Journal of Medical Ethics* 877.

Lewis, P. (1999) 'Feeding Anorexic Patients Who Refuse Food', 7 *Medical Law Review* 21.

Acknowledgements

We are grateful to the following for permission to reproduce copyright material:

Extract on page 91 from Cases, *Journal of Social Welfare and Family Law*, Vol. 26 (4), pp. 397–415 (Hitchings, E. 2004), Copyright © 2004 Routledge, reprinted by permission of the publisher (Taylor & Francis Ltd., http://www.tandf.co.uk/journals) and the author, Samantha Singer; Extract on page 118 from Secondary Iatrogenic Harm: Claims for Psychiatric Damage Following a Death Caused by Medical Error, *Modern Law Review*, Vol. 67 (4), pp. 561–587 (Case, P. 2004), Copyright © 2004 John Wiley and Sons, with permission of John Wiley and Sons; Extract on page 136 from Are the Courts Excessively Deferential to the Medical Profession?, *Medical Law Review*, Vol. 9 (1), pp. 1–16 (The Right Honourable The Lord Woolf 2001), by permission of Oxford University Press; Extracts Chapter 5 from *General Medical Council, Explanatory Guidance, Confidentiality* (2009) Copyright © General Medical Council 2009, www.gmc-uk.org/guidance/ethical_guidance.asp; Extract on page 260 from Medical Confidentiality Within the Family: The Doctor's Duty Reconsidered, *International Journal of Law, Policy and the Family*, Vol. 18 (2), pp. 195–213 (Gilbar, R. 2004), Copyright © 2004 Oxford University Press, by permission of Oxford University Press; Extract on page 387 from *Diagnostic and Statistical Manual of Mental Disorders*, Fifth Edition, American Psychiatric Association (2013) Copyright © 2013, reprinted with permission, all rights reserved; Extracts Chapters 8 and 10 from *Code of Practice, 8th Edition*, October 2011, Human Fertilisation and Embryology Authority http://www.hfea.gov.uk/code.html; Extract on page 507 from Hashmi and Whitaker: An Unjustifiable and Misguided Distinction, *Medical Law Review*, Vol. 12 (2), pp. 137–163 (Sheldon, S. and Wilkinson, S. 2004), by permission of Oxford University Press; Extracts Chapter 9 from Presumed consent in organ donation: is the duty finally upon us?, *European Journal of Health Law*, Vol. 17 (2), p. 149 (Cherkassky, L. 2010), used with permission of the publisher, Koninklijke Brill NV; Extract on page 600 from Two Concepts of Death Reconciled, *Medicine, Healthcare and Philosophy*, Vol. 2 (1), pp. 41–46 (Tannsjo, T. 1999), Copyright © 1999, Springer, with kind permission from Springer Science+Business Media and the author; Extracts Chapter 10 from *International Ethical Guidelines for Biomedical Research Involving Human Subjects*, World Health Organisation and Council for International Organisation of Medical Sciences (2002) http://www.cioms.ch/index.php/texts-of-guidelines:, CIOMS retains the copyright in respect to extracts from its guidelines.

In some instances we have been unable to trace the owners of copyright material, and we would appreciate any information that would enable us to do so.

Preface

Medicine is a hugely exciting area to study at any level of education, but the legal side to caring for patients can often be complicated and extensive. This new textbook is specially designed to guide the undergraduate, postgraduate and professional reader engagingly through the statute law, case law and professional regulations of medicine in the United Kingdom. It will explore court judgments and academic responses in detail, provide a critical analysis of legal decisions, and it will illustrate how the law works in practice to protect patients.

This textbook explores the most important areas of medical law and introduces some unique new ones. For example, the common areas of consent, confidentiality and mental health law are explored alongside more controversial topics such as organ transplantation, assisted conception, saviour siblings and feminism. Every chapter contains an extensive reading list to allow the reader to research their chosen area of interest, and a unique 'setting the scene' feature opens every chapter to give the reader a sense of context.

Finally, essay and case-study activities are placed at the end of every chapter to allow the reader to engage on a practical level with the law.

Lisa Cherkassky
Senior Lecturer in Medical Law
The University of Derby
(Spring 2014)

Table of cases

Table of statutes

Table of international legislation

Table of statutory instruments

Table of European treaties and conventions

1

The ethics of medical law

Chapter objectives

At the end of this chapter, you should have:

- An understanding of the difference between medical ethics and bioethics.

- An appreciation of human rights law and how it plays an important part in medical decisions regarding treatment, respect and autonomy.

- A good knowledge of religious bioethics and secular bioethics and how they help doctors and lawyers reach difficult decisions about medical treatment.

- An understanding of other medical ethics/bioethics that guide decisions in medicine, including utilitarianism, virtue ethics, principalism, casuistry, feminism, slippery slope and sanctity of life.

> **SETTING THE SCENE**
>
> A researcher in a university laboratory creates a miraculous new drug that tricks the male brain into thinking it is pregnant. The correct hormones are released from the brain to sustain a pregnancy. The doctor asks for a participant for a trial and a gay couple – who have been battling to adopt a child for over ten years with no success – step forward. A foetus is placed into one of the men and he begins his drug programme, his brain recognises the baby and it begins to grow. Eight months later the baby is successfully delivered via caesarean section and the researcher announces to the world that he has created the first male pregnancy. There is an immediate moral outcry that the baby will be emotionally disturbed at the thought of never having a birth mother, and that the boundaries of nature have been irrevocably blurred. How do lawyers, judges and the general public deal with the ethical issues that this scenario raises?

Introduction

The study of medical law would not be complete without understanding the ethical principles which have informed and helped shape the law into what it is today. Ethical codes have been guiding doctors for centuries, and their origins are rich and diverse. The Hippocratic Oath (see below) is an excellent example. Religion and culture, too, have played their part in how physicians should heal the diseased. Today, though, it is the law and its many regulatory bodies that govern doctors and their professional practice.

The growing emphasis on human rights law has seen a shift in the patient–doctor relationship, with patients increasingly aware of their rights in relation to treatment and evermore willing to challenge the once inviolable opinion of medical professionals if they feel their rights are being infringed or overlooked. As such, human rights considerations have come to play an important role in guiding medical practice.

The technology in hospitals has also progressed to such an extent that 'unnatural' practices have been happening for some time. The ethical quandaries that come with these practices are in need of some moral guidance, so as not to offend, repulse or mystify the general public.

This chapter will explore the wide range of ethical and moral approaches that can steer doctors and lawyers through the novel and controversial world of medicine.

Medical ethics and bioethics

Medical ethics

Ethics are the standards which regulate a person's conduct; they are what tells us whether a given action is 'right' or 'wrong'. As such, medical ethics are best described as those principles which govern the conduct of healthcare professionals in the execution of their duties. Ethics are often woven into law, for example it would be considered wrong to kill a patient and murder is also a crime. However, ethics and law do not always agree; many people would argue that terminating a foetus is ethically wrong, but it is lawful under certain circumstances. As such, medical ethics can be described as a set of principles that *run alongside* the law to guide and support it, but they do not always glide together and can sometimes steer off in completely different directions.

The Hippocratic Oath is among the earliest known ethical codes as applied to practising medicine, attributed to Hippocrates, a fifth century BC Greek physician. The Hippocratic Oath is still highly regarded today and the principles in it can be found in many international ethical codes of medical practice.

There are various versions of the Hippocratic Oath, but the most common translation generally available is understood to be as follows.

EXTRACT

The Hippocratic Oath

I swear by Apollo, the healer, Asclepius, Hygieia, and Panacea, and I take to witness all the Gods, all the Goddesses, to keep according to my ability and my judgment, the following Oath and agreement:

- To consider dear to me, as my parents, him who taught me this art; to live in common with him and, if necessary, to share my goods with him; to look upon his children as my own brothers, to teach them this art; and that by my teaching, I will impart a knowledge of this art to my own sons, and to my teacher's sons, and to disciples bound by an indenture and oath according to the medical laws, and no others.
- I will prescribe regimens for the good of my patients according to my ability and my judgment and never do harm to anyone.
- I will give no deadly medicine to any one if asked, nor suggest any such counsel; and similarly I will not give a woman a pessary to cause an abortion.
- But I will preserve the purity of my life and my arts.
- I will not cut for stone, even for patients in whom the disease is manifest; I will leave this operation to be performed by practitioners, specialists in this art.
- In every house where I come I will enter only for the good of my patients, keeping myself far from all intentional ill-doing and all seduction and especially from the pleasures of love with women or men, be they free or slaves.
- All that may come to my knowledge in the exercise of my profession or in daily commerce with men, which ought not to be spread abroad, I will keep secret and will never reveal.
- If I keep this oath faithfully, may I enjoy my life and practice my art, respected by all humanity and in all times; but if I swerve from it or violate it, may the reverse be my life.

In this extract we can see many themes which remain relevant to medical practice today. 'For the good of my patients' reflects the 'best interests' test – something routinely applied to ascertain the best treatment for a patient, particularly if they are unconscious, incompetent or otherwise unable to consent. We can see that euthanasia is addressed, in no uncertain terms: 'I will give no deadly medicine to anyone if asked', as is abortion – which remains a criminal offence today, although there do exist a handful of defences available to a doctor who performs a termination. We can also see precursors to modern notions of confidentiality ('I will keep secret and never reveal'), the imperative that a doctor acts only within the limitations of his expertise, and that a doctor should never be romantically involved with his patients.

If we fast-forward two-and-a-half thousand years and consider the General Medical Council's publication *Good Medical Practice 2013* (the guidelines which all doctors must follow) we see that many elements of the Hippocratic Oath remain relevant to medical practice in the twenty-first century.[1] The General Medical Council has also published other ethical codes, including the following:

- 0–18 years (2011)
- Child Protection (2012)
- Confidentiality (2010)
- Consent (2011)
- End of Life Care (2011)
- Raising Concerns about Patient Safety (2012)
- Medical Research (2010)

Clearly then, there remains a strong emphasis on good ethical practice in medicine. To suggest that the surrounding corpus of law and regulation around medicine somehow nullifies the importance of medical ethics is to miss the very heart of medical practice: they support high standards for patients and preserve the professional integrity of doctors.

Traditionally the doctor was at the heart of ethical decisions within medicine. A doctor's authority was seldom questioned and subsequently it was very rare for doctors to face criminal or civil charges. The main consequence was that the views of patients were largely ignored. Draper and Sorrell have highlighted the lack of input from patients because medical ethics were traditionally focused on the doctor.

EXTRACT

Heather Draper and Tom Sorrell, 'Patients Responsibilities in Medical Ethics' (2002) 16 *Bioethics* 335, at pages 335–51

In comparison to what it asks of doctors, mainstream medical ethics makes very few demands of patients, and these usually begin and end with consent. Traditionally medical ethics has asserted that, as autonomous agents, competent patients must be allowed to decide for themselves the course of their medical treatment, and even whether to be treated at all [...]. Little or nothing is said about what kinds of decisions patients ought to make. Nor is much said about their responsibilities for making good rather than bad decisions. Indeed [...] mainstream medical ethics implies that a competent patient's decision is good simply by virtue of having been made by the patient. At times it seems as though patients never make, or cannot make, bad decisions.

Draper and Sorrell submit that because medical ethics has traditionally ignored the patient, their responsibilities have been swept under the carpet.

Medicine has developed over the last few decades to include patient *and* doctor responsibilities. For example, the patient has a duty to be honest about her symptoms, to take responsibility for her health and to use the minimum amount of resources in our public healthcare system. The doctor has a duty to counsel, to support, to listen, to balance cost and benefit, to keep confidence, to honour a refusal and to act in accordance with her best interests. This will explain the wealth of ethical guidelines published by the General Medical Council over the last few decades (listed above).

---

[1] Their official website: www.gmc-uk.org.

● Bioethics

> **KEY DEFINITION**   **Bioethics**: theories to critically investigate the morality of medicine.

Bioethics takes a smaller but more specific role in helping doctors, researchers and lawyers to decide what would be the 'right' thing to do in a novel situation. Medicine can present the most controversial problems where there are no laws in place to offer a response. The courts may very easily accept a highly controversial practice (e.g. human cloning) without looking at the ethical issues, but this ignorance could overlook the *consequences* of the new practice and its *effects* on society. A bioethical theory can help us to discuss the pros and cons of a new practice, weigh up its consequences and give very good reasons for supporting or condemning it. Bioethics do not concern themselves with the duties of a doctor – they are more concerned about the morality of an act, particularly if it has not been done before. This is particularly relevant to modern medicine where new developments are taking place on a daily basis. A selection of past examples includes abortion, transplantation, fertility treatment, stem cell research, life support machines and contraceptives. These breakthroughs were highly invasive on the human body, bringing new ethical quandaries to the table that stretched far beyond the ambit of good medical practice. The courts were faced with very controversial questions that traditional medical ethics could not answer, such as: 'is this the right thing to do?', 'does this act go against God?', 'what will happen to the dignity of human beings?' or 'what would be the social consequences of this procedure?' Bioethics have stepped in to help us answer these questions. They do not always resolve the issue, but they do add a new dimension and can help to steer the courts in a certain direction or bring clarity if a decision cannot be reached. The case of *Airedale NHS Trust v Bland* [1993] AC 789 is an excellent example of this. The Court of Appeal decided that it was no longer in the best interests of a patient to be kept alive by artificial hydration and nutrition even though the law at the time clearly stated that the intentional removal of artificial hydration and nutrition was an act of murder. The courts were swayed by the moral arguments against keeping the patient alive when he was experiencing 'a living death' and they chose to ring the changes in the common law of murder based on these concerns. The *Bland* case shows us that the application of law could be a straightforward process, but an instinctive feeling that a decision is 'wrong' or 'unfair' inevitably leads to a discussion on bioethics. This happens more often in medical law than in any other area because autonomy, dignity and basic human rights are at stake. The following quote from *Bland* is an excellent illustration of this:

> This is not an area in which any difference can be allowed to exist between what is legal and what is morally right. The decision of the court should be able to carry conviction with the ordinary person as being based not merely on legal precedent but also upon acceptable ethical values.[2]

Bioethics clearly have a significant influence on the courts because they are highly critical in nature, and it is almost impossible to decide the outcome of a complex medical entanglement without referring to several ethical viewpoints to sort through the many consequences. They do not guide the relationship between the doctor and the patient, but they

---

[2] *Airedale NHS Trust v Bland* [1993] AC 789 per Lord Hoffmann.

do pick apart, dissect and evaluate controversial medical dilemmas to offer a far deeper understanding of the ethical issues. This is why it is impossible to learn about medical law without referring to bioethics.

THINKING POINT

A lawyer comes to you and asks for your advice about the following client. As a judge, you are aware that you have to justify your decision. Read the letter below and come to a decision, with *reasons* for your answer.

Dear Mr Lawyer,

We strongly and urgently need legal representation. My mother is dying of dementia and her memory is deteriorating every day. My sister and I would like to help her to pass away and we have purchased morphine off the internet to allow us to provide an overdose. We know that the current law forbids us from doing this and our actions will result in a murder charge, but our mother is too frightened of the consequences to do it herself (she is deeply religious). We need a lawyer who can help us to convince a judge in a court of law that we can legally murder our mother because we love her.

Human rights and religion

The word 'morality' comes from the Latin word 'customs'. A person will have his own personal set of morals depending on his social life, his religion, his upbringing and his environment, and they will dictate to him what is 'right' or 'wrong' in a certain situation. The problem with morality is that it is deeply personal. Medicine sees its fair share of controversies and many people react with their gut instinct by saying: 'I don't think that's right', but this is a *moral* perspective and doesn't help researchers, doctors or lawyers to decide a case. There must be a rationale *behind* the response to convince others that it is right or wrong and that is what bioethics can offer: a logical explanation. The message in this chapter is that 'morality' or a 'preference' for a particular view is not enough – there must be a logical rationale underpinning the argument in order to take the ethical discussion forward and reach a satisfactory conclusion.

Human rights

The European Convention on Human Rights was drafted by the Council of Europe in 1950 and it came into force in 1953. It was an international treaty to protect the human rights and fundamental freedoms of all European citizens, and there was an expectation that all member states would incorporate the Convention into their domestic jurisdictions as soon as possible.[3] It was incorporated into UK law via the Human Rights Act 1998.

A medical procedure can be highly invasive upon the body and mind and can invade social, emotional and bodily integrity. A breach of confidentiality could bring the medical profession into disrepute. In addition to this, the dying have argued that they have a right

---

[3] The European Convention on Human Rights (1953) is to be distinguished from the Universal Declaration of Human Rights (1948) which aimed to provide basic human rights to all citizens of the world after the atrocities of the Second World War.

to assisted suicide, anorexic patients have argued that they should not be force fed, incompetent patients have fought for their best interests, victims of medical negligence have pushed the boundaries of duties of care, gay couples have argued that they have a right to fertility treatment, the elderly have argued that they are entitled to shorter waiting times and teenagers have argued that they are entitled to refuse medical treatment. These cases would not be possible without the European Convention on Human Rights, the relevant principles of which are listed below.

These Articles do not look applicable to the practice of medicine on first glance, but a closer inspection will reveal their relevance.

Article	Application to medicine
2: Right to life	A doctor must not kill his patient (i.e. euthanasia). A patient has a right to life (i.e. her life should be preserved by medical treatment). Article 2 should not be confused with a right to die (i.e. assisted suicide).
3: Prohibition of torture	A doctor must not subject a patient to any treatment or harm that could equate to torture or inhumane treatment. A doctor must not leave a patient in a state that is degrading or impose a lengthy delay for treatment.
5: Right to liberty and security	A patient must not be trapped, forced or coerced into medical treatment. The exception is patients with a mental disorder, who can be detained and treated against their will under the Mental Health Act 1983.
8: Right to respect for private life	A patient is entitled to confidentiality and autonomy. A patient should not be turned away from medical treatment because of their personal lifestyle.
8: Right to respect for family life	A patient is entitled to seek contraceptive services. A patient is entitled to fertility treatment. A patient should not be excluded from any treatment that helps her create a family of her own or put in a position where her family life is jeopardised.
14: Prohibition of discrimination	A patient should not be excluded from medical treatment because of their characteristics. A patient should not be treated any differently to any other patients with the same condition.

It is clear that human rights are fundamental to the rights of patients and they could not exercise their autonomy without the support of human rights.

Religious bioethics

Religion and medicine have a chequered history. The healing of sick individuals used to be a religious and spiritual event where the local witchdoctor, chief or community leader would cast a spell or say a prayer or use other ancestral remedies to heal the ailment, which was often seen as a punishment from God. Centuries ago when there was little or no understanding of the anatomy, bacteria, infection or the human body generally, an illness and its adjoining cure was prescribed to bigger powers beyond our control. Christianity is an excellent example: it was wrong to practise surgical procedures on dead bodies and any kind of treatment that was not derived from nature or religion was untrustworthy.

The development of medicine as a field of *science* ran against these old traditions. Aromatherapy, for example, and other herbal remedies still claim to have a healing effect on particular ailments, and they may do, but the precision of science means that an infection can simply be given an antibiotic like Penicillin, which, ironically, comes from nature. The knowledge of the human body began to develop and it was learnt that a priest could not heal an infection as effectively as a doctor, so the two worlds began to separate. Religion viewed medicine as an interference, going against the will of God. This is understandable – it is not 'natural' for a baby to be conceived outside of the human body and it is not 'natural' for the organ of one man to be transplanted into the body of another – but these developments were exciting because they represented our ability as human beings to control our own lives.

The relationship between religion and medicine is much better today, because doctors are recognised as professionals in a field of science who cater for the best interests of the community. However, abortion and euthanasia are still contentious issues for religious groups because the termination of a life at any age is seen as a decision to be taken only by God. There are sometimes public announcements by religious leaders on scientific developments that threaten to overshadow the sanctity of life, but religion is regarded as a private matter so its influence is negligible. This is a loss, because religion has asked the deeper ethical questions for centuries that bioethics are only just beginning to ask now:

- What is the meaning of life?
- Where does life begin?
- Who controls life?
- What creates life?
- Does the human body have a meaning beyond the event of death?
- Who do our organs belong to?
- Is a foetus a human being?
- Is it wrong to prolong life when the body is ready for death?

Religion can offer an answer to all of the questions above, but the answer will often revert back to God. This can be a barrier to medical breakthroughs because religion often implies that doctors are 'playing God' by treating, amending and restoring the human body beyond what is naturally possible. Religious bioethics will judge these actions in terms of their rightfulness or wrongfulness but will probably not consider the consequences.

Religion places an element of 'awe' in the human body – we are created by a higher power – and therefore it is wrong to destroy it regardless of the reason. Abortion is an excellent example: many religions argue that it is deeply wrong to kill an unborn child because its mother cannot cope, but the consequence of the abortion, which religious bioethics frequently ignore, would mean supporting the mental health of the mother and an escape from financial destitution.

Individual patients who prescribe to a religion may refuse treatments, services or ideas that could 'interfere' with the will of God. A blood transfusion is the classic example, which is traditionally refused by Jehovah's Witnesses. Therefore, does religion rob a patient of his objectivity and dignity? The idea that 'life is a gift' could rob the patient of her freedom to do what she wants to her body, be it tattooing, opting for a caesarean, accepting a donated organ or seeking assisted suicide abroad.

RESEARCH ACTIVITY

Choose a well-known religion of your choice and research their approach to medical care and controversial treatments. How would that religion react to the 'setting the scene' scenario above regarding a pregnant man?

Secular bioethics: what is available?

Bioethics can be split into two groups: religious and secular (i.e. non-religious). Religious bioethics occupy very little space in law, but secular bioethics present many different views.

KEY DEFINITION

Religious bioethics: views on medicine that are founded in religious beliefs.
Secular bioethics: non-religious, non-sacred and non-spiritual views on medicine.

Secular bioethics (i.e. bioethics *without* a religious, sacred or spiritual motive) do not have a starting point and do not begin the discussion with an assumption, hypothesis or position (e.g. that life is a sacred gift). This means that the answer is open, the consequences can be explored, the effects can be deliberated and there may never be a solution. Medical law can work much better with secular bioethics than religious bioethics for these very reasons – the possibility of compromise, objectivity and rationality makes for a fuller and more detailed ethical debate.

What do secular bioethics offer?

- 'Secular' means non-religious, non-spiritual and non-sacred.
- They offer rational explanations, thoughts and ideas.
- They weigh up consequences and effects of a particular course of action.
- They deliberate alternative possibilities.
- They are not constrained to old teachings, texts or traditions.
- They are not emotional, personal, subjective or individual.
- They support the rights of the doctors and the patients (i.e. autonomy and respect).
- There is no motive, aim, coercion or force to manipulate the outcome.
- They will *justify* a decision as opposed to simply *reaching* a decision.
- They will always provide detailed and convincing reasons for adopting a view.

Secular bioethics can be split up into many different groups. The most notable ones seen frequently in medical law are explored in the remainder of this chapter.

KEY DEFINITION

Teleological: a secular bioethic that considers the *consequences* of an *action*.
Deontological: a secular bioethic that considers the *rights* of the *individual*.

Secular bioethic one: utilitarianism

Utilitarianism is the most well-known teleological theory in law and can be applied to complex medical law cases. It looks at the *consequences* of an action in order to ascertain whether it is right or wrong. Euthanasia is a classic example: if doctors were to begin killing their patients they would become 'angels of death' and public trust in the profession would disintegrate. This is a negative consequence that does not benefit the greater good, so therefore, according to the teleological theory of utilitarianism, it must be wrong.[4] Utilitarianism seeks to benefit the largest number of people. The solution with the most positive consequences for the greater public will be favoured. A small minority may suffer, but this is justified in order to please the majority. A good example is the flu vaccination: a small minority such as the weak and the frail may catch flu and possibly die from complications, but for the majority it is a safe way to protect the body from a potentially deadly virus. Therefore, as a result of the positive consequences for the majority, utilitarianism supports the flu vaccination.

Utilitarianism as a secular bioethic is not led by religious ideals and it is not subjective, individual, personal or biased – it literally operates an 'open door' policy to complex medical cases – coming to a conclusion only when *all* of the consequences have been explored. A researcher, doctor or lawyer who decides to apply utilitarianism to a complex medical problem must therefore weigh every eventuality before deciding on the most appropriate course of action. This can be timely and lead to delays in the health service, for example, but it means that the majority would benefit from the decision reached.

Utilitarianism has its downfalls as a secular bioethic. The 'right' or 'wrong' of an action is neither here nor there because it is so focused on the positive consequences of an action that the morality of it is set aside. To give a good example, a patient may have a unique form of cancer that requires specialist treatment at a great expense to public funds. Utilitarianism is only interested in benefiting the greater good, so in this case it would conclude that pouring money into a drug treatment programme for one patient would yield a negative consequence for the majority, and the request would be rejected. Utilitarianism as a secular bioethic is clearly not interested in patient need. A unique patient will be swallowed up by the bland majority. This poses a big problem in medical law because most of the developments are unique and the complex cases contain some kind of original problem. It becomes clear at this point that utilitarianism is only applicable to general medical procedures, such as vaccination programmes, but it cannot benefit 'hard cases' where an individual patient is fighting for her autonomy, dignity and respect.

Secular bioethic two: Kantianism

Immanuel Kant (1724–1804) argued that our decisions should be guided by *duties* as opposed to consequences. Kantianism is the most well known deontological theory (*deontos* is Greek for 'duty') and it can be applied as a secular bioethic through its belief that human beings are autonomous individuals with independence, freedom and rationality. We must not simply 'use' people as a means to an end, e.g. force someone to take part in a medical trial without their consent. Kantianism is said to be the opposite of utilitarianism because it puts the individual at the heart of the matter because he must be showed respect. It is not concerned with benefits, the majority or consequences. Euthanasia is the best example: if a doctor was to administer a lethal injection to a

---

[4] The pioneer of utilitarianism was Jeremy Bentham (1748–1832), his extensive literature on the subject is beyond the ambit of this chapter.

terminally ill patient on their request, Kantianism would uphold their autonomy, respect their view and administer the injection, whereas utilitarianism would condemn the action because the idea of doctors killing patients does not benefit the majority.

The main advantage to Kantianism is that any action that supports the autonomy of the patient is morally right, and any action that suppresses the autonomy of the patient is morally wrong. This would mean that euthanasia, abortion, confidentiality and honouring a refusal would be morally right, but forcing a patient to live, treating a patient against his wishes, breaching confidentiality or depriving the patient of the best resources would be morally wrong. The additional advantage to Kantianism is that, like utilitarianism, it brings an 'open door' policy to the table in regards to complex medical dilemmas. It is not led by religious ideals and it is not subjective, personal or biased – it comes to a conclusion only when *all* of the duties and rights have been investigated. A researcher, doctor or lawyer who decides to apply Kantianism to a complex medical problem must therefore consider the autonomy of the individual and the duty to uphold it before deciding on the most appropriate course of action. Kantianism was developed almost as a response to the teleological theory to counteract its unfairness to the individual. Therefore, as a bioethic it appears to go hand-in-hand with the general legal landscape where patient rights – and the adjoining duty to uphold those rights – are the cornerstone of good medical practice. However, there are problems with every theory, including Kantianism.

Firstly, the slippery slope argument will always rear its head by pointing out that one decision in support of autonomy could lead to a flood of cases from patients who demand the same treatment. Euthanasia is a good example of a practice that could spiral out of control to allow a doctor to kill any patient who asked for it. This is the main weakness of Kantianism: it places the emphasis on the individual at the expense of the consequences, which may not be considered in enough depth. Secondly, contrary to Kant's belief, not everyone in society is autonomous, independent and rational. In fact, when it comes to medical law, the opposite is often true. Patients who are suffering from a serious illness may be incapacitated, unable to make their own decisions and dependant upon those around them. This has been pointed out by commentators.

EXTRACT

Barbara Secker, 'The Appearance of Kant's Deontology in Contemporary Kantianism: Concepts of Patient Autonomy in Bioethics' (1999) 24 *Journal of Medicine and Philosophy* 43, at pages 85–112

The highly rationalistic, individualistic Kantian account appears to assume that all that patients need to qualify as autonomous, in addition to the requisite intrinsic capacities [...] is negative freedom. However, patients frequently are in vulnerable positions, are unable to act on their decisions, and require that positive measures be taken on their behalf. [...] If we appeal to the Kantian view (based on an ideal of the self as independent and exclusively rational), very few, if any, patients will be regarded as autonomous. Actual patients are likely to be dependant or interdependent, and their decision-making capacity is not always based (exclusively) on reason.

Secker argues that autonomy is not as strong in the medical environment as it would be in society. Decisions made will not always be rational because of the extraordinary, painful or urgent circumstances that the patient finds himself in. It is best, therefore, that Kantianism is only one of several secular bioethics to be considered in medical law.

 ## Secular bioethic three: virtue ethics

Morality is the key to virtue ethics. A person is 'virtuous' when he does the right thing for the right reason and behaves with integrity, decency, honesty, compassion and kindness. Aristotle (384–322 BC), the Greek philosopher, emphasised the importance of good personal morals and how they helped to shape the flourishing human race. There are no economic, social, environmental or religious considerations here. A person must simply do the right thing. A doctor is virtuous, for example, when he provides a patient with the medical treatment that she needs (i.e. doing the right thing) and he does it with an understanding of her medical needs (i.e. for the right reasons). This is similar to treating a patient in accordance with their best interests under the Hippocratic Oath.

The application of virtue ethics to medical law is incredibly difficult because the 'right thing' is not always clear. For example:

- Should a doctor offer a morphine overdose to an elderly patient who is suffering from an incurable disease and is begging to die?

- Should a doctor separate conjoined twins knowing that one will die if separated, but both will die without separation?

- Should a doctor perform an abortion on a happy, rich housewife who is traumatised at the prospect of childbirth?

- Should a doctor offer his only snake bite vaccination to a child patient when another three adult patients have also been bitten?

- Should a doctor tell his male patient that he is not the father to his two children after blood tests showed an unknown paternity?

There are no clear answers to the scenarios above, but as with other secular bioethics, virtue ethics can come to the table with an 'open door' policy: it is not led by religious ideals or bias and it will come to a conclusion only when the action has been found to be virtuous.

The advantages of virtue ethics as a secular bioethic are clear. They compel researchers, doctors and lawyers to do the right thing for the right reasons. In practical terms, this would oblige a doctor to give us the correct treatment, counsel us appropriately, conduct the necessary tests and write the correct prescription, and all with the best of intentions. This can lead to nothing but happy patients. However, the disadvantages to virtue ethics are numerous. Firstly, in order to do what is right, the doctor must act according to what *he feels* is right. This is a very subjective approach – it calls upon the instinct of a doctor and there is no objective benchmark against which to measure his approach. It is therefore the motives of the doctor that determine whether it is a good thing to do or a bad thing to do, resulting in the act itself becoming meaningless. Secondly, the consequences of an action are not considered. This is a great shame, because virtuous acts often have far-reaching consequences (e.g. putting a patient out of her misery with a lethal injection leads to the acceptance of euthanasia) and these should not be ignored. Thirdly, patient autonomy is overlooked by virtue ethics, rejecting the teachings of Kantianism. A religious patient may wish to reject a lifesaving blood transfusion but it would be the 'right' thing to do to save her, so the treatment would be carried out against her wishes. This forceful approach would be highly unethical in medicine today. Fourthly, a consent in virtue ethics would not count for anything because a particular treatment could be deemed 'not right' for the patient in the eyes of the surgeon (e.g. cosmetic surgery). The consequences of this are staggering. Fifthly, the law is a barrier to virtue ethics. The law dictates what a doctor can (and cannot) do and there are additional professional guidelines to regulate his practice, but he will ignore these in order to do what he feels is right for the right reasons. The doctor would thus become a law unto himself, making up the rules as he went along. The result would be an unregulated profession where the care received depended on the doctor and his moral compass. This leads to the sixth disadvantage, which is a disagreement over what is meant by 'virtuous' behaviour. This will inevitably differ from person to doctor to lawyer. An abortion would be the virtuous thing to do in certain circumstances according to some minds, whereas other minds would never view the killing of an unborn child as virtuous.[5] The final disadvantage is that certain immoral actions could be justified under virtue ethics simply because the motives behind them were good. A terrorist is a good example: he may have killed many innocent pedestrians with his suicide bomb, but his actions showed dedication to his faith and courageousness beyond belief.

In conclusion, the principles of autonomy and consent are the cornerstones of medical practice, but virtue ethics may override these (and the law) to simply do what it believes is 'right' at the time. In addition, virtue ethics does not solve a problem, it simply chooses an action. For example, let us say that there are not enough medical resources to go around and so the sickest patients are given the best medical facilities because that is the 'right' thing to do, but the next day there is a terrorist attack and a thousand more patients require the facilities? There is no solution to the problem.

Secular bioethic four: Principalism by Beauchamp and Childress

So far we have looked at utilitarianism (consequences), Kantianism (autonomy) and virtue ethics (morals), but doctors in particular are still faced with the same problem: what *is* the best course of action? Let us say that a female patient is refusing all medical treatment even though she is in labour and the prospects are very grave. The doctor can consider the consequences, her autonomy, or ignore them both and do what feels right, but how does he decide? It was thought by Tom Beauchamp and James Childress that a clear collection of principles (Principalism) could aid such a decision, and so autonomy, non-malfeasance, beneficence and justice have been suggested as the basic norms of common morality (known as Principalism).[6]

Autonomy

The word autonomy comes from the Greek words *autos* (self) and *nomos* (rule) and refers to the freedom that we have to choose for oneself what to do and how to do it. We are liberal bodies with free thoughts, we are entitled to privacy, to reject medical treatment, and to make any choice we wish when it comes to our behaviour, our morals and our destiny.

In the context of medical law, a patient exercises her autonomy when she visits her doctor, when she consents to a medical procedure, when she asks questions and when she rejects medical treatment. Autonomy is widely accepted in law and has helped to shape many different legal judgments where traditionally, the patient would not have been able to speak for herself. This is the positive effect of autonomy; it has taken a lot of the perceived power away from doctors who used to have complete control over the

---

[5] A classic example is given by Hursthouse in 'Virtue Theory and Abortion' (1991) 20 *Philosophy and Public Affairs* 223, where a woman who wants an abortion because the pregnancy would interfere with her holiday plans is not virtuous (and the doctor would not be virtuous if he acted upon it), whereas a teenager who cannot provide a decent life for her child may be acting virtuously in seeking the abortion (and the doctor would be virtuous if he provided it).

[6] Tom Beauchamp and James Childress (2008) *Principles of Biomedical Ethics*, sixth edition, Oxford University Press.

patient and her treatment. We must remember, however, that patients do not have a right to *demand* treatment. This is the common misconception to autonomy. In reality, a doctor will only provide the treatment that is in the *best interests* of the patient, and then it is for the patient to accept or reject that treatment. Autonomy can therefore be seen as a right to bodily integrity or personal freedom, but not power or control over others.

Non-malfeasance

The phrase non-malfeasance comes from the Latin term *primum non nocere* and means 'above all do no harm'. This is derived directly from the Hippocratic Oath which states: 'I will prescribe regimens for the good of my patients according to my ability and my judgment and never do harm to anyone'. A doctor must not do harm to his patient, it is as simple as that.

This may sound straightforward, but it is not. The term 'harm' has caused some confusion because patients are harmed in medicine quite frequently (i.e. surgically). The general rule is that an act is not considered to be 'harmful' if the doctor is acting in the best interests of the patient. For example, administering an injection may be harmful but it provides a cure from disease. Inevitably, there are rare cases where a patient is harmed with the best of intentions but she receives no benefit out of it, such as donating bone marrow to a sibling. This is not in the best interests of the patient because it does not 'treat' her, but the courts have manoeuvred round this complex issue by stating that the improved health of the recipient sibling is in the best interests of the patient donor: see *Re Y (Mental Patient: Bone Marrow Donation)* [1997] Fam 110.[7]

Beneficence

Beneficence refers to acting for the *benefit* of others. This principle is today known as the 'best interests' test and is widely applied in modern medicine. Beneficence and the best interests test are derived directly from the Hippocratic Oath, which states: 'I will prescribe regimens for the good of my patients according to my ability and my judgment'.

Beneficence is rumoured to have a second meaning that we are *all* under a duty to act in a way that benefits society as a whole. This is akin to a duty to rescue those who are less fortunate than us, like the good samaritan law in France, or to behave in a way that does not use up public healthcare resources. To be under such an obligation would take away our autonomy, our liberty and our freedom. However, this is only a moral obligation, so we are not under a *legal* duty to act in a way that benefits others in the same way as healthcare professionals.

Justice

The term 'justice' could stand for so much, but in reality it means very little. In theory, we could apply justice as a secular bioethic to medical cases by treating every patient fairly, sharing resources equally and respecting every decision (e.g. consent, refusal and autonomy). In practice, this is simply not possible. We cannot treat every patient fairly or equally because there are not enough resources to go around. In addition to this, the rights of every patient cannot always be respected, especially in cases of incompetence or emergency. Therefore, it is sometimes best to use 'justice' as a benchmark or a guiding factor when making decisions about medical treatment and patient care.

To conclude, there are clear benefits to Principalism. It is not steeped in theory, religion or history. It is also self-explanatory: a doctor must protect the autonomy of his

---

[7] This is an application of utilitarianism (i.e. consequences) and virtue ethics (i.e. the right thing for the right reason).

patient while treating her in accordance with her best interests. Principalism is also directly applicable to medicine. A doctor could potentially make a decision in a highly complicated case using these principles.

Principalism has one big drawback: a conflict between autonomy and beneficence (one supports freedom and one imposes a duty). The medical cases to reach the appeal courts are usually torn between these basic principles. There are numerous good examples:

- *Re P (A Child)* [2003] EWHC 2327: A teenager wished to refuse blood transfusions because of his religious beliefs, knowing that he would die. The courts did not allow this, and when he reached the age of majority he successfully refused.

- *Airedale NHS Trust* v *Bland* [1993] 1 All ER 821: The law was faced with a unique dilemma: should a doctor be exempt from the law of murder if he withdraws artificial nutrition and hydration from a patient who is not brain stem dead? The answer was yes.

- *South West Hertfordshire HA* v *KB* [1994] 2 FCR 1051: An anorexic patient wanted to refuse food and argued that she was competent to do so. The courts disagreed, stating the food was medical treatment for a mental disorder and thus it was in her best interests.

- *St George's Healthcare NHS Trust* v *S* [1999] Fam 26: A pregnant woman refused a caesarean section even though the prospects for herself and the baby were grave. A caesarean was performed anyway and she successfully argued in the courts that her autonomy had been breached.

- *Pretty* v *United Kingdom (2346/02)* (2002) 35 EHRR 1: A woman who was suffering from motor-neurone disease wished for her husband to assist her suicide when she was not able to do it herself. The courts told her that she did not have right to die under Article 2 (the right to life), and her husband would not be immune from a criminal charge on public policy grounds.

- *McFarlane* v *Tayside Health Board* [2000] 2 AC 59: When a woman becomes wrongfully pregnant at the hands of a doctor (i.e. incorrect statement of successful sterilisation), she cannot claim for the upbringing costs of the healthy child even though the rules of tort allow for all losses to be compensated.

The examples above illustrate very clearly how autonomy, i.e. freedom to make a decision without interference, can clash against beneficence, i.e. treating the patient in accordance with his best interests. The patient is also arguing that justice has not been done. How do we solve dilemmas like these? The answer appears to be to pick the principal that is most relevant to that particular case. To use the examples above, in *Bland* (1993) the patient was allowed to die by his doctors because he no longer had an interest in being kept alive (beneficence upheld), in *St George's* (1999) the patient successfully argued that her refusal for a caesarian was not respected (autonomy upheld), and in *Pretty* (2002) the courts wanted assisted suicide to remain illegal (justice upheld). It therefore depends on the issues in the case as to whether the principles of autonomy, beneficence and justice can provide an answer, but they *have* provided answers, unlike utilitarianism and virtue ethics which simply analyse the general issues. When a particular principle is chosen and applied by the courts, they will often justify why they did so. For example, in *Bland* it was decided that even though it was against the best interests of the patient to have his artificial hydration and nutrition removed, the courts concluded that he no longer had any best interests in being kept alive.

CASE EXTRACT

Airedale NHS Trust v *Bland* [1993] 1 All ER 821

Lord Browne-Wilkinson (at page 883): . . . if there comes a stage where the responsible doctor comes to the reasonable conclusion (which accords with the views of a responsible body of medical opinion) that further continuance of an intrusive life support system is not in the best interests of the patient, he can no longer lawfully continue that life support system: to do so would constitute the crime of battery and the tort of trespass to the person.

Lord Goff (at page 864): It is established that the principle of self-determination requires that respect must be given to the wishes of the patient, so that if an adult patient of sound mind refuses, however unreasonably, to consent to treatment or care by which his life would or might be prolonged, the doctors responsible for his care must give effect to his wishes, even though they do not consider it to be in his best interests to do so. On this basis, it has been held that a patient of sound mind may, if properly informed, require that life support should be discontinued.

The *Bland* case is an excellent example of when a single principle can change the law. This was the case that established our modern 'best interest' test and held that doctors do not commit murder when they effectively starve a patient who has no prospect of recovery.

Secular bioethic five: casuistry (i.e. case law)

A really good way to figure out what to do when a difficult medical case comes to court is to look at the previous case law. The formal title for this approach is casuistry, which means 'case-based reasoning' and has roots in Roman Catholic theology. Casuistry is not as much of a secular bioethic as utilitarianism, Kantianism or virtue ethics, but it is a judicial approach to ethical dilemmas and it can glean some positive results, although we must always be mindful that bad cases can make bad law through this approach. What is favourable about casuistry is that it follows previous rules, whereas the other secular bioethics try to establish a new rule. Casuistry is like judicial precedent in this respect, and as a secular bioethic there can be a lot said for taking such a methodical and analytical approach to medical dilemmas.

EXTRACT

John Arras, 'Getting Down to Cases: The Revival of Casuistry in Bioethics' (1991) 16 *Journal of Medicine and Philosophy* 29, at pages 29–51

Contrary to deductivist ethical theories, wherein principles are said to preexist the actual cases to which they apply, the new casuistry contends that ethical principles are 'discovered' in the cases themselves, just as common law legal principles are developed in and through judicial decisions in particular legal cases [...] Rather than stemming originally from some ethical theory, such as Utilitarianism, these principles are said to emerge gradually from reflection upon our responses to particular cases.

Arras argues that casuistry 'finds' relevant principles in case law. This is a logical way to approach complex cases. Judges will get far more use out of principles arising from cases than they would from moral, religious or legal principles that preexisted the cases. This is because principles such as utilitarianism must be manipulated in order to be applied to the law, whereas principles arising from cases are holistically entwined with the law. Casuistry works by drawing an analogy (i.e. a comparison) between previous cases and the current case. There may be similarities in past cases which can help to carve out a solution. This detailed analogy can draw a bigger picture as to the best course of action to take in the current case.

The main positive to casuistry is that judicial decisions are rarely decided purely on morality – there is usually a rational explanation for the final decision and a raft of legal authorities to support it – and this is a great help to future judges when faced with brand new medical cases. A second advantage is that case law can build a strong and secure precedent over time, consolidating an approach until it becomes the uncontroversial norm. A third advantage is the clarity provided by case law. The secular bioethics discussed above do not encourage a definitive decision, but the courts *must* reach a decision when confronted with a difficult case. There may, for example, be a clash between autonomy and beneficence. The judgment will typically adopt one approach over the other and justify its decision. This is very helpful to future cases, because the rationale for adopting a certain principle will assist future judges and doctors to apply it in practice. To give a good example, in *Airedale NHS Trust* v *Bland* [1993] AC 789 the lords explained why a persistent vegetative state patient no longer had an interest in being kept alive by artificial nutrition and hydration, and the phrase 'a living death' was used by Lord Goff. This is now a frame of reference for doctors: if any of their patients are experiencing similar symptoms, the precedent could offer a solution.

However, there are significant problems with casuistry. Firstly, casuistry cannot be used to solve a brand new ethical dilemma because previous authorities will provide no guidance whatsoever. *McFarlane* v *Tayside Health Board* [2000] 2 AC 59 is a good example of a major precedent that was set in the field of wrongful pregnancy despite barely a scrap of law to support the decision (further discussion can be found in Chapter 3). Secondly, to say that a legal judgment is representative of a collective moral response to a case is incorrect because it is a decision taken by judges, not the general public, and judges often dissent leading to split judgments with weak majorities. Thirdly, there is an old phrase which states: 'bad cases make bad law' and this has never been more prevalent than in the field of medicine. It only takes one judicial precedent to open the floodgates for one hundred claims, and it only takes one stretched interpretation by a judge to extend the rule to cover a new area of law. The law can become extended and distorted beyond recognition. *Donoghue* v *Stevenson* [1932] AC 562 is an excellent example whereby a common law duty of care between a manufacturer and a customer (a revolutionary idea from Lord Atkin) exploded into a whole new area of law that we know today as negligence. Fourthly, previous cases may be able to point judges in a *general* direction, but they have a habit of balancing on a very thin line. For example, in *An NHS Trust* v *B* [2006] EWHC 507 a baby was suffering from severe disabilities so a balance sheet of positives and negatives were drawn up by Holman J to ascertain whether it was in his best interests to be kept alive. This 'balance sheet' was felt to be the best approach to such an emotional case and it has been adopted in subsequent case law, but Holman J literally picked it out of nowhere because he did not know that else to do. Fifthly, there will always be exceptions to the rule. A unique case will come along to test the established precedent, it will make a new precedent, and the cycle starts again. Therefore, the moral standpoint of the court on a particular issue could change sporadically and there could be different rules for different types of cases in the same field. For example, the withdrawal of life support from a severely disabled baby was allowed in *K (A Child) (Medical Treatment: Declaration)* [2006] EWHC 1007 but it was continued in *An NHS Trust* v *B* [2006] EWHC 507. This is the big problem with case law: every case turns on its facts, and this inevitably leads to a patchwork quilt of medico-legal principles.

Secular bioethic six: feminism

The relatively new ethic of feminism is quite complicated. There are several views, e.g. liberal feminists, oppressive feminists and other feminists, all of which can be applied to medical practice. However, unlike casuistry, no clear answer is provided. Feminism is a secular bioethic like utilitarianism and virtue ethics in that it helps to discuss the pros and cons of an action and weigh up the consequences but it does not always resolve the issue or definitively conclude what is 'right' or 'wrong'.

Firstly, liberal feminists argue that there is an inequality between males and females in medicine. This idea can be applied mainly in the context of treatment and resources. For example, men could be getting the best resources and the best treatment. This may stem from the fact that men manage hospitals and control local authorities, so perhaps they are naturally offered the best of everything to recompense for their efforts in leadership? There is often statistical proof of this inequality to support the feminist view, but it may be because some ailments are suffered more by men than women (e.g. heart disease). In a wider context, pregnant women may be excluded from many things in life because of the risk to their health. Drugs or treatments often warn on the packaging: 'not suitable for pregnant women' because they are excluded from medical trials. However, there is not much of an argument to be formed here in terms of men and women being treated unequally, because only women can get pregnant. Secondly, oppressive feminists argue that women are either oppressed in medicine, or they are being taken advantage of by male doctors and this contributes to their oppression. This is a difficult standpoint to take because very few people in society feel strongly that women are oppressed in medicine. In fact, it would be safe to say that women are treated more frequently in medicine because they live longer, they have babies, they seek a medical diagnosis quicker and are more likely to follow advice. However, there are some medical treatments or procedures that are very invasive to women. Assisted conception is good example, where their eggs are harvested, fertilised in a dish, and then inserted back into the body. This is after a significant drug treatment programme to prepare the eggs for fertilisation. The oppressive feminists used to argue that this procedure – which was relatively new thirty years ago – was taking advantage of women and they were being exploited by men. However, it must be remembered that any women who undertakes *in vitro* fertilisation (IVF) treatment has *consented* to that treatment, and she may be taking advantage of science for her own gain (e.g. a longed-for family). It should also be remembered that men cannot undergo this procedure, so to say that women are being taken advantage of is inaccurate because they are the only possible candidates. Thirdly, other feminists argue that medicine has traditionally been too male-dominated, leading to an emphasis on control, order, process, consent, independence and autonomy. The other side to medicine – sympathy, love, support, care, dependency, vulnerability and need – are qualities that we deeply value at home but are very rarely factored into medical decisions. Females can offer these special qualities – this is represented by their roles as nurses, carers and mothers – but the perspectives of woman (according to feminists) have been shunned as worthless in the past, especially when it comes to hard cases. This may be because caring is traditionally seen as 'women's work' and so is taken for granted.

The positives to feminism are clear: it takes a holistic view to medicine. It is not all about duties, responsibilities and autonomy but about care, support and equality (or the lack thereof). Depending on the version of feminism chosen, a medical procedure can be unethical because it takes advantage of the woman (liberal), because it harms the woman (oppressive), or because it fails to recognise the deeper values and relationships of the patient (other). However, the disadvantages to feminism are also clear. Feminism as a secular bioethic can only lead to one outcome: the female must not be suppressed. This is not helpful to law, because female patients need to be suppressed for a few minutes to undergo cervical tests, childbirth and the fitting of contraceptives. The fact that the female patient *consents* to the procedure seems to matter little to oppressive feminists in particular. Feminism can be accused of bias. It comes to the table with pre-determined ideals on what is right and wrong and there does not appear to be any exceptions to the rule. This is the ultimate humiliation, because feminism was created to fight bias. Commentators have criticised feminism too, arguing that there is a lot to be said for good old reasoning, i.e. the traditional approach to problem solving and it should not be ignored when applying feminist theories.

EXTRACT

Helga Kuhse, 'Clinical Ethics and Nursing: "Yes" to Caring, But "No" to a Female Ethics of Care' (1995) 9 *Bioethics* 207, at pages 207–19

The assumption is that caring, in its sensitive attention to the particularities of the situation, can give the right answer. But this is not so. Sensitivity and particularity alone can not guide action [...] If women [...] excessively devalue reasoned argument, if they dismiss ethical principles and norms and hold that notions of impartiality and universalizability have no place in a female ethic of care, then they will be left without the theoretical tools necessary to condemn some actions or practices, and to defend others. Bereft of a universal ethical language, women will be unable to participate in ethical discourse.

Kuhse is arguing that being sensitive to patients and their needs is not enough – by rejecting reasoned argument, feminists are depriving themselves of the tools they need to engage in ethical discussions. This may sound far-fetched, but autonomy is one of the cornerstones of medicine, and if feminists choose to ignore it we may see the depersonalisation of medicine. Therefore, feminism in any of its guises it not much use as a secular bioethic if we must come to an objective decision.

ACTIVITY

In the case of *A (Children) (Conjoined Twins: Medical Treatment) (No.2), Re* [2001] 1 FLR 267, the Siamese twins Mary and Jodie were allowed to be separated despite the certain death of the weaker twin (Mary). The parents were strictly religious and did not consent, but the twins would die without treatment so the UK courts allowed the separation to go ahead using the defence of necessity (this had never been done before).

Find the case and pick out the ethical arguments put forward by the Lords during their deliberations. Then apply some of the secular bioethics listed above to come to your own conclusion. What would you decide if you were sitting in the House of Lords hearing the case and why?

Rejection of change

We have examined numerous secular bioethics and briefly looked at religious bioethics to understand the many different perspectives through which complex medical dilemmas can be resolved. We have learnt that consequences may count sometimes, intentions may count at other times, and between those, the basic principles of autonomy, beneficence and justice will steer the courts. There are clearly no right answers to complex cases, but there are tools available in the form of bioethics to help guide judges and doctors.

In response to bioethics, there are two common justifications for *not* changing the law, trialling a new medicine or respecting autonomy. They are formally known as the 'sanctity of life' and 'slippery slope' theories, and they argue that any change to the law or procedure will have a negative effect on society.

> **KEY DEFINITION**
>
> **Sanctity of life**: it is not our place to 'play God' with the human body.
> **Slippery slope**: the floodgates will open and the exception will become the rule.

Sanctity of life

The argument that we are interfering with the sanctity of life is a religious one. It was described above how religious bioethics regard human life as a 'gift from God' that should not be interfered with, this is particularly prevalent in Catholicism. This is very similar to the sanctity of life theory, which states that it is not our place to control, manipulate, injure, dissect, alter or kill a human being and we would be 'playing God' if we even attempted to do so.

The phrase 'playing God' is frequently quoted in social settings to express an objection, but what could it mean in a medical context? Firstly, it could mean that a doctor or a judge has too much power. Secondly, it could mean that a doctor or a judge should not attempt to control the processes of birth and death. Thirdly, it could mean that nature must be left alone to take its course. Fourthly, it could mean that doctors and judges are arrogant as to their position in society and they are not as powerful as they think they are. Fifthly, it could mean that doctors and judges have a disregard for human life. The five points listed above make good sense: if we are to support equality in society, then a handful of individuals with respected qualifications should not be able to control when we live, when we die and how our bodies are deprived of dignity. This is the main advantage of the sanctity of life argument: it may stand for rejection but it serves a useful purpose in that it reminds us of our roots and to remember who we are, where we come from and what is 'natural' in a world where science has blurred the boundaries.

However, the problem with sanctity of life is that on a strict reading of the theory, it prohibits medical practice in every form. An antibiotic that is prescribed to clear up an infection could be said to be interfering with the work of God. The sanctity of life theory has the potential to discredit almost any medical intervention on the grounds that it goes against nature. However, it is the most controversial and the most invasive medical procedures that will attract the attention of the theory. Abortion and euthanasia are the classic examples, but in vitro fertilisation (IVF) and organ donation also attracted criticism in the past. In the future, we can foresee several medical developments what will not go down very well in the sanctity of life camp:

- **Stem cell research**: this will probably develop in leaps and bounds over the next few generations to offer cures for degenerative illnesses such as Alzheimer's disease. This practice goes against the will of God in two ways: it uses embryos for their stem cells which could cheapen the value of life, and the idea of creating cures from embryos may be viewed as undignified and disrespectful.

- **Cloning**: it is currently illegal to clone a human being, but one day it will be a necessary and justified development in medicine. 'Saviour siblings' comes to mind, where a second child is born to provide life-saving material (i.e. bone marrow) for the first child. This is done already via IVF, but a full clone would be far easier.

- **Assisted suicide**: it is only a matter of time before Parliament allows for the suicide of terminally ill patients to be assisted in certain strict circumstances. It is almost primitive that we still allow human beings to suffer. However, the practice of assisted suicide goes against God in one big way: it ends human life without the consent of God.

- **Fertility**: we can already develop embryos outside of the human body which was controversial enough, but same sex male couples may be able to carry their own babies in the future with the help of science. A prosthetic uterus could be made and inserted into the man behind his bladder, and complete with a hormone course, he may be able to incubate a baby for nine months. This is hugely controversial for many bioethical camps but sanctity of life would have a field day: a pregnant man would almost certainly blur the boundaries of nature.

It is very unlikely that the sanctity of life argument will prevent medical developments in the future, but it is usually one of the first voices to be heard when a medical innovation is broadcast and the criticisms pour in. It serves as an excellent reminder that we constantly push the boundaries of nature, but if a medical innovation serves a good purpose (i.e. a cure for cancer) then it is usually justified in the eyes of the law and religion and can defeat most religious criticism.

There is often an element of 'dignity' interwoven throughout the sanctity of life argument, e.g. to terminate a life or to use an embryo for research would undermine its dignity. The idea of a man carrying a baby to full term is a good example of an act that would be contrary to natural life and thus the sanctity of life theory would label it as undignified. Dignity is a difficult term to define, because it is wider than human rights. We must, according to the sanctity of life theory, treat human beings with dignity at all stages of their life, including before birth (e.g. a foetus must not be destroyed) and after death (e.g. a dead body must not be abandoned). It is not clear what dignified behaviour is, but we recognise it when we see it and we recoil when it is forgotten. In the context of medical law, for example, it may refer to a lack of respect, a denial of autonomy, a curtailment of freedom, a rejection of independence, a lack of support and an absence of care. However, it is not as supportive of rights as it claims to be. Dignity is very restrictive in that it tells us what *must* be done at the expense of what *ought* to be done. This could lead to suppression and further suffering. For example, the sanctity of life argument would reject abortion because it is undignified, but it could save a pregnant mother from destitution or depression. It would also reject assisted suicide even though it could save an elderly patient from a slow and painful death, and it would reject stem cell research even though it could provide a cure for debilitating diseases. Therefore, sanctity of life – the very bioethic that *supports* dignity – could reject the breakthroughs that *restore* dignity to the most vulnerable patients in society.

Slippery slope

The slippery slope argument can be split into two depending on the scenario. The first meaning refers to the very existence of the slope, and the second argument refers to the dangers lurking at the bottom of the slope.

- **First meaning is 'floodgates'**: if we allow one exception, the rest will follow until the exception becomes the rule. This refers to the very existence of the slope.
- **Second meaning is 'culture change'**: a trickle of cases will lead to a dangerous culture change that we cannot control until a new culture is born. This refers to the dangers lurking at the bottom of the slope as time passes.

It clearly depends on the case under consideration as to whether the concern is 'floodgates' or 'culture change' but either way, the slippery slope argument is a teleological bioethic because it examines the *consequences* of an action when deliberating its rightfulness or wrongfulness. However, the slippery slope argument is also concerned with the danger to society. For example, a court may allow an anorexic patient to escape force-feeding under the Mental Health Act 1983. The case will turn on its facts as an exception to the rule and the effect on society will seem insignificant to the courts at the time. However, other anorexic patients will thereafter demand that their autonomy be respected and their forced feeding be withdrawn, leading to a wide expulsion of anorexia from the health system and a considerable number of deaths, not to mention desperate relatives who feel powerless to help their starving loved ones. This is the outcome that the slippery slope argument works hard to avoid because a dangerous culture shift might occur that cannot be controlled. This is a very paternalistic approach to the rejection of medicine, e.g. it is for the *protection of the people* that the procedure should not go ahead. There is some confusion as to when a slippery slope becomes 'slippery' in the sense that a single judgment on its own does not pose a significant threat. A unique case is only troublesome to the parties within it and the judges reading it, but it does not usually trouble the law itself. Therefore, when does the slippery slope begin to materialise? It appears to be when a handful of similar cases follows in the footsteps of the first case and threatens to widen the application of the exception. The anorexia scenario above is a good example. The practice of medicine is directly influenced by case law, and if judges allow a strict doctrine to be eroded through a trickle of controversial cases, the behaviour of healthcare professionals, patients and the general public will slowly but surely erode over time too.

The slippery slope argument could be viewed as irrational, because if the first case is decided with strict boundaries, then there should be no possibility subsequent cases sliding into a dangerous culture change. It is, after all, the *possibility* of danger as opposed to the *actual* danger that the slippery slope argument is concerned about, so as long as the factors that *cause* slippage are reigned in, the dignity of patients should remain intact, such factors that cause slippage could include human rights.

ACTIVITY

Apply the slippery slope argument to the 'setting the scene' scenario above (i.e. the possibility of pregnant men) and outline a legally possible response to this controversial medical development.

Chapter summary

- Bioethics are a recent development and can be described as ethical theories to critically evaluate the morality of medicine. They include: Hippocratic Oath, human rights, religious bioethics and secular bioethics (e.g. utilitarianism, Kantianism, virtue ethics, Principalism, casuistry and feminism). The case of *Airedale NHS Trust* v *Bland* [1993] AC 789 is an excellent example of morality blurring with the law to change medical practice.

- The Hippocratic Oath is an ancient Greek code of professional medical ethics. It is thought to originate from the fifth century BC. The principles have been embodied into the Declaration of Geneva (1948) and most newly qualified doctors still swear by some kind of ethical oath.

- The Human Rights Act 1998 plays an important part in medical practice, because it supports the patient in terms of treatment, respect and autonomy. A number of significant cases in medical law have hinged on a breach of respect for private life, and *Pretty* v *UK* (2002) 35 EHRR 1 confirmed that a right to life is not a right to die (i.e. assisted suicide).

- Religious bioethics derive from God. Catholicism, for example, argues that we 'play God' when we interfere with the human body and its natural processes. A good example is abortion, where it is argued that a termination of life goes against the will of God. Religious bioethics ask the difficult questions, such as 'when does life really begin?' and an answer to this question would, ironically, be very helpful to the law.

Chapter essay

'Discuss the different ways in which a controversial medical development can be rejected by bioethics.'

Chapter case study

The government is planning to introduce a compulsory contraceptive injection for all school girls between the ages of 12 and 18. This is hoped to cut the teenage pregnancy rate by half. In the UK the teenage pregnancy rate is currently the highest in Europe. The government proposes that if a parent or guardian refuses to take their daughter to the doctor and the daughter subsequently becomes pregnant, the child born will receive no financial help from the State. A small group of mothers from rich communities argue that they do not wish to take their daughters to the doctor for a contraceptive injection because they are too young, or it will sexualise them in the eyes of teenage boys. The government argues in response that the consequences of not having the injection are more dangerous. Can this argument be resolved using any of the bioethical approaches discussed above?

Further reading

Arras, J. (1991) 'Getting Down to Cases: The Revival of Casuistry in Bioethics', 16 *Journal of Medicine and Philosophy* 29.

Beauchamp, T. and Childress, J. (2008) *Principles of Biomedical Ethics*, 6th edn, Oxford University Press.

Draper, H. and Sorrell, T. (2002) 'Patients' Responsibilities in Medical Bioethics', 16 *Bioethics* 335.

Herring, J. (2007) 'Where are the Carers in Healthcare Law and Ethics?', 27 *Legal Studies* 51.

Veatch, R. (1988) 'The Danger of Virtue', 13 *Journal of Medicine and Philosophy* 13.

2

The allocation of healthcare resources

Chapter objectives

At the end of this chapter, you should have:

- An understanding of rationing in healthcare and why the National Health Service (NHS) needs to do it.
- An appreciation of the beginnings, the structure, the achievements and the pressures of the NHS.
- A knowledge of the ways in which healthcare resources can be rationed, including equality, cost effectiveness (also known as QALY), patient age (also known as the 'fair innings' argument), patient blame, lotteries, randomisation and going private (e.g. mass health insurance roll-out).
- An understanding of how the courts deal with disgruntled patients in judicial reviews of adverse funding decisions, including asylum seekers, claims for public funds for treatments abroad, and human rights.

SETTING THE SCENE

Jenna is aged 56 and has been diagnosed with stomach cancer. It is quite advanced and even though she is having chemotherapy, she is not showing signs of improvement. Her daughter researches the condition on the internet, and finds evidence of a new drug being piloted in France called KL09. Jenna visits her oncologist straight away and asks for the drug. Her oncologist says that the drug is not licensed in the United Kingdom, so her NHS trust will not fund it for her unless she is an 'exceptional' case. She consults you, a medical lawyer, to ask about a judicial review into the NHS trust policy and asks you what the courts are likely to tell her. She argues that she is an exceptional case because she is not responding well to the chemotherapy. How do you, as a medical lawyer, deal with this kind of plea?

Introduction

This chapter will primarily address the allocation of resources in the National Health Service (NHS) in England. However, private healthcare can often face the same problems in resource allocation. These problems require us to consider:

- Who should we treat first when there are more patients than staff?
- Which treatments/drugs should we make available to cancer patients?
- Who is more in need of surgery when theatres and surgeons are stretched?
- Should we provide the same care to the elderly than to younger patients?
- Patient A and Patient B both need the heart transplant – who should get it?

Sadly, there are not enough resources to go around in medicine, not even in private healthcare, although the waiting time is often shorter and the resources and staff may be less strained when paying for private care. The NHS has been taken advantage of by the general public for decades, and it is not coping very well. We do not pay enough taxes to ensure that every person has the bed, nurse, specialist and drugs that they require when they become sick. We are also living longer, putting an even greater strain on resources.

Citizens are usually required to pay for their medical treatment in developed countries, and medical insurance is a major market. In the United States, for example, a kidney transplant costs $259,000 and a combined heart and lung transplant can cost up to $1.1 million. In the UK, medical treatment is free at the point of delivery.

This chapter explores the ways in which public and private health services can ration their limited resources to ensure that the most deserving patients are treated first. Patients have previously taken their arguments to the courts (e.g. when a cancer drug is not funded because it is too expensive) because they feel that they are being deprived of adequate healthcare. As we shall see, such cases have rarely been successful and the courts have shown a significant reluctance to get involved in the daily workings of the NHS, especially in relation to the allocation of funds.

Citizens who do not belong to the United Kingdom (e.g. criminals awaiting deportation) have also had a hard time in the courts when requesting free healthcare at the taxpayers expense. They are usually rejected unless the deportation would result in a quicker and torturous death contrary to Article 3 of the European Convention on Human Rights.

Healthcare funding is, of course, a political issue too, and election manifestos frequently seek to improve the NHS. However, in the study of law we must sweep politics aside and focus on the real issue: the fair allocation of limited healthcare resources.

The National Health Service

The National Health Service (NHS) was born in 1948 as a result of the National Health Service Act 1946. It is the largest publicly funded health service in the world, and is seen by many countries as an excellent example because of its complexity and efficiency. Borne out of the rationing culture of the Second World War, within the NHS every person was entitled to an equal quota of medical treatment regardless of wealth, background, location and illness. The deprivation at the end of the war was to be shared equally across society to support the national good. These founding principles still remain at the heart of the NHS today. It was originally hoped that the NHS would nurse the postwar nation back to health until the need for medical treatment slowly shrank to a minimum. However, the opposite has happened. We are living twice as long and need far more resources than we ever could have predicted, especially at the end of life. The NHS is viewed by its critics as the master of its own downfall. A small number of charges have been introduced through the decades – such as prescription charges since 1952 (except for contraception), optical care and dental care – but the remainder of healthcare is free for every one of the 63 million citizens in the United Kingdom. In addition to the sheer number of treatments that are offered, the very idea that healthcare is 'free' does nothing but encourage patients to visit their doctor for illnesses that can be treated at home.[1] A painkiller, a better diet, exercise and less stress will banish most minor ailments. There is considerable concern that as we get older, we will simply drain even more resources from the already strained healthcare system. The UK is already the most obese nation in Europe and geographically, we are very small compared to other countries. The 'junk food generation' of children born between 1970–2020 may be unlikely to see a ripe old age because of our working hours, culture, diets, social lives and stresses, and we well exhaust the NHS with our addictions, obesity, stress, cancer and diabetes before we bow out.

The facts and figures below throw some light on how unique the NHS really is, and highlight some key milestones since its inception:

- The NHS employs 1.7 million people. The only organisations in the world to employ more are: The Chinese Army, Wal-Mart and Indian Railways.
- The 1.7 million workers include:
  - 39,780 general practitioners;
  - 370,327 nurses;
  - 18,687 ambulance staff;
  - 105,711 hospital and community staff.
- The NHS deals with 1 million patients every 36 hours.
- When the NHS was launched on 5 July 1948 in Park Hospital in Manchester it had a budget of £437 million per year.

---

[1] A classic example is tonsillitis – most patients seek antibiotics because there is infection on the tonsils – but it clears itself up with a week of rest and fluids.

- The approximate budget today is £109 billion per year.
- The NHS underwent some major changes on 1 April 2013 due to section 34 of the Health and Social Care Act 2012 including the abolishment of Primary Care Trusts, which transferred funding decisions to local authorities.
- A programme to vaccinate everyone under the age of 15 for polio and diptheria was launched in 1958.
- The contraceptive pill was made widely available in 1961 and is considered one of the major medical breakthroughs of the twentieth century.
- The first hip replacement was carried out in 1962 at Wrightington Hospital.
- The Abortion Act 1967 was introduced by MP David Steel and passed into law in April 1968, allowing access to safe and sanitary abortions on the NHS instead of dangerous backstreet procedures.
- The world's first test tube baby (Louise Brown) was born in London (Oldham) in 1978, changing fertility treatment forever.
- Keyhole surgery was introduced in 1980.
- The NHS organ donor register was established in 1994.
- NHS Direct was launched in 1998 to provide 24-hour advice over the phone.
- NHS walk-in centres were introduced in 2000.
- The NHS celebrated its sixtieth birthday in 2008.
- A cervical cancer vaccination was introduced for teenage girls in 2008.
- The NHS Constitution[2] was published in 2009 (updated in 2013) to promote its aims, duties and expectations of patients.
- Despite scares in the press, most patients are satisfied with their treatment.
- The Commonwealth Fund declared in 2010 that the NHS was the second best health-care system against Australia, Canada, Germany, Netherlands, New Zealand and the USA because of its efficiency, effective care, patient equality and safety.[3]

The NHS Constitution – published by the Department of Health – is briefly referred to in the staggering list of achievements above. It is a small document containing only general principles, but it outlines the aims and responsibilities of the NHS and its staff. It appears to be especially committed to equal access for everyone.

EXTRACT

The NHS Constitution, National Health Service, March 2013, Department of Health:

http://www.nhs.uk/choiceintheNHS/Rightsandpledges/NHSConstitution/Documents/2013/the-nhs-constitution-for-england-2013.pdf

Page 3, Principle 1: The NHS provides a comprehensive service, available to all irrespective of gender, race, disability, age, sexual orientation, religion or belief, gender reassignment,

→

---

[2] To access the NHS Constitution visit the NHS Choices website: http://www.nhs.uk/choiceintheNHS/rightsandpledges/NHSConstitution/pages/overview.aspx.

[3] For more facts and figures see the NHS Choices website: http://www.nhs.uk/NHSEngland/thenhs/about/Pages/overview.aspx#close.

pregnancy and maternity or marital or civil partnership status . . . It has a duty to each and every individual that it serves and must respect their human rights . . .

Page 3, Principle 2: Access to NHS services is based on clinical need, not an individual's ability to pay. NHS services are free of charge, except in limited circumstances sanctioned by Parliament.

Page 4, Principle 6: The NHS is committed to providing best value for taxpayers' money and the most effective, fair and sustainable use of finite resources. Public funds for healthcare will be devoted solely to the benefit of the people that the NHS serves.

Page 5: Everyone counts. We maximise our resources for the benefit of the whole community, and make sure nobody is excluded, discriminated against or left behind. We accept that some people need more help, that difficult decisions have to be taken – and that when we waste resources we waste opportunities for others.

[Interestingly, the constitution reminds patients that, because it is a free service, we also have a responsibility to help ourselves so as to release some of the pressure on an already strained system.]

Page 11, Principle 3b: You should recognise that you can make a significant contribution to your own, and your family's, good health and wellbeing, and take some personal responsibility for it.

The NHS Constitution is not enforceable, but it sets the standard for professional practice. It is also a stark reminder to the greater public that it is a free service and is battling to satisfy our excessive demands. In the forties when the National Health Service was in its infancy, patients simply visited their doctor, believed what he said, collected their medicine, or the recipe to make it at home, and left. It comes with little surprise that the NHS faced no legal challenges in its first thirty years of existence.

EXTRACT

Keith Syrett, 'Impotence or Importance? Judicial Review in an Era of Explicit NHS Rationing' (2004) 67 *Modern Law Review* 289, at page 293

For many years, rationing in the NHS was not a matter of significant political or public debate. This was in part because lower expectations in the early years of the Service led to acceptance that deficiencies in provision were simply a fact of life. More significantly, most rationing took place under cover of clinical judgment: that is, it was implicit, in that the reasoning involved was not clearly stated to anyone except [...] the person making the decision. Medical professionals effectively 'converted' political decisions on resource allocation into clinical decisions about treatment by 'internalising' resource limits and providing justification for denial on medical grounds by portraying the decision as optimal or routine in the specific circumstances. Suspicion that such decisions were in reality dictated by resource considerations tended to be minimal because of the existence of high levels of trust between doctors and patients, premised upon the belief that physicians possessed both expertise and access to all medical resources necessary for effective care and that they would act as dedicated patient advocates in attempting to secure these.

In the early days of the NHS, life expectancy was shorter. We did not live long enough for degenerative diseases such as dementia to take hold, and patients who had heart attacks and strokes could not be saved. There was no fertility treatment, no life support machines, no transplants, no palliative care and no detox. Sixty years later we see an array of different diseases, ailments and disorders from the most serious ones, such as HIV, to the most trivial ones, such as sprains. The modern healthcare system does not help itself by recognising new illnesses every day.

We might have caused our own discontent by raising our expectations to an unrealistic level. The internet (or 'Dr Web' as it is occasionally referred to) is now widely available to inform us of new disorders and the new wonder drugs available to treat them. We visit doctors with ailments in mind before our consultation has even finished, and we demand certain treatments that are not available or are not a benefit to us. The emphasis on doctors has completely changed in the last sixty years – doctors are not a law unto themselves anymore – they are viewed by many as prescription writers.

In light of these changes through the decades, perhaps we should accept that we will never have enough medical resources to treat everyone, and simply plan how to ration what we do have fairly instead of ploughing our energy into a deficiency that cannot be fixed? We may become very good at rationing – possibly the best in the world – making our public health system even better and more revered than it is today.

It must be remembered that rationing often occurs in emergencies where the difficult decision to leave one patient to treat another is normal. Emergency situations call for quick, instinctive and brutal decisions. A child will be saved over an adult. A stroke will be treated over a broken leg. It is also acceptable to see a doctor refusing to resuscitate an elderly patient because it is simply not in her best interests to do so (e.g. she has died of advanced cancer). This is indirect rationing: the main objective is to treat the patient in accordance with her best interests, but the knock-on effect is the saving of time and resources. Therefore, rationing appears to be more acceptable in emergencies.

THINKING POINT

We could always pour far more money into the NHS, but where could this come from? Should we increase taxes, and would the public be happy about this? Should we place new taxes on junk food? Or, should we allocate more of our current taxes to the NHS to the detriment of other public services? If so, which ones?

The structure of the National Health Service

The Department of Health publishes national guidelines, standards and codes of practice for the treatment of certain medical conditions, for example liver transplants, to ensure that the benchmarks for acceptable treatment, eligibility and aftercare are met. It also decides what to do with the funds given to it by the government. What part of healthcare should it invest in? These healthcare funds are made available to local authorities (i.e. your local council) and the local authority will then decide how to budget for healthcare in your region depending on the needs of the people in your particular area.[4]

---

[4] Primary Care Trusts – which used to control healthcare funds – were abolished by s. 34 of the Health and Social Care Act 2012 on 1 April 2013 and their role was replaced by local authorities to allow more freedom in expenditure at a local level.

The National Institute for Health and Care Excellence (NICE) was set up in 1999 by a statutory instrument under section 11 of the National Health Service Act 1977.[5] It aims to improve health and social care services nationwide by issuing guidelines on treatment, standards of care, technology appraisals and performance indicators. NICE has five distinct responsibilities:

1. the promotion of public health through guidance;

2. evaluating appropriate care for people with specific diseases and conditions;

3. issuing guidance on interventional procedures such as the safety of surgical procedures;

4. social care guidance to provide practical support to practitioners;

5. it is also responsible for recommending or rejecting new medicines or treatments based on clinical effectiveness and economical evidence in 'technology appraisals'. The published results of these appraisals are handed directly to the NHS which must find the money to incorporate the recommendations into practice (e.g. a new cancer drug).[6]

The many documents published by NICE are available on their website to promote transparency. There is also a Citizen's Council made up of 30 lay members to provide a public perspective on the moral and ethical issues of any guidance to be published. NICE is an independent body and it has been highly successful in developing strategies for budgeting, treatment and public guidance. It is accountable to the Department of Health, but for the most part it is independent from government and helps to keep the 'postcode lottery' under control by encouraging the implementation of new drugs, treatments and standards nationwide.[7] NICE does not play a very big role in rationing resources and cannot pull at the purse strings in any way; it simply selects drugs, treatments and procedures at random and investigates their cost effectiveness. There are many current treatments that have not been appraised by NICE, and so as a rationing tool it is meaningless.

The decisions taken by the government, the Department of Health and NICE are known as *macro* decisions – they take place at the very top of the hierarchy. General practitioners, nurses and other healthcare professionals make much smaller decisions about funding on the 'front line' of medicine. For example, a doctor may choose to prescribe an expensive drug for a rare infection, or he may decide to refer the patient to a costly specialist. These decisions are linked directly to expenditure and are known as *micro* decisions – they take place at the bottom of the hierarchy.

KEY DEFINITION   **Macro decisions**: made by the big bodies at the top.
Micro decisions: made by the little people at the bottom.

---

[5] The 1977 Act has since been repealed but NICE remains strong. The statutory instrument is: National Institute for Clinical Excellence (Establishment and Constitution) Order 1999 SI 1999/220.

[6] The NHS has a duty to fund the treatment recommended by NICE but the patient does not have a right to demand that treatment. See their webpage dedicated to technology appraisals: http://www.nice.org.uk/aboutnice/whatwedo/abouttechnologyappraisals/about_technology_appraisals.jsp.

[7] In practice, of course, now that local authorities are in control of healthcare budgets, the same treatment may be available everywhere but varying funds will be allocated to that treatment in different counties, making it more available in one postcode and less available in another.

It may be a good idea to allow local authorities and doctors to make decisions about funding, because they know their communities very well. They are qualified to paint an accurate picture of the health needs in their local area. A surgery in the middle of a busy city, for example, would probably deal with high levels of addiction. This contrasts to a surgery in a rural area, which would probably deal with diseases associated with old age. This is a stereotype, but it is well known that urban areas see far higher levels of addiction and unemployment, which in turn lead to stress-related illnesses, than rural communities. It can be argued, therefore, that doctors are already experienced at rationing. They can also decide which patient needs to see a specialist (costing a lot of money) and which patient needs to lie in bed for a few days (costing no money). They also take the 'wait and see' approach very frequently. For example, a young woman might visit her doctor for the first time in years suffering from suspicious chest pains. It transpires that the woman has started a stressful job. The doctor knows that chest pains are rather serious but because of the clean medical history and good health of the patient, he tells the woman to visit again in two weeks if the symptoms do not go away. In most instances, the patient does not return. This is an indirect form of rationing because the referral to a heart specialist and the array of medical tests would have cost a great deal of money, but the doctor identified a probable cause of the ailment and knew it would sort itself out on its own. The doctor is therefore the gatekeeper of rationing. He is the first step into the public healthcare system and he treats as many patients as possible to restrict the number of bodies walking through the hospital door and costing the health service even more money.

The changes to the funding system on 1 April 2013 caused much controversy. Doctors are trained to care for people, not to become accountants. We expect our doctors to treat us in accordance with our best interests, and they are legally obliged to do so, so it would be incredibly difficult for a doctor to ration funds by refusing a prescription, a test or a referral simply because there might be a 'better use' for the money. The patient would, in return, feel resentful and discriminated against, and the litigation would start. Academics believe that doctors do not want to make decisions about money or distinguish one patient from another for the purposes of funds.

EXTRACT

J.J.M. van Delden, 'Medical Decision-Making in Scarcity Situations' (2004) 30 *Journal of Medical Ethics* 207, at page 210

Physicians tend to primarily look to the government for making allocation decisions. In their view, their primary concern should be the interests of their patients. They accept that their decisions influence the distribution of means and are willing to take this into account, but choosing between patients is not their job.

To add to the concern, referral rates for doctors have always varied. Patients who simply do not get the answer they require from their doctor will simply check themselves into Accident and Emergency (A&E) and be seen within twelve hours. Interestingly, despite the unwillingness of the courts to get involved in these issues, there has been a small handful of quotes from the courts about the duties of doctors to consider *everyone* when doing their job.

R v North Derbyshire HA ex parte Fisher (1997) 38 BMLR 76

Dyson J: When deciding whether to prescribe treatment to a patient, a clinician has to have regard to many factors, including the resources available for that treatment and the needs of and likely benefit to that patient, as compared with other patients who are likely to be suitable for that treatment during the financial year.

Arthur J S Hall & Co v Simons [2002] 1 AC 615

Lord Hoffman (at page 690): The doctor, for example, owes a duty to the individual patient. But he also owes a duty to his other patients which may prevent him from giving one patient the treatment or resources he would ideally prefer.

To summarise, decisions about funding in healthcare clearly take place at macro *and* micro levels, and evidence of rationing can be seen very clearly at both levels. The Department of Health could not write a blank cheque to every local authority for the provision of healthcare services, and a doctor could not prescribe the most expensive contraceptive to every single female patient. Therefore, decisions about funding have to be selective, logical and justified *as well as* being in the best interests of the patient. This is a difficult task in a publicly funded health service where sources are limited. However, when it comes to micro decisions by doctors, honesty is clearly the best policy. We cannot go back to the old days when patients had an implicit trust in their doctor, because today we exercise our autonomy, our human rights and our right to search the internet for cures to our medical ailments.

'Healthwatch England' was also set up on 1 April 2013. What is it, and what does it do? How does it aim to help the allocation of resources in the NHS?

 ## How can we ration resources?

We have ascertained that there are currently not enough medical resources to go around. So, how do we ration/share the resources that we do have? Is there an accepted strategy for rationing? The short answer is yes: we treat those who are most in need if it is in their best interests, in line with the Hippocratic Oath. This strategy currently works well and is widely accepted because it contains a double filter for rationing: you must be an urgent case *and* you must benefit from the treatment. It can typically be seen in action in A&E departments where resources are particularly stretched.

'Need' is a difficult strategy to criticise, but it does have its problems. Firstly, there must be a hierarchy of 'need' in order to ascertain who deserves to be treated first, even in an emergency. A patient facing death will have the highest need of all, but what if their death is unpreventable or impending for example, a patient on a life support machine? Do they 'need' medical treatment in the true sense? Secondly, because medicine and science is moving so quickly, our 'needs' are expanding all the time. Sixty years ago we needed a bottle of medicine, whereas today we need an MRI scan, a blood test and a course of antibiotics. Thirdly, the calculation of 'need' does not mean anything if 'benefit' is not calculated too. A road accident victim with multiple organ failure would greatly benefit from medical treatment, thus increasing his need for it. A baby who is dying from advanced brain damage would not greatly benefit from treatment, thus *decreasing* her need for it. Fourthly, when dealing with diseases that do not carry a risk of death, how should 'need' be ranked? To take arthritis sufferers as an example, we could look at emotional distress, daily pain, inability to function normally, impact on employment or the cost of treatment in order to ascertain who 'needs' to be treated first. Who would be responsible for this decision and how would they know how the patient feels? Fifthly, basing a resource allocation system on 'need' removes a number of treatments from the NHS completely, including cosmetic surgery. It is true that most cosmetic surgery patients seek private care, but cosmetic procedures can be funded by the NHS if the doctor believes that it is in the best interests of the patient, for example if a physical abnormality is causing great distress or a breast cancer patient requires reconstructive surgery. Do these patients 'need' these treatments in the true sense? Are we happy to fund these treatments with our taxes? Sixthly, elderly patients are put in a difficult position when calculating need because they have so many. Additional factors such as age, general health, capacity, strength, support at home, drug regime, desire to get better and prognosis will have to be calculated too. Pensioners will need far more resources to counteract their higher mortality rate. Seventhly, a needs test would have to be subjective (i.e. consider the personal circumstances of the patient) not objective (i.e. a standard test for everyone). This is because a particular diagnosis could be a walk in the park for one patient and an absolute disaster for another depending on their family, social life, employment, age and wealth. In light of the problems above, we arrive at an important question: who will apply the subjective test? A doctor might not understand the daily struggle endured by a patient.

In conclusion, a needs-based rationing strategy is easy to apply in an emergency, but otherwise it is incredibly difficult and waiting lists are typically employed instead to ensure that everyone is treated equally.

There are other ways to ration healthcare resources that are worth exploring because of their ethical underpinnings. These include:

- Equality (i.e. every patient should have access to an equal number of resources).
- Cost effectiveness (i.e. QALY calculations).
- Age (i.e. 'good innings').
- Patient blame (i.e. virtue-based ethics state that some patients do not deserve treatment).
- Lotteries and randomisation (i.e. select patients at random if they suffer the same).
- Going private (i.e. abolish the NHS and purchase health insurance instead).

There are other factors to consider too, such as the definition of 'care' itself and public opinion, for example people are more likely to support expenditure on cancer drugs than alcohol detox.

Equality

The idea of equality brings comfort. The NHS Constitution confirms that our public healthcare system is 'available to everyone irrespective of gender, race, disability, age, sexual orientation, religion or belief' and we expect, when we need it, to have immediate access to it. This promise is technically fulfilled because anyone, regardless of age, belief, medical history, wealth and employment status, can walk into a hospital for treatment. In reality, however, access to medical care depends on distance, waiting lists, staffing numbers, costs of drugs, resources, access, research and equipment. Equality is therefore an excellent objective, but it cannot be achieved in a society with such diverse medical needs.

We could strive for equality in smaller groups of patients, such as bowel cancer patients or dementia patients. This would be easier to achieve, because they have the same needs, symptoms, treatments, waiting lists, resources and costs. The NHS works hard to meet this goal, and patients with the same disease usually have access to the same drugs, depending on the stage of the disease. To refuse access would be discriminatory and unlawful if it could not be justified. This is the closest we will get to equality, but it is surely as far as equality could go? After all, we could not treat a heroin addict equally to a baby with measles because their needs and costs would be completely different.

The only dilemma is when to compare patients and when to contrast patients in the same group. Lung transplant patients can be set apart by the *cause* of their disease. For example, we could put all smoking lung transplant patients into one subgroup and apply different funds, resources, drugs and waiting times to them, but how do we prove that their smoking *caused* their lung cancer? Additionally, how do we justify delaying life-saving treatment on the grounds that the patient *deserves* the delay? The NHS was definitely not designed to punish patients for their lifestyle choices, and the lung cancer is already assuming that role anyway.

Cost effectiveness (QALY calculations)

This might sound quite mathematical, but QALY stands for *Quality Adjusted Life Years* and it is a mathematical strategy to measure the cost of a treatment against its additional years of life offered to the patient. A patient should not only gain extra life, but it must be *quality* life. This strategy makes perfect sense in today's environment: why offer a drug for free on the NHS if it would cost the taxpayer a fortune and did not improve the quality of life of the patient? To use a practical example, a treatment that cost a lot of money and was relatively unsuccessful would have a low QALY (e.g. electric convulsive therapy) but a treatment that was relatively cheap and saved a lot of lives would have a high QALY (e.g. antibiotics).

NICE takes a very similar approach to the QALY strategy when appraising new medicines or evaluating old ones. It looks at the two following elements before recommending that a drug should be made available on the NHS or removed completely.

We base our recommendations on a review of clinical and economic evidence:

- **Clinical evidence** measures how well the medicine or treatment works.
- **Economic evidence** measures how well the medicine or treatment works in relation to how much it costs the NHS – does it represent value for money?[8]

In regard to rationing, the QALY strategy will ensure that healthcare funds are poured into affordable *and* beneficial treatments. The NHS will be able to treat as many patients as possible with its limited resources. In reality however, the QALY strategy cannot tell

---

[8] See their webpage dedicated to technology appraisals: http://www.nice.org.uk/aboutnice/whatwedo/abouttechnologyappraisals/about_technology_appraisals.jsp.

the NHS where to allocate healthcare resources, it would simply *categorise* treatments into 'expensive/successful', 'affordable/successful' or 'cheap/successful'. This is not overly helpful, and just because a treatment is categorised as 'expensive/successful' does not mean that it should be removed from public health. Cancer drugs and complicated surgical procedures are expensive but without them, many thousands of patents would die. Therefore, QALY could only ever be used to measure the cost effectiveness of small pockets of healthcare (e.g. all skin cancer drugs) as opposed to balancing the books across the board.

QALY has been criticised as a rationing tool. Firstly, the main aim of QALY is to generate the maximum number of quality years for the lowest cost. However, it appears to ignore our desire as taxpayers to treat more serious conditions with expensive drugs, such as rare cancers in children. Secondly, QALY ignores the patient as an autonomous individual with her own needs, choosing instead to focus on maximising health gains for society as a whole. This is strictly utilitarian, and even though objectivity is to be welcomed to a certain extent because it allows blind allocation of resources without discrimination or favouritism, surely the patient is the only person who is best equipped to accurately judge her quality of life, preferences and needs? The NHS was founded upon the principle that every citizen should have equal access to medical care, but this would go right out of the window if we implemented an objective and blind strategy such as QALY.[9] Thirdly, is it more cost effective to provide a pensioner with five quality years when a teenager could have two quality years? A teenager could do more with her life, could help others, could have a child of her own and could pay tax. It seems that the QALY strategy does not consider the age of the patient, the treatment required, the skill of the doctor, the aftercare available and the desires of the patient. The pensioner may not *want* to be treated. She may have lived for seventy good years and want to give her care to a younger patient instead, this is quite a common attitude among those at the very end of life. Fourthly, the QALY strategy discriminates against those who are very old and very sick, because they are likely to have low QALY scores. The cost of treating people with very serious illnesses is always going to be high – life support machines are very expensive – and their quality of life is rarely going to be improved if their condition is terminal. The NHS might be accused of cutting elderly and terminal patients out of their ambit of care altogether, and it is often these patients who have worked a full tax life.[10] Fifthly, the QALY strategy can be accused of favouring cheap healthcare over pioneering procedures. Stem cell research, for example, has the potential to reverse degenerative diseases, but the cost of this kind of experimental surgery means that QALY would not allocate funds to it. Surgeons often have to try new techniques out for themselves as part of research projects with desperate patients who have exhausted all other options, and if the technique works and a miracle cure is found, the lack of successful cases would still attract a low QALY score. It is not all negative, however. Keyhole surgery was a pioneering procedure in 1980, but now it is all but routine in smaller surgical procedures. This tells us that the more successful a pioneering procedure is, the more likely it will be condoned by NICE and thus funded by the local authorities, who are now in charge of healthcare budgets.

---

[9] The argument in response to this, of course, is that patients have never been equal because some of us need more care than others.

[10] The argument in response to this is that an elderly patient actually benefits more than a younger patient because their existing quality of life is already not very good: Rawlins and Dillon, 'NICE Discrimination' (2005) 31 *Journal of Medical Ethics* 683.

There are other ways to measure cost effectiveness without resorting to QALY. It is not just cheap medicine that contributes to the nation's health. We have vaccinations, better nutrition (except for junk food), a cleaner environment, better sanitation (e.g. less household sewerage in the streets), better benefits to reduce poverty and homelessness, happier social lives, better jobs (e.g. safety at work) and higher standards in healthcare generally (e.g. no more backstreet abortions or homemade concoctions for serious illnesses). To take a common example, a smoker can choose to stop smoking without seeing her doctor. This is cost effective in the short term (a saved appointment) and in the long term (a saved lung transplant or cancer drugs). The QALY makes no mention of these autonomous acts which are the most cost effective of all. The QALY strategy also calculates quality of life, but this is not just about additional years. It is about happiness too. A quality life can include a better home life, a happier family, a return to work or a recovering social life. The QALY does not measure these benefits because they would spread resources too wide and are subjective in nature, but without them, any additional years would surely be meaningless? A wider test to include these additional benefits would mean that dependants – such as children – would be included in the decision to treat the patient. This may sound strange, but if two identical patients were presented to a surgeon, and one has dependants and one does not, the surgeon is more likely to treat the patient with dependants because he will improve the quality of life of *several* people at once. John Harris, a critic of QALY, disagrees that we should consider the interests of dependants when calculating the quality of life of a patient.

EXTRACT

John Harris, *The Value of Life* (1985), Routledge, London, at pages 104–6

The feeling that it is somehow more important to rescue those with dependants, when elevated to the level of policy, amounts to a systematic preference of those with families over those without. Dependence is not simply dependence on parents, and grief and misery are not confined to family relationships. But even if they were, it is unclear that they would constitute adequate reasons for preferring to save one person rather than another. We should not forget that while the bereaved deserve sympathy, by far the greatest loss is to the deceased, and the misfortune of her friends and relations pales into insignificance besides the tragedy to the individual who must die. It seems as obviously offensive systematically to inflict this loss on the childless, and perhaps the friendless, as it would be to grade people in any other way.

In the view of this author, John Harris misses the point about two patients fighting for one resource: if they are identical in all but name, and it is an emergency situation, it might be perfectly fair and ethical to operate/treat the patient with dependants first if no other factors could separate them. There are problems with this approach: what if a mother does not speak to most of her children? The surgeon would have to conduct an intrusive and detailed examination of the patient's family history and social life before using 'dependants' as the justification for allocating scarce resources to one patient at the detriment of another. This 'dependants' approach is therefore not tenable unless the case was very clear.

The 'dependants' test may be a bit too controversial to be considered as part of the quality of life calculation, but there are good alternatives. We could measure a patient's contribution to society, employment, wealth, happiness, fitness and attitude when calculating quality of life. This might result in certain sectors of society (e.g. the workers) being allocated more healthcare resources than others (e.g. the unemployed), but one could argue that the workers are keeping the healthcare system running with their taxes and so deserve their elevated status. Social worth may also be factored into quality of life, but this is harder to measure unless the case was crystal clear (e.g. a convicted murderer spending life in prison). This may seem discriminatory, but perhaps if these rationing decisions were made at a macro level (i.e. very high up the chain) it would not feel like such a direct discrimination at micro level (i.e. on the front line of medicine). The founding principles of the NHS do not support this approach to rationing.

Age

The approach discussed here is blatantly discriminatory, but it is a reality in an overstretched public healthcare system. Age can be used as a rationing strategy. This is because resources are often wasted on patients at the end of life. The patient gains no real benefit from being kept alive for another few weeks or months if they are in pain or suffering from a terminal illness. This strategy does not always go against the values of elderly patients. It goes without saying that pain relief and a basic level of care is always provided for elderly patients, but new organs, blood transfusions, cancer drugs and complicated surgery may be futile if the elderly patient is so close to death or is so old that she has no chance of recovery. In a way, it is not just age that is the deciding factor in these cases – it is the *condition* of the patient too – and it just happens to be elderly patients who are in such a degenerative condition.

The 'fair innings' argument was first highlighted in such blatant terms by John Harris.

EXTRACT

John Harris, *The Value of Life* (1985) Routledge, London, at page 93

What the fair innings argument needs to do is capture and express in a workable form the truth while it is always a misfortune to die when one wants to go on living, it is not a tragedy to die in old age; but it is on the other hand, both a tragedy and a misfortune to be cut off prematurely.

The rationale behind the 'fair innings' argument is that a person, once he had reached a certain age, has lived a full life and experienced his quota of pleasures and pains. It is therefore not the worst thing in the world that he should meet his end. This sounds rather cruel, but elderly patients do take longer to recover and often have several ailments at the same time, meaning that they never really 'recover' in the true sense, just gradually get worse.

The arguments against using age as a rationing strategy are clear. Firstly, age has nothing to do with fitness and health. There are some pensioners who are fitter than teenagers. Therefore, as noted above, it is the *condition* of the patient that is considered when looking at the age of the patient, and this includes disease, medical history, prognosis, drugs, care and attitude. Secondly, using age as a rationing strategy could undervalue the old and frail in society. It sends a message that their lives are not worth saving. Pensioners already have a bad time in society – they are more vulnerable to crime and spiralling social costs – so to suggest that we will no longer treat them because they are a drain on public health resources is adding insult to existing injury. Other countries might also question the morality of the British people and our government if we showed such a derogatory attitude towards the elderly, who have paid taxes throughout their lives and are therefore more entitled to the free healthcare. The derogatory attitude may seep into other areas of society and we may start to deprive the elderly of food, housing, benefits and social care. This would be an absolute disaster and a step back into more deprived times.

Patient blame

Blame is no doubt a controversial rationing strategy. If a person causes their own illness through ignorance (e.g. 'it won't happen to me') or recklessness (e.g. 'I don't care') should we pay for their treatment? In these times of economic hardship many of us would say 'no' and it is easy to see why. The government has invested large amounts of money into promoting healthy eating, no smoking and the dangers of drugs. The number of people smoking has gone down dramatically in the last few generations, but obesity is a rising problem. The UK is currently the most obese nation in Europe, and this as a result leads to higher rates of diabetes, stroke, heart disease, cancer, skin conditions, infections, breathing difficulties and many other problems. Addicts are just as open to criticism when we consider the amount of social care that is ploughed into treating drug and alcohol abuse in the form of day centres, detox programmes and social care, not to mention social benefits. So, with all of this in mind, should we follow virtue-based ethics (see Chapter 1) and treat only the virtuous members of society?

The answer is that we can and we do . . . but it is done indirectly depending on the condition of the patient. A patient who is an addict, for example, may have no prospect of recovery because of advanced liver disease and has refused to remain abstinent. There is no point in treating this patient for his addiction because it will not be in his best interests to do so. However, the NHS is not refusing to treat him *because* he is an addict – they are refusing to treat him because his lifestyle as an addict makes the treatment *futile*. The treatment can be given to another addict who shows good prospects for recovery, who wants to remain abstinent and has a supportive environment at home. This is indirect rationing at a micro level.

Social responsibility is a big part of society today. We are held accountable for our actions.

As we saw above, the Principle 3b of the NHS Constitution makes reference to social responsibility by recognising that individuals should take some personal responsibility for the health of both themselves and their families.

In reality, there is not a *legal* duty to be kind to yourself or to protect the resources of others. However, it is not outside of the realms of possibility for the NHS to begin charging for A&E admissions in the future, just like we charge for prescriptions now. However, making patients take the blame for their general bad health is a controversial political topic. It cannot work in practice for four main reasons. Firstly, we cannot prove that the bad lifestyle *caused* the disease. The patient may have developed the disease anyway (i.e. genetic factors are involved). In addition to this, patients can cause their own car accidents by using mobile phones while driving and children are commonly reckless when they are playing with friends – do we turn them away too? Secondly, it is commonly the poorer in society who suffer from obesity, diabetes, addiction and general bad health, and so to withdraw public healthcare from this category of patients would lead to social disaster. Thirdly, the risk of bad health and death looms over a lot of these patients but it doesn't seem to stop them from behaving recklessly. A heroin addict, for example, faces a grave risk of death every time he injects, but a threat to withdraw healthcare is unlikely to impact upon his actions.[11] Fourthly, it has been suggested by many doctors that punishing the patient for the relaxed attitudes in society is not the answer. This is why the government have launched their 'Eat Right' and 'Five A Day' campaigns to re-educate patents about feeding their children healthy food and living healthy lives. We are becoming more obese because *society* is slipping towards obesity, not the individual himself.

Lotteries and randomisation

Picking patients at random, or using lotteries to treat patients, would be unpopular with the general public for one clear reason: we all instinctively know who needs treatment and who does not.

A healthcare lottery system for the allocation of medical resources does not occur anywhere in the world. There are two reasons for this: (1) most systems are private and so the patient can pay for her own treatment; and (2) a lottery system would completely ignore patient need. Let us imagine that the NHS implemented a lottery system for treatment. What would happen in the A&E department? The only argument in favour of a lottery-based healthcare system is that it does not discriminate and ensures that healthcare resources are shared out equally amongst society. This is the aim to strive for in the current publicly funded system, but we do not want to cause more deaths than is necessary by implementing a lottery system to meet this goal. The Hippocratic Oath is based on patient need, so it would go against the grain of the medical profession to ignore patient need and treat patients on a random basis. As we saw above, this is also ingrained within the NHS constitution.

We have all heard of a 'postcode lottery' in healthcare. This is where healthcare funds are allocated on a local level, leading to some treatments being more accessible in one region than they are in another. The West Midlands, for example, is the most obese county in the UK, thus requiring more funds for gastric bands. The 'postcode lottery' is even more prevalent since 1 April 2013 when local authorities took control of healthcare funds from Primary Care Trusts which have now been abolished.

The alternative is 'rationing by opinion poll' which would consist of asking the general public where they think the funds should be allocated. However, this is not a good idea for one clear reason: we are not medically qualified. We would not be able to accurately judge the effectiveness of treatments and our decisions may even be coloured by our personal experiences. For example, one community may like to plough funds into detox programmes, whereas another community will probably want to close such programmes down. Emotional decisions may even see an excess of funds to patients who 'deserve' sympathy but are terminal cases (e.g. children with cancer). The elderly and the frail may also be neglected to ensure that when our future grandchildren become ill, they will have access to enough funds.

Going private

This is an idea that is batted about frequently by the general public. Why not abolish the NHS and instal a private healthcare system like most other countries around the world? They seem to cope perfectly well and there is one major advantage: people would strictly

---

[11] It can be argued that the reckless die young and thus will use fewer medical resources throughout their lives, but this does not happen frequently enough these days to hold any weight. We are living longer in general, regardless of our addictions or behaviours.

pay for what they needed. There would be no waste, no unnecessary treatments and no taking advantage of a free system. Patients already choose to seek private fertility treatment because it is quicker and less hurried despite its 25% success rate. So, what is the problem?

Firstly, there are many people who cannot afford health insurance, so, as in the United States, free healthcare would have to be offered to the poorest in society anyway. The elderly in particular would see their insurance premiums shoot up because of the amount of medical care required towards the end of life, and they are the least likely to afford it. Secondly, if a trip to see the doctor cost us the same as an MP3 player, would we go so often? Would we simply wait and see if the symptoms cleared up on their own, thus risking our health and lives? The UK has a good record for medical care – especially the early diagnosis and treatment of cancer – but if we failed to see a doctor when we became unwell, the early diagnosis would never come, leading to an increase in terminal cases. Thirdly, insurance is based on health condition, not wealth (like the current tax system), so those who were sickest would have to pay more insurance. This means that the poorer people in society – such as the unemployed, addicts, the obese and the generally unhealthy – would be paying much more insurance than the wealthy. This is fair because they require more treatment, but they couldn't afford to do so. This leads us onto another problem – a handful of serious health conditions are uninsurable. What would patients with cancer or obesity do? They would have to be treated for free, as they are now, thus requiring the state to run a partial public health service for the increasing number in society who cannot find cover. Fourthly, it would be highly stressful being admitted to hospital knowing that as soon as you were discharged, you would have to pay for every piece of equipment you used, every member of staff who tended to you, and every drug you took. It is not unheard of for patients in the United States to discharge themselves out of hospital too early (or being discharged by staff) because they know that they simply cannot pay for their treatment. In the United Kingdom we have never experienced that concern, because we get our treatment for free.

It should also be remembered that in the UK the public and private sectors do work together. Private healthcare professionals carry out a lot of their work in public hospitals. They can also maintain their private practices. Therefore, a patient who wishes to be seen privately does not always have to move to a different hospital – there are private wards and private staff in some NHS hospitals.

So, is a patient entitled to pay for some private care whilst receiving public healthcare on the NHS? The answer is 'yes'. A patient can decide to pay for a certain aspects of her treatment privately (e.g. an expensive cancer drug that was deemed too expensive by NICE to fund on the NHS) while receiving general care on the NHS. These are known as 'top-up' payments by some professionals. The obvious difficulty with this strategy is the discrepancy between patients, which goes directly against the ethos of the NHS. To solve this problem, patients who choose to fund some of their care privately are kept as separate as possible from public patients (i.e. on a private ward). This is an inconvenience for the 'top-up' patient, but it shows respect to the other patients who cannot afford private care. There are many NHS hospitals that do not have any private facilities, meaning that the 'top-up' patient must travel in order to acquire the private element of her treatment, unless the 'top-up' patient is too sick to travel, in which case the doctor can allow private care to be provided in a public hospital. The NHS Choices webpage provides some invaluable information for patients on this matter.[12]

---

[12] See NHS Choices website: http://www.nhs.uk/choiceintheNHS/Pages/Choicehome.aspx.

You are the prime minister in 2040. You have been told by the NHS that it is about to implode because of excessive demand. You reach a decision to launch a partial NHS, meaning that 50% of the service must go private and invoices must be issued to patients when they check out (like a hotel). Which areas of healthcare are you going to remove from public funds, and how are you going to justify those removals to the furious public in your press conference on the matter?

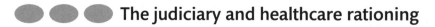 ## The judiciary and healthcare rationing

It has been stated several times already that the courts do not like to get involved in rationing decisions or any other healthcare funding decisions. However, judicial review is available if one of the following is suspected:

- The patient has been deprived of appropriate treatment.
- The decision to deprive was unlawful.
- The decision to deprive was outside of the statutory powers of the health authority.
- The decision to deprive was irrational and unreasonable.[13]
- The decision to deprive was a breach of human rights.

It is important to note that a judicial review cannot overturn a decision simply because it is deemed 'unfair' by the patient. There must be some unlawfulness or irrationality for a judicial review to take place. A patient must accept an unfair decision and the courts will reject cases where the rules were followed but the patient is simply disgruntled by the outcome. This is because public healthcare faces difficult decisions in regards to funding and the courts know they can do nothing about it. There were no legal challenges in the first thirty years of the NHS, suggesting that in recent times we have become more willing to complain, more aware of our rights, and more knowledgeable about treatments.

There is a long line of legal actions brought against health authorities for funding decisions. The timeline starts with *Hincks* (1980) where Lord Denning MR didn't think anything of a delay spanning several years.

CASE EXTRACT	*R v Secretary of State for Social Services ex parte Hincks* (1980) 1 BMLR 93

Facts: A patient had been on the waiting list for orthopaedic surgery for several years and sought a declaration that the Secretary of State was in breach of his duty under the National Health Service Act 1977 (now 2006) to 'provide throughout England and Wales to such extent as he considers necessary to meet all reasonable requirements (a) hospital accommodation and (c) medical services'.

Held: The action was dismissed.

Lord Denning MR: It cannot be supposed that the Secretary of State has to provide all the latest equipment. [...] It cannot be supposed that the Secretary of State has to

→

---

[13] In accordance with *Wednesbury* unreasonableness: no reasonable health authority could have come to the same decision. *Associated Provincial Picture Houses Ltd* v *Wednesbury Corp* [1948] 1 KB 223.

provide all the kidney machines which are asked for, or for all the new developments such as heart transplants in every case where people would benefit from them. It cannot be that the Secretary of State has a duty to provide everything that is asked for in the changed circumstances which have come about. That includes the numerous pills that people take nowadays: it cannot be said that he had to provide all these free for everybody. The Secretary of State says that he is doing the best he can with the financial resources available to him: and I do not think that he can be faulted in the matter.

This decision is intriguing. The lords would not come to this conclusion today because we have tests of reasonableness and proportion. The timeline continued with *Walker* (1987). There is a particularly strong feeling of opposition from the court in this case, who clearly felt protective of the NHS and did not want to interfere with their decisions to allocate resources.

CASE EXTRACT	*R v Central Birmingham Health Authority ex parte Walker* (1987) 3 BMLR 32

Facts: A premature baby required a non-urgent operation, but the surgery was postponed on a number of occasions because there was a shortage of nurses. The mother applied for a judicial review of the decisions.

Held: The Court of Appeal refused the application because sources were not infinite.

Sir John Donaldson MR: Resources are, and perhaps always will be, finite. It is not for this court, or indeed any court, to substitute its own judgment for the judgment of those who are responsible for the allocation of resources.

The reaction was even more hostile in the case of *Collier* (1988), which involved an intensive care unit.

CASE EXTRACT	*R v Central Birmingham Health Authority ex parte Collier* (1988) (unreported) Court of Appeal (Civ)

Facts: Matthew Collier (a young child) had already undergone a number of unsuccessful heart operations. He now needed open heart surgery. He was on the top of the waiting list but the operation was postponed several times because there was a lack of beds and nurses in the intensive care unit. The father sought a judicial review.

Held: The Court of Appeal rejected the review.

Sir Stephen Brown: This is not the forum in which a court can properly express opinions upon the way in which national resources are allocated or distributed. There may be very good reasons why the resources in this case do not allow all the beds in the hospital to be used at this particular time.

[...] From the legal point of view, in the absence of any evidence which could begin to show that there was a failure to allocate resources in this instance in circumstances which would make it unreasonable in the *Wednesbury* sense to make those resources available, there can be no arguable case. [...] The courts of this country cannot arrange the lists in the hospital, and, if it is not evidence that they are not being arranged properly due to some unreasonableness in the *Wednesbury* sense on the part of the authority, the courts cannot, and should not, be asked to intervene.

The cases of *Walker* and *Collier* show a strong reluctance on the part of the courts to intervene with the daily grind of the NHS, but if a similar case was heard today, the court would have no problem in deciding that the hospital should do more to make sure that the patient only has to wait a *reasonable* amount of time, including sending the patient to another hospital if necessary. The courts in the next case of *Re J* (1992) emphasised that if a court was to get involved in rationing decisions, it would be accountable for the lack of resources available to the other patients who needed access to that resource, and this was not fair on anyone.

CASE EXTRACT

Re J (A Minor) (Child in Care: Medical Treatment), Re [1992] 4 All ER 614

Facts: A toddler was brain damaged after a fall and there was an issue as to whether he should be placed on a life support machine when he ran into breathing difficulties.

Held: It was decided that he should be treated in accordance with the opinions of the specialists as to what was in his best interests and the courts could not tell the doctors what to do. This was not primarily a rationing case, but Lord Donaldson MR emphasised that there are not always enough resources to go around and they could not tell doctors what to make available.

Lord Donaldson MR: I would stress the absolute undesirability of the court making an order which may have the effect of compelling a doctor or health authority to make available scarce resources (both human and material) to a particular child, without knowing whether or not there are other patients to whom those resources might more advantageously be devoted.

This lack of support for patients continued in the case of *B* (1995), which was viewed as so strict that it attracted considerable media attention.

CASE EXTRACT

R v Cambridge DHA, ex parte B (No.1) [1995] 1 WLR 898

Facts: Jaymee Bowen was diagnosed with leukaemia when she was five and ten. The doctors agreed that the only possible treatment was intensive chemotherapy and a second bone marrow transplant, but they also agreed that they would be very unlikely to succeed and thus not in her best interests. A doctor in London was willing to treat her privately at the cost of £75,000. The father sought a referral from the

Cambridge Health Authority to pay for the treatment, but this was refused. The father sought a judicial review of this decision.

Held: Laws J (at first instance) asked the health authority to justify its decision to refuse funds in a case where the life of a ten-year-old child might be saved because 'tolling the bell of tight resources' was not enough of a reason. The Court of Appeal overturned this judgment. The health authority was found to have acted rationally and fairly so court intervention was therefore not appropriate.

Sir Thomas Bingham MR (at page 906): I have no doubt that in a perfect world any treatment with a patient, or a patient's family, sought would be provided if doctors were willing to give it, no matter how much it cost, particularly when a life was potentially at stake. It would however, in my view, be shutting one's eyes to the real world if the court were to proceed on the basis that we do live in such a world. It is common knowledge that health authorities of all kinds are constantly pressed to make ends meet. They cannot pay their nurses as much as they would like; they cannot provide all the treatments they would like; they cannot purchase all the extremely expensive medical equipment they would like; they cannot carry out all the research they would like; they cannot build all the hospitals and specialist units they would like. Difficult and agonising judgments have to be made as to how a limited budget is best allocated to the maximum advantage of the maximum number of patients. This is not a judgment which the court can make.

There is a line in Sir Thomas Bingham's judgment that raises a red flag: 'a limited budget is best allocated to the maximum advantage of the maximum number of patients' – this is a strictly utilitarian approach. The NHS does not take this approach when treating its patients. Rather, it treats patients according to their medical need if it is in their best interests to do so. The doctors of Jaymee Bowen came to the conclusion that the treatment was not in her best interests, so by phrasing his decision around utilitarian principles, Sir Thomas Bingham gave the impression that the referral was rejected because there was not enough money. However the Chief Executive of the Cambridge Health Authority argued that: (1) their refusal was not motivated by a shortage of money at all, (2) the case had nothing to do with healthcare rationing, and (3) the expert opinion was that the treatment requested by her father was ineffective and inappropriate.[14]

The tide started to turn in the lesser known case of *R v North Derbyshire HA, ex parte Fisher* (1997) 38 BMLR 76, where the courts criticised North Derbyshire Health Authority for failing to fund a particular drug (Beta-Interferon) unless it was part of a clinical trial and since there were no trials planned, it was effectively a blanket ban on the drug. The courts found that, according to *Wednesbury* reasonableness, North Derbyshire Health Authority had acted unreasonably in failing to prescribe the drug.

The first human rights case emerged at this point. There are several human rights that a patient could use to argue that they have been unfairly denied treatment:

---

[14] His argument was published: Stephen Thornton, 'The Child B Case – Reflections of a Chief' (1997) 314 *British Medical Journal* 1838.

- Article 2: the right to life.
- Article 3: protection from inhuman or degrading treatment and torture.
- Article 8: the right to a private and family life.
- Article 14: freedom from discrimination.[15]

Article 2 is a dual right in that a health authority must not cause a patient to die and it must do everything it can to support life.[16] However, it must not impose an impossible burden upon health authorities.[17] The Court of Appeal was quick to dismiss actions under remaining Articles 3, 8 and 14 in *Lancashire* (2000):

CASE EXTRACT

R v North West Lancashire HA, ex parte A [2000] 1 WLR 977

Facts: A (and two others) applied for judicial review of the health authority's decision not to fund gender reassignment (transsexual) surgery. It was argued that this breached Article 3, 8 and 14.

Held: At first instance it was held that the health authority had acted unlawfully because it failed to consider the most appropriate and effective treatment for the underlying illness. The health authority appealed. The appeal court found that human rights were not engaged in this case, but the health authority needed a clearer policy (appeal dismissed).

Buxton LJ (at pages 1001–2): It is plain that in this case there has occurred no interference with either the applicants' private life or with their sexuality. […] Such an interference could hardly be founded on a refusal to fund medical treatment. […] It is impossible to see how the applicants have been the victims of discrimination on grounds of sex. […] [Treatment] has been refused not because of that sexuality, but on grounds of allocation of resources.

This result may have been disappointing for the patients, but they were partially victorious. The appeal by the health authority was actually dismissed, because even though a policy to give gender reassignment a low priority was not *completely* irrational, such a policy should still consider individual needs and recognise the possibility of exceptional cases. The health authority had accepted transsexualism as an illness, but their policy was to support it using psychiatric intervention only. The policy did not reflect the clinical judgment upon which it was based (i.e. that transsexualism was an illness). This was a highly significant judgment and heralded a turning of the tide. Auld LJ provided further explanation and a legal test.

---

[15] The European Convention on Human Rights 1950, incorporated into UK law in the Human Rights Act 1998.

[16] This will include preventing a mentally ill patient from committing suicide if he is a known risk: *Savage v South Essex Partnership NHS Foundation Trust* [2008] UKHL 74.

[17] This was held in *Osman v United Kingdom (23452/94)* [1999] 1 FLR 193.

> **CASE EXTRACT**
>
> **Auld LJ** (at pages 991–2, 995): It is natural that each authority, in establishing its own priorities, will give greater priority to life-threatening and other grave illnesses than to others obviously less demanding of medical intervention. [...] Authorities might reasonably differ as to precisely where in the scale transsexualism should be placed and as to the criteria for determining the appropriateness and need for treatment of it in individual cases. [...] In my view, a policy to place transsexualism low in an order of priorities of illnesses for treatment and to deny it treatment save in exceptional circumstances such as overriding clinical need is not in principle irrational, provided that the policy genuinely recognises the possibility of there being an overriding clinical need and requires each request for treatment to be considered on its individual merits. However, in establishing priorities it is vital for an authority: (1) accurately to assess the nature and seriousness of each type of illness; (2) to determine the effectiveness of various forms of treatment for it; and (3) to give proper effect to that assessment and that determination in the formulation and individual application of its policy. [...] The authority should reformulate its policy to give proper weight to its acknowledgement that transsexualism is an illness, apply that weighting when setting its level of priority for treatment and make effective provision for exceptions in individual cases from any general policy restricting the funding of treatment for it.

Auld LJ recognised that health authorities are entitled to prioritise treatments for their local area. He also admitted that it would make sense for a health authority to register the treatment of transsexualism lower than the treatment for heart disease or kidney failure and confirmed that it is not completely irrational to give the treatment of trans-sexualism a low priority as long as the policy recognises an overriding clinical need (e.g. an exceptional case) and requires each case to be judged on its individual merits in order to reveal this clinical need. A three part test is thus established: a health authority must (1) assess the nature and seriousness of the illness; (2) determine the effectiveness of its treatments, and (3) give a proper assessment to reveal patient need, when justifying its priorities. The health authority in *Lancashire* had to reformulate its policy to recognise transsexualism as an illness and not a psychiatric disorder, apply that weighting when setting its level of priority, and make provision for exceptional cases if the general policy restricts the treatment. The *Lancaster* judgment is very important: it heralds the moment when blanket bans on certain treatments were ruled to be unlawful despite the stretched nature of NHS resources. However, a health authority can still refuse to fund a treatment as long as they justify their decision by assessing the illness, determining the effectiveness of the treatment, give a proper assessment of patient need and make allowances for exceptional cases. *Lancaster* therefore adds transparency to rationing decisions and forces health authorities to examine the fairness of their priorities.

The case law continues in *Coughlan* (2001), in which the Court of Appeal found that the health authority was obliged to keep its promise to provide a 'care home for life' even though it could no longer afford to run the expensive home and was going to provide a cheaper alternative.

CASE EXTRACT	*R v North and East Devon HA ex parte Coughlan* [2001] QB 213

Facts: The patient, Miss Coughlan, was severely disabled after a traffic accident and needed constant care. She was moved into Mardon House and was assured that it would be her 'home for life'. Three years later, the health authority stated that it had to close because of costs. The health authority accepted that it had made a commitment to the residents to provide a 'home for life' so it pledged to continue to finance the care of the residents. Miss Coughlan applied for a judicial review of the decision to close Mardon House.

Held: The residents were entitled to the benefit promised, which was a 'home for life' in Mardon House.

Lord Woolf MR (at pages 253–4): [The health authority] considered that [...] the provision of care services to the current residents had become 'excessively expensive' having regard to the needs of the majority of disabled people in the authority's area, [...] but the cheaper option favoured by the health authority misses the essential point of the promise which had been given. The fact is that the health authority has not offered to the applicant an equivalent facility to replace what was promised to her. The health authority's undertaking to fund her care for the remainder of her life is substantially different in nature and effect from the earlier promise that care for her would be provided at Mardon House. That place would be her home for as long as she chose to live there. We have no hesitation in concluding that the decision to move Miss Coughlan against her will and in breach of the health authority's own promise was in the circumstances unfair. It was unfair because it frustrated her legitimate expectation of having a home for life in Mardon House. There was no overriding public interest which justified it.

The judgment in *Coughlan* is bizarre. The health authority in this case could not afford to run the care home anymore, and they were entitled to decide to close it. The courts have previously held that they have no place to interfere in funding or rationing decisions made by health authorities. Therefore, the decision by the health authority in *Coughlan* to simply move the residents to another care home is perfectly legitimate, lawful and rational. What, then, upset Lord Woolf? It appears that the health authority made a promise to Miss Coughlan that she would live at Mardon House for the *rest of her life*, and Lord Woolf took offence to the breaking of this promise. The decision in *Coughlan* can be resigned to the 'oddities' drawer because *Wednesbury* reasonableness was clearly met but the courts chose to base their decision on the perspective of the patient instead, leading to a different outcome.

Article 3 – freedom from inhuman and degrading treatment and torture – was raised in the next case. Munby J was forced to deny that lengthy delays in healthcare were not inhuman.

CASE EXTRACT

R (on the application of Watts) v Bedford Primary Care Trust [2003] EWHC 2228

Facts: A patient had to wait a whole year for a hip replacement operation on the NHS, and this was argued to be inhuman and torturous because of the pain and suffering endured.

Held: The suffering while waiting for a hip replacement was not nearly as grave as the level of torture required to engage Article 3.

Munby J (at pages 725–6): Article 3 is not engaged unless the 'ill treatment' in question attains a minimum level of severity and involves actual bodily injury or intense physical or mental suffering. However, that is not this case. Making every allowance for the constant pain and suffering that the claimant was having to ensure – and I do not seek in any way to minimise it – the simple fact in my judgment is that nothing she had to ensure was so severe or so humiliating as to engage Article 3.

The patient in *Watts* must have been disappointed, but Bedford Primary Care Trust did not inflict any inhuman treatment upon her. It would have been different if, for example, Mrs Watts was in hospital and she was not looked after properly, leaving her with bed sores and unable to use the toilet.[18]

The remaining cases in the timeline focus on the availability of expensive cancer drugs. This is a controversial topic that has made a lot of national press and is a difficult issue for patients and their family members. Cancer drugs are notoriously expensive. The NHS cannot afford to pay for all of them using public funds. As we saw in *Lancashire* (2000), a health authority must make allowances for 'exceptional cases'. The case of *Swindon* questions whether this is fair.

CASE EXTRACT

R (on the application of Rogers) v Swindon Primary Care Trust [2006] EWCA Civ 392

Facts: Ann Rogers suffered from breast cancer and had a mastectomy. She asked to be treated with a new cancer drug called Herceptin. The drug was unlicensed and had not been appraised by NICE. Swindon Primary Care Trust decided that she was not an exceptional case because she was in the same position as all other breast cancer sufferers. She sought legal advice.

Held: The judicial review at first instance was rejected, but the Court of Appeal agreed with Ann Rogers that Swindon Primary Care Trust had acted irrationally. The test for exceptionality was meaningless because all women with breast cancer (at stage one) were exactly the same. It was a meaningless test.

Sir Anthony Clarke MR (at paras 63, 81, 82): The essential question is whether the policy was rational, and, in deciding whether it is rational or not, the court must consider whether there are any relevant exceptional circumstances which could justify the PCT refusing treatment to one woman within the eligible group but

➡

---

[18] It was confirmed in *Price v United Kingdom* (33394/96) (2002) 34 EHRR 1285 that if a patient is so badly looked after that they develop bed sores and cannot access the toilet it is degrading treatment under Article 3.

granting it to another. The PCT has not put any clinical or medical evidence before the court to suggest any such clinical distinction could be made. In these circumstances there is no rational basis for distinguishing between patients within the eligible group on the basis of exceptional clinical circumstances any more than on the basis of personal, let alone social, circumstances. For these reasons we have reached the conclusion that the policy of the PCT is irrational.

The rationale behind Sir Anthony Clarke's decision is clear: Swindon Primary Care Trust could not discriminate against Ann Rogers based on her personal characteristics and there were no clinical or medical circumstances to justify their decision to refuse to fund Herceptin for her. Therefore, the *Swindon* case establishes that, if a local authority or NHS trust[19] wishes to apply the exceptionality test to a patient, and this is inevitable as long as resources remain scarce and costly, they cannot use personal or non-clinical characteristics to justify their decision to refuse funding. The *Swindon* decision was seen by many patients as a victory for the lone man and it made the national news, but it does not provide an open-door policy to fund every cancer drug. The scarcity and cost of cancer drugs remains an issue and the exceptionality test is still used, but there are very few acceptable grounds upon which to say that one patient in an eligible group is more 'exceptional' than another in the same eligible group.

The next case illustrates what happens when the exceptionality test is accepted as rational by the courts, but it is not applied fairly to a cancer patient.

CASE EXTRACT

R (on the application of Otley) v Barking and Dagenham NHS Primary Care Trust [2007] EWHC 1927

Facts: Ms Otley was diagnosed with cancer and did not respond well to chemotherapy. A new drug, Avastin, was found on the internet and it was licensed for use in the United States and across Europe, but not in the United Kingdom. Ms Otley paid for five cycles of Avastin and she responded very well to it, but when her doctor (Dr Raouf) applied to the NHS Trust to fund another five prescriptions, it was refused. Ms Otley sought a judicial review.

Held: The exceptionality policy was found to be perfectly rational, but it had not been applied fairly to Ms Otley. The courts decided that she was an exceptional case because: there were no other options available to her, she was young and reasonably fit, she had not responded well to chemotherapy but had responded very well to Avastin, and another five cycles would be unlikely to jeopardise the ability to fund treatment for other similar patients.

Mitting J (at paras 20, 26, 27): Ms Otley was at the time when the decision was made, as she had been throughout, relatively fit. She was young by comparison with the cohort of patients suffering from this condition. Her reactions to other treatment, in particular to Irinotecan plus 5FU had been adverse. Her specific clinical history suggested that her reaction to a combination of chemotherapy and Avastin had been of benefit to her. By comparison with other patients, she, unlike many of those the subject of the studies, had suffered no significant side-effects from a cocktail which included Avastin.

→

---
[19] Primary Care Trusts were abolished on 1 April 2013.

I approach my task on a very conventional basis. The question which I have to ask is whether or not the reasoning and decision of the Panel was rational and so lawful on *Wednesbury* grounds. I have identified already respects in which in my view the decision of this panel was not rational. There were no other treatments in practice available to Ms Otley among those that could be prescribed within normal National Health Service standards which were likely to have any benefit for her. The Panel did not take into account the slim but important chance that treatment including Avastin could prolong Ms Otley's life by more than a few months. On any fair minded view of the exceptionality criteria identified in the critical analysis document, her case was exceptional. For those reasons, this Panel's reasoning was in my view flawed [...] [but] the policy is entirely rational and sensible.

The young and reasonably fit patient in this case was not responding to chemotherapy. Mitting J could list several clinical reasons why she should be placed in the 'exceptional' category and he supported the exceptionality policy – which he said was 'entirely rational and sensible' – but held that the decision to apply it to her and the decision not to fund her was flawed. An additional factor in favour of the patient was no doubt the cost of the drug: five cycles at £1,500 each was not thought by Mitting J to be significant enough to jeopardise funding for other patients.

In the final relevant case about expensive cancer drugs and exceptionality policies, Burnett J finally set out a test to be applied in cases such as these. It is not an exceptionality test, but it is a reminder of when to seek a judicial review. This is helpful to future patients and NHS trusts.

CASE EXTRACT

R (on the application of Murphy) v *Salford Primary Care Trust* [2008] EWHC 1908

Facts: The patient (M) applied for judicial review of the refusal by the NHS Trust (S) to provide funding for a drug to treat her cancer. The drug, which was too expensive to be ordinarily administered, could not cure her, but it might extend her life by a few months. The policy was that treatment which would otherwise be excluded could be considered in exceptional circumstances but on an examination of the patient, she was not exceptional and S refused to make the drug available. M submitted that the policy failed to consider her personal characteristics (e.g. psychiatric harm) before considering her case as a whole.

Held: Decision for M. The panel was not expected to strip down its decision but it should consider individual characteristics 'in the round'. The decision of the NHS Trust was quashed and the case was sent back to the panel to decide again (decision unknown).

Burnett J (at para 6): The legal principles that are in play are not controversial:

- When an NHS body makes a decision about whether to fund a treatment in an individual patient's case it is entitled to take into account the financial restraints on its budget as well as the patient's circumstances.
- Decisions about how to allocate scarce resources between patients are ones with which the Courts will not usually intervene absent irrationality on the part of the decision-maker. There are severe limits on the ability of the Court to intervene.
- The Court's role is not to express opinions as to the effectiveness of medical treatment or the merits of medical judgment.
- It is lawful for an NHS body to decide to decline to fund treatment save in exceptional circumstances, provided that it is possible to envisage such circumstances.

The current position is clear: the courts are reluctant to get involved in rationing decisions unless irrationality is suspected. The 'in the round' argument is interesting – it simply means that all clinical factors must be considered *together* as well as individually. This would make the decision *not* to fund a certain treatments easier for patients to understand, and it may prevent them from seeking a judicial review.

THINKING POINT

The cases above show two approaches to judicial review: *Wednesbury* reasonableness looks at the rationality of a decision, and the human rights cases look at the *proportionality* of the decision (e.g. the balance to be struck between the competing interests). Which approach do you think is better for the courts to use when investigating accusations of unfair rationing, and why?

Travelling for treatment: Brits and asylum seekers

Rationing decisions include non-citizens too. The rest of the world is aware of the British National Health Service and how it provides UK citizens with 'free' healthcare, leading to a number of sick tourists arriving in the United Kingdom to use our services for free. (Pregnant mothers are one example of 'healthcare tourist' that has been featured in the media recently.) Should we provide treatment for these tourists and asylum seekers, or should we make clear our refusal to provide treatment well before they reach UK hospitals?

Asylum seekers

Students are often surprised to learn that the courts are especially strict with asylum seekers when it comes to accessing our healthcare services. The answer has typically been 'no treatment' when the patient has taken their plea to court. The relevant law can be found in the National Health Service Act 2006, which states under section 175(2) that 'persons not ordinarily resident in Great Britain' can be charged for healthcare services.[20] This begs the question, what does 'resident' mean? Is an asylum seeker 'resident' in the UK as he awaits the decision on his status? This question was put before the courts as recently as 2010 by a failed asylum seeker in the *A* case.

CASE EXTRACT

R (on the application of A) v Secretary of State for Health [2010] 1 WLR 279

Facts: The Secretary of State appealed against a decision ([2008] EWHC 855) that a failed asylum seeker (X – a Palestinian) was ordinarily and lawfully resident in the United Kingdom for the purposes of obtaining NHS medical treatment. X, who suffered from a medical condition, was refused leave to enter. The issues were whether (i) a failed asylum seeker could ordinarily be resident in the UK; (ii) X was

→

---

[20] There are exceptions for Accident and Emergency services, compulsory mental health treatment and students from abroad. Tourists will normally have travel insurance.

lawfully resident in the UK; (iii) an NHS Trust had any discretion to withhold treatment from a failed asylum seeker. X argued that a person who claimed asylum had voluntarily adopted an abode in the UK and was in the UK for a settled purpose.

Held: The Court agreed that a health authority had discretion as to whether to treat a failed asylum seeker based on the facts (i.e. how likely it was that he could pay) and the words 'ordinarily resident' were to be given their ordinary meaning: the purpose of the 2006 Act was to provide a service for *the people of England* and that did not include those who ought not to be in the UK such as failed asylum seekers. An asylum seeker could also not establish ordinary residence when he was in a 'state of limbo' about his status.

Ward LJ (at paras 55, 59–62): The Secretary of State's duty prescribed by section 1 [of the National Health Service Act 2006] is to continue the promotion in England of a comprehensive health service designed to secure improvement in the health 'of the people of England'. Note that it is the people *of* England, not the people *in* England, which suggests that the beneficiaries of this free health service are to be those with some link to England so as to be part and parcel of the fabric of the place. [...] This strongly suggests that, as a rule, the benefits were not intended by Parliament to be bestowed on those who ought not to be here. [...] He is not free to come and go as he chooses. He may be at liberty – at large – but he is like a man on bail. [...] While he is at large he is liable to restrictions, e.g. as to his residence, and he is subject to further detention. [...] That being his position, can he fairly be said to establish his ordinary residence while in that state of limbo? In my judgment, whether he is an at-port applicant or an in-country applicant, he cannot. [...] Failed asylum seekers ought not to be here. They should never have come here in the first place and after their claims have finally been dismissed they are only here until arrangements can be made to secure their return, even if, in some cases, that return may be a long way off. Whereas exceptions affording free medical treatment are made under regulation 4(1)(c) of the [National Health Service (Charges to Overseas Visitors) Regulations 1989 (SI 1989/306)] for those accepted as refugees and those whose claims for asylum have not yet been finally determined, no exception is made for *failed* asylum seekers. [...] The result may be most unfortunate for those in ill-health like the claimant for they may now be at the mercy of the hospitals' discretion whether to treat them or not.

It was accepted by Ward LJ that 'immediately necessary treatment' can be given to an asylum seeker, regardless of his ability to pay, in order to enable him to return to his home country in accordance with the National Health Service (Charges to Overseas Visitors) Regulations 1989 (SI 1989/306). This will usually be life-saving treatment or childbirth. However, the general tone of the *A* case was that a failed asylum seeker, or an asylum seeker in limbo, could not claim free healthcare because he was not 'ordinarily resident' in the United Kingdom. NHS trusts have discretion as to whether to provide other types of treatments.

In slightly earlier cases the courts began to sharpen their knives in regards to the human rights of asylum seekers seeking free medical treatment. Article 3 was engaged in *D* v *United Kingdom*, where the asylum seeker was desperately ill. The courts were satisfied that because he was near death, his removal would have been torture. However, this case was shown to be the exception in the cases that followed it.

CASE EXTRACT

D v United Kingdom (3020/96) (1997) 24 EHRR 423

Facts: D, a national of St Kitts, was found in possession of cocaine upon his arrival in the UK and was convicted of illegally importing a controlled drug. By the time he was released from prison, he was in the advanced stages of AIDS and was provided with accommodation and care by a UK charity, as well as receiving medical treatment for his condition. The immigration authorities ordered D's removal to St Kitts. D applied to the ECHR, contending that his removal would breach Article 3 of the European Convention on Human Rights, as he would not receive adequate medical treatment at home and had no family in St Kitts who could care for him.

Held: Application allowed. States had the right to control the entry and residence of aliens and to impose severe sanctions for the commission of drug trafficking offences, but Article 3 was an absolute right and it applied regardless of the conduct of the individual concerned. Withdrawal of the care, support and treatment would have serious consequences for D, and his removal to St Kitts would expose him to a real risk that he would die in distressing circumstances amounting to inhuman treatment. D's case was exceptional and involved compelling humanitarian factors.

Judge Pettiti (at paras 51–3): The Court notes that the applicant is in the advanced states of a terminal and incurable illness. At the date of the hearing, it was observed that there had been a marked decline in his condition and he had to be transferred to a hospital. His condition was giving rise to concern. The limited quality of life he now enjoys results from the availability of sophisticated treatment and medication in the United Kingdom and the care and kindness administered by a charitable organisation. He has been counselled on how to approach death and has formed bonds with his carers. The abrupt withdrawal of these facilities will entail the most dramatic consequences for him. It is not disputed that his removal will hasten his death. There is a serious danger that the conditions of adversity which await him in St Kitts will further reduce his already limited life expectancy and subject him to acute mental and physical suffering. [...] There is no evidence of any other form of moral or social support, nor has it been shown whether the applicant would be guaranteed a bed in either of the hospitals on the island. [...] In view of these exceptional circumstances and bearing in mind the critical stage now reached in the applicant's fatal illness, the implementation of the decision to remove him to St Kitts would amount to inhuman treatment by the respondent State in violation of Article 3.

The European Court showed compassion for the patient in *D* (1997) because he was so close to death that he required palliative care. This case set a strong precedent: the patient must literally by *dying,* or have 'exceptional circumstances' in order for him to stay in the United Kingdom. This was reinforced in the cases of *Bensaid* (2001), *Razgar* (2004), *ZT* (2005) and *N* (2008).

CASE EXTRACT	*Bensaid v United Kingdom* **(44599/98) (2001) 33 EHRR 10**

Facts: B, an Algerian national, came to the UK in 1989 as a visitor and married a UK citizen in 1993. He began receiving treatment for schizophrenia on the NHS. The Secretary of State decided to remove B on the grounds that his marriage was one of convenience. B claimed that his removal would violate his human rights under Articles 3 and 8 because the difficulties in obtaining the necessary treatment in Algeria would amount to his suffering inhuman and degrading treatment and a violation of his right to respect for his private life.

Held: Refusing the application, B could obtain treatment for his condition at a hospital 75 kilometres from his home village and the fact that it would be harder to obtain was not conclusive for the purposes of Article 3, which had a very high threshold (Article 8 was not engaged, because his 'family life' was an illegal marriage).

Judge Costa (The President) (at paras 36–8, 41): In the present case, the applicant is suffering from a long-term mental illness, schizophrenia. He is currently receiving medication, olanzapine, which assists him in managing his symptoms. If he returns to Algeria, this drug will no longer be available to him free as an outpatient. He is not enrolled in any social insurance fund and cannot claim any reimbursement. It is, however, the case that the drug would be available to him if he was admitted as an inpatient and that it would be potentially available on payment as an outpatient. It is also the case that other medication, used in the management of mental illness, is likely to be available. [...] The difficulties in obtaining medication and the stresses inherent in returning to this part of Algeria, where there is violence and active terrorism, are alleged to endanger seriously his health. [...] The Court considers that the suffering associated with such a relapse could, in principle, fall within the scope of Article 3. The Court observes, however, that the applicant faces the risk of relapse even if he stays in the United Kingdom as his illness is long term and requires constant management. [...] The applicant has argued, in particular, that other drugs are less likely to be of benefit to his condition, and also that the option of becoming an inpatient should be a last resort. Nonetheless medical treatment is available to the applicant in Algeria. The fact that the applicant's circumstances in Algeria would be less favourable than those enjoyed by him in the United Kingdom is not decisive from the point of view of Article 3 of the Convention. [...] The Court finds, therefore, that the implementation of the decision to remove the applicant to Algeria would not violate Article 3 of the Convention.

The European Court in *Bensaid* seemed to be swayed by the fact that the claimant could receive very similar treatment in his home country and his risk of relapse could follow him there. In *Razgar* (2004) the health of the claimant was not sufficiently serious to engage Article 3, so he tried to argue that a withdrawal of healthcare for his post-traumatic stress disorder would engage Article 8 instead.

CASE EXTRACT

R (on the application of Razgar) v Secretary of State for the Home Department (No. 2) [2004] 2 AC 368

Facts: R was an Iraqi of Kurdish origin who had been refused asylum in Germany. In 1999 he travelled to the UK and claimed asylum. The Secretary of State proposed to remove R but he resisted removal on the grounds that it would violate his human rights under Article 8 because he was receiving psychiatric treatment for depression and post-traumatic stress disorder arising from his alleged ill treatment in Iraq and his fear of ill treatment in Germany.

Held: Dismissing the appeal by the Secretary of State, reliance could, in principle, be placed on Article 8 to resist a removal decision, because of the consequences on the mental health of the patient. However, the threshold of successful reliance was high (the case was to be placed before an adjudicator).

Lord Bingham (at paras 4, 9): Removal cannot be resisted merely on the ground that medical treatment or facilities are better or more accessible in the removing country than in that to which the applicant is to be removed. This was made plain in *D* v *United Kingdom* (1997) 24 EHRR 423. [...] I have no doubt that the court would adopt the same approach to an application based on Article 8. It would indeed frustrate the proper and necessary object of immigration control in the more advanced member states of the Council of Europe if illegal entrants requiring medical treatment could not, save in exceptional cases, be removed to the less developed countries of the world where comparable medical facilities were not available. [...] Reliance may in principle be placed on Article 8 to resist an expulsion decision, even where the main emphasis is not on the severance of family and social ties which the applicant has enjoyed in the expelling country but on the consequences for his mental health of removal to the receiving country. The threshold of successful reliance is high, but if the facts are strong enough Article 8 may in principle be invoked.

Baroness Hale (at para 59): There clearly must be a strong case before the Article is even engaged . . . only the most compelling humanitarian considerations are likely to prevail over the legitimate aims of immigration control or public safety. The expelling state is required to assess the strength of the threat and strike that balance. It is not required to compare the adequacy of the health care available in the two countries. The question is whether removal to the foreign country will have a sufficiently adverse effect upon the applicant.

The appeal by the Secretary of State may have been dismissed in *Razgar* because Article 8 could technically be engaged, but the courts made it clear that the claimant needed to prove a sufficiently serious detriment along the lines of *D* v *United Kingdom* (1997). The issue was to go to an adjudicator who could make a better decision as to the state of mind of the claimant (decision unknown).

The test of exceptionality is clearly hard to meet for asylum seekers, but this is because poor healthcare and disease is not 'exceptional' in their home countries. This point was made in *ZT* (2005) where the courts admitted it was almost impossible for a clamant to prove that suffering from HIV in a poorer county was exceptional.

CASE EXTRACT

ZT v *Secretary of State for the Home Department* [2005] EWCA Civ 1421

Facts: T, who was a citizen of Zimbabwe, had arrived in the UK as a visitor and shortly thereafter was diagnosed with HIV. She then started treatment which controlled the disease. She applied for leave to remain in the UK on the basis that such treatment would be difficult or impossible to obtain on her return to Zimbabwe – it had to be paid for personally and was not available from medical aid schemes. T appealed against the tribunal decision on the grounds that her case was exceptional but the tribunal had ignored this.

Held: The test that exceptional circumstances were required to prevent a removal was a matter for the tribunal to decide. Failure to accept that a case was exceptional did not amount to an error of law unless the tribunal had rejected a plain, obvious and uncontroversial issue.

Sedley LJ (at para 41): If HIV were a rare affliction [...] the courts would have little hesitation in holding removal of sufferers to [their home] countries to be inhuman treatment contrary to Article 3. It is the sheer volume of suffering now reaching these shores that has driven the Home Office, the Immigration Appellate Authority and the courts to find jurisprudential reasons for holding that neither Article 3 or Article 8 can ordinarily avail HIV sufferers who face removal.

In the last case of *N* (2008), Article 3 was raised by an asylum seeker with HIV. This case confirmed the status of *D* v *United Kingdom* (1997).

CASE EXTRACT

N v *United Kingdom* (2008) 47 EHRR 39 (European Court of Human Rights)

Facts: N, a Ugandan citizen, was admitted to hospital on entering the UK and was diagnosed with HIV and developed AIDS. However, after treatment in the UK, her condition stabilised and her life expectancy was very positive. If returned home to Uganda, her life expectancy would be less than one year. She appealed against the decision of an immigration tribunal to deport her on the grounds that Article 3 was engaged and that she would suffer inhuman and degrading treatment.

Held: Dismissing the appeal, N would be deprived her of life saving treatment, but it was not sufficiently 'extreme' to engage Article 3.

Judge Costa (The President) (at paras 42–4, 50): Aliens who are subject to expulsion cannot in principle claim any entitlement to remain in the territory of a contracting state in order to continue to benefit from medical, social or other forms of assistance and services provided by the expelling state. The fact that the applicant's circumstances, including his life expectancy, would be significantly reduced if he were to be removed from the contracting state is not sufficient in itself to give rise to breach of Article 3. The decision to remove an alien who is suffering from a serious mental or physical illness to a country where the facilities for the treatment of that

→

illness are inferior to those available in the contracting state may raise an issue under Article 3, but only in a very exceptional case, where the humanitarian grounds against the removal are compelling. In the *D* case the very exceptional circumstances were that the applicant was critically ill and appeared to be close to death, could not be guaranteed any nursing or medical care in his country of origin and had no family there willing or able to care for him or provide him with even a basic level of food, shelter or social support. The Court does not exclude that there may be other very exceptional cases where the humanitarian considerations are equally compelling. However, it considers that it should maintain the high threshold set in *D* v *United Kingdom* and applied in its subsequent case law, which it regards as correct in principle, given that in such cases the alleged future harm would emanate not from the intentional acts or omissions of public authorities or non-state bodies, but instead from a naturally occurring illness and the lack of sufficient resources to deal with it in the receiving country. [...] Advances in medical science, together with social and economic differences between countries, entail that the level of treatment available in the contracting state and the country of origin may vary considerably. [...] Article 3 does not place an obligation on the contracting state to alleviate such disparities through the provision of free and unlimited healthcare to all aliens without a right to stay within its jurisdiction. A finding to the contrary would place too great a burden on the contracting states. [...] The Court accepts that the quality of the applicant's life, and her life expectancy, would be affected if she were returned to Uganda. The applicant is not, however, at the present time critically ill. The rapidity of the deterioration which she would suffer and the extent to which she would be able to obtain access to medical treatment, support and care, including help from relatives, must involve a certain degree of speculation, particularly in view of the constantly evolving situation as regards the treatment of HIV and AIDS worldwide.

The European Court agreed in *N* that not only does *D* v *United Kingdom* (1997) establish a particularly high threshold for a breach of Article 3, but it would be unfair on the contracting state (i.e. the United Kingdom) if it imposed a duty upon us to care for failed asylum seekers simply because we have a better healthcare system. It is therefore not enough for an asylum seeker to argue that his home country does not have very good medical facilities; there must be an element of exceptionality to justify treatment in our country.

It is clear from the line of case law that the courts will apply the high standard of *D* v *United Kingdom* (1997) to cases in which asylum seekers try to claim free healthcare on our National Health Service. There must clearly be exceptional circumstances to invoke Articles 3 and 8 – such as imminent death – and an Immigration Appeal Tribunal have to consider the individual facts of each case before deciding that the Articles have been breached.

Brits going abroad

British patients also go abroad for medical treatment. A lot of us are able to travel around the world for healthcare because it is cheaper and quicker than in the United Kingdom. Fertility treatment, cancer treatment and cosmetic surgery are the best-known private examples, but what about public services or procedures? For example, should the NHS pay for us to go abroad for a hip replacement if the waiting lists are too long at home?

This very issue was raised in the case of *Watts* (2006). The current law states that throughout Europe, a member state cannot refuse to pay for medical treatment if it is available in their own country but the patient is waiting too long in light of his health and prognosis.

Article 22 of Council Regulation No. 1408/71

Authorisation may not be refused where the treatment in question is among the benefits provided for by the legislation of the member state on whose territory the person concerned resides and where he cannot be given such treatment within the time normally necessary for obtaining the treatment in question in the member state of residence, taking account of his current state of health and the probable course of the disease.

This means, in practice, that the NHS might have to pay for patients to be treated abroad if the patient is waiting too long for it. The Court of Appeal in *Watts* (2006) had to ask the European Court for clarification because the United Kingdom is unique in that it runs a publicly funded National Health Service, and the question was as follows:

Is the United Kingdom National Health Service entitled to refuse to authorise a patient's treatment in another Member State if it reasonably judges that to do so in the particular and similar cases would dislocate its system of administering priorities through waiting lists?[21]

The European Court responded in 2006 with a predictable response: it depended on the circumstances of the patient's case.

CASE EXTRACT

R (on the application of Watts) v *Bedford Primary Care Trust* (C-372/04) [2006] QB 667

Facts: Yvonne Watts needed a hip replacement operation but wanted it in France to avoid the NHS waiting time of one year. Bedford PCT refused to fund the operation abroad, so she challenged them quoting her right to free movement under EU law. The critical question was: is a one year waiting period long enough to reimburse the patient for treatment abroad?

Held: A patient could, pursuant to Council Regulation 1408/71 Article 22, to go to another member state for medical treatment and be reimbursed if there would, on an objective medical assessment of her medical circumstances, be an unacceptable delay before treatment could be provided in the UK. The delay must not exceed the period which was acceptable on the basis of the objective medical assessment. It cannot be refused simply because it would throw the NHS waiting lists (and thus its administration and priorities) into a state of disarray.

→

---

[21] *R (on the application of Watts)* v *Bedford Primary Care Trust and Another* [2004] EWCA Civ 166.

Grand Chamber (at paras 119, 145): A refusal to grant prior authorisation cannot be based merely on the existence of waiting lists enabling the supply of hospital care to be planned and managed on the basis of predetermined general clinical priorities, without carrying out in the individual case in question an objective medical assessment of the patient's medical condition, the history and probable course of his illness, the degree of pain he is in and/or the nature of his disability at the time when the request for authorisation was made or renewed. [...] [However], the requirements arising from Article 49 EC and Article 22 of Regulation Number 1408/71 are not to be interpreted as imposing on the member states an obligation to reimburse the cost of hospital treatment in other member states without reference to any budgetary consideration but, on the contrary, are based on the need to balance the objective of the free movement of patients against overriding national objectives relating to management of the available hospital capacity, control of health expenditure and financial balance of social security systems.

In the *Watts* judgment, there were several criteria laid down to authorise the payment of NHS treatment abroad:

- In favour of Mrs Watts, an 'objective medical assessment' was required to ascertain whether the delay was acceptable, and this included the history of her illness, the course of her illness, the degree of pain and the nature of the disability. Authorisation could not be refused simply because it would interrupt waiting lists (which enabled hospital care to be planned and managed).

- However, in favour of Bedford Primary Care Trust, Regulation 1408/71 does not impose an obligation to pay for NHS treatment abroad without balancing 'national objectives relating to management of the available hospital capacity, control of health expenditure and financial balance'. Therefore, Bedford Primary Care Trust still retained a lot of its control over its waiting lists.

It is understandable that a Primary Care Trust (now a local authority) would be concerned about this kind of legal action. A waiting list is there for a reason – it is a form of rationing – and it allows hospitals to plan their treatment at a pace that suits their capacity and ability. It is very common for patients to complain about waiting times on the NHS, but until our public health service has more funds, it cannot treat everybody as quickly as private hospitals. In the event that the European Court might have backed Mrs Watts, it would have turned the NHS into a bank from which to withdraw funds for private treatment, and this would have caused an administrative and financial meltdown.[22] It is therefore very positive that a local authority is still able to consider its objectives, capacity and finances before authorising treatment abroad.

---

[22] For example, hospitals may have been half empty and therefore too expensive to run, leading to closures.

THINKING POINT

In light of the *Watts* case above, there is clearly a lot of displeasure about waiting times in the NHS and it is a topical headline even today. The NHS does have to ration its resources, but can it do it another way? Can it introduce a fresh system? If so, what would the eligibility criteria be and why would they be fairer than the current system? How would it be enforced, and what would the appeals process be?

Chapter summary

- The National Health Service (NHS) was born in 1948 as a result of the National Health Service Act 1946, right at the end of the Second World War.

- The National Institute for Health and Care Excellence (NICE) underpins a lot of the decisions by the NHS. The new drugs and treatments on the market are appraised by NICE in terms of their cost effectiveness. The NHS will make the new drug or treatment available within a reasonable amount of time.

- A judicial review can be sought if the patient is unhappy with a decision not to fund a certain treatment, but the grounds for judicial review must be as follows:
  - the decision to deprive was unlawful;
  - the decision to deprive was outside of the statutory powers of the health authority;
  - the decision to deprive was irrational and unreasonable;
  - the decision to deprive was a breach of human rights.

- A local authority is entitled to refuse certain types of treatment if they cannot afford it, but they must always make room for exceptional cases in their policy and will be held to be acting unreasonably if they do not: *R v North West Lancashire Health Authority ex parte A* [2000] 1 WLR 977.

Chapter essay

'Discuss the ways in which the National Health Service can ration healthcare resources and describe the ethical problems that arise from each method.'

Chapter case study

Sheila requires brain surgery for a tumour and she is told that she has thirty months to live. The only brain surgeon in the United Kingdom who can help her is based in London. He can remove some of the tumour and offer her an extra year of quality life but he has a waiting list of eighteen months. Sheila asks her GP if the NHS can pay for her to travel to Germany to see the other specialist but he says no: the London specialist is closer and the waiting time is average. According to the case law, can Sheila ask the NHS to pay for her treatment in Germany? If so, what legal test is applied?

Further reading

Brazier, M. (1999) 'Regulating the Reproduction Business?', 7 *Medical Law Review* 166.

Davies, G. (2004) 'Health and Efficiency: Community Law and National Health Systems in the Light of Muller-Faure', 67 *Modern Law Review* 94.

Evans, H.M. (2007) 'Do Patients Have Duties?', 33 *Journal of Medical Ethics* 689.

Harris, J. (1995) 'Double Jeopardy and the Use of QALY's in Health Care Allocation', 21 *Journal of Medical Ethics* 144; (2005) 'The Age-Indifference Principle and Equality', 14 *Cambridge Quarterly of Healthcare Ethics* 93.

Light, D. (1997) 'The Real Ethics of Rationing', 315 *British Medical Journal* 112.

3

Medical negligence

Chapter objectives

At the end of this chapter, you should have:

- An understanding of how the tort of negligence is applied to a medical case.
- An appreciation of why it is so difficult to successfully bring a claim in medical negligence.
- Knowledge of the different types of action in medical negligence (i.e. before birth and after birth) and the range of defences available to healthcare professionals.
- An understanding of the NHS complaints procedure.

| SETTING THE SCENE | Jane was scheduled for complicated surgery. She was an NHS patient and was concerned that Countryshire NHS Trust – where she was booked in as a patient – had fallen below their standard of care over the last twelve months in relation to hospital infections. Jane had her surgery, and the seemed fine and was allowed home. A month later, she was found not only to have a blood infection, but also that her left leg was suffering from twinges and partial paralysis. She went back to her surgeon, but he told her that he had performed her surgery to a reasonable standard of care and that he could not help her. She then consulted legal advice. How would a medical lawyer explain the issues surrounding duty of care, breach, causation and consent to risk? |

Introduction

In medical law, a doctor has a duty of care over his patient.[1] When the duty of care is breached and it leads to harm, the tort of negligence is the most suitable legal route to take, although there may also be an opportunity in contract law if the healthcare was private. It must be proved that the doctor *owed a duty of care* to his patient, that he *breached* his duty, i.e. he fell below the reasonable standard of care for a doctor, and that his breach *caused* the damage, i.e. there is a clear chain of causation between the breach and the harm. A particular problem facing patients is proving that it was the doctor – not the underlying illness – that caused the injury to worsen, or new symptoms to arise.

A brief overview of the general principles of negligence will set a good foundation for the rest of the chapter.

The criteria for negligence

Negligence is a controversial area of law that was created by case law rather than Parliament. A claim in negligence will consist of one party (the claimant) arguing that he has suffered some sort of loss as a result of the careless behaviour of another party (the respondent). In medical law, for example, the patient will argue that he was the victim of negligent behaviour at the hands of a doctor and it has caused a physical injury. In *Donoghue* v *Stevenson* [1932] AC 562 it was established that there are three criteria to fulfil in order to claim that a person has been the victim of negligence:

1. There must be a **duty of care**.
2. There must be a **breach of that duty**.
3. The breach must **cause the damage**.

Duty of care

The general law on duty of care states as follows:

*   *Donoghue* v *Stevenson* **[1932] AC 562**: you do not need to be in a contract to bring a claim in negligence, it must simply be reasonably foreseeable that an act or omission would affect a neighbour (the 'neighbour principle').

---

[1] This was established by one case – *Donoghue* v *Stevenson* [1932] AC 562.

- *Caparo Industries Plc v Dickman* **[1990] 2 AC 605**: the harm must be *foreseeable*, there must be *proximity* between the parties (i.e. a close connection), and it must be *fair, just and reasonable* to impose a duty upon the respondent.

A duty of care in a medical context may read as follows: a patient visits the A&E department with a suspected broken arm. It is an NHS hospital not a private hospital, so no contract will come into existence. A doctor is called to treat the broken arm. The patient is harmed during the treatment because the doctor does not use a splint to keep the arm straight. The doctor will reasonably foresee that the patient would be affected by his negligence, and the patient is in his contemplation when he is doing his job (*Donoghue*). The harm is foreseeable, there is a close connection between the parties, and it is fair, just and reasonable to impose a duty of care upon the doctor (*Caparo*).

Breach of duty

The general law on breach of duty states as follows:

- *Bolam v Friern Hospital Management Committee* **[1957] 1 WLR 582**: the standard of care for doctors and other skilled professionals is: *the standard of the ordinary skilled man exercising and professing to have that special skill.*
- *Bolitho (Deceased) v City and Hackney HA* **[1998] AC 232**: the court can decide that the views of expert medical witnesses do not stand up to a *logical analysis.*
- *Bolton v Stone* **[1951] AC 850**; *Paris v Stepney BC* **[1951] AC 367**: if the risk of injury increases, the *standard* of care increases along with it and additional precautions are advised.
- *Latimer v AEC Ltd* **[1953] AC 643**: the respondent (doctor) must do everything that is *reasonable* to avoid the risk of injury, as long as the precautions are *in proportion* to the risk.

A breach of duty in a medical context may read as follows: a patient visits a specialist in physiotherapy for her back pain. The physiotherapist works with the patient for an hour, within which the patient hears her left hip joint click. The patient cannot stand up after the session, and it is learnt that the physiotherapist used an incorrect manoeuvre to treat the back pain. The physiotherapist must now be judged against the standard of an ordinary physiotherapist and must find other physiotherapists who would agree with her practice (*Bolam*). The courts are free to inform the physiotherapist that the evidence from her expert witnesses does not stand up to logic (*Bolitho*). If the patient had been elderly or vulnerable, a higher standard would have been required (*Bolton & Paris*) and any additional precautions should have been taken (*Latimer*).

Causing the damage

The general law on causation (in civil actions) states as follows:

- *Cork v Kirby Maclean Ltd* **[1952] 2 All ER 402**: the 'but for' test is applied to civil cases and the question is: *but for the respondent's actions, the damage would not have happened.*
- *Bonnington Castings Ltd v Wardlaw* **[1956] AC 613**: the respondent (doctor) does not need to be the only cause: it is enough to *contribute* to the damage as one of the causes.
- *Wilsher v Essex AHA* **[1988] AC 1074**: where there are *numerous* possible causes, causation is very difficult to establish on a balance of probabilities.

Causation in a medical context may read as follows: a very young patient is taken to hospital after suffering from domestic abuse injuries. She has a fractured skull, but her fracture is not life threatening. The medical team carry out several treatment errors, including wrapping the head tightly in thick bandages and injecting the patient with adrenaline when low blood pressure is mistaken for a cardiac arrest. The patient dies as a result of the mistreatment. The patient would not have died but for the mistreatment (*Cork*). The medical team do not need to be the only cause of death, but they must *contribute* to the patient's death (*Bonnington*). There are numerous potential causes of death in this scenario, including a fractured skull, pressure on the skull fracture, and an adrenaline injection. At least one of these incidents must be proved on a balance of probabilities to be the cause of death (*Wilsher*).

Damages

The general law on damages states as follows:

- *Rookes* v *Barnard* **[1964] AC 1129**: 'aggravated damages' are awarded *in addition* to regular damages when the initial harm is *made worse* by an aggravating factor, such as anxiety or distress.
- *Thompson* v *Commissioner of Police of the Metropolis* **[1998] QB 498**: aggravating factors can include humiliating circumstances or any conduct that is insulting, malicious or oppressive.
- *Law Reform (Personal Injuries) Act 1948, section 2(4)*: the claimant (patient) can choose to be compensated for private medical care.
- *H West & Son Ltd* v *Shephard* **[1964] AC 326**: the claimant (patient) can recover damages for loss of amenity, e.g. the ability to enjoy life like she did before, including sport or other pastimes, impairment of one of the five senses, reduction of marriage prospects, and destroyed holidays.

Damages in a medical context may read as follows: a patient undergoes surgery to relieve a trapped nerve in her back. She works as a lifeboat instructor. The surgery was carried out negligently and she is now paralysed from the waist down. She is successfully awarded pecuniary damages for her loss of earnings and medical care between the surgery and the trial ('special damages') and her estimated loss of earnings and estimated medical care for the rest of her life ('general damages'). She is also successfully awarded non-pecuniary damages for her distress. There are no aggravating factors (*Rookes, Thompson*), but she has opted for private medical care (1948 Act). She is also successfully awarded for loss of amenity because she cannot enjoy hobbies, walking, or her previous active family life (*West*).

Extras: economic loss through a negligent misstatement

Economic loss is not normally recoverable in negligence because it is more of a contractual issue than a tort issue. However, economic loss caused by a *negligent misstatement* can be claimed in negligence as long as special criteria from *Hedley* are in place.

The general law on economic loss through a negligent misstatement states as follows:

- *Hedley Byrne & Co Ltd* v *Heller & Partners Ltd* **[1964] AC 465**: economic loss cannot be claimed in the tort of negligence unless arising from a *negligent misstatement*: there must be a special relationship, the defendant must be specialised, the claimant must rely on the statement, the respondent must be aware of this reliance and the reliance must be reasonably foreseeable.

- *Goodwill* v *British Pregnancy Advisory Service* **[1996] 2 All ER 161**: when establishing a special relationship, the claimant (patient) must be *within the contemplation* of the respondent (doctor) at the time of the negligent misstatement.

- *Yianni* v *Edwin Evans & Sons* **[1982] 2 QB 438**: there must be sufficient proximity between the parties for a special relationship to be established.

- *Smith* v *Eric S Bush (A Firm)* **[1990] 2 WLR 790**: it must be reasonably foreseeable that the claimant (patient) will rely on the statement made by the respondent (doctor).

- *James McNaughton Paper Group Ltd* v *Hicks Anderson & Co* **[1991] 1 All ER 134**: additional factors to consider when applying *Hedley* can include: the purpose of the statement and the degree of knowledge of the respondent (doctor).

- *Henderson* v *Merrett Syndicates Ltd (No. 1)* **[1994] 3 All ER 506**: the respondent (doctor) must assume responsibility for the negligent misstatement.

Economic loss through a negligent misstatement in a medical context may read as follows: a patient visits a doctor about a vasectomy, because he and his wife already have six children and they cannot afford to care for any more. The doctor advises the patient that the vasectomy is '100% successful from day one', and that it reverses itself 'hardly ever'. The patient relies on this information, which is incorrect, and he has unprotected sex with his wife immediately after his recovery. She falls pregnant for the seventh time and they are struggling to make ends meet with the new addition to the family. The patient must give up his job to care for the children, leading to economic loss and psychiatric injury. There is a special relationship between the doctor and the patient, the doctor is a specialist, the patient relied on his statement and this reliance was reasonably foreseeable (*Hedley*). The patient (and his wife) are within the contemplation of the doctor when he is advising the patient (*Goodwill*), and there is sufficient proximity between the parties in order to establish a special relationship (*Yianni*). It is reasonably foreseeable that the patient (and his wife) would rely on this statement (*Smith*), and the knowledge of the doctor suggests that his statement should be informed and accurate (*James*). The doctor must now assume responsibility for his negligent misstatement (*Henderson*).

The rules of negligence when applied to medicine

The basic rules of negligence have been applied to medical cases on a number of occasions with some baffling results. A good example of this would be the rules on damages, which have not been followed in wrongful pregnancy cases, e.g. a patient has become pregnant as a result of a doctor's negligence. It is also not clear how far a duty of care can stretch, how high the standard of care must be, how causation is proved when there are several medical mishaps at the same time, and just how much reliance a patient must place on a misstatement for it to qualify as negligent.

This chapter will begin with a small section on liability for negligence before birth, and will move on to the much bigger area of liability for negligence after birth.

THINKING POINT

Medical negligence adopts all the rules of civil law, including the standard of proof of 'a balance of probabilities'. Does this make it easier for doctors to defend themselves, or easier for patients to prove cases against them? Should the standard be stricter in medical negligence cases than 51%? If so, how strict, and what implications would this have on both parties?

Liability for negligence *before* birth

It may sound a little odd to say that a doctor can be liable for medical negligence *before* a patient has been born, but there are a small number of civil actions that can arise from negligence during pregnancy. The following actions will be examined:

- **Wrongful pregnancy**: negligence has caused a pregnancy.
- **Wrongful birth**: negligence has caused a disabled birth (action brought by mother).
- **Wrongful life**: negligence has caused a disabled birth (action brought by child).
- **Injuries *in utero***: negligence has caused an injury *in utero* (action brought by child).

Action	Claim	Outcome/award
Wrongful pregnancy	Pregnancy not wanted	Costs of pregnancy only, 'extra' costs of disabled child, £15,000 for loss of autonomy
Wrongful birth	Disabled birth	Full damages awarded
Wrongful life	Abortion was deprived	No damages at all
Injuries *in utero*	Foetus injured before birth	Claim under Congenital Disabilities (Civil Liability) Act 1976

The mother will often seek expenses for pregnancy (e.g. pain, discomfort, clothes, loss of earnings etc.), birth, and the costs of raising the child, especially if the child is born disabled. The case law is not clear on the issue of damages, but it appears to have departed from the normal rules of negligence.

Wrongful pregnancy

In a wrongful pregnancy action, the mother (the claimant) is arguing that, as a result of a negligent misstatement from a doctor or a surgeon, she went through an unwanted pregnancy. The damages awarded to the mother will depend on the outcome of the wrongful pregnancy:

- *The wrongful pregnancy may end in a miscarriage*: damages can be awarded for pain and suffering, and the cost of pregnancy, although it is likely to be a small amount.
- *The wrongful pregnancy may end in an abortion*: damages can be awarded for pain and suffering, the cost of pregnancy, the cost of an abortion, and loss of earnings, although it is also likely to be a small amount.
- *The wrongful pregnancy may be carried to full term*: damages can be awarded for pain and suffering, the cost of pregnancy, the cost of birth, and loss of earnings.

Damages are not traditionally awarded for miscarriages, abortions or births because the pain and suffering that they cause are considered to be a normal, if unfortunate, part of life. However, they are awarded damages in cases of 'wrongful pregnancy' because the mother should not have been put in the position of facing these stressful events in the first place. The negligent doctor or surgeon is solely responsible for the pain and suffering that she is subjected to, and they should pay for their negligence.

Wrongful pregnancy in contract law

A 'wrongful pregnancy' action is usually pursued in the tort of negligence (below), but if the patient received a sterilisation (or fertility advice) in the private sector, the patient will have a contract with her hospital. This would be a breach of contract.

However, a contract for medical treatment will very rarely guarantee complete success. This is because it is not unknown for mistakes to happen, and the hospital would be exposing itself to a number of costly legal actions if it guaranteed complete success to every patient. Instead, a private hospital will traditionally promise 'reasonable care and skill' in performing the surgery and providing medical information. This criteria is clearly 'borrowed' from the tort of negligence. In practice, therefore, if a sterilisation operation does not work, the hospital will face no legal action if it was performed with reasonable care and skill. However, if it was not performed with reasonable care and skill, or the fertility advice was inaccurate, this is a breach of contract. There is a small handful of cases in this area confirming that private contracts do not guarantee complete success, but procedures or statements that are not carried out with reasonable care and skill can face legal action.

CASE EXTRACT

Eyre v *Measday* [1986] 1 All ER 488

Facts: The patient was a woman who decided not to have any more children. She consulted D, who was an experienced consultant gynaecological surgeon, about a sterilisation operation. D suggested a laparoscopy and emphasised to the patient that it was irreversible. D failed to advise her that there was a chance of 6 in 1,000 that she might become pregnant again. She agreed to the operation being carried out privately and signed a form consenting to the operation. After the operation she became pregnant and sued D for breach of contract. D admitted that the patient was advised that the operation was a permanent procedure and that she was not warned of the slight risk of failure.

Held: A contract does not guarantee that the patient will leave the hospital absolutely sterile, and any advice as to the 'irreversibility' of a procedure does not give rise to a warranty that the patient would be absolutely sterile. The reasonable man test should be applied to such conversations to figure out what was implied by the doctor or surgeon and a reasonable man would not infer a warranty of 100% success.

Slade LJ: The test thus does not depend on what either the plaintiff or the defendant thought were the terms of the contract in her or his own mind. It depends upon what the court objectively considers that the words used by the respective parties must be reasonably taken to have meant. [...] I think there is no doubt that the plaintiff would have been entitled reasonably to assume that the defendant was warranting that the operation would be performed with reasonable care and skill. That, I think, would have been the inevitable inference to be drawn, from an objective standpoint, from the relevant discussion between the parties. The contract did, in my opinion, include an implied warranty of that nature. However, that inference on its own does not enable the plaintiff to succeed in the present case. She has to go further. She has to suggest – and it is suggested on her behalf – that the defendant, by necessary implication, committed himself to an unqualified guarantee as to the success of the

→

particular operation proposed, in achieving its purpose of sterilising her, even though he were to exercise all due care and skill in performing it. The suggestion is that the guarantee went beyond due care and skill and extended to an unqualified warranty that the plaintiff would be absolutely sterile. [...] I do not think that any intelligent lay bystander (let alone another medical man), on hearing the discussion which took place, could have reasonably drawn the inference that the defendant was intending to give any warranty of this nature. It is true that in cross-examination he admitted that it would have been reasonable for the plaintiff to have gone away from his consulting rooms thinking that she would be sterilised. He did not, however, admit that it would have been reasonable for her to have left his consulting rooms thinking that he had given her a guarantee that after the operation she would be absolutely sterile; this, I think, is the really relevant point. [...] In my opinion, in the absence of any express warranty, the court should be slow to imply against a medical man an unqualified warranty as to the results of an intended operation, for the very simple reason that, objectively speaking, it is most unlikely that a responsible medical man would intend to give a warranty of this nature.

According to Slade LJ, the surgeon did not contract to render the patient absolutely sterile, he contracted to carry out a laparoscopy operation. The statement that the operation was *irreversible* did not give rise to a warranty that, as a result of the operation, the patient would be absolutely sterile. A test was clearly established: the 'intelligent lay bystander' on hearing the discussion would not reasonably infer that the surgeon was giving a warranty that the operation would be completely successful. This is rather unfair for the patient, who typically trusts the word of her doctor. However, as a result of *Eyre v Measday*, in the absence of any clear warranty the court will now be slow to imply against a medical man an absolute guarantee as to the results of an operation.

The law was confirmed in the next case of the same year.

CASE EXTRACT

Thake v Maurice [1986] QB 644

Facts: [T] and his wife wished to avoid having any more children and consulted a surgeon [M], with a view to T having a vasectomy. M carried out the operation, but subsequently, by a rare chance, T became fertile again and his wife conceived.

Held: A surgeon does not guarantee that surgery will achieve a particular result, but a contract does stipulate that the patient will receive reasonable care and skill.

Neill LJ (at page 685): It is the common experience of mankind that the results of medical treatment are to some extent unpredictable and that any treatment may be affected by the special characteristics of the particular patient. [...] Both the plaintiffs and the defendant expected that sterility would be the result of the operation and the defendant appreciated that that was the plaintiffs' expectation. This does not mean, however, that a reasonable person would have understood the defendant to be giving a binding promise that the operation would achieve its purpose or that the defendant was going further than to give an assurance that he expected and believed that it would have the desired result. Furthermore, I do not consider that a reasonable person would have expected a responsible medical man to be intending to give a guarantee. Medicine, though a highly skilled profession, is not, and is not generally regarded as being, an exact science. The reasonable man would have expected the defendant to exercise all the proper skill and care of a surgeon in that speciality; he would not in my view have expected the defendant to give a guarantee of 100% success. Accordingly, though I am satisfied that a reasonable person would have left the consulting room thinking that Mr Thake would be sterilised by the vasectomy operation, such a person would not have left thinking that the defendant had given a guarantee that Mr Thake would be absolutely sterile.

A surgeon does not guarantee that surgery will achieve a particular result if he promises to perform it with reasonable care and skill, and although the contract between a surgeon and a patient should require the surgeon to exercise reasonable care and skill, the fact that the desired result was not achieved did not mean that the surgeon was in breach of the contract. Neill LJ delivered a phrase that has been used in medical law ever since: 'medicine is not an exact science'. The courts realise that there is never a guarantee of 100% success.

The case law appears to be clear: a doctor cannot expressly imply a warranty into a private contract that a sterilisation operation, or any other surgical procedure for that matter, comes with a 100% guarantee of success. The use of the word 'irreversible' in a consultation used to mean exactly that – it could not be reversed – but this does not imply that the sterilisation will be permanent. Contracts must take account of the fact that medicine is not an exact science.

Wrongful pregnancy in the tort of negligence

It will be recalled that the tort of negligence requires three criteria to be satisfied: (i) there must be a duty of care; (ii) there must be a breach of duty; and (iii) the breach must cause the damage.

Duty of care

A patient in an NHS hospital will not be party to a private contract, so a common law duty of care will establish a legal connection between himself and his doctor instead. It is traditionally assumed that a doctor or a surgeon owes his patient a duty of care, so there will not usually be any legal complications in establishing a duty of care when the patient brings a claim for wrongful pregnancy. However, do doctors or surgeons have a duty of care over spouses or partners, who may find themselves out of pocket or extremely stressed as a result of the wrongful pregnancy? According to *Donoghue* v *Stevenson* [1932] AC 562, a claimant must be in the contemplation of the respondent at the time of the act or omission. This might be satisfied if a surgeon is performing a sterilisation procedure on a *married* man because the surgeon will foresee that his wife may suffer an unwanted pregnancy if the operation is performed negligently.

The case law in wrongful pregnancy actions supports this approach, confirming that if the claimant (i.e. the patient's wife) was in the contemplation of the surgeon, then it is fair, just and reasonable to impose a duty of care upon the surgeon for her wrongful pregnancy. It logically follows from this, as was seen in the *Goodwill* case (below), that if the wife came along a few years later, there is no duty of care because the surgeon did not contemplate her (she did not yet exist).

<table>
<tr><td>

CASE EXTRACT

</td><td>

Goodwill v British Pregnancy Advisory Service [1996] 1 WLR 1397

Facts: Goodwill [G] began her relationship with the male patient three years after he had undergone the vasectomy and been advised by BPAS that he no longer needed to use contraception. However, the vasectomy underwent a spontaneous reversal and G became pregnant. G argued that BPAS had breached their duty of care to her by failing to warn her partner, three years ago, of the possibility of reversal and claimed damages for financial loss.

Held: A partner who comes along *after* the procedure is not within the contemplation of the surgeon, and so there is no sufficient proximity to give rise to a duty of care.

Peter Gibson LJ (at pages 1403, 1405): The doctor is concerned only with the man (his patient), and possibly that man's wife or partner if the doctor intends her to receive, and she receives, advice from the doctor in relation to the vasectomy and the subsequent tests. [...] If the existence of that partner is known to the doctor, and the doctor is aware that she wishes not to become pregnant by the man and the vasectomy is carried out to meet her wish as well as the man's wish, it may be said that the doctor is employed to confer that benefit on her. But that is not this case. [...] [BPAS] could know nothing about the likely course of action of future sexual partners of Mr MacKinlay. In my judgment on [G]'s pleadings the defendants were not in a sufficient or any special relationship with [G] such as gives rise to a duty of care. I cannot see that it can properly be said of the defendants that they voluntarily assumed responsibility to [G] when giving advice to Mr MacKinlay. At that time they had no knowledge of her, she was not an existing sexual partner of Mr MacKinlay but was merely, like any other woman in the world, a potential future sexual partner of his, that is to say a member of an indeterminately large class of females who might have sexual relations with Mr MacKinlay during his lifetime. I find it impossible to believe that the policy of the law is or should be to treat so tenuous a relationship between the adviser and the advisee as giving rise to a duty of care, and there is no analogous situation recognised as giving rise to that duty. [...]

</td></tr>
</table>

The *Goodwill* case is significant. It confirms that a surgeon or doctor can have a duty of care over a partner or spouse to a patient if they are within the *contemplation* of the surgeon or doctor and if they are *sufficiently proximate* to the surgeon or doctor at the time of the negligent act.

Breach of duty

A breach of duty is the vital element in medical negligence. This is where the claimant (patient) will pinpoint the act or omission from the doctor or surgeon that led to her wrongful pregnancy. It has traditionally taken the form of two acts: a sterilisation operation that was performed negligently, or a negligent misstatement that was relied upon. According to *Bolam v Friern Hospital Management Committee* [1957] 1 WLR 582, the general law of negligence states that the standard of care for doctors and other skilled professionals is: 'the standard of the ordinary skilled man exercising and professing to have that special skill'. This rule was supplemented by *Bolitho v City and Hackney Health Authority* [1998] AC 232 which stated that the court can decide that the views of expert medical witnesses do not stand up to a logical analysis. A good example of an application of the *Bolam* test in a wrongful pregnancy case is *Newell* v *Goldenberg* [1995] 6 Med LR 371. In this case, it was argued by Mr Newell that his surgeon should have warned him that a vasectomy procedure can naturally reverse itself over time. Dr Goldenberg argued in return that even though he had failed to warn of this small risk, he had adopted the practice of a responsible body of medical opinion according to *Bolam*, which did not give warnings in such cases. The courts agreed: Dr Goldenberg had not fallen below the standard of care expected of a reasonably competent doctor who performs vasectomies.

It is widely accepted today that a vasectomy may reverse itself over time, although the risk of this is still quite low. The Royal College of Obstetricians and Gynaecologists have issued guidance to gynaecologists, advising them to always warn a patient about the risk of reversal or failure when it comes to sterilisation.

EXTRACT

Male and Female Sterilisation, Evidence-based Clinical Guideline Number 4, The Royal College of Obstetricians and Gynaecologists, (2004), at page 4:

http://www.rcog.org.uk/womens-health/clinical-guidance/male-and-female-sterilisation

Men and women requesting sterilisation should be given information about other long-term reversible methods of contraception. This should include information on the advantages, disadvantages and relative failure rates of each method . . . Women in particular should be informed that vasectomy carries a lower failure rate in terms of post-procedure pregnancy and there is less risk related to the procedure.

Although people requesting sterilisation should understand that the procedure is intended to be permanent, they should be given information about the success rates associated with reversal, should this procedure be necessary . . .

They should also be made aware that the longest period of follow-up data available for the most common method used in the UK . . . suggests a failure rate after ten years of two to three per 1000 procedures. The failure rate for vasectomy should be quoted as approximately one in 2000 after clearance has been given . . .

It is a good idea to advise patients of the *alternatives* as well as the risks, allowing the patient to become fully informed about the procedure and free to do his research.

The breach caused the damage

It is not enough for a doctor to breach his duty: the breach must also cause the damage, or at least be a contributing cause of the damage according to *Bonnington Castings Ltd* v *Wardlaw* [1956] AC 613. The doctrine of causation is difficult to apply in medical negligence cases because the number of potential causes can be significant. This was identified in *Wilsher* v *Essex Area Health Authority* [1988] AC 1074. Imagine, for example, that a patient takes a very bad turn after heart surgery and has a massive heart attack. Medical negligence is one possibility, but the patient could also have caused his own heart attack or an underlying illness could have made his condition worse.

In wrongful pregnancy cases, there are three possible causes of the unwanted conception: natural reversal of a sterilisation (nobody is liable), negligent performance of sterilisation surgery (surgeon is liable), or a negligent misstatement (doctor or surgeon liable). It must be proved, on a balance of probabilities, that the unwanted pregnancy was caused by the act or omission of the doctor or the surgeon. A *novus actus interveniens* (i.e. an intervening act) that is completely unforeseeable will break the chain of causation from the doctor or surgeon, but this is very rare.

The case of *Sabri-Tabrizi* (below) is a wrongful pregnancy case from Scotland, in which the doctors argued that, because the patient suspected that her sterilisation had failed, she broke the chain of causation when she decided to have unprotected sexual intercourse and became pregnant. The resulting pregnancy was, therefore, her own fault.

CASE EXTRACT

Sabri-Tabrizi v *Lothian Health Board* [1998] Rep LR 37

Facts: [S] underwent a sterilisation procedure but as a result of the negligent manner in which it was carried out, the procedure failed. S became pregnant. A termination was sought, but she became pregnant again and gave birth to a stillborn child. S raised an action for damages against [L]. L argued that the real cause of S's second pregnancy was not the failure of the sterilisation, but her decision to have intercourse in the knowledge that the sterilisation had failed, which amounted to a *novus actus interveniens*.

Held: S knew that there was a risk of her becoming pregnant after her termination, and so it was not reasonable for her to expose herself to that risk and her decision to do so constituted a *novus actus interveniens*. [...]

Lord Nimmo Smith (at paras 12, 14–15): The submissions on behalf of the defenders all appear to me to turn on the one point, which was that, if the pursuer had sexual intercourse with her husband at a time when she knew that the first sterilisation operation had been unsuccessful and that she was still fertile, the defenders could not be held liable for the ensuing pregnancy and the consequences thereof. [...] The acceptance of risk of injury after the original negligent act or omission can be effective to break the chain of causation as being a *novus actus interveniens*.

I think that it was unreasonable of her to expose herself to that risk. Accordingly I regard her decision to have sexual intercourse in the knowledge that she was not sterile as constituting a *novus actus interveniens*, breaking the chain of causation, with the result that the defenders cannot be held liable for the second pregnancy and the consequences thereof.

In *Sabri-Tabrizi*, the patient broke the chain of causation when she had unprotected sex with her husband *knowing* that her sterilisation had failed. However, does a patient break the chain of causation if she chooses to continue her pregnancy when she could have had an abortion? In other words, is a doctor or a surgeon absolved from liability for a wrongful pregnancy if the patient *chooses* to continue the pregnancy? The answer to this, according to Lord Steyn in the case of *McFarlane*, is 'no'.

McFarlane v Tayside Health Board [2000] 2 AC 59

Lord Steyn (at page 81): Counsel for the health board rightly did not argue that it is a factor against the claim that the parents should have resorted to abortion or adoption. I cannot conceive of any circumstances in which the autonomous decision of the parents not to resort to even a lawful abortion could be questioned. For similar reasons the parents' decision not to have the child adopted was plainly natural and commendable. It is difficult to envisage any circumstances in which it would be right to challenge such a decision of the parents. The starting point is the right of parents to make decisions on family planning and, if those plans fail, their right to care for an initially unwanted child. The law does and must respect these decisions of parents which are so closely tied to their basic freedoms and rights of personal autonomy.

The words 'freedom' and 'autonomy' are important in Lord Steyn's judgment. It means that if a patient is put in the position of going through an unwanted pregnancy, that patient is still entitled to her free choice to keep, abort or adopt that child. The patient's decision to integrate that child into the family does not take away from the fact that a wrongful pregnancy has been imposed upon her at the negligent hands of another. As a result of this passage from Lord Steyn, the decision to keep the unwanted pregnancy is not an intervening act that breaks the chain of causation in a wrongful pregnancy case.

Damages for wrongful pregnancy

The traditional principles of negligence begin to go awry when exploring the issue of damages. It will be recalled that, under the general rules of negligence, damages are a compensatory payment that aim to put the claimant back in her *original position* before the tort was committed. This can sometimes lead to very large payouts to cover a loss of current and future earnings, the cost of current and future medical expenses, and pain and suffering. A successful action for wrongful pregnancy – especially if it leads to the birth of a child – may involve the following costs: maternity clothes, medical expenses, loss of earnings, general costs of upbringing a child, private education, anxiety, stress, and pain and suffering. However, the courts have been reluctant to award large amounts of damages. A string of cases show how this small area of law has developed, and there is clearly a reluctance from the courts to compensate a mother for giving birth to a child (especially a healthy one). The reasons for this appear to be:

- A child is a blessing and cannot be calculated against its costs.

- It is not fair, just or reasonable for a doctor to pay towards the upbringing of a child.

It appears that the immediate economic costs of a wrongful pregnancy will be compensated (such as maternity clothes, loss of earnings, etc.), but it is highly unlikely that the courts will compensate for the general upbringing of the child. This strict approach by the courts is baffling, but it would not be appropriate to announce that pregnancy and birth are 'injuries' in civil law that can be compensated.

CASE EXTRACT

Udale v *Bloomsbury AHA* [1983] 1 WLR 1098

Facts: Mrs Udale [U] underwent a sterilisation operation. It was conducted negligently and she became pregnant. She suffered acute anxiety about whether the child would be born normally. The child was born perfectly healthy. She brought an action claiming damages for pain and discomfort, and also for the cost enlarging the family home and the cost of the child's upbringing to the age of 16. Bloomsbury [B] admitted liability, but the issue of damages arose.

Held: The measure of damages should reflect the disturbance to the family finances (economic loss was awarded at £8,000) but it was contrary to public policy that damages should be recoverable from the birth of a healthy child. The claim for upbringing and enlargement of the home were irrecoverable.

Jupp J (at pages 1109–10): The considerations that particularly impress me are these: (1) It is highly undesirable that any child should learn that a court has publicly declared his life or birth to be a mistake – a disaster even – and that he or she is unwanted or rejected. Such pronouncements would disrupt families and weaken the structure of society. (2) A plaintiff such as Mrs Udale would get little or no damages because her love and care for her child and her joy, ultimately, at his birth, would be set off against and might cancel out the inconvenience and financial disadvantages which naturally accompany parenthood. (3) Medical men would be under subconscious pressure to encourage abortions in order to avoid claims for medical negligence which would arise if the child were allowed to be born. (4) It has been the assumption of our culture from time immemorial that a child coming into the world, even if, as some say, 'the world is a vale of tears', is a blessing and an occasion for rejoicing. [...]

It seems to me that it is legitimate, without detracting from the above principles of public policy, to have some regard to the disturbance to the family finances which the unexpected pregnancy causes. One may look at the cost of the layette and the sudden necessity of having to find more ample accommodation in assessing the damages for the unwanted pregnancy, without regarding the child as unwanted. [...] Accordingly, in my view, it is proper to increase the award of damages with this in mind when awarding general damages for the pain, suffering, inconvenience, anxiety and the like, mentioned at the beginning of this judgment. I do so by awarding the sum of £8,000 for these matters together.

The case of *Udale* firmly shut the door in regards to the general upbringing costs of babies resulting from unwanted pregnancies. This issue was revisited in *Emeh* and in a radical departure from the Udale decision, full damages were awarded for financial loss.

CASE EXTRACT

Emeh v *Kensington and Chelsea AHA* [1985] 2 WLR 233

Facts: Mrs Emeh was negligently sterilised and became pregnant. She was not willing to undergo another abortion. She gave birth to a disabled child, and claimed full damages for financial loss, including future earnings, loss of amenity, and maintenance of the child (including the extra care required by a disabled child). The trial judge awarded damages only for pain and suffering until discovery of

→

the pregnancy, on the grounds that she could have had an abortion and her decision not to mitigated her damages.

Held: A health authority which performed a sterilisation operation negligently could not expect a woman to terminate a subsequent pregnancy (trial judge overruled). It would be liable for her full financial damages (this is a departure from *Udale* because the child in *Emeh* was disabled).

Waller LJ (at page 1022): In my judgment the court should not be too ready to lay down lines of public policy; and I would reject the argument in this case that public policy requires that damages should be confined. [...] So the result is that I would award £3,000 for pain and suffering up to the time of the trial, and £10,000 for the future loss of amenity and pain and suffering which is going to occur in the life of this child, who may require attention for many, many years, perhaps until the time she has grown up into adulthood.

Slade LJ (at page 1024): The judge held that the plaintiff's act in failing to obtain an abortion was, in the circumstances, so unreasonable as to eclipse the defendants' wrongdoing. With the greatest respect to the judge, I find myself in profound disagreement with him in this criticism of the plaintiff's conduct. The hospital authority had performed on her an operation which led her reasonably to believe it had rendered her incapable of having children. They had performed the operation so inefficiently that only some months later she discovered that she was again pregnant; nor did she make this discovery in the early stages of her pregnancy. She discovered it when the pregnancy had continued for some 17½ to 20 weeks. By that time the foetus would inevitably have grown to a considerable extent; according to the evidence of Sir John Dewhurst, an operation to terminate her pregnancy would have involved three days in hospital; the operation would not have been entirely without risk, and would no doubt have involved her in considerable pain and discomfort. Furthermore the child in this instance was that of her husband, and only some seven months before she had had to undergo a similar operation in hospital, which had no doubt been very disagreeable. [...] The judge, in saying that her failure to obtain an abortion was so unreasonable as to eclipse the defendants' wrongdoing, was, I think, really saying that the defendants had the right to expect that, if they had not performed the operation properly, she would procure an abortion, even if she did not become aware of its existence until nearly 20 weeks of her pregnancy had elapsed.

I do not, for my part, think that the defendants had the right to expect any such thing. By their own negligence, they faced her with the very dilemma which she had sought to avoid by having herself sterilised.

In *Udale*, Jupp J made it very clear that general financial losses arising out of a wrongful pregnancy can be compensated, but not the cost of upbringing a child. This decision is based on strong public policy reasons: it would have a very negative effect on society if children were to learn that they were the consequence of an unwanted pregnancy. The later decision of *Emeh* deliberately departs from the 'public policy' grounds in *Udale* by awarding full damages. There are two reasons for this: (1) the child in *Emeh* was disabled and so the 'joy' of a new baby may not have been so readily experienced; and (2) Kensington and Chelsea Health Authority argued that because Mrs Emeh refused an abortion, she had somehow broken the chain of causation and caused her own expenses. The lords felt overwhelmed to reject the respondents after hearing this.

Waller LJ and Slade LJ in *Emeh* did not state that their relaxed rule applied to disabled babies only. Therefore, as a result of *Emeh*, the doors were opened to unlimited damages for all wrongful pregnancy actions in negligence, and a doctor or surgeon who carried out the negligent sterilisation was liable to pay the full costs of the child's upbringing. This was consistent with the general principles of negligence, but it put a heavy strain on doctors, surgeons and the NHS. In *Benarr* v *Kettering* (1988) 138 NLJ Rep 179, this was extended to the private education of the child where: '*such education was proper and an ordinary feature of that particular family and its children*' (per Hodgson J). The expenses rolled out of control in *Allen* v *Bloomsbury* (below), in which the Health Authority was liable to pay all of the upbringing costs – including a garage extension – until the child was eighteen.

CASE EXTRACT

Allen v *Bloomsbury HA* [1992] PIQR Q50

Facts: Allen underwent a sterilisation operation at a hospital managed by Bloomsbury but shortly afterwards discovered that she was pregnant and that she had been four weeks pregnant at the time of the operation. She was concerned throughout the pregnancy that the sterilisation operation may have harmed the baby and suffered anxiety until she gave birth to a healthy daughter. She brought an action for damages against Bloomsbury claiming the cost and expense of bringing up her daughter until she was 18. They admitted liability and the only issue was quantum of damages.

Held: The respondents are liable to pay for all such expenses as may be reasonably incurred for the education and upkeep for the unplanned child, having regard to all the circumstances of the case and, in particular, to his condition in life and his reasonable requirements at the time the expenditure is incurred.

Brooke J (at pages 56–7, 61):

1. If a doctor fails to act towards his patient with the standard of care reasonably to be expected of him, and as a foreseeable result of the doctor's breach of duty a child is born whose potential for life would have been lawfully terminated but for the doctor's negligence, the law entitles the mother to recover damages for the foreseeable loss and damage she suffers in consequence of the doctor's negligence (*Emeh* v *Kensington and Chelsea and Westminster AHA* [1985] QB 1012, CA).

2. A plaintiff mother is entitled to recover general damages (and any associated financial special damage) for the discomfort and pain associated with the continuation of her pregnancy and the delivery of her child, although she must set off against this claim a sum in respect of the benefit of avoiding the pain and suffering and associated financial loss which would have resulted from the termination of her pregnancy under general anaesthetic, since in the events which have happened she has not had to undergo that operation.

3. She is also entitled to damages for economic loss unassociated with her own physical injury which falls into two main categories:

   (1) The financial loss she suffers because when the unwanted baby is born she has a growing child to feed, clothe, house, educate and care for until the child becomes an adult.

→

(2) The financial loss she suffers because she has lost or may lose earnings or incur other expense because of her obligation towards her child which she would have sought to avoid.

4. Although the law recognises that it is foreseeable that if an unwanted child is born following a doctor's negligence, a mother may suffer wear and tear and tiredness in bringing up a healthy child, the claim for general damages she might otherwise have had on this account is generally set off against and extinguished by the benefit of bringing a healthy child into the world and seeing one's child grow up to maturity. [...]

In my judgment in this type of case defendants are liable to pay for all such expenses as may be reasonably incurred for the education and upkeep for the unplanned child, having regard to all the circumstances of the case and, in particular, to his condition in life and his reasonable requirements at the time the expenditure is incurred.

The relaxed judgment in *Emeh* allowed for the full upbringing of a healthy child to be compensated for in the subsequent case of *Allen*, and the four grounds for damages in *Allen* were outlined by Brooke J as follows:

- A mother can recover damages for the foreseeable loss and damage she suffers in consequence of the doctor's negligence. This can, however, be criticised on the basis that although a doctor might foresee a wrong pregnancy, he may not foresee all of the costs of a child's upbringing.

- A mother is entitled to recover damages for the discomfort and pain associated with her pregnancy and birth, but this must be weighed against the benefit of avoiding the pain, suffering and financial loss of an abortion, which she has intentionally avoided.

- A mother can claim for economic loss unconnected to her own physical injury under two categories: (i) the financial loss she suffers because she has a growing child to feed, clothe, house, educate and care for until he becomes an adult; (ii) the financial loss she suffers because she has lost or may lose earnings or incur other expenses as a result of her obligation towards her child.

- A mother may suffer wear and tear and tiredness in bringing up a healthy child, but her claim for general damages on this matter is balanced against and extinguished by the benefit of bringing a healthy child into the world and seeing one's child grow up to maturity.

There is a 'balancing act' in the *Allen* judgment: the benefits of something (or the avoidance of something) are balanced against the injury or loss suffered in order to calculate damages. The *Allen* judgment is also full of mathematical calculations (omitted from above), and Brooke J explains in detail how much should be awarded in terms of general damages, special damages, and any mitigating factors balanced against the totals. General damages are more difficult to calculate, because they are only estimated amounts, but the grand total in this case came to £96,631.29; only £2,500 was allocated to pain and suffering, meaning that the majority of the award was for economic losses and general upbringing expenses.

The issue reached the House of Lords for the first time in the Scottish case of *McFarlane* (below), and the law was modified. Lord Slynn was the first of five lords to hand down the long and complex judgment. Firstly, he took the opportunity to confirm that pregnancy and birth can give rise to damages for economic loss and pain and suffering (this was supported by a majority). Secondly, he analysed the duty of care in detail, evaluating just how far it should stretch in wrongful pregnancy actions when it came to paying additional upbringing costs. He found that a fair calculation of upbringing costs was almost impossible, and so he was not willing to do it (this was also supported by a majority). In addition, under the traditional rules of economic loss in negligence (see *Caparo* v *Dickman* [1990] 2 AC 605) he found that it was not 'fair, just and reasonable' to impose a duty upon a doctor to compensate for the upbringing of a healthy child resulting from a wrongful pregnancy (this was also supported by a majority).

CASE EXTRACT

McFarlane v *Tayside Health Board* [2000] 2 AC 59

Facts: M's husband had a vasectomy. He was sent a letter advising him that his sperm count was zero, but M became pregnant and gave birth to a healthy baby girl. M sought damages of £10,000 for the pain and suffering arising out of the pregnancy and labour and £100,000 to maintain the child. The appealing party was Tayside Health Board, arguing that it was unfair to extend a doctor's duty to paying for the upbringing of a child.

Held: It was fair and reasonable to impose upon a doctor a duty of care to prevent an unwanted pregnancy, but it was unfair to extend that duty to include the costs of raising a child. It was impossible to value the pleasure received from the child's existence which would counteract the financial burden placed on the parents. M was, therefore, entitled to compensatory damages for the pain and discomfort caused by the unwanted pregnancy, but THB could not be held liable for any further economic loss suffered by M.

Lord Slynn (at pages 74–6): My Lords, I do not find real difficulty in deciding the claim for damages in respect of the pregnancy and birth itself. The parents did not want another child for justifiable, economic and family reasons; they already had four children. They were entitled lawfully to take steps to make sure that that did not happen, one possible such step being a vasectomy of the husband. It was plainly foreseeable that if the operation did not succeed, [...] the wife might become pregnant. [...] It seems to me that in consequence the wife, if there was negligence, is entitled by way of general damages to be compensated for the pain and discomfort and inconvenience of the unwanted pregnancy and birth and she is also entitled to special damages associated with both – extra medical expenses, clothes for herself and equipment on the birth of the baby. [...] To reduce the costs by anything resembling a realistic or reliable figure for the benefit to the parents is well-nigh impossible unless it is assumed that the benefit of a child must always outweigh the cost which, like many judges in the cases I have referred to, I am not prepared to assume. Of course, there should be joy at the birth of a healthy child, at the baby's smile and the teenager's enthusiasms but how can these be put in money terms and trimmed to allow for sleepless nights and teenage disobedience? If the valuation is

➡

made early how can it be known whether the baby will grow up strong or weak, clever or stupid, successful or a failure both personally and career-wise, honest or a crook? It is not impossible to make a stab at finding a figure for the benefits to reduce the costs of rearing a child but the difficulties of finding a reliable figure are sufficient to discourage the acceptance of this approach. [...] The doctor undertakes a duty of care in regard to the prevention of pregnancy: it does not follow that the duty includes also avoiding the costs of rearing the child if born and accepted into the family. Whereas I have no doubt that there should be compensation for the physical effects of the pregnancy and birth, including, of course, solatium for consequential suffering by the mother immediately following the birth, I consider that it is not fair, just or reasonable to impose on the doctor or his employer liability for the consequential responsibilities, imposed on or accepted by the parents to bring up a child. The doctor does not assume responsibility for those economic losses.

McFarlane concluded that the mother was entitled to damages for pain, suffering and economic loss arising from the wrongful pregnancy, but the damages did not extend to the costs of upbringing a healthy child. *Emeh* (1985) is now overruled, and *Udale* (1983) is affirmed. The decision in *McFarlane* was plagued by a difficult balancing act. Lord Slynn put the difficulty into clear terms when he said: 'there should be joy at the birth of a healthy child, at the baby's smile and the teenager's enthusiasms but how can these be put in money terms and trimmed to allow for sleepless nights and teenage disobedience?' The pleasures and burdens of a healthy baby were so hard to calculate that Lord Slynn decided not to do it. The traditional rules of negligence are now cast aside, because the mother is *not* put back into her original position before her wrongful pregnancy. The following critical questions must now be asked:

- A wrongful pregnancy case will now be split into two actions: liability for the short-term consequences (fair, just and reasonable) and liability for the long-term consequences (not fair, just and reasonable). This is a new approach, but why was it taken? Lord Slynn provided no logical explanation as to why he thought it was not fair, just and reasonable for a doctor to be liable for the long-term consequences of his negligent actions.

- The general rules of negligence state that the damage suffered by the patient must be *reasonably foreseeable* to the doctor (see *Morts Dock & Engineering Co v Overseas Tankship (UK) Ltd (The Wagon Mound)*). The answer to this question in *McFarlane* would have been 'yes' to the short-term and long-term damages, resulting in payment of full damages. Why was this law not applied?

McFarlane is a departure from the law of negligence and the general principles of civil law. The other three lords who agreed with Lord Slynn (namely Lord Steyn, Lord Hope and Lord Clyde) provided their own social and moral theories as to why the non-payment of long-term damages was justified. Lord Millett dissented, but he also provided very little in the way of law to justify his decision. What is especially difficult about the *McFarlane* case is that all five lords put forward differing rationales for their decision, even though four out of five reached the same conclusion:

Lord	Decision	Rationale
Lord Slynn	Refuse upbringing costs	The pleasures and burdens of a healthy child are incalculable for the purposes of damages. It is not fair, just or reasonable to award upbringing costs.
Lord Steyn	Refuse upbringing costs	The chain of causation is not broken by the decision to keep the baby, distributive justice requires burdens to be shared equally, commuters on the underground would not support the *McFarlane* claim, morality often shapes the common law.
Lord Hope	Refuse upbringing costs	The damages in this case are disproportionate to the minor negligent act, the damages are foreseeable but damage limitation is justified; the benefits and burdens of a child cannot be calculated.
Lord Clyde	Refuse upbringing costs	Moral and ethical policies are not helpful, it is not reasonable or just for a family to have their child maintained free of cost, a doctor does not reasonably foresee that he will undertake a duty to maintain a child.
Lord Millett	Award maintenance costs	There is no such distinction between pure economic loss and consequential losses, the upbringing costs are a direct and foreseeable consequence of the negligence, the transactional theory states that all benefits must be taken with their burdens, damages should be awarded for the costs of equipment disposed of as a result of the negligence.

Proportionality was a frequent feature in many of the judgments, but it is common-place to see large payouts in this area of law because of the long-term consequences of a negligent act on a patient. A handful of the judges also made reference to benefits and burdens of a child being incalculable, but again it is quite normal to make these kinds of estimates in the tort of negligence. The reliance on moral perspectives in this judgment is a concern because it suggests a lack of legal support. Distributive justice and a transactional theory were the notable theories, but as Lord Clyde stated, these do not lead to a confident solution.

McFarlane: *distributing justice*

McFarlane was a watershed case. Recent cases have felt obliged to follow *McFarlane* in holding that pure economic loss (i.e. long-term expenses) are not recoverable in wrongful pregnancy cases. *Greenfield* is a clear example.

CASE EXTRACT

Greenfield v *Irwin (A Firm)* [2001] 1 WLR 1279

Facts: Greenfield was not diagnosed as pregnant when she received the contraceptive injection, resulting in a pregnancy. She argued that had she been properly informed, she would have had an abortion. She claimed for loss of earnings during the upbringing of the child, as well as pain and suffering for wrongful pregnancy.

Held: *McFarlane* was applied: a healthy child was an incalculable benefit, and any compensation for lost employment was beyond the duty of care.

May LJ (at para 44): It is, I think, correct that the House of Lords in *McFarlane* did not have to decide in terms whether loss of earnings in claims of this kind was recoverable. But the House did in substance decide that it was not fair, just and reasonable to impose on the doctor or his employer liability for the responsibilities consequential on the birth of the child imposed on, or accepted by, the parents to bring up the child. The present claim for the loss of earnings is in my view plainly such a claim.

Laws LJ (at para 54): It is to be noted that if this lady were to obtain the damages she seeks, she would happily be in a position whereby she would look after her much loved child at home, yet at the same time in effect would receive the income she would have earned had she stayed at work. In my judgment that is not just compensation; it is the conferment of a financial privilege, which has nothing to do with just compensation.

The influence of *McFarlane* is clear in May LJ's judgment. The upbringing costs were held to be pure economic loss and therefore it was not fair, just or reasonable to impose these costs upon the doctors. *Greenfield* does not carry out a detailed analysis or examination of *McFarlane*, which is most unfortunate. However, such an analysis was carried out shortly after when, in *Parkinson*, a disabled child was born as a result of a wrongful pregnancy. The *McFarlane* criteria were developed in the context of a healthy child but did not calculate the damages payable to a disabled child. In the end, the 'extra costs' of bringing up a disabled child were awarded, but general upbringing costs were still refused.

CASE EXTRACT

Parkinson v *St James and Seacroft University Hospital NHS Trust* [2002] QB 266

Facts: St James appealed against a decision that Mrs Parkinson was entitled to compensation for the costs of providing for the child's special needs and care attributable to its disability. P cross-appealed against a finding that she could not recover damages for the basic costs of the child's maintenance.

Held: There was a direct causative link between the surgeon's negligence and the congenital abnormalities suffered by the child, so the tests of foreseeability and proximity enunciated in *Caparo Industries Plc* v *Dickman* [1990] 2 AC 605 were satisfied and the special upbringing costs associated with rearing a disabled child would be fair, just and reasonable. However, it would not be fair, just or reasonable to extend the scope of the dictum in *McFarlane* v *Tayside Health Board* [2000] 2 AC 59 by allowing recovery for basic child rearing expenses.

→

Brooke LJ (at paras 50, 53): My route would be as follows: (i) the birth of a child with congenital abnormalities was a foreseeable consequence of the surgeon's careless failure to clip a fallopian tube effectively; (ii) there was a very limited group of people who might be affected by this negligence, *viz* Mrs Parkinson and her husband; (iii) there is no difficulty in principle in accepting the proposition that the surgeon should be deemed to have assumed responsibility for the foreseeable and disastrous economic consequences of performing his services negligently; (iv) the purpose of the operation was to prevent Mrs Parkinson from conceiving any more children, including children with congenital abnormalities, and the surgeon's duty of care is strictly related to the proper fulfilment of that purpose; (v) parents in Mrs Parkinson's position were entitled to recover damages in these circumstances for 15 years between the decisions in *Emeh* and *McFarlane*, so that this is not a radical step forward into the unknown; (vi) for the reasons set out in (i) and (ii) above, tests of foreseeability and proximity are satisfied, and an award of compensation which is limited to the special upbringing costs associated with rearing a child with a serious disability would be fair, just and reasonable; (vii) if principles of distributive justice are called in aid, I believe that ordinary people would consider that it would be fair for the law to make an award in such a case, provided that it is limited to the extra expenses associated with the child's disability. [...]

I am concerned only with the loss that arises when the child's significant disabilities flow foreseeably from his or her unwanted conception.

Hale LJ (at paras 74, 87, 90, 92, 94): The whole object of the service offered to the claimant by the defendants was to prevent her becoming pregnant again. They had a duty to perform that service with reasonable care. They did not do so. She became pregnant as a result. On normal principles of tortious liability, once it was established that the pregnancy had been wrongfully caused, compensation would be payable for all those consequences, whether physical or financial, which are capable of sounding in damages. [...] At the heart of it all is the feeling that to compensate for the financial costs of bringing up a healthy child is a step too far. A child brings benefits as well as costs; it is impossible accurately to calculate those benefits so as to give a proper discount; the only sensible course is to assume that they balance one another out. [...] A disabled child needs extra care and extra expenditure. [...] This analysis treats a disabled child as having exactly the same worth as a non-disabled child. It affords him the same dignity and status. It simply acknowledges that he costs more. [...] I conclude that any disability arising from genetic causes or foreseeable events during pregnancy, such as rubella, spina bifida, or oxygen deprivation during pregnancy or childbirth, up until the child is born alive, and which are not *novus actus interveniens*, will suffice to found a claim. [...] The difference between a normal and a disabled child is primarily in the extra care that they need, although this may bring with it extra expenditure. It is right, therefore, that the parent who bears those *extra* burdens should have a claim.

Brooke LJ condensed his findings into seven criteria, some of which are baffling. The first, for example, states that a child's disabilities are a 'foreseeable consequence of the surgeon's careless failure to clip a fallopian tube effectively'. How can this be possible? A doctor might foresee pregnancy as a consequence, but certainly not disabilities. Brooke LJ finishes with a discussion about causation, which is important because according to *Cork* v *Kirby Maclean Ltd* [1952] 2 All ER 402 and *Barnett* v *Chelsea and Kensington*

Hospital Management Committee [1969] 1 QB 428, liability will not be established if: 'but for the doctor's action, the harm would still have occurred'. Unfortunately, Brooke LJ does not apply the traditional rule of causation and appears to assume, without explanation or justification, that the doctor, by negligently performing the sterilisation, caused the disability. This is not a correct application of the law. Hale LJ begins by outlining the traditional rules of negligence, which are clearly split into four elements: duty, breach, cause, and damages. She confirms that a 'benefits vs burdens' analysis is not possible, and this is in line with the judgment in *McFarlane*. She then goes on to explain that the benefits of a disabled child may be less likely because of the stresses and strains. However, she contradicts this observation by concluding: 'this analysis treats a disabled child as having exactly the same worth as a non-disabled child. It affords him the same dignity and status. It simply acknowledges that he costs more.' The rationale for awarding damages is not quite clear: is it because there are fewer benefits to a disabled child, or because he simply costs more? Hale LJ also addresses the issue of causation, but merely concludes that any disability arising out of pregnancy is foreseeable and can found a claim. This makes no sense: how did the doctor foresee the disability?

The conclusion in *Parkinson* does not shed any more light into this unique area of law, it simply poses more questions. However, what is clear is that disabled children are awarded differently to healthy children in wrongful pregnancy cases in terms of *extra* costs, not the general upbringing costs. This is despite a lack of causation between the doctor and the disability, in fact, it is probably easier to establish a causal link between the doctor and the upbringing costs in *McFarlane* than it is to establish a causal link between the doctor and the disability in *Parkinson*.

What is a disability?

Hale LJ in *Parkinson* was quite happy for the definition of 'disabled' under section 17 of the Children Act 1989 to apply, which states: 'a child is disabled if he is blind, deaf or dumb or suffers from mental disorder of any kind or is substantially and permanently handicapped by illness, injury or congenital deformity or such other disability as may be prescribed'. Brooke LJ added that any definition, in his opinion, should stretch to 'include disabilities of the mind (including severe behavioural disabilities) as well as physical disabilities' and should be 'decided by judges, if necessary, on a case by case basis'. It is likely that a case will arise in the future which requires a further explanation of just what a 'substantial' disability could be.

It has become clear in the subsequent case of *Groom* v *Selby* that the child must be born healthy for *McFarlane* to apply, and the child must be born disabled for *Parkinson* to apply. If a child is born healthy and *then* becomes disabled or injured, it does not qualify under the ambit of *Parkinson* because the doctor is probably not connected to it, i.e. there is no causation.

CASE EXTRACT

Groom v Selby [2002] PIQR P18

Facts: Dr Selby[S] had admitted to a negligent failure to diagnose or test for pregnancy at a consultation with Mrs Groom [G]. G was thus deprived of an opportunity to terminate the pregnancy. M was born premature and approximately four weeks later developed salmonella meningitis complicated by bilateral front brain abscesses, as a result of which she became severely handicapped. S contended that M was a healthy child at birth and that a subsequent infection could not found a claim for damages.

Held: M could not properly be described as a healthy child at birth since the bacterium responsible for the meningitis had already been present on her skin. There had been no *novus actus interveniens*. The birth of a premature child who developed salmonella meningitis as a result of her exposure to a bacterium during the normal birth process was a foreseeable consequence of S's admitted negligence, so G was entitled to recover damages for the 'extra' costs of raising the child on an application of *Parkinson* v *St James and Seacroft University Hospital NHS Trust* [2001] EWCA Civ 530.

Brooke LJ (at paras 23–4): We are concerned in the present case with a child whose severe handicap arose from the normal incidents of conception, intrauterine development and birth. Her prematurity (which made her particularly vulnerable) was not due to any new intervening event and her exposure to the bacterium which proved her downfall occurred during the process of birth. All the causes of her meningitis were in place when the umbilical cord was severed: all that remained was for the bacterium to penetrate a weak point in the child's skin or mucous membranes and the damage was done. […] If we go to the battery of tests to which I referred in paragraph 50 of my judgment in *Parkinson*, the route to the judge's conclusion in this case would be on the following lines:

(i)   in the absence of evidence of any new intervening act, the birth of a premature child who suffered salmonella meningitis through exposure to a bacterium during the normal processes of birth was a foreseeable consequence of Dr Selby's failure to advise the claimant that although she had been sterilised she was in fact pregnant;

(ii) there are no difficulties about proximity;

(iii) there is, as in *Parkinson*, no difficulty in principle in accepting the proposition that Dr Selby should be deemed to have assumed responsibility for the foreseeable and disastrous consequences of performing her services negligently;

(iv) Dr Selby knew that the claimant had been sterilised and wanted no more children (let alone children with serious handicaps) and Dr Selby's duty of care when advising on the symptoms of which the claimant made complaint must be deemed to include the purpose of ensuring that if the claimant was indeed pregnant again she should be informed of this fact, so as to enable her to take appropriate steps to prevent the birth of another child if she wished;

(v)   as in *Parkinson*, no radical step into the unknown is in question here;

(vi) as in *Parkinson*, an award of compensation which is limited to the special upbringing associated with rearing a child with a serious disability would be fair, just and reasonable.

The issues in *Groom* are interesting. Meningitis is a natural infection, caused by natural bacteria, and is a natural consequence of childbirth. Therefore, how did Brooke LJ come to the conclusion that the *doctor* caused the meningitis? They seemed to be in agreement that, because the doctor caused the wrongful pregnancy, he should foresee (and therefore caused) all of the consequences flowing from it: 'the birth of a premature child who suffered salmonella meningitis through exposure to a bacterium during the normal processes of birth was a foreseeable consequence of Dr Selby's failure to advise the claimant that although she had been sterilised she was in fact pregnant' (Brooke LJ).

This may not be entirely fair. Brooke LJ admitted that meningitis was an extremely rare event: 'the chain of events that took place in this case was foreseeable, even if it was extremely rare', and so it can be argued that when an outcome is extremely rare, it is probably not that foreseeable. However, Brooke LJ rejected the argument that the meningitis was an unforeseeable act that broke the chain of causation absolving the doctor from any liability, on the grounds that meningitis is a natural consequence flowing from the childbirth, as opposed to a new intervening act breaking the chain of causation. This leaves the law in a novel situation: a doctor who negligently performs a sterilisation operation foresees that a disabled child with meningitis will be born as a result.

It is not entirely fair to trace a naturally occurring infection back to the negligent act of the doctor.

A disabled pregnant mother

A wrongful pregnancy may occur to a disabled mother. This issue was not addressed in *McFarlane* or *Parkinson* because they dealt with claims from healthy parents, so when the case of *AD* v *East Kent Community NHS Trust* (2003) arose, the Court of Appeal took a particularly strict approach and held that no upbringing costs could be claimed because the baby was healthy even if the mother was not.

CASE EXTRACT

AD v *East Kent Community NHS Trust* [2003] PIQR P18

Facts: [A] was a disabled woman who became pregnant whilst living on a psychiatric ward. The grandmother (A's mother) took care of the healthy baby, but A claimed that the NHS Trust had negligently let her become pregnant, and claimed for 'extra' upbringing costs under the rule in *Parkinson*.

Held: There were no 'extra costs' under *Parkinson* because the child was healthy, and the case of *McFarlane* confirmed that general upbringing costs could not be claimed. The grandmother had also *volunteered* her own services, meaning that she could not be compensated for upbringing the child.

Judge LJ (at paras 20–2): The cost of rearing C is not 'additional' or 'extra' in the sense envisaged in *Parkinson*. For all practical purposes, they are the same costs, now being borne by someone other than the mother, the grandmother, gratuitously providing for her granddaughter in the same way as the child's mother would have done, if she had been fit. As a head of damages, on the authorities, these costs are not recoverable as part of the mother's claim. We must add that we do not accept that this child cannot and never will provide any possible benefit to her mother. [...] We naturally have great sympathy for [the grandmother] as well as considerable admiration for the way in which she has come to C's rescue and provided her with the love and care that she needs. We must, however, dismiss this appeal.

It is clear in *AD* v *East Kent* that disabled parents can be distinguished from disabled children when it comes to claiming extra costs: only a disabled child will be eligible for damages in wrongful pregnancy (both *McFarlane* and *Parkinson* applied).

The case of *Rees* (2003) surfaced at the same time on very similar facts, but it travelled up to the House of Lords. The lords were finally forced to revisit their decision in *McFarlane*. All seven lords who listened to the *Rees* appeal refused to overrule *McFarlane*. However, only a narrow majority ruled that Miss Rees could not recover the costs of upbringing her healthy child. The dissenting lords, who were veering away from the strict rule in *McFarlane*, appeared to be swayed by her visual disability.

CASE EXTRACT

Rees v *Darlington Memorial Hospital NHS Trust* [2003] UKHL 52

Facts: The claimant, who was severely visually handicapped and feared that her lack of sight would prevent her from being able to care for a child, underwent a sterilisation operation which was negligently performed at a hospital managed by the defendants. The claimant subsequently conceived and gave birth to a healthy child whose father did not wish to be involved with his upbringing. The trial judge held that she was not entitled to recover damages for any of the costs of providing for the healthy child (*McFarlane* applied). The Court of Appeal by a majority concluded that although damages could not be recovered in respect of costs arising from the birth of a healthy child under *McFarlane* it was, just as in the case of a child born with a disability, fair, just and reasonable for the parent who was disabled to recover by way of damages the additional costs attributable to her disability in bringing up the child. This was a wild stretch of the rule in *Parkinson* and the Trust appealed to the House of Lords.

Held: Considerations of what was fair, just and reasonable and principles of distributive justice prevented an award of damages against a doctor or health authority in respect of the costs of bringing up a normal healthy child. Her disability was irrelevant, but since she was the victim of a legal wrong which had denied her the opportunity to live in the way she had planned, it was unjust that she should be denied any recompense, so a modest award relating to her limitation of autonomy was awarded in the sum of £15,000.

Lord Bingham clearly stated that *McFarlane* would not be revisited. However, what does become clear throughout his judgment is that *McFarlane* may have been unfair in regards to failing to compensate the mother for her loss of freedom to choose the size of her family, and so compensation was awarded for a breach of autonomy. This was referred to as a 'gloss' on *McFarlane*.

Lord Bingham (at paras 1, 7–8): The claimant in these proceedings [Miss Rees] suffers a severe and progressive visual disability, such that she felt unable to discharge the ordinary duties of a mother, and for that reason wished to be sterilised. She made her wishes known to a consultant employed by the appellant NHS Trust, who carried out a sterilisation operation but did so negligently, and the claimant conceived and bore a son. The child is normal and healthy but the claimant's disability remains. She claimed as damages the cost of rearing the child. [...] I am of the clear opinion, for reasons more fully given by my noble and learned friends, that it would be wholly contrary to the practice of the House to disturb its unanimous decision in *McFarlane* given as recently as four years ago, even if a differently constituted committee were to conclude that a different solution should have been adopted. It would reflect no credit on the administration of the law if a line of English authority were to be disapproved in 1999 and reinstated in 2003 with no reason for the change beyond a change in the balance of judicial opinion. [...] Subject to one gloss, therefore, which I regard as important, I would affirm and adhere to the decision in *McFarlane*. [...] I question the fairness of a rule which denies the victim of a legal wrong any recompense at all beyond an award immediately related to the unwanted pregnancy and birth. [...] To speak of losing the freedom to limit the size of one's family is to mask the real loss suffered in a situation of this kind. This is that a parent, particularly (even today) the mother, has been denied, through the negligence of another, the opportunity to live her life in the way that she wished and planned. I do not think that an award immediately relating to the unwanted pregnancy and birth gives adequate recognition of or does justice to that loss. I would accordingly support the suggestion favoured by Lord Millett in *McFarlane*, that in all cases such as these there be a conventional award to mark the injury and loss, although I would favour a greater figure than the £5,000 he suggested (I have in mind a conventional figure of £15,000) and I would add this to the award for the pregnancy and birth. This solution is in my opinion consistent with the ruling and rationale of *McFarlane*. The conventional award would not be, and would not be intended to be, compensatory. It would afford some measure of recognition of the wrong done. And it would afford a more ample measure of justice than the pure *McFarlane* rule.

Lord Bingham does not want to disturb the 'unanimous' decision in *McFarlane* because it would 'reflect no credit on the administration of the law', but it is not entirely accurate to say that the judgment in *McFarlane* was unanimous because four of the five lords reached the majority decision on varying grounds. Besides, there is no reason to suggest that the law would not retain its 'credit' if it felt the need to overrule an unfair judgment only four years later. Lord Bingham clearly puts a 'gloss' on *McFarlane*, which is a financial award for the loss of the 'freedom to limit the size of one's family'. It was thought by Lord Bingham that £15,000 accurately represented the loss of freedom experienced by Miss Rees. This conventional award is paid *in addition* to the damages for wrongful pregnancy (e.g. pain, suffering, clothing and loss of earnings) and it is not meant to be compensatory but a *recognition* that a wrong was done. The courts do not typically compensate for the sole purpose of recognition in the tort of negligence – new rules relating to damages are a matter for Parliament.

Where does the law leave us after *Rees*? It was clearly accepted that *McFarlane* does not allow any of the upbringing costs to be claimed for a healthy baby borne out of a wrongful pregnancy, and this was applied in a straightforward fashion by the majority in *Rees*. The exception in *Parkinson* – that the extra costs of a disabled child can be claimed – was simply left alone but it was not stretched to cover disabled mothers. The 'gloss' in *Rees* took care of that indirectly, by providing a 'recognition payment' for a breach of autonomy. Lord Hope in *Rees* (not included above) pointed out that, under the traditional rules of tort, Miss Rees should have been compensated so as to put her back in her original position. The other lords ignored this view just as they did in *McFarlane* four years previously. The diversion from the normal rules of tort law in *McFarlane*, therefore, lives on. This controversial trail of case law considerably limits the amount of damages awarded to claimants in wrongful pregnancy cases. The NHS will no longer have to pay for the private education, for example, of a child who they negligently brought into existence. However, is a 'modest' acknowledgement of a civil wrong (regardless of income, parental disability or family circumstances) showing the law to be cheap and unsympathetic? Patients in medical negligence cases are entitled to be put back into their original position through an appropriate award of damages, so why are they limited to a standard award in wrongful pregnancy cases? It is not appropriate for the courts to exercise damage limitation simply because the money given to the claimants could be better used elsewhere. Lord Millett's original suggestion in *McFarlane* of a conventional sum of £5,000 (increased to £15,000 by Lord Bingham in *Rees*) aims to strike a balance between the needs of both parties, but in reality, it pleases only the NHS.

The academic response to wrongful pregnancy

It is perhaps an understatement to say that *McFarlane*, *Parkinson* and *Rees* have caused widespread confusion in civil law. It was *Udale* that first diverted from the established principle in tort to award full damages to place the claimant back in her original position. *McFarlane* simply followed suit at a higher level. *Parkinson* then developed an exception when the child was disabled, and *Rees* simply confirmed *McFarlane*. How have these cases been received by the wider academic community? Mullis showed an almost telepathic accuracy in the early 1990s when he commented that the courts should avoid being trapped by the 'floodgates' argument when calculating damages in medical negligence cases.

EXTRACT

Alastair Mullis, 'Wrongful Contraception Unravelled' (1993) 1 *Medical Law Review* 320, at pages 320–35

Where the doctor fails to exercise the required level of skill the patient should be entitled to recover damages to put him in the position he was in prior to the operation, so far as that is possible. The patient ordered his affairs in a particular way relying on the skill of the doctor, the doctor should, therefore, compensate him for any loss he suffers as a result of that reasonable reliance. [...] First, the number of potential plaintiffs is, in the usual case, limited to two and they can recover once only. Secondly, in most of these cases the woman will become pregnant fairly soon, usually within a year, after the operation. Finally, the amounts awarded have not usually been excessive and will of course be limited to the first child.

There has, since *McFarlane*, been far more criticism of the law from commentators.

EXTRACT

Tony Weir, 'The Unwanted Child' (2000) 59 *Cambridge Law Journal* 238 , at pages 238–41

For the fourteen years since *Emeh* the National Health Service, short of resources for curing the sick, has been disbursing large sums of money for the maintenance of children who have nothing wrong with them. [...] The result in *McFarlane* is quite right, and we should not be surprised if the reasoning is uneasy: whenever it enters the family home the law of obligations – not just tort, but contract and restitution as well – has a marked tendency to go pear-shaped.

Weir is clearly in support of *McFarlane* because it limits the amount of damages that an already pressed NHS service has to pay out to wronged patients. However, it can be argued that the decision in *McFarlane* does not sit 'uneasy' because it enters the family home – it sits uneasy because it does not follow the traditional rules of tort. Oppenheim suggests that the breach in *McFarlane* might be a breach of Article 8(1): the right to respect for private and family life. This would require a relevant exception under Article 8(2) to apply before damages were limited.

EXTRACT

Robin Oppenheim, 'The "Mosaic" of Tort Law: The Duty of Care Question' (2003) *Journal of Personal Injury Law* 151, at pages 151–71

The point of departure should be as Hale LJ suggests in *Parkinson*, that a wrongful conception or birth claim involves an invasion of bodily integrity. This raises issues that can be addressed under Article 8 of the Convention, which provide respectfully for the right to respect for a person's private and family life and home. [...] It is eminently arguable that the ability to regulate one's own fertility and plan the size of one's family, in the context of loss of autonomy and bodily integrity that unwanted pregnancy entails, falls within the ambit of this bundle of rights and where negligent advice has the consequence of disrupting that ability when conception takes place there is an infringement of Article 8(1). [...] If the limited recovery rule laid down by *McFarlane* is treated on the facts of a given case as an infringement of Article 8(1), the court must then go on to consider whether it fits within any of the restrictions under Article 8(2) that are necessary in a democratic society, namely whether it is a legitimate aim answering a pressing social need and applied proportionately. The only relevant exception is probably Article 8(2) on the basis that it was necessary 'for the protection of health or morals'. [...] It is difficult to see how non-recognition of a claim for economic loss could be said to be necessary for the protection of health or morals, as required by Article 8(2). There is no pressing need for this restriction.

Oppenheim may be wrong when he states that there is 'no pressing need' for a non-recognition of economic loss in this area of negligence. The health of the public could suffer considerably if massive amounts of damages are paid to completely healthy families in wrongful pregnancy cases, and this will be adequate justification for the UK courts to limit damages if and when they are faced with an action under Article 8.

The case of *Rees* has also come under fire from commentators, who claim that it wasted an opportunity to provide support for disabled parents.

EXTRACT

Samantha Singer, 'Case note: *Rees v Darlington*' (2004) in Emma Hitchings, Cases 26 *Journal of Social Welfare and Family Law* 403, at pages 403–15

By denying disabled parents damages for negligence – whether for the full expenses of bringing up the child or the additional costs – the risks that children in Ms Rees' son's situation will face being placed in care must increase. In turn, the fear of having their children removed often breeds reluctance in disabled parents to seek help in caring for their children. If this devastating end is avoided, the children of disabled parents often find themselves acting as carers for their parents. Indeed, Lord Millett used this fact as a reason for Ms Rees to be grateful for her surgeon's negligence:

> Once the child is able to go to school alone and be of some help around the house, his or her presence will to a greater or lesser extent help to alleviate the disadvantages of the parent's disability. And once the child has grown to adulthood, he or she can provide immeasurable help to an ageing and disabled parent.

It is surprising that such a naïve and unhelpful passage found its way into a speech in the House of Lords. What parent would wish this existence upon their child? Certainly not Karina Rees – this was part of her reason for being sterilised.

Singer clearly believes that the *Rees* judgment is unfair because of the long-term risks to the son, but it must be remembered that other blind parents bring up children with no payouts from the courts, so why should Miss Rees have her financial burdens eased when others do not? It is also not entirely true to say that disabled parents are reluctant to seek help to care for their children – there are benefits specifically for disabled people. The 'gloss' in *Rees* – that a conventional sum can be awarded to acknowledge a breach of autonomy – has been criticised at length by commentators.

EXTRACT

Alasdair Maclean, 'An Alexandrian Approach to the Knotty Problem of Wrongful pregnancy: *Rees* v *Darlington Memorial Hospital NHS Trust* in the House of Lords' [2004] 3 *Web Journal of Current Legal Issues* 1 at:

www.webjcli.ncl.ac.uk

The beauty of the conventional award is that it makes no unjustly arbitrary distinction between the claimants, all of whom will receive the same award. It will also make it considerably easier to come to an out of court settlement since there will be no need to haggle over the projected expenses of raising a child or the impact of a disability on those costs. It is, however, a bold but risky strategy. It is bold because, with one stroke, it destroys the knotty tangle weaved by the courts' ill-considered use of distributive justice. It is risky because it may end up pleasing no one, except perhaps the NHS. Given the potential costs involved in raising a child, the parents of a healthy child may still feel hard done by. Disabled parents may feel aggrieved because the comparatively small award is unlikely to meet the additional costs incurred because of their disability. Those in favour of a full award in line with corrective justice principles may feel that the solution fails to do justice and those who believe *McFarlane* was a wholly just decision may feel that the judgment has been undermined.

The new 'gloss' in *Rees* has given rise to a feeling that a wrongfully pregnant mother is 'hard done by'. The law awaits the next case, in which *McFarlane*, *Parkinson* and *Rees* are explored once more.

THINKING POINT

Having explored the case law in wrongful pregnancy cases and their relevant damages, would you advise a parent to pursue a claim for wrongful pregnancy in light of the ratios in *McFarlane*, *Parkinson* and *Rees*? Give reasons for your answer.

Wrongful birth

A mother can also bring an action for wrongful *birth* arising out of negligence. This is where the mother will typically argue: 'you caused me to give birth to a disabled child' as opposed to 'you caused me to conceive' as in a wrongful pregnancy case. Therefore, in wrongful birth actions, it is not the conception that occurred inexpertly, but the birth of a disabled child because the mother was deprived of a chance to have an abortion.

Typical scenarios could be as follows:

- The embryos created in fertility treatment may not be screened properly, leading to an embryo with a genetic disease or other disabilities being implanted into the mother.

- A married couple may undergo genetic testing before they plan a family, and they may be negligently informed that they do not carry genetic diseases.
- Tests taken during pregnancy fail to expose a disability or a disease, leading to the birth of a disabled baby and depriving the mother of an abortion.

The disabled babies born as a result of these scenarios could be prevented by using donor eggs or sperm, by not having children at all, or by having an abortion. If a mother claims that she was deprived of a chance to abort, the abortion must have been legal under the Infant Life (Preservation) Act 1929 or the Abortion Act 1967.[2]

Duty of care

The mother must first prove a duty of care. This will be straightforward: a medical professional who conducts genetic tests, screening, fertility treatment or other diagnostic tests will owe a duty of care to the patient. However, sometimes the person carrying out the test or recording the results may have never met the patient, so is there sufficient proximity to establish a duty of care in these scenarios? The following case says: 'yes – as long as they are patients'.

CASE EXTRACT

Farraj v *Kings Healthcare NHS Trust* [2010] 1 PTSR 1176

Facts: The patients [P] were carriers of a gene which could cause an inherited blood disorder. When the wife was pregnant she was advised to undergo DNA testing to detect whether the child would suffer from the disorder. A sample was taken and sent to the Trust's London hospital [KCH]. From there it was sent to an independent specialist cytogenetics laboratory [CSL] for foetal cells to be cultured. That was done and the sample returned to the hospital for testing. The test was negative. However, when the baby was born it was found to have the disorder. P sued the Trust and CSL. The trial judge held both defendants liable. The Trust appealed on liability, causation and apportionment.

Held: KCH appeal allowed. A hospital generally owed a non-delegable duty to its patients to ensure that they were treated with skill and care, but there was a significant difference between carrying out tests on a patient who had been admitted to hospital for treatment and carrying out tests on samples which were provided by a person who was not a patient. Since the claimants had not been admitted to the Trust's hospital for treatment and the hospital had undertaken no special responsibilities to the claimants, there was no basis for finding that it owed them a special non-delegable duty of care. The laboratory [CSL] was entirely responsible for the damages and solely liable to pay the claimants' costs.

Dyson LJ (at paras 88, 92): It is true that the extent to which a hospital owes a non-delegable duty to ensure that its patients are treated with due skill and care will depend on the facts of the particular case. [...] The rationale for this is that the hospital undertakes the care, supervision and control of its patients who are in special need of care. Patients are a vulnerable class of persons who place themselves in the care and under the control of a hospital and, as a result, the hospital assumes a particular

---

[2] This was confirmed by *Rance* v *Mid-Downs HA* [1991] 1 QB 587.

responsibility for their wellbeing and safety. To use the language of *Caparo Industries plc v Dickman* [1990] 2 AC 605, it is therefore fair just and reasonable that a hospital should owe such a duty of care to its patients in these circumstances. [...] [However] I do not consider that KCH owed the claimants a non-delegable duty to ensure that CSL carried out the task entrusted to it with due skill and care. [...] The claimants were not admitted to KCH for treatment. KCH has at all material times provided diagnostic and interpretative services for chorionic villus sampling. But there is no reason to suppose that these services could not have been provided by a specialist laboratory or testing house rather than a hospital. In my judgment, there is a significant difference between treating a patient who is admitted to hospital for that purpose and carrying out tests on samples which are provided by a person who is not a patient.

The *Farraj* case clearly tells us that, if a third party deals with test samples, they are connected to the patients and they can be found to have a duty of care towards the patients. The hospital was not found to have a special non-delegable duty of care because the patients were not being *treated* by the hospital and thus were not admitted as patients.

Breach of duty

The duty of care must be breached. According to *Bolam v Friern Hospital Management Committee* [1957] 1 WLR 582, the standard of care for doctors and other specialists is that of the ordinary skilled man exercising that special skill. In wrongful birth cases, a specialist who scans expectant mothers for abnormalities must display the same standard of care as a skilled person in that profession. A clear example of a breach occurred in *Lillywhite*.

CASE EXTRACT

Lillywhite v *University College London Hospitals NHS Trust* [2005] EWCA Civ 1466

Facts: The mother [P] had a scan on her foetus, performed by a radiologist [R] at the NHS Hospital. He failed to notice that certain brain structures were not present in the foetus. A second expert was approached at around the same time, and came to the same conclusion, although he admitted that he did not have a clear view. A daughter [D] was born with severe malformation of the brain. P alleged that R had been negligent when carrying out his ultrasound scan of D's brain before she was born in failing to detect the abnormalities. R argued in response that another expert had come to the same conclusion and so he had exercised proper care and skill.

Held: The duty of care owed by R demanded a high standard of care and skill. It was of vital importance for R to confirm the presence or absence of the normal brain structures. Although R carried out the ultrasound procedure carefully he could not have exercised reasonable care and skill in concluding on the basis of that examination that the relevant structures were present.

Latham LJ (at para 31): The duty of care owed by Professor Rodeck demanded a high standard of care and skill. [...] I do not understand the respondents to deny that. The issue was of vital importance. If the structures were indeed absent, that

→

would necessarily require consideration of a prompt intervention were Mrs Lillywhite to determine, as the judge found she would have done, to terminate the pregnancy. Equally, he would need to be confident of the absence of those structures in order to be able to advise Mrs Lillywhite as to termination, otherwise there would be the risk of aborting a healthy foetus.

The *Lillywhite* case confirms that it does not matter that the medical procedure is performed properly, what matters is that the care and skill was at an appropriate standard. Professor Rodeck was very careful when he performed the scan, but the fact that he did not identify the missing structures in the foetus brain meant that he did not display reasonable care and skill.

Breach must cause the damage

There must be a clear chain of causation between the negligent act and the disabled child for the breach to be said to cause the outcome. However, if there is an intervening act, such as dangerous substance abuse during pregnancy, this will probably break the chain of causation.

Damages: what can be compensated?

The ordinary principles of tort aim to put the claimant back in the position she was in before the breach took place. In wrongful pregnancy cases, damages were limited to the 'extra costs' of raising a disabled child according to *McFarlane, Parkinson* and *Rees*. In wrongful birth cases, how much can be recovered?

The mother in a wrongful birth case *wanted* to become pregnant, so recovery for the pain and suffering of pregnancy and childbirth is not possible. That leaves the upbringing costs. The mother wanted to bring up a healthy child, not a *disabled* child (she is arguing that she would have terminated if properly informed). Therefore, the damage appears to be purely economic; she is simply seeking the extra costs of raising a disabled child. The normal rules of tort apply to wrongful birth cases, meaning that full damages are awarded to place the claimant in her original position. For example, in the case of *FP* v *Taunton and Somerset NHS Trust* [2011] EWHC 3380, millions of pounds were awarded to help with the living arrangements of a child who had multiple disabilities as a result of wrongful birth. This appears to show that the strict damage limitation seen in wrongful pregnancy cases (*McFarlane, Parkinson* and *Rees*) has not applied to wrongful birth cases. What is also difficult about wrongful birth damages is that the mother must prove, had she been properly informed about the disability, that she would have terminated the pregnancy. How does a mother prove this retrospectively? It will depend on the facts of the case. For example, if there is evidence that the mother was highly concerned about foetal abnormalities and sought several tests to confirm her suspicions (as in *Lillywhite*), her lawyers may successfully argue on a balance of probabilities that she would have terminated if she had been properly informed. However, if there is no such evidence, then the judge is free to reject her claim.[3]

Wrongful birth actions are ethically difficult, and it is not hard to see why. The message sent out to society is disturbing: 'you must claim that you would have aborted your disabled child to be awarded compensation for its birth'. However, the case law appears to support wrongful birth claims, and the full amount of damages that comes with it.

___
[3] This happened in *Deriche* v *Ealing Hospital NHS Trust* [2003] EWHC 3104.

CASE EXTRACT

Hardman v Amin (2001) 59 BMLR 58

Facts: A doctor negligently failed to diagnose a rubella infection in a pregnant woman, leading to the birth of a severely handicapped baby boy.

Held: The action succeeded.

Henriques J (at para 11): If the commuters on the underground were asked whether the costs of bringing up Daniel (which are attributable to his disability) should fall on the claimant or the rest of the family, or the state, or the defendant, I am satisfied that the very substantial majority, having regard to the particular circumstances of this case, would say that the expense should fall on the wrongdoer.

CASE EXTRACT

Lee v Taunton and Somerset NHS Trust [2001] PNLR 11

Facts: A high resolution ultrasound was performed but it failed to detect spina bifida, a disease which affects a foetus.

Held: The action succeeded.

Toulson J: I do not believe that it would be right for the law to deem the birth of a disabled child to be a blessing, in all the circumstances and regardless of the extent to the child's disabilities; or to regard the responsibility for the care of such a child as so enriching in the ordinary nature of things that it would be unjust for a parent to recover the cost from a negligent doctor on whose skill that parent had properly relied to prevent the situation. If the matter were put to an opinion poll among passengers on the Underground, I would be surprised if a majority would support such a view.

The fact remains that in all the cited cases, before and after *McFarlane*, of birth of a disabled child after alleged negligence in failing to detect foetal abnormalities which would have led to a termination of the pregnancy, the courts have recognised the claimant's right to claim damages for the cost of meeting the child's special needs.

The 'underground' test originates from Lord Steyn in *McFarlane* (2000), where he used it to conclude that commuters on the underground would not support a claim for the upbringing costs of a healthy baby in a wrongful pregnancy. Henriques J in *Hardman* (2000) and Toulson J in *Lee* (2001) both use the test to conclude that commuters on the underground *would* support a claim for the upbringing costs of a disabled baby in a wrongful birth, probably because in wrongful birth actions the child is *always* born with abnormalities.

ACTIVITY

Draw up a comparison table for wrongful pregnancy and wrongful birth actions. Compare the ratios, legal support and damages in each case.

● Wrongful life

It is not just the mother who can bring an action against a negligent doctor or specialist. The child may be able to bring a claim if she is injured in some way. There are two potential actions available. The first action – a statutory action for prenatal injuries under the Congenital Disabilities (Civil Liability) Act 1976 – is widely accepted by the courts (examined further below). The second action – a common law action of 'wrongful life' – has been rejected by the courts. What is 'wrongful life' and why did the courts refuse the claim?

The essence of a wrongful life claim is that the mother was deprived of an abortion, leading to a birth which should never have happened.[4] The instances in which a claim for wrongful life might occur are the same as those for wrongful birth:

- The embryos created in fertility treatment may not be screened properly, leading to an embryo with a genetic disease or other disabilities being implanted into the mother.

- A married couple may undergo genetic testing before they plan a family, and they may be negligently informed that they do not carry genetic diseases.

- Tests taken during pregnancy fail to expose a disability or a disease, leading to the birth of a disabled baby and depriving the mother of an abortion.

The leading case on wrongful life is *McKay* (1982). In this case, the courts rejected the wrongful life claim and decided that it could not be pursued as a legal action in our jurisdiction. Stephenson LJ gave the most detailed judgment and the other judges provided unanimous support and felt the need to explain *why* they rejected the action with a detailed legal analysis.

CASE EXTRACT

McKay v *Essex AHA* [1982] QB 1166

Facts: The infant was born disabled as a result of an infection of rubella suffered by her mother during pregnancy. The child and mother alleged that but for the negligence of the defendant, the mother would have had an abortion. The child claimed damages on the grounds that she had 'suffered entry into a life in which her injuries are highly debilitating'.

Held: The doctor was under no legal obligation under the Abortion Act 1967 to the foetus to terminate its life, and the child's claim was contrary to public policy as a violation of the sanctity of human life. It was a claim which could not be recognised since the court could not evaluate damages for the denial of non-existence. It was an unreasonable action in law.

Stephenson LJ (at pages 1171, 1177–82, 1184): In this case we are unanimously of the opinion that the infant plaintiff's claim for what has been called 'wrongful life' discloses no reasonable cause of action. [...] Here the court is considering not 'ancient law' but a novel cause of action, for or against which there is no authority in any reported case in the courts of the United Kingdom or the Commonwealth. [...] If, as is conceded, any duty is owed to an unborn child, the authority's hospital laboratory and the doctor looking after the mother during her pregnancy undoubtedly owed the child a duty not to injure it, and if she had been injured as a result of lack of

➔

---

[4] The disability can be pursued by the child under the 1976 Act too (examined further below).

reasonable care and skill on their part after birth, she could have sued them. [...] But this child has not been injured by either defendant, but by the rubella which has infected the mother without fault on anybody's part. Her right not to be injured before birth by the carelessness of others has not been infringed by either defendant, any more than it would have been if she had been disabled by disease after birth. Neither defendant has broken any duty to take reasonable care not to injure her. [...] The only right on which she can rely as having been infringed is a right not to be born deformed or disabled, which means a right to be aborted or killed. The only duty which either defendant can owe to the unborn child infected with disabling rubella is a duty to abort or kill her or deprive her of that opportunity. [...] I am accordingly of opinion that though the judge was right in saying that the child's complaint is that she was born with deformities, without which she would have suffered no damage and have no complaint, her claim against the defendants is a claim that they were negligent in allowing her, injured as she was in the womb, to be born at all, a claim for 'wrongful entry into life' or 'wrongful life'. This analysis leads inexorably on to the question: how can there be a duty to take away life? How indeed can it be lawful? [...]

Because a doctor can lawfully by statute do to a foetus what he cannot lawfully do to a person who has been born, it does not follow that he is under a legal obligation to a foetus to do it and terminate its life, or that the foetus has a legal right to die. [...]

We have no exact information about the extent of this child's serious and highly debilitating congenital injuries – the judge was told that she was partly blind and deaf – but it is not and could not be suggested that the quality of her life is such that she is certainly better dead, or would herself wish that she had not been born or should now die. I am therefore compelled to hold that neither defendant was under any duty to the child to give the child's mother an opportunity to terminate the child's life. That duty may be owed to the mother, but it cannot be owed to the child. To impose such a duty towards the child would, in my opinion, make a further inroad on the sanctity of human life which would be contrary to public policy. It would mean regarding the life of a handicapped child as not only less valuable than the life of a normal child, but so much less valuable that it was not worth preserving. [...] The only way in which a child injured in the womb can be compensated in damages is by measuring what it has lost. [...] Judges have to pluck figures from the air in putting many imponderables into pounds and pence. Loss of expectation of life, for instance, has been held so difficult that the courts have been driven to fix for it a constant and arbitrary figure. [...] To measure loss of expectation of death would require a value judgment where a crucial factor lies altogether outside the range of human knowledge and could only be achieved, if at all, by resorting to the personal beliefs of the judge who has the misfortune to attempt the task. If difficulty in assessing damages is a bad reason for refusing the task, impossibility of assessing them is a good one. [...]

The defendants must be assumed to have been careless. The child suffers from serious disabilities. If the defendants had not been careless, the child would not be suffering now because it would not be alive. Why should the defendants not pay the child for its suffering? The answer lies in the implications and consequences of holding that they should.

Stephenson LJ clearly states at the very beginning of the judgment that it was a novel claim and worthy of exploration. There is no case law to look to for guidance in the United Kingdom or the entire Commonwealth (i.e. Australia, etc.). This gives a very big clue as to the complexity and unreasonableness of the action. The heart of the matter was whether a duty of care was owed to an unborn child, and Stephenson LJ confirmed that the hospital owed a duty not to injure it by applying reasonable care and skill. However, it was not the hospital that injured the child but the infection of rubella which occurred on its own, so the duty of care was not breached. A hospital only has a duty to offer the mother a chance to have an abortion, nothing more. The child is arguing that due to the negligence of the hospital she was born burdened with her deformities, but Stephenson LJ believed that they were only responsible for her being born, not her deformities (i.e. the elements were separated). This means that the heart of the action must be framed in the following terms in order to succeed: 'unborn disabled babies have a right to be aborted or killed by the hospital'. It is becoming clear why this action was eventually struck out for public policy reasons. Stephenson LJ accepts that there is such a duty towards the mother to offer her an abortion, but none towards the unborn child to offer it death. A foetus does not have a legal right to die even though it can be lawfully aborted under the Abortion Act 1967 under strict guidelines. Such an action, in the opinion of Stephenson LJ, would send out a message that disabled children were 'less valuable' or 'not worth preserving'. This may only be partially true, because we have carried out lawful abortions in the UK since the 1929 Infant Life (Preservation) Act and it has not devalued the life of a baby in any way. The biggest issue for Stephenson LJ was the impossible measurement of damages. To put the claimant (i.e. the child) back into its original position would be to abort her, which is impossible. A measurement of damages as a more plausible alternative was also impossible, because: 'to measure loss of expectation of death would require a value judgment where a crucial factor lies altogether outside the range of human knowledge and could only be achieved, if at all, by resorting to the personal beliefs of the judge who has the misfortune to attempt the task.' In other words, a judge cannot measure the 'imponderable' loss of a chance of death. In the end, Stephenson LJ decided that, even though a lack of precedent should not prevent a novel action, he had to prevent it on the grounds of public policy. The three lords who heard the *McKay* appeal (Stephenson LJ, Griffith LJ and Ackner LJ) raised valid justifications as to why a wrongful life claim could never succeed:

- It would be contrary to public policy to extend the common law duty of care to ensuring that a person did not exist.
- The sanctity of life would be undermined if doctors owed a duty to foetuses to prevent their lives.
- The fact that the foetus is born disabled is not something that the doctor should compensate for unless he actually caused the disability directly, there is a separate action for this known as 'injuries *in utero*' examined below.
- The action therefore centres around being brought into existence; and there is no legal duty to prevent this.
- If there was a duty to prevent this and a wrongful life claim did succeed, assessing the amount of damages is an impossible task on the grounds that they would have to compare existence to non-existence, and judges are not qualified or experienced to do this.
- Where would it end if wrongful life was actionable? In the future, could a child *sue her parent* for refusing an abortion, for example?

It is also misleading of the lords in *McKay* to suggest that existence cannot be balanced against non-existence, because this has been done in law before. In neonatal euthanasia cases (see Chapter 11), a 'balance sheet' of benefits and burdens has been drawn up to decide whether life sustaining treatment should be continued or withdrawn from severely disabled children (see: *An NHS Trust v B* [2006] EWHC 507). It has also been found on some occasions that it is in the best interests of the disabled child to withdraw its treatment leading to bring about its death: *Re J (A Minor) (Wardship: Medical Treatment), Re* [1991] 2 WLR 140; *Re C (A Minor) (Medical Treatment)* [1998] Lloyd's Rep Med 1 Fam Div *Re Wyatt (A Child) (Medical Treatment: Parents Consent)* [2004] EWHC 2247 (Fam), and *Re K (A Minor)* [2006] EWHC 1007. It is accepted that these cases did not require the quantification of damages and so were much easier for the lords to deliberate, but they do prove that it has been found, in the common law, to be in the best interests of a severely handicapped child to die. In this new light, perhaps there is a valid argument to be heard for 'wrongful life' actions after all? It has been argued by commentators that if the courts have no difficulty in awarding a mother full damages for the 'wrongful birth' of a disabled child, why is it such a difficult concept to compensate a *child* for her 'wrongful life' when she is born disabled?

EXTRACT

Tony Weir, 'Wrongful Life – Nipped in the Bud' (1982) 41 *Cambridge Law Journal* 225, at page 227

To assert that one cannot owe a duty to a foetus to kill it is plausible enough, but the plausibility fades a bit when one has to admit that a duty to kill the foetus may well be owed to the mother: if a duty is owed to one of the affected parties, why not to the other?

The actions are, in essence, exactly the same; the only difference is wrongful birth is claimed by the mother, whereas wrongful life is claimed by the child.

Action:	Wrongful birth	Wrongful life
Claimant:	Mother	Child
Claim:	'I should not have given birth to a disabled child'	'I am a disabled child that should not have been born'
Damages:	All upbringing costs	No case to answer

When looking at the comparison table above, the conclusion in *McKay* looks even more unsteady. What was the *real* reason for striking out the claim? There is clearly no compelling legal reason for doing so if wrongful birth cases are successful. Perhaps it is the way in which wrongful life claims are framed? The title 'wrongful life' implies that the life of the child is wrong. Teff has recognised that if the action was framed in a different way, the courts may have been more likely to consider it as a feasible claim.

EXTRACT

Harvey Teff, 'The Action for "Wrongful Life" in England and the United States' (1985) 34 *International & Comparative Law Quarterly* 423, at page 425

These labels are unfortunate not least in their bizarre, even macabre, overtones. One is not instinctively attracted to the cause of someone who appears to be impugning life itself. This aside, the terms are neither immediately intelligible nor readily distinguishable from each other. Though both signify claims for damages when negligent conduct has resulted in a child being born, they conceal a host of different legal and social implications, depending both on the circumstances leading up to the birth and on its consequences. Thus 'wrongful life', 'wrongful birth' and other expressions canvassed by courts and commentators are potentially a source of considerable confusion. It is scarcely surprising that the characterisation of 'birth' and 'life' as 'wrongful' has often prompted judicial hostility, if not sheer incredulity.

It is not clear where the title 'wrongful life' came from. The origins of the action, or its roots, are not traceable. What is clear, however, is that the title does no favours to the claimant, who will find her action rejected by the courts on the grounds of public policy because the very idea of claiming for 'wrongful life' goes against the sanctity of life. A less emotive title could prove to be more litigation-friendly, such as 'negligent birth' or 'wrongful disabled birth' instead of 'wrongful life'.

THINKING POINT

If *McKay* was decided differently and wrongful life had become actionable in negligence, what practical difference would this really make to medicine, the pressures on doctors and the people in society, if any?

Injuries *in utero*

The final action available for negligence before birth is for injuries *in utero*. This means any injury caused to the child *inside the uterus*. The main difference between this action and wrongful birth/life is that the disability is *directly caused* by the NHS trust, e.g. botched surgery or dangerous delivery. It is easier for the courts to find liability, sort through the ethical, moral and social issues, and award damages for the disabled existence of the child. This is a statutory claim under the Congenital Disabilities (Civil Liability) Act 1976, and it covers all babies born after 22 July 1976.

The 1976 Act is a very small Act, containing only six sections.

Congenital Disabilities (Civil Liability) Act 1976

Section 1: Civil liability to a child born disabled

(1) If a child is born disabled as the result of such an occurrence before its birth as is mentioned in subsection (2) below, and a person is under this section answerable to the child in respect of the occurrence, the child's disabilities are to be regarded as damage resulting from the wrongful act of that person and actionable accordingly at the suit of the child.

(2)   An occurrence to which this section applies is one which –

(a)   affected either parent of the child in his or her ability to have a normal, healthy child; or

(b)   affected the mother during her pregnancy, or affected her or the child in the course of its birth, so that the child is born with disabilities which would not otherwise have been present.

(3)   Subject to the following subsections, a person (here referred to as 'the defendant') is answerable to the child if he was liable in tort to the parent or would, if sued in due time, have been so; and it is no answer that there could not have been such liability because the parent suffered no actionable injury, if there was a breach of legal duty which, accompanied by injury, would have given rise to the liability.

(4)   In the case of an occurrence preceding the time of conception, the defendant is not answerable to the child if at that time either or both of the parents knew the risk of their child being born disabled, that is to say, the particular risk created by the occurrence; but should it be the child's father who is the defendant, this subsection does not apply if he knew of the risk and the mother did not.

(5)   The defendant is not answerable to the child, for anything he did or omitted to do when responsible in a professional capacity for treating or advising the parent, if he took reasonable care having due regard to then received professional opinion applicable to the particular class of case; but this does not mean that he is answerable only because he departed from received opinion.

(6)   [omitted]

(7)   If in the child's action under this section it is shown that the parent affected shared the responsibility for the child being born disabled, the damages are to be reduced to such extent as the court thinks just and equitable having regard to the extent of the parent's responsibility.

Section 1 may only have seven subsections, but they tell a complex story:

- Section 1(1): the occurrence must happen *before the birth* of the child at the hands of a person who is *not* the child's mother, e.g. a doctor or the hospital.

- Section 1(2): an 'occurrence' can include something that prevents a parent from conceiving a healthy child, e.g. botched surgery, or it can include something that happened during the pregnancy or birth, e.g. incorrect drugs or a dangerous delivery.

- Section 1(3): the defendant is answerable to the child if, in tort, he is answerable to the parent, e.g. duty, breach and cause, and it is no answer to say that the parent has escaped uninjured.

- Section 1(4): if the occurrence happened *before the conception* of the child, i.e. a botched sterilisation procedure or a sexually transmitted disease, the doctor or hospital is not answerable to the child if 'either or both parents' knew about the risk of disability created by that occurrence because they chose to conceive the child anyway . . .

- Section 1(4): . . . but if the *father* is the defendant, i.e. he caused the occurrence that led to a disabled child, the provisions under section 1(4) that the defendant is 'not answerable' do *not* apply and an action can be found against him if he knew of the risk of disability and didn't tell the mother.

- Section 1(5): the defendant is not answerable to the child for anything done or omitted if he was acting with reasonable care and in accordance with professional opinion at the time, although this will not *definitively* exclude him from liability.
- Section 1(7): if the parent who is affected shares some blame for the disabilities, i.e. misuse of prescription drugs during pregnancy, damages will be reduced by the courts.

It is helpful that, under section 1(2), occurrences *before the conception* of the child can be submitted as causes of the disability, opening the door for botched surgical procedures, sexually transmitted diseases or negligent medical care to be included as 'occurrences' under the Act. The mention of the father under section 1(4) is particularly strange. Parliament may have envisaged a scenario in which a father causes his own child to be disabled. The provision under section 1(4) seems confusing, but to put it in a nutshell, there is no action against a doctor for occurrences before conception if the *father* caused the occurrence. Bizarrely, this means that the child has an action against her own father for her disabilities under section 1(4) of the 1976 Act even though section 1(1) specifically excludes actions against the mother (explained below). There is another part to section 1(4): there is no action against the doctor – even though the occurrence was caused by his hands – when 'either or both' parents know of the risk of disability. This is because the parents themselves were aware of, and chose to run the risk of, conceiving a disabled child. The doctor cannot be blamed for this. This part of section 1(4) is unfair on the child of course, who has no avenue for damages in this situation and is disabled as a result of a doctor's negligence. It is made clear under section 1(3) that the doctor or trust must owe a duty of care over one of the parents which must be actionable in tort in order for the child to bring a claim under the 1976 Act. This means, in practical terms, that there must be a duty of care, a breach of that duty, and the breach must cause the damage (injury to the mother is not even necessary). This exact situation presented itself in the 'wrongful life' case of *McKay* (above). We know that the courts were quick to strike out this action on public policy and impossibility grounds (in terms of calculating damages), but it is a requirement under the 1976 Act for the child to prove that all of these criteria are in place in order to claim damages for her disability and this was done in *McKay*. What is the difference, if any, between these two actions?

A mother can cause disabilities to her own child just like a doctor or a father can, so why can't a child bring an action against her mother? The 1976 Act is only concerned with legal actions where there is a breach of a duty *owed to one of the parents*, clearly stated under section 1(3). This means that if the mother was responsible for the injuries *in vitro*, i.e. drug abuse or dangerous behaviour, then she was not under a duty of care from a doctor at the time. However, if the mother *contributed* to the disability *alongside the doctor* as part of his breach of duty, damages will be limited under section 1(7) of the 1976 Act because the doctor is not fully to blame. It is not a very good idea to allow a child to sue its mother. It might cause an intolerable strain within the family. The child would need to find someone else to represent her legally, and the mother would be paying damages to the child, which is odd when you consider that the mother pays to raise the child anyway. The child cannot do much with large amounts of money because it is the mother who provides clothes, food and extra care, so the mother would, in effect, be paying damages to herself.[5] If the Congenital Disabilities (Civil Liability) Act 1976 was to

---

[5] There is one exception to the liability of the mother: if she is driving she owes a duty of care to her unborn child just like she does to a pedestrian or a passenger. It follows that if she breaches that duty through her negligent driving, the child has an action for the disabilities that occur: section 2 of the 1976 Act.

be reformed to allow legal actions against the mother, there would be no end of dangerous social activities that would be listed under section 1. Science has still not established plausible connections between many dangerous social activities and the effects on an unborn child, from mobile phone use to eating eggs.

ACTIVITY

Kayleigh was expecting a baby at the unusual age of 48. It was her first child, having waited years for her career and finances to settle down. The doctor told her that she had a higher risk of giving birth to a brain damaged baby, and asked if she would like a test. Kayleigh consented. It involved taking a sample of the baby's blood using a big needle. It was a dangerous procedure that came with risks. The sample was taken, and the baby was fine. However, after birth, it was noted that the baby's breathing was not adequate, and it transpired that the doctor had pierced the baby's lungs *in utero*, which were clearly seen on the ultrasound screen, and the baby needed surgery to correct the damage. Kayleigh has come to you for advice on the 1976 Act and whether it applied to her.

Injuries *in utero*: the common law

The Congenital Disabilities (Civil Liability) Act 1976 covers all babies born after 22 July 1976. A child born before this date may still be able to use the old common law rules to bring an action on the condition that it was born alive with those disabilities. This situation might occur when the disability does not manifest itself until much later on in life. It is well established in common law that a baby cannot bring an action until after it is born.

CASE EXTRACT

Paton v British Pregnancy Advisory Service Trustees [1979] QB 276

Facts: A husband wanted to stop his wife from having an abortion and brought the action in the name of the foetus.

Held: A husband has no legal right to prevent an abortion and a foetus is not a legal entity in law.

Sir George Baker P (at page 279): The foetus cannot, in English law, in my view, have any right of its own at least until it is born and has a separate existence from the mother. That permeates the whole of the civil law of this country. [...] It was universally accepted, and has since been accepted, that in order to have a right the foetus must be born and be a child. [...] There can be no doubt, in my view, that in England and Wales, the foetus has no right of action, no right at all, until birth. [...]

It is well settled that a foetus does not have a legal personality. The law would be in an odd predicament if *Paton* was decided differently – a person would have to represent the foetus and give the foetus a voice and its own thoughts during a trial. The judges would then have to decide what was 'in the best interests' of that particular foetus, even though its disabilities could not be diagnosed until after its birth. The case of *Burton* (1993) confirmed that as soon as the child is born alive, the injuries inflicted *in utero* become real and actionable.

CASE EXTRACT

Burton v *Islington HA* [1993] QB 204

Facts: Two babies were born before the Congenital Disabilities (Civil Liability) Act 1976 came into force, and were disabled as a result of negligence to their mother during pregnancy and during birth. They wanted to bring claims for their disabilities under the common law of negligence.

Held: A child born suffering disabilities caused by medical negligence before birth can sue in negligence because, although not a person in the eyes of the law when the injury took place, a duty of care towards the child comes into existence when the child is born with his or her injuries.

Dillon LJ (at page 219): In law and in logic no damage can have been caused to the plaintiff before the plaintiff existed. The damage was suffered by the plaintiff at the moment that, in law, the plaintiff achieved personality and inherited the damaged body for which the health authority (on the assumed facts) was responsible. The events prior to birth were mere links in the chain of causation between the health authority's assumed lack of skill and care and the consequential damage to the plaintiff.

The common law, as illustrated by *Burton*, appears to be very accessible for children born disabled as a result of negligence. The duty of care is simply 'delayed' until birth. The Congenital Disabilities (Civil Liability) Act 1976 took a completely different route, insisting that there was a duty of care towards one of the *parents*. The common law is much simpler, placing the *child* at the centre of the action. The traditional test for negligence will thereafter apply (explored below):

(i)   duty of care;

(ii) breach of duty;

(iii) breach caused the outcome.

THINKING POINT

Do you think there are any moral or ethical issues relating to claiming damages for injuries *in utero* or before conception? In addition, how much compensation would be a fair amount for a negligent doctor to pay in these circumstances?

Liability for negligence *after* birth (i.e. general medical negligence)

We have learnt so far there is a three-part test to be satisfied for negligence to be established (duty, breach and cause). These three criteria must be proven – on a balance of probabilities – in a court of law for the NHS trust (representing the doctor) to be held responsible for the loss or injury to the patient.[6] This is when negligence becomes complicated. The three-part test is more difficult to satisfy than many people think. The first criterion requires a duty of care. This can be found in most cases, but what if a third party, such as the husband of a patient, wishes to take the hospital trust to court because they have suffered some harm too? The question here is: how far does a duty of care stretch in medical law? The second criterion requires a breach of that duty. There is a tangle of case law on this issue. What exactly does a 'breach' look like and what are the accepted standards of care for doctors and specialists? In addition, can the courts allow for human error in medical law, or are the slightest mistakes considered to be legally culpable? The third criterion requires a chain of causation to be complete. This is not so difficult in other areas of law where the pulling of a trigger and the resulting bullet wound is the clear cause of death. In medical law, the patient is already suffering from an illness at the time of the negligence, and this could be the cause of the harm just as much as the negligent act or omission. The courts must separate the potential causes in order to pinpoint the doctor as the main cause. This is not always possible and in reality a high number of medical negligence cases fall at this last hurdle.

THINKING POINT

Do you think the 'blame culture' is responsible for encouraging the public to pursue fruitless medical negligence actions? Does it lead to 'defensive medicine' or a lower standard of practice? How do you think your healthcare would be affected if your doctors or hospital trusts were constantly fearful of legal action?

A duty of care

A doctor, nurse, surgeon, counsellor, therapist, midwife and every other healthcare professional you can think of owes a duty of care to the patient they are treating. There does not need to be a contract in place these days, although in private medical care there is a formal contract to be signed, and this rule was developed in *Donoghue* v *Stevenson* (1932).

CASE EXTRACT

Donoghue v *Stevenson* [1932] AC 562

Facts: Mrs Donoghue was bought a bottle of ginger ale by a friend, and drank half the contents before a decomposing snail materialised from the bottle. Mrs Donoghue had severe gastroenteritis as a result, and wanted to sue the manufacturer (Stevenson). However, Mrs Donoghue did not have a contract connecting her to the manufacturer (her friend purchased the bottle) and so the question was: can a person sue a tortfeasor when no contract is in place?

→

---

[6] NHS trusts are vicariously liable for the doctors and surgeons working for them. This means that the NHS trust will fight the claim vicariously on behalf of the doctor or surgeon. The NHS Litigation Authority deals with these kinds of claims. GP's are a different matter – they are considered to be 'primary care' and nobody is vicariously liable for them – and so can be sued directly by the patient. GPs must therefore be insured by a medical defence union.

Held: A manufacturer owes a common law duty of care to his customers to make sure that their product does not cause any harm, illness or injury. No contract between the parties is necessary: only foreseeability and proximity are required.

Lord Atkin (at pages 578–80, 599): The question is whether the manufacturer of an article of drink sold by him to a distributor, in circumstances which prevent the distributor or the ultimate purchaser or consumer from discovering by inspection any defect, is under any legal duty to the ultimate purchaser or consumer to take reasonable care that the article is free from defect likely to cause injury to health. [...] You must take reasonable care to avoid acts or omissions which you can reasonably foresee would be likely to injure your neighbour. Who, then, in law is my neighbour? The answer seems to be persons who are so closely and directly affected by my act that I ought reasonably to have them in my contemplation as being so affected when I am directing my mind to the acts or omissions which are called in question. [...] My Lords, if your Lordships accept the view that this pleading discloses a relevant cause of action you will be affirming the proposition that by Scots and English law alike a manufacturer of products, which he sells in such a form as to show that he intends them to reach the ultimate consumer in the form in which they left him with no reasonable possibility of intermediate examination, and with the knowledge that the absence of reasonable care in the preparation or putting up of the products will result in an injury to the consumer's life or property, owes a duty to the consumer to take that reasonable care.

Even though the rule in *Donoghue* was only applicable to perishable goods at the time, it was eventually extended to people who offer services too, such as doctors, teachers and lifeguards . . . even drivers have a duty of care not to harm each other on the road. The basic rule was enhanced by a three-part test in *Caparo Industries* v *Dickman* [1990] 2 AC 605 a few decades later. This was a case involving financial loss through a negligent misstatement, but the lords considered whether the criteria for establishing a duty of care could be tightened up a bit. The result is as follows:

In order to ascertain whether a duty of care is owed:

1. There must be proximity between the parties.

2. The harm must be reasonably foreseeable.

3. It must be fair, just and reasonable to impose the duty of care.

The three-part test in *Caparo* is now applied to doctors, lawyers, teachers, road users . . . and every other person you can think of to ascertain whether they owe a duty of care to the victim, the tests for breach and cause were not enhanced in *Caparo*. The test is easily met. For example, if a doctor administers a lethal dose of morphine to a patient, there is *proximity* between the doctor and the patient, the harm to the patient is *reasonably foreseeable* and it is *fair, just and reasonable* to impose this duty upon the doctor.

(i) When does a duty of care begin?

It is not clear when a duty of care begins to take shape in a hospital setting. It is important to answer this question because a doctor may argue that the harm occurred before his duty of care began or after it expired, thus absolving him from all liability. The duty of care over a patient will typically begin as soon as the doctor assumes responsibility for his patient.[7] This can occur as soon as the doctor meets the patient in the hospital, i.e. when the patient walks into the consultation room or the doctor walks into the patient cubicle. The doctor will begin to advise the patient and the doctor is expected to take reasonable care so as to not injure the patient or anyone else within his contemplation by a negligent act or omission. A practical example of this occurred in *Barnett* (1969), a sad case in which a patient presented himself for treatment but the doctor negligently turned him away to his death.

CASE EXTRACT

Barnett v *Chelsea and Kensington Hospital Management Committee* [1969] 1 QB 428

Facts: Mr Barnett was one of three men visiting a hospital because they were feeling very unwell after drinking tea. A casualty officer, Dr Banerjee, was notified by a nurse but told them to return home and simply call a doctor. The men had severe arsenic poisoning and died, and Mrs Barnett (widow) brought a claim in negligence.

Held: The doctor had breached his duty of care by failing to examine the men, meaning that a duty of care must have come into being when Dr Banerjee was notified about the men and then imparted his bad advice (the action failed on causation).

Nield J (at pages 436–7): In my judgment, there was here such a close and direct relationship between the hospital and the watchmen that there was imposed on the hospital a duty of care which they owed to the watchmen. Thus I have no doubt that Nurse Corbett and the casualty officer were under a duty to the deceased to exercise that skill and care which is to be expected of persons in such positions acting reasonably. [...] Without doubt the casualty officer should have seen and examined the deceased. His failure to do either cannot be described as an excusable error as has been submitted, it was negligence. It is unfortunate that the casualty officer was himself at the time a tired and unwell doctor, but there was no one else to do that which it was his duty to do.

The *Barnett* case tells us that if a doctor refuses to examine a patient, he is considered not only to have a duty of care, but to have breached it too.

Can NHS trusts owe a direct duty of care to patients?

It was noted at the beginning of this section that all healthcare professionals owe a duty of care to patients. It has also been asked whether the NHS trust itself owes a direct duty of care to patients, as opposed to simply being vicariously liable for its doctors, nurses and surgeons etc. The answer, after a small trail of case law, appears to be 'yes', because sometimes there are bigger problems in a hospital, such as dangerous equipment, that cannot be pinned upon a doctor. The trail of cases began with *Wilsher* (1987).

CASE EXTRACT

Wilsher v *Essex AHA* [1987] QB 730

Facts: A premature baby was not given appropriate medical treatment in the special care baby unit leading to blindness (although the *actual* cause was not known).

Held: A health authority that fails to provide doctors of sufficient skill and experience may be directly liable in negligence to the patient. There is no reason why, in

---

[7] This was established in *R* v *Stone* [1977] QB 354 in relation to a caring relative.

principle, the health authority should not be liable if its organisation is at fault. A doctor with little experience cannot be held to be at fault if he consulted a senior colleague, and so vicarious liability is sometimes not an option.

Sir Nicolas Browne-Wilkinson (at pages 777–8): The general standard of care required of a doctor is that he should exercise the skill of a skilled doctor in the treatment which he has taken upon himself to offer. […] It is normally no answer for him to say the treatment he gave was of a specialist or technical nature in which he was inexperienced. […] But the position of the houseman in his first year after qualifying or of someone (like Dr Wiles in this case) who has just started in a specialist field in order to gain the necessary skill in that field is not capable of such analysis. […] In my judgment, such doctors cannot in fairness be said to be at fault if, at the start of their time, they lack the very skills which they are seeking to acquire. […]

In my judgment, a health authority which so conducts its hospital that it fails to provide doctors of sufficient skill and experience to give the treatment offered at the hospital may be directly liable in negligence to the patient. Although we were told in argument that no case has ever been decided on this ground and that it is not the practice to formulate claims in this way, I can see no reason why, in principle, the health authority should not be so liable if its organisation is at fault.

It is clear from *Wilsher* that if a junior expert takes on a job that he cannot yet do, any harm that results may not be his fault. This means that, theoretically, a Health Authority may be directly liable to the patient for the harm caused by staff shortages, inexperienced or insufficiently skilled staff, money problems and bad practice. Sir Nicolas Browne-Wilkinson did not think that the difficult questions raised by this kind of decision should prevent such findings in the future. A further successful case was *Bull* (1993), in which a baby was disabled due to a broken-down communication system at Devon Health Authority.

CASE EXTRACT

Bull v *Devon AHA* [1993] 4 Med LR 117

Facts: Mrs Bull was delivering twins, but the relevant professional was delayed by an hour because the system for urgently summoning her had broken down. The Health Authority argued that the delay was inevitable because the hospital operated on two sites.

Held: The system in place failed to provide an acceptable level of care to the patient, and it is not an excuse to make comparisons to 'centres of excellence' or 'large city hospitals' when providing a basic level of care.

Dillon LJ: We have had a certain amount of discussion in the course of the argument as to whether the law should impose, or a patient should have the right to expect, the same standard of care and treatment from a local district hospital such as the defendant's hospital in the present case as from a 'centre of excellence' – a major teaching hospital in London or Oxbridge or a large modern hospital in a large city. Obviously, there are highly specialised medical services which a district hospital does

→

not have the equipment to provide and does not hold itself out as ready to provide. But this case is not about highly specialised services like that. The Exeter City Hospital provides a maternity service for expectant mothers, and any hospital which provides such a service ought to be able to cope with the not particularly out of the way case of a healthy young mother in somewhat premature labour with twins.

In my judgment, the plaintiff has succeeded in proving, by the ordinary civil standards of proof, that the failure to provide for Mrs Bull the prompt attendance she needed was attributable to the negligence of the defendants in implementing an unreliable and essentially unsatisfactory system for calling the registrar.

The case of *Bull* clearly states that if a small hospital has specific facilities for expectant mothers, then that hospital should reasonably be expected to care for expectant mothers. It is no defence to say that the larger city hospital down the road has better facilities.[8] In the more recent case of *Garcia* (2006), the opposite decision was reached.

CASE EXTRACT

Garcia v St Mary's NHS Trust [2006] EWHC 2314

Facts: Mr Garcia lost consciousness following cardiac surgery, but it took thirty minutes for the on-call registrar to arrive at his bedside.

Held: This was not negligent because many duties exist between the Trust, the registrar and other patients. It is not unreasonable for the on-call registrar to be attending another emergency elsewhere.

Judge Shaun Spencer (at paras 94–5): Having the surgeon on site does not necessarily signify that he would be available for Mr Garcia.

I also have to bear in mind the rarity of the occurrence. Systems and resources obviously have to be designed in order to accommodate what is reasonably to be foreseen, always bearing in mind that the unexpected sometimes occurs, and, therefore, should come within the range of the foreseeable. I bear in mind that the Trust, operated under the provisions of the National Health Service, has a duty to Mr Garcia to take reasonable care of him and that that duty co-exists together with the duty which is owed to other patients, and also the duty as employers to its own staff.

Judge Shaun Spencer was quite strict in his judgment: he balanced the rarity of Mr Garcia's condition against the duty owed by the registrar to other patients, and concluded that an on-call registrar might not be within reach.

A small number of patients have also tried to bring actions in negligence against the Secretary of State or the Department of Health, arguing that they had a direct duty of care to provide safe healthcare. The first case, *Re HIV* (1990), saw Lord Bingham admit that there might be a legal action because a duty of care was theoretically present.

---

[8] This was confirmed in *A (A Child)* v *Ministry of Defence* [2004] EWCA Civ 641.

CASE
EXTRACT

Re HIV Haemophiliac Litigation, Re [1990] NJLR 1349

Facts: Patients received blood transfusions contaminated with HIV. They brought an action against the Secretary of State for failing to warn patients of the risks of contamination.

Held: The Court of Appeal decided that the issue could proceed to trial because there was an arguable case for a duty of care (the case was later settled by the government).

Bingham LJ (at page 249): Where, as here, foreseeability by a defendant of severe personal injury to a person such as the plaintiff is shown, and the existence of a proximate relationship between plaintiff and defendant is accepted, the plaintiff is well on his way to establishing the existence of a duty of care. He may still fail to do so if it is held that imposition of such a duty on the defendant would not in all the circumstances be just and reasonable, but it is by no means clear to me at this preliminary stage that the department's submissions on that aspect must prevail.

Lord Bingham provided temporary hope for patients, but the case of *Danns* (1998) eight years later put the issue to bed when a patient failed to bring an action against the Department of Health.

CASE
EXTRACT

Danns v Department of Health [1998] PIQR P226

Facts: Mr and Mrs Danns brought an action against the Department of Health for a failure to publicly acknowledge new findings about the reversibility of the vasectomy procedure, which affected 1.5 million people relying on it as their only form of birth control. The issue was whether the Department of Health owed Mr and Mrs Danns a duty of care.

Held: The Department of Health did not owe the claimants a duty of care.

Roch LJ (at page 233): The Department did not owe the plaintiff a duty at common law to take reasonable care, for the reason that there did not exist as between the plaintiffs and the defendants that degree of the proximity which the law requires. The plaintiffs were not the defendant's neighbours. [...] I agree with the [trial] judge when he said: 'I would also hold that requirements of fairness, justice and reasonableness do not require the Department to give to the public at large the warnings contended for by the plaintiffs in this action.'

This is a very strict judgment. It can be argued that Mr Danns was within the contemplation of the Department of Health as a patient of a vasectomy. The pool of patients is very large, but this does not mean that there is no proximity. To quote the decision of the trial judge as repeated by Roch LJ, it is apparently not fair, just and reasonable to let patients know of the risks of vasectomy reversibility. This does not sound fair, just or reasonable at all, and the decision by Roch LJ was probably an attempt to stem a flood of claims against the Department of Health.

How far can a duty of care stretch?

It is clear that a doctor (and all other healthcare professionals) owe a duty of care to their patients. However, what about third parties? There may be instances where the relative of a patient, such as a husband or a child, suffers some form of loss, harm or psychiatric injury as a result of the negligent treatment to their wife or mother.

Third parties: pregnant wife

It was confirmed earlier that if a man is negligently informed that he has become sterile after a vasectomy and his wife then becomes pregnant, she can claim for a wrongful pregnancy. She is a third party because her husband was the patient, but because she was in the contemplation of the doctor at the time of the procedure, she is able to claim for the loss arising from his negligent misstatement (i.e. time off work, maternity clothes and pain and suffering). It was also confirmed in *Goodwill* (1996) that future wives (or girl-friends) cannot claim against the doctor as a third party because they were not in the doctor's contemplation at the time of the negligent procedure or misstatement.

CASE EXTRACT

Goodwill v British Pregnancy Advisory Service [1996] 1 WLR 1397

Peter Gibson LJ (at pages 1403, 1405): The doctor is concerned only with the man (his patient), and possibly that man's wife or partner if the doctor intends her to receive, and she receives, advice from the doctor in relation to the vasectomy and the subsequent tests. [...] If the existence of that partner is known to the doctor, and the doctor is aware that she wishes not to become pregnant by the man, and the vasectomy is carried out to meet her wish as well as the man's wish, it may be said that the doctor is employed to confer that benefit on her. [...] I cannot see that it can properly be said of the defendants that they voluntarily assumed responsibility to [G] when giving advice to Mr MacKinlay. At that time they had no knowledge of her, she was not an existing sexual partner of Mr MacKinlay but was merely, like any other woman in the world, a potential future sexual partner of his.

Third parties: relatives with psychiatric injury

There may be occasions in which a relative of a patient witnesses negligent treatment – or the immediate aftermath of negligent treatment – and suffers a recognised psychiatric injury as a result. The relative may like to make a claim in negligence for psychiatric injury.[9] The law in this area originates from *McLoughlin* (1983).

CASE EXTRACT

McLoughlin v O'Brian [1983] 1 AC 410

Facts: The claimant's husband and children were involved in a car accident. She was told two hours later by a neighbour. However, when she eventually saw her husband and children at the hospital, they were still covered in oil and mud from the scene and she was told that her daughter had died.

---

[9] Post-traumatic stress disorder was a medically recognised psychiatric illness for the purposes of negligence in *Leach* v *Chief Constable of Gloucestershire* [1999] 1 WLR 1421, and pathological grief was also compensated in *Vernon* v *Bosley (No.1)* [1997] RTR 1.

Held: She successfully claimed for psychiatric injury: it was reasonably foreseeable that she would suffer psychiatric harm and the environment was sufficient to satisfy the 'immediate aftermath' criteria for proximity.

McLoughlin was heavily relied upon in subsequent cases that developed this area of law. The case of *Page* v *Smith* [1996] AC 155 established that there are two categories of victim in psychiatric injury claims: *primary* victims (i.e. the person who was harmed) and *secondary* victims (i.e. the witness to the harm). In medical negligence, a patient is the primary victim, and the relative of the patient is the secondary victim. The patient can claim for psychiatric injury through the normal rules of negligence, but the relative must satisfy additional criteria in addition to the normal rules of negligence.

CASE EXTRACT

Alcock v Chief Constable of South Yorkshire [1992] 1 AC 310

Facts: Relatives of the victims of the Hillsborough Disaster brought claims of psychiatric injury after witnessing the incident either at the stadium or watching on TV.

Held: A three-part test is established for secondary victims of psychiatric injury: it must be *reasonably foreseeable* that the claimant would suffer from a psychiatric injury, the claimant must have a *close tie* of love and affection to the victim and the claimant must be *proximate* to the accident in terms of space and time or its immediate aftermath.

Stocker LJ (at page 378): What has to be foreseeable is that someone may be present at the scene or its immediate aftermath who possesses that love and affection which a parent/spouse is assumed to possess, even if in fact that relative is less closely related to the victim than a parent or spouse.

Nolan LJ (at page 382): The defendant has admitted liability for negligence in respect of those who died or were physically injured at Hillsborough. That is to say, he has admitted that he owed them a duty of care, that he was in breach of that duty, and that their deaths or injuries resulted from the breach. If it could reasonably have been foreseen, as I think it could, that the crucial acts and omissions would not only be likely to lead to physical injury and death, but to a very large number of horrifying injuries and deaths, then to my mind it must inevitably follow that the defendant ought reasonably to have anticipated in addition the likelihood of nervous shock among those who were not physically but were mentally affected by the occurrence.

If the extent of the defendant's duty depended upon foreseeability alone, it would be almost infinite. It is well settled, however, that foreseeability alone, although essential to the existence of a duty of care, is not enough. In the familiar words of Lord Atkin in *Donoghue* v *Stevenson* [1932] AC 562, the duty is owed only to 'persons who are so closely and directly affected' by the defendant's act that he 'ought reasonably to have them in contemplation as being so affected' when directing his mind to the acts or omissions which are called in question.

In the context of medical negligence, *Alcock* tells us that the witness (i.e. the husband) must clearly be at the immediate aftermath of the negligence to the patient (i.e. his wife), but the lines are blurred as to what 'immediate aftermath' might be. The effects of medical negligence may not materialise for hours, days, weeks or even months later. There has been a small trail of cases which suggest that the negligence must be both immediate and shocking in order for a relative to claim as a secondary party for psychiatric injury.

CASE EXTRACT

Taylor v Somerset Health HA [1994] 5 Med LR; The Times, 10 June 1994

Facts: The Health Authority negligently failed to diagnose and treat T's husband's heart disease, as a result of which he had a heart attack at work and died. T visited the hospital and was informed of his death, which caused her shock and distress because she could not believe it, so she viewed the body which caused her further shock and distress. She claimed damages for nervous shock as a secondary party. The *Alcock* criteria were applied.

Held: The claim was dismissed. The main purpose in viewing the body in the mortuary in order to settle disbelief as to death was not capable of being 'immediate aftermath' and the viewing related to the *fact* of death, rather than the circumstances in which death *came about*.

Auld J (at page 267): Mr Hart, on behalf of the health authority, submitted first that there was no event on the facts of this case to which the proximity test could be applied. He maintained that the test required some external, traumatic event in the nature of an accident or violent happening. Here, he said, Mr Taylor's death long after the negligence which had caused it was the culmination of the natural process of heart disease, and the death, however unexpected and shocking to Mrs Taylor when she learnt of it, was not in itself an event of the kind to which the immediate aftermath extension could be attached. [...] In my judgment, Mrs Taylor's claim must fail. [...] There was no such event here other than the final consequence of Mr Taylor's progressively deteriorating heart condition which the health authority, by its negligence many months before, had failed to arrest. In my judgment, his death at work and the subsequent transference of his body to the hospital where Mrs Taylor was informed of what had happened and where she saw the body do not constitute such an event.

It is understandable that Mrs Taylor wanted to claim for psychiatric injury against the doctors who negligently treated her husband, because it could be concluded on the facts that his death (and thus her shock at seeing his death) was directly caused by their negligence. However, his death was not a sudden event and the cause of death was heart disease which happened progressively (he was being treated for months beforehand), and so the legal criteria were simply not satisfied. It is important to note that, as a result of *Taylor*, identifying a loved one in the morgue is not usually considered to be a shocking event, because it is confirmation of an earlier shocking event.

Taylor was confirmed in *Sion* (1994).

CASE EXTRACT

Sion v *Hampstead HA* [1994] 5 Med LR 170 & *The Times*, 10 June, 1994

Facts: A father stayed with his son in hospital after a serious motorbike accident. The son fell into a coma and died two weeks later. The father made a claim for psychiatric injury.

Held: He was not successful.

Staughton LJ: [There has been] no sudden appreciation by sight or sound of a horrifying event. On the contrary, the report describes a process continuing for some time, from first arrival at the hospital to the appreciation of medical negligence after the inquest. In particular, the son's death when it occurred was not surprising but expected.

The main barrier to success in *Sion* appears to be the lack of a sudden sight or sound of a horrifying event. The patient died a fortnight later after a coma, allowing a slow and painless death that might have brought the family some comfort compared to an agonising demise at the roadside. The father thus had time to adjust to his terrible situation. The next case involves a new baby who was treated negligently and a mother had very little time to adjust to her child's death, leading to a completely different outcome.

CASE EXTRACT

North Glamorgan NHS Trust v *Walters* [2003] PIQR P16

Facts: The hospital run by [N] had failed to diagnose Elliot's [E] acute hepatitis as a result of which he suffered a seizure witnessed by his mother Mrs Walters [W]. The hospital initially informed W that E had suffered no brain damage but, following his transfer and diagnosis at a second hospital, W was told that E had been severely brain damaged and would have no quality of life. W agreed to terminate life support and E died in her arms. N contended that the trial judge had erred in law by holding that the 36-hour period – from E's seizure to his death – could be categorised as one horrifying event. N further suggested that events had not been sudden but rather amounted to a gradual assault of the mind over a period of time.

Held: Applying *McLoughlin* and *Alcock*, W was entitled to damages as a secondary victim. A horrifying event was not confined to one moment in time.

Ward LJ (at paras 12, 20, 30, 37): The first question the [trial] judge had to ask himself was whether the claimant was a primary victim or a secondary victim. [...] He had no difficulty in concluding that Ms Walters was a secondary victim and there is no challenge to that finding. [...] The real and only issue in the case was whether [W's] illness had been caused by shock [arising] from the sudden appreciation by sight or sound of a horrifying event or its immediate aftermath. [...]

In my judgment on the facts of this case there was an inexorable progression from the moment when the fit occurred as a result of the failure of the hospital properly to diagnose and then to treat the baby, the fit causing the brain damage which shortly thereafter made termination of this child's life inevitable and the dreadful climax when the child died in her arms. It is a seamless tale with an obvious beginning and an equally obvious end. It was played out over a period of 36 hours, which for her

➔

both at the time and as subsequently recollected was undoubtedly one drawn-out experience. [...]

The question then is whether this entire event was 'horrifying'. For my part the facts only have to be stated for the test to be satisfied. This mother awakens to find her baby rigid after a convulsion. Blood is coming from his mouth. He is choking. Is that not as much an assault upon her senses as if her child had been involved in a road accident, suffered grievous head injuries as yet undetected and was found bleeding in the car seat? Her fear and anxiety was undoubtedly calmed not long afterwards when given an incorrect medical opinion that it was very unlikely and would be very unlucky if Elliot had suffered serious damage. [...] Her hopes were lifted then they were dashed and finally destroyed when shortly thereafter she was advised to terminate treatment on the life support machine. That she should have felt that 'this was a complete shock' seems to me to be inevitable.

Ward LJ clearly found that the collection of distressing events over the course of thirty-six hours were shocking enough for the mother to be a secondary victim.[10] The courts will clearly exercise their discretion on a case-by-case basis to ascertain whether the *Alcock* criteria have been satisfied. This was illustrated very clearly in the *Froggatt* (2002) case.

CASE EXTRACT

Froggatt v Chesterfield and North Derbyshire Royal Hospital NHS Trust [2002] QBD 13 December 2002

Facts: Mrs Froggatt, a married patient aged 28, underwent a mastectomy of her right breast following a misdiagnosis that she was suffering from cancer. She was mentally disturbed for a long time afterwards and had contemplated suicide. She was not happy with her reconstruction surgery and her husband was shocked when he first saw her naked after her mastectomy. Her son Dane [D] also overheard a telephone conversation about the situation that caused him great shock. It was Mr Froggatt and Dane who brought claims against the NHS Trust as secondary victims.

Held: They were able to claim damages for psychiatric harm as secondary victims, although they only received £6,000 between them compared to her £75,000 general damages.

Forbes J (at paras 77, 79, 80): It is common ground that neither Mr Froggatt nor Dane was a primary victim of the negligence in question. It was therefore common ground that each was a secondary victim and that, in order [...] to recover damages, each had to establish that [they] 'suffered psychiatric illness caused by the sudden appreciation, by sight or sound, of a horrifying event' [according to] Thomas J in *Walters* v *North Glamorgan NHS Trust* [2002] Lloyd's Med Reps 227 and *Alcock* v *The Chief Constable of South Yorkshire* (1992) AC 301 (in particular, the speeches of Lord Ackner at page 400 and Lord Oliver at pages 416 to 417). [...]

In Mr Froggatt's case, his sudden appreciation of the trauma that had been suffered by Mrs Froggatt as the result of the defendant's negligence occurred when he saw her

---

[10] *Ward* v *Leeds Teaching Hospitals NHS Trust* [2004] EWHC 2106 has since confirmed that the secondary party must witness an exceptionally horrifying event.

undressed for the first time after the mastectomy. He was quite unprepared for what he saw and he was profoundly and lastingly shocked by it. As a result, his sleep became fitful, he became generally agitated and he suffered an adjustment disorder that lasted for about one-and-a-half years. I am satisfied that, in his case, an award of £5,000 is appropriate. [...] In Dane's case, the sudden appreciation came as a result of overhearing his mother's telephone conversation and his immediate belief, based on the negligent advice that had been given to his mother and that she felt obliged to repeat to him, that she had cancer and was likely to die. He was completely unprepared for such a shock and, as a result, he suffered a moderate Post Traumatic Stress Disorder that affected his everyday life at home and at school. [...] Fortunately, the condition had largely resolved by March 2001. [...] In his case, I am satisfied that an award of £1,000 is appropriate.

Forbes J came to a very quick decision in this case: his judgment was mostly a regurgitation of facts with a handful of concluding paragraphs at the end which do little to justify the leniency of his judgment. There is no doubt that this judgment opens the floodgates for all traumatised relatives of breast cancer patients to come forward upon seeing a mastectomy. It is not particularly fair, just and reasonable on the NHS trust to award damages to a sleepless spouse and upset son when confronted with a grim prognosis of cancer because in reality, patients are diagnosed with cancer every day. It can be conceded, however, that in *Froggatt* it was the result of a negligent diagnosis and should never have happened and this could intensify the shock.

The final case in this trail of authorities is *Farrell*. The claimant (Mr Farrell) was a partner of the patient but was considered to be a primary victim because a negligent misstatement was spoken to him *directly*, causing him nervous shock. A secondary victim is not usually this directly involved and will typically *witness* the effects of the negligence rather than being directly instructed by a doctor.

CASE EXTRACT

Farrell v *Avon HA* [2001] Lloyd's Rep Med 458

Facts: [F] attended the hospital after receiving a telephone call from his child's mother – with whom he no longer had a relationship – informing him that she had given birth to their son. F was informed by staff that the baby had just died and he was given a deceased baby to hold. F kissed, cuddled and cried over the deceased baby, but was subsequently informed that there had been a mistake and that his son was in fact alive. F visited his living son but left after five minutes and was sick. F contended that the shock as a result of this incident had led him to develop post-traumatic stress disorder. F asserted that since grief at the death of a child was a reasonably foreseeable occurrence, he was entitled to recover damages for a reasonably unforeseeable but recognised psychiatric disorder.

Held: F was successful. He was a primary victim and the normal rules of negligence applied. The relevant test was whether Avon Health Authority ought reasonably to have foreseen that its conduct would expose F to the risk of a recognised psychiatric disorder. The answer was 'yes' because they believed him to be an ordinary, involved father. F had also established that his post-traumatic stress disorder, while delayed in onset, had been caused by the incident in question.

What is interesting about this judgment is that Avon Health Authority was judged according to what it believed rather than the facts. It believed that Mr Farrell was an ordinary involved father, and so it was deemed to have foreseen a risk of psychiatric injury as a result of its negligent actions. The facts were that Mr Farrell was not an involved father at all, and his risk of psychiatric injury was actually very low. In addition to this, Mr Farrell was shown to have lived a troubled life in the judgment, including unemployment, drug use and psychological problems, and so it was incredibly generous of Bursell J to accept the medical evidence that the hospital incident was the main cause of Mr Farrell's Post Traumatic Stress Disorder, proved on a balance of probabilities – 51%.

Commentators find this area of medical law interesting and have pointed out that relatives usually find it hard to claim for psychiatric injury when they have witnessed a loved one go through the trauma of medical negligence.

EXTRACT

Paula Case, 'Secondary Iatrogenic Harm: Claims for Psychiatric Damage Following a Death Caused by Medical Error' (2004) 67 *Modern Law Review* 561, at pages 561-87

The relative is unlikely to witness at first hand the 'sudden shocking event' currently required by English law as, unlike the typical accident environment, the hospital is a highly controlled space where the family's view of tragedy is often occluded by the intervention of hospital personnel. [...] The claimant (relative) will generally not witness the moment of their relative's demise and may rely on viewing the deceased's body after death as the 'shocking event' which caused the harm. Where the relative is absent during the events which caused the death of the deceased, an attempt to rely on identification of the body after death as the 'shocking event' is likely to fail. [...] In *Alcock*, their Lordships agreed that secondary victims must demonstrate that their injury be caused by a 'sudden appreciation by sight or sound of a horrifying event which violently agitates the mind'. The sudden shocking event requirement presents particular problems in hospital cases, because it might be argued by defendants that the 'suddenness' of the shocking event is negated by the reasons that brought the medical accident victim to hospital. In other words, the probability of deterioration is known merely by the fact that the medical accident victim was in hospital.

Despite the view by Case in this article, the test in *Alcock* appears to be perfectly adequate. It makes good sense that a relative should only be able to claim for psychiatric injury if they immediately experienced a shocking event, have a close tie of love and affection to the victim and their risk of psychiatric harm is foreseeable. It is not likely, as Case appears to argue, that most relatives would consider the moment of identification in the morgue as the shocking event. There are plenty of non-fatal negligent occurrences where the patient does not end up dead but significant grief is inflicted upon the relatives.

THINKING POINT

Do you think secondary victims should even be able to claim for psychiatric injury? Just because their harm is foreseeable, does that justify extending the duty of care upon a doctor's shoulders beyond the patient to his relatives?

Third parties: innocent members of the public

It is very rare, but sometimes it may be argued that a doctor owes a duty of care to members of the public. What if he negligently allows a patient to do something that she is not allowed to do? For example:

- An elderly patient is not told by her doctor that she is no longer fit to drive, so she leaves the surgery and drives home causing injuries to pedestrians.

- A doctor does not treat an infection that he knows will be quickly spread to the patient's partner or children, resulting in those people being infected.

- A young teenager has a clear mental health problem that must be assessed under section 2 of the Mental Health Act 1983, but the doctor negligently leaves her at home, leading to a neighbour being attacked.

In all of these instances, does the doctor owe the third party – pedestrians, partners, children and neighbours – a duty of care? The traditional common law tests from *Donoghue* v *Stevenson* (1932) and *Caparo* v *Dickman* (1990) should be applied to ascertain whether the doctor owes a duty of care:

- *Donoghue* v *Stevenson*: A doctor owes a common law duty of care to those in his reasonable contemplation to make sure that his care does not cause them any harm, illness or injury.

- *Caparo* v *Dickman*: There must be proximity between the parties; the harm must be reasonably foreseeable; and it must be fair, just and reasonable to impose the duty of care upon the doctor.

A third party is not usually within the contemplation of the doctor for him to owe a duty of care. For example, it is not enough that a patient drives home from her consultation and injures a pedestrian – there must be proximity (i.e. a sufficient connection) between the doctor and the pedestrian. Additionally, it will not be 'fair, just and reasonable' in the eyes of the courts to impose a duty of care upon a doctor for third parties that he is not made aware of. A spouse *may* be in the contemplation of the doctor (a good example is the infection scenario above) but a member of the public (i.e. a one night stand) would not be. There are not many cases in this area of law. The *Palmer* (1999) case did attempt to push the boundaries of duty, but the courts rejected the argument that a health authority had a duty of care over a mother for letting a dangerous patient out into society.

CASE EXTRACT

Palmer v *Tees HA* [1999] Lloyd's Re Med 351

Facts: A defendant with a long history of psychiatric problems abducted, sexually assaulted and murdered a 4-year-old girl, Rosie Palmer. Her mother argued that the local health authority had a duty of care to diagnose a real and foreseeable risk that he would be a danger to children, which they failed to do. She claimed damages for her post-traumatic stress disorder and pathological grief (as a primary victim).

Held: The health authority did not have a duty of care over Mrs Palmer. Even though the harm may have been foreseeable, there was insufficient proximity between the health authority and Mrs Palmer for there to be a common law duty of care over her. It was also not fair, just or reasonable to impose this duty of care.

Stuart-Smith LJ (at pages 12–13): An additional reason why in my judgment in this case it is at least necessary for the victim to be identifiable to establish proximity, is

→

that it seems to me that the most effective way of providing protection would be to give warning to the victim, his or her parents or social services so that some protective measure can be made. [...] It may be a somewhat novel approach to the question of proximity, but it seems to me to be a relevant consideration to ask what the defendant could have done to avoid the danger, if the suggested precautions [...] or treatment are likely to be of doubtful effectiveness, and the most effective precaution cannot be taken because the defendant does not know who to warn. This consideration suggests to me that the Court would be unwise to hold that there is sufficient proximity.

This judgment highlights that even when there is a strong moral argument for imposing a duty of care upon a health authority, the courts are unlikely to find it fair, just and reasonable to impose it unless sufficient proximity is found. Stuart-Smith LJ states that the health authority in this case were unable to take precautions because they did not know who to warn, and this appears to be the main ground for concluding that imposing a duty of care was not reasonable. A health authority does have a general duty of care to keep the public safe, but it does not have an additional duty of care to keep a particular member of the public safe if it cannot identify that particular member of the public and cannot establish a sufficient connection to that member of the public.

It is clear that there is a limit as to just how far the duty of care will stretch. The doctor or the health authority must be able to specifically identify the third party and be aware that she will be directly affected by any negligent act or omission. This is difficult to satisfy when the innocent member of the public is not connected to the patient or doctor in any way. However, in the case of infectious disease for example, the doctor may be made aware of a spouse at home. He is then under a duty of care to treat that patient appropriately and thus prevent his wife from contracting the infection too.

Third parties: parents of a child patient

A child is clearly owed a duty of care by her doctor because, regardless of her age, she is his patient and he must treat her in accordance with her best interests. This is confirmed in common law.

CASE EXTRACT

D v *East Berkshire Community Health NHS Trust* [2003] EWCA Civ 1151

Facts: A doctor was examining a child who was a suspected victim of child abuse. The legal issue was whether he owed the child a duty of care because he was asked to perform the service by another body.

Held: The doctor owes the child a duty of care as his patient.

Lord Phillips MR (at para 83): Where child abuse is suspected the interests of the child are paramount.

The *East Berkshire* case went up to the House of Lords because it was unclear whether the doctor, in a child abuse scenario, also owed a duty of care to the parents of the child too. Traditionally, the doctor would owe a duty of care over the parent as a third party, because when they bring their child into the doctor surgery they are proximate to the doctor and the doctor can identify the parent as a specific member of the public who might be harmed by his negligent act or omission. However, in a child abuse scenario, extra care must be taken to ensure that the best interests of the child are paramount. The House of Lords concluded that it would cause a conflict of interest if a duty of care were imposed for the child *and* her parents in a situation where the parents were suspected of abusing the child. The doctor owed a duty of care to the child alone.

CASE EXTRACT	**JD v *East Berkshire Community Health NHS Trust* [2005] AC 375**

Facts: It was questioned whether a doctor owed a duty of care to the parents of a child he was examining when they were suspected of abusing that child.

Held: In light of a conflict of interest, the doctor owed a duty of care to the child alone.

Lord Rodger (at para 10): In considering whether it would be fair, just and reasonable to impose such a duty, a court has to have regard, however, to all the circumstances and, in particular, to the doctors' admitted duty to the children. The duty to the children is simply to exercise reasonable care and skill in diagnosing and treating any condition from which they may be suffering. In carrying out that duty the doctors have regard only to the interests of the children. Suppose, however, that they were also under a duty to the parents not to cause them psychiatric harm by concluding that they might have abused their child. Then, in deciding how to proceed, the doctors would always have to take account of the risk that they might harm the parents in this way. There would be not one but two sets of interests to be considered. Acting on, or persisting in, a suspicion of abuse might well be reasonable when only the child's interests were engaged, but unreasonable if the interests of the parents had also to be taken into account. Of its very nature, therefore, this kind of duty of care to the parents would cut across the duty of care to the children.

The special circumstances of a child abuse case means that the duty of care owed to the parents would 'cut across' the duty to the child, and so any duty of care to the parents must be cancelled in the interests of the child.

ACTIVITY	

An off-duty doctor was waiting at a train station for his train home when he saw a passenger being pushed onto the live tracks after an argument. The off-duty doctor ran to her aid, but she had significant burns. He tried to treat her by the platform, but he had very little with him, meaning that her injuries were getting worse. The passenger was taken to hospital and delivered into the burns unit. The burns doctor was busy with another patient two corridors down and said that he 'would be over in a minute', but he never arrived. The patient died and her parents brought an action in negligence against the off-duty doctor for not treating her adequately and against the burns doctor for ignoring her. Who, if anybody, has a duty of care to the patient and on what grounds?

The duty has been breached

Once a duty of care has been established between the doctor and the injured party, the duty must be breached. The general law of tort will typically look for a 'standard of care' and then question whether the tortfeasor has fallen below that standard. The very early case of *Gerber* v *Pines* (1933) 79 SJ 13 confirmed that a failure to tell a patient that a needle had broken off during an injection was negligent practice. A breach of duty in medicine will depend on the circumstances of a particular case and the characteristics of the injured patient. It was established in *Wood* v *Thurston*, *The Times*, 25 May 1951 that a doctor should be able to recognise obvious symptoms, but if the patient does not tell the doctor how he is feeling then it will be very hard for the patient to establish a breach of duty, meaning that the patient must be honest.

Medical professionals are not judged according to the standard of care of the reasonable man on the street. They are judged according to the standard of a reasonable doctor exercising that particular skill. For example:

- Botched cosmetic surgery would see the surgeon being judged against the standard of a reasonable cosmetic surgeon.
- A negligent childbirth would see the midwife being judged against the standard of a reasonable midwife.
- A negligent house call would see the paramedic being judged against the standard of a reasonable paramedic . . . and so on.

There is a very specific reason why medical negligence is judged this way: they are *specialists*. They undergo rigorous training in a particular field. There would be no point in judging a specialist against an unqualified man on the street, because their qualifications, experience and judgment would be completely different. A slip in the standard of care will be much easier to identify this way, and it gives the courts an accepted 'standard' against which to measure the doctor's behaviour. After all, judges are not usually medically qualified. The leading case in this area is the classic *Bolam* (1957) case. The *Bolam* test (as it is commonly known) establishes that a doctor exercising a particular skill will be judged according to what another doctor exercising that particular skill would have done in the circumstances.

CASE EXTRACT

Bolam v Friern Hospital Management Committee [1957] 1 WLR 582

Facts: Mr Bolam was suffering from a mental illness. He was advised by a consultant at Friern Hospital to undergo electro-convulsive therapy. There was a small risk of fracture because it was a violent procedure, but he was not warned of this. In addition, he was not given relaxant drugs and was not physically restrained, two precautions which could have prevented fractures. Mr Bolam subsequently fractured his hip during the therapy. At the time, the medical opinion on this treatment was that it is sometimes a good idea to warn patients, but not always. The legal issue was: what was the standard of care and had it been breached?

Held: A doctor must exercise the same reasonable care and skill as another doctor who practices in that same art (i.e. brain surgery). It does not matter if there happens to be a contrary view on the matter.

McNair J (at pages 586–7): [Directing the jury] Where you get a situation which involves the use of some special skill or competence, then the test whether there has

→

been negligence or not is not the test of the man on the top of a Clapham omnibus, because he has not got this special skill. The test is the standard of the ordinary skilled man exercising and professing to have that special skill. [...] A man need not possess the highest expert skill; it is well established law that it is sufficient if he exercises the ordinary skill of an ordinary man exercising that particular art. [...] [A doctor] is not guilty of negligence if he has acted in accordance with a practice accepted as proper by a responsible body of medical men skilled in that particular art. [...] Putting it the other way round, a man is not negligent, if he is acting in accordance with such a practice, merely because there is a body of opinion that takes a contrary view.

McNair J dealt with the glaring problem of conflicting medical opinion very well in this case when he concluded that, as long as the defendant is acting in accordance with a body of medical men who practise that same art (called as 'expert witnesses'), it does not matter that a contrary opinion can be found.[11] In practice, the application of *Bolam* means that a doctor will not be guilty of medical negligence if he can find a body of medical men who practise his same skill and who can testify that they would have done the same thing. So . . . is the *Bolam* test a good or a bad thing?

It may be a bad thing. It suggests 'friends helping friends'. The courts will judge a medical breach of duty according to the reasonable doctor, and this is a test set by doctors. Much power is thus handed over to doctors to regulate themselves and judge their own breaches of duty *subjectively*. The medical profession was held in high regard during the *Bolam* years, and it was a time when doctors did not typically have to answer to anyone because they were specialists in their own field and thus a law unto themselves. This might go some way to explaining the rather 'easy' legal test for medical negligence. A small trail of cases after *Bolam* shows a reluctance from the courts to depart from the 'body of medical men' test as laid down by McNair J.

CASE EXTRACT	*Maynard v West Midlands RHA* [1984] 1 WLR 634

Facts: A patient was not happy with her doctor's decision to carry out an invasive operation for Hodgkin's disease. There was a risk of nerve damage, which materialised, even though the test was performed correctly. The patient argued that the *Bolam* test was not met because an alternative view had been found and the trial judge 'preferred' the alternative view in agreement with the patient. The health authority appealed.

Held: A judge may prefer one view over another but this does not justify the finding of negligence when the views of *both* sides are just as professionally valid. The *Bolam* test allows room for differing medical opinion.

Lord Scarman (at pages 638–9): I would only add that a doctor who professes to exercise a special skill must exercise the ordinary skill of his specialty. Differences of

➔

---

[11] *Bolam* was applied in *Defreitas v O'Brien* [1995] 6 Med LR 108 to confirm that the body of medical opinion does not have to be substantial (just four or five specialists in this case was sufficient).

> opinion and practice exist, and will always exist, in the medical as in other professions. There is seldom any one answer exclusive of all others to problems of professional judgment. A court may prefer one body of opinion to the other: but that is no basis for a conclusion of negligence. [...] I have to say that a judge's 'preference' for one body of distinguished professional opinion to another also professionally distinguished is not sufficient to establish negligence in a practitioner whose actions have received the seal of approval of those whose opinions, truthfully expressed, honestly held, were not preferred. If this was the real reason for the judge's finding, he erred in law even though elsewhere in his judgment he stated the law correctly. For in the realm of diagnosis and treatment negligence is not established by preferring one respectable body of professional opinion to another.

The phrase 'truthfully expressed and honestly held' is interesting. Lord Scarman is saying that the body of medical men who are found to support the tortfeasor must be true and honest in their views. This is obvious, but it also points to credibility. If, for example, the body of medical men are simply friends of the tortfeasor, e.g. they work together, their medical evidence may not be as truthful and honest as it first seems. This is something that the courts must be aware of, because doctors can be part of wider professional networks that can offer support for lesser known and risky procedures.

One case that famously rejected the *Bolam* principle was *Hucks* v *Cole* (below). It was unearthed and reported in 1993, but back in 1968 when it was heard in the Court of Appeal, the judges radically dismissed four expert witnesses for the defendant and found that he had been negligent in his practice as a doctor. This was a case of judges knowing better than doctors even though judges are not medically qualified.

CASE EXTRACT

Hucks v *Cole* (1968) 118 NLJ 469 & [1993] 4 Med LR 393

Facts: A pregnant woman had a sore on her finger and showed her doctor (Dr Cole). He gave her drugs which did not work, but failed to give her penicillin. The bacteria developed into septicemia and she nearly died. The doctor produced four expert witnesses of his own behalf to prove that he had acted in accordance with a body of medical men with the same skill.

Held: The doctor was negligent in not prescribing the penicillin, regardless of how many experts were called or what they said. The expert medical evidence did not stand up to legal analysis.

Sachs LJ: The fact that other practitioners would have done the same thing as the defendant practitioner is a very weighty matter to be put on the scales on his behalf; but it is not conclusive. The court must be vigilant to see whether the reasons given for putting a patient at risk are valid in the light of any well-known advance in medical knowledge, or whether they stem from a residual adherence to out-of-date ideas – a tendency which in the present case may well have affected the views of at any rate one of the defendant's witnesses, who, at a considerable age, seemed not to have any particular respect for laboratory results. Despite the facts that the risk could have been avoided by adopting a course that was easy, efficient and inexpensive, and which would have entailed only minimal chances of disadvantages to the patient, the evidence of the four defence experts to the effect that they and other responsible members of the medical profession would have taken the same risk in the same circumstances has naturally caused me to hesitate considerably [about] whether the failure of the defendant to turn over to penicillin treatment during the relevant period was unreasonable. I was in the end fully satisfied that failure to do this was not merely wrong but clearly unreasonable. The reasons given by the four experts do not to my mind stand up to analysis. Doctor Cole knowingly took an easily avoidable risk which elementary teaching had instructed him to avoid; and the fact that others say they would have done the same neither ought to nor can in the present case excuse him in an action for negligence however sympathetic one may be to him.

Sachs LJ shows a flagrant disregard for the *Bolam* test in this judgment, although it must be remembered that because *Bolam* was only a first-instance judgment it was not widely publicised until a later date. There are several important points to be taken from *Hucks* v *Cole* and they are relevant because the modern case law has taken a very similar approach and modified the *Bolam* test considerably. Sachs LJ states that the conclusion of negligence in this case will improve medical treatment for patients, thus encouraging judges to scrutinise medical practice for the good of the public. He felt that a practitioner may be able to support the defendant but this does not mean that the defendant is acting properly. A balance was struck between the 'reasons given for putting a patient at risk' and 'any well-known advance in medical knowledge'. No such balance was ever struck in *Bolam*, and this new legal test allows for the law to weigh up and scrutinise the facts and evidence, rather than leaving it to the doctors to decide what the proper outcome should have been. Sachs LJ also felt that if the practice stems from a 'residual adherence to out-of-date ideas' the witness is not likely to be credible. This is a direct contrast to *Bolam* which did not dare to question the judgment of traditional and experienced medical practitioners. It is also acceptable for the evidence of four medical practitioners to be struck out if the alternative course of action was 'easy, efficient and inexpensive' with 'minimal chances of disadvantages to the patient'. Sachs LJ concludes that the reasons given by the four expert witnesses as to why they would not have offered the penicillin 'did not stand up to analysis'. Legal analysis of medical evidence is a completely new approach that was not ever suggested in *Bolam* because judges are not qualified to do this. Finally, according to *Hucks* v *Cole*, when a doctor 'knowingly takes an easily avoidable risk which elementary teaching had instructed him to avoid', then the fact that 'others say they would have done the same' does not exonerate him from liability for negligence. This decision flies in the face of *Bolam* because it puts the powers back into the hands of the courts.

Despite the sweeping new approach in *Hucks* v *Cole* it was not widely reported, and *Bolam* was later supported by case law so it was *Bolam* that established the standard of care in medical negligence cases. However, the principles in *Hucks* v *Cole* made a re-appearance in *Bolitho* (1998), the leading case that began to chip away at the principles in *Bolam*.

Bolitho v *City and Hackney Health Authority* [1998] AC 232

Facts: Patrick Bolitho was a toddler admitted to hospital with breathing difficulties. He then had a heart attack leading to brain damage, and he died. The on-duty registrar did not see him, but she explained to the court that if she did, she would not have intubated him (i.e. put a tube into the patient), which was the only procedure that could have prevented the outcome. Medical evidence for each side had completely opposing views as to what a reasonably skilled registrar should have done.

Held: The registrar had not breached her duty, but the grounds upon which a court can find medical negligence needed to change. The medical evidence, in rare cases, may need to stand up to logical analysis by a court.

Lord Browne-Wilkinson (at pages 241, 243): In my view, the court is not bound to hold that a defendant doctor escapes liability for negligent treatment or diagnosis just because he leads evidence from a number of medical experts who are genuinely of opinion that the defendant's treatment or diagnosis accorded with sound medical practice. [...] In the vast majority of cases the fact that distinguished experts in the field are of a particular opinion will demonstrate the reasonableness of that opinion. In particular, where there are questions of assessment of the relative risks and benefits of adopting a particular medical practice, a reasonable view necessarily presupposes that the relative risks and benefits have been weighed by the experts in forming their opinions. But if, in a rare case, it can be demonstrated that the professional opinion is not capable of withstanding logical analysis, the judge is entitled to hold that the body of opinion is not reasonable or responsible. I emphasise that, in my view, it will very seldom be right for a judge to reach the conclusion that views genuinely held by a competent medical expert are unreasonable. The assessment of medical risks and benefits is a matter of clinical judgment which a judge would not normally be able to make without expert evidence. As the quotation from Lord Scarman [in *Maynard*] makes clear, it would be wrong to allow such assessment to deteriorate into seeking to persuade the judge to prefer one or two views both of which are capable of being logically supported. It is only where a judge can be satisfied that the body of expert opinion cannot be logically supported at all that such opinion will not provide the benchmark by reference to which the defendant's conduct falls to be assessed. I turn to consider whether this is one of those rare cases.

Lord Browne-Wilkinson is very careful in his wording of this judgment. He starts by stating that just because a defendant can find medical experts who agree with his act or omission, this does not mean that he has adhered to sound medical practice. This is in line with *Hucks* v *Cole* where it was held that even though four medical experts agreed with the defendant, he was still found to be negligent. Lord Browne-Wilkinson then moves on to establish a new legal test, which is: 'if, in a rare case, it can be demonstrated that the professional opinion is not capable of withstanding logical analysis, the judge is entitled to hold that the body of opinion is not reasonable or responsible'. This provides judges with a lot more power to question the medical profession. However, he also states that it is 'seldom right' for a judge to question medical experts without expert evidence, and that it would be 'rare' for a court to conclude that a professional body of opinion is not reasonable or responsible. He has opened the door to a logical analysis of professional medical opinion, but 'it is only where a judge can be satisfied that the body of expert opinion cannot be logically supported at all that such opinion will not provide the benchmark by which to assess the defendant's conduct'. In other words, the judge can dismiss the evidence if it does not stand up to any logical analysis whatsoever. The emphasis on 'seldom', 'rare' and 'evidence' in the judgment probably means that *Bolitho* will supplement rather than over-rule the test in *Bolam*. It is now perfectly possible for a judge to scrutinise a medical expert, and the medical profession are no longer given a free reign to decide for themselves what is reasonable practice. It seems that the courts no longer trust medical experts like they used to.

Sadly, it is not clear what is meant by 'logical analysis'. What has become clear in post-*Bolitho* case law is that it is still incredibly difficult to 'logically analyse' medical expertise. If a small handful of medical experts come forward and support the defendant, the *Bolam* test has technically been met, and because the judge has little in the way of medical qualifications or clinical evidence of his own to suggest the contrary, the doctor will be found to be working in accordance with accepted practice. It has, after all, been made clear in both *Maynard* and *Bolitho* that it is not acceptable for a judge to simply 'take sides' if both sides are just as professionally valid as each other. A good case example of this difficulty is *Wisniewski*, a very complicated case in which a well-regarded medical expert was initially thrown out by the trial judge, but it transpired that he was almost impossible to scrutinise and so the case did not fit into the 'rare' category as carved out by *Bolitho*.

CASE EXTRACT

Wisniewski v Central Manchester HA [1998] PIQR P324

Facts: A baby was born with the umbilical cord wrapped around its neck, leading to deprivation of oxygen and brain damage. It was argued that the defendant was negligent when failing to carry out a procedure to detect whether the cord was suffocating the child during childbirth, but the medical evidence differed. The trial judge rejected the defendant's expert witnesses and held that no responsible body of medical opinion would have behaved as the defendant did.

Held: The trial judge erred in rejecting expert medical evidence: the experts were well regarded and so this case did not fall into the 'rare' category as described in *Bolitho* as 'open to logical analysis' by the court. The defendant did cause the damage and he was liable.

Brooke LJ (at pages 336–7): *Hucks* v *Cole* itself was unquestionably one of the rare cases which Lord Browne-Wilkinson [in *Bolitho*] had in mind. […] In my judgment, the present case falls unquestionably on the other side of the line, and it is quite impossible for a court to hold that the views sincerely held by Mr Macdonald ('an eminent consultant and an impressive witness') and Professor Thomas cannot logically be supported at all. […] In my judgment, the judge was wrong to have concluded [for the patient] that any reasonably competent doctor would have resorted to this technique to eliminate the risk of cord prolapse, and the views expressed by Mr Macdonald and Professor Thomas [for the defence] were views which could be logically supported and held by responsible doctors.

This judgment is a warning to trial judges that expert witnesses cannot be dismissed out of hand simply because the trial judge does not agree with what they say. Lord Browne-Wilkinson clearly states in *Bolitho* that only if the body of expert opinion cannot be logically supported at all can the trial judge then dismiss it out of hand.[12]

Bolitho in action

Inevitably, there has been a *Bolitho* spring. There have been two notable cases – *Marriott* and *Reynolds* – in which the courts decided that the facts have fitted into the 'rare category' carved out by Lord Browne-Wilkinson, i.e. the expert medical opinion did not stand up to logical analysis.

CASE EXTRACT

Marriott v West Midlands RHA [1999] Lloyd's Rep Med 23

Facts: Mr Marriott had suffered a head injury but his symptoms – headaches and dizziness – were not taken as seriously as they should have been by doctors. Dr Patel was called out to the home, but after some brief tests did not send Mr Marriott to hospital. Mr Marriott had to undergo serious surgery and was left permanently disabled. There was medical evidence on both sides to suggest that Dr Patel should – and should not – have admitted Mr Marriott to hospital when he visited the house.

Held: The Court of Appeal decided that the expert witness for Dr Patel could not stand up to logical analysis, leading to the conclusion that Dr Patel had breached his duty.

Beldam LJ: The [trial] judge then identified the area of disagreement which lay, she said, in the element of discretion which a reasonably prudent doctor would exercise whether or not to advise readmission to hospital [...]:

> Furthermore, while a Court must plainly be reluctant to depart from the opinion of an apparently careful and prudent general practitioner, I have concluded that, if there is a body of professional opinion which supports the course of leaving a patient who has some seven days previously sustained a severe head injury at home in circumstances where he continues to complain of headaches, drowsiness etc., and where there continues to be a risk of the existence of an intracranial lesion which could cause a sudden and disastrous collapse, then such an approach is not reasonably prudent. It may well be that, if in the vast majority of cases, the risk is very small. Nevertheless, the consequence, if things go wrong, are disastrous to the patient. In such circumstances, it is my view that the only reasonably prudent course in any case where a general practitioner remains of the view that there is a risk of an intracranial lesion such as to warrant the carrying out of neurological testing and the giving of furt her head injury instructions, then the only prudent course judged from the point of view of the patient is to readmit for further testing and observation. [...]

It was open to the judge to hold that, in the circumstances as she found them to have been, it could not be a reasonable exercise of a general practitioner's discretion to leave a patient at home and not to refer him back to hospital.

---

[12] It was later confirmed in *Burne* v *A* [2006] EWCA Civ 24 that a trial judge was not free to ignore the views of experts on what was acceptable practice and rely on common sense until the experts had a chance to explain themselves and justify their practice.

Beldam LJ in *Marriott* takes the view of the trial judge that the medical evidence did not stand up to logical analysis. However, because this view flies in the face of *Bolam*, it should be scrutinised more closely. There are two key points worthy of analysis. Firstly, the trial judge looks at the facts and comes to the conclusion that: 'such an approach is not reasonably prudent'. It feels a little strange for a trial judge to tell a doctor that he is not doing his job prudently. The automatic response to such a statement would typically be: 'how do you know?' Secondly, the trial judge has looked at the situation through the eyes of the patient, and because the consequences of a breach would be 'disastrous' for the patient, it had to be concluded that 'in such circumstances the only reasonable prudent course . . . from the *point of view of the patient*, is to readmit for further testing and observation'. This patient-centred approach is new, but it is dangerous. Medical negligence should never be judged according to the standard or view of the patient: he is not only unqualified but he is completely subjective. It is not clear where the trial judge plucked this new test from, but this case must turn on its facts, because it would radically change the law if it was implemented on a wider scale.

The next case took the same approach.

CASE EXTRACT

Reynolds v *North Tyneside HA* [2002] Lloyd's Rep Med 459

Facts: The patient suffered from cerebral palsy as a result of a failure to examine her mother properly during childbirth (it happened during labour). The hospital had since closed, and the question was, did the nurse breach her duty of care when failing to perform a vaginal examination [VE] within twenty minutes of the patient's pregnant mother arriving at the hospital.

Held: The medical evidence did not stand up to scrutiny.

Gross J: In the circumstances, it was logical to conduct an immediate VE on admission. If, notwithstanding the above, there was a contrary body of opinion that would not have conducted VE's when the foetal head was 3/5 palpable (without other complications), then this was one of those rare cases where the Court could and should conclude that such body of opinion was unreasonable, irresponsible, illogical and indefensible. In any event, even if there was any contrary practice, or body of opinion, then the only reason articulated in its support for not conducting an immediate VE, namely the risk of infection, does not withstand scrutiny. The suggested contrary practice (or body or opinion) is neither defensible nor logical.

Gross J has been slightly clearer in *Reynolds* as to why the medical evidence was struck out. The reason that was given by the defence – infection – did not withstand logical scrutiny. This is probably because giving such examinations to women in labour is actually routine, and so even without medical qualifications Gross J was able to say that the medical evidence was 'unreasonable, irresponsible, illogical and indefensible'. He justified his decision by concluding that there was 'no proper basis' for the lacuna that he found in the medical practice, even if there was a 'contrary body of opinion' to argue otherwise. The facts of *Reynolds* clearly do fit within the *Bolitho* exception.

It can be concluded from both *Marriott* and *Reynolds* that only glaringly obvious mistakes will see a trial judge strike out the expert witness medical evidence. It is incredibly difficult in all other cases for a judge to say that a body of professional opinion does not stand up to logical analysis when he is not medically qualified himself, as confirmed in *M (A Child)* v *Blackpool Victoria Hospital NHS Trust* [2003] EWHC 1744, *Birch* v *University College London Hospital NHS Foundation* [2008] EWHC 2237 and *Norman* v *Peterborough and Stamford Hospital NHS Trust* [2008] EWHC 3266. If there is a conflict between experts, it was suggested in *Hanson* v *Airedale Hospital NHS Trust* [2003] CLY 2989 that the trial judge must say which expert he prefers and why, but Cranston J in *Birch* was far stricter: '. . . it would be folly for a judge with no training in medicine to conclude that one body of medical opinion should be preferred over another, when both are professionally sanctioned and both withstand logical attack'. The approach in *Birch* is preferred, simply because the exception carved out in *Bolitho* was meant to be exactly that: an exception. *Bolam*, therefore, is still good law, but *Bolitho* has created a rare exception that allows the most negligent of doctors to be found culpable of medical negligence even if they have located a remote witness to support their practice.

A varying standard of care

It is now clear that a breach of duty in medical law is measured by looking at the reasonable standard of care exercised by a body of medical men who practise the same skill (*Bolam*) and this body of medical men are exceptionally open to logical analysis by the courts (*Bolitho*). What has not yet been explored is the possibility of the standard of care increasing or, more controversially, decreasing, depending on the circumstances.

Standard of care: not enough resources to go around

The courts understand that there are often not enough resources, especially within the National Health Service to go around. There can be shortages in anything from beds to organs. There are, as a result, very few cases to refer to that make a claim of negligence against a hospital authority for not having enough resources to go around. The case of *Bull* (1993) is an exception.

CASE EXTRACT

Bull v *Devon AHA* [1993] 4 Med LR 117

Facts: During the birth of twins, the mother was left alone for sixty-eight minutes when she was in labour with the second twin in order for the staff to find a qualified medical practitioner. The birth was unassisted and the second twin suffered brain damage and was severely disabled.

Held: A minimum standard of care should always be met regardless of financial or resource limitations. It was unrealistic to have a registrar constantly available, but the delay in this case had been so substantial that the local authority were under an obligation in negligence to justify it (which they could not). They had been negligent.[13]

There is a prison case which may be of interest, because prisons must offer a standard of medical care too. The standard of care in prisons may be lower than that of a hospital for the simple reason that their primary purpose is to punish rather than treat. However, the case law does support a *minimum* standard of care, and this may increase further depending on the state of the prisoner (i.e. mentally ill).

---

[13] It was confirmed in the more recent case of *Garcia* v *St Mary's NHS Trust* [2006] EWHC 2314 that, generally, staffing levels were of no concern to the courts because staff cannot always attend promptly.

<table>
<tr><td></td><td>

Knight v Home Office [1990] 3 All ER 237

Facts: A mentally ill prisoner was not put on continuous observation because of insufficient resources. He therefore had the opportunity to hang himself.

Held: The prison doctors had not been negligent, but a lack of funds would not be a complete defence. Prisons are acknowledged to have slightly lower standards of care than proper hospitals, and it is Parliament who must deal with a lack of resources.

Pill J: It is not a complete defence for a government department any more than it would be for a private individual or organisation to say that no funds are available for additional safety measures. In making the decision as to the standard to be demanded the court must, however, bear in mind as one factor that resources available for the public service are limited and that the allocation of resources is a matter for Parliament.

I am unable to accept the submission that the law requires the standard of care in a prison hospital to be as high as the standard of care for all purposes in a psychiatric hospital outside prison. I am unable to accept that the practices in a prison hospital are to be judged in all respects by the standard appropriate to a psychiatric hospital outside prison. There may be circumstances in which the standard of care in a prison falls below that which would be expected in a psychiatric hospital without the prison authority being negligent.

</td></tr>
</table>

Pill J makes it very clear in his judgment that a prison hospital does not have to reach the same standards of care as a psychiatric hospital when dealing with mentally ill prisoners, but a minimal standard of care must obviously still be met.[14]

Standard of care: off-duty doctors in emergencies

Medical emergencies happen frequently. It may be something trivial, such as walking along the street and feeling dizzy, or a major train crash leading to a massive loss of life. Treatment may be carried out on the scene, or it may be carried out in a hospital which is completely overwhelmed by the sudden demand. The lack of equipment or the drop in the standard of care might adversely affect the victims. There is often a good Samaritan, and they may often be medically qualified, who will run to help. The doctor is technically off-duty at the time of his assistance, so will he then be judged according to the standards of an on-duty doctor?

A doctor is not under a legal obligation to assist a patient when he is not working. This is because omissions are not culpable in law unless you have a duty to act, and when a doctor is not working he is not under a duty to act. However, the General Medical Council do encourage doctors to help in an emergency, even if off-duty, and this tells us that he may face disciplinary action, but not legal action if he simply watches from the side-lines.

---

[14] A pregnant prisoner is entitled to the same standard of care as an ordinary pregnant woman: *Brooks* v *Home Office* [1999] 2 FLR 33, per Garland J.

EXTRACT

Good Medical Practice, (2013), General Medical Council, page 11:

http://www.gmc-uk.org/guidance/good_medical_practice.asp

Paragraph 26: You must offer help if emergencies arise in clinical settings or in the community, taking account of your own safety, your competence and the availability of other options for care.

Once a person assumes a duty of care over a victim, a duty of care has been legally established.[15] Walking away from a victim would be a clear breach of that duty, unless the emergency services or a properly qualified medical professional arrives to take over. The off-duty doctor must provide a reasonable standard of care, just like an ordinary doctor, but the courts will make allowances for the lack of equipment, the bustle of the emergency scene, and the ordinary risks inherent in treating a person at the roadside. This will inevitably mean that the standard of care will be lower than that of an ordinary doctor who has access to state-of-the-art equipment in an intensive care unit. This was noted in the judgment in *Wilsher* (1987).

CASE EXTRACT

Wilsher v *Essex AHA* [1988] AC 1074

Mustill LJ (at page 749): I accept that full allowance must be made for the fact that certain aspects of treatment may have to be carried out in what one witness called 'battle conditions'. An emergency may overburden resources and, if an individual is forced by circumstances to do too many things at once, the fact that he does one of them incorrectly should not lightly be taken as negligence.

Standard of care: the inexperienced doctor

Junior doctors must meet the same standard of care as senior doctors, as held in *Jones* v *Manchester Corp* [1952] 2 All ER 125. It is quite normal for junior doctors to learn 'on the job' through interaction with patients and colleagues, and if a junior doctor has to ask a senior doctor for help, then so be it. The case of *Wilsher* (1987) is the clearest example of this.

CASE EXTRACT

Wilsher v *Essex AHA* [1988] AC 1074

Facts: A junior doctor consulted with a senior doctor before wrongly inserting a catheter into a baby, resulting in too much oxygen, leaving the baby almost blind.

Held: The junior doctor had taken reasonable steps by asking a senior doctor what to do, and so the health authority was vicariously liable for the senior doctor (liability was later overturned by the House of Lords for lack of causation). There must, however, not be varying standards of care between doctors depending on experience. The same standards must apply to junior and senior doctors.

→

---

[15] *R* v *Stone* [1977] QB 354 is a clear example of this (they were not medical professionals but family members).

Glidewell LJ (at page 774): In my view, the law requires the trainee or learner to be judged by the same standard as his more experienced colleagues. If it did not, inexperience would frequently be urged as a defence to an action for professional negligence. If this test appears unduly harsh in relation to the inexperienced, I should add that, in my view, the inexperienced doctor called on to exercise a specialist skill will, as part of that skill, seek the advice and help of his superiors when he does or may need it. If he does seek such help, he will often have satisfied the test, even though he may himself have made a mistake.

Glidewell LJ takes a very strict approach but he clearly justifies his reasons. A junior doctor can always consult another colleague during his training. Additionally, it is vital that inexperience is *not* allowed by the law to be an excuse for negligence, otherwise all junior doctors will have a 'get out clause' for their mistakes and patients would only ever ask to be treated by senior staff, thereby destroying any chance of training 'on the job'.

Standard of care: alternative healers

Alternative medicine is a new area of medical law, and it has caused some confusion. The individuals who choose to practice alternative medicine – 'herbalists' or 'alternative healers' – can advise people about their ailments and how to treat them, just like a doctor might do, but they cannot write medical prescriptions. Additionally, patients often resort to alternative healers when their prescription drugs are simply not doing their job. A lot of trust is clearly bestowed into alternative healers, but how are they treated by the law? Interestingly, there is only one case to report and the normal rules of medical negligence were applied.

CASE EXTRACT

Shakoor (Administratix of the Estate of Shakoor) v *Situ (t/a Eternal Health Co)* [2001] 1 WLR 410

Facts: Abdul Shakoor had a skin condition and the only traditional treatment was surgery. Unwilling to do this, he visited Mr Situ, a practitioner of traditional Chinese herbal medicine. Abdul Shakoor took nine doses of the herbal remedy and died of liver failure.

Held: A practitioner in Chinese herbal medicine is to be judged against a practitioner practising that same art (*Bolam*), not against a regular doctor. He has a duty to ensure that the substances are not potentially harmful. The practitioner must read the relevant literature and be aware of the risks, and his practice is open to scrutiny the same as regular doctors (*Bolitho*). It is important that the patient rejected a regular doctor to seek the help of an alternative practitioner.

Bernard Livesey QC (at pages 414, 416, 417): As can be seen, there is not any dispute that the defendant owed to the deceased a professional duty to exercise reasonable care and skill in treating him and, in particular, a duty to take care not to cause him harm. But the extent of the duty is in dispute. [...] There is not any authority on this point in this country or, as far as I am aware after appropriate searches, in other common law jurisdictions. [...]

The Chinese herbalist, for example, does not hold himself out as a practitioner of orthodox medicine. More particularly, the patient has usually had the choice of going to an orthodox practitioner but has rejected him in favour of the alternative practitioner for reasons personal and best known to himself and almost certainly at some personal financial cost. [...] The decision of the patient may be enlightened and informed or based on ignorance and superstition. Whatever the basis of his decision, it seems to me that the fact that the patient has chosen to reject the orthodox and prefer the alternative practitioner is something important which must be taken into account. Why should he later be able to complain that the alternative practitioner has not provided him with skill and care in accordance with the standards of those orthodox practitioners whom he has rejected? On the other hand, it is of course obviously true to say that the alternative practitioner has chosen to practise in this country alongside a system of orthodox medicine and must abide by the laws and standards prevailing in this country. [...]

Where he prescribes a remedy which is taken by a patient it is not enough to say that the remedy is traditional and believed not to be harmful; he has a duty to ensure that the remedy is not actually or potentially harmful. [...] An alternative practitioner who prescribes a remedy must take steps to satisfy himself that there has not been any adverse report in such journals on the remedy which ought to affect the use he makes of it. [...] It should be enough if he subscribes to an 'association' which arranges to search the relevant literature and promptly report any material publication to him. [...] If he does not subscribe to such an association the practitioner will not have discharged his duty to inform himself properly and may act at his peril.

Accordingly, a plaintiff may succeed in an action against an alternative practitioner for negligently prescribing a remedy either by calling an expert in the speciality in question to assert and prove that the defendant has failed to exercise the skill and care appropriate to that art. [...] Alternatively, the plaintiff may prove that the prevailing standard of skill and care 'in that art' is deficient in this country having regard to risks which were not and should have been taken into account. [...] In these circumstances, I find that the defendant was not in breach of his duty to the deceased. I am satisfied that he acted in accordance with the standard of care appropriate to Chinese herbal medicine as properly practised in accordance with the standards required in this country. The fact that the deceased died in consequence of the medication, as the doctors have on a balance of probability agreed, is a tragic accident but not the fault of the defendant.

This judgment requires a deeper analysis because it is controversial, novel and based on very little legal and medical evidence. Firstly, Bernard Livesey QC admits that he cannot find any legal authority to help him make this decision and he has two choices: the defendant can be compared to a reasonable practitioner of Chinese herbal medicine, or a regular medical practitioner. It would clearly be unfair to compare a herbalist to a doctor, because their job, qualifications, knowledge and experience are completely different. The obvious option was therefore the former, rather than the latter. Secondly, if the patient rejects the help of a normal doctor, this 'must be taken into account'. Why must this be taken into account? The patient is *not* to blame when he dies at the hands of a herbalist simply because he did not choose orthodox (scientific) medicine. This statement should be revised by subsequent case law, because it suggests that the free will of the patient absolves the herbalist from any liability. Thirdly, Bernard Livesey QC states that it is fair to judge an alternative practitioner against the laws in our country. This is surely correct, but unfortunately the laws regarding herbalists are not clear. He begins to form his own legal test for herbalists. He states that they are under a duty to ensure that the remedy is 'not actually or potentially harmful'. The use of the word 'potentially' opens a considerable margin for error. A herbalist must meet this test by subscribing to relevant literature and an association. In real terms this test will do nothing to change the practice of the herbalist or the safety of the herbs he uses, because the practitioner could simply choose not to read all of the relevant material, or ignorantly believe that his knowledge is true and accurate. Bernard Livesey QC states that if the herbalist does not do this he has not discharged his duty, but it is a very weak foundation upon which to base a legal duty. Fourthly, and in conclusion, Bernard Livesey QC states that the defendant was not in breach of his duty. There is no solid explanation – legal or medical – to support this conclusion.

Standard of care: professional guidelines

In the days of *Bolam*, doctors were a law unto themselves and would not be questioned by the courts. In the 1990s, *Bolitho* encouraged judges to question expert medical evidence that could not stand up to logical analysis. Today, the leading regulatory health bodies are acutely aware of the growing confidence in patients to question the standard of care they have received. In response, a raft of regulations, guidelines and rules have been published for every kind of specialist and procedure. The courts today are finding it easier to locate and understand the standard of care required. The relevant guiding bodies include the following:

- The General Medical Council (official regulatory body for doctors).[16]
- The Department of Health (government department for public health and social care).[17]
- The Medical Research Council.[18]
- National Institute of Health and Care Excellence.[19]
- The Royal College of Medicine, Nursing, Surgeons, etc.

These regulatory bodies frequently publish good practice guidelines for the specialists who belong to their particular field to keep members up to date with the changing law and practice. Inevitably, judges are relying on these guidelines to determine an appropriate standard of care, but they can only read these guidelines through the eyes of an unqualified lay person.

Field J has confirmed that clinical guidelines are helpful to patients, doctors and judges by applying them directly in *Richards* (2007).

CASE EXTRACT

Richards v *Swansea NHS Trust* [2007] EWHC 487

Facts: The mother of a disabled child argued that the hospital was negligent in delaying her caesarean section, resulting in her son being born with cerebral palsy. It was standard to deliver the baby, in such circumstances, within thirty minutes, but it had taken fifty-five minutes overall.

→

---

[16] www.gmc-uk.org
[17] www.gov.uk/government/organisations/department-of-health
[18] www.mrc.ac.uk
[19] www.nice.org.uk

Held: The relevant guidelines clearly state that thirty minutes is the accepted time for delivery, and there was no evidence to support the fifty-five-minute delay. Judgment for the claimant (mother). [NICE: National Institute for Care Excellence; RCOG: Royal College of Obstetricians and Gynaecologists; NSCSAR: National Sentinel Caesarean Section Audit Report.]

Field J (at para 28): In my judgment once the decision had been taken to deliver Jac by emergency caesarean section, a decision which in the circumstances a reasonably competent obstetric registrar was entitled to make, the defendant owed a duty of care to Jac to deliver him as quickly as possible with the aim of trying to deliver him within thirty minutes. [...] This is the approach in the NSCSAR and the NICE/RCOG Caesarean section guideline and I am satisfied that the guidance set out in these reports reflects the approach that was operative in 1996.

Academic commentary: are standards of care clear?

The introduction of logical analysis in *Bolitho* rocked the medical world. It was the first time that an appeal court called into question the evidence of an expert medical witness (apart from *Hucks* v *Cole* of course, but that was not widely publicised at the time). The 'rare category' created in *Bolitho* is now encouraged by the many clinical guidelines made available to the public, allowing judges to read around a particular medical procedure and a description of its standard of care before walking into the court room and scrutinising the expert medical witness. This wealth of freedom and information may be a good thing, but could it have a negative impact on the medical profession?

A couple of pieces in the *Medical Law Review* have published opposing ideas as to whether this wealth of freedom and information for judges is a step in the right direction or not (below). Firstly, supportive comments have been penned by Lord Woolf as to the traditional ideals in *Bolam* being chipped away.

EXTRACT

Lord Woolf, 'Are the Courts Excessively Deferential to the Medical Profession?' (2001) 9 *Medical Law Review* 1, at pages 1–16

Until recently the courts treated the medical profession with excessive deference (i.e. respect and admiration), but recently the position has changed. It is my judgment that it has changed for the better. [...] What is it that has caused the change? I would identify the following causes:

First, today the courts have a less deferential approach to those in authority. [...] Secondly, [...] the courts became increasingly conscious of the difficulties which *bona fide* (i.e. genuine) claimants had in successfully establishing claims. Thirdly, there has developed an increasing awareness of patient rights. The public's expectations of what the profession should achieve have grown. [...] The move to a rights-based society has fundamentally changed the behaviour of the courts. Fourthly, [...] almost daily there are reports in the media suggesting that there is something amiss with our health treatment. Fifthly, our courts were aware that courts at the highest level of other Commonwealth jurisdictions, particularly Canada and Australia, were rejecting the approach of the English courts. They were subjecting the actions of the medical

→

profession to a closer scrutiny than the English courts. [...] [Sixthly omitted] Seventhly, recently a series of cases have come before the courts that raised fundamental questions of medical ethics. [...] The courts, having had to struggle with issues such as these, were prepared to adopt a more proactive approach to resolving conflicts as to more traditional medical issues.

Eighthly, [...] the incorporation into English domestic law of the European Convention on Human Rights.

Lord Woolf points to a small handful of causes what have influenced the case law in medical negligence. This shows understanding of patient concerns from the highest level, and sends a message to medical associations that the law is willing to support patients where necessary. The courts are also becoming aware of how other Commonwealth countries are rejecting our legal approach. The biggest influence appears to be changes in society. We now have human rights, and scandals have chipped away at the hard face of medicine to reveal it as a business prone to mistakes just like any other corporation.

The next piece argues that judges are better equipped than ever to deal with medical negligence cases.

EXTRACT

Margot Brazier and Jose Miola, 'Bye-Bye Bolam: A Medical Litigation Revolution?' (2000) 8 *Medical Law Review* 85, at pages 85–114

Most importantly, *Bolitho* has been decided at a time when other developments also point to a revolution in the way medical malpractice is judged. Medicine itself is changing with practitioners increasingly evaluating their own practice and seeking to develop evidence-based medicine. The traditional guardians of clinical standards, the Royal Colleges of Medicine, have over the last decade become more and more proactive, issuing guidelines about good practice with reference to treatments and procedures. [...] The National Institute for Clinical Excellence (NICE) has been established to develop guidelines for good practice, not just in the context of new drug treatments, but in a much wider sphere of reviewing all forms of therapies and procedures. [...] The judge confronted by individual experts who disagree about good practice will in certain cases be able to refer to something approaching a 'gold standard'. [...] The judge will have access to material, independent of the particular dispute before him, enabling him to assess the logic of the parties' cases. *Bolitho*, plus more ready access to clinical guidelines, suggests a more proactive role for judges assessing expert evidence. *Bolitho* demands that doctors explain their practice. Doctors themselves are developing tools which will enable judges to review those explanations.

Brazier and Miola make an interesting point: the wealth of clinical guidelines available today may be leading us towards a 'gold standard' in medical care. There is definitely a 'more proactive role for judges' in medical law today.

A contrasting piece notes that clinical guidelines are only meant to be used for general guidance and should not be applied to particular cases. They are not legal rules and contain irrelevant economic material, leading to the conclusion that they should not be relied upon so readily.

EXTRACT

Ash Samanta, et al, 'The Role of Clinical Guidelines in Medical Negligence Litigation: A Shift from the *Bolam* Standard' (2006) 14(3) *Medical Law Review* 321, at pages 321–66

Guidelines have a number of inherent limitations. There is a danger in applying the generalised prescription of guidelines in a rigid fashion to every patient. [...] There is always a need for flexibility in patient care, and although guidelines are designed to promote best practice, in any given clinical episode, the slavish adherence to guidelines may not be the best practice for that particular patient. [...] Additionally, guidelines are only as good as the underlying empirical evidence and the appropriateness of the conclusions reached on the basis of synthesis of evidence. The validity of guidelines may be undermined by weak research data as well as confounding factors and biases emanating from misconceptions, personal experiences and beliefs of the developers. [...]

Decisions reflected in some guidance might be motivated predominantly by economic considerations. NICE, for instance, has a specific remit to ensure the cost-effectiveness of treatment or interventional modalities, and its guidance is frequently against clinical interventions on the basis of cost. [...] If guidelines are perceived as a tool for rationing healthcare, it is less likely that they will be used by the court as a detriment of the legal standard.

Foster and Tingle put some very strong points forward to argue that clinical guidelines should not be relied upon so readily. Clinical guidelines are generalised because they focus on economic issues, cost-effectiveness and can be proved wrong over time in light of scientific developments. These guidelines, it is argued, are not much use when applied to individual patients who have personalised medical needs and as a result, judges will find little benefit from reading them.

Proving the breach: *res ipsa loquitur*

KEY DEFINITION   *Res ipsa loquitur*: the thing speaks for itself.

The Latin phrase *res ipsa loquitur* comes into play when something is so *obvious* that it speaks for itself, as held in *Gee* v *Metropolitan Railway Co* (1873) LR 8 QB 161. This may be applied in medical law, but it is very rare. It will typically be found where the cause of the negligence is so clear that very little evidence is needed. The maxim *res ipsa loquitur* does not mean that the claimant no longer has a burden of proof – he still must prove his case on a balance of probabilities (51%) – but it will be easier for him because the facts are so obvious. A few examples might be as follows:

- A patient goes into hospital to have her right arm amputated and leaves with her left arm amputated.
- A patient is given an overdose of a cleaning agent rather than a simple painkiller after her surgery.
- A patient suffers from chest pain after a routine procedure, only to find that surgical scissors were left in her body.

A judge may be willing to infer that a standard of care has not been met on very obvious facts because the events literally 'speak for themselves'. Lord Denning in *Cassidy* v *Ministry of Health* [1951] 2 KB 343 gave the example of a patient going into surgery with two stiff fingers and coming out with four. However, the claimant cannot turn up to court with no medical evidence whatsoever and simply assume that *res ipsa loquitur* will be applied, as the *Ratcliffe* (1998) case shows.

CASE EXTRACT

Ratcliffe v *Plymouth and Torbay HA* [1998] PIQR P170

Facts: Mr Ratcliffe had an operation on his ankle, which was successful, and was given a post-operative anaesthetic in his spine. He suffered from severe pain and a total loss of sensation in his leg. He argued that this must have meant that the anaesthetic was administered negligently.

Held: There is not to be an assumption of negligence in this case. There is not enough evidence to suggest that the anaesthetic was administered negligently.

Hobhouse LJ (at pages 186, 188): *Res ipsa loquitur* is no more than a convenient Latin phrase used to describe the proof of facts which are sufficient to support an inference that a defendant was negligent and therefore to establish a *prima facie* ['at first sight'] case against him. [...] The burden of proving the negligence of the defendant remains throughout upon the plaintiff. The burden is on the plaintiff at the start of the trial and, absent an admission by the defendant, is still upon the plaintiff at the conclusion of the trial. [...]

If the facts of the present case had been that the plaintiff had gone into the operating theatre to have an arthrodesis to his right ankle and had come out of the theatre with his right ankle untouched and an arthrodesis to his left ankle, clearly no expert evidence would be required to support an inference of negligence on the part of the claimants. [...] In practice, save in most extreme cases of blatant negligence, the plaintiff will have to adduce at least some expert evidence to get his case upon its feet.

Hobhouse LJ makes it clear in *Ratcliffe* that *res ipsa loquitur* is merely just a phrase with no real legal meaning. In reality, a judge can only infer that a standard of care has not been met without medical evidence in 'extreme cases of blatant negligence'. This test was not satisfied in Mr Ratcliffe's case.

ACTIVITY

Three rugby players were brought into accident and emergency after a national match, all suffering from severe head injuries. There were plenty of staff on duty, including five senior doctors and three junior doctors. Player number one – Andy – had concussion and was placed in his own quiet room awaiting a brain scan. Player number two – Paul – had bleeding on the brain and was awaiting surgery. Player number three – Mike – had swelling on the brain and was placed next to Andy awaiting a brain scan too. The senior doctors rushed off to arrange the scans and surgery, leaving the three junior doctors to prepare the three patients. The beds

→

were not labelled with patient numbers, so the patients were identifiable by clipboards on the bottom of the beds. The juniors picked the clipboards up, wondered around with them, and put them back down at a later point on the incorrect beds. Andy was given an anaesthetic for brain surgery, but it made his concussion worse. Paul was simply put on a drip. Mike was given a painkiller. Andy then went into surgery, but the surgeon could not find any bleeding. Paul died. Mike made a full recovery.

How many breaches of duty are there in this situation, if any, and on what grounds?

(c) The breach must cause the damage

A duty of care has been established and a breach of that duty has been proven through expert medical evidence. Finally, the patient must prove that the breach caused her injury. This is not as easy as it sounds. The chain of causation begins at the negligent act and finishes at the resulting injury. There must not be an intervening act or any other cause in between which may break this chain of causation. The difficulty with medical negligence is that the patient is usually already in hospital because of a pre-existing ailment, e.g. failing organs, headaches and sickness, numbness and dizziness or cuts and grazes, and if the patient was to leave hospital after her treatment in an even *worse* position than she was before, the doctor will simply argue that her pre-existing ailment is to blame rather than his negligence. There may even be multiple causes, or there may be no obvious cause.

Patient argument	Doctor argument
'I came into hospital for surgery for my back pain. You performed the surgery negligently. I now have even worse back pain. You had a duty of care which you breached and this caused my injury.'	'When you came into hospital you had back pain which worsened on its own. You were informed of the small risk of your back pain worsening after surgery but you consented. There was no negligence during surgery.'

The courts are sometimes put in the difficult position of having to guess what might have happened to the patient's condition had she not visited her doctor. Causation is therefore a vital tool in locating what actually *caused* the resulting injury, and it should be able to do this by separating the original ailment from the new injury through solid medical evidence, and this must be proven by the patient on a balance of probabilities at 51%. Civil causation is traditionally split into two areas: factual causation and remoteness.

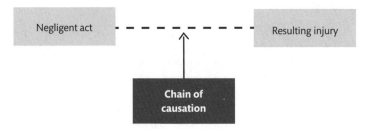

Figure 3.1

Factual causation

Factual causation is present if it is a physical fact that the patient would not have died if it was not for the doctor. This is often referred to as the 'but for . . .' test, as applied in the case of *Cork* v *Kirby Maclean Ltd* [1952] 2 All ER 402 per Lord Denning.

EXAMPLE

A doctor amputates the wrong limb: 'but for the doctor's actions, the wrong limb would not have been amputated'.

Barnett (1969) is a classic example of factual causation in a medical negligence context, and proof that if factual causation cannot be met, there is no case to answer.

CASE EXTRACT

Barnett v *Chelsea and Kensington Hospital Management Committee* **[1969] 1 QB 428**

Facts: Mr Barnett was one of three men who visited a hospital because they were feeling very unwell after drinking tea. A casualty officer, Dr Banerjee, was notified by a nurse but told them to return home and simply call a doctor. The men had severe arsenic poisoning and all died, and Mrs Barnett (widow) brought a claim in negligence.

Held: The doctor may have breached his duty of care by failing to examine the men, but even if Mr Barnett had been treated, it was far too late and he would have died anyway. The breach of duty by Dr Banerjee was *not* the cause of death.

Nield J (at pages 438–9): It remains to consider whether it is shown that the deceased's death was caused by this negligence or whether, as the defendants have said, the deceased must have died in any event. [...] I regard that evidence as very moderate, and that it might be a true assessment of the situation to say that there was no chance of [the drug] being administered before the death of the deceased. For these reasons, I find that the plaintiff has failed to establish, on the grounds of probability, that the defendants' negligence caused the death of the deceased.

The *Barnett* case is a clear application of factual causation: 'but for the doctor breaching his duty, the patient *still* would have died'. In other words, the doctor was *not* the factual cause of death and the legal action failed at the last hurdle.

Lord Reid concluded in *Bonnington Castings Ltd* v *Wardlaw* [1956] AC 613 (a health and safety case) that a tortfeasor does not need to be the only factual cause – it is enough for him to provide a *substantial contribution* to the outcome. This applies to doctors too. Additionally, if there are several causes that all play *more than a minimal* role in the resulting injury, it is almost impossible to prove factual causation on a balance of probabilities. The medical case of *Wilsher* (1988) is a classic example.

CASE EXTRACT

Wilsher v *Essex AHA* [1988] 1 AC 1074 (House of Lords)

Facts: A junior doctor consulted with a senior doctor before wrongly inserting a catheter into a baby (the plaintiff), resulting in too much oxygen, leaving the baby almost blind. There were a number of different factors that could have caused the blindness, and the medical treatment was the likely but not the definitive cause. The Court of Appeal [1987] 1 QB 730 said that the defendants were liable.

Held: The defendants were not liable because causation was wrongly decided. A number of different factors could have caused the condition, and there was no evidence and no presumption that it was the excess oxygen rather than one of the other factors which caused or contributed to the condition. Since there was a conflict of medical evidence, the issue of causation was remitted to a different judge to try (outcome unknown). [RLF: retrolental fibroplasias.]

Lord Bridge (at pages 1090–1): The onus of proving causation lies on the pursuer or plaintiff. [...] In the Court of Appeal in the instant case, Sir Nicolas Browne-Wilkinson, being in a minority, expressed his view on causation with understandable caution. But I am quite unable to find any fault with the following passage in his dissenting judgment [1987] QB 730, at page 779:

> [...] There are a number of different agents which could have caused the RLF. Excess oxygen was one of them. The defendants failed to take reasonable precautions to prevent one of the possible causative agents (e.g. excess oxygen) from causing RLF. But no one can tell in this case whether excess oxygen did or did not cause or contribute to the RLF suffered by the plaintiff. The plaintiff's RLF may have been caused by some completely different agent or agents, e.g. hypercarbia, intraventricular haemorrhage, apnoea or patent ductusarteriosus. In addition to oxygen, each of those conditions has been implicated as a possible cause of RLF. This baby suffered from each of those conditions at various times in the first two months of his life. There is no satisfactory evidence that excess oxygen is more likely than any of those other four candidates to have caused RLF in this baby. [...] A failure to take preventative measures against one out of five possible causes is no evidence as to which of those five caused the injury. [...]

In the absence of relevant findings of fact by the judge, there was really no alternative to a retrial.

Lord Bridge in the earlier Court of Appeal judgment was therefore correct when he held that just because preventative measures were not taken for one of five causes, does not mean that that cause was the factual cause. There must be medical evidence to prove which cause was the factual cause. *Wilsher* is more likely to be followed in medical negligence cases for public policy reasons.

CASE EXTRACT

Gregg v *Scott* [2005] 2 AC 176 (in detail below)

Lord Hoffman (at para 60): A wholesale adoption of possible rather than probable causation as the criterion of liability would be so radical a change in our law as to amount to a legislative act. It would have enormous consequences for insurance companies and the National Health Service.

Factual causation: intervening acts

Factual causation is not without its problems. There may be an unforeseen and unexpected intervening act that breaks the chain of causation. It is known in Latin as a *novus actus interveniens*.

KEY DEFINITION | *Novus actus interveniens*: new act intervening.

EXAMPLE

The patient is on the operating table and the doctor is using the wrong surgical tools to carry out an abortion. These dirty and old tools pose a grave risk of death and is a clear breach of duty. The patient suddenly has a heart attack on the table and dies. She is shown in the post-mortem to have contracted a deadly bacterial disease, but the heart attack was an unforeseeable intervening act that caused her death before the disease could reach her vital organs. This break in the chain of causation absolves the doctor from all liability. In other words, his breach of duty did not cause her death.

The intervening act must be *unforeseeable* for it to break the chain of causation. The *Home Office* v *Dorset Yacht Co Ltd* [1970] 2 All ER 294 case (non-medical) confirms that if an intervening act is 'very likely to happen' then it will not break the chain of causation, and if the damage is not too remote (i.e. not too far away), then the original tortfeasor will still be liable for it. The case of *Knightley* v *Johns* [1982] 1 WLR 349 (non-medical) confirms, in very clear terms, the following principles in regards to intervening acts:

- A doctor will only be held liable for injuries that are a *natural and probable* consequence of his negligent act or omission.

- The test is reasonable foreseeability, defined as: 'foreseeability of something *of the same sort* being likely to happen'. This allows a patient to claim that her injury, although not *exactly* what the doctor may have envisaged, should have been foreseen by him if it was very similar.

- A 'mere possibility' does not count, especially if it would 'never occur to the mind of a reasonable man or if it did would be neglected as too remote to impose liability'.

- In an emergency, allowances must be made for pressures on trained professionals, and he admitted that mistakes are to be expected when a human being acts in a crisis.

- In terms of medical negligence, it follows that positive acts are more likely to be viewed as causes of the injury, and failures to act are more likely to break the chain of causation.

- Stephenson LJ stated that the original tortfeasor (i.e. the doctor who began the chain of events) should not be able to escape all of the consequences of his original act simply because he believes they are 'improbable', but a *novus actus interveniens* can still be found if, as happened in *Knightley*, an injury occurs that is not a natural, probable and reasonably foreseeable consequence of the original act.

Remoteness

Factual causation may identify several causes of medical negligence, but it is not the only way to establish causation. 'Remoteness' is another consideration in negligence, and it is all about 'distance'. The lords will sometimes describe an outcome as 'too remote' to mean that it is 'too distant' or 'too "far away"' for it to be traced back to the original tortfeasor. The same principles apply in medical cases: if an injury is too remote, it means that it is too detached from the doctor's original act or omission to say that he caused it.

EXAMPLE

A doctor injects an overdose of morphine into a child as the child is being treated by the roadside. The child dies six months later as a result of injuries sustained from the collision, but it is not clear what the exact cause of death is. The injection of morphine has faded into the background as a potential cause of death – it is too far away – and so the courts will probably say it is 'too remote' to be a cause.

The leading case on remoteness is *Overseas Tankship (UK) Ltd* v *Morts Dock & Engineering Co (The Wagon Mound)* [1961] AC 388 (non-medical). It establishes that causation in civil law requires two things: the outcome must not only be a 'direct and natural' consequence of the negligent act or omission, but it must be 'foreseeable by a reasonable man' (an objective test). It would otherwise be unfair to hold a man liable for an outcome if he did not foresee the damage, or he did foresee the damage but it was not a direct and natural consequence of his negligent act or omission. In the context of medicine, any injury inflicted upon a patient must be a direct and natural consequence of the doctor's negligent act or omission, and a reasonable man should foresee that injury. The remoteness test was applied in the two medical cases of *Croydon* (1998) and *Creutzfeld–Jakob Disease* (2000).

CASE EXTRACT

R v Croydon HA [1998] PIQR Q26

Facts: The claimant had a chest x-ray before starting work at the health authority. The radiographer failed to alert her of an abnormality which could be worsened by pregnancy. She fell pregnant and experienced significant complications, leading her to retire early. She brought a claim for all of the costs arising from the pregnancy and birth.

Held: The courts dismissed her claim because there was not a sufficient connection between the radiographer and her personal circumstances (i.e. it was too remote).

Kennedy LJ (at page 32): The damage was, as is sometimes said, too remote. The chain of events had too many links. [...] We understand that the radiologist never actually saw the plaintiff, and he probably knew very little about her except her age. He would no doubt have accepted that, in so far as he failed to observe an abnormality which could have affected her fitness for work as an employee of the health authority in the immediate future, that was something for which he should be held accountable, but her domestic circumstances were not his affair.

The Creutzfeldt–Jakob Disease Litigation (No. 5), Re [2000] Lloyd's Rep Med 161

Facts: A group of children with a growth impairment underwent clinical research with a human growth hormone which may have infected them with the human form of mad cow disease. Psychiatric injury resulted. The issue was whether the psychiatric injury was too remote from the act of injection.

Held: The psychiatric injury was not too remote from the act of negligence in this case.

Morland J: I am satisfied that when the defendants breathed their duty of care to them by being responsible for injecting them with potentially lethal Hartree HGH they should have reasonably foreseen that, if deaths occurred from CJD caused by HGH contaminated with the CJD agent, some of the recipients of that HGH might well suffer psychiatric injury on becoming aware of the risk to them. The defendants as tortfeasors committed a wrong upon the Group B plaintiffs by imperilling their lives from a terrible fatal disease. It was reasonably foreseeable that, if the worst fears were realised and deaths from CJD occurred, Hartree HGH recipients, both those of normal fortitude and those more vulnerable, might suffer psychiatric injury. I cannot see in the facts and circumstances of this litigation why public policy, including social and economic policy considerations, should exclude them from compensation.

The cases above illustrate that if the resulting injury can be clearly traced back to the act of negligence, the tortfeasor (doctor) will be liable for it because it is not too remote.

The next case looks at the vulnerability of the victim and whether this can have an impact on causation. The case law states: you must take your victim as you find them and if they fall harder than expected, or hurt deeper than anticipated, the defendant cannot use this as a defence. This is known as the 'thin skull rule' and is seen in criminal law too.[20] This is connected to remoteness because, if a patient is particularly vulnerable, the doctor may argue that the victim caused her own injury through her frailty. The courts have taken the opposite view.

Smith v Leech Brain & Co [1962] 2 QB 405

Facts: Mr Smith was employed by the defendants to work with molten metal. He normally stood with his back to a firebrick wall and was provided with a sheet of corrugated iron with which to protect himself from the spattering of molten metal. A piece of molten metal struck him on the lower lip, causing a burn. The burn was the promoting agent of cancer, which developed at the site of the burn, and from which he died some three years later. His widow brought an action for damages in respect of his death. The issue was: had the employers *caused* his death?

Held: The risk of a workman receiving a burn from the molten metal while operating the overhead crane was one which any reasonable employer should have foreseen and the defendants were guilty of negligence at common law. Therefore, since the

➔

[20] The criminal case law is *R v Blaue (Robert Konrad)* [1975] 3 All ER 446.

cancer was merely an extension of the burn, which they should reasonably have anticipated, the defendants were liable in damages.

Lord Parker CJ (at pages 413, 415): I find that there was no visible sign of anything wrong with his lip before the accident. [...] I find that the burn was the promoting agency of cancer in tissues which already had a pre-malignant condition. In those circumstances, it is clear that the plaintiff's husband, but for the burn, would not necessarily ever have developed cancer. On the other hand, having regard to the number of matters which can be promoting agencies, there was a strong likelihood that at some stage in his life he would develop cancer. But that the burn did contribute to, or cause in part, at any rate, the cancer and the death, I have no doubt. [...] The test is not whether these employers could reasonably have foreseen that a burn would cause cancer and that he would die. The question is whether these employers could reasonably foresee the type of injury he suffered, namely, the burn.

This judgment is difficult to accept. Lord Parker CJ claims that cancer is merely an 'extension' of a small burn, but are these injuries really so closely connected as to impose full liability on the defendants? This decision draws a connection between a foreseeable injury (the burn) and a completely unforeseeable outcome (the cancer), going against the accepted principles of causation, i.e. 'reasonable foreseeability', 'natural and probable consequences' and 'remoteness'. Lord Parker CJ conveniently ignores these principles and the lack of medical evidence in his rather short judgment. However, the legal test is clear: as long as the tortfeasor can reasonably foresee the *type* of injury, then an *extension* of that injury will be attributed to his negligence too, even if it is unforeseen.

In medical negligence, a doctor must therefore foresee the *type* of injury resulting from his negligent act or omission but not the *seriousness* of it, and if a grave outcome happens to flow from a relatively trivial injury, the doctor will be held to have caused it.

Causation: the materialisation of a risk and 'loss of a chance'

Medical procedures pose risks, even when the procedure is performed correctly. These are known as 'inherent risks' because they are entrenched into the procedure whether it is performed perfectly or not. The surgeon or doctor must warn the patient about these risks so that the patient can provide an informed consent in return. The risks can materialise, but this is very rare.[21]

EXAMPLE

Jenna requires a caesarean section. She is told, before having the anaesthesia, that there is a very small risk of paralysis, brain damage or death. She consents to the general anaesthetic. She does not wake up: the very small risk has materialised.

---

[21] The doctor might *fail* to warn the patient of a risk which then materialises. The patient will argue that had she been warned of the risk, she never would have consented: see *Chester* v *Afshar* [2004] UKHL 41 in Chapter 4.

The main issue in this scenario is: is the doctor the cause of the injury, or did the injury happen without him? A common-sense approach would say that it was simply bad luck that the risk just happened to materialise for this particular patient, but technically, the anaesthetist would satisfy the factual causation test: 'but for the anaesthetist, Jenna would not be in a coma'. What does the law do in situations such as these, where the patient leaves hospital in a far worse condition than she entered because a risk materialised? The answer is: if the doctor warned her of the risk and she consented to it, it is simply bad luck, as long as he performed the procedure with reasonable care and skill.

An equally difficult case is one in which the doctor is negligent in diagnosing a patient, depriving the patient of a chance to heal. These are called 'loss of a chance' cases.

EXAMPLE

Jack falls off his bike and is taken to hospital. A sprain is diagnosed and he is sent home. He is taken back a week later and an x-ray is taken, to reveal shattered bone and a blood clot. Emergency surgery is now required. The original doctor is accused of causing the subsequent injury (surgery) because he deprived Jack of a proper diagnosis a week ago.

In situations such as these, the courts have previously calculated, in percentage terms, just how significant the loss of a chance was. The first case to acknowledge 'loss of a chance' as a head of damages was *Chaplin* v *Hicks* [1911] 2 KB 786, but the more recent case of *Hotson* (1987) explored the issue in detail. The lords ruled that the percentage calculations were a departure from the traditional rules of causation: loss of a chance does not exist in law and the doctor must cause the actual injury via the normal rules of causation.

CASE EXTRACT

Hotson v *East Berkshire HA* [1987] 1 AC 750

Facts: The plaintiff, then aged 13, fell twelve feet while climbing a tree and sustained an acute traumatic fracture of the left femoral epiphysis. He was taken to hospital, but his injury was not correctly diagnosed or treated for five days. In the event, he suffered avascular necrosis of the epiphysis, involving disability of the hip joint with the virtual certainty that osteoarthritis would later develop. He brought an action for damages against the defendant health authority, who admitted negligence in failing to diagnose and treat his injury promptly. Simon Brown J (the trial judge) found that even if the health authority had diagnosed the injury correctly and treated the plaintiff promptly, there had been a high probability – which he assessed as a 75% risk – that avascular necrosis would still have developed. He held that the plaintiff was entitled to damages for the loss of the 25% chance that he would have made a nearly full recovery and awarded him £11,500. The Court of Appeal dismissed an appeal by the health authority.

Held: The House of Lords allowed the appeal by the health authority. It is for the plaintiff (Hotson) to establish, on a balance of probabilities, that the delay in treatment had at least materially contributed to the development of the avascular necrosis (i.e. real loss, not loss of a chance). Full damages will then be awarded as per the usual rules of negligence, not calculated in percentages.

Lord Bridge (at page 782): The plaintiff's claim was for damages for physical injury and consequential loss alleged to have been caused by the authority's breach of their duty of care. In some cases, perhaps particularly medical negligence cases, causation may be so shrouded in mystery that the court can only measure statistical chances. But that was not so here. On the evidence there was a clear conflict as to what had caused the avascular necrosis. The authority's evidence was that the sole cause was the original traumatic injury to the hip. The plaintiff's evidence, at its highest, was that the delay in treatment was a material contributory cause. This was a conflict, like any other about some relevant past event, which the judge could not avoid resolving on a balance of probabilities. Unless the plaintiff proved on a balance of probabilities that the delayed treatment was at least a material contributory cause of the avascular necrosis he failed on the issue of causation and no question of quantification should arise.

Lord Ackner (at page 793): The deformed hip [...] was not caused by the admitted breach by the defendants [...] but was caused by the separation of the left femoral epiphysis when he fell. [...] I have sought to stress that this case was a relatively simple case concerned with the proof of causation, upon which the plaintiff failed, because he was unable to prove, on the balance of probabilities, that his deformed hip was caused by the authority's breach of duty in delaying over a period of five days a proper diagnosis and treatment. Where causation is in issue, the judge decides that issue on the balance of the probabilities. [...] Once liability is established, on the balance of probabilities, the loss which the plaintiff has sustained is payable in full.

The *Hotson* case tells us that in cases where there is an alleged 'loss of a chance', it is for the patient to prove, on a balance of probabilities (51%), that the doctor caused his *actual* injury. The patient is then paid in full for the whole injury, as per usual. The House of Lords clearly did not support the mathematical approach taken by the trial judge and the Court of Appeal, i.e. that the health authority contributed 25% to the injury, and the 'loss of a chance' must cause the injury at a probability of 51%. The only glaring problem with applying the traditional rules to 'loss of a chance' cases is that, if the doctor is proven by 51% to have caused the injury the patient has satisfied the burden of proof in civil law and is awarded full damages, but if the doctor is proven by 50% to have caused the injury the patient has not satisfied the burden of proof in civil law and will be awarded no damages. The Court of Appeal was clearly trying to be fairer to both parties by using the percentage method, but by sticking to the traditional burden of proof at 51%, the House of Lords have shut out many claims, including that of Stephen Hotson. This is very unfair to those patients who have been treated negligently but cannot prove that their loss of a chance contributed to more than 50% of their injury. They will not have a claim in law.

A strict application of *Hotson* was seen in the complicated case of *Gregg* v *Scott* (2005). The House of Lords confirmed that the patient must prove that his loss of a chance, i.e. a misdiagnosis or a delay, caused his resulting injury on a balance of probabilities (51%) and anything falling short of this was simply a 'possibility' that would not suffice for factual causation.

CASE EXTRACT	**Gregg v Scott** [2005] 2 AC 176

Facts: The appellant [G] (Malcolm Gregg) appealed against a decision (Court of Appeal: [2002] EWCA Civ 1471) that his medical negligence claim against the defendant doctor [S] (Dr Scott) failed. G had visited S because he had a lump under his arm. S negligently misdiagnosed G's condition as benign. A year later another general practitioner referred G to hospital for an examination and it was discovered that G had cancer of a lymph gland. By that time the tumour had spread to G's chest. G suffered pain, had to undergo a course of chemotherapy and was left with poor prospects of survival. G sued S, alleging that S should have referred him to hospital so the condition would have been diagnosed earlier and there would have been a high likelihood of a cure, the delay in diagnosis and treatment had caused physical injury in the shape of the spread of the cancer before his therapy began, and the losses he had suffered were consequential on that physical damage. The trial judge held that on the expert evidence the delay in diagnosis had reduced G's chances of surviving for more than ten years from 42% to 25%. However, he dismissed G's action because G had less than a 50% chance of surviving more than ten years anyway. The Court of Appeal also dismissed G's appeal.

Held: The appeal was dismissed again (although Lord Nicholls and Lord Hope dissented). A 'possibility' of factual causation will not suffice: the patient must prove, on a balance of probabilities, that the doctor's misdiagnosis caused an actual loss.

Lord Hoffman (at paras 79–80, 84–5, 90): Everything has a determinate cause, even if we do not know what it is. The blood-starved hip joint in *Hotson's* case [and] the blindness in *Wilsher's* case: [...] each had its cause and it was for the plaintiff to prove that it was an act or omission for which the defendant was responsible. [...] Similarly in the present case, the progress of Mr Gregg's disease had a determinate cause. [...] In the present case it is urged that Mr Gregg has suffered a wrong and ought to have a remedy. [...] There seem to me to be no new arguments or change of circumstances which could justify such a radical departure from precedent. [...] A wholesale adoption of possible rather than probable causation as the criterion of liability would be so radical a change in our law as to amount to a legislative act. It would have enormous consequences for insurance companies and the National Health Service.

Lord Phillips (at paras 72, 114, 177, 190): My Lords it seems to me that there is a danger, if special tests of causation are developed piecemeal to deal with perceived injustices in particular factual situations, that the coherence of our common law will be destroyed. [...] Under our law as it is at present, [...] a claimant will only succeed if, on balance of probability the negligence is the cause of the injury. If there is a possibility, but not a probability, that the negligence caused the injury, the claimant will recover nothing in respect of the breach of duty: *Hotson v East Berkshire Health Authority* [1987] AC 750; *Wilsher v Essex AHA* [1988] AC 1074. [...] I agree with Lord Hope that this case has been made peculiarly difficult to analyse by reason of the fact that, at least before this House, the only claim advanced has been a claim for loss of expectation of life. English law in relation to personal injury has yet to recognise a claim for the loss of a future prospect that is not consequent upon an established injury. [...] The complications of this case have persuaded me that it is not a suitable vehicle for introducing into the law of clinical negligence the right to recover damages for the loss of a chance of a cure. [...] Where medical treatment has resulted in an adverse outcome and negligence has increased the chance of that outcome, there may be a case for permitting a recovery of damages that is proportionate to the increase in the chance of the adverse outcome. That is not a case that has been made out on the present appeal. I would uphold the conventional approach to causation.

Firstly, the lords rejected the idea that a loss of a chance should be recoverable as a head of damages in medical negligence: the patient must prove, on a balance of probabilities, that the doctor's misdiagnosis caused an *actual* injury. Mr Gregg's claim was based on the loss of a chance of a cure, which was rejected. Lord Phillips doubted that a claim for a loss of a chance of a cure should exist in medical negligence because it did not require 'an established injury' to underpin it: 'English law in relation to personal injury has yet to recognise a claim for the loss of a future prospect that is not consequent upon an established injury'. Secondly, the lords were not comfortable with the idea that a 'possibility' of causation would suffice in cases of medical negligence. The main reason was that the burden of proof would change from 'probability' to 'possibility' and that would cause a radical upheaval in law. Lord Phillips admitted that there were already vaguely similar actions available in medical negligence: 'where medical treatment has resulted in an adverse outcome and negligence has increased the chance of that outcome, there may be a case for permitting a recovery of damages that is proportionate to the increase in the chance of the adverse outcome'. However, this was as far as he was willing to go. The present position, therefore, is that a loss of a chance does not exist as a head of damages in medical negligence.

Gregg was successfully applied in *Grieves* v *FT Everard & Sons Ltd* [2007] UKHL 39.

ACTIVITY

In the case of *Gregg* v *Scott* [2005] 2 AC 176, Lord Nicholls dissented against the decision and was very scathing about the 51% threshold in particular. Read his judgment and make notes on what he is suggesting as a way forward for patients who have suffered a loss. How would his suggestions change the law of medical negligence?

Defences to negligence

It has been established that in order to bring a claim for medical negligence, whether for occurrences before or after birth, there are three criteria to be proved: a duty of care, a breach of that duty, and the breach caused the damage.

A doctor can raise several defences in the law of negligence including denial, contributory negligence or consent.

Denial

The doctor can simply deny all charges. It is for the patient to prove, on a balance of probabilities, that the doctor had a duty of care, fell below the standard of duty, and caused her injury. The doctor can respond by arguing that he fulfilled the 'ordinary skill of an ordinary man exercising that particular art' test in *Bolam*. He can prove this by consulting other specialists who exercise the same skill. The expert evidence will, of course, need to stand up to logical analysis as a result of *Bolitho*, but it is not likely that a judge will question the integrity of medical practice unless it was obviously negligent.

Contributory negligence

The doctor may argue that the patient contributed to her injury. The Law Reform (Contributory Negligence) Act 1945 allows for damages to be reduced in proportion to the contribution made by the claimant.

The Law Reform (Contributory Negligence) Act 1945

Section 1: Apportionment of liability in case of contributory negligence

(1): Where any person suffers damage as the result partly of his own fault and partly of the fault of any other person or persons, a claim in respect of that damage shall not be defeated by reason of the fault of the person suffering the damage, but the damages recoverable in respect thereof shall be reduced to such extent as the court thinks just and equitable having regard to the claimant's share in the responsibility for the damage.

The courts may also find that there is no case to answer because the patient made a *complete* contribution to her own negligence. This may seem bizarre, but a case in the wrongful pregnancy section – *Sabri-Tabrizi* v *Lothian Health Board* [1998] Rep LR 37 – confirms that if a woman is aware of a risk of pregnancy because her sterilisation has failed and does not protect herself from becoming pregnant, she must take responsibility for her unwanted pregnancy.

Volenti non fit injuria

A doctor may raise the old defence of *volenti non fit injuria* – which translates as: 'to a willing person, no injury is done' – allows a doctor to argue that a patient willingly consented to his negligent medical care. It would be a very rare case in which this defence was presented by a doctor, because he would be admitting his negligence from the outset. However, it is plausible that, in desperate times, a patient may seek the help of a 'backstreet' doctor with inappropriate facilities, qualifications and tools, and consent to a procedure (an abortion or plastic surgery) that she could not get elsewhere.

THINKING POINT

Which defence is easier for a doctor to raise?

Limits to a claim

Legal claims do not stay open forever. There are good reasons for this: evidence may be lost or destroyed, relevant people may die or move on, and if a legal wrong does not show itself within a reasonable amount of time, it becomes increasingly difficult to say that the original defendant caused the outcome. The Limitation Act 1980 is the main weapon used by the courts to fend off late legal claims. The Act is split up into different areas of law, i.e. actions in tort, actions in contract, sums recoverable by statute, personal injury and death, recovering land and rent, etc. Medical negligence usually involves some form of personal injury, and these time limits are contained under section 11.

● Limitation Act 1980

Section 11: Special time limit for actions in respect of personal injuries

(1) This section applies to any action for damages for negligence, nuisance or breach of duty (whether the duty exists by virtue of a contract or of provision made by or under a statute or independently of any contract or any such provision) where the damages claimed by the plaintiff for the negligence, nuisance or breach of duty consist of or include damages in respect of personal injuries to the plaintiff or any other person.

(4) The period applicable is three years from –

  (a) the date on which the cause of action accrued; or

  (b) the date of knowledge (if later) of the person injured.

The time limit is clearly three years for negligence claims, although the three-year period begins depending on when the injury become known, referred to as 'the date of knowledge' under section 11(4)(b) above, or when the injury itself was done, referred to as 'accrued' under section 11(4)(a) above. Commentators have generally supported the limitation on claims.

EXTRACT

Richard Lewis, 'The Limitation Period in Medical Negligence Claims' (1998) *Medical Law Review* 62, at page 64

There is general agreement over the aims of the law of limitation. First, it provides finality so that sooner or later an incident or transgression which might have led to a claim can be safely treated as closed by all concerned. Secondly, it gives defendants a degree of protection from stale claims which they can no longer properly contest. And thirdly it provides an incentive to plaintiffs to commence proceedings without delay. This is closely related to the need to protect defendants from old claims but goes further in that it also recognises that the trial of disputes on complete or unreliable evidence is prejudicial to the public interest in the proper administration of justice. These objectives must of course be balanced against the interests of plaintiffs and the law now attaches very great weight to the need to give injured persons a fair chance to commence proceedings.

There are clear benefits to imposing limits on claims: the doctor will not have to worry about an old mistake coming back to haunt him, the lawyers will not have to worry about evidence being lost, and the patient will not have to worry about her claim dragging out for years and years.

Do you think it is morally and ethically right to impose a limit on medical negligence claims, considering the prolonged nature of some medical problems?

The criminal law

This chapter has mainly dealt with the criteria for negligence: duty of care, breach of duty, and cause. However, what if the negligence was *gross* (i.e. utterly extreme) resulting in the death of the patient? In these rare instances, the doctor will be charged with gross negligence manslaughter in criminal law *in addition* to negligence in civil law. The criteria for gross negligence manslaughter are almost identical to those for negligence (duty of care, which was breached and which caused a death), except for one major addition (the last criterion): the act or omission was so gross that it is criminal warranting a criminal charge *in addition* to the civil action.

It should be noted that it is not just doctors who can be charged with gross negligence manslaughter: anybody with a duty of care over someone else who breaches that duty to a gross level can be charged with it too, including teachers, parents, carers etc.[22]

Although there is little case law in this area, possible examples of situations where a medical professional could be charged with gross medical negligence include the following:

- A patient dies on the operating table because the surgeon cuts through the wrong artery even though it is clearly visible.

- A patient dies in childbirth because the doctor performs an appalling delivery leading to internal injuries.

- A patient dies of an overdose of a drug that should not have been anywhere near the patient.

Duty of care

The required duty of care is borrowed from civil law.[23] Therefore, Lord Atkin's 'neighbour principle' from *Donoghue* v *Stevenson* (1932) is applied to gross negligence manslaughter.

Typically, it is for the jury to decide whether the duty of care was present,[24] but in the context of medicine, the duty of care between a doctor and his patient is usually clear. The traditional duty issues, such as calculating how far the duty extends and whether a third party is covered, will still apply to a doctor who is accused of gross negligence manslaughter.

Breach of duty

In order to breach a duty of care the doctor must fall below the *reasonable standard of care* for someone exercising the same skill (*Bolam*). This is adopted from the civil law of negligence.

---

[22] The doctor will not be vicariously represented by his hospital trust – he will be charged individually and will appear in court as a criminal defendant.
[23] This was confirmed in the criminal case of *R* v *Wacker (Perry)* [2003] QB 1203.
[24] This was held in the criminal case of *R* v *Litchfield* [1998] Crim LR 508.

The breach caused the injury

The breach must cause the death. The traditional causal issues, such as factual causation, intervening acts and the thin skull rule will apply to a doctor who is accused of gross negligence manslaughter. However, it is important to note that the *criminal* versions of these tests will be applied, not the civil versions. For example, the leading case for factual causation in criminal law is *R* v *White (John)* [1910] 2 KB 124 (not *Cork* v *Kirby Maclean Ltd* [1952] 2 All ER 402), remoteness is replaced by 'legal causation' which looks for the *operating and substantial* cause of death, established by the criminal case of *R* v *Smith (Thomas Joseph)* [1959] 2 QB 35, and the thin skull rule is replaced by *R* v *Blaue* [1975] 3 All ER 446 (not *Smith* v *Leech Brain Ltd* [1962] 2 QB 405).

The conduct was so gross that it was criminal

The breach of duty will be examined in more detail here. If the doctor merely fell below a reasonable standard of care as required in the civil case of *Bolam*, then the criminal court cannot convict him of gross negligence manslaughter. However, if the defendant fell *grossly* below his standard of care in *Bolam*, then the jury are free to convict him of gross negligence manslaughter. The criminal case law has developed in a clear and simple manner, beginning with the very old case of *R* v *Doherty* (1887) 16 Cox CC 306 in which the breach was described as: 'culpable negligence of a grave kind', followed by *Bateman* (1927), *Andrews* (1937), *Adomako* (1995) and *Misra* (2005).

CASE EXTRACT

R v *Bateman (Percy)* [1927] 19 Cr App R 8

Facts: Dr Bateman was a qualified doctor who was called out to help deliver the baby of Mrs Harding. The baby was delivered dead and the mother was not taken to the hospital – on his orders – for some days, where she later died. The post-mortem showed that her bladder was ruptured, her colon was crushed, and most of her uterus was gone due to the botched delivery.

Held: There must be a duty of care, it must be breached, the breach must cause the death, and the negligence must show such disregard for the life and safety of others as to amount to a crime.

Lord Hewart CJ (at pages 11–12): *The negligence of the accused went beyond a mere matter of compensation between subjects and showed such disregard for the life and safety of others as to amount to a crime against the state and conduct deserving punishment.*

CASE EXTRACT

Andrews v *DPP* [1937] AC 576

Facts: Wilfred Andrews was charged with manslaughter after his dangerous driving caused the death of William Craven.

Held: This was a dangerous driving case but the requirements for manslaughter were discussed and *Bateman* was approved.

Lord Atkin (at page 583): *Simple lack of care as will constitute civil liability is not enough; For purposes of the criminal law there are degrees of negligence; and a very high degree of negligence is required to be proved.*

CASE EXTRACT

R v Adomako (John Asare) [1995] 1 AC 171

Facts: The defendant was a medical professional – an anaesthetist – and during an eye operation failed to notice that the tube from the ventilator had become disconnected. The patient suffered a heart attack and died.

Held: It is up to the jury to decide whether the breach was so gross that it amounted to a crime.

Lord Mackay (at page 187): The essence of the matter, which is supremely a jury question, is whether, having regard to the risk of death involved, the conduct of the defendant was so bad in all the circumstances as to amount in their judgment to a criminal act or omission.

CASE EXTRACT

R v Misra (Amit) [2005] 1 Cr App R 21

Facts: Two junior doctors failed to identify that a patient who had undergone surgery was seriously ill despite showing classic signs of an infection (the pulse, temperature and blood pressure were very abnormal). The infection was diagnosed too late and he died of toxic shock syndrome (an infection of the blood). Both doctors were charged with gross negligence manslaughter. The issue was, what was the correct jury test for grossness?

Held: The question for the jury was not whether D's negligence was gross and whether, additionally, it was a crime, but whether his behaviour was grossly negligent and consequently criminal.

Judge LJ (at paras 48, 64, 66): The decision of the House of Lords in *Adomako* clearly identified the ingredients of manslaughter by gross negligence. In very brief summary, the offence requires, first, death resulting from a negligent breach of the duty of care owed by the defendant to the deceased; second, that in negligent breach of that duty, the victim was exposed by the defendant to the risk of death; and third, that the circumstances were so reprehensible as to amount to gross negligence. [...] In our judgment the law is clear. [...] The jury concluded that the conduct of each appellant in the course of performing his professional obligations to his patient was 'truly exceptionally bad', and showed a high degree of indifference to an obvious and serious risk to the patient's life. Accordingly, along with the other ingredients of the offence, gross negligence too, was proved.

The offence of gross negligence manslaughter is not supported by all commentators, mainly because of its vagueness. It is, after all, the jury, who are not legally or medically qualified, who decide whether or not the conduct was so bad that it amounts to a crime. The offence also makes the medical profession uncomfortable and it may be that disciplinary procedures by a professional body – such as the General Medical Council – are enough when such tragic accidents happen.

⬤ Additional legal actions

- *The Corporate Manslaughter and Homicide Act* 2007: a hospital trust could be charged and prosecuted under this new law, but there are no such cases yet.
- *The Health and Safety at Work Act* 1974: a hospital trust can be charged and prosecuted under this older law for breaching their duty of care to persons not in their employment.[25]

ACTIVITY

It is, some argue, bad enough that doctors should face a civil action in negligence for a mistake, let alone criminal charges for manslaughter. Find the following article: Oliver Quick, 'Prosecuting "Gross" Medical Negligence: Manslaughter, Discretion and the Crown Prosecution Service' (2006) 33 *Journal of Law and Society* 421–50. What are the main reasons the author gives for abolishing the offence of gross negligence manslaughter, especially in relation to medical negligence?

⬤ ⬤ ⬤ The General Medical Council

The General Medical Council (GMC) is the regulatory body of general practitioners in the United Kingdom. All doctors must be registered with the GMC in order to practise. Its aim and purpose is to:

> '. . . protect, promote and maintain the health and safety of the public by ensuring proper standards in the practice of medicine'.[26]

The GMC was established by the Medical Act 1858. Its four main functions are outlined in the more recent Medical Act 1983:

- Keeping up-to-date registers of qualified doctors.
- Fostering good medical practice.
- Promoting high standards of medical education and training.
- Dealing firmly and fairly with doctors whose fitness to practice is in doubt.

The GMC have the power to control who practises medicine by governing entry onto the medical register and removing those who are found to be negligent if necessary. They also set standards for medical schools and postgraduate education and training, ensuring that all medical graduates adhere to the same set of principles. The GMC also publish good practice guides to ensure that ethical behaviour meets a consistent standard. They have now brought 'revalidation' into force, meaning that every five years a doctor must prove that he has worked according to good practice. He can do this by

---

[25] There is one case – *R* v *Southampton University Hospital NHS Trust* [2006] EWCA Crim 2971 – that stemmed from the prosecutions of the two junior doctors in *Misra*.

[26] www.gmc-uk.org

keeping evidence from his treatment of patients. The revalidation process was introduced across the UK in December 2012 with the hope that all doctors with licence to
practise will be revalidated by March 2016.[27] The GMC are completely independent of
the government, making them fully accountable for their own actions and allowing them
to exercise their own legal powers to protect patients (provided by the Medical Act
1983), who are their primary concern. A patient may be concerned that her doctor fell
below a reasonable standard of care, particularly if she was harmed. She can report the
doctor and the incident to the GMC. They will investigate all claims of professional misconduct. A 'Fitness to Practise Panel' will oversee the disciplinary investigations rather
than the courts, and an 'Interim Orders Panel' is available to decide whether a doctor
should be suspended during the investigation. There are several outcomes to such an
investigation:

- In the worst-case scenario, the doctor can be 'struck off' the register completely.
- The doctor can be suspended from practice for a certain amount of time.
- Conditions may be imposed upon practice, such as not to do a certain procedure.
- A warning may be issued.
- Training may be ordered.
- There may be no case to answer.

The civil standard of proof is applied by the GMC in its investigations, so negligence
must be proved on a balance of probabilities. It has been confirmed through case law that
'serious professional misconduct' does not have to be morally blameworthy, meaning
that an honest mistake could fall into this criteria.

CASE EXTRACT

McCandless v General Medical Council [1996] 1 WLR 167

Facts: Dr McCandless had been struck off the register for 'serious professional
misconduct'. He argued that, while he had been negligent, he had made an honest
mistake that was not morally blameworthy, and so that did not amount to 'serious
professional misconduct'.

Held: The public expect a high standard of care from doctors, and honest mistakes
are just as negligent as deliberate ones.

Lord Hoffman (at page 169): The public has higher expectations of doctors and
members of other self-governing professions. Their governing bodies are under a
corresponding duty to protect the public against the genially incompetent as well
as the deliberate wrongdoers.

It is not only patients who can report potential misconduct. A colleague – such as a
fellow doctor – may see or overhear something in his practice that causes him concern.
The GMC welcomes complaints from other healthcare workers because they are in a
better position to notice a poor standard of care.

---

[27] See www.gmc-uk.org for more information.

EXTRACT

General Medical Council, Good Medical Practice, Raising and Acting on Concerns about Patient Safety (2012):

http://www.gmc-uk.org/guidance/ethical_guidance/11860.asp

Paragraph 20: Concerns about patient safety can come from a number of sources, such as patients' complaints, colleagues' concerns, critical incident reports and clinical audit. Concerns may be about inadequate premises, equipment, other resources, policies or systems, or the conduct, health or performance of staff or multidisciplinary teams. If you receive this information, you have a responsibility to act on it promptly and professionally. You can do this by putting the matter right (if that is possible), investigating and dealing with the concern locally, or referring serious or repeated incidents or complaints to senior management or the relevant regulatory authority.

It is one thing to advise doctors to come forward with stories of misconduct about fellow colleagues, but it is quite another to do it in practice. 'Whistle blowing' is frowned upon in many big organisations because there is an understanding between colleagues that they will not 'tell tales' on each other. The medical profession in particular are a very closely-knit community. The Public Interest Disclosure Act 1998 protects employees who have disclosed information from dismissal by inserting new provisions into the Employment Rights Act 1996. The 1996 Act lists the kinds of disclosures that would qualify for protection.

Employment Rights Act 1996

Section 43B: Disclosures qualifying for protection

(1) In this Part a 'qualifying disclosure' means any disclosure of information which, in the reasonable belief of the worker making the disclosure, tends to show one or more of the following –

   (a) that a criminal offence has been committed, is being committed or is likely to be committed;

   (b) that a person has failed, is failing or is likely to fail to comply with any legal obligation to which he is subject;

   (c) that a miscarriage of justice has occurred, is occurring or is likely to occur;

   (d) that the health or safety of any individual has been, is being or is likely to be endangered;

   (e) that the environment has been, is being or is likely to be damaged; or

   (f) that information tending to show any matter falling within any one of the preceding paragraphs has been, is being or is likely to be deliberately concealed.

The doctor making the disclosure must have a 'reasonable belief' that one of the aforementioned circumstances have happened, making it an objective test, i.e. from the eyes of a reasonable man. This prevents colleagues who dislike each other from simply being spiteful and making false claims. The right of protection is located under section 47B.

> ## Employment Rights Act 1996
>
> **Section 47B: Protected disclosures**
>
> (1) A worker has the right not to be subjected to any detriment by any act, or any deliberate failure to act, by his employer done on the ground that the worker has made a protected disclosure.

Protection from dismissal is offered only if a 'protected disclosure' has occurred from the list under section 43B (above). There is a fear that even though legal protection is in place to prevent an unfair dismissal, doctors may feel victimised or pressured in the workplace after making a disclosure of potential misconduct. It may just be that the bigger the organisation (e.g. an NHS trust), the less likely the complaints will be heard.

EXTRACT

Julia Burrows, 'Telling Tales and Saving Lives: Whistleblowing – the Role of Professional Colleagues in Protecting Patients from Dangerous Doctors' (2001) 9 *Medical Law Review* 110, at pages 110–29

The nurses were given options to choose regarding the reasons they might not report concerns. The two most likely reasons to stop them reporting anything was a feeling it might not make a difference anyway . . . and a lack of trust in the authority or manager to take appropriate action. [...] Nearly one third of the nurses questioned said that during their career they had had concerns about GPs' performance to the extent they felt patients were at risk, yet over half of these did not report them. Of the 47 per cent who did report the concern, no action was taken in more than half of cases. [...] In my study, of the seven nurses who had raised their concern about specific GP performance, six of these (86 per cent) felt that the response they received was not adequate to protect patients. [...] Even among those who feel they would report a concern, there was little clarity about the correct procedures for doing this.

ACTIVITY

Visit the official General Medical Council website at www.gmc-uk.org and find out the processes for licensing and revalidation? Consider if these protect patients? If so, how?

● ● ● Making a complaint: NHS treatment

A patient is entitled to make a complaint if they are unhappy with their care or treatment. The NHS complaints system is open to patients and members of the public. According to www.nhs.uk, a patient (or a relative or a carer) has the following rights:

- To have a complaint dealt with efficiently and properly investigated.
- To know the outcome of any investigation into a complaint.

- To take a complaint to the independent Parliamentary and Health Service Ombudsman if a patient is not satisfied with the way the NHS has dealt with the complaint.
- To make a claim for judicial review if a patient thinks they've been directly affected by an unlawful act or decision of an NHS body.
- To receive compensation if a patent has been harmed.

The patient can complain directly to the service who treated her, or she can complain to the local authority who commissioned the service. There is a deadline of twelve months to make a complaint, or as soon as the matter first comes to the patients' attention.

The procedure for making a complaint

The procedure is very simple. There has been a two-stage process in place since April 2009:

- **First**: the patient should ask their hospital or trust for a copy of its complaints procedure, which will explain how to proceed.

This first step will normally be to raise the matter, which can be done in writing or verbally, with the doctor or nurse concerned, or with their organisation, which will have a complaints manager. If the patient does not want to do this, they can raise the matter with the local authority. This is called local resolution, and most cases are resolved at this stage.

- **Second**: if the patient is still unhappy, or does not feel that the hospital or local authority has dealt with the complaint appropriately, the patient can refer the matter to the Parliamentary and Health Service Ombudsman (PHSO), who is independent of the NHS and government.[28]

The role of the Parliamentary and Health Service Ombudsman (PHSO) is to consider complaints that accuse government departments, other public bodies, and the National Health Service of not acting properly or fairly or have provided a poor level of care. The PHSO offer a free service open to anyone, and most of their legal powers are drawn from the Health Services Commissioners Act 1993. The patient can only approach the PHSO once they have exhausted stage one of the complaints process, and the patient cannot approach the PHSO directly: they must ask a Member of Parliament to refer the complaint to the PHSO on their behalf. This may feel a little inaccessible, but the PHSO state on their website that it is important that the organisation complained about has a chance to respond and resolve the problem. The PHSO will not accept complaints about private healthcare or social care, but when they receive a complaint that they can take forward, they will assess it, make sure that local resolution has been exhausted, conduct a more detailed assessment, examine whether any injustice or hardship has occurred, and what can be achieved by investigating the matter. If all of these criteria are satisfied, they may launch a full investigation. Their official statistical figures show that, during the year 2010–2011, they received 23,442 complaints, resolved 23,667 complaints, and still had 1,378 complaints 'in-hand' (these statistics are for all government departments complained about, not just the NHS).[29]

If a patient has been a victim of medical negligence, it would be a better option to take a civil medical negligence action to court if compensation is required for extra medical expenses and living costs etc.

---

[28] See www.ombudsman.org.uk for more information.

[29] See http://www.ombudsman.org.uk/about-us/publications/annual-reports for more information.

The second stage of the complaints process is very strict – log onto www.ombudsman.org.uk and find their directions on what they do and how they deal with claims. Do you think, after your research, that a member of the public may be deterred from stage two and simply be forced to settle for the outcome of stage one instead?

Problems with the medical negligence system

There are a handful of significant complaints about the current medical negligence system.

Excessive costs

The civil law of negligence will order the doctor (through his NHS trust) to pay the patient a lump sum of damages to put her back in her original position before the negligence took place. This can cover: pain and suffering, loss of amenity, expenses, loss of earnings and future losses. Inevitably, this can add up to a considerable amount of money. Damages can be awarded in structured settlements under section 2 of the Damages Act 1996, and an interim payment – where the damages can later be increased if the patient can show that the losses are higher than anticipated – can also be awarded, as seen in *Kirby v Ashford and St Peter's Hospital* [2008] EWHC 1320 and *H v Thompson Holidays Ltd* [2007] EWHC 850.

The NHS Litigation Authority (NHSLA) handles all negligence claims and represent the NHS in negligence cases.[30] The compensatory payouts come from taxpayers money that should be spent on equipment and staff. There is no clear answer to this problem.

What do patients really want?

It is believed that those patients who push their claims all the way to court are seeking an *acknowledgement* that negligence occurred, and *apology* for the harm caused, an *explanation* of what went wrong and a *promise* that steps are being taken to ensure that it won't happen again. Despite the high number of claims received by the NHSLA, it is perfectly possible that many thousands of others are just sitting under the radar because the patient is too nervous about defensive responses, too apprehensive about stepping into the legal process, which can be very expensive, or simply anticipating a failure before the process has even begun. Additionally, patients who have been treated negligently are very vulnerable. They may have suffered additional injury at the hands of their doctor which they now have to struggle with on a daily basis, and the thought of going through court might add stress to an already tense situation. It is quite understandable that some patients, having realised that they were the victim of a 'medical mistake', simply want to avoid the confrontation. This would certainly be the easier option for the Department of Health.

Apologies are encouraged. It was once thought that an apology was an admission of guilt, and some motor insurance companies still advise drivers not to apologise after an

---

[30] See http://www.nhsla.com/Pages/Home.aspx

accident. However, doctors are encouraged to apologise when they cause harm or distress to a patient, and the law does not look upon an apology and/or an explanation from a doctor as an admission of guilt.

Compensation Act 2006

Section 2: Apologies, offers of treatment or other redress

An apology, an offer of treatment or other redress, shall not of itself amount to an admission of negligence or breach of statutory duty.

The General Medical Council supports this approach by stating in their Good Medical Practice guide that an apology and an explanation is the very least a doctor should do:

General Medical Council, Good Medical Practice (2013), http://www.gmc-uk.org/guidance/good_medical_practice.asp:

Paragraph 55: You must be open and honest with patients if things go wrong. If a patient under your care has suffered harm or distress, you should:

a. put matters right (if that is possible),

b. offer an apology,

c. explain fully and promptly what has happened and the likely short-term and long-term effects.

Paragraph 61: You must respond promptly, fully and honestly to complaints and apologise when appropriate. You must not allow a patient's complaint to adversely affect the care or treatment you provide or arrange.

This guidance is important because it recognises the need to alleviate any worry or concern immediately after an incident has occurred. It also builds trust between doctors and patients: if a doctor apologises straight away and offers an explanation, he will appear more genuine than a doctor who refuses to apologise for fear of being sued for negligence.

Our compensation culture

There has been a 'compensation culture' in the United States for quite some time, but it has been gathering pace in the United Kingdom over the last fifteen years. A compensation culture is bad news for medical care, for two main reasons. Firstly, the cost (as discussed earlier) of fighting a negligence claim is wasting hundreds of millions of NHS pounds every year. These funds could be spent on staff, equipment and treatments instead. Secondly, doctors will start practising 'defensive medicine'. This is where they become hesitant in practice because they are fearful of being sued. For example, a man with a brain tumour may require complicated and pioneering surgery. The surgeon may be frightened of a medical negligence claim in the event that things go wrong, so he tells the man that there is no cure, or moves him to another hospital, or gives him a drug alternative which is not very effective. The last thing patients need is healthcare professionals who are frightened to do their jobs or regulations that do not allow for creativity or innovation. The biggest breakthroughs in medicine often spring from risky procedures.

EXAMPLE

Dr Darren administered the wrong dose of a painkiller to a child patient. He has administered that particular painkiller only three times in his thirteen-year career and it was a genuine mistake. He should have asked a senior colleague and admits that he fell below a reasonable standard of care. The complaint was dealt with at local level before evolving into a full medical negligence action, so he has been allowed back to work on the condition that he takes training in painkillers, a condition set by the GMC. He is nervous at work, and will not deal with child patients. When he does, he is weary of giving painkillers of any kind, preferring to leave it until the child is in dire need of some assistance. He does not enjoy his job like he used to anymore, and he has become stressed as a result.

An alternative argument could be that, through fear of constant legal action, doctors take steps to improve their practice. For example, a doctor may provide more than what is necessary to ensure that all possibilities are covered. An x-ray may be performed when there is no need, or a decision may be taken to perform a caesarean section when there is still a small possibility for a natural birth. An application of the *Bolam* test may decide that the doctor performed an unnecessary procedure, but in reality, the doctor is likely to find a body of medical men to support his cautious approach, and it is hard to imagine that a patient would complain about an overly cautious doctor. It is far more likely that a patient would complain that a doctor did not do enough.

Parliament is aware of the problem of defensive medicine, and the Claims Management Regulator (CMR)[31] was set up by the Compensation Act 2006. It is part of the Ministry of Justice and it regulates all companies who provide claims management services (such as 'Claims Direct' for example). The CMR regulates personal injury claims among a handful of other areas, and it aims to protect and promote the interests of consumers.

THINKING POINT

Why do you think only 3.16% of medical negligence claims against the NHS are successful? What factors might be at play here?

Looking to the future in medical negligence

It seems rather radical, but a suggestion to replace the civil law of medical negligence with a better administrative system of identifying and learning from mistakes as met with some support. The strongest criticism of medical negligence came from a hospital inquiry which looked into a high rate of deaths for paediatric cardiac surgery at Bristol Royal Infirmary. The inquiry examined the bigger picture of medical negligence and whether it was causing more problems than solutions. (The conclusion of the inquiry found that it was.) The extract below focuses on the need for a reporting system and the real causes of negligence.

---

[31] http://www.justice.gov.uk/claims-regulation

EXTRACT

Bristol Royal Infirmary Inquiry, Final Report: Learning from Bristol: the report of the public inquiry into children's heart surgery at the Bristol Royal Infirmary 1984–1995; Chapter 26; July 2001, Cmnd 5207:

http://www.bristol-inquiry.org.uk/

Paragraph 19: There is a pressing need for research into some of the central questions about the type and extent of adverse events and near misses in the NHS. We need to be able to answer such fundamental questions as: what is the current scale of adverse events and (to the extent that it can be discovered) near misses? How do they arise? Can they be classified? How can they be guarded against? Such studies would be an invaluable source of information against which to measure progress. They are an essential part of the task of developing a coherent approach to safeguarding patients. They should be made a priority.

Paragraph 20: We fully support that there be a national system for reporting adverse healthcare events and certain specified near misses. Assuming such a system could be made to work, we have no doubt that it would provide an excellent means for identifying patterns of behaviour, for learning and for disseminating lessons throughout the NHS.

Paragraph 22: There are a number of causes which must be confronted. The first can be called the myth (or imperative) of infallibility. The idea of the healthcare professional as giver of life, restorer of health, or as one who does not make mistakes, is a dominant theme in the culture of healthcare. This makes it extremely difficult, particularly given the expectations placed upon professionals by the patient, for them to speak up and point out that things have not gone as expected. To admit this is to fail the myth and thus appear a failure. Professionals assume that the patient expects infallibility and consequently find it very hard to admit that they are fallible.

Paragraph 23: Secondly, in the particular case of errors, quite apart from any errors of their own, healthcare professionals find it difficult to speak up about the errors of others. There is what can be called a code of silence – that aspect of professional culture which causes 'tribal' groups to close ranks and keep problems within the group. As a consequence, junior staff, or those from other specialties or disciplines, are inhibited from speaking out.

Paragraph 24: Thirdly, fear of exposure and blame, whether in the press or through litigation, with the consequent loss of standing, career prospects, or even livelihood, is a further powerful inhibiting factor. Errors in the NHS, as elsewhere, are seen not as matters to learn from, but as moral lapses deserving of blame.

The inquiry clearly regards 'open reporting' as vital to safeguard patients, identify risks, reveal patterns of behaviour and build on success. The inquiry also reveals the real causes behind the current failing system of medical negligence: the myth that doctors are infallible makes it difficult for doctors to admit that they have made mistakes, and doctors are also unlikely to report the failings of their colleagues because of the 'tribal' nature of their relationships at work. To solve the problem of medical errors, it is becoming clear that there must be incentives or sanctions in place to encourage a systematic approach to identifying and eradicating errors, although this is unlikely as long as the threat of legal action hangs over the heads of healthcare professionals. The inquiry also recognises that if errors are not recorded and analysed then nothing can be learnt from them, and the current medical negligence system encourages doctors to keep quiet rather than manage and reduce errors because his or her reputation is at stake. The new approach, according to the inquiry, is to deal with such errors 'in house' by removing them from the legal system altogether. This is a good idea because an emphasis will be placed on identifying, analysing, learning from and preventing errors rather than naming and shaming individuals, but it is a bad idea because healthcare professionals will effectively be regulating their own behaviour. The threat of legal action will be removed, leading to a potential drop in the standard of care. Patient trust may also be knocked because they will no longer have the upper hand or be free to put a genuinely negligent doctor in the dock. These issues have been pointed out by commentators.

EXTRACT

Martin Smith and Heidi Foster, 'Morally Managing Medical Mistakes' (2000) 9 *Cambridge Quarterly of Healthcare Ethics* 38, at pages 38–53

Pertaining to rights-based reasoning, honest and candid communication followed by apology are a sign and a support of patients' rights to respectful treatment and care, and to self-determination. [...] A consideration of professional virtues or character traits also supports the general principle of disclosing mistakes with forthrightness. [...] The virtue of truthfulness is ultimately essential for an effective professional–patient relationship because relationships cannot endure failures of truthfulness for long. [...] Patients who [...] have greater clarity and understanding of the medical situation may make better healthcare decisions. [...] Honest disclosure can provide them with explanations and understanding, [...] give consolidation that lessons have been learnt, promote acceptance and closure about what transpired, and eliminate lawsuits filed to find out what really happened.

EXTRACT

Oliver Quick, 'Outing Medical Errors: Questions of Trust and Responsibility' (2006) 1 *Medical Law Review* 22, at pages 41-2

The focus on systems also risks diluting the notion of individual professional responsibility that has been central to medical autonomy and accountability. [...] In the medical context, if blaming the system becomes the default response, to what extent will this shelter the incompetent or poor performer? [...] Over-emphasis on the system . . . may mask individual failings.

The overall conclusion of the inquiry in regards to the current medical negligence system is that human error is there – and it will always be there – so instead of bucking a legal system that relies on personal responsibility and the concealment of mistakes, it is time to change to an administrative system that encourages open reporting, risk management and learning from mistakes. It might not be a good idea to remove the law altogether, but an increased culture of openness could radically change the approach to medical negligence.

THINKING POINT

Imagine that you are working in your dream job five years from now. Your close colleague is also your best friend. Your colleague makes a massive mistake at work, leading to a visitor being almost fatally injured. There is an investigation and you are interviewed. Are you likely to tell your boss the truth – that your colleague was in fact stupidly careless – or not? If not, why not? If so, what consequences might you be worried about, and how might all of these concerns affect doctors in the same position?

Private care: breach of contract

Negligence within the NHS typically leads to an action in the civil tort of negligence because there is a common law duty of care, etc. However, when there is a contract in place, the patient can sue for breach of contract instead. This does not make bringing a claim any easier, but it is an alternative route to legal action. Sometimes the contract will be with the hospital providing the services, and sometimes it will be with the doctor himself. All contracts contain terms that are implied by statute. We return goods back to shops because they are not 'satisfactory quality' or 'fit for purpose' under section 14 of the Sale of Goods Act 1979. These are known as our statutory rights and they are implied into all contracts. It is also impossible for a business to exclude liability for personal injury and death under section 2(1) of the Unfair Contract Terms Act 1977. However, contracts for healthcare are slightly more difficult in that there is no implied term of a guaranteed outcome. The contract merely enlists the services of a doctor or a surgeon. Therefore, if the outcome is not as expected, it is very difficult to enforce the contract against the doctor if he did provide the service that he was contracted to do. It is quite rare for a patient to bring an action against a doctor for a breach of contract. In private healthcare the tort of negligence is still preferred (there is still a common law duty of care, regardless of whether a contract is in place or not). However, the small handful of cases in contract law have shown that the courts are unwilling to imply terms into medical contracts that a certain outcome is guaranteed. This is because medicine is uncertain.

CASE EXTRACT

Thake v *Maurice* [1986] QB 644

Facts: Thake (T) and his wife wished to avoid having any more children and consulted Maurice (M), a surgeon, with a view to T having a vasectomy. M carried out the operation, but subsequently, by a rare chance, T became fertile again and his wife conceived.

Held: A surgeon does not guarantee that surgery will achieve a particular result, but a contract does stipulate that the patient will receive reasonable care and skill.

Neill LJ (at page 685): I do not consider that a reasonable person would have expected a responsible medical man to be intending to give a guarantee. Medicine, though a highly skilled profession, is not, and is not generally regarded as being, an exact science. The reasonable man would have expected the defendant to exercise all the proper skill and care of a surgeon in that speciality; he would not in my view have expected the defendant to give a guarantee of 100% success.

Thake v *Maurice* confirms that contracts will imply a term requiring the doctor to show proper care and skill when treating a patient, but the outcome is much less easier to guarantee because of the nature of medicine.[32] To take a practical example, in the facts of *Adomako* [1993] 4 All ER 935, the anaesthetist failed to spot that the oxygen had become detached during surgery, leading to the patient's death. This is a clear example of a doctor not showing 'all the proper care and skill' in the performance of his duty and would be grounds for a breach of contract. The outcome is, therefore, almost incidental. An action for a breach of contract is therefore quite similar to one in negligence because it must be shown that the doctor fell below a certain standard of care. However, in negligence the outcome is considered in more detail by the courts because it helps to measure just how grave the breach was and just how much damages should be awarded.

THINKING POINT

Is medical negligence better suited to contract-based actions? Would it improve the medical negligence system to found admission into hospital on a contract that stipulated that reasonable care and skill should be shown throughout the patient's visit? This would eliminate the resulting injury as a relevant factor (it would become incidental because the contract could not guarantee against a specific injurious outcome), but would it take account of patient need and might it affect the amount of damages awarded?

Chapter summary

- A wrongful pregnancy action can be brought as a breach of contract if the doctor does not carry out the sterilisation with reasonable care and skill: *Eyre* v *Measday* [1986] 1 All ER 488.

- A doctor must pay damages for the economic loss suffered as a result of the wrongful pregnancy but not for the child that results from it in terms of general upbringing costs: *McFarlane* v *Tayside Health Board* [2000] 2 AC 59.

- To impose a duty of care, there must be proximity, the harm must be reasonably foreseeable, and it must be fair, just and reasonable to impose that duty: *Caparo Industries* v *Dickman* [1990] 2 AC 605.

- A doctor must show in his defence that he exercised the same reasonable care and skill as another doctor who practices in that same art (i.e. brain surgery). It does not matter if there happens to be a contrary view on the matter: *Bolam* v *Friern Hospital Management Committee* [1957] WLR 582. The fact that a trial judge prefers one view over another is irrelevant: *Maynard* v *West Midlands Health Authority* [1984] 1 WLR 634.

---

[32] Nourse LJ in the same case noted an exception where the removal of a limb could be guaranteed if a patient was scheduled for an amputation.

Chapter essay

'Critically examine the current medical negligence system and its fairness to both doctors and patients.'

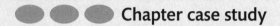

Chapter case study

Laura was desperate for a child so she visited her GP. Laura was told that she needed surgery to activate her ovaries which were otherwise perfectly fine, so she consented to the procedure and underwent surgery on the NHS with surgeon Dr Williams. She fell pregnant four months later, and the three-month scan showed no abnormalities. She was concerned at the six-month period when the baby stopped moving, so she visited a specialist – Dr Mohammed – who scanned the uterus. Laura told Dr Mohammed as he was setting up the equipment that she would never have a disabled child because she had waited so long to have a child of her own and she wanted everything to be perfect. Dr Mohammed found a heartbeat with normal blood pressure, so he sent Laura home. Three months later Laura booked in to have a caesarian section. The baby was delivered severely disabled, and the surgeon found that Laura's left ovary was irreparably damaged and all the eggs therein would probably be deformed. Laura was devastated and consulted a solicitor about her disabled child and her ovary damage. Advise Laura on whether she could bring a claim against her doctor.

Further reading

Cane, P. (2004) 'Another Failed Sterilisation', 120 *Law Quarterly Review* 189–93.

Hoyano, L. (2002) 'Misconceptions about Wrongful Conception', 65 *Modern Law Review* 883–906.

Morris, A. (2003) 'To Be or Not To Be: Is That The Question? Wrongful Life and Misconceptions', 11 *Medical Law Review* 197–93.

Quick, O. (2006) 'Outing Medical Errors: Questions of Trust and Responsibility', 22 *Medical Law Review* 41–2; (2006) 'Prosecuting "Gross" Medical Negligence: Manslaughter, Discretion and the Crown Prosecution Service', 33 *Journal of Law and Society* 421–50.

Samanta, A. (2006) 'The Role of Clinical Guidelines in Medical Negligence Litigation: A Shift from the *Bolam* Standard?', 14 *Medical Law Review* 321.

4

Consent

Chapter objectives

At the end of this chapter, you should have:

- An understanding of the rules relating to competence, incompetence and the ability to consent to medical treatment.
- An appreciation of the law regarding children and their ability to consent to medical procedures if found to be competent under the age of 16.
- Knowledge of the 'best interests test' under the Mental Capacity Act 2005 and how it helps the medical profession to ascertain how to treat incompetent patients who cannot consent to medical treatment.
- An understanding of the kind of legal action that can arise when a patient is not informed of the risks of a surgical procedure and consents to that procedure to find that the hidden risk has later materialised.

SETTING THE SCENE

Mary is an elderly lady in her 80s. She has been having severe back pain and she books an appointment to see her doctor. A multitude of tests are carried out and it transpires that she has pancreatic cancer. Her doctor prescribes very strong painkillers which have the effect of knocking her out for hours at a time, and when she does come round she is too drowsy and confused to speak coherently. Her daughter, Emily, is very worried. A specialist in pancreatic cancer contacts Emily and tells her about an innovative drug on the market called Pacreavita, which is designed to fight abnormal cells in the pancreas. It has been available for six years and has an 83% success rate. Emily takes Mary to see the specialist and he confirms that he must treat Mary in accordance with her 'best interests' because she is incompetent. Emily replies that she does not think her mother is incompetent, and conducts her own research as to what suffices as incompetence in medicine before she talks to the doctor again. Where must Emily look to ascertain the legal tests for competence?

● ● ● Introduction

Autonomy is the cornerstone of medicine. The freedom to consent to medical treatment forms the very foundation of this autonomy. A patient can also competently choose to refuse medical treatment, forcing those around her to respect her bodily integrity and her freedom of thought. The case law and regulatory bodies have summed up the issue concisely.

CASE EXTRACT

Chester v Afshar [2004] UKHL 41

Lord Steyn (at para 18): A rule requiring a doctor to abstain from performing an operation without the informed consent of a patient serves two purposes, [...] it tends to avoid the occurrence of the particular physical injury the risk of which a patient is not willing to accept. It also ensures that due respect is given to the autonomy and dignity of each patient.

CASE EXTRACT

R (on the application of Burke) v *General Medical Council* [2005] 3 WLR 1132

Lord Phillips MR (at para 30): Where a competent patient makes it clear that he does not wish to receive treatment which is, objectively, in his medical best interests, it is unlawful for doctors to administer that treatment. Personal autonomy or the right of self-determination prevails.

British Medical Association, *Withholding and Withdrawing Life-prolonging Medical Treatment: Guidance for Decision-Making*, 3rd edition, BMA: London, 2007

Paragraph 25.5: It is well established in law and ethics that competent adults have the right to refuse any medical treatment, even if that refusal results in their death.

In modern medicine, no treatment can take place without the consent of the patient. If the patient is incompetent, the doctors will treat him in accordance with his best interests, but even then the patient's values and beliefs must be sought from relatives as part of the best interests test. This chapter will explore the grey area between competence and incompetence. A competent refusal will be respected and an incompetent refusal will be overridden, but what if a doctor cannot decide whether a patient is competent or not? This could have disastrous consequences for the patient, such as undergoing invasive surgery or a blood transfusion, against his wishes. This chapter will also address how children are treated under the common law of consent.

What is consent?

The patient is free to consent to medical treatment of any kind. This is a long-established rule. The autonomy of the patient also allows for a full refusal of medical treatment and if this refusal is ignored, the professional who administered the treatment may face a civil action for trespass or a criminal charge of battery. It was famously announced in the US case of *Schloendorff* by Cardozo J that:

> . . . every human being of adult years and sound mind has a right to determine what shall be done with his own body; and a surgeon who performs an operation without his patient's consent, commits an assault.[1]

There are two very important key words in Cardozo J's speech. The first important phrase is 'adult years'. There is an assumption in medical law that a child cannot consent to his or her own medical treatment but there is an exception if the child is close to the age of majority, which in medical law is usually eighteen, and shows a high level of understanding. The second important phrase is 'sound mind' and this is particularly important. A patient must fully understand where he or she is, what is going to happen, what the treatment involves and what the outcome will be. This clear understanding is referred to as 'competency' and an adult patient must be fully competent in order to balance all the risks and consent to (or refuse) any medical treatment. A further criteria which Cardozo J did not mention is voluntariness. A patient's consent (or refusal) to medical treatment must not be subject to any external pressures or influences. However, as we will see from the case law, it is easier said than done to remove external influences, particularly if the patient is very close to his or her family. A final criteria that is vital to the element of consent is the idea that every decision must be fully informed. The patient

---

[1] *Schloendorff* v *Society of New York Hospital* (1914) 105 NE 92.

must be told everything he or she needs to know in order to make a balanced decision. This includes any significant risks that might materialise, the aims of the treatment, how it is performed, the quality of life after treatment, and the prognosis (i.e. the outlook). This is supported by the General Medical Council.

EXTRACT

General Medical Council, Good Medical Practice (2013):

www.gmc-uk.org

Paragraph 49: You must work in partnership with patients, sharing with them the information they will need to make decisions about their care, including:

a. Their condition, its likely progression and the options for treatment, including associated risks and uncertainties.

b. The progress of their care, and your role and responsibilities in the team.

c. Who is responsible for each aspect of patient care, and how information is shared within teams and among those who will be providing their care.

d. Any other information patients need if they are asked to agree to be involved in teaching or research.

If a patient is not fully informed of all the relevant facts, the consent may not be valid. This problem only really comes to light if the treatment goes wrong and the patient claims afterwards that: 'if I had been informed of this risk, I never would have consented'. There is a wealth of complex case law in this area, because it is not quite clear just how much a doctor must reveal in order for the patient to become informed.

THINKING POINT

What would medical care look like if doctor discretion still ruled in law and there was no such thing as patient autonomy (i.e. the patient simply 'let' the doctor treat her in accordance with his clinical judgment)? Would medical care be better or worse?

What does consent look like?

Consent can be provided in many ways in medical law. Implied consent is very common, where consent is 'assumed' through conduct. For example, if a doctor tells you that you must have a blood test to ascertain why you are always feeling dizzy, you go to have your blood test without signing any special form. Your attendance and cooperation is accepted as consent. There is no formal requirement to seek a patient signature for small procedures. The very thought of an official 'treatment contract' with a dotted signature line would probably scare many nervous patients away.

There is also a misconception that once you give your consent to treatment, you are bound by that decision and must see the treatment through to the end, no matter how much you hate it or how painful it is. This is not true. A patient may withdraw consent at any time. It is, of course, standard procedure to ask for a signature for serious procedures – such as surgery – as *proof* of consent, but it is not a legally binding contract. It is merely proof that the patient made a competent decision about his or her medical treatment, leaving the doctor free to administer the appropriate care. The patient can walk away at any stage, or ask for the treatment to be stopped at any time.

How does consent support autonomy?

The element of consent is vital. It puts the patient in control. It allows the patient to deliberate, choose, accept and reject every element of his or her medical care. It provides legal protection, self respect and bodily integrity. There have been a handful of cases in which doctors have sought permission from the courts to treat a competent adult who refuses lifesaving treatment. It is difficult for doctors and family members to understand or accept such decisions, but the courts have discussed this issue at length and every time they have decided that autonomy must prevail.

CASE EXTRACT

Airedale NHS Trust v Bland [1993] AC 789

Facts: Tony Bland was crushed in the Hillsborough disaster and was in a persistent vegetative state for a few years. There was no chance of him regaining consciousness but he was not brain dead. His parents and the doctors sought permission to remove his artificial hydration and nutrition. It would have been murder without court permission.

Held: The courts granted permission on several different grounds, but the discussion about patient autonomy inevitably reared its head during the difficult judgment.

Lord Mustill (at page 891): If the patient is capable of making a decision on whether to permit treatment, his choice must be obeyed even if on any objective view it is contrary to his best interests.

Lord Goff (at page 864): The principle of self-determination requires that respect must be given to the wishes of the patient, so that if an adult patient of sound mind refuses, however unreasonably, to consent to treatment or care by which his life would or might be prolonged, the doctors responsible for his care must give effect to his wishes, even though they do not consider it to be in his best interests to do.

Sir Bingham MR (at page 808): It is a civil wrong, and may be a crime, to impose medical treatment on a conscious adult of sound mind without his or her consent. A medical practitioner must comply with clear instructions given by an adult of sound mind as to the treatment to be given or not given in certain circumstances, whether those instructions are rational or irrational.

Butler-Sloss LJ (at page 816): The provision of treatment by a doctor without the consent of the patient other than in an emergency is likely to be a trespass.

Hoffman LJ (at page 827): A person of full age may refuse treatment for any reason or no reason at all, even if it appears certain that the result will be his death.

It follows from this judgment that a perfectly competent adult can refuse lifesaving treatment, even if the decision is not in his or her best interests, appears to be completely irrational or will lead to death. The *Re T* case also supports the notion of patient autonomy.

CASE EXTRACT

Re T (Adult: Refusal of Treatment) [1993] Fam 95

Facts: T was involved in a road traffic accident at 34 weeks pregnant. After talking to her mother, she refused a blood transfusion. She went into labour and after the birth of a stillborn baby her condition deteriorated. The doctors sought consent to give a blood transfusion. The courts gave permission for the transfusion because T had signed the refusal form in a moment of emergency without reading it, guided only by her mother, who exerted an undue influence over her decision.

Held: The mother had exerted an undue influence on the patient. However, despite the outcome of this particular case, the lords agreed that in all other cases, a fully informed refusal in medicine must be respected.

Lord Donaldson MR (at page 102): An adult patient who, like Miss T, suffers from no mental incapacity has an absolute right to choose whether to consent to medical treatment, to refuse it or to choose one rather than another of the treatments being offered. [...] This right of choice is not limited to decisions which others might regard as sensible. It exists notwithstanding that the reasons for making the choice are rational, irrational, unknown or even non-existent.

Butler-Sloss LJ (at page 116): A man or woman of full age and sound understanding may choose to reject medical advice and medical or surgical treatment either partially or in its entirety. A decision to refuse medical treatment by a patient capable of making the decision does not have to be sensible, rational or well-considered.

Staughton LJ (at pages 120–1): An adult whose mental capacity is unimpaired has the right to decide for herself whether she will or will not receive medical or surgical treatment, even in circumstances where she is likely or even certain to die in the absence of treatment. Thus far the law is clear.

The question of competence has also arisen in relation to pregnant women. This issue first arose in *Re S* (1992). The case is no longer legally binding, but it highlights a complex legal and ethical issue.

CASE EXTRACT

Re S (Adult: Refusal of Treatment) [1992] 4 All ER 671

Facts: A pregnant patient refused an emergency caesarean section despite the unborn baby becoming stuck and facing certain death within a matter of minutes. There was also a very high risk of the patient's uterus rupturing, which would have killed her too. Her refusal had the support of her husband, and was a result of their religious beliefs. The doctors sought a declaration from the courts to carry out the surgery.

Held: In a very short judgment (because of the emergency situation), Sir Stephen Brown P granted the declaration for surgery, supporting the evidence from the doctors that both mother and baby would die within minutes if the surgery did not go ahead.

This decision is not supported by subsequent cases (in detail below). Sir Stephen Brown J stated in his judgment that the patient was perfectly competent to make the decision despite her strong religious views, but ignored the refusal when he granted his declaration. This does not support patient autonomy. It may have been the urgent circumstances and the graphic evidence from doctors that swayed him into granting the declaration. Today, a declaration for surgery in identical circumstances to those in *Re S* (1992) would not be granted as held in *Re MB* (1997).

> **CASE EXTRACT**
>
> ## MB (Medical Treatment), Re [1997] 2 FLR 426
>
> **Butler-Sloss LJ**: A competent woman who has the capacity to decide may, for religious reasons, other reasons, for rational or irrational reasons or for no reason at all, choose not to have medical intervention, even though the consequence may be the death or serious handicap of the child she bears, or her own death.

The patient in *Re S* (1992) later appealed against the emergency caesarean section that was carried out. In light of *Re MB* (1997), it was held to be a trespass.

> **CASE EXTRACT**
>
> ## St George's Healthcare NHS Trust v S [1999] Fam 26
>
> **Facts**: S appealed against her emergency caesarean section in *Re S (Adult: Refusal of Treatment)* [1992] 4 All ER 671.
>
> **Held**: The procedure was a trespass to her person.
>
> **Judge LJ** (at page 50): In our judgment while pregnancy increases the personal responsibilities of a woman it does not diminish her entitlement to decide whether or not to undergo medical treatment. Although human, and protected by the law in a number of different ways, [...] an unborn child is not a separate person from its mother. Its need for medical assistance does not prevail over her rights. She is entitled not to be forced to submit to an invasion of her body against her will, whether her own life or that of her unborn child depends on it. Her right is not reduced or diminished merely because her decision to exercise it may appear morally repugnant.

Judge LJ confirmed not only that a pregnant woman is fully competent to refuse treatment, but that the rights of the foetus or the unborn baby do not override the autonomy of the mother. This may be 'morally repugnant' to many people, but the principle of autonomy was deemed to be supreme. The judgment of Sir Stephen Brown J in *Re S* (1992) is now resigned into the cupboard of legal history.

There are human rights to support the patient too. The right to make a fully autonomous decision – while pregnant or not – is supported by the Human Rights Act 1998. The particular Articles of the European Convention on Human Rights that may be applicable are the following:

- Article 3 – the right not to be subjected to inhuman or degrading treatment.
- Article 5 – the right to liberty.
- Article 8 – the right to respect for private and family life.
- Article 9 – the right to respect for religious views.

It is vital to note at this point that a patient cannot insist on, or demand, a medical treatment.

CASE EXTRACT

R (Burke) v General Medical Council [2005] 3 WLR 1132

Lord Phillips MR (at page 1147): Autonomy and the right of self-determination do not entitle the patient to insist on receiving a particular medical treatment regardless of the nature of the treatment. Insofar as a doctor has a legal obligation to provide treatment this cannot be founded simply upon the fact that the patient demands it.

The academic debate around the issue of autonomy is varied. Glick questions the disastrous effects of giving patients the power to effectively commit suicide in an emergency situation. Do they really refuse treatment, or are they simply giving up in a moment of fear?

EXTRACT

Shimon Glick, 'The Morality of Coercion' (2000) 26 *Journal of Medical Ethics* 393, at pages 393–5

Individuals under acute stress may make hasty tragic decisions which they subsequently, under more careful consideration, regret. [...] I would hope that even the most devoted advocates of autonomy might accept the premise that a patient who is frightened and stressed, may not be fully autonomous; his or her refusal should therefore be assigned less weight. It is tragic to accept such a patient's refusal automatically at face value, even if a team of psychiatrists and lawyers judge that person legally competent. [...] One is granting that person his short-term 'autonomous' wish while depriving him of his long term autonomy.

Is it true that in the heat of the moment, a patient can weaken and simply refuse medical treatment because it is the 'easiest' thing to do? It is likely that doctors are aware of the mixed emotions in these situations, and can usually judge when a refusal is strong and when it is weak. Relatives may also be consulted to help clarify the situation if the doctor has doubts that the refusal is not fully competent, but if there is no evidence to prove otherwise, a competent refusal – whether weak or strong – should be respected.

THINKING POINT

The principle of autonomy might support the patient, but it could cause her family endless grief if she makes a decision to refuse all lifesaving treatment in the heat of the moment. Does a patient's legal right to reject treatment clash with a moral obligation to take care of her family? Could the law address this imbalance, or should it be resigned to bad luck for the family?

The consent must be voluntary

A consent is only valid in law when it is given by the patient *voluntarily*. It is, of course, unthinkable that a doctor would force a patient to consent to treatment, but subtle forms of pressure can occur from family members and the illness itself.

An elderly patient is diagnosed with a serious illness at the end of her life. She knows that the only way to battle the illness is to consent to major surgery or a rigorous treatment programme that will leave her feeling drained, tired and depressed. She may feel as though she has no other choice but to consent to the treatment, especially when her family are by her bedside, awaiting her response.

A consent that is given reluctantly, under circumstances such as those above, is still a valid consent unless a very clear and identifiable undue influence can be spotted by the doctor. The courts must look at the facts to ascertain whether a relative, for example, exerted such a strong influence over the patient that her consent to treatment was not valid.

Where can pressure come from?

A patient is more likely to experience emotional blackmail from family members as opposed to force or threats, but conversations with a religious relative may be viewed as highly influential, particularly if the patient is also surrounded by confusion at the time of the decision.

CASE EXTRACT

Re T [1993] Fam 95

Facts: T was involved in a road traffic accident when she was thirty-four weeks pregnant. After receiving drugs and talking to her mother (who was a Jehovah's Witness), she refused a blood transfusion. She went into labour and a Caesarean section was performed but the baby was stillborn. Her condition deteriorated. A judge granted a declaration that in the circumstances it would be lawful for the hospital to administer a blood transfusion and they duly did so.

Held: The refusal was not effective or valid: she was unduly influenced, drugged and misled at the time of signing her refusal.

Lord Donaldson MR (at pages 113–4): A special problem may arise if at the time the decision is made the patient has been subjected to the influence of some third party. This is by no means to say that the patient is not entitled to receive and indeed invite advice and assistance from others in reaching a decision, particularly from members of the family. But the doctors have to consider whether the decision is really that of the patient. It is wholly acceptable that the patient should have been persuaded by others of the merits of such a decision and have decided accordingly. It matters not how strong the persuasion was, so long as it did not overbear the independence of the patient's decision. The real question in each such case is 'does the patient really mean what he says or is he merely saying it for a quiet life, to satisfy someone else or because the advice and persuasion to which he has been subjected is such that he can no longer think and decide for himself?' [...] When considering the effect of outside influences, two aspects can be of crucial importance. First, the strength of the will of the patient. One who is very tired, in pain or depressed will be much less able to resist having his will overborne than one who is rested, free from pain and cheerful. Second, the relationship of the 'persuader' to the patient may be of crucial importance. The influence of parents on their children or of one spouse on the other can be, but is by no means necessarily, much stronger than would be the case in other relationships. Persuasion based upon religious belief can also be much more compelling, and the fact that arguments based upon religious beliefs are being deployed by someone in a very close relationship with the patient will give them added force and should alert the doctors to the possibility that the patient's capacity or will to decide has been overborne.

The decision in *Re T* (1993) clearly states that a patient decision must be free from influence, particularly religious relatives. Lord Donaldson in particular highlights the 'compelling' nature of religious beliefs, particularly from someone close, and warns of a risk of a patient being 'overborne'. A two-part test to apply is as follows:

- What is the strength of will of the patient?
- What is the relationship of the persuader?

These criteria will apply to both consents and refusals, but doctors are more likely to question the influences surrounding a *refusal* of treatment, because the consequences of a refusal are far more serious.

THINKING POINT

Do you think that persuasion and pressure from family members can actually better inform a patient to consent?

The legal consequences of ignoring a competent refusal

The principle of autonomy means that a doctor cannot, even under grave circumstances, treat a patient if she competently refuses. If treatment is *still* administered against her wishes, she has been touched without consent and two legal consequences could follow: a prosecution in criminal law and an action in civil law.

The criminal law

It is widely accepted that a person can consent to an assault or a battery in criminal law. Therefore, if a doctor merely touches a patient, for example to feel for any swelling, a patient can consent to this and the doctor will not face any legal consequences.[2] A very serious harm, such as surgery, has been earmarked as an exception to the rule because it is in the best interests of the patient. Therefore, she can consent to it.

---

[2] This 'line of consent' was drawn in *R v Brown (Anthony Joseph)* [1994] 1 AC 212.

CASE EXTRACT

Attorney-General's Reference (No. 6 of 1980) **[1981] QB 715 (non-medical)**

Lord Lane CJ (at page 719): Nothing which we have said is intended to cast doubt upon the accepted legality of properly conducted games and sports, lawful chastisement or correction, reasonable surgical interference, dangerous exhibitions etc. These apparent exceptions can be justified as involving the exercise of a legal right, in the case of chastisement or correction, or as needed in the public interest, in the other cases.

CASE EXTRACT

Airedale NHS Trust v Bland **[1993] AC 789**

Lord Mustill (at page 891): Bodily invasions in the course of proper medical treatment stand completely outside the criminal law. The reason why the consent of the patient is so important is not that it furnishes a defence in itself, but because it is usually essential to the propriety of medical treatment.

CASE EXTRACT

R v Brown (Anthony Joseph) **[1994] 1 AC 212**

Lord Mustill (at page 266): Many of the acts done by surgeons would be very serious crimes if done by anyone else, and yet the surgeons incur no liability. Actual consent, or the substitute for consent deemed by the law to exist where an emergency creates a need for action, is an essential element of this immunity. [...] Proper medical treatment, for which actual or deemed consent is a prerequisite, is in a category of its own.

What can be taken from the case law above is that 'reasonable surgical interference' is an exception to the normal rules of consent in criminal law because of the 'public interest' invested in it. However, the word 'reasonable' is interesting. A patient may consent to an 'unreasonable' procedure by a medical student in a derelict garage but the courts will probably nullify the consent because it is an unreasonable interference and reaches beyond the assault/battery limit of consent. This is very rare.

The civil law

If a patient does not consent to medical treatment, the civil tort of battery (i.e. trespass to the person) may also be applicable. This requires hostile touching without consent. This is also very rare.

ACTIVITY

Darren was studying medicine and was keen to operate on a person. He had examined dead animals in the past, but this weekend his little nephew, Phillip, was coming to stay over. He was only 18 months old, but he was the perfect candidate for a medical experiment. Darren took Phillip to the woods and prepared to commence surgery. He waited until Phillip was asleep and cut through both layers of skin on Phillip's left arm (like a paper cut). Phillip began to scream so Darren had to tie him up. Darren then took pictures of the cut before applying glue to close it. Phillips cut became infected. What does the criminal law state in regards to criminal liability?

The 'scope' of competence

We have learnt that if a patient is competent, her consent or refusal is respected. However, if a patient is judged as incompetent, no matter how fleeting the incompetence may be, she can be treated without her consent in accordance with her best interests (more below). This may upset the patient if she becomes competent again the next day, e.g. she may have had an epileptic fit. It is therefore vital that the line between 'competent' and 'incompetent' is clear so that patient autonomy can be fully respected. Unfortunately, it is not clear at all.

> **KEY DEFINITION**
>
> **Competence**: the mind is fully able to make a clear decision.
> **Incompetence**: the mind is not able to make any kind of decision.

A patient who is incompetent to make a decision is someone who does not understand their condition, the situation, the medical treatment on offer or the risks involved. The law assumes that patients are competent unless it can be proved otherwise. The presumption of competence will be rebutted if valid proof can be found, such as a long-term mental health issue in a medical record (long term), or a drunken patient may be wheeled into Accident and Emergency (short term). The borderline of competence is clearly pivotal to patient autonomy, but where exactly does this crucial borderline lie? It is a very difficult grey area. Doctors simply have to deal with one patient at a time. The condition of the patient may provide a good starting point. For example, an elderly patient who is confused may be placed in the 'incompetent' category at first. The doctors will then have to ask her questions in order to ascertain her understanding and her level of capacity. The facts and risks may have to be explained in more detail, she may need relatives with her in order to help her to understand, and the doctors may ask searching questions as to why she has decided to accept (or reject) her treatment. However, just because a patient has a mental health problem, it does not mean that she cannot make a perfectly balanced decision about her own medical treatment.

> **EXTRACT**
>
> ### Michael Gunn, 'The Meaning of Incapacity' (1994) 2 *Medical Law Review* 8
>
> Capacity/incapacity are not concepts with clear *a priori* boundaries. They appear on a continuum which ranges from full capacity at one end to full incapacity at the other end. There are, therefore, degrees of capacity. The challenge is to choose the right level to set as the gateway to decision-making and respect for persons and autonomy.

An incompetent patient who *consents* to treatment is unlikely to be questioned because the treatment would have been carried out in her best interests anyway. However, it is slightly concerning that consents are not screened as frequently as refusals.

> **THINKING POINT**
>
> Why might it be a good idea to screen positive decisions more frequently, particularly if given from patients on the borderline of competency?

Adults: confirming incapacity

The Mental Capacity Act 2005 (MCA 2005) came into force in 2007. It applies to adults only, children are still governed by the old common law. It was designed to provide certainty and security to individuals and their families. It also comes with a very detailed Code of Practice to provide extra guidance and ensure that the provisions of the 2005 Act are implemented justly by the medical profession.

The basic principles of capacity

The MCA 2005 starts by listing the old common law principles on capacity. Section 1 begins with the old assumption that capacity should be assumed unless proved otherwise.

Mental Capacity Act 2005

Section 1: The principles

(2) A person must be assumed to have capacity unless it is established that he lacks capacity.

(3) A person is not to be treated as unable to make a decision unless all practicable steps to help him to do so have been taken without success.

(4) A person is not to be treated as unable to make a decision merely because he makes an unwise decision.

(5) An act done, or decision made, under this Act for or on behalf of a person who lacks capacity must be done, or made, in his best interests.

(6) Before the act is done, or the decision is made, regard must be had to whether the purpose for which it is needed can be as effectively achieved in a way that is less restrictive of the person's rights and freedom of action.

It can be seen from the provisions under section 1 that:

- Capacity is assumed.
- Incapacity must be proved.
- Practicable steps must be taken before the patient is rendered 'unable' to decide for himself.
- An unwise decision is not automatically an incompetent decision.
- All acts and decisions by other people must be based on the patient's best interests.
- The least restrictive method or decision must be used or taken.

The MCA 2005 puts the incompetent patient and his or her best interests first in all of its provisions. This shows support for the principle of autonomy (i.e. capacity is assumed unless proven otherwise), bodily integrity (i.e. the least restrictive action must be used), and the patients' rights, beliefs and values.

The definition of incapacity

The MCA 2005 introduced a two-stage test for incapacity which is much more technical than the old common law test.

Mental Capacity Act 2005

Section 2: People who lack capacity

(1) For the purposes of this Act, a person lacks capacity in relation to a matter if at the material time he is unable to make a decision for himself in relation to the matter because of an impairment of, or a disturbance in the functioning of, the mind or brain.

(2) It does not matter whether the impairment or disturbance is permanent or temporary.

The two-stage test is clear: the patient must be unable to make a decision for himself, and this must be caused by an impairment or disturbance of his or her mind or brain. The patient must not be able to 'make a decision for himself' and this allows for a competent patient to make a foolish decision and still be deemed competent. The patient must have an 'impairment or disturbance' in his 'mind or brain' and this could be an endless list of psychological or physical problems. The impairment or disturbance can be 'temporary' and this allows for treatment to be carried out on patients who would normally be perfectly competent, e.g. he or she is intoxicated for one night only. The use of the word 'impairment' alludes to a medical condition that can be *diagnosed*, meaning that many incompetent patients will not fall under the provisions of the section and thus be deemed competent when they are not. However, the word 'disturbance' widens the ambit of the test, and this alludes to a more short-lived state of distress that cannot be diagnosed.

The Code of Practice lists numerous conditions that will be covered by the two-stage test under section 2.

EXTRACT

The Mental Capacity Act 2005 Code of Practice (2007):

http://www.legislation.gov.uk/ukpga/2005/9/pdfs/ukpgacop_20050009_en.pdf

Paragraph 4.12: Examples of an impairment or disturbance in the functioning of the mind or brain may include the following:

- Conditions associated with some forms of mental illness.
- Dementia.
- Significant learning disabilities.
- The long-term effects of brain damage.
- Physical or mental conditions that cause confusion, drowsiness or loss of consciousness.
- Delirium.
- Concussion following a head injury.
- The symptoms of alcohol or drug use.

The list of conditions above show a wide assortment of circumstances in which a person can lack capacity. They range from organic brain damage to emotional confusion. Alcohol and drugs are well known for their incapacitating effects. The Code of Practice also wants to make it clear that just because a person agrees to a decision, does not mean that they are competent to make that decision.

EXTRACT

The Mental Capacity Act 2005 Code of Practice (2007):

http://www.legislation.gov.uk/ukpga/2005/9/pdfs/ukpgacop_20050009_en.pdf

Paragraph 4.45: . . . Does the person understand what decision they need to make and why they need to make it? . . . Be aware that the fact that a person agrees with you or assents to what is proposed does not necessarily mean that they have capacity to make the decision . . .

The Code of Practice appears to want to safeguard incompetent individuals from being misunderstood. Typically, a foolish decision will alert the doctors to a potential mental health issue, or a medical record may reveal a history of mental illness, but what if a patient is hallucinating or is simply wheeled into the hospital unconscious? The Code of Practice advises to wait until the patient comes back to full capacity (paragraph 4.45) if this is possible. Section 2(3) of the 2005 Act goes further to protect patients from stereotyping.

Mental Capacity Act 2005

Section 2(3): A lack of capacity cannot be established merely be reference to:

(a) a person's age or appearance, or;

(b) a condition of his, or an aspect of his behaviour, which might lead others to make unjustified assumptions about his capacity.

This provision reminds healthcare professionals that incapacity is not merely about assumptions – there must be some other evidence as to their inability to make competent decisions.[3] The Code of Practice provides some useful guidance on unjustified assumptions.

EXTRACT

The Mental Capacity Act 2005 Code of Practice (2007):

http://www.legislation.gov.uk/ukpga/2005/9/pdfs/ukpgacop_20050009_en.pdf

Paragraph 4.8: The Act deliberately uses the word 'appearance', because it covers all aspects of the way people look. So for example, it includes the physical characteristics of certain conditions (for example, scars, features linked to Down's syndrome or muscle spasms caused by cerebral palsy) as well as aspects of appearance like skin colour, tattoos and body piercings, or the way people dress (including religious dress).

Paragraph 4.9: The word 'condition' is also wide-ranging. It includes physical disabilities, learning difficulties and disabilities, illness related to age, and temporary conditions (for example, drunkenness or unconsciousness). Aspects of behaviour might include extrovert (for example, shouting or gesticulating) and withdrawn behaviour (for example, talking to yourself or avoiding eye contact).

---

[3] The courts agreed with this in: *Re B (Consent to Treatment: Capacity)* [2002] 1 FLR 1090.

'Unable to make a decision'

The phrase 'unable to make a decision' under section 2 of the MCA 2005 appears to be quite clear, but section 3 provides a four-part test to ensure that the patient cannot play any role in the decision-making process.

Mental Capacity Act 2005

Section 3: Inability to make decisions

(1) For the purposes of section 2, a person is unable to make a decision for himself if he is unable –

    (a) to understand the information relevant to the decision;

    (b) to retain that information;

    (c) to use or weigh that information as part of the process of making the decision; or

    (d) to communicate his decision (whether by talking, using sign language or any other means).

(2) A person is not to be regarded as unable to understand the information relevant to a decision if he is able to understand an explanation of it given to him in a way that is appropriate to his circumstances (using simple language, visual aids or any other means).

Section 3 appears to allow all forms of communication – no matter how slight – to constitute a competent statement. For example, a victim of a stroke may only be able to blink, but this may be enough to clearly communicate a 'yes' or a 'no' as to whether they would like to follow a particular method of treatment. This is supported by the Code of Practice, which offers some guidance as to how healthcare professionals, friends and family can assist the patient in communicating his or her wishes.

EXTRACT

The Mental Capacity Act 2005 Code of Practice (2007):

http://www.legislation.gov.uk/ukpga/2005/9/pdfs/ukpgacop_20050009_en.pdf

Paragraph 2.7: The kind of support people might need to help them make a decision varies. It depends on personal circumstances, the kind of decision that has to be made and the time available to make the decision. It might include:

- Using a different form of communication (for example, non-verbal communication);
- Providing information in a more accessible form (for example, photographs, drawings or tapes);
- Treating a medical condition which may be affecting the person's capacity or
- Having a structured programme to improve a person's capacity to make particular decisions (for example, helping a person with learning disabilities to learn new skills) . . .

Paragraph 4.20: . . . Items such as notebooks, photographs, posters, videos and voice recorders can help people record and retain information.

Many of the suggestions above would not be possible due to time constraints. However, doctors are obliged to help the patient to understand any decisions or procedures affecting them by using as many aids as possible.

The old common law

Prior to the coming into force of the Mental Capacity Act 2005 in April 2007, the common law had developed its own test for incapacity through a small handful of cases. The old test played a significant role in shaping the new statutory provisions, so it is worth exploring. *Re C* (1994) was the first in a collection of cases that devised a test for incapacity.

CASE EXTRACT

Re C (Adult: Refusal of Treatment) [1994] 1 WLR 290

Facts: The patient [C] suffered from paranoid schizophrenia. He was convinced that he had a successful career in medicine, which was not true. His leg became gangrenous and his doctor was of the view that, if the leg was not amputated, the patient faced an 85% chance of death. The patient was convinced that his leg would not be the cause of his death and he would never consent to amputation. Surgery was suggested, but the patient sought a declaration that the procedure could not go ahead without his consent.

Held: C was supported by the courts.

Thorpe J (at pages 293–5): It was clear to me that C was quite content to follow medical advice and to cooperate in treatment appropriately as a patient as long as his rejection of amputation was respected. […] C himself throughout the hours that he spent in the proceedings seemed ordinarily engaged and concerned. His answers to questions seemed measured and generally sensible. He was not always easy to understand and the grandiose delusions were manifest, but there was no sign of inappropriate emotional expression. His rejection of amputation seemed to result from sincerely held conviction. He had a certain dignity of manner. […] I consider helpful Dr Eastman's analysis of the decision-making process into three stages: first, comprehending and retaining treatment information, second, believing it and, third, weighing it in the balance to arrive at choice. […] Applying that test to my findings on the evidence, I am completely satisfied that the presumption that C has the right of self-determination has not been displaced. Although his general capacity is impaired by schizophrenia, it has not been established that he does not sufficiently understand the nature, purpose and effects of the treatment he refuses. Indeed, I am satisfied that he has understood and retained the relevant treatment information, that in his own way he believes it, and that in the same fashion he has arrived at a clear choice.

Outcome: He made a full recovery!

This judgment was very important in terms of providing guidance on how to deal with a mentally ill patient who refused medical treatment. The patient's schizophrenia was clearly diagnosed and his delusions were frequently on display, but this did not appear to alter his ability to 'sufficiently understand the nature, purpose and effects of the treatment' according to Thorpe J. In other words, this judgment was clear confirmation that a patient with a recognised mental disorder can still competently refuse his own medical treatment. A three-part test was supported by Thorpe J to help establish whether a mentally ill patient was capable of issuing a competent decision about his own medical treatment:

- First, comprehending and retaining treatment information;
- Second, believing it; and
- Third, weighing it in the balance to arrive at a choice.

These three criteria were taken to be the common law test for incapacity, and they appear to support the autonomy of patients with mental disorders.

A few years later, Thorpe J's test was approved in *Re MB* (1997).

CASE EXTRACT

Re MB (An Adult: Medical Treatment) [1997] 2 FLR 426

Facts: MB was informed that she might need a caesarean. She consented to the operation, but had a phobia of needles and refused to be anesthetised by an injection. MB was found to be temporarily incompetent as a result of her needle phobia.

Held: The lords agreed that it was in her best interests to use a needle against her will in order to deliver a healthy baby.

Butler-Sloss LJ: A person lacks capacity if some impairment or disturbance of mental functioning renders the person unable to make a decision whether to consent to or to refuse treatment. That inability to make a decision will occur when:

(a) the patient is unable to comprehend and retain the information which is material to the decision, especially as to the likely consequences of having or not having the treatment in question;

(b) the patient is unable to use the information and weigh it in the balance as part of the process of arriving at the decision.

Panic, indecisiveness and irrationality in themselves so not as such amount to incompetence, but they may be symptoms or evidence of incompetence.

It is this version of the common law incapacity test that was incorporated into the MCA 2005. However, at first glance, it appears that Thorpe J's three-part test from *Re C* has been amended by Butler-Sloss LJ into a different two-part test as follows:

• First, comprehending and retaining treatment information (especially consequences).

• Second, use the information and weigh it in the balance to arrive at a decision.

The tests laid down by both Thorpe J in *Re C* and Butler-Sloss LJ in *Re MB* were analysed by Munby J in *Local Authority X* v *M* (2007), and he found that the different wording did not alter the true meaning of the test, it simply restructured it.

CASE EXTRACT

Local Authority X v M [2007] EWHC 2003

Munby J (at paras 77, 81): It has generally been assumed [...] that the test as set out in *Re MB* applies not only where the question relates to capacity to consent to medical treatment, [...] but also where the question is whether a vulnerable adult has capacity to decide where she should reside, to decide whom she has contact with and to decide on issues concerning her care. [...] It will have been noticed that in *Re C* Thorpe J identified, as the second of three ingredients of the test, the ability or capacity to 'believe' the relevant information, whereas that ingredient is seemingly missing both from the formulation of the test in *Re MB* and from section 3(1) of the 2005 Act. [...] If one does not 'believe' a particular piece of information then one does not, in truth, 'comprehend' or 'understand' it, nor can it be said that one is able to 'use' or 'weigh' it. In other words, the specific requirement of belief is subsumed in the more general requirements of understanding and of ability to use and weigh information.

Munby J concludes that Thorpe J's second criteria from *Re C* is not *missing* from the test in *Re MB* – it is simply *absorbed* by it. In other words, for a patient to 'comprehend' information regarding his or her treatment, it can be assumed that he or she must therefore 'believe' it too.

Competent irrational v incompetent irrational

The difficulty remains in deciding which irrational decisions are competent and which irrational decisions are genuine evidence of incapacity. In *Re C*, the patient's irrational decision was deemed to be competent because he 'understood the nature, purpose and effect' of his treatment even though he had schizophrenia but in *Re MB,* the patient's decision was held to be incompetent because she had a phobia of needles even though she probably would have satisfied the two-part test to 'comprehend and retain' the information and then 'use it' to come to a decision. What is the point in having a test for incapacity if the courts can choose to ignore it on a case by case basis? There are a small number of cases that shed some light on how the courts deal with irrational medical decisions, whether using the common law or the 2005 Act.

CASE EXTRACT

X NHS Trust v T (Adult Patient: Refusal of Medical Treatment) [2004] EWHC 1279

Facts: The patient, who had a borderline personality disorder, submitted an advance directive to refuse any further blood transfusions, which she needed regularly to combat her self-harming. Her advance directive stated as follows: 'Should my blood volume or HB level fall low, I do not wish to be given a blood transfusion or iron. I make this decision for two reasons. First because I am caught in a vicious circle/set of circumstances too difficult for me to continue enduring. I am not aware of when I am cutting myself, and therefore cannot prevent my HB dropping very low periodically. Having a transfusion does not resolve this problem in the long term, only causes stress to myself. I believe my blood is evil, carrying evil around my body. Although the blood given in transfusions is perfectly healthy/clean once given to me it mixes with my own and also becomes evil. Contaminated by my own. Therefore the volume of evil blood in my body will have increased and likewise the danger of my committing acts of evil. I am fully aware that in refusing a blood transfusion I may die. At the time of writing this I have capacity and am mentally competent.' Her life was in danger if she did not receive her transfusion.

Held: The presumption of capacity was rebutted in this case by the evidence. Her belief that her blood was evil was enough to find a misconception of reality, which was accepted as a disorder of the mind and therefore evidence of incompetence. She did not have *Re MB* capacity when she signed her advance directive nor when she arrived in hospital for treatment.

Charles J (at paras 42, 61): In *Re B (Adult: Refusal of Medical Treatment)* [2002] 1 FLR 1090 the President dealt with 'the principle of autonomy', 'the sanctity of life', 'the presumption of mental capacity', 'assessing capacity' and 'ambivalence' and therefore covered many of the legal issues that arise in this case. At the end of her judgment she gave further guidance at 1116, in the following terms:

(v) If there are difficulties in deciding whether the patient has sufficient mental capacity, particularly if the refusal may have grave consequences for the patient, it is most important that those considering the issue should not confuse the

→

question of mental capacity with the nature of the decision made by the patient, however grave the consequences. The view of the patient may reflect a difference in values rather than an absence of competence and the assessment of capacity should be approached with this firmly in mind. The doctors must not allow their emotional reaction to or strong disagreement with the decision of the patient to cloud their judgment in answering the primary question whether the patient has the mental capacity to make the decision.

[...] It seems to me that this assertion and belief of Ms T [references to her blood being evil] is a misconception of reality which can more readily be accepted to be, and on the [...] present evidence should be accepted to be, a disorder of the mind and further or alternatively symptoms or evidence of incompetence.

Charles J came to the conclusion that the test for incapacity in *Re MB* was made out because the patient had a disorder of the mind. The advance directive – which in itself was supposed to be a document of autonomy – turned out to be the evidence of incapacity. This can be contrasted to *Re C* where the patient was convinced that he was medically qualified and successfully refused treatment despite an 85% risk of death. In both cases the patients had a mental illness of some kind and both patients understood the consequences of their refusal.

The Code of Practice recognises that a patient's mental illness might affect his or her ability to properly use any information about medical treatment and its benefits. An anorexic patient may, for example, comprehend and retain the reasons behind a course of counselling and regular meals in a controlled environment, but she may not be able to use this information to consent to the treatment because her judgment is clouded by the symptoms of her mental illness.

EXTRACT

The Mental Capacity Act 2005 Code of Practice (2007):

http://www.legislation.gov.uk/ukpga/2005/9/pdfs/ukpgacop_20050009_en.pdf

Paragraph 4.21: . . . Sometimes people can understand information but an impairment or disturbance stops them using it . . .

Paragraph 4.22: . . . A person with the eating disorder anorexia nervosa may understand information about the consequences of not eating. But their compulsion not to eat might be too strong for them to ignore . . .

This has been confirmed in cases too, where anorexic patients have refused treatment for their condition.

CASE EXTRACT

W (A Minor) (Medical Treatment: Court's Jurisdiction), Re [1993] Fam 64

Facts: The patient was a 16-year-old girl who suffered from anorexia nervosa. She refused treatment for her condition.

Held: The courts could override a refusal from a 16-year-old, especially if it was in her best interests. There was a risk of serious brain damage and damage to organs if the treatment was not carried out. The rejection was recognised as simply a symptom of the illness.

Lord Donaldson (at pages 80–1): I doubt whether Thorpe J [at first instance] was right to conclude that W was of sufficient understanding to make an informed decision. I do not say this on the basis that I consider her approach irrational. I personally consider that religious or other beliefs which bar any medical treatment or treatment of particular kinds are irrational, but that does not make minors who hold those beliefs any the less Gillick competent. They may well have sufficient intelligence and understanding fully to appreciate the treatment proposed and the consequences of their refusal to accept that treatment. What distinguishes W from them, [...] is that it is a feature of anorexia nervosa that it is capable of destroying the ability to make an informed choice. It creates a compulsion to refuse treatment or only to accept treatment which is likely to be ineffective. This attitude is part and parcel of the disease and the more advanced the illness, the more compelling it may become. Where the wishes of the minor are themselves something which the doctors reasonably consider need to be treated in the minor's own best interests, those wishes clearly have a much reduced significance.

Lord Donaldson believes that a refusal of medical treatment is 'part and parcel' of the disorder of anorexia. The patient could not weigh the information 'in the balance to arrive at a choice'. It was further held in *South West Hertfordshire HA* v *KB* [1994] 2 FCL 1051 that patients who suffer from anorexia nervosa do not have to consent to treatment anyway because it is a mental illness and can thus be treated in accordance with their best interests under the Mental Health Act 1983. The issue of treating anorexic patients without their consent has worried some commentators.

EXTRACT

Heather Draper, 'Treating Anorexics Without Consent: Some Reservations' (1998) 24 *Journal of Medical Ethics* 5, at pages 5-7

Let us take a step back from the emotionally charged issue of anorexia and consider a parallel case – that of a woman who knows that with a radical mastectomy and chemotherapy she has a good chance of recovering from breast cancer but who refuses to have the operation because, in her opinion, living with only one breast or no breasts at all will be intolerable. She is also making a decision based on her perception of her body image and we might think that this is an irrational perception. Nevertheless, operating without her consent is unthinkable.

The whole issue of anorexia nervosa and consent is now irrelevant after *KB* (above), because the condition is now considered to be a mental illness that can be treated without consent. However, if a patient with anorexia nervosa refuses a totally different kind of medical treatment (e.g. a blood transfusion) her refusal is in no way connected to her mental illness, so there is no reason why she would not be deemed competent to make that decision, just like the patient in *Re C*. It is the fact that her decision is *interwoven* with her mental illness that renders her decision incompetent.

ACTIVITY

Frank is homeless. He is dressed in rags and is mumbling random words rather than talking. He is asked where he lives and he says: 'on High Street'. He is asked about his life and he replies: 'Frank Coppola, 19 High Street, employee of Franks Cars from 1949 to 1999. Fifty years of service. Fifty years of good cars'. He is asked for his consent for surgery to fix an ingrown toenail that has become infected. He simply stares at the doctor without blinking and says absolutely nothing. How should a medical professional deal with him in terms of obtaining consent or ascertaining incompetence?

Treating incompetent adults

It was noted earlier that the Mental Capacity Act 2005 starts by listing the old common law principles of capacity. Under sections 1(5) and 1(6), those principles include the 'best interests' test and the 'least restrictive' rule.

Mental Capacity Act 2005

Section 1: The principles

(1)(5) An act done, or decision made, under this Act for or on behalf of a person who lacks capacity must be done, or made, in his best interests.

(1)(6) Before the act is done, or the decision is made, regard must be had to whether the purpose for which it is needed can be as effectively achieved in a way that is less restrictive of the person's rights and freedom of action.

These old common law principles are very important. If a patient is found *not* to be able to make his own decisions, his values and integrity are still kept intact by treating him in accordance with his best interests. The more invasive the procedure, the more appropriate it is that the patient should provide a competent consent. The least restrictive care is thus the best option for incompetent patients. For example, rather than sterilising a teenager with severe learning and social difficulties, providing a contraceptive injection will be far less invasive.

Calculating a patient's best interests

The MCA 2005 provides its own definition as to how the best interests of a patient should be calculated under section 4(6). The Code of Practice goes on to say that the section 4 checklist 'is only the starting point: in many cases, extra factors will need to be considered' (at paragraph 5.6).

Mental Capacity Act 2005

Section 4: Best interests

(2) The person making the determination must consider all the relevant circumstances and, in particular, take the following steps.

(3) He must consider:

  (a) whether it is likely that the person will at some time have capacity in relation to the matter in question, and

  (b) If it appears likely that he will, when that is likely to be.

(4) He must, so far as reasonably practicable, permit and encourage the person to participate, or to improve his ability to participate, as fully as possible in any act done for him and any decision affecting him.

(6) He must consider, so far as is reasonably ascertainable:

  (a) The person's past and present wishes and feelings and, in particular, any relevant written statement made by him when he had capacity;

  (b) The beliefs and values that would be likely to influence his decision if he had capacity; and

  (c) The other factors that he would be likely to consider if he were able to do so.

The 'best interests' test is contained in section 4(6) and contains three parts:

- The patient's past and present wishes and feelings.
- Any beliefs and values that would influence him.
- Any other factors.

The Code of Practice provides further guidance.

EXTRACT

The Mental Capacity Act 2005 Code of Practice (2007):

http://www.legislation.gov.uk/ukpga/2005/9/pdfs/ukpgacop_20050009_en.pdf

Paragraph 5.40: People who cannot express their current wishes and feelings in words may express themselves through their behaviour. Expressions of pleasure or distress and emotional responses will also be relevant in working out what is in their best interests. It is also important to be sure that other people have not influenced a person's views.

Paragraph 5.41: The person may have held strong views in the past which could have a bearing on the decision now to be made. All reasonable efforts must be made to find out whether the person has expressed views in the past that will shape the decision to be made. This could have been through verbal communication, writing, behaviour or habits, or recorded in any other way (for example, home videos or audiotapes).

The doctor must consider whether the patient will regain capacity under section 4(3)(a). If this is a possibility, and the decision can be put off for a short time, then it is best to wait. The doctor must also encourage a patient to participate and improve his ability to participate in any decisions and treatment under section 4(4). This goes slightly beyond ensuring that a patient can retain and weigh information under section 3(1). 'Beliefs and values' include cultural background, religious beliefs, political convictions and past behaviour or habits. However, how realistic are these provisions in terms of getting to know a patient and his true feelings in regards to serious medical treatment?

Best interests and temporary incapacity

The test for incapacity above in section 3(1) of the MCA 2005 – derived from *Re C* (1994) and *Re MB* (1997) – makes it clear that if patient cannot:

- understand the relevant information;
- retain that information;
- use or weigh that information; or
- communicate his decision (by any means) . . .

. . . then he or she is not able to make a decision about medical treatment. It was discussed above that there is a 'scope' of competence and that at one end, only temporary or fleeting conditions such as concussion or intoxication may make a patient incompetent. This temporary situation is reflected in the best interests test in section 4(3)(a) above, which recommends that a doctor should put off, if possible, the important decision about medical treatment until the patient regains capacity. This is an important provision because some patients may never regain their capacity and some may regain their capacity within a matter of minutes. This rule is derived from the old common law.

CASE EXTRACT

F v West Berkshire HA [1990] 2 AC 1

Lord Goff (at pages 76–7): Where, for example, a surgeon performs an operation without his consent on a patient temporarily rendered unconscious in an accident, he should do no more than is reasonably required, in the best interests of the patient, before he recovers consciousness. I can see no practical difficulty arising from this requirement, which derives from the fact that the patient is expected before long to regain consciousness and can then be consulted about longer term measures.

The 'temporary capacity' provision under section 4(3) may be very difficult to apply in an emergency. For example, a concussion injury may be coupled with bleeding on the brain. In this kind of situation, the best interests of the patient would be to receive immediate surgery to prevent death.

Best interests and the patient's wishes

Under section 4(6) of the MCA 2005, the best interests test contains three parts:

- The patient's past and present wishes and feelings.
- Any beliefs and values that would influence him.
- Any other factors.

If a patient's wishes, feelings, beliefs and values are in direct contrast to his or her best interests, it is likely that the doctor's clinical judgment will win through. A case has not decided this issue directly yet, but in *X NHS Trust* v *T* (2004) (above) an advance directive containing very strong views was refused. Although this was mainly because the patient wrote it and signed it when she was suffering from a disorder of the mind and referred to her blood as evil, she included some very logical reasons for refusing treatment. In the end, these were not relevant when deciding her best interests. The old common law did take the beliefs and values of patients into account, but the criteria for calculating best interests was not so clear. A 'balance sheet' of best interests was sometimes drawn up by the courts.[4] The main considerations appeared to be: (a) what would benefit the patient, and (b) what would the patient have wanted, had she been competent?

CASE EXTRACT

Ahsan v *University Hospitals Leicester NHS Trust* [2006] EWHC 2624

Facts: The patient (who was a devout Muslim) underwent a routine operation but was left in a permanent vegetative state after the procedure was performed negligently. The patient (through her family) sought damages from the Trust for her aftercare regime. The issue was whether the patient was better off in a private nursing and rehabilitation centre, paid for and supported by the Trust, or whether she should be cared for at home with her Muslim family in a Muslim environment with a dedicated team of care staff (also paid for by the Trust). The Trust argued that, while understanding her family's religious beliefs, the patient was now totally unaware of any spiritual or religious matters and could derive no provable benefit from being cared for in a Muslim environment, and that the court should proceed on the evidence available rather than on the basis of belief.

Held: The religious beliefs of an individual should not be disregarded in deciding how that person should be cared for in the unhappy event of supervening mental incapacity, and the wishes of the family should be taken into account.

Hegarty J (at paras 51, 54, 73): I do not think for one moment that a reasonable member of the public would consider that the religious beliefs of an individual and her family should simply be disregarded in deciding how she should be cared for in the unhappy event of supervening mental incapacity. On the contrary, I would have thought that most reasonable people would expect, in the event of some catastrophe of that kind, that they would be cared for, as far as practicable, in such a way as to ensure that they were treated with due regard for their personal dignity and with proper respect for their religious beliefs. [...] That approach appears to be entirely consistent with the scheme intended to be established by the Mental Capacity Act 2005. [...] I have no doubt whatever that if Mrs Ahsan had been asked her views before incapacity supervened, or if she had been able to form and express a view today as to her future treatment, she would have expressed a strong desire to be cared for at home once her condition had stabilised and, if possible, to die at home surrounded by her family. She would have wished, I am sure, to spend her remaining days in an environment where she would be confident that her spiritual needs were administered to and her physical requirements attended to in a manner compatible with the traditions of her culture. Likewise, I am quite satisfied that it is the sincere wish of Dr Ahsan and his family that his wife should be cared for at home rather than remain at Rushcliffe.

---

[4] This happened in: *Re A (Mental Patient: Sterilisation)* [2000] 1 FLR 549, *An LBC* v *BS* [2003] EWHC 1909, and *Re MM (An Adult)* [2007] EWHC 2003.

The sympathetic approach continued in *Ealing* (2008), where a patient's values and beliefs were supported despite her being deemed incompetent.

> **CASE EXTRACT**
>
> ### *Ealing LBC v S* [2008] EWHC 636
>
> **Facts**: The patient had a severe learning disability and a schizo-affective disorder. She required surgery to remove an ovarian cyst.
>
> **Held**: She was found to be incompetent. The surgery went ahead in her best interests, but the fitting of a contraceptive device at the same time was held not to be in her best interests because she was strongly opposed to IUDs.

The *Ealing* case highlights the usefulness of the best interests test under section 3(1) of the MCA 2005. A patient, however incompetent, may still have very strong views about his or her treatment. In previous cases (particularly *X NHS Trust* v *T*) these views were overlooked, but in *Ealing* they formed the basis of the decision. The facts of this case illustrate why it is important for doctors to consider the beliefs and values of an incompetent patient before deciding on the right course of action – it is a clear sign of respect for their dignity and integrity.

> **EXTRACT**
>
> ### Mary Donnelly, 'Best Interests, Patient Participation and the Mental Capacity Act 2005' (2009) *Medical Law Review* 1, at pages 1–29
>
> At a practical level, the participation requirement should, at a minimum, necessitate the acknowledgement that the person lacking capacity has an alternative preference. This in turn should lead to a rigorous scrutiny of the evidence presented in favour of the argument that the decision-maker should act against this preference. It cannot be enough for a decision-maker simply to acknowledge the views of the person lacking capacity before reaching a decision which takes no account of these views.

The views of Donnelly may be open to criticism. Firstly, just because a decision was reached that does not fully accord with the beliefs or values of the patient does not mean they were not taken into account. Secondly, in practice, doctors do not have the time, patience or training to undergo a rigorous review of every single patient decision. There is only time to take a decision at face value when the necessary statutory tests are applied.

Best interests and the views of relatives

What if the relatives of an incompetent patient disagree with his or her beliefs and values? For example, a patient may live as a converted Muslim having married into the faith, but her parents remain devout Catholics. In these kinds of instances, the doctor will glean all the relevant views and opinions before making his own decision. The best interests will always be decided by the doctor in the end.

EXTRACT

The Mental Capacity Act 2005 Code of Practice (2007):

http://www.legislation.gov.uk/ukpga/2005/9/pdfs/ukpgacop_
20050009_en.pdf

Paragraph 5.63: A decision-maker may be faced with people who disagree about a person's best interests. Family members, partners and carers may disagree between themselves. Or they might have different memories about what views the person expressed in the past. Carers and family might disagree with a professional's view about the person's care or treatment needs.

Paragraph 5.64: The decision-maker will need to find a way of balancing these concerns or deciding between them. The first approach should be to review all elements of the best interests checklist with everyone involved. They should include the person who lacks capacity (as much as they are able to take part) and anyone who has been involved in earlier discussions . . . Ultimate responsibility for working out best interests lies with the decision-maker.

A pushy or influential relative will raise a warning flag for doctors. This was the case in *P* (2008), which involved an adult male patient and his adoptive mother.

CASE EXTRACT

A Primary Care Trust v P [2008] EWHC 1403

Facts: The patient (P) was an adult male who suffered from severe and complex epilepsy. He was at risk of serious brain damage and even death. The Primary Care Trust was responsible for his treatment but the patient's mother (AH) was not complying. She was of the view that his epilepsy medication was making him worse, she was reducing his dosage, and she was reluctant to accept any medical advice. The deadlock needed to be broken urgently but there was a conflict as to the best way forward.

Held: Due to the closeness of the patient and his mother, it was not possible to determine whether his views about medical treatment were his own or an adoption of his mother's views.

Sir Mark Potter P (at para 19): The real difficulty in this case has been, and continues to be, that, such is the closeness of the relationship between P and AH, his mother and carer, that (1) there is real and unresolved doubt as to how far P's expressed views as to where, by whom, and in what manner he wishes or is prepared to accept treatment, are his own, and how far they are no more than simple adoption and repetition of his mother's views in a situation where he would otherwise be malleable and cooperative with the attempts of the experts to understand the true aetiology and interrelationship of his various symptoms and to relieve P from what is now largely a wheelchair bound existence. (2) In order to perform an overall assessment, reach an holistic diagnosis and set in train an appropriate course of treatment in respect of P's condition, it is necessary for him to be assessed as an in-patient over a substantial period, during which he is seen, observed and treated as an individual patient rather than on the basis of his symptoms and condition as reported or recounted in the presence and under the influence of his mother. This is particularly so because, despite her genuine and praiseworthy concerns, AH holds views which, so far as medical orthodoxy is concerned, are in many respects eccentric, misguided and, in the view of the experts, positively harmful rather than helpful in relation to the diagnosis and treatment of P.

Sir Mark Potter P came to the conclusion that if the mother did not comply within a week to place her son in the appropriate hospital ward, reasonable force would have to be used to place him there because his condition was very serious. Sir Mark Potter P also acknowledged that it would have been very distressing for both the patient and his mother to be separated, but in balance of the seriousness of his condition, it was in his best interests to provide him with an appropriate assessment in the correct environment. The ratio to be taken from *P* (2008) is that when a patient's medical condition is sufficiently serious, and a relative is suspected of standing in the way of the patient's best interests, both parties may be temporarily separated in order for healthcare professionals to monitor the patient alone and free from influence.

Best interests and missing relatives

It is not uncommon for patients to have no close friends or family. In this event, sections 35–37 of the MCA 2005 provide for the appointment of an Independent Mental Capacity Advocate (IMCA) to support and represent the incompetent patient when facing a serious decision. An IMCA *must* be appointed under section 37(3) of the 2005 Act if serious medical treatment is proposed by the NHS and there is no other close friend or relative to consult. The Mental Capacity Act 2005 (Independent Mental Capacity Advocate) (General) Regulations (2006) set out in detail how IMCA's are appointed. However, informative guidance about their function and role is also provided by the familiar Code of Practice.

EXTRACT

The Mental Capacity Act 2005 Code of Practice (2007):

http://www.legislation.gov.uk/ukpga/2005/9/pdfs/ukpgacop_20050009_en.pdf

Paragraph 10.4: The IMCA will:

- be independent of the person making the decision;
- provide support for the person who lacks capacity;
- represent the person without capacity in discussions to work out whether the proposed decision is in the person's best interests;
- provide information to help work out what is in the person's best interests; and
- raise questions or challenge decisions which appear not to be in the best interests of the person.

The guidance above is interesting. The IMCA will not know the patient personally, in fact, they are specifically independent of the patient and so any past beliefs or values will have to be dug out of any records or information that the IMCA may have access to.

IMCA's are usually called upon when serious medical decisions need to be made, although there may be no time to appoint an IMCA in an emergency. The following list of 'serious treatments' is listed by the Code of Practice.

EXTRACT

The Mental Capacity Act 2005 Code of Practice (2007):

http://www.legislation.gov.uk/ukpga/2005/9/pdfs/ukpgacop_20050009_en.pdf

Paragraph 10.43: Serious medical treatment is treatment which involves providing, withdrawing or withholding treatment.

Paragraph 10.45: . . . treatments that might be considered serious include:

- Chemotherapy and surgery for cancer.
- Electro-convulsive therapy.
- Therapeutic sterilisation.
- Major surgery (such as open-heart surgery or brain/neuro-surgery).
- Major amputations (for example, loss of an arm or leg).
- Treatments which will result in permanent loss of hearing or sight.
- Withholding or stopping artificial nutrition and hydration.
- Termination of pregnancy.

The list of treatments above are particularly invasive, and a doctor may be appreciative of a helping hand from a specially qualified IMCA when determining if any of these procedures are really in the incompetent patient's best interests.

Best interests of the relatives?

The best interests test under section 4(6) of the MCA 2005 is not confined to medical needs. The patient's social, emotional and welfare needs will also form part of the decision. For example, one patient may not be able to follow an aftercare programme because of a lack of funds or a lack of support. Another patient may have typically refused treatment because of social or religious reasons. These additional factors make the best interests test more complicated. In addition to social, emotional and welfare needs, healthcare professionals must sometimes consider the needs of relatives too. This may seem rather odd, but the Code of Practice gives a practical example of when blood is taken from an incompetent patient in order to screen it for genetic diseases that may affect other family members (at paragraph 5.48). The Code of Practice, by giving this example, is acknowledging that medical treatment can sometimes be provided to an incompetent patient in order to preserve the best interests of *another person*.

This is strange because the whole idea behind the section 4(6) 'best interests' test, even when it was developed by the common law was to administer medical treatment in a way that supported the best interests of the *incompetent patient*. A couple of cases (before the MCA 2005 was passed) illustrate how the courts have dealt with this controversial issue.

CASE EXTRACT

Re A (Medical Treatment: Male Sterilisation) [2000] 1 FLR 549

Facts: A, aged 28, had Down's syndrome and was on the borderline of severe impairment of intelligence. He was cared for by his mother, M. M was concerned that when, given her ill health, A moved into local authority care he might have a sexual relationship and be unable to understand the possible consequences. M applied for a declaration that a vasectomy was in his best interests.

Held: Male sterilisation on non therapeutic grounds could only be carried out if in the best interests of the patient, taking into account not just medical but emotional and all welfare issues. This was not the case just yet.

Dame Elizabeth Butler-Sloss P: It is necessary to focus upon the best interests of A himself. It is clear from the evidence of his mother that, as long as she cares for him, he will continue to be subjected to the present regime of close supervision. If sterilisation did take place, it would not save A from the possibility of exploitation nor help him cope with the emotional implications of any closer relationship that he might form. It is also clear from the evidence of those who care for him in the day centre that the level of supervision does not depend upon his fertility. His mother has raised her concerns with them over inappropriate behaviour with women attending the day centre. The supervisors stop inappropriate behaviour because it is conducted in a public place and, it would appear, will continue to do so whether or not he has the operation. If his quality of life were, however, to be diminished, that would be a reason to seek at that time a hearing before a high court judge to grant a declaration that sterilisation would then be in A's best interests.

In *Re A*, the mother of the patient argued that a vasectomy would be in her son's best interests because he could not handle the emotional turmoil of a relationship and pregnancy. However, the operation itself would not have actually *benefited* the patient in any way, except maybe to prevent a situation that might not even materialise. Dame Elizabeth Butler-Sloss did add onto the end of her judgment that the procedure may be in his best interests if his circumstances changed. There was a possibility that once his mother became elderly, the patient would be moved into local authority care and if he was restricted because of his fertility, and the quality of his life diminished, then it may have been of benefit to him to have a vasectomy. However, Dame Elizabeth Butler-Sloss pointed out that this would still not protect him from the emotional implications of a close relationship. What can be taken from this decision is that a surgical procedure must show a significant benefit to the incompetent patient in order for it to go ahead.

In the most controversial case in consent law, the best interests of the incompetent patient in *Re Y* (1997) (below) were calculated according to the best interests of her sister and her mother, and a surgical procedure with no therapeutic benefit to the incompetent patient was allowed to go ahead:

CASE EXTRACT

Re Y (Mental Patient: Bone Marrow Donation) [1997] Fam 110

Facts: Y, an adult, mentally and physically handicapped from birth, lived in a community home. She had lived with her parents and sisters in a close family until she was ten, and had since been regularly visited by them. Her mother's health was bad and her older sister, P [plaintiff], suffered from a bone marrow disorder. P's only

→

realistic prospect of recovery was a bone marrow transplant from a healthy compatible donor, and the option was Y. Her disabilities meant that Y was unaware of the situation and unable to consent to the operations required for a donation. P applied for declarations that they were lawful nonetheless.

Held: Since the donation of bone marrow by the patient would be likely to help to prolong the life of the mother as well as the plaintiff and to improve the patient's relationship with both of them, the patient would receive an emotional, psychological and social benefit from the operation and suffer minimal detriment.

Connell J (at pages 113, 115–16): I am satisfied that the root question remains, namely, whether the procedures here envisaged will benefit the [patient] and accordingly benefits which may flow to the plaintiff are relevant only in so far as they have a positive effect upon the best interests of the [patient]. [...] If the plaintiff dies, this is bound to have an adverse affect upon her mother who already suffers from significant ill-health. [...] Her ability to visit the [patient] would be handicapped significantly. [...] In this situation, the [patient] would clearly be harmed by the reduction in or loss of contact with her mother. Accordingly, it is to the benefit of the [patient] that she should act as donor to her sister, because in this way her positive relationship with her mother is most likely to be prolonged. Further, if the transplant occurs, this is likely to improve the [patient's] relationship with her mother who clearly wishes it to take place and also to improve her relationship with the plaintiff who will be eternally grateful to her. The disadvantages to the [patient] of the harvesting procedure are very small. [...] I should perhaps emphasise that this is a rather unusual case and that the family of the plaintiff and the [patient] are a particularly close family. It is doubtful that this case would act as a useful precedent in cases where the surgery involved is more intrusive than in this case, where the evidence shows that bone marrow is speedily regenerated and that a healthy individual can donate as much as two pints with no long term consequences at all. Thus, the bone marrow donated by the [patient] will cause her no loss and she will suffer no real long-term risk.

This judgment may turn on its facts (i.e. be a one off) but it is very controversial. The positive aspect of this case is that it shows an understanding for the wider interests that can affect a patient. Y would have indeed suffered emotionally if her sister were to die, because her mother would then struggle to visit her. Similarly, Y would have improved her relationship with both her mother and her sister, who would be 'eternally grateful' for the bone marrow. However, there are many negative aspects to this case. Firstly, it is not entirely clear whether Y would even be aware of the positive consequences of her endeavour, or of her sister's gratefulness. Secondly, for a sibling to be 'eternally grateful' is not an appropriate ground upon which to allow invasive surgery on an incompetent patient. Thirdly, collecting bone marrow may not be as invasive as organ donation, but it is still a serious procedure that breaks the patient's skin and removes some of her bodily matter. Fourthly, the principle of this case is potentially harmful: 'incompetent patients can be harvested to save their siblings'. Connell J is careful to say that this case should not set a precedent, but its existence is enough to begin a ball rolling. It is only a matter of time before another plaintiff, in almost identical family circumstances, comes forward wanting a declaration for the removal of a kidney from his or her incompetent sibling. On what grounds could a case like that be distinguished from *Re Y* (1997)?

The discussion (further above) about best interests and the views of relatives looks decidedly more dangerous in light of *Re Y* (1997). How can doctors be sure that the views of relatives – as sought under section 4(6) of the MCA 2005 in order to ascertain the best interests of the patient – are not simply their *own* wishes disguised as the patient's?

ACTIVITY

Jemima belonged to a lesser-known cult who believed that the sharing of bodily tissues was wrong because it crossed DNA in an artificial way. She believed this so strongly that she also refused to eat any meat products in case the animal DNA became a part of her body. Jemima was 19, so when she found that she needed a transfusion and slipped into unconsciousness, the doctor approached her parents. They never liked the strange cult that Jemima was a part of, and so they shared both their views and Jemima's views with the doctor. What might the doctor decide?

Refusing treatment through an advance directive

KEY DEFINITION

Advance directive: a decision made in advance (also referred to as an 'advance decision').

We have learnt that the best interests test under section 4(6) of the Mental Capacity Act 2005 does not only consider the medical needs of the patient, but wider interests such as social, emotional and welfare needs, including those of a sibling as seen in *Re Y* (1997). However, there is one way in which the best interests of a patient can be ignored at the request of the patient himself: advance directives are competent decisions (usually refusals) made *before* the patient becomes incapacitated, and they are legally binding should the patient later require medical treatment and has lost the capacity to issue his refusal for himself.

EXTRACT

The Mental Capacity Act 2005 Code of Practice (2007):

http://www.legislation.gov.uk/ukpga/2005/9/pdfs/ukpgacop_20050009_en.pdf

Paragraph 9.36: Where an advance decision is being followed, the best interests principle does not apply. This is because an advance decision reflects the decision of an adult with capacity who has made the decision for themselves. Healthcare professionals must follow a valid and applicable advance decision, even if they think it goes against a person's best interests.

However, there is a basic limitation.

EXTRACT

Paragraph 9.28: An advance decision cannot refuse actions that are needed to keep a person comfortable (sometimes called basic or essential care). Examples include warmth, shelter, actions to keep a person clean and the offer of food and water by mouth. [However] an advance decision can refuse artificial nutrition and hydration.

Advance directives feature under sections 24 and 25 of the MCA 2005. They play an important role in the treatment of incompetent patients in that they can overrule the best interests test:

Mental Capacity Act 2005

Section 24(1): 'Advance decision' is a decision made by a person [P] after he has reached 18 and when he has capacity to do so, that if:

(a) at a later time and in such circumstances as he may specify, a specified treatment is proposed to be carried out or continued by a person providing health care for him, and;

(b) at the time he lacks capacity to consent to the carrying out or continuation of the treatment;

. . . the specified treatment is not to be carried out or continued.

- The patient must be 18 or over for an advance directive to be effective.
- The patient must be fully competent at the time of making the advance directive.
- A treatment must be specified.
- The advance directive can apply to treatment that is proposed and treatment that is already being carried out.
- The advance directive will become effective when the patient lacks capacity to consent to the carrying out or continuation of treatment.

Advance directives only allow for competent *refusals* of medical treatment. A patient cannot *demand* a medical treatment, whether it be in an advance directive or not. A patient can *request* a particular treatment and this will be discussed with relatives when applying the best interests test under section 4(6) of the MCA 2005, but an advance *request* is not binding. The strict provisions surrounding advance directives have caused some problems for patients. It should be assumed, as a starting point, that the patient was fully competent when the advance directive was made (as required under section 24(1) of the 2005 Act). This assumption is supported by the Code of Practice.

EXTRACT

The Mental Capacity Act 2005 Code of Practice (2007):

http://www.legislation.gov.uk/ukpga/2005/9/pdfs/ukpgacop_20050009_en.pdf

Paragraph 9.8: . . . healthcare professionals should always start from the assumption that a person who has made an advance decision had capacity to make it, unless they are aware of reasonable grounds to doubt the person had the capacity to make the advance decision at the time they made it . . .

When a patient goes out of their way to make an advance directive, this is evidence that they feel particularly strongly about their medical treatment. What if, later on down the road, their behaviour indicates that they may have changed their mind? A case from

2003 dealt with this very issue, and even though the judgment was delivered before the Mental Capacity Act 2005 came into force (section 25(4)(c) deals with changes of heart), the principle of the case is still applicable to the new statutory provisions.

CASE EXTRACT

HE v A Hospital NHS Trust [2003] EWHC 1017

Facts: HE [the father] applied for a declaration that a blood transfusion could be given to his daughter[D]. D had been a Muslim until her mother separated from HE. D was then raised as a Jehovah's Witness by the mother. D signed an 'advance medical directive' in her 20s stipulating that because of her faith she did not consent to any treatment involving a blood transfusion. She later fell seriously ill and was hospitalised by the Trust. The doctors treating her diagnosed that she was very likely to die within hours without a blood transfusion. HE brought the current application, arguing that D would consent to treatment as she was now engaged to a Muslim man, had expressed a commitment to return to the Muslim faith and had ceased to worship as a Jehovah's Witness for some months before her illness.

Held: The treatment prescribed by D's doctor could be lawfully administered. D's change of faith had been a deliberate, implemented decision that was sufficient to effectively revoke and invalidate the directive.

Munby J (at paras 24, 37–8, 43, 45): Where, as here, life is at stake, the evidence must be scrutinised with especial care. The continuing validity and applicability of the advance directive must be clearly established by convincing and reliable evidence. […] In my judgment it is fundamental that an advance directive is, of its very essence and nature, inherently revocable. […] An advance directive is, after all, nothing more or less than the embodiment of the patient's autonomy and right of self-determination. […] Only the patient himself can revoke his own advance directive. […] No doubt there is a practical – what lawyers would call an evidential – burden on those who assert that an undisputed advance directive is for some reason no longer operative, a burden requiring them to point to something indicating that this is or may be so. It may be words said to have been written or spoken by the patient. It may be the patient's actions – for sometimes actions speak louder than words. It may be some change in circumstances. Thus, it may be alleged that the patient no longer professes the faith which underlay the advance directive; it may be said that the patient executed the advance directive because he was suffering from an illness which has since been cured; it may be said that medical science has now moved on; it may be said that the patient, having since married or had children, now finds himself with more compelling reasons to choose to live even a severely disadvantaged life. It may be suggested that, even though not revoked, […] the advance directive has not survived some material change of circumstances. But whatever the reasons may be, once the issue is properly raised, once there is some real reason for doubt, then it is for those who assert the continuing validity and applicability of the advance directive to prove that it is still operative. […] If there is doubt, that doubt falls to be resolved in favour of the preservation of life. So, if there is doubt the advance directive cannot be relied on and the doctor must treat the patient in such way as his best interests require. […] All I would add is that the longer the time which has elapsed since an advance directive was made, and the greater the apparent changes in the patient's circumstances since then, the more doubt there is likely to be as to its continuing validity and applicability.

Munby J believes that when a relative asserts that an advance directive is valid, that relative then has a duty to prove that this is the case. He also acknowledges that advance directives should be revocable. This means that, if a competent patient was to change his or her mind about refusing a specific medical treatment, they should be able to exercise their autonomy and alter or withdraw their advance direction. In addition to this, a patient's behaviour or lifestyle may be a good indicator as to whether the advance directive is still valid. Munby J gives the example of no longer professing a faith, or having a family. The Code of Practice supports this idea.

EXTRACT

The Mental Capacity Act 2005 Code of Practice (2007):

http://www.legislation.gov.uk/ukpga/2005/9/pdfs/ukpgacop_20050009_en.pdf

Paragraph 9.43: So when deciding whether an advance decision applies to the proposed treatment, healthcare professionals must consider:

- how long ago the advance decision was made;
- whether there have been changes in the patient's personal life (for example, the person is pregnant, and this was not anticipated when they made the advance decision) that might affect the validity of the advance decision; and
- whether there have been developments in medical treatment that the person did not foresee (for example, new medications, treatment or therapies).

The Code of Practice also encourages patients to regularly review and update their advance directives, because the longer they are left unchecked, the more it is likely that unforeseen circumstances or changes in behaviour and lifestyle may invalidate the directive.

EXTRACT

The Mental Capacity Act 2005 Code of Practice (2007):

http://www.legislation.gov.uk/ukpga/2005/9/pdfs/ukpgacop_20050009_en.pdf

Paragraph 9.16: It is a good idea to try to include possible future circumstances in the advance decision. For example, a woman may want to state in the advance decision whether or not it should still apply if she later becomes pregnant. If the document does not anticipate a change in circumstance, healthcare professionals may decide that it is not applicable if those particular circumstances arise.

Paragraph 9.29: Anyone who has made an advance decision is advised to regularly review and update it as necessary. Decisions made a long time in advance are not automatically invalid or inapplicable, but they may raise doubts when deciding whether they are valid and applicable . . .

Paragraph 9.30: Views and circumstances may change over time. A new stage in a person's illness, the development of new treatments or a major change in personal circumstances may be appropriate times to review and update an advance decision.

The Code of Practice appears to throw some doubt onto the rigidness of advance directives. They have been shown to be legally binding, but many obstacles lie in their way. A patient must update the advance directive regularly, to make the advance directive when fully competent, not behave in a way that might invalidate the advance directive, and to contemplate any future circumstances – whether personal, social or medical – that may change his or her mind in the future about rejecting that particular treatment. It was shown in *W* v *H* (2004) (below) that if there is any doubt as to the validity or applicability of an advance directive, the courts will fall in favour of preserving the patient's life.

CASE EXTRACT

W Healthcare NHS Trust v *H* [2004] EWCA Civ 1324

Facts: The appellants (H and P), who were the brother and daughter of the patient (K), appealed against a High Court decision to allow an NHS Trust [W] to reinsert a feeding tube to keep her alive. K was 59, had suffered from multiple sclerosis for thirty years and had been incapable of making informed decisions for twenty years. She had lived in a nursing home and for five years she had required feeding by tube. She was admitted into hospital [W] after her tube fell out. Her family unanimously did not want it to be reinserted, but W did. The High Court heard from K's family and friends that she had previously stated that she did not want to be kept alive and that she would now want to be allowed to die, but the initial judge decided that, in the absence of K's being able to make an informed decision or having made an advance directive which clearly amounted to a direction that she preferred to be deprived of food and drink until she died, it was in her best interests to reinsert the tube. The Court of Appeal were approached by the family.

Held: When a patient was incapable of taking decisions for herself and her doctors wished to treat her, the court's decision on whether to allow treatment should be based on the patient's best interests rather on its view of what she would have chosen if she were capable.

Brooke LJ (at para 21): I am of the clear view that the judge was correct in finding that there was not an advance directive which was sufficiently clear to amount to a direction that she preferred to be deprived of food and drink for a period of time which would lead to her death in all circumstances. There is no evidence that she was aware of the nature of this choice, or the unpleasantness or otherwise of death by starvation, and it would be departing from established principles of English law if one was to hold that there was an advance directive which was established and relevant in the circumstances in the present case, despite the very strong expression of her wishes which came through in the evidence.

The judgment of *W* v *H* is clear evidence that even an express wish throughout life to refuse life-sustaining treatment will not suffice as an advance directive if the refusal is not specifically recorded in a written directive. The value of life is regarded as so high by the courts that the courts will almost always find favour in preserving life rather than withdrawing the care which sustains it.

The Court of Protection

The Court of Protection was set up under section 45 of the Mental Capacity Act 2005. It has the same powers as the High Court, except it deals especially with incompetent adults:

- It can resolve disputes over capacity (in all areas of law).
- It can decide whether a person lacks capacity.
- It can conclude whether a treatment is in a person's best interests.
- It can rule on whether any treatment done (or about to be done) is lawful or unlawful.
- It can decide whether an advance directive is valid and applicable (listed under s. 15).

EXTRACT

The Mental Capacity Act 2005 Code of Practice (2007):

http://www.legislation.gov.uk/ukpga/2005/9/pdfs/ukpgacop_20050009_en.pdf

Paragraph 8.1: Section 45 of the Act sets up a specialist court, the Court of Protection, to deal with decision-making for adults (and children in a few cases) who may lack capacity to make specific decisions for themselves . . . The new court also deals with serious decisions affecting healthcare and personal welfare matters. These were previously dealt with by the High Court under its inherent jurisdiction.

Paragraph 8.2: The new Court of Protection is a superior court of record and is able to establish precedent (it can set examples for future cases) and build up expertise in all issues related to lack of capacity. It has the same powers, rights, privileges and authority as the High Court. When reaching any decision, the court must apply all the statutory principles set out in section 1 of the [2005] Act. In particular, it must make a decision in the best interests of the person who lacks capacity to make the specific decision.

The Court of Protection can decide whether an advance directive is still valid and applicable for an incompetent patient. However, it is unusual for things to get this far. A doctor will usually be able to treat the patient according to his or her best interests after consulting with relatives, or withdraw treatment from the patient in accordance with a clear advance directive. There are, however, a small number of highly controversial cases which should, as prescribed by the old common law, be brought before a Court (which would today be the Court of Protection).

EXTRACT

The Mental Capacity Act 2005 Code of Practice (2007):

http://www.legislation.gov.uk/ukpga/2005/9/pdfs/ukpgacop_20050009_en.pdf

Paragraph 8.18: Cases involving any of the following decisions should be brought before a Court:

- Decisions about the proposed withholding or withdrawal of artificial nutrition and hydration (ANH) from patients in a permanent vegetative state (PVS).
- Cases involving organ or bone marrow donation by a person who lacks capacity to consent.
- Cases involving the proposed non-therapeutic sterilisation of a person who lacks capacity to consent to this (e.g. for contraceptive purposes).
- All other cases where there is a doubt or dispute about whether a particular treatment will be in a person's best interests.

Withdrawing ANH from a PVS patient is particularly controversial because it could be the equivalent to murder. Organ and bone marrow donation is usually carried out for the benefit of *another* person (e.g. a relative), so the Court of Protection must be satisfied that the patient would gain at least *some* benefit from the procedure. Untested areas may set a precedent, so it is a good idea to take the issue to court to test their ideas as to which legal route would be the least controversial.

In relation to healthcare matters, an application to the Court of Protection should normally be made by the NHS trust (or other organisation) caring for the patient. A local authority can do so too if social care staff are concerned about the welfare of a person who lacks capacity; both scenarios are supported by paragraph 8.8 of the Code of Practice. The patient who is alleged to lack capacity can also apply, as can a family member in order to settle a dispute (paragraph 8.7).

THINKING POINT

Why do you think it is important to have a court that specifically deals with the best interests of incompetent individuals? What positive difference might this make to the treatment of patients?

Appointing a decision-maker

The Mental Capacity Act 2005 introduces another new feature to support the best interests of incompetent patients: proxy decision-making. This means that a person can be nominated by the patient to make his medical decisions for him.

KEY DEFINITION

Proxy decision-making: a person is nominated to make a decision on behalf of the patient.

The person nominated by the patient (the 'donor') is sometimes referred to as the 'donee' and has lasting power of attorney (also known as LPA). This means that the nominated person (the 'donee') can make legal decisions on behalf of the incompetent patient.

KEY DEFINITION

Donor: the patient.
Donee: the person nominated by the patient to make legal decisions.
Lasting power of attorney: the power to make legal decisions.

The legal powers of donees are contained under section 9 of the 2005 Act.

Mental Capacity Act 2005

Section 9: Lasting powers of attorney

(1) A lasting power of attorney is a power of attorney under which the donor ('P') confers on the donee (or donees) authority to make decisions about all or any of the following:

  (a) the patient's personal welfare or specified matters concerning the patient's personal welfare, and

  (b) the patient's property and affairs or specified matters concerning the patient's property and affairs,

  . . . and which includes authority to make such decisions in circumstances where the patient no longer has capacity.

Section 9(1) does not specifically mention medical decisions, but they are assumed under the term 'personal welfare'.

A donee with lasting power of attorney can accept or refuse treatment on behalf of the patient as long as that decision has satisfied all the criteria under the best interests test (s. 4(6)). However, there are restrictions as to just what a donee with lasting power of attorney can do.

Mental Capacity Act 2005

Section 11: Lasting powers of attorney: restrictions

(7) Where a lasting power of attorney authorises the donee to make decisions about the patient's personal welfare, the authority:

   (a) does not extend to making such decisions in circumstances other than those where P lacks, or the donee reasonably believes that P lacks, capacity;

   (b) cannot override an advance directive made by the patient to refuse medical treatment; and

   (c) extends to giving or refusing consent to the carrying out or continuation of a treatment by a person providing health care for P.

(8) But subsection (7)(c):

   (a) does not authorise the giving or refusing of consent to the carrying out or continuation of life-sustaining treatment, unless the instrument contains express provision to that effect.

The provisions under section 11 can be translated as follows (as supported by paragraph 7.27 of the Code of Practice):

- **Section 11(7)(a)**: A donee has no decision-making power if the donor can make their own treatment decisions.

- **Section 11(7)(b)**: An donee cannot consent to treatment if the donor has made a valid and applicable advance decision to refuse a specific treatment, but if the donor made an LPA after the advance decision, and gave the donee the right to consent to or refuse the treatment, the donee can choose not to follow the advance decision.

- **Section 11(7)(c) and (8)(a)**: An donee has no power to consent to or refuse life-sustaining treatment, unless the LPA document expressly authorises this.

It is very important that, if a patient wishes to refuse life-sustaining treatment, he expressly confers this power upon the donee as stipulated under section 11(8)(a). This will ensure that the donee is not simply 'putting the patient to death' but is complying with the express wish to refuse treatment. The best interests test under section 4(6) still applies to decisions of this nature, and an express authorisation from the patient to refuse treatment will be deemed good evidence that a refusal is in his best interests. This also means that the views of other family members and friends should be consulted under section 4(7)(e) before the final decision is made. The Code of Practice reminds doctors and relatives to keep a close eye on these kinds of decisions.

EXTRACT

The Mental Capacity Act 2005 Code of Practice (2007):

http://www.legislation.gov.uk/ukpga/2005/9/pdfs/ukpgacop_20050009_en.pdf

Paragraph 7.31: As with all decisions, an attorney must act in the donor's best interests when making decisions about such treatment. This will involve applying the best interests checklist and consulting with carers, family members and others interested in the donor's welfare. In particular, the attorney must not be motivated in any way by the desire to bring about the donor's death. Anyone who doubts that the attorney is acting in the donor's best interests can apply to the Court of Protection for a decision.

The patient can appoint more than one donee, and they can act jointly or severally under section10(4).

Court deputies

The Court of Protection can appoint a deputy to act on the patient's behalf. The power to do this lies under section 16(2)(b) of the MCA 2005. The Code of Practice confirms that this will only be necessary when there is a 'serious dispute' such as a family breakdown (under paragraphs 8.25 and 8.39), and section 16(4)(a) of the Act states that a deputy will be appointed by the Court when it would prefer a deputy to make the decision and this would support the patient's best interests.

A deputy appointed by the Court of Protection is *not* allowed to refuse consent to the beginning or continuation of life-sustaining treatment under section 17(1)(d) and section 20(5). This is probably because the deputy will not have known the patient on a personal level and so would not have been expressly granted the power to do so on behalf of the patient.

Restraining an incompetent patient

When a patient is judged to be incompetent under sections 2 and 3 of the Mental Capacity Act 2005, they are treated in accordance with their best interests under section 4(6). It has also been established that an advance directive made by the patient can refuse life-sustaining medical treatment, a donee with lasting power of attorney can be appointed on behalf of the patient to make medical decisions on their behalf, and a deputy can be appointed by the court to settle any other capacity issues. There are, therefore, many different ways in which a decision about the appropriate treatment for an incompetent patient can be reached (but it must always satisfy the best interests test).

A patient who lacks capacity might not know where they are and what is going on around them. It might be particularly distressing for relatives of the patient, who in his or her confused state, is adamant that he or she does not want that specific course of treatment. These issues could make the administration of treatment difficult. There are instances in which it might be acceptable to restrain an incompetent patient in order to treat them. The Mental Capacity Act 2005 provides specific directions on this matter.

Mental Capacity Act 2005

Section 6

(2) D [must] reasonably believe that it is necessary to do the act in order to prevent harm to the patient.

(3) The act is a proportionate response to:
   (a) the likelihood of the patient suffering harm, and
   (b) the seriousness of that harm.

(4) For the purposes of this section D restrains the patient if he:
   (a) uses, or threatens to use, force to secure the doing of an act which the patient resists, or
   (b) restricts the patient's liberty of movement, whether or not the patient resists.

Under section 6(2) the doctor must reasonably believe that the restraint is necessary. This is an objective test (i.e. the reasonable man would agree). Under section 6(2) the restraint must also be in order to prevent *harm* to the patient. What kind of harm? The thrashing around of the distressed patient, or the harm caused by his or her illness if the treatment is not administered? This is not clear. Under section 6(3), the *likelihood* and *seriousness* of the harm must justify the restraint, but without a definition of harm, this is almost impossible to define.

The Code of Practice provides additional guidance on the definition of 'harm' but it does not clearly identify what the restraint is supposed to prevent.

EXTRACT

The Mental Capacity Act 2005 Code of Practice (2007):

http://www.legislation.gov.uk/ukpga/2005/9/pdfs/ukpgacop_20050009_en.pdf

Paragraph 6.45: The Act does not define 'harm', because it will vary depending on the situation. For example:

- A person with learning disabilities might run into a busy road without warning, if they do not understand the dangers of cars.
- A person with dementia may wander away from home and get lost, if they cannot remember where they live.
- A person with manic depression might engage in excessive spending during a manic phase, causing them to get into debt.
- A person may also be at risk of harm if they behave in a way that encourages others to assault or exploit them (for example, by behaving in a dangerously provocative way).

In the context of medical care, there are many different types of harm that could be experienced by a patient. The vague terms used under section 6(2) mean that restraint can be justified in almost any situation as long as it prevents 'likely' and 'serious' harm. It is not clear whether restraint could be used to simply administer a treatment that a patient does not want, but it would probably be found to be 'preventing harm' in the long run to forcefully administer treatment to an unwilling incompetent patient. A donee with lasting power of attorney can even restrain a patient as long as the relevant criteria are satisfied.

Mental Capacity Act 2005

Section 11: Lasting powers of attorney: restrictions

(1) A lasting power of attorney does not authorise the donee to do an act that is intended to restrain the patient, unless three conditions are satisfied.

(2) The first condition is that the patient lacks, or the donee reasonably believes that the patient lacks, capacity in relation to the matter in question.

(3) The second is that the donee reasonably believes that it is necessary to do the act in order to prevent harm to the patient.

(4) The third is that the act is a proportionate response to:

(a) the likelihood of the patient suffering harm, and

(b) the seriousness of that harm.

The provisions for a donee with lasting power of attorney are almost identical to those given to medical professionals when wishing to use restraint; under section 5(1) the doctor must also be sure that the patient lacks capacity at the time and in relation to the specific matter. The Code of Practice makes it clear that the use of any restraint must be necessary, not simply convenient.

EXTRACT

The Mental Capacity Act 2005 Code of Practice (2007):

http://www.legislation.gov.uk/ukpga/2005/9/pdfs/ukpgacop_20050009_en.pdf

Paragraph 6.44: Anybody considering using restraint must have objective reasons to justify that restraint is necessary. They must be able to show that the person being cared for is likely to suffer harm unless proportionate restraint is used. A carer or professional must not use restraint just so that they can do something more easily. If restraint is necessary to prevent harm to the person who lacks capacity, it must be the minimum amount of force for the shortest time possible.

The word 'proportionate' is featured in paragraph 6.44 (above) and in section 6(3) (above). However, the term 'best interests' is nowhere to be found. It has been confirmed in common law that if the use of restraint is in fact impracticable because of the patient's condition, then the courts may declare it lawful to withdraw or cancel that treatment.[5]

The use of restraint does not breach a patient's right to freedom from inhuman and degrading treatment under Article 3 of the European Convention on Human Rights, because it is a therapeutic necessity. This was established in *Herczegfalvy v Austria* (1993) 15 EHRR 437 which called for a 'medical necessity' to be 'convincingly shown' to exist (more on this issue in Chapter 7).

---

[5] This was established in *D (Medical Treatment: Mentally Disabled Patient), Re* [1998] 2 FLR 22 in relation to kidney dialysis. The treatment could only be administered via general anaesthetic which was too dangerous.

A mistaken diagnosis of incapacity

There is a heavy burden upon a doctor when he is faced with a patient who appears to be flitting between competence and incompetence. The 'scope of competence' is a very grey area. Does he respect the consent or refusal of the patient even though she appears to be making an irrational and dangerous decision, or does he treat the patient according to her best interests and disregard her autonomy? If the doctor is mistaken, and a patient is found to be perfectly competent and has been treated against her wishes, a doctor can protect himself against criminal charges if he made an honest mistake. The Mental Capacity Act 2005 provides a test for doctors to satisfy when deliberating the capacity of an adult patient.

Mental Capacity Act 2005

Section 5: Acts in connection with care or treatment

(1) If a person (D) does an act in connection with the care or treatment of another person (P), the act is one to which this section applies if:

   (a) before doing the act, D takes reasonable steps to establish whether P lacks capacity in relation to the matter in question, and

   (b) when doing the act, D reasonably believes:

      (i)   that P lacks capacity in relation to the matter, and

      (ii) that it will be in P's best interests for the act to be done.

The three-part test can be described as follows:

- The doctor must take 'reasonable steps' to ascertain capacity;
- The doctor must 'reasonably believe' that the patient lacks capacity, and
- The doctor must 'reasonably believe' that the treatment is in the best interests of the patient.

The criterion of 'reasonable' is difficult to prove. To be on the safe side, any doctor or other medical professional should record any decisions made and the statutory provision against which it was made. For example, the statutory test for incapacity is under section 2, the statutory test for an inability to make decisions is under section 3 and the best interests checklist features under section 4(6) of the MCA 2005. These provisions should all be applied clearly and results recorded in the patient's file. Discussions with relatives should also be noted, as this is proof that the doctor took steps to ascertain capacity. An advance directive to refuse medical treatment must be also respected if it is found to be written when the patient was competent. Ignoring the advance directive will breach the patient's autonomy unless the doctor is *satisfied* that it didn't exist under section 26 of the MCA 2005.

Mental Capacity Act 2005

Section 26: Effect of advance decisions

(2) A person does not incur liability for carrying out or continuing the treatment unless, at the time, he is satisfied that an advance decision exists which is valid and applicable to the treatment.

Similarly, if a doctor withdraws treatment on the reasonable belief that an advance directive *did* exist, there is a defence available for that too.

Mental Capacity Act 2005

Section 26: Effect of advance decisions

(3) A person does not incur liability for the consequences of withholding or withdrawing a treatment from P if, at the time, he reasonably believes that an advance decision exists which is valid and applicable to the treatment.

A doctor can therefore have the following statutory defences in relation to making mistakes about advance directives:

- No liability will follow from continuing treatment *unless* he is satisfied that an advance directive exists – s. 26(2).
- No liability will follow from withdrawing treatment *if* he reasonably believes that an advance directive exists – s. 26(3).

These tests are easy to satisfy, particularly that of section 26(2). 'Satisfaction' is a very subjective concept. The doctor merely has to say that he was 'unsatisfied' as to whether there was a valid advance directive or not in order to ignore it and continue treatment. Perhaps this test is so easy to satisfy because *ignoring* an advance refusal is far less serious than believing an advance refusal existed. The consequences of the latter are extremely grave. The Code of Practice confirms that the burden of proof is on the doctor to show that he was satisfied or reasonably believed that an advance directive did or did not exist.

EXTRACT

The Mental Capacity Act 2005 Code of Practice (2007):

http://www.legislation.gov.uk/ukpga/2005/9/pdfs/ukpgacop_20050009_en.pdf

Paragraph 9.59: Healthcare professionals will be protected from liability for failing to provide treatment if they 'reasonably believe' that a valid and applicable advance decision to refuse that treatment exists. But they must be able to demonstrate that their belief was reasonable (section 26(3)) and point to reasonable grounds showing why they believe this. Healthcare professionals can only base their decision on the evidence that is available at the time they need consider an advance decision.

It may be argued that by providing healthcare professionals with these defences under section 26, the MCA 2005 has weakened the power of advance directives and scuppered patient autonomy.[6] In reality, we must recognise the pressurised environment of medical care and give allowances for healthcare professionals to make genuine mistakes.

---

[6] This was argued in Alasdair Maclean, 'Advance Directives and the Rocky Waters of Anticipatory Decision-Making' (2008) 16 *Medical Law Review* 1.

Rose is an elderly lady in her 70s. She has a long history of bad health, but is very traditional in her beliefs. She believes that modern technology does not work and prefers to treat her ailments with her great grandmother's old herbal remedies. She has no real knowledge of how the law or medicine works, but she does have a grandson who became a lawyer, and he taught her one or two things about her rights as a patient and a consumer over the years. She has secretly written an advance directive three years ago at the age of 71 because she could feel her health deteriorating.

Rose had a heart attack and she was taken to hospital. The doctor warned her family that she would need to take a particular concoction of drugs to stabilise her. Rose's family knew how strong her beliefs about modern medicine were, but they didn't want to interfere with the doctor's job so they merely mumbled that 'she wouldn't have liked that' before keeping quiet. The doctor treated Rose in accordance with her best interests by giving her a concoction of drugs to prolong her life, only to find, four days later when the grandson turned up, that Rose had written an advance directive prohibiting any medical intervention to prolong her life. Does the doctor have a defence against a criminal charge of battery or a civil action of trespass?

Children: incompetent

Children have a curious position in law. They are generally a 'minor' until the age of 18, which is known as the age of 'majority', but some areas of law will allow for certain acts to be committed at younger ages. For example,

- A 10-year-old can be criminally liable.
- A 16-year-old can marry.
- A 17-year-old can legally drive.

In medical law, there is no formal age of majority. It has been shown in the past that a child under the age of 18 is mature enough to consent to medical treatment, but the burden is on the child to prove this. In addition to this, the Mental Capacity Act 2005 does not cover children, so the old common law rules apply to minors.

Children are assumed to be incompetent because of the complexity of medical procedures. They may only take the short-term view and consider the pain of the procedure, without weighing up the long-term benefits. They may also lack life experience when it comes to the emotional strain of undergoing medical treatment, and they may not understand the doctor's instructions or diagnosis. It is therefore in their best interests that someone with more life experience and a better understanding of the treatment should make the decision for them.

(a) Who must consent?

A person with parental responsibility can consent to the child's medical treatment, right up until the age of 18. This includes legal guardians who have acquired parental responsibility by law. A parent can consent to the medical treatment without consulting the other parent because only one consent is needed (disagreements between parents are explored below). There are very few procedures in which the consent of both parents is required, but non-therapeutic circumcision is one of them. This is because it is a surgical procedure that will not benefit the patient in any medical way, so the parents must be sure that they are willing to put their child through surgery for no medical reason.

CASE EXTRACT

Re J (Specific Orders: Child's religious Upbringing and Circumcision) [2000] 1 FLR 571

Facts: The father, a Muslim, appealed against the refusal of his application for an order requiring the surgical circumcision of his 5-year-old son despite opposition from the child's mother. The father contended that the judge had failed to recognise that the child had been born a Muslim whatever his subsequent religious development.

Held: Dismissing the father's appeal, where there was a dispute concerning an important decision regarding a child, the matter should be referred to the court. Ritual circumcision was an irreversible operation which was not medically necessary, bearing physical and psychological risks and in such cases the Children Act 1989 section 2(7) stated that the consent of both parents was essential. The issue of what was in the best interests of the child would depend on the facts and, in the instant case, the judge had found that circumcision at the age of 5 which was not medically necessary was not in the child's best interests.

Lord Justice Thorpe (at para 15): Some recognise religion by some ceremony of induction or initiation, but the newborn does not share the perception of his parents or of the religious community to which the parents belong. A child's perception of his or her religion generally depends on involvement in worship and teaching within the family. From this develops the emotional, intellectual, psychological and spiritual sense of belonging to a religious faith.

Dame Elizabeth Butler-Sloss P (at paras 31–2): There is, in my view, a small group of important decisions made on behalf of a child which, in the absence of agreement of those with parental responsibility, ought not to be carried out or arranged by a one-parent carer although she has parental responsibility under section 2(7) of the Children Act 1989. Such a decision ought not to be made without the specific approval of the court. Sterilisation is one example. [...] The issue of circumcision has not, to my knowledge, previously been considered by this court, but in my view it comes within that group. The decision to circumcise a child on ground other than medical necessity is a very important one; the operation is irreversible, and should only be carried out where the parents together approve of it or, in the absence of parental agreement, where a court decides that the operation is in the best interests of the child.

It can be seen in *Re J* that when a non-therapeutic surgical procedure is suggested for a child, the courts are keen to receive consent from both parents. This is because the procedure has no medical benefit to the child and is irreversible. It should be noted that circumcisions at birth when both parents agree are less controversial, but the child in *Re J* was much older and the mother disagreed. The court will only get involved when one parent disagrees, and will rule in accordance with the child's best interests.

In *Re C* (2003), the issue of vaccination with the MMR injection (measles, mumps and rubella) was also considered to be within the 'small group of important decisions' where both parents must agree or the court will decide for them.

Re C (Welfare of Child: Immunisation) [2003] EWCA Civ 1148

Facts: The father wishes for the vaccinations to go ahead but the mother disagreed because of the controversy surrounding the MMR injection. The judge considered all of the medical evidence.

Held: Both parents must consent to the MMR vaccination before it can go ahead, or the courts will make the decision based on the child's best interests. Immunisation against childhood diseases is in the best interests of the child. If medical evidence conflicts, the judge must carry out a comprehensive survey of all the medical evidence and all the relevant factors.

Thorpe J (at para 17): In [Re J (2000)] the court held that the circumcision of the child should only be carried out where the parents agree or where a court, in settling the dispute between them, decides that the operation is in the best interests of the child. In my opinion this appeal demonstrates that hotly contested issues of immunisation are to be added to that 'small group of important decisions'.

In *Re C*, the father was not married to the mother and they did not live together at any time. However, despite his absence, he was still pivotal to the decision of whether or not to provide the vaccination.

Emergency situations

There may be an emergency in which no person with parental responsibility can be found, or no one with parental responsibility may be willing, to consent to a child's medical treatment. If this is the case, the doctors are entitled to treat the child without consent if the situation is critical. These thoughts were expressed during the judgment of *Gillick* (1984).

Gillick v West Norfolk and Wisbech AHA [1986] AC 112

Lord Templeman (at page 200): I accept that if there is no time to obtain a decision from the court, a doctor may safely carry out treatment in an emergency if the doctor believes the treatment to be vital to the survival or health of an infant and notwithstanding the opposition of a parent or the impossibility of alerting the parent before the treatment is carried out.

To put this judgment another way, if the parents can be found within a reasonable time, or if a court order can be obtained, a doctor should wait before administering treatment. If not, they can go ahead without consent.

Parents who refuse medical treatment

It is clear that a person with parental responsibility can consent to medical treatment on a child's behalf, but can they *refuse* medical treatment too? This is an extremely contentious area. A competent adult may be able to refuse medical treatment for *himself* and his autonomous decision will be respected, but a child must *always* be treated according to their best interests. Parents are assumed to be acting within the best interests of their children, so a refusal of medical treatment, especially life saving treatment, raises red flags amongst medical staff. Parents can sometimes be convinced that they know what is best for their children, but when the child is facing serious injury or death, the courts will intervene. Parental autonomy can, and has been, overruled by the courts in many high-profile cases. In *Re A* (2001) the courts authorised an operation to surgically separate Siamese twins. The parents were deeply religious and fought hard to stop the surgery, even though the twins were going to die without it.

CASE EXTRACT

A (Children) (Conjoined Twins: Surgical Separation), Re [2001] Fam 147

Facts: The parents of 6-week-old Siamese twins, Mary and Jody, appealed against a ruling granting medical staff to proceed with an elective surgical separation. M had severe brain abnormalities, no lung tissue and no properly functioning heart. The blood supply keeping M alive emanated from J who was functioning and developing normally. The judge at first instance held that the operation would be in the interests of both children on the basis that for J it afforded a good chance of a normal and independent life and that for M it offered relief from a potentially painful few months of life as J grew more active. In their appeal the parents contended that the judge had erred in his conclusions that the operation was both in the interest of each child and lawful.

Held: Dismissing the parent's appeal, that (1) while the wishes of the parents were entitled to great respect, the court was obliged to determine the issue on the basis that the welfare of the children was paramount; (2) the operation was clearly in the best interests of J since it would offer her the prospect of an independent existence and normal life expectancy, as opposed to almost certain death within a few months due to heart failure if she remained joined to M; (3) the operation would not constitute murder since the three components of the doctrine of necessity were satisfied, namely that (a) the act was required to avoid inevitable and irreparable evil; (b) no more would be done than was reasonably necessary for the purpose to be achieved; and (c) the evil to be inflicted was not disproportionate to the evil avoided.

The judgment in *Re A* is lengthy and complex, and it was handed down in an emergency situation. However, it is clear from the abstract above that one twin (the stronger twin) was treated in accordance with her best interests and the other twin (the weaker twin) was to be sacrificed to support these. The courts had not encountered a case like this before, and used the defence of necessity to authorise the killing of one of the twins through separation surgery. This is unique in medicine and law generally, and should a case like this occur again, it is unclear whether the courts would take the same approach or find a new one. In the equally unique case of *Re C* (2000), a mother did not want her child tested for HIV, but the courts overruled her objections.

CASE EXTRACT

Re C (A Child) (HIV Testing), Re [2000] Fam 48

Facts: A baby, C, was born to M, who was infected with the HIV virus. M, who was breast feeding the baby, refused to allow C to be tested for the presence of HIV infection due to her scepticism about conventional medical treatment for HIV and AIDS. She sought permission to appeal against a decision that it was in the interests of the baby's welfare that the test should take place (she was supported by the father too).

→

Held: The court overruled the mother.

Wilson J (at page 61): The mother said in evidence that, when the baby was older, she would talk to her about the possibility of infection, and, if she then wanted to take a test, she would allow her to do so. On the evidence before me, that is a hopeless programme for the baby's protection.

[...] The concluding words of the father's eloquent final submissions were these: 'Whatever the outcome of this case, we would have lost if we had not stood up for our rights.' But this case is not at its heart about the rights of the parents. And if, as he in effect suggested in his evidence, the father regards the rights of a tiny baby as subsumed within the rights of the parents, he is wrong. This baby has rights of her own. They can be considered nationally or internationally.

The judgment in *Re C* is a clear example of how the primary consideration for the court is the welfare of the child and not the rights of the parents. The advantages of the HIV test were overwhelming and it would not be in the best interests of the child to live in ignorance of the state of her health. She had both national and international rights of her own. The relationship between doctors and parents is summed up concisely by Holman J in the following case.

CASE EXTRACT

NHS Trust v *A (A Child)* [2007] EWHC 1696

Holman J (at para 40): (x) The views and opinions of both the doctors and the parents must be carefully considered. Where, as in this case, the parents spend a great deal of time with their child, their views may have particular value because they know the patient and how he reacts so well; although the court needs to be mindful that the views of any parents may, very understandably, be coloured by their own emotion or sentiment. It is important to stress that the reference is to the views and opinions of the parents. Their own wishes, however understandable in human terms, are wholly irrelevant to consideration of the objective best interests of the child save to the extent in any given case that they may illuminate the quality and value to the child of the child/parent relationship.

A doctor will not be expected to act against his own clinical judgment, especially if the demand comes from a parent, as seen in *Re J* (1991) regarding artificial ventilation.

CASE EXTRACT

Re J (A Minor) (Wardship: Medical Treatment) [1991] 2 WLR 140

Facts: The mother of a severely brain damaged baby wished for artificial ventilation to be administered if he was unable to breathe unaided. The doctors did not think this was appropriate because of the invasiveness of the procedure.

Held: It can sometimes be in a child's best interests to withhold ventilation if this experience would be completely intolerable and cause nothing but pain and suffering.

➜

Lord Donaldson MR (at pages 41, 46–7): The parents owe the child a duty to give or to withhold consent in the best interests of the child and without regard to their own interests. The court when exercising the *parens patriae* jurisdiction takes over the rights and duties of the parents, although this is not to say that the parents will be excluded from the decision-making process. Nevertheless in the end the responsibility for the decision whether to give or to withhold consent is that of the court alone. [...]

There is without doubt a very strong presumption in favour of a course of action which will prolong life, but, even excepting the 'cabbage' case to which special considerations may well apply, it is not irrebuttable. [...] Account has to be taken of the pain and suffering and quality of life which the child will experience if life is prolonged. Account has also to be taken of the pain and suffering involved in the proposed treatment itself. [...] People have an amazing adaptability. But in the end there will be cases in which the answer must be that it is not in the interests of the child to subject it to treatment which will cause increased suffering and produce no commensurate benefit, giving the fullest possible weight to the child's desire to survive.

The judgment in *Re J* highlights the power acquired by the courts when it comes to authorising the medical treatment of children: if a parent refuses treatment, a doctor can ask the courts to authorise it; if a parent and a doctor disagree about treatment, the court will make the final decision; and if a doctor is reluctant to administer treatment, the court can support his clinical judgment.[7] All of the issues above will be decided by the same principle: the court will do what is in the best interests of the child, and as seen in *Re J*, this may even mean withholding treatment.

There is one case which points the other way. In *Re T* (1997) the courts supported the parents when they refused consent for a liver transplant.

CASE EXTRACT

Re T (A Minor) (Wardship: Medical Treatment) [1997] 1 WLR 242

Facts: T was born with a life-threatening liver defect, which required a liver transplant if the child was to live. The mother, M, refused to consent to the operation as she considered it was in the child's best interests not to suffer stressful and painful invasive surgery. The judge at first instance considered medical evidence that the chances of success were good and held that M's decision was unreasonable and it was in the child's best interests for the operation to go ahead. M appealed.

Held: The mother was supported by the court on appeal.

Butler-Sloss LJ (at pages 250–1): In my view, the judge erred in his approach to the issue before the court. He accepted the unchallenged clinical opinion of the three consultants and assessed the reasonableness of the mother's decision against that medical opinion. Having held that the mother was unreasonable he accepted that the liver transplant would be likely to prolong the life of T. [...] Since he had already decided the mother's approach was unreasonable he did not weigh in the balance reasons against the treatment which might be held by a reasonable parent on much

$\rightarrow$

---

[7] See also: *R (Burke)* v *General Medical Council* [2005] 3 FCR 169.

broader grounds than the clinical assessment of the likely success of the proposed treatment. [...] The mother certainly told the judge that she recognised her son had only a short time to live if no operation was performed. She was focusing, it seems to me, on the present peaceful life of the child who had the chance to spend the rest of his short life without the pain, stress and upset of intrusive surgery against the future with the operation and treatment taking place. [...] The welfare of this child depends upon his mother. The practical considerations of her ability to cope with supporting the child in the face of her belief that this course is not right for him, the requirement to return probably for a long period to this country, either to leave the father behind and lose his support or to require him to give up his present job and seek one in England, were not put by the judge into the balance when he made his decision.

The case of *Re T* is an anomaly in medical law and will rarely be followed. It can be distinguished from the other cases in this area on several grounds. Firstly, to authorise treatment would be to throw the family into stressful disarray as they lived and worked internationally. Secondly, the parents were both healthcare professionals with knowledge of the effects of surgery on children. Thirdly, the trial judge did not adequately balance the medical evidence against non-medical factors. Fourthly, the reasonableness of the mother's decision was not examined, it was simply assumed to be unreasonable in the face of medical evidence.

Needless to say, the judgment in *Re T* has attracted criticism for the apparent overriding of the child's best interests in favour of the parent's needs.

EXTRACT

Marie Fox and Jean McHale, 'In Whose Best Interests?' (1996) 60 *Modern Law Review* 700, at pages 700–9

Although parents may legitimately object to proposed treatment where it is deemed 'heroic' in nature and parental opposition is rooted in the experimental, invasive and/or prolonged nature of the procedure, it would seem that this is not such a case. [...] It was a recognised clinical procedure, and one with a high success rate according to some experts. [...] We are given little evidence to support the Court's opinion that this mother was exceptionally devoted. Furthermore, even assuming that this representation is accurate, two troublesome issues arise. First, if we accept that Court's depiction of her as especially caring, it was surely incumbent upon the judges to examine why she was so reluctant to undertake the care of her son following a procedure which could save his life, particularly in view of her professional expertise in this area. Secondly, there is no exploration of the relationship between caring and reasonableness. It must be doubted whether the decisions of an exceptionally caring parent, even one who is a health professional herself, may automatically be deemed reasonable ones.

The issues left behind after this controversial trail of cases are as follows: can the courts undermine the authority of a parent? Who really knows best when it comes to the health and welfare of a child?

Powers of the court

The courts have three powers under which to authorise medical treatment on children:

- **Through wardship**: the child is taken in by the High Court under its power as *parens patriae*, and the court makes decisions on behalf of the child until the wardship ends.
- **By inherent jurisdiction**: a one-off decision using their jurisdiction as a court of law.
- **Under statute**: the court may have statutory powers to deal with a child in a specific way.

It is not only a doctor who can apply to a court if they have concerns over the medical treatment (or lack of it) of a child. In *Re D* (1976) the child's educational psychologist applied for the child to be a ward of court.

CASE EXTRACT

Re D (A Minor) (Wardship: Sterilisation) [1976] 2 WLR 279

Facts: D, a girl of 11, was born with a condition diagnosed as Sotos Syndrome. At age 10 it was clear that D had a lower than average intelligence and was substantially handicapped, but not so severely mentally retarded as to prevent her marrying in due course. D's parents feared that she might be seduced and give birth to an abnormal child and they arranged with a consultant paediatrician to have her sterilised. D's educational psychologist applied to have D made a ward of court. The courts then had to decide whether the procedure was in her best interests.

Held: It was held that it was not in her best interests.

Heilbron J (at pages 193–4, 196): The type of operation proposed is one which involves the deprivation of a basic human right, namely, the right of a woman to reproduce, and, therefore, it would be, if performed on a woman for non-therapeutic reasons and without her consent, a violation of such right. [...] I think this is the very type of case where this court should 'throw some care around this child', and I propose to continue her wardship which, in my judgment, is appropriate in this case. [...] I cannot believe, and the evidence does not warrant the view, that a decision to carry out an operation of this nature performed for non-therapeutic purposes on a minor can be held to be within the doctor's sole clinical judgment. [...]

A review of the whole of the evidence leads me to the conclusion that in a case of a child of 11 years of age, where the evidence shows that her mental and physical condition and attainments have already improved, and where her future prospects are as yet unpredictable, where the evidence also shows that she is unable as yet to understand and appreciate the implications of this operation and could not give a valid or informed consent, but the likelihood is that in later years she will be able to make her own choice, where, I believe, the frustration and resentment of realising (as she would one day) what had happened could be devastating, an operation of this nature is, in my view, contra-indicated.

For these, and for the other reasons to which I have adverted, I have come to the conclusion that this operation is neither medically indicated nor necessary, and that it would not be in D's best interest for it to be performed.

It is clear in *Re D* that once a child is made a ward of court, the court will do everything it can to protect the best interests of that child. This will include overriding the desires of the mother and the doctors to perform a non-therapeutic surgical procedure on that child. In the later case of *Re B* (1988), Lord Templeman confirmed that only the courts could authorise the non-therapeutic sterilisation of a child.

CASE EXTRACT

B (A Minor) (Wardship: Sterilisation), Re [1988] AC 199

Facts: B was a girl aged 17 and mentally handicapped. She was becoming sexually aware. The council in whose care she had been placed applied to have her made a ward of court so that leave could be given for a sterilisation operation because B could not understand that intercourse caused childbirth, the principles of contraception, could not cope with normal childbirth, and could not function as a mother.

Held: This is a decision for the High Court.

Lord Templeman (at pages 205–6): In my opinion sterilisation of a girl under 18 should only be carried out with the leave of a High Court judge. A doctor performing a sterilisation operation with the consent of the parents might still be liable in criminal, civil or professional proceedings. A court exercising the wardship jurisdiction emanating from the Crown is the only authority which is empowered to authorise such a drastic step as sterilisation after a full and informed investigation. [...] Expert evidence will be adduced setting out the reasons for the application, the history, conditions, circumstances and foreseeable future of the girl, the risks and consequences of pregnancy, the risks and consequences of sterilisation, the practicability of alternative precautions against pregnancy and any other relevant information. The judge may order additional evidence to be obtained. In my opinion, a decision should only be made by a High Court judge. In the Family Division a judge is selected for his or her experience, ability and compassion. No one has suggested a more satisfactory tribunal or a more satisfactory method of reaching a decision which vitally concerns an individual but also involves principles of law, ethics and medical practice. Applications for sterilisation will be rare.

In addition to making a child a ward of court and using inherent jurisdiction, a court can use statutory powers to enforce medical treatment upon a child. Under s. 8(1) the Children Act 1989, a court can grant the following two orders in relation to medical treatment:

- *A prohibited steps order*: a parent cannot do a certain act without the consent of the court.

- *A specific issue order*: directions to be followed in relation to parental responsibility.

If, for example, the courts wanted to authorise the vaccination of a child, as seen in *Re C* (2003) (above), they would issue a *specific issue* order. If, however, the courts wished to prevent a parent from consenting to non-therapeutic surgery, they would issue a *prohibited steps* order. The Children Act of 1989 is only relevant to medical law in small parts, but a fundamental principle under section 1(1) of the 1989 Act is applied to all areas of law that involve children, especially decisions in medicine. That principle is: 'the child's welfare shall be the court's paramount consideration'. The courts should consider a child's social, emotional, environmental, physical and clinical interests when deciding whether or not a particular treatment is in his or her best interests. The official checklist is contained in the Children Act 1989.

Children Act 1989

Section 1: Welfare of the child

(3) a court shall have regard in particular to –

    (a) the ascertainable wishes and feelings of the child concerned (considered in the light of his age and understanding);

    (b) his physical, emotional and educational needs;

    (c) the likely effect on him of any change in his circumstances;

    (d) his age, sex, background and any characteristics of his which the court considers relevant;

    (e) any harm which he has suffered or is at risk of suffering;

    (f) how capable each of his parents, and any other person in relation to whom the court considers the question to be relevant, is of meeting his needs;

    (g) the range of powers available to the court under this Act in the proceedings in question.

The General Medical Council provides additional guidance to doctors.

EXTRACT

General Medical Council, Explanatory Guidance, 0–18 years: Guidance for all Doctors (2007):

www.gmc-uk.org

Section 12: An assessment of best interests will include what is clinically indicated in a particular case. You should also consider:

a. the views of the child or young person, so far as they can express them, including any previously expressed preferences;

b. the views of parents;

c. the views of others close to the child or young person;

d. the cultural, religious or other beliefs and values of the child or parents;

e. the views of other healthcare professionals involved in providing care to the child or young person, and of any other professionals who have an interest in their welfare;

f. which choice, if there is more than one, will least restrict the child or young person's future options.

Cultural, social and religious views are clearly important, but they do not automatically decide the issue. The courts can also authorise the use of force against child patients, but, as with incompetent adults, only if it is in their best interests. *DB* (1997) is the accepted authority for this rule.

Wolverhampton MBC v DB (A Minor) [1997] 1 FLR 767

Facts: A teenager (B) was a cocaine addict and she was pregnant. She experienced serious complications but had a phobia of needles. She wanted to discharge herself from hospital.

Held: B had a right to refuse to give consent to medical treatment as she was over 16 years (she was 17 and so had not reached the age of majority), but that right could be overridden by the court or a person with parental responsibility for her. B's refusal was an important factor, but it carried little weight as it had been demonstrated that she could neither comprehend and retain information about her treatment, nor believe such information, and was unable to make a reasoned choice about her treatment. The local authority and her mother having parental responsibility could take steps to protect her best interests, which could permit the use of reasonable force in order to administer the correct treatment. An order would be made that the local authority was entitled to administer such treatment as was medically required with the use of reasonable force necessary to prevent her death or serious deterioration of health.

It is an uncomfortable thought that reasonable force can be used against a refusing teenage patient, but if the age of majority has not been met, and the teenager is showing signs of incompetence, it may be in her best interests to restrain her in order to save her and her unborn child.

Do you think that the courts are well equipped, in terms of common law rules and professional regulations, to fairly judge the best interests of a child?

 ## Children: competent

Despite the age of majority being widely accepted at 18, it was still not clear in law just how old a teenager could be before a consent to treatment could be acted upon by a doctor.

This is the issue in *Gillick* (1986), a case which radically changed the law. As a result of the judgment in *Gillick*, a minor aged 15 years or under, who is deemed to be competent, can *consent* to medical treatment without their parent's knowledge or permission.

Gillick v West Norfolk and Wisbech AHA [1986] AC 112

Facts: Mrs Gillick had several daughters under 16. She became aware of a Memorandum of Guidance, issued from the Department of Health and Social Security (DHSS), which allowed a doctor to give contraceptive advice and treatment to her daughters without her consent. She wrote to the local health authority seeking assurance that no contraceptive advice or treatment would be issued to her daughters without her knowledge or consent, and they refused. Mrs Gillick sought a declaration from the courts that the memorandum was unlawful.

Held: The Court of Appeal supported Mrs Gillick, but the House of Lords allowed the DHSS appeal.

Lord Fraser (at pages 169, 174): It seems to me verging on the absurd to suggest that a girl or a boy aged 15 could not effectively consent, for example, to have a medical examination of some trivial injury to his body or even to have a broken arm set. Of course the consent of the parents should normally be asked, but they may not be immediately available. Provided the patient, whether a boy or a girl, is capable of understanding what is proposed, and of expressing his or her own wishes, I see no good reason for holding that he or she lacks the capacity to express them validly and effectively and to authorise the medical man to make the examination or give the treatment which he advises. [...] The only practicable course is to entrust the doctor with a discretion to act in accordance with his view of what is best in the interests of the girl who is his patient. He should, of course, always seek to persuade her to tell her parents that she is seeking contraceptive advice, and the nature of the advice that she receives. [...] But there may well be cases, and I think there will be some cases, where the girl refuses either to tell the parents herself or to permit the doctor to do so and in such cases, the doctor will, in my opinion, be justified in proceeding without the parents' consent or even knowledge provided he is satisfied on the following matters: (1) that the girl (although under 16 years of age) will understand his advice; (2) that he cannot persuade her to inform her parents or to allow him to inform the parents that she is seeking contraceptive advice; (3) that she is very likely to begin or to continue having sexual intercourse with or without contraceptive treatment; (4) that unless she receives contraceptive advice or treatment her physical or mental health or both are likely to suffer; (5) that her best interests require him to give her contraceptive advice, treatment or both without the parental consent.

Lord Scarman (at pages 188–9): I would hold that as a matter of law the parental right to determine whether or not their minor child below the age of 16 will have medical treatment terminates if and when the child achieves a sufficient understanding and intelligence to enable him or her to understand fully what is proposed. It will be a question of fact whether a child seeking advice has sufficient understanding of what is involved to give a consent valid in law. Until the child achieves the capacity to consent, the parental right to make the decision continues save only in exceptional circumstances.

The case of *Gillick* consolidated several principles: a competent patient under 16 can consent to medical treatment without the knowledge or consent of her parents; it may be in a competent minor's best interests to consent to treatment without the knowledge or consent of her patents; there is a five-part test in order to ascertain '*Gillick* competence'; a doctor will not face criminal charges if he advises or treats a competent patient under the age of 16; and there may be social ramifications if a teenager could not visit her doctor in confidence and receive contraceptive advice and treatment. Lord Fraser's five-part test is as follows:

(1) the girl will understand the medical advice;
(2) the doctor cannot persuade her to inform her parents or allow him to inform the parents that she is seeking contraceptive advice;
(3) she is very likely to begin or to continue having sexual intercourse with or without contraceptive treatment;

(4) unless she receives contraceptive advice or treatment her physical or mental health or both are likely to suffer;

(5) her best interests require him to give her contraceptive advice, treatment or both without the parental consent.

This test is quite strict at first glance. It does not give a doctor a green light to simply dish out contraceptives for no apparent reason. The competent minor must be likely to suffer if she does not receive the advice or treatment and it must, of course, be in her best interests. This test is not completely new: case law has already shown that a court will put the best interests of a child over the views of the parents.

In 2006, the *Gillick* competence test was applied to abortion.

CASE EXTRACT

R (on the application of Axon) v *Secretary of State for Health* [2006] QB 539

Facts: This was a judicial review sought by parents of Department of Health Guidelines which allowed doctors to advise people under the age of 16 on contraception, sexually transmitted diseases and abortion. Mrs Axon, who had five children, claimed that the guidance was unlawful because it would permit a doctor to perform an abortion on one of her daughters without her knowledge. She also claimed that it was a breach of her family life under Article 8 of the European Convention on Human Rights.

Held: The procedure of abortion may have been more intrusive, but there was no reason why Lord Fraser's *Gillick* competence criteria could not be applied to another medical procedure.

Silber J (at page 569): The speeches of Lord Fraser, Lord Scarman and Lord Bridge [in *Gillick*] do not indicate or suggest that their conclusions depended in any way upon the nature of the treatment proposed because the approach in their speeches was and is of general application to all forms of medical advice and treatment.

Silber J in *Axon* was clearly persuaded by Lord Scarman's strong words in *Gillick* that a parental right to consent *terminates* when the child becomes competent because of the far-reaching consequences that could result (i.e. secrecy and teenage pregnancy) if their confidentiality was not respected. Mrs Axon's contention that her right to family life was breached was thrown out by Silber J, who concluded that the autonomy of a young person must undermine any Article 8 rights of a parent to family life.

How far does Gillick competence stretch?

The medical profession have recognised *Gillick* competence and enshrined it into all the relevant medical guidelines. For example, the General Medical Council states that when it comes to gleaning a competent consent from a child, the doctor must use the correct communication tools to achieve an honest answer. The following provisions are clearly derived from the criteria in *Gillick*.

EXTRACT

General Medical Council, Explanatory Guidance, 0–18 years: Guidance for all Doctors (2007):

www.gmc-uk.org

Paragraph 14: Effective communication between doctors and children and young people is essential to the provision of good care. You should find out what children, young people and their parents want and need to know, what issues are important to them, and what opinions or fears they have about their health or treatment. In particular you should:

(a) involve children and young people in discussions about their care;

(b) be honest and open with them and their parents, while respecting confidentiality;

(c) listen to and respect their views about their health, and respond to their concerns and preferences;

(d) explain things using language or other forms of communication they can understand;

(e) consider how you and they use non-verbal communication, and the surroundings in which you meet them;

(f) give them opportunities to ask questions, and answer these honestly and to the best of your ability;

(g) do all you can to make open and truthful discussion possible, taking into account that this can be helped or hindered by the involvement of parents or other people;

(h) give them the same time and respect that you would give to adult patients.

The General Medical Council places a duty upon on the doctor to ensure that the child patient can communicate effectively. These guidelines recognise that even competent children may need to be put at ease and encouraged to be honest before they can issue their consent. There should not, therefore, be an assumption that just because a child cannot express their views, they are automatically unable to consent for themselves. A procedure may be so overwhelming and confusing for the child that it is only until he or she sits down with a doctor who uses effective methods of communication that the child can reveal their honest thoughts about it all. Once the doctor has had an opportunity to talk to the child, he must be convinced that the child is *Gillick* competent.

EXTRACT

General Medical Council, Explanatory Guidance, 0–18 years: Guidance for all Doctors (2007):

www.gmc-uk.org

Paragraph 24: You must decide whether a young person is able to understand the nature, purpose and possible consequences of investigations or treatments you propose, as well as the consequences of not having treatment. Only if they are able to understand, retain, use and weigh this information, and communicate their decision to others can they consent to that investigation or treatment. That means you must make sure that all relevant information has been provided and thoroughly discussed before deciding whether or not a child or young person has the capacity to consent.

The *Gillick* judgment is clearly far-reaching and throws a lot of support behind minors who have 'sufficient understanding and intelligence' (as per Lord Scarman) to consent to their medical treatment. However, case law since *Gillick* has revealed that there are limits to *Gillick* competence. Minors do not have as much freedom as first thought:

- *Gillick* competence applies to issues of *consent* only: it will support a consent that is in the *best interests* of the minor.

- Refusals are *not* covered by *Gillick* competence: they will probably be deemed as proof of *incompetence*.

To put it another way, if a minor refused treatment, a competent parent (or a court) will simply consent on his behalf.[8] This is because, if a minor makes a foolish decision, it will be viewed as evidence that he or she does not have sufficient understanding or intelligence. These principles have come to light in a string of controversial cases concerning minors and life-saving treatment.

CASE EXTRACT

Re E (A Minor) (Wardship: Medical Treatment) [1993] 1 FLR 386

Facts: A 15-year-old patient was suffering from leukaemia (a cancer of the blood), and wanted to refuse his blood transfusion because he was a Jehovah's Witness. His parents supported this. The minor was clearly intelligent and met the *Gillick* criteria. The local authority made him a ward of court because he was in a critical condition.

Held: The *Gillick* criteria was not enough when making a decision this grave: an understanding of the manner of death and the extent of his family's suffering was required. It was in his best interests to have a blood transfusion.

Ward J: I find that A is a boy of sufficient intelligence to be able to take decisions about his own wellbeing, but I also find that there is a range of decisions of which some are outside his ability fully to grasp their implications. Impressed though I was by his obvious intelligence, by his calm discussion of the implications, by his assertion even that he would refuse well knowing that he may die as a result, in my judgment A does not have a full understanding of the whole implication of what the refusal of that treatment involves. I am quite satisfied that A does not have any sufficient comprehension of the pain he has yet to suffer, of the fear he will be undergoing, of the distress not only occasioned by that fear but also – and importantly – the distress he will inevitably suffer as he, a loving son, helplessly watches his parent's and his family's distress. They are a close family, and they are a brave family, but I find that he has no realisation of the full implications which lie before him as to the process of dying. He may have some concept of the fact that he will die, but as to the manner of his death and to the extent of his and his family's suffering I find he has not the ability to turn his mind to it nor the will to do so. If, therefore, this case depended upon my finding of whether or not A is of sufficient understanding and intelligence and maturity to give full and informed consent, I find that he is not. One has to admire – indeed one is almost baffled by – the courage of the conviction that he expresses. He is, he says, prepared to die for his faith. That makes him a martyr by itself. But I regret that I find it essential for his wellbeing to protect him from himself and his parents, and so I override his and his parents' decision.

---

[8] This was confirmed in *Re R (A Minor) (Wardship: Consent to Treatment)* [1992] Fam 11 CA.

Ward J's comments are interesting in that there appears to be an assumption that a minor would not understand the 'full implications as to the process of dying' but that an adult would. This is not the case. There are probably many adults who do not understand, or refuse to acknowledge, the process of dying and the inevitable pain and distress that a refusal will cause, but they are allowed in law to have their refusal respected as long as it is fully informed and competent. It appears from Ward J's judgment that if a minor had a deep-rooted and fully informed understanding of the pain, suffering and manner of death that would be endured by himself and his family as a result of his refusal, he might be more readily deemed as competent by the courts to make that decision. This would be rare, but is not impossible. However, support has been found for the decision in *Re E*.

> ## EXTRACT
>
> ### Nigel Lowe and Satvinder Juss, 'Medical Treatment – Pragmatism and the Search for Principle' (1993) 56 *Modern Law Review* 865, at pages 865–72
>
> If a doctor believes that a particular treatment is necessary for his patient, it is perfectly rational for the law to facilitate this as easily as possible and hence allow a '*Gillick* competent' child to give a valid consent, and also to protect the child against parents opposed to what is professionally considered to be in his best interests. In contrast, it is surely right for the law to be reluctant to allow a *child* of whatever age to be able to veto treatment designed for his or her benefit, particularly if a refusal would lead to the child's death or permanent damage. In other words, the clear and consistent policy of the law is to protect the child against wrong-headed parents and against himself.

The decision in *Re E* was followed in one year later in *Re S*.

> ## CASE EXTRACT
>
> ### *Re S (A Minor) (Wardship: Medical Treatment)* [1994] 2 FLR 1065
>
> **Facts**: A 15-year-old patient suffering from a serious illness no longer wanted to undergo monthly blood transfusions. This decision would have ended her life. She argued that she was *Gillick* competent to refuse her treatment.
>
> **Held**: She was not competent to make this decision.
>
> **Johnson J**: It does not seem to me that her capacity is commensurate with the gravity of the decision which she has made. It seems to me that an understanding that she will die is not enough. For her decision to carry weight she should have a greater understanding of the manner of the death and pain and the distress.

Johnson J in *Re S* did not expressly announce that *Gillick* did not apply to refusals. Rather, it appears that minors are deemed not to have sufficient understanding when it comes to making *grave* decisions. The nature of the pain and distress of death must be fully understood by the minor. The trail of cases continues with *Re L* (1998) in which another teenage minor refused a blood transfusion as a result of her religious beliefs.

CASE EXTRACT

Re L (Medical Treatment: Gillick Competence) [1998] 2 FLR 810

Facts: A 14-year-old minor (L) was critically injured had refused, on religious grounds, to consent to life saving medical treatment because it would involve blood transfusions. The hospital authority sought leave to carry out the treatment without her consent. The question for the court turned on whether L was competent to withhold consent within the rule in *Gillick*.

Held: Despite her maturity, L was still a child. Although her beliefs were sincere, they had not been developed through a broad and informed adult experience, but through her sheltered upbringing within the Jehovah's Witness community. She knew she would die without the treatment but had not been informed of the likely gruesome nature of her death (this was in fact deliberately held from her). She was therefore not *Gillick* competent and it was in her best interests for the treatment to be carried out.

Re L appears to ignore a fundamental element of the *Gillick* competence test: that the child has *sufficient understanding* of her medical treatment. L was deliberately kept in the dark as to the nature of her death, and so she was given insufficient information. The *Gillick* competency test should not apply unless the minor has been given *all* the relevant facts, although it should be noted that the patient in *Re L* had a strict religious upbringing and therefore was limited in her understanding the world. Commentators have noted this unfair decision.

EXTRACT

Andrew Grubb, 'Commentary on Re L (Medical Treatment: *Gillick* Competency)' (1999) 7 *Medical Law Review* 58, at page 60

The facts that L was ignorant of the detail that the court required her to understand was hardly her fault. This did not render her incompetent; rather, it left her uninformed. It cannot be right that a doctor may manipulate a patient's capacity to make a decision by failing to provide relevant information.

Despite the possible manipulation of the minor in *Re L*, the cases of *Re E* and *Re S* above illustrate that even when a minor is fully informed and perfectly intelligent, the court will still require a higher level of understanding in regards to the manner of pain, distress and death. It seems that *Gillick* competence is almost impossible to apply to refusals of life-saving treatment. This was confirmed in the more recent case of *Re P* (2003).

CASE EXTRACT

Re P (A Child) [2003] EWHC 2327

Facts: A 17-year-old patient (J) inherited a disease of weak blood vessels. His condition became critical and the hospital sought permission to administer a blood transfusion should he have a critical episode, but he refused as he was a Jehovah's Witness. His parent's supported his decision.

Held: J's best interests in the widest sense were met by permitting the doctors to administer blood as a last resort if J's situation became immediately life threatening.

→

Johnson J (at paras 9–12): There may be cases as a child approaches the age of 18 when his refusal would be determinative. A court will have to consider whether to override the wishes of a child approaching the age of majority when the likelihood is that all that will have been achieved will have been deferment of an inevitable death and for a matter only of months. [...] I have to seek to achieve what is best for John and I put at the forefront of my consideration his wishes. He is nearly 17. He is a young man with established convictions. He is undoubtedly a young man whose religious faith must surely demand the respect of all about him. In a world in which religious or indeed any other convictions are not commonly held, John is a young man to be respected. So too the wishes of his loving and committed parents. They do not wish him to die. They want what is best for him and their assessment of what is best for him is that he should be spared the administration of blood and blood products. Of course, cooperation between doctor and patient is at the heart of medical treatment if it is to be successful, and treatment which is imposed against the will of the patient is surely to be avoided wherever possible. I find there to be weighty and compelling reasons why this order should not be made. [...] Nonetheless, looking at the interests of John in the widest possible sense – medical, religious, social, whatever they be – my decision is that John's best interests in those widest senses will be met if I make an order in the terms sought by the NHS Trust with the addition of those extra words, 'unless no other form of treatment is available'.

This judgment is interesting in that Johnson J seems to have convinced himself that the order for treatment in this case should not be made, before finally making the order with no real evidence to support his decision. There is no mention of John failing to satisfy the *Gillick* competence test. It is almost as if there is a blanket assumption that, if the minor has not reached the age of majority, he or she cannot refuse life-saving treatment.

Commentators have argued that a right to consent automatically comes with a right to refuse. This is because, to understand a situation well enough to consent to it means that the consequences of refusal have also been well understood.

EXTRACT

John Harris, 'Consent and End of Life Decisions' (2003) 29 *Journal of Medical Ethics* 10, at page 12

The idea that a child (or anyone) might competently consent to a treatment but not be competent to refuse it is a palpable nonsense, the reasons for which are revealed by a moment's reflection on what a competent consent involves. To give an informed consent you need to understand the nature of the course of action to which you are consenting, which, in medical contexts, will include its probable and possible consequences and side effects and the nature of any alternative measures which might be taken and the consequences of doing nothing. So, to understand a proposed treatment well enough to consent to it is to understand the consequences of a refusal. And if the consequences of a refusal are understood well enough to consent to the alternative then the refusal must also be competent.

Gillick: consent vs refusal

The cases of *Re E*, *Re S*, *Re L* and *Re P* (above) came to the conclusion that, regardless of the desire of the teenage patient to refuse treatment, the authorisation of treatment was in the best interests of him and his family. In *Re E* and *Re P* in particular, the courts were persuaded by the intelligence and understanding of the minor, yet still felt that they were unable to support the refusal of treatment. None of these cases expressly stated that *Gillick* competence drew a clear line between consent and refusal. *Re R* (1992) took a clearer approach, and Lord Donaldson expressly stated that *Gillick* was applicable to consent only.

CASE EXTRACT	*Re R (A Minor) (Wardship: Consent To Treatment)* [1992] Fam 11 CA

Facts: A 15-year-old minor (R) suffered from bouts of violent and suicidal behaviour. During a competent spell, she said she did not consent to any further drug therapy. The local authority applied for permission to override her decision.

Held: When a minor is a ward of court, the court can override the consent or refusal of the minor, and the fluctuating nature of R's illness meant that she was not *Gillick* competent anyway.

Lord Donaldson MR (at pages 23–5): In a case in which the '*Gillick* competent' child refuses treatment, but the parents consent, that consent *enables* treatment to be undertaken lawfully. [...] In a case in which the positions are reversed, it is the child's consent which is the enabling factor and the parents' refusal of consent is not determinative. [...] In this case [...] the judges treated *Gillick* as deciding that a '*Gillick* competent' child has a right to refuse treatment. In this I consider that they were in error. Such a child can consent, but if he or she declines to do so or refuses, consent can be given by someone else who has parental rights or responsibilities. The failure or refusal of the '*Gillick* competent' child is a very important factor in the doctor's decision whether or not to treat, but does not prevent the necessary consent being obtained from another competent source.

Lord Donaldson MR is clear that if a child refuses medical treatment, consent can simply be gleaned from another competent source. This restricts the ambit of *Gillick* to just consent. Lord Donaldson MR returned a year later in *Re W* (1993) (below) to support his earlier ruling. This case also involved the Family Law Reform Act 1969, which states the following.

Family Law Reform Act 1969

Section 8

(1) The consent of a minor who has attained the age of sixteen years to any surgical, medical or dental treatment which, in the absence of consent, would constitute a trespass to his person, shall be as effective as it would be if he were of full age; and where a minor has by virtue of this section given an effective consent to any treatment it shall not be necessary to obtain any consent for it from his parent or guardian.

The provision under section 8(1) of the 1969 Act means that *Gillick* competence need only apply to minors aged 15 and under. However, note that section 8(1) covers consent only. It is silent as to the refusal of medical treatment.

CASE EXTRACT

Re W (A Minor) (Medical Treatment: Court's Jurisdiction), Re [1993] Fam 64

Facts: W, a girl of 16, was suffering from anorexia nervosa. Section 8(1) of the Family Law Reform Act 1969 states that a minor who has reached the age of 16 may consent to medical treatment without the consent of her parents. Treatment was authorised by the courts against W's wishes. The question was whether those with parental rights in respect of W could override her refusal.

Held: A refusal can be overridden if the patient has not reached the age of majority.

Lord Donaldson MR (at page 81): A feature of anorexia nervosa is that it is capable of destroying the ability to make an informed choice. It creates a compulsion to refuse treatment or only to accept treatment which is likely to be ineffective. This attitude is part and parcel of the disease and the more advanced the illness, the more compelling it may become. [...] There is ample authority for the proposition that the inherent powers of the court under its *parens patriae* jurisdiction are theoretically limitless and that they certainly extend beyond the powers of a natural parent. There can therefore be no doubt that it has power to override the refusal of a minor, whether over the age of 16 or under that age but '*Gillick* competent'.

Re R and *Re W* clearly state that a minor's refusal will be overruled by the court's jurisdiction up until the age of 18. This means that a refusal under the rules of *Gillick* has been rejected, and section 8(1) of the Family Law Reform Act 1969 allows a 16-year-old to consent only. However, the cases of *Re E*, *Re S*, *Re L* and *Re P* (above) did not view *Gillick* in this narrow way, and chose instead to focus on the minor's level of understanding and intelligence.

There has been plenty of commentary about Lord Donaldson's judgments and the implications they have on the autonomy of minors. To start off with, some have argued that the courts should simply be more open about the fact that the rights of minors are suppressed.

EXTRACT

Caroline Bridge, 'Religious Beliefs and Teenage Refusal of Medical Treatment' (1999) 62 *Modern Law Review* 585, at page 594

The law should openly declare that welfare reigns when grave decisions with momentous outcomes are considered and recognise that adolescent autonomy is, inevitably, circumscribed.

Andrew Grubb, 'Commentary on *Re L* (Medical Treatment: *Gillick* Competency)' (1999) 7 *Medical Law Review* 58, at pages 58–61

Clearly, the court is striving to act on its 'hunch' that society should not let children make a decision to die. [...] Until [the point of majority], the protective duty of society permits intervention. If this is the public policy of this country, it would be far better for the courts [...] simply to say so rather than to obfuscate matters by distorting the legal concept of competence.

John Eekelaar, 'White Coats or Flak Jackets? Children and the Courts Again' (1993) 109 *Law Quarterly Review* 182, at pages 182–7

Lord Donaldson seems to be reluctant to accept that the law should protect minors, even if competent, in the same manner. Rather, his primary concern is to fashion the law so as to minimise the risk of legal action against doctors.

To conclude this difficult area of medical law, the position can be stated as follows:

- Under section 8(1) of the Family Law Reform Act 1969 a minor aged 16 can consent to medical treatment.
- Under *Gillick* (1986) a minor aged 15 or under can be shown to be competent to consent to medical treatment.
- Under *Re R* (1992) and *Re W* (1993), section 8(1) and *Gillick* do not give a child a legal right to refuse treatment meaning that consent can simply be sought from another source.
- Under *Re E* (1993), *Re S* (1994), *Re L* (1998) and *Re P* (2003), in order to competently refuse life-saving treatment a child must show an additional level of understanding as to the pain, distress and manner of death that would result from a refusal.

For the minor, this all means that they do not have a legal right to refuse treatment until the age of majority (which is 18).

Terry is 17. He is sick of blood transfusions. He knows he will have to endure them every few weeks for the rest of his life because of a rare blood disorder. He wants to refuse any further treatment, knowing that it will end in his death. He expresses his thoughts to his parents but they are horrified and refuse to believe that Terry has adequately weighed up the consequences of his decision. He says he is 18 tomorrow, and is looking forward to refusing his next treatment. However, he is rushed into hospital the night before with complications and needs a transfusion, which is found at 23:52 pm. The doctor says he'll 'be back in a minute' to glean consent from the parents, but Terry is adamant that he does not want the transfusion and that he is perfectly clear in his mind what he wants and that he will 'have the same view in eight minutes time'. How are his doctors going to deal with him?

Consenting to risks

The notion that consent should be informed is an important one. A patient must be aware of the risks before consenting to the treatment. A patient must also be informed about anything else that might be relevant, such as alternatives to surgery, the chances of success and the prognosis after treatment (i.e. what effect will it have on the illness?). A patient does not need to be informed of every minor detail, but he or she must be 'adequately' informed. This is, of course, very difficult to measure and will depend on the kind of treatment being sought. The difficulty in this area of medical law is when one of those 'risks' transpires and the patient argues that had she known about that particular risk, she would not have consented to the treatment. A good example may be an operation on the spine which comes with a 2% risk of paralysis, and the patient wakes up paralysed. It is likely that a patient will argue that the doctor did not provide her with sufficient information and she was harmed as a direct result, meaning that he breached his duty of care and could face a claim in negligence. There are professional standards of care that a doctor must meet, and if a doctor falls below those professional standards, he may be found to have administered the treatment negligently. The law of tort looks for a 'reasonable standard of care' through its collection of case law (*Bolam*), and this is supplemented by professional medical guidelines which are very strict. The resulting law is not satisfactory, and it is not entirely clear just how much information is needed in order for consent to be 'fully informed'.

The duty to inform

An old case from 1767 highlighted that for very serious operations, the doctor usually sought consent.

CASE EXTRACT

Slater v *Baker & Stapleton* (1767) 95 ER 850

Facts: A patient had his leg re-fractured by a surgeon and then placed in a stretching apparatus to lengthen it during the healing process. This was in the days before anaesthetic, and it was incredibly painful for the patient who was not asked for his consent.

Held: It is reasonable that a patient should be told what is about to be done to him, that he may take courage and put himself in such a situation as to enable him to undergo the operation.

There was no clearly accepted rule on consent in medical law in 1767, but it was assumed to be good practice to ask the patient for consent before a serious procedure. This would allow, as the courts concluded, for the patient to 'prepare' himself for the procedure. The doctor in *Slater* was found to have improperly breached his professional conduct, but in the judgment there is no mention of patient autonomy, trespass to the person or a breach of trust. The principle of autonomy has only really developed in the last few decades.

The development of patient freedom

In medicine today, the patient takes an interest in his or her own needs, and is entitled to know all about the proposed treatment and related risks before consenting to it. Science has developed so quickly and real cures are so readily available that patients are becoming more interested in what is available to them. This transfers a lot of the power back onto the shoulders of the patient.

> ### EXTRACT
>
> ## Michael Jones, 'Informed Consent and Other Fairy Stories' (1999) 7 *Medical Law Review* 103, at page 129
>
> Patients expect to be at a disadvantage, because of their lack of knowledge, their lack of training, and sometimes because we want to believe desperately that the doctor is all knowing and all powerful and therefore will definitely make the correct diagnosis and provide a complete cure. Part of the imbalance between doctor and patient is due to the patient's lack of information, and, on one view, it is the function of the law to redress the imbalance by providing patients with the 'right' to be given that information, or perhaps more accurately imposing a duty on doctors to provide it.

We have already seen that a competent adult can refuse life-saving treatment, even if the decision is irrational, and a competent minor can consent to treatment without the knowledge or consent of her parents. Patients are also entitled to explore their many different treatment options, from surgical procedures to home remedies, and the internet makes research about alternative treatments, especially those that are available abroad, much more accessible. A patient cannot return to his doctor and demand a particular surgical treatment, but he can become clued-up as to the risks and any alternatives that might be available. The final decision rests with the patient.

A common misunderstanding

A patient, when diagnosed with a serious illness, may not fully understand what is involved despite various explanations from a doctor. This may happen for a number of reasons. The patient may feel particularly vulnerable and simply assume that her family members are listening to the complicated details on her behalf, or the panic of the diagnosis may have a negative effect on her ability to understand technical details clearly, or put them into perspective. It follows that just because a doctor explains the details and risks to a patient, it does not mean that the patient understands them. This is complicated by the fact that it is unclear just how much information is needed in order for a patient to be 'informed'. At the moment, doctors have to estimate how much information is enough to exclude them from liability, and in some instances they may give away too much information, having the effect of frightening the patient, magnifying the risks in their eyes and hampering communication rather than encouraging it.

> ### EXTRACT
>
> ## PDG Skegg, 'English Medical Law and "Informed Consent": An Antipodean Assessment and Alternative' (1999) 7 *Medical Law Review* 135–65, at page 138
>
> It is regrettable, although understandable, that it was not the expression 'sufficiently informed consent' which became so common. This would have alerted users to the fact that there is an issue of how informed it is necessary to be, in the context and for the purpose in question.

A patient will usually meet a doctor on one or two occasions to discuss the medical procedure or treatment, its benefits and risks, and a schedule for treatment before signing a consent form. This is usually the only opportunity to talk to the doctor about the risks.

Battery or negligence?

When a doctor fails to provide adequate information to a patient and as a result, that patient consents to a treatment and then finds that one of the unknown risks has transpired (e.g. paralysis), can the doctor face an action in criminal law (assault), civil law (trespass) or negligence? Technically, the answer is all three:

- **The crime of assault**: the doctor touched, treated or operated on the patient without a fully informed consent.
- **The tort of trespass**: the consent is invalid if it is not fully informed, meaning that the doctor trespassed upon the patient.
- **Negligence**: the doctor has breached his duty of care by not providing adequate information.

The criminal offence of assault is almost identical to the civil law of trespass in that the patient is touched without consent. However, this kind of action is very rare. It is far more common for a patient to pursue the negligence route. This is because, if a patient wishes to pursue a criminal assault or the tort of trespass, they must prove that their consent was not valid. This is extremely difficult, because in cases where the patient was given inadequate information, he or she *still consented* to the general procedure. Consent is not the main issue in negligence, it is the *breach of duty* which is the crux of the matter.

(e) The crime of assault and the tort of trespass

Although there have only been a small handful of 'inadequate information' cases under the tort of trespass, they are still worth exploring in order to identify where the boundaries of liability lie. It is important to stress that the cases in this area do not involve a complete lack of consent. Rather, the patient has been deceived or inadequately informed in some way and this has led to the consent being vitiated (i.e. cancelled). A civil trespass and a criminal assault are almost identical in terms of the physical act and mental element. It follows that any cases in which a civil trespass has been committed, it is very likely that a criminal assault has been committed too. The widely-known case in this area is *Tabassum* (a criminal case).

CASE EXTRACT

R v Tabassum (Naveed) [2000] 2 Cr App R 328

Facts: T examined the breasts of three women in a breast cancer survey in order to put together a software package to sell to doctors. The victims consented on the belief that he was medically qualified or had medical training, but he had neither. He was convicted of sexual assault. He argued on appeal that they had consented to his actions.

Held: Consent was given on a mistaken belief and so it was not valid.

Rose LJ (at pages 334, 336–7): [The defence lawyer] accepts that there will be no genuine consent if, in the present circumstances, a woman is misled either as to the identity of the man who does the acts complained of, or as to the nature and quality of the act done. But, he submits, the nature and quality of the act, [...] does not, as he put it, 'extend back' to the qualifications of the defendant. The nature and quality of the defendant's

→

acts in touching the breasts of women to whom, in sexual terms he was a stranger, was unlawful and an indecent assault unless the complainants consented to that touching. On the evidence, [...] consent was given because they mistakenly believed that the defendant was medically qualified [...] and that, in consequence, the touching was for a medical purpose. As this was not so, there was no true consent. They were consenting to touching for medical purposes not to indecent behaviour, that is, there was consent to the nature of the act but not its quality. [...] Whether the defendant had any sexual motive or intent was irrelevant. The only issues were consent and whether the defendant may have believed that the complainants were consenting.

In *Tabassum* a conviction of indecent assault was more appropriate because of the nature of the touching. Interestingly, in *R v Richardson (Diane)* [1999] QB 444, a dentist was no longer qualified to treat her patients but because the patients were fully aware of her identity and the nature and quality of the act, her convictions for assault occasioning actual bodily harm were overturned.

The leading case of *Chatterton* (1981) confirms the limits of liability regarding the tort of trespass.

CASE EXTRACT

Chatterton v *Gerson* [1981] QB 432

Facts: The patient underwent a first operation with only limited knowledge as to the potential risks (according to her), and then underwent a second operation with no further explanation of the risks because she had already undergone the first. She lost the feeling in her right leg and argued that her consent was vitiated because of inadequate information.

Held: The patient was not successful.

Bristow J (at pages 439, 441–3): I have come to the conclusion that on the balance of probability Dr Gerson did give his usual explanation about the [treatment] and its implications of numbness instead of pain plus a possibility of slight muscle weakness, and that the plaintiff's recollection is wrong. [...]The claim against him is put in two ways: (i) that her consent to the operation was vitiated by lack of explanation of what the procedure was and what were its implications, so that she gave no real consent and the operation was in law a trespass to her person, that is, a battery. (ii) That Dr Gerson was under a duty, as part of his obligation to treat his patient with the degree of professional skill and care to be expected of a reasonably skilled practitioner, [...] to give the plaintiff such an explanation of the nature and implications of the proposed operation that she could come to an informed decision on whether she wanted to have it, or would prefer to go on living with the pain which it was intended to relieve [and] that such explanation as he gave was in breach of that duty. [...] In my judgment what the court has to do in each case is to look at all the circumstances and say: 'was there a real consent?' I think justice requires that in order to vitiate the reality of consent there must be a greater failure of communication between doctor and patient than that involved in a breach of duty if the claim is based on negligence. When the claim is based on negligence the plaintiff must prove not only the breach of duty to inform, but that had the duty not been broken she would not have chosen to have the operation. [...] In my judgment once the patient is informed in broad terms of the nature of the procedure which is intended, and gives her consent, that consent is real, and the cause of the action on which to base a claim for failure to go into risks and implications is negligence, not trespass.

The judgment of *Chatterton* clearly establishes that: (1) if a doctor fails to explain the *general nature* of an operation, consent is vitiated and an action in trespass is available; (2) if a doctor fails to explain the *risks and implications* of an operation, he has fallen below his duty of care and may face an action in negligence, and (3) the doctor only faces an action in negligence if the patient can prove that she would not have consented to the operation had she received the adequate information. The table below summarises the law.

The tort of trespass	The tort of negligence
The doctor fails to explain the *general nature* of the operation	The doctor fails to explain the risks and implications of the operation
Consent is vitiated: trespass	Duty of care is breached: negligence
Why: the procedure is not consented to	Why: the procedure was consented to

The successful case in the area of trespass is that of *Appleton* v *Garrett* (1997). In this case, the defendant dentist was particularly deceptive and malicious, which encouraged the courts to find blame in the tort of trespass rather than the tort of negligence.

CASE EXTRACT

Appleton v *Garrett* [1996] PIQR P1

Facts: The defendant (G) performed completely unnecessary dental work on the patient for his own financial gain. He was struck off the Dental Register and the patient brought an action in negligence and trespass. G admitted liability in negligence but contested trespass.

Held: This was a trespass to the person in the civil law of tort because the patient could not be said to have consented at all.

Dyson J (at pages 3–4): The evidence undoubtedly establishes that none of these eight plaintiffs was given any information on which to base a suitably informed consent. None was told why Mr Garrett was of the view that massive restorative treatment was required often on perfect teeth. Typically the plaintiff went for a normal routine check-up, and was subjected to the course of treatment without any explanation at all. [...] Mr Garrett deliberately embarked on large scale treatment of these plaintiffs which he knew was unnecessary and that he deliberately withheld from them the information that the treatment was unnecessary because he knew that they would not have consented had they known the true position. [...] I find, therefore, that none of the plaintiffs consented at any rate to the treatment of those teeth that required no treatment, and that at least in relation to those teeth the tort of trespass to the person has been made out.

The intentional deception of these patients put the defendant in *Appleton* was the crucial factor in this case. It is incredibly rare to see a medical case contain such deceptive behaviour on the part of the healthcare professional.

In instances where the patient is not touched by the doctor (e.g. medicines are simply prescribed) but the patient received inadequate information as to the treatment which gave rise to a risk, harm or injury, the tort of trespass, or the crime of assault, cannot be pursued because there must be *physical contact* in order to satisfy the legal criteria. The correct action for this lies in the tort of negligence because it is a breach of duty to *inform* a patient.

The tort of negligence

It is clear that when a patient consents to the 'general' nature of a medical procedure, her consent is valid whether she was adequately informed or not. However, the tort of negligence offers an avenue for damages where a patient consents to the general procedure but receives inadequate information about risks that leads to harm. A successful claim in negligence will require the following components:

- The doctor had a duty to provide adequate information.
- The doctor breached that duty by providing inadequate information.
- The inadequate information caused the resulting harm.

The third criterion is particularly difficult for a patient to prove. The breach of duty must be directly linked to the outcome. To put it another way, the inadequate information from the doctor must have directly caused the injury.

Component 1: duty of care

It is widely accepted and understood that a doctor has a duty of care towards his patients. A doctor also has a duty to adequately inform a patient of the risks of treatment so that her consent can be fully informed. What is 'adequate' is unclear and so depends on the circumstances.

Component 2: the duty is breached

A duty is breached when a person falls below a certain standard of care. A doctor will breach his duty when he fails to *adequately inform* a patient about the risks of her treatment or procedure. It is therefore vital that the term 'adequate' is clear. This will allow a doctor to confidently decide when he has covered all the relevant risks, and it will also allow a patient to gather all the relevant information in order to make an informed decision. The leading case in this area was *Bolam* (1957). This case established that a doctor will breach his duty towards a patient if he falls below the standard of care that is accepted by a 'responsible body of medical men'.

CASE EXTRACT

Bolam v Friern Hospital Management Committee [1957] 1 WLR 582

Facts: The plaintiff sustained fractures during the course of electro-conclusive therapy treatment given to him while he was a voluntary patient at the defendants' mental hospital. He claimed damages against the hospital alleging that the defendants were negligent (1) in failing to administer any relaxant drug prior to the passing of the current through his brain; (2) since they had not administered such a drug, in failing to provide at least some form of manual restraint or control beyond that given; and (3) in failing to warn him of the risks involved in the treatment.

Held: A doctor is not guilty of negligence if he has acted in accordance with a practice accepted as proper by a responsible body of medical men skilled in that particular form of treatment; nor is he negligent merely because there is a body of opinion which would adopt a different technique. In deciding whether a doctor is negligent in failing to warn a patient of the risks involved in a particular treatment, it is appropriate to consider firstly whether good medical practice required that a warning should have been given to the patient before he submitted to the treatment, and, secondly, if a warning had been given, what difference it would have made. The defendants (FHMC) won.

→

McNair J (in directing a jury) (at pages 586–7, 590–1): In the ordinary case which does not involve any special skill, negligence in law means a failure to do some act which a reasonable man in the circumstances would do. [...] He is the ordinary man. But where you get a situation which involves the use of some special skill or competence, [...] the test is the standard of the ordinary skilled man exercising and professing to have that special skill. In the case of a medical man, negligence means failure to act in accordance with the standards of reasonably competent medical men at the time. [...] I myself would prefer to put it this way, that he is not guilty of negligence if he has acted in accordance with a practice accepted as proper by a responsible body of medical men skilled in that particular art. [...] You have to make up your minds whether it has been proved to your satisfaction that when the defendants adopted the practice they did (namely, the practice of saying very little and waiting for questions from the patient), they were falling below a proper standard of competent professional opinion on this question of whether or not it is right to warn. Members of the jury, though it is a matter entirely for you, you may well think that when dealing with a mentally sick man and having a strong belief that his only hope of cure is E.C.T. treatment, a doctor cannot be criticised if he does not stress the dangers which he believes to be minimal involved in that treatment.

If you do come to the conclusion that proper practice requires some warning to be given, the second question which you have to decide is: if a warning had been given, would it have made any difference? The only man who really can tell you the answer to that question is the plaintiff, and he was never asked the question. [...] You might well take the view that unless the plaintiff has satisfied you that he would not have taken the treatment if he had been warned, there is really nothing in this point.

Bolam was a hugely important case for the medical profession and negligence. It confirmed that a doctor is negligent if he has not: 'acted in accordance with a practice accepted as proper by a responsible body of medical men skilled in that particular art'. If the negligent act involves a failure to warn, the jury must also ask themselves: 'if a warning had been given, would it have made any difference?' The patient will have to answer 'yes' in order for the action to continue in negligence.

The later case of *Sidaway* (1985) clarified the situation. This was a case directly involved with a failure to warn the patient about the risks of surgery which later materialised.

CASE EXTRACT

Sidaway v *Board of Governors of the Bethlem Royal Hospital* [1985] AC 871

Facts: Mrs Sidaway was advised by the hospital to have an operation on her spinal cord to cure a painful neck. She was warned of danger to the nerve root, but not of danger to the spinal cord. In the event, damage to the spinal cord, a risk of less than 1%, took place, and she was left severely disabled. She claimed damages for failure to warn her of all possible risks.

Held: Her claim was dismissed. A doctor was merely bound to disclose such information as was reasonable to enable a patient to make a rational choice of whether or not to accept the treatment. In the present case, in view of the small degree of risk involved, the judge [and the Court of Appeal] had been right to dismiss her claim.

Lord Scarman (at pages 882, 885, 888–90): Known as the 'doctrine of informed consent', it amounts to this: where there is a 'real' or a 'material' risk inherent in the proposed operation (however competently and skilfully performed) the question whether and to what extent a patient should be warned before he gives his consent is to be answered not by reference to medical practice but by accepting as a matter of law that, [...] a patient has a right to be informed of the risks inherent in the treatment which is proposed. [...] On the *Bolam* view of the law, therefore, even if she established that she was so deprived by the lack of a warning, she would have no remedy in negligence unless she could also prove that there was no competent and respected body of medical opinion which was in favour of no warning. Moreover, the tort of trespass to the person would not provide her with a remedy, for Mrs Sidaway did consent to the operation. [...] Ideally, the court should ask itself whether in the particular circumstances the risk was such that this particular patient would think it significant if he was told it existed. [...] The doctor will not be liable if upon a reasonable assessment of his patient's condition he takes the view that a warning would be detrimental to his patient's health.

Lord Diplock (at page 895): To decide what risks the existence of which a patient should be voluntarily warned and the terms in which such warning, if any, should be given, having regard to the effect that the warning may have, is as much an exercise of professional skill and judgment as any other part of the doctor's comprehensive duty of care to the individual patient, and expert medical evidence on this matter should be treated in just the same way. The *Bolam* test should be applied.

Lord Bridge (at pages 888–900): I should perhaps add at this point, although the issue does not strictly arise in this appeal, that, when questioned specifically by a patient of apparently sound mind about risks involved in a particular treatment proposed, the doctor's duty must, in my opinion be to answer both truthfully and as fully as the questioner requires. [...] A very wide variety of factors must enter into a doctor's clinical judgment not only as to what treatment is appropriate for a particular patient, but also as to how best to communicate to the patient the significant factors necessary to enable the patient to make an informed decision whether to undergo the treatment. [...] The issue whether non-disclosure in a particular case should be condemned as a breach of the doctor's duty of care is an issue to be decided primarily on the basis of expert medical evidence, applying the *Bolam* test.

Lord Templeman (at pages 903–5): There is no doubt that a doctor ought to draw the attention of a patient to a danger which may be special in kind or magnitude or special to the patient. [...] An obligation to give a patient all the information available to the doctor would often be inconsistent with the doctor's contractual obligation to have regard to the patient's best interests. Some information might confuse, other information might alarm a particular patient. Whenever the occasion arises for the doctor to tell the patient the results of the doctor's diagnosis, the possible methods of treatment and the advantages and disadvantages of the recommended treatment, the doctor must decide in the light of his training and experience and in the light of his knowledge of the patient what should be said and how it should be said. [...] The patient is free to decide whether or not to submit to treatment recommended by the doctor and therefore the doctor impliedly contracts to provide information which is adequate to enable the patient to reach a balanced judgment, subject always to the doctor's own obligation to say and do nothing which the doctor is satisfied will be harmful to the patient. [...] At the end of the day, the doctor, bearing in mind the best interests of the patient and bearing in mind the patient's right of information which will enable the patient to make a balanced judgment must decide what information should be given to the patient and in what terms that information should be couched.

The judgment, above, in *Sidaway* is very clear in terms of what the doctor must do, and to what standard his disclosure must reach.

The law can be defined as follows: (1) it is up to the doctor, using his expertise, to decide what risks should be disclosed to the patient, and (2) his disclosure, if questioned as a breach of duty, shall be judged according to the *Bolam* test. There is clearly support to withhold certain risks from a patient if these would be to harm or deter the patient in some way. However, if the risk is a grave one, or as Lord Bridge put it, 'a substantial risk of grave consequences', it is likely that the courts will conclude that the doctor should disclose that risk or face an action in negligence for breaching their duty of care. The decision in *Sidaway* was later affirmed in *Gold* v *Haringey* (1988).[9]

The *Bolam* test was applied slightly differently in the later case of *Smith* v *Tunbridge Wells Health Authority* [1994] 5 Med LR 334, in which an emphasis was placed upon 'reasonable' and 'responsible' explanations of risks. This is a slight expansion of the law, because the *Bolam* test merely requires a 'responsible body of medical men' to agree that the concealment of a risk is accepted practice, and does not go into an objective test about what is 'reasonable'. In *Pearce* (1998), the size of the risk in comparison with the mental state of the patient was examined.

CASE EXTRACT

Pearce v *United Bristol Healthcare NHS Trust* (1999) ECC 167

Facts: Mrs Pearce was told to wait for a natural birth, despite begging for an induced labour or a caesarean. There was a 0.2% risk of stillbirth by waiting, but this risk was not disclosed to the patient. The baby died before birth a few days later.

Held: The risk was too small for the doctor to act.

Lord Woolf MR (at pages 174–5): In a case where it is being alleged that a plaintiff has been deprived of the opportunity to make a proper decision as to what course he or she should take in relation to treatment, it seems to me to be the law [...] that if there is a significant risk which would affect the judgment of a reasonable patient, then in the normal course it is the responsibility of a doctor to inform the patient of that significant risk, if the information is needed so that the patient can determine for him or herself as to what course he or she should adopt. [...] Turning on the facts of this case, the next question is, therefore, 'was there a significant risk?' [...] On any basis, the increased risk of the stillbirth of Jacqueline, as a result of additional delay, was very small indeed. [...] Even looked at comprehensively it comes to something like 0.1–0.2%. The doctors called on behalf of the defendants did not regard that risk as significant, nor do I. [...] Particularly when one bears in mind Mrs Pearce's distressed condition, one cannot criticise Mr Niven's decision not to inform Mrs Pearce of that very, very small additional risk. [...] This is a case where, in my judgment, it would not be proper for the courts to interfere with the clinical opinion of the expert medical man responsible for treating Mrs Pearce. As to what would have been the consequence if she had been told of this particularly small risk, it is difficult to envisage, [...] but my conclusion is that, in so far as it was possible for this court to make an assessment of this, the inference is that if Mrs Pearce had been able to understand what she had been told about the increased risk, her decision would still have been to follow, reluctantly, the advice of the doctor who was treating her.

---

[9] *Gold* v *Haringey HA* [1988] QB 481.

It is clear from *Pearce* that when a particular risk has less than a 1% chance of materialising, and the patient is in a state of distress, the courts will probably support the doctor if he chooses not to disclose that risk. This follows from *Sidaway*, in which Lord Bridge supported the idea that only 'a substantial risk of grave consequences' should be put to the patient. However, Lord Woolf in *Pearce* did not consider the patient's opinion, he simply *assumes* that she would have followed the doctor's recommendations. The unanswered question is: is it enough that the *doctor* views the risk as grave, or would it suffice for the *patient* to view it as grave?[10] In *Chester* (2004), Lord Steyn examined the decision in *Pearce* and came to the conclusion that a patient has a legal right to be informed of serious injuries as part of the duty of care.

CASE EXTRACT

Chester v *Afshar* [2004] UKHL 41 (below)

Lord Steyn (at paras 15–16): How a surgeon's duty to warn a patient of a serious risk of injury fits into the tort of negligence was explained by Lord Woolf MR in *Pearce* v *United Bristol Healthcare NHS Trust* [1999] PIQR P53. A surgeon owes a legal duty to a patient to warn him or her in general terms of possible [...] serious risks involved in the procedure. The only qualification is that there may be wholly exceptional cases where objectively in the best interests of the patient the surgeon may be excused from giving a warning. [...] In modern law medical paternalism no longer rules and a patient has a *prima facie* right to be informed by a surgeon of a small, but well established, risk of serious injury as well as result of surgery.

Lord Steyn in *Chester* came to the conclusion that a patient has a legal right to be informed of serious risks unless it would be in her best interests to conceal them from her. However, the main issue still seems to be unclear: what would constitute 'serious injury' and from whose perspective is it deemed 'serious'? Lord Steyn rejected the idea of 'medical paternalism' meaning that more freedom, control and information could be offered to patients, but to what extent? The trail of cases continued in *Birch* (2008). This case can be distinguished on the grounds that the doctor failed to inform the patient about a less dangerous alternative treatment, as opposed to warning her of the risks of her current treatment.

CASE EXTRACT

Birch v *University College London Hospital NHS Foundation Trust* [2008] EWHC 2237

Facts: Mrs Birch was warned that there was a one per cent risk of stroke with her treatment, but she was not informed that she could have an MRI scan instead without the risk of a stroke (although the results would be less exact). She had a stroke and claimed negligence on the grounds that she was inadequately informed.

Held: A patient should be made aware of alternatives with lower risks – there were special circumstances in the present case that justified the imposition of such a duty of care. The patient had therefore been subjected to an unnecessary procedure that resulted in harm.

---

[10] This was discussed in *Wyatt* v *Curtis* [2003] EWCA Civ 1779 and Sedley LJ came to the conclusion that doctors have a different (lower) perception of risks than patients.

Cranston J (at paras 74, 79): If patients must be informed of significant risks it is necessary to spell out what, in practice, that encompasses. In this case the defendant informed the patient of the probabilities, the one per cent, and the nature of the harm of this risk becoming manifest, the stroke. [...] Was it necessary for the defendant to go further and to inform Mrs Birch of comparative risk, how this risk compared with that associated with other imaging procedures, in particular MRI? No authority was cited to this effect but in my judgment there will be circumstances where consistently with Lord Woolf MR's statement of the law in *Pearce* v *United Bristol Healthcare NHS Trust* the duty to inform a patient of the significant risks will not be discharged unless she is made aware that fewer, or no risks, are associated with another procedure. In other words, unless the patient is informed of the comparative risks of different procedures she will not be in a position to give her fully informed consent to one procedure rather than another. [...] She was denied the opportunity to make an informed choice. [...] The failure to discuss with Mrs Birch these matters could not be described in law as reasonable, responsible or logical. [...] The failure to provide her with this information was in breach of duty.

The current position can now be described as follows:

- The *Bolam* (1957) test requires a responsible body of medical men to agree with the defendant's practice.
- *Sidaway* (1985) established that a substantial risk of grave consequences should be disclosed to the patient.
- In *Pearce* (1998), if a patient is distressed and unlikely to pursue an alternative treatment, a very, very small risk could be withheld.
- The patient has a legal right to be informed of serious risks, as held in *Chester* (2004).
- The patient also has a right to be informed about alternatives with lower risks, as held in *Birch* (2008).

The law is clearly unsatisfactory in that we do not know who should perceive the risk as 'serious' – the doctor or the patient? If the perception of the doctor is accepted, he may not view particular outcomes as necessarily grave, whereas the patient, who has to live with the consequence, may strongly disagree. This distinction makes all the difference as to what kinds of risks are disclosed. As a result of this ambiguity, it might sometimes be one person's word against another. The courts are no closer to clarifying this difficult issue, but the stream of cases suggests that the law is slowly coming around to the idea that a patient has a higher perception of risk that should be respected.

The General Medical Council provides assistance on this matter.

EXTRACT

General Medical Council, Explanatory Guidance, Consent: Patients and Doctors Making Decisions Together (2008):

www.gmc-uk.org

Paragraph 28: Clear, accurate information about the risks of any proposed investigation or treatment, presented in a way patients can understand, can help them make informed decisions. The amount of information about risk that you should share with patients will depend on the individual patient and what they want or need to know. Your discussions with patients should focus on their individual situation and the risk to them.

> **Paragraph 29**: In order to have effective discussions with patients about risk, you must identify the adverse outcomes that may result from the proposed options. This includes the potential outcome of taking no action.
>
> Risks can take a number of forms, but will usually be:
>
> a. side effects
>
> b. complications
>
> c. failure of an intervention to achieve the desired aim.
>
> Risks can vary from common but minor side effects, to rare but serious adverse outcomes possibly resulting in permanent disability or death.
>
> **Paragraph 31**: You should do your best to understand the patient's views and preferences about any proposed investigation or treatment, and the adverse outcomes they are most concerned about. You must not make assumptions about a patient's understanding of risk or the importance they attach to different outcomes. You should discuss these issues with your patient.

It appears that, in practice, the doctor and the patient work together to ascertain what is important to the patient. It is, after all, the patient who ultimately consents to, and lives with the consequences of, the medical treatment.

Component 3: the breach must cause the outcome

The patient may find it easy to claim that her doctor owed her a duty of care, and slightly harder to claim that he breached his duty by providing her with inadequate information, but even if she can successfully prove these two criteria, the final hurdle for a claim in negligence is the most difficult of all. She must prove that her injury, harm or loss was a *direct result* of the inadequate information disclosed by her doctor. The crux of her argument would probably be:

> The doctor **failed** to warn me of the alternative treatment or the risk of injury, I consented to the procedure **not knowing** about the alternative or the risk, and if I had known about the alternative or the risk, I would **not** have consented to this particular treatment.

There are big problems with causation. The patient may argue that she would have cancelled the operation on learning of the risks, but that is easy for her to say when the risk has since materialised. She was not to know, when sitting in the doctor's consultation room a few weeks or months ago, that the very small risk was to become a reality. She may now be influenced by her terrible misfortune. What exactly must the jury ask themselves as a causation test?

CASE EXTRACT

Smith v Barking, Havering and Brentwood HA [1994] 5 Med LR 285

Facts: The patient underwent a complex procedure and was not warned of the risks. The condition she was trying to prevent was in fact accelerated. She argued that she would not have underwent the procedure had she known of the risks.

Held: A two-part test is established for cases like these.

→

Hutchinson J: There is a peculiar difficulty involved in this sort of case – not least for the plaintiff herself – in giving, after the adverse outcome is known, reliable answers as to what she would have decided before the operation had she been given proper advice as to the risks inherent in it. Accordingly, it would, in my judgment, be right in the ordinary case to give particular weight to the objective assessment. If everything points to the fact that a reasonable patient, properly informed, would have assented to the operation, the assertion from the witness box, made after the adverse outcome is known, does not carry great weight unless there are extraneous or additional factors to substantiate it. By extraneous or additional factors I mean, and I am not doing more than giving examples, religious or some other firmly-held convictions; particular social or domestic considerations; [or] assertions in the immediate aftermath of the operation. In other words some particular factor which suggests that the plaintiff had grounds for not doing what a reasonable person in her situation might be expected to have done.

Hutchinson J in *Smith* seems to support a combination test of objective and subjective elements. For example:

- **Step 1 (objective)**: If a reasonable patient would have consented to the treatment with full knowledge of the risks . . .

- **Step 2 (subjective)**: . . . then the claimant must produce evidence to prove that *she* would have declined.

This approach was approved in *Sem* (2005) in which negligence was admitted by the surgeon but the patient could not provide evidence that she would have refused the treatment had she been adequately informed of the risks.

CASE EXTRACT

M v Mid Yorkshire Hospitals NHS Trust [2005] EWHC 3469

Facts: The patient was given a hysterectomy after a difficult medical history. She was not offered any less invasive alternatives and argued that had she known that there was a less invasive alternative, she would have taken it.

Held: The patient could not prove her claim.

Judge Peter Langan QC (at para 54): In my judgment, Mrs M, acting as a reasonable patient and even if one leaves out of the equation her particular psychiatric condition, would have been likely to follow the surgeon's advice. Patients do normally follow the advice of a consultant, and I cannot see in this case any factors which lead me to suppose that Mrs M would have done otherwise.

The law seems clear: a patient must provide evidence that she would have refused the treatment had she been adequately informed of the risks or alternatives. However, is the law fair? Why must a claimant, such as Mrs M in the case above, carry the burden of proving that she would have deviated? Commentators have argued that the need for evidence is vital.

EXTRACT

Tony Honore, 'Causation and Disclosure of Medical Risks' (1998) 114 *Law Quarterly Review* 52, at pages 52–5

The causal issue in such cases turns on a hypothesis about events that did not happen. Did one non-event – the doctor's failure to warn – cause another non-event – the patient's not deciding to have [treatment]? There may be little evidence available apart from that of the patient herself. She, after the event, is almost certain to say that, had she been warned, she would have reached a different decision. Otherwise she would not have sued. But her evidence, however honest, is speculative. We cannot know for certain what we would have done in circumstances with which we were never faced.

There are a small handful of cases that do not agree with the need for strict evidence of a different decision:

- *O'Keefe* v *Harvey-Kemble* (1999) 45 BMLR 74: the judge believed the patient when she said that had she been adequately informed about the risks of cosmetic surgery, she would not have had the procedure.

- *Birch* v *University College London Hospital NHS Foundation Trust* [2008] EWHC 2237: the judge accepted that Mrs Birch would have taken the alternative of an MRI scan had the option been made available to her.

A further concern regarding the causation test is when a patient admits, as Miss Chester did in *Chester* (2004), that if she had been adequately informed about the risks, she might still have consented to the procedure at a later date, but she would have used her newly acquired knowledge to do some research, take more time, consider alternatives and seek a second opinion. The courts held in *Chester* (on a close 3:2 majority) that the patient did not have to prove that had she known the risks, she would *never* have consented to the procedure for the rest of her life. It was enough to prove that she would have refused the procedure at *that particular time*.

CASE EXTRACT

Chester v Afshar [2004] UKHL 41

Facts: The patient underwent surgery for back pain and suffered a rare complication which she was not warned about by her surgeon. She argued that had she been warned, she would not have undergone the surgery at that time, but she admitted that she may have consented at a later time after thinking about it and researching her options and alternatives.

Held: The surgeon had deprived the patient of the right to choose for herself. The fact that she may have undergone the surgery at a later date is irrelevant because she would have had the opportunity to research the treatment and consider the risks properly. His appeal was dismissed.

Lord Hope (at paras 40, 86–7): The question of law which arises from these findings is whether it was sufficient for Miss Chester to prove that, if properly warned, she would not have consented to the operation which was in fact performed and which resulted in the injury, or whether it was necessary for her to prove also that she would never have had that operation. The issue is essentially one of causation. [...]

→

> The duty is owed as much to the patient who, if warned, would find the decision difficult as to the patient who would find it simple and could give a clear answer to the doctor one way or the other immediately. [...] The injury was intimately involved with the duty to warn. The duty was owed by the doctor who performed the surgery that Miss Chester consented to. It was the product of the very risk that she should have been warned about when she gave her consent. So I would hold that it can be regarded as having been caused, in the legal sense, by the breach of that duty.

Lord Hope's judgment places a significant emphasis on patient autonomy. A patient must be free to research and ponder the procedure for herself, and a failure to warn of the risks deprives the patient of that freedom. However, causation was a problem. Lord Steyn applied the traditional 'but-for' causation test.

CASE EXTRACT

Lord Steyn (at para 19): . . . but for the surgeon's negligent failure to warn the claimant of the small risk of serious injury, the actual injury would not have occurred when it did, and the chance of it occurring on a subsequent occasion was very small. It could therefore be said that the breach of the surgeon resulted in the very injury about which the claimant was entitled to be warned.

Lord Bingham, who strongly dissented, put what he thought of this application of the doctrine of causation in very clear terms:

CASE EXTRACT

Lord Bingham (at para 18): . . . in the ordinary run of cases, satisfying the 'but for' test is a necessary if not a sufficient condition of establishing causation. Here, in my opinion, it is not satisfied. Miss Chester has not established that but for the failure to warn she would not have undergone surgery. She has shown that but for the failure to warn she would not have consented to surgery on Monday, 21 November 1994. But the timing of the operation is irrelevant to the injury she suffered, for which she claims to be compensated. That injury would have been as liable to occur whenever the surgery was performed and whoever performed it.

In other words, the traditional doctrine of causation has not been satisfied. It was not conclusively proved by Miss Chester that Dr Afshar's inadequate information caused her injury, because the 2% risk of paralysis would have *still been there* had he adequately informed her. Lord Hoffman, who also dissented, agreed that causation had not been met.

CASE EXTRACT

Lord Hoffman (at paras 29–31): The burden is on a claimant to prove that the defendant's breach of duty caused him damage. Where the breach of duty is a failure to warn of a risk, he must prove that he would have taken the opportunity to avoid or reduce that risk. In the context of the present case, that means proving that she would not have had the operation. [...] The claimant argued that as a matter of law it was sufficient that she would not have had the operation at that time or by that surgeon, even though the evidence was that the risk could have been precisely the same if she had it at another time or by another surgeon. [...] The judge found as a fact that the risk would have been precisely the same whether it was done then or later or by that competent surgeon or by another. It follows that the claimant failed to prove that the defendant's breach of duty caused her loss. On ordinary principles of tort law, the defendant is not liable.

Chester has introduced a causative anomaly into the law. The lords stated in their judgment that Miss Chester was deprived of her autonomy, i.e. her right to make an informed decision, but they instead compensated her for *physical* harm which may have occurred anyway, meaning that she was overcompensated and her surgeon was found to be negligent when he performed the surgery correctly. A lot of support has thus been found from academics for the dissenting judges in *Chester*.

EXTRACT

Charles Foster, 'It Should Be, Therefore It Is' (2004) 154 *New Law Journal* 7151, at pages 1644–55

Causation is not established but, since it should be, it will be deemed to be. Where a duty exists for some reason that can be described in terms of human rights, [...] a breach will entitle the claimant to damages on policy grounds, even if causation cannot be proved. The House of Lords has stretched the rules of causation before, [...] but *Chester* goes much further: it abolishes the requirement for causation in any meaningful sense.

Causation in consent cases of the *Chester* type has always been difficult to prove. Now it will be easy. Claimant statements will in future, no doubt, say: 'if I had been properly warned, I would have gone off and pondered'. We have always thought of causation as a logical, almost mathematical business. To intrude policy into causation is like saying that two plus two does not equal four because, for policy reasons, it should not. After *Chester*, nothing seems unthinkable.

EXTRACT

Kumaralingam Amirthalingam, 'Medical Non-Disclosure, Causation and Autonomy' (2002) 118 *Law Quarterly Review* 540, at page 542

Causation is increasingly a proxy for moral accountability. While it was always meant to be a normative inquiry designed to fix liability on a responsible person, courts have been, for the most part, conscious of maintaining a causal link between breach and injury, whether through the traditional 'but for' test or the 'common sense' approach. Recently, causation has transcended its role in attributing causal responsibility and has been used instead to fix liability on a party who, in the court's eyes, ought to have been held accountable even if there were no evidence that that party actually caused the injury. The current mantra is that causation must be seen in the context of the purpose of the law and should not be separated from questions of liability. Effectively, this means that courts may find a defendant causally responsible if at the end of the day, despite the absence of actual evidence of a causal link, it is fair, just and reasonable that the defendant, rather than the plaintiff, should bear the loss. This confuses causation with the broader question of liability, more properly addressed at the duty or remoteness stage.

The legacy of *Chester* can be summed up as follows:

A patient has a right to make an autonomous decision about medical treatment, and this requires adequate knowledge of risks:

- A patient can seek damages even if she submits that, had she been informed of the risk, she may still have gone ahead with the procedure at another time.
- The burden of proof is on the patient to prove that she would have refused treatment had she known of the risks.

- It is irrelevant that the surgeon used proper care and skill when the risk materialised – the real issue is the deprivation of autonomy.

- It is open to debate as to whether the doctor really did 'cause' the materialisation of the risk by simply failing to inform the patient of it.

- *Chester* appears to hint that a doctor can be found liable for negligence because he simply deprived the patient of a chance to 'reflect' or 'research' her situation.

Additional communication problems

The three-part test for negligence appears to be quite simple at first glance: (i) a duty of care; (ii) a breach of that duty; and (iii) the breach must cause the damage. However, as illustrated by the cases above, this is a very grey area with no clear boundaries. The term 'adequate information' causes great confusion, because a doctor may not think too much of a particular risk and therefore not disclose it, whereas a patient may be vehemently against taking such a gamble and would be shocked to learn that she was not told. In legal terms, a doctor should disclose what a 'reasonable doctor' would disclose, but it appears that only a court can determine retrospectively whether or not the information was adequate, i.e. after the damage has been done. A doctor must therefore rely on his clinical judgment. The *Bolam* test places an emphasis on the *words* that a doctor said, but not on whether the patient *understands* the information. This test falls in favour of the doctor. However, it is easier in a court to determine what a reasonable doctor should have said as compared to what a reasonable patient would want to know. This is because every patient is different in terms of lifestyle, goals and strength, but every doctor must work in accordance to the same professional standard of care. In addition, many patients do not speak English as a first language. How far must a doctor go in order to communicate *adequate* information? If a doctor gives a patient too little information then her autonomy, her freedom to choose what is best for her, is deprived, but if he gives her too much information, she may be too frightened to consent or reject treatment, which also deprives her of her autonomy. This is an incredibly difficult balance to strike. In other jurisdictions such as the US, Canada, Australia and New Zealand, the 'reasonable doctor' test is replaced by the 'prudent patient' test, which requires a doctor to tell his patient what most patients in her position would want to know. This may encourage a doctor to get to know his patient properly in order to ascertain what is important to her in terms of risks, but the prudent patient test comes with the same problem as the reasonable doctor test: every patient is different and the importance of a particular risk will vary from patient to patient.

Therapeutic privilege

There is a doctrine in medical law known as 'therapeutic privilege', which allows a doctor to withhold information from a patient if it will harm her. This idea was briefly mentioned in the cases of *Sidaway* (1985), *Pearce* (1995) and *Chester* (2004):

- *Sidaway* **(1985) per Lord Scarman**: 'The doctor will not be liable if upon a reasonable assessment of his patient's condition he takes the view that a warning would be detrimental to his patient's health.'

- *Pearce* **(1998) per Lord Woolf MR**: 'Particularly when one bears in mind Mrs Pearce's distressed condition, one cannot criticise Mr Niven's decision not to inform Mrs Pearce of that very, very small additional risk.'

- *Chester* v *Afshar* (2004) per Lord Steyn: 'A surgeon owes a legal duty to a patient to warn him or her in general terms of possible serious risks involved in the procedure. The only qualification is that there may be wholly exceptional cases where objectively in the best interests of the patient the surgeon may be excused from giving a warning.'

Therapeutic privilege confuses matters in this area of law. There appears to be no legal duty to disclose information to a patient if it might be *harmful* to her. In *Pearce*, the patient was in a distressed state and Lord Woolf MR supported the doctor when he chose to conceal a 0.2% risk of stillbirth from her. This is the kind of situation to which therapeutic privilege would apply, but it is not clear how frequently this privilege is used. The doctrine of therapeutic privilege can trump the right to autonomy: a doctor can legally conceal information from a patient as long as he can show that, in his clinical judgment, it would have caused harm to the patient and he was justified in doing so. The General Medical Council makes it clear that the harm to the patient must be serious harm.

EXTRACT

General Medical Council, Explanatory Guidance, Consent: Patients and Doctors Making Decisions Together (2008):

www.gmc-uk.org

Paragraph 16: You should not withhold information necessary for making decisions for any other reason, including when a relative, partner, friend or carer asks you to, unless you believe that giving it would cause the patient serious harm. In this context 'serious harm' means more than that the patient might become upset or decide to refuse treatment.

Good communication

The General Medical Council states that doctors and patients should work together throughout the consultation process.

EXTRACT

General Medical Council, Explanatory Guidance, Consent: Patients and Doctors Making Decisions Together (2008):

www.gmc-uk.org

Paragraph 2: Whatever the context in which medical decisions are made, you must work in partnership with your patients to ensure good care . . .

Paragraph 3: For a relationship between doctor and patient to be effective, it should be a partnership based on openness, trust and good communication . . .

Paragraph 7: The exchange of information between doctor and patient is central to good decision-making. How much information you share with patients will vary, depending on their individual circumstances. You should tailor your approach . . .

Paragraph 8: You should not make assumptions . . .

A doctor must decide how and when to provide adequate information to patients. There are many circumstances to consider. A translator or interpreter may be required if the patient does not speak English or is hard of hearing. The minutes immediately before or after an operation are also not the appropriate time to be discussing such risks, as established by *Lybert* v *Warrington HA* [1996] 7 Med LR 71. It is difficult to say whether every single patient leaves her consultation with a full understanding of the procedure and the risks involved, but doctors must do all they can to facilitate that goal.

EXTRACT

General Medical Council, Explanatory Guidance, Consent: Patients and Doctors Making Decisions Together (2008):

www.gmc-uk.org

Paragraph 21: You should check whether the patient needs any additional support to understand information, to communicate their wishes, or to make a decision. You should bear in mind that some barriers to understanding and communication may not be obvious . . . You must make sure, wherever practical, that arrangements are made to give the patient any necessary support . . .

Paragraph 34: You must use clear, simple and consistent language when discussing risks with patients. You should be aware that patients may understand information about risk differently from you. You should check that the patient understands the terms that you use, particularly when describing the seriousness, frequency and likelihood of an adverse outcome. You should use simple and accurate written information or visual or other aids to explain risk, if they will help the patient to understand.

This guidance is supported by a case which established that doctors are not under an additional duty to *ensure* that a patient has understood, but they must take reasonable and appropriate steps to be *satisfied* that the patient has understood.

CASE EXTRACT

Al Hamwi v *Johnston* [2005] EWHC 206

Simon J (at para 69): Clinicians should take reasonable and appropriate steps to satisfy themselves that the patient has understood the information which has been provided; but the obligation does not extend to ensuring that the patient has understood.

● Patient questions

A patient is free to ask questions about risks, and a doctor should answer them the best he can. The case of *Poynter* v *Hillingdon HA* (1997) 37 BMLR 192 held that because the mother and father of a very ill child did not ask specific questions about the risk of serious disability of brain damage that came with a heart transplant, the medical team were under no duty to disclose what they viewed as a very small risk of it occurring. This case placed a duty upon the relatives of the patient to seek information rather than the doctor giving it to them freely. *Pearce* (1998) followed a year later, in which Lord Woolf MR said: 'if a patient asks a doctor about the risk, then the doctor is required to give an honest answer.'[11] The General Medical Council supports this:

---

[11] *Pearce* v *United Bristol Healthcare NHS Trust* (1998) 48 BMLR 118.

General Medical Council, Explanatory Guidance, Consent: Patients and Doctors Making Decisions Together (2008):

www.gmc-uk.org

Paragraph 12: You must answer patients' questions honestly and, as far as practical, answer as fully as they wish.

It follows from *Poynter*, *Pearce* and the GMC Guidance that a doctor must answer a patient honestly when it comes to the very serious risks, although this can be trumped by therapeutic privilege. A discussion of significant risks is usually a normal part of the consultation process, and most doctors would describe the risks as an intrinsic part of the procedure, e.g. 'when we do this, there is a risk of that . . .'. A patient may be understandably nervous in a consultation or may feel intimidated by a qualified doctor and the medical jargon, but this should not stop the patient from asking questions, and if it does, the doctor must still provide *adequate* information about risks according to the common law.

Wilful blindness

What if a patient refuses to accept any information about his or her procedure? This may sound strange, but some patients cope with serious illness by turning their heads away and prefer not to think about it. It is not unheard of for these patients to simply leave it up to their doctor to make the right decision. This is absolutely fine as long as the patient freely consents to any treatment that is given.

General Medical Council, Explanatory Guidance, Consent: Patients and Doctors Making Decisions Together (2008):

www.gmc-uk.org

Paragraph 15: If a patient insists that they do not want even this basic information, you must explain the potential consequences of them not having it, particularly if it might mean that their consent is not valid. You must record the fact that the patient has declined this information. You must also make it clear that they can change their mind and have more information at any time.

The only problem that may arise is when one of the risks materialises, and the patient complains that he or she was not told of the risks. The doctor may argue in response that the patient gave consent while voluntarily adopting wilful blindness to all the risks involved.

EXTRACT

U. Khilbom, 'Autonomy and Negatively Informed Consent' (2008) 34 *Journal of Medical Ethics* 146, at pages 146–9

A patient can take an autonomous decision to undergo a medical treatment without having (positive) knowledge of the treatment and risks . . . Furthermore, if I, as the patient, choose to let you, as the physician, determine my treatment, and I have well founded beliefs that you will choose the treatment that best promotes my values, and that the risks of the treatment you will choose, is in accordance with my attitudes towards different kinds of risks, I will exercise my autonomy, not waive my right to exercise it.

Khilbom is arguing that when a patient adopts a wilful blindness approach to any risks, she is still exercising autonomy by allowing the doctor to decide for her. This is a voluntary choice, and therefore, she is not robbed of her autonomy. However, it is not this straightforward. How can a doctor 'promote' the values and attitudes of a patient when choosing the correct treatment for her if she has chosen to close her eyes to the whole process?

ACTIVITY

Taylor needed brain surgery to remove a tumour. It was easy to access on the surface of her brain. However, it was attached to the mobility part of her brain, and the risk of her losing the ability to control her speech was 1%. Taylor was a public speaker by trade, working in politics and talking at numerous conferences every month. The doctor knew how keen Taylor was about the brain surgery because the procedure appeared straightforward, so he didn't bother mentioning the 1% risk of speech impairment. However, despite perfectly competent surgery, Taylor had impaired speech when she came around from surgery. She was horrified to learn that the surgery came with a 1% risk of speech impairment and said she would rather die of a brain tumour than give up her job as a public speaker.

Applying the three-part test in negligence, does Taylor have a case against her doctor?

Chapter summary

- A competent and fully informed consent or refusal must be respected in law: *Airedale NHS Trust* v *Bland* [1993] AC 789 and *Re T (Adult: Refusal of Treatment)* [1993] Fam 95.

- The Mental Capacity Act 2005 enshrines the common law principles on capacity, including the old maxim that an incompetent patient must be treated in accordance with his best interests under section 1(5).

- If both parents disagree as to whether an important vaccination (or any other treatment) should be given to their child, the court will decide for them in accordance with the child's best interests: *Re C (Welfare of Child: Immunisation)* [2003] EWCA Civ 1148.

- A child under the age of majority can *consent* to medical treatment when he achieves a sufficient intelligence to enable him to understand fully what is proposed: as per Lord Scarman in *Gillick* v *West Norfolk and Wisbech AHA* [1986] AC 112.

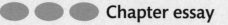 **Chapter essay**

'Critically analyse the protection afforded to incompetent adult patients when facing decisions about treatment in medical law.'

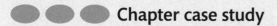 **Chapter case study**

Peter and Polly are twins and were born three months premature. They spent months in intensive care before being allowed home on a special regime of drugs. They had weak hearts and their mother, Cheryl, was warned that in their adolescent years, they may need further invasive treatment to rectify some heart tissue.

Peter and Polly reached the age of 15. Peter was strong and robust and suffered no long-term effects from his premature birth, but Polly was a weak teenager who collapsed frequently and suffered from heart compilations. Polly was finally admitted to hospital and many tests were conducted. She needed a bone marrow transplant and a heart transplant. Peter was an excellent match for bone marrow, but he refused to consent to the procedure. Polly's father Michael wanted her to have a heart transplant – she was tired of her bad health and wanted a fresh start – but her mother Cheryl did not want Polly to have a heart transplant because it was too invasive and too stressful for everybody concerned.

How will the law of consent apply to: (i) Peter's refusal, and (ii) Cheryl and Michael's divide over Polly?

Further reading

Fox, M. (1996) 'In Whose Best Interests?', 60 *Modern Law Review* 700–9.

Jones, M. (1999) 'Informed Consent and Other Fairy Stories', 7 *Medical Law Review* 103–34.

Lewis, P. (2002) 'Procedures That Are Against the Medical Interests of the Incompetent Person', 12 *Oxford Journal of Legal Studies* 575.

Michalowski, S. (2005) 'Advance Refusals of Life Sustaining Treatment: The Relativity of an Absolute Right', *Modern Law Review* 958.

Miola, J. (2009) 'On the Materiality of Risk: Paper Tigers and Panaceas', 17 *Medical Law Review* 76.

5

Confidentiality

Chapter objectives

At the end of this chapter, you should have:

- An understanding of the definition of confidentiality, where it comes from and how it applies to the doctor–patient relationship.

- An appreciation of the statute law on confidentiality as contained in the Data Protection Act 1998 and its exceptions.

- Knowledge of the common law of confidentiality and the exceptions allowing disclosure of medical records.

- An understanding of the relevant professional associations and bodies who have published guidelines to ensure that healthcare professionals deal with patient information in accordance with the law.

SETTING THE SCENE

Olga was a very old patient in a care home. She suddenly died of a very serious infection which could have been treated with antibiotics. Her son, Fred, was furious with the manager of the care home and the NHS trust (under which it was run) for their lack of care and attention over his mother's condition. He began legal proceedings against the NHS trust and the manager of the care home, and demanded that Olga's medical record be released to him immediately. The manager of the care home refused, stating that it was confidential information. Fred sought a solicitor's advice. How might you advise him, as a medical lawyer, about confidentiality law and the legal exceptions in place to justify a breach of confidentiality?

Introduction

Confidentiality is an extremely difficult area of law because the law itself is 'universal'. It is founded in a broad range of old doctrines and is applicable to every field of law, making it very difficult to apply to the particular area of medicine. To cope with the lack of clarity, the Department of Health, the General Medical Council and the British Medical Council have done their best to publish their own guidelines explaining to healthcare professionals the broad rules of confidentiality and how they apply in a medical context. It is these guidelines that most doctors rely on to steer them in the right direction. Human rights are also heavily involved in confidentiality.

The duty to keep information confidential is not absolute. There are some exceptions in law that allow a healthcare professional to release extracts of medical records. It may surprise readers to learn this, because the duty of confidentiality is viewed by many as 'absolute' to ensure that trust is maintained between doctor and patient. However, if doctors or nurses were forced into silence on every occasion, the patient or the general public may be at risk. It is also impossible to keep track of how many serious illnesses are diagnosed or how many medical procedures are performed if general clinical information is not fed back to the government or other health departments for audit purposes, and on a more practical level, a patient cannot be referred to a specialist if their medical record (or at least the relevant parts of it) are not shared within the healthcare system. Therefore, 'absolute' confidentiality would see limits placed on medical care and medical research.

A very delicate balance has to be struck between sharing patient information and not breaching confidentiality. It is incredibly hard to justify the disclosure of a medical record, because it is in the public interest to maintain confidentiality. To give a practical example, a patient may come forward with a blood infection as a result of his heroin use. Does his doctor inform the police, or does the duty of confidentiality override his instinct to disclose? The answer is, rather unhelpfully, 'it depends'. The law is so scattered and complicated that a doctor must literally decide for himself, with only a select few guidelines to help him, as to whether a disclosure in a particular case is justified. What is clear is that the patient must be informed of the disclosure if possible, and the doctor must justify why the disclosure should go ahead, but this is little consolation to the patient, who trusted his doctor only to find that his personal information has been passed on to another.

ACTIVITY

A paedophile, aged 40, visits his doctor because he was chasing a child out of a playground when he tripped over and cut his leg open. He received medical attention on the scene and has now returned to his doctor to have the stitches removed. The conversation between the doctor and the patient illuminates the patient's sexual desires for children. The doctor is concerned that his patient is a real danger to children and later on that day, when the doctor still cannot stop thinking about it, he consults the British Medical Association website and the General Medical Council website for advice. If you would like him to alert the police, how can you justify breaching confidentiality when no actual harm has occurred?

What is confidentiality and why is it important?

Confidentiality can be traced back to the Hippocratic Oath. The Oath is still highly regarded today and it has been enshrined into the Declaration of Geneva (1948) to ensure that all healthcare professionals perform their special skill with the best interests of their patients at heart. The relevant part of the Hippocratic Oath reads as follows.

The Hippocratic Oath (available generally)

I swear by Apollo, the healer, Asclepius, Hygieia, and Panacea, and I take to witness all the Gods, all the Goddesses, to keep according to my ability and my judgment, the following Oath and agreement:

- All that may come to my knowledge in the exercise of my profession or in daily commerce with men, which ought not to be spread abroad, I will keep secret and will never reveal.

It is interesting to note that in the Hippocratic Oath, the idea of daily conversations with friends and colleagues (i.e. 'men' generally) is considered to be a breach of confidentiality. This alludes to an obligation of silence that stretches beyond the boundaries of the workplace. However, it is clear that the duty of confidentiality is not absolute. The words 'which ought not to be spread abroad' can be read to include an exception to the rule that information *ought to* be spread abroad in certain circumstances. In other words, there may be exceptions. The relevant parts of the Declaration of Geneva (1948) (in Chapter 10) read as follows.

The Declaration of Geneva (1948) (as amended)[1]

At the time of being admitted as a member of the medical profession:

5. I will respect the secrets that are confided in me, even after the patient has died.

10. I will not use my medical knowledge to violate human rights and civil liberties, even under threat.

---

[1] World Medical Association: see www.wma.net under Publications: Policies: G for Geneva.

It is clear that the duty of confidentiality ranks very high on the list of professional medical ethics, and this is supported by the fact that it extends beyond death in The Declaration of Geneva. This is to protect the relatives of the patient from being shocked or distressed if a secret is revealed. It would not be ethical to tarnish the memory of a loved one by exposing their medical record and it would bring the integrity of the medical profession into disrepute.

The European Convention on Human Rights entitles us to respect for our private and family lives (Article 8). This is a human right that supports our freedom, security, autonomy and independence. A breach of our confidentiality would scupper all of these rights, leading to distrust, distress and restriction (i.e. we may not be free to live our lives in the usual way if others knew our secrets). Article 8 features in most of the case law in this chapter.

What is confidentiality?

The Oxford English Dictionary defines 'confidentiality' as follows:

1. Intended to be kept secret.
2. Entrusted with private information.

This definition is extremely broad, and not at all helpful to healthcare professionals. However, the case law appears to be quite settled with the fact that there is a duty of confidentiality owed to all patients.

CASE EXTRACT

Ashworth Security Hospital v MGN Ltd [2000] 1 WLR 515

Lord Phillips MR (at para 47): It is well settled that there is an abiding obligation of confidentiality as between doctor and patient, and in my view when a patient enters a hospital for treatment, whether he be a model citizen or murderer, he is entitled to be confident that details about his condition and treatment remain between himself and those who treat him.

In practice, the duty of confidentiality means that all of the information disclosed to a doctor must be kept confidential unless one of the legal exceptions (examined below) applies. It is, of course, up to the patient who else they tell about their condition but it is vital that this decision is made by the *patient*, not the doctor.

What makes the law of confidentiality especially difficult to define is the varying standards in patients. In medical negligence, for example, a doctor must fall below a reasonable standard of care for *every* patient. However, in cases of confidentiality, it will depend on the patient's perspective as to whether their confidentiality has been breached or not. For example, some patients will be quite happy to parade their broken leg cast and ask family members to autograph it, whereas other patients will not want a back injury, for example, to be broadcast (especially if it was attained in an embarrassing way). The ailments to be kept private will vary from one patient to another, and a doctor cannot foresee what kind of patient he has in front of him until a breach takes place. Similarly, x-rays or vaccinations will not be considered by some patients as confidential treatments, but a diagnosis and photographs will be considered to be very confidential to others. How can a doctor or a nurse be sure that they have maintained confidentiality when they are not even sure if the information they possess is confidential? Their answer seems to be: keep everything secret unless disclosure is encouraged by a legal exception. This way, it is up to the patient what is released and who it is released to, and the doctor does not have to worry about breaching his duty of confidence. Gilbar (below) argues that a *complete* confidence does not really exist in medicine, because patients like to tell their relatives about their ailment, their trips to the doctor, their symptoms and their medication. In addition, patients are often encouraged to bring a relative to the doctor surgery with them if the prognosis is particularly bad or the treatment is particularly invasive, so confidentiality is really just an illusion to encourage trust in the medical profession.

EXTRACT

Roy Gilbar, 'Medical Confidentiality Within the Family: The Doctor's Duty Reconsidered' (2004) 18 *International Journal of Law, Policy and the Family* 195, at pages 195–213

While the relationship between patients and employers or insurers is primarily confrontational, [...] the relationship with family members is generally based on care, commitment and mutual responsibility. Consequently, information is in most cases communicated more freely within the family than with other third parties. [...] Patients often consider the interests of their relatives and the implications of their decisions on their familial relationship, while doctors are willing to involve family members more than the law currently permits to help the patient cope with the bad news. In other words, doctors and patients value the patient's familial relationship as a separate and significant component in this area. Thus, the strict legal rule of medical confidentiality, which is adopted by many lawyers and policy makers, should be reconsidered. [...] If it is accepted that the gaps between law and practice should be bridged, then it can be argued that a doctor's duty of confidentiality must be qualified when it concerns the family. It must reflect awareness of familial solidarity and mutual responsibility and the reality that family members are inherently involved in the patient's well being and medical care. [...] Doctors in various areas of medicine have learnt to accept that the support and comfort that family members provide to the patient during all the stages of his or her illness is important, and that the family rather than the individual patient, should be considered as the unit of medical care. [...] Adhering to a strict rule of confidentiality may compromise the interests of the patient.

Gilbar argues that doctors disregard the strict laws of confidentiality to allow family members to play a part in supporting the patient. This is probably true, although a doctor would never divulge any information about a patient to a relative without that patient providing a fully informed consent (unless the patient is temporarily incompetent, in which case the best interests test from the Mental Capacity Act 2005 will be applied to ascertain whether a breach would be justified). To suggest that the law should be 'reconsidered' is a bit far-fetched, because it currently works quite well on the basis of doctor discretion combined with patient consent when it comes to family involvement. A floodgates scenario may unfold if the law were to be changed to allow familial access, and it would remove the power from the patient to decide for themselves what should be divulged to loved ones. It is not always the case that families get on: sometimes competent children seek medical treatment away from their parents, and sometimes spouses keep particularly distressing news from their partners in order not to worry them. Therefore, while recognising that familial solidarity is to be encouraged, removing patient autonomy is not a good idea as it could remove the 'individual' from medical care.

Why is confidentiality important?

The main argument in favour of confidentiality is that without a duty of confidence a patient would not confide in her doctor, and without all the facts, the doctor could not treat her effectively. This applies to all kinds of ailments, from a general infection to organ failure. Confidentiality is therefore in the best interests of the patient and society as a whole. A doctor is not asking such personal questions out of interest or nosiness; he is searching for a diagnosis and it must be as accurate as possible in order to locate the correct prescription. It can be disarming to many of us when a stranger asks an embarrassing question because we are not used to such an invasion of our privacy in our normal daily lives, but doctors deal with private details on a daily basis. Besides, we would be very likely to complain if our doctor took no interest in our ailment or its accompanying symptoms.

It is clear in the context of sexual health that a duty of confidentiality can benefit other people as well as the immediate patient. A student, for example, who seeks medical advice about her sexually transmitted disease is then educated by her doctor and prevented from passing the disease to a third person. A parent, to take another example, who takes her child to the doctor for a bruised arm may admit that her boyfriend is harming her child and the doctor will have to inform the police (this is one of the legal exceptions). This is a utilitarian perspective on confidentiality: by offering the promise of (or breaching) confidentiality to one patient, the greater good will feel the benefit of it.

EXTRACT

Chris Jones, 'The Utilitarian Argument for Medical Confidentiality: A Pilot Study of Patients' Views' (2003) 29 *Journal of Medical Ethics* 348, at pages 348–52

The utilitarian position receives considerable support from the views expressed in this study by patients. They clearly value confidentiality, see it as important in a medical consultation, and recognise that disclosure without consent would be likely to deter some patients from seeking treatment. To this extent it seems that the generally accepted view of the benefits of confidentiality can be justified. However for many people the utility of confidentiality appears to be outweighed by the benefits of disclosure in order to protect third parties. They were prepared to endorse disclosure of information at the same time as recognising that treatment might be impaired as a result.

A patient is, for the most part, in control of her medical record. She can request to see it (explored below), she can ask for inaccuracies to be amended and she can request that it remains confidential unless one of the following legal provisions apply.

Statutory exceptions

- Road Traffic Act 1972.
- Supreme Court Act 1981.
- Access to Health Records Act 1990.

- Data Protection Act 1998.
- Mental Capacity Act 2005.
- National Health Service Act 2006.

Common law exceptions

- The information is already in the public domain.
- The information is trivial in nature.
- There is a public interest in disclosure that outweighs the duty of confidentiality.

It is time to look at the general law of confidentiality, the legal exceptions therein, and how it is applied in a medical context. It will become apparent that confidentiality is not derived from an exact source: it has slowly developed through the decades using several obscure sources, and statutes and cases have often borrowed from each other in order to build the general provisions of confidentiality in a patchwork-quilt-style manner.

ACTIVITY

List the number of people and organisations who have your personal information on file.

The statute law on confidentiality

On 24 October 1995, European Directive 95/46/EC on the Protection of Individuals with Regard to the Processing of Personal Data and on the Free Movement of Such Data (the 'Data Protection Directive') was passed into EU law. It plays an important role in privacy law, and all member states were under an obligation to implement it within three years. In the UK, Parliament responded by updating the Data Protection Act 1984 to the Data Protection Act 1998. The 1998 Act contains provisions that are relevant to personal information – including medical records – and so a small part of it is relevant to medial law.[2] There are other lesser known statutes and statutory provisions dotted about in law that relate to confidential information (such as the Access to Health Records Act 1990), but the Data Protection Act 1998 is just about the only statute that deals wholly with sensitive and personal data. Healthcare professionals have access to guidelines to help interpret the Data Protection Act 1998 and explain how it applies in a medical context (examined below). The Data Protection Act 1998 is highly complex because it requires the detailed use of its Schedules as well as a Statutory Instrument (explored below) for it to have its full effect. However, the British Medical Association published a Confidentiality Toolkit (2009) and in it, there is a clear and concise description of what the Data Protection Act 1998 is designed to do and how it can protect patient confidentiality. This is an excellent place to start.

---

[2] The European Commission announced on 25 January 2012 that the European Directive 95/46/EC will be superseded by new European Data Protection Regulations to include foreign companies outside the EU, but we have no further details yet. This change will, in turn, alter the law in all member states.

EXTRACT

Confidentiality and Disclosure of Health Information Toolkit (2009), British Medical Association:

www.bma.org.uk/practical-support-at-work/ethics

Page 16 paragraph 5: Data protection Act 1998

. . . Patients are entitled to be informed that information is being held about them and of the purposes for which their information will be processed. They are entitled to have access to and a copy of their information, except where there are grounds for believing that access to that information would be likely to cause serious harm to the individual or a third party or where it would entail disclosure of another individual's identifiable data. They are also entitled to have information corrected when it is inaccurate.

The Data Protection Act 1998 clearly empowers the patient in terms of knowledge and control. However, like all statutory rights, there are exceptions which allow information to be released without consent.

The Data Protection Act 1998: basic definitions

The definition of 'data' clearly includes medical records.

Data Protection Act 1998

Section 1: Basic interpretative provisions

(1) In this Act, 'data' means information which:

(d) . . . forms part of an accessible record as defined by section 68.

Section 68(1)(a) defines an 'accessible record' as a health record, and section 68(2) defines a 'health record' as information relating to he physical or mental health or condition of an individual and has been made by or on behalf of a health professional in connection with the care of that individual. Your medical records are also categorised as 'sensitive personal data' under section 2.

Data Protection Act 1998

Section 2: Sensitive personal data

In this Act 'sensitive personal data' means personal data consisting of information as to:

(e) his physical or mental health or condition,

(f) his sexual life.

The Data Protection Act 1998 ensures that an individual is told when his personal information is being 'processed' and must be given a description of the data involved, the purposes of the process, the recipient of the information, and the reason behind the decision under section 7(1). The term 'processing' seems rather administrative, but it actually includes every conceivable handling of a piece of data.

Data Protection Act 1998

Section 1: Basic interpretative provisions

(1) In this Act, 'processing', in relation to information or data, means obtaining, recording or holding the information or data or carrying out any operation or set of operations on the information or data, including:

(a) organisation, adaptation or alteration of the information or data,

(b) retrieval, consultation or use of the information or data,

(c) disclosure of the information or data by transmission, dissemination or otherwise making available, or

(d) alignment, combination, blocking, erasure or destruction of the information or data.

When might a data controller process a person's sensitive personal data? He may have a request from an employer, a credit company or an insurance company. If the data controller cannot disclose the sensitive personal data without disclosing information about somebody else (e.g. a spouse), the data controller must have the consent of the spouse (or it must be reasonable in the circumstances to continue without their consent) under section 7(4). A person does have some element of control over how their sensitive personal data is disclosed. Section 10 allows a person to write to the data controller to prevent the disclosure.

Data Protection Act 1998

Section 10: Right to prevent processing likely to cause damage or distress

(1) Subject to subsection (2), an individual is entitled at any time by notice in writing to a data controller to require the data controller to cease, or not to begin, processing, or processing for a specified purpose or in a specified manner, any personal data in respect of which he is the data subject, on the ground that, for specified reasons:

(a) the processing of those data or their processing for that purpose or in that manner is causing or is likely to cause substantial damage or substantial distress to him or to another, and

(b) that damage or distress is or would be unwarranted.

(2) Subsection (1) does not apply:

(a) in a case where any of the conditions in paragraphs 1 to 4 of Schedule 2 is met, or

(b) in such other cases as may be prescribed by the Secretary of State by order.

It is interesting to note that a person must prove that 'substantial damage' or 'substantial distress' will be caused to himself or another if the disclosure was to take place. A disclosure could, for example, lead to unemployment, bankruptcy, distrust or divorce. There are exceptions, however, where disclosure can be made under Schedule 2 (consent, necessity, law and vital interests) or if the Secretary of State orders the disclosure. The data controller has twenty-one days to write to the person and tell him what the decision is under section 10(3). The court will become involved if the person is still not happy and will ask whether disclosure (or non disclosure) is justified under section 10(4). Compensation can be offered to the person under section 13 if it can be shown that damage or distress was caused by the contravention of the data controller, but the data controller can prove as a defence that in the circumstances he was reasonably required to comply with the order for disclosure under section 13(3). The court can also order that the data be rectified, blocked, erased or destroyed under section 14 if the data is shown to be inaccurate by the person.

Data Protection Principles

The Data Protection Act 1998 is best known for its 'Data Protection Principles' listed under Schedule 1. There are eight of them, and they aim to protect the privacy and integrity of the individual.

Data Protection Act 1998

Schedule 1: Part 1: The Data Protection Principles

1. Personal data shall be processed fairly and lawfully and, in particular, shall not be processed unless:

   (a) at least one of the conditions in Schedule 2 is met, and

   (b) in the case of sensitive personal data, at least one of the conditions in Schedule 3 is also met.

2. Personal data shall be obtained only for one or more specified and lawful purposes, and shall not be further processed in any manner incompatible with that purpose or those purposes.

3. Personal data shall be adequate, relevant and not excessive in relation to the purpose or purposes for which they are processed.

4. Personal data shall be accurate and, where necessary, kept up to date.

5. Personal data processed for any purpose or purposes shall not be kept for longer than is necessary for that purpose or those purposes.

6. Personal data shall be processed in accordance with the rights of data subjects under this Act.

7. Appropriate technical and organisational measures shall be taken against unauthorised or unlawful processing of personal data and against accidental loss or destruction of, or damage to, personal data.

8. Personal data shall not be transferred to a country or territory outside the European Economic Area unless that country or territory ensures an adequate level of protection for the rights and freedoms of data subjects in relation to the processing of personal data.

The principles above are relevant to medical records: the record should be obtained for a lawful purpose, data should be adequate and relevant, data should be accurate, data should not be kept for longer than necessary, etc. However, it is the first principle that we are most concerned with.

Section 1 in Schedule 1 stipulates that a medical record must be processed, i.e. obtained, held, organised, adapted, altered, retrieved, etc., fairly and lawfully. What does 'fairly' and 'lawfully' in this context mean? It appears that, as long as one condition in Schedule 2 is met and one condition in Schedule 3 is met, then a medical record (or any other kind of personal data) has been processed fairly and lawfully. Schedules 2 and 3 are provided below, although note that the conditions not relevant to medical law have been removed. Remember: one criteria from each Schedule must be satisfied for sensitive personal data . . .

Data Protection Act 1998

Schedule 2: Conditions Relevant for the Purposes of the First Principle: Processing of any Personal Data

1. The data subject has given his consent to the processing.

4. The processing is necessary in order to protect the vital interests of the data subject.

5. The processing is necessary:

   (a) for the administration of justice,

   (b) for the exercise of any functions conferred on any person by or under any enactment,

   (c) for the exercise of any functions of the Crown, a Minister of the Crown or a government department, or

   (d) for the exercise of any other functions of a public nature exercised in the public interest by any person.

6. (1) The processing is necessary for the purposes of legitimate interests pursued by the data controller or by the third party or parties to whom the data are disclosed, except where the processing is unwarranted in any particular case by reason of prejudice to the rights and freedoms or legitimate interests of the data subject.

   (2) The Secretary of State may by order specify particular circumstances in which this condition is, or is not, to be taken to be satisfied.

Consent is the first listing under condition one, and if consent is not offered by the individual, the data controller can justify the disclosure under any of the other five conditions. This is important, because the data controller must justify the disclosure if the individual has not consented to his personal data being released. Vital interests are listed under condition four, but it is not clear what this means. Perhaps 'vital interests' refer to a basic level of safety, health and wellbeing? It is not clear who decides this: the individual is likely to be too subjective (i.e. over dramatic), but the data controller is likely to be too objective. However, the disclosure must be 'necessary' to protect the vital interests, so mere convenience or interest in a disclosure will not suffice. This is a very important safeguard when the disclosure can take place without consent. The administration of justice is listed under condition five, and includes a wide range of bodies such as the Secretary of State, other public bodies (e.g. the NHS), the Crown (i.e. the law), or the public interest. If one of these conditions are satisfied it would probably be a very urgent matter (such as a murder inquiry, a virus breakout, or a terrorist matter, etc.), and so it would be difficult for the individual to argue that his privacy trumped the need to disclose. Condition six is an ambiguous one: what are the legitimate interests pursued by the data controller or a third party? This may include education, training or audit (e.g. statistics for cancer research), but it must be 'necessary' to disclose the information for these purposes. There is an exception listed under condition six, stating that if the processing is unwarranted or causes prejudice to the rights and freedoms of the individual, the disclosure is not justified.

In addition to one condition being met under Schedule 2, a second condition from Schedule 3, relating to sensitive and personal data such as medical records, must also be met.

Data Protection Act 1998

Schedule 3: Conditions Relevant for Purposes of the First Principle: Processing of Sensitive Personal Data

1. The data subject has given his explicit consent to the processing of the personal data.

3. The processing is necessary:

    (a) in order to protect the vital interests of the data subject or another person, in a case where:

        (i) consent cannot be given by or on behalf of the data subject, or

        (ii) the data controller cannot reasonably be expected to obtain the consent of the data subject, or

    (b) in order to protect the vital interests of another person, in a case where consent by or on behalf of the data subject has been unreasonably withheld.

7. (1) The processing is necessary:

    (a) for the administration of justice,

    (b) for the exercise of any functions conferred on any person by or under an enactment, or

    (c) for the exercise of any functions of the Crown, a Minister of the Crown or a government department.

8. (1) The processing is necessary for medical purposes and is undertaken by:

    (a) a health professional, or

    (b) a person who in the circumstances owes a duty of confidentiality which is equivalent to that which would arise if that person were a health professional.

    (2) In this paragraph 'medical purposes' includes the purposes of preventative medicine, medical diagnosis, medical research, the provision of care and treatment and the management of health care services.

Consent is once again listed under condition one. The individual can consent to his sensitive personal data being released, but if he does not consent, there are another nine conditions listed under Schedule 3 that will justify disclosure without his consent. Vital interests once again features as a justification for disclosure under condition three. However, it is expanded upon in Schedule 3 to include the vital interests of *another person*. For example, A has HIV but refuses to disclose his medical record even though it is in the vital interests of B – his wife – to do so. It must be 'necessary' to disclose this information without consent. Condition eight is directly relevant to medical law. A disclosure can take place for medical purposes if it is done by a medical professional or another person who owes a duty of confidentiality. This condition is rather wide in nature, because paragraph (2) describes 'medical purposes' as prevention, diagnosis, research, provision and management. This covers every area of medicine. It must, of course, be 'necessary' to disclose the information.

There are additional exceptions under Schedule 3 which are applicable to sensitive personal data such as medical records. They were set out by the Secretary of State in 2000 in a Statutory Instrument. The most relevant exception is number three, which aims to disclose sensitive personal information to protect the public against professional malpractice.

Data Protection (Processing of Sensitive Personal Data) Order (SI 2000/417)

3. (1) The disclosure of personal data:

    (a) is in the substantial public interest;

    (b) is in connection with:

        (i) the commission by any person of any unlawful act (whether alleged or established),

        (ii) dishonesty, malpractice, or other seriously improper conduct by, or the unfitness or incompetence of, any person (whether alleged or established), or

        (iii) mismanagement in the administration of, or failures in services provided by, any body or association (whether alleged or established);

    (c) is for the special purposes as defined in section 3 of the Act [journalism, art or literature]; and

    (d) is made with a view to the publication of those data by any person and the data controller reasonably believes that such publication would be in the public interest.

    (2) In this paragraph, 'act' includes a failure to act.

A disclosure of sensitive personal information can take place if it is in the public interest and it is in connection with an unlawful act or malpractice by a person or body. This includes individual doctors, teachers, lawyers, the NHS, companies, government departments, etc. The data controller must reasonably believe that the disclosure is in the public interest. This feels quite dangerous – the data controller has a lot of power – but the insertion of the word 'reasonably' instals an objective test: would a *reasonable man* also think it was in the public interest? The public interest must be 'substantial' for the disclosure to be justified. It must also be 'necessary' to disclose the information.

In practical terms, exception three may allow a medical record to be disclosed to the General Medical Council in a case of suspected medical malpractice, and this could subsequently be released to the press. However, sections 10, 13 and 14 of the Data Protection Act 1998 are still available to the patient, who can write to the data controller and ask that their sensitive personal details be withheld because it would cause damage and distress, they could also claim compensation for distress and damage caused, or ask the court to rectify, block, erase or destroy the data. A medical condition can certainly be anonymised for the purposes of reporting and journalism, and the newspapers would have to satisfy the common law tests on confidentiality if they received a medical record and wished to publish parts of it (see below).

Medical research in the Data Protection Act 1998

Medical research is a difficult area (see below for more detail and Chapter 10 generally). It is inevitable that some personal details will need to be disclosed to research bodies if medical research is to develop. The second and fifth 'Data Protection Principles' under Schedule 1 of the Data Protection Act 1998 are relevant here, and include the following provisions:

Data Protection Act 1998

Schedule 1

2. Personal data shall be obtained only for one or more specified and lawful purposes, and shall not be further processed in any manner incompatible with that purpose or purposes.

5. Personal data processed for any purpose or purposes shall not be kept for longer than is necessary for that purpose or those purposes.

Section 33 allows for medical research using personal data. It stipulates under section 33(1)–(3) that as long as the data is not processed in a way that supports an individual nor in such a way as to cause substantial damage or substantial distress, then the further processing of data is compatible with the second data protection principle. The fifth data protection principle is also complied with if the data is kept indefinitely.

Additional statutory provisions

There are a very small handful of other statutory provisions that govern confidential personal information. For example, under abortion law, the Chief Medical Office must be notified of every termination. This is for audit purposes.

Abortion Regulations 1991/499

Regulation 4: Notice of termination of pregnancy and information relating to the termination

(1) Any practitioner who terminates a pregnancy in England or Wales shall give to the appropriate Chief Medical Officer:

(a) notice of the termination, and

(b) such other information relating to the termination,

and shall do so by sending them to him or her within 14 days of the termination either in a sealed envelope or by electronic communication transmitted by an electronic communications system solely used for the transfer of confidential information to him or her.

Similarly under the Human Fertilisation and Embryology Act 1990, there is a strict duty of confidentiality over those working at the licensed centres not to disclose information about the individuals seeking treatment under section 33A (added by the 2008 reform).

There are legal rights to view the medical record of a deceased patient under the Access to Health Records Act 1990 (see below).

The Senior Courts Act 1981 allows the High Court to hand down an order to a doctor or a hospital to release the medical files of a patient who is about to embark on a legal case or some other form of litigation (e.g. medical negligence). The patient can apply for the order under section 33(2) of the 1981 Act, but the documents have to be handed to the legal advisor of the patient.

The Care Quality Commission is under a statutory obligation to publish a code of practice about its use of confidential personal information under section 80 of the Health and Social Care Act 2008. The Care Quality Commission is the independent regulator of health and adult social care in England and as part of its role it comes into contact with a lot of sensitive and personal data, including medical records.[3]

ACTIVITY

Draw a flow chart of the provisions of the Data Protection Act 1998 and the different tests that must be satisfied before your medical record can be 'released' to a person or company at the bottom of the diagram.

● ● ● The common law on confidentiality

It is old law that doctors have a duty of confidentiality over their patients, but it has also long been accepted that it can be breached depending on the circumstances. *Hunter* v *Mann* (1974) is a good example, where a doctor was prosecuted for not helping the police. This case illuminates the difficult conflict of interest experienced by doctors when it comes to their duty of confidentiality and their duty to abide by the law.

CASE EXTRACT

Hunter v Mann [1974] QB 767

Facts: The defendant, a doctor, had information which might have led to the identification of the driver of a stolen car who was alleged to be guilty of dangerous driving. A police officer, acting under section 168(2)(b) of the Road Traffic Act 1972, asked the defendant (the doctor) to give the information. He refused on the grounds that the information had been obtained solely through the relationship of doctor and patient and to divulge it would be a breach of professional confidence and the code of conduct. The doctor was convicted of contravening section 168(3).

Held: Dismissing the doctor's appeal, he had a statutory duty imposed upon him to give the information and the justices were correct to convict him.

→

---

[3] They successfully published their code of practice two years later: *Code of Practice on Confidential Personal Information*, December 2010, Care Quality Commission, at www.cqc.org.uk.

Boreham J (at pages 772, 774): In common with other professional men, for instance a priest and there are of course others, the doctor is under a duty not to disclose, without the consent of his patient, information which he, the doctor, has gained in his professional capacity, save in very exceptional circumstances. [...] I appreciate the concern of a responsible medical practitioner who feels that he is faced with a conflict of duty. That the defendant was conscious of a conflict and realised his duty both to society and to his patient is clear from the finding of the justices, but he may find comfort, although the decision goes against him, from the following. First, that he has only to disclose information which may lead to identification and not other confidential matters; secondly, that the result, in my judgment, is entirely consistent with the rules that the British Medical Association have laid down and from which I have quoted in the course of this judgment.

In *Hunter* v *Mann* it is made clear that the duty of confidentiality upon a doctor is not absolute, and he may find that, particularly in relation to statutory duties, he may have to breach his duty of confidentiality to help the police. The good news is that the doctor only needs to disclose information that could lead to the *identity* of the patient, not the medical record itself. This does, in the most part, protect the confidentiality of the patient.

The next significant case is *Gillick*, which confirmed that young people under 16 are entitled to seek medical advice and treatment without their parents' consent. This requires a duty of confidentiality to the child.

CASE EXTRACT

Gillick v West Norfolk and Wisbech AHA **[1986] AC 112**

Facts: Mrs Gillick had several daughters under 16. She became aware of a Memorandum of Guidance, issued from the Department of Health and Social Security (DHSS), which allowed a doctor to give contraceptive advice and treatment to her daughters without her consent. She wrote to the local health authority seeking assurance that no contraceptive advice or treatment would be issued to her daughters without her knowledge or consent, and they refused. Mrs Gillick sought a declaration from the courts that the memorandum was unlawful.

Held: The Court of Appeal supported Mrs Gillick, but the House of Lords allowed the DHSS appeal. There is a duty of confidentiality owed to children.

Lord Fraser (at pages 169, 174): It seems to me verging on the absurd to suggest that a girl or a boy aged 15 could not effectively consent, for example, to have a medical examination of some trivial injury to his body or even to have a broken arm set. Of course the consent of the parents should normally be asked, but they may not be immediately available. Provided the patient, whether a boy or a girl, is capable of understanding what is proposed, and of expressing his or her own wishes, I see no good reason for holding that he or she lacks the capacity to express them validly and effectively and to authorise the medical man to make the examination or give the treatment which he advises. [...] The only practicable course is to entrust the doctor with a discretion to act in accordance with his view of what is best in the interests of the girl who is his patient.

Lord Scarman (at pages 188–9): I would hold that as a matter of law the parental right to determine whether or not their minor child below the age of 16 will have medical treatment terminates if and when the child achieves a sufficient understanding and intelligence to enable him or her to understand fully what is proposed. It will be a question of fact whether a child seeking advice has sufficient understanding of what is involved to give a consent valid in law. Until the child achieves the capacity to consent, the parental right to make the decision continues save only in exceptional circumstances.

The case of *Gillick* consolidated several principles: (1) a competent patient under 16 can consent to medical treatment without the knowledge or consent of her parents; and (2) there is a test in order to ascertain *Gillick* competence and with this competence comes the duty of confidentiality. Lord Fraser's test for *Gillick* competence (and its adjoining confidentiality) is as follows:

- The minor will understand the medical advice.
- The doctor cannot persuade her to inform her parents that she is seeking the advice.
- Unless she receives the sought-after advice or treatment her physical or mental health or both are likely to suffer.
- Her best interests require the doctor to give her the advice, treatment or both without the parental consent.

What is important is that according to *Gillick*, not only must the child be *competent*, but it must be in her *best interests* to be advised or treated without her parents' knowledge.

The case law becomes rather technical at this point, because it is based on 'general' law as opposed to the specific area of medical law. The High Court is one of the most senior civil courts in the land, dealing with hugely important cases in its three divisions: the Queen's Bench Division (i.e. contract and personal injury), the Chancery Division (business and equity) and the Family Division (divorce and medical treatment). It is the Chancery Division in the High Court that has the power to hand down injunctions to prevent confidential information from being disclosed because it deals with equitable matters (i.e. justice, fairness, balance and restoration). In order to hand down an injunction, the appeal courts have had to define, as best they could, what confidentiality is, when a duty to protect it may arise, and where the limits are drawn. The leading case of *AG* v *Guardian Newspapers* (1990) does not offer a definition of confidentiality, but it does identify a 'general equitable duty of conscience' to pinpoint when a duty of confidentiality begins. Lord Bingham took the time to ponder where the duty originated from, whereas Lord Goff listed the three exceptions to a duty of confidence that are still used today (known as the 'common law exceptions'). This advice was thought to aid future judges when deciding whether there was a duty of confidentiality and whether there was a justification for the subsequent breach. *AG* v *Guardian Newspapers* is the first in a trail of cases and has been applied in most of them (listed below).

CASE EXTRACT

AG v Guardian Newspapers (No.2) (1989) 2 FSR 181

Facts: A former member of M.I.5 went to live in Tasmania and wrote the book 'Spycatcher' about his time at the security service. He was making allegations about unlawful activities. The book could not be published in the United Kingdom because of the Official Secrets Act 1911, but he found a publisher in Australia and it was going to be published in the United States. The UK newspapers 'The Observer' and 'The Guardian' published pieces about the legal actions that ensued, and 'The Sunday Times' then published extracts from the book two days before its publication in the United States. The Attorney-General sought an injunction against 'The Sunday Times' from publishing any more extracts of the book.

Held: A person who finds himself acquiring information in confidence is under a duty of confidence until the information is released to the general public or the duty is outweighed by a public interest in disclosure (exceptions stated by Lord Goff).

Lord Bingham (at pages 287–8): The cases show that the duty of confidence does not depend on any contract, express or implied, between the parties. If it did, it would follow on ordinary principles that strangers to the contract would not be bound. But the duty 'depends on the broad principle of equity that he who has received information in confidence shall not take unfair advantage of it'. [...] A third party coming into possession of confidential information is accordingly liable to be restrained from publishing it if he knows the information to be confidential and the circumstances are such as to impose upon him an obligation in good conscience not to publish.

Lord Keith (at pages 306–7): The law has long recognised that an obligation of confidence can arise out of particular relationships. Examples are the relationships of doctor and patient, priest and penitent, solicitor and client, banker and customer. The obligation may be imposed by an express or implied term in a contract but it may also exist independently of any contract on the basis of an independent equitable principle of confidence. [...] The right to personal privacy is clearly one which the law should in this field seek to protect. [...] Further, as a general rule, it is in the public interest that confidences should be respected, and the encouragement of such respect may in itself constitute a sufficient ground for recognising and enforcing the obligation of confidence even where the confider can point to no specific detriment to himself.

Lord Goff (at page 332): A duty of confidence arises when confidential information comes to the knowledge of a person (the confidant) in circumstances where he has notice, or is held to have agreed, that the information is confidential, with the effect that it would be just in all the circumstances that he should be precluded from disclosing the information to others.

Confidentiality is not based in contract. Lord Bingham explained that this was vital because if confidentiality was dependent on a contract, a third party who was not privy to the contract would not be under a duty of confidence if confidential information happened to fall into his hands. Lord Bingham accepts that a duty of confidence stems from a 'broad principle of equity' which stipulates that if a person receives confidential information, it is not just, fair or reasonable to take advantage of it. It is important that the courts are seen to uphold these old equitable principles. Lord Bingham also placed a burden upon the defendant to maintain his duty of confidence 'if he knows' that the information is confidential. This is important – it means that the defendant will have to justify his breach. The information must be 'confidential' but sadly there is no clear definition in law (especially medical law) of what that could include. The circumstances must point to a duty of confidence and a moral obligation (i.e. 'good conscience') to keep the information secret. This is a wide test – whispering a piece of information could satisfy this test – so it will be up to the claimant (e.g. the patient) to prove that, when the information was disclosed to the defendant (e.g. the press), the circumstances were such that the defendant should have known that he was receiving confidential information. The use of the phrase 'good conscience' is very interesting: there is a moral duty to keep secrets and the law will support it. Lord Keith lists the many examples of a duty of confidence, including between doctor and patient, and confirms that this duty may arise through an 'independent equitable principle'. He adds that it is in the public interest to respect the duty of confidence and to encourage that respect we must 'enforce the obligation of confidence' even if there is no clear detriment to the claimant. Lord Goff adds that the defendant must 'have notice' that the information is confidential and that the circumstances should prevent the defendant from disclosing it. The ratio from *AG* v *Guardian Newspapers* has since been enshrined into the General Medical Council's guidance on confidentiality:

> You must make sure that anyone you disclose personal information to understands that you are giving it to them in confidence, which they must respect. All staff members receiving personal information in order to provide or support care are bound by a legal duty of confidence, whether or not they have contractual or professional obligations to protect confidentiality.[4]

Lord Goff added some further 'limiting principles' to identify when the duty of confidentiality has extinguished.

CASE EXTRACT	**Lord Goff** (at pages 333–4): There are three limiting principles. […] The first […] is that the principle of confidentiality only applies to information to the extent that it is confidential. In particular, once it has entered what is usually called the public domain (which means no more than that the information in question is so generally accessible that, in all the circumstances, it cannot be regarded as confidential) then, as a general rule, the principle of confidentiality can have no application to it. […] The second limiting principle is that the duty of confidence applies neither to useless information, nor to trivia. […] The third limiting principle is of far greater importance. It is that, although the basis of the law's protection of confidence is that there is a public interest that confidences should be preserved and protected by the law, nevertheless that public interest may be outweighed by some other countervailing public interest which favours disclosure. […] It is this limiting principle which may require a court to carry out a balancing operation, weighing the public interest in maintaining confidence against a countervailing public interest favouring disclosure.

---

[4] *Confidentiality* (2009) General Medical Council, Explanatory Guidance, page 13, paragraph 28, www.gmc-uk.org.

Lord Goff lists the common law exceptions that allow for a breach of confidence. These exceptions are valid in law today and relate to all kinds of confidential information, whether it be medical or financial, personal or private:

- **Exception 1**: the information must actually be confidential and if it is in the public domain, it probably isn't.
- **Exception 2**: any useless or trivial information is not protected by a duty of confidentiality.
- **Exception 3**: even though there is a public interest in maintaining confidentiality, there may be a greater public interest in disclosure.

There are two questions that spring to mind when reading the common law exceptions. Firstly, it is not clear what 'useless or trivial' information is. Your personal information may be trivial to your next door neighbour, but you may see the disclosure of it as a breach of confidence. Secondly, Lord Goff refers to a 'balancing operation' to ascertain whether the duty to keep information confidential has been outweighed by a duty to disclose that information. This will be decided by judging what is in the public interest. This is a difficult test for any judge, let alone a doctor, to apply and it is now becoming clear that the law of confidentiality is general, universal and difficult to understand in the context of medicine.

The medical case of *W* v *Edgell* (1990) came to court on a matter of patient confidentiality in the same year. The case of *AG* v *Guardian Newspapers* was applied, confirming that not only does a doctor have a duty of confidentiality over a patient, but when there is a danger to the public, one of Lord Goff's common law exceptions must be satisfied before the relevant patient information could be released.

CASE EXTRACT

W v *Edgell* [1990] Ch 359

Facts: The plaintiff (W) who was suffering from paranoid schizophrenia, shot and killed five people and injured two others in 1974. At his trial, the court ordered that he be detained without limit in a secure hospital. In 1986, W's medical officer recommended to the Secretary of State that W be transferred to a regional secure unit which could eventually lead to him returning to the community. The Secretary of State refused consent. The plaintiff then applied to a mental health review tribunal and to support his application he sought a report from the defendant E (Dr Egdell) as an independent consultant psychiatrist. E's report did not support W's application – it disclosed that W had a long standing and continuing interest in homemade bombs – and E did not accept the view that W was no longer a danger to the public. W withdrew his application to the tribunal and refused to consent to E disclosing the report to the medical officer at the secure hospital. E disclosed the report to the medical officer and copies were subsequently sent to the Secretary of State and the Department of Health and Social Security.

Held: The public interest in maintaining that confidence had to be balanced against the public interest in protecting others against possible violence. The nature of the crimes committed by W made it a matter of public interest that those responsible for treating and managing him had all the relevant information concerning his mental state before considering his release from hospital.

Bingham LJ (at page 419): It has never been doubted that the circumstances here were such as to impose on Dr Egdell a duty of confidence owed to W. He could not lawfully sell the contents of his report to a newspaper. [...] Nor could he, without a breach of the law as well as professional etiquette, discuss the case in a learned article or in his memoirs or in gossiping with friends, unless he took appropriate steps to conceal the identity of W. [...] The decided cases very clearly establish: (1) that the law recognises an important public interest in maintaining professional duties of confidence; but (2) that the law treats such duties not as absolute but as liable to be overridden where there is held to be a stronger public interest in disclosure. Thus the public interest in the administration of justice may require a clergyman, a banker, a medical man, a journalist or an accountant to breach his professional duty of confidence.

Bingham LJ went on to explain how the 'public interest' exception might be fulfilled in cases such as these.

CASE EXTRACT

Bingham LJ (at pages 422–4): The parties were agreed, as I think rightly, that the crucial question in the present case was how, on the special facts of the case, the balance should be struck between the public interest in maintaining professional confidences and the public interest in protecting the public against possible violence. [...]

There is one consideration which in my judgment, as in that of the judge, weighs the balance of public interest decisively in favour of disclosure. It may be shortly put. Where a man has committed multiple killings under the disability of serious mental illness, decisions which may lead directly or indirectly to his release from hospital should not be made unless a responsible authority is properly able to make an informed judgment that the risk of repetition is so small as to be acceptable. A consultant psychiatrist who becomes aware, even in the course of a confidential relationship, of information which leads him, in the exercise of what the court considers a sound professional judgment, to fear that such decisions may be made on the basis of inadequate information and with a real risk of consequent danger to the public is entitled to take such steps as are reasonable in all the circumstances to communicate the grounds of his concern to the responsible authorities.

The *Egdell* case illustrates how the general rules on confidentiality can be applied in the context of medicine. It is not always this straightforward – the judges would usually have engaged in a lengthy 'balancing operation' to ascertain whether the public interest in disclosure outweighed the public interest in keeping medical reports private – but the threat of violence appears to be one area in which the courts have no problem in finding in favour of disclosure. The phrases 'possible violence', 'multiple killings' and 'consequent danger to the public' in the judgment were enough to justify a disclosure in the public interest. This judgment did not, therefore, attract much criticism.[5] A case like *Egdell* puts psychiatrists in a difficult position, because they may deal with violent patients (or

---

[5] Interestingly, in the US case of *Tarasoff* v *Regents of the University of California* 551 P 2d 334 (Cal 1976) it was held that if a therapist comes into knowledge that a student is under threat from another student, the therapist is under a duty to disclose that risk to the student (who was subsequently killed).

patients who fantasise about violence) on a regular basis. It appears that if the patient poses a real threat of violence, a disclosure is justified in the public interest. Does this undermine the whole point of visiting a psychiatrist? A dangerous patient may refrain from visiting a psychiatrist for fear of being exposed, thus *increasing* the danger to the public.

When the Human Rights Act 1998 was passed into UK law, it heralded a new era for confidentiality cases. It incorporated the European Convention on Human Rights into our legal system and suddenly, it became apparent to patients, celebrities and businesses that breaches of confidentiality could be pursued under a treble layer of protection:

- Layer 1: the UK common law under *AG* v *Guardian Newspapers* (1990).
- Layer 2: the Data Protection Act 1998.
- Layer 3: the European Convention on Human Rights (Article 8).

Article 8 of the European Convention is a double right in that it is split into two: a right to respect for private life *and* a right to respect for family life. A breach of confidentiality can be likened to an intrusion of privacy, and therefore it is Article 8 that appears to offer the prefect legal protection. However, it is a 'qualified' right, meaning that an exception is written into the Article itself (otherwise it would be referred to as an 'absolute' right).

> ## European Convention on Human Rights
>
> **Article 8(1)**: Everyone has the right to respect for his private and family life, his home and his correspondence.
>
> **Article 8(2)**: There shall be no interference by a public authority with the exercise of this right except such as is in accordance with the law and is necessary in a democratic society in the interests of national security, public safety or the economic wellbeing of the country, for the prevention of disorder or crime, for the protection of health or morals, or for the protection of the rights and freedoms of others.

What is very disappointing about Article 8 is the scope of the exceptions. There are many ways in which a person's private and family life can be interfered with, including the following:

- If it is 'in accordance with the law' in the UK (e.g. section 172 of the Road Traffic Act 1988).
- If it is necessary to maintain a democratic society (e.g. a public inquiry into a serious crime may require the publication of mental health information).
- In the interests of national security (e.g. raiding the home of a suspected terrorist).
- In the interests of public safety (e.g. disclosing a patient with a rare contagious disease – there was a case of Rabies in the UK in 2012).
- For economic wellbeing (e.g. emails exchanged between corrupt bankers bragging about Bollinger were famously broadcast in the UK in 2012).
- For the prevention of disorder or crime (e.g. a defendant's name, address and date of birth are broadcast when he goes on the run).
- For the protection of health or morals (e.g. the courts may have to release a legal judgment with full medical details to justify why they have refused to legalise assisted suicide).
- For the protection of others (e.g. a teenage patient may have been raped and had an abortion – this must be forwarded to the police).

This extensive list of exceptions makes it almost impossible to imagine a scenario in which the UK (or European) courts will uphold the claimant's submission that his confidentiality has been breached. To put it another way, it appears to be very easy for public authorities to breach their duty of confidentiality. One of the first notable human rights cases was *Z* v *Finland*, a case concerning medical records and HIV.

CASE EXTRACT

Z v Finland (2209/93) (1998) 25 EHRR 371

Facts: The applicant, Z, was a Swedish national married to X, whom she had met in Africa. During an investigation of X for a number of sexual offences, it was discovered that he was HIV positive. He was consequently tried on several counts of attempted manslaughter. It was not clear that he had knowledge of his medical condition at the time of the sexual assaults. In attempting to discover this, orders were issued obliging the medical advisers treating both X and Z to give evidence. The police seized medical records concerning Z and added them to the investigation file. X was convicted by the City Court and on two further counts by the Court of Appeal, which disclosed both Z's identity and her medical data in the course of its judgment. The applicant (Z) complained that there had been violations of her right to respect for private and family life under Article 8.

Held: The orders requiring the applicant's medical advisers to give evidence and the seizure of the applicant's medical records and their inclusion in the investigation file did not give rise to a violation of Article 8; but unanimously, that the disclosure of the applicant's identity and medical condition by the Helsinki Court of Appeal did constitute a breach of Article 8.

European Court (at pages 405–6, 411–12): Respecting the confidentiality of health data is a vital principle in the legal systems of all the Contracting Parties to the Convention. It is crucial not only to respect the sense of privacy of a patient but also to preserve his or her confidence in the medical profession and in the health services in general. Without such protection, those in need of medical assistance may be deterred from revealing such information of a personal and intimate nature as may be necessary in order to receive appropriate treatment and, even, from seeking such assistance, thereby endangering their own health and, in the case of transmissible diseases, that of the community. [...]

The above considerations are especially valid as regards protection of the confidentiality of information about a person's HIV infection. The disclosure of such data may dramatically affect his or her private and family life, as well as social and employment situation, by exposing him or her to opprobrium and the risk of ostracism. For this reason it may also discourage persons from seeking diagnosis or treatment and thus undermine any preventive efforts by the community to contain the pandemic. The interests in protecting the confidentiality of such information will therefore weigh heavily in the balance in determining whether the interference was proportionate to the legitimate aim pursued. Such interference cannot be compatible with Article 8 of the Convention unless it is justified by an overriding requirement in the public interest. In view of the highly intimate and sensitive nature of information concerning a person's HIV status, any state measures compelling communication or disclosure of such information without the consent of the patient call for the most careful scrutiny on the part of the Court, as do the safeguards designed to secure

→

an effective protection. At the same time, the Court accepts that the interests of a patient and the community as a whole in protecting the confidentiality of medical data may be outweighed by the interest in investigation and prosecution of crime and in the publicity of court proceedings. [...]

The court was informed by X's lawyer about her wishes that the confidentiality order be extended beyond ten years. It evidently followed from this that she would be opposed to the disclosure of the information in question to the public. In these circumstances, the Court does not find that the impugned publication was supported by any cogent reasons. Accordingly, the publication of the information concerned gave rise to a violation of the applicant's right to respect for her private and family life as guaranteed by Article 8.

The European Court in *Z* v *Finland* applied the exception in Article 8(2) to the letter, finding that it was in the public interest to disclose medical information for the purposes of investigating and prosecuting a serious crime. This was described as a 'legitimate aim' and so the public interest outweighed the protection of confidentiality in medical law. However, the applicant (Z) did win on one ground – there was no need to disclose her identity and HIV infection in the Court of Appeal judgment. It was not justified, and Z had already made it clear during proceedings that the ten-year limit of anonymity was not long enough.

The next case involved the disclosure of private statements made by a nurse during a police investigation when a patient died in her care. The issue was: are the police allowed to disclose private statements without the consent of the person under investigation when the purpose is to aid a professional body in an investigation? The answer is 'yes'.

CASE EXTRACT

Woolgar v Chief Constable of Sussex [2000] 1 WLR 25

Facts: The appellant, a registered nurse, was matron of a nursing home. After the death of a patient in her care, allegations were made relating to over-administration of drugs which led to her being arrested and interviewed by the police. The matter was referred to the disciplinary committee of the United Kingdom Central Council for Nursing, Midwifery and Health Visiting (UKCC). The UKCC contacted the police for relevant information. The police, in accordance with their normal practice, asked the appellant for authority to disclose her statements. She indicated that her agreement would not be forthcoming. The police then indicated that they proposed to disclose the requested material. The appellant sought an injunction to restrain the police from disclosing the contents of her interview to the UKCC.

Held: There was a public interest in this disclosure.

Kennedy LJ (at pages 36–7): In my judgment, where a regulatory body such as the UKCC, operating in the field of public health and safety, seeks access to confidential material in the possession of the police, being material which the police are reasonably persuaded is of some relevance to the subject matter of an inquiry being conducted by the regulatory body, then a countervailing public interest is shown to exist which, as in this case, entitles the police to release the material to the regulatory

→

body on the basis that save in so far as it may be used by the regulatory body for the purposes of its own inquiry, the confidentiality which already attaches to the material will be maintained. [...] I would accept, that disclosure is 'necessary in a democratic society in the interests of . . . public safety or . . . for the protection of health or morals, or for the protection of the rights and freedoms of others' [Article 8 exception]. [...]

In order to safeguard the interests of the individual, it is, in my judgment, desirable that where the police are minded to disclose, they should, as in this case, inform the person affected of what they propose to do in such time as to enable that person, if so advised, to seek assistance from the court. In some cases that may not be practicable or desirable, but in most cases that seems to me to be the course that should be followed.

Kennedy LJ was clearly encouraged by the fact that the UKCC was a regulatory body in the field of public health and safety. A 'countervailing' public interest can trump the right to confidentiality if the police are reasonable persuaded of some relevance to the inquiry. This judgment appears to be applicable only to inquiries by regulatory bodies. Kennedy LJ invokes the exception to Article 8, which allows a disclosure to take place if it is 'necessary in a democratic society' for public safety, health and morals. The police should still notify the person that their private information is about to be disclosed to a regulatory body, even if consent is not forthcoming, and a court is on hand to offer advice.[6]

The security of medical records was explored in the next relevant case of *Ashworth Hospital Authority* (2002). Ian Brady (one of the Moors Murderers) was keen to inform the public about his ill treatment in prison (he was on hunger strike in protest), and an employee leaked his medical notes to a newspaper. Ashworth Prison (one of three high security prisons in the UK) sought an order requiring the newspaper to identify the person responsible for the breach. The courts had no trouble in condemning the breach of confidentiality and ordered the colleague to be disclosed in order to uphold patient confidentiality. What is strange about this case is that Ian Brady – the patient – *wanted* his notes to be released. This begs the question: why was confidentiality even an issue if the patient consented?

CASE EXTRACT

Ashworth Hospital Authority v *Mirror Group Newspapers Ltd*
[2002] 1 WLR 2033

Facts: A convicted murderer detained in custody at a secure hospital managed by the claimant authority was on hunger strike and conducting a media campaign about his treatment. An article was published in the defendant's newspaper containing extracts from the patient's medical records. The information had been supplied by an intermediary, who had been paid for it, and it was probable that an employee at the

→

---

[6] There appears to be agreement that there is a public interest in the proper administration of professional disciplinary hearings in medicine, according to Thorpe LJ in *A Health Authority* v *X (No.1)* [2001] EWCA Civ 2014 at paragraph 19.

hospital had supplied the intermediary with a printout from the hospital's computer database. The employee would in so doing have been in breach of his duty of confidentiality under his contract of employment. The hospital authority, having attempted unsuccessfully to identify the informant, applied for orders against the defendants (i) requiring them to deliver up to all medical records or copies or extracts in their possession relating to the hospital's care or treatment of the patient, (ii) restraining them from publishing, distributing or otherwise disseminating information contained in those records and (iii) requiring them to explain how they had come to be in such possession or control and identifying any employee and others involved.

Held: In view of the need for the integrity of the authority's records to be protected and the authority's need to identify and punish the informant, the disclosure ordered by the initial judge had been justified.

Lord Woolf (at pages 2037, 2052–3): The importance of confidentiality of medical records is emphasised when a new member of staff is engaged at Ashworth. The contract of employment contains a clause:

> Disclosure of information. You must not whilst you are employed or after your employment ends disclose to any unauthorised person information concerning the authority's business or the patients in its care nor must you make any copy, abstract, summary or précis of the whole or of a document relating to the authority.

It is part of the agreed facts that leaks to the press have a detrimental effect on security; treatment of patients and staff morale, because they may inhibit proper recording of information about patients; may deter patients from providing information about themselves; may damage the patient–doctor relationship which rests on trust; may lead to assaults by patients on a patient about whom information is disclosed; may create an atmosphere of distrust amongst staff which is detrimental to efficient and cooperative work; and give rise to fear of future (and potentially more damaging) leaks. [...]

The situation here is exceptional, [...] as it has to be, if disclosure of sources is to be justified. The care of patients at Ashworth is fraught with difficulty and danger. The disclosure of the patient's records increases that difficulty and danger and to deter the same or similar wrongdoing in the future it was essential that the source should be identified and punished. This was what made the orders to disclose necessary and proportionate and justified. The fact that Ian Brady had himself disclosed his medical history did not detract from the need to prevent staff from revealing medical records of patients.

Ashworth tells us that a hospital can bring an action for breach of confidentiality even though the information disclosed was *supported* by the victim of the disclosure. This is to protect the running of the hospital as a public service and to ensure that the morale, trust and security of the hospital was not destroyed. In support of this finding, Lord Woolf lists many reasons why hospital records should be protected – including bad morale, lack of security, risk of assault and distrust of staff – and they are all very good reasons for identifying the employee, but the real justification for the order appears to be the need to punish the employee who breached his contractual duty. This is most unusual, because it is not usually justified in civil law to reveal the identity of a person for the sole purpose of punishing him. Lord Woolf has probably made the right decision because caring for dangerous prisoners could well be made more difficult in light of security breaches, but he has worded the judgment in such a way as to be misinterpreted as a witch hunt. Hopefully, this rather strong judgment will simply turn on its facts, that is, be a one off.[7]

A further balancing act was played out in the well known case of *Campbell* v *Mirror Group Newspapers Ltd* (2004). This was a confidentiality case brought by supermodel Naomi Campbell against *The Mirror*, and had very little to do with medical law. However, it added a lot to the law on confidentiality, and so it is often cited alongside *AG* v *Guardian Newspapers* (1990). Article 10 – freedom of expression – made a significant appearance in this case, turning it into a human rights battle between a right to privacy (Article 8) and a right to publish (Article 10). Article 10 is also a qualified right, meaning that an exception is written into the Article itself (otherwise it would be an absolute right).

European Convention on Human Rights

Article 10(1): Everyone has the right to freedom of expression. This right shall include freedom to hold opinions and to receive and impart information and ideas without interference by public authority and regardless of frontiers. This Article shall not prevent States from requiring the licensing of broadcasting, television or cinema enterprises.

Article 10(2): The exercise of these freedoms, since it carries with it duties and responsibilities, may be subject to such formalities, conditions, restrictions or penalties as are prescribed by law and are necessary in a democratic society, in the interests of national security, territorial integrity or public safety, for the prevention of disorder or crime, for the protection of health or morals, for the protection of the reputation or rights of others, for preventing the disclosure of information received in confidence, or for maintaining the authority and impartiality of the judiciary.

In the *Campbell* case, the courts decided that an article about meetings at Narcotics Anonymous could ruin the treatment and pose a risk of harm to the fragility of the celebrity.

CASE EXTRACT

Campbell v *Mirror Group Newspapers Ltd* [2004] 2 AC 457

Facts: The defendant newspaper published articles which disclosed Naomi Campbell's (C) drug addiction and the fact that she was receiving therapy, gave details of group meetings she attended and showed photographs of her in a street as she was leaving a group meeting. C sought damages against the newspaper for breach of confidentiality. She accepted that the newspaper was entitled to publish her drug addiction and the fact that she was receiving treatment (these were in the public interest because she had lied about it), but alleged that the newspaper had

→

---

[7] The case trailed all the way up to the Court of Appeal when only the journalist (Ackroyd) – not the employee – was revealed, and the Court of Appeal confirmed that the journalist did not have to reveal his source after all: *Mersey Care NHS Trust* v *Ackroyd (No. 2)* [2007] EWCA Civ 101.

acted in breach of confidence by obtaining and publishing the additional details of her therapy at the group meetings and the photographs, which had been taken covertly. The newspaper denied the claim on the grounds that it was entitled, in the public interest, to publish the information in order to correct her misleading public statements and asserted that the information published was minor and not sufficiently significant to amount to a breach of the duty of confidence.

Held: The details of C's therapy for her drug addiction related to the condition of her physical and mental health and the treatment she was receiving for it – they were akin to the private and confidential information contained in a medical record – and their publication required specific justification. C's right pursuant to Article 8 to respect for her private life outweighed the newspaper's right pursuant to Article 10 to freedom of expression.

Lord Hope (at pages 483–4): Views may differ as to what is the best treatment for an addiction. But it is well known that persons who are addicted to the taking of illegal drugs or to alcohol can benefit from meetings at which they discuss and face up to their addiction. The private nature of these meetings encourages addicts to attend them in the belief that they can do so anonymously. The assurance of privacy is an essential part of the exercise. The therapy is at risk of being damaged if the duty of confidence which the participants owe to each other is breached by making details of the therapy, such as where, when and how often it is being undertaken, public. I would hold that these details are obviously private. [...]

Where the person is suffering from a condition that is in need of treatment one has to try, in order to assess whether the disclosure would be objectionable, to put oneself into the shoes of a reasonable person who is in need of that treatment. Otherwise the exercise is divorced from its context. [...] The context was that of a drug addict who was receiving treatment. It is her sensibilities that needed to be taken into account. Critical to this exercise was an assessment of whether disclosure of the details would be liable to disrupt her treatment. It does not require much imagination to appreciate the sense of unease that disclosure of these details would be liable to engender, especially when they were accompanied by a covertly taken photograph. [...] I would expect a drug addict who was trying to benefit from meetings to discuss her problem anonymously with other addicts to find this distressing and highly offensive.

The mind that has to be examined is that, not of the reader in general, but of the person who is affected by the publicity. The question is what a reasonable person of ordinary sensibilities would feel if she was placed in the same position as the claimant and faced with the same publicity. [...]

Baroness Hale (at pages 499–502): The Court of Appeal in this case held that the information revealed here was not in the same category as clinical medical records. That may be so, in the sense that it was not the notes made by a doctor when consulted by a patient. But the information was of exactly the same kind as that which would be recorded by a doctor on those notes: the presenting problem was addiction to illegal drugs, the diagnosis was no doubt the same, and the prescription was therapy, including the self-help group therapy offered by regular attendance at Narcotics Anonymous. [...] The risk of harm is what matters at this stage, rather than the proof that actual harm has occurred.

Lord Hope and Baroness Hale delivered the leading judgments in the *Campbell* case, and both contain interesting amendments to the law on confidentiality. Lord Hope established a clear test for when information can be categorised as 'private' and it reads like this.

The 'privacy' test

The mind that has to be examined is that, not of the reader in general, but of the person who is affected by the publicity. The question is what a reasonable person of ordinary sensibilities would feel if she was placed in the same position as the claimant and faced with the same publicity.

Lord Hope makes his reasons behind this test clear: in order to assess whether a disclosure is objectionable, the judge or jury must put themselves in the position of the person requiring treatment. He concluded that a disclosure of the nature seen in this case could disrupt treatment, would be distressing and highly offensive, and the therapy (which is based on confidential discussions with other addicts) could be damaged.

Baroness Hale approached the issue from a slightly different view, assuming from the very beginning that the information was confidential and using the judgment to explore the *effect* of the disclosure on the patient. Baroness Hale likened a meeting with Narcotics Anonymous to a medical record because it concerned information about the mental condition of the patient and the treatment required, and this should automatically attract a very high level of confidentiality. Baroness Hale also found that whether a piece of information was confidential or not depended on whether it carried a *risk of harm* to the patient (which does not have to materialise).

The 'confidentiality' test

The risk of harm is what matters at this stage, rather than the proof that actual harm has occurred.

The justification for this new test is the fragility of the patient: a breach of confidence during treatment for a mental condition may make the situation even worse. This is a useful addition to the law, because so far the courts have only defined *when* a piece of information becomes confidential and the *exceptions* to a duty of confidentiality (in *AG* v *Guardian Newspapers*). We now know that there is more likely to be a breach of confidentiality if there is a *risk of harm* to the patient. It will be up to the patient to prove this risk. Baroness Hale also confirmed that medical information can be construed as a medical record if the content of the disclosure is something that a doctor would write down.

Campbell has since been followed by a medical case. In *Stone* (2006) a convicted murderer (S) wanted to stop the publication of a homicide inquiry because it contained a lot of information about his mental health and treatment. He did not find much sympathy from the courts, mainly because, as a convicted murder, he had put himself in a difficult situation. There was a clear balance between a right to privacy (Article 8) and a right to freedom of expression (Article 10) in this case, and inevitably, the history of S meant that there was a public interest in disclosure. The grounds of this judgment are worth criticising. Does a patient ever 'deserve' disclosure of his entire medical history because of his criminal acts?

CASE EXTRACT

Stone v South East Coast SHA (formerly Kent and Medway SHA) [2006] EWHC 1668

Facts: The defendant (Michael Stone – S) was convicted of the murders of a mother and a daughter (and the attempted murder of a second daughter). An independent inquiry into his care, treatment and supervision was launched, because he was found to have health problems before the murders took place. S cooperated fully with the inquiry panel and released his medical records. In 2005, he indicated through his lawyers that he objected to the report in its full form being published to the world at large. He accepted that the full version of the report may be provided to health professionals and relevant professional bodies and similar agencies (who would be under a duty of confidentiality with regard to its contents) and he also accepted that *some* version of the report properly could, indeed should, be placed before the public, but he asserted that the extensive citations from his private medical record would, if publicised, be a disproportionate and unlawful interference with his private life, contrary to Article 8 of the European Convention on Human Rights.

Held: S did have a right to privacy, and a publication of his medical details may deter future patients from cooperating with inquiry panels, but this was outweighed by the public interest in knowing about his medical treatment and how the loopholes therein (if any) would be fixed in the future. S had also caused his own predicament by committing murder in the first place, and because of the sheer amount of publicity surrounding the case, many of his details were already in the public domain. The report could not be summarised, and if it was the public might suspect a cover up, so all of the details could be released.

Davis J (at paras 34, 36, 39, 44–55): In a case such as the present an ultimate balance has to be struck not only by weighing the considerations for and against a restriction on the right to privacy by reference to Article 8 itself but also by weighing the considerations for and against a restriction on publication by reference to Article 10. [...]

The defendants [South East Coast] decided that, notwithstanding the best efforts of the journalist involved, [a] summary was not appropriate for publication: it was unable to cover all the fundamental points; it could not contain the amount of detail needed for the report to be of sufficient value to persons reading it; and its effect, by reducing the text, was to distort the report itself and to devalue its conclusions. [...]

I consider that there is a degree of force in the observation that publication of a summary or redacted version of this kind might be viewed with scepticism by the public, who might even suspect a cover-up. [...] It is not practicable to publish a report without disclosing details of Mr Stone's private medical information. [...]

So far as Mr Stone is concerned, the most weighty point in his favour, as it seems to me, is his very entitlement to claim a right of privacy. [...] Further, that is reinforced by other and wider considerations of the public interest: first, that persons may talk freely with their doctors, probation officers and other such persons without being deterred by risk of subsequent disclosure; [...] second, that such persons may give access to such information for the purposes of an inquiry without being deterred from doing so through fear of such matters later being released into the public domain.

But it seems to me that the force of those points is significantly outweighed by a number of other considerations. [...]

→

There is a true public interest in the public at large knowing of the actual care and treatment supplied (or not supplied) to Mr Stone: and knowing, and being able to reach an informed assessment of, the failures identified and steps that may be taken to address identified deficiencies. [...] [The] community has a reasonable and justified expectation that an inquiry undertaken after such a high profile case as the present will be publicised in full, so that the public is not left in the dark (or in the shade) about how it happened or left to speculate about the lessons that have been or should be learnt and about the recommendations made, with a view to implementation, to reduce the risk of such occurrences in the future. [...]

It is of importance as a justification for restricting Mr Stone's right to privacy in this context that this inquiry, and all this publicity, have arisen out of Mr Stone's own acts – acts found to have been criminal. He has, as it were, put himself in the public domain by reason of those criminal acts, which inevitably created great publicity. [...]

I also think it a point of considerable importance as a justification for restricting Mr Stone's right to privacy in this context that a great deal of information relating to the background, treatment and mental health of Mr Stone has already been put in the public domain, and at a significant level of detail. The essential nature of his observed mental and personality disorders is already known.

Davis J clearly outlines the grounds upon which full disclosure of a medical record can be made in this case, and all of them appear to trace back to the wrongful behaviour of the patient as if it is justification for disclosure. It was found that a summary of the report was not appropriate because it could lead to distortion, insufficient coverage, and suspicion of a cover up. Davis J does recognise the importance of the entitlement to privacy because dangerous patients need to talk freely with their doctors and probation officers, and they may be deterred from communicating with inquiries in the future if they knew their private medical information may not be safeguarded. However, this was outweighed by the public interest in knowing about his mental care before the killings and any failings in the system. They key phrase in the judgment to justify the public interest in disclosure came in paragraph 45.2 when Davis J said:

> the existence of potentially dangerous persons at liberty in the community affects the entire community. That community has a reasonable and justified expectation that an inquiry undertaken after such a high profile case as the present will be publicised in full, so that the public is not left in the dark . . .

Davis J reverts back to one of the older justifications for disclosure listed by Lord Goff in *AG* v *Guardian Newspapers*: if information is already in the public domain, the duty of confidence is extinguished and it can be disclosed. This is unfair on the patient because it is not what the exception states: just because some information is already released, this does not justify the release of *even more*. The case of *Stone* may turn on its facts because it involved a very public murder inquiry, but the 'balancing exercise' and 'issue of proportionality' that Davis J refers to in his judgment have not been applied as strictly as they might have been if the patient was a law abiding patient.

Overview of the common law

There are other confidentiality cases in other areas of law, but the notable cases – *AG* v *Guardian Newspapers*, *W* v *Egdell*, *Z* v *Finland*, *Ashworth* v *Mirror Group Newspapers*,

Campbell v *Mirror Group Newspapers* and *Stone* v *South East Coast* – all show us how the general common law of confidentiality (mainly established in *AG* & *Campbell*) applies to the disclosure of medical details (in *Egdell*, *Finland*, *Ashworth* and *Stone*). It remains to be seen how the common law on confidentiality will develop. The current rules can be summarised as follows:

- *Hunter* v *Mann* [1974] QB 767
    - A duty of confidentiality is not absolute.
- *Gillick* v *West Norfolk and Wisbech Health Authority* [1986] AC 112
    - A duty of confidentiality is owed to a young person under sixteen if that child is deemed to be competent.
- *AG* v *Guardian Newspapers (No.2)* [1990] AC 109
    - The duty of confidentiality arises from the equitable principle of good conscience.
    - A duty of confidence exists if the holder 'ought to know' that the information is confidential.
    - The circumstances surrounding the disclosure can also point to a duty of confidence.
    - There are three exceptions to a duty of confidence: already in the public domain, trivial details, or a public interest in disclosure.
- *W* v *Egdell* [1990] Ch 359
    - A balancing act must be performed between the public interest in maintaining confidentiality and the public interest in ensuring a safe society.
- *Z* v *Finland* (22009/93) (1998) 25 EHRR 371
    - It is in the public interest to disclose medical information when investigating and prosecuting a serious crime.
    - This meets the exception under Article 8.
    - The patient's personal details do not need to be included in the court judgment for the public to see.
- *Woolgar* v *Chief Constable of Sussex* [1999] 3 All ER 604
    - The police can disclose private information to a regulatory body.
    - The regulatory body must be conducting an inquiry.
    - The inquiry must be in the interests of public health and safety.
- *Ashworth Hospital Authority* v *Mirror Group Newspapers Ltd* [2002] 1 WLR 2033
    - A hospital can claim a breach in confidentiality when their patient records are duplicated and released.
    - This is even if the patient consented to the release.
    - It is vital that patient records are kept secure for security reasons.
    - The need to punish the employee is also a factor to be considered.
- *Campbell* v *Mirror Group Newspapers Ltd* [2004] UKHL 22
    - The test for whether information is 'private' is based on a person in the position of the patient/celebrity faced with the same publicity/disclosure.
    - Medical information in a newspaper article is the same as a medical record if it cites mental illness and its treatment.
    - The test for whether information is confidential depends on whether its disclosure comes with a risk of harm to the patient/celebrity.

- *Stone v South East Coast SHA (formerly Kent and Medway SHA)* **[2006] EWHC 1668**
  - A summary report or limited medical details may raise suspicion in the public eye.
  - It is in the public interest to know about the mental health and treatment of a convicted murderer before he killed the victims in order to ascertain what is being done about it and how their safety is being supported by the State.
  - A patient who commits a murder cannot then complain that his personal details are exposed to the media.
  - If extensive personal details are exposed to the media already, this may justify further disclosure (however *Stone* may turn on its facts on this point because it was a famous murder inquiry).

ACTIVITY

Imagine that Peter Sutcliffe, the Yorkshire Ripper, brings a legal action against Bradford Prison because the details of his parole hearing are broadcast to the nation on the evening news, which contains information about his mental disorders. He did argue that he was schizophrenic at his murder trial in the 1980s, but the jury convicted him anyway. Do you think his confidentiality has been breached under the common law?

The guidelines on confidentiality

It may have become clear at this point that the law on confidentiality is scattered. It would be completely unreasonable to expect doctors and other healthcare professionals to trawl through the complex provisions of the Data Protection Act 1998 and the common law to ascertain what the current law on confidentiality looks like. To this end, the various medical associations and authorities – the British Medical Association, the Department of Health and the General Medical Council – have published a wide range of confidentiality guidelines to assist the medical profession. The result is a larger collection of guidelines than usual:

- **The Department of Health**
  - The Caldicott Committee (1997)
  - Confidentiality: Code of Practice (2003)
  - The NHS Constitution (2013)
- **British Medical Association**
  - Access to Health Records (2008)
  - Confidentiality Tool Kit (2009)
- **General Medical Council**
  - Good Medical Practice (2013)
  - Confidentiality (2009)

It is impossible to set out all of the provisions, but most of them restate the rules of the common law in a way that is user-friendly for healthcare professionals. It must be noted at this point that if a patient wishes to complain about a breach of confidentiality, the guidelines are not legally enforceable. Rather the general law on confidentiality will apply.

The Department of Health[8]

The Department of Health is a governmental department, so any medical guidelines handed down by the government are likely to form the basis for other professional guidelines (e.g. from the General Medical Council).

The Caldicott Committee

In 1997 a report was published by the Department of Health on the use of patient identifiable information. It was chaired by Fiona Caldicott and is known as the 'Caldicott Committee Report'.[9] It called for greater awareness of patient confidentiality and proposed stronger security measures for the storage of patient identifiable information. It made a total of sixteen recommendations on the use of information in the NHS, and these included:

- **Recommendation 3**: A senior person, preferably a health professional, should be nominated in each health organisation to act as a guardian, responsible for safeguarding the confidentiality of patient information.[10]

- **Recommendation 4**: Clear guidance should be provided for those individuals/bodies responsible for approving uses of patient identifiable information.

- **Recommendation 8**: The NHS Number should replace other identifiers wherever practicable, taking account of the consequences of errors and particular requirements for other specific identifiers.

- **Recommendation 10**: Where particularly sensitive information is transferred, privacy enhancing technologies (e.g. encrypting identifiers or patient identifying information) must be explored.[11]

Patient identifiable information was identified as follows:[12]

Surname	Forename
Initials	Address
Postcode	Date of Birth
Date of diagnosis or death	Gender
NHS number	National Insurance Number
Hospital or GP Practice	Ethnic group
Occupation	(A combination of any of the above)

The Caldicott Committee also published six general principles to ensure good practice when accessing patient identifiable information:

---

[8] www.gov.uk/government/organisations/department-of-health.

[9] Report on the Review of Patient Identifiable Information: The Caldicott Committee, December 1997, The Department of Health (archived): http://webarchive.nationalarchives.gov.uk/20130107105354/ http://www.dh.gov.uk/en/publicationsandstatistics/publications/publicationspolicyandguidance/ DH_4068403.

[10] This is known as a 'Caldicott Guardian'.

[11] The sixteen recommendations are outlined on pages iv–v of the introduction.

[12] Listed on page 89 of the report.

1. Justify the purpose(s) for which the information is required.

2. Do not use patient identifiable information unless it is absolutely necessary.

3. Use the minimum necessary patient identifiable information.

4. Access to patient identifiable information should be on a strict need to know basis.

5. Everyone with access to patient identifiable information should be aware of their responsibilities.

6. Understand and comply with the law.[13]

These six general principles have now been incorporated into the NHS Code of Practice for Confidentiality (2003). The Caldicott Committee concluded that the NHS in general showed a lack of awareness for the importance of confidentiality, and that trust was a vital element to patient care.

EXTRACT

Report on the Review of Patient Identifiable Information: The Caldicott Committee, December 1997, The Department of Health (archived):

http://webarchive.nationalarchives.gov.uk/20130107105354/ http://www.dh.gov.uk/en/publicationsandstatistics/publications/ publicationspolicyandguidance/DH_4068403

Paragraph 2.1.1: The need to safeguard the confidentiality of the information that patients give to clinicians about their condition, their personal circumstances, their family and their way of life, is fundamental to the relationship between patients and health care professionals.

Paragraph 4.1.4: We concluded that whilst there was no significant evidence of unjustified use of patient identifiable information, there was a general lack of awareness throughout the NHS at all levels of existing guidance on confidentiality and security, increasing the risk of error or misuse. Problems posed by poor access controls were identified . . .

The Caldicott Committee believed that any release of patient identifiable information should be 'robustly justified' and proper technology should be used to safeguard such sensitive information.

EXTRACT

Paragraph 4.6.5: Where particular items of information, such as date of birth or postcode, are required for purposes other than confirmation of identity, there may be sufficient justification, on practical grounds, for these specific items to accompany the NHS number. Such exceptions should be robustly justified.

Paragraph 4.6.8: . . . there is concern that the new NHS number may not be a sufficiently secure main/sole identifier for information flows of a particularly sensitive nature for example from clinicians to the Public Health Laboratory Service where HIV/AIDS is involved . . . The use of appropriate privacy enhancing technologies, for example encryption of the NHS number, must be explored as a matter of urgency.

---

[13] Listed on page 17 of the report.

The Code of Practice for Confidentiality

In light of the Caldicott Committee Report (1997), the Department of Health published a Code of Practice for Confidentiality (2003) to incorporate the Caldicott principles throughout the entire NHS. It is considered to be the current authority on confidentiality in medical practice and it is very thorough.[14] However, it describes the law in a way that is accessible to healthcare professionals. For example, the Code of Practice helpfully defines what is meant by a 'duty of confidence' in a medical context.

EXTRACT

Confidentiality: NHS Code of Practice, November 2003, Department of Health:

https://www.gov.uk/government/publications/confidentiality-nhs-code-of-practice

Page 7 paragraph 9: A duty of confidence arises when one person discloses information to another (e.g. patient to clinician) in circumstances where it is reasonable to expect that the information will be held in confidence.[15] It:

a. Is a legal obligation that is derived from case law;

b. Is a requirement established within professional codes of conduct;[16] and

c. Must be included within NHS employment contracts as a specific requirement linked to disciplinary procedures.

The Code of Practice then moves on to describe confidentiality in a medical context, the boundaries of consent, the legal exceptions to a duty of confidentiality and the issues that lie on the boundaries (e.g. medical research).

EXTRACT

Confidentiality: NHS Code of Practice, November 2003, Department of Health:

https://www.gov.uk/government/publications/confidentiality-nhs-code-of-practice

Page 7 paragraph 11: . . . information that can identify individual patients must not be used or disclosed for purposes other than healthcare without the individual's explicit consent, some other legal basis, or where there is a robust public interest or legal justification to do so.[17]

Page 8 paragraph 13: Many current uses of confidential patient information do not contribute to or support the healthcare that a patient receives. Very often, these other uses are extremely important and provide benefits to society – e.g. medical research, protecting the health of the public, health services management and financial audit . . .

→

---

[14] It is still applicable today, but there was Supplementary Guidance published in November (2010).

[15] This is taken directly from *AG* v *Guardian Newspapers (No.2)* [1990] AC 109.

[16] This is a reference to the General Medical Council, examined below.

[17] These are the common law exceptions from *AG* v *Guardian Newspapers (No.2)* [1990] AC 109.

Paragraph 15: . . . explicit consent is not usually required for information disclosures needed to provide . . . healthcare. Even so, opportunities to check that patient's understand what may happen should be taken . . .

Paragraph 16: Where the purpose is not directly concerned with the healthcare of a patient however, it would be wrong to assume consent.

It may seem obvious, but if a patient consents to his or her confidential information being released, there is not a legal problem. This is because the act of consent absolves the doctor from his duty to provide confidentiality.[18] The NHS Code of Practice on Confidentiality (2003) has outlined what is required when it comes to both explicit and implicit consent. Generally speaking, a healthcare professional must obtain the consent (implicit or explicit) of the patient when disclosing their confidential information. However, it depends on the kind of disclosure as to what kind of consent is required. The Code of Practice states that where the disclosure is *directly related* to their healthcare, only implied consent is required.

EXTRACT

Confidentiality: NHS Code of Practice, November 2003, Department of Health:

https://www.gov.uk/government/publications/confidentiality-nhs-code-of-practice

Page 21 paragraph 8: . . . Examples might be:

- In respect of a referral letter – 'I am writing to the consultant to let them know about your medical history and the abdominal pains you are having';
- With electronic records – 'The hospital specialist is able to view your health records to understand your medical history and the tests we have arranged to date before he examines you'; or
- In respect of other agencies – 'I will tell Social Services about your dietary needs to help them arrange Meals on Wheels for you'.

A doctor is clearly justified in passing on confidential information if he is satisfied that the patient *understands* what he is doing. This is implied consent, because the patient is presumed to know that a disclosure of her confidential information is imminent to allow her treatment to go ahead. It places an emphasis on the doctor to explain the process properly. A badly informed patient who does not understand what is going on cannot be assumed to be consenting. It is well established that third parties are included in implied consent (e.g. the laboratory staff would be the third party) and this was confirmed in the case of *Kapadia* (2000).

---

[18] This was confirmed in a divorce case of *C* v *C* [1946] 1 All ER 562 when both parties consented to the release of a medical record.

Kapadia v Lambeth LBC (2001) 57 BMLR 170

Facts: The patient (K) brought an action of discrimination under the Disability Discrimination Act 1995. He was in a dispute with his employers and underwent a medical examination to prove his disability, but he did not want the report released to his employers until he had seen it.

Held: Consent to a medical examination is implied consent to the disclosure of that examination to the relevant parties. It was expedient to the legal case and good practice to allow the disclosure of the report and this did not require the consent of the patient.

Pill LJ: On the facts the Court knows, the report should, in my judgment, have been disclosed by the doctor to the employers. No further consent was required from the claimant. By consenting to being examined on behalf of the employers the claimant was consenting to the disclosure to the employers of a report resulting from that examination. A practice under which a person who has agreed to be examined in circumstances such as these, but then claims a veto upon disclosure of the report to those who obtained it is not, in my view, a good practice. Indeed it is an impediment to the fair and expeditious conduct of litigation.

The decision in *Kapadia* may be uncomfortable for some. It seems as though Mr Kapadia could not stop his own information from being released to his employer simply because he consented to a medical examination at an earlier date. It does, of course, make perfect sense to release a medical record if it is at the centre of a legal action, but surely the patient is free to withdraw consent, even if it was implied? This is the problem with implied consent: it can sometimes be 'implied' further down the line where the patient has no control over what happens to his information.[19]

Where the disclosure is *not* directly related to patient healthcare (e.g. police investigation), the Code of Practice makes it clear that explicit consent must be sought (or one of the statutory or common law exceptions can be applied).

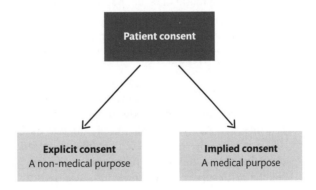

Figure 5.1

---

[19] *Kapadia* has since been applied in *Chang-Tave v Haydon School* (2010) WL 3694340 (Westlaw).

The NHS Code of Practice provides more details to healthcare professionals on gleaning explicit consent.

EXTRACT

Confidentiality: NHS Code of Practice, November 2003, Department of Health:

https://www.gov.uk/government/publications/confidentiality-nhs-code-of-practice

Page 32 paragraph 16: Explicit consent

When seeking explicit consent from patients, the approach must be to provide:

a. Honest, clear, objective information about information uses and their choices – this information must be multi-layered, allowing patients to seek as much detail as they require; . . .

c. Reasonable time (and privacy) to reach decisions;

d. Support and explanations about any form that they may be required to sign;

e. A choice as to whether to be contacted in the future about further uses, and how such contacts should be made; and

f. Evidence that consent has been given, either by noting this within a patient's health record or by including a consent form signed by the patient.

Paragraph 17: The information provided must cover:

a. A basic explanation of what information is recorded and why, and what further uses may be made of it;

b. A description of the benefits that may result from the proposed use or disclosure of the information;

c. How the information and its future uses will be protected and assured, including how long the information is likely to be retained, and under what circumstances it will be destroyed;

d. Any outcomes, implications or risks, if consent is withheld (this must be honest, clear, and objecting – it must not be or appear to be coercive in any way); and

e. An explanation that any consent can be withdrawn in the future (including any difficulties in withdrawing information that has already been shared).

The gleaning of explicit consent is complex to allow the patient time to understand that his medical record is about to be released for non-medical purposes.[20] The Code of Practice casts its eye over the public interest exception, as derived from common law. The provisions are explained to healthcare professionals in a very simple way, and it is clear that they are under an obligation to perform a balancing act if they are contemplating the disclosure of confidential information.

---

[20] A patient awaiting a serious surgical procedure abroad may be asked for explicit consent for his records to be released to the foreign hospital. If he refuses this will halt the surgery, but the patient clearly has a right to withdraw his consent to disclosure in the guidelines (above).

> **EXTRACT**
>
> Confidentiality: NHS Code of Practice, November 2003, Department of Health:
>
> **https://www.gov.uk/government/publications/confidentiality-nhs-code-of-practice**
>
> **Page 34 paragraph 30**: Under common law, staff are permitted to disclose personal information in order to prevent and support detection, investigation and punishment of serious crime and/or to prevent abuse or serious harm to others where they judge, on a case by case basis, that the public good that would be achieved by the disclosure outweighs both the obligation of confidentiality to the individual patient and the broader public interest in the provision of a confidential service.
>
> **Paragraph 32**: Wherever possible the issue of disclosure should be discussed with the individual concerned and consent sought. Where this is not forthcoming, the individual should be told of any decision to disclose against his/her wishes. This will not be possible in certain circumstances, e.g. where the likelihood of a violent response is significant or where informing a potential suspect in a criminal investigation might allow them to evade custody, destroy evidence or disrupt an investigation.

It is clear that doctors have to deal with quite serious matters as part of their job. A number of health complaints stem from criminal activities (e.g. rape, drug use and offences against the person). A doctor is clearly under a common law duty to disclose the information if, after the balancing exercise, it is in the public's best interests to disclose the information.[21] Examples of criminal offences are provided by the Department of Health in its Code of Practice on confidentiality.

> **EXTRACT**
>
> Confidentiality: NHS Code of Practice, November 2003, Department of Health:
>
> **https://www.gov.uk/government/publications/confidentiality-nhs-code-of-practice**
>
> **Page 35 figure 7**: The definition of serious crime is not entirely clear. Murder, manslaughter, rape, treason, kidnapping, child abuse or other cases where individuals have suffered serious harm may all warrant breaching confidentiality. Serious harm to the security of the State or to public order and crimes that involve substantial financial gain or loss will also fall within this category.
>
> The risk of child abuse or neglect, assault, a traffic accident or the spread of an infectious disease are perhaps the most common that staff may face.

It is a sad fact that healthcare professionals have to treat children who are subject to domestic abuse, but after a number of high profile cases of children dying in the home because social services did not take action quickly enough, these guidelines allow healthcare professionals to disclose personal information to satisfy themselves that nothing

---

[21] Medical records are considered to be 'excluded material' under section 11 of the Police and Criminal Evidence Act 1984, meaning that the police do not have free access to them.

untoward is going on.[22] If the healthcare professional is unsure of what to do, the supplementary advice recommends consulting with other colleagues who can offer objectivity.

EXTRACT

Confidentiality: NHS Code of Practice, November 2003, Department of Health:

https://www.gov.uk/government/publications/confidentiality-nhs-code-of-practice

Page 10 paragraph 17: The decision to disclose must take account of the likelihood of detriment (harm, distress or loss of privacy) to the individuals concerned, but a proportionate disclosure may be acceptable where there is clear benefit to the public.

Paragraph 18: However, since there is little case law in this area it is recommended that advice is sought from the National Information Governance Board (NIGB).

Paragraph 19: The key factors in deciding whether or not to share confidential information are necessity and proportionality (Article 8). Such a defence is only applicable in limited circumstances; public interest does not mean 'of interest to the public'.

Page 10–11 paragraph 20: A fair balance must be struck between the rights of the patient, and the rights of other affected persons. Account should also be taken of the risk of a breakdown in trust between the patient and the NHS, and of the risk of loss of confidence amongst the public of the confidentiality of NHS services.

Page 11 paragraph 21: Health professionals must objectively assess public interest (e.g. through conferring with colleagues and by accessing independent advice) and not their own subjective views of what constitutes a public interest. Seeking such advice may not be practicable in cases where the decision is urgent and there are no suitable colleagues available.

It is clear that there are no obvious answers when it comes to the 'public interest' exception: the grey areas and borderline cases are the ones that cause the most difficulty (e.g. the *possibility* of a crime as opposed to an *actual* crime). A lot of consultation and balancing may be required, but the final decision, whatever it is, must be justified.

Finally, the Code of Practice also casts its eye over security arrangements.

EXTRACT

Confidentiality: NHS Code of Practice, November 2003, Department of Health:

https://www.gov.uk/government/publications/confidentiality-nhs-code-of-practice

Page 18 Annexe A paragraph 4: This section covers both manual and electronic records. Staff should not leave portable computers, medical notes or files in unattended cars or in easily accessible areas. Ideally, store all files and portable equipment under lock and key when not actually being used . . .

→

---

[22] 'Baby Peter' and Victoria Climbie are the most shocking examples in recent times.

Page 19 figure 5: Keeping patient information secure

For all types of records, staff working in offices where records may be seen must:

- Shut and lock doors and cabinets as required;
- Wear building passes and ID if issued;
- Query the status of strangers;
- Know who to tell if anything suspicious or worrying is noted;
- Not tell unauthorised personnel how the security systems operate;
- Not breach security themselves.

With electronic records, staff must:

- Always log out of any computer system or application when work on it is finished;
- Not leave a terminal unattended and logged in;
- Not share logins with other people;
- Not reveal passwords to others;
- Change passwords at regular intervals to prevent anyone else using them;
- Avoid using short passwords or using names or words that are known to be associated with them; . . .
- Always clear the screen of a previous patient's information before seeing another;
- Use a password-protected screen-saver to prevent casual viewing of patient information by others.

This advice may seem obvious in today's world, but there are many rural doctor surgeries that still rely on paper-based medical records (especially in dental surgeries).

The NHS constitution

The Department of Health must publish a constitution (a set of principles) to guide the NHS every few years. It is a small document containing only general guidelines, but it outlines the aims and responsibilities of the NHS and its staff. It appears to be especially committed to respect for the individual and their autonomy.

EXTRACT

The NHS Constitution, National Health Service, March 2013, Department of Health:

https://www.gov.uk/government/publications/the-nhs-constitution-for-england

Page 5 Respect and dignity: We value every person [...] as an individual, respect their aspirations and commitments in life, and seek to understand their priorities, needs, abilities and limits. We take what others have to say seriously. We are honest about our point of view and what we can and cannot do.

Unsurprisingly, the duty to maintain confidentiality is outlined very clearly.

EXTRACT

The NHS Constitution, National Health Service, March 2013, Department of Health:

https://www.gov.uk/government/publications/the-nhs-constitution-for-england

Page 8 You have the right: to privacy and confidentiality and to expect the NHS to keep your confidential information safe and secure.

You have the right: of access to your own health records . . .

The NHS also commits: . . . to share with you any letters sent between clinicians about your care.

Page 14 [Staff] have a duty: . . . to protect the confidentiality of personal information that you hold.

The NHS Constitution is also keen to point out that patients have duties to divulge information too.

EXTRACT

The NHS Constitution, National Health Service, March 2013, Department of Health:

https://www.gov.uk/government/publications/the-nhs-constitution-for-england

Page 11 Please provide: accurate information about your health, condition and status . . .

Please ensure: that those closest to you are aware of your wishes about organ donation . . .

The NHS Constitution is not enforceable, but it sets the standard for the rules, regulations, guidelines and codes of practice that bind the NHS together. It also serves as a powerful weapon to remind the NHS (and the public and the press) of their own pledges, especially when they fall short.

British Medical Association[23]

The British Medical Association (BMA) is the trade union for the medical profession. It provides guidance, training, publications, research support and an arena for the exchange of views. It has published two notable documents on the topic of confidentiality.

Access to Health Records

The first document of relevance is the *Access to Health Records* (2008) leaflet. It outlines the provisions for access to medical records and who may be exempt from such a privilege.

---

[23] Official website: www.bma.org.uk.

These provisions will be explored below in relation to deceased patients, but the concise definition of a medical record is worth stating here.

EXTRACT

Access To Health Records: Guidance for Health Professionals in the United Kingdom, December 2008, British Medical Association:

http://bma.org.uk/practical-support-at-work/ethics/confidentiality-and-health-records

Page 2 paragraph 2: What is a health record?

A health record is any record which consists of information relating to the physical or mental health or condition of an individual made by a health professional in connection with the care of that individual. It can be recorded in a computerised form, in a manual form or a mixture of both. Information covers expression of opinion about individuals as well as fact. Health records may include notes made during consultations, correspondence between health professionals such as referral and discharge letters, results of tests and their interpretation, x-ray films, videotapes, audiotapes, photographs and tissue samples taken for diagnostic purposes. They may also include internal memoranda, reports written for third parties such as insurance companies, as well as theatre lists, booking-in registers and clinical audit data, if the patient is identifiable from these.

It is quite surprising how much information can be contained in one medical file. Clearly, the disclosure of some of these contents could harm a patient or his relatives. A living patient who wishes to access their own medical record will find their power to do so under section 7 of the Data Protection Act 1998[24] and if the data controller fails to comply with the request the court can order him to comply.

Data Protection Act 1998

Section 7: Right of Access to Personal Data

(7) An individual making a request under this section may, in such cases as may be prescribed, specify that his request is limited to personal data of any prescribed description.

(9) If a court is satisfied on the application of any person who has made a request under the foregoing provisions of this section that the data controller in question has failed to comply with the request in contravention of those provisions, the court may order him to comply with the request.

There is an exception to section 7(7) if serious harm may be caused to the patient or another person.

---

[24] This includes 'personal data consisting of information as to the physical or mental health or condition of the data subject' under paragraph 3 of the Data Protection (Subject Access Modification) (Health) Order (2000) SI 2000/413.

EXTRACT

Data Protection (Subject Access Modification) (Health) Order (2000) SI 2000/413

Paragraph 5: Exemptions from section 7

(1) Personal data to which this Order applies are exempt from section 7 in any case to the extent to which the application of that section would be likely to cause serious harm to the physical or mental health or condition of the data subject or any other person.

The British Medical Association in its guidance on Access To Health Records (2008) states that a competent patient (or the parties formally representing them) may apply for access to a health record.

EXTRACT

Access To Health Records: Guidance for Health Professionals in the United Kingdom, December 2008, British Medical Association:

http://bma.org.uk/practical-support-at-work/ethics/confidentiality-and-health-records

Page 3 paragraph 4.1: Who may apply for access?

4.1.1 Competent patients

. . . competent patients may apply for access to their own records, or may authorise third parties such as lawyers, employers, or insurance companies to do so on their behalf. Competent young people may also seek access to their own health records. It is not necessary for competent patients to give reasons as to why they wish to access their records.

Notice that a person does not have to give a reason as to why they wish to see their medical record. This is supportive of patient autonomy. Interestingly, a competent child can trump the request of a parent, and a father can seek access unbeknown to the mother.

EXTRACT

Access To Health Records: Guidance for Health Professionals in the United Kingdom, December 2008, British Medical Association:

http://bma.org.uk/practical-support-at-work/ethics/confidentiality-and-health-records

Pages 3–4 paragraph 4.1.3: Parents

Parents may have access to their children's records if this is not contrary to a competent child's wishes. A common enquiry to the BMA concerns a child who lives with his or her mother and whose father applies for access to the child's records. In such circumstances there is no obligation to inform the child's mother that access has been sought . . .

The holder of the record is entitled to refuse access to a parent, or an individual with parental responsibility where the information contained in the child's records is likely to cause serious harm to the child, or another person.

There are limits, however. The guidelines state that 'next of kin' have no access to your medical records.

EXTRACT

Access To Health Records: Guidance for Health Professionals in the United Kingdom, December 2008, British Medical Association:

http://bma.org.uk/practical-support-at-work/ethics/confidentiality-and-health-records

Page 4 paragraph 4.1.5: Next of kin

Despite the widespread use of the phrase 'next of kin' this is not defined, nor does it have formal legal status. A next of kin cannot give or withhold their consent to the sharing of information on a patient's behalf. A next of kin has no rights of access to medical records.

This provision may come as a surprise to many people because the phrase 'next of kin' is heard very frequently in hospitals, but on a practical level, if a person was to claim that they were your 'next of kin' in order to gain access to your medical records – and then they did gain access to your medical records – it is unlikely that you would be happy about it. It would breach your autonomy and your confidentiality. The old case law supports the notion that a patient can have access to his own records.

CASE EXTRACT

R v Mid Glamorgan Family Health Services ex parte Martin [1995] 1 WLR 110

Facts: Martin had been a patient in a number of different hospitals and he wanted to see his medical records. The hospitals were happy to provide them, but not to the patient directly, choosing medical advisors instead.

Held: The Court of Appeal stated that the hospitals owned the medical records, but they could only be withheld from the patient if it was in his best interests. Therefore, the offer to disclose to medical advisors was adequate in the case.

Sir Roger Parker LJ (at pages 119–20): I regard as untenable the proposition that, at common law, a doctor or health authority has an absolute property in medical records of a patient, if this means, which it appears to do, that either could make what use of them he or it chose. Information given to a doctor by a patient or a third party is given in confidence and the absolute property rights are therefore necessarily qualified by the obligations arising out of that situation. [...]

In my view the circumstances in which a patient or former patient is entitled to demand access to his medical history as set out in the records will be infinitely various, and it is neither desirable nor possible for this or any court to attempt to set out the scope of the duty to afford access or, its obverse, the scope of the patient's rights to demand access. Each case must depend on its own facts.

The decision in this case conflicts with section 7 of the Data Protection Act 1998, which does not state that a medical record has to be handed to an advisor. The benefits to releasing medical records directly to patents are numerous. The accuracy of the records would improve, the quality of the records would improve, inappropriate comments about patients would be kept in check, it would relieve patient anxiety, it would help with patient confusion, it would increase trust between doctors and patients because it provides transparency, and it may improve communication.

Finally, the British Medical Association's guidelines on *Access to Health Records* (2008) also provides guidance on police access,[25] solicitor access,[26] time limits[27] and fees.[28]

Confidentiality Toolkit

The British Medical Association has published one of the most helpful and accessible guides to confidentiality in a medical context: the *Confidentiality Toolkit* (2009). It lays out, in the simplest terms, where the law lies for all types of situations. It is particularly helpful to healthcare professionals, but it is just as easy to understand for patients. The Toolkit includes a clear warning to professionals that there are consequences for breaching confidentiality:

EXTRACT

Confidentiality and Disclosure of Health Information Toolkit (2009), British Medical Association:

http://bma.org.uk/practical-support-at-work/ethics/confidentiality-and-health-records

Page 15 paragraph 2: Professional standards

All healthcare professionals must maintain the standards of confidentiality laid down by their professional body, such as the GMC, or risk complaint for professional misconduct. This may result in a warning, restriction of practice or removal from the register.

The General Medical Council standards will be examined directly below, but they do have the power to discipline doctors for breaches of confidentiality. Breaches of confidentiality rarely make it to court because such misconduct can be handled in-house by the regulatory authority. This is quicker and cheaper for all the parties.

The General Medical Council[29]

The final body to publish regulations on confidentiality is the General Medical Council (GMC). The GMC has the power under the Medical Act 1983 to register all practising doctors in the UK and to suspend or remove a practising licence from a doctor if misconduct is

---

[25] They have powers under section 29 of the Data Protection Act 1998 if they do not have a court order or a warrant – paragraph 4.1.6.

[26] They need the consent of their client (who is the patient) and a standard form must be completed which is attached to the back of the guidelines – paragraph 4.1.7.

[27] The time limit for release is forty days – paragraph 4.2.

[28] It costs £10 for computer records and £50 for manual records – paragraph 4.6.

[29] Official website: www.gmc-uk.org.

proved. In addition to this, the GMC can protect and promote the health and safety of the general public by training and educating doctors and by publishing authoritative guidelines on *Good Medical Practice* (2006) which all doctors are legally obliged to follow.

Confidentiality is mentioned only briefly in the *Good Medical Practice* (2006) guidelines, but a second publication – *Confidentiality* (2009) – provides far more advice to doctors and is the ultimate authority for good practice when dealing with private information in a doctor–patient situation.

Good Medical Practice (2006)

Confidentiality is described briefly in the *Good Medical Practice* (2006) guidelines but the position is clear: the duty of confidentiality extends beyond death.

EXTRACT

Good Medical Practice (2013):

www.gmc-uk.org

Page 17 paragraph 50: You must treat information about patients as confidential. This includes after a patient has died.

It might seem odd that a duty of confidentiality can extend beyond death, but the surviving relatives stand to be hurt or offended if any confidential details are released about the deceased. The fact that this rule has transcended into GMC guidelines shows that it is well established.

Confidentiality (2009)

The definitive guide for doctors is the General Medical Council's guidance on *Confidentiality* (2009). A large volume of the Department of Health's *Code of Practice on Confidentiality* (2003) has been enshrined into this guidance. The guidance begins with the importance of confidentiality and the legal exceptions to a duty of confidentiality, which are outlined very clearly as follows.

EXTRACT

General Medical Council, Explanatory Guidance, Confidentiality (2009):

www.gmc-uk.org/guidance/ethical_guidance.asp

Page 6 paragraph 6: Confidentiality is central to trust between doctors and patients. Without assurances about confidentiality, patients may be reluctant to seek medical attention or to give doctors the information they need in order to provide good care. But appropriate information sharing is essential to the efficient provision of safe, effective care, both for the individual patient and for the wider community of patients.

Paragraph 8: Confidentiality is an important duty, but it is not absolute. You can disclose personal information if:

- It is required by law (e.g. statutory exceptions);
- The patient consents (e.g. explicitly or implicitly);
- It is justified in the public interest (e.g. common law exceptions).

In light of the common law handed down in *AG* v *Guardian Newspapers (No. 2)* [1990] AC 109, the General Medical Council provides doctors with advice on the 'public interest' exception and suggests a 'weighing up' exercise between the duty of confidentiality and the benefit to the patient or society when contemplating a disclosure.

EXTRACT

General Medical Council, Explanatory Guidance, Confidentiality (2009):

www.gmc-uk.org/guidance/ethical_guidance.asp

Page 16 paragraph 36: There is a clear public good in having a confidential medical service. The fact that people are encouraged to seek advice and treatment, including for communicable diseases, benefits society as a whole as well as the individual. However, there can also be a public interest in disclosing information: to protect individuals or society from risks of serious harm, such as serious communicable diseases or serious crime, or to enable medical research, education or other secondary uses of information that will benefit society over time.

Paragraph 37: Personal information may, therefore, be disclosed in the public interest, without patients' consent, and in exceptional cases where patients have withheld consent, if the benefits to an individual or to society of the disclosure outweigh both the public and the patient's interest in keeping the information confidential. You must weigh the harms that are likely to arise from non-disclosure of information against the possible harm, both to the patient and to the overall trust between doctors and patients, arising from the release of that information.

This guidance is clear evidence of the common law influencing the practice of doctors: a balancing exercise should be able to reveal whether disclosure is justified in the public interest or not, but it is up to the doctor. If one of the legal exceptions are present (e.g. it is found to be in the public interest to disclose), then the personal information can be released but only in accordance with the following guidelines.

EXTRACT

General Medical Council, Explanatory Guidance, Confidentiality (2009):

www.gmc-uk.org/guidance/ethical_guidance.asp

Page 7 paragraph 9: When disclosing information about a patient, you must:

- Use anonymised or coded information if practicable and if it will serve the purpose;
- Be satisfied that the patient:
  - Has ready access to information that explains that their personal information might be disclosed for the sake of their own care, or for local clinical audit, and that they can object, and
  - Has not objected.
- Get the patient's express consent if identifiable information is to be disclosed for purposes other than their care or local clinical audit, unless the disclosure is required by law or justified in the public interest.
- Keep disclosures to the minimum necessary, and
- Keep up to date with, and observe, all relevant legal requirements, including the common law and data protection legislation.

It is always a good idea to attain the consent of the patient anyway, even if a disclosure is in the public interest. However, doctors are advised by the General Medical Council not to seek consent under the following circumstances.

EXTRACT

General Medical Council, Explanatory Guidance, Confidentiality (2009):

www.gmc-uk.org/guidance/ethical_guidance.asp

Page 17:

- The patient is not competent to give consent, in which case you should consult the patient's welfare attorney, court appointed deputy, guardian or the patient's relatives, friends or carers;
- You have reason to believe that seeking consent would put you or others at risk of serious harm;
- Seeking consent would be likely to undermine the purpose of the disclosure, for example, by prejudicing the prevention or detection of serious crime;
- Action must be taken quickly, for example, in the detection or control of outbreaks of some communicable diseases and there is insufficient time to contact the patient.

Paragraph 39: You should inform the patient that a disclosure will be made in the public interest, even if you have not sought consent, unless to do so is impracticable, would put you or others at risk of serious harm, or would prejudice the purpose of the disclosure. You must document in the patient's record your reasons for disclosing the information without consent.

If, however, the patient is the only party at risk of serious harm, the General Medical Council does advise doctors to respect their wishes not to disclose their information.

EXTRACT

General Medical Council, Explanatory Guidance, Confidentiality (2009):

www.gmc-uk.org/guidance/ethical_guidance.asp

Page 21 paragraph 51: It may be appropriate to encourage patients to consent to disclosures you consider necessary for their protection, and to warn them of the risks of refusing to consent; but you should usually abide by a competent adult patient's refusal to consent to disclosure, even if their decision leaves them, but nobody else, at risk of serious harm. You should do your best to provide patients with the information and support they need to make decisions in their own interests, for example, by arranging contact with agencies that support victims of domestic violence.

This advice is strange in light of the raft of other guidelines that encourage disclosure in dangerous situations, and in reality a doctor would probably be afraid for his own practising licence if he failed to reveal this information.

The guidance from the General Medical Council is very helpful. It appears that the somewhat scattered statute and common law provisions on confidentiality have been enshrined by the General Medical Council into a small collection of helpful bullet points for healthcare professionals *and* patients to understand. The provisions above can be traced back to a mixture of the Data Protection Act 1998, the common law, the Human Rights Act 1998 (Article 8), the Department of Health's Code of Practice on Confidentiality and the Caldicott Committee. This is hugely important because not only to doctors who do not have time to trawl through the legal quagmire, but to patients who can clearly identify what their legal rights are.

RESEARCH ACTIVITY

The following case study was taken from the Department of Health's Supplementary Guidance for the Code of Practice for Confidentiality (2010):

Mrs Jones arrives at the Accident and Emergency Department with a number of cuts and bruises and stab wounds of some kind (from a screwdriver or penknife). She is very shaken up and anxious. Whilst treating the patient, A&E staff discover that this is the third time in three months that Mrs Jones has presented at A&E with injuries. It is also noted that Mrs Jones has a ten-year-old son. She tells the staff that she is very clumsy and keeps having accidents. However, the injuries this time are not consistent with a clumsy accident, and the A&E staff are concerned that she may be the victim of assault, and that her son might also be at risk.[30]

What does the guidance above suggest that the healthcare professionals looking after Mrs Jones do next?

Patients who lack capacity

The provisions relating to incompetent adults and children in the area of confidentiality are even more convoluted than the general law relating to confidentiality. This is because incompetent adults and children are often not able to visit doctors themselves, and so a third person must also be privy to their medical information (usually a parent, a sibling or a carer). This appears to contradict the concept of confidentiality, where a patient is entitled to keep their personal information to themselves. The same applies to children who may be too young to understand. It is, therefore, not realistic to apply the usual rules of confidentiality to these patients, because their healthcare would be delayed indefinitely.

Incompetent adults

It shall be recalled in Chapter 4 that the definition of incapacity was described as a two-part test under the Mental Capacity Act 2005.

---

[30] Confidentiality: NHS Code of Practice: Supplementary Guidance: Public Interest Disclosures (2010), Department of Health, page 14: https://www.gov.uk/government/publications/confidentiality-nhs-code-of-practice-supplementary-guidance-public-interest-disclosures.

Mental Capacity Act 2005

Section 2: People who lack capacity

(1) For the purposes of this Act, a person lacks capacity in relation to a matter if at the material time he is unable to make a decision for himself in relation to the matter because of an impairment of, or a disturbance in the functioning of, the mind or brain.

(2) It does not matter whether the impairment or disturbance is permanent or temporary.

The two-stage test is clear: the patient must be unable to make a decision for himself, and this must be caused by an impairment or disturbance of his mind or brain. If this is the case, what happens to that patient's confidentiality? Section 4 of the MCA 2005 states that a healthcare professional can consult with a person responsible for the patient to help with decisions relating to that patient.

Mental Capacity Act 2005

Section 4: Best interests

(4) [The person making the decision] must, so far as reasonably practicable, permit and encourage the person to participate, or to improve his ability to participate, as fully as possible in any act done for him and any decision affecting him.

(6) [The person making the decision] must consider, so far as is reasonably ascertainable:

    (a) The person's past and present wishes and feelings (and, in particular, any relevant written statement made by him when he had capacity);

    (b) The beliefs and values that would be likely to influence his decision if he had capacity; and

    (c) The other factors that he would be likely to consider if he were able to do so.[31]

(7) [The person making the decision] must take into account, if it is practicable and appropriate to consult them, the views of:

    (a) anyone named by the person as someone to be consulted on the matter in question or on matters of that kind;

    (b) anyone engaged in caring for the person or interested in his welfare;

    (c) any donee of a lasting power of attorney granted by the person; and

    (d) any deputy appointed for the person by the court, as to what would be in the person's best interests.

It is clear that a doctor can approach a family member for advice, but this does not mean that the entire medical file of the incompetent patient will be opened for the family member to see. Only the relevant information relating to the immediate care of the

---

[31] This is the 'best interests' test – s. 4(6) of the MCA 2005.

incompetent patient will be divulged to the family member if a decision needs to be made. That will ensure not only that the consent is fully informed but that the confidentiality of the incompetent patient has not been breached. The Code of Practice to the Mental Capacity Act 2005 provides a wealth of guidance on how to interpret the provisions of the 2005 Act. It addresses the issue of confidentiality when treating incompetent patients.

EXTRACT

The Mental Capacity Act 2005 Code of Practice (2007):

http://www.legislation.gov.uk/ukpga/2005/9/pdfs/ukpgacop_20050009_en.pdf

Paragraph 5.56: Decision-makers must balance the duty to consult other people with the right to confidentiality of the person who lacks capacity. So if confidential information is to be discussed, they should only seek the views of people who it is appropriate to consult, where their views are relevant to the decision to be made and the particular circumstances.

Paragraph 5.57: There may be occasions where it is in the person's best interests for personal information (for example, about their medical condition, if the decision concerns the provision of medical treatment) to be revealed to the people consulted as part of the process of working out their best interests. Healthcare and social care staff who are trying to determine a person's best interests must follow their professional guidance, as well as other relevant guidance, about confidentiality.

Paragraph 16.27: Whenever a carer gets information, they should treat the information in confidence, and they should not share it with anyone else (unless there is a lawful basis for doing so). In some circumstances, the information holder might ask the carer to give a formal confirmation that they will keep information confidential.

The guidance above establishes four things:

- There must be a balance struck between the duty of confidentiality and the need to consult with other people.
- A person who is consulted must be relevant to the care of the incompetent patient in the circumstances.
- It might be in the best interests of the incompetent patient to share medical information with healthcare staff but the staff must still adhere to the professional guidance on confidentiality.
- A carer of an incompetent patient is under the same duty of confidentiality as that of a healthcare professional treating a competent patient.

The importance of confidentiality to incompetent adults was discussed in *R v Plymouth City Council*, where medical notes were disclosed to the mother of a patient. The incompetent patient did not have any objection to his mother seeing his files and his welfare was not at risk by the disclosure.

CASE EXTRACT

R (on the application of S) v Plymouth City Council [2002] 1 WLR 2583

Facts: A 27-year-old man [C] was suffering from serious learning and behavioural difficulties. The local authority wanted to remove the mother as 'nearest relative' in order to place the patient in a residential care environment. The mother, in turn, wanted to remove the local authority as guardian. She sought access to his files, but was refused.

Held: The local authority had been under an obligation, both at common law and under the Human Rights Act 1998, to allow the mother's request for confidential information about her son so she could fight her case.

Hale LJ (at pages 2598–99): Article 8 confers a right to respect for private life. Adults such as C have that right as much as anyone else. Indeed, many would think them more at risk, and therefore more worthy of respect by the authorities if, because of their mental disabilities, they are unable to protect it for themselves. But both his and his mother's right to respect for their family life under Article 8, and the mother's right to a fair trial under Article 6, would [justify] interference with C's right to respect for his private life, provided as always that the interference was proportionate. [...] C's interest in protecting the confidentiality of personal information about himself must not be underestimated. It is all too easy for professionals and parents to regard children and incapacitated adults as having no independent interests of their own: as objects rather than subjects. [...] C also has an interest in being protected from a risk of harm to his health or welfare which would stem from disclosure. [...] There is no suggestion that C has any objection to his mother and her advisers being properly informed about his health and welfare. There is no suggestion of any risk to his health and welfare arising from this. The mother and her advisers have sought access to the information which her own psychiatric and social work experts need in order properly to advise her. That limits both the context and the content of disclosure in a way which strikes a proper balance between the competing interests.

Hale LJ makes the interesting point that incompetent patients are entitled to a higher level of respect to their confidentiality because they are less able to protect themselves and are still viewed as 'objects rather than subjects'. This is probably true. He ruled that the mother's interference with the patient's right to private life was justified because it was proportionate in all the circumstances: he did not register an objection to such a disclosure; there was no risk to his health or welfare; and she required the information in order to satisfy her own human right under Article 6. This collection of circumstances may have also satisfied the best interests test under section 4 of the MCA 2005.

It is incredibly difficult for doctors to differentiate between competent decisions and incompetent decisions at the end of life, especially when degenerate diseases are beginning to show. It is perhaps best to allow the doctor some discretion in regards to confidentiality when it comes to treating patients with diseases that effect memory loss, because a relative will often bring the patient to the doctor surgery to alleviate their own concerns. The doctor can decide for himself whether the patient is capable of retaining all of the information, or whether he needs to share certain aspects of her care with the relative. It has even been suggested that the diagnosis of Alzheimer's could depress a particularly vulnerable patient and so it is best to only tell the carer.[32] The NHS Code of

---

[32] See: Pucci, E. 'Relatives Attitudes Towards Informing Patients about the Diagnosis of Alzheimer's Disease' (2003) 29 *Journal of Medical Ethics* 51.

Practice on *Confidentiality* (2003) advises that the best interests of the patient will determine whether any personal information is to be disclosed.

EXTRACT

Confidentiality: NHS Code of Practice, November 2003, Department of Health:

https://www.gov.uk/government/publications/confidentiality-nhs-code-of-practice

Page 31 paragraph 11: If a patient is unconscious or unable, due to a mental or physical condition, to give consent or to communicate a decision, the health professionals concerned must take decisions about the use of information. This needs to take into account the patient's best interests and any previously expressed wishes, and be informed by the views of relatives or carers as to the likely wishes of the patient. If a patient has made his or her preferences about information disclosures known in advance, this should be respected.

Paragraph 13: Where the patient is incapacitated and unable to consent, information should only be disclosed in the patient's best interests, and then only as much information as is needed to support their care. This might, however, cause unnecessary suffering to the patient's relatives, which could in turn cause distress to the patient when he or she later learnt of the situation. Each situation must be judged on its merits, and great care taken to avoid breaching confidentiality or creating difficulties for the patient. Decisions to disclose and the justifications for disclosing should be noted in the patient's records. Focusing on the future and care needs rather than past records will normally help avoid inappropriate disclosures.

The General Medical Council also provide very useful advice to doctors in their *Confidentiality* (2009) guidelines. The key considerations are as follows.

EXTRACT

General Medical Council, Explanatory Guidance, Confidentiality (2009):

www.gmc-uk.org/guidance/ethical_guidance.asp

Page 23 paragraph 59: When making decisions about whether to disclose information about a patient who lacks capacity, you must:

- Make the care of the patient your first concern;
- Respect the patient's dignity and privacy; and
- Support and encourage the patient to be involved, as far as they want and are able, in decisions about disclosure of their personal information.

A doctor must also consider: whether the incapacity is permanent or temporary, if he can reasonably wait until capacity returns, any previously expressed wishes, the views of anyone relevant to the patient, the preferences, feelings, beliefs and values of the patient, and what the rest of the healthcare team know about the patient.[33] It is becoming clear

---

[33] See *Confidentiality* (2009) at page 23–24, paragraph 60.

that in order to ascertain whether disclosure is in the best interests of the patient, the doctor must gather as many facts about the patient as possible in addition to what is best for her healthcare. The doctor can overrule an incompetent patient if she tries to prevent disclosure, but it must be in the best interests of the patient to do so.[34] If, in the rare event that some of the patient's medical information needs to be disclosed to relatives, the General Medical Council is very clear that this does not allow *full* access.

EXTRACT

General Medical Council, Explanatory Guidance, Confidentiality (2009):

www.gmc-uk.org/guidance/ethical_guidance.asp

Page 24 paragraph 62: You may need to share personal information with a patient's relatives, friends or carers to enable you to assess the patient's best interests. But that does not mean they have a general right of access to the patient's records or to have irrelevant information about, for example, the patient's past healthcare.

Interestingly, it is quite safe to assume that a patient who lacks capacity would wish for her closest relatives to be kept informed about her general condition. This is most likely to be the case if incapacity has happened suddenly, e.g. in the event of a stroke or an accident.[35] The incompetent patient may not get on with certain relatives. This places the doctor in an incredibly difficult situation, especially if, before becoming incompetent, the patient asked the doctor not to speak to certain relatives about her treatment and it later transpires that the doctor did speak to – and took advice from – that relative.

EXTRACT

General Medical Council, Explanatory Guidance, Confidentiality (2009):

www.gmc-uk.org/guidance/ethical_guidance.asp

Page 26 paragraph 66: If anyone close to the patient wants to discuss their concerns about the patient's health, you should make it clear to them that, while it is not a breach of confidentiality to listen to their concerns, you cannot guarantee that you will not tell the patient about the conversation. You should not refuse to listen to a patient's partner, carers or others on the basis of confidentiality. Their views or the information they provide might be helpful in your care of the patient. You will, though, need to consider whether your patient consider you listening to the concerns of others about your patient's health or care to be a breach of trust, particularly if they have asked you not to listen to particular people.

This is incredibly difficult. A patient might say: 'do not listen to my daughter, she does not know what she is talking about and has no experience of my condition' but the daughter may be the primary carer of the patient and may be able to help the doctor ascertain what is in the best interests of her mother. The British Medical Association's Toolkit on *Confidentiality* (2008) adds some interesting advice on the rights of next of kin: the BMA can provide valuable information, but that's about it. It has no control over the patient's right to confidentiality.

---

[34] See *Confidentiality* (2009) at page 24, paragraph 61.
[35] Ibid at page 26, paragraph 65.

> ### EXTRACT
>
> Confidentiality and Disclosure of Health Information Toolkit (2009), British Medical Association:
>
> **http://bma.org.uk/practical-support-at-work/ethics/confidentiality-and-health-records**
>
> ### Page 31 paragraph 3: Next of kin
>
> Such a person may provide valuable information about the patient's wishes to staff caring for the patient. However, the nominated person cannot give or withhold consent to the sharing of information about the patient and has no rights of access to the patient's medical records. The patient may nominate anyone as next of kin – spouse, partner, family member or friend. In the absence of such a nomination, no one can claim next of kin.

This will inevitably disappoint some relatives, who are convinced that they have the right to control the medical care of an elderly relative, or have a say in how her medical information is disclosed. This will be the doctor's decision in accordance with the patient's best interests.[36]

Children

The courts see children as their own beings with their own legal rights, and in any medical law case where the parents have argued against medical treatment, the courts have always put the children first because their needs are paramount.[37] In *Re C* it was made very clear by Wilson J that children have their own legal rights – they are not simply an extension of their parent.

> ### CASE EXTRACT
>
> ### *Re C (A Child) (HIV Testing)* [2000] Fam 48
>
> **Facts**: A baby, C, was born to a mother who was infected with HIV. She was breast feeding the baby and refused to allow the baby to be tested for the presence of HIV due to her scepticism about conventional medical treatment.
>
> **Held**: A child has its own legal rights separate from its parents.
>
> **Wilson J** (at page 61): The mother said in evidence that, when the baby was older, she would talk to her about the possibility of infection, and, if she then wanted to take a test, she would allow her to do so. On the evidence before me, that is a hopeless programme for the baby's protection. [...] The concluding words of the father's final eloquent submissions were these: 'whatever the outcome of this case, we would have lost if we had not stood up for our rights'. But this case is not at its heart about the rights of the parents. And if, as he in effect suggested in his evidence, the father regards the rights of a tiny baby as subsumed within the rights of the parents, he is wrong. This baby has rights of her own. They can be considered nationally or internationally.

---

[36] Under the Mental Capacity Act 2005, a patient over 18 may appoint a person to make decisions for them in the event that they become incompetent. The Court of Protection can appoint a deputy too. Even then, only relevant medical information will be disclosed. This is discussed in more detail in Chapter 4.

[37] The watershed case for this is the conjoined twins case of Mary and Jodie: *Re A (Children) (Conjoined Twins: Separation)* [2001] Fam 147. See Chapter 4.

The judgment in *Re C* is a clear example of how the rights of the child can trump the rights of the parent. This must be the way forward in law because parents are often subjective in their decisions. This was summed up perfectly by Holman J in *The NHS Trust* case.

CASE EXTRACT

The NHS Trust v A (A Child) [2007] EWHC 1696

Holman J (at para 40): (x) The views and opinions of both the doctors and the parents must be carefully considered. Where [...] the parents spend a great deal of time with their child, their views may have particular value because they know the [child]; [...] although the court needs to be mindful that the views of any parents may, very understandably, be coloured by their own emotion or sentiment. It is important to stress that the reference is to the views and opinions of the parents. Their own wishes, however understandable in human terms, are wholly irrelevant to consideration of the objective best interests of the child.

In relation to confidentiality, the same approach has been taken. The child patient is entitled to confidentiality just as an adult patient is entitled to confidentiality.

CASE EXTRACT

Venables v News Group Newspapers Ltd [2001] 2 WLR 1038

Dame Elizabeth Butler-Sloss P: [...] Children, like adults, are entitled to confidentiality in respect of certain areas of information. Medical records are the obvious example.

It will, of course, depend on the age of the child. A primary school child might not fully understand her medical treatment. However, a secondary school child may well be able to understand her treatment. It is safe to say that when it comes to very young children (i.e. toddlers), the doctor has a joint duty to the parent *and* the child (or whoever brings the child into the consultation room). It is also safe to say, when the child is old enough to understand the details of her condition and her treatment, she will be deemed *Gillick* competent and will be entitled to confidentiality away from her parents.

CASE EXTRACT

Gillick v West Norfolk and Wisbech AHA [1986] AC 112

Lord Fraser (at page 169): It seems to me verging on the absurd to suggest that a girl or a boy aged 15 could not effectively consent, for example, to have a medical examination of some trivial injury to his body or even to have a broken arm set. [...] Provided the patient, whether a boy or a girl, is capable of understanding what is proposed, and of expressing his or her own wishes, I see no good reason for holding that he or she lacks the capacity to express them validly and effectively and to authorise the medical man to make the examination or give the treatment which he advises.

Lord Scarman (at pages 188–9): I would hold that as a matter of law the parental right to determine whether or not their minor child below the age of 16 will have medical treatment terminates if and when the child achieves a sufficient understanding and intelligence to enable him or her to understand fully what is proposed. It will be a question of fact whether a child seeking advice has sufficient understanding of what is involved to give a consent valid in law.

In the context of confidentiality, the case of *Gillick* consolidated several principles:

- A competent patient under 16 can consent to medical treatment without the knowledge or consent of her parents.
- This will be a question of fact (i.e. it will depend on the individual child).
- This moment will see the rights of the parent 'terminated' in terms of medical advice and treatment.
- This will inevitably require confidentiality between the doctor and the patient under 16.

The later case of *Axon* confirmed that children are entitled to confidentiality when seeking abortion services. Silber J applied *Gillick* directly when coming to the decision that a duty of confidentiality was present.

CASE EXTRACT

R (on the application of Axon) v *Secretary of State for Health* [2006] QB 539

Silber J (at pages 543, 561): This application raises a tension between two important principles of which the first is that a competent young person under 16 years of age (who is able to understand all aspects of any advice, including its consequences) is an autonomous person, who first should be allowed to make decisions about his or her own health and second is entitled to confidentiality about such decisions even *vis-à-vis* his or her parents. The second principle is that . . . there is evidence that without the guarantee of confidentiality, some of these young people might not seek advice or treatment from medical professionals on sexual matters with potentially disturbing consequences . . . the very basis and nature of the information which a doctor or a medical professional receives relating to the sexual and reproductive health of any patient of whatever age deserves the highest degree of confidentiality and this factor undermines the existence of a limitation on the duty of disclosure.

Silber J in *Axon* was clearly persuaded by Lord Scarman in *Gillick* that a parental right to consent 'terminates' when a child becomes competent. This comes with an adjoining duty of confidentiality to the child. The first issue was whether a young person under sixteen was autonomous, and the decision was 'yes'. The second issue was whether the duty of confidentiality was her own or her that of her parents, and the decision was 'her own'. Silber J noted the 'disturbing consequences' if the answer were to be 'her parents'. This is because the highest degree of confidentiality is required for issues of sexual and reproductive health, and if a young person under 16 knew that her confidentiality was subsumed within that of her parents, she would be unlikely to visit the doctor at all.

The Department of Health in their *Confidentiality* (2003) Code of Practice states that a child of 16 is entitled to the same confidentiality as an adult, and a child under 16 can be *Gillick* competent.[38] Interestingly, if a *Gillick* competent child refuses medical treatment, this can be overruled.

---

[38] See *Confidentiality: Code of Practice* (2003) Department of Health, page 30 at paragraph 9.

EXTRACT

Confidentiality: NHS Code of Practice, November 2003, Department of Health:

https://www.gov.uk/government/publications/confidentiality-nhs-code-of-practice

Page 31 paragraph 9: Where a competent young person or child is refusing treatment for a life threatening condition, the duty of care would require confidentiality to be breached to the extent of informing those with parental responsibility for the child who might then be able to provide the necessary consent to the treatment.

This guidance is in line with the current law because *Gillick* only offered young people under 16 the right to *consent* to medical treatment, not the right to *refuse* it.

An incompetent or competent child can sometimes be in danger, or a parent may refuse to share relevant information with authorities. In cases such as these, the best interests of the child will always be considered first, and the disclosure will be authorised under the common law exception to protect the child from harm.

EXTRACT

Confidentiality and Disclosure of Health Information Toolkit (2009), British Medical Association:

http://bma.org.uk/practical-support-at-work/ethics/confidentiality-and-health-records

Page 36: Where an individual who has parental responsibility refuses to share relevant information with other health professionals or agencies and the health professional considers that it is not in the best interests of the child (for example, it puts the child at risk of significant harm), disclosure may take place in the public interest without consent.

Page 37: Where there is any doubt as to whether disclosure is in the child's best interests, it is recommended that the health professional discusses the matter anonymously with an experienced colleague, the Caldicott Guardian, their professional body or defence body.

These provisions confirm that the best interests of the child are always paramount and will trump the interests of the parents if the child is at risk of harm. However, it is ironic that in order to decide whether a breach of confidentiality is in the best interests of the young patient, so many people have to be consulted about the facts of the case before a decision is made.

ACTIVITY

Margaret, a 46-year-old woman, takes her forgetful mother Daisy to the doctors for an Alzheimer's test. Daisy, who is 86 years old, clearly does not want to be there and refuses to cooperate. Dr Williams is not quite sure where the law on confidentiality places him, because the patient is uncooperative he does not know whether she is competent or not. Advise him.

The rights of deceased patients

Does the duty of confidentiality survive death? The legal answer used to be 'no', until very recently. This is because once a patient had died he no longer complained of a breach of confidentiality, and therefore the courts were never in a position to discuss it and never under pressure to change it.

However, there have been two cases in the last few years that have altered the legal landscape. In *Lewis* (2008), a doctor was reluctant to release the medical records of deceased patients, and the court had to decide whether a duty of confidentiality existed after death. The issue was first decided in the lesser known tribunal case of *Bluck* only one year before *Lewis*. It was not legally binding because it was a tribunal decision, but because it influenced the court in *Lewis* it is worth reading.

CASE EXTRACT

Bluck v Information Commissioner (2007) 98 BMLR 1

Facts: Pauline Bluck – the mother of Karen Davies, a 33-year-old woman who died in hospital – sought the release of her daughter's medical files after it transpired five years later that the hospital was responsible for the death and the widower was paid a substantial compensation payment. Pauline Bluck wrote to the relevant Trust but they stated that the medical records were confidential and the widower had to consent to the release but he refused. Pauline complained to the Information Commissioner, who also decided that they should not be disclosed because the obligation of confidence survived the death of the patient.

Held: The duty of confidence survived the death of the patient.

Deputy Chairman Chris Ryan (at paras 13, 19, 20–1, 30): The Appellant's case is that there is a clear public interest in the disclosure of information in cases where a hospital has been negligent in its treatment of a patient, leading to that patient's death. Her counsel emphasised the importance of poor treatment being recognised and avoided in the future and of the public being made aware of the treatment of diseases. He also submitted that disclosure of such information would facilitate communication between medical staff and the relatives of a deceased person, whose grieving may be assisted if they receive a full medical explanation. The Trust accepted that circumstances may arise where disclosure may be justified, including the need for public scrutiny of the activities of a public authority, but both the Trust and the Information Commissioner argued that the factors in favour of disclosure are outweighed by the need to ensure that patients retain trust in the confidentiality of information they impart to doctors. They argue that if a patient is aware that the information he gives his doctor may be disclosed to the public after his death he may not make full disclosure, with the result that medical staff may be unable to make a correct diagnosis or provide appropriate treatment. [...] We believe that the public interest in maintaining confidentiality in the medical records of a deceased outweighs, by some way, the countervailing public interest in disclosure.

The Appellant's case [also argued] that a duty of confidence has to be owed to someone and that, once that person has died, there is no one capable of enforcing it.

→

It was accepted that there might be continuing ethical, moral or professional duties requiring a doctor to maintain confidentiality [...] but that no legal obligation survived. [...] It was suggested that it would remain unconscionable to [disclose information] after the death of the person to whom the information related and that the duty must therefore survive death. It should not come to an end simply because it could be said that there was no one able to enforce it or capable of demonstrating harm resulting from its breach. The Information Commissioner also invited us to consider the unacceptable practical consequence if the duty did come to an end on death. Any medical practitioner would then be legally entitled to publish information from the records of a deceased patient, possibly for financial gain. We think that this is a powerful point. [...]

We also agree with the Trust and the Information Commissioner that, as a matter of principle, the basis of the duty in respect of private information lies in conscience. [...] In these circumstances we conclude that a duty of confidence is capable of surviving the death of the confider and that in the circumstances of this case it does survive. [...] We have concluded, therefore, that the Trust would breach the duty of confidence owed to Karen Davies if it disclosed the medical records.

Pauline Bluck argued that there was a public interest in disclosure of her daughter's records because the hospital had been negligent and this resulted in the death of her daughter. Although the trust conceded that this was a good justification for disclosure, both the trust and the Information Commissioner said that the 'factors in favour of disclosure are outweighed by the need to ensure that patients retain trust in the confidentiality of information they impart to doctors'. The basis for this counter argument is that if a patient knew their medical records could be released upon death to immediate relatives, they would not make full disclosures to doctors. This would delay the 'correct diagnosis and appropriate treatment' of the patient. Pauline Bluck also argued that once a person has died, there is no one to enforce the duty of confidence and thus there was no existing legal obligation to maintain it. This argument was rebutted by the Tribunal on the grounds that there was an 'equitable obligation' to maintain confidentiality. The Tribunal said it was 'unconscionable' for doctors to breach their trust to patients, whether alive or dead. The ratio from the Tribunal is as follows: 'the duty must therefore survive death. It should not come to an end simply because it could be said that there was no one able to enforce it or capable of demonstrating harm resulting from its breach.' This is a clear indication that the law is beginning to favour the moral obligation to maintain confidence after death. A 'powerful point' was made by the Information Commissioner that if the duty of confidentiality came to an end on death, records could be published for a financial gain. This seems a bit far fetched and many doctors would probably strenuously deny that they would behave this way, but it illuminates the possibility of abuse.

The *Bluck* case may not have been legally binding, but its clear and reasonable decision was certainly a big help to Foskett J in *Lewis*, when he was faced with the same question in the High Court a year later.

CASE EXTRACT

Lewis v *Secretary of State for Health* [2008] EWHC 2196

Facts: A doctor was reluctant to disclose patient records after their death to the Redfern Inquiry, which was investigating the removal of tissue samples from individuals who worked at a Sellafield nuclear plant to see if they contained radionuclide. There were two questions to be answered: (1) was there still a duty of confidentiality and (2) if there was, did any of the common law exceptions apply to allow disclosure?

Held: There was still a duty of confidentiality in place because the nature of the examination was sensitive enough to impose a high degree of confidentiality even after death, but the disclosures were justified in the public interest.

Foskett J: There is no doubt that it is the view of those who administer the medical profession, both in the United Kingdom and worldwide, that the professional obligation of the doctor is to maintain the medical confidences of the patient after the patient's death. The Hippocratic oath, the Declaration of Geneva ('I will respect the secrets that are confided in me, even after the patient has died') and guidance given by the General Medical Council all point to this professional obligation. [...] In the course of argument, I ventured the proposition that if anyone is asked whether they thought that something said in confidence to their doctor would remain confidential after their death, the answer would almost certainly be 'yes'. That seems to me to accord with contemporary notions of what is accepted practice and indeed it might even reflect notions of what the law, not merely professional ethics, may require. [...] The Information Tribunal in *Bluck* v *Information Commissioner* (2007) 98 BMLR 1 is not, of course, binding upon me, it does, if I may say so with respect, set out clearly and lucidly the competing arguments and reaches a conclusion which, for my part, I would be content to adopt. [...] The more intimate and sensitive the type of examination, and the more sensitive the kind of results obtained, the more onerous and prolonged would be the obligation to maintain confidence. [...] In my judgment, the kind of examination that appears to have been conducted in this case would certainly rank high in the league of intimacy and sensitivity. Obtaining tissues from a dead body reflects a unique form of intimacy and the results of any examination that might reveal exposure to ionising radiation, with the connotations that such exposure will have in the minds of those exposed to it or of those related to the person who had been so exposed, make the results extremely sensitive. [...] [T]he presumption must be that those matters are sufficiently sensitive to require a high degree of confidentiality and one that endures for many years after the death of the individual concerned. [...] I have not the slightest doubt that this is an appropriate case in which to hold that the public interest in disclosure of the material sought outweighs the other public interest, namely, that of maintaining the confidentiality of medical records and information, provided, of course, proper safeguards are put in place to ensure that no inappropriate information becomes public. In support of this conclusion I would merely say that there is plainly a public interest [...] in determining what happened.

Foskett J is of the opinion that there is a professional understanding worldwide that there is a duty to maintain confidentiality after death. He uses the Hippocratic Oath and the Declaration of Geneva to confirm this. This means that there was no legal obligation to maintain confidentiality after death – there was a moral and ethical one – which has now become enshrined into English common law via this judgment. Foskett J uses a reasonable man test to justify his finding, by stating: 'if anyone is asked whether they thought that something said in confidence to their doctor would remain confidential after their death, the answer would almost certainly be "yes".' This has not always been the best approach to take in complex medical law cases, but in this instance, there is no actual law to support his decision and the result seems relatively uncontroversial. Foskett J says he is 'content to adopt' the decision in *Bluck*, which very clearly stated that a duty of confidentiality is 'capable of surviving the death' of the patient. The examinations undertaken by the patients in *Lewis* were 'intimate and sensitive' and Foskett J was of the opinion that these circumstances 'rank high in the league of intimacy and sensitivity' because they made the 'results extremely sensitive'. These are all clear indicators that a duty of confidentiality should be retained after death. Foskett J came to the conclusion that the public interest in disclosure outweighed the public interest in maintaining confidentiality, and stipulated that there should be no inappropriate information disclosed, therefore applying the regular rules of confidentiality to the deceased.

It might not have been clear in law that there was a duty of confidentiality after death, but it has been clear in ethics for some time. It was stated clearly in *Bluck* and *Lewis* that ethical obligations stem back to the Hippocratic Oath, and this was probably why the trust in *Bluck* and the doctor in *Lewis* were so reluctant to release the medical records. The many guidelines published by the relevant medical bodies support a duty of confidentiality after death. The Department of Health kicks it off in their *Confidentiality* (2003) Code of Practice by stating that even though a legal obligation does not exist (this was written before *Lewis*), the ethical duty is firmly in place.

EXTRACT

Confidentiality: NHS Code of Practice, November 2003, Department of Health:

https://www.gov.uk/government/publications/confidentiality-nhs-code-of-practice

Page 13 paragraph 28: Whilst law and ethics in this area are largely in step, the law provides a minimum standard that does not always reflect the appropriate ethical standards that the government and the professional regulatory bodies require. For example, the Department of Health and the General Medical Council are in agreement that, whilst there are no clear legal obligations of confidentiality that apply to the deceased, there is an ethical basis for requiring that confidentiality obligations, as outlined in this document, must continue to apply.

The General Medical Council in their *Confidentiality* (2009) guidance clearly state the legal provisions and considerations when contemplating the release of a deceased patient's medical record.

EXTRACT

General Medical Council, Explanatory Guidance, Confidentiality (2009):

www.gmc-uk.org/guidance/ethical_guidance.asp

Page 28 paragraph 70: Your duty of confidentiality continues after a patient has died. Whether and what personal information may be disclosed after a patient's death will depend on the circumstances. If the patient had asked for information to remain confidential, you should usually respect their wishes. If you are unaware of any instructions from the patient, when you are considering requests for information you should take into account:

- Whether the disclosure of information is likely to cause distress to, or be of benefit to, the patient's partner or family;
- Whether the disclosure will also disclose information about the patient's family or anyone else;
- Whether the information is already public knowledge or can be anonymised or coded; and
- The purpose of the disclosure.

The reasons provided by the GMC for the release of medical records include: to help a coroner with an inquest, when the disclosure is required by statute or common law, when it is justified for education, research or local clinical audit, for public health surveillance (it should be anonymised or coded), when a parent asks abut the causes of their child's death, when a partner or close relative asks for information and there is no reason to believe that the patient would have objected, and when the inquiring person has a right under the Access to Health Records Act 1990.[39] This statutory provision can be called into action when a person (a relative) requires confidential information about the patient for a legal action. It might be an action against the hospital for the negligent death of the patient, for example. A solicitor or the courts will commonly use the powers of access under the Access to Health Records Act 1990, but they are also available to the surviving relative if they are party to the legal action. There are limits to what can be disclosed: only confidential information directly related to the legal action can be disclosed. The British Medical Association published a document entitled: *Access To Health Records* (2008) to clarify the situation in regards to deceased patients.

EXTRACT

Access To Health Records: Guidance for Health Professionals in the United Kingdom, December 2008, British Medical Association:

http://bma.org.uk/practical-support-at-work/ethics/confidentiality-and-health-records

Page 8 paragraph 5: Deceased patients

The ethical obligation to respect a patient's confidentiality extends beyond death. The Information Tribunal in England and Wales has also held that a duty of confidence attaches to the medical records of the deceased under s. 41 of the Freedom of Information Act 2000.[40]

➜

---

[39] See *Confidentiality* (2009) General Medical Council, pages 28–29.
[40] This is a reference to *Bluck* v *Information Commissioner* (2007) 98 BMLR 1.

However, this duty of confidentiality needs to be balanced with other considerations, such as the interests of justice and of people close to the deceased person. Health professionals should therefore counsel their patients about the possibility of disclosure after death and solicit views about disclosure where it is obvious that there may be some sensitivity.

Paragraph 5.1: Are there any rights of access to a deceased patient's record?

Statutory rights of access are set out in the Access to Health Records Act 1990.

Paragraph 5.2: Who can apply for access?

Unless they requested confidentiality while alive, a patient's personal representative and any other person who may have a claim arising out of the patient's death has a right of access to information in the deceased person's records directly relevant to the claim.

There appears to be considerable freedom to access the medical records of a deceased patient if there is a legal action regarding his death. However, there are strict limits as to what can be released (just as with living patients).

EXTRACT

Access To Health Records: Guidance for Health Professionals in the United Kingdom, December 2008, British Medical Association:

http://bma.org.uk/practical-support-at-work/ethics/confidentiality-and-health-records

Paragraph 5.2: Who can apply for access?

It is the BMA's opinion that under s. 5(4) of the Access to Health Records Act 1990, no information which is not directly relevant to a claim should be disclosed to either the personal representative or any other person who may have a claim arising out of the patient's death.

Pages 9–10 paragraph 5.5: What information should not be disclosed?

Information should not be disclosed if:

● It identifies a third party without that person's consent unless that person is a health professional who has cared for the patient; or

● In the opinion of the relevant health professional, it is likely to cause serious harm to a third party's physical or mental health; or

● The patient gave it in the past on the understanding that it would be kept confidential.

No information at all can be revealed if the patient requested non-disclosure.

These provisions pose the question that many grieving relatives probably ask: can we be granted access to the medical records of our loved one to simply relieve our minds on the cause of death? The answer seems to be: 'it depends'. There is no legal obligation to disclose, but it is a good idea to alleviate suspicion.

EXTRACT

Access To Health Records: Guidance for Health Professionals in the United Kingdom, December 2008, British Medical Association:

http://bma.org.uk/practical-support-at-work/ethics/confidentiality-and-health-records

Page 10 paragraph 5.6: Are relatives entitled to information about the deceased's last illness?

While there is no legal entitlement, health professionals have always had discretion to disclose information to a deceased person's relatives or others when there is a clear justification. A common example is when the family requests details of the terminal illness because of anxiety that the patient might have been misdiagnosed or there might have been negligence. Disclosure in such cases is likely to be what the deceased person would have wanted and may also be in the interests of justice. Refusal to disclose in the absence of some evidence that this was the deceased patient's known wish exacerbates suspicion and can result in unnecessary litigation. In other cases, the balance of benefit to be gained by the disclosure to the family, for example of a hereditary or infectious condition, may outweigh the obligation of confidentiality to the deceased.

It appears that according to the British Medical Association, discretion can be exercised when a grieving relative simply wants to know how the patient died. This is a sensitive way of dealing with the death of a patient whilst at the same time ensuring that the hospital avoids legal actions based on nothing but suspicion.

It is, of course, better for everyone if medical records are kept confidential after death. An elderly person, for example, may have procedures and treatments stemming back to her teenage days that she does not want her surviving family to know about (e.g. an abortion at the beginning of her marriage). A younger person may be just as embarrassed if he knew that his family could find out about his sexually transmitted disease during his university years. A person who disagrees with these rules (such as Pauline Bluck – a parent) could argue that the patient is no longer living and therefore would not be harmed by the disclosure. This is correct, but there are many others who could be harmed. The surviving family would be the first to be distressed, and their memories of the deceased could be tarnished forever. Thereafter, the medical profession would suffer greatly from a lack of trust from their living patients, who may even take to suffering in silence until the condition becomes unbearable simply because they do not want an embarrassing 'blot' on their medical record. This is not to say that the rights of the deceased are greater than the rights of the living, but the rights of the living are strangely protected by ensuring the confidentiality of the dead.

RESEARCH ACTIVITY

Locate the Access to Health Records (2008) guidelines on the British Medical Association website and find the standard Law Society form used by solicitors to access the medical records of their clients. What do you think of it?

●●● Contractible diseases, anonymity and research

Two key issues relating in this area will now be explored. Firstly, patients and healthcare workers with HIV are subject to their own rules (although their confidentiality is still highly regarded), and secondly, if confidential information is anonymised, it can be used for research and audit without consent.

● Patients and healthcare workers with HIV/AIDS

The issue of HIV raises difficulties for confidentiality. A doctor may find out through laboratory tests that his patient is HIV positive. What happens to this information? It must, of course, be passed on to the patient, but what about his partner? It is understandable that she would want to know about the risk to her health, but if patients knew that their doctor could contact their partner at home and disclose their test results, patients who suspected that they had contracted HIV may stop going to their doctors, preferring instead to live in ignorance for fear of being discovered. The General Medical Council has decided in their *Confidentiality* (2003) guidance that disclosure is sometimes justified if the circumstances are serious.

> **EXTRACT**
>
> ## General Medical Council, Explanatory Guidance, Confidentiality (2009):
>
> **www.gmc-uk.org/guidance/ethical_guidance.asp**
>
> **Page 21 paragraph 53**: Disclosure of personal information about a patient without consent may be justified in the public interest if failure to disclose may expose others to a risk of death or serious harm. You should still seek the patient's consent to disclose if practicable and consider any reasons given for refusal.

The General Medical Council published a supplementary document to their *Confidentiality* (2009) guidance on disclosing information about serious diseases. The supplementary guidance advises doctors to disclose an HIV diagnosis to a partner only if the patient refuses to cooperate.

> **EXTRACT**
>
> ## Confidentiality: disclosing information about serious communicable diseases (2009), Supplementary Guidance, General Medical Council:
>
> **http://www.gmc-uk.org/guidance/ethical_guidance/confidentiality.asp**
>
> **Paragraph 9**: You should explain to patients how they can protect others from infection, including the practical measures they can take to avoid transmission, and the importance of informing sexual contacts about the risk of transmission of sexually transmitted serious communicable diseases.
>
> **Paragraph 10**: You may disclose information to a known sexual contact of a patient with a sexually transmitted serious communicable disease if you have reason to think that they are at risk of infection and that the patient has not informed them and cannot be persuaded to do so. In such circumstances, you should tell the patient before you make the disclosure, if it is practicable and safe to do so. You must be prepared to justify a decision to disclose personal information without consent.

It is clear from the supplementary guidance above that a doctor is only entitled to inform a partner of a patient about HIV if the patient is refusing to tell that partner himself. In reality, of course, the patient could always lie to the doctor in order to keep the doctor satisfied, but in the rare event that the patient is honest about his intentions to keep his disease to himself, the doctor can intervene. This is because, without a modification in behaviour, a close sexual partner of the patient is at risk of catching a very serious disease.

What if a healthcare worker contracts HIV? They can continue to work in their regular job as a doctor or a nurse, but is there a duty to inform the patient that they are being treated by a member of staff with HIV? The Department of Health have published guidance on this issue: *HIV Infected Health Care Workers* (2005). The risk of transmission appears to be very small, so the confidentiality of the healthcare worker will be upheld unless the risk of contraction is increased in some way.

EXTRACT

HIV Infected Health Care Workers: Guidance on Management and Patient Notification (2005), Department of Health (archived):

http://webarchive.nationalarchives.gov.uk/20130107105354/
http://www.dh.gov.uk/en/Publicationsandstatistics/Publications/
PublicationsPolicyAndGuidance/DH_4116415

Page 10 paragraph 1.5: All health care workers are under ethical and legal duties to protect the health and safety of their patients. They also have a right to expect that their confidentiality will be respected and protected.

Page 10-11 paragraph 1.6: Provided appropriate infection control precautions are adhered to scrupulously, the majority of procedures in the health care setting pose no risk of transmission of the human immunodeficiency virus (HIV) from an infected health care worker to a patient.

Page 11 paragraph 1.7: The circumstances in which HIV could be transmitted from an infected health care worker to a patient are limited to exposure prone procedures in which injury to the health care worker could result in the worker's blood contaminating the patient's open tissues. HIV infected healthcare workers must not perform any exposure prone procedures. The majority of health care workers do not perform exposure prone procedures.

Page 19 paragraph 4.7: A healthcare worker who has any reason to believe they may have been exposed to infection with HIV, in whatever circumstances, must promptly seek and follow confidential professional advice on whether they should be tested for HIV. Failure to do so may breach the duty of care to patients.

Page 37 paragraph 10.2: Every effort should be made to avoid disclosure of the infected worker's identity, or information which would allow deductive disclosure. This should include the use of a media injunction as necessary to prevent disclosure of a health care worker's identity. The use of personal identifiers in correspondence and requests for laboratory tests should be avoided and care taken to ensure that the number of people who know the worker's identity is kept to a minimum. Any unauthorised disclosure about the HIV status of an employee or patient constitutes a breach of confidence and may lead to disciplinary action or legal proceedings.

Paragraph 10.3: The duty of confidentiality, however, is not absolute. Legally, the identity of infected individuals may be disclosed with their consent, or without consent in exceptional circumstances, where it is considered necessary for the purpose of treatment, or prevention of spread of infection. Any such disclosure may need to be justified.

It is clear from the guidance above that:

- Healthcare workers are under a duty of care to protect their patients from harm, but they also have the same right to confidentiality as patients do.
- The risk of catching HIV from a healthcare worker in the routine treatment of patients is very, very small.
- The only potential risk of contamination from an infected healthcare worker is an exposure prone procedure such as surgery, and infected workers are not allowed to perform these procedures.
- It is recommended that only if the infected worker is performing an exposure prone procedure should the patient be warned about the risk of HIV transmission (this will be very rare).
- A healthcare worker who fears that they have been contaminated with HIV has a duty of care over their patients to seek help as soon as possible.
- The identity of the infected worker should not be revealed in most other circumstances and all steps should be taken to protect their identity, including press injunctions, if necessary.
- Legal action can result if an unjustified disclosure is made.
- The duty of confidentiality is not absolute, and a disclosure can be made if it is *necessary* for the purpose of treatment or the prevention of the spread of infection, but this disclosure must be clearly justified.

There have been two noteworthy cases in this area. They both confirm that the identity of the healthcare worker should be preserved in the interests of confidentiality (these cases helped to shape the guidelines above). The first case is from 1988, the decade that saw the rise of HIV as the 'unnamed disease' before it was fully understood.

CASE EXTRACT

X Health Authority v Y [1988] RPC 379

Facts: A national newspaper had discovered the identity of two general practitioners who had AIDS (this is the developed version of the HIV virus). The newspaper had already published an article on the matter and was going to publish more, but this time with enough information to allow the doctors to be identified. The Health Authority sought an injunction.

Held: The public interest in preserving the confidentiality of hospital records identifying actual or potential AIDS sufferers outweighed the public interest in the freedom of the press to publish such information. Accordingly, the plaintiffs were entitled to a permanent injunction restraining the defendants from publishing that information in any form

Rose J (at pages 384–5, 395–6): The most important treatment [for HIV] today is counselling which benefits the patient and the public: it benefits the patient in promoting a positive attitude and improving the quality of life – for many patients can live an essentially normal life for long periods; [...] it benefits the public because the patient can be advised to avoid activities likely to put others at risk of infection. Clearly such counselling cannot be given unless those who are infected seek medical help and to this end confidentiality is vital. [...] There are eleven known cases of the infection being transmitted from patients to health care workers. There are no known cases anywhere in the world of the infection being transmitted from health care workers (which includes doctors) to patients. The risk of such transmission is extremely small. [...]

On the one hand, there are the public interests in having a free press and an informed public debate; on the other, it is in the public interest that actual or potential AIDS sufferers should be able to resort to hospitals without fear of this being revealed, that those owing duties of confidence in their employment should be loyal and should not disclose confidential matters and that, *prima facie*, no one should be allowed to use information extracted in breach of confidence from hospital records even if disclosure of the particular information may not give rise to immediately apparent harm. [...] But in my judgment those public interests are substantially outweighed when measured against the public interests in relation to loyalty and confidentiality both generally and with particular reference to AIDS patients' hospital records.

Rose J was very clear in his judgment when he justified the injunction against the press. There was a balance to be struck between the freedom of the press and the confidentiality of infected healthcare individuals, and the public interest in loyalty and confidentiality 'substantially outweighed' the publication of confidential information. The basis for this decision was two-fold: (i) counselling was thought to be a significant treatment for the disease and this could be harmed if patients knew that their details could be disclosed; and (ii) the risk of transmission from doctor to patient was 'extremely small' at the time (and it still is today).

The more modern case of *Associated Newspapers Ltd* (2002) went into a little more detail about the particular details that could/could not be released to the public.

CASE EXTRACT

H (A Healthcare Worker) v Associated Newspapers Ltd [2002] EMLR 23

Facts: A healthcare worker (H) was diagnosed with HIV. His employer, the health authority (N), wanted to perform a 'look back' exercise to notify all of the previous patients about the risk of infection and offer them advice and an HIV test. The worker claimed that this would be unlawful. The *Mail on Sunday* (ANL) wanted to publish a story about the legal action against the health authority. The worker sought an injunction prohibiting the release of his details, in particular his identity, his whereabouts and his specialism.

Held: The Court of Appeal supported the injunction but the specialism of the worker could be revealed. There was not a realistic chance that this would identify the worker, and the public interest justified the disclosure of this detail.

Lord Phillips MR (at pages 435–6): ANL have accepted that they should not identify H or publish information that would lead to his identification. We think that they were right to do so. H disclosed to N the fact that he was HIV positive in confidence. His right to confidentiality was one which could properly be protected by injunction. [...] The consequences to H if his identity were to be disclosed would be likely to be distressing on a personal level. More than this, there is an obvious public interest in preserving the confidentiality of victims of the AIDS epidemic and, in particular, of healthcare workers who report the fact that they are HIV positive. Where a look back exercise follows, it may prove impossible to preserve the identification of the worker.

The underlying justification in this judgment for allowing the injunctions was to encourage infected healthcare workers to disclose their disease to their employers (the health authorities). There was a stronger interest in protecting the victims of the HIV/AIDS epidemic than there was to release the identifiable details of one particular healthcare worker. Besides, Lord Phillips noted that the healthcare worker had disclosed his disease to his employer *in confidence*, and that was the way it should stay.

Research and audit: anonymity

We need to train healthcare professionals and we need to take an audit of what treatments are being prescribed and what ailments are being diagnosed, but how can we do this if confidential information requires consent before it can be disclosed? We anonymise the information. These are known as 'secondary uses' of confidential information by the many regulations and guidelines in this field.

Clinical audits are vital to the health service, because they allow clinics, local authorities and the government to build a picture of the nation's health. The General Medical Council in their guidance on Confidentiality (2009) advise doctors that implied consent will suffice for an audit, but if any personal information is released to external teams that is not anonymised there must be explicit consent.

EXTRACT

General Medical Council, Explanatory Guidance, Confidentiality (2009):

www.gmc-uk.org/guidance/ethical_guidance.asp

Page 13 paragraph 30: All doctors in clinical practice have a duty to participate in clinical audit and to contribute to National Confidential Inquiries. If an audit is to be undertaken by the team that provided care, you may disclose identifiable information, provided you are satisfied that the patient:

- Has ready access to information that explains that their personal information may be disclosed for local clinical audit, and that they have the right to object, and
- Has not objected.

Page 14 paragraph 32: If clinical audit is to be undertaken, but not by the team that provided care or those who support them, the information should be anonymised or coded. If this is not practicable, or if identifiable information is essential to the audit, you should disclose the information only if you have the patient's express consent.

It appears that anonymised information does not require consent from the patient for it to be disclosed. This is supported by the Department of Health.

EXTRACT

Confidentiality: NHS Code of Practice, November 2003, Department of Health:

https://www.gov.uk/government/publications/confidentiality-nhs-code-of-practice

Page 29 paragraph 3: Once information is effectively anonymised it is no longer confidential. [Footnote 12:] effective anonymisation generally requires more than just the removal of name and address. Full postcode can identify individuals, NHS Number can be a strong identifier and other information, e.g. date of birth, can also serve as an identifier, particularly if looked at in combination with other data items.

This is hugely helpful to the medical profession, because if consent was required for a disclosure of anonymised information there would be a lack of materials for training, a lack of statistical information for audit, and research into diseases would come to a standstill. As we have already seen, the Caldicott Committee Report (1997) published a list of what they considered to be 'patient identifiable' information including the following information:[41]

- Name, including Surname, Forename and Initials
- Address
- Date of Birth
- Date of diagnosis or death
- Gender
- NHS number
- National insurance number
- Hospital or GP Practice
- Ethnic group
- Occupation

The fact that the data is anonymous means that there is no harm done to the patient and his confidentiality is not breached. Therefore, the common law does not have to be applied and a balancing act does not have to be performed.[42]

The Data Protection Act 1998 is relevant here. Anonymous data is not covered by the 1998 Act because the patient is not identifiable by the data, but the process of anonymisation includes the *processing* of confidential data and this does come under the 1998 Act. This is how it would apply:

- Under the first Data Protection Principle, the processing of the information must be done 'fairly and lawfully'.
- The patient can expressly consent to this processing.
- If the patient does not consent, it must be 'necessary' under Schedule 2.
- If the patient does not consent and it is sensitive personal data (e.g. a medical record), it must also be done for 'medical purposes' under Schedule 3.
- Medical purposes are defined under Schedule 3 as 'preventative medicine, medical diagnosis, medical research, the provision of care and treatment and the management of health care services'.

If the patient does not consent to their confidential information being anonymised, the other criteria would not be difficult to meet. It would probably be considered 'necessary' to anonymise data for medical research, medical audit or even medical training purposes. The case law has been helpful in this area, which stems from *Source Informatics* (2001). This case established that it is possible to anonymise confidential information and this will not be a breach of confidence.

---

[41] Listed on page 89 of the report: Report on the Review of Patient Identifiable Information: The Caldicott Committee, December 1997, The Department of Health (archived): http://webarchive.nationalarchives.gov.uk/20130107105354/http://www.dh.gov.uk/en/publicationsandstatistics/publications/publicationspolicyandguidance/DH_4068403.

[42] If a disclosure for research purposes includes personal information and it cannot be anonymised, it must be justified in the public interest if the patient does not consent (i.e. the normal rules of confidentiality apply).

CASE EXTRACT	*R v Department of Health ex parte Source Informatics Ltd* [2001] QB 424

Facts: Source Informatics paid doctors and pharmacists for the information on prescription forms, but the names of the patients were not included. This information was then sold on to pharmaceutical companies who used it for marketing purposes. The Department of Health warned doctors and pharmacists that the removal of patient names did not remove the duty of confidence and that the scheme should be ignored. Source Informatics sought a judicial review because they believed the Department of Health was incorrect.

Held: The Court of Appeal supported Source Informatics on appeal.

Simon Brown LJ (at pages 439–40): To my mind the one clear and consistent theme emerging from all these authorities is this: the confidant is placed under a duty of good faith to the confider and the touchstone by which to judge the scope of this duty and whether or not it has been fulfilled or breached is his own conscience, no more and no less. One asks, therefore, on the facts of this case: would a reasonable pharmacist's conscience be troubled by the proposed use to be made of patients' prescriptions? Would he think that by entering Source's scheme he was breaking his customers' confidence, making unconscientious use of the information they provide? [...]

In my judgment the answer is plain. The concern of the law here is to protect the confider's personal privacy. That and that alone is the right at issue in this case. The patient has no proprietorial claim to the prescription form or to the information it contains. [...] If, as I conclude, his only legitimate interest is in the protection of his privacy and, if that is safeguarded, I fail to see how his will could be thought thwarted or his personal integrity undermined. [...] In a case involving personal confidences I would hold [...] that the confidence is not breached where the confider's identity is protected.

The Data Protection Act 1998 was in force when this case was heard. It should have been applied because it involved the processing of personal information that could identify the patient. This case was not about proprietorial interests as Simon Brown LJ appears to think, but about the provisions of the Data Protection Act 1998 and whether the information was processed fairly and lawfully. The test is not whether the pharmacist's conscience was troubled as Simon Brown LJ states, but whether confidential medical information has been properly anonymised and if it has not, its release must be necessary and for a medical purpose under Schedules 2 and 3 of the 1998 Act. It is not clear whether the purpose of the release in *Source Informatics* was 'necessary' under Schedule 2 because it was not for training, research or audit. It is also not clear whether it was for 'medical purposes' under Schedule 3 because it the information was sold to a pharmaceutical company for marketing purposes. The *Source Informatics* case looks more like a financial gain. *Source Informatics* is a strange case: it is the leading authority on the issue of anonymising patient information, but it was not decided using the principles of the Data Protection Act 1998, which should have been applied.

There are bigger problems to tackle when it comes to the release of personal data for training, research or audit. It is accepted that completely anonymised information can be disclosed without consent because it does not breach confidentiality (*Source Informatics*), but complete anonymisation of data could be damaging to research activities. It would also make it impossible to check whether data has not been duplicated, and unless it has been codified in some way (e.g. an identifiable marker) it cannot be updated either. The research into cancer is an excellent example. Scientists in university hospitals often look into the characteristics of sufferers to pinpoint the causes of cancer in some patients but not others. Personal characteristics such as height, age, weight, environment, prescriptions, medical history, habits and location need to be included in medical research otherwise scientists would have no material to work with. This kind of research is pivotal to finding a cure, and the results of such studies are often published in medical journals and in the national press. It is not possible to do this kind of medical research if every record was anonymised. However, not every patient would consent either. Consent acts as a barrier to medical research because it excludes particular groups of patients: incompetent patients, children, those who do not understand, those who cannot be reached, those who were worried about breaches of confidentiality, those who were scared of another diagnosis and those who refuse. It is therefore more accurate and more believable to conduct research on the data of *everyone* who suffered from cancer as opposed to the data of *select groups* in society. It does state, of course, in the Data Protection Act 1998 that patient identifiable information can be disclosed without consent as long as it is 'necessary' and for 'medical purposes' under Schedules 2 and 3, but it is not clear whether medical research into cancer treatments is necessary as a medical purpose (i.e. the disclosure does not treat a patient, it simply helps researchers to figure out how to treat society generally). Section 251 of the National Health Service Act 2006 was passed to enable patient identifiable information to be released without consent for medical research, just in case the provisions under the Data Protection Act 1998 could not be satisfied. This provision is known as a loophole filler to enable medical researchers and scientists to get on with their job using confidential information without having to worry about breaches of confidentiality.

National Health Service Act 2006

Section 251: Control of patient information

(1) The Secretary of State may by regulations make such provision for and in connection with requiring or regulating the processing of prescribed patient information for medical purposes as he considers necessary or expedient –

   (a) in the interests of improving patient care, or

   (b) in the public interest.

(4) Regulations under subsection (1) may not make provision requiring the processing of confidential patient information for any purpose if it would be reasonably practicable to achieve that purpose otherwise than pursuant to such regulations, having regard to the cost of and the technology available for achieving that purpose.

Section 251 allows the Secretary of State to make regulations which allow the disclosure of confidential information without consent if it supports 'necessary or expedient' NHS activity. He is only allowed to do this if: (a) it is in the interests of improving patient care; (b) it is in the public interest; (c) it is for medical purposes; (d) if it is not reasonable practicable to do it without using regulations; (e) it doesn't cost too much;

(f) if the relevant technology is available; and (g) if, of course, anonymous information will not suffice.

In light of section 251, there needs to be an advisory body to help direct the Secretary of State. The Patient Information Advisory Group (PIAG) were initially set up to advise on whether the disclosure of patient information was appropriate without consent. This helped to safeguard the right to confidentiality. This role was taken over by the Ethics and Confidentiality Committee (ECC) as part of the National Information Governance Board for Health and Social Care (NIGB) in 2009, and was passed to the NHS Health Research Authority in 2013. The Confidentiality Advisory Group (CAG) consider up to 100 applications a year. A number of factors are taken into account by the CAG when deliberating whether it would be ethical to disclose confidential information to the NHS. They state on their website that:

> The key purpose of the CAG is to promote and protect the interests of the patient whilst at the same time facilitating appropriate use of confidential patient information for purposes beyond direct patient care.[43]

This is supported by the Department of Health in their Code of Practice on Confidentiality (2003), which states that any disclosure for the purposes of research must have ethical approval and it must be in the public interest, not merely an interest to the public.

EXTRACT

Confidentiality: NHS Code of Practice, November 2003, Department of Health:

https://www.gov.uk/government/publications/confidentiality-nhs-code-of-practice

Page 35 paragraph 34: When the public good that would be served by disclosure is significant, there may be grounds for disclosure. The key principle to apply here is that of proportionality (from Article 8). Whilst it would not be reasonable or proportionate to disclose confidential patient information to a researcher where patient consent could be sought, if it is not practicable to locate a patient without unreasonable effort and the likelihood of detriment to the patient is negligible, disclosure to support the research might be proportionate. It is important not to equate 'the public interest' with what may be 'of interest' to the public.

Generally speaking, it is a good idea to allow confidential information to be made available for the purposes of NHS research if the disclosure has been approved by the ECC, and the Department of Health are clearly concerned about the patient's right to be informed, if possible, about the disclosure and its limits. However, section 251 could be viewed as a statutory exception to the duty of confidentiality and this raises difficult ethical questions. The law of confidentiality only allows confidential medical information to be released if a well established exception applies, so is it ever justifiable to release confidential information for utilitarian purposes, for example for the greater good? The answer from some commentators has been 'no'.

---

[43] See their official website: www.hra.nhs.uk. A strong objection from the patient would probably influence the decision of the CAG considerably.

EXTRACT

Paula Case, 'Confidence Matters: The Rise and Fall of Informational Autonomy in Medical Law' (2003) 11 *Medical Law Review* 208, at pages 208–36

The implications [...] for patient trust and the therapeutic relationship will be felt at two levels. First of all, it has been widely anticipated that the therapeutic relationship between doctors and patients will be scarred. Patients apprised of the possibility of disclosure of their records to government departments may be less frank with their doctors with implications for the quality of their healthcare. That discretion may be exercised so as to protect confidence and to withdraw from the information supply chain as much as possible. Trust in health care institutions is also implicated. [...] Not only might hospitals and relevant government departments be regarded by some as part of the conspiracy to deprive patients of informational autonomy, but the whole system of government and legislation are coloured by these reforms. The fact that Parliament has passed ostensibly contradictory legislation – protecting individual rights with the much applauded Human Rights Act and Data Protection Act – and biting chunks out of those protections in the next legislative breath, might be regarded as damning evidence of untrustworthiness.

Paula Case has a very clear view of the powers under section 251 (which were known as section 60 of the Health and Social Care Act 2001 at the time this article was published): it is detrimental to patient trust, it may hinder the amount of personal information passed on to doctors, there may appear to be a conspiracy between health institutions, and the legislation contradicts itself by protecting confidentiality in one hand and breaching it in the other. These are all believable arguments, but is it not possible that patients would be happy to contribute their details to medical research if they knew it was for a good cause? This may justify the disclosure of their details without their consent.

The importance of medical research into serious diseases means that disclosures under s. 251 are still vital. They would simply be hindered indefinitely if the barrier of patient consent were to be introduced. The law in this area is finely summarised by the British Medical Association's *Confidentiality Toolkit* (2009).

EXTRACT

Confidentiality and Disclosure of Health Information Toolkit (2009), British Medical Association:

http://bma.org.uk/practical-support-at-work/ethics/confidentiality-and-health-records

Pages 53–54 paragraph 2: When can information be disclosed for secondary uses?

Patient data may be disclosed to an appropriate and secure authority and used for secondary purposes if:

- They have been effectively anonymised or pseudonymised;
- They are required by law;
- The patient has given explicit consent;

$\longrightarrow$

- The health professional is satisfied, in some limited circumstances, that the patient is aware of the use and has not objected to it and so has effectively provided implied consent;

- Disclosure is authorised by ECC under s. 251 of the National Health Service Act 2006;

- The health professional is satisfied that the legal and professional criteria for disclosure without consent in the 'public interest' have been met and has sought advice from the Caldicott Guardian, professional body or defence organisation in the case of any doubt.

Page 54: In the absence of patient consent, anonymised data should be used for any secondary purpose where it is practicable to do so.

What do you think would happen if every patient was required to consent to their identifiable details being used in medical research? It is likely that they would offer their consent anyway, but as the guidelines prove, this cannot ever be assumed.

RESEARCH ACTIVITY

Locate the Ethics and Confidentiality Committee website and research what an application under section 251 is, who may make it and what they must do for their research study to be approved.

Remedies for a breach of confidentiality

A remedy for a breach of confidence does not exist in the traditional sense. A breach of confidence is tantamount to a broken promise. There is no tangible injury and no economic loss. It may be a breach of contract on certain occasions, but there is still no measurable loss to be replaced with an award of damages. It is accepted law that the courts do not award compensation for mere distress alone.[44]

If the breach has already taken place, there could be an action under defamation law if the disclosure ruins a reputation. Alternatively, if the disclosure leads to a diagnosed psychiatric illness, there may be an avenue in the tort of negligence (duty, breach and cause – see Chapter 3). However, not much else is available to the patient, except for an apology by the relevant person for causing distress when disclosing the information (and a possible investigation by the General Medical Council following a patient complaint). If the breach is impending, there is another option: an injunction could prevent the disclosure from going ahead. This would require the patient to know who, what, where and why in regards to the disclosure.

There is only one known case which has awarded damages for the injury to the claimant's feelings for a breach of confidentiality, and that is *De Taranto* (2001). This case was interwoven with defamation, so perhaps this was why it was easier for the judge to award damages.

---

[44] The civil case of *Kralj* v *McGrath and St Theresa's Hospital* [1986] 1 All ER 54 confirmed that distress will not be compensated as a psychiatric injury.

CASE EXTRACT

Cornelius v De Taranto [2001] EMLR 12

Facts: The female claimant, a teacher, was suffering stress at work and consulted solicitors with a view to claiming constructive dismissal. In order to establish that her illnesses were work-related the solicitors advised the her to obtain an expert's report. The defendant, who was then a senior registrar in forensic psychiatry, was instructed to prepare a report. There was a dispute as to whether at the end of the interview the claimant consented to being referred to a consultant psychiatrist for treatment (as the defendant contended) or whether the claimant refused to consent to a referral (as the claimant contended). Subsequently the defendant prepared a report which she sent to the claimant's G.P. and a consultant psychiatrist. The report became part of the claimant's NHS records and she was unable to secure its removal despite repeated attempts to do so. The claimant brought proceedings against the defendant for libel and breach of an implied contractual obligation of confidence.

Held: Giving judgment for the defendant on the libel claim and for the claimant on the breach of contract claim, the claimant received £3,750 damages for injury to feelings caused by the unauthorised disclosure of her medical records (the appeal by defendant was dismissed in [2001] EWCA Civ 1511).[45]

Morland J (at pages 344–5, 348): In this case an injunction or order for delivery of all copies of the medico-legal report against the defendant will be of little use to the claimant. The damage has been done. The details of the claimant's private and family life are within the archives of the National Health Service and she has been unable to retrieve them. [...]

In the present case in my judgment recovery of damages for mental distress caused by breach of confidence, when no other substantial remedy is available, would not be inimical to considerations of policy but indeed to refuse such recovery would illustrate that something was wrong with the law. Although the object of the contract was the provision of a medico-legal report, that object could not be achieved without the defendant's examination and assessment of confidential material relating to the claimant's private and family life. The duty of confidence was an essential indeed fundamental ingredient of the contractual relationship between the claimant and the defendant which she breached. [...]

My conclusion is that I am entitled to award damages for injury to feelings caused by breach of confidence. Although it is a novel instance of such a remedy, it is in accord with the movement of current legal thinking. My decision is incremental rather than revolutionary. In my assessment of damages I must be careful to ensure that the claimant is only compensated for the injury to her feelings caused by the defendant's unauthorised disclosure of the medico-legal report. I have no doubt that the claimant suffered acute distress and injury to her feelings when on October 10, 1995 she read the report for the first time. The report contained defamatory matters, inaccuracies, embarrassing details about her private and family life and her medical history. It revealed that her G.P. notes had been sent without her consent to the defendant who had set out in the report details from the notes and made use of them in reaching her conclusions. This revelation has been a cause of continuing annoyance and anger to the claimant.

---

[45] The case went to appeal and the issue of compensation was not discussed, meaning that the claimant was still awarded the damages and the House of Lords did not think anything of it: [2001] EWCA Civ 1511.

An injunction or the delivery of all copies of the report to the claimant would have been little use to her because the damage had already been done, but according to the current law that was the only compensation Morland J could offer. Morland J accepted that the claimant suffered from mental distress as a result of the disclosure and he was of the view that an injunction or a delivery of copies would not be an adequate remedy for this: 'such recovery would illustrate that something was wrong with the law'. The duty of confidence was 'an essential indeed fundamental ingredient' to the report, meaning that its breach would be felt heavily. Morland J decides to award damages for 'injury to feelings' knowing that this is a 'novel' decision by the courts, but he is careful to mention that the damages awarded are for the *unauthorised disclosure*, not the defamation complained of by the claimant. Morland J also comments that the disclosure caused 'continuing annoyance and anger' to the claimant, but it is highly unlikely that these emotions will be grounds for damages in future cases.

The *De Taranto* case is unique, and it was mentioned by *Lady Archer* v *Williams* [2003] EWHC 1670 (QB) but is has not been followed or applied to date. This may be for the best, because as soon as the floodgates open for patients to claim damages for the mental distress caused by breaches of confidential information in the healthcare arena, health authorities may not be able to cope with the amount of additional litigation.

Under the Data Protection Act 1998, compensation can be offered to a claimant under section 13 if it can be shown that damage or distress was caused by disclosure by a data controller, but the data controller can prove as a defence that in the circumstances he was reasonably required to comply with the order for disclosure under section 13(3). The court can also order that the data be rectified, blocked, erased or destroyed under section 14 if the data is shown to be inaccurate by the claimant.

THINKING POINT

What would you offer a patient in terms of compensation if, for example, their confidentiality was breached in a hospital setting where relatives were privy to a private conversation with a doctor? Would this amount differ if a celebrity was photographed coming out of a sexual health clinic? If so, why? Would you award any damages at all for a breach of confidentiality in medicine?

Chapter summary

- The duty of confidentiality in medicine stems from the Hippocratic Oath and was consolidated in the Declaration of Geneva (1948).

- Common law exceptions to a duty of confidentiality are listed in three criteria: (1) the information is already in the public domain; (2) the information is trivial in nature; (3) there is a public interest in disclosure that outweighs the public interest in maintaining confidentiality (e.g. a grave risk of injury to the patient).

- Department of Health published a Code of Practice on Confidentiality in 2003 and it underpins the practice of confidentiality throughout the whole NHS. It is supplemented by Supplementary Guidance on the 'public interest' common law exception (published in 2010).

- A duty of confidence survives the patient: *Pauline Bluck* v *The Information Commissioner* (2007) 98 BMLR 1 and *Lewis* v *Secretary of State for Health* [2008] EWHC 2196.

Chapter essay

'Critically analyse the current professional guidelines provided to general practitioners to help them decide whether to disclose the personal information of a patient in the public interest.'

Chapter case study

Kelly has to take her daughter, Trixie, to see the family doctor because she has been crying constantly for three weeks. Dr Samantha Rogers sees Trixie on Thursday afternoon, and is concerned about Trixie's swollen arm. An x-ray is taken, and it turns out that Trixie has a broken wrist and torn ligaments which could only have been caused by pulling hard on her arm (e.g. swinging her around the room by her hand). Dr Samantha Rogers tells Kelly about the injuries and Kelly breaks down, confessing that she lives with an abusive partner. She is scared that he will punch her if the police come to the house. Dr Samantha Rogers consults the guidelines from the Department of Health, the British Medical Association and the General Medical Council because she wants to breach Kelly's and Trixie's confidentiality and report the incident to the police. What do the guidelines and laws state that Dr Samantha Roger should do?

Further reading

Andorno, R. (2004) 'The Right Not To Know: An Autonomy Based Approach', 30 *Journal of Medical Ethics* 435.

Case, P. (2003) 'Confidence Matters: The Rise and Fall of Informational Autonomy in Medical Law', 11 *Medical Law Review* 208.

Gibbons, S. (2009) 'Regulating Biobanks: A Twelve-Point Typological Tool', 19 *Medical Law Review* 1.

Moreham, N. (2005) 'Privacy in the Common Law: A Doctrinal and Theoretical Analysis', 121 *Law Quarterly Review* 628.

Sandland, R. (2007) 'Freedom of the Press and the Confidentiality of Medical Records', 15 *Medical Law Review* 400.

6

Abortion

Chapter objectives

At the end of this chapter, you should have:

- An understanding of the history of abortion.
- An appreciation of the difference between the morning-after pill and abortion and why the difference matters in law.
- Knowledge of the current statutory provisions of abortion, where they come from, what they cover and the defences therein.
- An understanding of the case law on abortion and the rights of the foetus.

> **SETTING THE SCENE**
>
> Alice visits her doctor. She is pregnant and wants an abortion. She pleads with her doctor that she is about to be made homeless and has been dumped by her partner, leaving her financially and emotionally unsupported. The doctor agrees to carry out the abortion under section 1(1)(a) of the Abortion Act 1967 on the grounds that Alice is mentally unstable because of her poor environment. When Alice turns up for her abortion three days later, she is wearing expensive designer clothes and an engagement ring. The doctor still performs the abortion, but his practice manager questions whether it has been performed in good faith according to the statute. The practice manager consults the law – what does it say?

Introduction

The law of abortion is steeped in history and religion. Abortions have been performed throughout the centuries, often through the use of odd or dangerous techniques such as ingesting poisonous herbs or applying pressure to the abdomen. As far back as the second century, the Greeks suggested ways in which a woman could prevent herself from getting pregnant and ways in which a miscarriage could be procured, e.g. energetic exercise or riding animals. It was Pope Sixtus V back in 1585 who first suggested that abortion was homicide. In the nineteenth century, the United Kingdom passed criminal laws (the Offences Against the Person Act 1861) to ensure that abortions remained illegal and that those who carried them out were punished. Nevertheless 'backstreet' abortions continued to exist in Victorian England, often leading to infections and even death.

Today, the old nineteenth-century criminal laws are still active, but Parliament has passed the Abortion Act 1967 to ensure that medical professionals have a statutory defence. The advances in technology, scans and medical care enable very premature babies to survive without significant defects. As a result, the central issue around abortion has slowly evolved from: 'should abortion be illegal?' to: 'should the old abortion laws be reformed to take account of the advances in medical care?' The most interesting question to be asked is why abortion laws exist in the first place. The foetus is not recognised as a person in law, meaning that an abortive treatment, in legal terms, is simply a medical procedure. This chapter will start by exploring the very recent debate about morning-after pills and whether they are abortions or not. This is significant, because if they do bring about an abortion, they are subject to the Abortion Act 1967, implying potential delays for the patient if she cannot find a doctor. If, however, it is a contraceptive, then it can simply be purchased over the counter and it narrowly escapes the fierce moral and legal debates surrounding abortion.

What is the morning-after pill?

The morning-after pill was introduced in the United Kingdom thirty years ago, and the most recognised brand is Levonelle. The Levonelle pill is recommended to be ingested orally up to seventy-two hours after sex and is designed to *prevent* a pregnancy, not *terminate* one. It can do this in a number of ways:

- It may stop an egg from being released by the ovary.
- It may prevent sperm from fertilising a released egg.
- It may stop a fertilised egg from attaching to the lining of the womb.[1]

---

[1] See www.levonelle.co.uk for more information.

If a fertilised egg has already implanted itself into the lining of the womb, a pregnancy has occurred and the morning-after pill will not work. Because it is considered to be a form of contraception rather than abortion, Levonelle is currently available over the counter at particular pharmacies. However, there has been a legal debate as to whether the morning-after pill, by preventing a pregnancy from developing, is acting as an abortifacient. In criminal law, the Offences Against the Person Act 1861 (the statute that criminalises abortion) defines abortion as 'procuring a miscarriage' so in order for the morning-after pill to be an abortifacient, it must cause a miscarriage. What exactly is the legal definition of a miscarriage? The term 'miscarry' has not been defined in law, but it is understood to mean that the foetus was already being 'carried' (i.e. implanted) when it was lost. In addition to this, a woman's body only begins to produce pregnancy hormones after the egg has implanted. The Human Fertilisation and Embryology Act 1990 takes the view that implantation leads to pregnancy for the purposes of assisted conception.

The Human Fertilisation and Embryology Act 1990

Section 2(3): For the purposes of this Act, a woman is not to be treated as carrying a child until the embryo has become implanted.

The law seems to have settled on the belief that until an egg is implanted, a woman is not pregnant. Therefore, a miscarriage cannot occur until implantation has taken place. This did not stop a case on behalf of the Society for the Protection of Unborn Children (SPUC) from reaching the High Court to argue that the morning-after pill was an abortifacient.

CASE EXTRACT

R (on the application of Smeaton) v *Secretary of State for Health* [2002] EWHC 610

Facts: The morning after pill was given the green light to be dispensed over the counter by pharmacists *without* a prescription. SPUC argued that the pill was an abortifacient, and as a result, the woman taking the pill and the pharmacists dispensing it were committing criminal offences under the 1861 Act.

Held: The pill was not an abortifacient because implantation had not taken place, it was a form of contraception instead.

Munby J (at paras 74, 350, 353, 394): If SPUC were to succeed in this challenge, the result would be, as I have said, that Levonelle could be prescribed only by doctors who had complied with the requirements of the Abortion Act 1967. This in turn would mean that:

(i) Levonelle would tend to be administered either not at all or at a later stage, when the expert evidence is that it is less effective and more likely to operate post-fertilisation;

(ii) There would inevitably be an increase in the number of abortions as conventionally understood, a result which, Schering [the manufacturer] suggests, SPUC would presumably not welcome.

Applying the principles to be found, the correct approach can be set out in the form of four propositions:

(i)   the 1861 Act is an 'always speaking' Act;

(ii)   the word 'miscarriage' is an ordinary English word of flexible meaning which Parliament in 1861 chose to leave undefined;

(iii) it should accordingly be interpreted as it would be *currently* understood;

(iv)   it should be interpreted in the light of the best current scientific and medical knowledge that is available to the court.

[...] Prior to implantation there is no true carriage. It may be theoretically possible to argue that carriage can occur when the embryo is free floating in the fallopian tube or in the uterus. However, the much the more natural meaning involves not merely presence in the woman's body and interaction with it, but attachment to it in a real sense such as occurs only with implantation. [...] There would in my judgment be something very seriously wrong, indeed grievously wrong with our system – by which I mean not just our legal system but the entire system by which our polity is governed – if a judge in 2002 were to be compelled by a statute 141 years old to hold that what thousands, hundreds of thousands, indeed millions, of ordinary honest, decent, law abiding citizens have been doing day in day out for so many years is and always has been criminal. I am glad to be spared so unattractive a duty.

Munby J examined the many different moral, social and legal aspects of abortion in the *Smeaton* case. It was on those numerous grounds that he came to a conclusion. The most interesting element of the judgment is the inference of 'implantation' from the word 'carriage'. Munby J also veered off into social considerations and based his decision not only on medical grounds, but on social grounds too. The only real issue in *Smeaton* was whether a fertilised egg constituted a pregnancy, but had he supported SPUC, his decision would have constituted a radical change in society and how individuals conduct their private lives.

What is an abortion?

Clearly, the morning-after pill is not deemed in medicine or in law to be an abortifacient because the fertilised egg has not implanted itself into the lining of the womb. An abortion by definition is the intentional termination of a pregnancy, meaning that the fertilised egg must have implanted into the wall of the uterus before it is removed. An abortion can be performed in several different ways depending on the stage of pregnancy:

- **The abortion pill**: a pill is taken in early pregnancy to cause a miscarriage by blocking particular hormones.
- **Dilation and evacuation**: dilation and suction can be used to empty the contents of the womb but this is only necessary when the abortion pill is no longer efficient.
- **Dilation and curettage**: dilation and scraping of the womb can procure an abortion but this is only necessary when the pregnancy has developed.

- **Intact dilation and extraction (IDX)**: the head of the foetus is compressed before being evacuated. If the foetus is particularly developed, an injection may be used to stop the foetus's heart beating first. This is quite rare and is typically required in the later stages of pregnancy.

RESEARCH ACTIVITY

Find the full judgment of Munby J in R (John Smeaton on Behalf of Society for the Protection of Unborn Children) v The Secretary of State for Health [2002] EWHC 610 and list the four main points to be taken from his judgment.

The history of abortion

In UK law, abortion was founded in the common law up until 1803, and the common law was founded upon the religious notion that life was a gift from God and that killing was a universal wrong. After 1803, statutes were passed to illegalise abortion, and although the statutory provisions became more and more complex through the years, particular words and phrases were repeated in the many reforms, including the term 'miscarry'.

The common law[2]

In the thirteenth century, Bracton said in his *De Legibus et Consuetudinibus Angliae* (On the Laws and Customs of England) that:

> If one strikes a pregnant woman (*mulierem praegnantem*) or gives her poison in order to procure an abortion (*abortivum*), if the foetus is already formed or quickened, especially if it is quickened (*iam formatum vel animatum fuerit, et maxime si animatum*), he commits homicide.

The word 'quickened' means that the foetus has begun to move inside the mother. Quickening made the offence of abortion much more serious, because the foetus was beginning to show signs of life. In the seventeenth century, Coke in his Institutes of the Laws of England said that:

> If a woman be quick with childe, and by a potion or otherwise killeth it in her wombe; or if a man beat here, whereby the child dieth in her body, and she is delivered of a dead child, this is a great misprision, and no murder . . . herein the law is grounded upon the law of God.

Blackstone said much the same thing in the eighteenth century in his Commentaries on the Laws of England:

> 'Life is the immediate gift of God, a right inherent by nature in every individual; and it begins in contemplation of law as soon as an infant is able to stir in the mother's womb. For if a woman is quick with child, and by a potion, or otherwise, killeth it in her womb; or if any one beat her, whereby the child dieth in her body, and she is

---

[2] The following laws are taken from a detailed breakdown of the history of abortion law in the United Kingdom in the judgment of Munby J in R (on the application of Smeaton) v Secretary of State for Health [2002] EWHC 610 (Admin).

delivered of a dead child; this, though not murder, was by the antient law homicide or manslaughter. But at present it is not looked upon in quite so atrocious a light, though it remains a very heinous misdemeanor.'

On reading the old common law above, it becomes clear that the attitudes towards abortion were strong. The word 'God' was used as recently as the nineteenth century, and emotive words such as 'homicide', 'killeth', 'dieth' and 'dead child' all suggest that although the abortion did not amount to murder, it was a very serious and shocking crime.

Statute law

Lord Ellenborough's Act of 1803 created two statutory criminal offences. Section I made abortion a felony (a serious crime) punishable by death:

> . . . if any person . . . shall wilfully, maliciously and unlawfully administer to, or cause to be administered to or taken by any of his Majesty's Subjects, any deadly Poison, or other noxious and destructive Substance or Thing, with Intent . . . thereby to cause and procure the Miscarriage of any Woman then being quick with Child.

For the first time, section II of Lord Ellenborough's Act of 1803 also made it an offence to abort a foetus *before* quickening (meaning that the woman may not even be pregnant):

> And whereas it may sometimes happen that Poison or some other noxious and destructive Substance or Thing may be given, or other Means used, with Intent to procure Miscarriage or Abortion where the Woman may not be quick with Child at the Time, or it may not be proved that she was quick with Child . . . if any Person or Persons . . . shall wilfully and maliciously administer to, or cause to be administered to, or taken by any Woman, any Medicines, Drug, or other Substance or Thing whatsoever, or shall use or employ, or cause or procure to be used or employed, any Instrument or other Means whatsoever, with Intent thereby to cause or procure the Miscarriage of any Woman not being, or not being proved to be, quick with Child at the Time of administering such Things or using such Means, . . . then [a felony is committed].

Section II provides considerable detail as to what the defendant must do, and intend to do, in order to be convicted under this section. The use of instruments has been added to the law under section II. The criminal sanctions available under section II were a fine, imprisonment, the Pillory, whipping or transportation for up to fourteen years. One problem with section II was that it did not require proof that a woman was pregnant at the time. In *R v Phillips* (1811) 3 Camp 73 this was no defence, whereas in the later case of *R v James Scudder* (1828) 1 Mood CC 216 it was a defence. The 1803 Act was repealed by Lord Lansdowne's Offences Against the Person Act 1828, but very few changes were made to the 1803 version of abortion. Abortion was still split into two separate offences and many of the same words and phrases were carried down. It also adopted the death penalty for an abortion after quickening.

The 1828 Act was radically reformed in 1837, turning abortion into one offence and abolishing the death penalty altogether:

> whosoever, with Intent to procure the Miscarriage of any Woman, shall unlawfully administer to her or cause to be taken by her any Poison or other noxious Thing, or shall unlawfully use any Instrument or other Means whatsoever with the like Intent.

The penalty for this new single offence of abortion was transportation for life or imprisonment. The reasons for simplifying the offence of abortion were explained clearly by Commissioners Appointed to Inquire Into the State of the Criminal Law in 1837:

By the present Law, this offence is divided into two classes: the capital offence being where the woman shall be quick with child. Having taken away the capital punishment, we have omitted this distinction, which we consider will be advantageous as removing a difficulty in evidence, and as obviating the necessity of discussing a question respecting which considerable doubt must always exist.

In other words, by taking away the death penalty for abortion, there was no longer the need for the 'quickening' distinction. There was simply one offence of abortion and it applied to instances both before *and* after the foetus began to show signs of life. In addition, evidence was still not required to prove that the woman was even pregnant. This was confirmed by *R* v *Mary Goodhall* (1846) 1 Den CC 187, which stated that proof of pregnancy was not necessary. The Offences Against the Person Act was amended again in 1861, separating abortion out into several offences under sections 58 and 59. This old law is still in force today. This means that abortion is still a criminal offence, but medical practitioners may use defences under the Abortion Act 1967 to justify their actions.

RESEARCH ACTIVITY

Read the old abortion laws above, which represented the old legal position on abortion, and make some notes as to how the law developed from the thirteenth century to the eighteenth century. What elements were added – and removed – to the common law offence as the centuries progressed? What does the 1837 reform suggest in regards to the moral and legal value of the foetus?

The law of abortion (development)

The Offences Against the Person Act 1861 is well known by law students from their criminal studies because it contains the provisions for actual bodily harm (section 47), malicious wounding (section 20), and malicious wounding with intent (section 18). However, few people know that the criminal offence of abortion is also housed under this Act, and can be found at sections 58 and 59.

Section 58 of the Offences Against the Person Act 1861

When it came to the 1861 reform of the Offences Against the Person Act, Parliament decided to complicate the offence of abortion by splitting it up. Section 58 of the 1861 Act (still in force) provides the following.

Offences Against the Person Act 1861

Section 58: Administering drugs or using instruments to procure an abortion

Every woman, being with child, who, with intent to procure her own miscarriage, shall unlawfully administer to herself any poison or other noxious thing, or shall unlawfully use any instrument or other means whatsoever with the like intent, and whosoever, with intent to procure the miscarriage of any woman, whether she be or not with child, shall unlawfully administer to her or cause to be taken by her any poison or other noxious thing, or shall unlawfully use any instrument or other means whatsoever with the like intent, shall be guilty of felony (up to life in prison).

Section 58 can be split into two: a woman can procure her own miscarriage *and* a third party can be liable for procuring a miscarriage. The new provision allowing for the conviction of a woman who procures her *own* miscarriage is an interesting statutory development. The following new words and phrases are of particular interest:

- **Being with child**: the term 'quickening' has now been abolished from the statute and it only matters that the woman is pregnant. How far along she is in the pregnancy is irrelevant.

- **With intent**: the old term 'maliciously' has disappeared from the offence. This means that a simple intention will suffice, whether it be malicious or charitable (e.g. the mother already has five children and cannot afford to raise any more).

- **Procure her own miscarriage and administer to herself**: for the first time, the pregnant woman herself could be guilty of procuring (i.e. 'bring about') her own abortion. This is a completely new provision and imposes a new restriction upon the pregnant woman.

- **Unlawfully administer and unlawfully use**: the insertion of the word 'unlawfully' (which was seen as early as the 1803 Act) suggests that there is a 'lawful' alternative.

- **Felony**: this is a serious offence.

- **Whether she be or not with child**: for another person to be guilty under section 58, the woman does not have to be pregnant.

Section 59 of the Offences Against the Person Act 1861

Section 59 provides the following.

Offences Against the Person Act 1861

Section 59: Procuring drugs to cause abortion

Whosoever shall unlawfully supply or procure any poison or other noxious thing, or any instrument or thing whatsoever knowing that the same is intended to be unlawfully used or employed with intent to procure the miscarriage of any woman, whether she be or not be with child, shall be guilty of a misdemeanor (up to five years in prison).

Section 59 is less serious than the two offences in section 58. Not only is it described as a 'misdemeanor' rather than a 'felony', but the person charged under section 59 does not carry out an abortion, he merely *supplies* or *procures* a poison or an instrument to a third party so they can carry out an abortion. The key words and phrases are as follows:

- **Supply and procure and used and employed**: a person is only guilty under section 59 if his actions reflect one of these key words (e.g. he 'supplies' a drug knowing it is for abortive purposes).

- **Knowing**: the person charged under section 59 must know that the poisons or instruments he is gathering and handing over to a third party are to be used to procure an abortion.

- **Whether she be or not with child**: the woman in question does not have to be pregnant for a person to be guilty under section 59.

Notice that in both sections 58 and 59, the pregnant woman or another person must 'intend to procure a miscarriage' (whether it is successful or not). Therefore, if a miscarriage is caused recklessly, this does not come under the ambit of the statute. In addition to this, the pregnant woman or other person must have completed key actions under sections 58 and 59 to be guilty, such as 'administer', 'use', 'taken', 'supply', 'procure' and 'employ', but the death of the foetus is not a necessary requirement.

It was stated above that the word 'unlawful' appeared not only in the 1861 Act but as far back as Lord Ellenborough's 1803 Act. This can be interpreted as meaning that an abortion may be 'lawful' in certain circumstances. This commonly understood rule was later enshrined into the Infant Life (Preservation) Act 1929, allowing a lawful defence to a charge under sections 58 and 59 of the Offences Against the Person Act 1861.

The Infant Life (Preservation) Act 1929

Section 1(1) provides the following.

Infant Life (Preservation) Act 1929

Section 1: Punishment for child destruction

(1) Any person who, with intent to destroy the life of a child capable of being born alive, by any wilful act causes a child to die before it has an existence independent of its mother, shall be guilty of felony, to wit, of child destruction, and shall be liable on conviction thereof on indictment to penal servitude for life:

Provided that no person shall be found guilty of an offence under this section unless it is proved that the act which caused the death of the child was not done in good faith for the purpose only of preserving the life of the mother.

The Infant Life (Preservation) Act 1929 makes it a criminal offence to kill a child that is capable of being born alive (akin to aborting a 'quickened' child centuries ago). It is, of course, difficult to tell when exactly a child is capable of being born alive as medical developments are allowing premature babies to survive for longer than ever before. Childbirth, of course, could occur at any stage of pregnancy, but it was thought that a child was 'capable of being born alive' from about 28 weeks.

The 1929 Act lays down a clear defence to liability under the Offences Against the Person Act 1861: if the mother's life is in grave danger, the act of killing a child that is capable of being born alive will not attract criminal liability under sections 58 and 59.

The first leading case in abortion appears at this point, creating a new *common law defence* to abortion which was a based on a wide interpretation of the 1929 Act.

CASE EXTRACT

R v Bourne [1939] 1 KB 687

Facts: Aleck Bourne, an obstetric surgeon, performed an abortion on a 14-year-old girl after she suffered a violent rape. He was charged under section 58 of the Offences Against the Person Act 1861. The only defence available at the time was section 1(1) of the Infant Life Act 1929, but the girl's life was not in grave danger. Dr Aleck Bourne argued that the pregnancy would have posed a serious risk to the girl's *mental* health.

→

Held: There is a new common law defence to the criminal offence of abortion: if the mother is to become a 'physical or mental wreck' during pregnancy then it is best that it does not continue (later adopted as the 'social ground' under section 1(1)(a) of the Abortion Act 1967).

Macnaghten J [...]: It is true that [the Infant Life (Preservation) Act 1929] provides for the case where a child is killed by a wilful act at the time when it is being delivered in the ordinary course of nature, but in my view the proviso that it is necessary for the Crown to prove that the act was not done in good faith for the purpose only of preserving the life of the mother is in accordance with what has always been the common law of England with regard to the killing of an unborn child. No such proviso is in fact set out in section 58 of the Offences Against the Person Act, 1861; but the words of that section are that any person who 'unlawfully' uses an instrument with intent to procure miscarriage shall be guilty of felony. In my opinion the word 'unlawfully' is not, in that section, a meaningless word. I think it imports the meaning expressed by the proviso in section 1(1) of the Infant Life (Preservation) Act 1929. [...] What then is the meaning to be given to the words 'for the purpose of preserving the life of the mother'. There has been much discussion in this case as to the difference between danger to life and danger to health. [...] If the doctor is of opinion, on reasonable grounds and with adequate knowledge, that the probable consequence of the continuance of the pregnancy will be to make the woman a physical or mental wreck, the jury are quite entitled to take the view that the doctor who, under those circumstances and in that honest belief, operates, is operating for the purpose of preserving the life of the mother. [...] No doubt you will think it is only common sense that a girl who for nine months has to carry in her body the reminder of the dreadful scene and then go through the pangs of childbirth must suffer great mental anguish.

Macnaghten J introduced a new common law defence to abortion in this judgment using a wide interpretation of section 1(1) of the Infant Life (Preservation) Act 1929. It is today known as the 'social ground' defence, i.e. the mother would become a physical and emotional wreck if the pregnancy continued. He also confirmed that the 'preserving of life' defence in the 1929 Act could be used against a charge under section 58 of the Offences Against the Person Act 1861 (this was the first case to test the law). He based his decision on several grounds:

- The doctor's actions and intentions appeared to be charitable.
- The 'preserving of life' defence contained in section 1(1) of the Infant Life Preservation Act 1929 should be used against a charge of section 58 of the 1861 Act.
- 'Preserving the life' could be construed to mean 'preserving the health'.
- Performing an abortion to prevent the patient from becoming a 'physical or mental wreck' will qualify as 'preserving the life' of the mother.
- Medical evidence supports the view that it would be detrimental to allow for young girls to carry a pregnancy to full term.
- It is common sense to conclude that a pregnancy, as a result of a violent sexual attack, would cause great mental anguish.

Macnaghten J took a very wide interpretation of the law to allow for abortions to be carried out in certain circumstances. The position after *Bourne* could thus be described as follows:

Old law before *R v Bourne* (1939)	New law after *R v Bourne* (1939)
Abortions were illegal under sections 58 and 59 of the Offences Against the person Act 1861.	Abortions were still illegal under sections 58 and 59 of the Offences Against the person Act 1861.
The Infant Life (Preservation) Act of 1929 allowed for a pregnancy to be terminated in order to 'preserve the life of the mother'. Other exceptions: none.	The Infant Life (Preservation) Act of 1929 still allowed for a pregnancy to be terminated in order to 'preserve the life of the mother'. New exception: 'preserving the life of the mother' can include performing an abortion to prevent her from becoming a 'physical or mental wreck' and this exception can be used against a charge under section 58 of the 1861 Act.

The Infant Life (Preservation) Act 1929 is of little relevance today because any defences to abortion are now contained within the Abortion Act 1967 (below). However, the unique case of *Bourne* led to a significantly lenient common law defence that softened the law of abortion considerably. Doctors knew that if they performed an abortion they could still face prosecution under section 58 (and 59) of the Offences Against the Person Act 1861 but they could have a defence in common law. They had to prove the following:

- The continuance of the pregnancy would make a woman a physical or mental wreck.
- The doctor must form this opinion on reasonable grounds.
- The doctor must form this opinion with adequate knowledge.
- The physical or mental wreck must be a probable consequence of the pregnancy.
- The doctor must perform the procedure with the honest belief that he is preserving the mother's life.

Notice how the term 'physical or mental wreck' can be interpreted according to the facts of each individual case (i.e. Macnaghten J gave no further definition or guidance). Sometimes, doctors may have performed abortions simply because the woman was showing signs of distress or anxiety rather than becoming a 'mental wreck'. The patient in *Bourne* could also be distinguished from other pregnant women on the grounds that she was only 14 years old when she fell pregnant as a result of a violent rape. The 'mental wreck' criteria must only be a 'probable consequence' of the pregnancy, not an 'actual' consequence, leading doctors to employ foreseeability in their decision-making even though some patients they may never have seen before.

After *Bourne*

The *Bourne* defence was loose and ambiguous, but it allowed many more women to terminate their pregnancies if they were suffering severe physical or mental stress that was not quite grave in nature. It also heralded a more sympathetic approach within the law. Gone were the days in which pregnant women seeking abortion were merely viewed as reckless prostitutes – the law was beginning to recognise that all cases were different – and it would be much to fairer to the patient if they were decided on their own merits. However, there was still a significant problem. Because abortion was still a very serious criminal offence attracting a life sentence under section 58 of the Offences Against the

Person Act 1861, many doctors were extremely reluctant to perform the procedure. Pregnant women who showed signs of severe physical or mental distress were easier cases to decide, but other women were still seeking terminations for other reasons, and these were not legal. 'Backstreet' abortions were therefore an open secret, and they were very dangerous. Unqualified individuals would perform abortions for considerable amounts of money, meaning that the poorer women in society had to carry their pregnancy to full term. Those who could afford abortions faced a high mortality rate in unsanitary conditions. In response to this problem, David Steel MP brought an Abortion Bill to Parliament in the mid-1960s to radically reform the law. It was proposed that the abortion procedure should remain a criminal offence under sections 58 and 59 of the Offences Against the Person Act 1861, but clearer and more accessible defences should be introduced for medical practitioners. The result was the hugely successful Abortion Act 1967 (examined below).

ACTIVITY

Kim and Tanya are both sisters and they are both pregnant. They are only 14 and 15 years old, and so do not want their babies. They seek abortions.

Kim, who is 14, tells her friend, Daniel, at school. Daniel offers to push down hard on Kim's stomach to cause a miscarriage. He does so, but it does not work. Later, Daniel returns with ten raw eggs and tells Kim to eat them, which she does, and she is very sick, but still does not miscarry.

Tanya, who is 15, goes running on a 25-mile trek in an attempt to miscarry. It fails. She then travels to a backstreet abortion clinic. They are not regulated or sanitary. The owner of the premises, Michael, wants £400 for the procedure. Tanya pays him. Michael performs an abortion on Tanya with the help of his assistant Ben, who simply passes instruments to Michael.

> Question 1: is Kim guilty of an offence under sections 58 or 59?
>
> Question 2: is Daniel guilty of an offence under sections 58 or 59?
>
> Question 3: is Tanya guilty of an offence under sections 58 or 59?
>
> Question 4: is Michael guilty of an offence under sections 58 or 59?
>
> Question 5: is Ben guilty of an offence under sections 58 or 59?

The law of abortion (present): the Abortion Act 1967

The Abortion Act 1967 was one of the most successful private members' bills put forward by a Member of Parliament (David Steel MP). It provides statutory defences to sections 58 and 59 of the Offences Against the Person Act 1861 meaning that abortion was still a criminal offence, but medical practitioners can use a statutory defence to shield them from criminal liability.

Why was the Abortion Act 1967 passed?

David Steel did not simply suggest the Abortion Bill for the sake of causing controversy. The situation regarding 'backstreet' abortions was out of control before 1967 and many women who sought abortion were physically maimed or died as a result of unqualified and unsanitary practices. They were also taken advantage of by greedy and unscrupulous individuals who offered their services for large amounts of money. The new Bill in 1967 was thus designed to bring qualified doctors out from the shadows to perform safe and clean medical procedures. The new law was not designed to give women a right to an abortion. This 'right' does not exist because abortion is still illegal under the 1861 Act. The new law was instead designed to ensure that any abortions that did take place were performed safely, at the hands of professionals, in an appropriate place and for the right reasons. The Bill left it to two doctors to decide whether an abortion was appropriate, taking the woman out of the decision-making process. A case confirmed this ten years later.

CASE EXTRACT

Paton v British Pregnancy Advisory Service Trustees [1979] QB 276

Facts: Mr Paton sought an injunction preventing his wife from having abortion.

Held: A husband/father of the child could not prevent his wife from having an abortion – the doctors were the only people qualified to make the decision.

Sir George Baker (at pages 281–2): My own view is that it would be quite impossible for the courts in any event to supervise the operation of the Abortion Act 1967. The great social responsibility is firmly placed by the law upon the shoulders of the medical profession: see *per* Scarman LJ in *Reg.* v *Smith (John)* [1973] 1 WLR 1510 at 1512. […] The two doctors have given a certificate. It is not and cannot be suggested that the certificate was given in other than good faith and it seems to me that there is the end of the matter in English law. […] This certificate is clear, and not only would it be a bold and brave judge who would seek to interfere with the discretion of doctors acting under the Abortion Act 1967, but I think he would really be a foolish judge who would try to do any such thing, unless, possibly, where there is clear bad faith and an obvious attempt to perpetrate a criminal offence.

The *Paton* case established that only the two medical professionals carrying out the abortion under the 1967 Act had a right to decide whether the procedure should be carried out. The mother and the father of the child could not demand an abortion, and the father could not stop an abortion. This is a significant affront to patient autonomy.

What does the Abortion Act 1967 do?

The Abortion Act 1967 provides for four defences to a charge under sections 58 and 59 of the Offences Against the Person Act 1861. Any abortions that are performed outside of these four grounds are illegal and the doctor or other unqualified individual who performed, or attempted to perform, the abortion will face prosecution under the 1861 Act.

Abortion Act 1967

Section 1: Medical termination of pregnancy

(1) Subject to the provisions of this section, a person shall not be guilty of an offence under the law relating to abortion when a pregnancy is terminated by a registered medical practitioner if two registered medical practitioners are of the opinion, formed in good faith –

→

(a) that the pregnancy has not exceeded its twenty-fourth week and that the continuance of the pregnancy would involve risk, greater than if the pregnancy were terminated, of injury to the physical or mental health of the pregnant woman or any existing children of her family; or

(b) that the termination is necessary to prevent grave permanent injury to the physical or mental health of the pregnant woman; or

(c) that the continuance of the pregnancy would involve risk to the life of the pregnant woman, greater than if the pregnancy were terminated; or

(d) that there is a substantial risk that if the child were born it would suffer from such physical or mental abnormalities as to be seriously handicapped.

(2) In determining whether the continuance of a pregnancy would involve such risk of injury to health as is mentioned in paragraph (a) or (b) of subsection (1) of this section, account may be taken of the pregnant woman's actual or reasonably foreseeable environment.

Notice how under section 1(1), a 'registered medical practitioner' must terminate the pregnancy. In addition, a *second* registered medical practitioner must confirm that one of the four grounds are made out, which are simplified in the table below:

Section of Abortion Act 1967	Ground for legal abortion
Section 1(1)(a)	Risk of injury to physical or mental health of the mother or any existing children.[3]
Section 1(1)(b)	To prevent grave permanent injury to physical or mental health of woman.[4]
Section 1(1)(c)	Continuance of pregnancy involves greater risk to woman's life than a termination.
Section 1(1)(d)	Substantial risk of physical or mental abnormalities leading to serious handicap.

Some of the legal grounds for an abortion listed in the box above may seem a bit odd. Why are the needs of existing children considered? What is a serious handicap? What is the difference between sections 1(1)(b) and 1(1)(c)? We will investigate these below.

Ground 1: section 1(1)(a)

Section 1(1)(a) of the Abortion Act 1967 states the following:

Abortion Act 1967

Section 1: Medical termination of pregnancy

(1)(a): that the pregnancy has not exceeded its twenty-fourth week and that the continuance of the pregnancy would involve risk, greater than if the pregnancy were terminated, of injury to the physical or mental health of the pregnant woman or any existing children of her family.

---

[3] This a reference to the *R* v *Bourne* [1939] 1 KB 687 common law defence of 'physical and mental wreck'.
[4] This is a reference to the original statutory defence under the Infant Life (Preservation) Act 1929.

Section 1(1)(a) is known as the 'social ground' and contains a time limit. Pregnancies that have reached 24 weeks can no longer be aborted under this section. This is because section 1(1)(a) is the most lenient ground under the 1967 Act: it does not require a grave risk to the mother, nor does it require the foetus to be seriously handicapped. Women who simply find themselves pregnant at the wrong time of life or are in financial or personal trouble seek legal abortions under this ground, and this is why it is not available for advanced pregnancies. Parliament did not consider the reasons under section 1(1)(a) as being strong enough to terminate a full term pregnancy.[5]

The time limit

There is a time limit under section 1(1)(a) to prevent late abortions for social reasons, but it poses a problem. Doctors can not accurately predict when a pregnancy begins, meaning that the time limit cannot be enforced with accuracy. Currently, doctors will consider the date of the woman's last period as the start of the pregnancy, even though sexual intercourse and conception probably occurred two weeks later. If a woman has irregular periods, this whole process becomes much more difficult, and scans will be able to show just how big the foetus is. Until medicine becomes more exact, it is accepted that a margin of uncertainty occurs under the section 1(1)(a) time limit. It is actually quite rare for a woman to seek an abortion under section 1(1)(a) if she is over 20 weeks gestation. The Department of Health publish annual statistics on abortion, outlined below. It shows, among other things, that only 1% of abortions are carried out at 20 weeks gestation:

EXTRACT

Abortion Statistics: England and Wales 2012, published July 2013, Department of Health:

https://www.gov.uk/government/organisations/department-of-health/series/abortion-statistics-for-england-and-wales

- There were 185,122 abortions in the UK in 2012:
    - 182,239 abortions were carried out under section 1(1)(a):
    - 190 abortions were carried out under sections 1(1)(b) and (c);
    - 2,692 abortions were carried out under section 1(1)(d).
- 841 abortions were carried out on women aged under 15.
- 689 abortions were carried out on women aged 45 and older.
- 81% of the women were single.
- 76% of the women were white (10% were Asian and 9% were black).
- 37% had at least one abortion before.
- 97% of abortions were funded by the NHS.

---

[5] The 24-week time limit was added to the 1967 Act in 1990 by the Human Fertilisation and Embryology Act 1990.

Considerably more abortions were performed under section 1(1)(a) in 2011 than any other section (and this result is similar in all previous years). This means that the overwhelming majority of women seeking abortions are doing so for social, rather than medical, reasons. If it was not for the 1967 Act, these women would have no choice but to carry their pregnancy to full term. The time limit under section 1(1)(a) has made little practical difference to the law of abortion. As can be seen from the statistics above, only a very small number of abortions were carried out after 20 weeks gestation under section 1(1)(a). This may be for two reasons:

- Most women have decided by 20 weeks which course of action to take.
- Doctors may be reluctant to perform abortions so close to the time limit.

However, the existence of the time limit itself has caused controversy, especially as ultrasound and neonatal technology develops. There are many social, religious and medical reasons why the abortion time limit should be lower than 24 weeks, but campaigners in favour of abortion argue that the small minority who seek an abortion beyond 20 weeks have good reasons for doing so. For example, not only might they be oblivious to the fact that they are pregnant, they may have had a drastic change of circumstances at the last minute, they may not have had good access to medical services, or they may have found it emotionally difficult to seek an abortion. It is argued, therefore, that a legal abortion should still be available to these women, even though they are a very small minority.

Viability (i.e. survival)

The time limit under section 1(1)(a) of the Abortion Act 1967 has come under increased scrutiny in recent years after 4D ultrasound scanning was introduced. A foetus can now be shown in considerable detail. Facial muscle contractions can be mistaken for smiles, and hand movements can be mistaken for waves. This kind of technology gives a foetus a personality all of its own before it has been born. The point of viability (i.e. the point at which a baby can be born alive and survive on its own) is commonly understood to be 24 weeks. This limit was adopted into the 1967 Act. However, babies are now being born earlier than 24 weeks and surviving with the help of advanced neonatal care. This technology, combined with 4D ultrasound scanning, has led some people to argue that the time limit under section 1(1)(a) should be lowered to 22 weeks, or perhaps lower. This is because 'social abortions' under section 1(1)(a) are not justified on medical grounds in the same way that abortions under paragraphs (b), (c) and (d) are. The main argument, therefore, is: should we be aborting babies under paragraph (a) who, at 24 weeks, are today capable of being born alive, simply because the mother would be a mental wreck?

What is 'physical or mental injury to women or children'?

Under section 1(1)(a), a pregnancy can be terminated if the continuance of the pregnancy poses a risk to the physical or mental health of the mother or any existing children. This can be split into two categories: the health of the mother, and the health of her children.

The pregnant woman's physical or mental health need not be in grave danger under paragraph (a), there must simply be a 'risk' to her physical or mental health but it is not clear how serious or trivial this risk must be. Section 1(1)(a) is commonly understood to refer to a woman's wellbeing. For example, a pregnant woman may argue that a new baby would cause considerable emotional distress because of ongoing financial problems. Two medical practitioners must confirm, in good faith, that the grounds under section 1(1)(a) have been made out, and they must also take into account the woman's reasonably foreseeable environment. An abortion will not, therefore, be granted if the pregnant woman is simply worried about missing a holiday date. These safeguards are in place to prevent against 'needless' abortions.

The 'children' criteria under section 1(1)(a) is interesting. A pregnant woman can argue that the physical or mental health of her existing children will suffer as a result of another child being born. It is not likely that new child will *physically* harm any existing children – it is more likely that the family as a whole would be put under a considerable financial or emotional strain. The rights of any existing children would, therefore, override the rights of the foetus in order to keep the family unit stable.

Sex selection?

If a pregnant woman finds out that she is expecting a girl, should she be allowed to abort the pregnancy under ground 1(1)(a) if it causes her mental anguish? There appears to be a preference for boys worldwide, particularly in India, and many developed countries will allow abortions on request (or at least on social grounds). To use an example, let us say that a pregnant woman already has five boys and they are all under the age of 5. They have Attention Deficit Hyperactivity Disorder and she cannot cope with the prospect of another son. When she finds out that her sixth pregnancy is another boy, she wants an abortion. Technically, if two medical practitioners believe that she will become a mental wreck as a result of her sixth pregnancy, she will satisfy the grounds for an abortion under section 1(1)(a) of the 1967 Act.

Ground 2: section 1(1)(b)

Section 1(1)(b) of the Abortion Act 1967 states the following:

Abortion Act 1967

Section 1: Medical termination of pregnancy

(1)(b): that the termination is necessary to prevent grave permanent injury to the physical or mental health of the pregnant woman.

Section 1(1)(b) is the ground which allows for an abortion, at *any time* during the pregnancy, if the pregnant woman's physical or mental health is in grave danger. The key words in this section are 'necessary' and 'grave' – the circumstances must be extremely serious. The 'grave' criterion under section 1(1)(b) has been a legal ground for abortion since the Infant Life (Preservation) Act 1929. In a grave situation, the life of the mother will trump the life of the foetus. Grave permanent injury is not defined by the Abortion Act 1967. Pregnancy is a fragile and sometimes dangerous condition and it is foreseeable that a very small minority of women will experience life-threatening complications which require their pregnancies to be terminated. However, note how the statistical evidence shows that very few abortions are carried out under this section. If a pregnant woman's life is found to be in grave danger and the pregnancy is close to full term, a caesarean section to deliver a live baby is the preferred option. Life-threatening complications usually occur towards the end of the pregnancy, and the option of a caesarean may explain the low rates of abortion under paragraph (b).

What was not found in the Infant Life (Preservation) Act 1929 was the term 'mental health'. Before 1939, doctors were only allowed to terminate a pregnancy for the purposes of 'preserving the life of the mother' under the 1929 Act. This did not include considerations of mental health. *R v Bourne* [1939] 1 KB 687 (examined above) later extended the law to allow for an abortion to prevent the patient from becoming 'a physical or mental wreck'. Mental health considerations are now an intrinsic part of the laws on abortion. Despite these legal developments, it is unlikely that section 1(1)(b) will be enforced to prevent grave *mental* injury, it is more likely to be grave *physical* injury.

Ground 3: section 1(1)(c)

Section 1(1)(c) of the Abortion Act 1967 states the following:

Abortion Act 1967

Section 1: Medical termination of pregnancy

(1)(c): that the continuance of the pregnancy would involve risk to the life of the pregnant woman, greater than if the pregnancy were terminated.

Section 1(1)(c) allows for an abortion *at any time* during the pregnancy if the pregnant woman's life is put *at risk* because of her pregnancy. The 'grave and permanent' criteria is not present in paragraph (c) as it is in paragraph (b). Section 1(1)(c) is also interesting in that it does not separate the risk into physical or mental injuries – it is assumed that section 1(1)(c) only covers a physical risk to life. Therefore, section 1(1)(c) is distinguished from section 1(1)(b) on the grounds that a termination under paragraph (b) will save the pregnant woman's life, whereas a termination under paragraph (c) will only *decrease the risk* to a woman's life.

Ground 4: section 1(1)(d)

Section 1(1)(d) of the Abortion Act 1967 states the following:

Abortion Act 1967

Section 1: Medical termination of pregnancy

(1)(d): that there is a substantial risk that if the child were born it would suffer from physical or mental abnormalities as to be seriously handicapped.

Aside from 'social' abortions under section 1(1)(a), section 1(1)(d) is the most controversial ground for abortion under the 1967 Act. It allows for an abortion, at any time during the pregnancy, if there is a substantial risk of the child being born seriously handicapped. The statistics show that very few abortions are carried out under paragraph (d).

EXTRACT

Abortion Statistics: England and Wales 2012, published July 2013.
Department of Health:

https://www.gov.uk/government/organisations/department-of-health/series/abortion-statistics-for-england-and-wales

- 185,122 abortions in 2012;
- 2,692 of these under section 1(1)(d):
  - 607 abortions because of nervous system malformations;
  - 1012 abortions because of chromosomal malformations.

The key words under section 1(1)(d) are 'substantial risk' and 'seriously handicapped'. No medical evidence is required for paragraph (d) to be met – there must simply be a substantial risk of a serious handicap and this must be the opinion of two medical practitioners in good faith. Medical evidence will, however, show that the doctors have been able to form an opinion in good faith as opposed to simply 'guessing' the health of the baby. Campaigners against abortion argue that a termination on the grounds of physical or mental abnormalities is not justified: just because pregnant women expect a healthy, intelligent baby does not mean it is legally or morally right to terminate a baby that does not live up to these standards. Pro-choice groups argue in return that terminating pregnancies with foetal abnormalities is vital to ensure the mental health of the pregnant women and to save the potential child from an unhappy and sub-standard quality of life.

'Substantial risk'

The 'substantial risk' criteria is controversial. Even though neonatal technology is advancing rapidly, advanced diagnostic techniques are still not available to detect serious abnormalities with accuracy. Even if abnormalities are found during pregnancy it is sometimes only clear once the baby is born just how serious the abnormality is. This is particularly true of mental abnormalities, which may surface during pre-school years. As a result, doctors cannot calculate an 'actual risk' of handicap, it must only be a 'substantial risk'. This leaves room for error. Potentially, an abortion can take place under section 1(1)(d) when there is no real handicap at all if the two medical practitioners form the opinion, in good faith, that there is.

'Serious abnormalities'

A specific list of 'physical or mental abnormalities' does not exist under section 1 of the Abortion Act 1967. Doctors are left with the burden of deciding for themselves whether ground (d) is made out. Some pregnant women are happy to raise a child with a particular physical or mental handicap, whereas other women do not feel that they could emotionally or financially cope with the burden or responsibility. An Act of Parliament could not determine this issue for every individual woman. In the end, this decision is highly subjective, i.e. it is made on a personal basis during discussions between the doctor and patient. Some foetal abnormalities are deemed to be more serious than others, and inevitably some borderline cases have caused controversy.

A well-known case arose in 2003. An abortion under paragraph (d) took place on a baby with a cleft palate (where the two skull plates that form the roof of the mouth do not join properly). The baby was also over 24 weeks gestation.

CASE EXTRACT

Jepson v Chief Constable of West Mercia [2003] EWHC 3318

Facts: Reverend Joanna Jepson complained to West Mercia Police when she learned of an abortion under section 1(1)(d) of the Abortion Act 1967 being carried out on a foetus with a cleft palate that was over 24 weeks gestation. West Mercia Police referred the matter to the Crown Prosecution Service but no prosecution followed, so Joanna Jepson took legal action. Her main argument was that paragraph (d) under the 1967 Act was only ever intended for very serious abnormalities. She sought several declarations, two of them being (1) that 'seriously handicapped' was to be understood with reference to whether it could be treated), and (2) that a foetus over 24 weeks gestation has a right to life under Article 2.

Held: A judicial review was necessary.

Jackson J (at paras 15–17): For my part, having listened to the competing submissions of counsel, it does seem to me that the claimant in these proceedings faces substantial evidential hurdles and substantial legal hurdles. [...] Nevertheless, I am persuaded, having listened to the submissions of counsel, that this case does raise serious issues of law and issues of public importance which cannot be properly or fully argued in the context of a permission application. For all these reasons, in my view, permission to proceed with this claim for judicial review ought to be granted.

Jackson J anticipated that Reverend Joanna Jepson would face many obstacles in her legal battle, but he believed that her case raised serious issues of law and public importance. The CPS re-opened the case and conducted a more thorough investigation, but in 2005 they came to the conclusion that the law had not been broken.

EXTRACT

'CPS decides not no prosecute doctors following complaint by Rev. Joanna Jepson' 16 March 2005:

http://www.cps.gov.uk/news/latest_news/117_05/index.html

The Chief Crown Prosecutor for West Mercia CPS, Jim England, said: 'This complaint has been investigated most thoroughly by the police and the CPS has considered a great deal of evidence before reaching its decision. The issue is whether the two doctors who had authorised the termination were of the opinion, formed in good faith, that there was a substantial risk that if the child were born it would suffer from such physical and mental abnormalities as to be seriously handicapped. I consider that both doctors concluded that there was a substantial risk of abnormalities that would amount to the child being seriously handicapped. The evidence shows that these two doctors did form this opinion and formed it in good faith. In these circumstances I decided there was insufficient evidence for a realistic prospect of conviction and that there should be no charges against either of the doctors.'

In the end, only a very small number of abortions are carried out under paragraph (d), and a smaller amount of those are terminated after 24 weeks gestation. It is worth maintaining paragraph (d) as a separate ground for abortion for the small minority of women who discover a serious foetal abnormality but have missed the section 1(1)(a) time limit of 24 weeks.

Diseases and the future of section 1(1)(d)

Genetic testing is a rapidly advancing area of medicine. We are able to tell more accurately than ever if a foetus has inherited a serious generic disorder. This may have far-reaching implications for abortions under section 1(1)(d) of the 1967 Act. Many genetic disorders transpire later in life, so could it justify an abortion under paragraph (d)? Although blood tests will show an 'actual risk' of an abnormality as opposed to a 'substantial' risk, what if the foetus was destined to enjoy his or her first forty or fifty years of life without major health complications? Would we be saving individuals from an unpleasant demise later in life? Taking the argument one step further, could abortion for inherited genetic disorders be a form of 'genetic cleansing'? This might have a devastating effect on society.

Emergencies: section 1(4)

Section 1(4) of the Abortion Act 1967 states the following:

Abortion Act 1967

Section 1: Medical termination of pregnancy

(1)(4): So much of subsection (1) as relates to the opinion of two registered medical practitioners, shall not apply to the termination of a pregnancy by a registered medical practitioner in a case where he is of the opinion, formed in good faith, that the termination is immediately necessary to save the life or to prevent grave permanent injury to the physical or mental health of the pregnant woman.

If a life-threatening emergency arises, and there is no time to send the pregnant woman to an approved NHS Hospital – a requirement under section 1(3) – for a termination, then a medical practitioner can perform the abortion alone as long as certain criteria are met. The term 'mental health' is inserted into section 1(4) of the 1967 Act. This term could be interpreted rather widely, allowing for a medical practitioner to perform an emergency abortion for reasons that are not connected to the pregnant woman's physical health.

THINKING POINT

Why do you think abortions for foetal abnormalities are legally allowed under section 1(1)(d) of the 1967 Act? Should it be amended to include medical evidence of a serious handicap, thus making the 'substantial' risk, rather than an 'actual' risk? Give reasons for your answer.

Problems with section 1 of the 1967 Act

The Abortion Act 1967 sets out a relatively simple procedure: if two medical practitioners believe, in good faith, that one of the four statutory grounds are met, then an abortion can be carried out. However, loopholes can be found in the statute.

The 'good faith' ambiguity

The term 'good faith' is highly ambiguous. It may be Parliament's way of ensuring that the doctor carrying out the abortion is doing so with true and honest intentions, i.e. fairly and professionally, rather than maliciously. The terms 'opinion' and 'good faith' in section 1(1) are connected to each other: any opinion formed by doctors must be formed in good faith. There is no requirement for medical evidence under section 1(1) to allow the doctors to come to an accurate decision: the doctors must simply believe, or be of the opinion that, one of the grounds are met. This lack of medical evidence confirms that it falls to the doctor to decide whether the abortion should be carried out. The lack of medical evidence also begs the question: what exactly is 'good faith'? One case has emerged inside this loophole.

CASE EXTRACT

R v Smith [1973] 1 WLR 1510

Facts: A 19-year-old girl became pregnant with a man she did not want to marry. She was referred to Dr Smith. Dr Smith asked her why she wanted an abortion and she explained that she was not in love and that she was frightened of childbirth. Dr Smith asked for £150 and the girl handed the money over a week later and had her abortion. Dr Smith did not undertake an internal examination, did not ask about her medical history, and did not seek a second opinion.

Held: It does not matter that the decision is illogical, the decision *must* be taken in good faith. It was not in this case, and he was convicted (appeal against conviction dismissed).

Scarman LJ (at pages 15–12, 1515–16, 1518): The [1967] Act, though it renders lawful abortions that before its enactment would have been unlawful, does not depart from the basic principle of the common law as declared in *Rex v Bourne* [1939] 1 KB 687, namely, that the legality of an abortion depends upon the opinion of the doctor. It has introduced the safeguard of two opinions: but, if they are formed in good faith by the time the operation is undertaken, the abortion is lawful. Thus a great social responsibility is firmly placed by the law upon the shoulders of the medical profession. [...] An opinion may be absurd professionally and yet formed in good faith: conversely an opinion may be one which a doctor could have entertained and yet in the particular circumstances of a case may be found either to have been formed in bad faith or not to have been formed at all. [...] The sequence of events was such as to call for very careful consideration as to whether it was possible to believe that Dr Smith had formed in good faith, or at all, the opinion necessary to give him the protection of the Abortion Act. Had he, or had he not, abused the trust reposed in him by the Act of Parliament?

All this was faithfully explained to the jury by the recorder. We quote only one passage towards the end of the summing up:

You have to wonder in the case of Dr Smith whether such a view could genuinely be held by a medical man, whether it was held in the case of Miss Rodgers in particular. The only indication on the case notes about any danger to her mental or physical health was the word 'depressed', 'not willing to marry and depressed'. Those are the only words about it on the case notes. You have to ask yourselves, was there any balancing of the risks involved in allowing the pregnancy to continue and allowing the pregnancy to be terminated, or was this a mere routine abortion for cash? Was there any real contemplation or thought that a second opinion was necessary?

'Good faith' is clearly an intrinsic part of the decision-making process under section 1(1) of the Abortion Act 1967. Even if a decision is 'absurd professionally' according to Scarman LJ, all that matters is that it was formed in good faith. It also emerged from *Smith* that if the medical evidence is sparse on the ground, it is less likely that the opinion was formed in good faith and more likely that it was performed for money or other reasons (as stated in the passage by the Recorder in the first instance, Judge Sir Carl Aarvold). Dr Smith had very little medical evidence before him, making it unlikely that his opinion was formed in good faith. Dr Smith's appeal against his conviction was dismissed.

As a result of *Smith*, it is not entirely clear what role medical evidence plays under section 1(1) of the 1967 Act. However, it is clear that complete discretion – and the power to decide whether an abortion shall go ahead – is left with the doctor. Medical evidence can reinforce that a decision was made in good faith, but medical evidence is not, according to section 1(1), a compulsory requirement.

The 'two doctors' criteria

Two doctors must confirm whether one of the legal grounds in section 1(1) of the Abortion Act 1967 has been made out. This is a safeguard, inserted into the 1967 Act by Parliament back in the 1960s, to ensure that abortions were carried out according to the law and that unscrupulous individuals were not simply left on their own to interpret the statute in any way they liked. There could arise two problems from this requirement. Firstly, the second doctor probably does not know the patient, making his signature a 'rubber stamp exercise', which, clinically, serves no real point. Secondly, this rubber stamp exercise may cause considerable delay, forcing a woman to carry her pregnancy to full term if she has missed the 24-week deadline under section 1(1)(a).

The 'too much power' concern

Section 1(1) gives the power and discretion to doctors to decide whether an abortion should take place or not, allowing the medical profession to control the practice of abortion. The decisions in *R v Smith* [1973] 1 WLR 1510 and *Paton v British Pregnancy Advisory Service Trustees* [1979] QB 276 confirm this, and the criminal law is not to intervene unless a criminal offence is committed. The cumulative result is that the pregnant woman is left without a voice. Should the pregnant woman play more of a role in her decision to have an abortion? If so, what role would she take and what safeguards would be in place if her decision was not in her best interests? The answer is not clear, but it poses a fascinating ethical question.

The 'environment' requirement

Another notable controversy under section 1 of the 1967 Act is section 1(2), which makes reference to a pregnant woman's 'actual or reasonably foreseeable environment'. In practical terms, it means that when a doctor is determining whether a pregnant woman will suffer injury to her physical or mental health under paragraph (a) or grave injury under paragraph (b), be must consider her environment. The term 'environment' can be interpreted as widely, or as narrowly, as a doctor will allow, and it may include the woman's social, financial, emotional, personal, physical and psychological circumstances, or it may include none of these.

It is easy to understand why the 'environment' requirement was added to section 1(1) (a). This ground for abortion is known as the 'social ground' and it requires a woman to explain the ways in which she will become a physical or mental wreck if the pregnancy was to continue. This will include the effect on her environment by the baby (or, conversely, the effect of the environment *on* the baby).

It is less easy to understand why the 'environment' requirement was added to paragraph (b), which allows for legal abortions if there is a risk of grave permanent injury to the physical or mental health of the pregnant woman. Paragraph (b) contains the most urgent ground for an abortion, so it seems rather odd that a doctor would need to consider the environment of his patient before allowing the abortion if she is facing a grave and permanent injury to her health.

ACTIVITY

Lauren visited her doctor for an abortion. She explained that she was finishing university and could not afford to raise a child, and that she would suffer great mental anguish if she became a parent at this stage in her life. Her doctor looked at her current environment, and the fact that she was studying to become a pilot in the Royal Air Force, and decided that an abortion would be legal under paragraph (a).

Jenny also visited her doctor for an abortion. She was also finishing university and could not afford to raise a child. She also argued that she would suffer a great mental anguish if she became a parent before her career got off the ground. Jenny's doctor looked at her environment. Jenny was training to become a scientist. Jenny's doctor decided that Jenny could probably give a child a comfortable life in the foreseeable future. He did not allow the abortion as he did not believe that ground (a) was made out.

Question 1: is either doctor wrong in their decision?

Question 2: Do you think that section 1(2) of the 1967 Act could be amended to allow for greater consistency? If so, in what way?

Barriers to abortion

So far we have examined the criminal statutes that make abortion illegal in the UK, we have analysed the defences to abortion under the Abortion Act 1967, and we have criticised section 1 of the Abortion Act 1967 in terms of loopholes and impracticality. Now it is time to look at the other legal barriers to abortion. Abortion as an area of medicine is embroiled in moral, ethical, social and religious controversies. Although most of these issues are outside the ambit of medical law, the strong feelings surrounding the subject of abortion sometimes exert an influence on how the Abortion Act 1967 is applied in practice. A typical example of this would be an objection by a family member, a doctor or another person.

The doctor objects

Doctors do not have to participate in authorising an abortion if they do not want to. This is called a 'conscientious objection' because they are objecting on the grounds of their conscience, i.e. they believe that abortions are wrong. A conscientious objection can also be used by doctors who participate in early abortions but are not comfortable with very late abortions. Section 4 of the Abortion Act 1967 contains the relevant provision.

Abortion Act 1967

Section 4: Conscientious objection to participation in treatment

(1) Subject to subsection (2) of this section, no person shall be under any duty, whether by contract or by any statutory or other legal requirement, to participate in any treatment authorised by this Act to which he has a conscientious objection.

(2) Nothing in subsection (1) of this section shall affect any duty to participate in treatment which is necessary to save the life or to prevent grave permanent injury to the physical or mental health of a pregnant woman.

Under section 4 a doctor cannot object to an abortion if it is required under section 1(1)(b) of the 1967 Act, i.e. to prevent grave permanent injury to the pregnant woman. This means that a doctor only has a limited right to refuse to participate. The phrase 'participate in any treatment' can be interpreted quite widely. A doctor may not wish to sign the consent form, or he may not want to carry out the procedure itself. If a doctor does not wish to sign the relevant form he must refer the patient to another doctor. This must be done without delay.

Insightful guidelines have been published by the General Medical Council to guide doctors who have a conscientious objection to abortion. They emphasise the need to protect the pregnant woman's right to an abortion by helping her to find a doctor who *will* participate:

EXTRACT

General Medical Council, Good Medical Practice (2013):

www.gmc-uk.org

Paragraph 52: You must explain to patients if you have a conscientious objection to a particular procedure. You must tell them about their right to see another doctor and make sure they have enough information to exercise that right. In providing this information you must not imply or express disapproval of the patient's lifestyle, choices or beliefs. If it is not practical for a patient to arrange to see another doctor, you must make sure that arrangements are made for another suitably qualified colleague to take over your role.

It is clear from the professional guidance above that a conscientious objection by a doctor will play a very limited role in access to abortion services. The patient can simply go elsewhere. If the patient lives in an area where accessibility is difficult, e.g. in a rural area, then her doctor must aid her search. It follows from this that if a doctor objects to abortion because of religious or moral reasons, his view will be respected, i.e. he does not have to participate, but if a doctor objects because he believes that abortions are wrong generally, then his view will not be respected, as he is required to help the patient find another more willing doctor to carry out the procedure. In addition, section 4 of the 1967 Act requires a doctor to carry out an abortion under grave circumstances regardless of his beliefs, placing the life of the patient before the beliefs of the doctor.

The administration objects

Sometimes, other medical professionals may object to the abortion too. This may include nurses and administrative staff. Administrative staff are not directly involved in the abortion procedure. They are usually sorting the relevant paperwork and passing on the relevant forms and documents to the relevant people. Admittedly, abortion procedures could not happen without their administrative input. However, what if a member of administrative staff refuses to help with the administrative side of abortion because of a conscientious objection? Is section 4 open to administrative staff who are not directly involved in the abortion procedure? The answer is 'no'.

CASE EXTRACT

R v Salford HA, ex parte Janaway [1989] AC 537

Facts: Janaway was a receptionist at a medical centre. She was asked to type a letter of referral for a doctor. The letter was intended to refer a patient to a consultant for a possible termination. Janaway refused to type the letter, stating that she was exercising her right to a conscientious objection under section 4 of the Abortion Act 1967. She was dismissed from her post.

Held: The right to a conscientious objection is not open to administrative staff who simply write referral letters. This is not enough of a participation in the abortion procedure.

Lord Keith (at page 150): On a proper construction the word 'participate' in section 4(1) did not import the whole concept of principal and accessory residing in the criminal law, but in its ordinary and natural meaning referred to actually taking part in treatment administered in a hospital or other approved place in accordance with section 1(3), for the purpose of terminating a pregnancy. [...] The majority of the Court of Appeal accepted the main thrust of the applicant's argument, [...] but decided against her on the ground that her intention in typing a letter of referral would not be to assist in procuring an abortion but merely to carry out the obligations of her employment. In their view the typing of such a letter by the applicant would not be a criminal offence in the absence of section 1(1).

Lord Keith came to the conclusion that in order for a conscientious objection under section 4 of the 1967 Act to be honoured and protected, the person refusing must actually be 'participating' in the medical treatment. Typing a letter, for example, is not 'assisting' an abortion, it is simply an employment duty. This was confirmed by the fact that the act of typing the letter would not have attracted any criminal charges.

The 'medical practitioner' does not participate

Section 1(1) of the Abortion Act 1967 states that only a registered medical practitioner can carry out an abortion. If, for example, the pregnancy is in its early stages and a pill is prescribed to the pregnant woman to take orally, this must be prescribed by a medical practitioner. All surgical abortions must also be carried out by a medical practitioner. Nurses, therefore, can not carry out abortions under the 1967 Act. The *Royal College of Nursing* case determined that the medical practitioner requirement was vital to ensure that a professional person was present to oversee the whole procedure. However, as long as the medical practitioner was there, a nurse could participate too.

CASE EXTRACT

Royal College of Nursing of the United Kingdom v Department of Health and Social Security [1981] AC 800

Lord Diplock (at pages 828–9): In my opinion in the context of the Act, what it requires is that a registered medical practitioner, whom I will refer to as a doctor, should accept responsibility for all stages of the treatment for the termination of the pregnancy. The particular method to be used should be decided by the doctor in charge of the treatment for termination of the pregnancy, he should carry out any physical acts, forming part of the treatment, that in accordance with accepted medical practice are done only by qualified medical practitioners, and should give specific instructions as to the carrying out of such parts of the treatment as in accordance with accepted medical practice are carried out by nurses or other members of the hospital staff without medical qualifications. To each of them, the doctor, or his substitute, should be available to be consulted or called on for assistance from beginning to end of the treatment. In other words, the doctor need not do everything with his own hands; the requirements of the subsection are satisfied when the treatment for termination of a pregnancy is one prescribed by a registered medical practitioner carried out in accordance with his directions and of which a registered medical practitioner remains in charge throughout.

Lord Diplock agreed that a doctor does not have to perform the whole procedure on his own. As long as he is supervising, he is considered to be playing an active role in the abortion. The phrase 'terminated by a registered medical practitioner' under section 1 of the 1967 Act has thus been interpreted rather widely to mean that a registered medical practitioner can simply observe proceedings in order to legally carry out an abortion.

Approved hospitals

According to section 1(3) of the Abortion Act 1967, all abortion procedures (except emergency abortions) must be carried out in an approved place, typically in an NHS hospital.

Abortion Act 1967

Section 1: Medical termination of a pregnancy

(3) Except as provided by subsection (4) of this section, any treatment for the termination of pregnancy must be carried out in a hospital vested in the Secretary of State for the purposes of his functions under the National Health Service Act 2006 or the National Health Service (Scotland) Act 1978 or in a hospital vested in a Primary Care Trust or a National Health Service Trust or an NHS Foundation Trust or in a place approved for the purposes of this section by the Secretary of State.

This requirement could pose a considerable barrier to abortion. Many patients cannot gain easy access to an approved abortion hospital. There may be a number of reasons for this:

- The patient may be disabled or incapacitated.
- The patient may live in a rural area.
- The patient may not understand English.
- The patient may not have access to any form of transport.
- The patient may be scared and unsupported.

Parliament's intentions under provision 1(3) are clear – abortions must be carried out in a safe and professional environment. The backstreet abortions of the nineteenth century were dangerous and unregulated. By allowing for abortions to only be carried out in approved hospitals, this sends a firm message that unqualified practices – whether in public or in the home – are illegal. This is in the interests of patient safety.

ACTIVITY

Dr Adams tells his patient Lorena (aged 15) that he has a conscientious objection to her abortion because the foetus is perfectly healthy. Lorena then visits Dr McConnell, who states that he has a conscientious objection to the abortion because she is perfectly capable of bringing up a child. According to the GMC guidelines, do either of Lorena's doctors submit a valid conscientious objection? If you are unsure, how would you tighten-up the guidelines?

Patients who lack capacity

Earlier in Chapter 4, we looked at issues of capacity. In law, if a patient lacks capacity, that patient will be treated according to his or her best interests. It was also explained in Chapter 4 that children are not competent to consent, but if the parent refuses medical treatment they can be overruled by the courts to preserve the child's best interests. If a child is *Gillick* competent, she can consent to her own medical treatment. Abortion works in the same way:

- A competent pregnant woman: she can consent to the abortion.
- An incompetent pregnant woman: she is treated according to her best interests.
- A *Gillick* competent child: she can consent to the abortion but *Gillick* does not cover refusals so a parent can override a refusal).
- An incompetent child: parents can consent or the court can decide a parental refusal.

Pregnant women

As discussed in Chapter 4, the Mental Capacity Act 2005 is used to treat an incompetent adult in accordance with her best interests. The best interests test also includes considerations of values, beliefs and feelings.

Mental Capacity Act 2005

Section 4: Best interests

(6) [The decision-maker] must consider, so far as is reasonably ascertainable –

    (a) the person's past and present wishes and feelings (and, in particular, any relevant written statement made by him when he had capacity),

    (b) the beliefs and values that would be likely to influence his decision if he had capacity, and

    (c) the other factors that he would be likely to consider if he were able to do so.

The best interests criteria under section 4(6) of the MCA 2005 is particularly relevant to abortion. A doctor must consider an incompetent pregnant woman's wishes, feelings, beliefs and values when deciding whether an abortion would be in her best interests. This is a difficult question. In practical terms, if an incompetent pregnant woman has previously held strong views against abortion, it might not be in her best interests to perform the procedure on her. There is one case from 2002 in which it was held not to be in her best interests to perform an abortion.

CASE EXTRACT

SS (Medical Treatment: Late Termination), Re [2002] 1 FLR 445

Facts: S was a 34-year-old schizophrenic of Indian origin, detained in a psychiatric hospital under the Mental Health Act 1983. She was 24 weeks pregnant, the limit for a termination under the Abortion Act 1967 section 1(1)(a). She argued that she was incapacitated and that an abortion was in her best interests. In response, expert evidence showed that the procedure used for a late termination would be as stressful as a normal birth. Further, that the child would be of mixed race, giving rise to attendant adoption difficulties.

Held: It was not in the best interests of the patient to perform an abortion on her.

Wall J: The applicant has previously had a child removed from her care either at birth or shortly afterwards, and placed for adoption. I do not underestimate the stress of that process. However, there is no evidence that it caused a radical deterioration in her mental or physical health. It is for these reasons . . . that I came to the conclusion that, on a fine balance, the continuation of the pregnancy carried the lesser detriment to the applicant, and that, accordingly, a termination of pregnancy in these circumstances was not in her best interests.

The decision in *SS* is unusual in that it rejected medical treatment (i.e. the abortion) because it was not in the best interests of the patient. It is not clear why Wall LJ came to this decision: perhaps the method of abortion at 24 weeks would be too stressful for a schizophrenic patient?

Pregnant children

Pregnancy can occur in a child under 16. Out of the 185,122 abortions carried out in the UK in 2012, 841 were performed on patients under 15 years old.[6] Sexual abuse may also play a role in pregnancies in children under 16, making the procedure of abortion far more likely. Children who are aged 15 or under can consent to an abortion if they are *Gillick* competent. *Axon* (2006) confirmed that *Gillick* competency applies to the procedure of abortion.

CASE EXTRACT

R (on the application of Axon) v *Secretary of State for Health* [2006] QB 539

Silber J (at pages 565, 567): The young person who was pregnant might well be deterred from obtaining advice and so she would be unable to decide if she wanted an abortion or she might be forced to seek the assistance of an unqualified abortionist. [...]

In the light of this change in the landscape of family matters, in which rights of children are becoming increasingly important, it would be ironic and indeed not acceptable now to retreat from the approach adopted in *Gillick* and to impose additional new duties on medical professionals to disclose information to parents of their younger patients.

What about children who are not *Gillick* competent? Medical decisions are usually left up to the parents unless the child is made a ward of court and then the court will decide what is in the best interests of the child. The child may have very strong views about her medical treatment, e.g. she may not want an abortion. This is not a decisive factor but it is considered. The next case illustrates what happens to a child who is not deemed to be *Gillick* competent but requires an abortion and her parent(s) refuse the procedure:

CASE EXTRACT

Re B (Wardship: Abortion) [1991] 2 FLR 426

Facts: B was a 12-year-old girl who had fallen pregnant. Her boyfriend was 16. She lived with her grandparents who supported her decision to seek an abortion. B's mother did not provide consent to the procedure, as she disapproved of abortion. The local authority made B a ward of court and sought to have B's pregnancy terminated because the continuation of the pregnancy carried great risks to B's physical and mental wellbeing.

Held: The court will override the parent(s) if their decision is not in the child's best interests, and in this case it was in her best interests to have an abortion.

Hollis J: The court, in its wardship jurisdiction, has been called in in this case to make the decision on the principle that the interests of the ward are first and paramount. Thus, it seems to me that the ward's wishes are not decisive but are, in

---

[6] Statistical Bulletin: Abortion Statistics: England and Wales 2012, published July 2012. Department of Health: https://www.gov.uk/government/organisations/department-of-health/series/abortion-statistics-for-england-and-wales.

my view, a part of the evidence which it is important to take into consideration. If the mother's view is to prevail, it means that this girl will be forced to continue with her pregnancy against her own expressed wishes. One can easily imagine the mental turmoil she may thus suffer.

In the end, I came to the clear conclusion that it would be in the ward's best interests to have her pregnancy terminated and that, having balanced all the risks, a continuance of the pregnancy would involve risk to the ward greater than if the pregnancy were terminated, of injury to her physical and mental health.

Re B shows us that even if a child is not *Gillick* competent to consent to a medical procedure, her opinions will hold weight against a parent who does not act in accordance with her best interests.

THINKING POINT

Do you think a court should step in when a mother does not want her child to have an abortion? Do you think the outcome in *Re B* would have been different if the mother was living with B and was willing to help B raise her baby? Give reasons for your answer.

Fathers and foetuses: legal and moral rights

Even though it is only women who can fall pregnant, carry a child and give birth, other parties have, in the past, fought hard in this area of law to have their rights recognised. Fathers in particular feel that their participation in the creation of a foetus bestows upon them a legal right to prevent a woman from having an abortion. After all, a foetus is exactly 50% of each parent. We have learnt that under section 1(1) of the Abortion Act 1967, two medical practitioners must form the opinion, in good faith, that the pregnant woman meets one of the four statutory grounds for a legal abortion. Given the lack of autonomy that a pregnant woman has in this area of law, it is hardly surprising that fathers have faced big legal challenges. The European Convention on Human Rights has inevitably become involved in this complex area.

The rights of the father

When a pregnant woman decides that she would like to seek an abortion under grounds 1(1)(a) or (d) of the 1967 Act, it is understandable that some fathers become frustrated. Sometimes fathers are perfectly willing to raise a baby – whether handicapped or not – on their own. In the *Paton* case, a husband sought an injunction preventing his wife from having an abortion. The courts had to establish whether he or the foetus had any rights under the Abortion Act 1967. The answer is: neither.

> **CASE EXTRACT**
>
> ### *Paton v British Pregnancy Advisory Service Trustees* [1979] QB 276
>
> **Sir George Baker** (at pages 279, 281): The first question is whether this plaintiff has a right at all. The foetus cannot, in English law, in my view, have a right of its own at least until it is born and has a separate existence from its mother. [...]
>
> The two doctors have given a certificate. It is not and cannot be suggested that the certificate was given in other than good faith and it seems to me that there is the end of the matter in English law. The Abortion Act 1967 gives no right to a father to be consulted in respect of a termination of a pregnancy. True, it gives no right to the mother either, but obviously the mother is going to be right at the heart of the matter consulting with the doctors if they are to arrive at a decision in good faith, unless, of course, she is mentally incapacitated or physically incapacitated (unable to make any decision or give any help) as, for example, in consequence of an accident. The husband, therefore, in my view, has no legal right enforceable in law or in equity to stop his wife having this abortion or to stop the doctors from carrying out the abortion.

Mr Paton's consent was not required for the abortion to go ahead under the 1967 Act – only two medical practitioners are entitled to authorise the procedure and this had been done properly according to the facts. Therefore, Mr Paton took his argument to the European Court of Human Rights.

> **CASE EXTRACT**
>
> ### *Paton v United Kingdom* (8416/78) (1981) 3 EHRR 408
>
> **Facts**: Mr Paton argued that the unborn child had a right to life under Article 2, and that by failing to consult him about the abortion there was no respect for his family life under Article 8.
>
> **Held**: His case was dismissed.
>
> **Mr C.A. Norgaard** (at pages 416–17): As regards the principal complaint concerning the permission of the abortion, the Commission recalls that the pregnancy of the applicant's wife was terminated in accordance with her wish and in order to avert the risk of injury to her physical or mental health. [...] The Commission therefore finds that this decision, in so far as it interfered in itself with the applicant's right to respect for his family life, was justified under paragraph (2) of Article 8 as being necessary for the protection of the rights of another person. The Commission has next considered the applicant's ancillary complaint that the Abortion Act 1967 denies the father of the foetus a right to be consulted, and to make applications, about the proposed abortion. It observes that any interpretation of the husband's and potential father's right, under Article 8 of the Convention, to respect for his private and family life, as regards an abortion which his wife intends to have performed on her, must first of all take into account the right of the pregnant woman, being the person primarily concerned in the pregnancy and its continuation or termination, to respect for her private life. [...] In the present case the Commission, having regard to the right of the pregnant woman, does not find that the husband's and potential father's right to respect for his private and family life can be interpreted so widely as to embrace such procedural rights as claimed by the applicant, i.e. a right to be consulted, or a right to make applications, about an abortion which his wife intends to have performed on her.

The European Court concluded that Mr Paton's arguments were inadmissible on the following three grounds: firstly, Article 2 was subject to an implied limitation which justified the termination of a pregnancy if the pregnant woman's life or health was in danger; secondly, the exception under Article 8 was relevant, i.e. that an interference upon somebody's respect for family life was justified on the grounds that it was necessary to protect the rights of the pregnant woman; and thirdly, the pregnant woman is the main person concerned and her rights will override the rights of the father. What is surprising about this judgment is how direct the Court was about the pregnant woman's rights overriding the rights of the father. By stating: 'the Commission does not find that the father's right to respect for his private and family life can be interpreted so widely as to embrace such procedural rights as claimed by the applicant', the Court is concluding that the rights of the pregnant woman will 'trump' the rights of the father, and that the procedure of abortion has no direct influence on the father's private or family life, even though the baby belongs equally to both parents.

The rights of the foetus

The ethical debate surrounding abortion is outside of the ambit of this book. However, the moral status of the foetus deserves attention. In criminal law, the crime of murder can only be committed against a 'person' and this does not include a foetus. The following case made that very clear.

CASE EXTRACT

Attorney-General's Reference (No. 3 of 1994) [1998] AC 245

Facts: A man stabbed his pregnant girlfriend, injuring her and the foetus. The foetus was born but then died a few weeks later.

Held: The defendant was charged with murder, but he could not be prosecuted for killing a foetus because it was not a person in law. However, once the baby was born and then subsequently died of its injuries, an unlawful act manslaughter had been committed instead.

Lord Mustill (at pages 255–6): The foetus does not (for the purposes of the law of homicide and violent crime) have any relevant type of personality but is an organism *sui generis* lacking at this stage the entire range of characteristics both of the mother to which it is physically linked and of the complete human being which it will later become. [...] I would, therefore, reject the reasoning which assumes that since (in the eyes of English law) the foetus does not have the attributes which make it a 'person' it must be an adjunct of the mother. Eschewing all religious and political debate I would say that the foetus is neither. It is a unique organism.

As a result of *Attorney-General's Reference*, a foetus is accepted as having no legal rights to speak of in English law. However, many argue that a foetus has moral rights.

A foetus is a moral entity

One theory argues that a person is created at the moment of conception. This is because the chromosomes from the egg and the sperm fuse together to create new chromosomes which develop into a new person.[7] However, if a foetus *was* to be classed as a person

---

[7] This theory has been put forward by John Finnis, 'The Rights and Wrongs of Abortion: A reply to Judith Thomson' (1973) 2 *Philosophy and Public Affairs* 117–45.

under this theory, it still cannot override the rights of the pregnant woman, i.e. if her life is at risk, an abortion is usually justified and the foetus is sacrificed to save her life.

A foetus is not a person

An opposing theory may argue that a foetus only becomes a person when it develops human qualities. These may include the following things:

- Communicative abilities.
- Self-awareness and the recognition of concepts and beliefs.
- The ability to take part in activities.
- The presence of consciousness.
- The recognition of pain.
- The ability to reason, think, analyse, solve and evaluate.

It is believed by some that these criteria, and there may be more constitute a complete person in morality and in law.[8] However, there is a loophole in these criteria, because they exclude persons with limited capacity for communication, understanding, consciousness and mobility. This could be offensive. The middle road is taken by many members of the public when it comes to the issue of abortion and the rights of the foetus. This is illustrated in the table below.

Left theory	Middle theory	Right theory
'The foetus becomes a person from the moment of conception and has moral integrity as a being.'	'The foetus becomes a baby sometime throughout the pregnancy.'	'The foetus is a collection of indistinct cells until it is born and only then does it become a person in law.'

The rights of the mother

Although it was made clear earlier that the Abortion Act 1967 does not confer any legal right upon a woman to demand an abortion, should a pregnant woman be forced to carry a baby to full term if she does not want to? To ask an even more blunt question, can a woman be 'burdened' by a pregnancy? This theory is all about a woman being 'occupied' by a baby and her right not to be occupied.[9] In a more wider context, does society assume that all women want to become mothers? If so, how does this alter our view of women who choose not to have children? A woman has a right not to be burdened or occupied by a baby without her consent, but a woman, when having unprotected sex and knowing that unprotected sex leads to pregnancy, was probably consenting to the risk of becoming pregnant and the adjoining burdens of her actions.

The Abortion Act 1967 meets somewhere in the middle on this issue. Seriously handicapped foetuses, for example, are legally aborted under section 1(1)(d) partly because of the burden that they place on their parents and the health system. Social abortions under section 1(1)(a), however, are not allowed beyond 24 weeks. It appears that an

---

[8] One such theory was presented by Mary Ann Warren, 'On the Moral and Legal Status of Abortion' (1973) 1 *The Monist* 43–61.

[9] A theory first put forward by Margaret Olivia Little in 'Abortion, Intimacy, and the Duty to Gestate' (1999) 2 *Ethical Theory and Moral Practice* 295–312.

emotional burden will not justify an abortion in the later stages of pregnancy, but a physical burden will justify an abortion in the later stages of pregnancy.

Human rights and the foetus

The European Court of Human Rights has not seen very many abortion cases. The *Paton* case (1980) considered human rights in relation to a foetus (Article 2) and a father's right to prevent an abortion (Article 8). No other human rights Articles have been pursued in the interests of the foetus. This is probably because the fact that a foetus is not a person in law is a settled issue in most member states. A widely recognised abortion case emerged from France in 2005. In the *Vo v France* case, Article 2 was argued to confer a right to life onto a foetus. The European Court took this opportunity to clarify the European consensus regarding the protection of the foetus.

CASE EXTRACT

Vo v France (53924/00) (2005) 40 EHRR 12

Facts: The claimant made a criminal complaint that her doctor had negligently aborted her baby when removing her contraceptive device. The criminal complaint was not pursued by the French authorities because in French law a foetus is not a person. She appealed to the European Court on the ground of Article 2, that her foetus had a right to life.

Held: The legal status of the foetus is unclear. Its legal rights are currently limited.

Wildhaber J (at pages 290, 293–5): Article 2 of the [European] Convention is silent as to the temporal limitations of the right to life and, in particular, does not define 'everyone' whose 'life' is protected by the Convention. The Court has yet to determine the issue of the 'beginning' of 'everyone's right to life' within the meaning of this provision and whether the unborn child has such a right. [...] It follows [...] that in the circumstances examined to date by the Convention institutions – that is, in the various laws on abortion – the unborn child is not regarded as a 'person' directly protected by Article 2 of the Convention and that if the unborn do have a 'right' to 'life', it is implicitly limited by the mother's rights and interests. [...] At European level, the Court observes that there is no consensus on the nature and status of the embryo and/or foetus, although they are beginning to receive some protection in the light of scientific progress and the potential consequences of research into genetic engineering, medically assisted procreation or embryo experimentation. At best, it may be regarded as common ground between states that the embryo/foetus belongs to the human race. The potentiality of that being and its capacity to become a person – enjoying protection under the civil law, moreover, in many states, such as France, in the context of inheritance and gifts, and also in the United Kingdom – require protection in the name of human dignity, without making it a 'person' with the 'right to life' for the purposes of Article 2.

Wildhaber J states that the European Court can find 'no consensus' on the nature and status of the embryo or foetus. However, he does acknowledge that they are beginning to receive some recognition as reproductive technology develops. Articles 9 and 10 have also been invoked in a more recent abortion case involving a person with strong religious views who was opposed to abortion.

CASE EXTRACT

Connolly v DPP [2007] 2 Cr App R 5

Facts: Connolly was a practising Christian and believed that abortion was murder. She sent pictures of dead foetuses to three pharmacies that sold the morning-after pill. She was convicted under the Malicious Communications Act 1988 for sending 'indecent or grossly offensive' articles with a purpose to 'cause distress or anxiety'. Connolly argued that the pictures were not offensive and were meant to be educational, but the Crown Court rejected her appeal. She appealed to the High Court and invoked Article 9 and Article 10, arguing that she had a freedom of religion and a freedom of expression.

Held: The freedom of expression was not absolute – there were limits to that right which must be respected.

Dyson J (at pages 48, 53): [The DPP] accepts that Article 10 is engaged. He is right to do so. The sending of the photographs was an exercise of the right to freedom of expression. It was not the mere sending of an offensive article: the article contained a message, namely that abortion involves the destruction of life and should be prohibited. Since it related to political issues, it was an expression of the kind that is regarded as particularly entitled to protection by Article 10. [The DPP] submits, however, that the interference with Mrs Connolly's freedom of expression is justified as being 'for the protection of health' and/or 'for the protection of the rights of others' within the meaning of Article 10(2). [...]

In my judgment, the persons who worked in the three pharmacies which were targeted by Mrs Connolly had the right not to have sent to them material of the kind that she sent when it was her purpose, or one of her purposes, to cause distress or anxiety to the recipient. Just as members of the public have the right to be protected from such material (sent for such a purpose) in the privacy of their homes, so too, in general terms, do people in the workplace. But it must depend on the circumstances. The more offensive the material, the greater the likelihood that such persons have the right to be protected from receiving it. [...] It seems to me that such a doctor would be less likely to find the photographs grossly offensive than the pharmacist's employees. [...] In my view, the fact that they are employed by pharmacists that sell the 'morning after pill' is not of itself sufficient to deny to them the right to be protected from receiving grossly offensive photographs of abortions at their place of work, where the photographs are sent for the purpose of causing distress of anxiety. I would hold that the right not to receive such material when sent for such a purpose is a 'right of others' within the meaning of Article 10(2) of the Convention.

Mrs Connolly was found to be entitled to her freedom of religion and her freedom of expression under Articles 9 and 10, but her freedom of expression under Article 10 was curtailed because of public safety reasons. Article 10 provides:

(1) Everyone has the right to freedom of expression. This right shall include freedom to hold opinions and to receive and impart information and ideas without interference by public authority and regardless of frontiers. This Article shall not prevent States from requiring the licensing of broadcasting, television or cinema enterprises.

(2) The exercise of these freedoms, since it carries with it duties and responsibilities, may be subject to such formalities, conditions, restrictions or penalties as are prescribed by law and are necessary in a democratic society, in the interests of national security, territorial integrity or public safety, for the prevention of disorder

or crime, for the protection of health or morals, for the protection of the reputation or rights of others, for preventing the disclosure of information received in confidence, or for maintaining the authority and impartiality of the judiciary.

Notice that there are many exceptions under Article 10(2) to a person's freedom of expression. Mrs Connolly impinged upon the 'rights of others' when she sent the offensive material to three pharmacies, and for this reason, the limitation under Article 10(2) was applied to her freedom of expression. You could also argue that she was offending public morals.

RESEARCH ACTIVITY

Do you think the following expressions are subject to a limitation under Article 10(2)?

1. A priest puts a large poster of an aborted foetus up in the middle of a marketplace.
2. A doctor publishes a leaflet about how to access morning-after pills.
3. A student loudly protests from the roof of Parliament about how the abortion time limit should be lowered.
4. An anti-abortion pressure group would like to air an advertisement about how an abortion harms a foetus on prime time TV.
5. A doctor preaches his religious beliefs and tells his patients that foetuses feel pain when patients seek advice on abortion.

Abortion tourism

Abortion laws differ greatly all over the world as a result of political and religious issues. Even within the European Union, some countries are surprisingly liberal when it comes to abortion, whereas other countries are very restrictive. Abortions on social grounds are particularly difficult to measure from country to country. For pregnant women living in the restrictive countries, this means travelling abroad to terminate their pregnancies, if they can afford it. In the UK, the Abortion Act 1967 applies to Scotland, England and Wales. Northern Ireland and Ireland are excluded from the 1967 Act.

Northern Ireland

The Offences Against the Person Act 1861 applies in Northern Ireland, meaning that abortion is illegal under sections 58 and 59. There are no statutory defences available in Northern Ireland, making the legal situation unclear. However, *R v Bourne* [1939] 1 KB 687 (above) is commonly understood to offer a medical practitioner a defence against a criminal charge if the pregnant woman is predicted to become a 'mental wreck'. To put it another way, the best interests of the pregnant woman will prevail.

Legal ground for abortion in Northern Ireland	Availability
To save the pregnant woman's life.	*Available under Bourne.*
To preserve the mental or physical health of the mother.	*Available under Bourne.*
The foetus is handicapped.	Not available.
There would be a detrimental effect on existing children.	Not available.
Any other social, financial or moral reason.	Not available.

The only widely-accepted ground for abortion in Northern Ireland is that of saving the pregnant woman from grave and serious risk to her health under *Bourne*. As a result, abortion is very difficult to attain in Northern Ireland.

Ireland

Ireland poses a unique set of circumstances. The Offences Against the Person Act 1861 applies in Ireland, making abortion illegal under sections 58 and 59. However, Ireland also has its own Constitution, which states that the pregnant woman and her foetus have an equal right to life. An Irish case in 1992 shed some light on what exactly was accepted in Ireland as a lawful defence to abortion. There are not many legal grounds available.

CASE EXTRACT

Attorney General v *X* [1992] 2 CMLR 277

Facts: X was a 14-year-old girl who was raped by her friend's father and became pregnant. She and her mother travelled to England to have an abortion. The Irish Attorney General found out and issued an injunction, stopping them from seeking the procedure. X returned to fight the injunction. The Irish High Court first held that under Article 40.3.3 of the Irish Constitution, the restriction of abortion services included a restriction on travelling abroad to seek an abortion. X appealed to the Irish Supreme Court.

Held: There must be a real and substantial risk to the life of the mother.

Finlay CJ (at page 30): I conclude that the proper test to be applied is that if it is established as a matter of probability that there is a real and substantial risk to the life as distinct from the health of the mother, which can only be avoided by the termination of her pregnancy, that such termination is permissible, having regard to the true interpretation of Article 40.3.3 of the Constitution.

McCarthy J (at page 323): It is not a question of setting one above the other but rather of vindicating, as far as practicable, the right to life of the mother (Article 40.3.2), whilst [...] vindicating, as far as practicable, the right to life of the unborn (Article 40.3.3). If the right to life of the mother is threatened by the pregnancy, and it is practicable to vindicate that right, then because of the due regard which must be paid to the equal right to life of the mother, it may not be practicable to vindicate the right to life of the unborn.

O'Flaherty J (at page 330): I believe that the law in this State is that surgical intervention which has the effect of terminating pregnancy *bona fide* undertaken to save the life of the mother where she is in danger of death is permissible under the Constitution and the law. The danger has to represent a substantial risk to her life though this does not necessarily have to be an imminent danger of instant death. The law does not require the doctors to wait until the mother is in peril of immediate death.

Egan J (at page 334): In my opinion the true test should be that a pregnancy may be terminated if its continuance as a matter of probability involves a real and substantial risk to the life of the mother. The risk must be to her life but it is irrelevant, in my view, that it should be a risk of self-destruction rather than a risk to life for any other reason. The evidence establishes that such a risk exists in the present case.

The *X* case shows how difficult it is to balance a pregnant woman's rights against the rights of a foetus. When exactly is it appropriate – legally and morally – for one right to prevail over the other? Because a foetus can enjoy legal rights in Irish law, the mothers' life can be sacrificed for the foetus just the same as the foetus can be sacrificed for the mother. This is controversial because it cannot be predicted how long a foetus will survive. It may not even see the end of the pregnancy and may never become a breathing person in society.

RESEARCH ACTIVITY

Access the full judgment of *Attorney General* v *X* [1992] 2 CMLR 277 and write your own definitions of what Finlay J, McCarthy J, O'Flaherty J and Egan J decided. What implications do their decisions have on pregnant women in Ireland?

Chapter summary

- The morning-after pill has been confirmed through case law as a contraceptive rather than an abortifacient: *R (on the application of Smeaton)* v *Secretary of State for Health* [2002] EWHC 610.

- A doctor could, according to the common law developments, also perform an abortion if the patient was predicted to become a 'physical or mental wreck' according to *R* v *Bourne* [1939] 1 KB 687.

- The Abortion Act 1967 was passed to prevent any more women dying or becoming infected from dangerous backstreet abortions. The contraceptive pill was also launched in the 1960s, leading to a more liberal attitude to sex and pregnancy.

- The 1967 Act does not provide a woman with a 'right' to have an abortion – it is still a criminal offence under the 1861 Act. It provides doctors with four defences to a criminal charge under the 1861 Act.

Chapter essay

'Critically analyse the law of abortion in the United Kingdom.'

Chapter case study

Alice is suffering from ME (a chronic fatigue syndrome). She frequently experiences cognitive, psychological and physical problems such as disorientation, depression, seizures, paralysis, blackouts, abdominal pains and frequent flu-like symptoms. Alice falls pregnant after moving in with her partner Karl, who also has ME. She visits her doctor and her doctor informs her that the symptoms will get much worse as the pregnancy continues. Alice asks about an abortion. Which ground for abortion – (a), (b) or (c) – is most appropriate for Alice and why?

Further reading

Jackson, E. (2000) 'Abortion, Autonomy and Prenatal Diagnosis', 9 *Social and Legal Studies* 467–94; (2008) 'Degendering Reproduction', 16 *Medical Law Review* 346–68.

Keown, J. (2005) '"Morning After" Pills, "Miscarriage" and Muddle', 25 *Legal Studies* 296–319.

Kirklin, D. (2004) 'The Role of Medical Imaging in the Abortion Debate', 30 *Journal of Medical Ethics* 426.

Sheldon, S. and Wilkinson, S. (2001) 'Termination of Pregnancy for Reason of Foetal Disability: Are There grounds for a Special Exception in Law?', 9(2) *Medical Law Review* 85–109.

Wyatt, J. (2001) 'Medical Paternalism and the Foetus', 27 *Journal of Medical Ethics* 15.

7

Mental Health Law

Chapter objectives

At the end of this chapter, you should have:

- An understanding of the 'autonomy anomaly' in mental health law in regards to the forceful treatment of patients without their consent.

- An appreciation of the history of mental health law all the way up until the pioneering Mental Capacity Act 2005 which incorporated the 'best interests' test into UK law.

- Knowledge of what 'sectioning' means for the patient and where the powers to section a patient for assessment and treatment are stored.

- An understanding of how human rights can aid patients with mental health problems.

SETTING THE SCENE

Frank is a single man in his 50s. He works for a mechanical engineering company and has been sent home because his frequent dizzy spells are causing concern among his colleagues and employers. He is sent to see the company doctor the next day. Frank cannot concentrate on simple questions and loses his balance several times. He also becomes uncharacteristically aggressive towards the doctor when his ability to work is called into question. The company doctor detains him under section 2 of the Mental Health Act 1983 for a further mental assessment. A brain scan reveals some abnormalities and a psychiatrist uncovers severe behavioural problems and possible depression. Frank refuses to be treated for any of his conditions, claiming that: 'if it is my time, then it is my time'. Frank is therefore forcibly treated for his mental disorders under section 3 of the Mental Health Act 1983. There is no real evidence of his mental disorders getting any better, and Frank is worried that he will be in hospital forever. As his lawyer, how can you advise him as to his legal rights once in the mental health system?

Introduction

Mental health law is a highly complex area of medical law. It is regulated by the Mental Health Act 1983 for the most part (as amended in 2007), but the statute is intricate and controversial. The process of reforming the 1983 Act took over ten years. The main controversy in this area of law centres around the principle of patient autonomy. Under the Mental Health Act 1983, a *competent* patient who refuses treatment can be detained and treated *against her wishes* for a mental disorder. As seen earlier in Chapter 4, a competent patient can refuse medical treatment and this decision is acknowledged and respected by the medical profession. So why, then, do competent patients with a mental disorder not have access to this right?

The treatment of mentally ill patients stems back to the days of asylums and workhouses. In those days, there was a very different perception of people with mental disorders. They were treated without their consent because it was 'for their own good' or because they were 'a danger to society' and the principle of treating mentally ill people without their consent has been carried down through the centuries. The majority of patients who have a mental disorder are perfectly competent and do consent to treatment without any complications. An incompetent patient will be treated according to their best interests under the Mental Capacity Act 2005. However, there are a very small handful of competent patients who refuse treatment and whose disorder may be dangerous to their safety or the safety of others, and this is where the Mental Health Act 1983 applies. These patients will be detained and treated against their will for as long as they are suffering from their mental disorder. There are three important points to remember:

Mental condition	Response to treatment	Action in law
Competent with disorder	Consent	Treated as normal
Competent with disorder	Refuse	Treated with force: 1983 Act
Incompetent with disorder	No response	Best interests test: 2005 Act

Human rights have also become tangled up in mental health law because the detention and treatment of patients without their consent could potentially constitute several breaches of the European Convention on Human Rights. There are safeguards in place to protect patients who are forcibly deprived of their liberty for the purposes of receiving medical treatment, but these are not without their critics. To add further confusion to this area of law, some commentators doubt that there is such a thing as a mental illness, e.g. mental health laws are just another way of controlling strange behaviour. This suggestion, of course, would mean that patients with severe mental disorders would be free to walk amongst us in the street, but only a very, very small percentage of patients with a mental disorder are considered to be a danger to others.

THINKING POINT

What do you think about the forced detention and treatment of competent patients for the purpose of treating mental disorders? Do you agree that mental health law should be an exception to the rule on autonomy? If not, why not?

The 'autonomy anomaly' in mental health law

As noted briefly above, the chief controversy in mental health law is that a competent patient who refuses medical treatment can be detained and treated against his or her will simply because he or she is diagnosed with a mental disorder. The legal definition of a 'mental disorder' will be analysed further below. First, it will be helpful to learn where this controversy comes from, why mentally ill patients are treated differently to other patients and which other laws and regulations underpin this controversial area of medicine.

The dark history of mental health law

In the middle of the eighteenth century, people who appeared to be mentally ill were assumed to be cared for by family members or locked up in a madhouse – a private house whose owner was paid to detain mentally ill people (known legally as lunatics). No doctors or medical professionals were involved in the detention of these people, and the living conditions inside the madhouses were terrible. Insane people were also prosecuted and simply sent to jail (labelled criminally insane).

The Madhouses Act 1774 (later updated by the Madhouses Act 1832) required all madhouses to be licensed by a Committee of The Royal College of Physicians. The licence would allow the house owner to accommodate lunatics in one private dwelling which would be inspected by the Committee once a year. The Committee also kept a register of all detainees and the owner was fined £100 for accepting a lunatic without a certificate from a doctor, placing the first emphasis on medical diagnosis. Formal asylums were created for the criminally insane and other mentally ill people by the County Asylums Act 1808. However, by 1827 only nine asylums had opened across the country, leaving most mentally ill people in jail, in workhouses or madhouses. As a result, two co-dependant Acts were passed: the Lunacy Act 1845 and the County Asylums Act 1845. These Acts in conjunction with each other established the Lunacy Commission, a public body to oversee the operation of asylums and the treatment and welfare of mentally ill people. The Commission had considerable powers: it monitored the treatment, condition and discharge of patients in asylums and moved mentally ill people from workhouses and prisons into asylums for appropriate treatment. Those who couldn't be moved were monitored by the Commission. Asylums also had to be formally registered with the Commission, had to present written regulations, and had to employ a resident physician. Even though patients were still denied access to the legal system, the 1845 Acts adopted the term 'patient' for the first time, and gave asylums the authority to detain 'lunatics, idiots and persons of unsound mind', thus categorising mentally ill patients into separate groups. In 1890 a new Lunacy Act came into force, introducing Reception Orders. These orders authorised the detention of mentally ill people in asylums for a period of one year. The order was made by a specialist Justice of the Peace (a magistrate in today's terms). The orders could thereafter be renewed at intervals until the patient was cured by filing a medical report to the Lunacy Commission.

The Mental Deficiency Act 1913 renamed the Lunacy Commission as the Board of Control and increased its powers, and introduced the terms 'feeble-minded people' and 'moral defectives' into the law. A few years later, the Mental Treatment Act 1930 radically changed how people viewed mentally ill people and psychiatrists. The 1930 Act permitted voluntary admission to, and outpatient treatment within, proper mental hospitals, which were renamed from 'asylums' by this Act. There was a notable shift towards 'medicalism' rather than 'legalism', where proper treatments were beginning to emerge and psychiatrists were viewed as doctors rather than jailers.

Following the Second World War and the change of opinion of mental disorders as a result of war injuries, the first Mental Health Act was passed in 1959. This Act placed an emphasis on the short-term detention of patients and voluntary admission, and the Board of Control was abolished. The Act aimed to provide informal treatment for the majority of patients suffering from mental disorders and made local councils responsible for the care of mentally ill people in the community. A legal framework was also provided to ensure that if necessary, people could be detained against their will. By this time, psychiatric medications, electroconvulsive therapy and psychosurgery were common treatments for mental disorders, and a proper legal framework was still needed to regulate exactly when a hospital could impose treatment upon a patient. The Mental Health Act 1959 was thereby replaced by the Mental Health Act 1983, which aimed to provide more protection and rights for mentally ill patients. The Mental Health Act 2007 was passed after more than ten years of consultation. It was meant to herald a new approach to the care of mentally ill patients, but instead it simply updated the 1983 Act. The Mental Health Act 1983 is rather draconian in nature, even after the 2007 amendments. For example, it will detain and treat a competent mentally ill patient according to what her health or safety requires or for the protection of others. This is a controversial provision because competent patients can usually refuse medical treatment regardless of what their health or safety requires, and even incompetent patients have access to a best interests test under the Mental Capacity Act 2005 to consider the wishes, feelings, values and beliefs of the patient before commencing any medical treatment. Additionally, the Mental Health Act 1983 makes no mention of competency or autonomy when detaining or treating competent mentally ill patients. This has created considerable concern because competent patients could be stripped of their autonomous rights and treated like incapacitated individuals, leading to stigmatisation and discrimination. The Mental Health Act 1983 does come with a Code of Practice and contains a set of principles, but these principles are not incorporated into the statute itself. This gives the principles therein slightly less influence.

EXTRACT

Department of Health, Mental Health Act 1983, Code of Practice, (2008) (archived):

http://webarchive.nationalarchives.gov.uk/20130107105354/
http://www.dh.gov.uk/en/Publicationsandstatistics/Publications/
PublicationsPolicyAndGuidance/DH_084597

Purpose principle at paragraph 1.2: Decisions under the Act must be taken with a view to minimising the undesirable effects of mental disorder by maximising the safety and wellbeing (mental and physical) of patients, promoting their recovery and protecting other people from harm.

Least restriction principle at paragraph 1.3: People taking action without a patient's consent must attempt to keep to a minimum the restrictions they impose on the patient's liberty, having regard to the purpose for which the restrictions are imposed.

Respect principle at paragraph 1.4: People taking decisions under the Act must recognise and respect the diverse needs, values and circumstances of each patient, including their race, religion, culture, gender, age, sexual orientation and any disability. They must consider the patient's views, wishes and feelings (whether expressed at the time or in advance), so far as they are reasonably ascertainable, and follow those wishes wherever practicable and consistent with the purpose of the decision. There must be no unlawful discrimination.

Participation principle at paragraph 1.5: Patients must be given the opportunity to be involved, as far as is practicable in the circumstances, in planning, developing and reviewing their own treatment and care to help ensure that it is delivered in a way that is as appropriate and effective for them as possible. The involvement of carers, family members and other people who have an interest in the patient's welfare should be engaged and their views taken seriously.

The following phrases from the principles (above) are in line with the best interests of a patient:

- Minimising the undesirable effects of the mental disorder.
- Maximising the safety and wellbeing of the patient.
- Promoting the patient's recovery.
- Restrictions on liberty must be kept to a minimum.
- Restrictions must serve a relevant purpose.
- Diverse needs, values and circumstances must be recognised and respected.
- Race, religion, culture, gender, age, sexual orientation and any disability must be recognised and respected.
- Views, wishes and feelings must be considered and followed when reasonably practicable.
- No unlawful discrimination is allowed.
- The opportunity for the patient to be involved must be offered.
- Patients can plan, develop and review their treatment programme.
- Carers and family members can express their views and these must be taken seriously.

These principles look promising, but they are not included within the 1983 Act itself. To come out of the draconian era, the 1983 Act would need to implement these principles into the statute itself, which would afford far more protection to detained patients. The last chapter in the history of mental health law was the Mental Capacity Act 2005, which includes a best interests test for patients who lack capacity to make their own decisions.

Public fear

Another interesting element to mental health law is the public perception of mentally ill people. Press coverage of mentally ill people who commit violent crimes is often excessive and frightening, and this does nothing to help change the perception of mentally ill people from the last century. The current statistics appear to demonstrate that mental disorders are surprisingly common, and that far from fearing people with mental disorders, we may actually be faced with one ourselves throughout our lifetime. A mental disorder can include neurotic disorders such as mixed anxiety and depressive disorders, panic disorders, obsessive compulsive disorders, eating disorders and phobias. These can be added to other 'minor' mental disorders such as sleep problems, fatigue, irritability, worry and forgetfulness:

- The NHS has found that one in four adults have a psychiatric disorder of some kind. Additionally, in people over 75 years of age, 12% of women had a common mental disorder compared to 6% of men.[1]

- According to MIND, postnatal depression is now so common it is named 'baby blues' and it is estimated that it effects up to 85% of women, 1 in 4 people will have a mental illness each year, 1.5 million people may have an eating disorder, and up to 13% of adults could have a personality disorder.[2]

Statistics from mental health charities also show us that the perception of danger is misguided:

- People with mental health problems are more dangerous to themselves than they are to others: 90% of people who commit suicide in the UK are experiencing mental distress, people with serious mental illness are more likely to be the *victim* of a violent crime than the perpetrator and one study found that more than one in four people with a severe mental illness had been a victim of crime in one year.[3]

- Out of the 13,315 homicides committed between January 2000 and December 2010, a total of 1,210 (27%) were identified as patient homicide, i.e. the person had been in contact with mental health services in the twelve months before committing the homicide.[4]

Commentators seem to agree that the public perception of danger is wrong.

---

[1] Adult Psychiatric Morbidity in England 2007: results of a household survey. Published January 2012. See http://www.hscic.gov.uk/article/1813/Publications-Calendar-April-2008---March-2009.

[2] Mind: For Better Mental Health (charity). See: http://www.mind.org.uk/mental_health_a-z/8105_mental_health_facts_and_statistics.

[3] See note above.

[4] National Confidential Inquiry into Suicide and Homicide by People with Mental Illness. The University of Manchester. Annual Report: England and Wales. 2012, page 20. See: http://www.bbmh.manchester.ac.uk/cmhr/research/centreforsuicideprevention/nci.

EXTRACT

Nancy Wolff, 'Risk, Response and Mental Health Policy: Learning from the Experience of the United Kingdom' (2002) 27 *Journal of Health Politics, Policy and Law* 801, at pages 801–32

The high risk group is comparatively small. [...] Evidence on homicides in England and Wales suggests that 0.05 per cent of persons with severe mental illness pose the greatest risk of homicidal violence. [...] Behaviours that deviate from social norms, such as dishevelled and unkempt appearance, talking to oneself, sleeping on public sidewalks, may be interpreted by the public as evidence of menace potential. Guided by fear, the public may misinterpret and overreact to the behaviour or appearance of persons with mental illness, if such indicators of social nuisance confirm stereotypical beliefs.

According to Wolff, it may be possible that the public fear of mentally ill people is supporting the forced detention and treatment of these individuals. The Royal College of Psychiatrists has commented on the public perception of mentally ill people and published a report regarding the forced detention and treatment of patients, hinting that forced detention and treatment might actually exacerbate the problem:

EXTRACT

Royal College of Psychiatrists, College submission to the Joint Committee on the Draft Mental Health Bill, *Evidence Submitted to the Joint Committee on the Draft Mental Health Bill*, RCP: London, 2004 (no longer available) at pages 33–34

The percentage of homicides committed each year by the mentally ill, as a percentage of the total, is falling. The following figures are not intended to minimise the importance of each death but may help to put the matter into perspective. For each citizen killed by a mentally ill person:

- 10 are killed by corporate manslaughter;
- 20 by people who are not mentally ill;
- 25 by passive smoking;
- 125 by NHS hospital acquired infection.

The starting point in risk reduction is encouraging patients to seek help and talk about their thoughts and feelings. It is hard to believe that potential patients will not be deterred from the services if they know that psychiatrists will have a duty to enforce treatment on them, not only in hospital but also in the community, even when they are perfectly able to make decisions for themselves.

The Royal College of Psychiatrists make a valid point in their evidence: if patients with mental illnesses know that they are going to be detained and treated against their will, why would they contact the mental health services? The deprivation of liberty is certainly a significant deterrent against patients who feel they should seek help for their condition.

> ### THINKING POINT
>
> How do you feel about the way mental health law has developed? Do you think the practice of forcible detention and treatment of mentally ill patients harms the public perception of the medical profession and the role of the doctor?

What is a mental disorder?

In order for the Mental Health Act 1983 to be legally enforced against a mentally ill person, the term 'mental disorder' must be defined. This allows for patients with a diagnosed mental disorder to be subject to the detention and treatment provisions within the statute.[5] Because the detention and treatment of competent patients without their consent is controversial, it is especially important that the definition of mental disorder is clinical and fair. This is because the deprivation of liberty is a very serious offence, and the law must have a good reason to detain somebody against their will for a set amount of time without their consent.

Statutory definition of 'mental disorder'

The 1983 Act has defined a mental disorder, which is provided below.

> ### Mental Health Act 1983
>
> **Section 1: Application of Act: 'mental disorder'**
>
> (2)   In this Act, 'mental disorder' means any disorder or disability of the mind;
>
> (2A) But a person with learning disability shall not be considered by reason of that disability to be –
>
>   (a)   suffering from mental disorder . . .
>
>   (b)   requiring treatment in hospital for mental disorder . . .
>
> Unless that disability is associated with abnormally aggressive or seriously irresponsible conduct on his part.
>
> (3)   Dependence on alcohol or drugs is not considered to be a disorder or disability of the mind for the purposes of subsection (2) above.
>
> (4)   In subsection (2A) above, 'learning disability' means a state of arrested or incomplete development of the mind which includes significant impairment of intelligence and social functioning.

Notice how the term 'mental disorder' includes 'any disorder or disability of the mind'. The word 'any' makes this definition potentially limitless in its application. This is why the draconian provisions of the Mental Health Act 1983 are so controversial. In practice, should a competent person who is suffering from a phobia – who may put his own safety at risk by running away from something he is afraid of – be forcibly detained and treated alongside a severely mentally ill incompetent schizophrenic patient who is

---

[5] Remember, competent patients who have a mental disorder and refuse treatment are treated forcefully under the 1983 Act, whereas incompetent patients are treated according to their best interests under the Mental Capacity Act 2005.

genuinely dangerous? Interestingly, the Mental Health Act 1983 specifically states that a learning disability in particular is exempt from its provisions, and is defined as 'a state of arrested or incomplete development of the mind which includes significant impairment of intelligence and social functioning'. It is impossible to know what this definition means in practice and what borderline disorders are included within the definition. However, a learning disability is only exempt from the 1983 Act if it is *not* associated with 'abnormally aggressive' or 'seriously irresponsible' conduct. This means that a person with a learning disability alone will not be subject to the provisions within the Mental Health Act 1983; a person with a learning disability who shows signs of aggressive or irresponsible behaviour may find himself detained and treated under the 1983 Act.

One final interesting point to note about the section 1(2) definition of a mental disorder is that alcohol and drugs is specifically excluded from the definition. This is because alcohol and drug use is seen as a social problem, not a mental health problem, and there are other kinds of treatment available for alcohol and drug use. However, if a patient develops a mental disorder because of his substance abuse, that disorder will come under the section 1(2) definition.

Kinds of 'mental disorder'

The Code of Practice for the Mental Health Act 1983 contains a list of clinically recognised conditions which it claims could fall under the definition of mental disorder. The list (provided below) is not included within the Act itself, but it can provide a guide as to what kind of disorder may require detention and treatment if a person (or the public) is at risk.

EXTRACT

Department of Health, Mental Health Act 1983, Code of Practice, (2008) (archived):

http://webarchive.nationalarchives.gov.uk/20130107105354/
http://www.dh.gov.uk/en/Publicationsandstatistics/Publications/
PublicationsPolicyAndGuidance/DH_084597

Clinically recognised conditions which could fall within the Act's definition of mental disorder:

- Affective disorders, such as depression and bipolar disorder.
- Schizophrenia and delusional disorders.
- Neurotic, stress-related and somatoform disorders, such as anxiety, phobic disorders, obsessive compulsive disorders, post-traumatic stress disorder and hypochondriacal disorders, organic mental disorders such as dementia and delirium however caused.
- Personality and behavioural changes caused by brain injury or damage however acquired.
- Personality disorders.
- Mental and behavioural disorders caused by psychoactive substance use.[6]
- Eating disorders, non-organic sleep disorders and non-organic sexual disorders.
- Learning disabilities.[7]
- Autistic spectrum disorders including Asperger's syndrome.
- Behavioural and emotional disorders of children and adolescents.

---

[6] Detention and treatment is not authorised for substance use alone, but is allowed for the mental effects and disorders stemming from the substance use (Code of Practice paragraphs 3.8–3.12).

[7] People with learning disabilities alone (i.e. no mental disorder to speak of) are exempt from being detained from treatment, but they can be detained for assessment (Code of Practice paragraphs 3.13–3.15).

This list is rather startling. Not only are stress-related disorders very common in society, but personality, behavioural and emotional disorders are also subject to forced detention and treatment. A common perception of mental disorders is that they are organic, i.e. they are physical and come from inside the brain, but personality, behavioural and emotional disorders are not organic, they are simply behavioural, meaning that it is unlikely that a psychiatric hospital could offer any medical treatment for these disorders. This is also the case for sleep disorders and sexual disorders, also listed above. So why have they been included within the ambit of the 1983 Act?

It is interesting to note that the Code of Practice also includes phobias, anxiety, obsessive compulsive disorders and eating disorders. These may well be mental disorders, but if they are, can (or should) they be treated by forced detention and treatment in a psychiatric hospital?

Discrimination and mental disorders

Centuries ago, all kinds of people ended up in madhouses and asylums. Sometimes, people who were perfectly competent and healthy but engaged in immoral behaviour were detained without consent and simply left in a cell. This could have included prostitutes, pregnant teenagers, religious, political and violent people. They were not wanted by society, so the simple solution was to detain them out of sight. This cannot happen anymore. A patient must have a mental disorder as described by the 1983 Act and according to the Code of Practice, the 1983 Act cannot be used in a discriminatory manner.

EXTRACT

Department of Health, Mental Health Act 1983, Code of Practice, (2008) (archived):

http://webarchive.nationalarchives.gov.uk/20130107105354/
http://www.dh.gov.uk/en/Publicationsandstatistics/Publications/
PublicationsPolicyAndGuidance/DH_084597

Paragraph 3.6: 'Difference' should not be confused with 'disorder'. No-one may be considered to be mentally disordered solely because of their political, religious or cultural beliefs, values or opinions, unless there are proper clinical grounds to believe that they are the symptoms or manifestations of a disability or disorder of the mind. The same is true of a person's involvement, or likely involvement, in illegal, anti-social or 'immoral' behaviour.

This guidance is not enshrined into the statute itself, where it would have much more authority. However, this guidance may have been left out of the statute because in practice it is unworkable. The values or opinions of a person are almost impossible to separate from their potential mental disorder. Those with non-organic disorders such as eating disorders will have very strong opinions as to what is best for them.

Personality disorders

The Mental Health Act 1983 is controversial for the inclusion of personality disorders. The Code of Practice clearly lists personality disorders as a clinically recognised condition (above). An example of a personality disorder might include paedophilic tendencies, which may also explain why non organic sexual disorders are also included within the Code of Practice (above). It appears that dangerous sexual predators can be detained and treated under the Mental Health Act 1983. This is a good example of how the Mental Health Act 1983 is used to prevent harm to others as well as to treat individuals. A personality disorder which is dangerous enough to warrant the forced detention and treatment of the sufferer is known as a Dangerous and Severe Personality Disorder (DSPD). The question that remains is: can a DSPD be a mental disorder that requires forced admission into a psychiatric hospital?

There have been several attempts worldwide to define personality disorders. The World Health Organisation has produced a document entitled: International Statistical Classification of Diseases and Related Health Problems, in which it recognises a 'dissocial personality disorder'. The document is also known as ICD-10 (which stands for International Classification of Diseases, tenth revision). The American Psychiatric Association has also had a go, producing its Diagnostic and Statistical Manual of Mental Disorders (fifth edition). It is also known as DSM-V. The American Psychiatric Association has published a list containing various forms of antisocial behaviour and recommends that if three or more forms are found in an individual, he or she can be diagnosed with an antisocial personality disorder.

EXTRACT

American Psychiatric Association, Diagnostic and Statistical Manual of Mental Disorders, Fifth edition (2013), Copyright © 2013, reprinted with permission, all rights reserved:

www.psych.org/practice/dsm

1. Failure to conform to social norms with respect to lawful behaviours as indicated by repeatedly performing acts that are grounds for arrest.

2. Deceitfulness, as indicated by repeatedly lying, use of aliases, or conning others for personal profit or pleasure.

3. Impulsivity or failure to plan ahead.

4. Irritability and aggressiveness, as indicated by repeated physical fights or assaults.

5. Reckless disregard for safety of self or others.

6. Consistent irresponsibility, as indicated by repeated failure to sustain consistent work behaviour or honour financial obligations.

7. Lack of remorse, as indicated by being indifferent to or rationalising having hurt, mistreated, or stolen from another.

These antisocial behaviours are not uncommon, but it may be a rather low threshold to state that only three of the behaviours (above) could amount to an antisocial personality disorder. How would we treat antisocial personality disorders? Education and counselling may be the answer, but they are already widely available in the community. Detention under the 1983 Act may not be necessary, and it may turn psychiatrists into law enforcers.

EXTRACT

Alex Carlile, 'Legislation to Law: Rubicon or Styx?' (2005) *Journal of Mental Health Law* 107

Naturally there is a desire at large to anticipate and limit the damage DSPD cases may cause (Dangerous and Severe Personality Disorders). The stories make good news copy, lend themselves to exaggeration in terms of the mental health treatment potential available, and worst of all excite all too easily demands by elected politicians that 'something should be done', usually equated with the assumption that something can be done. [...] Where there is treatment available and a degree of therapeutic benefit, compulsory powers may well have a part to play in DSPD. [...] However . . . hospitals and their clinical staff should not be placed in the position of least worst jailers without any realistic medical intervention taking place.

There is a feeling amongst commentators that the detention and treatment of antisocial individuals is simply an alternative way to remove them from the streets, thus turning the medical profession into 'jailers'. However, if left on the streets, these individuals may not volunteer for education and counselling, leaving the antisocial behaviour in some communities to spiral. A difficult balance has to be made between treatment and safety.

ACTIVITY

According to the criteria above, who below has a mental disorder?

1. Henry is dyslexic. He becomes very frustrated with his disorder, because it means that his school work is messy but he can't help it. He has tantrums in his classroom because of his dyslexia and he is prone to throwing things at other students who laugh at him. He has hurt students before during his tantrums.

2. James has severe Downs Syndrome. He lives with his mother at home. He is unable to work and he cannot interact with people. He breaks things at home and is aggressive towards his family, especially if he comes off his medication. Sometimes his mother has to confine him to one room to ensure the safety of the other members of the family.

3. Hayley is 23 and has just experienced a relationship break up. She is devastated because she was engaged to her partner and she was planning their wedding. Her partner left her for someone else. She has signed off sick from work and has contemplated suicide a few times.

4. Rick is 38 and is a convicted sex offender. He lives near a primary school and watches the children play. He has been convicted of rape of a minor and possession of indecent images. He is planning on taking a child from the playground.

5. Shola was hit by a car two months ago. She only sustained minor injuries, but her head hit the road quite hard. She is beginning to hallucinate. She sees giant spiders and is experiencing blurred vision. She has run into oncoming traffic a few times to escape from her hallucinations.

Detention under the Mental Health Act 1983 (assessment)

Under the Mental Health Act 1983, a person can be forcibly detained for assessment under section 2 (known commonly as 'being sectioned'), and once assessment is complete and the need for treatment is identified, they can be forcibly treated under section 3. Patients are entitled to voluntarily admit themselves into the mental health system so there is no need to use force against them. This section deals with detention for assessment under section 2 of the 1983 Act.

Section 2 of the Mental Health Act 1983

Section 2 states the following:

Mental Health Act 1983

Section 2: Admission for assessment

(1) A patient may be admitted to a hospital and detained there for the period allowed by subsection (4) below . . .

(2) An application for admission for assessment may be made in respect of a patient on the grounds that –

(a) he is suffering from a mental disorder of a nature or degree which warrants the detention of the patient in a hospital for assessment (or for assessment followed by medical treatment) for at least a limited period; and

(b) he ought to be so detained in the interests of his own health or safety or with a view to the protection of other persons.

(3) An application for admission for assessment shall be founded on the written recommendations in the prescribed form of two registered medical practitioners, including in each case a statement that in the opinion of the practitioner the conditions set out in subsection (2) above are complied with.

(4) A patient admitted to hospital in pursuance of an application for admission for assessment may be detained for a period not exceeding 28 days beginning with the day on which he is admitted.

According to section 2, a patient may be detained for up to 28 days to allow medical professionals to assess him for a mental disorder. In order to justify the deprivation of his liberty, the 'nature or degree' of his disorder must warrant forced detention, and the detention is in the interests of 'his own health and safety' or to 'protect others'.

It all seems straightforward, but there are ambiguities. What nature or degree must the disorder take to warrant forced detention for assessment? Also, how must the patient's health or safety be at risk? The Mental Health Act 1983's Code of Practice attempts to flesh out these issues at paragraph 4.3 and 4.6:

'Nature'	The chronicity and prognosis of the disorder and the patient's response to previous treatment.
'Degree'	The current manifestation of the disorder.
'Patient health or safety'	Risk of suicide, self-harm, self-neglect, jeopardising health or safety accidentally, recklessly or unintentionally, patient's mental health will deteriorate.

The phrase 'nature or degree' was explored in the following case and it was decided that they can be read and applied separately.

CASE EXTRACT

R v Mental Health Review Tribunal for South Thames region, ex parte Smith (1999) 47 BMLR 104

Facts: Smith was a paranoid schizophrenic. During his detention, he was displaying neither positive or negative symptoms and asked the Mental Health Review Tribunal to give him a conditional discharge from hospital. They refused on the grounds that while the 'nature' of his condition did not warrant detention, the 'degree' of his condition was such that detention was necessary. S appealed, arguing that 'nature or degree' should be read conjunctively.

Held: He was detained.

Popplewell J: 'Nature or degree' was not to be read conjunctively. Although Smith's condition was static at present, the nature of his condition meant that it might not continue to be so. He should therefore still be detained.

The Code of Practice warns against using the powers of detention excessively. For example, alternative treatments should be sought first and detention should be a last resort.

EXTRACT

Department of Health, Mental Health Act 1983, Code of Practice, (2008) (archived):

http://webarchive.nationalarchives.gov.uk/20130107105354/
http://www.dh.gov.uk/en/Publicationsandstatistics/Publications/
PublicationsPolicyAndGuidance/DH_084597

Paragraph 4.4: Before it is decided that admission to hospital is necessary, consideration must be given to whether there are alternative means of providing the care and treatment which the patient requires. This includes consideration of whether there might be other effective forms of care or treatment which the patient would be willing to accept, and of whether guardianship would be appropriate instead.

The Code of Practice goes further to list a collection of considerations similar to the best interests test under the Mental Capacity Act 2005.

EXTRACT

Department of Health, Mental Health Act 1983, Code of Practice, (2008) (archived):

http://webarchive.nationalarchives.gov.uk/20130107105354/
http://www.dh.gov.uk/en/Publicationsandstatistics/Publications/
PublicationsPolicyAndGuidance/DH_084597

Paragraph 4.5: In all cases, consideration must be given to:

- The patient's wishes and views of their own needs.
- The patient's age and physical health.

- Any past wishes or feelings expressed by the patient.
- The patient's cultural background.
- The patient's social and family circumstances.
- The impact that any future deterioration or lack of improvement in the patient's condition would have on their children, other relatives or carers, especially those living with the patient, including an assessment of these people's ability and willingness to cope.
- The effect on the patient, and those close to the patient, of a decision to admit or not to admit under the Act.

Consideration must be given to the wishes and views of the patient, but the patient has no power to negotiate his forced detention under section 2 unless he voluntarily admits himself into the mental health system (even then, if he refuses treatment he will be sectioned). In addition, the effect of the disorder on family members will be considered. This principle does not sit well with the principle of autonomy where the competent patient usually decides for himself what treatment he will accept or reject, and the influence of family members is not usually relevant to allow for the decision to be autonomous. A competent patient's social circumstances or his family's ability to cope should also have no effect on whether he or she is forcibly detained and treated for a mental disorder. The detention and treatment of a patient for the protection of others is preventative detention and does not seek to treat the patient according to what is best for him. Finally, the detention and treatment of a patient for the patient's own good is paternalistic. It is not for the law to tell people what is best for them, and this is why the principle of autonomy, i.e. the freedom to make your own choice about treatment, is usually so well respected in medicine. Thankfully, these guidelines are not enshrined in the statute.

Safeguard

There are provisions (albeit brief) in place to allow for detained patients to make an application to a tribunal to question and overturn their application for detention under section 2.

Mental Health Act 1983

Section 66(1)(a)(i): Where a patient is admitted to a hospital in pursuance of an application for admission for assessment, an application may be made to the appropriate tribunal within the relevant period by the patient.

Section 66(2)(a): In subsection (1) above 'the relevant period' means 14 days beginning with the day on which the patient is admitted as so mentioned.

Just because the patient is allowed to appeal, however, does not mean that the patient is discharged. The Mental Health Review Tribunal (MHRT) will decide what happens to the patient, as long as this is within a reasonable time.

> **CASE EXTRACT**
>
> ### SS (Medical Treatment: Late Termination), Re [2005] UKHL 60
>
> **Facts**: M, who was severely mentally disabled, had been detained in hospital under section 2 of the 1983 Act. She had not applied to the Mental Health Review Tribunal within the first 14 days, as was her right. The hospital wished to arrange for M to be received into their guardianship but M's mother objected. The unfolding legal proceedings took longer than expected, which meant that M was detained under the section 2 order well beyond the usual 28 days. M brought judicial review proceedings challenging the compatibility of section 2 with Article 5 of the Human Rights Act 1998, particularly where a patient had a right to make an application to a Mental Health Review Tribunal but was incapable (because of incapacity) of exercising the right on his own initiative.
>
> **Held**: Every sensible effort should be made to enable the patient to exercise his right to apply to a tribunal if there was reason to think that he would wish to do so. The system tried hard to give patients and relatives easy access to a Mental Health Review Tribunal which was designed to meet their needs. Hospital managers had a statutory duty to take steps to ensure that a patient understood his rights under the provisions of his detention. Even if a patient's nearest relative had no independent right of application, there was much that the relative could do to put the patient's case before a judicial authority.

The case of *MH* clearly states that a patient who is detained under section 2 of the 1983 Act must have access to a timely tribunal should she wish to question her detention.

> **ACTIVITY**
>
> Who below can be detained for assessment under section 2 of the 1983 Act and are you comfortable with the answers?
>
> 1. Shelly has a phobia of spiders and refuses to use public toilets.
> 2. Matthew's brother has recently died in a car accident and he has been contemplating suicide. He has purchased a large amount of drugs to help him with this.
> 3. Betty has an advanced form of dementia and is beginning to injure herself around the home.
> 4. Claire is anorexic. She has eaten one apple over the period of five days and is beginning to have heart palpitations.

Detention under the Mental Health Act 1983 (treatment)

Once a patient has been forcibly detained and assessed under section 2 of the 1983 Act and is found to have a mental disorder that puts his health or safety (or the safety of others) at risk, he can be forcibly admitted into hospital for treatment under section 3. Again, a competent patients' consent is not required.[8]

---

[8] This is only for the first three months. Thereafter, section 58 allows for a registered medical practitioner to administer treatment against the patient's wishes if it is still 'appropriate to be given'. See below.

Section 3 of the Mental Health Act 1983

Section 3 states as follows.

Mental Health Act 1983

Section 3: Admission for treatment

(1) A patient may be admitted to a hospital and detained there for the period allowed by the following provisions of this Act . . .

(2) An application for admission for treatment may be made in respect of a patient on the grounds that –

   (a) he is suffering from mental disorder of a nature and degree which makes it appropriate for him to receive medical treatment in hospital; and

   (b) [repealed in 2008]

   (c) it is necessary for the health or safety of the patient or for the protection of other persons that he should receive such treatment and it cannot be provided unless he is detained under this section; and

   (d) appropriate medical treatment is available for him.

(3) An application for admission for treatment shall be founded on the written recommendations in the prescribed form of two registered medical practitioners, including in each case a statement that in the opinion of the practitioner the conditions set out in subsection (2) above are complied with; and each such recommendation shall include –

   (a) [omitted]

   (b) a statement of the reasons for that opinion so far as it relates to the conditions set out in paragraph (c) of that subsection, specifying whether other methods of dealing with the patient are available and, if so, why they are not appropriate.

(4) In this Act, references to appropriate medical treatment, in relation to a person suffering from mental disorder, are references to medical treatment which is appropriate in his case, taking into account the nature and degree of the mental disorder and all other circumstances of his case.

Under section 3, no period of time for treatment is specified. It is in fact located at section 20(1) of the 1983 Act, and it is six months. The order for detention and treatment can also be renewed under section 20(2) for another six months once that has expired, and then annually after that. Potentially, under section 20(2), a patient can be detained for the rest of his or her life. In order to justify the detention of a patient for treatment under section 3, it must be appropriate for him to receive his treatment within a hospital environment. This alludes to a particularly aggressive or severe mental disorder. The provision: 'it cannot be provided unless he is detained' can be read as saying: 'the treatment is available, but we must detain him against his will to give him it'. Even on this simple interpretation, section 3 looks considerably draconian and unethical. A patient with a mental disorder can only be forcibly detained and treated for his disorder if there is treatment *available* for his disorder. Otherwise, the patient is simply being detained for no reason, and this is a deprivation of his liberty under Article 5. To put it another way, if the mental health system cannot treat his disorder, they must let him go. The consideration of 'other methods' acts as a safeguard from abuse to ensure that the forced detention and treatment of the patient is a last resort, but the medical practitioner must justify why the other available methods are not appropriate. Finally, any treatment proposed must be tailored to the patient's needs after taking into account the nature and degree of his mental disorder. He must not be given excessive or inappropriate treatment for his disorder.

Finally, under section 2 above, the justification given for forcibly detaining and treating the patient is that: 'it is necessary for the health or safety of the patient or for the protection of other persons.' This removes the patient from the fundamental principles of medicine because he is being detained and treated for the benefit of others, not for his own benefit.

Safeguard

There are, again, brief provisions in place to allow for detained patients to make an application to a tribunal to question and overturn their application for treatment under section 3.

Mental Health Act 1983

Section 66(1)(b)(i): Where a patient is admitted to a hospital in pursuance of an application for admission for treatment, an application may be made to the appropriate tribunal within the relevant period by the patient.

Section 66(2)(b): In subsection (1) above 'the relevant period' means six months beginning with the day on which the patient is admitted as so mentioned.

The Mental Health Review Tribunal (MHRT) will decide what happens to the patient.

ACTIVITY

Who can be detained for treatment under section 3 of the 1983 Act and are you comfortable with the answers?

1. Mike is assessed for a mental disorder and brain abnormalities are found, but they cannot diagnose him.
2. Freddy is assessed and he is found to have the early stages of dementia.
3. Jill is assessed and she is suffering from acute depression.

Detention under the Mental Health Act 1983 (emergency and other)

The procedure for detaining and assessing a person under section 2 may cause unnecessary or undesirable delay. What if much quicker action is needed to detain him or her for assessment? In an emergency, a person can be fast-tracked through section 2 in what is known as an 'emergency application'. The powers to do this are under section 4.

Mental Health Act 1983

Section 4: Admission for assessment in cases of emergency

(1) In any case of urgent necessity, an application for admission for assessment may be made in respect of a patient in accordance with the following provisions of this section, and any application so made is in this Act referred to as 'an emergency application'.

(2) An emergency application may be made either by an approved mental health professional or by the nearest relative of the patient; and every such application shall include a statement that it is of urgent necessity for the patient to be admitted and detained under section 2 above, and that compliance with the provisions of this Part of this Act relating to applications under that section would involve undesirable delay.

(3) An emergency application shall be sufficient in the first instance if founded on one of the medical recommendations required by section 2 above, given, if practicable, by a practitioner who has previous acquaintance with the patient . . . and verifying the statement referred to in subsection (2) above.

(4) An emergency application shall cease to have effect on the expiration of a period of 72 hours from the time when the patient is admitted to the hospital unless:

  (a) the second medical recommendation required by section 2 above is given and received by the managers within that period.

The 'emergency application' provisions are interesting. Unlike section 2, any admission for assessment under section 4 must be supported by written recommendations from only one medical practitioner who must also provide a statement confirming that the criteria, i.e. a risk to health or safety, are met. The Code of Practice for the 1983 Act states that section 4 should be used only in a genuine emergency, where the patient's need for urgent assessment outweighs the desirability of waiting for a second doctor (paragraph 5.4). Also, either the approved mental health professional or the nearest relative must make a statement explaining why following the usual section 2 procedure would cause undesirable delay.

What kind of situation might be so urgent as to warrant a short cut via section 4? The Code of Practice provides some advice.

EXTRACT

Department of Health, Mental Health Act 1983, Code of Practice, (2008) (archived):

http://webarchive.nationalarchives.gov.uk/20130107105354/
http://www.dh.gov.uk/en/Publicationsandstatistics/Publications/
PublicationsPolicyAndGuidance/DH_084597

Paragraph 5.6: An emergency may arise where the patient's mental state or behaviour presents problems which those involved cannot reasonably be expected to manage while waiting for a second doctor. To be satisfied that an emergency has arisen, the person making the application and the doctor making the supporting recommendation should have evidence of:

- an immediate and significant risk of mental or physical harm to the patient or to others;
- danger of serious harm to property; or
- a need for physical restraint of the patient.

It is clearly not necessary that the medical practitioner knows the patient personally, but he must verify the statement that there is an emergency. Also, notice how under section 2, a patient can be detained for assessment for 28 days, whereas under an emergency assessment under section 4, only 72 hours is permitted. If, however, the second medical practitioner comes forward and provides his recommendation and statement within those 72 hours, then we have a standard section 2 admission for assessment which will last 28 days.

Other important details

A combination of section 4(5) and 11(5) read together to state that 'none of the applications shall be made by any person in respect of a patient unless that person has personally seen the patient within the previous 24 hours'. In practical terms, if a parent wishes to section her aggressive son under section 2 but it is felt that the procedure under section 2 would cause considerable delay and she wishes to use section 4, she must have seen her son within 24 hours before making her application. This simply confirms the emergency status.

Alternative routes to admission

Apart from section 2 and section 4, there are a small handful of alternative routes into the mental health system:

- **Section 5: Application in respect of patient already in hospital**: a patient who is already voluntarily in hospital who needs to be compulsorily admitted may be detained for 72 hours. If the patient is in hospital receiving treatment for a mental disorder and it appears to a nurse that he should be immediately restrained from leaving hospital, she can detain him for six hours until a medical practitioner arrives.

- **Section 135: Warrant to search for and remove patients**: a Justice of the Peace, on evidence submitted by a mental health professional, may issue a warrant allowing a constable to break into a premises and take a suspected mentally ill person to a place of safety if he is ill-treated or neglected or unable to care for himself. He can be detained for 72 hours.

- **Section 136: Mentally disordered persons found in public places**: if a constable finds a person in a public place who appears to be suffering from a mental disorder, the constable may move that person to a place of safety for the protection of the individual or other persons for 72 hours (a place of safety can include a hospital, a care home, or local social services).

THINKING POINT

Has Parliament covered every eventuality with their emergency provisions? If so, is the emphasis placed on public safety or patient safety?

Detention of incompetent patients

Patients who lack capacity are treated in accordance with their best interests under the Mental Capacity Act 2005. Their deprivation of liberty is therefore in their best interests.

This might sound unfair, but the Deprivation of Liberty Safeguards have now been implemented into the Mental Capacity Act 2005 (inserted by the Mental Health Act 2007) to allow this to happen lawfully.[9]

Case law

The Deprivation of Liberty Safeguards originate from two cases.

CASE EXTRACT	**JE v DE [2006] EWHC 3459**

CASE EXTRACT

JE v DE [2006] EWHC 3459

Facts: D was 76 and a major stroke had left him blind and with significant short-term memory impairment. He was disorientated and needed assistance. There was evidence strongly suggesting that he lacked the capacity to consent to his confinement. He had known J for many years but had only been married to her for a few months when he was placed into care homes (X and Y) by the local authority following an incident in which J had shut him out of the house claiming she could not care for him. According to his care notes, he repeatedly told staff at the home that he wanted to live with J and that he was being held against his will. The local authority contended that D was merely subjected to restrictions on his liberty that were in his own best interests, and that he was not being deprived of his liberty.

Held: An incompetent patient can be deprived of his liberty under Article 5. A restriction did not breach human rights if it was in the patient's best interests.

Munby J (at paras 115, 124): The fundamental issue in this case, in my judgment, is whether D was deprived of his liberty to leave the X home and whether D has been and is deprived of his liberty to leave the Y home. And when I refer to leaving the X home and the Y home, I do not mean leaving for the purpose of some trip or outing [...] by those managing the institution; I mean leaving in the sense of removing himself permanently in order to live where and with whom he chooses, specifically removing himself to live at home with J. [...]

In the light of this substantial and consistent volume of material it seems to me that D quite plainly was not 'free to leave' the X home and has not been and is not 'free to leave' the Y home, with the consequence, in my judgment, that he has been and continues to be 'deprived of his liberty' – a state of affairs that has continued since 4 September 2005 and is still continuing. The fact is that D has repeatedly expressed his wish to be living at home with J and has made it clear that he is in the Y home, as previously the X home, 'against his will'. It is suggested that he would not have been prevented from leaving had he actually tried to. That, in my judgment, simply will not wash.

JE v DE established that an incompetent patient can be deprived of his liberty against Article 5 of the European Convention on Human Rights because it is in his best interests. It also made a distinction between mere 'restriction' of liberty (which may be in the patient's best interests) and 'deprivation' of liberty, which is a breach of human rights. However, in another case immediately thereafter, a different decision was reached.

---

[9] This section refers to *incompetent* patients with mental disorders. They are treated under the Mental Capacity Act 2005 instead of the Mental Health Act 1983.

CASE EXTRACT

L LBC v *G* [2007] EWHC 2640

Facts: T suffered from poor health and had been resident in a care home, but the placement had been terminated. Before an alternative home could be found, T fell ill and was admitted to hospital. J and K (daughter and granddaughter) had put themselves forward as carers for T on the basis that he would live with them on his discharge. However, the local authority considered that T required full-time care in a residential home, and a suitable one was found. Before T's placement was achieved, he was discharged by the hospital to the care of J and K. The local authority made a without notice application for orders designed to achieve T's transfer to the care home. J and K submitted that the local authority had no right to bring the case in the first place and that the order amounted to a breach of Article 5 (among others).

Held: The patient was not deprived of his liberty under Article 5.

McFarlane J (at paras 103, 105, 108): LLBC submits that the circumstances of T's placement at Towerbridge fall outside Article 5 and seeks to draw the distinction between 'deprivation of liberty' and 'a restriction of liberty'; the distinction between the two being one of degree or intensity and not one of nature or substance. [...] In making this determination the court must look at all the circumstances of the individual's placement. When that is done, [LLBC] submits that, whilst T's circumstances may be close to the borderline, it does not cross into Article 5 territory. Of the submissions made on this point the following seem to have particular weight:

(i)   Towerbridge was an ordinary care home where only ordinary restrictions of liberty applied;

(ii) The family were able to visit T on a largely unrestricted basis and were entitled to remove him from the home for outings;

(iii) T was personally compliant and expressed himself as happy at Towerbridge. He had lived in a local authority care home for over three years and was objectively content with his situation there;

(iv) There was no occasion when he was objectively deprived of his liberty.

[...] Whilst I agree that the circumstances of the present case may be near the borderline between mere restriction of liberty and Article 5 detention, I have come to the conclusion that, looked at as a whole and having regard to all the relevant circumstances, the placement of T in Towerbridge falls short of engaging Article 5.

The main difference between *JE* v *DE* and *LLBC* v *G* is that the patient in the former case was not happy in his care home and was told he could not leave, whereas the patient in the latter case was perfectly happy where he was and did not try to leave. This is a shaky distinction: does it mean that a patient who tries to leave is deprived of his liberty (which is actionable), whereas a patient who does not try to leave is simply restricted of his liberty (which is not actionable)?

The Deprivation of Liberty Safeguards: brief overview

Regardless of this shaky distinction, the definition of a 'deprivation of liberty' emerged shortly afterwards in a mini Code of Practice to supplement the Mental Capacity Act 2005.

EXTRACT

Department of Health, Deprivation of Liberty Safeguards, Code of Practice to supplement the main Mental Capacity Act 2005 Code of Practice (2008) (archived):

http://webarchive.nationalarchives.gov.uk/20130107105354/
http://www.dh.gov.uk/en/Publicationsandstatistics/Publications/
PublicationsPolicyAndGuidance/DH_085476

Paragraph 2.5: The following factors can be relevant to identifying whether steps taken involve more than restraint and amount to a deprivation of liberty. It is important to remember that this list is not exclusive.

- Restraint is used, including sedation, to admit a person to an institution where that person is resisting admission.
- Staff exercise complete and effective control over the care and movement of a person for a significant period.
- Staff exercise control over assessments, treatment, contacts and residence.
- A decision has been taken by the institution that the person will not be released into the care of others, or permitted to live elsewhere, unless the staff in the institution consider it appropriate.
- A request by carers for a person to be discharged to their care is refused.
- The person is unable to maintain social contacts because of restrictions placed on their access to other people.
- The person loses autonomy because they are under continuous supervision and control.

The phrase 'deprivation of liberty' usually produces an image of a person being locked in a cell, but this is clearly not the case. It is all about the whereabouts and confines of the patient. The Mental Capacity Act 2005 was amended to make it lawful to deprive an incompetent patient of his or her liberty. The new provisions are contained within Schedule A1 of the Mental Capacity Act 2005 and medical professionals are obliged to follow them.

Mental Capacity Act 2005

Schedule A1: Hospital and Care Home Residents: Deprivation of Liberty

Paragraph 1: Application of Part

(1) [omitted]

(2) The first condition is that a person (P) is detained in a hospital or care home – for the purpose of being given care or treatment – in circumstances which amount to deprivation of the person's liberty.

(3) The second condition is that a standard or urgent authorisation is in force.

Paragraph 2: Authorisation to deprive P of liberty

The managing authority of the hospital or care home may deprive P of his liberty by detaining him as mentioned in paragraph 1(2).

→

Paragraph 13: The relevant person meets the age requirement if he has reached 18.

Paragraph 14(1): The relevant person meets the mental health requirement if he is suffering from mental disorder within the meaning of the Mental Health Act 1983.

Paragraph 15: The relevant person meets the mental capacity requirement if he lacks capacity.

Paragraph 16(1): The relevant person meets the best interests requirement if all of the following conditions are met:

(2)   He is, or is to be, a detained resident.

(3)   It is in the best interests of the relevant person for him to be a detained resident.

(4)   In order to prevent harm to the relevant person, it is necessary for him to be a detained resident.

(5)   It is a proportionate response to:

    (a)   the likelihood of the relevant person suffering harm, and

    (b)   the seriousness of that harm,

. . . for him to be a detained resident.

The patient must be detained in a hospital or a care home, not a residential place or in any other public place. This is to ensure that he is being cared for by medical or mental health professionals in a safe environment. He must also be receiving care or treatment. If he is being detained for any other reason, this Act/Schedule cannot apply to him. The professionals responsible for the patient must apply for authorisation before they can deprive the patient of his or her liberty. This is important because it protects against 'casual' deprivations of liberty, e.g. in the home by relatives, which provide no legal protection for the patient. Schedule A1 is only for incompetent adult patients. The patient must be suffering from a mental disorder as defined by section 1 of the Mental Health Act 1983. Remember, this includes personality disorders too, as listed in the Mental Health Act 1983 Code of Practice. The patient must 'lack capacity' – if the patient is fully competent to make autonomous medical decisions, the Mental Health Act 1983 will apply to him and he will be detained under section 2 as normal. It must be in the 'best interests' of the patient to be detained. This is controversial. On the one hand, a deprivation of liberty may cause even more distress to the patient who is already confused but on the other hand, because an incompetent patient cannot consent, sometimes the only way to care for a patient is to detain him (this argument holds particular weight if the detention is life-saving). An incompetent patient can be deprived of their liberty in accordance with *their* best interests, whereas we have learnt that competent patients can be detained, assessed and treated to protect the safety of *others*. The 2005 Act therefore places an emphasis on caring for the patient himself, and it provides a stronger justification for the deprivation of liberty than sections 2 and 3 of the 1983 Act in relation to competent patients. If any restraint is to be used during the deprivation of liberty, the restraint used must be in proportion to the violence or resistance displayed by the patient. The harm that he poses to himself must be very serious indeed to justify the deprivation of liberty. The restraint must, of course, be in the patient's best interests.

The Deprivation of Liberty Safeguards are complex and open to criticism: before a deprivation of liberty can be authorised the patient must be assessed and in practical terms this could mean the assessment of the tens of thousands of people in care homes and hospitals who have lost their capacity. However, when such an important breach of human rights is at stake, it is important to ensure that each and every deprivation of liberty is fair and justified. There is not usually a quick and easy way to do this.

Is the Mental Health Act 1983 ever relevant to incompetent patients?

For the most part, the Mental Capacity Act 2005 will suffice to care for incompetent patients. However, the Mental Health Act 1983 can be enforced if the Mental Capacity Act 2005 cannot be used. There are several instances when this might be the case. It is important to remember that the Mental Capacity Act 2005 does not *enforce* detention, assessment or treatment like the Mental Health Act 1983 does, it simply ensures that it is in the *best interests* of the patient. It is true that Schedule A1 of the Mental Capacity Act 2005 does allow for an appropriate use of restraint, but this is only in relation to depriving the patient of his liberty when it is in his best interests. Therefore, if medical staff need to use force which is not in the best interests of the patient, they might have to turn to the Mental Health Act 1983 section 3 which, it might be recalled, takes no account of best interests.

EXTRACT

The Mental Capacity Act 2005 Code of Practice (2007):

http://www.legislation.gov.uk/ukpga/2005/9/pdfs/ukpgacop_20050009_en.pdf

Paragraph 13.12: It might be necessary to consider using the Mental Health Act 1983 rather than the Mental Capacity Act 2005 if:

- It is not possible to give the person the care or treatment they need without carrying out an action that might deprive them of their liberty.
- The person needs treatment that cannot be given under the Mental Capacity Act 2005 (for example, because the person has made a valid and applicable advance decision to refuse all or part of that treatment).
- The person may need to be restrained in a way that is not allowed under the Mental Capacity Act 2005.
- It is not possible to assess or treat the person safely or effectively without treatment being compulsory (perhaps because the person is expected to regain capacity to consent and will then refuse).
- The person lacks capacity to decide on some elements of the treatment but has capacity to refuse a vital part of it – and they have done so.

It is hoped that there will be very few occasions in which healthcare professionals will have to apply force to an incompetent patient which is not in his best interests. The examples given by the Code of Practice (above) can all be said to satisfy the patient's best interests in some way and if they do not, it seems inappropriate that the law should allow them to be carried out by 'swapping statutes'.

ACTIVITY

Choose the statute that is most applicable to each patient below. The three options are: the Mental Health Act 1983, the Mental Capacity Act 2005, or a move from one to the other to suit the patient's capacity status.

1. Jackie is a competent 40-year-old patient who is suffering from severe depression. She has begun to self-harm and is contemplating suicide. Her family are worried for her safety.

2. Freddie is 20 and suffers from severe learning disabilities. He lashes out at his brothers and he threatens his mother with a knife. He is very aggressive and will not take his medication.

3. Emily is unconscious after a car accident. She is treated in hospital with a blood transfusion. She wakes up and becomes competent but she still has a head injury that causes her to hallucinate. She refuses any further blood but medical staff fear she is suffering from an organic mental disorder.

The mental disorder must be 'treatable'

Section 3(2)(d) of the Mental Health Act 1983 (see above) states very clearly:

An application for admission for treatment may be made in respect of a patient on the grounds that appropriate medical treatment is available for him.

This provision is known as the 'treatability' requirement and it is controversial. It means that a competent patient can only be detained and treated against his will if there is medical treatment available to him. On the face of it, this seems encouraging, because it means that if a hospital cannot treat a person's mental disorder, he cannot be deprived of his liberty and he must be freed. However, it is not as simple as that. Before the 2007 reforms to the Mental Health Act 1983, the previous law stated the following:

Mental Health Act 1983 (original)	Mental Health Act 1983 (after 2007 reform)
Section 3: 'Treatment is likely to alleviate or prevent a deterioration of his condition.'	Section 3: 'On the grounds that appropriate medical treatment is available for him.'

As you can see from the table above, the old law stated that a person could be detained and treated under section 3 only if the treatment available to him was likely to alleviate or prevent a deterioration of his mental disorder. In practical terms, a person could only be detained if the treatment *helped* his disorder. After the 2007 reforms, there is no need for these requirements to be met. Instead, a patient may simply be detained if medical treatment is *available* – it does not have to alleviate or prevent a deterioration of his mental disorder. This is controversial because a person can now be detained when the treatment he is receiving is doing him no good at all.

Why was the law changed in this way?

At the time of the 2007 reforms, the government were concerned about individuals with Dangerous and Severe Personality Disorders (DSPD) such as paedophilia and other sexual disorders. It was thought appropriate to detain and treat these individuals under the newly amended Mental Health Act 1983. Section 2(2) of the Mental Health Act 1983 defines a mental disorder as 'any disorder or disability of the mind' and this definition clearly includes dangerous and severe personality disorders. The Code of Practice also lists 'personality disorders' as a mental disorder, meaning that individuals with DSPD are now at risk of being detained and treated under the 1983 Act. However, there is a problem. A personality disorder may not accepted by some as a mental disorder. In fact, some may go as far as to say that personality disorders cannot be treated at all. Under the old section 3, a hospital could not detain a person unless they could alleviate his condition. A patient with a personality disorder was therefore released. This was unsatisfactory, so in order to enable hospitals to detain individuals with personality disorders, the terms 'alleviate' and 'prevent a deterioration' were removed from section 3 and the phrase 'medical treatment is available' was slotted in.

Mental Health Act 1983 (original)	Mental Health Act 1983 (after 2007 reform)
Section 3: 'Treatment is likely to alleviate or prevent a deterioration of his condition.'	**Section 3**: 'On the grounds that appropriate medical treatment is available for him.'
Potential 'untreatable' disorders: schizophrenia, dementia, brain damage, brain tumour, personality disorder, behavioural disorder, severe learning disability, etc.	
Treatment result: released.	Treatment result: detained.

A patient who is detained simply because he is anticipated to be dangerous is enduring preventative detention, i.e. he is detained to prevent him from being violent, and it is illegal – a person cannot be detained if he or she has done nothing wrong. Unfortunately, mental health law operates in a system that looks an awful lot like preventative detention. The 1983 Act has thus created a loophole. There has been a large amount of debate about the role of medical professionals in the mental health system when detaining patients: does preventative detention turn doctors into law enforcers? A positive aspect of the new amendment is that the treatment that must be available is medical (it did not have to be medical pre-reform).

'Medical treatment'

The Mental Health Act 1983 provides a further definition as to 'medical treatment' for the purposes of detaining and treating a patient.

Mental Health Act 1983

Section 145(4): Any reference in this Act to medical treatment, in relation to mental disorder, shall be construed as a reference to medical treatment the purpose of which is to alleviate, or prevent a worsening of, the disorder or one or more of its symptoms or manifestations.

The terms 'alleviate' and 'prevent the worsening of' are included in the definition of medical treatment above, but it should be noted that the treatment must only have this as a *purpose* (every treatment has a purpose) – it does not actually have to show these effects on the patient. This is in direct contrast to the old version of section 3 where 'alleviation' and 'prevention' must have been shown to be *likely*. The Code of Practice provides further information on the definition of medical treatment. It makes for very interesting reading, particularly in relation to what is meant by 'appropriate' medical treatment:

EXTRACT

Department of Health, Mental Health Act 1983, Code of Practice (2008) (archived):

http://webarchive.nationalarchives.gov.uk/20130107105354/
http://www.dh.gov.uk/en/Publicationsandstatistics/Publications/
PublicationsPolicyAndGuidance/DH_084597

Paragraph 6.4: 'Purpose' is not the same as 'likelihood'. Medical treatment may be for the purpose of alleviating, or preventing a worsening of, a mental disorder even though it cannot be shown in advance that any particular effect is likely to be achieved;

Paragraph 6.6: It should never be assumed that any disorders, or any patients, are inherently or inevitably untreatable. Nor should it be assumed that likely difficulties in achieving long-term and sustainable change in a person's underlying disorder make medical treatment to help manage their condition and the behaviours arising from it either inappropriate or unnecessary;

Paragraph 6.8: This medical treatment must be appropriate, taking into account the nature and degree of the person's mental disorder and all their particular circumstances, including cultural, ethnic and religious considerations;

Paragraph 6.12: Medical treatment need not be the most appropriate treatment that could ideally be made available. Nor does it need to address every aspect of the person's disorder. But the medical treatment available at any time must be an appropriate response to the patient's condition and situation;

Paragraph 6.13: Medical treatment must actually be available to the patient. It is not sufficient that appropriate treatment could theoretically be provided;

Paragraph 6.17: Simply detaining someone – even in a hospital – does not constitute medical treatment;

Paragraph 6.19: In particular, psychological therapies and other forms of medical treatments which, to be effective, require the patient's co-operation are not automatically inappropriate simply because a patient does not currently wish to engage with them. Such treatments can potentially remain appropriate and available as long as it continues to be clinically suitable to offer them and they would be provided if the patient agreed to engage.

Paragraph 6.6 is interesting – by stating that it should 'never be assumed' that a particular disorder is untreatable, the Code of Practice is encouraging hospital trusts to provide an appropriate treatment for *every* patient, even those with untreatable personality disorders. Next to this is the recommendation that difficulties in sustaining long-term results should not be taken as proof that the treatment is unnecessary. This could be read as encouragement to detain untreatable patients even when no progress is shown following treatment. Paragraph 6.19 supports this idea by including 'psychological therapies' into the ambit of medical treatment and stating that even if the patient does not cooperate with such therapies, as long as they are available, the patient can be detained until his cooperation is forthcoming.

What do the 2007 reforms mean for patients who are sectioned under the 1983 Act for treatment?

Treating the mentally ill

It has been explained so far that in mental health law, the following rules apply:

Patient capacity	Patient decision	Outcome
Competent	Consents to treatment for mental disorder	Normal principles of medical law apply when treating competent patients
Competent	Refuses treatment for mental disorder	Detained and treated under the 1983 Act
Incompetent	N/A	Treated according to best interests under the Mental Capacity Act 2005

It will be remembered that a patient will only be detained and treated under the Mental Health Act 1983 if he is diagnosed with a mental disorder which is dangerous to his health or safety (or the safety of others). The 'autonomy anomaly' in mental health law was discussed in detail above and refers to the idea that a perfectly competent patient is not able, under the Mental Health Act 1983, to refuse medical treatment. This is an autonomy anomaly because a patients' autonomous refusal of treatment is highly respected in every other area of medical law. It is therefore a good idea at this point to investigate the very provisions in the Mental Health Act 1983 that make this 'autonomy anomaly' possible.

Section 63: the root source of the 'autonomy anomaly'

It is section 63 which contains the provision that consent is not required from a competent patient once he has been detained and assessed under the Mental Health Act 1983.

Mental Health Act 1983

Section 63: Treatment not requiring consent

The consent of a patient shall not be required for any medical treatment given to him for the mental disorder from which he is suffering [not being a form of treatment to which section 57, 58 or 58A above applies], if the treatment is given by or under the direction of the approved clinician in charge of the treatment.

Section 63 does not require a second opinion from any approved clinician, or a test of competence, nor does it refer to the best interests of the patient. In its simplest form, section 63 supports an overwhelming breach of patient autonomy. This is one of the most highly contentious provisions in the whole of medical law, and for good reason.

EXTRACT

Genevra Richardson, 'Autonomy, Guardianship and Mental Disorder: One Problem, Two Solutions' (2002) 65 *Modern Law Review* 702, at pages 702–23

The Mental Health Act 1983 permits a person suffering from a mental disorder of the necessary degree to be detained in hospital and treated for that disorder against her competent wishes. No assessment of competence is required. Although the wishes of the patient may be relevant to the treatment decision taken on her behalf, statute allows that decision to be driven by beneficence and social protection. [...] In relation to treatment of mental disorder of sufficient severity, statute requires patient autonomy to cede to the values of paternalism and social protection. [...] It is therefore interesting to note that the statutory powers of compulsion are limited to treatment for mental disorder; compulsory patients can still refuse treatment for physical disorder. [...] Much, therefore, turns on the meaning given to mental disorder and if it is interpreted too generously there is a danger that a competent patent could be forced to accept treatment for a condition which has little or no bearing on his or her mental state.

Genevra Richardson makes a noteworthy point: patients can refuse treatment for a physical condition, but the very same competent patient cannot refuse treatment for her mental disorder. The reasons for this are completely unclear. The most logical explanation appears to be social protection.

Can force be used when providing treatment?

The short answer to this is: 'yes'. If a competent patient refuses medical treatment for his mental disorder and a statutory provision enables an approved clinician to treat the patient without his consent, the natural result is that sometimes treatment will be forced. This may be traumatising for perfectly competent patients who refuse treatment. A case visited this issue back in the late 1990s.

CASE EXTRACT

R v Broadmoor Special Hospital Authority, ex parte S, The Times, **17 February 1998**

Auld LJ: Sections 3 [and 37] of the 1983 Act provide for detention, not just for its own sake, but for treatment. Detention for treatment necessarily implies control for that purpose. [...] [The relevant] statutes leave unspoken many of the unnecessary incidents of control flowing from a power of detention for treatment, including: the power to restrain patients, to keep them in seclusion, to deprive them of their personal possessions for their own safety and to regulate the frequency and manner of visits to them.

Auld LJ may be suggesting that the statutory provisions in mental health law are illusive because they fail to contain details about the exact measures required to administer treatment to a competent patient who refuses. It follows that any force used by an approved clinician (s. 63) is discretionary. This may be a dangerous level of discretion, open to abuse.

In what circumstances can forced treatment be justified?

Section 63 also makes it clear that any treatment that is provided must be: 'for the mental disorder from which he is suffering'. This means that the approved clinician cannot simply force *any* treatment upon the patient – it must be directly relevant to the disorder. To add to this, the medical treatment must have the purpose to: 'alleviate, or prevent a worsening of, the disorder or one or more of its symptoms or manifestations' under section 145(4) (as examined above). Putting these provisions together, it becomes clear that an approved clinician can forcibly administer treatment to a competent and refusing patient only if that treatment is relevant to his disorder and has the purpose of alleviating his disorder or one of its symptoms (it was also noted above that the treatment might not have an effect on the patient as long as its *purpose* is to do so). The cases below provide further clarity regarding what exactly is meant by appropriate treatment for mental disorders and when it is justifiable to force that treatment upon a competent patient.

CASE EXTRACT

South West Hertfordshire HA v KB [1994] 2 FCR 1051

Facts: KB was an adult patient who was suffering from anorexia nervosa. She was a competent patient but refused to eat and had been sectioned under the Mental Health Act 1983. The hospital authority wanted a declaration from the court as to the lawfulness of naso-gastric feeding without KB's consent. The issue was whether force-feeding was 'medical treatment' (which could be forced) or simply food (which could not be forced).

Held: Force feeding was medical treatment for this condition and therefore it was justified.

Ewbank J: Anorexia nervosa is an eating disorder and relieving symptoms is just as much a part of treatment as relieving the underlying cause. If the symptoms are exacerbated by the patient's refusal to eat and drink, the mental disorder becomes progressively more and more difficult to treat and so the treatment by naso-gastric tube is an integral part of the treatment of the mental disorder itself. It is also said that the treatment is necessary in order to make psychiatric treatment of the underlying cause possible at all. Feeding by naso-gastric tube in the circumstances of this type of case is treatment envisaged under section 63 and does not require the consent of the patient.

A collection of medical, social and ethical complexities spring from this case. Anorexia nervosa is a well-known and well-established mental disorder concerning the sufferer's perception of his or her own body. The most dominant symptom of anorexia nervosa is the refusal of food. It therefore follows that the forced feeding of an anorexia nervosa sufferer will simply exacerbate the problem. Ewbank J attempted to justify naso-gastric feeding by suggesting that treating a symptom is akin to treating the cause, but this is not true of many mental disorders and this case shows a worrying trend towards forcing treatment upon patients without consulting mental health specialists about what kind of medical care each mental disorder requires. Unsurprisingly, academics have commented on this issue.

EXTRACT

Penney Lewis, 'Feeding Anorexic Patients Who Refuse Food' (1999) 7 *Medical Law Review* 21, at pages 21–37

The anorexic's holy grail is control. [...] Force-feeding crushes the patient's will, destroying who the patient is. This is the antithesis of what a successful, therapeutic treatment must be. [...] The patient may be force-fed up to a more healthy weight and then discharged from hospital, free to return to her previous eating pattern and to lose the weight she has been forced to gain. [...] The gain has been short term, rather than long term. The immediate crisis has been averted, but long-term damage has been done. Forcing treatment upon a young sufferer of anorexia merely reinforces her lack of self-confidence by taking this decision out of her control, and denies her the capacity for self-directed action which must be developed if she is to recover from this illness.

Unfortunately, the rationale in *South West Hertfordshire HA* v *KB* was applied less than a year later in another force-feeding case but with an even more bizarre judgment.

CASE EXTRACT

B v Croydon HA [1995] Fam 133

Facts: B was a 24-year-old woman suffering from a psychopathic disorder (a borderline personality disorder combined with post-traumatic stress disorder) as a result of sexual abuse as a child. She was detained under section 3 of the 1983 Act. One of her symptoms was a compulsion to harm herself. She stopped eating and her weight fell to a dangerous level. The threat of force-feeding was made. B made an application to the High Court for an injunction to restrain the health authority from tube feeding her without her consent. The issue was whether tube feeding was treatment for B's mental disorder.

Held: Force-feeding was treatment for a mental disorder meaning it could be administered with force.

Hoffmann LJ: It does not, however, follow that every act which forms part of that treatment within the wide definition in section 145(1) must in itself be likely to alleviate or prevent a deterioration of that disorder. Nursing and care concurrent with the core treatment or as a necessary prerequisite to such treatment or to prevent the patient from causing harm to himself or to alleviate the consequences of the disorder are in my view all capable of being ancillary to a treatment calculated to alleviate or prevent a deterioration of the psychopathic disorder.

Neill LJ: I also agree. I am satisfied that the words in section 63 of the Mental Health Act 1983 'any medical treatment given to him for the mental disorder from which he is suffering' include treatment given to alleviate the symptoms of the disorder as well as treatment to remedy its underlying cause. In the first place it seems to me that it would often be difficult in practice for those treating a patient to draw a clear distinction between procedures or parts of procedures which were designed to treat the disorder itself and those procedures or parts which were designed to treat its symptoms. In my view the medical treatment has to be looked at as a whole, and this approach is reinforced by the wide definition of 'medical treatment' in section 145(1) as including 'nursing' and also 'care, habilitation and rehabilitation under medical supervision'.

The distinguishing features of *South West Hertfordshire* and *Croydon HA* are clear: both cases reached the same conclusion – that force-feeding was treatment for a mental disorder – but both cases justified this decision on different grounds. Ewbank J in *South West Hertfordshire* equated the treatment of a physical symptom to the treatment of the mental disorder itself, whereas Hoffmann LJ in *Croydon HA* justified force-feeding on the grounds that some forms of treatment were a prerequisite to the core treatment and were therefore necessary to 'alleviate the consequences of the disorder'. This approach was also taken by Neill LJ, who noted that it is often difficult to draw a clear line between a disorder and its symptoms and so the term 'medical treatment' should be 'looked at as a whole'.

A third case confirmed that force-feeding is indeed treatment for a mental disorder.

CASE EXTRACT

R v Collins ex parte Ian Stewart Brady, QBD, [2000] MHLR 17

Facts: Ian Brady – one of the Moors Murderers – went on hunger strike because of ill treatment in prison. He had a personality disorder, but it was unrelated to his hunger strike. He sought a judicial review of the decision of his medical officer to force-feed him. The legal issue fell under section 63: 'the consent of a patient shall not be required for any medical treatment given to him for the mental disorder *from which he is suffering*'.

Held: Maurice Kay J reasoned that the decision of Brady to go on hunger strike was a feature or manifestation of his personality disorder and accordingly his force-feeding had constituted necessary medical treatment for his mental disorder under section 63 of the 1983 Act.

The decision in *Brady* appears to represent a rather wide definition of section 63. Unlike the two cases above, the nature of the refusal of food in *Brady* was wholly different. *KB* and *B* were suffering from mental disorders from which their refusal of food flowed as a 'symptom', whereas Brady's hunger strike was motivated by political reasons. However, it is impossible to prove that Brady's hunger strike did not arise from his personality disorder. Commentators have tried to make sense of this trilogy of cases:

EXTRACT

Sameer Sarkar and Gwen Adshead, 'Treatment over Objection: Minds, Bodies and Beneficence' (2002) *Journal of Mental Health Law* 105, at pages 105–18

An ordinary person who decides to starve themselves to death (for example, a prisoner), or a terminally ill person who is not eating during the final stages of life, cannot be force fed against their will. [...] If, however, food-refusing individuals can be deemed to be suffering from a mental disorder, then they can be force fed, even if they are deemed to be competent. The 'not eating' is understood as a symptom, which is secondary to the mental disorder, and forced feeding is the appropriate treatment for that symptom. This was the case in *B v Croydon Health Authority* where, although B's treatment refusal was deemed to be competent, she could be force fed in the face of her refusal because she was detained for treatment of a mental disorder.

The bottom line is, these cases do not make legal sense. Force-feeding is not treatment for a mental disorder, but because the patients were sectioned under the Mental Health Act 1983 for a mental disorder the courts have felt justified in stating that force-feeding can be administered as treatment against their will because it alleviates a symptom of their mental disorder.

Section 63: other 'treatment' cases

More cases regarding section 63 of the Mental Health Act 1983 have emerged in recent years. These cases do not only involve force-feeding or even the treatment of symptoms of a mental disorder. The following case, for example, involves treatment via a caesarean section for schizophrenia.

CASE EXTRACT

Tameside and Glossop Acute Services NHS Trust v CH (A Patient) [1996] 1 FLR 762

Facts: The patient, who was detained under section 3 of the Mental Health Act 1983, suffered from paranoid schizophrenia and was at times incapable of making a balanced and rational decision about her treatment. Tests carried out at the 38th week of her pregnancy indicated that unless labour was induced very shortly the foetus was likely to die *in utero*. The patient was wavering in her consent to the medical procedures. Her doctor's opinion was that it was in her interests to have a live baby, but the patient was delusional and believed that the medical staff were a threat to her child.

Held: A still-birth would have a deleterious effect on her health, so producing a live child would lead to optimum treatment of her mental state and was therefore linked to the outcome of her psychiatric recovery.

Wall J: At first blush, it might appear difficult to say that performance of a caesarean section is medical treatment for [CH's] mental disorder. There are several strands in the evidence which, in my judgment, bring the proposed treatment within section 63 of the Act. Firstly, if necessary the birth by caesarean section is to prevent a deterioration on [CH's] mental state. Secondly, there is clear evidence of Dr M that in order for the treatment of her schizophrenia to be effective, it is necessary for her to give birth to a live baby. Thirdly, the overall structure of her treatment has been necessarily interrupted by her pregnancy and cannot be resumed until her child is born. It is not, therefore, I think stretching language unduly to say that achievement of a successful outcome of her pregnancy is a necessary part of the overall treatment of her mental disorder. I am therefore satisfied that the treatment of [CH's] pregnancy proposed by Dr G is within the broad interpretation of section 63 of the Mental Health Act approved by the Court of Appeal in *B v Croydon Health Authority*.

What is extraordinary about this judgment is that the Mental Health Act 1983 was combined with what looks like a best interests test. Even though CH was detained under section 3 of the Mental Health Act 1983, she was actually found to be incompetent because she failed to comprehend, believe and weigh the information about her prospective treatment. Once a patient is judged incompetent, she must be treated according to her *best interests* and the forced treatment provision under section 3 of the Mental Health Act 1983 is no longer required. For Wall J to state that the caesarean section was treatment for her mental disorder and came within the definition of medical treatment under section 63 of the 1983 Act was surely a stretch into the realms of fiction – CH's schizophrenia simply confirmed that she was incompetent and so the caesarean was simply in her best interests.

Although the held in *CH* (1996) has not been formally overruled, a very similar case emerged only two years later and the courts showed much more caution when applying section 63.

CASE EXTRACT

St George's Healthcare NHS Trust v S [1998] 3 WLR 936

Facts: At 36 weeks into her pregnancy, S was diagnosed with pre-eclampsia and advised of the risk to her health and that of the unborn child unless she was admitted to hospital for urgent medical treatment. When S rejected that advice, her social worker obtained the consent of two doctors for S's compulsory admission to hospital for assessment under section 2 of the Mental Health Act 1983. The caesarean was performed after a judge dispensed her consent. S appealed against the order dispensing with her consent, and applied for judicial review against the social worker in respect of her detention under section 2, and against the hospital trust in relation to the decision to make the application, the transfers, detention and medical treatment administered.

Held: A competent patient is entitled to refuse medical treatment.

Judge LJ (at pages 950, 957–8): Even when his or her own life depends on receiving medical treatment, an adult of sound mind is entitled to refuse it. This reflects the autonomy of each individual and the right of self-determination. [...] In our judgment, while pregnancy increases the personal responsibilities of a woman it does not diminish her entitlement to decide whether or not to undergo medical treatment. [...] She is entitled not to be forced to submit to an invasion of her body against her will, whether her own life or that of her unborn child depends on it. Her right is not reduced or diminished merely because her decision to exercise it may appear morally repugnant. The declaration in this case involved the removal of the baby from within the body of her mother under physical compulsion. Unless lawfully justified this constituted an infringement of the mother's autonomy. [...] The Act cannot be deployed to achieve the detention of an individual against her will merely because her thinking process is unusual, even apparently bizarre and irrational, and contrary to the views of the overwhelming majority of the community at large.

In the final analysis a woman detained under the Act for mental disorder cannot be forced into medical procedures unconnected with her mental condition unless her capacity to consent to such treatment is diminished.

This decision is much more in line with the normal principles of medical law. A perfectly competent patient can refuse treatment, including a caesarean section. This has nothing to do with the Mental Health Act 1983, which cannot be invoked simply because the patient's views do not accord with the views of society. Even more importantly, a patient detained under the Mental Health Act 1983 cannot be forced into any medical treatment that is in no way connected to his or her mental disorder unless the patient's capacity is diminished (after which it becomes a best interests consideration outside of the Mental Health Act 1983).

A summary of section 63

- A perfectly competent patient can refuse lifesaving treatment as per the normal principles of medical law.
- A refusal of life-saving treatment does not justify the sectioning of somebody under the Mental Health Act 1983.
- The Mental Health Act 1983 cannot be used to administer treatment that is not connected to a mental disorder.
- When a patient becomes incompetent, the Mental Capacity Act 2005 will apply.

A further case on section 63 raised an interesting question: can a patient be treated for a mental disorder that does not form the grounds for his detention (i.e. it was diagnosed *after* his detention for another disorder)? The answer is: 'yes'.

CASE EXTRACT

R (on the application of B) v Ashworth Hospital Authority [2005] 2 AC 278

Facts: B had been convicted of manslaughter and detained under a hospital order under the Mental Health Act 1983. B was classified as suffering from schizophrenia. Eventually, having concluded that B's mental illness was being successfully controlled by medication and after further tests, B was transferred to a ward particularly designed to address traits of personality disorder. The new regime was less agreeable to B than the one he had previously enjoyed. B argued that he should not have been transferred to a ward for patients with psychopathic disorder.

Held: A second disorder can also be treated even though it did not form the grounds for the original detention.

Baroness Hale of Richmond (at pages 290, 292–3): The Act's definition of 'mental disorder' encompasses [...] the broader concepts of 'arrested or incomplete development of mind' and 'any other disorder or disability of mind'. Thus, the natural and ordinary meaning of the words is that the patient may be treated without consent for any mental disorder from which he is suffering, and any treatment ancillary to that. [...] The words of section 63 mean what they say. They authorise a patient to be treated for any mental disorder from which he is suffering, irrespective of whether this falls within the form of disorder from which he is classified as suffering in the application, order or direction justifying his detention. [...] It is not easy to disentangle which features of the patient's presentation stem from a disease of the mind and which stem from his underlying personality traits. The psychiatrist's aim should be to treat the whole patient. [...] Once the State has taken away a person's liberty and detained him in a hospital with a view to medical treatment, the State should be able (some would say obliged) to provide him with the treatment which he needs.

What Baroness Hale has effectively decided in this judgment is that a person can be detained and treated under the Mental Health Act 1983 for one mental disorder, but when another disorder is identified, they can be treated against their will for this one too, even though it did not form the grounds for detention and may not even come under the provisions of the 1983 Act.

Exceptions to section 63?

Section 63 does not apply across the board: there are one or two notable exceptions to section 63 where either consent is required from the patient or there is simply a time limit on how long section 63 can operate.

Exceptions	
Section 57	Brain surgery requires consent
Section 58	Section 63 has a three-month time limit
Section 58A	Electro-convulsive therapy requires consent if competent
Section 62	Treatment under s. 57, s. 58 and s. 58A may be given in an emergency

These exceptions to section 63 are important because they represent a line in the sand which the Mental Health Act 1983 cannot cross. Brain surgery, for example, cannot be performed without consent unless the patient's life is at risk, and this is a very rare occurrence.

Exception 1: section 57

Section 57 states as follows:

Mental Health Act 1983

Section 57: Treatment requiring consent and a second opinion

(1) This section applies to the following forms of medical treatment for mental disorder –

    (a) any surgical operation for destroying brain tissue or for destroying the functioning of brain tissue.

(2) Subject to section 62 below, a patient shall not be given any form of treatment to which this section applies unless he has consented to it and –

    (a) a registered medical practitioner and two other persons appointed by the regulatory authority have certified in writing that the patient is capable of understanding the nature, purpose and likely effects of the treatment in question and has consented to it; and

    (b) the registered medical practitioner referred to in paragraph (a) above has certified in writing that it is appropriate for the treatment to be given.

Brain surgery requires patient consent, the professional opinion of one registered medical practitioner and two further qualified professionals. The registered medical practitioner in subsection (2)(a) has been specifically nominated by the Care Quality Commission to provide his second opinion, and will sometimes be referred to as a SOAD (Second Opinion Appointed Doctor). This is a statutory addition, built in to ensure that treatment plans are reviewed independently. Notice how the SOAD must also consult two further professionals. Section 57 is a very strict provision.

Exception 2: section 58

Section 58 imposes a time limit upon section 63. It states as follows:

> ## Mental Health Act 1983
>
> ### Section 58: Treatment requiring consent or a second opinion
>
> (1) This section applies to the following forms of medical treatment for mental disorder –
>
>   (b) the administration of medicine to a patient by any means (not being a form of treatment under section 57 above or section 58A below) at any time during a period for which he is liable to be detained as a patient if three months or more have elapsed since the first occasion in that period when medicine was administered to him by any means for his mental disorder.
>
> (3) Subject to section 62 below, a patient shall not be given any form of treatment to which this section applies unless:
>
>   (a) he has consented to that treatment and either the approved clinician in charge of it or a registered medical practitioner has certified in writing that the patient is capable of understanding its nature, purpose and likely effects and has consented to it; or
>
>   (b) a registered medical practitioner appointed as aforesaid has certified in writing that the patient is not capable of understanding the nature, purpose and likely effects of that treatment or being so capable has not consented to it but that it is appropriate for the treatment to be given.

Section 58 is interesting. A patient who is receiving treatment does not have to consent for the first three months. Thereafter, several options present themselves under section 58:

Option 1	The patient can consent to the treatment after the first three months.
Option 2	The patient is not able to consent but treatment must still be carried out.
Option 3	The patient is competent and has refused treatment but it must still be carried out.
Option 4	The patient is competent and has refused but treatment no longer needs to be carried out – he is free to go.

Section 58 does not provide as much hope for competent patients as it first appears. Once the first three months of treatment have passed, the patient, if competent, will still be forced to undergo treatment if the registered medical practitioner believes that the treatment should still be given. This provision may be used even if the treatment does not improve the patient's condition (treatment must simply be 'available' – see section 3 of the 1983 Act). There is concern that three months is too long to treat a competent patient without their consent.

EXTRACT

Mental Health Act Commission, Twelfth Biennial Report – Risk, Rights and Recovery, 2005–2007, Care Quality Commission, (no longer available) paragraph 6.29, page 202, see:

http://archive.cqc.org.uk/_db/_documents/pdf%2012th%20biennial%20report.pdf

We are sympathetic to calls for the reduction of the three-month period. Many detained patients will never have their treatment subjected to the scrutiny of a statutory Second Opinion, because they are discharged within three months of treatment commencing. Some such patients may have repeated admissions to hospital which cumulatively amount to long periods of treatment under the Act without this safeguard applying to them. Others who remain in hospital and go on to see a Second Opinion doctor may quite justifiably wonder where that safeguard has been for the initial period of their detention.

Exception 3: section 58A

Section 58A concerns another extreme form of medical treatment: electro-convulsive therapy.

Mental Health Act 1983

Section 58A: Electro-convulsive therapy

(1) This section applies to the following forms of medical treatment for mental disorder –

    (a) electro-convulsive therapy.

(2) Subject to section 62 below, a patient shall not be given any form of treatment to which this section applies unless he falls within subsection (3) or (5) below –

(3) A patient falls within this subsection if –

    (a) has attained the age of 18 years;

    (b) has consented to the treatment in question; and

    (c) either the approved clinician in charge of it or a registered medical practitioner has certified in writing that the patient is capable of understanding the nature, purpose and likely effects of the treatment and has consented to it.

(5) A patient falls within this subsection if a registered medical practitioner or the approved clinician in charge of the treatment in question has certified in writing –

    (a) that the patient is not capable of understanding the nature, purpose and likely effects of the treatment; but

    (b) that it is appropriate for the treatment to be given; and

    (c) that giving him the treatment would not conflict with –

        (i) an advance decision which the registered medical practitioner concerned is satisfied is valid and applicable; or

        (ii) a decision made by a donee or deputy or by the Court of Protection.

Section 58A requires the consent of a patient unless he is incompetent, in which case a registered medical practitioner can state that treatment is still appropriate and he must confirm that there is not an advance directive from the patient refusing treatment. In contrast to section 58, a competent patient under section 58A can refuse electro-convulsive therapy (consent is clearly required if the patient understands the nature and purpose of the procedure). It is a concern, however, that electro-convulsive treatment can be given to an incompetent patient without considering his best interests under subsection (5). The test is simply whether the treatment would be 'appropriate'.

Who is the 'SOAD'?

The doctor appointed by the Care Quality Commission to give a second opinion (Second Opinion Appointed Doctor) is a safeguard for mentally ill patients – he protects their interests and provides an objective review of their treatment plan once the three-month time limit under section 63 has expired (see s. 58). This is especially vital for competent patients, because they may be vehemently opposed to their treatment plan. Traditionally, a SOAD will 'rubber stamp' treatment plans laid down by the patient's doctor, but case law has since decided that his role entails much more than this. He is independent and must give reasons for his decisions:

CASE EXTRACT

R (on the application of Wilkinson) v Broadmoor Special Hospital Authority [2001] EWCA Civ 1545

Simon Brown LJ (at para 33): Whilst, of course, it is proper for the SOAD to pay regard to the views of the [responsible medical officer] who has, after all, the most intimate knowledge of the patient's case, that does not relieve him of the responsibility of forming his own independent judgment as to whether or not 'the treatment should be given'. And certainly, if the SOAD's certificate and evidence is to carry any real weight in cases where, as here, the treatment plan is challenged, it will be necessary to demonstrate a less deferential approach than appears to be the norm.

Hale LJ (at para 71): The more difficult question is whether it is enough that the relevant pieces of paper are signed. In my view that cannot possibly be enough. I agree with both Simon Brown and Brooke LJJ that the SOAD has to form his own independent opinion upon the existence of the statutory criteria. At the very least, he must act in good faith and with reasonable care in forming his judgment.

CASE EXTRACT

R (on the application of Wooder) v Feggetter [2002] ACD 94

Brooke LJ (at paras 15, 19): The law will not require a SOAD to dot every i and cross every t when giving reasons for his opinion. So long as he gives his reasons clearly on what he reasonably regards as the substantive points on which he formed his clinical judgment, this will suffice. [...] The court granted a declaration that fairness demands that a SOAD should give in writing the reasons for his opinion when certifying under section 58 of the Mental Health Act 1983 that a detained patient should be given medication against his will, and that these reasons should be disclosed to the patient unless the SOAD or the RMO considers that such disclosure would be likely to cause serious harm to the physical or mental health of the patient or any other person.

Exception 4: section 62

So far, we have learnt that: brain surgery cannot be conducted without consent, there is a three-month time limit on section 63, and electro-convulsive therapy cannot be provided unless the patient consents or a registered medical practitioner agrees to it. The final exception is section 62. You may have noticed above that sections 57, 58 and 58A all contain the phrase 'subject to section 62 below'. The provisions in sections 57, 58 and 58A can be overridden by section 62, but this can only happen if a situation of urgency presents itself:

Mental Health Act 1983

Section 62: Urgent treatment

(1)   Sections 57 and 58 above shall not apply to any treatment –

    (a) which is immediately necessary to save the patient's life; or

    (b) which (not being irreversible) is immediately necessary to prevent a serious deterioration of his condition; or

    (c) which (not being irreversible or hazardous) is immediately necessary to alleviate serious suffering by the patient; or

    (d) which (not being irreversible or hazardous) is immediately necessary and represents the minimum interference necessary to prevent the patient from behaving violently or being a danger to himself or to others.

(1A) Section 58A above, in so far as it relates to electro-convulsive therapy, shall not apply to any treatment which falls within paragraph (a) or (b) of subsection (1) above.

Section 62 allows for brain surgery (s. 57), all other medical treatment (s. 58) and electro-convulsive therapy (s. 58A) to be given when criteria (a) to (d) above are satisfied (although note at subsection (1A) that electro-convulsive therapy is exempt from criteria (a) and (b)). In reality, it is very rare for brain surgery and electro-convulsive therapy to be given without consent under this 'urgent' provision.

THINKING POINT

Should patients with eating disorders be treated as mentally ill? What treatment do you think is appropriate for them and is the law getting it right at the moment? Give reasons for your answer.

●●● Mental health and human rights

When the Human Rights Act 1998 was passed into UK law, the Mental Health Act 1983 was faced with a dilemma. Was it a breach of human rights to detain a competent person and forcibly treat them without their consent?

The article that has seen the most activity in mental health law is Article 3. This article is directly applicable to the forced detention and treatment that occurs in the mental health system. However, other articles have been brought before the courts too and commentators note the progress in this area of law so far.

EXTRACT

Jill Stavert, 'Mental Health, Community Care and Human Rights in Europe: Still an Incomplete Picture?' (2007) *Journal of Mental Health Law* 182

Over the last two decades we have come some way in Europe towards recognising that those suffering from mental illness require enforceable rights so that they are not subjected to abuse and neglect. These rights are, however, mainly civil rights which are applicable to the patient-institution relationship. If care takes place outside institutions, a far greater emphasis on socio-economic rights is required.

Article 2: the right to life

Sometimes, a mentally ill patient may be at risk of committing suicide. If this is the case, must a hospital trust, which detains the patient under the Mental Health Act 1983, do all it can to protect the patient from committing suicide? If the patient manages to escape and commit suicide, has the hospital trust breached its obligation under Article 2 to protect this patient's life?

CASE EXTRACT

***Savage v South Essex Partnership NHS Foundation Trust* [2009] 1 AC 681**

Facts: A mental patient with a long history of mental illness was detained for treatment for paranoid schizophrenia under section 3 of the Mental Health Act 1983 on an open acute psychiatric ward in an NHS hospital. After several attempts to leave she succeeded in absconding from the hospital and committed suicide. Her daughter brought an action against the NHS Trust responsible for the hospital for breach of the deceased's right to life under Article 2 of the Convention.

Held: There is an obligation to protect the life of a suicidal patient.

Lord Roger of Earlsferry (at pages 704, 709): Plainly, patients who have been detained because their health or safety demands that they should receive treatment in the hospital, are vulnerable. [...] They are vulnerable to exploitation, abuse, bullying and all the other potential dangers of a closed institution. [...] The hospital authorities are accordingly responsible for the health and wellbeing of their detained patients. Their obligations under Article 2 include an obligation to protect those patients from self-harm and suicide. [...] When deciding on the most appropriate treatment and therapeutic environment for detained patients, medical staff would have to take proper account of the risk of suicide. [...] Those who presented a greater risk would need to be supervised to an appropriate extent, while those presenting the highest risk would have to be supervised in a locked ward. [...] Finally, Article 2 imposes a further 'operational' obligation on health authorities and their hospital staff. [...] The operational obligation arises only if members of staff know or ought to know that a particular patient presents a 'real and immediate' risk of suicide. In these circumstances Article 2 requires them to do all that can reasonably be expected to prevent the patient from committing suicide. If they fail to do this, not only will they and the health authorities be liable in negligence, but there will also be a violation of the operational obligation under Article 2 to protect the patient's life.

This decision is clear. If a patient detained under the Mental Health Act 1983 presents a 'real and immediate' risk of suicide, then the hospital staff have an additional obligation under Article 2 to do all that they can to protect that patient's life.

Article 3: the right to protection from torture, inhuman or degrading treatment

Patients detained under the Mental Health Act 1983 have argued that forced detention and treatment constitutes torture, inhuman and degrading treatment. This is an absolute right without qualification, meaning that there are no 'exceptions' to justify a breach of Article 3. The case law has shown that the courts have applied Article 3 rather leniently.

CASE EXTRACT

Herczegfalvy v Austria (A/242-B) (1993) 15 EHRR 437

Facts: H was a convicted criminal who was transferred to a mental hospital for 'deranged offenders'. Amongst other issues, the applicant complained that the lawfulness of his arrest did not conform with conditions of his detention and amounted to inhuman or degrading treatment contrary to Article 3.

Held: A measure which is therapeutic and necessary does not breach Article 3.

European Court (at paras 81–2): In the Government's opinion, the measures were essentially the consequence of the applicant's behaviour, as he had refused medical treatment which was urgent in view of the deterioration in his physical and mental health. [...] It proved to be necessary to feed him artificially, in view of his extremely weak state caused by his refusal to take any food. [...] Similarly, it was only his resistance to all treatment, his extreme aggressiveness and the threats and acts of violence on his part against the hospital staff which explained why the staff had used coercive measures including the intramuscular injection of sedatives and the use of handcuffs and the security bed. [...] Their sole aim had always been therapeutic, and they had been terminated as soon as the state of the patient permitted this. [...] The Court considers that the position of inferiority and powerlessness which is typical of patients confined in psychiatric hospitals calls for increased vigilance in reviewing whether the Convention has been complied with. While it is for the medical authorities to decide, on the basis of the recognised rules of medical science, on the therapeutic methods to be used, if necessary by force, to preserve the physical and mental health of patients who are entirely incapable of deciding for themselves and for whom they are therefore responsible, such patients nevertheless remain under the protection of Article 3, the requirements of which permit of no derogation. The established principles of medicine are admittedly in principle decisive in such cases; as a general rule, a measure which is a therapeutic necessity cannot be regarded as inhuman or degrading. The Court must nevertheless satisfy itself that the medical necessity has been convincingly shown to exist.

Prior to the *Herczegfalvy* case, there was no established exception to Article 3. With this in mind, it is a cause for concern that the European Court of Human Rights can announce that necessary therapeutic measures cannot be regarded as inhuman or degrading. Is this the birth of a new common law exception to Article 3? This new exception could have a profound effect on mental healthcare.

Nearly a decade later, the *Herczegfalvy* case was applied to a competent patient. The 'convincing medical necessity' test was held to be just as applicable to competent patients.

CASE EXTRACT

R (on the application of Wilkinson) v *Broadmoor Hospital Authority* [2001] EWCA Civ 1545

Facts: The defendant was a convicted criminal and was detained at Broadmoor for many years. He was assessed and was found to require anti-psychotic medication. Under section 63 of the Mental Health Act 1983 his consent was not required for the first three months. Thereafter, the defendant refused consent. His responsible medical officer said that under section 62 the treatment can be provided urgently if the defendant was not competent. The injections were forced upon the defendant and he sought a judicial review, claiming Article 3 had been breached.

Held: If any inhuman or degrading treatment is 'convincingly shown' to be medically necessary, it will not breach Article 3, regardless of whether the patient is competent or not.

Simon Brown LJ (at para 30): If in truth this claimant has the capacity to refuse consent to the treatment proposed here, it is difficult to suppose that he should nevertheless be forcibly subjected to it. [...] Even, moreover, if the claimant is incompetent, the court will need to be satisfied, in the language of the European Court of Human Rights in *Herczegfalvy*'s case, 'that the medical necessity has been convincingly shown to exist . . .' according to the psychiatric principles generally accepted at the time.

Hale LJ (at paras 79–80): One can at least conclude from this that forcible measures inflicted upon an incapacitated patient which are *not* a medical necessity may indeed be inhuman or degrading. The same must apply to forcible measures inflicted upon a capacitated patient. [...] I do not take the view that detained patients who have the capacity to decide for themselves can never be treated against their will.

Whilst Simon Brown LJ referred to the 'convincing medical necessity' test in relation to incompetent patients, Hale LJ took this further and said that the same principles apply to patients with capacity. In practice, therefore, if any inhuman or degrading treatment is 'convincingly shown' to be medically necessary, it will not breach Article 3, regardless of whether the patient is competent or not.

The phrase 'convincingly shown' – which was used in both *Herczegfalvy* and *Broadmoor* – was under dispute in the next case.

CASE EXTRACT

R (on the application of N) v *M* [2002] EWCA Civ 1789

Facts: M, the responsible medical officer, presented N with a treatment plan which included administering the medication by injection for the prevention or alleviation of her psychiatric illness. N did not consent to that treatment. The SOAD stated that N was suffering from paranoid psychosis or severe personality disorder and required anti-psychotic drugs. N contended that she was suffering from an untreatable personality disorder and that an independent opinion contended that the proposed treatment was not in her best interests. It had not, therefore, been 'convincingly shown' to be necessary.

Held: The patient was unsuccessful.

Dyson J (at para 16): The [trial] judge was right to say that he had to be satisfied that the proposed treatment was both in the claimant's best interests and 'medically necessary' as that phrase should be understood and applied for the purposes of Article 3 of the Convention.

In the light of the [*Herczegfalvy*] decision, it is common ground that the standard of proof required is that the court should be satisfied that medical necessity has been 'convincingly' shown. There is but a single question: has the proposed treatment been convincingly shown to be medically necessary? The answer to that question will depend on a number of factors, including (a) how certain is it that the patient does suffer from a treatable mental disorder, (b) how serious a disorder is it, (c) how serious a risk is presented to others, (d) how likely is it that, if the patient does suffer from such a disorder, the proposed treatment will alleviate the condition, (e) how much alleviation is there likely to be, (f) how likely is it that the treatment will have adverse consequences for the patient and (g) how severe may they be? N's submission on analysis involves the proposition that, in a case where there is a responsible body of opinion that a patient is not suffering from a treatable condition, then it *cannot* be convincingly shown that the treatment proposed is medically necessary. We reject this submission. It is too well known to require stating that a professional person is not guilty of negligence if he has acted in accordance with a practice accepted as proper by a responsible body of persons who practise the same art, merely because there is a body of opinion who would take a contrary view.

Dyson J added to the 'convincing medical necessity' test in *Herczegfalvy* considerably. In addition to the new (a)–(g) criteria, Dyson J announced that even if a patient can show through an independent opinion that her medical treatment is not necessary, this does not mean that she has 'convincingly shown' it to be the case. In fact, it appears that an independent opinion has no influence on the 'convincing' element of the test at all. The exception under Article 3 is considerably difficult for mentally ill patients to overturn. This is completely unfair considering there should not be any exceptions to Article 3 at all.

Most recently, it was established that even if a patient's treatment was a medical necessity, it did not have to work.

CASE EXTRACT

R (on the application of B) v Haddock (Responsible Medical Officer) [2006] HR LR 40

Facts: B had been detained in a high security hospital under the 1983 Act. He had been classified as suffering from a psychopathic disorder. H, who was B's responsible medical officer, considered that B required anti-psychotic medication. This was forcibly administered. Subsequent reports from a psychiatrist and a psychologist maintained that B was not suffering from any mental illness or mental disorder, and that the treatment was not necessary. B then lodged the claim for judicial review, submitting that the test of 'medical necessity' derived from *Herczegfalvy* required H to establish convincingly that he suffered from a particular form of mental disorder, that the treatment proposed was for that condition, and that he would benefit from the treatment.

Held: The treatment does not *have* to work, but it must be likely to work.

Auld LJ (at paras 12, 41–2): The section 58(3) power to treat a patient capable of consent against his will or a patient incapable of consent is potentially a violation of his Article 3 right not to be subjected to degrading treatment. [...] However, it is common ground that, while the risk of infringement of those rights may be greater when the patient is capable of giving or refusing consent, it is not necessarily an infringement to treat him against his will where such treatment can be convincingly shown to be medically or therapeutically necessary. [...] The clinical reality for psychiatrists is that the precise forms of mental disorder are not always readily diagnosable one from the other; there is overlap and there is often co-morbidity. [...] And, as to whether the treatment will do any good, it is unreal to require psychiatrists, under the umbrella of a requirement of medical or therapeutic necessity, to demonstrate sureness or near sureness of success. [...] Accordingly I do not consider that the requirement on a court to be convinced, in this context, of medical necessity in the light of the medical evidence and other evidence, is capable of being expressed in terms of a standard of evidential proof. It is rather a value judgment as to the future – a forecast – to be made by a court in reliance on medical evidence according to a standard of persuasion. If it is to be expressed in forensic terms at all, it is doubtful whether it amounts to more than satisfaction of medical necessity on a balance of probabilities, or as a 'likelihood' of therapeutic benefit.

In light of *Haddock*, there is now a much lower burden of proof when applying the 'convincing medical necessity' test: as long as the suggested treatment is 'likely' to show a therapeutic benefit, it is medically necessary. To put it another way, the test could now be called the 'likely medical necessity' test. Clearly, the exception to Article 3 is becoming wider. Article 3 contains a fundamental human right, but in order for hospital trusts to justify inhuman and degrading treatment, they simply have to show that the necessary medical treatment is *likely* to show a benefit, not definitely or probably. Can treatment even be described as 'necessary' if it is only 'likely' to work?

EXTRACT

Peter Bartlett, 'A Matter of Necessity? Enforced Treatment under the Mental Health Act' (2007) 15 *Medical Law Review* 86, at pages 86–98

This is an odd argument from a human rights standpoint, as it suggests that the fact that an area is fraught with uncertainty is a justification for restricting human rights protection within that area. If we are serious that treatment without consent constitutes an 'invasion', to use Auld LJ's word, it would instead seem that enforced interventions in such uncertain circumstances ought to be approached with particular caution. If we accept that enforced treatment is a constitutional question, it is far from clear that the State is more justified in restricting an individual's rights in cases where the knowledge base of the intervention is so fluid. [...] The outcome of the *Haddock* case would appear to be that any rights under Articles 3 or 8 of the ECHR to be free from involuntary treatment are to be subject to the professional practice of the psychiatric profession: that is not to be subject to significant scrutiny.

Article 5: the right to liberty and security of person

Article 5 provides that everyone has a right to liberty and security of the person. However, there is a well-known exception to Article 5 allowing for 'persons of unsound mind' to be deprived of their liberty. In practical terms, this exception supports the detention of mentally ill patients simply because they are mentally ill. Article 5 does not, for example, state that persons of unsound mind must be treated whilst detained. The subsequent case law has had to fill in these gaps. According to the Mental Health Act 1983 Code of Practice, detention must be a final resort.[10] Back in 1979, a case was brought under Article 5 that signalled the first real development of the Article in relation to the detention of mentally ill patients.

CASE EXTRACT

Winterwerp v The Netherlands (1979) 2 EHRR 387

Facts: The applicant, who had been compulsorily detained under the relevant Netherlands legislation dealing with mentally ill persons, complained that Article 5 of the European Convention on Human Rights had been violated. He had been detained by court orders renewed periodically, but had not been notified that the proceedings were in progress or allowed to appear or be represented. On several occasions, his requests for release were not forwarded to the court by the public prosecutor. As a result of his detention, the applicant automatically lost the capacity to administer his property.

European Court (at pages 403, 409): In the Court's opinion, except in emergency cases, the individual concerned should not be deprived of his liberty unless he has been reliably shown to be of 'unsound mind'. The very nature of what has to be established before the competent national authority – that is, a true mental disorder – calls for objective medical expertise. Further, the mental disorder must be of a kind or degree warranting compulsory confinement. What is more, the validity of continued confinement depends upon the persistence of such a disorder. [...] It is essential that the person concerned should have access to a court and the opportunity to be heard either in person or, where necessary, through some form of representation, failing which he will not have been afforded 'the fundamental guarantees of procedure applied in matters of deprivation of liberty'. Mental illness may entail restricting or modifying the manner of exercise of such a right, but it cannot justify impairing the very essence of the right.

The European Court held that in order to detain a person of unsound mind, a person must have a true mental disorder and a kind or degree of disorder that warrants detention. This was an important development for Article 5 – the phrase 'unsound mind' took on a more medical meaning. Although Mr Winterwerp was found to be detained lawfully under Article 5 because he had an unsound mind according to the relevant mental health legislation in the Netherlands, he was not given the appropriate opportunities to exercise his right to be heard. This is a safeguard under Article 5 which applies to all detainees.

Article 5 safeguard (4)

Everyone who is deprived of his liberty by arrest or detention shall be entitled to take proceedings by which the lawfulness of his detention shall be decided speedily by a court and his release ordered if the detention is not lawful.

This safeguard is important as it ensures that a patient (or any individual) is not detained needlessly and without justification. A handful of UK cases have confirmed that this safeguard under Article 5 must be executed effectively and speedily.

---

[10] Department of Health, Mental Health Act 1983, Code of Practice, (2008), (archived), paragraph 4.4. See: http://webarchive.nationalarchives.gov.uk/20130107105354/http://www.dh.gov.uk/en/Publicationsandstatistics/Publications/PublicationsPolicyAndGuidance/DH_084597.

CASE EXTRACT	*R (on the application of C) v Mental Health Review Tribunal* [2002] 1 WLR 176

Facts: C, who suffered from schizophrenia and had been detained in hospital under section 3 of the Mental Health Act 1983. He requested a judicial review of the practice of the Mental Health Appeal Tribunal of listing hearings of applications for discharge eight weeks after the application had been made. C submitted that the practice was both arbitrary and did not satisfy the Human Rights Act 1998 Schedule 1 Part I Article 5(4) which specified that the lawfulness of a detention should be determined 'speedily'.

Held: He was successful.

Lord Phillips MR (at pages 187–8): Miss Lieven [lawyer] submitted that it would be impossible to arrange dates at shorter notice, having regard to the fact that members of the Tribunal [...] would have to identify periods of common availability within crowded diaries. I am not prepared to accept this without cogent evidence. [...] My conclusion is that the practice of fixing hearing dates eight weeks after the date of application is bred of administrative convenience, not of administrative necessity. There is nothing inconsistent with Article 5(4) of the ECHR in having a target date of eight weeks maximum. The circumstances of some cases may well require eight weeks' preparation for the hearing. In such cases an eight week period will not conflict with the requirement of Article 5(4) that the decision on the application must be obtained speedily. [...] I do not consider lawful a practice which makes no effort to see that the individual application is heard as soon as reasonably practicable, having regard to the relevant circumstances of the case.

CASE EXTRACT	*Hutchison Reid v United Kingdom* (2003) 37 EHRR 9

Facts: H, a Scottish mental patient, complained that his continued detention in a mental hospital constituted a breach of his rights under the European Convention on Human Rights 1950 Article 5(1) and that the procedures which had been adopted for effecting a review of that detention violated Article 5(4).

Held: A person does not have to be receiving treatment to be detained under Article 5.

Judge Ress (at para 5): For the purposes of Article 5(1)(e), an individual cannot be deprived of his liberty as being of 'unsound mind' unless the following three minimum conditions are satisfied: first, he must reliably be shown to be of unsound mind; secondly, the mental disorder must be of a kind or degree warranting compulsory confinement; thirdly, the validity of continued confinement depends upon the persistence of such a disorder.

Detention in a mental hospital was conditional on the illness or condition being of a nature or degree amenable to medical treatment. There is no such requirement imposed by Article 5(1)(e) of the Convention. The Court's case law refers rather to the applicant being properly established as suffering from a mental disorder of a degree warranting compulsory confinement. Such confinement may be necessary not only where a person needs therapy, medication or other clinical treatment to cure or alleviate his condition, but also where the person needs control and supervision to prevent him, for example, causing harm to himself or other persons.

An entitlement to a review arises both at the time of the initial deprivation of liberty and, where new issues of lawfulness are capable of arising, periodically thereafter. In the review procedure, the competent courts are required to reach their decisions 'speedily'. The question of whether periods comply with the requirement must – as with the reasonable time stipulation in Article 5(3) – be determined in the light of the circumstances of each case.

In *Mental Health Review Tribunal* Lord Phillips supported the term 'speedily'. In *Hutchison*, Judge Ress confirmed that a person's detention under Article 5 was *not* conditional on him receiving treatment – Article 5 says no such thing – the patient must simply be suffering from a mental disorder that requires confinement. You may notice that preventative detention is listed by Judge Ress as one of the additional instances in which a patient can be detained under Article 5, i.e. to prevent harm to others. To ensure that the exception to Article 5 does not become too unfair to patients, other cases have developed Article 5 to ensure that patients are eligible for release if community care can be offered.

CASE EXTRACT

R (on the application of H) v Secretary of State for the Home Department [2003] UKHL 59

Facts: H, a restricted patient, contended that his detention during a two-year period had been unlawful and had violated his human rights under the Human Rights Act 1998 Article 5 because of a series of delays and the fact that psychiatrists had not provided supervision for him.

Held: Just because Article 5 mentions nothing about conditional releases, does not mean they cannot be tried.

Lord Bingham (at para 26): What Article 5(1)(e) and (4) require is that a person of unsound mind compulsorily detained in hospital should have access to a court with power to decide whether the detention is lawful and, if not, to order his release. [...] Nothing in Article 5 suggests that discharge subject to conditions is impermissible in principle, and nothing in the Convention jurisprudence suggests that the power to discharge conditionally (whether there are specific conditions or a mere liability to recall), properly used, should be viewed with disfavour. Indeed, the conditional discharge regime, properly used, is of great benefit to patients and the public, and conducive to the Convention object of restricting the curtailment of personal liberty to the maximum, because it enables tribunals to ensure that restricted patients compulsorily detained in hospital represent the hard core of those who suffer from mental illness, are a risk to themselves or others and cannot be effectively treated and supervised otherwise than in hospital. If there is any possibility of treating and supervising a patient in the community, the imposition of conditions permits that possibility to be explored and, it may be, tried.

Lord Bingham acknowledges that Article 5 includes nothing about conditional releases, but he supports them because they limit the need to deprive an individual of his liberty.

Article 8: the right to respect of private life the right to respect of family life

There are exceptions to Article 8, including the 'protection of health'. It follows from this, that if a patient is found to be receiving treatment that is deemed to be 'medically necessary' and it is 'likely' to show a therapeutic benefit, it will not be a breach of Article 8.

CASE EXTRACT

R (on the application of PS) v G (Responsible Medical Officer) [2003] EWHC 2335

Facts: PS was detained under the Mental Health Act 1983 upon his conviction for the manslaughter of his mother and son. PS was vulnerable to a recurrence of depression. G, the responsible medical officer, considered that the proposed treatment was justified and should be given. W, the SOAD, certified under section 58 that the treatment should be administered. PS had the capacity to make decisions and he did not wish to have the proposed treatment. He applied for judicial review of a decision to administer treatment by way of anti-psychotic medication to him without his consent. Additionally, the administration of the treatment would infringe his rights under Article 8.

Held: There must be a balance of interests when Article 8 is involved.

Silber J (at paras 133–4): The defendants contend that any breach of Article 8(1) is justifiable under Article 8(2) in this case because the proposed treatment was 'in accordance with the law and is necessary in a democratic society . . . for the protection of health'. [...] This approach is logical because inherent in the interpretation of the Convention is its aim to strike a 'fair balance between the demands of the general interest of the community and the requirements of the protection of the individual's fundamental rights'. Any restriction on a guaranteed freedom, such as that set out in Article 8(1) of the Convention, must be proportionate to the legitimate aim pursued. [...]

I agree that without the medication, PS will continue to pose a danger to others if he is outside a hospital, especially he is in a stressful situation. Thus I conclude that the administration of the proposed medication 'is necessary in a democratic society for the protection of health'.

This judgment clearly states that a breach of Article 8 can be justified if a balance is struck. Currently, if a patient is detained and treated under the Mental Health Act 1983, he can be forcibly treated under section 63 for the first three months, and then forcibly treated under section 58(3)(b) if a registered medical practitioner believes it is appropriate for the treatment to continue. The *PS* case confirms that this will not constitute a breach of Article 8 because the medical treatment will be deemed a 'fair balance' between the interests of the community and the 'individual's fundamental rights', and the treatment is in proportion to its aim (which is to rehabilitate the patient).

RESEARCH ACTIVITY

In light of the decisions in *Herczegfalvy v Austria, R (on the application of Wilkinson) v Broadmoor Hospital, R (on the application of N) v M* and *R (on the application of B) v Haddock (Responsible Medical Officer)*, do you believe that the forced detention and treatment of mentally ill patients – both competent and incompetent – is 'inhuman and degrading'? Give reasons for your answer.

● ● ● Releasing patients from detention and treatment

So far, we have investigated the legal grounds upon which a person with a mental disorder can be detained for assessment, treated without consent, and the human rights which will serve to protect him from inhuman and degrading treatment and a deprivation of liberty. It is now time to turn our attention to the legal rules governing the release of mentally ill patients.

● The current law

It was explained in detail above that a patient can only be detained under section 3 of the Mental Health Act 1983 if appropriate medical treatment is available to him. It follows that if no treatment is available to the patient, he is being unlawfully detained under section 3 of the 1983 Act and he must be released. Cases brought under Article 5 have confirmed that if a patient is being deprived of his liberty he must have a mental disorder of a kind or degree that warrants detention, and his disorder must persist. The *Winterwerp* case discussed Article 5 and the instances in which a mentally ill person (or a person of 'unsound mind') could be released.

CASE EXTRACT	*Winterwerp* v *The Netherlands* (1979) 2 EHRR 387 at paragraph 39
	In the Court's opinion, except in emergency cases, the individual concerned should not be deprived of his liberty unless he has been reliably shown to be of 'unsound mind'. The very nature of what has to be established before the competent national authority – that is, a true mental disorder – calls for objective medical expertise. Further, the mental disorder must be of a kind or degree warranting compulsory confinement. What is more, the validity of continued confinement depends upon the persistence of such a disorder.

The *Winterwerp* case confirms that a patient's mental disorder must *persist* in order to justify his deprivation of liberty. In *Hutchison*, Judge Ress confirmed that a person may be detained under article 5 for the purpose of protecting others (preventative detention), but the patient must still have a mental disorder at the material time.

CASE EXTRACT	*Hutchison Reid* v *United Kingdom* (2003) 37 EHRR 9 at paragraph 51
	Judge Rees: The Court's case law refers rather to the applicant being properly established as suffering from a mental disorder of a degree warranting compulsory confinement. Such confinement may be necessary not only where a person needs therapy, medication or other clinical treatment to cure or alleviate his condition, but also where the person needs control and supervision to prevent him, for example, causing harm to himself or other persons.

It can be taken from these two European Court of Human Rights cases and section 3 of the Mental Health Act 1983 that as soon as a mentally ill patient no longer has a mental disorder, his deprivation of liberty is unjustified and he must be released.

The process of review

If hospital trusts are to ensure that they are detaining and treating mentally ill patients within the law (both domestic and European law) then each patient must be continuously reviewed to establish how their condition is progressing. Some patients may not be responding to treatment, but according to section 3 of the Mental Health Act 1983 this does not matter – as long as treatment is 'available' to him he can be detained for treatment.

Time limits

Under section 2 of the Mental Health Act 1983, a patient can only be detained for assessment for 28 days. Thereafter, if he is not detained under section 3, he will be released. Under section 3 of the Mental Health Act 1983, a patient can be detained for treatment for six months (this is confirmed under section 20(1)). The order for detention and treatment can be renewed under section 20(2) for another six months, and then annually after that for an indefinite amount of time.

Hospital manager duty to review

When a patient is detained under section 3, the hospital manager in charge of that patient must bring the patient's case to a Mental Health Review Tribunal within six months and then three years (if the patient has not done so already).

Mental Health Act 1983

Section 68: Duty of managers of hospitals to refer cases to tribunal

(1) This section applies in respect of the following patients –

   (b) a patient who is admitted to a hospital in pursuance of an application for admission for treatment.

(2) On expiry of the period of six months beginning with the applicable day, the managers of the hospital shall refer the patient's case to the appropriate tribunal.

(6) The managers of the hospital shall also refer the patient's case to the appropriate tribunal if a period of more than three years has elapsed since his case was last considered by such a tribunal, whether on his own or otherwise.

A patient's right to review

A patient is entitled to review his or her detention under sections 2 and 3 of the Mental Health Act 1983.

The Mental Health Act 1983 (review of section 2 detention)

Section 66(1)(a)(i): Where a patient is admitted to a hospital in pursuance of an application for admission for assessment, an application may be made to the appropriate tribunal within the relevant period by the patient.

Section 66(2)(a): In subsection (1) above 'the relevant period' means 14 days beginning with the day on which the patient is admitted as so mentioned.

The Mental Health Act 1983 (review of section 3 detention)

Section 66(1)(b)(i): Where a patient is admitted to a hospital in pursuance of an application for admission for treatment, an application may be made to the appropriate tribunal within the relevant period by the patient.

Section 66(2)(b): In subsection (1) above 'the relevant period' means six months beginning with the day on which the patient is admitted as so mentioned.

It is important that a patient can exercise this right to review, because competent patients especially can be detained, assessed and treated against their wishes under the Mental Health Act 1983 and they might strongly oppose their treatment plan. Incompetent patients may not find it so easy to exercise this right. In *R (on the application of H) v Secretary of State for Health* [2005] UKHL 60, the House of Lords decided that Article 5(4) of the European Convention on Human Rights allows for individuals to 'take proceedings' but this is not the same as an obligation to promptly place every patient before a court. The House of Lords simply noted that hospital managers have to do (and already do) the best they can to make the patient's rights practical and effective and that it was up to the patient to put the matter before a court or tribunal.

Who are the Mental Health Review Tribunal (MHRT)?

The Mental Health Tribunals Service is an independent judicial body. Each Mental Health Review Tribunal contains one legal, one medical and one lay member. The judges on each panel are chosen by the Lord Chancellor and the other tribunal members are chosen by the Secretary of State for Health.[11]

EXTRACT

Department of Health, Mental Health Act 1983, Code of Practice (2008) (archived):

http://webarchive.nationalarchives.gov.uk/20130107105354/
http://www.dh.gov.uk/en/Publicationsandstatistics/Publications/
PublicationsPolicyAndGuidance/DH_084597

Paragraph 32.2: The Tribunal is an independent judicial body. Its main purpose is to review the cases of detained, conditionally discharged, and supervised community treatment (SCT) patients under the Act and to direct the discharge of any patients where it thinks it appropriate.

The tribunal judge chairs (controls) the tribunal. He is responsible for making sure that the law (i.e. the Mental Health Act 1983) is followed correctly. He draughts the tribunal decision and signs the record. The medical tribunal member must examine the patient before the hearing to help him decide whether the patient should still be detained. He is usually an experienced psychiatrist. This member provides balance to the tribunal as a representative of the community who is neither legal or medical. Most third tribunal members will have a background in health and welfare, e.g. experience working for the NHS.

---

[11] The Mental Health Tribunals Service has its own website: www.mhrt.org.uk.

The grounds for discharge

The Mental Health Review Tribunal must discharge a patient if certain criteria are not proved to exist by the persons detaining the patient.

Mental Health Act 1983

Section 72: Powers of tribunals

(a) the tribunal shall direct the discharge of a patient liable to be detained under section 2 above if it is not satisfied –

   (i)   that he is then suffering from mental disorder or from mental disorder of a nature or degree which warrants his detention in a hospital for assessment (or for assessment followed by medical treatment) for at least a limited period; or

   (ii) that his detention as aforesaid is justified in the interests of his own health or safety or with a view to the protection of other persons; (b) the tribunal shall direct the discharge of a patient liable to be detained otherwise than under section 2 above if it is not satisfied –

      (i)   that he is then suffering from mental disorder or from mental disorder of a nature or degree which makes it appropriate for him to be liable to be detained in a hospital for medical treatment; or (ii) that it is necessary for the health of safety of the patient or for the protection of other persons that he should receive such treatment; or

      (iia) that appropriate medical treatment is available for him.

Section 72(a) refers to detention for assessment under section 2, whereas section 72(b) refers to detention for treatment under section 3. The emphasis is upon the shoulders of those who wish to detain the patient to prove that the patient must still be detained. If they cannot prove their case, the MHRT will discharge the patient. The patient does not have to prove anything. An important phrase within section 72 is 'nature or degree'. If a patient is suffering from a mental disorder which, by its very nature or degree, warrants detention in hospital, then the detention will continue. 'Nature' and 'degree' do not have to be proved in conjunction with each other – it can be one or the other. It follows that a patient can be detained because the 'nature' of her illness is serious, even though the 'degree' of her illness may not require detention at that exact moment.

Even though section 72 provides a safeguard for patients detained against their will, the tribunal process itself has not been short of criticism. The tribunal will examine whether the patient satisfies all the criteria for detention under the 1983 Act, but it does not examine whether the patient's detention in lawful or unlawful. The emphasis, therefore, is on the patient's medical condition at the time of the hearing and not the lawfulness of her detention.

CASE EXTRACT

R (on the application of Care Principles Limited) v Mental Health Review Tribunal [2006] EWHC 3194

Facts: X, who had a mild form of learning disability, was detained in hospital under section 2 of the 1983 Act for assessment owing to his behaviour, which included significant threats to social workers. X appealed to a Mental Health Review Tribunal, which decided that he should be discharged but that, as he needed a comprehensive support package, discharge should be delayed by three days. The social workers were concerned that full information had not been put before the tribunal and Care Ltd took the view that the tribunal's decision was flawed, and they lodged an application for judicial review.

Held: There must be an error in law for the court to intervene in a decision by the MHRT.

Collins J (at paras 18, 34): An important word in section 72(1)(a)(i) is the word 'then', because this establishes that the Tribunal is concerned with the condition of the patient when the Tribunal considers the matter. Whether or not he was properly taken into hospital is not material for that consideration. When I say 'properly', I mean whether there was indeed material which justified the admission, or indeed the other way round, whether at the time it was clearly justified. The question before the Tribunal is: is the detention proper now? The burden is upon the hospital, or those who seek his continued detention, to establish that that detention is necessary and within the terms of the Act. [...] That is what the Mental Health Review Tribunal is there to do, and it does sometimes reach decisions which do not accord with the views of the hospital psychiatrists or the social worker or whoever. There is no appeal on fact. This court does not and cannot sit as an Appeal Tribunal from the Mental Health Review Tribunal. It is only if there is an error of law that this court can intervene.

This decision is interesting, because it confirms that a patient can only appeal against a tribunal decision if there has been an error of law (this right is enshrined into section 78 of the 1983 Act). The Mental Health Review Tribunal is, therefore, not a safeguard but more of a review. The tribunal must give reasons for its decision. Sometimes, several witness will be called and all of the witnesses will produce different evidence. If the tribunal follows one witness over all others, it must explain, in simple terms, why it has done so. The tribunal cannot simply say that it preferred the evidence of one doctor over the evidence of the other five or six doctors.[12]

Timely reviews

We examined Article 5 of the European Convention on Human Rights above and saw that 'persons of unsound mind' were exempt from Article 5 and could, therefore, be deprived of their liberty according to domestic laws (i.e. the Mental Health Act 1983). However, there is a safeguard under Article 5 which states that:

> Everyone who is deprived of his liberty by arrest or detention shall be entitled to take proceedings by which the lawfulness of his detention shall be decided speedily by a court and his release ordered if the detention is not lawful.

According to this safeguard, Mental Health Review Tribunals must be undertaken speedily. This was confirmed by Lord Phillips MR in *R (on the application of C) v Mental Health Review Tribunal* [2002] 1 WLR 176 as discussed above. Other cases have also ruled that delays in tribunal procedures are unacceptable.

---

[12] This was confirmed in *R v Ashworth Hospital Authority ex parte H* [2003] 1 WLR 127.

CASE EXTRACT

R (on the application of KB) v Mental Health Review Tribunal [2002] EWHC 639

Facts: A number of patients who had been detained under the Mental Health Act 1983 experienced a delay between making an application to the MHRT for a review of their detention and the hearing of their applications. One patient waited twenty-seven weeks for a hearing.

Held: This was an unacceptable delay.

Stanley Burton J (at para 8): Delays in Tribunal hearings may result in the unjustified detention of patients who, if their cases had been considered earlier, would have been discharged. Even when discharge is not directed (and it is only in a relatively small percentage of cases that the Tribunal directs discharge), the delay prolongs the period of uncertainty for the patient. Cancellations of hearings, particularly if repeated, have other consequences: distress and disappointment for the mentally vulnerable patient, the risk of damage to his or her relationship with the psychiatrists and staff of his or her hospital, loss of trust in the tribunal system, and the waste of scarce resources.

The fact that a patient's case is perceived to be unmeritorious does not deprive him of his right to a speedy hearing; and similarly, if there is unjustified delay before the hearing, the fact that his case is belatedly held to be unmeritorious does not excuse the infringement of that right.

CASE EXTRACT

R (on the application of B) v Mental Health Review Tribunal [2002] EWHC 1553

Facts: B, a restricted patient who had been recalled to hospital by the Secretary of State under the Mental Health Act 1983 section 42(3), sought judicial review of a decision of the Mental Health Review Tribunal to adjourn the hearing of his case. He waited a total of eight months for a tribunal hearing because of evidence issues.

Held: The delay was too long.

Scott Baker J (at paras 39, 49, 53): A delay does not of itself give rise to a breach of Article 5(4), but it does give rise to the need for an explanation. [...] Whilst in my judgment some of the delay may have been caused by the failure of those representing B to ensure their evidence was available more promptly and to have pressed for an earlier hearing date (albeit the detailed facts are somewhat obscure), the underlying problem is the lack of case management on the tribunal's part. [...] The longer the delay that has occurred the more aggressive the directions will need to be to ensure early disposal of the case. [...] The delay in this case of eight and a half months is so long as to call for an explanation by the State (represented in this instance by the tribunal). No adequate explanation has been forthcoming, albeit it is plain that with effective case management the substantive hearing would have taken place a great deal earlier without in any way prejudicing B's right to a fair hearing. I have come to the conclusion that the lawfulness of B's detention was not decided speedily in this case and that therefore there is a breach of Article 5(4) of the ECHR.

The two cases above illustrate how the 'speedy' safeguard under Article 5 actually works in practice, and it is encouraging to see both decisions in favour of the patient, regardless of whether their cases were 'meritorious' or not.

Overriding the Mental Health Review Tribunal

Once a patient is discharged, he or she is free to leave (although the discharge may be deferred to find suitable accommodation). What if the responsible clinician in charge of the patient disagrees with the Tribunal's decision and wishes to re-admit the patient under section 3 for treatment? This is not allowed, because it would undermine the power of the Tribunal and render it ineffective. A significant case in 2003 looked at this issue in detail.

CASE EXTRACT

R (on the application of von Brandenburg) v East London and the City Mental Health NHS Trust [2003] UKHL 58

Facts: B applied for a Mental Health Review Tribunal hearing and on 31 March 2000 the tribunal ordered his discharge with effect from April 7, the delay being to allow a care plan to be made and accommodation to be found. On April 6, B, who had not left the hospital, was readmitted under section 3. B contended that there had been no change of circumstances since the tribunal hearing. The approved social worker contended that B had declined to continue taking his medication with the result that his condition had significantly deteriorated. The issue of law was whether it was lawful to readmit a patient under section 2 or section 3 when a Mental Health Review Tribunal had ordered his discharge, and when it could not be demonstrated that there had been a relevant change of circumstances.

Held: A patient cannot be readmitted once discharged.

Lord Bingham (at para 10): An Approved Social Worker (ASW) may not lawfully apply for the admission of a patient whose discharge has been ordered by the decision of a Mental Health Review Tribunal of which the ASW is aware unless the ASW has formed the reasonable and *bona fide* opinion that he has information not known to the tribunal which puts a significantly different complexion on the case as compared with that which was before the tribunal. It is impossible and undesirable to attempt to describe in advance the information which might justify such an opinion.

Lord Bingham makes it very clear in *Brandenburg* that a patient, once discharged by the MHRT, cannot be re-admitted by a responsible clinician unless new information emerges which changes the whole complexion of the case.

ACTIVITY

Pauline is suffering from schizophrenia. She has not showed any symptoms for a long time but she was detained five years ago because she threatened to kill her husband. Under section 72, and in light of *R (on the application of Care Principles Limited) v Mental Health Review Tribunal*, will the MHRT still detain her? If so, under which ground?

Mentally ill patients in the community

Preventative detention is illegal. A mentally ill person cannot be detained simply to prevent him or her from harming themselves or the public at large. This would be a breach of Article 5 of the European Convention on Human Rights. According to sections 2 and 3 of the Mental Health Act 1983, a patient can only be detained for assessment or treatment if: the nature or degree of his disorder warrants detention, he is a risk to his own safety or to the safety of others, it is appropriate and necessary for him to receive treatment in hospital, and that medical treatment is available to him. When the 1983 Act was reformed in 2007, a strong emphasis was placed on care in the community. Typically, this is where a local authority will provide a mentally ill patient with appropriate medical care without the need for detention in a hospital. The Mental Health Act 1983 contains specific provisions in section 117 relating to 'aftercare' including what it is, who provides it, and when it ceases to operate.

Mental Health Act 1983

Section 117: Aftercare

(2) It shall be the duty of the Primary Care Trust or Local Health Board and of the local social services authority to provide, in co-operation with relevant voluntary agencies, aftercare services for any person to whom this section applies until such time as the Primary Care Trust or Local Health Board and the local social services authority are satisfied that the person concerned is no longer in need of such services (but they shall not be so satisfied in the case of a community patient while he remains such a patient).[13]

Section 117 is applicable to patients who were detained for treatment under section 3 but it is no longer appropriate to deprive them of their liberty. Section 117 is also applicable to patients on supervised community treatment (below).

What does 'aftercare' look like?

The Mental Health Act 1983 Code of Practice contains a wealth of information about section 117 and what is has to offer newly released patients. The first task is to draft an aftercare plan.

EXTRACT

Department of Health, Mental Health Act 1983, Code of Practice (2008) (archived):

http://webarchive.nationalarchives.gov.uk/20130107105354/
http://www.dh.gov.uk/en/Publicationsandstatistics/Publications/
PublicationsPolicyAndGuidance/DH_084597

Paragraph 27.12: In order to ensure that the aftercare plan reflects the needs of each patient, it is important to consider who needs to be involved, in addition to patients themselves. This may include:

- The patient's responsible clinician;
- Nurses and other professionals involved in caring for the patient in hospital;
- A clinical psychologist, community mental health nurse and other members of the community team;
- The patient's GP and primary care team;
- Subject to the patient's views, any carer who will be involved in looking after them outside hospital, the patient's nearest relative or other family members;

→

---

[13] Primary Care Trusts ceased to exist after 1 April 2013.

- A representative of any relevant voluntary organisations;
- In the case of a restricted patient, the probation service;
- A representative of housing authorities, if accommodation is an issue;
- An employment expert, if employment is an issue;
- An independent mental health advocate, if the patient has one;
- An independent mental capacity advocate, if the patient has one;
- The patient's attorney or deputy, if the patient has one; and
- Any other representative nominated by the patient.

There are clearly many people involved in a patient's aftercare once he is released from hospital. The local social services authority will need to carefully consider what is the best way forward for the patient when drafting his aftercare plan, as they will not only want the patient to remain stable, but to regain confidence and rejoin society. It can be a potentially dangerous exercise releasing mentally ill patients back into the community, as the exposure to daily pressures and a lack of authority could lead a patient to harm himself (or, in rare instances, others). Therefore, the Code of Practice outlines what factors should be considered when drafting a patients' aftercare plan.

EXTRACT

Department of Health, Mental Health Act 1983, Code of Practice (2008) (archived):

http://webarchive.nationalarchives.gov.uk/20130107105354/
http://www.dh.gov.uk/en/Publicationsandstatistics/Publications/
PublicationsPolicyAndGuidance/DH_084597

Paragraph 27.13: A thorough assessment is likely to involve consideration of:

- Continuing mental healthcare, whether in the community or on an out-patient basis;
- The psychological needs of the patient and, where appropriate, of their family and carers;
- Physical healthcare;
- Daytime activities or employment;
- Appropriate accommodation;
- Identified risks and safety issues;
- Any specific needs arising from, for example, co-existing physical disability, sensory impairment, learning disability or autistic spectrum disorder;
- Any specific needs arising from drug, alcohol or substance misuse (if relevant);
- Any parenting or caring needs;
- Social, cultural or spiritual needs;
- Counselling and personal support;
- Assistance in welfare rights and managing finances;
- The involvement of authorities and agencies in a different area, if the patient is not going to live locally;
- The involvement of other agencies, for example the probation service or voluntary organisations;
- For a restricted patient, the conditions which the Secretary of State for Justice or the Tribunal has imposed or is likely to impose on their conditional discharge; and
- Contingency plans (should the patient's mental health deteriorate) and crisis contact details.

The list above is detailed and wide-ranging, but it is not exhaustive. Many other personal factors will also need to be considered, including the patient's emotional ability to cope with the pressures of ordinary life.

Power and control over released patients

There has been recent debate surrounding how exactly the Mental Health Act 1983 can control patients who are released from hospital into community care. Are they forced to attend community care and uphold their aftercare plan if they are no longer detained in hospital? The answer is: 'no'.

CASE EXTRACT

R (on the application on H) v Mental Health Review Tribunal [2007] EWHC 884

Facts: H had been made subject to hospital and restriction orders under the 1983 Act following his conviction for the manslaughter of his wife. The tribunal subsequently ordered H's conditional discharge under section 73 of the Act. One of the conditions was that H 'shall comply' with medication prescribed by his responsible medical officer. After two years of adhering to the conditions, H made an application seeking his absolute discharge. The tribunal refused his application. H contended that although he intended to continue to take the medication in question, the condition should be quashed so that he would be able to express his willingness and eagerness to take the medication free from a requirement that he should do so.

Held: The patient was successful.

Holman J: An adult of full capacity has an absolute right to choose whether to consent to medical treatment. That applies to every aspect of treatment and every occasion of treatment. Thus in this case, on each occasion that H attends, or should attend, for his fortnightly depot injection he has an absolute right to choose whether to consent to it or not. The treating doctor or nurse must, on each occasion, satisfy himself that the apparent consent is a real consent and that the independence of the patient's decision or his will has not been overborne.

This decision highlights the 'autonomy anomaly' in mental health law. According to the current law, a competent patient can be detained and treated under section 3 against his will. This was described above as the 'autonomy anomaly' because it goes against the ordinary principles of consent in law. However, once the patient can no longer be detained, the ordinary principles of consent come back into force and he can refuse all medical treatment once more, despite still harbouring a mental disorder. There seems little point in devising a detailed aftercare plan if the patient can simply refuse to accept it. Despite the decision in *R (on the application on H) v Mental Health Review Tribunal*, there is still a strong emphasis upon care in the community, as it is a more modern approach to treating mental disorders as opposed to the madhouses used centuries ago. The community care is also provided free of charge, after a case in 2002 established that local authorities could not charge patients for services under section 117.[14]

---

[14] See *R (on the application of Stennett) v Manchester City Council* [2002] UKHL 34.

It was established back in 1993 that local health authorities had a *duty* to provide aftercare services. This is a legal duty that a patient can enforce in a court of law:

CASE EXTRACT

R v *Ealing DHA ex parte Fox* [1993] 1 WLR 373

Facts: On the review of an order restricting a patient's discharge from hospital, the review tribunal directed a conditional discharge pending satisfactory arrangements for the provision of aftercare by the health authority. The health authority doctors opposed the scheme to discharge the patient and refused to provide the necessary supervision. The patient remained in hospital.

Held: There is a duty to treat discharged patients should they need the care.

Otton J (at page 385): I consider section 117(2) as mandatory: 'It shall be the duty of the district health authority' to provide aftercare services for any person to whom the section applies. [...] Thus, the duty is not only a general duty but a specific duty owed to the applicant to provide him with aftercare services until such time as the district health authority and local social services authority are satisfied that he is no longer in need of such services. [...] I consider a proper interpretation of this section to be that it is a continuing duty in respect of any patient who may be discharged and falls within section 117, although the duty to any particular patient is only triggered at the moment of discharge.

Otton J's judgment in *Fox* is encouraging, particularly for competent mentally ill patients who find themselves discharged from hospital but are still fearful that they are not yet fully recovered from their mental disorder and wish to continue with some form of medical treatment. However, Otton J's judgment was eroded somewhat in 2001 when the *Camden* case came along to state that sometimes, a local authority cannot accommodate every patient who comes their way.

CASE EXTRACT

R (on the application of K) v *Camden and Islington HA* [2001] EWCA Civ 240

Facts: K had challenged the health authority's failure to provide her with supervision from a consultant forensic psychiatrist following a decision by a Mental Health Review Tribunal that she could be conditionally discharged to reside at her parent's home. K contended that section 117 of the 1983 Act imposed an absolute obligation upon the health authority to comply with the requirements set by the tribunal as a condition of discharge but no psychiatrist was willing to take her case.

Held: There is not an absolute duty to follow the requirements of the MHRT depending on the circumstances.

Lord Phillips (at paras 26, 29–30): Otton J declared [...] that a District Health Authority was under a duty under section 117 to provide after care services when a patient left hospital and acted unlawfully in failing to seek to make practical arrangements for after care prior to that patient's discharge from hospital. Thus the judgment held that the Health Authority was under a duty to use all reasonable endeavours to satisfy the Tribunal conditions, not that it had an absolute obligation

---

→

so to do. [...] In my judgment section 117 imposes on Health Authorities a duty to provide after care facilities for the benefit of patients who are discharged from mental hospitals. The nature and extent of those facilities must, to a degree, fall within the discretion of the Health Authority which must have regard to other demands on its budget. [...] I can see no justification in interpreting section 117 so as to impose on Health Authorities an absolute obligation to satisfy any conditions that a Tribunal may specify as prerequisites to the discharge of a patient. The section does not expressly impose any such requirement, nor is it reasonable to imply such a requirement. The Appellant's suggested interpretation would place upon Health Authorities a duty which, on occasion, would be impossible to perform. [...] An interpretation of section 117 which imposed on Health Authorities absolute duties which they would not necessarily be able to perform would be manifestly unreasonable.

Lord Phillips clearly states in *Camden* that a local health authority does not have an 'absolute obligation' to meet the requirements of a Tribunal's conditional discharge. Therefore, in regards to *K's* argument, just because her Mental Health Review Tribunal stated that she could be discharged subject to observation by a consultant psychiatrist, this does not mean that the local health authority has an absolute obligation to find one if it is proving a difficult task. Lord Phillips went on to say that because a consultant psychiatrist could not be found for *K*, and because the psychiatrist observation was a condition of her discharge, i.e. she was still sufficiently ill enough to require further care, she was still sufficiently mentally disordered to justify detaining her under Article 5 of the European Convention on Human Rights.

Lord Phillips at paragraphs 33–4

Whether or not it is necessary to detain a patient in hospital for treatment may well depend upon the level of facilities available for treatment within the community. If a Health Authority is unable, despite the exercise of all reasonable endeavours, to procure for a patient the level of care and treatment in the community that a Tribunal considers to be a prerequisite to the discharge of the patient from hospital, I do not consider that the continued detention of the patient in hospital will violate the right to liberty conferred by Article 5.

This portion of Lord Phillip's judgment is difficult to justify. If *K* was well enough to be released on a conditional discharge subject to observation, some might say that she was already being needlessly (and therefore unlawfully) detained – and will be again – because the local health authority could not find the appropriate support in the community. The European Court confirmed this when *K* appealed to Strasbourg.[15]

Community treatment orders

It is clear from the discussion above that unless a patient is detained, he or she is simply free to refuse all medical treatment once released from hospital. This may lead to a vicious circle: a patient is sectioned for assessment, treated, released, refuses further treatment,

---

[15] *Kolanis v United Kingdom* (517/02) (2006) All ER 227.

and is then sectioned again. This differs to a community treatment order (CTO). A CTO is not something that a patient can refuse because it is a form of supervised community treatment (SCT), and since the 2007 reforms it has been a new and innovative way to ensure that released patients continue their treatment once their liberty has returned. If the patient breaches his or her CTO, they are detained again. The Mental Health Act 1983 Code of Practice provides the following definition of supervised community treatment.

EXTRACT

Department of Health, Mental Health Act 1983, Code of Practice, (2008) (archived):

http://webarchive.nationalarchives.gov.uk/20130107105354/
http://www.dh.gov.uk/en/Publicationsandstatistics/Publications/
PublicationsPolicyAndGuidance/DH_084597

Paragraph 25.2: The purpose of SCT is to allow suitable patients to be safely treated in the community rather than under detention in hospital, and to provide a way to help prevent relapse and any harm – to the patient or to others – that this might cause. It is intended to help patients to maintain stable mental health outside hospital and to promote recovery.

Paragraph 25.3: SCT provides a framework for the management of patient care in the community and gives the responsible clinician the power to recall the patient to hospital for treatment if necessary.

CTOs are only available to patients who have been detained and treated under section 3 of the 1983 Act. Section 2 patients, i.e. patients detained for assessment only, are not eligible. Section 17A introduces CTOs into the 1983 Act and gives responsible clinicians the power to discharge a detained patient from hospital with a CTO, with support from an approved mental health professional.

Mental Health Act 1983

17A: Community treatment orders

(5) The relevant criteria are –

  (a) the patient is suffering from a mental disorder of a nature or degree which makes it appropriate for him to receive medical treatment;

  (b) it is necessary for his health or safety or for the protection of other persons that he should receive such treatment;

  (c) subject to his being liable to be recalled as mentioned in paragraph (d) below, such treatment can be provided without his continuing to be detained in a hospital;

  (d) it is necessary that the responsible clinician should be able to exercise the power under section 17E(1) below to recall the patient to hospital; and

  (e) appropriate medical treatment is available for him.

The provisions of section 17A are interesting in that they provide the opportunity for many detained patients with potentially serious mental disorders to be freed into the community. This is one way to overcome preventative detention and it supports the idea that a deprivation of liberty should really be a last resort. According to section 17A, to be eligible for a CTO the patient must show:

- A mental disorder.
- The nature or degree of the disorder must be significant enough to require medical treatment.
- Treatment is necessary for the safety of the patient; or
- Treatment is necessary for the protection of others.
- The patient doesn't have to be detained in order to receive such treatment.
- A clinician must be available to recall the patient if necessary.
- Appropriate treatment is available to him (although as discussed above it doesn't have to alleviate the patient's condition).

Recalling patients from community care back into hospital

Community treatment orders allow for patients to live without restriction, but they also ensure that they continue to take their medical treatment in a comfortable environment. A responsible clinical can recall a patient if he or she breaches the CTO, and this allows for compulsory treatment to resume under section 3. The power of recall under section 17E is an important safeguard against releasing dangerous or reckless mentally ill patients back into the community. If, for example, a patient with schizophrenia who shows no sign of violence suddenly decides once he is released to live without medication, he might pose a danger to himself or others and his responsible clinician can take him back into hospital.

Mental Health Act 1983

17E: Power to recall to hospital

(1) The responsible clinician may recall a community patient to hospital if in his opinion –

    (a) the patient requires medical treatment in hospital for his mental disorder;

    (b) there would be a risk of harm to the health or safety of the patient or to other persons if the patient were not recalled to hospital for that purpose.

Technically, these criteria are considerably wide. There is no indication in section 17E that a patient must simply stop taking his medication; there must simply be a requirement for treatment in hospital or a risk of harm to the patient or others. Under section 17F, once a patient has been recalled, a responsible clinician can detain the patient for 72 hours. During this time, the patient can be treated. After the 72 hours have elapsed, the responsible clinician can release the patient back into the community with the CTO still active, or the CTO can be revoked completely, meaning that the patient is detained for treatment under section 3.[16] Patients released with CTO's who are recalled, treated, released and recalled for treatment again may settle into a disturbing pattern.

---

[16] Patients are not required to consent to supervised community treatment, but ideally, they play a role in decisions about treatment. See paragraph 25.14 of the Mental Health Act 1983, Code of Practice (2008), (archived). At: http://webarchive.nationalarchives.gov.uk/20130107105354/http://www.dh.gov.uk/en/Publicationsandstatistics/Publications/PublicationsPolicyAndGuidance/DH_084597.

Community treatment orders with conditions

When a patient is discharged with a CTO, he or she must ensure that the terms of the CTO are followed, otherwise they risk being recalled back into hospital. The responsible clinician in charge of the patient may insert some conditions into the CTO to control the patient's behaviour further. The power to add conditions into a CTO is provided under section 17B.

Mental Health Act 1983

17B: Conditions

(1) A community treatment order shall specify conditions to which the patient is to be subject while the order remains in force.

(2) But, the order may specify conditions only if the responsible clinician, with the agreement of the approved mental health professional, thinks them necessary or appropriate for one or more of the following purposes –

   (a) ensuring that the patient receives medical treatment;

   (b) preventing risk of harm to the patient's health or safety;

   (c) protecting other persons.

The purposes listed above under criteria (a), (b) and (c) are vital to ensure that a patient is not controlled needlessly by a condition that has no direct relevance to his or her mental disorder. Any condition must be related to the patient's treatment and is implemented to ensure the health and safety of the patient and others. It is not clear under section 17B what form the CTO conditions can take. It appears that, as long as the conditions are 'necessary or appropriate' to the patient's medical treatment or the health and safety of the patient or others, the responsible clinician can insert any conditions into the CTO as he sees fit. The Code of Practice gives further detail, but discretion remains with the clinician.

EXTRACT

Department of Health, Mental Health Act 1983, Code of Practice (2008) (archived):

http://webarchive.nationalarchives.gov.uk/20130107105354/
http://www.dh.gov.uk/en/Publicationsandstatistics/Publications/
PublicationsPolicyAndGuidance/DH_084597

Paragraph 25.32: In considering what conditions might be necessary or appropriate, the responsible clinician should always keep in view the patient's specific cultural needs and background.

Paragraph 25.33: The conditions should:

- be kept to a minimum number consistent with achieving their purpose;
- restrict the patient's liberty as little as possible while being consistent with achieving their purpose;
- have a clear rationale;
- be clearly and precisely expressed, so that the patient can readily understand what is expected.

→

Paragraph 25.34: The nature of the conditions will depend on the patient's individual circumstances. They might cover matters such as where and when the patient is to receive treatment in the community; where the patient is to live; and avoidance of known risk factors or high-risk situations relevant to the patient's mental disorder.

Redress

Under section 66(1)(cb), a patient may, within six months, make an application to a Mental Health Review Tribunal if their community treatment order is revoked. The MHRT has the power under section 72(1)(c) to discharge a community patient.

Criticisms of supervised community care

CTOs are the governments way of enhancing supervised community care for mentally ill patients. However, the comparisons to aftercare show a significant discrepancy between levels of care. For example, CTOs are potentially highly restrictive. Responsible clinicians have discretion as to what conditions are inserted into the CTO, and under section 17E a CTO patient can be recalled to hospital, treated without consent, and released again. This merry-go-round cannot be beneficial for a patient with mental health problems. Competent patients in particular will dislike their autonomy being revoked at a moment's notice for the purposes of compulsory medical treatment, only to be released again a short time later. Some commentators may refer to supervised community treatment as 'compulsion in the community':

EXTRACT

Patricia Walton, 'Reforming the Mental Health Act 1983: An Approved Social Worker Perspective' (2000) 22 *Journal of Social Welfare and Family Law* 410, at pages 410–14

Approved Social Workers are strongly opposed to compulsion in the community on social and human rights grounds: some people find the drug effects intolerable; some people find relentless awareness of their circumstances intolerable; the risks of suicide and other effects of unwanted long-term drug treatment have not been considered; psychiatric treatments can be harmful; the impact of forcible treatment on the family and within the community have not been considered; a person's home should be a safe haven; people ultimately have the right to choose ill health. [...] In [our] experience many, possibly most, people on long-term medication choose to come off it from time to time, to be free of side-effects or to achieve a feeling of autonomy.

The view above from Walton, a social worker, is rather worrying. Patients who are released into the community are likely to relinquish their treatment in order to win their autonomy back. Without healthcare professionals around, this new found freedom cannot be monitored.

Guardianship

Guardianship is an interesting exception to supervised community treatment. A guardian can be appointed to look after the patient under section 7 of the 1983 Act. Although guardianship is still, technically, a way for the Mental Health Act 1983 to control discharged mentally ill patients, control is minimal because the patient is in the care of a relative or an approved mental health professional. The patient does not have to receive treatment; the aim of guardianship is to provide a safe place for the patient. It follows that guardianship is not used when patients need urgent medication or are non-compliant.

Mental Health Act 1983

Section 7: Application for guardianship

(1) A patient who has attained the age of 16 years may be received into guardianship.

(2) A guardianship application may be made in respect of a patient on the grounds that –

    (a) he is suffering from mental disorder of a nature or degree which warrants his reception into guardianship under this section; and

    (b) it is necessary in the interests of the welfare of the patient or for the protection of other persons that the patient should be so received.

(3) A guardianship application shall be founded on the written recommendations in the prescribed form of two registered medical practitioners.

(5) The person named as guardian in a guardianship application may be either a local social services authority or any other person (including the applicant himself).

Notice also, how there is no 'treatability' requirement under section 7. Guardianship is not about treatment, it is about providing a safe and caring environment. However, a patient under guardianship can still informally seek medical treatment if he or she wishes. Section 7 also mentions 'welfare' – a term not used too frequently in the Mental Health Act 1983 – indicating that section 7 is veering towards supporting the best interests of the patient, rather than simply treating a patient without consent.

Under section 8, a guardian can exercise certain powers over the patient.

Mental Health Act 1983

Section 8: Effect of guardianship application

(1) Where a guardianship application, the application shall confer on the authority or person named in the application as guardian, to the exclusion of any other person –

    (a) the power to require the patient to reside at a place specified by the authority or person named as guardian;

    (b) the power to require the patient to attend at places and times so specified for the purpose of medical treatment, occupation, education or training;

    (c) the power to require access to the patient to be given, at any place where the patient is residing, to any registered medical practitioner, approved mental health professional or other person so specified.

It is encouraging to see the terms 'treatment, occupation, education or training' inserted into section 8. This supports the notion that guardianship is not just a 'holding house' for the mentally ill but an environment in which patients can rehabilitate themselves and develop their skills. Guardianship is similar to a parental role, except sometimes a local social services authority can take guardianship of a patient if the patient's relatives are not suitable or unwilling to do so. Guardianship is not indefinite; it must be renewed after six months, and annually after that, under section 20(2) of the Mental Health Act 1983.

THINKING POINT

What effect might a CTO have on competent mentally ill patients and their position in society? Can you suggest any changes to the relevant legal provisions to make CTOs more patient friendly?

Mentally ill prisoners

Mentally ill people rarely commit serious crimes. However, if a mentally ill person commits murder, they have two defences available to them:

Criminal defence	Criteria of defence
'Persons Suffering from Diminished Responsibility' under section 52 of the Coroners and Justice Act 2009	An abnormality of mental functioning which arose from a recognised medical condition and substantially impaired the defendants ability to (a) understand the nature of his conduct; (b) to form a rational judgment; (c) to exercise self-control
Insanity	Defect of reason from a disease of the mind, defendant did not know the nature and quality of his act, or did not know that what he was doing was wrong (R v *McNaughten* (1843) 8 ER 718)

The existence of these defences in criminal law proves that there is a need to provide separate defences for mentally ill people. It is also an acknowledgement that mentally ill people may not be aware of what they were doing when they committed the crime, i.e. they had no malice at the time. What is unique about the defence of insanity is that the verdict, if used successfully, will be 'not guilty by reason of insanity' and the defendant will be sent to a high-security hospital for medical treatment (Ashworth, Broadmoor and Rampton are the three high-security psychiatric hospitals in England and Wales). This is when potentially dangerous defendants come into contact with the mental health system. Commentators argue that mentally ill prisoners do not belong in traditional police cells.

EXTRACT

Ian Bynoe, quoted in Andrew Cole, 'Overuse of Police Cells for Detaining People with Mental Health Problems "Intolerable"' (2008) *337 British Medical Journal* 1635

Police custody is an unsuitable environment for someone with mental illness and may make their condition worse, particularly if they are not dealt with quickly and appropriately and don't receive the care they need. The continued use of cells not only diverts police resources from fighting crime but criminalises behaviour that is not a crime. A police cell should only be used when absolutely necessary, for example, when someone is violent and not as a convenience.

Assessing accused individuals

Under section 35(1) of the Mental Health Act 1983, an accused defendant who is awaiting trial can be sent to hospital by a Magistrates or a Crown Court for a report on his mental condition.

Sending defendants to hospital for treatment

Convicted criminals of less serious offences may also require treatment for a mental disorder and can be diverted by the courts into the mental health system under section 37 of the 1983 Act.

Mental Health Act 1983 Section 37: Powers of courts to order hospital admission or guardianship

(1) Where a person is convicted before the Crown Court of an offence punishable with imprisonment, or is convicted by a Magistrates' Court of an offence punishable on summary conviction with imprisonment, the court may by order authorise his admission to and detention in such hospital as may be specified in the order.

(2) The conditions are that –

    (a) the court is satisfied, on the written or oral evidence of two registered medical practitioners, that the offender is suffering from mental disorder and that either –

        (i) the mental disorder from which the offender is suffering is of a nature or degree which makes it appropriate for him to be detained in a hospital for medical treatment and appropriate medical treatment is available for him; or

        (ii) in the case of an offender who has attained the age of 16 years, the mental disorder is of a nature or degree which warrants his reception into guardianship under this Act.

    (b) the court is of the opinion, having regard to all the circumstances including the nature of the offence and the character and antecedents of the offender, and to the other available methods of dealing with him, that the most suitable method of disposing of the case is by means of an order under this section.

It is important to note that under section 37(2)(b) above, the court must consider all of the relevant circumstances, including the nature of the offence, the character of the offender and the other methods available. An order to hospital must be the most suitable method. This means that admission into the mental health system is a last resort.

According to the MIND charity, antisocial personality disorders are the most common form of mental disorders amongst convicted criminals:

- Up to 39% of male prisoners and 75% female prisoners have some kind of neurotic problem;
- Up to 10% of female and 6% of male prisoners self harm during their time in prison;
- The risk of suicide is ten times higher for the prison population than it is for the general population;

- 18% of prisoners are diagnosed with schizophrenia;
- 18% of prisoners are diagnosed with psychosis;
- During 2007/8, 1,400 people were sent to hospital for treatment by the courts under the Mental Health Act 1983;
- During 2007/8, 7,500 convicted criminals were sent to high-security hospitals for treatment under the Mental Health Act 1983.[17]

If antisocial personality disorders are included within the definition of mental disorder, then a vast number of the prisoners suffer from a mental disorder. Appropriate help may not be available to these prisoners if they remain in prison.

Transferring prisoners

Sometimes, prisoners can begin their sentence in a regular prison and then later be transferred into a high-security hospital for treatment for their mental disorder under section 47 of the 1983 Act.

Mental Health Act 1983

Section 47: Removal to hospital of persons serving sentences of imprisonment

(1) If in the case of a person serving a sentence of imprisonment the Secretary of State is satisfied, by reports from at least two registered medical practitioners –

(a) that the said person is suffering from mental disorder; and

(b) that the mental disorder from which that person is suffering is of a nature or degree which makes it appropriate for him to be detained in a hospital for medical treatment; and –

(c) that appropriate medical treatment is available for him;

the Secretary of State may, if he is of the opinion having regard to the public interest and all the circumstances that it is expedient so to do, by warrant direct that that person be removed to and detained in such hospital as may be specified in the direction; and a direction under this section shall be known as 'a transfer direction'.

This 'transfer direction' is important, because it allows for prisoners who have a mental disorder to be treated in a hospital environment during their time in custody. It is far removed from the asylums of the old days where mentally ill people were simply locked up without any medical provisions whatsoever. However, there is a safety concern. Section 47 includes the phrase: 'having regard to the public interest'. The public may be angry to find that a serial offender – or even a murderer – is removed from prison to a much more comfortable environment to receive medical treatment.

---

[17] Mind: For Better Mental Health (charity). See: http://www.mind.org.uk/mental_health_a-z/8105_mental_health_facts_and_statistics.

EXTRACT

Robert Francis, 'The Michael Stone Inquiry – A Reflection' (2007)
Journal of Mental Health Law 41

Governmental thinking still appears to be informed by a belief that persons with personality disorders are denied treatment which is available and effective and is more than mere detention. [...] A risk of using the mental health legislation for non-clinical purposes is that hospitals will become as full as the prisons now, with the consequent adverse effect on the care and supervision of those already within that system, to the detriment not only of the patients themselves, but to the public who deserve properly focused and informed protection.

Using the MHA 1983 to keep prisoners detained

When a prisoner's sentence is about to run out but he is still perceived to be a danger to the public, the Mental Health Act 1983 can be used to detain the prisoner, under section 3, for treatment. This is not an ideal scenario, because if the prisoner was genuinely suffering from a mental disorder he would have received treatment before his release deadline. This 'moving around' of prisoners results in the mental health system being used as a stop-gap for prisoners who are formally free to leave jail but are still deemed to be dangerous.

THINKING POINT

Can you think of any instances where it would not be in the public interest to treat a prisoner for a mental disorder? If not, is the mental health system simply being used as a crutch for the criminal justice system to keep the public safe from dangerous individuals?

Voluntary admission into the mental health system

So far, this chapter has focused on the detention of mentally ill patients and the 'autonomy anomaly', i.e. competent patients being detained against their will and forced to accept treatment. Most commentators focus on this small but controversial element of mental health law because it goes against the well-established principles of medicine. However, there is another, simpler side to mental health law. The majority of sufferers of a mental disorder are quite happy to seek treatment for their disorder, and can thus voluntarily admit themselves into the mental health system without the need for forced detention.

Informal admission

Under the Mental Health Act 1983, a patient can admit themselves into the mental health system voluntarily. Because they have not been detained under section 3, they cannot be forced to receive treatment. For competent patients, this means that he or she has full autonomy to refuse all suggested medical treatment.

Mental Health Act 1983

Section 131: Informal admission of patients

(1) Nothing in this Act shall be construed as preventing a patient who requires treatment for mental disorder from being admitted to any hospital or registered establishment in pursuance of arrangements made in that behalf and without any application, order or direction rendering him liable to be detained under this Act, or from remaining in any hospital or registered establishment in pursuance of such arrangements after he has ceased to be so liable to be detained.

When a patient is admitted informally (i.e. voluntarily), he is less likely to reject or refuse medical treatment. The relationship between doctor and patient is also less likely to be strained. However, notice how in section 131 above, the phrase 'being admitted' is included. This means that another party can admit the patient. For example, a mentally handicapped patient may require treatment for a mental disorder, so his carer *voluntarily* admits him into the mental health system. The patient would not have to be detained under section 3 because he is being admitted voluntarily and he is assumed to be compliant with all methods of treatment. Commentators are sceptical of informal admissions:

EXTRACT

Phil Fennell, 'Doctor Knows Best? Therapeutic Detention under Common Law, the Mental Health Act and the European Convention' (1998) 6 *Medical Law Review* 322, at pages 322–53

Even if there were an unlimited right for informal patients to leave hospital, to speak of mentally incapacitated patients having it makes little sense. There may be nowhere else capable of providing the care which the patient needs, he may have no home to go to and be too dependent to survive in sheltered accommodation. [...] Not being detained does not make an informal patient 'freer'.

In 2005, section 131 was heavily scrutinised in *HL v United Kingdom* (below). In particular, it was questioned whether a breach of Article 5 could occur if a patient who *voluntarily* admits himself for treatment under section 131 is subsequently controlled by medical staff. It is important to note that the patient in this case was incompetent, and was thus admitted 'voluntarily' into the hospital by someone else.

CASE EXTRACT

HL v United Kingdom (455508/99) [2005] 40 EHRR 32

Facts: H, who suffered from autism, lacked the capacity to consent to medical treatment. H became extremely agitated whilst attending a day centre. He was assessed by two doctors as requiring in-patient treatment but he was not admitted to hospital under the Mental Health Act 1983 because he did not resist admission. The health care professionals appeared to exercise complete control over him whilst he was in care and movements. H contended that his detention was unlawful under Article 5(1)(e).

Held: Liberty must not be deprived unless the Mental Health Act 1983 is engaged.

Judge Pellonpaa (at pages 793–5): It is clear from the above-noted correspondence that the applicant's contact with his carers was directed and controlled by the hospital, his carers visiting him for the first time after his admission on November 2, 1997. Accordingly, the concrete situation was that the applicant was under continuous supervision and control and was not free to leave. Any suggestion to the contrary was, in the Court's view, fairly described by Lord Steyn as 'stretching credulity to breaking point' and as a 'fairy tale'. [...] The Court therefore concludes that the applicant was 'deprived of his liberty' within the meaning of Article 5(1) of the Convention from July 22, 1997 to October 29, 1997. [...] It is recalled that an individual cannot be deprived of his liberty on the basis of unsoundness of mind unless three minimum conditions are satisfied: he must reliably be shown to be of unsound mind; the mental disorder must be of a kind or degree warranting compulsory confinement; and the validity of continued confinement depends upon the persistence of such a disorder.

Judge Pellonpaa established two important criteria in his judgment above: (1) if a patient is controlled under section 131, his liberty is deprived, and (2) for the deprivation of liberty to be lawful, the patient must be admitted into the hospital under the provisions of the Mental Health Act 1983. Judge Pellonpaa did not stop here. When analysing section 131 of the Mental Health Act 1983, he was unhappy about the lack of procedural rules in place to allow for the safe and voluntary admission of incapacitated patients. How can it be that another party can voluntarily admit an incompetent patient? Can the patient be said to be 'voluntarily' admitting himself?

CASE EXTRACT

Judge Pellonpaa (at paragraph 120): In this latter respect, the Court finds striking the lack of any fixed procedural rules by which the admission and detention of compliant incapacitated persons is conducted. The contrast between this dearth of regulation and the extensive network of safeguards applicable to psychiatric committals covered by the 1983 Act is, in the Court's view, significant. In particular and most obviously, the Court notes the lack of any formalised admission procedures which indicate who can propose admission, for what reasons and on the basis of what kind of medical and other assessments and conclusions. There is no requirement to fix the exact purpose of admission (for example, for assessment or for treatment) and, consistently, no limits in terms of time, treatment or care attach to that admission. Nor is there any specific provision requiring a continuing clinical assessment of the persistence of a disorder warranting detention.

As a result of the scathing judgment in *HL* v *United Kingdom*, the mental health law in the UK had to change. The 2007 reforms to the Mental Health Act 1983 created a new provision at section 64D, which enables an authorised person to provide treatment to a 'community' patient who lacks capacity. This cannot be done with force, so if force is required, the patient should be sectioned under section 4 (emergency admission for assessment), or the usual section 2 detention for assessment may be enforced.

ACTIVITY

Apply Judge Pellonpaa's criteria from *HL* v *United Kingdom* (45508/99) [2005] 40 EHRR 32 to the patient below – has Mary been deprived of her liberty?

Mary is an old lady aged 96. She is suffering from a mild form of dementia. She lives with her daughter Louise in a small terraced house. Recently, Mary has become agitated and aggressive towards her daughter Louise, and Louise fears for her and her mother's safety. Louise takes her mother to the mental hospital down the road and voluntarily admits her mother for assessment under section 131 of the Mental Health Act 1983. Mary becomes distressed when Louise leaves the hospital to do the school run and tries to leave the hospital. The medical staff in the hospital secure Mary to her chair to ensure that she doesn't escape. Mary is left in her chair until Louise returns.

Chapter summary

- The definition of a 'mental disorder' under section 1 of the Mental Health Act 1983 has been examined closely. The definition is very wide and includes personality and behavioural disorders.

- The powers of detention for assessment (s. 2) and treatment (s. 3) have been scrutinised. They allow for the forced detention and treatment of patients who are fully competent.

- The relevant human rights Articles are 2, 3, 5 and 8. Article 3 – a right to protection from torture and inhuman treatment – is supposed to be applied without exception, but the courts have applied it very leniently. Article 5 – a right to liberty – is the most implemented Article in this area of law, and it contains a safeguard which the courts have applied to mentally ill patients in European cases.

- The Mental Health Review Tribunal plays a big part in releasing mentally ill patients back into the community under section 72. The Mental Health Act 1983 also allows for aftercare (s. 117) and community treatment orders (s. 17A). These patients can be recalled, however, for further treatment under section 17E, causing concern that they are never really 'free' from the mental health system once released.

 **Chapter essay**

'Critically analyse the provisions under the Mental Health Act 1983 that allow for the forced detention and treatment of mentally ill patients.'

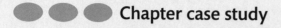 **Chapter case study**

Lucy is a troublesome teenager. At the age of 13, her mother caught her self-harming in her bedroom and she needed emergency medical treatment. At the age of 15 she was convicted of criminal damage and was sentenced to three months community service. A mental health assessment uncovered disturbing behavioural patterns at the time and possible attention deficit hyperactivity disorder, but Lucy refused counselling services. At the age of 17, Lucy has stopped eating. Her mother is very worried because she keeps fainting and is failing her A-Levels. A doctor is called to the family home when Lucy is too weak to get out of bed. She complains of seeing creatures, hearing voices and feeling sudden bouts of anger. She finally hits out at the doctor and breaks his spectacles. The doctor informs Lucy's mother that he wishes to section Lucy.

Lucy is about to enter the mental health system involuntarily. What will happen to her and which legal provisions will oversee the whole process?

Further reading

Bartlett, P. (2003) 'The Test of Compulsion in Mental Health Law: Capacity, Therapeutic Benefit and Dangerous as Possible Criteria', 11 *Medical Law Review* 326; (2006) 'Psychiatric Treatment in the Absence of Law?', 14 *Medical Law Review* 124–31; (2007) 'A Matter of Necessity? Enforced Treatment Under the Mental Health Act', 15 *Medical Law Review* 86.

Laing, J. (2000) 'Rights versus Risk? Reform of the Mental Health Act 1983', 8 *Medical Law Review* 210.

Large, M. (2008) 'The Danger of Dangerousness: Why We Must Remove the Dangerousness Criterion from our Mental Health Acts', 34 *Journal of Medical Ethics* 877.

Lewis, P. (1999) 'Feeding Anorexic Patients Who Refuse Food', 7 *Medical Law Review* 21.

Szasz, T. (2005) 'Idiots, Infants and the Insane: Mental Illness and Legal Incompetence', 31 *Journal of Medical Ethics* 78.

8

Assisted conception

Chapter objectives

At the end of this chapter, you should have:

- An understanding of the origins of fertility treatment and how it developed through the decades.
- An appreciation of the current facts and figures regarding fertility treatment today, the types of treatment available, the success rates and the types of couples coming forward for treatment.
- Knowledge of the legal assignment of parentage to couples seeking fertility treatment, including same-sex couples.
- An understanding of the laws relating to cloning, screening for diseases, sex selection and surrogacy.

SETTING THE SCENE	Chris and Jo are married and cannot have children. Jo was a prostitute before she met her husband Chris, and as a result of a sexually transmitted infection during her working days, her ovaries are damaged and she cannot have children. Chris and Jo have now been married for eleven years and even though they agreed that they would be quite happy to have a childless marriage, Chris is approaching 40 and wants more to life than his full-time job. Jo still does not work after she gave up her old job. Chris suspects that she visits her old clubs and her old contacts, but he turns a blind eye because he loves her very much. They take all of their concerns (and chequered history) to a fertility clinic and seek advice on assisted conception. Will the law allow them to access IVF treatment?

Introduction

Assisted conception is an example of how science and medicine can come together to create miracles that were never thought possible a few hundred years ago. A life can now be created *outside* of the human body, and what is more, the embryo can be screened for diseases before its implantation back into the body. It allows infertile couples to have children and it allows the next generation to be free of some debilitating diseases. However, there are major criticisms. The creation of life is, in the religious world, a natural act between a husband and a wife. The resulting child that is born is viewed as a gift from God. It may come as no surprise to learn that scientists are accused of playing God. It is not possible to turn back because infertile couples will once again be faced with the heart breaking reality of not having a biological child of their own, and with infertility on the rise and the acceptance of gay couples in civil partnerships, it is perhaps best to focus on the positive results that science can bring, rather than the moral complexities, and there are many in this field.

This chapter is going to explore the types of assisted conception available, the laws and regulations that allow them to be provided, the use of donor gametes (i.e. eggs and sperm), screening (i.e. saviour siblings and sex selection), human cloning and surrogacy. The law has covered assisted conception relatively well, but surrogacy is still largely unregulated. Cloning is currently illegal between humans, but the existence of identical twins proves that society does not fall into disarray when two babies are born sharing the same physical and genetic profile. The main statutory provision in this chapter is the Human Fertilisation and Embryology Act 1990, which was reformed in 2008, and the regulatory body that it produced: the Human Fertilisation and Embryology Authority (HFEA). It will become clear very quickly that in the world of assisted conception, consent is pivotal to treatment. In addition to this, the best interests of any child born is always taken into consideration before providing fertility treatment.

The history behind assisted conception

The idea of assisted conception is accepted today without a second thought, but back in 1978 when the first IVF baby was born (Louise Brown in Oldham, United Kingdom) it was a shocking scientific breakthrough. An egg and a sperm are brought together in a glass dish (*in vitro* is Latin for 'in glass') and the conceived egg was then placed back inside the mother to continue the pregnancy. There had been many failed attempts to create an embryo outside the human body, but the birth of Louise Brown heralded an end to heartbreak for millions of infertile couples. It is still a relatively unsuccessful procedure, but this does not put people off. The practice of IVF has also paved the way for the screening of embryos before implantation to ensure that they are free from disease or can cure the disease of another, i.e. saviour siblings. This is still a relatively new procedure, but it is becoming increasingly common, for example sex selection is a form of screening and is popular in the United States. It is understandable that certain religious groups were repelled a few decades ago when the first baby was born without the act of intercourse. This was considered unnatural, and a strictly religious person may argue that a scientific conception removes the quality of 'blessing' from the new arrival. However, the infertile couple would probably argue in response that the child was even more of a blessing considering they were infertile. The history of assisted conception is hard to pin down because it is not well documented, i.e. it was full of failures for a very long time, and it has only gathered pace over the last thirty years. It is estimated that, since Louise Brown was born in 1978, 5 million babies have been born worldwide after IVF treatment and in the UK alone, 224,196 babies have been born after IVF treatment between 1991 (when record began) and 2011.[1] The current desire for fertility treatment is undeniable: the waiting lists are long and the costs – both emotional and financial – are significant.

The facts: infertility today

The following types of assisted conception are available:

Term	Treatment
IVF	*In vitro* fertilisation: the egg and sperm are collected from the partners (or donors) and mixed together in a laboratory to fertilise them outside the body. The resulting embryos are transferred back into the female patient.
DI	Donor insemination: donor sperm is placed inside the woman in the uterus, cervix or vagina. Fertilisation of her egg is hoped to take place inside the body naturally. This allows a lesbian couple to have a baby.
PGD	Preimplantation genetic diagnosis: during IVF treatment one or two cells are removed from an embryo to test it for hereditary disorders. This is referred to as 'screening'.

IVF is a phrase that is relatively well known, but many do not understand how it works. A woman's eggs are removed from her ovaries after a rigorous drug programme and are combined with removed sperm in a laboratory (often by injecting the sperm directly into the egg). The embryos develop in the laboratory for a few days and are then transferred back into the woman's body in the hope that they lead to a pregnancy. The success rate (i.e. a live birth) is 25%. The removal of eggs and the implantation of embryos are both highly invasive procedures for the woman. The table below contains some of the outcomes that are measured by the HFEA:

---

[1] Fertility Treatment in 2012: Trends and Figures. Human Fertilisation and Embryology Authority, page 46 (2013), http://www.hfea.gov.uk/104.html.

Live birth	A baby is born with signs of life (it may later die)
Miscarriage	A pregnancy is lost before 24 weeks
Still birth	A pregnancy is lost after 24 weeks

The facts and figures on assisted conception are collected and published by the Human Fertilisation and Embryology Authority (HFEA) as the sole regulator of fertility treatment in the United Kingdom. The National Institute for Health and Care Excellence (NICE) has also published guidelines on the provision of fertility treatment in the NHS. The guidelines are not legally binding but they provide a very helpful benchmark as to what kind of assessment and treatment should be provided for certain fertility problems and what would be considered 'best practice' in the field. The following facts paint a broad picture of this field.

NICE guidelines

- It is estimated that infertility affects one in seven heterosexual couples.
- 50% of infertility is caused by unexplained fertility and ovulatory disorders.
- Fertility treatment falls into three categories: medical (i.e. drugs), surgical and assisted.
- Over 80% of couples conceive within their first year of trying for a baby.[2]

HFEA statistics

- 62,155 IVF cycles are performed in UK licensed clinics each year.
- 65.5% of women were aged under 37 at the time of treatment.
- 60% of IVF cycles were funded privately.
- 83.8% of donor insemination cycles were funded privately.
- The live birth rate for IVF treatment is 25% (this is the success rate).
- The success rate when records began in 1991 was only 14%.[3]

NICE guidelines on fertility treatment

The definition of infertility is provided as follows:

A woman of reproductive age who has not conceived after one year of unprotected vaginal sexual intercourse. In the absence of any known cause of infertility, should be offered further clinical assessment and investigation along with her partner.[4]

---

[2] Fertility: Assessment and Treatment for People with Fertility Problems, National Institute for Health and Clinical Excellence, National Health Service, pages 5–6. February 2013, http://publications.nice. org.uk/fertility-cg156.

[3] Fertility Treatment in 2012: Trends and Figures. Human Fertilisation and Embryology Authority, page 14, 15 and 46 (2013), http://www.hfea.gov.uk/104.html.

[4] Fertility: Assessment and Treatment for People with Fertility Problems, National Institute for Health and Clinical Excellence, National Health Service, pages 9 and 17. February 2013 http://publications. nice.org.uk/fertility-cg156.

An earlier referral to a specialist is offered if the woman is aged 36 or over, or there is a known clinical cause of infertility.[5] There is no additional provision for same-sex couples who cannot engage in vaginal intercourse, leaving the guidelines open to criticism for discrimination. A couple who are concerned about delays in conception should be offered an initial assessment, but this involves a 'specific inquiry' about lifestyle and sexual history.[6] This might not sit very well with some partners, but fertility treatment is a very invasive procedure. It is important to note that couples must be seen together because both partners are affected by the investigations. Counselling plays a large role in seeking fertility treatment because of the psychological stress that it can cause, and counselling is offered to both partners before, during and after the fertility procedures.[7]

The provision of IVF is outlined by NICE. Patients are warned that the overall chance of a live birth following IVF treatment falls as the number of unsuccessful cycles increases,[8] and the outcome of previous IVF treatment is taken into account when assessing the likely effectiveness and safety of any further IVF treatment.[9] However, as long as a woman is within a certain age bracket, the following treatment can be provided:

EXTRACT

Fertility: Assessment and Treatment for People with Fertility Problems, National Institute for Health and Clinical Excellence, National Health Service:

http://publications.nice.org.uk/fertility-cg156/introduction

Pages 32–33 paragraph 1.11.1.3: In women aged under 40 years who have not conceived after 2 years of regular unprotected intercourse, . . . offer 3 full cycles of IVF . . . If the woman reaches the age of 40 during treatment, complete the current full cycle but do not offer further full cycles.

Paragraph 1.11.1.4: In women aged 40–42 years who have not conceived after 2 years of regular unprotected intercourse . . . offer 1 full cycle of IVF . . . provided the following 3 criteria are fulfilled:

- They have never previously had IVF treatment;
- There is no evidence of low ovarian reserve;
- There has been a discussion of the additional implications of IVF and pregnancy at this age.

The guidelines above are clear: a woman up to the age of 40 can have three cycles of IVF on the NHS, but a woman between 40–42 can only have one cycle of IVF on the NHS. Private clinics can offer discretion and may heighten or lower these criteria depending on the patient and her circumstances. Paragraph 1.11.1.4 regarding women aged 40–42 was only added to the guidelines in 2013 (updated from 2004) and it caused significant

---

[5] See note above, at pages 9 and 18.
[6] At page 16.
[7] At page 13.
[8] At page 31.
[9] At page 33.

controversy. Critics argued that if a woman over 40 wanted to conceive a child, she simply had to accept that her time had passed or seek private treatment so as not to deprive other patients in the NHS. The defending argument was that, not only are women living longer, but the women aged 40–42 who are seeking IVF treatment typically have solid careers, homes and incomes and since they have paid tax all of their lives, they are entitled to the treatment.

A person who is undergoing treatment for cancer can choose to have their eggs, sperm and embryos frozen, because chemotherapy can often lead to infertility. The provisions for allowing this were added to the NICE guidelines during the 2013 reforms and read as follows.

EXTRACT

Fertility: Assessment and Treatment for People with Fertility Problems, National Institute for Health and Clinical Excellence, National Health Service:

http://publications.nice.org.uk/fertility-cg156/introduction

Pages 42–43 paragraph 1.16.1.3: When deciding to offer fertility preservation to people diagnosed with cancer, take into account the following factors:

- Diagnosis;
- Treatment plan;
- Expected outcome of subsequent fertility treatment;
- Prognosis of the cancer treatment;
- Viability of stored/post thawed material.

Page 43 paragraph 1.16.1.10: Offer oocyte (egg) or embryo cryopreservation (freezing) as appropriate to women of reproductive age (including adolescent girls) who are preparing for medical treatment for cancer that is likely to make them infertile if:

- They are well enough to undergo ovarian stimulation and egg collection, and
- This will not worsen their condition, and
- Enough time is available before the start of their cancer treatment.

It is clearly important that the woman who is about to undergo treatment for cancer has enough time and strength to consent to the drug programme for the collection of her eggs before her cancer treatment starts. This is the same for men and sperm collection (although they do not need a drug programme).

HFEA statistics on fertility treatment

It is now time to look at the facts and figures of assisted conception. The Human Fertilisation and Embryology Authority (HFEA) publishes a statistical document every year to inform the public of its work and success. It is also helpful for potential patients who are considering IVF treatment and are unsure of their chances of success. The relevant facts and figures are as follows:

EXTRACT

Fertility Treatment in 2012: Trends and Figures. Human Fertilisation and Embryology Authority (2013):

http://www.hfea.gov.uk/104.html

Page 13:

- 77 clinics licensed by the HFEA performed IVF treatment in 2012;
- 72 clinics performed DI treatment.

Pages 13–14:

- 47,422 women had 62,155 cycles of IVF in 2012; 3.5% of these had an egg sharing agreement to produce eggs or embryos for donation;
- 2265 women had 4452 cycles of DI in 2012.

Page 15:

- The average age of an IVF patient was 35 years old;
- The average length of time trying to conceive was 4.7 years;
- The average age of a DI patient was 35 years old;
- The average length of time trying to conceive was 3.8 years (this may not include gay couples).

Page 21:

- A total of 86,466 embryos were transferred during 2012;
- 17,135 of these embryos were thawed.

Page 26:

- IVF treatment with fresh eggs resulted in 13,786 pregnancies (not births) in 2012;
- his translates into a 34.6% success rate.

Page 38:

- 2,225 cycles of DI were performed in 2011 leading to 776 live births.

It is clear from the statistics above that babies are big business. The overall success rate for live births is only 25%, meaning that 75% of couples are left without children after IVF treatment.[10] This is a big pressure for both scientists and the couples to deal with.

---

[10] Fertility Treatment in 2011: Trends and Figures. Human Fertilisation and Embryology Authority, page 4 (2012), http://www.hfea.gov.uk/104.html.

However, on the basis that a quarter of treatments do lead to success, it is time to look at the law governing the practice of assisted conception.

Bioethics and fertility

There are some medical ethics entwined into the area of assisted conception to illustrate the rights of each party.

Reproductive liberty

Fertility treatment is a private matter. The state should not interfere with the decision to have children, should not prevent a bad mother from becoming pregnant, and should not prevent a childless mother from seeking fertility treatment. It is widely accepted that any woman can get pregnant and decide to keep her child after a reckless one night stand. The State should not interfere with this, or the decision to have an abortion, according to the theory of reproductive liberty. In real life, the State *does* remove children from bad mothers, and the State *does* prevent bad mothers from using fertility treatment services.

Reproductive autonomy

Fertility treatment is still a private matter, but the State is under an obligation to *support* the autonomy of the woman wherever possible. Therefore, fertility services must be provided, access must be easy, the NHS should be obliged to treat infertility and those suffering from infertility shall not be judged. A woman who conceived during a one-night stand should receive state support for her decision to either raise the child or abort the child. This theory is like reproductive liberty but with an additional layer of support for autonomy. In real life, we cannot afford to treat infertility like we treat diseases, but reproductive autonomy would support this very approach.

RESEARCH ACTIVITY

Find the NICE and HFEA documents explored above and read the introductions in each publication: where do these bodies see fertility treatment going in the future?

The law on assisted conception

In light of the birth of Louise Brown in 1978, the Department of Health and Social Security set up an inquiry to investigate the developments in assisted conception. The resulting report was entitled the 'Report of the Committee of Inquiry into Human Fertilisation and Embryology' and was chaired by Mary Warnock. It was published in 1984 (known as the Warnock Report) and it concluded that even though the embryo should be protected, embryonic research and IVF should be allowed if the appropriate safeguards were in place.[11]

---

[11] The report is analysed in detail in Chapter 10 in relation to embryonic research.

EXTRACT

The Warnock Report, *Report of the Committee of Enquiry into Human Fertilisation and Embryology*, Department of Health and Social Security, July 1984, Her Majesty's Stationery Office:

http://www.hfea.gov.uk/2068.html

Page 32 paragraph 5.10: We have reached the conclusion that IVF is an acceptable means of treating infertility and we therefore recommend that the service of IVF should continue to be available subject to the same type of licensing and inspection as we have recommended with regard to the regulation of [assisted insemination with a donor]. For the protection and reassurance of the public this recommendation must apply equally to IVF within the NHS and in the private medical sector. At the present time IVF is available on a limited scale within the NHS and we recommend that IVF should continue to be available within the NHS.

Page 62 paragraph 11.15: We found that the more generally held position is that though the human embryo is entitled to some added measure of respect beyond that accorded to other animal subjects, that respect cannot be absolute, and may be weighed against the benefits arising from research. Although many research studies in embryology and developmental biology can be carried out on animal subjects, and it is possible in many cases to extrapolate these results and findings to man, in certain situations there is no substitute for the use of human embryos. This particularly applies to the study of disorders occurring only in humans, such as Down's syndrome, or for research into the processes of human fertilisation, or perhaps into the specific effect of drugs or toxic substances on human tissue.

The Human Fertilisation and Embryology Authority

The Human Fertilisation and Embryology Bill made it to Parliament in 1989, and it passed into law as the Human Fertilisation and Embryology Act 1990. The 1990 Act launched the Human Fertilisation and Embryology Authority (HFEA) under section 5.[12] It has a number of functions, including:

- Regulating fertility treatment using eggs, sperm and embryos.
- Regulating embryonic research.
- Setting standards for practice in fertility clinics.
- Inspecting clinics for safety and compliance.
- Authorising licences for fertility treatment and embryonic research.
- Maintaining a register of fertility and its success rate.
- Providing information to the general public, including patients and donors.
- Determining legal and ethical policies in fertility issues.

The HFEA must also publish a Code of Practice (2011), and it is highly detailed to assist professionals and the public alike in reading and understanding the provisions of the Act. It is updated frequently because of the speed of developments in assisted conception and provides optimum flexibility where the statute can not. A breach of the Code of Practice is not, as usual, a criminal offence, but it is pivotal when deciding who should be issued

---

[12] It has an official website: www.hfea.gov.uk.

a licence to practise fertility treatment or embryonic research. The HFEA must also publish an Annual Report to the Secretary of State for Health outlining its annual activities,
aims, objectives, activities and accounts (under section 7 of the 1990 Act). There appears
to be a lot of roles for the HFEA to handle, but it means that the provisions, standards and
licences for assisted conception are found in one place. This makes matters clear and
straightforward for professionals and patients. It is there to protect several vulnerable
parties, including:

- The embryo and any potential person derived therefrom.
- Patients such as the infertile woman, the partners, the husband, the donors and the
  surrogates.
- Society and the wider public interest.
- The fertility team treating the patient, including nurses, general practitioners, scientists
  and counsellors.

The HFEA is a public body, meaning that their decisions are subject to a judicial review
if it leads to concern or controversy (or fails to take account of human rights law). One
of the first cases to question a decision of the HFEA was *R and Another* v *HFEA* (2002), in
which the courts were satisfied that the decision was rational and thus the court did not
need to intervene.

CASE EXTRACT

R (on the application of Assisted Reproduction and Gynaecology Centre) v Human Fertilisation and Embryology Authority [2002] EWCA Civ 20

Facts: A clinic sought permission to seek judicial review of a decision by HFEA not
to authorise the implantation of more than three embryos into a particular patient.
The HFEA Code of Practice stipulated that no more than three embryos were to be
implanted in a woman in any single fertilisation cycle. A contended that, whilst the
general prescription on the numbers of embryos to be transferred was reasonable,
it was nevertheless appropriate to authorise a departure from the normal rule in the
case of a patient who had undergone eight previous unsuccessful attempts at in vitro
fertilisation.

Held: Advice given or decisions taken by the Human Fertilisation and Embryology
Authority could only be challenged where the Authority had abused or exceeded its
powers or responsibilities or where the decision taken was irrational.

Wall LJ (at paras 62, 65): We likewise see nothing irrational in the Authority's position.
The members thought that future treatment for Mrs H was likely to fail but that, if she
did succeed in becoming pregnant, there would be a higher risk of multiple pregnancy
if five embryos had been transplanted rather than three. The Authority therefore
considered that the possible marginal improvement in the chances of pregnancy
were outweighed by the albeit small risk of multiple pregnancy. Two scientists may
disagree over that proposition, but in our judgment it is impossible to describe it as
irrational. [...] It is an area of rapidly developing science in which judicial review has
a limited role to play. Disagreements between doctors and scientific bodies in this
pioneering field are inevitable. The United Kingdom, through the Act, has opted for a
system of licensing and regulation. The Authority is the body which is empowered by

→

Parliament to regulate. Like any public authority, it is open to challenge by way of judicial review, if it exceeds or abuses the powers and responsibilities given to it by Parliament; but where, as is manifest here from an examination of the facts, it considers requests for advice carefully and thoroughly, and produces opinions which are plainly rational, the court, in our judgment, has no part to play in the debate, and certainly no power to intervene to strike down any such decision. The fact that the appellants may disagree with the Authority's advice is neither here nor there.

The court powers are limited when it comes to challenging the decisions of a public authority that is exercising its powers under an Act of Parliament. The HFEA is best placed to enter into discourse about assisted conception because it is a rapidly developing area of science. The courts should not enter into scientific discussions to control Board decisions – the courts can only intervene if the Authority 'exceeds or abuses the powers and responsibilities' given by Parliament. The decision by the Authority was not irrational considering the facts of the case because the risk of multiple pregnancy outweighed the improved chance of pregnancy and if an Authority produces a decision that is carefully and thoughtfully made, the court has no power to strike down the decision. A disagreement as to the advice of the Authority is not relevant.

Activities that must be licensed by the HFEA

According to sections 3 and 4 of the 1990 Act, a person cannot deal with a human embryo or the gametes that make up a human embryo without a licence.

Human Fertilisation and Embryology Act 1990

Section 3: Prohibitions in connection with embryos

(1) No person shall bring about the creation of an embryo except in pursuance of a licence.

(2) No person shall place in a woman:

    (a) an embryo other than a permitted embryo (as defined by section 3ZA), or

    (b) any gametes other than permitted eggs or permitted sperm (as so defined).

(3) A licence cannot authorise:

    (a) keeping or using an embryo after the appearance of the primitive streak,

    (b) placing an embryo in any animal, or

    (c) keeping or using an embryo in any circumstances in which regulations prohibit its keeping or use.

(4) For the purposes of subsection (3)(a) above, the primitive streak is to be taken to have appeared in an embryo not later than the end of the period of 14 days beginning with the day on which the process of creating the embryo began, not counting any time during which the embryo is stored.

Section 4: Prohibitions in connection with gametes

(2) A licence cannot authorise storing or using gametes in any circumstances in which regulations prohibit their storage or use.

(3) No person shall place sperm and eggs in a woman in any circumstances specified in regulations except in pursuance of a licence.

A number of the activities above are criminal offences and can result in up to ten years in prison (under section 41 of the 1990 Act). The HFEA has the power to grant a licence under section 16(1) as long as the storage, use and destruction of gametes and embryos is legitimate and necessary. A licence can be granted for the following purposes:

- Fertility treatment.
- Storage of gametes and embryos.
- Research using gametes and embryos (these are listed under section 11 of the 1990 Act).

Schedule 2 provides more detail on what can be authorised under a licence for the purposes of treatment, and as you can see, this includes everything from creation to distribution:

Human Fertilisation and Embryology Act 1990

Schedule 2. Paragraph 1: Licences for treatment

(1) A licence under this paragraph may authorise any of the following in the course of providing treatment services:

(a) bringing about the creation of embryos *in vitro*;

(b) procuring, keeping, testing, processing or distributing embryos;

(c) procuring, testing, processing, distributing or using gametes;

(ca) using embryos for the purpose of training persons in embryo biopsy, embryo storage or other embryological techniques;

(d) other practices designed to secure that embryos are in a suitable condition to be placed in a woman;

(e) placing any permitted embryo in a woman.

(4A) A licence under this paragraph cannot authorise the use of embryos for the purpose mentioned in sub-paragraph (1)(ca) unless the Authority is satisfied that the proposed use of embryos is necessary for that purpose.

(5) A licence under this paragraph shall be granted for such period not exceeding five years as may be specified in the licence.

(6) In this paragraph, references to a permitted embryo are to be read in accordance with section 3ZA.

The term 'in vitro' means that the embryo was created in the laboratory ('in glass') as opposed to inside the body naturally. The provisions under Paragraph 1 refer to the use of embryos and gametes for fertility treatment and it is clear that embryos and gametes can be legitimately created, kept, processed, distributed and placed into a woman for the purposes of this treatment. Notice that embryos can also be used for 'embryological techniques' under paragraph 1(1)(ca), but the HFEA must be satisfied that this is a 'necessary' use of the embryo. A 'permitted' embryo is an unaltered embryo using egg and sperm which have not had their nuclear or mitochondrial DNA altered, as defined under section 3ZA of the 1990 Act. Only 'permitted' embryos – not altered or artificial embryos – are allowed to be placed into a woman for the purposes of treatment. The licence can last for a maximum of five years.

Human Fertilisation and Embryology Act 1990

Schedule 2. Paragraph 2: Licences for storage

(1) A licence under this paragraph or paragraph 1 or 3 of this Schedule may authorise the storage of gametes or embryos or both.

(3) A licence under this paragraph shall be granted for such period not exceeding five years as may be specified in the licence.

There is no use of the term 'permitted' in paragraph 2 meaning that altered gametes and embryos are included under this provision. An embryo and gametes can be stored for up to five years for the purposes of treatment (defined in paragraph 1). There is no 'necessary' requirement for the storage of gametes and embryos.

We can clearly see from the provisions above that the creation, storage, testing, processing and distribution of embryos and gametes are regulated by strict statutory provisions. This is to be expected when the treatment is so controversial. It is clearly illegal under section 3(3) to keep or use an embryo 14 days after the gametes have been mixed because the 'primitive streak' has begun to form inside the embryo (this is a thin bead of cells that will become the spinal column). This was considered by the Warnock Report (1984) to be the beginnings of a human being, and implantation beyond this point would be unethical.

EXTRACT

The Warnock Report, *Report of the Committee of Enquiry into Human Fertilisation and Embryology*, Department of Health and Social Security, July 1984, Her Majesty's Stationery Office:

http://www.hfea.gov.uk/2068.html

Page 66 paragraph 11.22: We accordingly recommend that no live human embryo derived from *in vitro* fertilisation, whether frozen or unfrozen, may be kept alive, if not transferred to a woman, beyond fourteen days after fertilisation, nor may it be used as a research subject beyond fourteen days after fertilisation. This fourteen day period does not include any time during which the embryo may have been frozen. We further recommend that it shall be a criminal offence to handle or to use as a research subject any live human embryo derived from *in vitro* fertilisation beyond that limit.

There are standard licensing conditions which must be complied with when using gametes or embryos for fertility treatment. These include the following:

- Activity should only be carried out on the premises in the licence – section 12(1)(a).
- A member of the HFEA can inspect the property at a reasonable time – section 12(1)(b).
- Schedule 3 (consent) must be complied with – section 12(1)(c).
- Money shall not be given or received for gametes or embryos – section 12(1)(e).

- Information to trace the gametes or embryos must be recorded – section 12(3).
- Patient details, their treatment and the outcome must be recorded – section 13(2).
- The welfare of the future child must be considered before treatment – section 13(5).
- Proper counselling shall be provided before treatment commences – section 13(6).
- A patient must not be discriminated against for a serious illness – section 13(9).
- A patient must not be discriminated against for a gender related illness – section 13(10).
- The licence must allocate a 'person responsible' (PR) for the activity – section 16(2).
- The PR must be suitably qualified and have two years' experience – section 16(2)(c).
- The PR must have the 'character' required to perform the tasks – section 16(2)(cb).
- The premises must be appropriate for the activity – section 16(2)(d).
- The PR must ensure proper equipment, storage, practice and compliance – section 17(1).

The PR is normally the head scientist who leads the treatment or research project. He is to be accountable for the storage, use and disposal of the gametes and embryos, as well as ensuring that all other provisions are followed. It has been established in case law that a PR is not vicariously liable for the criminal offences committed by his staff.

CASE EXTRACT

Attorney General's Reference (No. 2 of 2003), Re [2004] EWCA Crim 785

Facts: The defendant was the 'person responsible' for the supervision of the activities authorised by licences at the clinics. At the relevant time, the sole embryologist at both clinics was a man of apparently high reputation and skill. Unfortunately he was dishonest. He was convicted of making false claims for the cost of thawing frozen embryos, procedures which he had not carried out. In effect, he had kept these embryos when he should not have done so. He was further convicted of assaulting and occasioning actual bodily harm to female patients who did not have their own embryos implanted. The legal issue was, did the 'person responsible' carry any liability for the embryologist's criminal activities?

Held: No vicarious liability – criminal liability was not extended vicariously under the 1990 Act. The embryologist was responsible for his own actions.

Judge LJ (at pages 2066–7): In summary, anyone lacking an appropriate licence, or acting outside the ambit or in breach of the terms of a licence, is prohibited from keeping or using an embryo. If he does so, he commits an offence contrary to section 41(2)(a). The offence, however, is committed by the person who contravenes section 3(1). The language is simple. It is difficult to see how it extends to create criminal liability for keeping an embryo otherwise than authorised by the licence to an individual who, notwithstanding his statutory responsibilities, does not in fact keep the embryo at all. If it had been intended that the person responsible should, as a matter of law, have been criminally liable for any contravention of section 3(1) by anyone else, or for administrative failures within the clinic in relation to the keeping and use of embryos, this could have been achieved, if Parliament had so intended, by clear language. Such language is not used. [...] Accordingly, the answer to the question in the reference, which is exclusively concerned with a proposition of law, not one of fact, is 'No'.

A licence can, of course, be revoked if serious misconduct such as this is discovered. The powers to do so are found under sections 18 and 19, and they include the following grounds for revocation:

- Information upon which the licence was based was false or misleading.
- The PR failed to use proper equipment, store or use the materials appropriately.
- The premises are not or no longer suitable for the activity.
- The PR is no longer a suitable person to hold a licence.
- The PR dies or is convicted of an offence under the 1990 Act (list found under s. 18).

When a licence is about to be varied or revoked, the HFEA must notify the PR and he has 28 days to provide an oral or written representation (under section 19). A decision to revoke a licence must be a reasonable one. According to the case law of *Associated Provincial Picture Houses* v *Wednesbury Corporation* [1948] 1 KB 223, a public body can still be overruled by a court if they come to a decision that is so unreasonable that no other public body would have supported it. The requirement of licences is somewhat frowned upon in other countries. A government should not interfere with science, and it is quite abnormal to limit the research of scientists in some Eastern countries. British couples often seek fertility treatment in India because the regulations are far more relaxed (this is known as reproductive tourism), and come back expecting triplets and quads because the number of embryos to be implanted is limitless. However, despite the differences between the UK and India (amongst other countries), the UK system is considered to be the model system for the regulation of fertility treatment, and it has been implemented in many Western countries.

Confidentiality

It is important to register the details of the patients who undertake a course of fertility treatment for a number of reasons. Firstly, the Department of Health can keep tabs on how many couples are seeking fertility treatments in this country (and in which counties). Secondly, if something goes wrong, that couple can be contacted. Thirdly, if a baby results, this can be added to the number of success stories. Fourthly, the baby is entitled to know where it came from when it reaches the age of majority.

The HFEA is obliged under section 31(2) of the 1990 Act to keep a register of the following things:

- The provision for any identifiable individual of treatment services.
- The keeping of the gametes of any identifiable individual or of an embryo taken from any identifiable woman.
- The use of the gametes of any identifiable individual.
- The use of an embryo taken from any identifiable woman.
- Information that shows any identifiable individual is a relevant individual.

Section 33A(1) (added by the 2008 reform) stipulates that anybody working for the HFEA cannot disclose any confidential information falling within the description of section 31(2) (above) unless one of the legal exceptions under section 33A(2) apply. It was also learnt in Chapter 5 that confidential information can be disclosed for the purposes of medical research under section 251 of the National Health Service Act 2006. This provision has been incorporated into the Human Fertilisation and Embryology Act 1990 in section 33D.

Human Fertilisation and Embryology Act 1990

Section 33D: Disclosure for the purposes of medical or other research

(1) Regulations may:

   (a) make such provision for and in connection with requiring or regulating the processing of protected information for the purposes of medical research as the Secretary of State considers is necessary or expedient in the public interest or in the interests of improving patient care, and

   (b) make such provision for and in connection with requiring or regulating the processing of protected information for the purposes of any other research as the Secretary of State considers is necessary or expedient in the public interest.

It must clearly be 'necessary' or 'in the public interest' to disclose personal information for the purposes of medical research. This will probably be quite rare, such as a medical breakthrough or a cure for a disease.

ACTIVITY

Dr Starling has travelled over from Germany to conduct his own research. He wants to set up his own lab in the English University where he now works and begin research into 'the quickest way to create a viable embryo using human and animal materials' but he comes to you to ask about the current law and regulations in this field. Advise him on the restrictions imposed upon him by the common law, statute law and the HFEA.

Who can seek assisted conception?

This is a difficult question. There is not a simple answer because of the welfare tests and the complexity of family relationships (e.g. gay couples and single women). The attitudes of society have softened over the last few decades and there are provisions in place to protect patients from discrimination, but fertility treatment is still not offered to *everyone* who seeks it.

Barrier 1: the 'welfare' test

The Human Fertilisation and Embryology Act 1990 was quite liberal in nature. It allowed for any person to receive fertility treatment in the UK. There was no clear limit on age, and no barrier to sexual orientation or marital status. However, there was one clear provision under section 13(5) which read:

> A woman shall not be provided with treatment services unless account has been taken of the welfare of any child who may be born as a result of the treatment (including the need of that child *for a father*), and of any other child who may be affected by the birth.[13]

---

[13] Italics added to show the old provision which has now been removed.

The italics above draw attention to the one condition that appeared to limit fertility treatment. There must have been a *father* for the child (or at the very least, the child's *need* for a father had to be considered). This provision allowed clinics to turn away single women and lesbian couples who sought fertility treatment using donor sperm. The Act was passed with this provision because it was seen as supportive of the family unit. However, critics claimed that it discriminated against single women and lesbian couples who could both adopt children under the Adoption and Children Act 2002 and lesbian couples could enter into a civil partnership under the Civil Partnership Act 2004. The new Bill came before Parliament in 2007 and it was suggested that the 'father' clause be removed. Society has moved on since 1990, and many mothers are now bringing up children alone because of divorce or separation, which do not carry the stigma they used to. The alternative for a single woman or a lesbian couple who wanted to have a baby was to get pregnant through a 'one-night stand', despite this carrying the threat of disease and no sure identity of the father. The removal of the clause was highly controversial and it upset a lot of people including Members of Parliament and the general public, because it removed the role of the father from conception and childhood. However, the removal went ahead, and as a result of the 2008 reform section 13(5) now reads:

> A woman shall not be provided with treatment services unless account has been taken of the welfare of any child who may be born as a result of the treatment (including the need of that child for supportive parenting), and of any other child who may be affected by the birth.

The need for 'a father' has been replaced by the need for 'supportive parenting' to allow for single women and lesbian couples to access fertility treatments. Groups in favour of the removal argue that it is not always guaranteed that a father will stick around and children raised by same-sex couples show no significant side effects.[14] Groups in favour of the 'father' clause have been horrified that children are now brought into the world without a father *intentionally*, instead of losing their father through death, divorce or separation. The 'supportive parenting' clause is all about the *welfare* of the child. For example, instead of her need for a father, the clinics (and courts) consider her need for a stable and healthy environment. There are some groups who argue that this is a better test, because the presence of a father does not guarantee a safe and healthy environment. It is true that men are more likely to lose their temper when a young child tests their patience and this is proved by the significant number of domestic violence incidents every year caused by men rather than women. There are other groups who argue that this is a vague test that allows the role of the father in society to be slowly extinguished. The Human Fertilisation and Embryology Authority's Code of Practice (2008) explains in detail how section 13(5) is to be interpreted.

EXTRACT

Code of Practice, 8th edition, October 2013, Human Fertilisation and Embryology Authority:

http://www.hfea.gov.uk/code.html

Paragraph 8.2: The centre should have documented procedures to ensure that proper account is taken of the welfare of any child who may be born as a result of treatment services, and any other child who may be affected by the birth.

---

[14] This will not be entirely clear until our generation of children in same-sex families grow up and look back on their childhoods compared to the childhoods of their own children to see whether they missed out, and even then, they know no any different to be able to compare their experience.

Paragraph 8.3: The centre should assess each patient and their partner (if they have one) before providing any treatment, and should use this assessment to decide whether there is a risk of significant harm or neglect to any child referred to in 8.2.

Paragraph 8.7: Those seeking treatment are entitled to a fair assessment. The centre is expected to consider the wishes of all those involved, and the assessment must be done in a non-discriminatory way. In particular, patients should not be discriminated against on grounds of gender, race, disability, sexual orientation, religious belief or age.

Paragraph 8.9: The centre should take a medical and social history from each patient and their partner (if they have one). Where appropriate, the patient and their partner may be interviewed separately.

Paragraph 8.10: The centre should consider factors that are likely to cause a risk of significant harm or neglect to any child who may be born or to any existing child of the family. These factors include any aspects of the patient's or (if they have one) their partner's:

(a) past or current circumstances that may lead to any child mentioned above experiencing serious physical or psychological harm or neglect, for example:

    (i) previous convictions relating to harming children

    (ii) child protection measures taken regarding existing children, or

    (iii) violence or serious discord in the family environment

(b) past or current circumstances that are likely to lead to an inability to care throughout childhood for any child who may be born, or that are already seriously impairing the care of any existing child of the family, for example:

    (i) mental or physical conditions

    (ii) drug or alcohol abuse

    (iii) medical history, where the medical history indicates that any child who may be born is likely to suffer from a serious medical condition, or

    (iv) circumstances that the centre considers likely to cause serious harm to any child mentioned above.

Under paragraph 8.2, the welfare of any child born and any *existing children* must be taken into account. This is radical: it is not often that the needs of relatives and/or siblings are considered when providing medical treatment to a patient. It shows a rounded view of the family and acknowledges that medical treatment can effect more than just the patient. In addition to this, each centre should have 'documented procedures' in place to assess the welfare of any child born. This provides significant discretion to centres to develop their own assessment procedures, as long as they roughly follow the Code of Practice guidelines. Under paragraph 8.3, each partner is to be assessed to provide the foundation for the welfare test. The 'assessment' is contained under paragraph 8.10. Under paragraph 8.7, the assessment must be fair. The 1990/2008 Act does not elaborate on the meaning of fairness, but according to the Code of Practice it must be a non-discriminatory assessment. The grounds of gender, race, disability, sexual orientation, religious belief or age should not pose a barrier to fertility treatment. Age is, however, dealt with in other regulations by NICE. Under paragraph 8.9, the medical and social history of each partner is considered. This is interesting. Medical history is important for the success of the fertility treatment, but *social* history is used solely as a benchmark to measure good parenting. This will no doubt include criminal convictions, employment status, relationship history and education. The patients can be interviewed separately, allowing for secrets or inconsistencies to be revealed. Under paragraph 8.10, the risk factors are listed in detail. These help to ascertain the welfare of any child born or any existing child. These include serious physical or psychological harm and an inability to care for the child or existing children. It is disappointing that the words 'serious', 'abuse' and 'convictions' are used to measure the suitability of patients. It appears that the patient and her partner must be *significantly* unsuitable candidates before they can be turned away from fertility treatment.

The welfare test under section 13(5) is clearly used as a guideline to ascertain the suitability of the patients as prospective parents. The Code of Practice does provide further guidance on how to apply it in practice but it has its difficulties, not least because it is so vague. It is not possible for healthcare professionals working in fertility clinics to accurately judge how good a patient would be at raising a child. There are no home visits or specialist training. It is also not clear what would happen if a clinic failed to assess a couple properly. Who would bring a claim and what would the damage be? 'Wrongful life' claims by children have not been accepted by the courts because the child is arguing that it had a right to be aborted or killed and a court will not award damages for the *birth* of a child: *McKay* v *Essex AHA* [1982] QB 1166. As a result, the welfare test under section 13(5) is very difficult to regulate in practice.

There may not be any need for the welfare test at all. It has been suggested that, because many teenage mothers conceive a baby through carelessness, infertile couples unfairly burden a rigorous and sometimes intrusive assessment process when they are probably more dedicated, better educated, emotionally settled and considerably wealthier than the average teenage mother.[15]

Barrier 2: turning away 'unsuitable' characters

It has been known for disappointed patients to seek judicial review when they have been rejected for fertility treatment. In the case of *Harriott*, the patient had previous convictions for prostitution and was removed from the IVF waiting list. Her request for a judicial review was rejected because any other reasonable consultant or ethics committee would have come to the same conclusion, therefore it was not discriminatory.

CASE EXTRACT

R v *Ethical Committee of St Mary's Hospital, ex parte Harriott* [1988] 1 FLR 512

Facts: The applicant, unable to conceive a child, had an application to adopt refused because of her criminal record for offences related to prostitution. She then sought an *in vitro* fertilisation. She saw a consultant who then became aware of the refused adoption application and the reasons for refusal. For that reason and for other reasons the consultant decided that IVF treatment should not be given. The Infertility Services Ethical Committee of the hospital, a body set up to give advice and guidance, referred to the applicant's case and took the view that the decision was one for the medical team to make. The applicant applied for judicial review, contending

---

[15] See E. Jackson (2002) 'Conception and the Irrelevance of the Welfare Principle' 65 *Modern Law Review* 176.

that the committee was obliged to investigate the matter and give the applicant an opportunity to be heard before it gave guidance or advice.

Held: The committee had no duty to investigate the matter; it was an informal body that could not be compelled by the court to investigate or give advice. Accordingly the court would be slow to force the committee to hear representations before deciding to give advice. Judicial review may lie in appropriate cases where the advice was illegal or discriminatory but that was not so here.

As a result of *Harriott*, it is clear that previous convictions for non-violent crimes, such as prostitution, could be a barrier to fertility treatment. Is this fair? After all, if the patient in *Harriott* was able to conceive naturally, she could easily become pregnant as many times as she liked and may even be an excellent mother. The *Harriott* case was decided before human rights were incorporated into UK law. As a result of the Human Rights Act 1998, the following human rights are now available to patients who feel they have been unfairly refused fertility treatment:

- Article 8: a right to respect for private life.
- Article 8: a right to respect for family life.
- Article 12: a right to found a family.
- Article 14: the right to be free from discrimination.

These rights have been used by patients in two notable prison cases where the male partners were incarcerated and not allowed to seek fertility treatment.

CASE EXTRACT

R v Secretary of State for the Home Department, ex parte Mellor [2001] HR LR 38

Facts: M, a prisoner serving a life sentence for murder, appealed against the dismissal of his application for judicial review ([2000] 2 FLR 951) of the refusal by the Secretary of State to grant him the opportunity to conceive a child with his wife via the aid of artificial insemination. M contended that the refusal infringed his right to respect for his private and family life and his right to found a family, contrary to the Human Rights Act 1998.

Held: Dismissing the appeal, the Secretary of State had not acted in breach of M's right to respect for his family life in refusing him access to the facilities he had requested. One aspect of the punishment meted out to M was the denial of precisely those rights which he now sought to avail himself of. No interference with those rights would amount to a breach of his fundamental rights, provided that it was proportionate under Article 8(2) to the aim of operating a penal system designed for both punishment and deterrence.

Lord Phillips MR (at pages 798–9, 804): Mr Pannick QC makes the following submissions on behalf of the appellant. [...] [Semen] could be taken from the prisoner within the prison without undue dislocation of the prison regime. Alternatively it could be provided by escorting the prisoner to a clinic, which would

→

involve no greater administrative burden than that involved when a prisoner is taken to a funeral of a close relative, or to a hospital for treatment. It follows that artificial insemination provides a method by which a prisoner can exercise his right to found a family which is compatible with his imprisonment. That is a fundamental right which the prisoner ought to be permitted to exercise in the absence of a cogent reason for interfering with it. Miss Rose for the Secretary of State challenges this analysis. She submits that the purpose, or at least a purpose, of imprisonment is to punish the criminal by depriving him of certain rights and pleasures which he can only enjoy when at liberty. Those rights and pleasures include the enjoyment of family life, the exercise of conjugal rights and the right to found a family. Imprisonment is inconsistent with those rights not merely as a matter of practical incompatibility but because part of the object of the exercise is that it should preclude the exercise of those rights. [...]

I consider that the jurisprudence [...] supports Miss Rose's submission. The Commission noted with sympathy the facilitating of conjugal visits in several European countries, but concluded that *for the present time* the refusal of such visits should continue to be regarded as *justified for the prevention of disorder or crime*. [...] It does not follow from this that it will always be justifiable to prevent a prisoner from inseminating his wife artificially, or indeed naturally. The interference with fundamental human rights which is permitted by Article 8(2) involves an exercise in proportionality. Exceptional circumstances may require the normal consequences of imprisonment to yield, because the effect of its interference with a particular human right is disproportionate. [...] I would simply observe that it seems to me rational that the normal starting point should be a need to demonstrate that, if facilities for artificial insemination are not provided, the founding of a family may not merely be delayed, but prevented altogether.

Lord Phillips MR was clearly of the opinion that, in accordance with proportionality under Article 8(2), as long as the prospect of parenthood was simply delayed and not prevented altogether, then the human rights of the prisoner have not been breached when he was prevented from providing a semen sample for the purposes of artificial insemination. It does seem rather strange that Mrs Mellor could not wait until the release of Mr Mellor to conceive a child when they would have both still been in their early 30s at the time (murderers can have parole).

The issue rose again in *Dickson* a few years later in the Grand Chamber of the European Court of Human Rights, and this time there was a chance that parenthood could be prevented altogether by a delay in fertility treatment because the prisoner's wife would be aged 50. The UK policy in *Mellor* was given a significant stripping down by Judge Rozakis.

CASE EXTRACT

Dickson v United Kingdom (74025/01) (2008) 46 EHRR 41

Facts: The complainants (D) argued that a refusal of access to artificial insemination was in breach of their rights under the European Convention on Human Rights 1950 Article 8. D had been married while they were serving prisoners. The wife had since been released, but the earliest expected release date for the husband, who was convicted of murder, was 2009, when she would be 50. D had applied to the Secretary of State for facilities for artificial insemination arguing that, because of her age, they would be unlikely to conceive naturally after his release. That application was refused on grounds of public policy and permission for judicial review was refused. D brought a complaint before the European Court of Human Rights, which held that it had not been shown that the refusal of facilities for artificial insemination was arbitrary or unreasonable. The United Kingdom government put forward three grounds justifying the policy reasons for the Secretary of State's refusal, namely that (i) losing the opportunity to beget children was an inevitable and necessary consequence of imprisonment; (ii) to allow prisoners guilty of certain serious offences to conceive children would undermine public confidence in the prison system by circumventing punitive and deterrent elements of the sentence; (iii) the long-term absence of a parent would have a negative impact on any child conceived, and therefore on society as a whole.

Held: Complaint upheld. Article 8 was applicable because the refusal of artificial insemination facilities concerned private and family life, which incorporated the right to respect for their decision to become genetic parents. A person retained his Convention rights on imprisonment, so any restriction on those rights had to be justified. Prisoners' rights should not be automatically forfeited based purely on what might offend public opinion.

Judge Rozakis (at pages 941, 948, 950): Only the right to liberty was automatically removed by a sentence of imprisonment. A state had to justify the limitation of any other rights. The starting-point of the policy was therefore wrong and should be reversed: the policy should be that prisoners had a right to procreate unless there were compelling reasons against. This inversed structure prevented any real assessment of each individual case: it was necessary to show that, but for artificial insemination, conception would be impossible and, thereafter, exceptional circumstances had to be demonstrated. The odds were thereby so stacked against the grant of facilities that there was no real individual assessment and the result was a foregone conclusion so that the policy amounted to a blanket ban. [...] As to the applicants' interests, it was accepted domestically that artificial insemination remained the only realistic hope of the applicants, a couple since 1999 and married since 2001, of having a child together given the second applicant's age and the first applicant's release date. The Court considers it evident that the matter was of vital importance to the applicants. [...] Whilst the inability to beget a child might be a consequence of imprisonment, it is not an inevitable one, it not being suggested that the grant of artificial insemination facilities would involve any security issues or impose any significant administrative or financial demands on the State. [...] In particular, and having regard to the judgment of Lord Phillips MR in the *Mellor* case and of Auld LJ in the present case, the policy placed an inordinately high 'exceptionality' burden on the applicants when requesting artificial insemination facilities. [...] The policy set the threshold so high against them from the outset that it did not allow a balancing of the competing individual and public interests and a proportionality test by the Secretary of State or by the domestic courts in their case, as required by the Convention. [...] Further, since the policy was not embodied in primary legislation, the various competing interests were never weighed, nor were issues of proportionality ever assessed, by Parliament. Indeed, the policy was adopted, as noted in the judgment of the Court of Appeal in the *Mellor* case, prior to the incorporation of the Convention into domestic law.

The European Court of Human Rights (ECHR) acknowledged that imprisonment did not deprive the prisoner of his human rights (except his liberty) but it did mean that some rights would be limited and controlled. The UK's aims of maintaining public confidence in the penal system and the welfare of any child born from fertility treatment were legitimate aims to pursue. However, the argument by the UK that the prisoner's right to be a parent were an exception rather than the norm was not compatible with the European Convention on Human Rights. The UK had to justify why a prisoner could not have access to his other human rights apart from his liberty, and the norm should be that a prisoner had a right to procreate unless there were compelling reasons against (not the other way around). The policy in the UK prevented any real assessment of the individual case and it was not appropriate that the prisoner had to show that, without artificial insemination, conception would be impossible. The UK policy therefore amounted to a blanket ban and it should not have used the interests of the wider public as a justification for their policy. The age and the release date in this case should have been considered, because they were important to the claimants. There were no clear security issues, administrative issues or financial demands to providing a semen sample (although the possibility of another child being raised on the State because its mother was a single parent and its father was a convicted criminal was not considered by Judge Rozakis). The UK policy 'placed an inordinately high exceptionality burden on the applicants when requesting artificial insemination facilities' and this threshold was so high that it did not allow for the balancing of individual and public interests as required by the Convention. The UK policy was not embodied in UK legislation or assessed by Parliament, rendering it invalid in light of the Convention.

The *Dickson* case opened the door for prisoners to engage in artificial insemination during their incarceration unless there was a compelling reason against the treatment. There is no evidence to suggest that there has been a tidal wave of fertility services for prisoners, but it is now available.

THINKING POINT

The removal of a 'need for a father' in the HFEA 1990/2008 created considerable controversy. Should we turn away single women from fertility treatment services? If so, are single women who seek fertility treatment any different to the single women who raise children alone as a result of becoming pregnant after a one-night stand? Give reasons for your answer.

Eggs, sperm and embryos

The use of eggs and sperm (known as 'gametes' by the legislation) is fundamental to fertility treatment, and provisions for consent and donation have been drawn up to enable fertility treatment to go ahead. This is the case whether our own gametes are being used or the donated gametes of another are being used in our own treatment.

Consenting to using our own gametes and embryos

A man and a woman can consent to their own sperm and eggs being used in their own fertility treatment as long as they are healthy (otherwise a donor can be used). The Human Fertilisation and Embryology Act 1990 has been amended several times (most recently in 2008) to keep up with scientific developments such as screening, but the basic definitions for embryos, eggs and sperm under section 1 remain the same.

Human Fertilisation and Embryology Act 1990

Section 1: Meaning of 'embryo', 'gamete' and associated expressions

(1) In this Act –

   (a) embryo means a live human embryo, and

   (b) references to an embryo include an egg that is in the process of fertilisation or is undergoing any other process capable of resulting in an embryo.

(4) In this Act –

   (a) references to eggs are to live human eggs, including cells of the female germ line at any stage of maturity;

   (b) references to sperm are to live human sperm, including cells of the male germ line at any stage of maturity, and

   (c) references to gametes are to be read accordingly.

An egg which is 'in the process' of being fertilised is considered to be an embryo. The egg and sperm can be at any stage of maturity and the egg and sperm must be 'live' but there is no requirement for them to remain unaltered by science, i.e. the use of an altered egg and sperm appears to be acceptable. The egg and sperm are usually referred to as 'gametes' in this area of medical law.

The provisions of consent are housed under Schedule 3 of the 1990 Act. The giving of consent (or a withdrawal of consent) must be in writing and signed by the person giving it or withdrawing it (under paragraph 1). Paragraph 2(4) lists all the activities for which consent must be attained, and these include the following.

Human Fertilisation and Embryology Act 1990

Schedule 3. Paragraph 2: Consent

(4) A consent under this Schedule may apply –

   (a) to the use or storage of a particular embryo or human admixed embryo, or

   (b) in the case of a person providing gametes or human cells, to the use or storage of –

   (i) any embryo or human admixed embryo whose creation may be brought about using those gametes or those cells, and

   (ii) any embryo or human admixed embryo whose creation may be brought about using such an embryo or human admixed embryo.

(5) In the case of a consent falling within sub-paragraph (4)(b), the terms of the consent may be varied, or the consent may be withdrawn in relation to –

   (a) a particular embryo or particular embryos, or

   (b) a particular human admixed embryo or particular human admixed embryos.

The 1990 Act clearly gives donors the freedom to choose what happens to their gametes and embryos because the storage and use of these materials requires their consent. In addition, under paragraph 2(5) (above) a donor can vary or withdraw his consent at any time. Paragraph 2(1) provides more detail on consent for the use of embryos.

Human Fertilisation and Embryology Act 1990

Schedule 3. Paragraph 2: Consent

(1) A consent to the use of any embryo must specify one or more of the following purposes –

    (a) use in providing treatment services to the person giving consent, or that person and another specified person together;

    (b) use in providing treatment services to persons not including the person giving consent;

    (ba) use for the purpose of training persons in embryo biopsy, embryo storage or other embryological techniques, or

    (c) use for the purposes of any project of research,

and may specify conditions subject to which the embryo may be so used.

Paragraph 6: *in vitro* fertilisation and subsequent use of embryo

(1) A person's gametes or human cells must not be used to bring about the creation of any embryo *in vitro* unless there is an effective consent by that person to any embryo, the creation of which may be brought about with the use of those gametes or human cells, being used for one or more of the purposes mentioned in paragraph 2(1)(a), (b) and (c) above.

Paragraph 8: storage of gametes and embryos

(1) A person's gametes must not be kept in storage unless there is an effective consent by that person to their storage and they are stored in accordance with the consent.

(2) An embryo the creation of which was brought about *in vitro* must not be kept in storage unless there is an effective consent, by each relevant person in relation to the embryo, to the storage of the embryo and the embryo is stored in accordance with those consents.

The provisions above show us that a donor may consent to his or her embryo being used for a range of activities, including the treatment of others, training and research. The treatment of others under paragraph (1)(b) would typically occur when, at the end of an IVF cycle, there are unwanted embryos left and a couple consent to donating their embryos to another couple who cannot make embryos of their own. An interesting addition to Schedule 3 is the need for counselling. Paragraph 3 states that an opportunity to receive 'proper counselling' must be offered to the person who gives consent.

Human Fertilisation and Embryology Act 1990

Schedule 3. Paragraph 3: Procedure for giving consent

(1) Before a person gives consent under this Schedule –

    (a) he must be given a suitable opportunity to receive proper counselling about the implications of taking the proposed steps, and

    (b) he must be provided with such relevant information as is proper.

It is not clear why this requirement features in Schedule 3, but the likely aim is to inform a donor, for example, that he or she may be handing a 'potential human being' over to either another couple to use in treatment, or to a scientist for the purposes of medical research. A married couple may see their unused embryos as potential children and twenty years after the donation of the embryo they should be prepared for their child turning up wanting to know who they are. The HFEA published a Code of Practice to be read in conjunction with the 1990 Act, and it provides insightful guidance as to what couples (and donors) should be told *before* they offer consent.

EXTRACT

Code of Practice, 8th edition, October 2013, Human Fertilisation and Embryology Authority:

http://www.hfea.gov.uk/code.html

Paragraph 5.8: The centre should ensure that consent is:

(a) given voluntarily (without pressure to accept treatment or agree to donation);

(b) given by a person who has capacity to do so, as defined by the Mental Capacity Act 2005 (England and Wales); . . . and

(c) taken by a person authorised by the centre to do so.

Paragraph 5.9: The centre should ensure that anyone giving consent declares that:

(a) they were given enough information to enable them to understand the nature, purpose and implications of the treatment or donation;

(b) they were given a suitable opportunity to receive proper counselling about the implications of the proposed procedures;

(c) they were given information about the procedure for varying or withdrawing consent; and

(d) the information they have given in writing is correct and complete.

The couple seeking fertility treatment (or the donor) must provide voluntary consent with full capacity to a person in authority. This consent must be fully informed as to the nature, purpose and implications of the treatment or donation, they must have had an opportunity for counselling, and their consent must be based on complete information provided to them in writing. These many consent provisions stem from case law (see Chapter 4). The first significant case involving consent to the use of gametes was *Blood* (1997). This case illustrates just how a loophole in the law of consent can leave a female partner deprived of sperm for fertility treatment.

CASE EXTRACT

R v *Human Fertilisation and Embryology Authority ex parte Blood* [1997] 2 CMLR 591

Facts: The applicant [B] and her husband had been actively trying to start a family when he became ill and was admitted to hospital. His condition deteriorated rapidly, and when he went into a coma samples of sperm were taken from him at the applicant's request so that she might be artificially inseminated. He died shortly thereafter. The Human Fertilisation and Embryology Authority informed the applicant that section 4 of and Schedule 3 to the Human Fertilisation and Embryology Act 1990 together with the authority's Code of Practice prohibited the storage of the sperm since her husband had not given written consent, and further that the sperm could not be exported for use abroad. The applicant sought judicial review of the authority's decision.

Held: The storage of the husband's sperm had been unlawful because of the lack of consent. Once a donor had died the use of his sperm in the course of providing treatment services to a woman could not be regarded as being provided for 'the woman and the man together' within the meaning of section 4(1)(b) so the applicant could not lawfully receive treatment in the United Kingdom. However, allowing the appeal despite the unlawful storage of sperm, the applicant had a directly enforceable right to receive medical treatment in another Member State unless interference with that right was justified.

Lord Woolf MR (at pages 598–9, 601, 606): Section 4(1) [of the HFEA 1990] makes it clear that [storage] must always be pursuant to a licence. That means that storage can only take place lawfully in accordance with the requirements of the licence which for the present purposes are those contained in Schedule 3. This means that there must be a consent in writing [...] before the storage can lawfully take place. [...] It follows that Mr Blood's sperm should not in fact have been preserved and stored. Technically therefore an offence was committed by the licence holder as a result of the storage by the licensee. There is however no question of any prosecution being brought in the circumstances of this case and no possible criticism can be made of the fact that storage has taken place because [the scientist] was acting throughout in close consultation with the authority in a perfectly *bona fide* manner, in an unexplored legal situation where humanity dictated that the sperm was taken and preserved first, and the legal argument followed. [...] The next question is therefore whether the obtaining of the sperm amounted to treatment services which were being provided for Mr and Mrs Blood together in the sense that section 4(1)(b) refers to the provision of services 'for the woman and man together'. [...] It is really not possible to regard treatment as being together for the purposes of section 4(1)(b), once the man who has provided the sperm has died. [...] The absence of the necessary written consent means that both the treatment of Mrs Blood and the storage of Mr Blood's sperm would be prohibited by the Act of 1990. The authority has no discretion to authorise treatment in the United Kingdom. [...] It has already been pointed out that the Act of 1990 in section 24(4) gives a discretion to the Authority as to when and subject to what conditions to permit any person to whom a licence applies to export sperm in any particular case. [...] Parliament by the Act of 1990 had left issues of public policy as to export to be determined by the Authority.

It does indeed state under section 4(1)(a) that gametes must not be stored without a licence, and under section 12(1)(c) it clearly states that a licence must comply with the provisions under Schedule 3 (i.e. consent). Mr Blood did not consent to his gametes being preserved and stored in the way that they were, and so it was unlawful storage. The HFEA used this unlawful act to justify preventing Mrs Blood from exporting the sperm to Belgium (she couldn't seek treatment in the UK). Lord Woolf MR decided that, even though the licensee had committed an unlawful act by storing the gametes without consent, he did it in good faith ('bona fide'). It also states under section 4(1)(b) that any gametes must be used in a service 'for the woman and the man together' and as Lord Woolf MR points out, Mr and Mrs Blood would not be seeking services 'together' if he is deceased. Paragraph 2(2)(b) of Schedule 3 makes allowances for death: 'a consent to the storage of any gametes or any embryo must state what is to be done with the gametes or embryo if the person who gave consent dies or is unable because of incapacity to vary the terms of the consent or to revoke it, and may specify conditions subject to which the gametes or embryo may remain in storage.' Mr Blood did not state what he wanted to do in the event of his death, but patents today will be asked by their clinician. It was left up to the HFEA to decide, on a case by case basis, whether it would allow such exports to go ahead or not (despite a criminal offence being committed). It does indeed state under section 24(4) that: 'directions may authorise any person to whom a licence applies to receive gametes or embryos from outside the United Kingdom or to send gametes or embryos outside the united Kingdom in such circumstances and subject to such conditions as may be specified in the directions.' Lord Woolf MR believed that Mrs Blood's right to seek medical treatment in other European countries was not appropriately considered by the HFEA. The HFEA was invited to reconsider its decision, and because they were the ones who stored the gametes without consent and failed to acknowledge the rights of their patient, they changed their mind so as to not set a precedent for these facts to happen again.

The exact same issue was raised again in *L* (2008). The facts were very similar to those of *Blood*, and a precedent had clearly been set that allowed the unlawful storage of gametes to enable treatment to take place abroad.

CASE EXTRACT

L v Human Fertilisation and Embryology Authority [2008] EWHC 2149

Facts: L sought IVF advice six days before her husband (H) suddenly died during surgery. They already had one child, but wanted another. There was no written consent from H so the storage of the gametes and treatment using the gametes would not be lawful in the UK.

Held: The judge believed that the HFEA had a wide discretion after *Blood* to permit export of gametes to another country for treatment (this is despite the storage of the gametes being unlawful without consent).

Charles J (at para 29): I have concluded that: (1) The bases for the declarations sought by the claimant that continued storage of H's sperm is lawful do not exist, and I therefore refuse to make them. (2) The issue of whether or not H's sperm can be exported for use in treatment of L is a matter to be decided by the HFEA as the statutory decision-maker.

This case is unsettling. The precedent established is as follows: a man must consent to his sperm being stored and if he dies suddenly and does not consent, the storage is unlawful. However, his female partner can take his unlawfully stored sperm to another country under section 24(4) of the HFEA 1990. The courts will turn a blind eye to the unlawfulness of the storage for the purposes of export. This is surely not correct. There will, no doubt, be other similar cases until the HFEA realises that it is condoning unlawful storage of gametes. It is bringing its own integrity into disrepute when exercising this level of discretion.

The use of embryos is slightly different when it comes to consent. The embryo is a fusion of both gametes – the sperm and the egg – and so both the male and the female must consent to the use of the embryo. It is clear in the provisions laid out above (paragraphs 2, 6 and 8 of Schedule 3) that both parties must consent to the treatment, research and storage of the embryo. A disagreement between the partners (i.e. a break up) will complicate the matter considerably. A woman's eggs can be frozen, but this is not very successful. The storage of embryos is much more likely to result in a child one day. Therefore, if a woman was to undergo chemotherapy treatment for cancer, she may be advised to freeze embryos with her partner rather than her eggs alone. This puts her in a difficult position if they break up and he withdraws his consent further down the line – she will lose her only chance of becoming a biological parent. Paragraph 4 of Schedule 3 confirms that either party can withdraw their consent to the use of their gametes or embryos, which effectively brings the whole process to an end.

Paragraph 4: Variation and withdrawal of consent

(1) The terms of any consent under this Schedule may from time to time be varied, and the consent may be withdrawn, by notice given by the person who gave the consent to the person keeping the gametes or embryo to which the consent is relevant.

(2) The terms of any consent to the use of any embryo cannot be varied, and such consent cannot be withdrawn, once the embryo has been used:

(a) in providing treatment services;

(b) for the purposes of any project of research.

The idea that only one withdrawal can bring the process to an end is supportive of patient autonomy, but in real life, it doesn't quite work this way. A woman may find herself pregnant after a one-night stand (e.g. an ex-partner), who later rejects the pregnancy when he finds out about it. The woman can still choose to have the baby without his support or consent. However, in the course of fertility treatment, the man must consent to the pregnancy otherwise the embryos will be destroyed. This was made painfully clear in the famous *Evans* case.

CASE EXTRACT

Evans v United Kingdom (74025/01) (2008) 46 EHRR 34

Facts: Natalie Evans (E) was diagnosed with ovarian cancer. She froze six embryos with her partner Howard Johnston (J). The was successfully treated and could still carry a baby but did not have any eggs, so the six embryos were her last chance to have a biological child. They separated and Howard Johnston withdrew his consent. Natalie sought a declaration that the provisions of the HFEA Act 1990 was incompatible with her human right to found a family (Article 8). She failed at first instance, in the Court of Appeal, in the European Court of Human Rights and in the Grand Chamber.

Held: The 1990 Act was clear in regards to consent to storage: a clinic was only entitled to store an embryo if both the parties who had provided the gametes which had produced the embryo consented to the embryo being stored. If one party withdrew consent, the embryos had to be destroyed.

Judge Rozakis (at pages 750–3, 755): It is not disputed between the parties that Article 8 is applicable and that the case concerns the applicant's right to respect for her private life. [...] The dilemma central to the present case is that it involves a conflict between the Article 8 rights of two private individuals: the applicant and J. Moreover, each person's interest is entirely irreconcilable with the other's, since if the applicant is permitted to use the embryos, J will be forced to become a father, whereas if J's refusal or withdrawal of consent is upheld, the applicant will be denied the opportunity of becoming a genetic parent. In the difficult circumstances of this case, whatever the solution the national authorities might adopt would result in the interests of one or the other parties to the IVF treatment being wholly frustrated. [...] While the applicant contends that her greater physical and emotional expenditure during the IVF process and her subsequent fertility entail that her Article 8 rights should take precedence over J's, it does not appear to the court that there is any clear consensus on this point either. [...]

As regards the balance struck between the conflicting Article 8 rights of the parties to the IVF treatment, the Grand Chamber, in common with every other court which has examined this case, has great sympathy for the applicant, who clearly desires a genetically related child above all else. However, given the above considerations, including the lack of any European consensus on this point, it does not consider that the applicant's right to respect for the decision to become a parent in the genetic sense should be accorded greater weight than J's right to respect for his decision not to have a genetically-related child with her.

The phrase 'forced to become a father' is interesting: many men in society are 'forced' into becoming fathers because their wives, girlfriends or one-night stands unexpectedly become pregnant and they refuse to have an abortion. Judge Rozakis tried to balance J's right to autonomy against E's right to become a parent and could not come to a clear consensus, but some would argue that a right to become a parent trumps the right of the father to reject the child as long as that father is not significantly harmed in any way by the denial of his autonomy. Judge Rozakis finally decided that E's right to become a parent could not be accorded any greater weight than J's right not to become a parent but it is not clear how these rights can be compared to each other and the outcome fall in J's favour: E is clearly suffering a larger detriment than J.

The Grand Chamber was happy with the UK law: the HFEA Act 1990 is clear on consent and this was the intention of Parliament. The last thing a patient needs in the complex process of fertility treatment is for the law to turn out to be vague, ambiguous and unsupportive of his or her rights. There is a public policy element to the *Evans* judgment: the law must have clarity and patient autonomy (of the father) must be respected. There are many criticisms that can be directed towards Howard Johnston and the provisions that protected him. First of all, Howard Johnston could easily have provided consent and not had anything to do with the child. Secondly, the provisions of the 1990 Act do not allow for sensitive cases such as *Evans* where one partner is clearly about to suffer a greater detriment than the other. Should an exception be made in certain circumstances to allow for the overruling of a withdrawal? This would be a significant breach of autonomy, but surely the right to *found* a family is greater than the right to *prevent* a family? The *Evans* case was well publicised and criticised by commentators (below). Sally

Sheldon argues that Natalie Evans and Howard Johnston should have talked through the implications of their treatment before creating embryos, whereas Craig Lind criticises the priority given to Howard Johnston. These are good arguments, but there are flaws in each.

EXTRACT

Sally Sheldon, Case Commentary: Revealing Cracks in the 'Twin Pillars'?' (2004) 16 *Child and Family Law Quarterly* 437

On the facts of this case, the robustness of the consent obtained from each party is surely open to question. The lack of space for confidential, private discussions between each party and clinic staff on the one hand, and between the two parties themselves, on the other, makes for rather less than the quality of consent which might be thought desirable. While the courts seem cognisant of the necessity of a 'bright line rule' to offer certainty to clinics, the consenting procedures in this case were such as potentially to leave Ms Evans and Mr Johnston in a position of considerable uncertainty about the implications of their treatment.

EXTRACT

Craig Lind, '*Evans v United Kingdom* – Judgments of Solomon: Power, Gender and Procreation' (2006) 18 *Child and Family Law Quarterly* 576

It is deeply ironic that, in the context of assisted reproduction, men are given such complete control over their procreative capacity. Mr Johnston is said to have had a fundamental objection to there being a child of his in the world which he was not actively raising with the child's mother. Yet, if he had fathered a child accidentally during sexual intercourse, he would have been denied the level of control over his procreation that the statute gives him. He would have had to support any child born as a result of that activity (even if it were of the briefest, most meaningless kind). His involvement in a clinical infertility venture is, however, a much more deliberate move to procreate than a casual sexual encounter is. However, only the latter can lead to substantial support obligations. [...] After this series of decisions I am left with the abiding question: do we really believe that a greater injustice would have been done to Mr Johnston in 'foisting' an unwanted child on him than is done by preventing Ms Evans from ever having a child of her own?

Sally Sheldon argues that Natalie Evans and Howard Johnston were not given enough time to discuss the implications of freezing their embryos in advance. The flaw in this argument, however, is that most couples cannot see into the future and would probably choose to freeze embryos over eggs because the success rate is higher. Craig Lind argues in comparison that if we were to compare Howard Johnston's deliberate participation in fertility treatment to a casual sexual encounter leading to a child, Howard Johnston has been accosted far more freedom in the former scenario than he would have in the latter. This may be true, but if the law were to take such a comparison into account, Howard Johnston would be deprived of his autonomy because the courts would almost certainly overrule his withdrawal.[16] The *Evans* case did change the law. There is now a cooling-off period of twelve months which was added to Schedule 3 as a result of the 2008 reforms.

---

[16] It was confirmed only two years later that frozen sperm is the property of the man: *Yearworth v North Bristol NHS Trust* [2010] QB1 (see Chapter 9).

Human Fertilisation and Embryology Act 1990

Paragraph 4A: Variation and withdrawal of consent

(2) The person keeping the embryo must as soon as possible take all reasonable steps to notify each interested person in relation to the embryo of P's withdrawal of consent.

(4) Storage of the embryo remains lawful until:

   (a) the end of the period of 12 months beginning with the day on which the notice mentioned in sub-paragraph (1) was received from P, or

   (b) if, before the end of that period, the person keeping the embryo receives a notice from each person notified of P's withdrawal under sub-paragraph (2) stating that the person consents to the destruction of the embryo, the time at which the last of those notices is received.

It is not clear how useful a cooling off period of twelve months will be. In the *Evans* case, the embryos were stored for much longer than that as the case trailed through the appeal courts. However, some couples may reconcile or come to an amicable conclusion through discussion and compromise.

Consenting to using a donor's gametes and embryos

It is far more likely for a couple to use their own, fresh gametes in fertility treatment rather than the gametes of a donor. However, donated gametes are used in fertility treatment when either the male or the female cannot provide healthy eggs or sperm. The statistics for the use of donated gametes are as follows.

EXTRACT

Fertility Treatment in 2012: Trends and Figures. Human Fertilisation and Embryology Authority, 2013:

http://www.hfea.gov.uk/104.html

Page 19:

- 72 clinics performed donor insemination treatment in 2012.

Page 14:

- 2265 women had 4452 cycles of donor insemination in 2012.

Page 38:

- A total of 2225 cycles of fresh own egg IVF were performed in 2011 using donated sperm resulting in 776 live babies being born; This gives an overall live birth rate of 28.8% using donated sperm.

The process of donation is more complicated than people think. It is not as simple as providing a sperm donation and leaving the clinic with expenses paid. There must be detailed checks into the background of the donor, including his medical history, and he must be of a certain age. Since 2005, the donor will also be identifiable to any child born when she reaches 18, so his personal details must be taken too. The HFEA Code of Practice, 8th Edition, explains in more detail what must be investigated:

EXTRACT

Code of Practice, 8th edition, October 2013, Human Fertilisation and Embryology Authority:

http://www.hfea.gov.uk/code.html

Paragraph 11.2: (NOTE): Current professional guidelines state that eggs should not be taken from donors aged 36 or over, and sperm should not be taken from donors ages 41 or over.

Paragraph 11.6: Gametes for the treatment of others should not be taken from anyone under the age of 18.

Paragraph 11.7: The recruiting centre should take reasonable steps to verify the identity of the prospective donor by asking for appropriate identification (e.g. passport or photo card driving licence). Failure to obtain satisfactory evidence of identity should be taken into account in deciding whether to accept their gametes or embryos for treatment.

Paragraph 11.9: Before a prospective donor provides gametes, the recruiting centre should take their medical and family histories, and details of previous donations. The centre should encourage prospective donors to provide as much other non-identifying biographical information as possible, so that it may be available to prospective recipients, parents and resulting children. If a prospective donor cannot give a full and accurate family history, the centre should record this fact and take it into account in deciding whether or not to accept their gametes or embryos for treatment.

Paragraph 11.14: Before accepting gametes for the treatment of others, the recruiting centre should consider the suitability of the prospective donor. In particular, the centre should consider:

(a)   personal or family history of heritable disorders

(b)   personal history of transmissible infection

(c)   the level of potential fertility indicated by semen analysis (where appropriate)

(d)   the implications of the donation for the prospective donor and their family, especially for any children they may have at the time of donation or in the future, and

(e)   the implications for any children born as a result of the donation, in the short and long term.

The proposed age limits of prospective donors is interesting. It is clear that the quality of female eggs depletes quicker than the quality of male sperm. It is also interesting to see medical and family histories taken into account, in addition to infection history, implications for the donor and implications for any children born, e.g. if the donor is a rich and famous celebrity this may have implications further down the line. It is not possible for the HFEA to be completely accurate, and the motives of the donor will have to be taken as correct. There are also a significant number of hereditary diseases that we cannot yet screen for. It is not an exact science, and there are no reliable legal authorities to show whether an action could be brought against the HFEA for using damaged gametes in IVF treatment.

The donor is, of course, required to consent under paragraph 5 of Schedule 3 to the donation of his or her gametes before they can be used in the course of fertility treatment.

Human Fertilisation and Embryology Act 1990

Schedule 3. Paragraph 5: Use of gametes for treatment of others

(1) A person's gametes must not be used for the purposes of treatment services or non-medical fertility services unless there is an effective consent by that person to their being so used and they are used in accordance with the terms of the consent.

(2) A person's gametes must not be received for use for those purposes unless there is an effective consent by that person to their being so used.

The donor may also dictate how many families can use his or her donated gametes (although there is a limit). This provides the donor with a considerable amount of control over his or her donation.

EXTRACT

Code of Practice, 8th edition, October 2013, Human Fertilisation and Embryology Authority:

http://www.hfea.gov.uk/code.html

Paragraph 5.18: Consent to the use of gametes or embryos for the treatment of others should state the number of families that may have children using the donated gametes or embryos.

The difficulty with donated gametes is the knowledge of the child. Anonymity used to be the norm for donated eggs and sperm to ensure peace of mind for the donor, but it is not anymore. This is because there is a risk that genetic diseases could be passed on to the child from the donor, and the child is entitled to know who they are related to. It is also not fair on the donor to retain anonymity. A sperm donor, for example, may have a successful child with his features, characteristics and talents who he has never met. The psychological need to uncover one's heritage was summed up in *R (on the application of Rose)* v *Secretary of State for Health* [2002] EWHC 1593 by Scott Baker J when he said: 'everyone should be able to establish details of his identity as a human being'. Parliament passed the Human Fertilisation and Embryology Authority (Disclosure of Donor Information) Regulations 2004/1511 in 2005 to allow children born as a result of donated gametes to be able to trace their heritage at the age of 18:

- At the age of 16 the child can ask the HFEA whether they are related to a sexual partner or prospective spouse under section 31ZB(2).

- At the age of 16 the child can ask the HFEA for the following information about their donor parent: physical description, year and country of birth, ethnicity, genetic siblings, occupation, religion and interests if provided, marital status, medical history, skills, reason for donating, a goodwill message and a description of themselves under section 31ZA(2)(a) in conjunction with the 2004 Regulations at paragraph 2(2).

- At the age of 18 the child can ask the HFEA for the following additional information about their donor parent: full name, previous names, date of birth, last known postal address under section 31ZA(2)(a) in conjunction with the 2004 Regulations at paragraph 2(3).

- The donor can request the following information about any children born as a result of his donated gametes or embryos: the number of children born, their sex and their year of birth under section 31ZD(3).

A child born as a result of donated gametes can now clearly trace their genetic parent(s). A donor from pre-2005 is able to reregister as identifiable. Couples seeking fertility treatment using donated gametes are advised of this, and they are also advised to tell their child that they were conceived using donated gametes.

EXTRACT

Code of Practice, 8th edition, October 2013, Human Fertilisation and Embryology Authority:

http://www.hfea.gov.uk/code.html

Paragraph 20.7: The centre should tell people who seek treatment with donated gametes or embryos that it is best for any resulting child to be told about their origin early in childhood. There is evidence that finding out suddenly, later in life, about donor origins can be emotionally damaging to children and to family relations.

Paragraph 20.8: The centre should encourage and prepare patients to be open with their children from an early age about how they were conceived. The centre should give patients information about how counselling may allow them to explore the implications of treatment, in particular how information may be shared with any resultant children.

These provisions may upset the couple seeking fertility treatment via donated gametes, because they may have planned to raise their child in complete ignorance of its genetic history. The reaction will no doubt be worse as the child becomes older, as acknowledged by the HFEA in the Code of Practice (above), who clearly support an open attitude to gamete donation. Parliament had discussed the idea of recording the donated gamete on the birth certificate, but a parent could simply choose to hide this or it could be found at an inopportune moment. NICE has therefore recommended counselling for donors and recipients of eggs and sperm.

EXTRACT

Fertility: Assessment and Treatment for People with Fertility Problems, National Institute for Health and Clinical Excellence, National Health Service, February 2013:

http://publications.nice.org.uk/fertility-cg156

Page 40 paragraph 1.14.2.2: Couples considering donor insemination should be offered counselling from someone who is independent of the treatment unit regarding all the physical and psychological implications of treatment for themselves and potential children.

→

Paragraph 1.14.3.2: All potential semen donors should be offered counselling from someone who is independent of the treatment unit regarding the implications for themselves and their genetic children, including any potential children resulting from donated semen.

Page 42 Paragraph 1.15.3.2: Oocyte recipients and donors should be offered counselling from someone who is independent of the treatment unit regarding the physical and psychological implications of treatment for themselves and their genetic children, including any potential children resulting from donated oocytes.

Paragraph 1.15.3.3: All people considering participation in an 'egg sharing' scheme should be counselled about its particular implications.

The parents can, of course, choose not to tell the child about their donated origin, but this is not fair to the child if other relatives know, and in the future when the screening of genetic diseases becomes better, it may be viewed as deeply unethical and a potential breach of the child's human rights. It has been noted by one commentator that children born to lesbian couples using donated sperm know by default that there is a third party involved in their heritage because the father is absent, so children born to heterosexual couples using donated sperm may be discriminated against.[17]

Donors are not allowed to be paid in the UK for their gamete donations. This is to prevent a 'price' being attached to the value of life, as well as the possibility of a distasteful 'market' in eggs, sperm and embryos. The prohibition of payment is confirmed in the 1990 Act.

Human Fertilisation and Embryology Act 1990

Section 12: General conditions

(1) The following shall be conditions of every licence granted under this Act:

    (e) that no money or other benefit shall be given or received in respect of any supply ofgametes, embryos or human admixed embryos unless authorised by directions.

Section 41: Offences

(8) Where a person to whom a licence applies or the holder of the licence gives or receives any money or other benefit, not authorised by directions, in respect of any supply of gametes, embryos or human admixed embryos, he is guilty of an offence.

(9) A person guilty of an offence under subsection (8) above is liable on summary conviction to imprisonment for a term not exceeding six months or a fine not exceeding level five on the standard scale or both.

The phrase 'authorised by directions' allows for expenses to be paid to the donor. The HFEA Code of Practice, 8th edition, provides further details as to what can be reimbursed.

---

[17] Andrew Bainham, 'Arguments about Parentage' (2008) 67 *Cambridge Law Journal* 322.

EXTRACT

Code of Practice, 8th edition, October 2013, Human Fertilisation and Embryology Authority:

http://www.hfea.gov.uk/code.html

Paragraph 13.3: Donors may be compensated with a fixed amount of money, as specified in HFEA Directions, which reasonably covers any financial losses incurred in connection with donating gametes provided to that centre.

Paragraph 13.4: If donors have incurred expenses (not including loss of earnings) that exceed the amounts specified in HFEA Directions, the centre may compensate donors with excess expenses in line with HFEA Directions.

Paragraph 13.5: The centre should ensure that donors understand that donating gametes and embryos is voluntary and unpaid and that they may be compensated only in line with relevant HFEA Directions.

Paragraph 13.6: If an egg donor becomes ill as a direct result of donating, the centre may also reimburse their reasonable expenses arising from the illness.

There is clearly an obligation to see that the donor is not taken advantage of in any way: adequate compensation is provided to ensure that the donor is placed back in their original position before the donation in terms of money and expense. However, the process of egg donation is far more intrusive than sperm donation. It might well be that the lack of donated eggs is a direct consequence not of the intrusive nature of the procedure but of the unwillingness to *compensate* for the intrusive nature of the procedure.

There are many critics of the payment system because it encourages more donations to take place (see Chapter 9 for detailed arguments for and against organ markets). What is the problem with donation? The donation of sperm and eggs poses a unique psychological problem for the donor: every child that passes on the street with similar features could belong to the donor. Perhaps even more difficult is the egg sharing scheme, where a woman undergoing IVF treatment donates her own eggs to another woman undergoing IVF treatment, and later finds out that while her own treatment failed, her eggs resulted in a child for another woman. In the United States, egg donation is big business and donors are paid thousands of dollars for their eggs (the sums can soar depending on the donor's privileged position in life). It has been argued that an egg donation can still be a gift even if it is sold at a price, but surely a price changes the donor's motive from 'gift' to 'sale'?[18]

ACTIVITY

Gregg and Callum are a gay couple who seek IVF to start a family. Gregg's sister Tia has volunteered to be the surrogate, so all they need now is a donated egg. The clinic says that they have donated embryos from other couples. Gregg and Callum refuse these, saying they want the child to be biologically related to one of them. A donor egg is found and Greg's sperm is used to create an embryo. Advise Gregg and Callum of the implications of using donated gametes.

---

[18] David Resnik, 'Regulating the Market in Human Eggs' (2001) 15 *Bioethics* 1.

Who are the legal parents?

The question of 'who is the parent?' is a legal one, not a social or emotional one, and not as simple as it seems, especially when donated gametes are used. The law has made provisions for parentage to pass from donor to recipient for both men and women, but there are still unconventional scenarios that don't quite fit within the regulations. A surrogate mother, for example, is the legal mother, even though she is to hand the baby over to the 'real' mother whose egg was implanted into the surrogate. This is problematic for couples seeking surrogacy arrangements (examined further below), and they are not the only couples who face problems with legal parentage.

> **KEY DEFINITION**
>
> **Maternity**: the mother's parentage.
> **Paternity**: the father's parentage.

The legal mother

It is well established in law that the woman who gives birth to the baby is the legal mother. This is confirmed under section 27 of the HFEA 1990 and sections 33 and 47 of the HFEA 2008 (both statutes run alongside each other).

> ## Human Fertilisation and Embryology Act 2008
>
> **Section 33: Meaning of 'mother'**
>
> (1) The woman who is carrying or has carried a child as a result of the placing in her of an embryo or of sperm and eggs, and no other woman, is to be treated as the mother of the child.
>
> **Section 47: Woman not to be other parent merely because of egg donation**
>
> A woman is not to be treated as the parent of a child whom she is not carrying and has not carried.

It is clear that the woman who gives birth is the legal mother and this will remain the case until the child is legally adopted by another parent or parenthood is transferred through a parental order. Parliament have worded this provision to allow for women undergoing IVF treatment with donor eggs or embryos to become the legal mother of the child when it is born. The mother and the child will not be genetically related, but the woman who sought IVF will give birth to the child. The statute specifically excludes the egg donor as the mother under section 47 to ensure that there is no confusion. This provision does not work for two types of women: surrogate mothers (the surrogate is the legal mother because she goes through the birth) and lesbian couples (only the partner who gives birth is the legal mother).

The legal father if married (own sperm)

A husband who used his own sperm in the IVF treatment of his wife is the legal father (both legally and genetically). There is a legal presumption of paternity in law if the couple are married because they 'forsake all others' in their marriage vows. A legal presumption can be rebutted, of course, if there is evidence to support it (e.g. a DNA test). This presumption is confirmed under section 28(5) of the 1990 Act.

The legal father if married (donor sperm)

A presumption of paternity can also apply if donated sperm is used (as long as the husband consents to this) under section 28(2) of the 1990 Act. The presumption of paternity for married couples (whether own or donor sperm) also features under section 38 of the 2008 Act.

Human Fertilisation and Embryology Act 1990

Section 28: Meaning of 'father'

(1) This section applies in the case of a child who is being or has been carried by a woman as the result of the placing in her of an embryo or of sperm and eggs or her artificial insemination.

(2) If:

    (a) at the time of the placing in her of the embryo or the sperm and eggs or of her insemination, the woman was a party to a marriage, and

    (b) the creation of the embryo carried by her was not brought about with the sperm of the other party to the marriage,

    then, subject to subsection (5) below, the other party to the marriage shall be treated as the father of the child unless it is shown that he did not consent to the placing in her of the embryo or the sperm and eggs or to her insemination (as the case may be).

(5) Subsection (2) above does not apply:

    (a) to any child who, by virtue of the rules of common law, is treated as the legitimate child of the parties to a marriage.

Section 28(5) above confirms the existence of the presumption of paternity within a marriage, and section 28(2) confirms the presumption of paternity in a marriage if donated sperm are used. An astonishing case was brought under this provision in 1996, and the courts – thankfully – held firm to the presumptions of paternity and to the spirit of the statute.

CASE EXTRACT

Re CH (Contact: Parentage) [1996] 1 FLR 569

Facts: The issue was whether, after the marital breakdown, the father should have contact with his daughter, who had been born by artificial insemination; he was not the biological father.

→

Held: applying the Human Fertilisation and Embryology Act 1990 section 28, that where a child had been carried by the mother as a result of artificial insemination and the donor was not the other party to the marriage, the other party should be treated as the father of the child, unless he had withheld his consent to the insemination. The father had given his consent, had been present at the birth and was registered as the child's father and so was to be treated in law as the father of the child. There existed a statutory presumption.

It was foolish of the woman in *Re CH* to ask the courts to remove paternity from the father simply because they were divorced. Paternity – whether a donor is used or not – is not disposable simply because the shape of the family unit takes an unforeseen turn. A more shocking case under section 28(2) occurred in 2003. There was a mix up in the fertility clinic and the sperm from Mr B was accidently given to couple A, resulting in mixed-race twins. The A couple were naturally devastated, and Mr A needed to know if he could become the father of the twins via section 28(2) because, technically, donor sperm (from Mr B) had been used. The courts said 'no' – Mr A had not consented to his wife being treated by donor sperm so had to adopt the twins instead.

CASE EXTRACT

L Teaching Hospitals NHS Trust v *A* [2003] EWHC 259

Dame Elizabeth Butler-Sloss P (at paras 24–5, 28–9, 56–7): Looking specifically at section 28(2), it might appear that Mr A could be the legal father of the twins, since, at the time of the placing in Mrs A of the embryo, Mrs A was a party to the marriage with Mr A and the creation of the embryo carried by her was not brought about with the sperm of Mr A. The application of subsection (2), however, is subject to two provisos. The first is contained in section 28(5) and provides for the common law presumption of legitimacy of a child born to a mother during her marriage. In the present case, that presumption is displaced by the DNA tests which established that Mr B is the biological father of the twins. The second proviso, contained in subsection (2) itself, is the requirement of the husband's consent. Subsection (2) applies unless it is shown that Mr A 'did not consent to her insemination'. […] The question is whether Mr A consented to the insemination of Mrs A by a third person. […] On the clear evidence provided in the consent forms Mr A plainly did not consent to the sperm of a named or anonymous donor being mixed with his wife's eggs. This was clearly an embryo created without the consent of Mr and Mrs A. […] I am satisfied that, on the proper interpretation of section 28(2) Mr A did not consent to the placing in his wife of the embryo which was actually placed. Accordingly, section 28(2) does not apply. […] In my judgment the twins' rights to respect for their family life with their mother and Mr A can be met by appropriate family or adoption orders. […] To refuse to recognise Mr B as their biological father is to distort the truth about which some day the twins will have to learn through knowledge of their parental identity.

This case is clearly a nightmare scenario for patients undergoing IVF, but it is very rare for this to happen. Dame Butler-Sloss applied section 28(2) to the letter, and because Mr A did not consent to the use of Mr B's sperm in his wife's eggs, Mr A could not be the legal father of the twins (and a DNA test already proved that he was not the biological father anyway). This approach is justified because, as Dame Butler-Sloss points out, if the presumption of paternity had been applied, the twins would have been living in fiction.

The legal father if deceased during IVF treatment

A man who consents to his wife using his own sperm under section 28(2) and subsequently dies before the child is born is still to be referred to as the legal father, unless he withdrew his consent before death, under section 39(1) of the 2008 Act. This applies to donated sperm too under section 40(1) of the 2008 Act, and if they are not married he can use section 40(2) of the 2008 Act for the same presumption.

The legal father if unmarried (donor sperm)

Section 36 of the 2008 Act provides that an unmarried man, e.g. the boyfriend of the woman undergoing treatment, can be the legal father of a child conceived using donated sperm as long as he was alive at the time and the 'agreed fatherhood conditions' under section 37 are fulfilled. The 2008 Act added 'agreed fatherhood conditions' to the law to ensure that both the man and the woman, e.g. the boyfriend and girlfriend, undergoing treatment agree to the man being the legal father in the event that donated sperm is used. The 'agreed fatherhood conditions' read as follows.

Human Fertilisation and Embryology Act 2008

Section 37: The agreed fatherhood conditions

(1) The agreed fatherhood conditions referred to in section 36(b) are met in relation to a man ('M') in relation to treatment provided to W (woman) under a licence if, but only if:

    (a) M has given the person responsible a notice stating that he consents to being treated as the father of any child resulting from treatment provided to W under the licence,

    (b) W has given the person responsible a notice stating that she consents to M being so treated,

    (c) neither M nor W has, since giving notice under paragraph (a) or (b), given the person responsible notice of the withdrawal of M's or W's consent to M being so treated,

    (d) W has not, since the giving of the notice under paragraph (b), given the person responsible –

        (i) a further notice under that paragraph stating that she consents to another man being treated as the father of any resulting child, or

        (ii) a notice under section 44(1)(b) stating that she consents to a woman being treated as a parent of any resulting child, and

    (e) W and M are not within prohibited degrees of relationship in relation to each other (i.e. an incestuous relationship).

(2) A notice under subsection (1)(a), (b) or (c) must be in writing and must be signed by the person giving it.

There is a clear emphasis on consent from *both* parties under section 37. In real terms, it states that a boyfriend must consent to the legal fatherhood of any baby born if his girlfriend used donated sperm, and the girlfriend must consent to her boyfriend obtaining legal fatherhood.

A lesbian couple (non-civil)

A woman who is not in a civil partnership but would like her girlfriend to be the 'second legal parent' of her child born using donated sperm can do so under section 43 of the 2008 Act.

Human Fertilisation and Embryology Act 2008

Section 43: Treatment provided to woman who agrees that second woman to be parent

If no man is treated by virtue of section 35 as the father of the child and no woman is treated by virtue of section 42 as a parent of the child but:

(a) the embryo or the sperm and eggs were placed in W, or she was artificially inseminated, inthe course of treatment services provided in the United Kingdom by a person to whom a licence applies,

(b) at the time when the embryo or the sperm and eggs were placed in W, or W was artificially inseminated, the agreed female parenthood conditions (as set out in section 44) were met in relation to another woman, in relation to treatment provided to W under that licence, and

(c) the other woman remained alive at that time, then, subject to section 45(2) to (4), the other woman is to be treated as a parent of the child.

The law now allows lesbian couples who are not in a civil partnership to be legal parents to a child born through IVF using donor sperm. Notice that the girlfriend of the woman undergoing IVF will be known as the 'parent' rather than a 'second mother' or a 'father'. There are 'agreed female parenthood conditions' for female couples just as there are 'agreed fatherhood conditions' for heterosexual couples who are unmarried.

Human Fertilisation and Embryology Act 2008

Section 44: The agreed female parenthood conditions

(1) The agreed female parenthood conditions referred to in section 43(b) are met in relation to another woman ('P') in relation to treatment provided to W under a licence if, but only if:

(a) P has given the person responsible a notice stating that P consents to P being treated as aparent of any child resulting from treatment provided to W under the licence,

(b) W has given the person responsible a notice stating that W agrees to P being so treated,

→

(c)   neither W nor P has, since giving notice under paragraph (a) or (b), given the person responsible notice of the withdrawal of P's or W's consent to P being so treated,

(d)   W has not, since the giving of the notice under paragraph (b), given the person responsible –

(i)   a further notice under that paragraph stating that W consents to a woman other than P being treated as a parent of any resulting child, or

(ii)   a notice under section 37(1)(b) stating that W consents to a man being treated as the father of any resulting child, and

(e)   W and P are not within prohibited degrees of relationship in relation to each other.

Lesbian couples have used these provisions to create their own families. The statistics from the Human Fertilisation and Embryology Authority speak for themselves.

EXTRACT

Fertility Treatment in 2012: Trends and Figures. Human Fertilisation and Embryology Authority (2013):

http://www.hfea.gov.uk/104.html

Page 39:

- A total of 766 cycles of IVF were performed in women who registered with a female partner in 2011;
- This was an increase of approximately 205 on the year before;
- It resulted in 265 babies being born and a live birth rate of 29.1%;
- A total of 1271 cycles of donor insemination were performed in women who registered with a female partner in 2011;
- This resulted in 161 babies being born and a live birth rate of 11.6%.

A lesbian couple (civil)

A lesbian couple who have entered into a civil partnership are treated the same as a married couple, so there is a presumption that the civil partner of the woman undergoing IVF is going to be the legal parent (as long as she consents to this).

Human Fertilisation and Embryology Act 2008

Section 42: Woman in civil partnership at time of treatment

(1)   If at the time of the placing in her of the embryo or the sperm and eggs or of her artificial insemination, W was a party to a civil partnership, then subject to section 45(2) to (4), the other party to the civil partnership is to be treated as a parent of the child unless it is shown that she did not consent to the placing in W of the embryo or the sperm and eggs or to her artificial insemination (as the case may be).

It is clear from the many provisions above that female couples (whether in a civil partnership or not) can create a family using IVF treatment and donor sperm. The law now permits a child to have two female parents. This has inevitably attracted criticism, because the female partner who did not provide the egg is merely undertaking parental responsibility but is not an actual 'parent' in the traditional sense and it would be unfair on the child to suggest that she was.

EXTRACT

Andrew Bainham, 'Arguments about Parentage' (2008) 67 *Cambridge Law Journal* 322, at pages 322–51

The argument, therefore, is that while it may be appropriate to give to the lesbian partner and other social parents parental responsibility (depending on the extent to which the individual actually performs parenting functions), it is inappropriate to make that person the legal parent because this is to distort and misrepresent kinship. The lesbian partner's mother and father, for example, would become the child's grandparents and her brothers and sisters the child's uncles and aunts. [...] The concept of parentage should rather be confined, to reflect as far as possible the unique position of biological parents and, through the child's filiation with them, the wider kinship links to the extended maternal and paternal families.

Not everyone agrees with Andrew Bainham: gay couples engaging in fertility treatment (of both sexes) will argue that they have enough love for the child to fill any void left by the absent parent. However, until heterosexual people stop having sexual intercourse, same-sex parents will represent the minority in society.

A doctor can refuse to treat a patient if he does not believe that the treatment is appropriate. The 'conscientious objection' clause is contained under section 38 of the 1990 Act, which states:

Human Fertilisation and Embryology Act 1990

Section 38(1): No person who has a conscientious objection to participating in any activity governed by this Act shall be under any duty, however arising, to do so.

It is not clear how much a doctor can object to, but technically, since there are no limitations to section 38(1), he could potentially object to everything (i.e. assessment and treatment). This will be a bit difficult for the HFEA, because it appears to have passed regulations that call section 38(1) into disrepute.

Code of Practice, 8th edition, October 2013 Human Fertilisation and Embryology Authority:

http://www.hfea.gov.uk/code.html

Paragraph 29.9: A staff member's views about the lifestyle, beliefs, race, gender, age, sexuality, disability or other perceived status of a patient, patient's partner or donor should not affect that individual's treatment or care.

Paragraph 29.11: The person responsible should satisfy themselves that the staff member has a conscientious objection to providing a particular licensed activity, and is not unlawfully discriminating against a patient on the basis of their race, disability, gender, religion or belief, sexual orientation or age.

If a doctor cannot conscientiously object to assessment or treatment on the grounds of race, disability, gender, religion, belief, sexual orientation or age, what grounds does he have left? The HFEA guidelines cannot overrule the law, so if push came to shove, the doctor could enforce his right under section 38(1). There is no case law to confirm as of yet.

Single women

It is open for single women to seek IVF treatment (or donor insemination) using donated sperm. This may occur when a woman has followed a highly successful career and never met her spouse, or had failed marriages which resulted in no children. They will be interviewed by the clinic and will have to ensure that the welfare of the child is satisfied under section 13(5) of the 1990 Act (i.e. there should be a supportive family environment). The clinic can decide for themselves whether the provisions under section 13(5) have been met, but there is nothing else stopping a single woman from undergoing fertility treatment. She will be the legal mother because she gives birth to the baby, but the baby will have no legal father.

ACTIVITY

Sheila and Sally have been in a civil partnership for three years and now want to start a family. Sally has always wanted to be pregnant and have a baby, so Sheila agrees to this and they contact a fertility clinic. The clinic advises Sheila that they have stores of donated sperm. Sheila agrees to this. Sally undergoes donor insemination at the clinic. Sheila is worried that she will be pushed out of the family because she is not biologically related to the child. Advise Sheila about how parentage is assigned in law to couples like her and Sally.

Embryo testing and screening

There are extraordinary developments happening in embryonic/fertility research. We are now able to screen embryos for genetic abnormalities. A few cells are taken from the embryo without harming it and they are tested for a gender or disease. This enables sex selection. It also enables the option to dispose of IVF embryos which carry a serious, hereditary disease. This process is called Preimplantation Genetic Diagnosis (PGD) because it is offered to IVF patients before the embryos are implanted. It is especially helpful to couples who know they carry a hereditary disease and do not want to pass it on to their child. The other option would be diagnosis during pregnancy and, if the disease or abnormality is serious, an abortion. The Human Fertilisation and Embryology Authority has published a list of all the disorders it is currently able to screen for. This list is extensive.[19] 18 clinics provided PGD in 2012, making a total of 523 IVF cycles.[20] PGD was incorporated into the Human Fertilisation and Embryology Act 1990 by the 2008 reform. It is authorised in certain circumstances, but not in others.

Human Fertilisation and Embryology Act 1990

Schedule 2: Activities for which licences may be granted

Paragraph 1ZA(1): A licence under paragraph 1 cannot authorise the testing of an embryo, except for one or more of the following purposes:

(a) establishing whether the embryo has a gene, chromosome or mitochondrion abnormality that may affect its capacity to result in a live birth,

(b) in a case where there is a particular risk that the embryo may have any gene, chromosome or mitochondrion abnormality, establishing whether it has that abnormality or any other gene, chromosome or mitochondrion abnormality,

(c) in a case where there is a particular risk that any resulting child will have or develop:

    (i) a gender-related serious physical or mental disability,

    (ii) a gender-related serious illness, or

    (iii) any other gender-related serious medical condition,

    establishing the sex of the embryo,

(d) in a case where a person ('the sibling') who is the child of the persons whose gametes are used to bring about the creation of the embryo (or of either of those persons) suffers from a serious medical condition which could be treated by umbilical cord blood stem cells, bone marrow or other tissue of any resulting child, establishing whether the tissue of any resulting child would be compatible with that of the sibling, and

(e) in a case where uncertainty has arisen as to whether the embryo is one of those whose creation was brought about by using the gametes of particular persons, establishing whether it is.

The provisions above can be split into six categories: (1) PGD can screen for a fatal gene, chromosome or mitochondrion abnormality under paragraph 1ZA(1)(a); (2) PGD can screen for the presence of a *risk* of a gene, chromosome or mitochondrion abnormality under paragraph 1ZA(1)(b) but this risk must be a 'significant risk of a serious physical or mental disability' according to paragraph 1ZA(2) (not shown above); (3) testing for 'carrier status' is not provided for under Schedule 2; (4) PGD can screen for the sex of the embryo if it is at risk from developing a gender-specific disease under paragraph 1ZA(1)(c) but sex selection for social reasons is not provided for under Schedule 2; (5) PGD can screen for compatibility with a sibling if there is potential to treat the sibling with umbilical

[19] http://www.hfea.gov.uk/preimplantation-genetic-diagnosis.html.

[20] Fertility Treatment in 2012: Trends and Figures. Human Fertilisation and Embryology Authority, (2013) http://www.hfea.gov.uk/104.html.

cord blood cells, bone marrow or other tissue under paragraph 1ZA(1)(d) but this does not include a 'whole organ' of the child born under paragraph 1ZA(4) (not shown above); and (6) PGD can screen for a DNA match to the parents under paragraph 1ZA(1)(e).

It may surprise some readers to learn that sex selection for social reasons is not allowed. The practice is well established in the United States. The UK will only allow sex screening for the benefit of the *embryo* (e.g. to establish whether it is carrying a particular disease). It is probably only a matter of time before sex selection is allowed in the UK as part of the IVF process. It is foreseeable that parents of a large family of boys, for example, may argue that their human rights are breached because they are unable to choose a girl when the scientific technology is available to allow them to do so.

PGD for serious diseases

It is clear that embryos can be screened for abnormalities that could result in fatal injuries or a significant risk of a serious physical or mental disability. However, it is difficult to establish the dividing line between 'significant risk' and 'a mere risk'. The Code of Practice for the 1990 Act provides further directions for screening. It suggests that the views of the parents should be taken into account in addition to the seriousness of the disease and the treatments available for it.

EXTRACT

Code of Practice, 8th edition, October 2013, Human Fertilisation and Embryology Authority:

http://www.hfea.gov.uk/code.html

Paragraph 10.5: When deciding if it is appropriate to provide PGD in particular cases, the centre should consider the circumstances of those seeking treatment rather than the particular heritable condition.

Paragraph 10.6: The use of PGD should be considered only where there is a significant risk of a serious genetic condition being present in the embryo. When deciding if it is appropriate to provide PGD in particular cases, the seriousness of the condition in that case should be discussed between the people seeking treatment and the clinical team. The perception of the level of risk for those seeking treatment will also be an important factor for the centre to consider.

Paragraph 10.7: The centre should consider the following factors when deciding if PGD is appropriate in particular cases:

(a) the views of the people seeking treatment in relation to the condition to be avoided, including their previous reproductive experience

(b) the likely degree of suffering associated with the condition

(c) the availability of effective therapy, now and in the future

(d) the speed of degeneration in progressive disorders

(e) the extent of any intellectual impairment

(f) the social support available, and

(g) the family circumstances of the people seeking treatment.

There is no clear benchmark against which to justify or refuse PGD. It may develop in the future to include many trivial disabilities and abnormalities, and this has concerned some writers. It might not be ethical to reject embryos for such trivial reasons, and it could herald the beginning of the pursuit of a 'perfect race' in our society. For example, the BRCA1 gene is included in the list of diseases published by the HFEA and if faulty can reveal an 80% risk of developing breast cancer in later life. Should we reject embryos if they are susceptible to breast cancer when one in three people already die of cancer? The HFEA may have to exercise caution when adding particular diseases to their blacklist. We must be careful not to allow IVF treatment to slowly turn into 'embryo cleansing' as our quest for perfection deepens. Parliament predicted the opposite use for PGD. The 2008 reform suggested that patients may like to use PGD to locate a specific abnormality and select *that* embryo for implantation instead of a healthy one. This may sound bizarre, because it is highly unusual for parents to wish for a disabled child, but there was a story in 2008 about deaf parents who did not wish to reject embryos with a hearing abnormality.[21] The story posed an interesting question: if parents wish for their child to be disabled like them, should we let them? The 1990 Act (as a result of the 2008 reform) has said 'no':

Human Fertilisation and Embryology Act 1990

Section 13: Conditions of licences for treatment

(9) Persons or embryos that are known to have a gene, chromosome or mitochondrion abnormality involving a significant risk that a person with the abnormality will have or develop:

(a)   a serious physical or mental disability,

(b)   a serious illness, or

(c)   any other serious medical condition,

must not be preferred to those that are not known to have such an abnormality.

An abnormal embryo cannot be preferred. This falls short of a complete ban on selecting abnormal embryos because some couples may only be able to produce embryos with abnormalities and it may be their only chance of being biological parents (subject to the 'welfare test' under section 13(5) of the 1990 Act). Julian Savulescu has argued that it is about balance – it is better to be born with an abnormality than to not be born at all – therefore what is the harm in selecting a deaf embryo, for example?

EXTRACT

Julian Savulescu, 'Deaf Lesbians, Designer Disability and the Future of Medicine' (2002) 325 *British Medical Journal* 771, at pages 771–3

What if a couple has *in vitro* fertilisation and Preimplantation genetic diagnosis and they select a deaf embryo? Have they harmed that child? Is that child worse off than it would otherwise have been (that is, if they had selected a different embryo)? No – another (different) child would have existed. The deaf child is harmed by being selected to exist only if his or her life is

→

---

[21] Robin McKie and Gaby Hinsliff, 'This Couple Want a Deaf Child. Should We Try to Stop Them?' *The Observer*, 9 March 2008.

so bad it is not worth living. Deafness is not that bad. Because reproductive choices to have a disabled child do not harm the child, couples who select disabled rather than non-disabled offspring should be allowed to make those choices, even though they may be having a child with worse life prospects. [...] Reproduction should be about having children who have the best prospects. But to discover what are the best prospects, we must give individual couples the freedom to act on their own value judgment of what constitutes a life of prospect.

Julian Savulescu puts forward a dangerous argument that it is up to the *parents* to decide the prospects of the child. This is surely up to the child once he reaches adulthood. Besides, to say that a child has not been harmed by specifically selecting it because it has a disability is erroneous. A person who causes another person to have a disability will face a criminal court for grievous bodily harm in normal circumstances because their life has been irreparably damaged, so why should embryo selection be any different?

The controversy of PGD has been briefly noted above in regards to the creation of a 'perfect race' in society.

A market in eugenics could lead to disparities of wealth and social class, and it could lead to preferred skin colour. These views are not founded on evidence: there is already a disparity between rich and poor in society and probably always will be regardless of the developments in fertility treatment, and it is not clear how the selection of skin colour would change society from what it already is (i.e. multicultural). PGD is not often carried out because it is very complicated and expensive, and it may still not be successful. It also comes with a raft of emotional hardship – parents seeking PGD are likely to be carriers of a disease themselves and are seeking a healthy embryo – so it can be a very stressful time for couples. To say that PGD is simply a 'market in eugenics' underestimates the scientific value of the procedure.

PGD for sex selection

Many parents have preferences as to whether they welcome a boy or a girl. The emergence of the new social term SMOG (Smug Mothers of Girls) occurred in the media in 2012. It can be a great disappointment to have a family full of boys when there is an overwhelming desire for a girl (and the other way around), so can fertility treatment end the woe for parents? The answer is 'yes' but not in the UK. It is clear from Schedule 2 paragraph 1ZA(1)(c) that the sex of the embryo can only be established if it is to discover a gender-related disease, disability or serious illness:

Human Fertilisation and Embryology Act 1990

Schedule 2: Activities for which licences may be granted

Paragraph 1ZA(1): A licence under paragraph 1 cannot authorise the testing of an embryo, except for one or more of the following purposes:

(c) in a case where there is a particular risk that any resulting child will have or develop:

    (i)   a gender-related serious physical or mental disability,

    (ii) a gender-related serious illness, or

    (iii) any other gender-related serious medical condition,

    establishing the sex of the embryo.

Social sex selection, therefore, is not provided for. The Human Fertilisation and Embryology Authority compiled a report about sex selection in 2003. Their consultation was based on research into safety, techniques and public opinion in the matter. They came to the somewhat bizarre conclusion that there was widespread public opposition to sex selection for social reasons. One of their justifications is provided below.

EXTRACT

Sex Selection: Options for Regulation. The Human Fertilisation and Embryology Authority (2003):

http://www.hfea.gov.uk/517.html

Page 34 paragraph 139: In our view the most persuasive arguments for restricting access to sex selection technologies, beside the potential health risks involved, are related to the welfare of the children and families concerned. There was considerable alarm among consultation respondents that children selected for their sex alone may be in some way psychologically damaged by the knowledge that they had been selected in this way as embryos. Some consultation respondents expressed concerns that such children would be treated prejudicially by their parents and that parents would try to mould them to fulfil their expectations. Others saw a potential for existing children in the family to be neglected by their parents at the expense of the sex-selected children.

The findings in this report were put on a statutory footing in the 2008 reform. The 1990 Act now reads as follows.

Human Fertilisation and Embryology Act 1990

Schedule 2: Activities for which licences may be granted

Paragraph 1ZB: *Sex selection*

(1) A licence under paragraph 1 cannot authorise any practice designed to secure that any resulting child will be of one sex rather than the other.

The HFEA has also developed licensing conditions prohibiting social sex selection.

EXTRACT

Code of Practice, 8th edition, October 2013, Human Fertilisation and Embryology Authority:

http://www.hfea.gov.uk/code.html

Licence condition T88: With respect to any embryo testing programme involving biopsy the centre must ensure that:

b. any information derived from tests on an embryo, or any material removed from it or from the gametes that produced it, is not used to select embryos of a particular sex for social reasons.

These provisions are hugely disappointing. It is highly unlikely that a child will be 'psychologically damaged' from learning that their parents *wanted* a boy or a girl and took steps to ensure this. It is also not clear how parents would try to 'mould' their children after birth: if the child is born in the preferred gender, what else is there to change? The HFEA shows a lack of understanding when it comes to the desires of parents. Parents require a certain sex of child for many different reasons, the main ones being to equal the family unit or a lifelong preference. It seems almost offensive that PGD can be available to parents to produce saviour siblings (i.e. they were only conceived to help a brother or sister) whereas it is not available for sex selection (i.e. where the child is wanted for being itself). However, there is a surprisingly large amount of criticism to be found on sex selection from commentators.

EXTRACT

Jonathan Berkowitz and Jack Snyder, 'Racism and Sexism in Medically Assisted Conception' (1998) 12 *Bioethics* 25, at pages 25–44

To choose a boy or a girl, parents must have preconceived notions, however vague, about the ramifications of having a certain sexed child: notions which are fundamentally sexist as they are predicated upon anticipated gender based behaviour. Preconceptive sex selection is disturbing because it can be used as a vehicle for parents to express spoken or unspoken sexual prejudice. [...] Furthermore, by making a choice, parents must essentially prefer one sex over another. This emphasis upon sex is in direct conflict with larger societal goals directed against sexism and which urge individuals to be sex-blind. Preconceptive sex-selection represents sexism in its purest most blatant form as prior to conception, before parents can possibly know anything about their child, a child's worth is based in large part upon its sex.

Berkowitz and Snyder believe that a parent can discriminate when selecting the sex of their child. For example, selecting a girl will discriminate against boys and place an emphasis on female goals and female worth. This view is a bit far-fetched: many mothers naturally conceive the girl they have always wanted and do not show a derogatory attitude towards boys or force their girls to play certain roles in life. Alternatively, a prejudiced mother will remain so whether she conceives naturally or through PGD sex selection.

McDougall argues that a parent should love its child unconditionally, thus rendering sex selection useless to truly virtuous parents.

EXTRACT

R. McDougall, 'Acting Parentally: An Argument Against Sex Selection' (2005) 31 *Journal of Medical Ethics* 601, at pages 601–5

Because a child's characteristics are unpredictable, acceptance is a parental virtue. [...] Accepting one's child, regardless of his or her particular current characteristics, is already perceived as a necessary characteristic of the good parent. [...] In acting on a preference to parent only a child of a particular sex, the sex selecting agent fails to act in accordance with the parental virtue of acceptance.

McDougall raises a valid point: a virtuous parent would be accepting of its child's character traits and this includes the sex of the child. However, to say that a virtuous parent is wholly accepting of their child's characteristics is misguided. There are many characteristics that are completely unacceptable to parents, including disrespectful and violent behaviour. A child is often punished to change its characteristics. This is still a virtuous parent. Arguments in favour of sex selection take many forms: freedom to choose, positive selection and family balancing.

EXTRACT

David McCarthy, 'Why Sex Selection Should be Legal' (2001) 27 *Journal of Medical Ethics* 302, at pages 302–7

In a pluralistic democratic society built upon the ideals of free and equal citizenry, there is always a presumption in favour of liberty. The burden of proof is always on those who want to restrict the liberty of others. Defenders of the legality of sex selection are not seeking to restrict anyone's liberty, whereas opponents are. So the burden of proof is on the opponents to show that those whose liberties they propose to restrict cannot reasonably reject this restriction. What must be established is that the behaviour they are trying to restrict itself results in something like significant harm to others or infringement of their basic liberties or significant social costs. In the case of sex selection, I have argued that no such grounds have been established.

David McCarthy argues that it is for the opponents of sex selection to prove that it is harmful to society in order for liberty to be curtailed, and there is no real evidence to suggest that this is the case. John Harris has instead chosen to criticise the HFEA and its decision not to allow PGD sex selection.

EXTRACT

John Harris, 'Sex Selection and Regulated Hatred' (2005) 31 *Journal of Medical Ethics* 291, at pages 291–4

The HFEA in effect rely on the following very limited arguments against gender selection. The first is set out in paragraph 139 where they say 'in our view the most persuasive arguments for restricting access to sex selection technologies, beside the potential health risks involved, are related to the welfare of the children and families concerned'. The HFEA then glosses this concern for children by noting that, 'children selected for their sex alone may be in some way psychologically damaged by the knowledge that they had been selected in this way as embryos'. This is a very tendentious and unwarranted way of putting the point. [...] The suggestion that sons or daughters would be so unloved and treated so unacceptably badly that it would cause psychological damage is a piece of reckless speculation.

John Harris accuses the HFEA of being reckless by speculating that a sex-selected child could be psychologically harmed by learning that it was chosen because of its sex. This criticism is surely correct: a child would be pleased that it was wanted so badly that its parents took extra steps to ensure that it arrived.

Family balancing is another argument in favour of PGD sex selection. A family with two boys might like two girls too. This would remove the concern about discrimination because the family would be equal. The children will also know how to interact with the opposite sex before they get to school, which can only be in their best interests.

PGD for saviour siblings

A relatively new – and controversial – development in embryonic research is tissue typing (known as saviour siblings). A cell is taken from an embryo before it is implanted and it is tested for a genetic match to an older sibling. A match will allow the blood from the umbilical cord to be used to treat the older sibling. The child born to help the older sibling is known as the 'saviour sibling' and its parents specifically chose the embryo because it was a match to the older brother or sister. A bone marrow transplant is a good example of a procedure that can be helped along by the matching blood of an umbilical cord from a saviour sibling. This is viewed, by some, as a distasteful reason to bring a child into the world and goes against the spirit of fertility treatment. A pressure group named CORE (Comment on Reproductive Ethics led by Josephine Quintavalle) brought an application for judicial review. It argued that tissue typing for the purposes of saving a sibling was not supported by the 1990 Act. The case reached the House of Lords and they decided to interpret the 1990 Act very widely, allowing the Human Fertilisation and Embryology Authority to licence the procedure.

CASE EXTRACT

R (on the application of Quintavalle) v Human Fertilisation and Embryology Authority [2005] UKHL 28; affirming [2004] QB 168

Facts: The appellant (Q) appealed against the decision ([2004] QB 168) that the respondent authority (H) had the power to authorise examination of human leukocyte antigens, known as tissue typing, in order to assist a woman in bearing a tissue compatible child. It involved the creation and use of embryos and therefore required a licence under the Human Fertilisation and Embryology Act 1990. H submitted that tissue typing was a practice designed to secure that an embryo was suitable for the purpose of being placed in a woman within Sch. 2 para. 1(1)(d) to the 1990 Act because the mother in the instant case [Mrs Hashmi] was entitled to regard an embryo as unsuitable unless it was both free of abnormality and tissue compatible with the sibling and it was desirable for the purpose of providing her with in vitro fertilisation treatment services within Sch. 2 para. 1(3) that she should be able to make such a choice.

Held: Dismissing the appeal, that Preimplantation genetic diagnosis and tissue typing could lawfully be authorised by H as activities to determine the suitability of the embryo for implantation within the meaning of Sch. 2 para. 1(1)(d) to the 1990 Act. Parliament had intended to leave it to H to decide whether activities such as tissue typing could be permitted. The concept of suitability included taking into account the particular wishes and needs of the mother. Therefore H could authorise tests to determine whether the embryo was in that sense suitable for implantation in her womb.

Lord Hoffman (at pages 567–8, 570): In this case we are particularly concerned with the activities which may be authorised to be done in the course of providing

→

treatment services. 'Treatment services' are defined by section 2(1) to mean, among other things, medical services provided to the public for the purpose of assisting women to carry children. IVF is of course such a service. [...] So the question is whether PGD and HLA typing are activities which the authority can authorise to be done 'in the course' of providing her with IVF treatment. The authority may authorise tests to determine whether the embryo is in that sense suitable for implantation in her womb. It may, but of course it is not obliged to do so. [...] It may consider that allowing the mother to select an embryo on such grounds is undesirable on ethical or other grounds. [...] The licensing power of the authority is defined in broad terms. Paragraph 1(1) of Schedule 2 enables it to authorise a variety of activities (with the possibility of others being added by regulation) provided only that they are done 'in the course of "providing IVF services to the public" and appear to the authority "necessary or desirable" for the purpose of providing those services. Thus, if the concept of suitability in subparagraph (d) of 1(1) is broad enough to include suitability for the purposes of the particular mother, it seems to me clear enough that the activity of determining the genetic characteristics of the embryo by way of PGD or HLA typing would be "in the course of" providing the mother with IVF services and that the authority would be entitled to take the view that it was necessary or desirable for the purpose of providing such services'.

Lord Brown (at pages 575–6, 579): Is it acceptable to follow a procedure resulting in the birth of a child designed to secure the health of a sibling and necessarily therefore intended to donate tissue (including perhaps bone marrow) to that sibling? Is this straying into the field of 'designer babies' or, as the celebrated geneticist, Lord Winston, has put it, 'treating the offspring to be born as a commodity?' These are just some of the questions prompted by this litigation. [...]

IVF treatment is a fast moving medical science. It is clear that when the 1990 Act was passed PGD was expressly foreseen but tissue typing was not. It is your Lordships' task to decide whether by the 1990 Act, Parliament was conferring power upon the newly created authority to take whatever decisions arose from such unforeseen possibilities as tissue typing, or whether Parliament must rather have been contemplating the need for further primary legislation to deal with whatever ethical questions arose out of such future discoveries. [...] PGD with a view to producing a healthy child assists a woman to carry a child only in the sense that it helps her decide whether the embryo is 'suitable' and whether she will bear the child. Whereas, however, suitability is for the woman, the limits of permissible embryo selection are for the authority. In the unlikely event that the authority were to propose licensing genetic selection for purely social reasons, Parliament would surely act at once to remove that possibility.

Lord Hoffman decided that tissue typing for the purposes of creating saviour siblings was 'in the course of' providing fertility treatment. He also decided that it was 'necessary and desirable' to take account of the mother's reasons for tissue typing. Lord Brown did not think it was realistic to suppress the power of the HFEA at this point; they had discretion as to what activities they wished to license. He was also of the opinion that when social tissue typing (i.e. designer babies) became an issue, Parliament would legislate against it. The *Quintavalle* case is the leading case on tissue typing for the purposes of creating saviour siblings, and it confirms that the HFEA have the power to license the technique because it falls within the statutory provisions of the 1990 Act. There is a grey line between saviour siblings and designer babies: Mrs Hashmi *is* asking for a designer baby and the fact that his umbilical cord blood will be used to save his brother or sister does not change the fact that he was born with 'designed' genetics.

Tissue typing was incorporated into the Human Fertilisation and Embryology Act 1990 by the 2008 reform.

Human Fertilisation and Embryology Act 1990

Schedule 2: Activities for which licences may be granted

Paragraph 1ZA(1): A licence under paragraph 1 cannot authorise the testing of an embryo, except for one or more of the following purposes:

(d) in a case where a person ('the sibling') who is the child of the persons whose gametes are used to bring about the creation of the embryo (or of either of those persons) suffers from a serious medical condition which could be treated by umbilical cord blood stem cells, bone marrow or other tissue of any resulting child, establishing whether the tissue of any resulting child would be compatible with that of the sibling, and

(e) in a case where uncertainty has arisen as to whether the embryo is one of those whose creation was brought about by using the gametes of particular persons, establishing whether it is.

(4) In sub-paragraph (1)(d) the reference to 'other tissue' of the resulting child does not include a reference to any whole organ of the child.

There is clearly permission to take umbilical blood stem cells, bone marrow or tissue from a saviour *sibling* (not a parent or any other relative) when it is born in order to save the older sibling. Whole organs are not allowed, and this will disappoint many parents who require a matching kidney for an older sibling. This does not, however, prevent the younger sibling from being tested for a match later on and donating a kidney when it is older (with court approval). This is a lot of material to take from a child born with a view to saving another. It is not clear how this is in the best interests of the child born either, although case law has stated that the saving of an older sibling will *add to the happiness* of the younger sibling: *Re Y (Mental Patient: Bone Marrow Donation)* [1997] Fam 110.

Saviour siblings have caused a great deal of controversy. Would you like to be informed by your parents that you were only brought into the world to save your older brother or sister from a deadly disease? It is almost shocking that the House of Lords in *Quintavalle* have allowed this technique to go ahead. It opens the door for designer babies, who are probably less controversial than saviour siblings because they are born for their own sake, not for the purposes of saving another. Commentators have addressed the potential psychological issues of being a saviour sibling.

Susan Wolf, et al, 'Using Preimplantation Genetic Diagnosis to Create a Stem Cell Donor: Issues, Guidelines and Limits' (2003) 31 *Journal of Law, Medicine and Ethics* 327

We know almost nothing about the psychological impact of being conceived to serve as an HLA-matched donor and save a sibling's life. The effects on the donor child are potentially profound. Indeed, if the cord blood transplant fails or the donor child is otherwise repeatedly considered for harvest over a prolonged period of time, there may be a potential for serious effects. The potential may be all the greater if the donor child comes to resist or refuse further procedures. [...]

Moreover, even if one debates whether using PGD solely to conceive an HLA-matched donor may be said to harm the donor child, this use of PGD exclusively to create an opportunity for later harvesting may be wrong on other grounds, such as violating the ethical injunction to respect each individual and avoid using persons as mere means. [...]

The donor child is at lifelong risk of exploitation, of being told that he or she exists as an insurance policy and tissue source for the sibling, of being repeatedly subjected to testing and harvesting procedures, of being used this way no matter how severe the psychological and physical burden, and of being pressured, manipulated, or even forced over protest.

Susan Wolf puts forward a good argument that the saviour sibling is merely used as a means to an end, and may be forever 'harvested' to ensure the stability of the older sibling. This is not fair to the saviour sibling, who may be constantly reminded that he was not born for his own sake. It is, of course, only natural for the parents of the saviour sibling to love him unconditionally and incorporate him into the family, but he may never be able to shake off the reality that he was created to serve the needs of his brother or sister, forever living in their shadow.

A supporting argument has been put forward that because saviour siblings *prevent* the death of their older brother or sister, it is in their best interests to be born via this technique:

Sally Sheldon and Stephen Wilkinson, 'Hashmi and Whitaker: An Unjustifiable and Misguided Distinction' (2004) 12 *Medical Law Review* 137, at pages 137–63

Banning the use of PGD and tissue typing to select saviour siblings would lead to the avoidable deaths of existing children. As such, it seems appropriate to assume that the onus of proof rests with the prohibitionists who must demonstrate that these consequences are less terrible than the results of allowing this particular use of PGD. [...]

The first prohibitionist argument is that a saviour sibling would be 'a commodity rather than a person' and would be wrongfully treated as a means rather than an end in itself. [...] This argument fails to say what is wrong with creating a child as a saviour sibling, when creating a child for a number of other 'instrumental' purposes is widely accepted. Given that

→

(for example) attempting to conceive a child in order to provide a playmate for an existing child is seen as reasonable, how would we distinguish this from the reasons advanced [for saviour siblings]? [...]

We turn now to the idea that saviour siblings will by psychologically harmed. [...] Even if we concede for the sake of argument that it would be hurtful or upsetting for a selected sibling (A) to discover that she had been conceived for the primary purpose of saving the life of an existing child (B), is it really plausible to suppose that A would be less happy than another, randomly selected sibling (C) who was unable to act as a tissue donor? For it could surely be argued that A would benefit from B's company and may well derive pleasure from knowing that she has saved B's life. In contrast, imagine the psychological impact on C, born into a bereaved family, later to discover that she was a huge disappointment to her parents because of her inability to save B's life. [...] We can at least say that it is far from obvious that child welfare considerations should count against, rather than for, the practice of saviour sibling selection.

There is no guarantee that the saviour sibling will prevent the death of the older brother or sister. This is an untold pressure to place on the child. What if the saviour sibling feels like a failure for the rest of their adult lives because they could not save their older brother or sister?

THINKING POINT

List the social, psychological and legal disadvantages to screening for sex selection. How many are there? Now list the social, psychological and legal disadvantages to screening for saviour siblings. How many are there? If you find that saviour siblings has more disadvantages than sex selection, draft a letter to the Health Secretary explaining why the law has got it the wrong way round and explain why.

Human cloning

Cloning works by inserting the DNA of the person wishing to be cloned into an empty egg and using stimulation in a laboratory to help it develop. It is an exact clone because no other person's DNA is present in the egg. Dolly the Sheep changed cloning forever. She was first mammal to ever be cloned.[22] The UK media had a field day, speculating whether we could now raise the dead through cloning. Parliament had never acted so swiftly to legislate and passed the Human Reproductive Cloning Act in 2001, making it a criminal offence under section 1(1) to place a human embryo inside a woman which was created otherwise than by fertilisation. The Human Fertilisation and Embryology Act 2008 created a new offence and inserted it into the older 1990 Act, so the 2001 Act is now obsolete.

---

[22] Dolly the Sheep was born as a complete replica of her mother in the UK in February 1997.

Human Fertilisation and Embryology Act 1990

Section 3: Prohibitions in connection with embryos

(2) No person shall place in a woman:

  (a) an embryo other than a permitted embryo (as defined by section 3ZA), or

  (b) any gametes other than permitted eggs or permitted sperm (as so defined).

(3) A licence cannot authorise:

  (c) keeping or using an embryo in any circumstances in which regulations prohibit its keeping or use.

Section 3 of the 1990 Act (as amended) makes it clear that only 'permitted' embryos may be placed inside a woman. A cloned embryo is not a 'permitted' embryo, so they are now outlawed. The House of Lords published a research report on human cloning in light of the scientific developments. They shunned the idea of a human clone and even suggested an international ban on the practice.

EXTRACT

House of Lords Stem Cell Research Committee, (2002):

http://www.publications.parliament.uk/pa/ld/ldstem.htm

Paragraph 5.21(a): Given the high risk of abnormalities, the scientific objections to human reproductive cloning are currently overwhelming;

Paragraph 5.21(b): There are further strong ethical objections in addition to those based on the risk of abnormalities, although not all the arguments deployed against reproductive cloning are equally valid. The most powerful are the unacceptability of experimenting on a human being and the familial and child welfare considerations arising from the ambiguity of the cloned child's relationships.

Paragraph 7.18: Nevertheless, despite the difficulties, we believe that there would be advantage in seeking to secure international agreement on prohibiting reproductive cloning. It would send a powerful signal of international opposition to the practice; it would put moral pressure on countries not to permit facilities in their jurisdictions to be used for this purpose; and it would afford further reassurance to the public that there was protection against the use of CNR for research purposes becoming a slippery slope to reproductive cloning.

Paragraph 7.19: We have not examined in detail what would be the most appropriate international body to negotiate such an agreement, but it should be a world-wide rather than a regional body, which points to the United Nations. The enforcement of an agreement, which might take the form of a Convention, would be the responsibility of the States party to it.

Notice in paragraph 5.21(b) that there is an issue with child welfare and ambiguity of relationships. Where do these concerns come from? The very fact that a cloned child is created would suggest that the adult – who asked for the clone – *wanted* the child to be born. Saviour siblings who are a genetic match are already legal, and naturally conceived twins who share identical DNA have no welfare problems, so why do the House of Lords have such a problem with cloning?

Positive aspects of cloning

The positive aspects of cloning can be split into two categories: medical and emotional.

Medical benefits

- Any organs, tissues, cells or blood derived from a clone would be an exact match to the recipient, thus solving the organ shortage.
- A couple who wanted a child and required fertility treatment could ensure that any child born was an exact replica of either one of them rather than a hash-up of both.
- Making it legal in the UK would prevent grief-stricken or childless couples from venturing overseas for the treatment.
- A couple who could not have their own children at all because of damaged eggs or sperm could still have their own child without using a complete stranger to fill the gap (i.e. a donor).

Emotional benefits

- A child who has suddenly died can be recreated in the laboratory and the parents can have another child who looked exactly like the earlier deceased child (i.e. it would be a more accurate replacement than a regular sibling).
- The clone and its 'mother' would have an unbreakable bond because not only are they an exact DNA match, but the clone would live in the comforting knowledge that its 'mother' asked for it to be specifically created.

An infertile couple would benefit significantly from a cloned child. For example, let us say that a husband has damaged sperm and the only possibility of a biological child is using a sperm donor. The husband does not want his wife to have another man's child, so what else can they do? They can create an exact clone of his wife, or, using one of his skin cells, an exact clone of the husband.[23]

The list above does not include the obvious clones already in existence. Twins are identical genetic replicas of each other. However, their personalities are different because thoughts and emotions cannot be cloned. This is how a human clone would behave: a DNA match with its own personality. In light of the acceptance of natural twins, what is wrong with clones? The clone would have a biological parent, it would be the result of fertility treatment and it would be loved like many other children. It may be suggested that the hostile attitude towards clones is simply out of ignorance, fear, recklessness, religion or watching too many sci-fi movies. Saviour siblings are an excellent example of a highly controversial and uneasy medical practice that has been accepted by the House of Lords because a clear benefit can be derived from it. A human clone would have this exact benefit too. There is actually a very blurred line between saviour siblings (*implanted* for their genetic match) and human clones (*created* for their genetic match).

Negative aspects of cloning

The main problem with cloning is the technique used. It is not safe enough to trial on humans and it will not be safe for a long time. However, those who argue that the

---

[23] Sperm can also have their DNA replaced, so this couple can have a child matching both of them if they wanted to. This technique is still in its early stages.

wastage of eggs and embryos is unethical may like to consider the wastage in natural conception: over three quarters of pregnancies naturally miscarry before the three-month stage and many babies born end up severely disabled. Therefore, natural conception and birth carries just as much of a risk to the mother and the child as cloning does. It must also be remembered that IVF only carries a 25% success rate, meaning that wastage in fertility treatment is also considerable and very costly to couples. The success rates, safety concerns and arguments on wastage should not prevent trials of human cloning completely – they should simply inform scientists of the risks.

There are other reasons for outlawing cloning. Firstly, religious groups will argue that the technique of cloning plays God to an unacceptable degree. The beginning of life is meant to be a mysterious and sacred process not to be tampered with. However, IVF prompted an angry outcry but it is now commonplace for infertile couples. Secondly, cloning may be criticised for stripping one person of their own identity because it is simply 'borrowed' from another, but identical twins have their own personalities because their thoughts and feelings cannot be cloned, so this is a weak argument against cloning. Anne McLaren agrees:

EXTRACT

Anne McLaren, 'Commentary on Ethical Aspects of Cloning Techniques' (1998) 7 *Cambridge Quarterly of Healthcare Ethics* 192, at page 193

It has been argued that the unique identity of human beings must be protected; but monozygotic twins are at least as identical genetically as any deliberately cloned human beings would be, while all the important influences of upbringing and environment that make monozygotic twins not identical would ensure that individuals produced by nuclear transfer were still more different from one another and from their donor. If we do not wish to impugn the unique identity of each monozygotic twin, it is hard to base a convincing argument against cloning on this concept.

Thirdly, the clone will be brought up with the expectation that it will behave and achieve the same as its 'mother' but in reality, because it has its own thoughts and feelings, it may stray down a completely different path and disappoint everyone.

EXTRACT

Alexander Morgan Capron, 'Placing a Moratorium on Research Cloning to Ensure Effective Control over Reproductive Cloning' (2002) 53 *Hastings Law Journal* 1057

Given the uniqueness of each individual's environmental experience, from the earliest embryonic moment onwards, it's true that if Mozart were cloned, you wouldn't get another Mozart. But, so long as the impulse to act otherwise exists, the failure of the Mozart clones to measure up to expectations is likely to be a source of harm rather than a benefit for them, as their makers' expectations – and elaborate plans or fantasies – are disappointed. [...] Were medicine to sanction cloning as a legitimate way of getting the child you want, it would exacerbate rather than reduce the drive to regard children as objects to fulfil parental wants rather than as individuals who are entitled to their own, self-directed lives.

Alexander Capron makes a good point: a clone is more likely to be regarded as an 'object' because it is born with expectations on its shoulders. The element of 'surprise' is something that a cloned baby could not offer. The second they are born, cloned babies are expected to look, talk and behave in a certain way. It is the reason why they were cloned in the first place – to behave as a 'copy' of someone already in existence. This is unfair to the clone. A natural conception allows the element of surprise in relation to looks, features, behaviour, aspirations and destiny.

Fourthly, it could be argued that if one parent is cloned, e.g. the wife in the marriage, the husband could not have a normal father–daughter relationship with his child because it is a copy of his wife. This is a disturbing concept.

EXTRACT

Alexander Morgan Capron, 'Placing a Moratorium on Research Cloning to Ensure Effective Control over Reproductive Cloning' (2002) *Hastings Law Journal* 1057

My wife and I have nothing but sons. If we wanted to have a daughter, probably our best method would be to clone my wife. Now, suppose we did that and then, tragically, my wife died. Would her clone, who has no biological relationship to me, be a suitable replacement for my now dead spouse (assuming the clone were by then old enough to marry)? She would be the embodiment of the woman I had married, which is exactly the kind of 'replacement' that people who want to use cloning to replace a dead child are talking about.

Alexander Capron paints a rather controversial picture, but it must be remembered that some children are naturally born so identical to one of their parents that relatives struggle to tell them apart as the years advance. It may simply make the family unit closer.

Fifthly, cloning enables lesbian couples to have children without men, but the child would only be biologically related to one of the parents. This is the same as donor insemination which uses one egg and donor sperm. Lesbian couples who wish to have a clone may argue that cloning eliminates the need for sperm altogether. Sixthly, the law would have a problem in allocating parentage to a cloned child: (1) the egg donor could be the mother, although because the nucleus has been removed she would not be a DNA match; (2) the person who contributed their DNA and had it placed into the egg could be the mother, and it is likely that this is the person who asked for the clone of themselves; (3) the surrogate mother who carried the clone and gave birth the clone is currently the legal mother. Seventhly, cloning allows a parent to 'make a copy' of a deceased child. This was listed as a positive aspect of cloning (above), but it clearly presents a significant disadvantage for the cloned child. The cloned child will be expected to live up to the grand expectation of filling the gap left behind by the sudden death of their older sibling. It is highly unlikely that the cloned child will be an exact copy because his thoughts and feelings cannot be cloned, so the parents may end up bitterly disappointed or may try to push the cloned child into the path lived by the older sibling, only to find resistance and argument. This is a huge burden to place on a cloned child, and it deprives the child of a chance to let his own personality shine and to live his own life.

Surrogacy

Surrogacy is where a surrogate mother carries a baby for a couple, before handing the baby over to the couple when it is born. There are clearly controversial issues with surrogacy, namely using the mother as a carriage, and depriving the child of its birth. However, there are two types of surrogacy, partial and full, that can be explored.

Partial surrogacy

This is where the female inseminates herself with the male sperm by either engaging in sexual intercourse with him or depositing the sperm sample herself at home, using some kind of instrument. This is a very unsafe form of surrogacy, leading to possible infection or injury. There is no formal way to regulate or record these kinds of arrangements. There is no welfare test, history screening or counselling.

Full surrogacy

The baby is conceived *in vitro* and the embryo(s) are transferred into the woman in a fertility clinic, just the same as IVF treatment. This ensures that no sexual intercourse takes place, and is considered to be more 'above board' than partial surrogacy. The normal rules and regulations regarding fertility treatment (IVF) apply, so, under section 13(5) of the HFEA 1990, a welfare test must be applied to the commissioning couple. This is standard if the commissioning couple are a husband and wife and the surrogate mother is a sister who has kindly come forward to help in their desire to have a child. However, if the commissioning couple are a gay couple, the clinic must be especially sure of the welfare of any child born and the availability of a supportive environment (i.e. a female influence would be beneficial).

There are two types of surrogacy but this does not mean that they are accepted or regulated in law, because they are neither. A full surrogacy arrangement can be regulated to a certain extent by the Human Fertilisation and Embryology Authority because the use of a donor egg and the transfer of embryos represents normal IVF treatment and takes place in a licensed fertility clinic. The outcome of the treatment will be recorded for statistical purposes, and the child can trace its donor mother when it reaches the age of eighteen. However, the law has not made any legal provisions for surrogacy arrangements. They are not prohibited, but they are not enforceable either. They sit under the radar, and it allows straight/gay couples to arrange surrogacy agreements socially with no hope of legal enforcement if the surrogate mother goes back on her word and keeps the baby plus her expenses. It is estimated that only 180 surrogacy arrangements are made in the UK every year, resulting in approximately 80 live births. Statistics show that half of all surrogate mothers are known to the commissioning couple, and include biological sisters, sisters-in-law and best friends.[24] Parliament has never felt the need to legislate to protect the parties in surrogacy arrangements (full or partial) and the low numbers may be one of the reasons why.

The law on surrogacy

It was stated above that the law contains no regulations in regards to surrogacy. This is still true today, but this has not stopped the courts from dismissing surrogacy out of hand in the odd case that did come along. In 1978, the courts showed a shocking level of contempt for surrogacy arrangements in *A* v *C*.

CASE EXTRACT

A v *C* (1978); [1985] FLR 445 CA

Facts: The case concerned a baby boy who had been conceived through artificial insemination. F [father] lived with a lady who was unable to have any more children. He made an agreement with a girl, aged 19, who was artificially inseminated with F's sperm. During the pregnancy the girl changed her mind and felt unable to hand over the child. After the birth F started wardship proceedings to obtain custody.

Held: The situation between F and the girl had been wholly artificial, there being no bond between F and the child except a biological one. Any advantage that F could confer was wholly and obviously outbalanced by the disadvantage to the welfare of the child of a constant reminder of the whole sordid story. The best way was to let the girl lead as normal a life as possible with the child without interference from an obsessive father who was still passionately anxious to get care and control of the child.

Ormrod LJ: It is a simple, logical, but totally inhuman proceeding, and shows, in my view, very grave defects in his character and, indeed, in the characters of all three participants, because the lady with whom he was living was definitely involved in the plan, no doubt now to her great regret. One can feel very sorry for her in that she must feel that it was her fault in a sense that the father was in the position in which he was, so that she felt obliged to help him and take part in the most extraordinary and irresponsible arrangement. It is unnecessary to make any more comment on the irresponsibility shown by all three of the adults in this case, which is perhaps only rivalled by the irresponsibility of the person who performed the insemination on the mother.

In this case we have a situation where there is no bond between the father and the child except the mere biological one, there has never been any association, except of the most exiguous character, between the father and the mother. There has never been anything between them except a sordid commercial bargain. This was a wholly artificial situation from the very beginning which should never have happened and which no responsible adult should ever have allowed to happen.

Cumming-Bruce LJ: [This is] a kind of baby-farming operation of a wholly distasteful and lamentable kind.

Stamp LJ: [This is] an ugly little drama.

---

[24] There was a report commissioned into surrogacy in 1998 and it presented some interesting facts and figures, but they are impossible to confirm. The Brazier Report: Margaret Brazier, Alastair Campbell and Susan Golombok, *Surrogacy:Review for Health Ministers of Current Arrangements for Payments and Regulation* (1998) London, Her Majesty's Stationery Office, Command 4068, paragraph 6.22 on page 54. Archived by the Department of Health: http://webarchive.nationalarchives.gov.uk/+/www.dh.gov.uk/en/Publicationsandstatistics/Publications/PublicationsLegislation/DH_4009697.

It is not clear in *A v C* what made the lords so mad, but they had a very low opinion of what now appears to be perfectly acceptable. The arrangement in *A v C* was between a heterosexual couple and a female surrogate, so imagine what the response might have been to a *gay* couple! The law moved on very quickly, but surrogacy was still not made legal. The courts in *Re C* in 1985 decided to leave the morality of surrogacy to one side and concentrate on the best interests of the child. This is the accepted approach today.

CASE EXTRACT

Re C (A Minor) (Wardship: Surrogacy) [1985] FLR 346

Facts: A heterosexual couple commissioned a female surrogate from America, but the arrangement did not go according to plan and the baby ended up in wardship of the court.

Latey J: [The] difficult and delicate problems of ethics, morality and social desirability [are not relevant]. The baby is here. All that matters is what is best for her now that she is here and not how she arrived. If it be said (though it has not been said during these hearings) that because the father and his wife entered into these arrangements it is some indication of their unsuitability as parents, I should reject any such suggestion.

There is a recognition in *Re C* that just because you seek a third woman to carry your baby, it does not make you a bad parent. This is clearly a far better opinion of the commissioning couple than that of Ormrod LJ in *A v C*.

It was around this time that the Human Fertilisation and Embryology Act 1990 was being discussed in Parliament, and when it was passed it inserted section 1A into the Surrogacy Arrangements Act 1985 which confirms that surrogacy arrangements – of all kinds – are not enforceable in law.

Surrogacy Arrangements Act 1985

Section 1A: Surrogacy arrangements unenforceable

No surrogacy arrangement is enforceable by or against any of the persons making it.

In practice, this small and insignificant section has major implications for childless couples. The commissioning couple (i.e. the couple who seek out a surrogate) cannot take the surrogate to court if she decides after the birth to keep the baby for herself. The commissioning couple would have paid a lot of expenses to the surrogate mother for medical tests, visits to hospitals and time off work, and they will probably not get their money back if the surrogate mother defaults from the agreement. A contract may have even been formed, but the courts will not enforce it no matter how clearly it is written and no matter how many times it is signed. This puts the commissioning couple in a very vulnerable position and they are positioned to lose everything – including their own child if their egg or sperm are used – if the surrogate mother changes her mind and keeps their baby. She is, after all, the legal mother because she gave birth to the child. She would have formed a bond with the child, whether it belonged to her or not (i.e. donor egg might have been used). This vulnerability can also be applied to the surrogate mother if the commissioning couple change their mind. What if the baby is born disabled? Or it is the wrong sex? The commissioning couple can walk away from the agreement just as easily as the surrogate mother can, leaving her with a child that she does not want, cannot pay for and does not love.

The remaining provisions of the Surrogacy Arrangements Act 1985 require a closer look. The 1985 Act was originally passed to ban commercial involvement in surrogacy (i.e. advertising), initiation of surrogacy arrangements and negotiation of surrogacy arrangements. Section 1A was added in the wake of the HFEA 1990, and further polishing was provided by the HFEA 2008. Section 2(1) of the Surrogacy Arrangements Act 1985 (as amended) bans all commercial negotiations with a view to forming surrogacy arrangements (this applies to persons who seek to gain a profit). Section 3(1) also bans all advertising of surrogacy arrangements if they come under section 2(1) (i.e. for a profit).

Surrogacy Arrangements Act 1985

Section 2: Negotiating surrogacy arrangements on a commercial basis

(1) No person shall on a commercial basis do any of the following acts in the United Kingdom, that is:

(a) initiate any negotiations with a view to the making of a surrogacy arrangement,

(aa) take part in any negotiations with a view to the making of a surrogacy arrangement,

(b) offer or agree to negotiate the making of a surrogacy arrangement, or

(c) compile any information with a view to its use in making, or negotiating the making of, surrogacy arrangement;

and no person shall in the United Kingdom knowingly cause another to do any of those acts on a commercial basis.

Section 3: Advertisements about surrogacy

(1) This section applies to any advertisement containing an indication (however expressed):

(a) that any person is or may be willing to enter into a surrogacy arrangement or to negotiate or facilitate the making of a surrogacy arrangement, or

(b) that any person is looking for a woman willing to become a surrogate mother or for persons wanting a woman to carry a child as a surrogate mother.

(2) Where a newspaper or periodical containing an advertisement to which this section applies is published in the United Kingdom, any proprietor, editor or publisher of the newspaper or periodical is guilty of an offence.

Things become a little complicated under section 2(2). The 1985 Act was reformed by the HFEA 2008, allowing for a surrogate mother – and a father seeking a surrogate mother – to do the acts listed under section 2(1). This is because the arrangement will *not* be for profit, and it allows for a sister or friend to offer their surrogacy services to their brother or friend.

Surrogacy Arrangements Act 1985

Section 2: Negotiating surrogacy arrangements on a commercial basis

(2)   A person who contravenes subsection (1) above is guilty of an offence; but it is not a contravention of that subsection:

   (a)   for a woman, with a view to becoming a surrogate mother herself, to do any act mentioned in that subsection or to cause such an act to be done, or

   (b)   for any person, with a view to a surrogate mother carrying a child for him, to do such an act or to cause such an act to be done.

Section 2(2) is somewhat contradictory because it accepts that a woman may wish to offer her surrogacy services and a father may seek out her services as long as it is not for profit under section 2(1), yet under section 1A any arrangement is unenforceable in law! In real terms, a surrogacy arrangement can go ahead socially (partial surrogacy) or via IVF (full surrogacy), but it will not be enforced by a court.

The situation becomes a little more confused under section 2(2A) following the reform by the HFEA 2008. Section 2(2A) now allows for a non-profit making body (e.g. a woman offering surrogacy or a father seeking a surrogate) to claim or pay for the expenses surrounding the surrogacy. This is to enable a woman to offer her services in the peace of mind that any lost earnings or travel expenses can be reimbursed and the courts can enforce these because they are not banned under the 1985 Act.

Surrogacy Arrangements Act 1985

Section 2: Negotiating surrogacy arrangements on a commercial basis

1. (2A)   A non-profit making body does not contravene subsection (1) merely because:

   (a)   the body does an act falling within subsection (1)(a) or (c) in respect of which any reasonable payment is at any time received by it or another, or

   (b)   it does an act falling within subsection (1)(a) or (c) with a view to any reasonable payment being received by it or another in respect of facilitating the making of any surrogacy arrangement.

  (2C)   Any reference in subsection (2A) or (2B) to a reasonable payment in respect of the doing of an act by a non-profit making body is a reference to a payment not exceeding the body's costs reasonably attributable to the doing of the act.

In view of section 2(2) and section 2(2A) of the 1985 Act, it becomes clear that the attitude towards surrogacy has softened somewhat compared to the attitude in *A* v *C* (1978). There is a clear acknowledgement that women can offer their surrogacy services to friends or relatives of infertile couples or friends (e.g. a gay couple) and expenses can be sought as a result of the surrogacy arrangement (which can be enforced in a court) . . . but the surrogacy arrangement itself is still not enforceable in law under section 1A.

Assigning maternity in surrogacy

When discussing IVF treatment above, it was made clear that the woman who gives birth to the child is the legal mother. This is to enable a woman who uses a donor egg as part of her IVF treatment to be the legal parent of the child born, even though she is not genetically related to the child.

Human Fertilisation and Embryology Act 2008

Section 33: Meaning of 'mother'

(1)   The woman who is carrying or has carried a child as a result of the placing in her of an embryo or of sperm and eggs, and no other woman, is to be treated as the mother of the child.

Section 47: Woman not to be other parent merely because of egg donation

A woman is not to be treated as the parent of a child whom she is not carrying and has not carried.

It is immediately clear that these legal provisions cause a significant problem for commissioning couples taking part in surrogacy arrangements. The surrogate mother does not want to be the legal mother – she is having the baby for someone else – but if the surrogacy arrangement falls through and the surrogate mother refuses to give up the baby or the commissioning couple reject the baby, the only advantage is that the baby is already assigned a legal mother: the surrogate. The position of the commissioning mother is bleak: she must apply for a parental order or go through a challenging adoption process in order to legally acquire the child. Wallbank argues that a new law should be created to allow the child to have a relationship with its surrogate mother and its commissioning mother in one big family, rather than taking the either/or approach to having one legal mother.

EXTRACT

Julie Wallbank, 'Too Many Mothers? Surrogacy, Kinship and the Welfare of the Child' (2002) 10 *Medical Law Review* 271, at pages 271–94

It is my view that by continuing to forward the traditional two-parent family as the paradigmatic form for children's welfare and by denying the interested parties an input into the child's life, we merely reify the social standing of children born through surrogacy as somehow deviant. It may well be the time to institute into surrogacy law and social practice the idea that children can and should have knowledge of and contact with all interested parties whether we call them 'mother', 'father' or some other appropriate epithet. [...] My own proposal is [...] that there should be no need to decide cases based on the either/or approach. The paramountcy principle is not inimical to child sharing, rather, it is the entrenchment of the ideology that children's interests are best served by the private nuclear family that continues to proscribe alternative ways of being a family. [...] We need to centralise the welfare of the child in these cases rather than subordinate it to the adults involved and ensure that the welfare principle encompasses a thorough consideration of the basic need for children to have knowledge of their birth origins and where possible their wider kinship network.

Wallbank makes a staggering suggestion. She believes that a child born from a surrogacy should not have one mother, but acknowledge two separate mothers in a 'wider kinship network'. This is unworkable for two reasons and unnecessary for a third reason. Firstly, the commissioning mother would want to be referred to as the child's mother, and it is unfair to deprive her of the title if she is bringing the child up. Secondly, the majority of children have one 'mother' figure (this could include a step-mother or a grandma who raises the child), so it would be discriminatory to deprive a surrogate child of her own 'mother'. Thirdly, a surrogate child will probably know from an early age that she is the result of a special arrangement or that a close family friend carried her during pregnancy. This knowledge of the surrogacy is not to be confused with the need to be *involved* with both mothers. The surrogate mother may not want anything to do with the child once it is born.

Assigning paternity in surrogacy

It has been confirmed under section 4(1) of the Children Act 1989 that a father who is unmarried to the birth mother (i.e. the commissioning father) can be registered as the father of the baby if there is an agreement between himself and the birth mother that he should acquire parental responsibility for the child or the court orders that he should acquire parental responsibility for the child. The use of a sperm donor means that the commissioning father is not the biological father, so the commissioning father must instead apply for a parental order under section 54 of the Human Fertilisation and Embryology Act 2008 (if a full surrogacy) or apply for adoption (if a partial surrogacy).

We cannot use the standard paternity provisions (sections 28 of the 1990 Act and section 37 of the 2008 Act) to assign legal paternity to a commissioning father in a surrogacy arrangement because they only apply in instances where the *wife or girlfriend* of the man is undertaking fertility treatment with his sperm or a donor sperm. There is no reference to surrogate mothers or surrogacy arrangements in the 1990/2008 Act. The 1990/2008 provisions, if applied, lead to an odd result: the husband of the surrogate mother – if he consents to the IVF treatment upon his wife – is the legal father of the child even though he has absolutely nothing to do with the arrangement.[25]

Parental orders

The commissioning couple can apply for a parental order under the Human Fertilisation and Embryology Act 2008. This only applies to *full* surrogacy arrangements (i.e. IVF). The child will be registered a second time to the commissioning couple, but the original birth certificate (if it contains different names) will be made available once the child turns 18.

Human Fertilisation and Embryology Act 2008

Section 54: Parental orders

(1) On an application made by two people ('the applicants'), the court may make an order providing for a child to be treated in law as the child of the applicants if:

→

---

[25] This happened in *Re G (Surrogacy: Foreign Domicile)* [2007] EWHC 2814 and it proves the need for clear surrogacy laws.

> (a)　the child has been carried by a woman who is not one of the applicants, as a result of the placing in her of an embryo or sperm and eggs or her artificial insemination,
>
> (b)　the gametes of at least one of the applicants were used to bring about the creation of the embryo, and
>
> (c)　the conditions in subsections (2) to (8) are satisfied.
>
> (2)　The applicants must be:
>
> (a)　husband and wife,
>
> (b)　civil partners of each other, or
>
> (c)　two persons who are living as partners in an enduring family relationship and are not within prohibited degrees of relationship in relation to each other.
>
> (3)　Except in a case falling within subsection (11), the applicants must apply for the order during the period of 6 months beginning with the day on which the child is born.
>
> (4)　At the time of the application and the making of the order: (a) the child's home must be with the applicants, and
>
> (b)　either or both of the applicants must be domiciled in the United Kingdom or in the Channel Islands or the Isle of Man.
>
> (5)　At the time of the making of the order both the applicants must have attained the age of 18.
>
> (6)　The court must be satisfied that both:
>
> (a)　the woman who carried the child, and
>
> (b)　any other person who is a parent of the child but is not one of the applicants, i.e. the sperm donor or the egg donor,
>
> have freely, and with full understanding of what is involved, agreed unconditionally to the making of the order.
>
> (7)　Subsection (6) does not require the agreement of a person who cannot be found or is incapable of giving agreement; and the agreement of the woman who carried the child is ineffective for the purpose of that subsection if given by her less than six weeks after the child's birth.
>
> (8)　The court must be satisfied that no money or other benefit (other than for expenses reasonably incurred) has been given or received by either of the applicants for or in consideration of:
>
> (a)　the making of the order,
>
> (b)　any agreement required by subsection (6),
>
> (c)　the handing over of the child to the applicants, or
>
> (d)　the making of arrangements with a view to the making of the order, unless authorised by the court.

The parental order can only be made if a surrogate mother was used and she was treated through artificial insemination under section 54(1)(a). The embryo must be genetically related to at least one of the commissioning parents under section 54(1)(b). This removes the possibility for a parental order if a donor egg *and* sperm were used, leaving adoption the only other option. The commissioning couple can be married (legally or civilly) or be in an 'enduring family relationship' under section 54(2). There is a six-month deadline to apply for the parental order under section 54(3). The child must be living with the commissioning couple under section 54(4). The commissioning couple must be aged 18 under section 54(5). The surrogate mother and any other parent of the child, e.g. a donor, who are not part of the order must agree to the order taking place under section 54(6). The surrogate mother can only consent to the order six weeks after the birth under section 54(7). The only payment that can exchange hands is expenses under section 54(8). It is interesting to note that an egg donor or a sperm donor can be used with a surrogate mother and this can result in a parental order, but if both gametes are donated a parental order is no longer available because the commissioning couple are not biologically related to the child. This is a simple case of adopting an unrelated child.

These provisions are only applicable to full surrogacy arrangements, i.e. IVF in a proper clinic, meaning that partial surrogacy arrangements, e.g. an agreement between social friends or relatives, require adoption. The child must also be living with the commissioning parents, indicating that the surrogate mother has already handed the baby over. This shows that she is agreeable with the order being made.

Expenses and parental orders

The courts clearly have the power under section 2(2A) of the Surrogacy Arrangements Act 1985 to enforce expenses as part of a surrogacy arrangement (not the arrangement itself). There have been a small handful of cases regarding expenses to surrogates and the courts have allowed considerably large payments to be validated, but they have felt uneasy about doing so. Section 30 of the 1990 Act (before it was repealed by the 2008 reform) allowed for 'expenses reasonably incurred' to be paid but a parental order could not be made until the high expenses had been paid. This put the courts in a highly difficult position, because they wanted to make the parental orders to satisfy the best interests of the child born as a result of the arrangement.

CASE EXTRACT	*Re C (Application by Mr and Mrs X under s. 30 of the Human Fertilisation and Embryology Act 1990)* [2002] EWHC 157[26]

Facts: H and W applied for a parental order under the Human Fertilisation and Embryology Act 1990 section 30. The applicants were childless and were introduced to a surrogate mother, S, through an organisation Childlessness Overcome Through Surrogacy, COTS. The applicants and S signed a memorandum under which they agreed that conception would take place by artificial insemination using the male applicant's semen and that S would part with the child at birth. The memorandum also included an agreement that S would be paid £12,000 expenses, including S's loss of earnings. It later transpired that S had been in receipt of income support (i.e. benefits). S conceived and the child lived with the applicants from birth. The questions raised were whether the £12,000 was for expenses reasonably incurred and, if not, whether the court had the power retrospectively to authorise the payment.

Held: It was reasonably clear that S had not incurred £12,000 in expenses and loss of earnings. However, the applicants had acted in good faith throughout. The sum involved was high but not disproportionately greater than the sum they were advised

→

---

[26] Section 30 of the 1990 Act is now repealed – it related to parental orders and gamete donors.

by COTS to pay for expenses. They did not find out that S was receiving income support until after she was pregnant, they were committed to make the payment. The court could not make a parental order unless the payments were authorised by the court. It was manifestly in the child's best interests that she should be treated in law as the child of the applicants and that they should have parental responsibility for her. In the circumstances, the payment of £12,000 was authorised and a parental order under section 30 of the Act was made.

Wall LJ (at paras 20–1, 34–5): What is important, I think, is that on all the evidence it is clear that the memorandum was entered into by Mr and Mrs X in good faith, and without any corrupt intent. They were not paying £12,000 to buy a baby. They were paying a figure for expenses which they had been advised was on the high side, but which was not disproportionate. Nonetheless, it must follow that money other than for 'expenses reasonably incurred' has been given by Mr and Mrs X to SM as a consequence of the memorandum, and that the court cannot make a parental order unless the payments are 'authorised' by the court. [...] The factors which seem to me to weigh in the scales when considering the degree to which Mr and Mrs X are tainted by the transaction are the following:

(1) The sum of £12,000 required of them was not disproportionate, given the usual figure quotes by COTS and Mr and Mrs X's wish to ensure that SM did not take employment during her pregnancy. (2) Mr and Mrs X did not know that SM was claiming income support until after it was confirmed that SM was pregnant. At that point it was plainly too late for them to withdraw. (3) Mr and Mrs X are plainly a genuine couple who have spent many years attempting to conceive a child; they entered into the memorandum in good faith and without any corrupt intent. (4) If SM was defrauding the Department of Social Security by not disclosing the sums Mr and Mrs X were paying her, the responsibility for that behaviour is hers alone. There is no suggestion that Mr and Mrs X encouraged or aided and abetted her to do so in any way. (5) It is very clear that C is a much loved and cherished child. It is manifestly in her interests that she should be treated in law as the child of Mr and Mrs X, and that both should have parental responsibility for her.

For all these reasons, I authorised the payment of £12,000 by Mr and Mrs X to SM and make a parental order under section 30 of the Act.

It is interesting to note that, although SM appeared to be defrauding the Department of Social Security by not declaring the £12,000 when she was claiming benefits, Wall LJ felt obliged to make the parental order for the following reasons: the £12,000 was not disproportionate, the commissioning couple did not know that SM was receiving income support and they came across as a genuine couple who simply wanted a child for themselves, the fraudulent activity was the responsibility of SM and therefore the commissioning couple were not involved in it, and it was in the best interests of the child to grant the parental order. The difficulty in this case was, because the payment of £12,000 was part of the memorandum, the court could not make the parental order without the expenses being paid (this was the rule under section 30 at the time). This case appears to lay down a new common law test for authorising surrogacy expenses as part of a surrogacy agreement.

The sum of £12,000 was mere pennies compared to *Re X & Y* where the courts showed the same unease at being shoehorned into validating expenses to allow a parental order to be made.

CASE EXTRACT

X (Children) (Parental Order: Foreign Surrogacy), Re [2008] Fam 71[27]

Facts: The applicants applied for a parental order pursuant to the Human Fertilisation and Embryology Act 1990 section 30. The applicants were a married couple. They had entered into an agreement with a married Ukrainian woman who was interested in being a surrogate mother. The agreed terms included a monthly payment to the surrogate mother during pregnancy and a lump sum of €25,000. The surrogate mother was implanted with embryos conceived with donor eggs, the donor being anonymous, and fertilised by the male applicant's sperm. In due course she conceived and gave birth to twins. It was argued that this amount of money exceeded 'expenses reasonably incurred'.

Held: It was effectively conceded that the sums paid to the surrogate mother significantly exceeded 'expenses reasonably incurred' within section 30(7) of the 1990 Act. It followed that the section 30 application could not succeed unless the court retrospectively authorised the payments which exceeded expenses. It was clearly a policy decision that commercial surrogacy agreements should not be lawful, but there was a recognition that sometimes there might be reasons to do so. In the instant case the court authorised the payments made under section 30(7) of the 1990 Act. The welfare of the children, with a lifelong perspective, would best be served by the making of the parental order sought by the applicants.

Hedley J (at pages 80–1): I feel bound to observe that I find this process of authorisation most uncomfortable. What the court is required to do is to balance two competing and potentially irreconcilably conflicting concepts. Parliament is clearly entitled to legislate against commercial surrogacy and is clearly entitled to expect that the courts should implement that policy consideration in its decisions. [...] The difficulty is that it is almost impossible to imagine a set of circumstances in which by the time the case comes to court, the welfare of any child (particularly a foreign child) would not be gravely compromised (at the very least) by a refusal to make an order.

What Hedley J is saying is that Parliament, on the one hand, wishes to outlaw payments for surrogacy, but on the other hand the welfare of the child must also be considered and the courts cannot do this without authorising the agreed payments.

The situation is made even worse when a couple from abroad enlist the help of a surrogate mother in the UK, expecting to simply take the child back to their country once it is born. They are not eligible for a parental order because they are not domiciled in the UK. Adoption is available but again, they are not domiciled in the UK, making the process extremely difficult. This happened in *Re G*, where McFarlane J hurled a raft of criticism at the organisation (COTS: Childlessness Overcome Through Surrogacy) which set up the arrangement for its lack of legal foresight.

---

[27] This case was heard just before the 2008 reform repealed section 30 of the 1990 Act.

CASE EXTRACT

Re G (Surrogacy: Foreign Domicile) [2007] EWHC 2814

Facts: The applicants (H and W), a husband and wife, applied for a parental order under the Human Fertilisation and Embryology Act 1990 section 30. H and W were Turkish nationals, domiciled in Turkey. They had approached a British surrogacy agency, which had introduced them to a potential surrogate mother (J). Using sperm from H and an egg from J, the process of insemination resulted in the birth of a girl (M). J was named as M's mother and H as her father. H and W promptly filed their application for a parenting order. J was willing to abide by the terms of the memorandum. The issues for the court were whether it could grant the order pursuant to section 30, notwithstanding that H and W were not domiciled in the UK. The surrogacy agency [COTS] gave evidence to the effect that it did not consider the non-UK domicile of the commissioning parents to be an impediment to the making of a parenting order under section 30 and that it was aware of cases where the parents had been able to take the child back with them to their country of domicile without objections.

Held: The application was refused. It was clear from section 30(3)(b) that H and W were required to be domiciled in the UK for the court to make the order. It was of concern that the agency was facilitating surrogacy arrangements where the commissioning couple was domiciled overseas without understanding the legal position. The simplest course was for the court to make an order under section 84 of the Adoption and Children Act 2002 granting H and W parental responsibility with the aim of facilitating M's subsequent adoption in Turkey (this was successful).

McFarlane J (at paras 27–9, 40): It is a matter of significant concern that COTS has, albeit naively, been involved in the activities that I have described which are, and have long been, outside the law. For an agency working in the surrogacy field not to be aware of one of the basic requirements needed to obtain a parental order is a matter of some real concern. [...] The court's understanding is that surrogacy agencies such as COTS are not covered by any statutory or regulatory umbrella and are therefore not required to perform to any recognised standard of competence. I am sufficiently concerned by the information uncovered in these two cases to question whether some form of inspection or authorisation should be required in order to improve the quality of advice that is given to individuals who seek to achieve the birth of a child through surrogacy. Given the importance of the issues involved when the life of a child is created in this matter, it is questionable whether the role of facilitating surrogacy arrangements should be left to groups of well-meaning amateurs. [...] The one enormously positive feature in this case is that young M is said to be an absolute delight, who is well settled in the care of Mr and Mrs G who are turning out to be fine parents. The aim of the court has therefore been to identify and establish the most effective legal structure, short of a parental order, that can facilitate Mr and Mrs G in due course adopting M in their home country.

There are clearly difficulties when surrogacy arrangements are multi-national. McFarlane J was moved to criticise the lack of knowledge, expertise and regulation of COTS for arranging these agreements. It is no wonder, looking at the complexities of these cases, that section 30 was eventually repealed by the 2008 Act. There is still no regulation of surrogacy agencies, however, because surrogacy agreements are not enforceable in the UK.

A parental order may not be the best way forward in some cases. The time limit may expire, for example, or there may be some other delay. Adoption is the only other option.

Adopting a child

This section will approach adoption from the perspective that a surrogacy arrangement has gone wrong and the commissioning couple are fighting to acquire their child from the surrogate mother.[28]

The Adoption and Children Act 2002 governs this area of law. In order to be eligible to adopt a child from an uncooperative surrogate (or from the social care system) the commissioning couple must undergo a rigorous and invasive investigation by the local authority and its social workers over a long period of time. It may be made more difficult if the surrogate mother changed her mind completely and wanted to keep the child from the commissioning couple as opposed to simply running out of time to sign a parental order. The solution, according to section 52(1) of the Adoption and Children Act 2002 is that the parent of the child (e.g. the surrogate mother) must consent to the adoption of the child unless the best interests of the child requires her consent to be overridden, e.g. because she is unsuitable or incapacitated.

Adoption and Children Act 2002

Section 52: Parental consent

(1) The court cannot dispense with the consent of any parent or guardian of a child to the child being placed for adoption or to the making of an adoption order in respect of the child unless the court is satisfied that:

    (a) the parent or guardian cannot be found or lacks capacity (within the meaning of the Mental Capacity Act 2005) to give consent, or

    (b) the welfare of the child requires the consent to be dispensed with.

It might sound controversial to 'dispense with' the consent of the surrogate mother, but sometimes it is for the best that the child is adopted out. The surrogate mother may lack competence, for example, or she may be deceased or missing. The courts are unlikely to dispense with the consent of the surrogate mother if the child is still living with her and has since formed a bond with her. A small trail of cases illustrates this. In *Re P (Minors) (Wardship: Surrogacy)* the child had already lived with the surrogate mother for five months, so the courts could not justify its removal to the commissioning couple.

CASE EXTRACT

Re P (Minors) (Wardship: Surrogacy) [1987] 2 FLR 421

Facts: A woman agreed to act as a surrogate mother for a professional couple who agreed to pay a lump sum to adopt the child. Following artificial insemination, the woman gave birth to twins. She changed her mind about giving the children up.

→

---

[28] The general laws of adoption are covered in more detail in family law textbooks.

The local authority made the children wards of court to deal with the matter. By the time of the hearing the surrogate mother had cared for the children for five months.

Held: The welfare of the children was the paramount consideration. The father and his wife (i.e. the commissioning couple) could provide a superior material and intellectual background for the child but when considering the bond that the children had formed with the surrogate mother over the past five months, the court would still award care and control to the surrogate mother.

Sir John Arnold P: It is said, and quite correctly, that the shape of the B family is the better shape of a family in which these children might be brought up, because it contains a father as well as a mother and that is undoubtedly true. Next, it is said that the material circumstances of the B family are such that they exhibit a far larger degree of affluence than can be demonstrated by Mrs P. That, also, is undoubtedly true. Then it is said that the intellectual quality of the environment of the B's home and the stimulus which would be afforded to these babies, if they were to grow up in that home, would be greater than the corresponding features in the home of Mrs P. That is not a matter which has been extensively investigated, but I suspect that that is probably true. Then it is said that the religious comfort and support which the B's derive from their Church is greater than anything of that sort available to Mrs P. How far that is true, I simply do not know. I do know that the B's are practising Christians and do derive advantages from that circumstance, but nobody asked Mrs P about this and I am not disposed to assume that she lacks that sort of comfort and support in the absence of any investigation by way of cross-examination to lay the foundations for such a conclusion. Then it is said, and there is something in this, that the problems which might arise from the circumstance that these children who are, of course, congenitally derived from the semen of Mr B and bear traces of Mr B's Asiatic origin would be more easily understood and discussed and reconciled in the household of Mr and Mrs B, a household with an Asiatic ethnic background than they would be if they arose in relation to these children while they were situated in the home of Mrs P, which is in an English village and which has no non-English connections. As regards the other factors, they are, in the aggregate, weighty, but I do not think, having given my very best effort to the evaluation of the case dispassionately on both sides, that they ought to be taken to outweigh the advantages to these children of preserving the link with the mother to whom they are bonded and who has, as is amply testified, exercised over them a satisfactory level of maternal care, and accordingly it is, I think, the duty of the court to award the care and control of these babies to their mother.

Sir John Arnold P was clearly balancing all the relevant factors – including finances, environment and religion – in order to ascertain who could provide the best upbringing for the child, but in the end it will always be in the best interests of the child to remain with the parent who it has bonded with as long as that parent has provided a suitable upbringing so far. It is not about wealth, it is about love and care. Mr and Mrs B were foolish to think that their considerable wealth and affluence could sway the court's decision: a child of five months is not interested in – and has no need for – these kinds of material things. This can be contrasted to the case of *Re MW* (below) where the surrogate mother was dispensed with because her uncooperative behaviour was not supportive of the child.

CASE EXTRACT	**Re MW (Adoption: Surrogacy) [1995] 2 FLR 789**[29]

Facts: M (surrogate mother) entered into a surrogacy agreement with F and his wife (the applicants). It was drafted by solicitors, whereby M would bear F's child for a fee of £7,500 on condition that M supported the adoption process. The applicants cared for the child from its birth. A dispute arose between M and the applicants over contact and M launched a publicity campaign in the press and on television, which distressed the applicants. M also opposed the adoption application.

Held: Granting the adoption application, the court's primary duty was to safeguard and promote the welfare of the child. The child had lived with the applicants for two and a half years and there were independent, glowing reports about his progress. The court would make an adoption order and authorise the payments under Adoption Act 1976, section 57(3) retrospectively. M was dispensed with, as on any objective view she was unreasonably withholding her agreement, and an order was granted restraining her from contact with the child during its minority.

Callman J: I have had no evidence in this case, in any shape or form, of anything other than beneficial consequences flowing from the care lavished upon M. I think the mother now wants to undo what she did but the wish to undo this is for her benefit. To introduce uncertainty, to disturb the present position, is contrary to the welfare and interests of this small boy. I have found that her withholding of consent under the circumstances of this case is not what a reasonably objective parent would want to do for her child. Under the circumstances I am prepared to dispense with the mother's consent in this case, bearing in mind that she had previously given her consent and plainly had entered into this arrangement from the beginning with the advice of a solicitor. The reality is that sad as it is for the mother I must make an adoption order. It is a sad case, but the mother in the last resort has mainly herself to blame about it. The reality is that I have to guard M's interests.

In *Re MW* the surrogate mother was making life difficult for everyone because she refused to comply with the adoption order and the request for contact was confusing for the child. The court therefore dispensed with her and even prevented her from seeing the child during its minor years. This is the harsh reality of surrogacy arrangements when they go wrong. The courts were clearly swayed by the fact that the child lived with the commissioning couple and his development was progressing nicely. This logic was followed by the courts in *Re N (A Child)* in which the child had lived with its surrogate mother for its first eighteen months, but was moved via a residence order to its commissioning father because the commissioning mother was shown to be a vindictive woman who had always intended on keeping the baby to herself to simply extend her own family.

---

[29] This case was decided using old adoption legislation, but the points about dispensing consent are still applicable today.

CASE EXTRACT

Re N (A Child) [2007] EWCA Civ 1053

Facts: The appellant (the surrogate mother 'P') appealed against a decision transferring residence of an 18-month-old child (N) to the respondent (the commissioning father 'SJ'). N was born as a result of a surrogacy agreement between P and SJ and had lived with P since birth. The trial judge rejected P and commended the responsibility of SJ, finding in particular that P had deliberately embarked on a path of deception driven by a compulsive desire to bear further children and had no other objective than to obtain insemination by surrogacy with the single purpose of obtaining another child. P appealed.

Held: P's appeal was dismissed.

Thorpe LJ (at paras 1, 4): N is approximately 18 months of age and he was born to Mrs P who, with her husband, were what might be said to be the first contenders, since they had cared for N over the first 18 months of his life and had clearly given him high standards of care. The rival contenders were Mr SJ, the biological father, together with his wife, TR. [...] The [trial] judge's findings in relation to the history are perhaps largely superfluous for this afternoon's disposal of the appeal, but in very broad terms he rejected the evidence of the P's and commended the responsibility of the J's. In particular, and crucially, he found that the P's had deliberately embarked on a path of deception, driven by Mrs P's compulsive desire to bear a child or further children, and that she had never had any other objective than to obtain insemination by surrogacy with the single purpose of acquiring for herself, and her family, another child. This was crucially important, since it informed the review of the experts and the review of the judge of the medium and long-term future of N, if the responsibility for his future care were left with the P's.

Re N (A Child) is a unique case because it is highly unlikely that a court would remove a baby from adequate and established care, especially if the adequate carer was also its biological mother. However, the deceitfulness of the surrogate mother was the deciding factor in this case, and it was easier to move the baby to the commissioning couple because the baby was only 18 months old. A baby older than this would see the courts struggling to justify the residence order, whether the mother was vindictive or not.

Arguments in favour of surrogacy

There is one big argument in favour of surrogacy: the gift of life. Surrogacy is like organ donation in that it brings new hope to a family who are in desperate need of a child. The act of providing an organ is selfless and charitable, and the same goes for a baby to an infertile couple. The positives of surrogacy are listed below:

- It is a selfless and unparalleled gift.
- It helps childless couples to realise their dream.
- It brings families closer together.
- IVF allows the commissioning couple to be the biological parents of the child, lessening the chances of the surrogate mother forming a bond with the child and changing her mind.
- Women have autonomy to choose to do as they wish with their bodies.

It is quite common for the surrogate mother to be a member of the same family as the commissioning couple (e.g. a sister-in-law), because she understands the heartache of that couple to have a child of their own. The whole family can watch the child grow into an adolescent and watch the family unit become complete. Autonomy is a strong second argument in favour of surrogacy. A woman has the right to choose whether or not she becomes pregnant. Woman have many different reasons for becoming pregnant: starting a family, a one night stand, extending their family, passing on their family business to the next generation, or surrogacy for a childless family member. A prohibition on surrogacy arrangements would violate the right to liberty and remove the freedom to exercise autonomy. This is not what medical law purports to do. It would go against the fundamental principles of medicine to prevent a woman from becoming pregnant, for any reason. There is every possibility that, in the future, Parliament will recognise the increasing popularity of surrogacy because of the growing emergence of gay couples wanting to start families. There may be a system of regulation in place to interview the surrogate mother and to screen her medical history, motives and family environment (these are particularly important because research has shown that they can affect a growing child during pregnancy). Specialist lawyers could advise the surrogate mother on the true implications of handing over a child and that there will be no turning back once she has become pregnant. Specialist counsellors could also be able to advise on the emotional trauma of handing a baby over to a commissioning couple if it is part related to the surrogate mother (e.g. it used her egg).

Arguments against surrogacy

The problems posed by surrogacy are clear when read in conjunction with the statute and case law outlined above:

- The enforcement of surrogacy arrangements may not be allowed but the payment of expenses will validate the agreement, and the courts – through a string of cases – have validated surrogacy agreements by ordering the expenses to be paid (although their hands were tied under the old section 30 rule). This puts them in a contradictory (and difficult) situation not seen in any other area of law.

- The allocation of maternity and paternity to commissioning couples is not as simple as we would like for two reasons: a commissioning couple who use donor sperm will find that paternity is allocated to the husband or boyfriend of the *surrogate* mother under the HFEA 2008 if he consents to the IVF treatment, and the legal mother is the birth mother.

- Surrogacy arrangements are not regulated, meaning that multi-national surrogacy arrangements face immigration and parentage difficulties. This is not fair to the child.

Why is the law in this state?

- Reason 1: it is unethical to create a market in children.
- Reason 2: human beings are not a commodity to be passed around.
- Reason 3: a market in children would cheapen the value of children.
- Reason 4: it interferes with human nature to have three or four parents.
- Reason 5: it may psychologically harm a child to learn that he has a surrogate mother who gave him up for expenses.
- Reason 6: surrogacy allows rich commissioning couples to take advantage of poor surrogate mothers.

- Reason 7: the surrogate mother, aware of her power over the commissioning couple once becoming pregnant, can make endless and unfair demands for attention and money.
- Reason 8: a surrogate mother who already has children may unsettle their security by becoming pregnant and then simply giving the baby away.
- Reason 9: using a woman as a surrogate simply treats the woman as a means to an end.
- Reason 10: it shows coldness and it is unnatural to hand over a child after the trials and bonding of pregnancy.

The following quote from the Warnock Report sums this up.

EXTRACT

The Warnock Report, *Report of the Committee of Enquiry into Human Fertilisation and Embryology*, Department of Health and Social Security, July 1984, Her Majesty's Stationery Office:

http://www.hfea.gov.uk/2068.html

Page 45 paragraph 8.10: It is inconsistent with human dignity that a woman should use her uterus for financial profit and treat it as an incubator for someone else's child.

This attitude may be out of date. The payment issue appears to create the most controversy in surrogacy, and it has been widely debated. Freeman argues that if payment was banned, it would simply chase surrogacy underground, not prevent it altogether.

EXTRACT

Michael Freeman, 'Does Surrogacy Have a Future After Brazier?' (1999) 7 *Medical Law Review* 1, at pages 1–20

The Brazier Report fails to appreciate that withdrawing remuneration from surrogates will only drive potential surrogates away from regulated surrogacy into an invisible and socially uncontrolled world where the regulators will be more like pimps than adoption agencies. There is every reason to control surrogacy and to guard against perceived problems, but most women will expect to be rewarded. Brazier agrees and believes that surrogacy will rarely be undertaken by strangers once its recommendations are implemented. This prognosis is misplaced: surrogacy will continue; it will probably grow as infertility increases; it will go underground and the fees will become larger. We cannot stop women exercising their autonomy, nor can we persuade them that being paid aggravates their exploitation, when common sense tells them the reverse.

Freeman addresses the issue of payment in surrogacy, and believes that the situation is only going to get worse as infertility increases. What he fails to mention is that women rarely enter into surrogacy agreements for the money alone. It is often family members – such as sisters – who offer to be a surrogate for their brothers or sisters who have found themselves in a childless marriage. The offer to provide a family member with such a precious gift can sometimes be the only payment that the surrogate mother needs. A woman who is not related to the commissioning couple will also have other motives than money: she may be exercising her autonomy as a woman, or may genuinely wish to help an infertile couple. On this note, Arneson argues that the idea that poor women are exploited in surrogacy is a myth.

EXTRACT

Richard Arneson, 'Commodification and Commercial Surrogacy' (1992) 21 *Philosophy and Public Affairs* 132, at pages 132–64

Notice that the mere observation that the women who choose commercial surrogacy tend to be poor and to have few if any minimally attractive work options other than surrogacy is not a reason to ban commercial surrogacy unless one believes that these women are choosing incompetently. No matter how restricted one's life options, the idea that the narrow range of one's options unacceptably constrains one's choice is not a reason to limit further one's range of choice. [...] My point is simply that a concern that some people are forced to choose their lives from an unfairly small menu of options is a reason to expend not restrict the range of options from which these people must choose. [...] The thought that commercial surrogacy should be banned because the poor working women who mostly choose it are too incompetent to be entrusted to make their own decisions in this sphere has an ugly, elitist sound.

The two articles above try to release surrogacy from its critics, but Anderson (below) argues that the children already born will be harmed by their mother acting as a surrogate.

EXTRACT

Elizabeth Anderson, 'Is Women's Labour a Commodity?' (1990) 19 *Philosophy and Public Affairs* 71, at pages 71–92

She and the couple who pay her to give up her parental rights over her child thus treat her rights as a kind of property right. They thereby treat the child itself as a kind of commodity, which may be properly bought and sold. [...] The unsold children of surrogate mothers are also harmed by commercial surrogacy. The children of some surrogate mothers have reported their fears that they may be sold like their half-brother or half-sister, and express a sense of loss at being deprived of a sibling. Furthermore, the widespread acceptance of commercial surrogacy would psychologically threaten all children. For it would change the way children are valued by people (parents and surrogate brokers) – from being loved by their parents and respected by others, to being sometimes used as objects of commercial profit-making.

Anderson makes a valid comment about siblings feeling deprived. They may be too young to understand that the baby belongs to another couple, so as far as they are concerned they are awaiting the happy arrival of a new brother or sister. To then see the new arrival given away could be deeply shocking and could begin a mourning period for the children. The thought of this is very uncomfortable. However, the rest of the points made by Anderson – about children being objects – does not ring true. We have had surrogacy arrangements for generations – and adoption for even longer – and children are still valued regardless of how many parents they have. This argument originates from the idea that babies, through surrogacy arrangements, are simply turned into a commodity to be bought and sold like objects, leading to society to talk of surrogate children like we talk of cars at a dealership. A market in surrogacy may put a price on children, leading ordinary people to measure their worth in society. This is a frightening prospect, but it is nothing new. We already measure our worth in terms of money, career and success. Additionally, IVF costs up to £8,000 per cycle yet we do not see babies born as a result of IVF wearing a price tag around their wrist. It must be remembered, when reading criticisms about money, that surrogacy is not about exchanging a baby for money. The payments by the commissioning couple are merely *compensation* for any expense that is incurred during the pregnancy. This includes travel costs, loss of earnings and maternity clothes. There should never be an exchange of money for the baby itself because the baby is, of course, priceless.

Consent is another issue that has concerned critics. If a surrogate mother is backed into a corner by her dire financial situation, is her consent to surrogacy voluntary, valid and informed? Or, has her arm been twisted into the surrogacy agreement by the circumstances around her? It is also possible for a fertile family member to feel 'obliged' to help out a childless sibling if that family member has children of her own. Could you say no to your married and childless brother or sister if you had several children and they had none? This argument may paint a picture of 'invalid' or 'coercive' surrogacy arrangements but in real life, a surrogacy arrangement is never going to be completely devoid of emotion. The surrogate mother will be emotionally engaged with the commissioning couple if they are related, and if they are not related, the surrogate mother will still feel the pressure to complete a successful pregnancy to fulfil the dreams of the commissioning couple. Therefore, as long as the surrogate mother has all the information she requires, as well as knowledge of the risks involved, then her consent to being a surrogate will be the same as any other consent in medical law: voluntary but laced with emotion.

Finally, if surrogacy arrangements were enforceable in law, what would that mean for the child if the arrangement broke down? It is said that surrogacy agreements are like contracts for services, so the remedy enforced by the courts would be specific performance, rather than compensation. This means that the surrogate mother would be forced to perform her specific part of the contract, i.e. handing the child over. This is not as bad as it sounds, because the case law has already illustrated the courts are willing to remove a child from its surrogate mother if a bond has not been formed or she is behaving inappropriately. It would also add a rather serious tone to surrogacy arrangements, encouraging the surrogate mother to play fair and not to abuse, or take advantage of, the commissioning couple who are subject to extortion under the current law because the surrogate mother can ask for spiralling costs or pull out of the arrangement at the last minute, leaving them with nothing.

THINKING POINT

Write a list of ten disadvantages to surrogacy (you can use the points provided above to help you), then write an argument in response to each disadvantage explaining why it is not a valid criticism of surrogacy.

Chapter summary

- The Warnock Report (1984) was the first report of its kind to examine the future of fertility treatment and embryonic research in the UK. It accepted that there was a future of progress, so a new law had to be implemented alongside a regulatory body. This led to the Human Fertilisation and Embryology Act 1990 (amended in 2008). Section 5 of the 1990 Act established the Human Fertilisation and Embryology Authority with its helpful Code of Practice.

- A woman shall not be provided with treatment services unless account has been taken of the welfare of any child who may be born as a result of the treatment (including the need of that child for *supportive parenting*), and of any other child who may be affected by the birth: section 13(5) HFEA 1990. This is the 'welfare test' and the 2008 amendment saw the term 'father' being removed.

- The case law precedent has now been set to allow the wives of deceased husbands to take their unlawfully stored gametes abroad to use fertility treatment: *L v Human Fertilisation and Embryology Authority* [2008] EWHC 2149.

- It is acceptable, according to the common law, to use preimplantation genetic diagnosis (PGD) during fertility treatment to find an embryo with a genetic match to an existing sibling in order to save their life: *R (on the application of Quintavalle) v Human Fertilisation and Embryology Authority* [2005] UKHL 28; affirming [2004] QB 168. This is known as a 'saviour sibling' because its blood, bone marrow or tissue can treat the older sibling and potentially save its life.

Chapter essay

'Critically explain the need for clear and enforceable surrogacy laws in the United Kingdom.'

Chapter case study

Mike and David have been dating for thirteen years. They entered into a civil partnership two years ago, and their whole family joined the ceremony, wishing them well. They were a very well-suited couple, but they desperately want a child to make their family complete. Stephanie, David's sister, offered to carry a baby for them, but said it could only be using Mike's sperm, otherwise she would effectively be having her brother's child. Mike and David were not happy with this, because David was the younger and healthier partner and they both agreed some years ago if they ever had a child, that it would be using David's sperm. They therefore seek a surrogate through an agency, which they find, and they meet up with her. She is happy to give them a child for expenses of approximately £10,000, but she will not seek IVF treatment in a clinic because it is too invasive – she wants David to socially impregnate her instead. Describe the main differences between partial surrogacy (proposed by S) and full surrogacy (proposed by Mike and David), including the transferral of parental responsibility.

Further reading

Laing, J. and Oderberg, D.S. (2005) 'Artificial Reproduction, the Welfare Principle and the Common Good', 13 *Medical Law Review* 328.

McMillan, J. (2003) 'NICE, the Draft Fertility Guideline and Dodging the Big Question', 29 *Journal of Medical Ethics* 313.

Sheldon, S. (2005) 'Fragmenting Fatherhood: The Regulation of Reproductive Technologies', 68 *Modern Law Review* 523.

Wallbank, J. (2002) 'Too Many Mothers? Surrogacy, Kinship and the Welfare of the Child', 10 *Medical Law Review* 271.

Wilkinson, S. (2008) 'Sexism, Sex Selection and Family Balancing', 16 *Medical Law Review* 369.

9

Organs

Chapter objectives

At the end of this chapter, you should have:

- An understanding of the history of organ transplantation from experimental procedures centuries ago to the astonishing scientific developments of the present day.

- An appreciation of the primary legislation in this area – the Human Tissue Act 2004 (and its Human Tissue Authority) – which stemmed from the Alder Hey scandal.

- Knowledge of the controversies surrounding elective ventilation and our opt-in system of organ donation.

- An understanding of the controversies of organ donation in a legal, social and moral context.

SETTING THE SCENE

Johnny, 21, was in a car accident. His injuries are very serious and he is taken to hospital unconscious. The doctors order a brain stem death test because his breathing is being supported by a life support machine. His family are approached about organ donation. They have no idea what to say because Johnny never had a view on organ donation. He had a rare blood type and there was a shortage of organs with his blood type. His family decide to donate his organs but they want to know all about the donation and transplant procedure, including the relevant laws and regulations, before they consent. How can you advise them?

Introduction

The world of organ donation and transplantation has surprised medicine in the last six decades. One hundred years ago, it was unthinkable that an internal organ from one person could be used to give life to another person. In some cases, several organs can be used at once, and transplants have become a routine treatment in the case of some illnesses (e.g. liver failure). The technique of organ transplantation is actually incredibly cost effective. NHS Blood and Transplant has published some statistics in regards to kidney transplants.

EXTRACT

Cost-effectiveness of Transplantation, NHS Blood and Transplant, October 2009[1]

- Kidney transplants save a lot of NHS money because a patient on hospital haemodialysis could cost the NHS up to £35,000 a year.
- The average cost of a kidney transplant is £17,000 and the immunosuppressant drugs required afterwards cost £5,000 per patient per year.
- The cost benefit of kidney transplantation compared to dialysis over a period of ten years is £241,000 per patient.
- In 2008–2009, there were 2,497 kidney transplants, and these transplants are now saving the NHS £50.3 million in dialysis costs each year for every year that the kidney functions.
- At the end of March 2009, the UK Transplant Registry had records of over 23,000 people in the United Kingdom with a functioning kidney transplant, and these patients will save the NHS over £512 million per year in the dialysis costs that they would need if they did not have a functioning kidney transplant.

However, the world of organ donation and transplantation has been plagued with two major problems that continue to inhibit progress. Firstly, there are not enough organs to go around. Organs currently come from deceased donors on life support machines or altruistic living donors, and there are not nearly enough to go around (there are approximately 7,500 patients on the transplant waiting list at any one time).[2] A previous source

---

[1] http://www.organdonation.nhs.uk/newsroom/fact_sheets/cost_effectiveness_of_transplantation.asp.
[2] See the homepage for statistics at: www.organdonation.nhs.uk.

of organs was fatal car accidents, but fewer people are dying on the road because of European safety regulations in the car manufacturing industry. We do not allow a market in organs, although black markets exist in poorer countries, and we have rejected the 'assumed consent' system in the United Kingdom, meaning that an organ will only be donated if consent is attained from the donor (living or dead). Xenotransplantation (animal organs) has not been successful either, so what can we do to fill the supply gap? Secondly, the issue of consent is a touchy one in this area, because dead donors have to consent through their relatives who may disagree with the procedure, and living donors may feel pressured into consenting if their own family member needs a new organ. Consent cannot be valid unless it is free from duress, so are there any safeguards in place to ensure that family members are not *forced* into parting with their organs?

This chapter will look at the history of organ donation and transplantation first, before providing a brief overview of the organ transplant procedure, e.g. the waiting list system. The law regarding living donation will be explored in detail, e.g. the typical procedure here would be kidney donation to a relative, followed by the law regarding deceased donors. Finally, the issues outlined above – such as black markets, donor consent and ownership in the body – will close this chapter, illustrating just how problematic this area of medicine really is. What is unique about this area of medical law compared to others is the *lack* of law. The Human Tissue Act 2004 will be referred to frequently because it covers the consent of removal, storage and use of human tissue and organs, but there are very few cases and even fewer additional statutes. The relevant organ donation and transplantation authority – NHS Blood and Transplant – has the power to create its own organ allocation regulations, so it is mainly in-house guidelines and protocols that govern this area of medicine. However, there is an abundance of academic commentary, because the ethical issues in this field of medicine are significantly controversial. The topics that will come under particularly close ethical scrutiny are: (i) the definition of death (i.e. the point at which it is legal to take the organs out); (ii) elective ventilation (i.e. keeping a body on a life support machine just to keep the organs fresh); and (iii) financial incentives to donate.

 ## The history of organ donation and transplantation

> **KEY DEFINITION** **Autograft**: tissues are transplanted back into or onto the same body (e.g. skin graft).
> **Allograft**: an organ or tissue is transplanted into another body of the same species (e.g. between humans).

The history of organ donation and transplantation is highly experimental, with roots that can be traced all the way back to the second century BC, long before the real science of transplantation and immune rejection was even known. It appears that resourceful scientists from centuries ago quickly figured out that skin and limbs could potentially be transferred from one body to another in order to help the healing process.

What can be transplanted today? (D = deceased donor only)

- **Thoracic (i.e. chest) organs**
  - Heart (D)
  - Lung
  - Heart and lung domino transplant (D)

- **Abdominal organs**
  - Kidney
  - Liver
  - Pancreas (D)
  - Intestine
  - Stomach (D)
- **Tissues and other**
  - Hand and arm (D)
  - Foot and leg (D)
  - Cornea (D)
  - Skin
  - Face (D)
  - Pancreas cells
  - Bone marrow
  - Blood transfusion
  - Heart valve (traditionally a xenograft from a pig or cow)
  - Bone.

Allotransplants (a tissue or organ transplant between two individuals of the same species) have existed in history for some time, although the records are not very specific and may refer to spiritual ideas rather than actual procedures. It is more likely that the real science began with autografts (tissue being retransplanted back onto or into the same person). There is a reference from the second century BC of a legendary Indian surgeon – named Sushruta – performing a skin autograft during a nose reconstruction (the first recorded plastic surgery).[3] The success of these autografts was not clear, but centuries later an Italian surgeon – named Gaspare Tagliacozzi – recorded successful skin autografts and was very active in the field of plastic surgery. He could not succeed with allografts (a tissue or organ transplant from one person to another) and before he died in 1599 he wrote the book *De Curtorum Chirurgia per Insitionem* in which he suggested that some form of 'rejection' was taking place. This was extraordinary, because the human immune system was still centuries away from being discovered and it still poses a barrier to organ transplantation today. Allografts became far more successful in the twentieth century when the first successful human cornea transplant took place in 1905, performed by ophthalmologist Eduard Zirm in the Czech Republic between an adult and a child (both living). The recipient regained the sight in one of his eyes and returned to work. This success opened up the possibility of organs being transplanted into humans, but immune rejection was still a mystery.

The First World War (1914–1918) allowed surgeons to develop skin autograft techniques on injured soldiers. The Second World War (1939–1945) allowed reconstructive surgery on soldiers to be developed further. However, despite the sharpening of surgical techniques between 1914–1945, the problem of immune rejection was still not solved and allograft organ transplants were still not successful. Sir Peter Medawar identified immune rejection in 1951 and suggested that drugs could be used to allow allograft organ transplants between humans to take place. Scientists began to experiment with

---

[3] He was known as the 'father of medicine' and authored the book *Sushruta Samhita* in which he described hundreds of surgical procedures and surgical instruments.

immunosuppressant drugs right away, even though their main side effect was the suppression of the immune system. There were a few drugs available to surgeons over the following few decades that had varied levels of success, including Cortisone and Azathioprine, but the immunosuppressant properties of Cyclosporine were discovered in 1972 (approved for clinical use in 1983) and it is now widely used as one of the most powerful immunosuppressant drugs in human allograft transplants. Tacrolimus is also available (approved for clinical use in 1994). These drugs may have high success rates, but there are post-transplant complications such as common viruses attacking the patient when their immune system is weakened, leading to organ failure in particularly elderly or frail patients. This is not ideal.

The first successful organ transplant was performed by Dr Joseph Murray and Dr John Harrison in Boston in 1954. It was a kidney transplant between identical twins, and because their immune system was identical the issue of immune rejection did not arise. Dr James Hardy attempted to follow this success in Mississippi in 1963 with the first lung transplant, but the patient died after eighteen days from kidney failure. A few months later he tried again in 1964 with the first xenograft heart transplant between a chimpanzee (a close genetic match) and a human. The patient, Mr Boyd Rush, was a 68-year-old man very close to death, and he died after ninety minutes. Dr James Hardy was criticised for this experiment as some thought it was immoral, grotesque and cruel, but it opened up the possibility of a heart transplants between humans, which was the ultimate prize for pioneering transplant surgeons. The moment finally came in 1967 in South Africa when Dr Christiaan Barnard performed an allograft heart transplant between Louis Washkansky, a 57-year-old grocer suffering from heart disease and Denise Darvall, a young woman who was brain damaged and on a life support machine after being hit by a car. The operation lasted nine hours and required a team of thirty people. He injected Denise Darvall's heart with potassium to paralyse it with her father's permission (effectively killing her), and it was successfully transplanted into Louis Washkansky. He survived for eighteen days, finally succumbing to pneumonia because of his immunosuppressant drugs. This was frustrating, but it was proof that a human being could survive a heart transplant. Dr Christiaan Barnard continued his work in 1968, where his next heart transplant patient survived for nineteen months, and his biggest success story was patient Dirk van Zyl, who received a heart transplant in 1971 and lived for twenty-three years. Dr Thomas Starzl paved the way for liver transplantation, performing the first unsuccessful liver allograft transplant in Denver in 1963 but finding success with the same procedure in 1967 when the patient survived for a year. Success rates steadily increased in the eighties, and liver transplantation is now the accepted treatment for liver failure. Surgeons all over the world were becoming more brave with their procedures as a result of the increased effectiveness of immunosuppressant drugs, and were beginning to perform multiple organ transplants. Dr Denton Cooley performed the first unsuccessful heart-lung transplant in 1968, but it was successful in 1981 at the hands of Dr Bruce Reitz in Stanford, USA, who credited Cyclosporine as the key to his success.[4] Dr Roy Calne performed the first liver, heart and lung transplant in 1987, and the first successful stomach, intestine, pancreas, liver and kidney cluster transplant in 1994.

Other notable achievements in history

- 1902: Alexis Carrel demonstrates the method of joining blood vessels to make organ transplants a possibility.

---

[4] Dr Denton Cooley was also the first surgeon to perform a total artificial heart transplant in 1969.

- 1918: Blood transfusions are performed.
- 1966: First successful pancreas transplant by Dr Richard Lillehei and Dr William Kelly (Minnesota, USA).
- 1981: First UK donor card to include kidneys, corneas, heart, liver and pancreas was launched.
- 1983: First successful lung lobe transplant by Dr Joel Cooper (Toronto, Canada).
- 1984: First successful double organ transplant by Dr Thomas Starzl and Dr Henry Bahnson (Pittsburgh, USA).
- 1986: First successful double-lung transplant by Dr Joel Cooper (Toronto, Canada).
- 1994: The NHS Organ Donor Register is established in the UK.
- 1998: First successful live-donor partial pancreas transplant by Dr David Sutherland (Minnesota, USA).
- 1998: First successful hand transplant (France).
- 2005: First successful partial face transplant (France).
- 2006: First jaw transplant to combine donor jaw with bone marrow from the patient by Dr Eric Genden (New York, USA).
- 2008: First successful full double arm transplant by Dr Edgar Biemer, Dr Christoph Höhnke and Dr Manfred Stangl (Munich, Germany).
- 2008: First baby born from transplanted ovary by Dr James Randerson.
- 2010: First full facial transplant by Dr Joan Barret (Barcelona, Spain).
- 2011: First womb transplant in Derya Sert, aged 22, from a deceased donor (Turkey).
- 2011: First double leg transplant, by Dr Cavadas (Valencia, Spain).[5]

What are the future developments?

There are two scientific developments that could potentially change the organ transplantation system forever: they are 'regenerative medicine' and 'artificial organs'.

Regenerative medicine is a modern term that refers to the regeneration of human cells, tissues and organs using stem cells, which are blank cells that can rebuild and repair the tissue around them. They could hold the key to the development of new human tissues and organs in the future. There are numerous ways to harvest stem cells, including embryos, umbilical cords and bone marrow, but what is important is that the stem cells come from the patient herself, so if a new organ was to be grown from them in a laboratory, the immune system would be a perfect match. This is referred to as 'tissue engineering' because new tissues are grown from blank cells that have been engineered or 'encouraged' to multiply in a laboratory. Full organs – such as hearts and livers – have not been grown or transplanted yet but science is moving fast. Dr Anthony Atala of Wake Forest University in the USA broke the news in 2006 that he had developed the first laboratory-grown bladder from engineered human cells and had successfully transplanted it back into the patient.[6] His team are now trying to develop several tissues and organs in their laboratories using the same method. In addition to this, Professor

---

[5] http://www.organdonation.nhs.uk/about_transplants/transplantation_milestones/.
[6] Atala, A. 'Tissue-engineered autologous bladders for patients needing cystoplasty', *The Lancet*, 15 April 2006, vol. 367, no. 9518, page 1241.

Macchiarini at the University of Barcelona performed the first tissue-engineered trachea, i.e. windpipe, transplant in 2008. The trachea itself was from a deceased donor, but adult stem cells were extracted from the patient's bone marrow, grown into a large mass in the laboratory, matured into cartilage cells and then seeded into a segment of the trachea that had been decellularised (it was free from the donor's cells). Four days later the trachea was transplanted into the patient, and within a month all of the blood vessels had grown back. These two exciting developments are different from each other: the 2006 procedure created a whole new organ, whereas the 2008 procedure simply turned a donated organ into an immune match. However, this is a rapidly developing field of medicine and it is only a matter of time before either a full organ is developed in the laboratory and transplanted back into its immune-matching host, or a donated organ is turned into an immune match to suit its new host.

Artificial organs are nothing new, but they are getting better in every decade. They are man-made devices that can either restore an old function (such as sight or mobility) or bridge the transplantation gap between an old heart and a new heart (artificial hearts last for about eighteen months and originate from the USA). The earliest version of an artificial limb goes back centuries – children will recognise the old 'peg leg' cartoon caricature in story books. However, these limbs were not very practical or flexible, and continued to be so for centuries. What is clever about modern artificial organs (such as pacemakers) is that they are not powered by a main power supply – they must work on their own and in tandem with the human body once they have been implanted. This is why a dialysis machine cannot be labelled as an artificial kidney: even though they replace the functions of the kidney perfectly well, they need to be plugged into the main power supply and the patient often lives a miserable existence while connected to the machine waiting for a kidney transplant. The history of organ transplantation has led us to a rather frustrating position. Current sufferers of organ failure cannot expect to receive an artificial organ because they have not been invented yet, nor can they expect to receive their own 'created' organ either because they do not have time to wait for a team of scientists to develop one from their stem cells in a laboratory. This is frustrating because there are glimpses of breakthroughs every few years, but progress is very slow. In one hundred years' time, it will probably be routine to have stem cells from an umbilical cord stored for 'future use' and organs grown from them in a laboratory. For the meantime, we have to rely on organs from donors and immunosuppressant drugs, which is still considered to be quite an amazing feat in itself.

The current law in the United Kingdom

Parliament acted retrospectively when it came to our current law on organ transplantation. The Human Tissue Act 2004 was a legislative reaction to a massive hospital scandal involving Bristol Royal Infirmary and Liverpool's Alder Hey Children's Hospital in the 1990s where it emerged that both hospitals had kept child organs without the consent or knowledge of the parents. This was a highly emotive controversy, and the Department of Health published a consultation document with a view to changing the law in the area. The following principles were suggested as the foundation of any new law in transplantation.

EXTRACT

Human Bodies Human Choices: The Law on Human Organs and Tissue in England and Wales – A Consultation Report (July 2002), Department of Health (archived):

http://webarchive.nationalarchives.gov.uk/20130107105354/ http://www.dh.gov.uk/en/Publicationsandstatistics/Publications/ PublicationsPolicyAndGuidance/DH_4109272, page 14, paragraph 2.3

- Respect;
- Understanding;
- Informed consent;
- Time and space;
- Skill and sensitivity;
- Information;
- Cultural competence;
- A gift relationship.

Parliament passed a new law that was very clear about the storage and use of human tissue and organs and the need for consent, which is the fundamental basis of the Human Tissue Act 2004. The 2004 Act covers all kinds of things to do with donating parts of the human body, including research, post-mortems, anatomy and public display, although it does not cover every single human tissue (sperm and eggs are not included – see Chapter 8 for the relevant law on assisted conception). Most importantly, the Human Tissue Act 2004 set up the Human Tissue Authority (HTA) which plays a very big role in the donation, storage and use of human bodies, tissues and organs.[7] It issues licences for these purposes to ensure that they are performed legally, although organs and tissues donated for transplantation are not stored for long enough to require a licence. The HTA has issued nine Codes of Practice in total, and these Codes provide a wealth of additional information in regard to:

- Code 1: Consent.
- Code 2: Donation of solid organs for transplantation.
- Code 3: Post-mortem examination.
- Code 4: Anatomical examination.
- Code 5: Disposal of human tissue.
- Code 6: Donation of allogeneic bone marrow and peripheral blood stem cells for transplantation.
- Code 7: Public display.
- Code 8: Import and export of human bodies, body parts and tissue.
- Code 9: Research.

---

[7] Official website: www.hta.gov.uk.

Most of these Codes were updated in September 2009, and further amendments can take place whenever and wherever the HTA feels it is necessary. The Human Tissue Act 2004 covers the following activities which are listed under section 1 and under Schedule 1.

Human Tissue Act 2004

Section 1: Authorisation of activities for scheduled purposes

1. (1) The following activities shall be lawful if done with appropriate consent:

   (a) the storage of the body of a deceased person for use for a purpose specified in Schedule 1;

   (b) the use of the body of a deceased person for a purpose so specified;

   (c) the removal from the body of a deceased person, for use for a purpose specified in Schedule 1, of any relevant material of which the body consists or which it contains;

   (d) the storage for use for a purpose specified in Part 1 of Schedule 1 of any relevant material which has come from a human body;

   (f) the use for a purpose specified in Part 1 of Schedule 1 of any relevant material which has come from a human body.

Schedule 1 (part 1) of the Human Tissue Act 2004

- Anatomical examination;
- Determining the cause of death;
- Establishing after a person's death the efficacy of any drug or other treatment administered to him;
- Obtaining scientific or medical information about a living or deceased person which may be relevant to any other person (including a future person);
- Public display;
- Research in connection with disorders, or the functioning, of the human body;
- Transplantation.

The storage of a deceased body for one of the purposes under Schedule 1 is lawful under section 1(1)(a). The use of a deceased body for one of the purposes under Schedule 1 is lawful under section 1(1)(b). The removal of organs and tissues from a deceased body for one of the purposes under Schedule 1 is lawful under section 1(1)(c). The storage of organs and tissues from a body (living or deceased) for one of the purposes under Schedule 1 is lawful under section 1(1)(d) and the use of organs and tissues from a body (living or deceased) for one of the purposes under Schedule 1 is lawful under section 1(1)(f).

It is interesting to see that consent for the *removal, storage* and *use* of organs and tissues from a *deceased* person are covered under the 2004 Act, but only consent for the *storage* and *use* of organs and tissues from a *living* person are covered by sections 1(1)(d) and (f). This means that a living donor must consent to their *removal* under the common law of consent (see Chapter 4). The current legal situation can be summarised as follows:

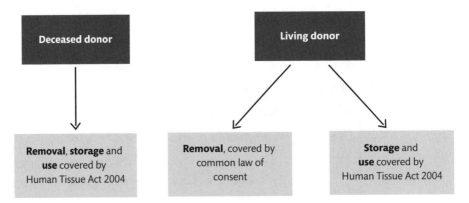

Figure 9.1

It is finally worth noting that under section 5(1) of the 2004 Act, anyone who removes, stores and uses organs and tissues without appropriate consent commits a criminal offence unless he reasonably believes that he has appropriate consent. This is a hard thing for the defendant to prove. The maximum penalty is three years in prison.

RESEARCH ACTIVITY

Enter the term 'tissue engineering' into an internet search engine. What are the latest developments? Do you think that this is the best way forward, or might there be a better way that scientists haven't yet thought of?

The organ transplant procedure

The general public may regard organ transplantation as a simple procedure: get onto the waiting list and wait for an organ. It is not as simple as that. There are several stages to organ transplantation. The Human Tissue Act 2004 is the leading piece of legislation in this area, governing consent, removal, storage and use of human organs and tissues.

Stage one: donation

There must be an organ available, so the first stage of the process is donation. This can occur from a living donor (e.g. kidney, bone marrow, blood) or a dead donor (heart, liver, stomach). An organ begins to deteriorate as soon as it is removed from the human body, meaning that there is only a very small window of time before it becomes unusable. In some instances, the organ must travel up or down the country to reach the matching recipient. A valid consent is appropriate for both living and dead donors. Living donations typically go to a pre-selected recipient (e.g. a sister), but deceased organs are usually anonymous. NHS Blood and Transplant is the organ donation and transplantation organisation for the United Kingdom.[8] When a donor organ becomes available, its duty

---

[8] Official website: www.nhsbt.nhs.uk.

office is notified immediately and staff verify whether there are any urgent cases in the UK transplant centres, that is the major hospitals around the country that carry out transplant procedures. There are different matching criteria for each organ but generally, the level of urgency, a blood match, location and age compatibility will be considered when searching the National Transplant Database (where all waiting recipients are listed) for a match. The organs may go to Europe if no match can be found in the United Kingdom. NHS Blood and Transplant (NHSBT) states that, between 1 April 2014 and 20 May 2014, the following procedures took place:

- 170 people have donated organs;
- 301 additional people have donated corneas;
- 433 people have received the gift of sight;
- 430 people have received transplants;
- 6,934 people are still waiting for a transplant.[9]

This illuminates just how grave the shortage of organs is. These figures, of course, are small change compared to the USA. The Organ Procurement and Transplantation Network (OPTN) controls the national patient waiting list in the USA and on 20 May 2014 it reported the following:

- 122,702 people are waiting for a transplant;
- 4,577 transplants have taken place between Jan–Feb 2014;
- 2,283 people have donated organs between Jan–Feb 2014.[10]

Stage two: candidate assessment

It is a myth that when a patient suddenly finds that he needs an organ transplant, he is automatically placed on the organ waiting list. This is not true: transplant candidates must be assessed by a multi-disciplinary transplant team made up of surgeons, healthcare specialists, therapists, dieticians, social carers and nurses. The patient will find the following characteristics – in addition to his failing health – under the microscope:

- Social history (e.g. housing and quality of life);
- Employment history;
- Habits (e.g. drug or alcohol abuse);
- Psychiatric condition (e.g. past compliance with medical care);
- Marital status;
- Past medical history;
- Current health stats (e.g. height, weight, blood pressure, temperature, etc.);
- Microbiology assessment (e.g. MRSA);
- Detailed blood tests (e.g. calcium, creatine, thyroid, HIV, syphilis).

The assessment criteria listed above may be rigorous, but an organ transplant is a very serious procedure. The transplant team must be sure that the candidate can physically,

---

[9] www.organdonation.nhs.uk accessed on 20 May 2014.
[10] http://optn.transplant.hrsa.gov/ accessed on 20 May 2014.

mentally and socially handle the surgery and the post-operative care. This is the nature of organ transplantation. The classic argument that alcoholics should not be allowed liver transplants seems too discriminatory to be implemented in real life, but the assessment process actually does a good job of weeding out those candidates who will abuse their new organs with the same old bad habits. The assessment team and their questions will change slightly depending on the organ required, but the full regulations for each organ are made public to allow for fairness and inequality, and are posted on the NHSBT website.[11] A patient may win his place on the waiting list, but this is not the end of his journey: he still needs to be matched to an organ as they slowly trickle into the system. Sadly, the journey does end on the waiting list for many patients: between April 2012 and March 2013 a total of 466 patients died whilst they were waiting for an organ.[12]

Stage three: organ allocation

NHS Blood and Transplant (NHSBT) is determined to ensure that our organ allocation system is fair, unbiased and based on need. Patients who make it through the assessment process are listed on the National Transplant Database (this is socially known as 'the waiting list'). NHSBT is governed by the Department of Health, but it can publish its own regulations for organ allocation. A website page is dedicated to each organ. The assessment and allocation procedures are often set out in the same document, which is helpful for patients wishing to research their condition. However, some organs have their own allocation schemes.[13] There used to be concern that organs were allocated to the 'best' patients in terms of social standing or wealth, but this is not true. Medical criteria are far more prominent in the assessment/allocation process than social criteria. A patient's living conditions are only relevant in terms of his ability to access post-operative care.

Stage four: surgery and post-operative care

The final stage of organ transplantation is the surgery itself, which can be complex. However, transplant surgeons are highly skilled specialists and if anything was to go wrong, they would be judged according to what a highly skilled transplant surgeon would have done (*Bolam* v *Friern Hospital Management Committee* [1957] 1 WLR 582). Surgery will take a few hours, and more than one organ can be transplanted at once. The patient will be taking immunosuppressant drugs so his body does not reject the new organ during the recovery stage. Success rates are steadily improving. NHSBT claims on its website that one year after surgery:

- 94% of kidney transplants from living donors are functioning well;
- 88% of kidney transplants from dead donors are functioning well;
- 86% of all liver transplants are functioning well;
- 84% of all heart transplants are functioning well.[14]

---

[11] http://www.organdonation.nhs.uk/about_transplants/organ_allocation/.

[12] Taken from: Transplant Activity in the UK – Activity Report, 2012/13, NHS Blood and Transplant, at page 2. See: http://www.organdonation.nhs.uk/statistics/transplant_activity_report/.

[13] http://www.organdonation.nhs.uk/about_transplants/organ_allocation/.

[14] http://www.organdonation.nhs.uk/about_transplants/success_rates/, accessed on 20 May 2014.

ACTIVITY

The following two patients need a transplant. Can you reach a decision that is fair to both the patient and the thousands of other people waiting for the same organ, i.e. should they be listed for a transplant or should they be sent home?

1. Kerry is 24 and has heart disease. She has lived a healthy lifestyle all of her life, but heart disease runs in her family and she was found to have a particularly weak heart when she was born. Kerry has just graduated from her teaching degree and had been working as a primary school teacher for five months when she had a cardiac arrest. She is in a serious condition and a heart transplant within two months is her only option for survival. She is single with no dependants and has no funds, but her parents are very supportive.

2. Deborah is 43 years old and has cancer of the stomach. The chemotherapy did not work and she is suffering from a particularly aggressive form of cancer, meaning she must have a stomach transplant as soon as possible. Deborah is overweight but not obese. She does not eat well but she does not smoke or drink. She has a very stressful job which contributed to her illness. She cannot give up her job because it pays the mortgage, but the doctor warned her that she must leave work for several months. She has one teenage child, who also causes significant stress.

Living donor transplantation

A living donor can donate:

- A lung lobe;
- A kidney;
- Liver segments;
- Intestinal segments;
- Skin;
- Pancreas cells;
- Bone marrow;
- Blood;
- Bone.

Living donation is a significant lifeline for many patients. The NHSBT website confirms that between April 2012 and March 2013, there were 969 living kidney donations and 30 living liver donations.[15] Living donation can take two forms:

- **Directed donation**: a healthy person donates organs or tissues to a specific recipient;
- **Altruistic non-directed donation**: a donation is made selflessly to be given away anonymously to an unknown recipient.

The Human Tissue Authority (HTA) must approve living organ donation (especially a kidney donation where the full organ is donated intact), and the following criteria must be satisfied.

---

[15] http://www.organdonation.nhs.uk/statistics/downloads/annual_stats.pdf.

EXTRACT

Code of Practice 2: Donation of Solid Organs for Transplantation, Human Tissue Authority (2013):

http://www.hta.gov.uk/legislationpoliciesandcodesofpractice.cfm

Paragraph 34: Before the HTA can approve such cases, the Regulations require that the Authority must be satisfied that:

1. No reward has been, or is to be, given;
2. Consent to removal for the purpose of transplantation has been given (or removal for that purpose is otherwise lawful);
3. An Independent Assessor (IA) has conducted separate interviews with the donor (and if different from the donor, the person giving consent) and the recipient (or the person acting on behalf of the recipient) and submitted a report of their assessment to the HTA.

Additionally in cases of directed genetically or emotionally related donation, the HTA requires evidence of relationship to be provided, so that it can be satisfied the relationship between donor and recipient is as stated.

Paragraph 58: As required by the Regulations, the HTA must approve all cases of living organ donation (except domino donations) for transplantation. The HTA undertakes this role through an independent assessment process.

The Independent Assessor (IA) must put the following things in his report to the HTA if the living donation is to go ahead.

EXTRACT

Code of Practice 2: Donation of Solid Organs for Transplantation, Human Tissue Authority (2013):

http://www.hta.gov.uk/legislationpoliciesandcodesofpractice.cfm

Paragraph 36: The Regulations also specify the matters to be covered in the report submitted by the IA to the HTA, which are:

1. The information given to the potential donor (or other person giving consent) as to the nature of the medical procedure and the risk involved;
2. The full name of the person who gave that information to the potential donor (or other person giving consent), and their qualification to give it;
3. The capacity of the potential donor (or other person giving consent) to understand the nature of the medical procedure and the risk involved and that consent may be withdrawn at any time before the removal of the organ or part organ;
4. Whether there is any evidence of duress or coercion affecting the decision to give consent;
5. Whether there is any evidence of an offer of a reward;
6. Whether there were any difficulties in communicating with the person interviewed (e.g. language, hearing), and if so, an explanation of how these difficulties were overcome.

It is clearly important that a reward is not provided for the living donation, otherwise a donor may feel pressured into going through with the procedure simply because of the prize at the end if it, e.g. help to pay bills. There is a strong emphasis on the correct information being passed on to the donor too, and this requires adequate communication. If this is a problem for the donor, the IA must make it clear to the HTA that it has been overcome. There are certain serious procedures that must be decided by an HTA Panel, and these include.

EXTRACT

Code of Practice 2: Donation of Solid Organs for Transplantation, Human Tissue Authority (2013):

http://www.hta.gov.uk/legislationpoliciesandcodesofpractice.cfm

Paragraph 38: A decision on a transplant must be made by an HTA panel:

1. If the donor is a child;
2. If the donor is an adult who lacks capacity to consent to removal of an organ or part organ;
3. In all cases of paired and pooled donation;
4. In all cases of altruistic non-directed donation.

Paragraph 39: All other cases can be approved by the HTA transplant approvals team, although they can also refer complex or novel cases to a panel where required.

These procedures must be agreed to be lawful by a HTA Panel because of their controversial nature. For example, a paired donation is when a pair (donor and recipient) who do not match are introduced to another pair (donor and recipient) who do not match in order for a swap to take place. This direct 'exchange' of organs should not be validated without strict authorisation because it resembles a marketplace-type scenario. Similarly, when organs or tissues are taken from adults who lack capacity, there must be every imaginable safeguard in place to protect the best interests of the incompetent patient who is undergoing a surgical procedure that is without her consent and not in her best interests.

Consent

Living donation is a bit of an anomaly in law in that it is governed by both common law and statute. This may have been an oversight by Parliament, but the Human Tissue Act 2004 does *not* cover the *removal* of organs and tissues from a living person, it merely covers the *storage* and *use* of organs and tissues from a living person under section 1(1)(d) and (f). This means that consent to *removal* is still covered by the common law.

EXTRACT

Code of Practice 2: Donation of Solid Organs for Transplantation, Human Tissue Authority (2013):

http://www.hta.gov.uk/legislationpoliciesandcodesofpractice.cfm

Paragraph 30: Consent for the removal of organs from living donors, whether for transplantation or otherwise, is outside the scope of the HT Act. It is instead covered by the common law (competent patients) and the Mental Capacity Act 2005 (incompetent patients) where appropriate.

The position for living donors can be summarised as follows:

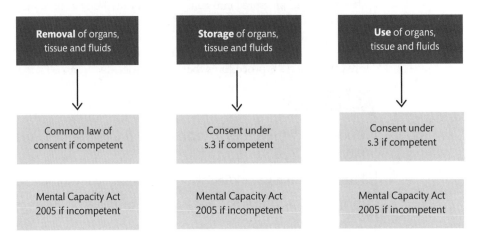

Figure 9.2

The Human Tissue Authority provides guidance on what consent should look like and what information should be provided to the donor before consent is given.

EXTRACT

Code of Practice 2: Donation of Solid Organs for Transplantation, Human Tissue Authority (2013):

http://www.hta.gov.uk/legislationpoliciesandcodesofpractice.cfm

Paragraph 72: Obtaining valid consent presupposes that there is a process in which individuals, including their partners, relatives or close friends where appropriate, may discuss the issue fully, ask questions and make an informed choice. Sufficient time should be allowed for questions and discussion. Surgeons should always check before surgery that the person still consents to the procedure, and be clear that consent has not been withdrawn before they proceed.

Paragraph 87: Potential donors must be provided with sufficient information for them to reach an informed decision about whether they wish to give consent.

Paragraph 89: The following information should be explained in full to the donor:

1. The surgical procedures and medical treatments involved for the donor and the risks involved in both the short-and long-term;
2. The chances of the transplant being successful and any possible side-effects or complications for both donor and recipient;
3. The right to withdraw consent at any time, and the implications of doing so;
4. Their right to be free of any kind of coercion or threat against them or anyone else (for example, family or friends) and that consent seen to be given under any such pressure will not be validated;
5. The fact that it is an offence to seek or receive payment or any other reward for providing organs or part organs for transplantation, and that this offence is subject to significant penalties;
6. Donors are able to seek reimbursement of expenses, such as travel costs and loss of earnings that are reasonably attributable to and directly result from donation.

The guidance above highlights the additional problems – coercion and illegal payments – that living donors bring to the table, because deceased donors cannot be misled, coerced or bribed. This is why it is important for living donors to have sufficient time to talk to their families, ask questions, and make an informed choice. The Independent Assessor for the Human Tissue Authority must be satisfied that all of these concerns have been eliminated and the final consent is voluntary, informed and free. If the criteria above have been met to the satisfaction of the Independent Assessor, then the donor is now free to consent to the *removal* of her organs and tissues through the common law, and to the *storage* and *use* of the organs and tissues for transplantation purposes under section 3(2) of the 2004 Act.

Human Tissue Act 2004

Section 3: 'Appropriate consent': adults

(2) Where the person concerned is alive, 'appropriate consent' means his consent.

The Human Tissue Authority provides an overview in their relevant Code of Practice of what can constitute 'appropriate consent'.

EXTRACT

Code of Practice 1: Consent, Human Tissue Authority (2009):

http://www.hta.gov.uk/legislationpoliciesandcodesofpractice.cfm

Paragraph 30: The giving of consent is a positive act. For consent to be valid it must be given voluntarily, by an appropriately informed person who has the capacity to agree to the activity in question.

Paragraph 32: For consent to be valid, the person should understand what the activity involves and, where appropriate, what the risks are.

Paragraph 39: Consent may be withdrawn at any time. Withdrawal should be discussed at the outset when consent is being sought. The practicalities of withdrawing consent and the implications of doing so should be made clear, for example, for potential recipients if the donated tissue is for clinical use.

Paragraph 60: Consent is valid only if proper communication has taken place. Particular consideration should be given to the needs of individuals and families whose first language is not English. Any difficulties in communicating with the person interviewed (e.g. because of language, literacy or hearing difficulties), and an explanation of how these difficulties were overcome (e.g. through an independent translator), should be recorded.

Paragraph 30 (above) contains four key words: valid, voluntary, informed and capacity. It is also important that allowances are made for donors who do not understand English (paragraph 60). The medical professionals involved are clearly under an obligation to solve and language barriers that may be effecting the validity of consent. The donor is free to withdraw her consent at any time (paragraph 39), but what is difficult about the field of organ donation is that if a donor withdraws consent from a procedure, rather than putting *herself* at risk as she would do in any other area of medicine, she is putting *another person* at risk. For example, a granddaughter volunteers her kidney and bone marrow to her beloved grandmother because they are an excellent match. The granddaughter goes through with the bone marrow procedure, but cannot face undergoing surgery and have an organ removed when she has so much of life left to live. The granddaughter will then be faced with the guilt of watching her beloved grandmother die of kidney failure and the anguish of her entire family knowing that the cure lay in her hands and she refused to give it over. This is enormous pressure for a donor to carry, and the HTA are well aware of this, encouraging open discussions about the consequences of withdrawal from a very early stage.

Further provisions in the Code of Practice address the very fine line between competent consent and confused or unwise decisions. The line between competence and incompetence is not very clear at all in medical law, but there should always be an assumption of competence, thus allowing a patient to retain their autonomy until it is almost impossible for them to make their own decision.

EXTRACT

Code of Practice 1: Consent, Human Tissue Authority (2009):

http://www.hta.gov.uk/legislationpoliciesandcodesofpractice.cfm

Paragraph 124: If an adult has the capacity to make the decision in question, then only they are permitted to give consent.

Paragraph 132: It should always be assumed that an adult has the capacity to make a decision unless there is reason to believe otherwise.

Paragraph 135: A person must not be treated as unable to make a decision unless all practicable steps to help them do so have been taken without success, nor must they be treated as being unable to make a decision merely because they make an unwise decision.

Paragraph 136: The ability of adults with learning difficulties, or with limited capacity to understand should not be underestimated. Where appropriate, someone who knows the individual well, such as a family member or carer, should be consulted, as they may be able to advise or assist with communication.

Paragraph 146: To give consent, the individual should understand the nature and purpose of what is proposed and be able to make an informed decision. They should be told of any 'material' or 'significant' risks inherent in the way the sample will be obtained, how the tissue will be used and any possible risks or implications of its use, e.g. genetic tests.

Paragraph 147: Some people may not be interested in knowing the full details about the proposed use of the tissue and it is good practice to record this in the notes. People should nevertheless have all their options explained to them and be provided with an appropriate level of information.

It is encouraging to see that adults with learning difficulties will not be struck off as incompetent straight away (resulting in their autonomy being taken away). Similarly, unwise decisions are also recognised as competent, unless proved otherwise. This is the position of the common law and the HTA has supported this practice. There is an additional mention of 'material' or 'significant' risks in paragraph 146 – patients must be told about material or significant risks inherent within their medical treatment in order for their consent to be informed and valid (see Chapter 4), and the HTA clearly support this practice too. Paragraph 147 is an interesting reference to 'wilful blindness' (i.e. donors who don't want to know). It is not uncommon for a patient to consent to a procedure but to say they do not want to hear about the risks and the details, instead choosing to completely trust the doctor. It is arguable whether this is really informed consent, so doctors are advised by the HTA to still provide an 'appropriate level' of information and record the wilful blindness in the record. This will then protect the doctor from later allegations that: 'if I had been told of this particular risk, I never would have consented'.

The common law limits to consent

A living donor must consent to the removal of her organs and tissues according to the rules of the common law. It was learnt in Chapter 4 that a patient can consent to surgical procedures because they are an exception outside of the normal rules of criminal law. There is a small trail of cases (outlined below) to confirm this line of consent: it lies between battery (i.e. a physical examination) and actual bodily harm (bruising). These cases also list the exceptions to the rule, including medical treatment.

CASE EXTRACT

Attorney-General's Reference (No. 6 of 1980) [1981] QB 715

Lord Lane CJ (at page 179): Nothing which we have said is intended to cast doubt upon the accepted legality of properly conducted games and sports, lawful chastisement or correction, reasonable surgical interference, dangerous exhibitions etc. These apparent exceptions can be justified as involving the exercise of a legal right, in the case of chastisement or correction, or as needed in the public interest, in the other cases.

CASE EXTRACT

Airedale NHS Trust v Bland [1993] AC 789

Lord Mustill (at page 891): Bodily invasions in the course of proper medical treatment stand completely outside the criminal law. The reason why the consent of the patient is so important is not that it furnishes a defence in itself, but because it is usually essential to the propriety of medical treatment.

CASE EXTRACT

R v Brown (Anthony Joseph) [1994] 1 AC 212

Lord Mustill (at page 266): Many of the acts done by surgeons would be very serious crimes if done by anyone else, and yet the surgeons incur no liability. Actual consent, or the substitute for consent deemed by the law to exist where an emergency creates a need for action, is an essential element of this immunity. [...] Proper medical treatment, for which actual or deemed consent is a prerequisite, is in a category of its own.

Lord Jauncey (at pages 244–5): Consent of the victim is no answer to anyone charged with [section 47 ABH or section 20 wounding] unless the circumstances fall within one of the well-known exceptions such as organised sporting contests and games, parental chastisement or reasonable surgery.

Lord Lane CJ in *Attorney-General's Reference* supports the listed exceptions, i.e. sports, chastisement, tattooing and surgery, on the grounds that they are in the 'public interest'. Therefore, patients can consent to surgery because it is in their best interests to receive surgical treatment. Lord Mustill and Lord Jauncey agree with this in the subsequent cases of *Bland* and *Brown*, adding that surgery has immunity from the normal rules of criminal law on the condition that it takes the form of 'proper medical treatment'. This puts living donors in a difficult position. They do not benefit from the surgical removal of their organs or tissues, and a nephrectomy (kidney removal) is almost certainly a grievous bodily harm. They have no best interests in undergoing the operation, and it may even put the donor in a worse position. Therefore, is the consent to the removal of organs and tissues even valid in common law? There was a case in the United States[16] where a father wanted to donate his second kidney to his daughter, who already had his first one but it had failed. He would have survived the surgery and simply lived on dialysis until his own donors came along, but there were major ethical issues: he would face a substantial deterioration to his own health and quality of life. It was unlikely that a surgeon could be found to perform such a dangerous procedure on a patient that had no benefit to his health anyway. This is a clear example of the limits to autonomy: the patient will be prevented from undergoing a surgical procedure if he will be significantly harmed by it and will experience no benefit from it. It is, therefore, assumed that a donor can consent to her organs and tissues being removed for the purposes of transplantation as long as she does not put herself in any grave danger. There is no case law to confirm this rule, but it appears to be acceptable at the moment on the condition that the Human Tissue Authority is happy with the circumstances.

Adults who lack capacity

It may be surprising to learn that organs and tissues can be donated from adults who lack capacity. The Mental Capacity Act 2005 was passed to allow relatives to consent on their behalf to medical treatment, as long as it is in their best interests. It is, therefore, debatable whether donation is in the best interests of the incompetent patient or the best interests of someone else, i.e. the receiving relative. Regardless of this ethical complexity, the Human Tissue Act 2004 includes incompetent patients in its provisions under section 6, meaning that the law allows organs and tissues to be donated by this particularly vulnerable group of patients:

Human Tissue Act 2004

Section 6: Activities involving material from adults who lack capacity to consent

Where –

(a) an activity of a kind mentioned in section 1(1)(d) or (f) involves material from the body of a person who –

   (i)   is an adult, and

   (ii) lacks capacity to consent to the activity, and

(b) neither a decision of his to consent to the activity, nor a decision of his not to consent to it, is in force,

there shall for the purposes of this Part be deemed to be consent of his to the activity if it is done in circumstances of a kind specified by regulations made by the Secretary of State.

---

[16] Sauder, R. and Parker, L. (2001) 'Autonomy's Limits: Living Donation and Health-Related Harm' 10 *Cambridge Quarterly of Healthcare Ethics* 399–401.

The 'regulations made by the Secretary of State' is a reference to the Statutory Instrument: The Human Tissue Act 2004 (Persons who Lack Capacity to Consent and Transplants) Regulations 2006. This additional document works together with the 2004 Act to flesh out the role of the Human Tissue Authority and its powers to authorise organ donations and transplants. The incompetent donor's best interests are enshrined under regulation 3.

The Human Tissue Act 2004 (Persons who Lack Capacity to Consent and Transplants) Regulations 2006

Regulation 3: Deemed consent to storage and use of relevant material: England and Wales

(1) This regulation applies in any case falling within paragraphs (a) and (b) of section 6 of the Act (storage and use involving material from adults who lack capacity to consent).

(2) An adult ('P') who lacks capacity to consent to an activity of a kind mentioned in section 1(1)(d) or (f) of the Act (storage or use of material for purposes specified in Schedule 1) which involves material from P's body, is deemed to have consented to the activity where:

    (a) the activity is done for a purpose specified in paragraph 4 or 7 of Part 1 of Schedule 1 to the Act (transplantation) by a person who is acting in what he reasonably believes to be P's best interests.

It is clear that in order for a surgeon or any other relevant healthcare professional to store or use any organs or tissues donated from an incompetent donor, they must 'reasonably believe' that these actions are in his best interests. A detailed analysis of the Codes of Practice (below) will show that the courts – followed by a Human Tissue Authority Panel – will decide if this is the case.

The law regarding incompetent patients is covered by the Mental Capacity Act 2005. The Code of Practice to the Human Tissue Act 2004 confirms this.

EXTRACT

Code of Practice 1: Consent, Human Tissue Authority (2009):

http://www.hta.gov.uk/legislationpoliciesandcodesofpractice.cfm

Paragraph 126: The Human Tissue Act 2004 does not specify the criteria for considering whether an adult has capacity to consent.

Paragraph 129: The Mental Capacity Act 2005 governs decision-making on behalf of adults (aged 16 and over) who lack capacity if unable to make a decision in relation to a matter at the relevant time because of an impairment of, or disturbance of, the mind or brain, whether permanent or temporary.

Paragraph 130: All decisions must be made in the person's best interests, as laid out in Chapter 5 of the Mental Capacity Act 2005 Code of Practice.

Court approval must be sought if any organs or tissues are to be donated by an incompetent adult. This is an important safeguard because it ensures that vulnerable adults are not taken advantage of. Court approval must be given before the issue can go to a HTA Panel, as explained below.

EXTRACT

Code of Practice 2: Donation of Solid Organs for Transplantation, Human Tissue Authority (2013):

http://www.hta.gov.uk/legislationpoliciesandcodesofpractice.cfm

Paragraph 50: Where an adult lacks the capacity to consent to the removal of an organ or part organ, the case must be referred to a court for a declaration that the removal would be lawful. Donation may then only proceed if court approval has been obtained and following court approval the case is referred to, and approved by, an HTA panel.

Paragraph 68: HTA panels consist of three Authority members.

EXTRACT

Mental Capacity Act 2005, Code of Practice (2007):

http://www.legislation.gov.uk/ukpga/2005/9/resources

Paragraph 6.18: The Court of Protection must be asked to make decisions relating to:

- cases where it is proposed that a person who lacks capacity to consent should donate an organ or bone marrow to another person;
- cases where there is a dispute about whether a particular treatment will be in a person's best interests.

The Court of Protection was set up under section 45 of the Mental Capacity Act 2005. It has the same powers as the High Court, but it deals specifically with incompetent adults and vulnerable children. Medical treatment falls under their ambit, meaning they have the power to make the final legally binding decision as to whether a treatment (or a withdrawal of treatment) would be lawful and in accordance with best interests. The Mental Capacity Act 2005 and its adjoining Code of Practice both confirm the powers of the Court.

Mental Capacity Act 2005

Section 15: Power to make declarations

(1) The court may make declarations as to –

   (a) whether a person has or lacks capacity to make a decision;

   (b) whether a person has or lacks capacity to make decisions on such matters;

   (c) the lawfulness or otherwise of any act done, or yet to be done, in relation to that person.

Mental Capacity Act 2005, Code of Practice (2007):

http://www.legislation.gov.uk/ukpga/2005/9/resources

Paragraph 8.2: The new Court of Protection is a superior court of record and is able to establish precedent and build up expertise in all issues related to lack of capacity. In particular, it must make a decision in the best interests of the person who lacks capacity to make the specific decision.

Paragraph 8.17: The court can also make a declaration as to whether a specific act relating to a person's care or treatment is lawful. This power to decide on the lawfulness of an act is particularly relevant for major medical treatment cases where there is doubt or disagreement over whether the treatment would be in the person's best interests.

Organ and tissue donation is usually carried out for the benefit of a third party, so the Court of Protection must be satisfied that the donor would gain at least *some* benefit from the procedure in order for the 'best interests' test (under s. 4(6) of the MCA 2005) to be satisfied. It would be very unusual indeed for an incompetent donor to benefit from undergoing a surgical procedure and having parts of his body removed to save someone else's life. What kind of instance might satisfy the Court of Protection?

The MCA Code of Practice has deliberated this issue, and believes that an incompetent donor could benefit from donating organs or tissues to a third party in a return for a happier family environment:

Mental Capacity Act 2005, Code of Practice (2007):

http://www.legislation.gov.uk/ukpga/2005/9/resources

Paragraph 8.20: Cases involving organ or bone marrow donation by a person who lacks capacity to consent should also be referred to the Court of Protection. Such cases involve medical procedures being performed on a person who lacks capacity to consent but which would benefit a third party. However, sometimes such procedures may be in the person's overall best interests. For example, the person might receive emotional, social and psychological benefits as a result of the help they have given, and in some cases the person may experience only minimal physical discomfort.

This provision is quite controversial, because it appears to justify the harvesting of bodily materials from an incompetent donor on the grounds that an intangible benefit, i.e. a state of happiness, might be experienced by the donor. There are no well-known cases in which this has happened (with the exception of *Re Y* examined below) and so it can safely be said that it would be an incredibly rare event for an organ or tissues to be taken from an incompetent patient. However, in the event that it does occur, it is suggested that any benefit experienced by the incompetent donor must be glaringly obvious to everyone involved and evidenced in some form, such as a psychiatric report, before the procedure can go ahead. The Code of Practice is able to discuss this controversial issue as a result of a deeply problematic bone marrow case – *Re Y* (1997) – in which the best interests of an incompetent donor were calculated in combination with the best interests of her sister, who needed the transplant, and her mother. An invasive surgical procedure with no therapeutic benefit to the incompetent donor was justified on this occasion.

CASE EXTRACT

Re Y (Mental Patient: Bone Marrow Donation) [1997] Fam 110

Facts: Y, an adult mentally and physically handicapped from birth, lived in a community home. She had lived with her parents and sisters in a close family until she was 10, and had been regularly visited by them. Her mother's health was bad and her older sister, P, suffered from a bone marrow disorder. P's only realistic prospect of recovery was a bone marrow transplant from a healthy compatible donor, and the option was Y. Y's disabilities meant that Y was unaware of the situation and unable to consent to the operations required for a donation. P applied for declarations that they were lawful nonetheless.

Held: Since the donation of bone marrow by the patient would be likely to help to prolong the life of the mother as well as the sister and to improve the donor's relationship with both of them, the donor would receive an emotional, psychological and social benefit from the operation and suffer minimal detriment.

Connell J (at pages 113, 115–16): I am satisfied that the root question remains, namely, whether the procedures here envisaged will benefit the [donor] and accordingly benefits which may flow to the [sister] are relevant only in so far as they have a positive effect upon the best interests of the [donor]. [...] If the [sister] dies, this is bound to have an adverse effect upon her mother who already suffers from significant ill-health. [...] Her ability to visit the [donor] would be handicapped significantly. [...] In this situation, the [donor] would clearly be harmed by the reduction in or loss of contact with her mother. Accordingly, it is to the benefit of the [donor] that she should act as donor to her sister, because in this way her positive relationship with her mother is most likely to be prolonged. Further, if the transplant occurs, this is likely to improve the [donor's] relationship with her mother who clearly wishes it to take place and also to improve her relationship with [her sister] who will be eternally grateful to her. The disadvantages to the [donor] of the harvesting procedure are very small. [...] I should perhaps emphasise that this is a rather unusual case and that the family of the [sister] and the [donor] are a particularly close family. It is doubtful that this case would act as a useful precedent in cases where the surgery involved is more intrusive than in this case, where the evidence shows that bone marrow is speedily regenerated and that a healthy individual can donate as much as two pints with no long term consequences at all. Thus, the bone marrow donated by the [donor] will cause her no loss and she will suffer no real long term risk.

This judgment may turn on its facts, but it is controversial. Firstly, it must be made clear that the donor will benefit from the procedure. The evidence required is not made clear in the judgment: Y may not notice the slightest difference to her daily life after the procedure; she has simply prevented a reduction in visits from her mother. This is not a benefit, it is a continuation of the status quo. Secondly, it can be argued that it is not appropriate to allow an invasive surgical procedure to be inflicted upon an incompetent donor simply because a relative will be 'eternally grateful'. Thirdly, whilst it is admitted that collecting bone marrow may not be as invasive as organ donation, it is still a serious medical procedure in which the donor's skin is broken and some of her internal tissues are removed. Connell J was very careful to note that surgery would be outside of the ambit of his decision because it was far more invasive, but the nature of case law is that it can be flexible in emergency situations so there is every possibility that the ratio in *Re Y* could be extended one day to cover a situation in which a dying brother or sister is in desperate need of a new kidney from their disabled sibling. Fourthly, the principle of this case is potentially harmful, which could be phrased as: 'incompetent patients can be harvested for their organs and tissues to save their siblings'. Fifthly, Connell J appears to distinguish this case from others on the grounds that the family is very close. This should not make any difference – a court should not base such decisions on whether the donor's family appear to be well connected or not.

The MCA Code of Practice clearly uses the decision in *Re Y* to support its provisions.

EXTRACT

Mental Capacity Act 2005, Code of Practice (2007):

http://www.legislation.gov.uk/ukpga/2005/9/resources

Paragraph 8.21: A prime example of this is the case of *Re Y* where it was found to be in Y's best interests for her to donate bone marrow to her sister. The court decided that it was in Y's best interests to continue to receive strong emotional support from her mother, which might be diminished if her sister's health were to deteriorate further, or she were to die.

The decision in *Re Y* was relevant only to bone marrow, so it may cover future cases regarding blood donation (and possibly eggs or sperm) but not a kidney. It remains to be seen which direction the law will turn. It was supported in the USA in the older case of *Strunk* v *Strunk* (1969) 445 SW 2d 145, in which the courts approved the donation of a kidney to the incompetent donor's brother on the grounds that the brother's death would have caused the donor more psychological injury than the surgical procedure itself. This is a logical rationale because it weighs up the potential benefits and burdens to the incompetent donor, but it is also a concern, highlighting just how easy it is to justify a highly invasive surgical procedure upon an incompetent donor.

This section has no associated Explanatory Memorandum.

Children

Children can be donors of organs and tissues too. A child is defined as a person under the age of 18 under section 54(1) of the Human Tissue Act 2004. It should be remembered that only the *storage* and *use* of organs and tissues from a living body – as listed under section 1(1)(d) and (f) – is included under the 2004 Act. This means that a living child donor must consent to their *removal* under the normal common law rules of consent just like adults (see Chapter 4 for the common law of consent). The Mental Capacity Act 2005 is not available for children like it is for incompetent adults, so the position can be summarised as follows:

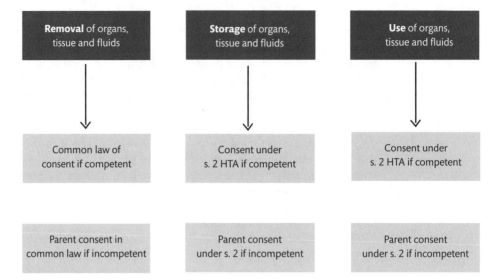

Figure 9.3

The Human Tissue Act 2004 has made provisions for children to consent as living donors under section 2 (this is in regards to *storage* and *use* of organs and tissues only).

Human Tissue Act 2004

Section 2: 'Appropriate consent': children

(1) This section makes provision for the interpretation of 'appropriate consent' in section 1 in relation to an activity involving the body, or material from the body, of a person who is a child or has died a child ('the child concerned').

(2) Subject to subsection (3), where the child concerned is alive, 'appropriate consent' means his consent.

(3) Where –

    (a) the child concerned is alive,

    (b) neither a decision of his to consent to the activity, nor a decision of his not to consent to it, is in force, and

    (c) either he is not competent to deal with the issue of consent in relation to the activity or, though he is competent to deal with that issue, he fails to do so,

'appropriate consent' means the consent of a person who has parental responsibility for him.

Section 2 appears to be very open minded at first glance when it comes to child consent – the child himself is allowed to consent to the storage and use of his organs and tissues under section 2(2). However, the child can only consent if, according to section 2(3), he is alive, his consent is in force at the time, he is competent to deal with the issue and does deal with the issue. If, however, the child does not satisfy any of the above criteria from section 2(3) then his parents will consent for him. The Human Tissue Act 2004 Code of Practice defines the current situation in this way.

EXTRACT

Code of Practice 1: Consent, Human Tissue Authority (2009):

http://www.hta.gov.uk/legislationpoliciesandcodesofpractice.cfm

Paragraph 142: Under the Children Act 1989, a person who has parental responsibility for the child may consent on their behalf only if the child has not made a decision either way; and the child:

1. is not competent to do so; or
2. is competent to do so, but is unwilling to make that decision.

A closer look therefore reveals that the child may not have full autonomy after all, because section 2(3) states that if the child is competent to deal with the issue and then fails to do so his parents can consent for him.

A 'competent' consent was developed by *Gillick*, a case which radically changed the common law of consent. The judgment allows for a child aged 15 years or under, who is deemed to be competent, to consent to medical treatment without their parent's knowledge. This is the law used to allow a child donor to consent to the *removal* of his organs and tissues under common law.

CASE EXTRACT

Gillick v *West Norfolk and Wisbech AHA* [1986] AC 112

Facts: Mrs Gillick had several daughters under 16. She became aware of a Memorandum of Guidance, issued from the Department of Health and Social Security (DHSS), which allowed a doctor to give contraceptive advice and treatment to her daughters without her consent. She wrote to the local health authority seeking assurance that no contraceptive advice or treatment would be issued to her daughters without her knowledge or consent, and they refused. Mrs Gillick sought a declaration from the courts that the memorandum was unlawful.

Held: The Court of Appeal supported Mrs Gillick, but the House of Lords allowed the DHSS appeal.

Lord Fraser (at page 169): It seems to me verging on the absurd to suggest that a girl or a boy aged 15 could not effectively consent, for example, to have a medical examination of some trivial injury to his body or even to have a broken arm set. [...] Provided the patient, whether a boy or a girl, is capable of understanding what is proposed, and of expressing his or her own wishes, I see no good reason for holding that he or she lacks the capacity to express them validly and effectively and to authorise the medical man to make the examination or give the treatment which he advises. [...] Accordingly, I am not disposed to hold now, for the first time, that a girl aged less than 16 lacks the power to give valid consent to contraceptive advice or treatment, merely on account of her age.

Lord Scarman (at pages 188–9): I would hold that as a matter of law the parental right to determine whether or not their minor child below the age of 16 will have medical treatment terminates if and when the child achieves a sufficient understanding and intelligence to enable him or her to understand fully what is proposed. It will be a question of fact whether a child seeking advice has sufficient understanding of what is involved to give a consent valid in law. [...] It is not enough that she should understand the nature of the advice which is being given: she must also have a sufficient maturity to understand what is involved.

The case of *Gillick* consolidated that a competent child under 16 can consent to medical treatment without the knowledge or consent of her parents. Lord Scarman said that when the child achieves a 'sufficient understanding and intelligence' to enable her to 'understand fully' what is proposed, then she can consent to the procedure. There must also be 'sufficient maturity' from the child to enable her to understand what is involved. This may be easy to satisfy when contraception is the treatment sought (as was the case in *Gillick*), but this judgment was not delivered with organ or tissue donation in mind. A child may have sufficient maturity to understand the consequences of a blood donation to a sibling (e.g. one-hour bed rest), but not the consequences of a kidney donation (e.g. surgery, risks, immobility, weakness, etc.). The additional problem in applying *Gillick* competence to the removal of organs and tissues should now become clear: the child donor will be consenting to an invasive procedure which will not fulfil any of her best interests, in fact, her health is likely to suffer if she goes through with the procedure. The *Gillick* criteria are therefore not satisfied. However, this does not seem to have prevented the courts from applying *Gillick* competence to any other area of medicine or law. It has not been applied to organ donation in a high profile case yet. Despite this, the Human Tissue Authority has taken full advantage of the decision in *Gillick*, referring to the judgment in its Code of Practice 1: Consent. There appears to be a clear assumption that *Gillick* competence will apply to living child organ and tissue donation.

EXTRACT

Code of Practice 1: Consent, Human Tissue Authority (2009):

http://www.hta.gov.uk/legislationpoliciesandcodesofpractice.cfm

Paragraph 140: Children may consent to a proposed medical procedure (i.e. removal) or the storage and use of their tissue if they are competent to do so. In the *Gillick* case, the court held that a child was considered competent to give valid consent to a proposed intervention if they had sufficient intelligence and understanding to enable them fully to understand what was involved.

The Code of Practice adds that if a parent can be consulted too, this would be a good idea, but the child must be informed of this.

EXTRACT

Code of Practice 1: Consent, Human Tissue Authority (2009):

http://www.hta.gov.uk/legislationpoliciesandcodesofpractice.cfm

Paragraph 145: Even if the child is competent to consent, it is good practice to consult the person who has parental responsibility for the child and to involve them in the process of the child making a decision. However, it should be emphasised that, if the child is competent, the decision to consent must be the child's. Information about a competent young person should only be disclosed to the person with parental responsibility for the child with the child's consent. It is also essential to make sure that a child has consented voluntarily and has not been unduly influenced by anyone else.

This is a very liberal application of the *Gillick* principle as it gives the child a lot of autonomy. Organ and tissue donation are very serious procedures, and to give a child this much power over the donation of his own organs and tissues is quite extra-ordinary considering that the judgment in *Gillick* has not been applied by the courts to this kind of medical procedure. The Code of Practice is clear that the court should still be involved:

EXTRACT

Code of Practice 1: Consent, Human Tissue Authority (2009):

http://www.hta.gov.uk/legislationpoliciesandcodesofpractice.cfm

Paragraph 144: Where there is any dispute between persons with parental responsibility or any doubt as to the child's best interests, the matter should be referred to court for approval.

The requirement of court approval is actually very important to living child donation. The idea that the courts should approve surgical procedures on children that are not in their best interests was clearly laid down by *Re B* (1988). It may have been a case involving sterilisation, but the principle is applicable generally:

CASE EXTRACT

B (A Minor) (Wardship: Sterilisation), Re [1988] AC 199

Lord Templeman (at pages 205–6): In my opinion [sterilisation] of a girl under 18 should only be carried out with the leave of a High Court judge. [...] A court exercising the wardship jurisdiction emanating from the Crown is the only authority which is empowered to authorise such a drastic step as sterilisation after a full and informed investigation.

This was followed by *Re W* (1993), a case in which organ donation was specifically mentioned:

CASE EXTRACT

W (A Minor) (Medical Treatment: Court's Jurisdiction), Re [1993] Fam 64

Nolan LJ (at page 94): Where major surgical or other procedures (such as an abortion) were proposed, and where the parents or those in *loco parentis* were prepared to give consent but the child (having sufficient understanding to make an informed decision) was not, the jurisdiction of the court should always be invoked. I would say the same of a case in which a child of any age consented to donate an organ.

The more recent case of *Re J* (2000) confirmed that there is 'a small group' of medical procedures that must seek court approval, and one of them is a surgical procedure that does not support the best interests of the child.

CASE EXTRACT	*Re J (Specific Orders: Child's religious Upbringing and Circumcision)* [2000] 1 FLR 571

Dame Elizabeth Butler-Sloss P (at paras 31–2): There is, in my view, a small group of important decisions made on behalf of a child which, in the absence of agreement of those with parental responsibility, ought not to be carried out. […] Such a decision ought not to be made without the specific approval of the court. Sterilisation is one example. […] The issue of circumcision has not, to my knowledge, previously been considered by this court, but in my view it comes within that group. The decision to circumcise a child on ground other than medical necessity is a very important one; the operation is irreversible, and should only be carried out where the parents together approve of it or, in the absence of parental agreement, where a court decides that the operation is in the best interests of the child.

As a result of the common law (above), it is threaded throughout the Human Tissue Act 2004 Code of Practice that court approval must be sought before a Human Tissue Authority Panel can examine a child donor case.

EXTRACT

Code of Practice 2: Donation of Solid Organs for Transplantation, Human Tissue Authority (2013):

http://www.hta.gov.uk/legislationpoliciesandcodesofpractice.cfm

Paragraph 47: Children can be considered as living organ donors only in extremely rare circumstances. In accordance with common law and the Children Act 1989, before the removal of a solid organ or part organ from a child for donation, court approval should be obtained.

Paragraph 48: Living donation by a child under the HT Act can only go ahead with the approval of an HTA panel. Such cases should only be referred to the HTA for decision after court approval to the removal has been obtained.

It is particularly important in cases of living child donation that court approval is sought in addition to the views of a HTA Panel. This is because of the complex relationship between the donor and the recipient. It is an unfortunate fact that living child donors usually *know* their recipient, i.e. their brother or sister, although the Code of Practice states that this event is still quite rare (Paragraph 47 above). Therefore, when a living child donor comes forward, this means that the parent has probably played a hand in taking that child to the hospital to enquire about donation, and has even put that child forward for the procedure. The possibility of coercion in this kind of situation is incredibly high indeed, because the mother wants to save the life of her recipient child. Therefore, it is vital that the court is allowed to assess the donor child's interests *separately* from the recipient child.

EXTRACT

Code of Practice 2: Donation of Solid Organs for Transplantation, Human Tissue Authority, Appendix A (2013):

http://www.hta.gov.uk/legislationpoliciesandcodesofpractice.cfm

Paragraph A11: If the court is asked to consider the matter, the welfare of the prospective donor child will be the court's paramount consideration and not the welfare of the recipient. The 'welfare checklist' which is set out in the Children Act 1989 will be considered by the court in determining the application.

The court will clearly have to balance many different factors using the checklist in the Children Act 1989 as a starting point (provided below). It is encouraging to see under paragraph A11 that the welfare of the *recipient* will not be included. This is a good thing because the recipient, i.e. a brother or sister, will often face grave health or even death if a donor is not found, making the surgical interference forced upon the donor child to look very trivial indeed. The interests of the recipient would therefore always trump the best interests of the child donor.[17] The courts will take the following child interests into account:

Children Act 1989

Section 1: Welfare of the child

(3) A court shall have regard in particular to –
  (a) the ascertainable wishes and feelings of the child concerned (considered in the light of his age and understanding);
  (b) his physical, emotional and educational needs;
  (c) the likely effect on him of any change in his circumstances;
  (d) his age, sex, background and any characteristics of his which the court considers relevant;
  (e) any harm which he has suffered or is at risk of suffering;
  (f) how capable each of his parents, and any other person in relation to whom the court considers the question to be relevant, is of meeting his needs;
  (g) the range of powers available to the court under this Act in the proceedings in question.

The General Medical Council add to the above criteria with their own considerations when advising doctors and other medical professionals on how to deal with child consent.

EXTRACT

General Medical Council, Guidance of Good Practice: Ethical Guidance, Guidance for all doctors: Assessing Best Interests, 0–18 years (2007):

www.gmc-uk.org

Paragraph 12: An assessment of best interests will include what is clinically indicated in a particular case. You should also consider:

a. the views of the child or young person, so far as they can express them, including any previously expressed preferences;
b. the views of parents;
c. the views of others close to the child or young person;
d. the cultural, religious or other beliefs and values of the child or parents;
e. the views of other healthcare professionals involved in providing care to the child or young person, and of any other professionals who have an interest in their welfare;
f. which choice, if there is more than one, will least restrict the child or young person's future options.

---

[17] The courts will also override the wishes of the parents in favour of the best interests of the child: *Re J (A Minor) (Child in Care: Medical Treatment)* [1991] 2 WLR 140 and *Re C (A Child) (HIV Test)* [2000] Fam 48.

The courts clearly have to balance several emotional and social factors, including the child's background, his feelings, his religious views, his education and any other characteristics. This is an all-encompassing assessment of what is best for the child donor. Tissue donation, e.g. blood or bone marrow, may not impact on these interests too heavily, but a kidney donation certainly will: every aspect of the child's life will be disturbed as a result of undergoing a serious surgical procedure. The courts may also be influenced by the innocent and vulnerable mind of the child. For example, the child may not want to undergo surgery because they associate it with death, monsters, horror films or the unknown, and this might have a psychological impact on the child that could last for years, not to mention the resentment felt towards the recipient family member who caused the donor child to experience pain and suffering with no real reward or mark of gratitude. The UK appeal courts have not yet dealt with a living child kidney donation case. *Hart v Brown* (1972) 289 A 2d 386 was a case of living child organ donation in the USA, in which a full organ was donated to an identical twin sister on the grounds that the prolonged relationship between the twins would outweigh the risks of donation. This case could be distinguished from all other potentially similar cases in the future on the grounds that the recipient and donor were identical twins, who are notorious for living closely together throughout their lives and would thus yield a great benefit from keeping each other alive.

It has already been made clear by the HTA Code of Practice that an Independent Assessor (IA) will make a report to the Human Tissue Authority on whether the 2004 Act provisions are met (see paragraph 36 in Code of Practice 2: Donation of Solid Organs for Transplantation, above). There are specific interview provisions for children, which are especially important if the child knows the recipient.

EXTRACT

Code of Practice 2: Donation of Solid Organs for Transplantation, Human Tissue Authority (2013):

http://www.hta.gov.uk/legislationpoliciesandcodesofpractice.cfm

Paragraph 62: The IA's responsibility is to interview the donor and recipient to assess whether the requirements of the HT Act and Regulations have been met. Separate interviews must be carried out with the donor and recipient, and IAs also interview the donor and recipient together.

Paragraph 63: The exceptions to this are:
when the recipient is a child, the donor will be interviewed separately.

Paragraph 64: Following the interview the IA must prepare a report for the HTA which states whether they are satisfied that the relevant requirements of the HT Act and Regulations have been met.

Paragraph 63 states that the child donor will be interviewed alone *and* with the person with parental responsibility. This will even be the case if the person with parental responsibility is the recipient of the organ or tissue. Such a complex situation must be handled very carefully by the Independent Assessor, taking into account any evidence of pressure, any promises of rewards, and the true level of understanding displayed by the child. A parent may simply tell their child that: 'it will be alright' and then the child will consent, but this does not indicate that the child fully understands all of the risks. The IA will then write a report (paragraph 64) and make a recommendation to the HTA.

It can be concluded that child donors can offer their own *Gillick* competent consent to the removal, use and storage of their organs and tissues, but a refusal will be overridden by a parent. In addition, once a child has consented to the procedures, a court will have to validate the surgical procedure because it is not in the best interests of the child. Thereafter, a HTA Panel will refer to the Independent Assessor's report to decide whether they are happy for the donation to go ahead. There is plenty of protection offered to the child donor, but coercion is always a major concern where a child donor is saving the life of a sibling.

The ethics of living donation

In living donation so far we have looked at the provisions for consent, the common law limits of consent and the methods of achieving consent from living donors who are incompetent or children. There are clearly some difficult issues to deal with: relative coercion is the biggest concern, closely followed by the understanding of the donor and the ethics of harvesting organs and tissues from individuals who do not understand what is going on. Are we taking advantage of vulnerable groups of patients?

Living donors are an important source of organs. Kidneys are more likely to be successful if they are taken from a living donor because as soon as a person dies the organ begins to deplete in quality. The statistics paint a supportive picture: it is estimated that only 2% of living kidney donors will experience major health problems after donation.[18] In addition to this, living donors can provide a much better match to their related recipients, blood and bone marrow can be harvested from living donors will little discomfort, and they can be regenerated by the body quite quickly with no long-term harm. In light of these advantages, what is the problem with living donation? The risk to the living donors has been a concern for researchers and commentators in this area of medical law. Kidney donation risks may be low, but liver segment donation risks are much higher with an estimated 40–60% chance of health problems for living donors.[19] In addition to this, in the small number of studies that have been undertaken in the late 1990s, up to 15% of donors believed that donation had resulted in a negative impact upon their heath, and a small number had regretted the procedure.[20] There is always a risk that things will go wrong, or that the act of donation did not turn out to be the positive altruistic experience that was anticipated, but these studies show that the majority of living donors do not suffer from any major complications (physically or mentally). It could be argued that the older the donor, the more altruistic and positive the experience, because it would be akin to 'handing something down' to the younger generations in the family. Interestingly, woman are more likely to donate organs,[21] and more women (54%) than men (46%) have signed up to the NHS Organ Donor Register.[22]

A more extreme argument against living donation would be that a doctor, by carrying out an altruistic donation procedure, is actually inflicting harm upon one patient for the

---

[18] See: Neuberger, J. and Price, D. (2003) 'Role of Living Liver Donation in the United Kingdom' 327 *British Medical Journal* 676–9.

[19] See note above.

[20] See: Schover, L.R. (1997) 'The Psychological Impact of Donating a Kidney: Long Term Follow-Up from a Urology Based Center' 157 *Journal of Urology* 1596–601; Johnson, E.M. (1997) 'Living Kidney Donation: Donor Risks and Quality of Life' *Clinical Transplantation* 231–40.

[21] This was shown in a German study in 2002, but more research into this area would be particularly valuable in terms of advertising for organ donors (living or dead). See: Biller-Andorno, N. (2002) 'Gender Imbalance in Living Organ Donation' 5 *Medicine, Health Care and Philosophy* 199–204.

[22] http://www.organdonation.nhs.uk/newsroom/fact_sheets/did_you_know.asp.

benefit of another. It logically follows that the recipient, by accepting the organ, is supporting and encouraging that harm.

There is always going to be a difficult moral issue when a surgeon carries out a procedure that has no benefit to the patient on the operating table, but in the field of organ donation it is widely accepted that the altruistic nature of the donation offsets the questionable morality of the procedure. The surgeon can still have the best interests of the patient at heart by exercising due care and skill during the procedure. A life will be saved in the end.

Living donors are also faced with extraordinary pressure from relatives, leading to emotional coercion to consent to a highly intrusive surgical procedure. It is important to remember that unless the donation is 100% altruistic, i.e. it is selflessly donated to an autonomous recipient for no reason except to save a life, then the donor will know (and probably love) the recipient, making a true consent almost impossible. How would a sister cope with the family fallout if she refused to donate her blood, bone marrow or her kidney to her dying brother? It would be easier for her to reluctantly consent to keep the peace, and this kind of scenario has caused great concern among commentators because consent *must* be voluntary to be valid:

EXTRACT

Ryan Sauder and Lisa Parker (2001) 'Autonomy's Limits: Living Donation and Health-Related Harm', 10 *Cambridge Quarterly of Healthcare Ethics* 399, at page 403

Frequently, a prospective donor, particularly a parent or sibling of the prospective recipient, will experience the decision to donate as automatic. They frequently report feeling that they had no choice but to donate, and proceed to offer their organs willingly and without hesitation, sometimes even before hearing of the risks involved in such a donation. Disclosure of risks frequently has no effect on the decision to donate. These decisions hardly seem to meet the traditional requirements of informed consent. Failing to take risks of an intervention into account when deciding whether to consent to it, and feeling compelled to consent, are typically hallmarks of a failure of the informed consent process. Yet we are reluctant to suggest that these prospective donors are not making autonomous decisions to donate and, consequently, that their decisions (and organs) should not be accepted.

Sauder and Parker are arguing that in a family scenario, the consent provided by a donor is not valid because of the pressures surrounding him. This may be true, but can it be argued in response that the emotional circumstances surrounding a family illness exacerbate the urgency and make the consent even stronger?

Altruistic donation, of course, does not have this problem, because the donor does not know the recipient. The consent, therefore, is voluntary, free from coercion, and valid.

EXTRACT

Walter Glannon and Lainie Ross (2002) 'Do Genetic Relationships Create Moral Obligations in Organ Transplantation?', 11 *Cambridge Quarterly of Healthcare Ethics* 153, at pages 153–9

An altruistic donor has no obligation to donate. The decision to donate goes beyond the obligatory and permissible to the supererogatory, and a decision not to donate does not invite or warrant moral criticism because there is no moral basis on which to criticise not performing an act that would have been beyond the call of duty. In contrast, the family member who is a potential donor has a *prima facie* obligation to donate because of the nature of relationships within the family.

It will be recalled that in *Re Y (Mental Patient: Bone Marrow Donation)* [1997] Fam 110 the extraction of bone marrow from an incompetent patient was held to be in her best interests because the visits from her mother would continue if the unwell sister was treated. This justification could not be applied to altruistic donation. The unknown donor does not glean *any* benefit from donation *at all*, except possibly a feeling of gratification that they have saved an anonymous person from ill health or death.

In living child donation, there is an additional concern that parents cannot not appropriately calculate the best interests of their children. For example, in a scenario where a mother is the parent of the donor *and* the recipient, who will she look out for in terms of preserving the best interests of the child? The donor who must undergo a minor procedure, or the recipient who may die? In these cases the donor child is put at a significant disadvantage, finding himself categorised as a 'source' of life for his brother and sister. The parent, who would never normally consent to her child undergoing a needless surgical procedure, is now very keen to sign the consent form. This is why the courts must rule on child donor cases before the Human Tissue Authority Panel can assess them. Tissue donation will almost never be a problem for the courts, because the extraction of blood and bone marrow is the equivalent of an injection to the donor child, resulting in minimal physical and emotional harm. However, organ donation – which is yet to be ruled on by our courts – is an entirely different matter. The donor child will suffer significant harm, which may last a lifetime, and all to meet the best interests of a third party (e.g. his sister). The smartest of parents will find it incredibly difficult to reconcile their competing interests when both of their children are caught up in an organ donation situation.

Despite all of these concerns, it would not be a very good idea to eliminate living donation as a source of organs and tissues completely, because so many recipients benefit from it and it is only natural for some family members to want to help each other out in times of need.

ACTIVITY

Jack and Jenny are brother and sister. Jenny is 5 years old and was very weak when she was born. She requires a bone marrow donation and Jack, who is 13 years old, is a perfect match. Their mother, Debra, brought them both to hospital to enquire about the procedure. Jack folds his arms and says he does not want to have a needle. Debra says she will consent for him. What is the legal procedure that must now be followed if Jack is to be a child donor, and what may the physical, emotional and moral consequences be?

Dead donor transplantation

The majority of organs used in transplantation come from dead donors. The following organs and tissues can be donated from a dead donor:

- **Thoracic (i.e. chest) organs:**
  - Heart
  - Lungs
  - Heart and lung domino transplant.
- **Abdominal organs:**
  - Kidneys
  - Liver

- Pancreas
- Intestine
- Stomach
- **Tissues and other:**
  - Hand and arm
  - Foot and leg
  - Cornea
  - Skin
  - Face
  - Pancreas cells
  - Bone marrow
  - Blood transfusion
  - Heart valve
  - Bone.

Many of the organs and tissues listed above can only come from dead donors (i.e. heart, liver, pancreas, stomach, hands, legs and face). There is a better choice of organs and tissues from dead donors, but they are in short supply. It is true that people die every day, but most of them are not healthy. Cancer, heart disease, old age, diabetes, obesity and substance abuse will rule out many dead bodies as donor candidates because their organs will be damaged, overworked or in bad condition. Traditionally, dead organ donors had been healthy people who suddenly died as a result of head injuries, car accidents, brain haemorrhages or some other form of sudden death. Their organs may have remained unaffected by the trauma but road traffic laws, car manufacturing regulations and advanced healthcare means that fewer people in these categories are dying.[23]

Organs deplete very quickly after the oxygen supply stops – particularly the heart and lungs – and so it is preferred to keep these particular candidates on an artificial ventilator (i.e. life support machine) for a short while after they have died. This allows extra time for consent to be attained and it also enables the blood to continue to flow to the organs. The act of keeping dead donors 'alive' on ventilators will be examined in detail further below because it is viewed by some as a grotesque and unethical way of harvesting organs.

Statistics

> **KEY DEFINITION**   **Circulatory death**: the patient died on his own without medical intervention.
> **Brain death**: the patient died while on a life support machine (a controlled death).

NHSBT confirm in their Annual Transplant Activity Report that between 1 April 2012 and 31 March 2013, there was an 11% increase in the number of deceased donors to 1,212. The number of donors after brain death increased 8% to 705, and the number of donors after circulatory death increased 16% to 507.[24] The statistics are quite complicated, but the important figures can be simplified as follows:

---

[23] http://www.organdonation.nhs.uk/newsroom/fact_sheets/did_you_know.asp.

[24] Taken from: Transplant Activity in the UK – Activity Report, 2012/13, NHS Blood and Transplant, at page 2. See: http://www.organdonation.nhs.uk/statistics/transplant_activity_report/.

Donation after brain death	Donation after circulatory death[25]
Total deaths: 28,966	
55 donors not able to donate	3,403 donors not able to donate
88 donor families were not approached	1,298 donor families were not approached
68 donors did not donate	482 donors did not donate

It is clear from the data above that brain dead donors are the most efficient source of organs because a circulatory death means that the donor has died without hospital intervention and has already begun to degenerate, but they are not a long term source or a reliable source because there are simply not enough to go around.

Health checks

It is quite rare, but dead donors may carry diseases, conditions or infections which, during an interview, would be disclosed by a living donor. Therefore, as soon as the possibility of donation arises, the dead donor must be tested for a selection of things that could be harmful to the recipient. There is a very small window of opportunity to consult with relatives about the donor's living conditions, social lifestyle, employment, criminal history and health problems, and this may still not provide a full picture of the donor's life. The Department of Health has provided guidelines to help with the clinical investigations of dead donors. The *Guidance on the Microbiological Safety of Human Organs, Tissues and Cells used in Transplantation* was published in 2000 by the Advisory Committee on the Safety of Blood, Tissues and Organs. It was updated in February 2011. It points out that screening for infections is particularly important because, should the recipient catch an infection after transplantation, the diet of immunosuppressant drugs means that she cannot fight it.

EXTRACT

Guidance on the Microbiological Safety of Human Organs, Tissues and Cells used in Transplantation (2011), Department of Health, page 9, see:

http://www.dh.gov.uk/en/Publicationsandstatistics/Publications/PublicationsPolicyAndGuidance/DH_121497

Paragraph 2.1: Transplantation has been one of the great success stories in health care. However, there have been repeated reports of transmissions of viruses, bacteria, fungi, protozoa and prions following transplantation of organs, tissues and cells. These transmissions can be difficult to manage as the recipients may be immunosuppressed and thus more susceptible to becoming ill from the infection. The risk of infection during the whole process of transplantation can never be completely removed. This guidance sets out precautions that should help to keep the risk as low as is reasonably possible whilst at the same time facilitating the maximum clinical benefit from transplantation.

The risk of infection is difficult to remove completely, but the aim is to make transplantation as safe as possible. Recipients will be informed of the small risk of catching an infection or a genetic condition that cannot be traced, but this is part of the organ transplant process.

---

[25] See note above, at page 113.

There appears to be a two-stage process for the assessment of dead donors. Firstly, an interview should take place with the relatives of the dead donor to ascertain the donor's suitability for donation. A family doctor can also be consulted to provide a more accurate picture, and a physical examination might also hold clues:

EXTRACT

Guidance on the Microbiological Safety of Human Organs, Tissues and Cells used in Transplantation (2011), Department of Health, page 18, see:

http://www.dh.gov.uk/en/Publicationsandstatistics/Publications/ PublicationsPolicyAndGuidance/DH_121497

Paragraph 4.2: The first component comprises a clinical risk assessment based upon an interview, which addresses the likelihood of a donor having been exposed to a variety of infection risks. In the case of deceased donors the most relevant life partner or close relative should be interviewed to ascertain the medical, behavioural and travel history. Additional information may be available from the referring clinician, the primary healthcare practitioner, the donor's GP, post-mortem and/or examination at the time of tissue procurement or organ retrieval.

Paragraph 4.3: A physical examination of the deceased potential donor should be undertaken at the time of organ and tissue retrieval. This may indicate extra risks of infection. For example, needle marks on the potential donor could indicate possible risk behaviour and should be taken into account when assessing the donor suitability.

In stage one, detailed information is required on the following matters (paragraph 4.4):

- Any treatment received before donation;
- Any previous or current immunosuppression (by disease or drugs);
- Any travel history outside of the UK to assess the risk of potential transmission of exotic infections, e.g. malaria, West Nile virus and rabies;
- Any other medical history: pituitary-derived growth hormone, brain and spinal surgery, and progressive neurological degenerative diseases;
- Any history of malignancy, recent infectious disease or exposure to an infectious disease that may affect the safety of donation;
- Any behavioural history that could have put the donor at risk of blood-borne viruses, including questions about risk behaviours such as recreational drug use, men who have sex with men, and risks such as accidental body fluid exposure;
- Results of any recent microbiological tests must be made available and should be reviewed.

Stage two involves microbiology tests.

EXTRACT

Guidance on the Microbiological Safety of Human Organs, Tissues and Cells used in Transplantation (2011), Department of Health, page 18, see:

http://www.dh.gov.uk/en/Publicationsandstatistics/Publications/ PublicationsPolicyAndGuidance/DH_121497

Paragraph 4.5: The second component comprises appropriate microbiological testing. Whilst medical and behavioural assessment will be similar for all donors, the actual microbiological assessment will vary for different types of donors.

The microbiology tests will focus on bacteria in the blood. There are guidelines available to advise on the finding of common infections, and it may be surprising to learn that if the donor is found to have influenza, the lungs and the bowel cannot be donated.

EXTRACT

Guidance on the Microbiological Safety of Human Organs, Tissues and Cells used in Transplantation (2011), Department of Health, pages 47–48, see:

http://www.dh.gov.uk/en/Publicationsandstatistics/Publications/ PublicationsPolicyAndGuidance/DH_121497

Paragraph 9.54: Lungs and bowel should not be used from donors with confirmed influenza infection.

Paragraph 9.76: Organs, tissues and cells from donors with superficial fungal infection of the skin or mucosa (thrush) are acceptable for donation.

Paragraph 9.80: Expert microbiological advice should be sought when considering using organs, tissues or cells from donors who have had unusual infections in the past, including those acquired outside of Western Europe. This should include infections common in immuno-compromised patients (e.g. listeriosis, nocardiosis) or infections which lie dormant or are difficult to eradicate (e.g. brucellosis, Lyme disease, typhoid).

All of the data collected from stage one (interviews, history, physical examination) and stage two (microbiology) will be handed to the transplant surgeon, and it is he who makes the final decision as to whether the risks/benefits lean towards donation.

EXTRACT

Guidance on the Microbiological Safety of Human Organs, Tissues and Cells used in Transplantation (2011), Department of Health, page 18, see:

http://www.dh.gov.uk/en/Publicationsandstatistics/Publications/ PublicationsPolicyAndGuidance/DH_121497

Paragraph 4.6: The balance of risk and benefit is carried out by the recipient's transplant surgeon, who must be able to assess correctly the risk of a potential donor having an infection, or having been exposed to an infection. The risk benefit analysis will consider different factors depending on the type of donor and whether organs, tissue or cells were donated.

It may often be the case that, as a result of the two-stage assessment process, a dead donor is revealed as unsuitable for donation. This is more likely when circulatory death has occurred, because of the rapid depletion in the quality of organs.

Unusual donations

It has not escaped our attention that in recent years, face transplants have become the new procedure on the block. The world press was very keen to broadcast the first partial face transplant in 2005. The first full-face transplant occurred shortly afterwards in

2010. These are procedures of fantasy: only in the movies could a person wake up with a new face. The shock is exacerbated by the thought of the procedure: a face has been removed from a dead person and sewn onto a living person. The general public may find it macabre and shocking, but doctors and recipients view it as a medical marvel that could give hope to thousands of disfigured people in the future. The possibility of failure must be particularly haunting for a face transplant recipient, who will have no identity if the new face fails to graft to her own flesh. This would leave her in an even worse position than before, because what was left of her old face would have been removed to make way for the new one. The ethical issues are new and unexplored, but some fascinating questions do arise:

- **Question 1**: is a face transplant an organ donation in the traditional sense, or does it sit in a new category of organ donation?
- **Question 2**: since a face transplant does not 'treat' the recipient, can this procedure be justified on the grounds of best interests?
- **Question 3**: what are the psychological implications of receiving an anonymous external body part (e.g. face, hand, etc.) and adopting it as your own to see and use every day?

A person seeking a face transplant will be in an extraordinary position. She would have suffered severe burns, for example, or a very serious injury, which means not only that her skin was destroyed (which could have been treated by a skin graft), but her muscle structure was destroyed too. This is incredibly rare. The first partial face transplant was performed on Isabelle Dinoire, a 38-year-old woman in France, who had the lower half of her face bitten off by her pet dog. A triangle of face tissue – the nose, the lips and the lower cheeks – were taken from a donor who had committed suicide and was declared brain dead. The procedure was successful. Isabelle has since said that she has regained a lot of the feeling and movement in her lower face, but she finds it difficult to accept her new face when she looks in the mirror. This is one of the ethical difficulties of face transplants: should we bring dead people back to life by transplanting their faces onto others?

The first full face transplant was performed on a man in Spain who was shot in the face, leaving him unable to breath properly, swallow or talk. The cheekbones, nose, lips and jaw were all taken from a dead donor. It was the first known procedure to transplant the whole face including some of the bones of the face. It was a complex procedure, taking twenty-two hours and a team of thirty surgeons, involving surgery with nerves, blood vessels, veins, arteries, skin, muscles and bone. The unnamed recipient will have to take drugs for the rest of his life to ensure that his body does not reject the graft, but he is reportedly satisfied.[26]

Face transplants are difficult to categorise. A face is not a 'vital' organ that gives life, it is a shield from the world outside and a primary means of identification for human beings. A face transplant could be described as a form of reconstructive surgery, except it uses materials taken from another person. Therefore, it could be renamed 'cosmetic donation' or 'reconstructive donation'. This is a very efficient use of natural resources, but from an ethical point of view it is especially important that the donor (or his family) gives full and voluntary consent to his face being brought back to life after his death. A face is quite different to an internal organ that is not seen: it is external, animated, alive and expressive. The deceased person continues to speak, blink, eat, sleep, greet, cry and smile. This would have an astonishing impact on his family, who have already mourned his departure. The Royal College of Surgeons explored the area of facial transplantation

---

[26] See: http://news.bbc.co.uk/1/hi/health/8639437.stm.

some years ago, and published a report about their concerns. It was established that extra care must be taken to support the psychological welfare of the face transplant recipient and ethical questions are inevitably raised about the morality of the procedure. There was a particular concern about the psychological effects on the families involved, both donor and recipient.

EXTRACT

Facial Transplantation: Working Party Report (2006), Royal College of Surgeons, 2nd edition:

http://www.rcseng.ac.uk/publications/docs/facial_transplant_report_2006.html

Paragraph 5.5.3: Teams should be vigilant for signs of psychological rejection of the donor face, for example, lack of interest in looking at the face in the mirror, or indications that the patient feels the new face is 'not the real me'. The recipient may need assistance to resolve complex feelings about the donor (for example, curiosity about the sort of person, guilt about the donor's death, gratitude to the family).

Paragraph 5.6: Post-operatively, family members should be monitored for signs of excessive stress and anxiety. They may experience distress in relation to the immediate post-operative appearance and lack of facial functioning in the patient. Strategies may be needed to encourage acceptance of the new face.

Paragraph 5.7: Transplant teams should also offer psychological support to donor families. The decision to donate a face of a close relative is likely to be made in the immediate and highly stressful aftermath of the death of a loved one. As the face is so closely aligned with recognition and identity, the motivation for donation may be more complex than in organ donation (for example, the family may believe that the donation will mean the relative will 'live on' in some tangible way).

It is a valid point that donor families may donate the face of their loved one to simply see their loved one alive after his death. This would not be the correct motivation for donating a face. What if, for example, the donor family feel attached to the recipient?

EXTRACT

Michael Freeman and Pauline Jaoude (2007) 'Justifying Surgery's Last Taboo: The Ethics of Face Transplants' 33 *Journal of Medical Ethics* 76, at pages 76–81

The donor will die and in a disembodied form live on. What was the stuff of drama to earlier generations is set for contemporary realisation. Should we therefore question a donor's motivation? Should it matter what this is? Should offers to donate be ruled out if the motivation is less altruistic than, literally, face saving? A form of 'life after death', a 'second coming', self-aggrandisement? Perhaps even a desire to haunt family, friends and colleagues? [...] The deceased's family is likely to think of him or her in terms of his or her face. This may be especially so where the deceased is a child or a young person. In such cases there may even be a desire for continuing a quasi-relationship by means of contact. [...] It is most unlikely, indeed, undesirable, that any right to contact will develop. But denial could lead to frustration, anger and trauma, in extreme cases perhaps even to a macabre form of stalking.

It is very likely that a mother, who has donated her young son's face for donation, will feel a very strong connection to the recipient when wearing her son's face. This is a very complex ethical problem which has not been researched in any great detail (probably because the procedure itself is still quite rare). The Royal College of Surgeons have noted the importance of faces as a form of human identity, and they worry that a face transplant will permanently alter the recipient to her friends and family.

EXTRACT

Facial Transplantation: Working Party Report (2006), Royal College of Surgeons, 2nd edition:

http://www.rcseng.ac.uk/publications/docs/facial_transplant_report_2006.html

Paragraph 5.2: The face is central to our understanding of our own identity. Faces help us understand who we are and where we come from with markers of genetic inheritance over many generations providing evidence of parentage, ancestry and racial identity. Disruption of one's facial appearance, especially, the inability to recognise oneself, represents a profound disruption of body image and may constitute a major life crisis.

The Royal College of Surgeons also need a recipient to be emotionally strong. Not only will her identity change, but her entire life will change, and the reactions from others (whether family or strangers) will be trying for even the most resilient of characters.

EXTRACT

Facial Transplantation: Working Party Report (2006), Royal College of Surgeons, 2nd edition:

http://www.rcseng.ac.uk/publications/docs/facial_transplant_report_2006.html

Paragraph 5.5.1.3: The prospective patient should be sufficiently resilient to cope with the considerable stress associated with the transplant, including the 'unknown' associated with a new procedure of this nature, the complex immunological and behavioural post-operative regimen, the risks of rejection and intrusive media interest.

Paragraph 5.5.4.1: Recipients will have to deal with the reactions of family and friends, both to their changed appearance and to any changes in previous patterns of non-verbal communication. There will be initial uncertainty concerning the extent to which the new facial appearance will be accepted. In the case of strangers the recipient will have to develop coping strategies to explain any visible signs of surgery, or any deficits in nonverbal communication that may accompany the transplant.

The Facial Transplantation Report was published in 2006, before the first full face transplant had taken place in Spain in 2010 to include the full face and bone structures. The Royal College of Surgeons could only guess as to the risks and benefits of such procedures because it was merely experimental, and informed consent was a particular area of concern. The general risks of facial transplantation (i.e. graft rejection) are significant and very serious but the unknown psychological risks cannot yet be passed onto the recipient, so there was a discussion as to whether the consent could ever really be fully informed when the surgeons themselves did not know what the risks would be.

EXTRACT

Facial Transplantation: Working Party Report (2006), Royal College of Surgeons, 2nd edition:

http://www.rcseng.ac.uk/publications/docs/facial_transplant_report_2006.html

Paragraph 6.1.3: Given the fact that facial transplantation is experimental and involves high levels of both known and unknown risks, the capacity of patients just to understand appropriate information of such complexity is an insufficient criterion of competence to provide valid consent.

The competence of a face transplant recipient must clearly be of a higher standard than that of a regular organ transplant recipient. The Royal College of Surgeons decided that because of the experimental nature of the procedure, it should be subject to an ethical evaluation by an appropriate Research Ethics Committee (see Chapter 10).

A serious surgical procedure is legally justified on the grounds that it is in the best interests of the patient, but is a face transplant in the best interests of the patient? The face is not a vital organ, so the procedure could be likened to cosmetic surgery rather than medical treatment. Patients can consent to cosmetic surgery on the grounds that it would benefit them *psychologically*, and this is probably what a face transplant would do for the recipient. The recipient would have to take a regimen of drugs for the rest of her life to ensure that her body did not reject the graft, but she would have been informed of this. The psychological issues taunting these recipients cannot be underestimated. Reconstructive surgery will usually be attempted first, but even the effects of this can be long lasting:

EXTRACT

A. Clarke (1999) 'Psychological Aspects of Facial Disfigurement' 4 *Psychology, Health and Medicine* 127, at pages 127–42

[Facial disfigurement involves] visual and verbal assaults, and a level of familiarity from strangers, naked stares, startled reactions, double takes, whispering, remarks, furtive looks, curiosity, personal questions, advice, manifestations of pity or aversion, laughter, ridicule and outright avoidance.

There has been some discussion as to whether the need for face transplants is actually derived from our inability to accept disfigured people in society. This is not a very strong argument, considering that the recipients of face transplants are usually always physically disabled in some way (i.e. they cannot eat, breathe, talk, etc.). It is therefore very unlikely to be vanity alone that warrants the procedure. However, the argument is still interesting, because face transplants inevitably connect to the way we interact with the world.

EXTRACT

Richard Huxtable and Julie Woodley (2005) 'Gaining Face or Losing Face? Framing the Debate on Face Transplants' 19 *Bioethics* 505, at pages 505–22

In an important sense, one must query whether the 'patient' is actually society, and in particular image-conscious Western society. [...] This apparent obsession with beauty is probably one of the strongest reasons for permitting this procedure and also ironically one of the main reasons why it gives cause for concern. Ideally, of course, society would celebrate, rather than alienate, such diversity. There nevertheless lingers the suspicion that the influence of societal norms amounts to a form of coercion, which might again threaten the validity of any consent. Furthermore, we wonder whether alternative responses to disfigurement, such as counselling, would suffer once the transplantation doors are opened. As Strauss has pointed out, 'when something is correctable, our willingness to accept it as untouched is reduced'.

Counselling could certainly be offered to facial transplant recipients as Huxtable and Woodley suggest, but the disfigurement may be so extreme in these cases that counselling will not solve the matter, especially if the recipient is disabled in some way as a result of their disfigurement (e.g. can't breathe properly). Relatives and friends have been telling recipients of cosmetic surgery for decades that they 'look fine the way they are' but no amount of love, support and encouragement can persuade a candidate to love their flaws. This may be the case for face transplant recipients too, particularly once they learn that the procedure is available and successful. The law requires their consent to be voluntary and their best interests to be met, so as long as these two criteria are satisfied, there should not be a legal issue.

It is not unusual for external limbs to be transplanted, as attempts have been made by surgeons for centuries to reattach legs after bloody battles, or hands after accidents. Captain Hook settled for a metal hook, but the idea of hand transplants (and all other external limb transplants) have been around for a while. They were never successful, of course, because the immune system of the recipient would reject the limb, leaving the recipient in an even worse state than before. The first successful hand transplant came as late as 1998 in France, although the recipient regretted his decision and it was removed a few years later because he failed to take his immunosuppressant drugs and it was rejected. However, once it was proved that limb transplants could work, the ethical questions arose again. Firstly, like a facial transplantation, a limb is not a vital organ so it can be referred to as a 'reconstructive donation'. It is safe to say, however, that the similarities stop there, because there is nothing *cosmetic* about a hand donation – the recipient is clearly disabled because of the loss of his hand and so the transplant should provide him with a sufficient amount of mobility to live a relatively normal life. Secondly, the procedure is easier to justify in law because it is in the best interests of the recipient to have a functioning hand. Thirdly, the psychological implications are not too serious with limb transplants compared to face transplants because the recipient will still be recognised by himself, his family, his colleagues and friends. In addition, the donor family will be less likely to have a morbid fascination in the outcome of the hand transplant, because the hand does not really play a part in the identification of a deceased human being. However, the issue of hand/limb transplants is not that simple. We have personal relationships with our limbs: our legs take us places and our hands help us to connect to those around us, and to see another person's hand touching a loved one may be incredibly difficult for some recipients to accept. The donor must be dead in order to donate a hand, an arm, a foot or a leg, and so the recipient will forever see a deceased person's hand at the end of his arm. It would almost be like the dead donor was picking things up for him, writing letters for him, texting for him, and touching his relatives for him. The psychological impact of this should not be underestimated.

There are mainly psychological reasons why we should reject unusual limbs, organs and faces for transplantation. This is due to a lack of research into the social and emotional effects of face and limb transplantation on recipients, donors, and their families. However, this is not a reason for banning the procedures completely – it is simply a reason for surgeons to carefully pick the correct recipients and donors. In the years before heart transplants were successful, there were fears that carrying the heart of another man would transfer his thoughts, feelings, dreams and memories into the new body. This was because the human heart was always considered to be the core of a man's existence. These days we know that an organ is simply an organ with no conscious memory, but its presence is still difficult to accept. The unidentified hand transplant recipient in 1998 was not happy with his new hand and refused to undertake his post-operative care until it led to a rejection, illustrating the importance of nominating a resilient personality who is totally dedicated to the graft and has a complete understanding of the procedure.

Consent: adults

The removal of organs and tissues from a dead donor is much simpler, because the rules of consent for dead donors are covered completely by the Human Tissue Act 2004. There is no need to divert into the common law of consent, as was necessary for donation by living donors, and there is no need to consider incompetent donors separately. The Code of Practice will still provide additional guidance. It is worth reminding ourselves of the main provisions of the Human Tissue Act 2004, which are listed under section 1 and under Schedule 1.

Human Tissue Act 2004

Section 1: Authorisation of activities for scheduled purposes

(1) The following activities shall be lawful if done with appropriate consent:

   (a) the storage of the body of a deceased person for use for a purpose specified in Schedule 1;

   (b) the use of the body of a deceased person for a purpose so specified;

   (c) the removal from the body of a deceased person, for use for a purpose specified in Schedule 1, of any relevant material of which the body consists or which it contains;

   (d) the storage for use for a purpose specified in Part 1 of Schedule 1 of any relevant material which has come from a human body;

   (f) the use for a purpose specified in Part 1 of Schedule 1 of any relevant material which has come from a human body.

Schedule 1 (part 1) of the Human Tissue Act 2004

- Anatomical examination;
- Determining the cause of death;
- Establishing after a person's death the efficacy of any drug or other treatment administered to him;

→

- Obtaining scientific or medical information about a living or deceased person which may be relevant to any other person (including a future person);
- Public display;
- Research in connection with disorders, or the functioning, of the human body;
- Transplantation.

Critical analysis

- The **storage** of a deceased body for one of the purposes under Schedule 1 is lawful – s. 1(1)(a);
- The **use** of a deceased body for one of the purposes under Schedule 1 is lawful – s. 1(1)(b);
- The **removal** of organs and tissues from a deceased body for one of the purposes under Schedule 1 is lawful – s. 1(1)(c);
- The **storage** of organs and tissues from a body (living or deceased) for one of the purposes under Schedule 1 is lawful – s. 1(1)(d);
- The **use** of organs and tissues from a body (living or deceased) for one of the purposes under Schedule 1 is lawful – s. 1(1)(f).

The **removal**, **storage** and **use** of organs and tissues from a deceased body are all covered under sections 1(1)(a),(b),(c),(d) and (f) of the 2004 Act. The current legal situation can be summarised as follows:

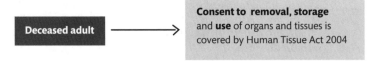

Figure 9.4

Parliament has made life much easier for doctors and relatives by including consent for the removal, storage and use of organs and tissues from dead donors within the ambit of the 2004 Act. It acts as a 'one stop shop' for consent. There are several ways for a dead donor to consent to his organs and tissues being removed, stored and used under section 3. The relevant provisions read as follows:

Human Tissue Act 2004

Section 3: 'Appropriate Consent': adults

(6) Where the person concerned has died, 'appropriate consent' means –

(a) if a decision of his to consent to the activity, or a decision of his not to consent to it, was in force immediately before he died, his consent;

(b) if –

(i) paragraph (a) does not apply, and

(ii) he has appointed a person or persons under section 4 to deal after his death with the issue of consent in relation to the activityconsent given under the appointment;

(c) if neither paragraph (a) nor paragraph (b) applies, the consent of a person who stood in a qualifying relationship to him immediately before he died.

The three ways to offer consent are as follows:

1. The donor can consent (or refuse) before his death under s. 3(6)(a).
2. The donor can nominate someone to consent for him under s. 3(6)(b).
3. A qualifying person can consent on the (incompetent) donor's behalf under s. 3(6)(c).

It is worth exploring these provisions in more detail. Firstly, the donor can consent for himself. He can, for example, join the organ donor register at www.organdonation.nhs.uk or carry a donor card. When first-time drivers collect their new licences, they are asked whether they would like to join the organ donor register because traditionally, most organs were derived from motor accidents. The donor can also express his wishes to his family. If any of these criteria are satisfied, then the dead donor can consent to the removal, storage and use of his own organs and tissues after his death. The wishes of the dead donor may not be immediately clear on the event of his death and if this is the case, a doctor can ask relatives or friends about any conversations that the donor may have had about the issue. Religious beliefs or cultural background can also point to consent or refusal. The Code of Practice provides further guidance. Firstly, it is confirmed that the dead donor can consent to the removal, storage and use of his tissues and organs, meaning that relatives do not have the legal power to veto (i.e. overrule) his consent.

EXTRACT

Code of Practice 1: Consent, Human Tissue Authority (2009):

http://www.hta.gov.uk/legislationpoliciesandcodesofpractice.cfm

Paragraph 74: Where an adult has, whilst alive, given valid consent for any particular donation or the removal, storage or use of their body or tissue for scheduled purposes to take place following their death, then that consent is sufficient for the activity to be lawful.

Paragraph 75: If those close to the deceased person object to the donation, for whatever purpose, when the deceased person (or their nominated representative) has explicitly consented, the healthcare professional should seek to discuss the matter sensitively with them. They should be encouraged to accept the deceased person's wishes and it should be made clear that they do not have the legal right to veto or overrule those wishes.

It is especially helpful if a discussion about consent can take place before the donor has died, and this is encouraged by the Code of Practice. The issue of consent must, of course, be handled very carefully with relatives *before* death, i.e. the patient is on a life support machine and the prognosis is grave, otherwise doctors could look like insensitive vultures, circling around hospital beds, waiting for death to be confirmed.

EXTRACT

Code of Practice 1: Consent, Human Tissue Authority (2009):

http://www.hta.gov.uk/legislationpoliciesandcodesofpractice.cfm

Paragraph 45: Where possible, it is good practice to seek the person's consent to the proposed procedure in advance. Sufficient time should be allowed for questions and discussion.

Paragraph 46: Equally, discussions with families may often take place in hospital before a person's death. They may know the person's wishes in respect of, for example, donating organs for transplantation.

Paragraph 47: The seeking and obtaining of consent from patients before death or from those close to them after their death requires sensitivity.

The relatives have a responsibility to accurately describe the donor's wishes to the doctor, even if they disagree with them. When relatives do disagree, the doctor must remember that every case is different and a little flexibility is suggested when disagreements are very strong.

EXTRACT

Code of Practice 2: Donation of Solid Organs for Transplantation, Human Tissue Authority (2009):

http://www.hta.gov.uk/legislationpoliciesandcodesofpractice.cfm

Paragraph 100: Once it is known that the deceased person consented to donation, the matter should be discussed sensitively with those close to the deceased. They should be encouraged to recognise the wishes of the deceased and it should be made clear, if necessary, that they do not have the legal right to veto or overrule their wishes. There may nevertheless be cases in which donation is considered inappropriate and each case should be assessed individually.

The Code of Practice clearly recognises (in Paragraph 100) that sometimes it would not be appropriate to order the donation if the relatives strictly object. This will be decided on a case-by-case basis, but it leaves the law in a very flexible position.

Secondly, a nominee can be appointed by the dead donor under section 4 of the 2004 Act. This allows the dead donor to hand the power of consent over to a person who he trusts in the event that he cannot decide for himself.

Human Tissue Act 2004

Section 4: Nominated representatives

(1) An adult may appoint one or more persons to represent him after his death in relation to consent for the purposes of section 1.

(2) An appointment under this section may be general or limited to consent in relation to such one or more activities as may be specified in the appointment.

(3) An appointment under this section may be made orally or in writing.

(7) An appointment under this section may be revoked at any time.

(9) A person appointed under this section may at any time renounce his appointment.

Section 4 is particularly beneficial when the donor is aware of divided views within the family. Rather than leaving the decision up to a person in a 'qualifying relationship' who disagrees with his views on donation, e.g. his mother is strictly religious, he can nominate a relative who agrees with his views on donation, e.g. one of his open-minded and educated children. The nominated representative can, however, renounce, i.e. walk away from, his responsibility under section 4(9), meaning that a relative is not forced to make a decision on donation. This puts the doctor in a difficult position because he cannot remove, store or use donated organs from the deceased patient without consent. However, the fact that Parliament has given dead donors the option to nominate a representative means that consent to donation can be provided in the event that the donor cannot decide for himself. This should, in theory, increase the number of dead donations.

Thirdly, a person in a 'qualifying relationship' can consent for the donor. This can happen if: the donor did not appoint a nominee, under section 3(7) the nominated representative cannot give consent, or under section 3(8) it is not reasonably practicable to communicate with the nominated representative within the time available. 'Qualifying relationships' are ranked under section 27, and the hierarchy means that the doctor will simply start from the top and work his way down.

Human Tissue Act 2004

Section 27: Provision with respect to consent

(4) The qualifying relationships should be ranked in the following order –

    (a) spouse [and civil partner] or partner;

    (b) parent or child;

    (c) brother or sister;

    (d) grandparent or grandchild;

    (e) child of a person falling within paragraph (c);

    (f) stepfather or stepmother;

    (g) half-brother or half-sister;

    (h) friend of longstanding.

Organs and tissues degenerate very quickly once the donor dies because the blood flow and oxygen supply leaves the organs within a few minutes. Therefore, it is vitally important that the doctor can reach someone on this list of qualifying relationships, and the higher the better. This 'leapfrogging' allows doctors to seek consent to dead donation much more effectively. There are a few additional provisions to look out for when seeking someone in a qualifying relationship: under section 27(5), the 2004 Act states that: 'relationships in the same paragraph of subsection (4) should be accorded equal ranking'. This means that if both a parent and a child are located by the doctor, they are both entitled to give consent (although the doctor only needs consent from one of them). The potential for family arguments gets worse under section 27(7), which states that: 'if the relationship of each of two or more persons to the [donor] concerned is accorded equal highest ranking in accordance with subsections (4) and (5), it is suffi-cient to obtain the consent of any of them.' This means that if a number of persons come forward in the same category, e.g. three grown children, or a pervious spouse and a new partner, then consent from any of them will do. This has the potential to be an emotional minefield, but as far as the doctor is concerned, in order to remove, store and use the organs and tissues from the dead donor, he only needs consent from one of these indi-viduals regardless of the strength of the objections from the others. The Code of Practice provides further guidance on this difficult issue. It discusses ranking and authority in particular, and confirms that the law only requires one consent from the *highest ranking* person.

EXTRACT

Code of Practice 2: Donation of Solid Organs for Transplantation, Human Tissue Authority (2013):

http://www.hta.gov.uk/legislationpoliciesandcodesofpractice.cfm

Paragraph 102: If the deceased person's wishes are not known, and they had not appointed a nominated representative, consent can be given by a person who was in a qualifying relationship immediately before the death.

Paragraph 109: Consent is needed from only one person in the hierarchy of qualifying relationships and should be obtained from the person ranked highest. If a person high up the list refuses to give consent, it is not possible to act on consent from someone further down the list. For example, if a spouse refuses but others in the family wish to give consent, the wishes of the spouse must be respected.

Paragraph 110: While the HT Act is clear about the hierarchy of consent, the person giving consent should be encouraged to discuss the decision with other family members – this may include people not on the list, for example, an aunt or uncle.

Paragraph 111: Relationships listed together, for example 'brother or sister', are accorded equal ranking, in which case it is sufficient to obtain consent from just one of them, provided they are ranked equal highest. For example, if the deceased person has no spouse or partner, but has several children, the consent of only one child is required.

Paragraph 112: Where there is a conflict between those accorded equal ranking, then this needs to be discussed sensitively with all parties, whilst explaining clearly that so far as the HT Act is concerned, the consent of one of those ranked equally in the hierarchy is sufficient for the procedure to go ahead.

The relatives are not legally provided with the power to veto the consent, but in the event of a unanimous rejection to donation the doctor may not be acting responsibly if he authorised the donation in the face of strong family criticism. This rejection of consent could be viewed as a 'back door erosion' of the donor's autonomy and it would be discouraging to all future potential donors to learn that their families could override their consent if they kicked up enough of a fuss, but the procedure could add great distress to an already aggrieved family (especially if the donor is young). The Code of Practice agrees that flexibility may be required.

EXTRACT

Code of Practice 1: Consent, Human Tissue Authority (2009):

http://www.hta.gov.uk/legislationpoliciesandcodesofpractice.cfm

Paragraph 76: Healthcare professionals should also consider the impact of going ahead with a procedure in light of strong opposition from the family, despite the legal basis for doing so.

It might, therefore, be for the best if a doctor decided to respect the wishes of significantly distressed relatives and ignored the donor's (or the nominated representative's) consent. There are two clear reasons why a doctor might do this. Firstly, negative publicity could do a lot of harm to the national donation programme, leading to a drop in consent rates from relatives. Secondly, a typical doctor may also feel compassion for the relatives if they were particularly traumatised by the death of a loved one, and so it may be best not to aggravate their grief. This flexibility begs an important question: do relatives possess an informal power to veto a donor's consent? The answer should be 'no': patient autonomy is one of the cornerstones of medical law and a donor is entitled to donate his own organs and tissues, whether dead or alive, as long as he has provided his own valid and fully informed consent. Besides, just because a donor has died does not mean that his wishes should be rejected in favour of those who are still alive. The opt-out system in Austria, for example, is particularly strict, allowing for organs to be taken from donors who have not opted out *regardless* of the objections from relatives. This may upset some relatives, because it could be argued that they make the bigger sacrifice. A donor is physically altered after donation – parts of him are removed and continue to live on in someone else – and this process might leave the relatives in a strange 'transitional' state of grief where they cannot properly mourn the death of their loved one who, in their mind, has been changed forever. In light of this, perhaps relatives should, therefore, have the power to veto consent because they are the ones who will be deeply affected by the donation? There may not be anything to worry about, as statistics from NHS Blood and Transplant show that most relatives would consent to the removal, storage and use of organs and tissues anyway. Relatives of donors who suffered brain death consented at a rate of 32%, and relatives of donors who suffered circulatory death consented at a rate of 49%.[27]

Consent: children

The Human Tissue Act 2004 also allows a dead child donor to consent to the removal, storage and use of his organs and tissues (as long as the child is *Gillick* competent). The provisions are listed under section 2 of the 2004 Act.

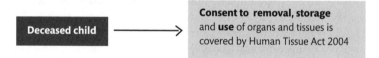

Figure 9.5

Human Tissue Act 2004

Section 2: 'Appropriate consent': children

(7) Where the child concerned has died and the activity is not one to which subsection (5) applies, 'appropriate consent' means –

(a) if a decision of his to consent to the activity, or a decision of his not to consent to it, was in force immediately before he died, his consent;

(b) if paragraph (a) does not apply –

(i) the consent of a person who had parental responsibility for him immediately before he died, or

(ii) where no person had parental responsibility for him immediately before he died, the consent of a person who stood in a qualifying relationship to him at that time.

---

[27] Taken from: Transplant Activity in the UK – Activity Report, 2012/13, NHS Blood and Transplant, at page 114. See: http://www.organdonation.nhs.uk/statistics/transplant_activity_report/.

The three ways to offer consent are as follows:

1. The child can consent (or refuse) before his death under s. 7(a).
2. A person with parental responsibility for him can consent on his behalf under s. 7(b)(i).
3. A person in a qualifying relationship can consent on his behalf under s. 7(b)(ii).

These provisions are very similar to those for dead adult donors in that if the donor does not offer his own consent, somebody else in a trusted position can do it for him. However, there is one subtle difference. A child cannot nominate a representative to consent for him, meaning that if he does not consent, his parent will simply do it for him. The benefit of the nominated representative system is that the donor can select a person who has similar beliefs on organ donation to him, but a child donor cannot do this – his parents will override him regardless of whether their beliefs match or not. This is not necessarily a bad thing in most cases, but the 'child' may be a teenager, in which case he may have strong views on certain things which his mother may like to override. There are three issues that must now be clarified using the Codes of Practice: (a) does the dead child donor need to be *Gillick* competent under common law? (b) are the consenting parents under any restrictions? and (c) what are qualifying relationships?

Firstly, if a dead child can consent to the removal, storage and use of his organs and tissues before his death, then he must be competent to do so. It is a significant legal power to bestow upon a child, so he must understand the implications of his consent. The provisions regarding consent (listed above for dead adult donors) are all applicable to dead child donors too, including sufficient information about risks (paragraph 32 under Code 1), seeking consent before death to allow for discussion and questions (paragraph 45 under Code 1), discussions with family before death (paragraph 46 under Code 1), and sensitivity should be used when seeking consent from patients before death (paragraph 47 under Code 1). A child is defined by the Code of Practice as a person under the age of 18 (paragraph 89 under Code 1, and s. 54(1) of the 2004 Act). The Code of Practice is very clear that a child can provide his consent as long as he is *Gillick* competent, and this will allow healthcare professionals to treat him like an adult.

EXTRACT

Code of Practice 1: Consent, Human Tissue Authority (2009):

http://www.hta.gov.uk/legislationpoliciesandcodesofpractice.cfm

Paragraph 90: The position of a child who, before they died, was competent to reach a decision and gave consent for one or more scheduled purposes to take place after their death, is no different from that of an adult. Their consent is sufficient to make lawful the removal, storage or use of tissue for that purpose. In the *Gillick* case, the court held that a child was considered competent to give valid consent to a proposed intervention if they had sufficient intelligence and understanding to enable them fully to understand what was involved.

Paragraph 91: If a child consents to a procedure, then this consent carries over into adulthood unless they withdraw their consent.

This provision appears to give a lot of power to children to choose what happens to their own deceased bodies, but the power may only be a theory, because the Code of Practice goes on to confirm that a person who has parental responsibility should be consulted in order to ascertain whether the child is *Gillick* competent. The parent of a strong-willed teenager who has withdrawn from the family religion may well be tempted to say no.

EXTRACT

Code of Practice 2: Donation of Solid Organs for Transplantation, Human Tissue Authority (2013):

http://www.hta.gov.uk/legislationpoliciesandcodesofpractice.cfm

Paragraph 115: Clearly, in any case where a child has given consent to donation, especially if the child has self-registered on the Organ Donor Register it is essential to discuss this with the child's family, and take their views and wishes into account before deciding how to proceed. In some cases it may also be advisable to establish with the person who had parental responsibility for the deceased child, whether the child was competent to make the decision.

It is safe to say that a child's consent will certainly be heard and considered, but a discussion with the parents will help direct the doctor towards a *final* decision.

Secondly, the person who has parental consent can be approached by the doctor if a consent is not in place at the time of death. The Code of Practice acknowledges that this may not always be the biological parent, because step parents, carers or guardians may also be responsible for a child. The doctor only needs to seek *one* consent. This may cause problems.

EXTRACT

Code of Practice 1: Consent, Human Tissue Authority (2009):

http://www.hta.gov.uk/legislationpoliciesandcodesofpractice.cfm

Paragraph 93: A person who has parental responsibility will usually, but not always, be the child's parent.

Paragraph 94: If a child did not make a decision, or was not competent to make a decision, the HT Act makes clear that the appropriate consent will be that of a person with parental responsibility for the child. The consent of only one person with parental responsibility is necessary.

Paragraph 95: The issue should be discussed fully with relatives and careful thought should be given as to whether to proceed if a disagreement arises between parents or other family members. Any previously stated wishes of the deceased child should be considered, taking into account their age and understanding.

The Code of Practice clearly encourages doctors to have a discussion with all of the relatives involved to ensure that if a consent is accepted, those who disagree to it understand why it was taken and the benefits it can bring. However, if the dissenting statements are very forceful, the doctor is clearly not under any obligation to remove the organs. He can judge for himself whether it would cause too much upset to a particular family. This freedom is important, because if families felt that their dead child was being violated against their wishes, the support for organ donation would decrease.

Thirdly, if a person with parental responsibility is not available, a person with a qualifying relationship to the child can consent on their behalf instead.

EXTRACT

Code of Practice 2: Donation of Solid Organs for Transplantation, Human Tissue Authority (2013):

http://www.hta.gov.uk/legislationpoliciesandcodesofpractice.cfm

Paragraph 117: If there is no person with parental responsibility (e.g. if the parents have also died, perhaps at the same time as the child), then consent for organ donation should be sought from someone in a qualifying relationship.

As with dead adult donors, 'qualifying relationships' are ranked under section 27, and the hierarchy means that the doctor will simply start from the top and work his way down.

Human Tissue Act 2004

Section 27: Provision with respect to consent

(4) The qualifying relationships should be ranked in the following order –

   (a)   spouse [and civil partner] or partner;

   (b)   parent or child;

   (c)   brother or sister;

   (d)   grandparent or grandchild;

   (e)   child of a person falling within paragraph (c);

   (f)   stepfather or stepmother;

   (g)   half-brother or half-sister;

   (h)   friend of longstanding.

In the event that the doctor cannot find a competent brother or sister (the dead child donor will not have a spouse, partner or child) then the grandparents or step-parents are the next places to look for consent. The window for organ retrieval is very small, and so it might be difficult to contact the qualifying relationship in a reasonable amount of time. The provisions regarding qualifying relationships (listed above for dead adult donors) are all applicable to dead child donors too, including the need to find only one person from the hierarchy who is placed as high as possible (paragraph 110 under Code 2), the rule that if one person rejects, a lower person cannot override their rejection (paragraph 110 under Code 2), the person giving consent should discuss this with other people who may or may not have qualifying relationships (paragraph 111 under Code 2), relationships with equal ranking such as brother and sister have equal say but only one consent will do (paragraph 112 under Code 2), and where there is a conflict between equal ranking relationships, the issue must be discussed sensitively with all of the relevant parties with the view to seeking one consent (paragraph 113 under Code 2). The provisions may be the same for adult and child dead donors, but the emotions involved are quite different.

Children are vulnerable in nature because they are smaller, less experienced and more fragile than adults. It is only natural for the adults around them to protect them. Donating organs and tissues from a dead child may grate against the protective instinct that goes hand in hand with raising or guarding children. The doctors must be sensitive to this, and make it clear that any organs or tissues from the child donor will go to help another child recipient.

ACTIVITY

Charlie is a 15-year-old and has joined a gothic cult at school. His mother, Elaine, is a strict Catholic and is uncomfortable with his clothing and music, which often refer to death. Charlie has very strong views against blood transfusions, believing that his 'life blood' should not be mixed with another's, but he never mentioned his views on organ donation or transplantation. Charlie was killed in a shooting at his school, and his organs were prime candidates for transplantation. Elaine was approached by the doctor. What laws are in place to protect Charlie's views, and if his views are not clear enough, what can the doctor legally do?

The definition of death

This might seem a strange topic to include in an organs chapter because organ donation is traditionally about giving life to another, but the definition of death is more important in this field of medicine than in any other. Why? The reason is simple: the dead donor must be clinically dead before his organs can be removed. If he is not dead but simply in a comatose state, then the surgeon is committing murder on the removal of the organs.

The definition of death that we apply is therefore vitally important. When does a person meet his death? This is a legal, moral, religious and ethical question. Centuries before any medical technology was developed (even the stethoscope), a patient was deemed to be dead when he had stopped breathing. In the nineteenth century when scientists had a better understanding of human bodies, a patient was deemed to be dead when he no longer showed a pulse. It is now possible to bring dead people back to life through resuscitation, suggesting that a definition of death based on pulse and breathing is not entirely accurate. Sadly, this old definition of death is still applied today in very poor countries and shockingly, there are often reported incidents of people waking up in morgues after natural disasters when rescue teams did not have a proper opportunity to confirm death. In developed countries, medical technology can help to ascertain brain activity, and it has long been established that a patient is clinically dead when his brain stem shows no activity. This definition of death (outlined in detail below) clearly excludes patients who are in a persistent vegetative state. This is because their brain stem and lower brain is still alive, but they are not able to move or communicate because their upper brain – which controls their capacity for consciousness – has died. This is bad news for the purposes of organ donation, because the organs would be in a much better condition if they could be removed from a living donor. Artificial ventilators, i.e. life support machines, can perform the function of breathing when the patient cannot do it on his own. The patient will be removed from the life support machine after a brain stem death test has confirmed his death. The organs will be well preserved using this method (these donors are sometimes referred to as 'heartbeating donors'), but it can lead to confusion and distress for families to receive a diagnosis of death when the patient appears to be alive, and the key ethical issue is: should we maintain dead donors on valuable life support machines to simply harvest their organs? The courts have adopted the medical definition of death for convenience, and this is a very good idea. The court system would confuse matters considerably if they were to apply their own definition of death. Anthony Bland (a victim of the Hillsborough Disaster) was in a persistent vegetative state when his parents and doctors wanted to switch his life support machine off, thereby killing him. They sought court approval, and the courts stated that because his brain stem was still alive, *he* was still alive.

CASE EXTRACT

Airedale NHS Trust v *Bland* [1993] AC 789

Lord Goff (at page 863): I start with the simple fact that, in law, Anthony is still alive. It is true that his condition is such that it can be described as a living death; but he is nevertheless still alive. This is because, as a result of developments in modern medical technology, doctors no longer associate death exclusively with breathing and heartbeat, and it has come to be accepted that death occurs when the brain, and in particular the brain stem, has been destroyed. [...] The evidence is that Anthony's brain stem is still alive and functioning and it follows that, in the present state of medical science, he is still alive and should be so regarded as a matter of law.

The rest of the *Bland* judgment is difficult to forget: he was experiencing 'a living death' with no prospect of recovery so, according to the lords, he had no best interests in being kept alive anymore and the duty to feed him was extinguished. Anthony Bland would have been an ideal candidate for organ donation, because his organs were functioning right up until the moment of his death. In reality, death probably happens in different stages. Depending on how the patient has died, e.g. old age, disease, trauma etc., the heart may stop beating first, or the brain may stop working first, but the other organs are likely to fail shortly afterwards because their blood and oxygen supply has slowly come to a stop. Religious groups may argue that the human does not really die at all because the soul lives on. This theory – if true – would make organ donation, postmortems and even burial impossible to perform because the patient would still be 'alive'. It is much easier, for now, to adopt the medical definition of brain stem death for legal purposes.

The history of the brain stem death test

Brain function has not always been considered as an indicator of death, but developments in technology in the twentieth century allowed doctors to measure brain activity. It was especially important to create a formal definition of death after it was learnt that a human being could be brought back to life (whether fully or partially) after the heart apparently stopped beating, and this is when the brain became the focus of death. Harvard Medical School set up an ad hoc committee in 1968 and defined brain death for the first time.

EXTRACT

A Definition of Irreversible Coma, Ad Hoc Committee of the Harvard Medical School to Examine the Definition of Death (1968) 205 *Journal of the American Medical Association* 85–8, at page 85

Our primary purpose is to define irreversible coma as a new criterion for death. There are two reasons why there is a need for a definition: (1) Improvements in resuscitative and supportive measures have led to increased efforts to save those who are desperately injured. Sometimes these efforts have only partial success, so that the result is an individual whose heart continues to beat but whose brain is irreversibly damaged. The burden is great on patients who suffer permanent loss of intellect, on their families, on the hospitals, and on those in need of hospital beds already occupied by these comatose patients. (2) Obsolete criteria for the definition of death can lead to controversy in obtaining organs for transplantation.

The concept of brain death has been accepted in many countries and the reasons why are clear: technology enables us to keep patients 'alive' after their brain has died, leading to an 'artificial' state of life which must be diagnosed as dead in order to remove organs. The test for brain death differs according to which country the patient is in. In the UK (and in India) doctors are interested in the brain *stem* when diagnosing death. This is the 'stalk' at the base of the brain that connects to the spinal cord and the nervous system. Death in these countries will be diagnosed and legally accepted when brain stem activity has ceased, but in most other parts of the world (including the USA) the *whole* brain must be dead for death to be diagnosed. The human brain is split into two: the upper brain regulates consciousness and the lower brain regulates bodily functions, and in order for a brain to be completely dead, the activity in the upper brain and the lower brain must have ceased. The UK test is therefore seen as 'restrictive' and 'unethical' in some jurisdictions, because it only focuses on the brain stem. It does mean, however, that death can be diagnosed and organs can be removed when other parts of the brain are still functioning.

The brain stem death test began to gather pace back in 1976, when the Conference of Medical Royal Colleges first published some brain stem test criteria in response to concerns that deeply comatose patients were being kept alive by artificial ventilators but showing no signs of recovery. The aim of the Conference was: 'to establish diagnostic criteria of such rigour that on their fulfilment the mechanical ventilator can be switched off, in the secure knowledge that there is no possible chance of recovery'.[28] The published criteria indicated that life support could be withdrawn from patients who showed no response to a number of bedside tests, and these criteria were deemed to be 'sufficient to distinguish between those patients who retain the functional capacity to have a chance of even partial recovery and those where no such possibility exists'. An academic commentator – Pallis – published a piece in the British Medical Journal in 1982 suggesting that 'brain stem death' was the correct term for the test.[29] The Department of Health took the opportunity to publish its first Code of Practice for 'brain death' in 1983 in relation to harvesting organs from dead donors.[30] A review was then undertaken in 1995 by a Working Group of the Royal College of Physicians of London and the term 'brain stem

---

[28] Conference of Medical Royal Colleges and their Faculties in the UK (1976) 2 *British Medical Journal* 1187.

[29] Pallis, C. 'From Brain Death to Brain Stem Death' (1982) 1 *British Medical Journal* 285.

[30] *Cadaveric Organs for Transplantation: A Code of Practice Including the Diagnosis of Brain Death*. London, 1983, HMSO (no longer available on the Department of Health Website).

death' was supported but this time with a clear new definition: 'the irreversible loss of the capacity for consciousness, combined with irreversible loss of the capacity to breathe' and that 'brain stem death is equivalent to the death of the individual'.[31] The Conference of Medical Royal Colleges adopted this new definition of brain stem death and the definition has changed very little since. The Department of Health updated its Code of Practice in 1998, recognising the new definition in a document entitled: A Code of Practice for the Diagnosis of Brain Stem Death (below). The addition of the word 'stem' in the title was a clear indication that the accepted definition of death was now based firmly on the brain stem death test. This was explained clearly in the introduction to the updated Code of Practice.

EXTRACT

A Code of Practice for the Diagnosis of Brain Stem Death (1998), Department of Health (archived), at page 2:

http://webarchive.nationalarchives.gov.uk/20130107105354/
http://www.dh.gov.uk/en/Publicationsandstatistics/Publications/
PublicationsPolicyAndGuidance/DH_4009696

The 1983 Code of Practice carried in its sub-title the phrase 'including the diagnosis of brain death'. The requirement for the removal of organs for transplantation is not death of the whole brain but 'brain stem death' have been satisfied, there is no prospect of survival and cessation of the heart beat will then occur. It is important that this is fully explained to the relatives. The evidence for this approach is given in the review by a Working Group convened by the Royal College of Physicians on behalf of the UK Conference of Medical Royal Colleges and their Faculties, and endorsed by the Conference. It is because the term 'brain death' has led to real confusion, that we take the view that it should be replaced by 'brain stem death'.

The definition of brain stem death quickly followed under paragraph 1.

EXTRACT

A Code of Practice for the Diagnosis of Brain Stem Death (1998), Department of Health (archived), at page 3:

http://webarchive.nationalarchives.gov.uk/20130107105354/
http://www.dh.gov.uk/en/Publicationsandstatistics/Publications/
PublicationsPolicyAndGuidance/DH_4009696

1. The Definition of Death

Death entails the irreversible loss of those essential characteristics which are necessary to the existence of a living human person. Thus, it is recommended that the definition of death should be regarded as 'irreversible loss of the capacity for consciousness, combined with irreversible loss of the capacity to breathe'.

The current position in law is that there is no statutory definition of death in the United Kingdom. Subsequent to the proposal of the 'brain death criteria' by the Conference of Royal Colleges in 1976 and 1979, the courts in England and Northern Ireland have adopted these criteria, as part of the law, for the diagnosis of death. There is no reason to believe that courts in other parts of the United Kingdom would not follow this approach.

---

[31] 'Criteria for the Diagnosis of Brain Stem Death' (1995) 29 *Journal of the Royal College of Physicians of London* 381.

Brain stem death was clearly defined as a two-part test:

- **Part 1**: irreversible loss of the capacity for consciousness.
- **Part 2**: irreversible loss of the capacity to breathe.

These two elements must be combined, so it is not sufficient, for example, for a patient to be incapable of breathing for himself but still conscious. In 2008, the Academy of Medical Royal Colleges published an updated Code to include important developments and more scientifically rigorous criteria for confirming brain stem death.[32] The word 'stem' has been removed from the title of the 2008 Code (which is currently in force), but this is merely cosmetic – the brain stem death test is still an accepted method of confirming death in the UK and the changes are relatively minor.

The current tests for determining death

According to the Academy of Medical Royal Colleges in its 2008 Code, entitled: A Code of Practice for the Diagnosis and Confirmation of Death, death can be diagnosed after two separate events: (i) following cessation of cardiorespiratory function, and (ii) following the irreversible cessation of brain stem function.[33]

(i) **Cessation of cardiorespiratory function.** A patient may have died at home, in a care home, or at the scene of an accident. In these instances, cardio (heart) and respiratory (lung) function has ceased (i.e. 'cardiorespiratory'), and this is an indication that the brain has also ceased or is about to cease, because it cannot function without an oxygen and blood supply. A qualified medical practitioner can diagnose death if enough time has passed and there are no responses (breathing, heartbeat and pupil responses) from the patient.

(ii) **Irreversible cessation of brain stem function.** A patient on an artificial ventilator will have his lungs filled with oxygen causing his heart to beat. There may be several reasons for his comatose state – from disease to head injury – but this does not mean that he is brain stem dead. A significant number of patients in a comatose state, for example after a car accident, regain consciousness after being on a life support machine and make a full recovery. However, in some instances, the brain stem may die. When it does, a healthcare professional will notice certain symptoms, such as no pupil reaction to light, changes in blood pressure and heart rate, and no reaction to stimulus.[34] This is when a brain stem death test will occur, to confirm that the brain has died. This is the ideal time to approach relatives about organ donation if the patient's organs are relatively unharmed. The heart will continue to beat for a short while on the artificial ventilator, but because the 'nerve centre' has died, the heart will stop beating eventually too. There is only a limited amount of time for donation.

Confirming death after cessation of cardiorespiratory function

Sadly, there is no standardised test for confirming death following the cessation of cardiorespiratory function, e.g. an elderly person in a care home succumbs to heart

---

[32] A Code of Practice for the Diagnosis and Confirmation of Death (2008) Academy of Medical Royal Colleges, http://www.aomrc.org.uk/publications/reports-a-guidance.html.

[33] See note above, paragraphs 2.1 and 2.2, at page 11.

[34] See note 32, Appendix 5 at page 34.

disease, meaning that the moment of death and the accuracy of the diagnosis may be blurred. This does not prove to be too much of a problem in most scenarios, but if the deceased is a potential organ donor, it is likely that too much time has passed for the organs to be removed. The Academy of Medical Royal Colleges recognises that in instances of cessation of cardiorespiratory function, there needs to be a standard approach for confirming death in the event that the patient may be a potential non-heartbeating donor.

EXTRACT

A Code of Practice for the Diagnosis and Confirmation of Death (2008), Academy of Medical Royal Colleges, at page 12:

http://www.aomrc.org.uk/publications/reports-a-guidance.html

Unlike confirmation of death using neurological assessment of cessation of brain stem reflexes, there are currently no standardised criteria for the confirmation of death following irreversible cessation of cardiorespiratory function. As a result current practice varies from confirming death as soon as the heart stops of its own accord, or when attempts at cardiopulmonary resuscitation are abandoned, to waiting ten minutes or longer after the onset of asystole (absence of heartbeat) and apnoea (absence of breathing). While such practice continues to be appropriate, particularly within primary care, the increasing practice of non-heartbeating organ donation has also focussed attention on the need in a hospital setting for a standard approach to confirming death.

A patient who died of cardiorespiratory arrest clearly has to show several different symptoms before death can be announced. By the time the doctor reaches the scene, the organs may have been deprived of oxygen for some time. Similarly, patients who die of cardiorespiratory arrest are not usually the healthiest of patients. These patients will have died of old age, disease or injury. They will not be useful for organ donation, unless the death was sudden, the patient was young and healthy, and the event of death involved very little trauma to be body. There are not many scenarios in which these criteria would be met in a cardiorespiratory arrest situation.

Confirming death after cessation of brain stem function

Death resulting from irreversible cessation of brain stem function is announced after a much more scientific test. It is vital that the patient (now referred to as a 'heartbeating donor') is confirmed to be brain stem dead when taken into surgery for donation because if he is not, the surgeon will be killing him. The artificial ventilator of an organ donor is not switched off when brain stem death is announced: the heart and lungs must still be working during the removal to ensure that the organs have a sufficient blood supply. It is now clear why the brain stem death test (examined below) must be thoroughly accurate. The Academy of Medical Royal Colleges is aware of the controversy surrounding the narrow scope of the brain stem death test, and move to justify it by explaining that the death of the brain stem must surely equate to the death of the individual.

EXTRACT

A Code of Practice for the Diagnosis and Confirmation of Death (2008), Academy of Medical Royal Colleges, at page 11:

http://www.aomrc.org.uk/publications/reports-a-guidance.html

The definition of death should be regarded as the irreversible loss of the capacity for consciousness, combined with irreversible loss of the capacity to breathe.

The irreversible cessation of brain stem function . . . will produce this clinical state (i.e. death) and therefore irreversible cessation of the integrative function of the brain stem equates with the death of the individual and allows the medical practitioner to diagnose death.

The Academy of Medical Royal Colleges goes on to publish three notable points of concern when using the brain stem test to confirm death in a patient.

EXTRACT

A Code of Practice for the Diagnosis and Confirmation of Death (2008), Academy of Medical Royal Colleges, section 2.1, at page 11:

http://www.aomrc.org.uk/publications/reports-a-guidance.html

First, the irreversible loss of the capacity for consciousness does not by itself entail individual death. Patients in the vegetative state (VS) have also lost this capacity.

Second, the diagnosis of death because of cessation of brain stem function does not entail the cessation of all neurological activity in the brain. Where such residual activity exists (i.e. the ability to feel, to be aware of, or to do, anything), it will not do so for long due to the rapid breakdown of other bodily functions.

Third, residual reflex movement . . . is independent of the brain and is controlled through the spinal cord, it is neither indicative of the ability to feel, be aware of, or to respond to, any stimulus, nor to sustain respiration or allow other bodily functions to continue.

These three points are interesting. Firstly, PVS patients are excluded from the brain stem death test. This is because their brain stem is still alive so it would not be appropriate – at least according to the Academy – to label them as dead. Secondly, the Academy admits that some brain activity will still be present when the brain stem ceases to function, meaning that the patient may still be able to 'feel, be aware of, or do, anything' when death is confirmed. This does not make for comfortable reading. The Academy justifies this approach by stating that such residual activities 'do not last long', but without any detailed research into the process of death (which the Academy admits is 'a process rather than an event'[35]), then how do we know that the patient is really dead at this point? Thirdly, the rejection of residual reflex movements as a sign of life is simply a way to bring relief to families and relatives, who may be confused by sudden movements of the legs, arms or face when death has already been diagnosed.

The Academy rejects these reflex movements as having no moral bearing on the diagnosis of death.

---

[35] See note 32, at page 12.

EXTRACT

A Code of Practice for the Diagnosis and Confirmation of Death (2008), Academy of Medical Royal Colleges, section 2.1, at page 11:

http://www.aomrc.org.uk/publications/reports-a-guidance.html

In short, while there are some ways in which parts of the body may continue to show signs of biological activity after a diagnosis of irreversible cessation of brain stem function, these have no moral relevance to the declaration of death for the purpose of the immediate withdrawal of all forms of supportive therapy. It is for this reason that patients with such activity can no longer benefit from supportive treatment and legal certification of their death is appropriate.

It is not for the Academy to decide matters of morality and as we shall see later, many commentators disagree with the narrow scope of the current brain-stem death test. The test for brain stem death involves reflex actions and nerve reactions (e.g. touching the cornea, shining a light into the eye and a gag reflex amongst others) and is clearly more scientific. It does not accurately provide a time of death, but it provides a larger picture of how the brain stem is functioning. The Academy of Medical Royal Colleges makes it clear that two doctors must perform the brain stem death test.

EXTRACT

A Code of Practice for the Diagnosis and Confirmation of Death (2008), Academy of Medical Royal Colleges, section 6.3, at page 19:

http://www.aomrc.org.uk/publications/reports-a-guidance.html

The diagnosis of death by brain stem testing should be made by at least two medical practitioners who have been registered for more than five years and are competent in the conduct and interpretation of brain stem testing. At least one of the doctors must be a consultant. Those carrying out the tests must not have, or be perceived to have, any clinical conflict of interest and neither doctor should be a member of the transplant team. Testing should be undertaken by the nominated doctors acting together and must always be performed on two occasions.

It is interesting that both doctors must not be part of the transplant team. This is because it may lead to bias or an enthusiasm to diagnose death too readily. The Academy also advises on the legal time of death.

EXTRACT

A Code of Practice for the Diagnosis and Confirmation of Death (2008), Academy of Medical Royal Colleges, section 6.3, at page 19:

http://www.aomrc.org.uk/publications/reports-a-guidance.html

If the first set of tests shows no evidence of brain stem function there need not be a lengthy delay prior to performing the second test. A short period of time will be necessary after reconnection to the ventilator. Although death is not confirmed until the second test has been completed the legal time of death is when the first test indicated death due to the absence of brain stem reflexes.

What is strange is that the time of death is recorded after the *first* test, even though a second test is required to confirm death. This poses some ethical questions: when is the patient considered to be dead? What if the second test shows a sign of life? Why is the second test even required if the time of death has already been recorded?

The Academy makes a final point at the very end of their 2008 Code about elective ventilation: a patient must *never* be put on an artificial ventilator simply to preserve his organs because he is receiving medical treatment that is not in his best interests (and is being forced to live to serve the best interests others).[36] This is a highly unethical practice, but as we shall see below, commentators have questioned its potential for the purposes of organ donation.

The controversy surrounding brain stem death

An artificial ventilator is commonly referred to as a 'life support machine'. When patients are attached to artificial ventilators to help them breathe, many of them go on to make a full recovery from their injuries. However, some patients die whilst on the ventilator, or it transpires after initial tests that they were already dead when placed on the ventilator. These patients are then removed from the ventilator, or taken into surgery (with the ventilator) for organ donation. There are ethical problems surrounding artificial ventilators. The relatives are 'fooled' into thinking that the patient is still alive because his heart is beating (although this will cease in time) and he is still breathing (but only because oxygen is being pumped into his lungs). The thought of a breathing patient – whose heart is still beating – being diagnosed as dead has not settled well with many commentators, and the idea of removing organs from these patients is even more macabre because it looks like the surgeon is killing the patient for his organs (even though a test has already declared him as dead). We would not bury or cremate a person whose heart is still beating, so is it ethical to remove organs from these patients when their brain stem is dead but their heart and lungs are still working?

A novel argument has previously proposed that brain stem dead patients should be anaesthetised before their organs are removed to ensure that they feel no pain. However, some commentators have rejected this argument because it is akin to anaesthetising a dead person.

EXTRACT

Robert Truog, 'Brain Death – Too Flawed to Endure, Too Ingrained to Abandon' (2007) *Journal of Law, Medicine and Ethics* 273, at pages 273–81

Most interesting is a debate that has occurred in the European anaesthesia literature regarding the question of whether brain dead patients should receive an anaesthetic during organ procurement. Some argue that the brain death criterion is insufficient to be absolutely sure that patients are incapable of experiencing pain, even if only at a rudimentary level, and so should receive 'the benefit of the doubt' and be given an anaesthetic. Others respond, not by defending the criterion itself, but by arguing that administration of anaesthesia to these patients will send a message to society that we are uncertain whether brain death is truly a state of permanent unconsciousness. As such, they argue, administration of an anaesthetic to these patients will undermine the trust of the public and jeopardise the organ transplantation enterprise.

Truog makes a good point: if we were to anaesthetise brain dead patients, it gives the impression that the medical profession do not believe the accuracy of their own brain stem death test. There are some commentators who doubt the validity of the brain stem death

---

[36] See note 32, section 7.3, at page 21.

test altogether, arguing that the test was simply designed for the purposes of organ transplantation to ensure that the organs were as fresh as possible on removal. It is, after all, a concept designed by humans for humans. We do not refer to animals as brain stem dead – we can generally tell when an animal is dead and when it is alive. The human patient is therefore not really dead in the traditional sense, but by conveniently dangling him between life and death we can do more with him, including donating his organs to others. The parties who benefit from this 'dangling' between life and death are recipients awaiting organs, transplant surgeons, the general public who fear they may one day need a transplant, and the government (in cost-saving terms). This looks like the utilitarian approach to diagnosing death: it sacrifices the rights of the minority (the deceased donor) to benefit the majority.

Artificial ventilators have also opened up the possibility of death itself being redefined to allow for a new 'control centre' for the human body. The brain was considered to be the control centre because it was responsible for the many functions of the body, but now it appears that a person can remain 'alive' for weeks or even months on an artificial ventilator even though their brain, i.e. 'control centre', has died, leading to confusion as to when a human passes into a state of death and whether we can now delay death when it was once viewed as 'the inevitable'.

Modern technology in hospitals has clearly blurred the boundary between life and death. In poor countries where artificial ventilators are not available, the patient simply dies when his body can no longer maintain life. This is a very traditional and natural death, and there is no need for a brain stem test to confirm death. In developed countries, we attach patients to artificial ventilators to aid recovery. What is to stop us from abolishing these complicated machines and returning to traditional medicine, thus abolishing the brain stem death test along with them? Well, many patients survive after being maintained on artificial ventilators, so they do save a lot of lives. It would be a very big step backwards in terms of pioneering medical treatment if we were to abolish artificial ventilators simply because they blur the boundary between life and death. In truth, it could be argued that the boundary between life and death has never been settled anyway. When does a person die? When their brain is dead? When their heart stops beating? When they are decomposing? When their spirit leaves their body? When they are in a coma? When they no longer derive any pleasure out of life? We do not know the answer and it varies depending on profession and belief, but medicine requires a definition of death for legal reasons and so the brain stem is what we have adopted. It might be a better idea to view death as a process, and ascertain at which part of the process is it ethically and legally acceptable to remove vital organs. This is more difficult than it sounds. In order to maintain public trust in the organ transplant system, it must be made clear that organs are removed when the donor is deceased, and that surgeons do not play a part in 'killing' the donor in order to remove a fresh heart, liver or stomach. It is argued in the three extracts below that we should simply accept that some dead donors are still alive, but this does not sit right with medicine, society, religion or the law.

EXTRACT

Julian Savulescu, 'Death, Us and Our Bodies: Personal Reflections' (2003) 29 *Journal of Medical Ethics* 127, at pages 127–30

Since I believe we die when our meaningful mental life ceases, organs should be available from that point, which may significantly predate death. At the very least, people should be allowed to complete advance directives that direct that their organs be removed when their brain is severely damaged or they are permanently unconscious.

EXTRACT

R. Truog and W. Robinson, 'Role of Brain Death and the Dead Donor Rule in the Ethics of Organ Transplantation' (2003) 31 *Critical Care Medicine* 2391, at pages 2391–6

In some circumstances we believe that the harm of dying is sufficiently small that patients or surrogates should be allowed to voluntarily accept it to be able to donate organs. For example, some might say that if they were ever diagnosed as being permanently unconscious they would accept the harm of dying if this would make it possible for them to donate their organs to others. Similarly, some patients who are imminently dying might be willing to have their life shortened by a few minutes or hours if this would make organ donation possible. [...] Proposals similar to ours have been suggested by others over the years. All involved shifting the key ethical question from 'is the patient dead?' to 'are the harms of removing life-sustaining organs sufficiently small that patients or surrogates should be allowed to consent to donation?'

EXTRACT

M. Potts and D. Evans, 'Does it Matter that Organ Donors are Not Dead? Ethical and Policy Implications' (2005) 31 *Journal of Medical Ethics* 406, at pages 406–9

Truog and Robinson's proposals that unpaired vital organs be removed from 'brain dead' and other classes of patients can be seen as the endorsement of killing people for their organs. One difficulty with this is that once utilitarian considerations are used to justify killing ventilator/dependant patients who are dying, those same considerations could also be used to justify killing non-ventilator/dependant patients or patients who are not dying. [...] Currently, the statement on organ donor cards asserts that organs may be taken 'after my death'. We believe that such wording should be changed to reflect the fact that 'brain dead' individuals are not dead in the usual understanding of what death is. Explanatory literature accompanying organ donor cards should be frank that a 'brain dead' donor's heart is beating during part of the organ removal surgery.

Savulescu believes that we die when 'meaningful mental life ceases', but this includes elderly people, patients who have had strokes, patients who are in a coma, patients who suffer from degenerative mental diseases and children with severe mental disorders. This is an extreme view, purporting that organs should be removed from vulnerable and disabled people, which is entirely inappropriate. Truog believes that two groups of patients – those who are permanently unconscious and those who are imminently dying – should have their organs removed, thus shortening their lives by a few minutes or hours. The word 'shortened' is a gentle word for 'killed' which is rather difficult to justify. This is almost like a form of euthanasia, where the patient consents to being killed by a medical professional. In real life this would be rare in any event, because a person who is imminently dying is clearly fatally diseased or injured, making her organs inappropriate for donation. Truog also proposes to conveniently 'shift the ethical question' but ethical questions cannot simply be 'shifted' to allow for previously unethical practices to be accepted – it doesn't work that way. Potts criticises Truog for condoning the killing of the patient at the hands of the surgeon, and rightly argues that it will inevitably form a slippery slope into euthanasia, where patients are being killed regardless of whether or not they are dependent on artificial ventilators. Potts proposes a change to donor cards, which are quite outdated now but are still carried around by a few people. They should be changed to state that deceased donors are sometimes heartbeating donors, i.e. they are still connected to their life support machine at the time of donation. This would probably alarm the public, but it is a true statement which may lead to a drop in support for the organ donation programme.

One suggestion to overcome the difficulty of defining the moment of death has been to accept two definitions of death: when the person dies, and when the body dies. This seems a bit far-fetched, but because it is better to remove organs from a body where the blood supply is still working, perhaps this approach will answer some of the ethical questions surrounding heartbeating donors?

EXTRACT

TorbjornTannsjo, 'Two Concepts of Death Reconciled' (1999) 2 *Medicine, Healthcare and Philosophy* 41, at pages 41–6

We can now define death of a person as the point at which the person in question ceases to exist. This happens when there is too little psychological continuity and connectedness left over. If there is no consciousness at all, then there is no person at all. And we can define the death of the body as the point at which the body ceases to function as a unified organism. This means that bodies, in contradistinction to persons, often continue to exist after their death. [...] But could it not be objected that to have a beating heart is to be a person? I do not think that this is a plausible move. First of all, it could simply be rejected on linguistic grounds. Most of us would not call someone without a working brain, someone whose brain had irreversibly ceased to exist, a 'person'. Secondly, and more importantly, even if some would do so, they would still have to admit that something of importance was gone once someone's brain had ceased to exist. In particular, even those who reject the brain death criterion do typically accept that we stop ventilating people whose brains have irreversibly ceased to function. What they object to as manipulative is merely the saying that these people are 'dead'.

Tannsjo puts forward a very clear rationale for splitting the process of death into two: a 'person' can be distinguished from a 'body' on the grounds that the body continues to exist for many thousands of years, whereas the personality is long gone. However, as logical and as believable as this distinction is, the general public simply wouldn't buy it. We instinctively recognise a dead person. A relative is dead in our eyes when they have no signs of life – their breathing has stopped, their heartbeat has stopped, and their personality has gone too. To redefine death as a two-part process may be to go against our natural instincts.

Expanding the general definition of death: anencephalic babies, vegetative patients and elective ventilation

The controversy surrounding the brain stem death test is that it is too narrow, i.e. a person is not necessarily clinically dead when their brain stem has ceased to function. This differs to the policy in most other developed countries (including the USA) where the whole brain must be dead to diagnose death. In the event that the brain stem death test does not accurately diagnose death, which some argue that it does not, should we openly admit this and widen the definition of death to include patients whose brain stem is alive and do not need an artificial ventilator but appear to be experiencing a living death? There are two categories of patients who fall into this category: persistent vegetative state patients and anencephalic babies.

In persistent vegetative state patients, the top half of the brain which controls the capacity for consciousness has died but the bottom half of the brain which controls the capacity to breathe is still alive, and so the brain stem is also still alive. This means that not only to they fail the brain stem death test, but they can often breathe on their own without a ventilator. They will probably not wake up and must be fed through a tube so they are still alive in the clinical sense, but they will no longer 'live' in the social sense. Anencephalic babies are very similar in that they are born with significant parts of the brain missing, but the brain stem is still alive, meaning that they will never become conscious and must feed through a tube. Two questions will now be asked: (i) should we modify the definition of death to include this small group of patients, who often have a full collection of healthy organs to donate, or (ii) should we place them onto an artificial ventilator at the moment of death to maintain the quality of their organs, even though this would not be in their best interests?

Firstly, it has been suggested that the definition of death should be expanded to include patients who are not brain dead but who are experiencing a living death, or are permanently unconscious. This would ensure that more organs can be harvested and that they are in a very good condition. A supportive argument for this suggestion would be that, once the capacity for consciousness has permanently ceased, the patient cannot experience pain. Therefore, the patient will not be harmed by the removal of her organs. They also have no best interests in being alive, and so if the law can permit the withdrawal of life-sustaining treatment, e.g. a feeding tube as in *Bland*, then why not remove their organs too? There are several problems with this argument. Firstly, the removal of the organs would kill the patient. Secondly, it is not universally agreed that a persistent vegetative patient has no best interests in being alive, so to remove their organs on this ground would be equally controversial. Thirdly, to harvest unconscious patients for their organs shows a significant disrespect to them as human beings. They are not simply 'recyclable materials' that we can dispose of when we wish. They are living people with beating hearts, breathing lungs and grieving families, who would be very unlikely to consent to the donation in these circumstances anyway. Fourthly, the slippery slope argument rears its head again, reminding us that once we begin to expend the definition of death to include persistent vegetative patients and anencephalic babies, we will eventually include others. This could cover the elderly, people suffering from severe mental illnesses, or other disabled members of society. Where will the list stop? It might expand over the next one hundred years to eventually include all 'distasteful' characters in society such as prisoners, paedophiles and the poor. This would have a terrible effect on the doctor–patient relationship leading to distrust, suspicion and a radical shift in power. Doctors would become the guardians of society, taking 'damaged' people off the streets and disposing of them for their organs. This utilitarian approach to organ donation could spiral out of control. Fifthly, it is not a good idea to expand the definition of death simply to ensure that we can recover a good number of organs. The definition of death should be based on medical criteria only, and if we were ever to get lost in the many definitions of death to achieve different goals, we should look to the animal kingdom to remind us of how simple and natural the definition of death should be.

Secondly, it has been suggested that we should place permanently unconscious patients or anencephalic babies onto artificial ventilators when they are very close to death to maintain the quality of their organs. The rationale behind this idea is that the patient is almost dead anyway, so why not keep them alive a little longer in order to harvest their organs? When they eventually die (via brain stem death), they are already hooked up to the machine and ready to go into surgery. The massive criticism to this suggestion is that medical treatment must only be given to a patient if it is in her *best interests*, and if it is not it should be withdrawn at once (this is the law). The patient will not benefit from elective ventilation if she has absolutely no chance of recovery, and so it is merely benefiting a third party (i.e. the organ recipient). This is unlawful medical treatment and will constitute an assault (in criminal law) or a trespass to the person (in civil law). In the words of Lord Browne-Wilksinson in *Airedale NHS Trust v Bland*:

> If there comes a stage where the responsible doctor comes to the reasonable conclusion that further continuance of an intrusive life support system is not in the best interests of the patient, he can no longer lawfully continue that life support system: to do so would constitute the crime of battery and the tort of trespass to the person.[37]

The Academy of Royal Medical Colleges has already confirmed that anencephalic babies and adults (who are removed from ventilators because their condition is grave) should not be placed on elective ventilation to maintain their organs.

EXTRACT

A Code of Practice for the Diagnosis and Confirmation of Death (2008), Academy of Medical Royal Colleges, section 7.3, at page 21:

http://www.aomrc.org.uk/publications/reports-a-guidance.html

It may become clear that, whether or not death of the brain has actually occurred, the patient's condition is inevitably going to be fatal. In such a case, withdrawal of ventilator support, ideally following discussion with the patient's relatives, may be the most appropriate course. The patient will usually start to make some respiratory effort for a period of time following withdrawal of ventilator support. In this situation, although further active treatment is inappropriate, transfer to a Critical Care Unit may allow the family to spend time with their dying relative, during which palliative care can be provided (i.e. painkillers) in an environment that is dignified for the patient and supportive for the relatives. A similar situation exists in the case of a spontaneously breathing baby with a lethal congenital anomaly such as anencephaly. In both these situations endotracheal intubation and artificial ventilation of the patient should only be initiated and maintained to further the patient's benefit and not as a means of preserving organ function.

Elective ventilation is not practical for a few reasons. Firstly, if we were to move all of the gravely ill patients into Intensive Care units and connect them to artificial ventilators and wait for them to die for their organs, this would be a waste of NHS resources. An artificial ventilator is an expensive piece of equipment and there is always a shortage of such things in hospitals. It could and should be used to treat other patients who have a much better prospect of recovery. The alternative view, of course, is that the dying patient will in fact save several lives when she donates her organs and this will, in turn, save the government a lot of money in healthcare costs, so the use of the bed and equipment to ventilate a dying patient could be justified. Secondly, what if the doctors are wrong in their prognosis? What if, instead of dying, the patient falls into a persistent vegetative state with no prospect of recovery? This would be a disaster: not only would we be ventilating a patient who does not need it, treating him against his best interests

---

[37] See Lord Browne-Wilkinson in *Airedale NHS Trust v Bland* [1993] AC 789, at page 884.

and prolonging his death, but we may even be harming him. In real life it would be very unlikely for this scenario to occur because a patient in a persistent vegetative state has a living brain stem, whereas a patient moved into Intensive Care following a grave prognosis is probably on the cusp of death. However, it is not an impossibility. Thirdly, the patient may wake up and make a full recovery and learn that his family elected for him to receive medical treatment that was not in his best interests to preserve his organs. Who is to know what psychological effect this may have on a patient? Fourthly, the patient may succumb to an unexpected hospital or viral infection whilst in Intensive Care (which is not uncommon), making his organs unsuitable for donation after all. A patient can escape all of these traumatic possibilities by making an advance directive, refusing all medical treatment in the event of grave injury or disease.

It is not outside the realms of possibility that one day, in the foreseeable future, the courts may see the elective ventilation of a dying patient as supportive of his best interests. For example, in *Re Y (Mental Patient: Bone Marrow Donation)* [1997] Fam 110 the courts allowed a bone marrow donation to take place on an incompetent patient. This was found to be in her best interests because she was saving her sister which in turn enabled the mother to continue her visitation. This was not really in the best interests of the patient – it was in the best interests of the sister and mother – so this precedent runs against the grain of accepted medical law. However, the courts could one day use *Re Y* to bend the rules on elective ventilation and allow for a dying patient to be placed on a ventilator in order to preserve her organs to benefit a whole host of third parties. This outcome may be even more likely if the patient is found to have no best interests in being alive, as confirmed in *Airedale NHS Trust v Bland* [1993] AC 789. The only other way in which elective ventilation could escape the 'best interests' debate was if the patient was attached to the artificial ventilator after the moment of death. A deceased person does not have any legal rights and there is no longer an obligation to treat the patient in accordance with his best interests, so it would technically be lawful because it would not be classed as 'treatment'.

ACTIVITY

The concept of elective ventilation is highly controversial because it provides unnecessary treatment to benefit not the patient but a third party. Imagine that you sit in the House of Lords and a hospital trust has asked for permission to electively ventilate a mother – who has been in a serious car accident – to save her son, who is on the liver transplant waiting list. Write a judgment to legalise elective ventilation. How will you legally handle the 'best interests' issue?

How can we increase the number of donated organs?

This chapter has explored the organ allocation procedure, the rules regarding consent and the definition of death so far, and one thing is still abundantly clear: there is a shortage of human organs available for donation. It has been shown that between April 2012 and March 2013 a total of 466 patients died while waiting on the organ donor register.[38] Key statistics relating to organ donation are shown below:

---

[38] Taken from: Transplant Activity in the UK – Activity Report, 2012/13, NHS Blood and Transplant, at page 2. See: http://www.organdonation.nhs.uk/statistics/transplant_activity_report/.

- The number of people needing a transplant is expected to *rise steeply* over the next decade due to an ageing population, an increase in kidney failure and scientific advances resulting in more people being suitable for a transplant.
- Black people are *three times* more likely than the general population to develop kidney failure.
- The need for organs (kidneys in particular) in the Asian community is *three to four times* higher than that of the white community. This is because conditions such as diabetes and heart disease – that can result in organ failure – occur more often in the Asian population.[39]
- Asian and African-Caribbean patients make up 23% of the kidney waiting list, but they represent only 8% of the population, showing a significant shortage in organs for certain ethnic groups.
- Only 3% of deceased donors are Asian or African Caribbean. It would be interesting to know why this was, but research is currently thin on the ground.[40]

NHS Blood and Transplant (NHSBT) states that, between 1 April 2014 and 20 May 2014, the following procedures took place:

- 170 people have donated organs;
- 301 additional people have donated corneas;
- 433 people have received the gift of sight;
- 430 people have received transplants;
- 6,934 people are still waiting for a transplant.[41]

We are a long way from the point of mass production of human organs in the laboratory. There are several ways in which the number of donated organs could potentially be increased, and they are explored in this section.

The UK and the organ donor register

In the UK, the general public can voluntarily register their consent to donation on the Organ Donor Register. This is known as the 'opt-in system' and will be explored in detail below. The Organ Donor Register is the official way of registering a desire to donate organs on the event of death, but a person is free to remove their details at any time. There are several ways to join the Organ Donor Register, including through the Boots Advantage Card, the European Health Insurance Card, through a General Practitioner, when applying for a driving licence with the Driver and Vehicle Licensing Authority (DVLA), when applying for a passport with the Passport Agency, and via the Organ Donation and Transplantation website. Some 58% of registrations come through the DVLA route.[42] There are statistics available to illustrate how important the Organ Donor Register is to the organ transplant programme:

---

[39] http://www.organdonation.nhs.uk/newsroom/fact_sheets/did_you_know.asp.

[40] Organs for Transplants: A Report from the Organ Donation Taskforce, Department of Health, January 2008, (archived), at page 4: http://webarchive.nationalarchives.gov.uk/20130107105354/http://www.dh.gov.uk/en/Publicationsandstatistics/Publications/PublicationsPolicyAndGuidance/DH_082122.

[41] www.organdonation.nhs.uk, accessed on 20 May 2013.

[42] Taken from: Transplant Activity in the UK – Activity Report, 2012/13, NHS Blood and Transplant, at page 108. See: http://www.organdonation.nhs.uk/statistics/transplant_activity_report/.

- Repeated surveys show that the majority of the public support organ donation. The last survey conducted in 2003 for UK Transplant showed that 90% of people support organ donation.

- All the major religions support organ donation and many actively promote it.

- 30% of people on the NHS Organ Donor Register are aged between 16 and 25 when they join, and a further 24% are aged between 26 and 35.9% are 65 or over when they join.[43]

The number of people on the Organ Donor Register is slowly but steadily increasing. In 2012/13 for example, the grand total was over 19.5 million names (31% of the population).[44] The number of patients on the waiting list is steadily rising by approximately 8% every year but there is still a long way to go and the gap between donors and recipients is widening.[45] Interestingly, of the 1,212 deceased organ donors in 2012/13, only 38% of them were registered on the Organ Donor Register.[46] This illustrates just how effective transplant teams are at finding additional sources of organ donations from patients in hospitals who have not registered their names for organ donation but their families are willing to consent for them. There are interesting statistics available on the type of people who join the register:

- It was shown that by the end of March 2013, the highest proportion of registrations were in the 21–30 age group, of which 22% were males and 24% were females.

- The lowest proportion of registrations were for children between 11–15 years old.

- A larger proportion of women (52%) than men (48%) have signed up to the NHS Organ Donor Register.[47]

The Organ Donor Register was launched in 1994 following a campaign by a donor family – John and Rosemary Cox – whose son Peter died in 1989 following a brain tumour. Peter expressed a wish to donate his organs upon his death to help others, but there was no formal system in place to register consent to organ donation. The register now contains the forename, surname, date of birth, sex and address of all registered donors, and individual records are matched with NHS numbers to avoid duplication. Donors can opt to donate all organs and tissues or specific organs only, including kidneys, heart, lungs, liver, pancreas and eyes. By the end of 1995, more than 2 million donors had registered their details. This soared to 8 million by the millennium, 12 million in 2005 and 16 million by 2009, which was the original government target set in 2001.[48] There are currently 20,333,750 donors on the register as of 20 May 2014, and this might seem impressive but it is only 31% of the UK population, and many of these donors will probably not be suitable for donation at the time of death anyway because of injury, old age or disease.[49]

---

[43] http://www.organdonation.nhs.uk/newsroom/fact_sheets/did_you_know.asp.

[44] Taken from: Transplant Activity in the UK – Activity Report, 2012/13, NHS Blood and Transplant, at page 105. See: http://www.organdonation.nhs.uk/statistics/transplant_activity_report/.

[45] Organs for Transplants: A Report from the Organ Donation Taskforce, Department of Health, January 2008 (archived) at page 4: http://webarchive.nationalarchives.gov.uk/20130107105354/http://www.dh.gov.uk/en/Publicationsandstatistics/Publications/PublicationsPolicyAndGuidance/DH_082122.

[46] Taken from: Transplant Activity in the UK – Activity Report, 2012/13, NHS Blood and Transplant, at page 108. See: http://www.organdonation.nhs.uk/statistics/transplant_activity_report/.

[47] See note above, at page 110.

[48] http://www.organdonation.nhs.uk/newsroom/fact_sheets/nhs_organ_donor_register_a_history.asp.

[49] See the official homepage: http://www.organdonation.nhs.uk/.

The UK and its 'opt in system' for donation

KEY DEFINITION	**Opt-in system**: the general public can choose to be organ donors. **Opt-out system**: the general public are assumed to be donors until they issue a refusal. **Hard opt-out system**: only the donor can opt out. **Soft opt-out system**: the donor's relatives can be consulted and can opt him out. **Hard opt-in system**: only the donor can opt in. **Soft opt-in system**: the donor's relatives can be consulted and can opt him in.

In the UK we can choose to join the Organ Donor Register. This is known as an 'opt-in system' and means that, for the majority of us, we can freely choose to donate our organs and tissues in the event of our death. For the small selection of people who do not make a decision during their lifetime, i.e. incompetent patients or children, they may find that their relatives will make the decision for them. The opt-in system of organ donation supports the principles of consent and autonomy by giving the patient the freedom to decide what she wants to do with her body (although consultation of relatives may erode this).

The opt-in system is a potential problem for NHS Blood and Transplant, because it does not have nearly enough organ donors to cater for the thousands of patients on the transplant waiting list. However, contrary to common belief, this shortage of organs is not just down to the opt-in system. The potential influences on low donation rates include: fewer fatal car accidents, public awareness is not as comprehensive as it could be, religion may impose a personal restriction to donation, cultural attitudes may also form a barrier to donation, people do not want to discuss or be confronted by their own death, more of us are living longer, although this is likely to change with the 'junk-food' generation, many dead patients are not suitable for donation because of injury or disease, and in the next few decades we will see the sickest elderly generation ever with record levels of heart disease, diabetes and obesity. It is therefore debatable whether switching to an opt-out system – where everyone is automatically listed for donation until they remove their name – would change the organ donation landscape drastically, but it is worth exploring as a real possibility.

Opt-in system (i.e. patient chooses to consent/register for donation)	Opt-out system (i.e. patient assumed to consent until they refuse)
USA	Spain
Ireland	Austria
Denmark	Portugal
Canada	Belgium
UK	France
Netherlands	Italy
Germany	Finland
Australia	Norway
Switzerland	Poland
New Zealand	Sweden
Japan	Israel

Brazil does not feature in the list above but it has an interesting story. In 1997 it moved from the 'opt-in system' to a strict 'opt-out system' where every donor was assumed to consent to the removal of all organs and tissues unless he registered an official objection.

The new law was repealed only one year later as a result of significant mistrust in the medical system and a massive opt-out movement.[50]

Improvements to the UK organ donation system

Can the UK do anything to improve its own donation rates? This issue has been investigated thoroughly in recent years. In January 2008, the Organ Donation Taskforce published an independent report containing fourteen recommendations for increasing our donation rate by a staggering 50% within five years (from 2008 to 2013). The idea was to provide an additional 1,200 transplants every year by improving our current system.[51] The report claimed that such an increase in organ donation depended on three key issues: donor identification and referral, donor coordination and organ retrieval arrangements.[52] In order to improve these systems, the following matters were earmarked for attention: legal and ethical issues, the role of the NHS, organisation of coordination and retrieval, training, public recognition and public promotion of donation.[53] The recommendations were administrative rather than sweeping, and would have no doubt required a lot of money to put into practice. The economic downturn had not properly manifested itself when this report was published in 2008, so it was not clear how many of the recommendations had been implemented. It was announced in 2013 that NHSBT has in fact met their objective of a 50% rise in donations.

Should we switch to 'opt-out'?

The Organ Donation Taskforce completed further research to investigate whether or not an opt-out system would be practicable in the UK. It published a second independent report in November 2008 which explored the potential legal, ethical and procedural implications of such a radical shift in policy. The report bizarrely concluded that it was not the right time to implement an opt-out system, despite most of the top ten transplant countries using the very same system to harvest significantly higher numbers of organs:

Top ten organ donation countries	
1. Spain	6. Ireland (opt in)
2. Austria	7. France
3. Portugal	8. Italy
4. Belgium	9. Finland
5. USA (opt in)	10. Norway.[54]

---

[50] 'The Potential Impact of an Opt Out System for Organ Donation in the UK, An Independent Report from the Organ Donation Taskforce', Department of Health, November 2008 (archived) at page 23: http://webarchive.nationalarchives.gov.uk/20130107105354/http://www.dh.gov.uk/en/Publicationsandstatistics/Publications/PublicationsPolicyAndGuidance/DH_090312.

[51] Organs for Transplants: A Report from the Organ Donation Taskforce, Department of Health, January 2008 (archived) at page 3: http://webarchive.nationalarchives.gov.uk/20130107105354/http://www.dh.gov.uk/en/Publicationsandstatistics/Publications/PublicationsPolicyAndGuidance/DH_082122.

[52] See note above.

[53] See note above, at page 5.

[54] The Potential Impact of an Opt Out System for Organ Donation in the UK, An Independent Report from the Organ Donation Taskforce, Department of Health, November 2008 (archived) at page 23, http://webarchive.nationalarchives.gov.uk/20130107105354/http://www.dh.gov.uk/en/Publicationsandstatistics/Publications/PublicationsPolicyAndGuidance/DH_090312.

The reasons for rejecting an opt-out system were numerous, as detailed below.

> ## EXTRACT
>
> ### The Potential Impact of an Opt Out System for Organ Donation in the UK, An Independent Report from the Organ Donation Taskforce, Department of Health, November 2008 (archived):
>
> http://webarchive.nationalarchives.gov.uk/20130107105354/
> http://www.dh.gov.uk/en/Publicationsandstatistics/Publications/
> PublicationsPolicyAndGuidance/DH_090312
>
> **Paragraph 1.5:** [We] revealed an apparent correlation between high donation rates and opt out systems in countries around the world. However, presumed consent alone does not explain the variation in organ donation rates between the different countries. Many other factors affect donation rates.
>
> **Paragraph 1.9:** [We] heard persuasive arguments from health professionals about the potentially negative implications for clinical practice, especially the potential to damage the vital relationship of trust between clinicians caring for people at the end of life, their patients and their families.
>
> **Paragraph 1.10:** Recipients of organs stressed their need to know that organs had been freely given by donors and their families . . . donor families often find great comfort in being an active part of the decision to donate.
>
> **Paragraph 1.11:** It became increasingly clear that it would be both complex in practical terms and also costly to put in place an opt out system that could command the trust of professionals and members of the public. There would need to be a significant and sustained communications programme to ensure that all members of society knew about the new system and what it would mean for them. Real concerns were expressed about the security of information on an opt out register, this issue would need to be addressed by using a robust and secure IT system.
>
> **Paragraph 1.12:** [There is a] perception that assuming consent from silence belongs to a more paternalistic era. Some felt that an opt out system could be 'dehumanising'. Given that current trends in healthcare place great emphasis on choice and responsiveness, this is an important consideration.
>
> **Paragraph 10.15:** Given the lack of awareness about organ donation among the general public, the Taskforce believes that there are simpler and easier ways of substantially increasing the numbers of organs available for donation, without the complexity and difficulties of trying to implement an opt out system.
>
> **Paragraph 11.5:** The Taskforce is not confident that the introduction of opt out legislation would increase organ donor numbers, and there is evidence that donor numbers may go down (e.g. Brazil).
>
> **Paragraph 15.2 (conclusion):** Taskforce members had a wide range of views at the outset. However, after examining the evidence, the Taskforce reached a clear consensus in recommending that an opt out system should not be introduced in the UK at the present time. The Taskforce concluded that such a system has the potential to undermine the concept of donation as a gift, to erode trust in NHS professionals and the Government, and negatively impact on organ donation numbers. It would distract attention away from essential improvements to systems and infrastructure and from the urgent need to improve public awareness and understanding of organ donation. Furthermore, it would be challenging and costly to implement successfully. Most compelling of all, we found no convincing evidence that it would deliver significant increases in the number of donated organs.

Many of the reasons for rejection listed above are not, it can be argued, serious enough to warrant a complete rejection of the opt-out system. For example, there is no need to distrust NHS professionals if donors can still voluntarily remove their names from the register and family members can still be consulted (i.e. *soft* opt-out system). In addition, there is nothing to suggest that the Organ Donor Register for an opt-out system needs to be any more secure than the current opt-in register. There is no difference between the two. Finally, it is all very well basking in the glow of receiving a 'gift' of an organ, but if we wish to save more lives we may have to move away from 'altruism' and focus on 'treatment'.

'Opt-out system' = presumed consent

The opt-out system of organ donation is often referred to as 'presumed consent' by commentators, and it is a highly controversial approach to organ donation. Traditionally, consent is a free and voluntary act in medical law, but an opt-out system will allow organ donation to take place on an *assumption* of consent instead, i.e. no real consent has been provided. The Taskforce erred on the side of caution and did not express a view either way, but some commentators are very clear in their opinions.

EXTRACT

The Potential Impact of an Opt Out System for Organ Donation in the UK, An Independent Report from the Organ Donation Taskforce, Department of Health, November 2008 (archived):

http://webarchive.nationalarchives.gov.uk/20130107105354/
http://www.dh.gov.uk/en/Publicationsandstatistics/Publications/
PublicationsPolicyAndGuidance/DH_090312

Paragraph 4.3: A system of presumed consent is often described as consent for the disorganised. Many argue that having such a system would more accurately reflect majority wishes, allowing donation to become the default position. This is a powerful argument for the introduction of presumed consent. On the other hand, some people are concerned that a proportion of the population who would not have wished to donate their organs, but never got round to registering an objection, could mistakenly be considered as willing donors under an opt out system.

EXTRACT

L. Cherkassky, 'Presumed consent in organ donation: is the duty finally upon us?' [2010] 17(2) *European Journal of Health Law* 149, at pages 157–158

The doctrine of presumed consent assumes not only that every individual in the land is consenting to a particular procedure, but that every such individual is aware of what he is consenting to. This is a dangerous assumption. There are many groups of people, from many cultures and backgrounds, who may not understand such a law. The influx of migrant workers in the UK from other European countries means that many of our inhabitants may have difficulty comprehending the new legislation. Others may not wish to be a part of the new law but do not understand how to register an objection, some may not have ever heard of the new law, and others may be too lethargic to investigate the law. Individuals may feel pressured into consenting to donation simply because the act of opting-out could be viewed as anti-social.

The argument that people who object to donation may be 'too disorganised' to remove their name from the register does not hold much force when we consider that this already happens in our current opt-in system: a person may register his name, change his mind ten years later, and forget to remove his name again. However, let us assume for a moment that presumed consent is a bad thing because it allows organs to be taken from dead donors without their free and informed consent. Why is this a problem when the donor is dead? He cannot bring a criminal or legal action against the clinical staff for performing an unlawful medical procedure upon his body, so perhaps for this category of patients, an assumed consent is sufficient? There may be legal implications, as explored by the Taskforce below, in the guise of successful challenges under the European Convention on Human Rights if a presumed consent system was adopted.

EXTRACT

The Potential Impact of an Opt Out System for Organ Donation in the UK, An Independent Report from the Organ Donation Taskforce, Department of Health, November 2008 (archived):

http://webarchive.nationalarchives.gov.uk/20130107105354/
http://www.dh.gov.uk/en/Publicationsandstatistics/Publications/
PublicationsPolicyAndGuidance/DH_090312

Paragraph 6.2: The legal group concluded that simply having a register where people could record their decision (opting either in or out) during their lifetime, without involving families at the time of death, would probably be insufficient to ensure compliance with the ECHR because in an opt out system, it could result in organs being taken from those who had not yet managed to register an objection, perhaps because they were simply busy or disorganised. Therefore, any system must allow for taking evidence from family members about the deceased's wishes and beliefs. If the law were to be changed to an opt out system, this would be necessary to enable the presumption of consent to be rebutted if there was evidence that the deceased did not wish to be a donor, even though they had not recorded this decision on a register. If this were not provided for, the Legal Working Group considered that there would be a significant risk of successful legal challenge.

It is not clear who would make a legal claim and what would be achieved by it, especially if the donor had the option to remove his name from the register and simply never did so. This would mean that the surgeon was acting lawfully. It is accepted that relatives may become upset if organs are taken from their loved one in the face of their firm objections and so legal actions may arise out of hurt and anger, but the courts are not likely to sympathise unless the donor was incapacitated in some way and was thus taken advantage of. It is anticipated that special provisions would be put in place for vulnerable donors anyway, or they could be exempt from the system altogether – discussed below. There are certainly no legal problems in Austria who operate a hard opt-out system, i.e. relatives are not consulted at all, and boast a very high donation rate.

The ethics of an opt-out system

The ethical complications of an opt-out system must also be explored. The opt-out system enables surgeons to remove organs from donors who did not freely and voluntary consent in the traditional sense, meaning that a shift in power (from patient to surgeon) could lead to an erosion of trust and a change in how medical care is perceived and performed.

EXTRACT

The Potential Impact of an Opt Out System for Organ Donation in the UK, An Independent Report from the Organ Donation Taskforce, Department of Health, November 2008 (archived):

http://webarchive.nationalarchives.gov.uk/20130107105354/
http://www.dh.gov.uk/en/Publicationsandstatistics/Publications/
PublicationsPolicyAndGuidance/DH_090312

Paragraph 8.2: A presumption of consent might make families feel that they were being pressured and erode the relationship of trust between clinician and family. Many people had concerns that their best interests might be jeopardised if they were seen to be potential organ donors. The fear that you might not actually be dead, with doctors 'jumping in too quickly' before 'someone is "definitely gone"' was one that was widely expressed. A system of decision-making which is based on respecting the known wishes of the patient is the one that is most likely to maintain the integrity of the relationship between doctors and patients and between doctors and the wider public, and maintain trust and confidence in the donation system.

Paragraph 8.4: There is an argument, advanced by some, that a system of presumed consent would relieve families of the burden of making a decision in the absence of any indication as to the deceased's wishes. The Taskforce finds this is a somewhat paternalistic view, at odds with the ethos of today's NHS. Further, our evidence from donor families was that they stressed the importance to them of being involved in the decision to donate and of being allowed to make the decision that was right for them at the time.

It is not clear how families will feel pressure if an opt-out system was adopted in the UK. The emphasis is on the *donor* to remove his name from the register, and the family should, in practice, have very little else to do with the process. In a soft opt-out system the families may be approached by the doctor to confirm the donor's views, but this is all. If anything, our current soft opt-in system applies much more pressure on families to consent to donation because the donor has not registered his views on the Organ Donor Register. If we are to 'respect the known wishes' of the donor, then surely we should refer to his decision to keep his name on the register, rather than ask his family what they think (in case they disagree with his decision). Families want to be involved with the decision to donate (Paragraph 8.4), but this does not support the autonomy of the donor. Organ donation is not a family decision, they are merely supporting evidence of the donor's decision. The Taskforce have not recognised that by refusing an opt-out system, they give far more control to families and far less control to donors.

The following piece illustrates just how an opt-out system would support the *donor's* autonomy:

EXTRACT

V. English and A. Sommerville, 'Presumed Consent for Transplantation: A Dead issue after Alder Hey?' (2003) 29 *Journal of Medical Ethics* 147, at pages 147–52

Arguably, simply changing the default position could have huge benefits. Not least for relatives themselves who, at a time of emotional upheaval and bereavement, may not relish being asked to decide in the absence of any indication of the wishes of the deceased. One of the advantages of a presumed consent system is that the main burden of making this decision is lessened for the relatives although they would still be involved. […] The possibility of relatives refusing donation when the deceased person actually wished to donate has already been mentioned. The opposite can also happen. Currently, individuals who strongly object to donation lack any formal mechanism for registering that objection and the decision to donate may ultimately be made by distant relatives. Under the opt in system, there are no guarantees that relatives will not act contrary to the strongly held views of a deceased person, either through lack of knowledge or lack of agreement with them. In this way, an opt out system where objections can be registered and must be respected, would enhance individual autonomy for those who do not want to be donors.

If the UK were to ever switch to an opt-out system of organ donation it would probably be the soft version, meaning that the family would be consulted and may, in some cases, have the final say. This may not seem too dissimilar to our current opt-in system, but there would be a subtle change in how doctors handle the situation. For example, in our current *soft opt-in system*, the family may make the decision if the patient is not listed. However, in a *soft opt-out system*, the patient has already been listed and the family simply confirm that no strong dissenting feelings have been aired before death. This could lead to a significant increase in consent rates from families because the pressure has been taken off them to make the final decision.

Barriers to an opt-out system

The barriers to implementing an opt-out system are considered by the Taskforce to be considerable and costly, but there is no evidence to support this. The smaller difficulties (listed below) can easily be overcome.

EXTRACT

The Potential Impact of an Opt Out System for Organ Donation in the UK, An Independent Report from the Organ Donation Taskforce, Department of Health, November 2008 (archived):

http://webarchive.nationalarchives.gov.uk/20130107105354/
http://www.dh.gov.uk/en/Publicationsandstatistics/Publications/
PublicationsPolicyAndGuidance/DH_090312

Paragraph 10.8: There is an assumption that those with strong objections to organ donation are likely to register their wishes, but this is not an assumption backed by evidence, and the disorganised may be as disadvantaged in an opt out system as in an opt in system.

Paragraph 10.9: There would need to be an initial public awareness programme, targeted so that it reached every UK adult. In addition, an on-going education and public awareness programme would be essential.

Paragraph 12.11: [The public] felt that it would give the State too much control and 'ownership' over people's organs, rather than giving individuals the right to choose what to do with their own bodies.

Paragraph 12.13: A small number believed that there was even a danger that donation rates might actually go down, for example if people opt out because they resent government interference, or to be on the 'safe side' if they have not fully understood the system.

It is likely that those with strong objections *would* register their objections, because they would want to 'make a stand' against the whole system of presumed consent. However, the State would not 'own' the organs and tissues of every adult – it should be made clear that a rejection can be registered at any GP surgery, town hall, etc.

Vulnerable donors will need to be carefully considered if an opt-out system were to be implemented. The following groups of people may be taken advantage of if they are not able to register their objection:

- People with mental illnesses.
- Minors.
- The elderly.
- The poor/uneducated.
- Prisoners.
- The homeless.
- Disabled or handicapped people.
- People with strong religious preferences.
- People with learning disabilities.
- Non-citizens from all over the world.
- Other groups of people (e.g. teenagers who have joined cults).

The Taskforce notes that good communication is the key to protecting such vulnerable people (see their suggestion below), but is it right that such vulnerable donors are still to be 'presumed' to be consenting to organ donation when ordinarily they would be deemed incompetent to consent to a medical procedure? After all, just because a homeless person, for example, is told how to opt out, does not mean that he will find the means or the strength to do so.

EXTRACT

The Potential Impact of an Opt Out System for Organ Donation in the UK, An Independent Report from the Organ Donation Taskforce, Department of Health, November 2008 (archived):

http://webarchive.nationalarchives.gov.uk/20130107105354/
http://www.dh.gov.uk/en/Publicationsandstatistics/Publications/
PublicationsPolicyAndGuidance/DH_090312

Paragraph 14.1: Were an opt out system to be introduced, a communications strategy would need to be devised to ensure that all those people who wished to opt out entirely, or to opt out of the donation of particular organs or tissues, knew how to do so. In addition, communications would be needed to outline arrangements for special groups such as children, those lacking capacity and visitors to the UK. Consideration would need to be given to the information needs of ethnic minorities, those with English as a second language, and hard-to-reach groups, such as the homeless. The media campaign would need to be extensive both in its use of different forms of media and in its duration (over at least two years, prior to and after enactment of legislation). Such a campaign would require considerable resource (at least £45 million initially, with further reminder campaigns every few years).

EXTRACT

Cherkassky, L., 'Presumed consent in organ donation: is the duty finally upon us?' [2010] 17(2) *European Journal of Health Law* 149, at page 160

It is thought that those who are most unlikely to 'consent' are mentally impaired children and adults, non-citizens, and religious individuals. It also seems unlikely that non-citizens would consent to donating their organs to a strange country. If our Government were to procure their organs upon their death – thus 'presuming' their kindness towards us as hosts – this could be seen as simply taking advantage of international visitors.

It is very important that certain vulnerable groups are either removed from the opt-out system altogether or protected with extra regulations (i.e. family control). It is unlikely that a £45 million campaign would be required when a bulletin on the six o'clock news would reach most of the public, and leaflets in all supermarkets/shops/surgeries would reach the rest.

Improving our opt-in system

The Taskforce slowly talk their way out of adopting an opt-out system throughout their report, and begin to focus instead on what is wrong with our current opt-in system and how they could improve it.

EXTRACT

The Potential Impact of an Opt Out System for Organ Donation in the UK, An Independent Report from the Organ Donation Taskforce, Department of Health, November 2008 (archived):

http://webarchive.nationalarchives.gov.uk/20130107105354/
http://www.dh.gov.uk/en/Publicationsandstatistics/Publications/
PublicationsPolicyAndGuidance/DH_090312

Paragraph 1.5: [There is an] extremely low awareness of the Organ Donor Register. If a person's name is on this register, 90% of families consent to donation, compared with a general consent rate of about 60%. There is a clear need to publicise the register and to make the process of registering easier and more widely understood.

Paragraph 4.3: This illustrates a problem of inertia familiar to us all: always meaning to get round to doing something that is not top of the 'to do' list.

Paragraph 10.13 (recipient family view): 'We need to bring it into the national curriculum, perhaps as part of personal and social education issues. I think if we get children thinking about it when they are young, then at least they will have an opinion on it.'

Paragraph 12.6: A number of barriers to donation were identified, including lack of awareness, laziness, unwillingness to think about death and concerns about donation in practice. Many felt that these could be overcome within the current legal system with better publicity and education (including in schools) to dispel myths about organ donation, to encourage families to discuss the issues and to make registration easier. There is strong support from all for such changes.

Paragraph 12.7: Those who did not wish to register voiced a number of concerns, the chief of which were that you might not actually be dead when organs were retrieved and that there would be less effort to keep you alive if it was known that you were a potential donor. Older people thought it was not worth them registering as their organs would be 'worthless'.

It is a major concern that very few people know about the Organ Donor Register, and many people are afraid that they will not be dead when their organs are removed. There is clearly a need for better education on the issue of organ donation, no matter which system of consent we adopt in this country. The overall feeling is that, according to the Taskforce, there is much more to be done with our current opt-in system before we change to an opt-out system of presumed consent. Interestingly, the Taskforce sign off with a promise to revisit the issue if their target is not met.

EXTRACT

The Potential Impact of an Opt Out System for Organ Donation in the UK, An Independent Report from the Organ Donation Taskforce, Department of Health, November 2008 (archived):

http://webarchive.nationalarchives.gov.uk/20130107105354/
http://www.dh.gov.uk/en/Publicationsandstatistics/Publications/
PublicationsPolicyAndGuidance/DH_090312

Paragraph 15.7: The Taskforce shares the same passion for increasing the number of organ donors as those calling for presumed consent. It simply concludes that there is a way of getting to the same place by a different, less risky route. Only if donor numbers have not grown by 50% by 2013 should the question of opt out be revisited. Meanwhile, every effort should be made to deliver the potential for increase within the current legal system.

It transpired that they did reach their target in 2013 of a 50% increase, but a formal report has not been published as of June 2013 to explain in what way the donations have increased.

Mandated choice and required request

Mandated choice is like an election: the general public would be required to make a decision. There would be two options available if mandated choice was enforced: 'yes' to organ donation or 'no' to organ donation. The idea behind mandated choice is that everybody makes a decision at the same time, and indecision would thus be removed as a barrier to organ donation. No one would be forced into donation, but they would be forced to make a decision about donation. This would inevitably increase the number of names on the Organ Donor Register because indecision is a significant problem (only 29% of us are registered on the Organ Donor Register).[55] However, some people might not take kindly to being pressured into making a decision about such a personal matter, leading to a high number of rejections as a statement against the mandate. There is also another significant problem: people naturally change their minds as time goes on. Family tragedies may encourage someone to change their refusal to consent, and impending old age may encourage a pensioner to change her consent to a refusal. There would need to be an easily accessible database where changes could be registered daily, and this could be a significant expense if the whole country was required to register a decision, i.e. approximately 60 million people. Commentators have correctly submitted that a mandated choice will require considerable public education, otherwise how would they know what they were consenting to?

EXTRACT

P. Chouhan and H. Draper, 'Modified Mandated Choice for Organ Procurement' (2003) 29 *Journal of Medical Ethics* 157, at pages 157–68

Mandated choice requires competent adults to decide whether they wish to donate their organs after their deaths. Individuals are free to choose whether to donate, and even which organs they would like to donate: what they are not permitted to do is to fail to register their wishes. Individuals can also choose to let their relatives have the final say. Unless they are granted this right, however, the relatives have neither power nor opportunity to veto an individual's decision, whether it was for or against decision. [...] A move to mandated choice would also have to be accompanied by extensive public education so that when making their choices, people are sufficiently informed about both the need for choice and the implications of their decision. Finally, choices, though binding would also be revocable: indeed, people could change their minds as often as they wish, and the most recent choice would prevail. [...] To avoid coercion, registered choices would be confidential and no privileges would accrue from the particular choice made.

There are clearly many potential advantages to a mandated choice, including confidentiality, autonomy and clarity. However, there are smaller sections of society who cannot make a mandated choice, such as incompetent patients and children (who face the biggest shortage of all). The Taskforce was not supportive of mandated choice, and it listed the practical reasons why.

---

[55] See the homepage for statistics at: www.organdonation.nhs.uk.

EXTRACT

The Potential Impact of an Opt Out System for Organ Donation in the UK, An Independent Report from the Organ Donation Taskforce, Department of Health, November 2008 (archived):

http://webarchive.nationalarchives.gov.uk/20130107105354/
http://www.dh.gov.uk/en/Publicationsandstatistics/Publications/
PublicationsPolicyAndGuidance/DH_090312

Paragraph 6.5: There is some support for the concept of 'mandated choice', in which people would be legally obliged to opt in or opt out of organ donation at some point in their lives.

Paragraph 6.6: However, it would not resolve all potentially difficult issues; for example:

- Where a person dies having changed their mind but not having registered a revised decision;
- Where a person fails to comply with the requirement to choose, but nevertheless wished to donate; and
- Whether the feelings or views of the donor's family should carry any weight.

Paragraph 6.7: In general in the UK, we do not require people to make choices. For example, we do not make voting mandatory as it is in Australia. We encourage UK citizens to make choices but also allow them the right not to make choices. A system of mandated choice on organ donation would be a significant departure from established UK norms.

Paragraph 6.8: It is debateable whether such a system would be effective in practice, since it would be difficult to force people to make a decision if they do not want to. The Taskforce was uncomfortable with the idea of a legal sanction if people did not make a choice. Moreover, the Taskforce was concerned that if people were forced to choose, this might cause resentment and have a negative impact on organ donation rates.

It is a shame that the Taskforce rejects the option of mandated choice (in Paragraph 6.9) because of these practical difficulties. They are rather trivial obstacles and would be simple to overcome.

A similar option to mandated choice is 'required request'. This is where medical practitioners are under a duty to ask relatives about organ donation, and it is quite popular in the United States. In an emergency, it can be quite difficult for a practitioner, e.g. in intensive care, to approach a family and ask about donation and it can be very distressing for the relatives because it brings the prospect of death even closer to their door. However, by imposing a duty upon practitioners to raise the issue, many more organs could potentially be harvested. There are no clear statistics available to prove whether required request has significantly increased the number of donated organs in the United States, but it is believed that many potential donations are lost in the United Kingdom because practitioners often use their clinical discretion in an emergency situation and decide not to inflame the emotions of the relatives by asking about donation.[56]

The ethical problem is clear: a medical practitioner should not be forced to ask particularly distressing questions, especially in an emergency when emotions are high.

---

[56] One study was done some time ago, and did not yield any significant results: D. Gentleman, J. Easton and B. Jennet, 'Brain Death and Organ Donation in a Neurosurgical Unit: Audit of Recent Practice' (1990) 301 *British Medical Journal* 1203.

The relatives of the patient may interpret a question about donation as a confirmation of death. However, there must be a balancing act between protecting the feelings of relatives and saving another person's life. The distress of the relatives will pass, but the organ recipient will be forever thankful.

Conditional donation

The idea of conditional donation is a controversial one. It is where an organ is donated but with conditions attached to it, such as: 'only donate this to a white recipient' or 'only donate this to a young recipient'. This strange form of clinical discrimination is something we want to avoid, but it raises an interesting question: if we could donate our organs conditionally, would more people sign the donor register?

This issue raised its head for the first time in 2000 when the Department of Health set up an investigation into conditional donation.[57] A patient in July 1998 was in a critical condition in an intensive care unit and after his brain stem death test his family consented to organ donation on the condition that any organs retrieved from him would go to white recipients.[58] It just so happened that the recipients who were most in need of his liver and his kidneys were white, and so the donations took place without discrimination. However, the publicity surrounding the case indicated to the Department of Health that an investigation was required, because the threat of discrimination could send the altruistic world of organ donation toppling down. The Department of Health concluded that, even though no one was disadvantaged in this case, the organs should not have been accepted in the first place.

EXTRACT

An Investigation into Conditional Organ Donation: The Report of the Panel, February 2000, Department of Health (archived):

http://webarchive.nationalarchives.gov.uk/20050203020616/
http://www.dh.gov.uk/PublicationsAndStatistics/Publications/
PublicationsPolicyAndGuidance/PublicationsPolicyAndGuidanceArticle/fs/
en?CONTENT_ID=4002934&chk=WrD3WR

Paragraph 6.1: This was a very unfortunate incident. It should not have happened. In the Panel's view to attach any condition to a donation is unacceptable, because it offends against the fundamental principle that organs are donated altruistically and should go to patients in the greatest need. The Panel consider that racist conditions are completely abhorrent, as well as being unacceptable under the Race Relations Act. As far as the Panel have been able to ascertain, such conditions have never been accepted before. None of those who gave information to the Panel was aware of any precedents.

In transplantation it has long been understood that the donor does not *own* his organs, whether legally or otherwise, and therefore he cannot dictate how they will be used after his death. A relative would certainly have no authority to attach such conditions. The conditional donation in 1998 should be resigned to the cupboard of history because it could

---

[57] An Investigation into Conditional Organ Donation: The Report of the Panel, February (2000), Department of Health (archived) at: http://webarchive.nationalarchives.gov.uk/20050203020616/ http://www.dh.gov.uk/PublicationsAndStatistics/Publications/PublicationsPolicyAndGuidance/ PublicationsPolicyAndGuidanceArticle/fs/en?CONTENT_ID=4002934&chk=WrD3WR.
[58] See note above, at page 16.

easily lead to a slippery slope if it was accepted in practice, but a compelling argument has come forward to illustrate the benefits of conditional donation. Wilkinson suggests that a form of conditional donation already exists in living kidney donation, where the kidney goes to an identified recipient, i.e. a family member. There are no significant ethical problems and the recipient clearly benefits, so why not extend this practice to cadaveric donation too?

EXTRACT

T.M. Wilkinson, 'What's Not Wrong with Conditional Organ Donation?' (2003) 29 Journal of Medical Ethics 163–4

Is it really so bad to attach a condition to an organ donation? Of course it was bad in the case of the racist. The motive there was some mix of hatred and contempt and there is nothing to be said for it. But what about the condition that an organ go to a relative? There seems nothing morally wrong about agreeing to donate a kidney, say, on condition that it go to a sibling, whether the donation is to be from a living person or a dead one. [...]

The [Department of Health] panel claims that conditional donation 'offends against the fundamental principle that organs are donated altruistically and should go to patients in the greatest need'. Altruism in its normal sense refers roughly to a non-self-interested concern for the interests of others. Importantly, a wide variety of other-regarding motives can be regarded as altruistic, such as a special concern for children, or the deaf, or the poor.

Wilkinson raises a good point: altruism can take many forms. A donor may wish to benefit a certain corner of society as opposed to the whole of society. In addition to this, a donor may wish to attach a condition that his organs only go to minority recipients because, as a minority person himself, he understands the significant shortage of organs. This could be labelled as 'positive discrimination' to a certain extent.

However, the glaring practical problem with conditional donation is that cadaveric donations are often taken from donors who did not foresee their sudden death, for example in a road accident or by suffering a brain haemorrhage. It is very unlikely, in the context of conditional donation to a sibling, that the surviving brother or sister will need the newly available liver or kidney. The Human Tissue Authority was forced to release a statement to the press on the issue in 2008 when a patient – Laura Ashworth – wanted to donate a kidney to her mother but she suddenly died and was treated as a routine dead donor, meaning her kidneys were donated to anonymous recipients. There was wide public criticism. The Human Tissue Authority stated:

> The central principle of matching and allocating organs from the deceased is that they are allocated to the person on the UK Transplant waiting list who is most in need and who is the best match with the donor. This is regardless of gender, race, religion or any other factor. The ethics of this position have long been supported by the government and professionals working in the field. In line with this central principle, a person cannot choose to whom their organ can be given when they die, nor can their family. However, the HTA recognises that there may be exceptional situations when this rule might be reconsidered, but the importance of maintaining the central principle means that such exceptional situations would need to be considered with the greatest care before any part of the current rules were to be changed.[59]

---

[59] Human Tissue Authority Press Release, 12 April 2008, http://www.hta.gov.uk/newsandevents/htanews.cfm/411-HTA-statement-on-directed-donation-of-organs-after-death.html.

The Department of Health has since announced in a report entitled: Requested Allocation of a Deceased Donor that it may consider 'requested donation' to a family member or a friend but only where there are no others in urgent clinical need.[60] This is highly unlikely.

Financial incentives (dead donors)

The most difficult suggestion of all is payment for organs. A 'market' of body parts. This is dangerous for four reasons:

1. The altruism of the donor and the relatives to donate organs becomes worthless.
2. The best organs go to the highest bidders.
3. The human body becomes a product that can be bought and sold at a price.
4. The money would fall into the hands of surviving relatives who may have consented to donation simply to pay off their own debts.

The four reasons listed above are not practical barriers to payment for organs – a market could be set up relatively easily – they are ethical barriers to payment for organs. A pressing concern for commentators and practitioners is the shunning of altruistic donation. The donation of an organ is traditionally a selfless deed to save the life of another. It restores faith in human kind and confirms the old adage that we are valuable beings in our own right, not a cave of treasures to be mined upon death. To learn that donors were joining the Organ Donor Register simply because they would earn money out of it would cheapen the meaning of organ donation. A recipient could be less appreciative upon learning that the donor did not *want* to donate his organs, he simply *had* to because his family were in financial trouble.

The event of death could also be taken advantage of by greedy relatives. For example, a family member may consent to your organ donation to use the money to pay for her own bills and burdens. You would not receive any money because you would be dead, so it would have to go to your relative or a third party. In light of this fact, perhaps a market in organs is not such an attractive idea after all?

This use of deceased relatives to 'settle bills' is clearly not ethical (unless it was funeral costs in which case a payment could be quite helpful). A little research has been done, and the reaction was, perhaps predictably, negative.

EXTRACT

G. Haddow, '"Because You're Worth It?" The Taking and Selling of Transplantable Organs' (2006) 32 *Journal of Medical Ethics* 324, at pages 324–8

Offering a payment of £20 to register proved to be the least popular of all options [amongst potential donors]. Approximately 40% of respondents reacted positively to the grants after death of £2,000 payment per organ to the family, to a favourite charity, or towards funeral costs. We found certain groups to be more favourable towards incentives, especially the 16–24 age cohort and men. [...] Importantly, there is a prominent level of 'would make no difference' response to all options – even the favoured 'cash for relatives' option. Therefore, the overall reaction to any of the financial options was decidedly tepid. Among donor families, [...] sixteen of seventeen donor relatives were opposed. [...] The response to financial incentives was [that] it was 'immoral'.

---

[60] Requested Allocation of a Deceased Donor Organ, Department of Health, March 2010, (archived) at: http://wales.gov.uk/docs/dhss/publications/100330finalguidanceen.doc.

It is not surprising that out of the potential donor respondents, the younger generation and the men were more likely to donate their organs if their relatives were handed a £2,000 grant. The idea of a grant is a practical approach to donation that could help to settle the finances of the deceased. It is also not surprising that out of the seventeen donor family respondents, sixteen of them thought that financial incentives were immoral. This may be because they have recently been through the process of donating a loved one's organs and they sought comfort in the fact that it was altruistic, i.e. his final act of kindness.

The law has settled the issue for us. Under section 32(1) of the Human Tissue Act 2004, payment for human organs is prohibited. The maximum penalty for any of these crimes is three years in prison under s. 32(4)(b).

Human Tissue Act 2004

Section 32: Prohibition of commercial dealings in human material for transplantation

(1) A person commits an offence if he –
   (a) gives or receives a reward for the supply of, or for an offer to supply, any controlled material;
   (b) seeks to find a person willing to supply any controlled material for reward;
   (c) offers to supply any controlled material for reward;
   (d) initiates or negotiates any arrangement involving the giving of a reward for the supply of, or for an offer to supply, any controlled material;
   (e) takes part in the management or control of a body of persons corporate or unincorporate whose activities consist of or include the initiation or negotiation of such arrangements.

It is not just organ traffickers who commit an offence under section 32(1) – it appears that anyone who engages in payment for organs is guilty under this provision. A person who gives a reward is liable, a person who receives a reward is liable, a person who seeks out a willing donor is liable, an offer to supply organs is liable and a person who initiates or negotiates an arrangement (i.e. donor, recipient and relatives) is liable.

The Human Tissue Act 2004 has clearly tried to cover every possibility of supply and payment of organs by every conceivable party. There are other offences relating to publishing and distributing advertisements under section 32(2). The maximum penalty for any of these crimes is 51 weeks in prison under section 32(5).

Human Tissue Act 2004

Section 32: Prohibition of commercial dealings in human material for transplantation

(2) Without prejudice to subsection (1)(b) and (c), a person commits an offence if he causes to be published or distributed, or knowingly publishes or distributes, an advertisement –
   (a) inviting persons to supply, or offering to supply, any controlled material for reward, or
   (b) indicating that the advertiser is willing to initiate or negotiate any such arrangement as is mentioned in subsection (1)(d).

There are some exceptions to the law. A hospital, for example, as a licence holder will not be prosecuted for receiving a payment of money where it enables the transporting, removing, preparing, preserving or storing of organs under section 32(6). A reward for the supply of organs does not include money for reimbursing expenses incurred in transporting, removing, preparing, preserving or storing organs under section 32(7), and this includes the costs incurred by the living donor for any travel or loss of earnings connected to the donation. This is *not* compensation for donating the organ and it is *not* payment for the organ, it is more of a 'replacement' for the costs incurred whilst donating the organ.

A market for organs (living donors)

Let us assume that the law (stated above) was to be amended in light of the shortage of organs to introduce a market for organs from living donors. What could be the main barriers to this? In addition to the ethical barriers raised above in relation to dead donors – i.e. no more altruism, best organ to the highest bidder and the body becomes a product – there is the added concern of the living donor volunteering his own organs for a simple financial reward. The notion of altruistic donation would slowly shrivel away, leaving us with a cold meat market that would not even be referred to as 'donation' anymore, paving the way for 'marketing' or 'selling' or 'transferring' instead.

The main practical problem is putting a price on certain organs. How much would you pay for a kidney? The answer should be: enough to pay for the costs, pain and suffering incurred by the donor, similar to the damages paid to victims of personal injury in negligence. This may seem straightforward, but wrapped up in this seemingly practical solution to the organ shortage is a persuasive ethical counter-argument: it is not virtuous to sell one of your organs, no matter how desperate you are.

EXTRACT

Barbo Bjorkman, 'Why We Are Not Allowed to Sell That which We Are Encouraged to Donate' (2006) 15 *Cambridge Quarterly of Healthcare Ethics* 60, at pages 60–70

Virtue ethics rejects commodification of organs because it fails to make us flourish, not because it has bad consequences or breaks some rule. [...] Virtuous persons would not sell their organs but rather donate them because they wish to help their less fortunate fellow man, they 'see' that this is fine, noble, and worthwhile. The fact that this is not the current practice in society today only shows that people in general are not virtuous. The way to redeem the problems of organ shortage in a given society is not to create a market but rather to increase the sense of virtue.

The ideals put forward by Bjorkman are all well and good but in these difficult economic times, an extra £5,000 for a kidney could be a very welcome relief to a family who were living on the poverty line. In addition to this, the 'virtuous man' is typically rich, noble and comfortable and can afford to be generous. The 'poor man' needs every penny he can get.

The black market in organs is already rife in some very poor countries, and rich patients can take advantage of this by travelling over to impoverished countries to pay a modest amount of money for an organ and the accompanying surgery. The only way to solve this problem is to eradicate poverty (or at least the most degrading forms of poverty where money for organs is the only option left), but we have been working on this for decades already to no avail.

In reality, the sale of a kidney will do very little to help an impoverished family in India, especially at the knock-down price of £300 to £500 (which is probably close to what they are sold for). The family will probably suffer temporarily anyway because the donor (who will probably be the mother) will need to recover from her surgery. She will be weaker in the long term, and be susceptible to illnesses and injury. In our country, the price tag will inevitably be higher for a kidney at an estimated £5,000, but this will not spread very far in our economy and will probably be spent on recovery. A person only has two kidneys and must keep at least one, so selling organs does not look like a very good idea for long-term financial prosperity regardless of the social standing of the donor.

A market in organs also raises a few other unique ethical barriers. Firstly, the idea of payment may negate consent. This is because, if a very poor donor knew that he would receive £5,000 for donating a kidney, he may care little about the risks and begin to fantasise about his new untold wealth as he is signing on the dotted line. This is not consent in the true sense because it does not represent a fully informed and voluntary consent: it is simply the materialisation of a dream. A critic of a market in organs may go as far as to say that payment to a very poor donor was tantamount to coercion. Secondly, it would make for a very crooked society if we paid our fellow citizens to undergo a surgical procedure, pain and suffering for our benefit. This is taking advantage of the vulnerable in the most crudest sense. Thirdly, what would a poor person do if they suddenly needed a kidney transplant? For example, an impoverished mother of four children developed a kidney infection and was told by her doctor that she needed to buy a kidney from the national organ market. Where would she find £5,000? The most obvious solution, if she was living in a very bad environment and had no family to turn to, would be to prostitute herself for the money if she was well enough. Fourthly, pushy or domineering relatives could put pressure on a younger or vulnerable family member to give up their organ for a larger share of the inheritance, or the keys to the house, or enough money to buy a new car.

EXTRACT

J. Harvey, 'Paying Organ Donors' (1990) 16 *Journal of Medical Ethics* 117, at pages 117–19

There is financial pressure when the potential donor is in poverty. And perhaps it may be argued that this alone is sufficient for banning all paid-for donations. But then, in consistency, the same reasoning should be applied to related donors: since *some* of them are open to heavy psychological and emotional pressure (for example, perhaps by being the submissive and 'guilt'-ridden offspring of an extremely domineering and now ailing parent), then all donations from relatives should be forbidden. The difficult task of distinguishing between truly vulnerable relatives and those not vulnerable is undertaken. This would point to our attempting the analogous task in the case of paid for donations, namely the task of distinguishing between the truly financially vulnerable and those not so.

A market in organs appears to be surrounded by an ethical minefield. The NHS would become a purchaser of organs as opposed to the givers of free care, human body parts would have a price, organs are already tested for HIV where possible and their provenance is already known, vulnerable or poor people may still be coerced into selling their kidney or bone marrow to the NHS to scrape together some emergency money, and the 'strict controls and penalties' referred to are already in place in the form of criminal liability under section 32 of the Human Tissue Act 2004 (as outlined above). However, as negative as all of this sounds, the ethical barriers to a market in organs do not have to be so problematic. Firstly, if the NHS was to purchase organs instead of the recipient himself, this would ensure that the donor was not forced into donation by a pushy buyer with a fat wad of cash. Secondly, a market in organs can still be altruistic. A mother may like to donate a kidney to her niece, for example. This will make her an altruistic person and she will receive payment as a 'thank you' for her time, pain and suffering. Thirdly, the fact that donation is dangerous should not be a reason to prevent payment because it is dangerous *anyway* regardless of whether money is exchanged or not. Fourthly, the third world market in organs could be quite a lucrative one for the countries involved. The developed countries have a shortage of organs and would pay a significant price for a kidney or a bone marrow transplant. The developing countries, in return, have an abundance of kidneys and bone marrow to be harvested. It is a win–win situation. Fifthly, patient autonomy is the cornerstone of medicine, and so it would be very paternalistic of us to deny a patient the right to donate a kidney for money when she is also allowed to refuse medical treatment which could endanger her own life. Sixthly, the pressure from pushy or domineering relatives to sell an organ would be rooted out during the interview process that every living donor must go through, particularly if the organ is being sold to a family member. The Human Tissue Authority is well aware of the blackmail and emotional entanglements that could take place. There is, therefore, still room for a market in organs if we put the correct provisions in place or change our attitudes about certain things.

The idea of a European market in organs was explored very recently by the House of Lords in 2008. They put together a European Union Committee to address the shortage of human organs across the European Union, and the final Report in July 2008 showed strong support for an extension of our domestic system to include neighbouring countries who boasted better donation rates. There would also be an opportunity for a larger financial infrastructure, research collaboration across Europe, and significant expansion of the organ pool.

EXTRACT

Increasing the Supply of Donor Organs within the European Union, European Union Committee, House of Lords, July 2008, Volume 1: Report, at:

http://www.publications.parliament.uk/pa/ld200708/ldselect/ldeucom/ldeucom.htm

Paragraph 25: At present, the five member States that comprise the Eurotransplant area (Austria, Belgium, Luxembourg, the Netherlands and Slovenia) have entered into collaborative agreements relating to organ exchange. While the Commission has not suggested that this area should be extended to include any further Member States, it does argue that a Community framework would be desirable for setting quality and safety criteria with respect to the procurement, transport and use of organs across the Community.

Paragraph 175: We recommend that the Government should support the Commission in its development of an Action Plan relating to organ donation and transplantation. The action plan should provide financial and infrastructure support for information exchange and research collaboration between Member States, both reinforcing and expanding existing successful collaborations, and enabling the development of new initiatives which will address the shortage of organs for donation across the EU.

The Report places an emphasis on 'sharing expertise' to 'identify the best of the models and support its application throughout the EU, while respecting cultural and organisational diversity.'[61] One of the recommendations of the Report was to introduce a European Directive which would impose minimum standards for a safe organ transplant system but would not be too bureaucratic.

EXTRACT

Increasing the Supply of Donor Organs within the European Union, European Union Committee, House of Lords, July 2008, Volume 1: Report, at:

http://www.publications.parliament.uk/pa/ld200708/ldselect/ldeucom/ldeucom.htm

Paragraph 124: We recommend that the Government should support the introduction of an EU directive on the quality and safety of organ donation and transplantation in a form which provides minimum standards across the EU, but is not overly bureaucratic and which does not impose requirements beyond those which are clinically justified.

The Report makes for interesting reading because it also covers organ quality, patient care, alternative forms of consent, ethnic aspects, cultural differences and the views of several faiths. However, the push for such a sweeping change was put on hold by the Report until the Organ Donation Taskforce published its findings on the potential impact of an 'opt-out' system for organ donation in the UK. The Taskforce concluded that there should *not* be a presumed consent system in our country, so the plan to implement any sweeping changes appears to have been shelved to focus on improving our donation rates in our current 'opt-in' system by 50% in five years (2008–2012).[62]

Preference to donors

There is one other way in which donors could be encouraged to donate their organs whilst alive or dead: they could be given preference when they need an organ themselves. Organs are typically allocated using a points system, i.e. points are awarded for time waiting, urgency, and sometimes blood match depending on the organ sought. However, a patient who has already donated in his lifetime could be awarded an additional few points to give him a slight advantage. This would not override the needs of the other patients because urgency is still the main factor in organ allocation, but it may be enough to encourage more donors to come forward. Commentators have been supportive of this cheap and effective suggestion to increase the number of organs available, although Jarvis proposes that *only* donors (or potential donors) should be eligible for organs.

---

[61] Increasing the Supply of Donor Organs within the European Union, European Union Committee, House of Lords, July 2008, Volume 1: Report, at paragraph 33.

[62] The Potential Impact of an Opt Out System for Organ Donation in the UK, An Independent Report from the Organ Donation Taskforce, Department of Health, November 2008 (archived) at paragraph 15.7: http://webarchive.nationalarchives.gov.uk/20130107105354/http://www.dh.gov.uk/en/Publicationsandstatistics/Publications/PublicationsPolicyAndGuidance/DH_090312. This goal has recently been met, but we are awaiting a report to confirm.

EXTRACT

Rupert Jarvis, 'Join the Club: A Modest Proposal to Increase Availability of Donor Organs' (1995) 21 *Journal of Medical Ethics* 199, at pages 199–204

I suggest that legislation governing organ donation be amended such that all and only those who identify themselves as potential donors (perhaps by a card similar to the one currently in use, or by registration on a central computer) are eligible themselves to receive transplant organs. [...] We are presented, then, with what appears to be a thoroughly attractive option, by sacrificing our minimal post mortem interests we guarantee our inclusion on the waiting list for the donor organ which might save or vastly improve the quality of our own life. [...] It hardly seems fanciful to suggest that the vast majority of people would elect to join the scheme, since it is so clearly in their interests to do so, with the potential gain (life) being infinite and the potential loss being zero.

Jarvis may go a bit too far: he suggests that *only* those who are registered on the organ donor register should be eligible for an organ transplant. This would be unethical for one clear reason: the medical profession would have to turn away dying patients and that is not acceptable in our country. It also goes against the ethic of care: doctors are supposed to care for those in need, not turn them away because their name is not on a register. It is also questionable whether everyone in the UK would sign up to the Organ Donor Register if this legislative change was made. Apathy would be a big problem – people simply don't have the time these days to 'get round to it' – and many others will not see it as important because they are presently healthy. Besides, far more people need an organ than become eligible to donate after a sudden and unexpected death, so there would probably still be a shortage. Perhaps unsurprisingly, Jarvis attracted a strong response to his proposal, and Gillon argued that medical need should be the overarching priority when allocating organs.

EXTRACT

Raanan Gillon, 'On Giving Preference to Prior Volunteers When Allocating Organs for Transplantation' (1995) 21 *Journal of Medical Ethics* 195, at page 196

Here seems to be the Achilles heel of Mr Jarvis's proposal. For even if such non-volunteers can properly be said to have only themselves to blame for their predicament; even if they can properly be said to have deliberately and autonomously made their choice and rejected the opportunity to give themselves priority for receipt for transplanted organs; even if they can properly be said to have been selfish, and/or inconsiderate and/or foolish, even immoral, in refusing to pre-volunteer their own organs, nonetheless there is an important countervailing moral tradition in medicine. It is that patients should be given treatment in relation to their medical need, and that scarce medical resources should not be prioritised on the basis of a patient's blameworthiness. [...] If the fault and/or inconsiderateness of not previously volunteering his or her organs for transplantation were to justify withholding scarce life-saving resources from a patient, then all other prior faults and inconsiderateness of equal or greater weight could, logically, also be regarded as morally relevant and potentially justificatory for withholding scarce life-saving medical resources from patients. Such a prospect hardly bears contemplation.

Gillon interprets Jarvis as rejecting all organ recipients who have behaved immorally. This is not what Jarvis proposed, but there may be a slippery slope. For example, the rejection of recipients who are not listed on the register may, over time, expand to a rejection of patients who have caused their own organ failure, etc. A fresh option would be to implement the 'opt-out' system and make it clear to donors who opt out of the Organ Donor Register that they will not be eligible for an organ, as Eaton explains:

EXTRACT

Stephanie Eaton, 'The Subtle Politics of Organ Donation: A Proposal' (1998) 24 *Journal of Medical Ethics* 166, at page 168

Where people still choose to opt-out knowing that this constitutes free-riding, they should be made aware that they may be disadvantaged in the future if they should ever become potential recipients of organs. [...] Publicity that promotes the idea that an opted-out person may be less likely to receive a transplant if he or she ever needs one, forces opters-out to reconsider their own moral standards. It is hoped that the unease that will be felt when opting-out is acknowledged as being a form of free-riding will have the consequence that few people will choose to opt out.

Eaton proposes that we rely on moral pressure when donors turn up at a local town hall to remove their name from the Organ Donor Register. This is not the most ethical way to glean medical resources because it is a form of manipulation, and we have the same ethical problem as presented in the Jarvis proposal: the medical profession would have to turn away dying patients.

Your organs are a public resource

The final way in we could increase the number of donated organs – and by far the most controversial – is to consider organs as a public resource that should be harvested upon our death and dispatched amongst society to those who are most in need. This would remove consent as an issue completely: the organs would be removed regardless of who you are or what your beliefs are, no questions asked. This is controversial because it treats human beings as objects and it robs us of our autonomy. McGuinness and Brazier argue that the human body is not simply an object to be used as a means to an end after death.

EXTRACT

S. McGuinness and M. Brazier, 'Respecting the Living Means Respecting the Dead Too' (2008) 28 *Oxford Journal of Legal Studies* 297, at page 297–316

Death is not akin to a switch that once 'off' means that the dead person ceases to matter at all. Death is described by some as, and can traditionally be seen to be, a socially constructed event. Death rituals have formed an important part of the grieving process. Throughout history there has been an expectation that in death the body will be respected as a symbol of the living person. Death of someone close to you is difficult to accept. We struggle to adjust to an understanding that the person is gone. Identifying with the dead is so hard that we think of the dead body as a symbol of the pre-mortem person. The dead infant, the wife succumbing to breast cancer at 35, the elderly father dying suddenly of a heart attack, do not change their nature for their mother, husband or daughter. They remain Susannah, Lucy and Dad. They are not simply things.

What is difficult about this argument is that the human body is personalised when, technically, the personality is no longer present. This view can also significantly harm the view of organ donation as 'taking away' from a person, even though they are already 'gone'. Glannon takes this argument to the extreme and suggests that we have a right to say what happens to our bodies after death, and this right far outweighs the rights of those waiting for an organ.

EXTRACT

W. Glannon, 'Do the Sick Have a Right to Cadaveric Organs?' (2003) 29 *Journal of Medical Ethics* 153, at page 154

Because the body is so closely associated with who we are, we can have an interest in what is done to it even after we cease to exist. The fact that my whole body is mine and is essential to my life plan means that I have a deep interest in what is done to it. If it is treated in a way that does not accord with my wishes or interests, then in an important respect this can be bad for me and I can be harmed. The special relationship between humans and their bodies can make it wrong for others to ignore the expressed wish that one's organs not be harvested at death, despite their viability for transplantation. [...] Given the special relation between humans and their bodies, the moral importance of individual autonomy in having a life plan, and that what happens to one's body after death is part of such a plan, the negative right to bodily integrity after death outweighs any presumed positive right of the sick to receive organs from those who did not consent to cadaver donation.

Glannon's argument requires some analysis. He argues that his body is so closely connected to his 'life plan' that he is entitled to have a say in what happens to it when he dies. The clear fallacy in this argument is the use of the word 'life' – once you are deceased, your 'life plan' has expired and there is no longer an interest in your own body. In addition to this, he argues that he 'can be harmed' if his body is used in a way that disagrees with him, but this is literally impossible if he is no longer alive.

Your organs are your own resource

It is believed by the majority of the general public that we own our bodies, tissues and organs. This would be highly beneficial to the organ donation programme. We would be legally entitled to sell our bodies, body parts, organs and tissues to needy recipients or researchers. It would also be easier for us to claim that our bodies, body parts, organs and tissues were mistreated, abused or exploited if we were to learn that they were used in a way that did not match our consent. We could pursue a legal action to get them back or seek compensation and this would deter traffickers, smugglers and thieves from breaking the law. Most importantly, we would be able to control what happened to our bodies, body parts, organs and tissues after our death and our interests would be harmed if our wishes were ignored. This supreme level of control would no doubt empower many individuals to donate all of their bodies, body parts, organs and tissues to 'the greater good' when we die. However, while it is true that we have a say in how our bodies are used during our lifetime and this gives us the impression that we stake a legal claim in our bodies, in reality, we do not have any such claim. We are allowed to tattoo our bodies, feed or starve our bodies, change our bodies, reproduce with our bodies and take risks with our bodies, for example by skydiving, overeating or by taking drugs, but we have no legal ownership of our bodies, organs or tissues at all. The law has been clear on this matter for a while: we do not own our bodies. The current legal picture looks like this: some parts of the body (once detached) and some tissues or fluids (once extracted) are property that can be stolen for the purposes of theft if they have had a skill applied to them. However, a person does not own his complete body in law because there is no statute or case in existence to confirm this legal right. The relevant trail of cases as to body parts and the 'application of skill' is provided below.

In the Australian case of *Doodeward v Spence* (1908) 6 CLR 906 it was confirmed that under the common law we do not have any proprietary rights in our bodies, but that could be altered if a skill was applied.

CASE EXTRACT

Doodeward v Spence (1908) 6 CLR 406

Griffiths CJ (at page 414): A human body, or a portion of a human body, is capable by law of becoming the subject of property. It is not necessary to give an exhaustive enumeration of the circumstances under which such a right may be acquired, but I entertain no doubt that, when a person has by the lawful exercise of work or skill so dealt with a human body or part of a human body in his lawful possession that it has acquired some attributes differentiating it from a mere corpse awaiting burial, he acquires a right to retain possession of it, at least as against any person not entitled to have it delivered to him for the purpose of burial, but subject, of course, to any positive law which forbids its retention under the particular circumstances.

The ratio from *Doodeward* was applied in two English authorities (below) to confirm that when a sample from the body is destroyed, it is theft:

- A man was convicted of theft in *R v Welsh* [1974] RTR 478 when he poured his *own* urine sample down the sink at a police station.

- A man was convicted of theft in *R v Rothery (Henry Michael)* [1976] RTR 550 for stealing his *own* blood sample in a police station.

The case law became interesting in *R v Kelly* (1999). Body parts were traditionally viewed as ownerless, but when a skill is applied to them, this turns them into property capable of being stolen.

CASE EXTRACT

R v Kelly (Anthony Noel) [1999] QB 621

Facts: The appellant Kelly, who was an artist, had privileged access to the premises of the Royal College of Surgeons in order to draw anatomical specimens held on display and used for training surgeons. The other appellant (Lindsay) was employed by the college during that period as a junior technician. Kelly asked Lindsay to remove a number of human body parts from the college. Some 35 to 40 such parts, including three human heads, part of a brain, six arms or parts of an arm, ten legs or feet, and part of three human torsos were removed and taken to Kelly's home. He made casts of the parts, some of which were exhibited in an art gallery. Neither appellant intended to return the body parts, many of which Kelly buried in a field

→

in the grounds of his family home. Part of a leg was kept in the attic of his home. The remaining parts were recovered from the basement of a flat occupied by one of Kelly's friends. They argued that human body parts were not items capable of being stolen under the Theft Act 1968 and thus had not acted dishonestly.

Held: Although neither a corpse nor parts of a corpse were in themselves capable of being property protected by rights, the parts of a corpse could be 'property' for the purposes of section 4 of the Theft Act 1968 if they had acquired different attributes by virtue of the application of skill, such as dissection or preservation techniques, for exhibition or teaching purposes.

Rose LJ (at pages 630–1): We return to the first question, that is to say whether or not a corpse or part of a corpse is property. We accept that, however questionable the historical origins of the principle, it has now been the common law for 150 years at least that neither a corpse nor parts of a corpse are in themselves and without more capable of being property protected by rights: see, for example, Erle J, delivering the judgment of a powerful Court for Crown Cases Reserved in *Regina v Sharpe* (1857) Dears & B. 160, 163, where he said: 'Our law recognises no property in a corpse, and the protection of the grave at common law as contradistinguished from ecclesiastic protection to consecrated ground depends on this form of indictment.' He was there referring to an indictment which charged not theft of a corpse but removal of a corpse from a grave. If that principle is now to be changed, in our view, it must be by Parliament, because it has been express or implicit in all the subsequent authorities and writings to which we have been referred that a corpse or part of it cannot be stolen. To address the point as it was addressed before the trial judge and to which his certificate relates, in our judgment, parts of a corpse are capable of being property within section 4 of the Theft Act 1968 if they have acquired different attributes by virtue of the application of skill, such as dissection or preservation techniques, for exhibition or teaching purposes: see *Doodeward* v *Spence*, 6 CLR 406, in the judgment of Griffith CJ. [...] Accordingly the trial judge was correct to rule as he did. Furthermore, the common law does not stand still.

What is strange about the *Kelly* judgment is that it does not make much legal sense. The earlier ratio of Griffiths CJ in *Doodeward* was adopted to confirm that, once a skill is applied to body parts, they are property capable of being stolen. Rose LJ in *Kelly* did not question the logic behind this ratio, nor did he add to it or try to rationalise it. This is a shame, because it does not make sense that a body part cannot be stolen unless a skill has been applied to it. What if the defendant in *Kelly* had stolen all of the body parts and then decided, once retuning home, that he didn't want them anymore and didn't make casts of them after all? According to Rose LJ, this would not be theft.

- In *Dobson v North Tyneside HA* [1996] 4 All ER 474 it was confirmed that removing a brain during a post-mortem and preserving it in paraffin was not an application of a skill that transformed the brain into property.

- It was confirmed in the criminal case of *DPP v Smith* [2006] 1 WLR 1571 that the hair is an attributable part of the body and cutting a ponytail off constitutes 'bodily harm' for the purposes of a conviction of actual bodily harm under section 47 of the Offences Against the Person Act 1861.

In the most recent case of *Yearworth* (2010), the law in this area was revisited and deeply criticised.

CASE EXTRACT

Yearworth v North Bristol NHS Trust [2010] QB 1

Facts: Six men who were undergoing chemotherapy were advised to store sperm samples in case the treatment affected their fertility. They did so, but the storage temperature meant that the samples thawed too early and the samples were destroyed. The men brought actions in personal injury.

Held: The samples were no longer part of the body, so the personal injury route was not successful. However, the samples could be their 'property' as an alternative route. The Court held that the samples were the property of the six men and that old rule in *Doodeward* needed an urgent rethink.

Judge LJ (at pages 11, 19–20, 23): We agree with the judge that the damage to, and consequential loss of, the sperm did not constitute 'personal injury'. Although we understand the contrary argument, it would be a fiction to hold that damage to a substance generated by a person's body, inflicted after its removal for storage purposes, constituted a bodily or 'personal' injury to him. [...]

We conclude:

(a) In this jurisdiction developments in medical science now require a re-analysis of the common law's treatment of and approach to the issue of ownership of parts or products of a living human body, whether for present purposes (*viz* an action in negligence) or otherwise. [...]

(c) For us the easiest course would be to uphold the claims of the men to have had ownership of the sperm for present purposes by reference to the principle first identified in the *Doodeward* case 6 CLR 406. We would have no difficulty in concluding that the unit's storage of the sperm in liquid nitrogen at minus 196°C was an application to the sperm of work and skill which conferred on it a substantially different attribute, namely the arrest of its swift perishability.

(d) However, as foreshadowed by Rose LJ in *R v Kelly* [1999] QB 621, we are not content to see the common law in this area founded upon the principle in the *Doodeward* case 6 CLR 406, which was devised as an exception to a principle, itself of exceptional character, relating to the ownership of a human corpse. Such ancestry does not commend it as a solid foundation. Moreover a distinction between the capacity to own body parts or products which have, and which have not, been subject to the exercise of work or skill is not entirely logical. Why, for example, should the surgeon presented with a part of the body, for example, a finger which has been amputated in a factory accident, with a view to re-attaching it to the injured hand, but who carelessly damages it before starting the necessary medical procedures, be able to escape liability on the footing that the body part had not been subject to the exercise of work or skill which had changed its attributes? [...]

(f) In our judgment, for the purposes of their claims in negligence, the men had ownership of the sperm which they ejaculated. (i) By their bodies, they alone generated and ejaculated the sperm. (ii) The sole object of their ejaculation of the sperm was that, in certain events, it might later be used for their benefit. [...] The absence of their ability to 'direct' its use does not in our view derogate from their ownership. [...] By its provisions for consent, the [Human

→

Fertilisation and Embryology] Act assiduously preserves the ability of the men to direct that the sperm be *not* used in a certain way: their negative control over its use remains absolute. [...]

In the above circumstances we conclude without hesitation that there was a bailment of the sperm by the men to the unit and that, subject to the resolution of factual issues yet to be determined, the unit is liable to them under the law of bailment as well as under that of tort.

Judge LJ in *Yearworth* makes it clear that the old law in *Doodeward* is out of touch with modern medicine. He held that ownership was established because: the samples originated from the six claimants, the purpose of storing the samples was to provide the claimants with children and the Human Fertilisation and Embryology Act 2008 preserved the control of the claimants via the consent mechanism. This judgment makes better legal sense because it takes all of the surrounding factors into account to establish ownership (as opposed to relying solely on an 'application of skill'). However, *Yearworth* does not completely change the law, it simply provides very strong encouragement to begin veering away from *Doodeward*.

The law has not developed further to shed any more light on exactly when we own parts of our bodies once they have been detached, removed or extracted. It seems to be important that all six claimants generated the samples themselves, but there were several other factors to consider too, such as the *purpose* of the storage, a *duty* to store, and the *rules of consent* surrounding the storage. *Yearworth* suggests that it is a combination of factors, which makes the law even more difficult to untangle, but it is clear that an erosion of *Doodeward* has begun.

ACTIVITY

Having read all the suggestions for increasing the number of donated organs in this country, draft your very own new law to increase the number of organs using one of the suggestions above.

Chapter summary

- The Human Tissue Act 2004 was set up to clarify the law on organ donation and transplantation after the Alder Hey scandal. It also launched the Human Tissue Authority, which publishes guidelines to regulate the donation, storage and use of tissues and organs.

- The removal, storage and use of human organs and tissues from *deceased* donors is covered by section 1(1)(a)(b)(c)(d) and (f) of the Human Tissue Act 2004.

- The storage and use of human organs and tissues from *living* donors is covered by section 1(1)(d)(f) of the Human Tissue Act 2004 (removal was omitted from the statute and is still governed by the common law of consent).

- The Department of Health set up the Organ Donation Taskforce to investigate the effect of an 'opt out' system in the UK. The 2008 (November) Report concluded that we would be better off increasing donation rates in our current 'opt in' system by 50% between 2008–2012 before we change to an 'opt out' system (this was met).

Chapter essay

'Discuss whether the medical values of autonomy and consent have hampered attempts to increase the number of donated organs in the UK.'

Chapter case study

Laura is a mother with two young children. She would like to offer her elderly mother, Doreen, a kidney to ease the pain of dialysis. Medical tests are undertaken and they are found to be a match. They now find themselves in the living organ donation system and find it all quite bewildering. Describe and evaluate the legal and regulatory system of living organ donation.

Further reading

Brazier, M. (2002) 'Retained Organs: Ethics and Humanity', 22 *Legal Studies* 550–69; (2003) 'Organ Retention and Return: Problems of Consent', 29 *Journal of Medical Ethics* 30–3; (2004) 'Human Tissue Retention', 72 *Medico-Legal Journal* 39.

Charles, E. and Harris, J. (2003) 'An Ethical Market in Human Organs', 29 *Journal of Medical Ethics* 137.

Cherkassky, L. (2010) 'Presumed Consent in Organ Donation: is the duty finally upon us?', 17(2) *European Journal of Health Law* 149; (2010) 'Rational Rejection? The Ethical Complications of Assessing Organ Transplant Candidates in the UK and the USA', 18(1) *Journal of Law and Medicine* 156; (2011) 'Does The U.S. Do It Better? A Comparative Analysis of Liver Allocation Protocols in the United Kingdom and the United States', 20(3) *Cambridge Quarterly of Healthcare Ethics* 1; (2011) 'The Secret World of Liver Transplant Candidate Assessment', 11(2) *Medical Law International* 23; (2011) 'A Fair Trial? The Assessment of Liver Transplant Candidates with Psychiatric Illnesses', 37(12) *Journal of Medical Ethics* 739–742.

Jones, M. (1995) 'Elective Ventilation of Potential Organ Donors: The Legal Background', 310 *British Medical Journal* 717.

McHale, J.V. (1995) 'Elective Ventilation – Pragmatic Solution or Ethical Minefield?', 2 *Professional Negligence* 24.

10

Medical research

Chapter objectives

At the end of this chapter, you should have:

- An understanding of the history of medical research, which is of mixed character, leading to the Nuremberg Code (1947) and the Declaration of Helsinki (1964) which are regarded as the primary ethical codes for medical research on humans.

- An appreciation of the law in the UK, which is governed by the Medicines for Human Use (Clinical Trials) Regulations (2004), incorporating the Declaration of Helsinki (1964) into the practice of medical research.

- Knowledge of the kinds of research that can take place on humans, the use of placebos, the patients who are exempt, and what happens when it all goes wrong.

- An understanding of the pioneering medical research on eggs, sperm, embryos and stem cells.

SETTING THE SCENE

Ella was 9 years old and had a rare blood disorder. She was getting weaker and her immune system was failing, but doctors and specialists could not figure out why. There was no diagnosis and no cure, but a small handful of drugs did appear to alleviate some of the less serious symptoms, such as tiredness and nausea. Ella's doctor suggested that she take part in a clinical trial with a new HIV drug to boost her immune system. It was the last hope. Ella's mother Terri wanted to say yes, but she was unsure about the procedures of consent and she was also worried about the harm that Ella might be subjected to during the trial. She comes to you as a medical lawyer – how do you explain the laws surrounding medical research and the legal protection in place for participants?

Introduction

Medical research is one of the most controversial areas of medical law. The concept of administering potentially dangerous medical treatment to a volunteer is contrary to the very purpose of medicine, which is to treat a patient in accordance with his best interests. The risks involved are usually minor, but these are often measured against the benefits of the research in order to justify the trial taking place.

We need medical research in order to develop new medicines. There would not be painkillers if volunteers did not offer to take them as part of a clinical trial, and there would not be keyhole surgery if patients did not consent to take part in radical new surgical procedures. We all need a prescription from time to time, and as we get older our ailments often become more serious, amplifying our need for safe and effective medical treatments. This is why medical research is vital. However, we do not want to subject ourselves to unnecessary harm. Critics argue that if we are willing to take prescription drugs to fight our own illnesses we should be willing to give back by participating in medical research to benefit others, but in reality the utilitarian approach is commonly adopted in this area of medicine: the risk to a small few will lead to a benefit for many.

The Second World War highlighted the need for an ethical code for medical research following the practices in concentration camps. The Nuremberg Code (1947) placed voluntary consent at the top of its list of priorities, ensuring that any participant in a clinical trial could walk away as soon as the process became too uncomfortable. Consent has since slipped down the list of priorities and when the Declaration of Helsinki (1964) was composed, incompetent patients and minors were included within the ambit of potential participants, but only in certain circumstances. The Medicines for Human Use (Clinical trials) Regulations (2004) incorporates the Declaration of Helsinki into UK law.

Clinical trials are not just restricted to pills: it can include surgical techniques, therapies, all kinds of invasive treatments and statistical gathering. In poor countries where healthcare provisions are scarce, the need for medical research comes hand-in-hand with the obligation to offer the new treatment to the community itself. This is an example of when medical research really does help the participants and the population, but scientists in poor countries must ensure that they do not take advantage of particularly vulnerable participants, especially when they are in the grip of a pandemic. The participants in clinical trials must be told that they are taking part in a clinical trial, but there is a concern that a 'therapeutic misconception' will lure particularly vulnerable patients into the trial in the hope that they might be cured of a serious illness. In addition to this, the elderly, minors and pregnant women are all underrepresented in clinical trials because of the higher risk of harm. The result is that many products on the market still contain the advice 'do not take if pregnant or breastfeeding' because the results (if any) are not known.

Stem cell research is the most controversial practice of all. It is governed by the Human Fertilisation and Embryology Act 1990. Stem cells are 'blank' cells taken from embryos, which opens an ethical minefield. The hotly debated question is: should scientists be using 'potential' human beings to supplement their own research? The answer seems to be that there is a greater benefit to the general public to justify embryonic research. The use of admixed embryos, i.e. an animal egg and a human nucleus, makes this area of medical law a little more unsettling, but there is a shortage of human eggs making admixed embryos a good alternative.

The international ethical codes

Experimentation on humans is a concept that has been around for a long time. Vaccinations were tested on slaves as far back as the eighteenth century. These experiments would not require the consent of the victims, or inform them of the potential risks, and patient autonomy did not exist. Edward Jenner famously tested his smallpox vaccine on his son and other children. In the twentieth century, the world of medicine began to develop very quickly, strengthening the need for more medical experiments on human beings. However, there was still no real push for an international code of research ethics, because there were plenty of incompetent and imprisoned humans who could be subject to medical experiments.

EXTRACT

Margot Brazier, 'Exploitation and Enrichment: The Paradox of Medical Experimentation' (2008) 34 *Journal of Medical Ethics* 180–83

Edward Jenner, injected an eight-year-old boy, James Phipps, with cowpox. Months later, he injected the boy with smallpox. The vaccination 'took' and the boy survived. Jenner's experiment has saved millions of lives and led to the virtual eradication of smallpox. [...] It has often been said no modern ethics committee would have sanctioned such an experiment. Consider the case – the experiment used a child subject, who was too young to consent for himself, in non-therapeutic research where there was a high risk of death or disfigurement. The 'exploitation' of James Phipps undoubtedly saved the lives of some of us reading this.

Nuremberg

Germany has been at the forefront of the development of international codes of research ethics. In 1900, Dr Albert Neisser infected prostitutes with venereal diseases without their consent. The public disagreed with his experiments because the victims had not been informed. Guidelines were then issued by the minister for religious, educational and medical affairs, stating that all medical interventions (except diagnosis, healing and immunisation) were not allowed if the victim was a minor, incompetent, or did not give unambiguous consent. This was, however, not enshrined into law. In the Second World War, the Nazi regime allowed doctors and other individuals to conduct inhuman medical experiments upon prisoners in concentration camps. These included deliberately infecting humans with diseases, finding effective ways to torture and kill human beings, finding ways to sterilise humans, and experiments on children (particularly twins in order to conduct joint autopsies). It is not clear how many humans died as a result of medical experiments, but thousands died in concentration camps alone. In addition to this, the Unit 731 Complex of the Imperial Japanese Army in Pingfang, China, was the site of biological, nuclear, radiological and chemical warfare experimentation during the Second World War. These included infecting victims with germs and diseases, killing victims by radiation, spinning and vivisection, burying and burning them alive, and removing organs and limbs whilst alive. Over 600,000 humans died in field experiments alone, but most of the doctors and scientists were pardoned in return for classified information. It was clear that there was a glaring need for an international code of research ethics to ensure that human beings were never again subjected to torturous medical experiments.

The Nuremberg Trials followed the Second World War in 1946, in which a handful of German doctors and scientists were prosecuted for their role in the unethical treatment of humans in medical experiments in concentration camps (including one of Hitler's personal doctors, Karl Brandt). Out of the twenty-three defendants, some of them were respected internationally and others were incompetent and simply took advantage of the situation. Their defence was that there was no international law stating that medical experimentation on humans was illegal (in the Nuremberg Trials, fifteen of the defendants were convicted, seven were executed, nine were sent to prison and seven were acquitted). Dr Leo Alexander (an American psychiatrist) was a key medical advisor during the Nuremberg trial and helped to draft a document outlining the proposed limits of legitimate medical research, which later became known as the Nuremberg Code.[1] The Code emphasises the need for voluntary consent, avoiding unnecessary pain and suffering, and a belief that the experiment will not end in death or disability. The Code did not formally make it into international law, but it provides powerful ethical guidance, and its provisions (laid out below) have formed an important basis for all subsequent international ethical codes. At the very least, it started the ball rolling.

Nuremberg Code (1947)

Paragraph 1: The voluntary consent of the human subject is absolutely essential.

Paragraph 2: The experiment should be such as to yield fruitful results for the good of society, unprocurable by other methods or means of study, and not random and unnecessary in nature.

Paragraph 3: The experiment should be so designed and based on the results of animal experimentation and a knowledge of the natural history of the disease or other problem under study that the anticipated results will justify the performance of the experiment.

Paragraph 4: The experiment should be so conducted as to avoid all unnecessary physical and mental suffering and injury.

---

[1] Different from the more general 'Nuremberg Principles' which provide the definition of a war crime.

Paragraph 5: No experiment should be conducted where there is an *a priori* reason to believe that death or disabling injury will occur; except, perhaps, in those experiments where the experimental physicians also serve as subjects.

Paragraph 6: The degree of risk to be taken should never exceed that determined by the humanitarian importance of the problem to be solved by the experiment.

Paragraph 7: Proper preparations should be made and adequate facilities provided to protect the experimental subject against even remote possibilities of injury, disability or death.

Paragraph 8: The experiment should be conducted only by scientifically qualified persons. The highest degree of skill and care should be required through all stages of the experiment of those who conduct or engage in the experiment.

Paragraph 9: During the course of the experiment the human subject should be at liberty to bring the experiment to an end if he has reached the physical or mental state where continuation of the experiment seems to him to be impossible.

Paragraph 10: During the course of the experiment the scientist in charge must be prepared to terminate the experiment at any stage, if he has probable cause to believe, in the exercise of the good faith, superior skill and careful judgment required of him, that a continuation of the experiment is likely to result in injury, disability or death to the experimental subject.

Consent is clearly the top priority, making any forced medical experiments upon humans completely unethical. The good of society is a consideration, suggesting that the suffering of a minority will benefit the majority (utilitarianism). The experiment must not be possible any other way except through human experimentation and the experiment must not be random in nature, possibly because random experiments show a lack of purpose. The results should justify the performance of the experiment, although inevitably, some results may be completely unknown until the experiment is carried out. All unnecessary physical and mental suffering and injury must be avoided, although this leaves open a new question of what *is* necessary. Experiments resulting death or disabling injury are allowed if the physicians also take part, suggesting that those who perform medical experiments on humans should be directly involved in the real dangers. The degree of risk should not be higher than the seriousness of the humanitarian problem to be solved and proper preparations and adequate facilities are expected to protect against 'even remote' possibilities of injury allowing for a high level of protection for research subjects. Scientifically qualified persons must show a high degree of skill and care throughout the experiment, although it is not clear what exactly they must do skilfully and carefully. Vitally, the human subject can bring the research to an end, but strangely, only when he feels it is *impossible* to carry on – this is a very high threshold. The scientist must exercise his good faith when bringing an experiment to an end, suggesting that unscrupulous scientists can not allow their experiment to carry on in the face of grave risks.

The Nuremberg Code might not have been enshrined into law, but it symbolised a historical moment in medical research. For the first time, an international ethical code was available to guide scientists and other medical professionals as to when human medical experiments may be unethical and what the boundaries of such unethical research might be. The Code was developed as a result of the Nuremberg Trials where the main issue was murder, but its ambit stretches far beyond that and is applicable to all kinds of human medical experiments.

Geneva

The Declaration of Geneva followed shortly after in 1948. It was adopted by the General Assembly of the World Medical Association in Geneva, Switzerland. Its main aim is to enshrine the ethical ideals of the Hippocratic Oath into an international ethical code and to consolidate the humanitarian goals of the medical profession, which was vital in light of the Nazi activities of that decade). It has been amended several times over the years to keep up with the changing attitudes and developments in modern medicine, but the essence of the document remains the same, outlining the ethical duties of a doctor towards his patient. The amended version of the Declaration of Geneva from 2006 reads as follows.

The Declaration of Geneva (1948) (as amended)[2]

At the time of being admitted as a member of the medical profession:

Paragraph 1: I solemnly pledge to consecrate my life to the service of humanity.

Paragraph 2: I will give to my teachers the respect and gratitude that is their due.

Paragraph 3: I will practice my profession with conscience and dignity.

Paragraph 4: The health of my patient will be my first consideration.

Paragraph 5: I will respect the secrets that are confided in me, even after the patient has died.

Paragraph 6: I will maintain by all the means in my power, the honour and the noble traditions of the medical profession.

Paragraph 7: My colleagues will be my sisters and brothers.

Paragraph 8: I will not permit considerations of age, disease or disability, creed, ethnic origin, gender, nationality, political affiliation, race, sexual orientation, social standing or any other factor to intervene between my duty and my patient.

Paragraph 9: I will maintain the utmost respect for human life.

Paragraph 10: I will not use my medical knowledge to violate human rights and civil liberties, even under threat.

Paragraph 11: I make these promises solemnly, freely and upon my honour.

These guidelines are ethical in nature, placing an emphasis on trust, honour and integrity. Medical experiments are not specifically mentioned, but the principles within the Declaration can be applied to the behaviour of scientists during medical experiments.

---

[2] See: http://www.wma.net/en/30publications/10policies/index.html.

Helsinki

Two decades later, the Declaration of Helsinki became the ultimate cornerstone of medical research ethics. It was adopted by the eighteenth World Medical Association assembly in Helsinki, Finland in 1964, and is the first real effort on the part of the international medical community to publish a detailed collection of ethical guidelines that relate to medical research involving humans. It has not been enshrined into international law, but it is considered to be the leading authority on ethical human experimentation. It has been amended eight times, and there are currently thirty-five paragraphs (a selection follow).

The Declaration of Helsinki (1964) (as amended)[3]

Paragraph 2: Although the Declaration is addressed primarily to physicians, the World Medical Association (WMA) encourages other participants in medical research involving human subjects to adopt these principles.

Paragraph 3: It is the duty of the physician to promote and safeguard the health of patients, including those who are involved in medical research.

Paragraph 6: In medical research involving human subjects, the wellbeing of the individual research subject must take precedence over all other interests.

Paragraph 7: The primary purpose of medical research involving human subjects is to understand the causes, development and effects of diseases and improve preventive, diagnostic and therapeutic interventions (methods, procedures and treatments).

Paragraph 10: Physicians should consider the ethical, legal and regulatory norms and standards for research involving human subjects in their own countries as well as applicable international norms and standards.

All medical professionals must adhere to the ethical standards adopted in the declaration of Helsinki. The doctor must promote the health of his patients, adding a deeper element to the Nuremberg rule that injury, disability or death should simply be avoided. The wellbeing of the patient takes precedence over all other interests, showing a strong commitment to patient autonomy, bodily integrity and the social, emotional and religious needs of the patient. The purpose of the research must be to *understand* and *improve* medicine, thus excluding inhuman experiments to simply satisfy curiosity. National and international legal and ethical standards must be considered, allowing for vulnerable communities to be protected.

The Declaration of Helsinki (continued)

Paragraph 11: It is the duty of physicians who participate in medical research to protect the life, health, dignity, integrity, right to self-determination, privacy, and confidentiality of personal information of research subjects.

Paragraph 12: Medical research involving human subjects must conform to generally accepted scientific principles, be based on a thorough knowledge of the scientific literature, other relevant sources of information, and adequate laboratory and, as appropriate, animal experimentation.

➜

[3] See note above.

Paragraph 14: The design and performance of each research study involving human subjects must be clearly described in a research protocol.

Paragraph 15: The research protocol must be submitted for consideration, comment, guidance and approval to a research ethics committee before the study begins. The committee must be independent of the researcher, the sponsor and any other undue influence. It must take into consideration the laws and regulations of the country or countries in which the research is to be performed as well as applicable international norms and standards. No change to the protocol may be made without consideration and approval by the committee.

Paragraph 16: Medical research involving human subjects must be conducted only by individuals with the appropriate scientific training and qualifications.

Paragraph 17: Medical research involving a disadvantaged or vulnerable population or community is only justified if the research is responsive to the health needs and priorities of this population or community and if there is a reasonable likelihood that this population or community stands to benefit from the results of the research.

It was a new idea that doctors should protect the dignity and integrity of a patient undergoing a medical experiment, completely irradiating the idea that prisoners, incompetent people and the elderly were 'easy targets' for research. There must be a research protocol and an objective ethics committee must validate it, and this is vital to ensure that all trials are logged and observed. Following on from the Nuremberg Code, the doctors involved must be scientifically qualified. In an interesting addition to the Nuremberg Code, and possibly a premonition into future clinical trials abroad, a vulnerable community must benefit from the research conducted upon them, encouraging specific clinical trials to respond to specific needs.

The Declaration of Helsinki (continued)

Paragraph 18: Every medical research study involving human subjects must be preceded by careful assessment of predictable risks and burdens to the individuals and communities involved in the research in comparison with foreseeable benefits to them and to other individuals or communities affected by the condition under investigation.

Paragraph 20: Physicians must immediately stop a study when the risks are found to outweigh the potential benefits or when there is conclusive proof of positive and beneficial results.

Paragraph 21: Medical research involving human subjects may only be conducted if the importance of the objective outweighs the inherent risks and burdens to the research subjects.

Paragraph 22: Participation by competent individuals as subjects in medical research must be voluntary.

Paragraph 24: In medical research involving competent human subjects, each potential subject must be adequately informed of the aims, methods, sources of funding, any possible conflicts of interest, institutional affiliations of the researcher, the anticipated benefits and potential risks of the study and the discomfort it may entail, and any other relevant aspects of the study. The potential subject must be informed of the right to refuse to participate in the study or to withdraw consent to participate at any time without reprisal. If the consent cannot be expressed in writing, the non-written consent must be formally documented and witnessed.

There must be a careful assessment of the risks and burdens and these must be compared to the benefits. This develops the Nuremberg request for 'proper preparations' in 'adequate facilities', but there is no further detail in Helsinki as to what the outcome of the assessment should be. A doctor must stop when the risks outweigh the objective, but this means that the risks can still be as high as the patient will allow. A doctor must stop on conclusive proof of positive results. This is a vital addition to the Nuremberg Code as it prevents patients from being subjected to medical experiments when there is no longer a need to do so. Consent must be valid, from the patient herself, and completely voluntary, enshrining the number one principle from the Nuremberg Code. Interestingly, the patient must be informed of the aims, methods, benefits and risks. This is a radical enhancement of the principles in the Nuremberg Code, and turns the clinical research process into an equal agreement between doctor and patient. It is encouraging to see that a patient can still refuse to participate in a study and that this is enshrined into the Declaration of Helsinki directly from the Nuremberg Code.

The Declaration of Helsinki (continued)

Paragraph 27: For a potential research subject who is incompetent, the physician must seek informed consent from the legally authorised representative. These individuals must not be included in a research study that has no likelihood of benefit for them unless:

- it is intended to promote the health of the population represented by the potential subject,
- the research cannot instead be performed with competent persons, and
- the research entails only minimal risk and minimal burden.

Paragraph 29: Research involving subjects who are physically or mentally incapable of giving consent, for example, unconscious patients, may be done only if the physical or mental condition that prevents giving informed consent is a necessary characteristic of the research population. If no such representative is available and if the research cannot be delayed, the study may proceed without informed consent provided that the specific reasons for involving subjects with a condition that renders them unable to give informed consent have been stated in the research protocol and the study has been approved by a research ethics committee.

Paragraph 30: Authors, editors and publishers all have ethical obligations with regard to the publication of the results of research. Authors have a duty to make publicly available the results of their research on human subjects and are accountable for the completeness and accuracy of their reports. They should adhere to accepted guidelines for ethical reporting. Negative and inconclusive as well as positive results should be published or otherwise made publicly available. Sources of funding, institutional affiliations and conflicts of interest should be declared in the publication.

Paragraph 32: The benefits, risks, burdens and effectiveness of a new intervention must be tested against those of the best current proven intervention, except in the following circumstances:

- The use of placebo, or no treatment, is acceptable in studies where no current proven intervention exists; or
- Where for compelling and scientifically sound methodological reasons the use of placebo is necessary to determine the efficacy or safety of an intervention and the patients who receive placebo or no treatment will not be subject to any risk of serious or irreversible harm. Extreme care must be taken to avoid abuse of this option.

Paragraph 33: At the conclusion of the study, patients entered into the study are entitled to be informed about the outcome of the study and to share any benefits that result from it, for example, access to interventions identified as beneficial in the study or to other appropriate care or benefits.

Paragraph 35: In the treatment of a patient, where proven interventions do not exist or have been ineffective, the physician, after seeking expert advice, with informed consent from the patient or a legally authorised representative, may use an unproven intervention if in the physician's judgement it offers hope of saving life, re-establishing health or alleviating suffering. Where possible, this intervention should be made the object of research, designed to evaluate its safety and efficacy. In all cases, new information should be recorded and, where appropriate, made publicly available.

In a significant departure from the Nuremberg Code, which states from the outset that 'voluntary consent' is 'absolutely essential', the Declaration of Helsinki allows for incompetent patients to engage in medical research as long as a legal representative is found to consent on their behalf. There are strict criteria to meet: the research must benefit others with the same problem; it wouldn't work on competent patients (meaning the research will probably be illness-specific), and there must be minimal risk and minimal burden. This is a controversial guideline because of the lack of voluntary consent, so perhaps 'minimal distress' could be added too? Consent is not even necessary if the incompetent patient requires the research to be carried out urgently (e.g. a new drug). This is only allowed if the legal representative cannot be found and the reason for the lack of consent (e.g. a rare brain disease) is listed in the protocol as *the ailment to be researched*. This is a huge departure from the Nuremberg Code, which does not contemplate incompetent patients or urgent treatment. It is noted that negative and inconclusive results should be published as well as positive results, in order to prevent any similar trials and additional suffering for no reason. Risks and effectiveness must be judged against the best current intervention (i.e. the best current treatment). This is important because it encourages clinical trials to find a treatment that is *better* than the current option. The use of a placebo (i.e. a fake treatment) is controversial because the patient will not experience any benefit from the trial. The Declaration of Helsinki requires the use of a placebo to be justified, that is 'compelling and scientifically sound methodological reasons', but ideally, a placebo should only be an option where *no* current treatment exists at all. It is very useful that patients should benefit from the outcome of the study. An unproven intervention may only be used when nothing else is available, and the patient (or representative) must consent. This could happen when a rare disease is diagnosed and there are no drugs available. Doctors may offer a consenting patient an unknown and untested drug to simply see what happens. The results must, of course, be recorded because it is medical research.

Ethical problems with the ethical codes?

The Declaration of Helsinki (1964) may be the cornerstone of international medical research ethics, but it contains some controversies. The Nuremberg Code strongly endorsed voluntary consent, but this idea has been undermined by the introduction of legal representatives, including the right to perform urgent research on incompetent patients without the representative being present. This is a step backwards in time. In addition, the Nuremberg Code focussed on 'fruitful' results but now, with the use of a placebo, researchers can deprive a patient of the best current treatment and cause unnecessary suffering. The Declaration of Helsinki would be more ethically sound if it supported the use of a placebo only in circumstances where *no* other treatment was available.

Progress has certainly been made since the days of the Nuremberg Trials. In medicine today, any medical research involving human subjects must now be scientifically valid, must be performed by qualified professionals, must seek the voluntary consent of the competent patient, must place the wellbeing of the patient at the forefront of all considerations, should provide a benefit to the patient, must be approved by an ethics committee, must be stopped when the risks outweigh the benefits, and must inform the patient of the outcome. There are still elements of utilitarianism throughout the provisions of Helsinki, particularly in paragraphs 17, 18, 27 and 29 where the risks to the human subject are balanced against the benefits for the community or the general objective of the research. The subject can also withdraw from a study if he becomes uncomfortable, but this option is only available to competent patients.

It is admirable that under paragraph 33 a subject is allowed to share any benefits that result from the study, but this might be dangerous. What if long-term effects are not yet known? In addition to this, what if the patient is tempted into a false sense of promise that his suffering will be rewarded in the end? This might not always be the case. In the UK, there are a number of regulations, codes and guidelines that will be able to shed more light on exactly how the Helsinki provisions have been implemented in the UK (below).

ACTIVITY

Dr Wells is a cardiovascular scientist and is running a large NHS research project. She wishes to research a new heart drug for older patients with angina. She does not know what the risks will be because the new drug has not been tested on elderly men before, and she does not know what the benefits will be, for the same reason.

Dr Valkerie is a biological scientist and is also running a large NHS research project into a common strain of winter flu. He wishes to research the effects of a recently rejected drug for flu sufferers. He knows what the risks will be because it was tested last year, and he anticipates that the benefits will be barely noticeable in the general population.

According to the Declaration of Helsinki in regards to the balancing of risks against benefits, who is proposing to perform unethical research on human subjects and why?

The UK approach to medical research

In the UK, there is one particularly significant statutory instrument that governs this area of law. The Medicines for Human Use (Clinical Trials) Regulations 2004 implements the relevant European standards in this area into UK law. It provides a definition for human medical experiments, it lays down the responsibilities of Ethics Committees and it describes good clinical practice. Importantly, 'medical experiments' are now referred to as 'clinical trials', and there is a definition of this and of 'subject' under regulation 2.

Medicines for Human Use (Clinical Trials) Regulations 2004

Part 1

Regulation 2(1): In these regulations 'clinical trial' means any investigation in human subjects, other than a non-interventional trial, intended:

(a) to discover or verify the clinical, pharmacological or other pharmacodynamic effects of one or more medicinal products,

(b) to identify any adverse reactions to one or more such products, or

(c) to study the absorption, distribution, metabolism and excretion of one or more such products.

In these regulations, 'subject' means, in relation to a clinical trial, an individual, whether a patient or not, who participates in a clinical trial:

(a) as a recipient of an investigational medicinal product or of some other treatment or product, or

(b) without receiving any treatment or product, as a control.

There is clearly an emphasis on clinical research under regulation 2, allowing for studies into how medicines react in the human body and whether they are effective at preventing diseases. This principle is in line with the Declaration of Helsinki (paragraph 7). In addition, according to the 2004 Regulations, a subject is still part of clinical research even if he receives no treatment, suggesting that a placebo may be used.

The Declaration of Helsinki is more expressly referred to in Schedule 1 of the 2004 Regulations, which outlines the conditions and principles which apply to all clinical trials. This is an important part of the Schedule because it establishes the boundaries of ethical medical research. A selection of these principles are provided below.

Medicines for Human Use (Clinical trials) Regulations (2004)

Schedule 1, Part 2

Paragraph 1: The rights, safety and wellbeing of the trial subjects shall prevail over the interests of science and society.

Paragraph 3: Clinical trials shall be scientifically sound and guided by ethical principles in all their aspects.

Paragraph 6: Clinical trials shall be conducted in accordance with the principles of the Declaration of Helsinki.

For the first time, the interests of the subject must prevail *over* the interests of society, showing a move away from the utilitarian ideal that a minority should suffer to benefit the majority. All the principles under the Declaration of Helsinki (1964) apply to clinical research in the UK (paragraph 6 above), meaning that the scientists must be scientifically qualified, a protocol should describe the clinical research and be put before an ethics committee, and all information should be recorded.

> ## Medicines for Human Use (Clinical trials) Regulations (2004)
>
> ### Schedule 1, Part 2
>
> **Paragraph 10**: Before the trial is initiated, foreseeable risks and inconveniences have been weighed against the anticipated benefit for the individual trial subject and other present and future patients. A trial should be initiated and continued only if the benefits justify the risks.
>
> **Paragraph 12**: A trial shall be initiated only if an ethics committee and the licensing authority comes to the conclusion that the anticipated therapeutic and public health benefits justify the risks and may be continued only if compliance with this requirement is permanently monitored.
>
> **Paragraph 14**: Provision has been made for insurance or indemnity to cover the liability of the investigator and sponsor which may arise in relation to the clinical trial.

The familiar suggestion from the Declaration of Helsinki that a scientist must weigh risks against benefits (at paragraph 18) has clearly been transferred into the UK regulations, but it is a new requirement that the benefits must *justify* the risks. This is a stricter approach because it requires the scientist to give *good reasons* for subjecting a patient to risks. The benefit can be felt by the participant and future patients, and it is also a very good idea that a clinical trial is permanently monitored. For the first time, there must be insurance in place to pay the subject compensation should anything go wrong.

> ## Medicines for Human Use (Clinical trials) Regulations (2004)
>
> ### Schedule 1, Part 3
>
> **Paragraph 2**: The subject has been informed of his right to withdraw from the trial at any time.
>
> **Paragraph 3**: The subject has given his informed consent to taking part in the trial.
>
> **Paragraph 4**: The subject may, without being subject to any resulting detriment, withdraw from the clinical trial at any time by revoking his informed consent.

As far back as the Nuremberg Code, the voluntary consent of the patient was crucial. We should however remember that nowadays there is a split between competent and incompetent subjects and different rules apply to each group (more below).

Who is the licensing authority?

There is a brief mention of a 'licensing authority' within the provisions of the 2004 Regulations (above). It is a formal requirement under regulation 17 that the 'sponsor', the person in charge of initiating, organising and financing the research, must request permission from a licensing authority to conduct his clinical trial. In the UK, the licensing authority is currently the Medicines and Healthcare Products Regulatory Agency (MHRA), which was set up by the government to ensure that medicines and medical devices are safe to use.[4] It does this by ensuring that:

- the design and conduct of clinical trials for medicines and medical devices provides acceptable levels of protection for subjects;

- a new medicine or device will be allowed on the market only if the benefits outweigh the risks;

- enough reliable information is received from healthcare professionals, patients, the public and companies about the adverse effects of a medicine or device;

- if new information becomes available about a benefit, a risk, the quality or the supply, a warning will be issued to the public and the manufacturer or it will be withdrawn from the market;

- and good advice can be issued to the public and the manufacturer if adverse effects result from the medicine or device being inappropriately or incorrectly used, cleaned or maintained.

Any suspected unexpected serious adverse reactions during the course of a clinical trial which could be fatal or life threatening *must* be recorded and reported to the licensing authority (the MHRA) as soon as possible (under regulation 33). It is a criminal offence to fail to do so (under regulation 49), and the person who does so may face criminal sanctions such as a term of imprisonment or a fine (under regulation 52).

Who is the ethics committee?

There is also a brief mention of an 'ethics committee' within the provisions of the 2004 Regulations (above). There is a complex history behind ethics committees, but they form an important part of clinical research, especially in light of the Declaration of Helsinki (1964) which encouraged the active involvement of independent and objective ethics committees to authorise research protocols (under paragraph 15).

The UK government recognised the need for boards of medical professionals to authorise clinical trials in light of the Declaration of Helsinki, and it asked regional health authorities and hospitals to set up research ethics committees (RECs). Lord Warner reviewed the system of ethics committees in his report entitled: Ad Hoc Advisory Group on the Operations of NHS Research Ethics Committees (2005).[5] As a result, the National Research Ethics Service (NRES) was set up in 2007 as a branch of the NHS.[6] It is designed to protect the rights, safety, dignity and wellbeing of research participants who take part in clinical trials. To do this, it maintains a national ethical review system through its NHS Research Ethics Committees (NHS RECs). There are approximately eighty NHS RECs all around the UK who review research applications and give an ethical opinion as to the proposed involvement of the participant. The applicants range from pharmaceutical companies and healthcare professionals to prison health researchers. NHS RECs are completely independent of the research, which allows them to put the needs of the participant first. There are some clinical trials that present more complex ethical problems than others. For example, anything that requires drugs or invasive procedures will certainly raise ethical questions, whereas record collecting may not be so controversial.

---

[4] See their official website: www.mhra.gov.uk.
[5] Lord Warner, Ad Hoc Advisory Group on the Operations of NHS Research Ethics Committees, 6 June 2005, http://www.ops.org.bo/textocompleto/iet26345.pdf.
[6] See: http://www.nres.nhs.uk/applications/approval-requirements/ethical-review-requirements/.

The Medicines for Human Use (Clinical Trials) Regulations 2004 state that a clinical trial cannot proceed without permission from an ethics committee and a licensing authority under regulation 12(3). There are numerous matters which the ethics committee must consider, listed below.

Medicines for Human Use (Clinical trials) Regulations (2004)

Regulation 15(5): In preparing its opinion, the committee shall consider, in particular, the following matters:

(a) the relevance of the clinical trial and its design;

(b) whether the evaluation of the anticipated benefits and risks is satisfactory and whether the conclusions are justified;

(c) the suitability of the investigator and supporting staff;

(d) the investigator's procedure;

(e) the quality of the facilities for the trial;

(f) the adequacy and completeness of the information given, and the procedure to be followed, for the purpose of obtaining informed consent to the subjects' participation in the trial;

(g) if the subjects are to include persons incapable of giving informed consent, whether the research is justified having regard to the conditions and principles specified in Schedule 1, Part 5;

(h) provision for indemnity or compensation in the event of injury or death attributable to the clinical trial.

An ethics committee would be expected to pay particular attention to the ethical promises enshrined into the Nuremberg Code, the Declaration of Geneva, and in particular, the Declaration of Helsinki. Perhaps there could be more of an emphasis on the *need* for the research, the *intensity* of the research, the exact risks (if known), the justification for these, the benefit to the participant and the level of distress that could be caused to the participants? The aim of the REC, however, is clear: they must review the protocol and decide whether the clinical trial is set to an acceptable ethical standard. The chief investigator of the clinical trial, i.e. the person responsible for the conduct of that trial at the trial site, must apply to the ethics committee for an opinion under regulation 14(1). The NHS REC must come to a decision within 60 days normally, although for special cases it may be 180 days under regulation 15(10). This strict timeline may be a way of encouraging research to be authorised quickly when a widespread public need for a drug or antidote suddenly becomes apparent.

The constitution of NHS RECs is described under Schedule 2 of the 2004 Regulations as a collection of no more than eighteen members from mixed backgrounds, including healthcare professionals and lay members who have never worked in medicine (regulation 3).

UK medical research guidelines

There are numerous medical bodies who are free to publish their own guidelines. These include:

- General Medical Council.[7]
- Department of Health.[8]
- Medical Research Council.[9]

The General Medical Council publishes the highly regarded: Good Medical Practice (2006) which provides all qualified doctors with professional guidance on life and death, maintaining standards, the patient relationship, confidentiality and consent, working with colleagues and maintaining boundaries. The GMC also publishes supplementary ethical guidelines, including a research guide entitled: Good Practice in Research (2010) for those doctors who choose to initiate or contribute to a clinical trial. A select few paragraphs are provided below.

EXTRACT

Good Practice in Research (2010), General Medical Council:

http://www.gmc-uk.org/guidance/ethical_guidance/5992.asp

Paragraph 5: To protect participants and maintain public confidence in research, it is important that all research is conducted lawfully, with honesty and integrity, and in accordance with good practice.

Paragraph 8: You must make sure that the safety, dignity and wellbeing of participants take precedence over the development of treatments and the furthering of knowledge.

Paragraph 9: You must make sure that foreseeable risks to participants are kept as low as possible. In addition, you must be satisfied that:

- the anticipated benefits to participants outweigh the foreseeable risks, or
- the foreseeable risks to participants are minimal if the research only has the potential to benefit others more generally.

Paragraph 13: You must keep your knowledge and skills up to date. If you lead a research team, you must make sure that all members of the team have the necessary skills, experience, training and support to carry out their research responsibilities as effectively as possible.

Paragraph 15: You must stop research where the results indicate that participants are at risk of significant harm or, in research involving treatment required by a patient, where no benefit can be expected.

Paragraph 24: You must report research results accurately, objectively, promptly and in a way that can be clearly understood.

Paragraph 27: You must not allow your judgement about a research project to be influenced, or be seen to be influenced, at any stage, by financial, personal, political or other external interests.

Paragraph 28: You must get consent from participants before involving them in any research project. You must have other valid authority before involving in research adults who lack capacity, or children or young people who cannot consent for themselves.

Paragraph 29: You must make sure that people are informed of, and that you respect, their right to decline to take part in research and to withdraw from the research project at any time, with an assurance that this will not adversely affect their relationship with those providing care, or the care they receive.

---

[7] www.gmc-uk.org.
[8] www.dh.gov.uk.
[9] www.mrc.ac.uk.

There are references to the Declaration of Geneva in that the doctor must conduct his research with honesty and integrity, and make sure that the wellbeing of the patient presides over all else. If the research is to benefit the majority, the risks to the patient (who receives no benefit) must be minimal. This is the utilitarian approach taken from the Declaration of Helsinki. The doctor must ensure that his whole team is skilled, qualified and experienced. This was not included in the Declaration of Helsinki (or any other regulation) and adds an additional duty upon the doctor to oversee his staff as well as his subjects. The clinical research must not be influenced by personal or external interests. This may seem obvious, but this was not expressly mentioned in the Nuremberg Code, the Declaration of Geneva, the Declaration of Helsinki or the Medicines for Human Use (Clinical Trials) Regulations 2004. The use of incompetent subjects is supported by the requirement for valid consent from a 'valid authority' – an idea from the Declaration of Helsinki that has clearly been widely accepted into practice.

There appears to be a stronger emphasis on good ethical behaviour and less mention of the regulatory nature of clinical trials, such as risk assessments, in the GMC research guidelines. The GMC guidelines do, however, refer frequently to the 2004 Regulations and the MHRA as the legal authorities for clinical trials, and encourage doctors to adhere to the legal provisions at all times.

THINKING POINT

Ethics committees are clearly important to clinical research, but how well do you think an NHS REC can judge whether a clinical trial is ethical? Visit the National Research Ethics Service website and find out how they work in practice before answering this question.

What is research?

Medical research can take many different forms. It can be as simple as collecting statistical data from a database in one afternoon, to as complex as trialling a new drug on individual patients diagnosed with that particular illness over a long period of time. What should be remembered is that, regardless of the kind of research that is undertaken, the Declaration of Helsinki (1964), the Medicines for Human Use (Clinical trials) Regulations (2004), and the General Medical Council Guidelines (2010) should be followed at all times. This is especially important in regard to putting the welfare of the patient at the forefront of the study, and respecting their right to withdraw from the research at any time.

Statistical research

It may be useful to collect medical research on the general population. This could help with designing a clinical trial because statistical facts and figures can put a medical issue into perspective by answering a lot of questions. For example:

- Is this illness/condition a real problem in society?
- How widespread is it?
- How many people are being treated for it, and with what?
- What are the current prospects if diagnosed?

- Has any research been carried out before?
- What is really needed in terms of treatment or therapy to help this illness/condition?

This kind of information can be gathered in statistical form only, showing such results as:

- How many males/females are suffering from it.
- The age ranges of sufferers.
- The current drugs used to alleviate it.
- The location of the population suffering from it (e.g. city areas).
- The symptoms.
- The number of sufferers.
- The number of deaths.
- Any trends.

When a matter of public health is at stake (examples in our lifetime include foot and mouth disease, bird flu and swine flu), this kind of statistical information can illustrate how urgent the need for medical research is, what the symptoms are, how fast it is spreading, what precautions can be taken and who would benefit most from a cure. Potential statistical projects could be:

- How many people suffered from swine flu last winter?
- How many men over the age of 50 have heart disease?
- What are the current drugs for ovarian cancer and how effective are they?
- Do patients living in the countryside receive adequate access to cancer care?
- How many toddlers have been treated for measles in the last twelve months?
- How many new cases of HIV/AIDS have been diagnosed in the last three months?

Patients do not have to consent to their statistical data being used if it is made anonymous. For example, personal and identifiable details are removed from the record, such as name and address. The date of birth is important as it shows the age of the patient, and the general location of the patient (e.g. 'Gloucestershire') gives the researcher a basic idea of the medical health of that particular area. Chapter 5 deals with patient confidentiality in more detail.

Clinical trials for new drugs

The most valuable medical research is that which tests new drugs on patients with a specific medical ailment, such as cancer drugs on cancer patients, HIV drugs on patients with HIV, and so on. There would be no point in giving chemotherapy to healthy volunteers who do not have cancer, and besides, the risks will outweigh the benefits and this goes against the Declaration of Helsinki (1964), the Medicines for Human Use (Clinical trials) Regulations (2004) and the General Medical Council Guidelines (2010). These clinical trials are properly planned, funded, licensed and supervised in accordance with the regulations and declarations listed above, and on completion they allow a new drug to be licensed for public consumption. They happen in several different phases:

- **Phase I**: a small number of healthy volunteers are brought forward and the researchers will investigate how the drug is absorbed by the body and whether it proves to be toxic to the volunteer.

- **Phase II**: the drug, once proved safe, is given to patients with a specific medical ailment to measure its effectiveness. An example may be a new drug that is intended to lower blood pressure in pregnant women.

- **Phase III**: the drug, once proved safe with phase II patients, will be tested on a wider group of patients with the ailment. This phase will take longer to complete because long-term side effects must also be looked into.

These phases are intended to gather information as opposed to treating patients, but it is clear that patients in phases II and III may well find that their ailment is being treated as a consequence of being part of the trial. Patients should be warned not to *expect* benefits automatically, but that they *could* occur unexpectedly. Phase I could therefore be described as non-therapeutic, because it does not treat the volunteers, whereas phases II and III could be described as therapeutic, because they may provide treatment. Once the three phases are complete the drug will be licensed for public use in specific doses, but it will still be monitored. This is because, during the three phases, certain categories of patient may not have been tested, such as pregnant women, adults with certain other ailments, or children. The new drug will also not have been comprehensively tested alongside other drugs, which is important because some drugs – once ingested – can alter the way other drugs work inside the body.

In 2006, there was a well-publicised incident involving eight healthy men in a phase I trial at Northwick Park Hospital, in which they received a new antibody called TGN 1412 for the treatment of arthritis, leukaemia and multiple sclerosis. Primate studies showed no adverse effects, but six of the men suffered multiple organ failure, whereas the other two had received a placebo (a drug that does nothing). A report was published after the incident by the Department of Health on direction from the Secretary of State for Health, entitled: The Expert Group on Phase One Clinical Trials: Final Report (2007). The report found that extra caution had to be taken when introducing new agents into the human body for the first time. In the extract below, a phase I trial is also referred to as a 'first-in-man' trial:

EXTRACT

The Expert Group on Phase One Clinical Trials: Final Report (2007) (no longer available), The Department of Health, at pages 84–98

There may be circumstances where healthy volunteers are more appropriate subjects in a phase one clinical trial. The decision whether to conduct a first-in-man trial in healthy volunteers should be carefully considered and fully justified, taking into account all factors relevant to the safety of the subjects and the value of the scientific information that is likely to be obtained.

The paramount factors should always be the safety, rights and well-being of the volunteers, whether patients or healthy individuals, and the value of what can be learnt from the clinical trial. First-in-man trials should be conducted in appropriate clinical environments supervised by staff with appropriate levels of training and expertise and an understanding of the trial agent, its target and mechanism of action. There must be immediate access to facilities for the treatment of medical emergencies (such as cardiac emergencies, anaphylaxis, cytokine release syndrome, convulsions, hypotension), facilities for stabilising individuals in an acute emergency and ready availability of ITU facilities.

A thorough assessment of risk should always be carried out before first-in-man trials. The risk assessment should be clearly described in the trial documents and be fully examined by the regulator. When there is significant doubt, higher risk should always be assumed.

Therapeutic v non-therapeutic

It is important to distinguish between therapeutic research and non-therapeutic research for one simple reason: it is much easier to enrol incompetent patients on a therapeutic clinical trial because they will 'benefit' from the experience. If they find themselves on a non-therapeutic clinical trial, the risks must be minimal according to the Declaration of Helsinki (1964), the Medicines for Human Use (Clinical Trials) Regulations (2004) and in particular the General Medical Council Guidelines (2010), but this is difficult to prove when a new drug is being tested for the first time. In a therapeutic trial, when the risks equate to serious harm or the risks override the proposed benefits, the researcher must stop the trial according to the regulations and declarations above, and this applies to competent and incompetent patients alike. A reference to 'therapeutic' research is ambiguous, because the researcher does not know for sure that there will be any positive results from his trial. He is merely *speculating* that there will be positive results, and this puts patients – whether competent or incompetent – in a precarious situation. The Research Ethics Committees are in place to scrutinise the research protocol before the trial begins, and they must agree that the clinical trial is in line with all the relevant regulations and declarations before it begins.

Placebos in clinical trials

A placebo is a drug that has no effect, like a sugar pill. They are vital in clinical trials because they allow researchers to directly compare patients who have ingested the new drug against patients who have not. The secret is to not tell the controlled patients that they have received the placebo. This secrecy is vital because, when a patient knowingly takes a pill for a complaint (such as aspirin for headaches or drugs for depression), he may be tricked into thinking that the drug is working when he is simply getting better on his own. To allow placebo's to be used, researchers split patients into two groups and the 'controlled' group gets a placebo. These kinds of clinical trials are known as randomised controlled trials because the patients are randomly placed into their group:

- **Active group**: they receive the new drug but are not told.
- **Control group**: they receive the placebo but are not told.

These kinds of clinical trials (which make up the majority of clinical trials) are plagued with ethical difficulties. The first ethical problem with random allocation into a control group is that if a patient is suffering from a serious illness such as cancer, it would go against his best interests to receive a placebo which does nothing, when he could be receiving prescription drugs. The second ethical difficulty is that it would also go against the moral duty of a doctor to put his patient forward for a treatment that might not be in his best interests. The third ethical difficulty is that if the new drug shows signs of working in the active group, the control group are now placed at a disadvantage. They are not receiving any prescription drugs *or* the new and more effective drug, but stopping the trial would mean that valuable research is lost. The fourth ethical difficulty relates to consent: how can a patient consent to a treatment that he does not know he is receiving?

The relevant regulations and declarations in this field address the use of placebos. If there is no current treatment on the market, then a placebo does not pose an ethical problem. However, if there is a treatment available on the market, referred to as a 'best current proven intervention', the control group *must* receive that instead of the placebo. In this way, their best interests are still being met, and they are not missing out on any treatment or suffering any loss. This is probably a more effective way of conducting randomised control trials, because the researchers can then compare the effects of the old drug against the new drug. The Declaration of Helsinki (1964) and the Medicines for Human Use (Clinical Trials) Regulations (2004) both support this approach:

Declaration of Helsinki (1964)

Paragraph 32: The benefits, risks, burdens and effectiveness of a new intervention must be tested against those of the best current proven intervention, except in the following circumstances:

- The use of placebo, or no treatment, is acceptable in studies where no current proven intervention exists; or
- Where for compelling and scientifically sound methodological reasons the use of placebo is necessary to determine the efficacy or safety of an intervention and the patients who receive placebo or no treatment will not be subject to any risk of serious or irreversible harm. Extreme care must be taken to avoid abuse of this option.

Medicines for Human Use (Clinical trials) Regulations (2004)

Schedule 1, Part 2

Paragraph 6: Clinical trials shall be conducted in accordance with the principles of the Declaration of Helsinki.

Placebos are clearly a contentious subject when placed alongside the duty to treat patients in accordance with their best interests, but two things should be remembered when faced with the many ethical difficulties:

- The use of placebos in clinical trials leads to more effective results.
- The patients consent to the randomised control trial, so technically, they do consent to receiving no treatment at all.

Surgery as a placebo

In controlled clinical trials, i.e. active group v controlled group, the risks for the controlled group increase to far beyond 'more than minimal' when they undergo surgery with no therapeutic effect.

EXAMPLE

- The active group undergo a new style of laser brain surgery on a brain tumour.
- The control group undergo placebo surgery which has no effect at all.

Even though the risks in surgical clinical trials are much higher to both groups of patients, it is just as useful to carry out placebo surgery as it is to carry out placebo drug trials. This is because the outcome of the new surgical treatment can be compared to the placebo surgery in order to measure a genuine improvement. In addition to this, the field of medicine would greatly benefit from new and innovative surgical techniques. Keyhole surgery, for example, saves time, money, distress and recovery. The problem is that the controlled patients in particular are undergoing a very serious procedure with the miniscule benefit of gathering 'useful information', and this is not only an unfavourable utilitarian approach to clinical trials, i.e. the greater good will benefit from the misery of an individual, but it means that the risk to the patient outweighs the benefit and this breaches several declarations, regulations and guidelines in this area which state the following:

Nuremberg Code (1947)

Paragraph 4: The experiment should be so conducted as to avoid all unnecessary physical and mental suffering and injury.

Paragraph 5: No experiment should be conducted where there is an *a priori* reason to believe that death or disabling injury will occur; except, perhaps, in those experiments where the experimental physicians also serve as subjects.

The Declaration of Geneva (1948)

Paragraph 13: The health of my patient will be my first consideration.

The Declaration of Helsinki (1964)

Paragraph 6: In medical research involving human subjects, the wellbeing of the individual research subject must take precedence over all other interests.

Paragraph 21: Medical research involving human subjects may only be conducted if the importance of the objective outweighs the inherent risks and burdens to the research subjects.

Paragraph 32: The benefits, risks, burdens and effectiveness of a new intervention must be tested against those of the best current proven intervention, except in the following circumstances:

- The use of placebo, or no treatment, is acceptable in studies where no current proven intervention exists; or
- Where for compelling and scientifically sound methodological reasons the use of placebo is necessary to determine the efficacy or safety of an intervention and the patients who receive placebo or no treatment will not be subject to any risk of serious or irreversible harm. Extreme care must be taken to avoid abuse of this option.

Medicines for Human Use (Clinical trials) Regulations (2004)

Schedule 1, Part 2

Paragraph 1: The rights, safety and wellbeing of the trial subjects shall prevail over the interests of science and society.

Paragraph 10: Before the trial is initiated, foreseeable risks and inconveniences have been weighed against the anticipated benefit for the individual trial subject and other present and future patients. A trial should be initiated and continued only if the benefits justify the risks.

EXTRACT

Good Practice in Research (2010), General Medical Council:

http://www.gmc-uk.org/guidance/ethical_guidance/5992.asp

Paragraph 9: You must make sure that foreseeable risks to participants are kept as low as possible. In addition, you must be satisfied that:

- the anticipated benefits to participants outweigh the foreseeable risks, or
- the foreseeable risks to participants are minimal if the research only has the potential to benefit others more generally.

Paragraph 15: You must stop research where the results indicate that participants are at risk of significant harm or, in research involving treatment required by a patient, where no benefit can be expected.

The international declarations are ambiguous on the use of placebos, stating only that a placebo is acceptable where no current intervention exists (Helsinki). However, the UK regulations are much stricter, stating that the benefits must *justify* the risks (2004 Regulations) and the benefits must *outweigh* the risks (2010 guidance). It could be argued by a scientist that the risks of undergoing placebo surgery is justified because it brings a benefit to many millions of sufferers. This is a strict utilitarian approach which goes against the health of the patient (Geneva), but there is nothing in any of the rules above to suggest that a utilitarian approach cannot be used in clinical trials as long as a benefit of some sort can be measured. The General Medical Council (2010) do suggest that the risk should be *minimal* if the procedure simply 'benefits others more generally' and a scientist who is willing to carry out placebo surgery could argue that his placebo surgery carries only a minimal risk, which would satisfy the guidelines.

Perhaps if the competent patient understood the risks, the use of a surgical placebo might be more acceptable, both ethically and legally?

EXTRACT

R.L. Albin, 'Sham Surgery Controls: Intercerebral Grafting of Foetal Tissue for Parkinson's Disease and Proposed Criteria for Use of Sham Surgery Controls' (2002) 28 *Journal of Medical Ethics* 322, at pages 322–5

The result [of unevaluated surgical techniques] can be exposure of substantial numbers of patients to procedures that incur significant risks and have no benefit. In addition to becoming a public health hazard, inadequately evaluated surgical methods can consume valuable societal resources. [...] Use of sham surgery is unattractive because the increased risk to control subjects is not accompanied by any possibility of benefit. In some cases, however, sham surgery controls are strongly preferred on scientific grounds and may be necessary to answer the key questions. Sham surgery controls cannot be prohibited absolutely but their use must be balanced carefully against the safety of research subjects. Because of the necessity of minimising risk for research subjects, sham surgery controls should not be the default method of constructing human clinical trials involving surgical interventions. Sham surgery controls should be used only with careful justification and I believe that these circumstances will be rare.

Trialling something new

There are instances where medical research involves treating an unknown ailment with a new drug. This may happen when a new disease has been recognised by scientists and there is no known cure, or a patient consults his doctor about mystery symptoms, and the doctor does not know what to suggest (this is more common than people realise). There are several options available to doctors:

- The doctor can prescribe a traditional drug to treat the mystery symptoms and monitor the results. This is medical research because the traditional drug has not been used to treat the mystery symptoms before.

- The doctor can prescribe a new drug that has just come onto the market for a similar ailment and monitor the results. This is also medical research because nobody can predict what might happen.

In instances like this, medical research is not just about gathering statistical information – it is about *treating* a patient at the same time. The patient must consent to the treatment and must be made aware that it is simply 'trial and error'. If a patient is particularly sick, he may be willing to try any suggestion. The usual standard in medical research, according to the regulations and declarations, is that there must be a benefit to either the patient or his group of sufferers (and the benefits must be weighed against the risks). Medical research involving trial and error is therefore only ethical when no better intervention exists, and this is clearly stated in the Declaration of Helsinki and the Medicines for Human Use (Clinical Trials) Regulations (2004).

The Declaration of Helsinki (1964)

Paragraph 35: In the treatment of a patient, where proven interventions do not exist or have been ineffective, the physician, after seeking expert advice, with informed consent from the patient or a legally authorised representative, may use an unproven intervention if in the physician's judgement it offers hope of saving life, re-establishing health or alleviating suffering. Where possible, this intervention should be made the object of research, designed to evaluate its safety and efficacy. In all cases, new information should be recorded and, where appropriate, made publicly available.

Medicines for Human Use (Clinical trials) Regulations (2004)

Schedule 1, Part 2

Paragraph 6: Clinical trials shall be conducted in accordance with the principles of the Declaration of Helsinki.

The key phrases in the paragraph above include: 'do not exist', 'ineffective', 'expert advice', 'informed consent', 'unproven intervention', 'physician's judgment', 'alleviating suffering' and 'object of research'. Clearly, an unproven drug can be trialled on a human if he consents and there is no other alternative. However, in order to ensure that the patient is not being taken advantage of, a medical expert must be consulted and the purpose of the trial must be to save his life, re-establish his health or alleviate his suffering. The results must be recorded properly so any new knowledge can be shared with the rest of the medical population. This kind of 'trial and error' medical research is not like a formal clinical trial with funding, equipment and licensing issues. A patient is simply offered a prescription drug by his doctor that may help him with his symptoms. The drug offered has already been through its clinical trials and has been deemed safe for human consumption in its specified doses. An excellent example of this kind of 'trial and error' medical research happened in *Simms* v *Simms* (2002), involving the human form of mad cow disease which is rare and extremely dangerous.

CASE EXTRACT

Simms v *Simms* [2003] 2 WLR 1465

Facts: Two minor patients were suffering from Creutzfeldt–Jakob disease and there was evidence that a new treatment known as PPS had slowed the progress of a similar disease in mice. The research had not extended to humans. The parents of the minors wished for their children to receive the treatment (i.e. surgery) anyway, and sought a declaration from the courts that it would be lawful, because surgery was not deemed to be in the best interests of the children (and therefore unlawful) if there was no clear benefit.

Held: As long as the risks appeared to be low in comparison with the benefits, it was acceptable to treat patients with a *potential* cure when no other cure was available. The doctor must work in accordance with a responsible body of medical opinion as prescribed by the *Bolam* test.

Dame Elizabeth Butler-Sloss P (at pages 95–8): To the question: 'is there a responsible body of medical opinion which would support the PPS treatment within the United Kingdom?' the answer in one sense is unclear. This is untried treatment and there is so far no validation of the experimental work done in Japan. [...] Mr T is a very experienced and clearly very responsible neurosurgeon. He has carefully thought through at considerable length in his two reports, the research, its implications, the uncertainties, the risks and the doubts about the benefits to these two patients. He has come to the conclusion that 'it is in the best interests of [JS and JA] to be treated and I would personally be prepared to carry out that treatment'. [...] I am satisfied, consistent with the philosophy that underpins the *Bolam* test [1957] 1 WLR 582, that there is a responsible body of relevant professional opinion which supports this innovative treatment. That is, in my view, subject to the seriousness of the risks involved and the degree of benefit that might be achieved. [...]

There may not be any obvious benefit or any benefit at all. None of the medical witnesses entirely ruled out the possibility of some benefit. Even though the patients will not recover, it seems to me that the concept of 'benefit' to a patient suffering from vCJD does encompass an improvement from the present state of illness, or a continuation of the existing state of illness without deterioration for a longer period than might otherwise have occurred, or the prolongation of life for a longer period than might otherwise have occurred. The medical evidence that I heard provided for the possibility of one of those three benefits occurring. [...] Where there is no alternative treatment available and the disease is progressive and fatal, it seems to me to be reasonable to consider experimental treatment with unknown benefits and risks, but without significant risks of increased suffering to the patient, in cases where there is some chance of benefit to the patient. [...] I consider that even the prospect of a slightly longer life is a benefit worth having for each of these two patients. There is sufficient possibility of unquantifiable benefit for me to find that it would be in their best interests to have the operations and the treatment subject to an assessment of the risks. There is no alternative treatment available.

Dame Elizabeth Butler-Sloss highlights several important issues when it comes to 'trial and error' type medical research on human patients: (1) the risks to the patient if the treatment is not given must be very serious; (2) the benefits may be slight, or there may be no benefit at all, but the risks must be low; (3) the doctor must still act in accordance with a responsible body of medical opinion; and (4) if the patient was old enough, he would have consented (omitted from above).

It is important to allow research like this to be carried out on consenting patients. This is how some major medical breakthroughs have been achieved in the past. It should be noted, however, that the parents wished for the treatment to go ahead, and the risks were thought to be low. The reason why this particular instance of 'trial and error' medical research had to seek court permission was because it involved surgery. Surgical treatment with no benefit to the patient is simply unlawful.

ACTIVITY

Geraldine has a brain tumour. She has tried drugs and radiotherapy but nothing has worked. Her doctor tells her about a clinical trial at the local hospital. She understands that they are using pioneering surgical techniques to remove cancerous cells from the brain with a local anaesthetic to ensure that speech and motor skills are not impaired. She signs up for the clinical trial right away, and her surgery is scheduled for four days time. Geraldine tells her daughter Gemma, who is concerned about the fact that it is a clinical trial. How would you advise Geraldine and Gemma in regards to their expectations?

 **Participating in clinical research**

It is clear when looking at the declarations, regulations and guidelines in this area of medicine that there are risks involved. The experimental nature of clinical research means that the patient, and the scientist or doctor, does not know for sure what will happen as a result of the trial. There might be a terrible reaction to a new drug, or it might be a miracle cure. The declarations, regulations and guidelines do their best to protect patients, but willing participants in clinical trials are still consenting to potentially harmful treatments with no benefit at all (unless, of course, there is a current intervention, in which case they will be given that instead of a placebo, as stipulated by paragraph 32 of Helsinki 1964). So where do these participants come from, and why do they volunteer? The main reason is to gain access to cutting-edge medical treatment for their ailment. HIV sufferers, for example, may wish to put themselves forward for clinical trials involving anti-retroviral drugs to stop the HIV virus from developing into AIDS. Alternatively, cancer patients may also like to access new and untested cancer drugs. Studies in these areas are ongoing and they always need research participants.

Benefits

- Access to a pioneering cure.
- Improvement of painful and debilitating symptoms.
- Helping fellow sufferers in the future.
- Hope that there may be a treatment after being told that there wasn't one.
- Something to do whilst on permanent sick leave.
- Shorter waiting times for drugs.

However, a difficult ethical issue is raised. If the participants are volunteering for the clinical trials in order to access innovative drugs, what if they are, unknown to them, placed in the control group and given a useless placebo instead? Is it ethical for doctors and scientists to accept these participants into their trials, knowing that half of them will be receiving no treatment at all (or simply the best current intervention, which they are probably already taking)? There may be cancellations, false starts, last minute changes, bad reactions, injuries, no reactions or confusing reactions. Participants may feel used or short-changed if they enter into a clinical trial whilst suffering from a serious ailment and come out with nothing. It might be a good idea for the researcher to:

- Explain clearly in the moments before consent that the participant is not receiving treatment but undergoing research.
- Explain clearly that the research has no proven results, whether good or bad.
- Explain clearly that the aim of the research is to *understand*, not to *treat*.
- Explain clearly that there is a control group using placebos or the best current intervention, and the participant could be placed into that group at random.
- Explain clearly that it can sometimes take years to yield a good result, if at all.

Should I participate?

Research participants are usually from the same corners of society. This may sound strange, but some groups of people are more exposed to medicine and clinical trials than others:

Frequently represented in clinical trials:

- Sick, ill, frail, diseased and weak individuals.
- Medical students.
- Junior medical staff.
- Poor individuals.
- Unemployed.

Frequently not represented in clinical trials:

- Healthy individuals.
- Wealthy individuals.
- Incompetent individuals.
- Children.
- Employed.

The first set of bullet points may seem a bit odd, but there are good reasons why these particular groups of individuals are often overrepresented in clinical trials. Firstly, sick patients are more useful in phase II and phase III trials where the new drug is tested against the ailment it is designed to cure. Secondly, medical students and staff are more accustomed to the world of medicine and clinical trials, and as a result are less fearful of the process. Thirdly, poor and unemployed individuals may enter into clinical trials to earn money, which is often paid to participants. It is not enough to constitute a full-time wage, but it may make things easier. The Declaration of Helsinki (1964) was the first international protocol to raise the issue of over-participation. The General Medical Council has also briefly discussed using colleagues or students as participants in clinical trials. This could point to a financial, personal or political interest and it would discredit the results of the trial.

The Declaration of Helsinki (1964)

Paragraph 26: When seeking informed consent for participation in a research study the physician should be particularly cautious if the potential subject is in a dependent relationship with the physician or may consent under duress. In such situations the informed consent should be sought by an appropriately qualified individual who is completely independent of this relationship.

EXTRACT

Good Practice in Research (2010), General Medical Council:

http://www.gmc-uk.org/guidance/ethical_guidance/5992.asp

Paragraph 27: You must not allow your judgement about a research project to be influenced, or be seen to be influenced, at any stage, by financial, personal, political or other external interests.

The facts listed above about groups of participants raise an interesting question: why should certain corners of society bear the brunt of clinical trials when all of us reap the benefits of new drugs? Should participation in clinical trials be more evenly spread in society? If so, how do we achieve proportionate participation?

Uneven participation: problems and theories

The main problem with uneven participation is the uncertainty of the effectiveness of the drug when it is licensed for general sale. Scientists will know for sure that a new drug works on young unemployed males, for example, but what about elderly females with arthritis? Clinical research will inevitably be restricted in terms of its applicability to ailments and users when only certain groups of participants step forward. An ethics committee could, of course, state at the very beginning of the process that the trial proposal is simply not detailed enough to justify its commencement. It would then be up to the sponsor or investigator of the trial to find a more diverse pool of participants to take part in his research. Another problem with uneven participation is that the burdens and risks are not distributed evenly or ethically. Financial rewards bring the poor and unemployed to the fore, but how could we entice the wealthy and employed to participate in clinical trials?

- We could pay them the equivalent of a day's wages for a day in the lab.
- We could promise them free medication for five years.
- We could give them continued access to the trial drug if it works (as per Helsinki).

To take it one step further, should we impose a duty upon society generally to participate in medical research? The rationale behind this idea is that, if we are willing to benefit from the research, we should be willing to take part in it. This would, of course, only ever be a *moral* duty, like the moral duty to donate to charity. It would not be ethical to *force* individuals to submit to clinical trials through law, especially when patient autonomy and the right to refuse medical treatment is the cornerstone of modern medicine.

Clinical research could be viewed as a mandatory act for the social and public good, like jury service or paying tax. The rationale behind this idea is that we would all benefit from a society in which medical research is cheap, fast-moving and effective. If we were to participate on the false understanding that we would achieve a direct benefit to ourselves, many of us would be disappointed and none of us would offer our time.

Receiving payment for participation

The issue of payment was mentioned briefly above. It is not uncommon to pay participants to take part in medical research. This may explain why there are far more unemployed and poor participants coming forward than employed and wealthy (although free time may also be an issue).

Why should we pay?

- Participants would willingly come forward.
- It would encourage a participant to undergo something he would normally refuse.
- It gives the impression of an 'exchange' of some sort.

Why should we not pay?

- Participants are 'volunteers' and should be treated as such.
- Participation should be altruistic.
- Payment may put pressure on the participant to perform.
- Is consent really valid when it has been achieved through payment?
- Payment attracts the disadvantaged, the unemployed and the poor.
- Participants could hide health problems in order to take part.

There are good reasons for paying clinical trial participants. Firstly, the participants can be viewed as providing a service, and it follows that they should be paid for their time. There are many individuals who work with dangerous machinery and to compensate them for taking a daily risk, they are paid for it. There is no real difference between dangerous jobs and volunteering for clinical research, except that the former are wages and the latter are an acknowledgement of participation. It would not, of course, be right to regard participants as 'employees' and afford them employee rights during a clinical trial, because they are not doing a job or being entered into a contract of employment. The participants are simply volunteering their time and are *free to leave* at any time. Besides, medical law legislation works perfectly well to protect the best interests of patients without employment law complicating things. Secondly, participation in clinical trials may be time consuming, uncomfortable, fruitless and inconvenient, making payment necessary to attract a sufficient number of participants. There is no intention to *coerce* the participants into a trial that they do not want to take part in, there is simply an intention to *compensate* the participant for their time and patience.

EXTRACT

Martin Wilkinson and Andrew Moore, 'Inducement in Research' (1997) 11 *Bioethics* 373, at pages 373–89

Some researchers would find it worthwhile to pay inducements in order to attract enough subjects. Those who would accept this reward would not do so unless it were worthwhile to them. As a result of offering the reward, the researchers get the subjects they want. As a result of participating, the subjects get the reward they want. Both are better off. No one is worse off. Inducement is thus a good thing. [...]

Many people would not work if they were not paid; in that sense wages are inducements. Few people think that, as a result, it is wrong to offer wages. Those that do have concerns about the existing wage system usually object that wages are too *low*, not that they are too high, or that they are offered at all. [...]

Coercion usually takes the form of threats, which restrict people's options. Inducements are offers, not threats, and they expand people's options.

It is not entirely true that the participants are not 'worse off' – the commentators seem to have forgotten about the risks faced by the participants in clinical trials. The payment should not be compared to formal wages either: it is not a 'job' to submit oneself to medical experiments! Payment might not be a threat to partake in research, but the lack of money when bills have to be paid is definitely a threat, and the commentators also ignore this very significant issue when it comes to poorer participants.

It is lawful to pay participants to engage in research, but the amount paid should be capped at a moderate level when balanced with the time spent and risks taken otherwise participants would simply submit to *anything* to make a few thousand pounds, and this would border on unethical practice (and almost definitely coercion of poorer participants). If payment is capped at a sufficiently low level, the participant will be more likely to make decisions based on his own logic as opposed to a clouded fantasy because of the money to be won at the end of the process. This allows for altruistic motives to still shine through. There are, however, plenty of reasons why payment for participation in medical research is unethical and dangerous. McNeill argues that the lure of payment would attract only certain corners of society:

Paul McNeill, 'Paying People to Participate in Research: Why Not?' (1997) 11 *Bioethics* 391, at pages 391–6

It is already the poor and socially disadvantaged who volunteer for most research yet it is typically the better off members of society who benefit from research. The offering of financial inducement simply exacerbates this inequity and adds further to the risks for those disadvantaged people. [...]

The basis of my argument against inducement is that it encourages people to expose themselves to risk of harm. This encouragement is greater for the impecunious. [...]

There is something repugnant about offering money to relatively poor people, impecunious students, travellers and others, to take part in research, which, by its nature, exposes them to risks of harm. The poor in our societies already have higher risks of poor health and other adverse life events. Inducement to take part in experimentation should not be allowed where it adds to those risks.

Firstly, there is no concrete proof in this piece (or anywhere else) that only the rich benefit from medical research. Drugs are prescribed to all patients regardless of their wages. Following from this, the poor, the elderly, students and the unemployed receive financial help for their prescriptions anyway. Secondly, the poor in our society may be more likely to suffer from bad health, but this makes them more likely to benefit from the research, take the drugs, and thus make them good candidates for clinical trials. Thirdly, experimentation which adds to the risk to the participant will be scrutinised by an ethics committee and all of the declarations, regulations and guidelines in this area of medicine stipulate that the benefits and risks must be balanced and justified.

There are ethical problems flowing on from the act of payment. For example, what if a poor participant, who knew that he could earn £5,000 from a three-month clinical trial, lied about his other ailments in order to be registered on the trial? What if he really took heroin and needed money to fund his drug habit? This kind of participant would render the results of the trial useless, and he could put himself in grave danger. Another problem to flow from the act of payment is that of participants signing up to risks that would normally repulse them. For example, let us say that a middle-aged woman was afraid of needles, and the very sight of them normally sent her into shock. If she was receiving payment to accept a needle, what psychological or physical state might she be in during the trial if she forced herself to accept one or more injections?

J.P. Bentley and P.G. Thacker, 'The Influence of Risk and Monetary Payment on the Research Participation Decision-Making Process' (2004) 30 *Journal of Medical Ethics* 293, at pages 293–8

This study suggests that monetary payment increases respondents' willingness to participate in research regardless of the level of risk; higher levels of payment make respondents more willing to participate, even if the study is relatively risky. [...] Monetary payments appeared to influence respondents' propensity to neglect to tell researchers about restricted activities they have

→

engaged in either before or during a study, with higher payment levels leading to a higher propensity to neglect to tell.

This study also showed that higher levels of monetary payment may influence subjects' behaviours regarding concealing information about restricted activities. If such activities were actually engaged in, the results of the hypothetical studies may have been distorted (that is, alcohol, caffeine, medications, herbal products may all affect the pharmacokinetics of a study drug).

Research has therefore shown that participants may lie about their pre-existing ailments, may accept higher risks than normal and may lie about consuming alcohol or drugs in order to receive payment. As a result, it is in the best interests of clinical trials that participation is altruistic and that participants volunteer out of the kindness of their hearts to help others. This is a more ethical way to conduct research, because the participant is fully aware that there may be no medical benefit to themselves and their consent is not influenced by external factors. However, there are few altruistic participants available.

Is anybody excluded from clinical trials?

Controlled clinical trials can clearly be dangerous, so there have traditionally been certain groups of society that have been refused entry into a clinical trial in order to protect their best interests. Women are excluded from clinical trials more frequently than men. There are good clinical reasons for this. Firstly, if an ailment affects only men (i.e. prostate cancer drugs) then women are not needed. This can, of course, work the other way round, as in ovarian cancer trials. Secondly, women undergo hormonal fluctuations week by week in their childbearing years, which can complicate results. This is not a reference to heightened emotional responses, but a reference to different levels of chemicals in the bloodstream which can affect skin, muscles, blood, tissues and physical sensitivity. The problem for doctors is clear: to find a consistent female response to a new drug, far more women would need to be recruited in order to eliminate the hormonal fluctuations from the research, costing more money and taking more time. Thirdly, women might become pregnant during the trial, which would alter their physical reactions and blood test results and potentially harm the unborn baby. This is why so many drugs state on the back of the packaging: 'consult your doctor when pregnant' or 'do not take if pregnant or breastfeeding' – because sufficient trials have not been conducted on pregnant women. Doctors are very careful when issuing drugs to pregnant women as a result of this lack of clinical research. It may sometimes be left up to the pregnant woman to decide for herself: 'should I take this risk or not?' This is unsatisfactory. However, pregnant women are understandably cautious when submitting to clinical trials, and researchers are probably just as cautious about accepting them. Men are probably, therefore, easier research participants. The outcome of the exclusion of women is not positive. Far more drugs are tested on men than women, leading to higher numbers of adverse reactions in women when the new drugs are passed into the general market. This is unnecessary: not all women are fertile, in their childbearing years, or trying to get pregnant. It is in society's best interests to include more women in clinical trials for drugs that are prescribed to men *and* women.

There is another group of society commonly excluded from medical research. Elderly people pose significant health risks in clinical trials. This is ironic, because the elderly population take more medication than the rest of us. The reason for their widespread exclusion is that they usually have other ailments to deal with, such as angina, inconsistent blood pressure, organic mental illnesses, arthritis, bad sight and hearing, and general frailty. This causes several problems for scientists:

- The medication taken for current ailments may interfere with the new drug.
- The current medication may battle with the new drug, causing an adverse reaction.
- The current medication may be cancelled out by the new drug.
- The new drug cannot be measured in combination with other drugs.
- The elderly patient cannot stop taking her current medication.
- The elderly patient may be unable to measure new reactions alongside old niggles.
- The elderly patient may die before the trial is complete.
- The elderly patient is not strong or robust enough to deal with an adverse reaction.
- The scientist may look as though he is taking advantage of weak participants.

There are benefits to allowing elderly patients into clinical trials too: their lack of other commitments and their relevance to medical research, i.e. they would benefit greatly, make them excellent candidates. However, because their reactions to a new drug might be complicated with the use of other drugs, very little useful information could be derived from the research unless the patient could stop all current medication. In addition, there are not many elderly people who are relatively fit. Even with no formal ailments, an 'all clear' 70-year-old man is still weaker than an 'all clear' 40-year-old man. The Royal College of Physicians recognises this and asks ethics committees to keep an eye open for discrimination.

EXTRACT

Guidelines on the Practice of Ethics Committees in Medical Research with Human Participants, 4th edition (2007), Royal College of Physicians, at pages 64–5:

http://www.rcplondon.ac.uk/bookshop/g

Paragraph 8.55: The RCP recognises that the greatest burden of disease in the developed world falls upon older people and that research activity should reflect this.

Paragraph 8.58: The assumption that older people are more vulnerable undermines autonomy. Evidence suggests that older people may be more willing to participate in research. Transport and mobility problems, social isolation and communication difficulties secondary to visual or hearing impairments are all problems that may need to be surmounted. RECs should therefore examine protocols to ensure that applications address such practical difficulties and should regard exclusion on arbitrary and unjustified age restrictions as unethical.

Interestingly, the declarations, regulations and guidelines stay silent on the issue of excluded participants, but the Department of Health have issued some vague directions. In their publication, *Research Governance Framework for Health and Social Care* (2005), they have suggested that research participants should reflect the multicultural population of society (below), but they do not explain why certain members may be excluded from clinical trials.

EXTRACT

Research Governance Framework for Health and Social Care, 2nd edition (2005), Department of Health:

https://www.gov.uk/government/publications/research-governance-framework-for-health-and-social-care-second-edition

Paragraph 2.2.7: Research, and those pursuing it, should respect the diversity of human society and conditions and the multicultural nature of society. Whenever relevant, it should take account of age, disability, gender, sexual orientation, race, culture and religion in its design, undertaking, and reporting. The body of research evidence available to policy makers should reflect the diversity of the population.

This suggestion is all very well, but it is easier said than done to ensure that a multicultural group of participants steps forward for a clinical trial. It depends on the ailment and the nature of the trial. Some religious teachings may frown upon clinical trials because they are essentially medical experiments on humans. Particular trials may also be race, age, weight, gender or culture specific. Generally, it is clear that not everybody could play a part in clinical trials, even if they wanted to. This is, of course, for their own benefit, but the important question remains: is exclusion of particular groups of people actually doing the progress of medicine more harm than good?

ACTIVITY

You are a scientist and are ready to launch your own clinical trial for an alternative to paracetamol. You need a wide range of research participants in order to glean accurate results for your new vitamin pill. Write an advert for your local doctor surgery for clinical trial volunteers. Make sure your advert is worded in a way that attracts as diverse a participant as possible.

 ## Consent

Taking part in a clinical trial is a dangerous venture. The results are unknown, but the scientists and doctors are keen to measure whether a new drug has a positive or a negative effect on the human body. Human participants are a lot like guinea pigs in this respect – they are taking part in an experiment. It follows that voluntary and fully informed consent is *vital*.

EXTRACT

Consent to Research (2010), General Medical Council:

http://www.gmc-uk.org/guidance/ethical_guidance/5993.asp

Paragraph 1: Seeking consent is fundamental in research involving people. Participants' consent is legally valid and professionally acceptable only if they have the capacity to decide whether to take part in the research, have been properly informed, and have agreed to participate without pressure or coercion.

There are concerns over consent to participation in clinical trials. First of all, as explored above, payment might coerce a particularly poor participant into consenting, but the consent is still technically voluntary in that the participant signs the contract wilfully with the knowledge that he can walk away at any time. However, some patients may consent on the understanding that they might *benefit* from the trial when they may not. This is known as a 'therapeutic misconception'. They may be consenting for the wrong reasons. This issue will be explored further in this section. Finally, there are vulnerable participants who may succumb to clinical trials because of their situation or environment (e.g. prisoners). It may be unethical to use these participants in clinical trials. In a category all on their own, incompetent patients provide a unique problem. They are just as important to medical research as competent patients, but providing consent on their behalf is a delicate exercise and is open to abuse, particularly when no benefit is to be gained by their participation.

Informed consent

One of the cornerstones of modern medicine is that all patients must provide their informed and voluntary consent to any medical procedure.[10] The risks must be explained to the patient in general terms[11] and it is up to the doctor to judge, using his medical expertise, what risks should be disclosed to the patient.[12] It is therefore vital that the participant is informed that he is taking part in a clinical trial and not simply checking-in for regular treatment. This mix-up would certainly vitiate consent because the nature and quality of the treatment is not what the patient/participant is consenting to. As explained earlier, in the concentration camps of the Second World War the medical experiments that took place were against the wishes of the victims. It was because of this lack of consent that the scientists were allowed to get away with terrible crimes. Many of the medical experiments ended in death. As a result of this 'free-for-all' approach to medical research on humans, the Nuremberg Code (1947) states as its number one priority that voluntary consent is essential.

Nuremberg Code (1947)

Paragraph 1: The voluntary consent of the human subject is absolutely essential.

From Nuremberg onwards, the relevant declarations, regulations and guidelines in this area all claim that voluntary consent is essential to medical research on humans, but it has dropped down the list of priorities.

The Declaration of Helsinki (1964)

Paragraph 22: Participation by competent individuals as subjects in medical research must be voluntary.

---

[10] *Re T (Adult: Refusal of Treatment)* [1993] Fam 95.
[11] *Chatterton v Gerson* [1981] QB 432.
[12] *Sidaway v Board of Governors of the Bethlem Royal Hospital* [1985] AC 871.

Medicines for Human Use (Clinical trials) Regulations (2004)

Schedule 1, Part III

Paragraph 3: The subject has given his informed consent to taking part in the trial.

EXTRACT

Good Practice in Research (2010), General Medical Council:

http://www.gmc-uk.org/guidance/ethical_guidance/5992.asp

Paragraph 28: You must get consent from participants before involving them in any research project.

How much must the participant be told in order for his consent to be 'informed'? The answer is: it depends. In medical law, the doctor or surgeon can generally exercise his professional discretion when informing the patient of risks and in medical research, it is just as ambiguous:

The Declaration of Helsinki (1964)

Paragraph 24: In medical research involving competent human subjects, each potential subject must be adequately informed of the aims, methods, sources of funding, any possible conflicts of interest, institutional affiliations of the researcher, the anticipated benefits and potential risks of the study and the discomfort it may entail, and any other relevant aspects of the study.

Medicines for Human Use (Clinical Trials) Regulations (2004)

Schedule 1

Part I

Paragraph 3(1): A person gives informed consent to take part in a clinical trial only if his decision:

(a) is given freely after that person is informed of the nature, significance, implications and risks of the trial.

Part III

Paragraph 1: The subject has had an interview with the investigator, or another member of the investigating team, in which he has been given the opportunity to understand the objectives, risks and inconveniences of the trial and the conditions under which it is to be conducted.

Paragraph 5: The subject has been provided with a contact point where he may obtain further information about the trial.

EXTRACT

Good Practice in Research (2010), General Medical Council:

http://www.gmc-uk.org/guidance/ethical_guidance/5992.asp

Paragraph 22: You must be open and honest with participants when sharing information about a research project. You must answer questions honestly and as fully as possible.

EXTRACT

Consent to Research (2010), General Medical Council:

http://www.gmc-uk.org/guidance/ethical_guidance/5993.asp

Paragraph 4: You must give people the information they want or need in order to decide whether to take part in research. How much information you share with them will depend on their individual circumstances. You must not make assumptions about the information a person might want or need, or their knowledge and understanding of the proposed research project.

There is clearly an emphasis on honesty and disclosure, but how much? A grey area remains in relation to the level of risk that should be disclosed. Additionally, what if the risks are genuinely not known? This grey area expands even further in light of Helsinki: must the participant be told of the relevant motivations, professional benefits and financial dealings that flow from the clinical trial? If so, what difference would this make? If not, would the participant be misinformed? There are no further definitions available to help with this. Researchers should explain the main issues in a way that helps the participant to understand. After all, simply providing information does not mean that the participant has absorbed, processed and consented to the trial. Researchers should answer questions honestly,[13] but they are not under an obligation to take extra steps *beyond what is reasonable* to ensure that a participant understands everything.[14]

EXTRACT

Consent to Research (2010), General Medical Council:

http://www.gmc-uk.org/guidance/ethical_guidance/5993.asp

Paragraph 7: You must make sure that people are given information in a way that they can understand. You should check that people understand the terms that you use and any explanation given about the proposed research method. If necessary, you should support your discussions with simple and accurate written material or visual or other aids.

---

[13] *Pearce v United Bristol Healthcare NHS Trust* (1998) 48 BMLR 118.
[14] *Poynter v Hillingdon Health Authority* (1997) 37 BMLR 192.

The mechanics of consent

Patients who sign up for medical treatment often believe that consent is like a contract: consent is given at the beginning, and the treatment is provided thereafter. As explored in Chapter 4, this is not true. Consent is an ongoing concept in medical law, and can be revoked at *any* time. The contract that is signed is not a legally binding document, it is simply proof that consent has been given and a patient is not forced to complete the contract if he changes his mind. This is specifically provided for in all of the relevant declarations, regulations and guidance in this area.

Nuremberg Code (1947)

Paragraph 9: During the course of the experiment the human subject should be at liberty to bring the experiment to an end if he has reached the physical or mental state where continuation of the experiment seems to him to be impossible.

The Declaration of Helsinki (1964)

Paragraph 24: The potential subject must be informed of the right to refuse to participate in the study or to withdraw consent to participate at any time without reprisal.

Medicines for Human Use (Clinical Trials) Regulations (2004)

Schedule 1, Part III

Paragraph 2: The subject has been informed of his right to withdraw from the trial at any time.

EXTRACT

Good Practice in Research (2010), General Medical Council:

http://www.gmc-uk.org/guidance/ethical_guidance/5992.asp

Paragraph 29: You must make sure that people are informed of, and that you respect, their right to decline to take part in research and to withdraw from the research project at any time, with an assurance that this will not adversely affect their relationship with those providing care, or the care they receive.

The participant must be informed of all of the developments in order for his consent to be ongoing. This may not be too difficult in practice, because if a participant experiences a negative reaction or a helpful benefit, he will know about it and can choose at that moment whether or not to continue. The real problem occurs when a participant exercises his right to revoke his consent. The trial is not finished so all the data (and the time, money and resources) will be lost. This is a big disadvantage to allowing patients to revoke their consent at any time, but it is a small price to pay to ensure that participants in clinical trials are not taken advantage of again as they were in the medical research conducted during the Second World War. The relevant UK regulations give a simple definition of informed consent for the purposes of medical research, which is described as follows.

Medicines for Human Use (Clinical Trials) Regulations (2004)

Schedule 1, Part I

Paragraph 3(1): A person gives informed consent to take part in a clinical trial only if his decision:

(b) (i) is evidenced in writing, dated and signed, or otherwise marked, by that person so as to indicate his consent, or (ii) if the person is unable to sign or to mark a document so as to indicate his consent, is given orally in the presence of at least one witness and recorded in writing.

This simple definition is derived from the Declaration of Helsinki:

The Declaration of Helsinki (1964)

Paragraph 24: If the consent cannot be expressed in writing, the non-written consent must be formally documented and witnessed.

The usual queries arise from this simple definition: what does 'nature', 'significance', 'implications' and 'risks' mean in terms of fully informing a participant? No further definitions are given.

The 'therapeutic misconception'

In phase II and phase III trials, the participants are usually suffering from the specific ailment that the new drug is trying to cure. In many clinical trials, this ailment can be quite a common problem, such as headaches or flu, but in other instances, it is a rare and very serious ailment, such as a rare form of cancer with no cure. If the latter is the case, the participant might be desperate to take part in the clinical trial in order to access an innovative treatment which could save her life. Does this kind of participant provide a properly informed and voluntary consent? There is a concern that even if the scientist explains to the participant that she could be placed in the controlled group of the trial (and thus receive a placebo), she would still consent in the desperate hope of surviving a bit longer. This is known as the 'therapeutic misconception' because she is signing up to take part in a trial under the misconception that she is going to receive a therapeutic advantage. The ethical issue becomes clear: the lure of a cure could potentially coerce a participant into a clinical trial far quicker than a large amount of money if it meant the chance of life.

EXTRACT

Franz Ingelfinger, 'Informed (But Uneducated) Consent' (1972) 287 *New England Journal of Medicine* 466

Incapacitated and hospitalised because of the illness, frightened by strange and impersonal routines, and fearful for his health and perhaps life, he is far from exercising a free power of choice when the person to whom he anchors all his hopes asks, 'say, you wouldn't mind, would you, if you joined some of the other patients on this floor and helped us to carry out some very important research we're doing?' When informed consent is obtained, it is not the student, the destitute bum, or the prisoner to whom, by virtue of his condition, the thumb screws of coercion are most relentlessly applied; it is the most used and useful of all experimental subjects, the patient with disease.

Doctors have a duty of care to treat patients in accordance with their best interests, and according to the Declaration of Geneva (1948), the health of the patient is the doctor's first consideration (paragraph 4). It follows that if a patient is put forward, by her doctor, to take part in a clinical trial, she might assume that it is in her best interests to participate (i.e. it will help her). A doctor might even explain very clearly what the trial is trying to achieve, i.e. a cure for the condition, but the patient may interpret this as 'a cure for *my* condition' and thus sign up with misguided ideals. If the patient has already tried all of the other available drugs on the market to no avail, the desire to take part in the trial may be even stronger. A doctor should make it very clear to the patient that clinical trials have controlled groups, where placebos are given at random. He should also make it very clear that clinical trials are developed to *gather* information, not to *cure* the participants. This information might enable the patient to think clearly about whether she really wants to participate in a trial. It is assumed, of course, that doctors already give clear information on these matters, but for the small handful of patients who are terminally ill and running out of options, they may misinterpret the phrase 'clinical trial' for something far more promising. The process of consenting to a clinical trial does not help. The standard consent forms may describe what the trial is trying to achieve without explaining to the participant herself that she might not achieve anything. In research done on this issue, it was found that participants were unaware of control groups.

EXTRACT

Katie Featherstone and Jenny Donovan, 'Why Don't They Just Tell Me Straight, Why Allocate It? The Struggle to Make Sense of Participating in a Randomised Controlled Trial' (2002) 55 *Social Science and Medicine* 709, at pages 709–19

It was difficult for these men to believe that such a haphazard procedure was reasonable, particularly when they had completed so many questionnaires about their symptoms and undergone clinical tests, some of which were very invasive. The men reasoned that the data from the questionnaires and clinical tests must be useful, not just for research purposes, but also for clinicians to make individualised treatment decisions – hence the unacceptability of randomisation. [...]

→

Even when trials adhere to strict informed consent procedures and ensure that 'simple language' is used, this does not guarantee that subjects will fully understand the implications of participation and that they may still have unrealistic treatment expectations. [...] It has been suggested that potential trial participants should be informed specifically about the components of research that constitute a change from the standard doctor-patient relationship – randomisation and blinding.

This level of misunderstanding from participants is a concern. However, there is no need for this situation to arise today as a result of the Medicines for Human Use (Clinical Trials) Regulations (2004), in combination with the Declaration of Helsinki (1964) and the General Medical Council Guidance (2010).

The Declaration of Helsinki (1964)

Paragraph 24: In medical research involving competent human subjects, each potential subject must be adequately informed of the aims, methods, sources of funding, any possible conflicts of interest, institutional affiliations of the researcher, the anticipated benefits and potential risks of the study and the discomfort it may entail, and any other relevant aspects of the study.

The Medicines for Human Use (Clinical Trials) Regulations (2004)

Schedule 1, Part III

Paragraph 1: The subject has had an interview with the investigator, or another member of the investigating team, in which he has been given the opportunity to understand the objectives, risks and inconveniences of the trial and the conditions under which it is to be conducted.

Paragraph 5: The subject has been provided with a contact point where he may obtain further information about the trial.

EXTRACT

Good Practice in Research (2010), General Medical Council:

http://www.gmc-uk.org/guidance/ethical_guidance/5992.asp

Paragraph 22: You must be open and honest with participants and members of the research team, including nonmedical staff, when sharing information about a research project. You must answer questions honestly and as fully as possible.

The declarations, regulations and guidance above sends a very strong message to researchers and doctors who are conducting clinical trials: the participants must be fully informed about all aspects of the research, otherwise their consent is not valid.

Vulnerable participants

The following participants may be viewed as particularly vulnerable even though they are able to provide their competent consent:

- Medical students.
- Medical staff (especially junior staff).
- Colleagues.
- Elderly.
- Children (referred to as 'minors').
- Poor.
- Unemployed.
- Prisoners.

These groups of participants are vulnerable because they may have a specific reason for participating in clinical research beyond their desire to simply volunteer. For example, they may receive payment, they may receive a pioneering cure before anyone else, or they may feel the need to support a colleague who is launching a trial. The General Medical Council warns doctors and researchers to keep an eye out for vulnerable participants.

EXTRACT

Good Practice in Research (2010), General Medical Council:

http://www.gmc-uk.org/guidance/ethical_guidance/5992.asp

Paragraph 17: You should make sure that participants are not encouraged to volunteer more frequently than is advisable or against their best interests. You should make sure that nobody takes part repeatedly in research projects if it might lead to a risk of significant harm to them. You should make sure that any necessary safeguards are in place to protect anybody who may be vulnerable to pressure to take part in research.

EXTRACT

Consent to Research (2010), General Medical Council:

http://www.gmc-uk.org/guidance/ethical_guidance/5993.asp

Paragraph 21: Some adults with capacity may be vulnerable to pressure to take part in research. You should be aware that their health or social circumstances might make them vulnerable to pressure from others. Vulnerable adults may be, for example, living in care homes or other institutions, or have learning difficulties or mental illnesses. In these circumstances, it is particularly important that you check whether they need any additional support to understand information or to make a decision. You must make sure that they know they have the right to decline to participate in research, and that they are able to decline if they want to.

Prisoners used to be a good option for medical research a few centuries ago (just like slaves used to be). They did not have any human rights, they were not regarded as 'decent' individuals because they committed crimes and they were separated from normal society, so no one noticed that medical experiments were carried out upon them. In a practical sense, prisoners were also ideal because they were guaranteed to be in one place all of the time and they could be manipulated and controlled by threats or violence. However, in today's medical environment, prisoner participants are seen as a particularly vulnerable group for all of the reasons above: they are unable to escape their environment, they may simply be bored, they may have self-harming tendencies which would make an invasive clinical trial all the more attractive, they may feel threatened or coerced into the trial, they may mistakenly believe that they will be released early or receive privileges for their participation and even a small financial reward might seem significant to them if they have scant access to luxury items. As a result of these issues, the Royal College of Physicians has suggested some guidelines as to when it might be appropriate to conduct medical research on prisoners. The guidelines give the impression that it would only ever be ethical to enlist prisoners into medical research when the research is directly related to prison life.

EXTRACT

Guidelines on the Practice of Ethics Committees in Medical Research with Human Participants, 4th edition (2007), Royal College of Physicians, at pages 63–4:

http://www.rcplondon.ac.uk/bookshop/g

Paragraph 8.47: Research that can be conducted on patients or healthy volunteers who are not in prison should not be conducted on prisoners. Incarceration in prison creates a constraint which could affect the ability of prisoners to make truly voluntary decisions without coercion to participate in research. Accusations of exploitation or violation of human rights could easily arise. Additional safeguards are therefore warranted.

Paragraph 8.48: Research studies in prisons should normally be limited to:

- Studies of the possible causes, effects, and processes of incarceration, and of criminal behaviour, provided that the study presents no more than minimal risk and no more than inconvenience to the participants.

- Research on conditions particularly affecting prisoners as a class (for example, vaccine trials and other research on hepatitis which is much more prevalent in prisons than elsewhere; and research on social and psychological problems such as alcoholism, drug addiction, and sexual assaults).

- Research on practices, both innovative and accepted, which have the intent and reasonable probability of improving the health or wellbeing of a prisoner.

- Studies of prisons as institutional structures or of prisoners as incarcerated persons, provided that the study presents no more than minimal risk and no more than inconvenience to the participants.

It is clear from the guidelines above that prisoners would make ideal participants in research that directly involves their way of life, their mental health or their environment, but research that can be conducted on healthy volunteers should not be conducted on prisoners.

Incompetent participants

One of the reasons why medical research conducted in the Nazi concentration camps was so heinous was because researchers did not glean consent from the victims, who were subject to experiments against their will. Children and the mentally ill could not refuse because they did not understand (although a refusal would not have made much of a difference at the time). It was this lack of consent that allowed the researchers to exert their power over vulnerable victims, and this was the first issue to be addressed by the Nuremberg Code.

Nuremberg Code (1947)

Paragraph 1: The voluntary consent of the human subject is absolutely essential.

As discussed above, the requirement of voluntary consent has since dropped in the list of priorities. This may be because in today's society we have human rights to protect vulnerable patients, allowing for any new research codes to focus on other issues. The term 'voluntary' only has a limited application today, because research on incompetent patients can be justified in certain circumstances. This would, no doubt, horrify the writers of the Nuremberg Code, but there is a good reason why incompetent patients are important to research. The laws do put safeguards in place, but it is not clear whether they are effective. The main problem in this area can be split into two:

- In medical law, an incompetent patient is treated according to his best interests. Non-therapeutic medical research in particular would subject him to risks without clear benefits, which is not in his best interests.

- Consent from the participant usually justifies the use of humans in medical research, but incompetent participants cannot offer this consent. Therefore, is this research unjustifiable?

The utilitarian approach to research is rather problematic when dealing with incompetent participants. A participant who is unable to consent to medical research will be subject to risks that he will not benefit from therefore, researchers could be accused of using them as simply 'a means to an end'. This was certainly the approach taken in the concentration camps in the Second World War. A commentator has argued that this approach should only be necessary in restricted circumstances, because otherwise, the dignity of the participant would be infringed:

EXTRACT

Penney Lewis, 'Procedures that are Against the Medical Interests of Incompetent Adults' (2002) 22 *Oxford Journal of Legal Studies* 575, at pages 575–618

In the context of non-therapeutic research, the existence of an international 'consensus', supporting the participation of incompetent persons, is used to avoid providing a justification for a utilitarian calculation that allows the use of vulnerable members of society in order to benefit others. [...]

Judicial approval is generally considered desirable for organ and tissue donation from incompetents and for their non-therapeutic sterilisation. It is not, however, encouraged for the approval of non-therapeutic research with incompetent subjects. To obtain judicial approval for all research projects would be overly burdensome on both the judiciary and the research community. A separate system has evolved of research ethics committees, which approve research projects. These committees may be more willing than judges to engage in utilitarian balancing of the interests of society against the interests of the incompetent prospective research subject.

Lewis claims that ethics committees may be willing to justify the use of incompetent participants in medical research. This theory is quite strange, because ethics committees were specifically designed to ensure that all medical research involving human beings is conducted ethically and in accordance with the appropriate regulations. However, the regulations are quite ambiguous, meaning that an ethics committee may have a lot of freedom when deciding whether the use of an incompetent participant in a non-therapeutic clinical trial, for example, is in fact acceptable or not.

Why use incompetent participants?

The 'good reason' why incompetent participants should be used in medical research is: we want to learn how to treat their conditions. Researchers cannot test drugs for incompetent participants on competent participants: what would they measure? The only way of achieving accurate results is to try the new drug on a participant who is suffering from the ailment that the drug is meant to cure. This rationale does not only apply to serious diseases which require drugs. It applies to all kinds of learning difficulties and behavioural disorders too. Attention Deficit Hyperactivity Disorder is an excellent example: both drugs and therapies have been explored in the treatment of this condition. We do not want to provide incompetent patients (or children) with inadequately tested drugs and therapies. The medical profession want to know how effective a treatment really is in order to offer the best that they can.

The law regarding incompetent participants

The Nuremberg Code does not allow for medical research on incompetent participants as a result of the Second World War, which was still very prevalent in the minds of medical and legal professionals when the Code was drafted.

Nuremberg Code (1947)

Paragraph 1: The voluntary consent of the human subject is absolutely essential.

The Declaration of Geneva followed immediately after, where a clear emphasis was placed on the best interests of patients and respect for patients.

The Declaration of Geneva (1948)

Paragraph 4: The health of my patient will be my first consideration.

Paragraph 9: I will maintain the utmost respect for human life.

These international rules are very clear. The Declaration of Helsinki must have been viewed as rather liberal when it came along two decades later, because for the first time, incompetent participants are named as a potential source of research subjects.

The Declaration of Helsinki (1964)

Paragraph 27: For a potential research subject who is incompetent, the physician must seek informed consent from the legally authorised representative. These individuals must not be included in a research study that has no likelihood of benefit for them unless:

- it is intended to promote the health of the population represented by the potential subject,
- the research cannot instead be performed with competent persons, and
- the research entails only minimal risk and minimal burden.

There is now a requirement for a 'legally authorised representative' to consent on behalf of an incompetent participant. It is acceptable to use incompetent participants when:

- it will benefit others with the same condition (a utilitarian approach);
- it cannot be performed on competent participants;
- there will be only a *minimal* risk and burden.

The Declaration of Helsinki is clearly a significant departure from the Nuremberg Code. However, it does contain two positive provisions. Firstly, it states that incompetent participants are *only* to be used in medical research when the research cannot be conducted on competent participants. This is a safeguard to prevent researchers from taking advantage of vulnerable individuals when competent participants will not come forward for a clinical trial. Secondly, the risk and burden must be *minimal*. However, this is a grossly ambiguous term and will vary according to the nature of the research. For example, the minimal risks in a therapeutic clinical trial for headache tablets may result in headaches, whereas the minimal risks in a non-therapeutic clinical trial involving brain surgery may result in paralysis. The negative provision in the Declaration of Helsinki is the reference to 'population represented'. It appears to be justifiable to include incompetent participants in medical research if it is to simply gather information about a particular a group of people. This 'means to an end' approach is not in the best interests of the participant, because there will be no benefit to him. The researcher must therefore explain to the ethics committee that his research can *only* be conducted on incompetent participants, he must explain the benefit and he must prove that the risks will be minimal. The Medicines for Human Use (Clinical Trials) Regulations (2004) incorporated this liberal approach from Helsinki and has dealt with incompetent participants in a completely separate section (Part 5). It clearly supports the inclusion of these individuals in medical research.

Medicines for Human Use (Clinical Trials) Regulations (2004)

Schedule 1, Part 5

Paragraph 12: Informed consent given by a legal representative to an incapacitated adult in a clinical trial shall represent that adult's presumed will.

Notice how the decision of the legal representative is accepted as the 'presumed will' of the incompetent participant under paragraph 12. Unfortunately, if the participant is completely incompetent, e.g. in a coma, then the legal representative will have no other choice than to 'presume' his will to participate in a clinical trial. However, if the participant is fighting against the process, it is more difficult to say that the consent given by the representative is in fact the 'presumed will' of the participant. In addition to this, if an incompetent participant expresses clear views that he does not want to participate in the research, this holds little influence with the researcher who is conducting the trial.

Medicines for Human Use (Clinical Trials) Regulations (2004)

Schedule 1, Part 5

Paragraph 7: The explicit wish of a subject who is capable of forming an opinion and assessing the information to refuse participation in, or to be withdrawn from, the clinical trial at any time is considered by the investigator.

A particular concern is the phrase: '*considered* by the investigator'. Medical research may involve blood tests, and if an incompetent participant refuses to submit to one, he may well be forced. This is usually only acceptable in medical law if the blood test is in the *best interests* of the patient. To do this to an incompetent participant in a clinical trial seems almost like a step back in time. The General Medical Council accepts that incompetent participants can be used in medical research, but is far more supportive of an incompetent wish to withdraw from research and these are the regulations that are more likely to be followed.

EXTRACT

Good Practice in Research (2010), General Medical Council:

http://www.gmc-uk.org/guidance/ethical_guidance/5992.asp

Paragraph 28: You must have other valid authority before involving in research adults who lack capacity.

EXTRACT

Consent to Research (2010), General Medical Council:

http://www.gmc-uk.org/guidance/ethical_guidance/5993.asp

Paragraph 25: You must only undertake research involving an adult who lacks capacity if it is related to their incapacity or its treatment. You must not involve in research adults who lack capacity if the same or similar research could be undertaken by involving only people with capacity.

Paragraph 30: You must make sure that a participant's right to withdraw from research is respected. You should consider any sign of objection, distress or indication of refusal, whether or not it is spoken, as implied refusal.

There is clearly a widespread consensus in the modern regulations and guidelines that the inclusion of incompetent participants in medical research is acceptable as long as certain provisions are in place.

Risks versus benefits

When it comes to incompetent participants, it is vital that the risks are kept to a *minimum*. This principle stems from the Declaration of Helsinki (1964) under paragraph 27, and the basic principle features in all of the relevant regulations and guidelines today (although it might be worded in a different way). The reason why this is so important is because when the participant cannot voluntarily consent to taking part in medical research, it would be taking advantage of him to subject him to hurt, pain or discomfort. Further guidance on the acceptable level of risk is provided in the 2004 Regulations.

Medicines for Human Use (Clinical Trials) Regulations (2004)

Schedule 1, Part 5

Paragraph 6: The subject has received information according to his capacity of understanding regarding the trial, its risks and its benefits.

Paragraph 9: There are grounds for expecting that administering the medicinal product to be tested in the trial will produce a benefit to the subject outweighing the risks or produce no risk at all.

Paragraph 11: The clinical trial relates directly to a life-threatening or debilitating clinical condition from which the subject suffers.

Paragraph 13: The clinical trial has been designed to minimise pain, discomfort, fear and any other foreseeable risk in relation to the disease and the cognitive abilities of the patient.

Paragraph 14: The risk threshold and the degree of distress have to be specially defined and constantly monitored.

Paragraph 15: The interests of the patient always prevail over those of science and society.

The incompetent participant only has to *receive* information regarding the trial and its risks and benefits and if a medicinal product is administered, there is an assumption that a benefit will be produced that outweighs any risks. This is slightly different to Helsinki, in that the risks no longer need to be *minimal*, they must now be *outweighed*. There must clearly be a benefit and this benefit must be 'to the subject' himself, rejecting the utilitarian 'means to an end' approach. The trial must also relate to a debilitating clinical condition and this narrows the scope considerably for the inclusion of incompetent participants in clinical trials, although it depends on the accepted definition of 'debilitating' (none is given). The trial must *minimise* pain, discomfort, fear and risk, which is an idea taken from Helsinki. Interestingly, the minimising process must be *in relation to* the cognitive abilities of the patient. This means a sliding scale of pain, discomfort, fear and risk in connection with what the patient can understand and tolerate. It might be very difficult for a researcher to 'specially define' the degree of distress because each participant is different. Interestingly, the incompetent participant is referred to as a 'patient' under paragraph 15, alluding to the fact that the participant may already be in the healthcare system. Finally, the participant comes before the interests of society, effectively abolishing non-therapeutic medical research on incompetent participants.

The General Medical Council guidelines on medical research are not specific when it comes to incompetent participants, instead choosing to settle for the more general 'minimal risk' rule taken from Helsinki and the 'benefits outweigh burdens' rule taken from the 2004 Regulations.

EXTRACT

Good Practice in Research (2010), General Medical Council:

http://www.gmc-uk.org/guidance/ethical_guidance/5992.asp

Paragraph 9: You must make sure that foreseeable risks to participants are kept as low as possible. In addition, you must be satisfied that:

- the anticipated benefits to participants outweigh the foreseeable risks, or
- the foreseeable risks to participants are minimal if the research only has the potential to benefit others more generally.

EXTRACT

Consent to Research (2010), General Medical Council:

http://www.gmc-uk.org/guidance/ethical_guidance/5993.asp

Paragraph 26: You should only involve in research adults who lack capacity, including clinical trials of investigational medicinal products, if the research is expected to provide a benefit to them that outweighs the risks. Research, not including clinical trials of investigational medicinal products, may also involve adults who lack capacity if the research is not expected to provide a direct benefit to them but is expected to contribute to the understanding of their incapacity, leading to an indirect benefit to them or others with the same incapacity, and if the risks are minimal. This means that the person should not suffer harm or distress by taking part. In all research involving adults who lack capacity, you must make sure that the foreseeable risks are kept as low as possible.

The ethics committee

If a researcher wishes to include incompetent participants in his clinical trial, the ethics committee will be especially careful when validating a medical research protocol according to the Medicines for Human Use (Clinical Trials) Regulations 2004. This is in order to protect vulnerable individuals from being taken advantage of by scrupulous or unethical researchers.

> ## Medicines for Human Use (Clinical Trials) Regulations (2004)
>
> **Part III**
>
> **Paragraph 15(5)**: In preparing its opinion, the committee shall consider, in particular, the following matters:
>
> (h) if the subjects are to include minors or persons incapable of giving consent, whether the research is justified having regard to the conditions and principles specified in Part 5 of Schedule 1.
>
> **Paragraph 15(7)**: If:
>
> (a) any subject to the clinical trial is to be an adult incapable by reason of physical and mental incapacity to give informed consent to participation in the trial; and
>
> (b) the committee does not have a member with professional expertise in the treatment of:
>
>   (i) the disease to which the trial relates, and
>
>   (ii) the patient population suffering that disease,
>
> it shall, before giving its opinion, obtain advice on the clinical, ethical and psychosocial problems in the field of that disease and patient population which may arise in relation to that trial.

The ethics committee will seek advice from an experienced professional who has knowledge of the incompetent participant's relevant illness before making its decision, showing a desire to understand what effect the research will have on the participant and whether any unnecessary suffering could result from the trial.

Emergencies

In medical law, emergency treatment can be carried out on *any* patient, but *only* if it is to save their life or prevent grave injury.

> ## EXTRACT
>
> Consent: Patients and Doctors Making Decisions Together (2008), General Medical Council, at page 32:
>
> **http://www.gmc-uk.org/guidance/ethical_guidance/consent_guidance_index.asp**
>
> **Paragraph 79**: When an emergency arises in a clinical setting and it is not possible to find out a patient's wishes, you can treat them without their consent, provided the treatment is immediately necessary to save their life or to prevent a serious deterioration of their condition.

If an incompetent participant, and this includes unconscious patients too, is to take part in an emergency clinical trial, e.g. research into how to control sudden cardiac arrests or seizures, consent must be sought from the legal representative. If this person is not available, there is a problem. The Declaration of Helsinki supports medical research on incompetent participants in emergency situations, as long as certain safeguards are in place:

The Declaration of Helsinki (1964)

Paragraph 29: Research involving subjects who are physically or mentally incapable of giving consent, for example, unconscious patients, may be done only if the physical or mental condition that prevents giving informed consent is a necessary characteristic of the research population. If no such representative is available and if the research cannot be delayed, the study may proceed without informed consent provided that the specific reasons for involving subjects with a condition that renders them unable to give informed consent have been stated in the research protocol and the study has been approved by a research ethics committee.

The provision above can be simplified as follows:

- The use of unconscious participants is only justified if the unconsciousness is a characteristic of the illness that the researcher is trying to treat.
- In an urgent situation, research can still go ahead as long as the research protocol included the factor that renders the participant unable to consent, and an ethics committee has approved this.

The General Medical Council supports this approach.

EXTRACT

Consent to Research (2010), General Medical Council:

http://www.gmc-uk.org/guidance/ethical_guidance/5993.asp

Paragraph 33: You may want to undertake urgent research into procedures or treatments used in emergencies when a person is unconscious or otherwise unable to make a decision. In an emergency situation it is not always possible to get consent to involve a person in research using the standard consent procedures.

Paragraph 34: You can start a clinical trial of investigational medicinal products when it needs to be undertaken urgently if you cannot get the consent of a legal representative, as long as a research ethics committee has given approval for such action.

The 2004 Regulations used to require a consultation to take place with a legal representative before emergency research could be carried out, but this was too time consuming and prevented further research. As a result, new regulations were passed to ease the situation. The Medicines for Human Use (Clinical trials) Amendment (No. 2) Regulations 2006 allowed for an incompetent participant to be subject to emergency research *before* consent is obtained by the legal representative, but only on strict conditions. The 2004 Regulations now read as follows:

Medicines for Human Use (Clinical Trials) Regulations (2004)

Schedule 1, Part 1

Paragraph 15: (6) Sub-paragraph (7) (below) applies if treatment is being, or is about to be, provided for a subject who is an incapacitated adult as a matter of urgency and, having regard to the nature of the clinical trial and of the particular circumstances of the case:

(a) it is necessary to take action for the purposes of the clinical trial as a matter of urgency; but

(b) it is not reasonably practicable to meet the conditions set out in paragraphs 1 to 5 of Part 5.

(7) Where this sub-paragraph applies, paragraphs 1–5 of Part 5 shall not apply in relation to the subject if the action specified in sub-paragraph (6) is carried out in accordance with a procedure approved by an ethics committee or by an appeal panel appointed under Schedule 4 at the time it gave its favourable opinion.

This provision seems rather complex, but a much simpler version is as follows:

- paragraph 15(7) of the 2004 Regulations applies when urgent treatment is about to be given to an incapacitated adult;
- the nature of the clinical trial and the circumstances of the case must be considered;
- action is necessary and urgent;
- the conditions in Part 5 cannot be met in time;
- Part 5 will no longer apply as long as the procedure has already been approved.

If the procedure has been approved by an ethics committee, then, technically, it would be ethical, but these new legal powers are not as broad as they seem. Emergency research can only be carried out if it is 'necessary' and 'urgent'. This would suggest a life-threatening situation. In addition to this, the circumstances and nature of the trial must justify the emergency research. Therefore this new provision appears to stay within the lines of the current common law as described by the General Medical Council (2008, paragraph 79, above): emergency treatment can only be given if it is to prevent grave injury, and anything beyond that is subject to the normal rules of consent. It is vital to carry out emergency medical research. There are many life-saving devices and techniques that can only be tested out in an emergency situation. This would be an excellent example of therapeutic research, i.e. a benefit to the incompetent participant.

Children as research participants

In medical law, children lack capacity to make their own decisions. This is because there is a realistic chance that they will not understand the nature of the treatment or the consequences of refusal. However, a child can be found *Gillick* competent under the common law. Medical research on children is a difficult issue. They are particularly vulnerable to adult control. However, they are often sick and there needs to be assurance from the medical profession to parents that any medication prescribed to children is good for them:

- Children have illnesses that adults don't have.
- Children take different doses to adults.
- Children have different bodies and immune systems to adults.
- Children react differently to drugs and environments.
- Children are still growing and drugs may interfere with the process.

If a child is put forward for a clinical trial, it is probably a therapeutic trial in which the child hopes to achieve a benefit. This might happen where a child suffers from a mystery illness, or has a collection of symptoms that an expert cannot diagnose. There may be no cure, or the current interventions have not worked. This would be the ideal opportunity for the family doctor to say: 'would you like to try this new drug as part of a trial?' It is almost unthinkable that a child would be put forward for non-therapeutic medical research, because this would mean him undergoing a risk to his health for the benefit of another, and children *must* be treated in accordance with their best interests according to the common law. To begin with the international laws in this area, the Nuremberg Code (1947) and the Declaration of Helsinki (1964) do not refer to minors in their provisions. The Medicines for Human Use (Clinical Trials) Regulations 2004 do specifically refer to minors, who are dealt with under Part 4 of Schedule 1.

Medicines for Human Use (Clinical Trials) Regulations (2004)

Schedule 1, Part 4

Paragraph 4: [A] person or legal representative has given his informed consent to the minor taking part in the trial.

Paragraph 5: [A] person with parental responsibility or the legal representative may, without the minor being subject to any resulting detriment, withdraw the minor from the trial at any time by revoking his informed consent.

Paragraph 6: The minor has received information according to his capacity of understanding, from staff with experience with minors, regarding the trial, its risks and its benefits.

Paragraph 7: The explicit wish of a minor who is capable of forming an opinion and assessing the information to refuse participation in, or to be withdrawn from, the clinical trial at any time is considered by the investigator.

Paragraph 9: The clinical trial relates directly to a clinical condition from which the minor suffers or is of such a nature that it can only be carried out on minors.

Paragraph 10: Some direct benefit for the group of patients involved in the clinical trial is to be obtained from that trial.

Paragraph 13: Informed consent given by a person with parental responsibility or a legal representative to a minor taking part in a clinical trial shall represent the minor's presumed will.

Paragraph 14: The clinical trial has been designed to minimise pain, discomfort, fear and any other foreseeable risk in relation to the disease and the minor's stage of development.

Paragraph 15: The risk threshold and the degree of distress have to be specially defined and constantly monitored.

Paragraph 16: The interests of the patient always prevail over those of science and society.

The general principles for minors under the 2004 Regulations are almost identical to those for incompetent adults in the following ways:

- A legal representative has complete control over the informed consent.
- A legal representative can withdraw informed consent at any time.
- The minor must receive information about the risks and benefits.
- A refusal may only be *considered* by the researcher.
- The research is of a nature that can only be carried out on minors.
- The informed consent of the legal representative is assumed to represent the will of the participant.
- The trial must be designed to *minimise* pain, discomfort, fear and risk.
- The threshold of risk must be *defined* and monitored.
- A rejection of the utilitarian approach, putting the interests of the minor over those of society.

When it comes to the 'risk and benefit' balance for minors the 2004 Regulations are ambiguous, but when read as a whole they do clearly distinguish between the following three groups of people:

- Competent adults: benefits must *justify* the risks.
- Incompetent adults: benefits must *outweigh* the risks.
- Minors: there must simply be a *direct benefit*.

The 2004 Regulations (Schedule 1, Part 4, Paragraph 10, above) specifically state that minor participants should obtain a *direct benefit* from the trial. This definitively rules out non-therapeutic research on minors. However, there is no further information. There is no reference to *measuring* risks, *minimal* risks or *outweighing* risks. This seems rather odd. The trial must be designed to *minimise* pain, discomfort, fear and risk (paragraph 14), and the threshold of risk must be defined and monitored (paragraph 15), but this does not mean that the minor will not be subject to a *disproportionate* risk. There is therefore no scale against which to measure the risks to minors. The General Medical Council gives a bit more guidance, referring to a 'minimal or low' risk of harm to minors and any benefit must *outweigh* the risks, which are to be 'kept low'. This is derived from the guidance on incompetent participants and is much fairer to minors.

> ## EXTRACT
>
> ### 0–18 Years: Guidance for All Doctors, (2007), General Medical Council:
>
> **http://www.gmc-uk.org/guidance/ethical_guidance/children_guidance_index.asp**
>
> **Paragraph 36**: Research involving children and young people can benefit all children; but they may be vulnerable because they cannot always recognise their best interests, express their needs or defend their rights.
>
> **Paragraph 37**: Children or young people should be involved in research only when research on adults cannot provide the same benefits. They can be involved in research that has either:

(a)   potential benefits for children or young people generally, as long as the research does not go against their best interests or involves only minimal or low risk of harm;

(b)   potential therapeutic benefits for them that outweigh any foreseeable risks, which should be kept as low as possible.

Paragraph 38: Children and young people should not usually be involved in research if they object or appear to object in either words or actions, even if their parents consent. If they are able to consent for themselves, you should still consider involving their parents, depending on the nature of the research.

Paragraph 39: You must not put pressure on children, young people or their parents to consent to research in the expectation of therapeutic, financial or any other benefit.

Minors are still left in an awkward position. It is not clear if a minor can still be taken advantage of by an unscrupulous researcher who wishes to subject her to a distressing procedure as long as the risk is outweighed by the direct benefit to be achieved. Should children be included in research at all? Miller and Kenny argue that leaving children out of medical research will only harm them even more:

EXTRACT

Paul Miller and Nuala Kenny, 'Walking the Moral Tightrope: Respecting and Protecting Children in Health-Related Research' (2002) 11 *Cambridge Quarterly of Healthcare Ethics* 217, at pages 217–29

Ironically, the protective impulse to shield children entirely from the harms of research participation has the potential to cause them significant harm. History tells of the dangerous consequences of presuming treatments tested on adults to be safe and effective for children. [...] For scientific and ethical reasons, children should receive wherever possible only those treatments that have been adequately evaluated on children. [...] Reliance on the results of research involving adults as the knowledge base from which to develop the care of children may make the provision of such care unnecessarily dangerous.

Miller and Kenny raise a valid point: we may be doing children more harm by giving them medical treatments that have only been tested on adults. However, it is understandable why parents do not put their children forward for medical research (even if it is therapeutic): it could be a frightening experience, the benefit might not materialise and there is no formal requirement that the risks should be *outweighed* or *justified* by the benefits. Children are subject to risks every day, but a parent does not usually place a child in a risky situation unless, more than likely, it would save the life of that child. There is one significant way in which the rules for minors can be distinguished from the rules for incompetent adults. The phrase 'stage of development' is included for minors. An expert in child development may be consulted by the ethics committee to ensure that the child will come to no future harm as a result of the trial.

A 'best interests' anomaly

All other kinds of medical research involving incompetent participants which is *not* included under the Medicines for Human Use (Clinical Trials) Regulations 2004 can be governed by the Mental Capacity Act 2005 instead. This is quite rare, because the definition of a 'clinical trial' under the 2004 regulations is very wide indeed so it will cover most types of medical research:

Medicines for Human Use (Clinical Trials) Regulations 2004

Part 1

Paragraph 2(1): In these regulations, 'clinical trial' means any investigation in human subjects, other than a non-interventional trial, intended:

(a) to discover or verify the clinical, pharmacological or other pharmacodynamic effects of one or more medicinal products,

(b) to identify any adverse reactions to one or more such products, or

(c) to study the absorption, distribution, metabolism and excretion of one or more such products.

If any medical research was to fall outside of the ambit of the 2004 Regulations, the 2005 Act provides far stricter provisions:

Mental Capacity Act 2005

Section 31: Requirements for approval

(2) The research must be connected with:

    (a) an impairing condition affecting P, or

    (b) its treatment.

(5) The research must:

    (a) have the potential the benefit P without imposing on P a burden that is disproportionate to the potential benefit to P, or

    (b) be intended to provide knowledge of the causes or treatment of, or of the care of persons affected by, the same or a similar condition.

(6) If the research falls within paragraph (b) of subsection (5) but not within paragraph (a), there must be reasonable grounds for believing:

    (a) that the risk to P from taking part in the project is likely to be negligible, and

    (b) that anything done to, or in relation to, P will not:

        (i)   interfere with P's freedom of action or privacy in a significant way, or

        (ii) be unduly invasive or restrictive.

The provisions under section 31(6) is a concern, because it allows for research with a higher burden than benefit to be carried out on the condition that the risk is negligible and will not interfere with the freedom, privacy or body of the participant. The anomaly is clear: the Medicines for Human Use (Clinical Trials) Regulations 2004 would not allow the risks to outweigh the benefits, whereas the Mental Capacity Act 2005 would allow the risks to outweigh the benefits (albeit under strict criteria). It should not be justifiable to subject an incompetent participant to a disproportionate burden.

However, the Mental Capacity Act 2005 does provide some more understanding provisions. Under section 32(4), the person in charge of the research project must consult a carer on behalf of the participant and ask whether (a) the participant should take part, and (b) what the participant's wishes and feelings would have been about the project had he been competent. This provision shows a greater understanding for the needs of the incompetent participant, and this understanding is not provided for in the 2004 Regulations. The 2005 Act goes even further, and states under section 33 that an incompetent participant can be withdrawn from the medical research if he indicates *in any way* that this is his wish.

Mental Capacity Act 2005

Section 33: Additional safeguards

(2) Nothing may be done to, or in relation to, him in the course of the research:

    (a) to which he appears to object (whether by showing signs of resistance or otherwise) except where what is being done is intended to protect him from harm or to reduce or prevent pain or discomfort,

(4) If he indicates (in any way) that he wishes to be withdrawn from the project he must be withdrawn without delay.

The provision under section 33(4) of the 2005 Act is particularly generous when comparing it to the alternative provision in the 2004 Regulations.

Medicines for Human Use (Clinical Trials) Regulations (2004)

Schedule 1, Part 5

Paragraph 7: The explicit wish of a subject who is capable of forming an opinion and assessing the information referred to in the previous paragraph to refuse participation in, or to be withdrawn from, the clinical trial at any time is considered by the investigator.

An important question must be asked: why does the Mental Capacity Act 2005 take clear steps to respect an incompetent participant's wish to withdraw from medical research, whereas the Medicines for Human Use (Clinical Trials) Regulations 2004 does not? It is most unfortunate that the 2004 Regulations cover most types of medical research, because it leaves only a minority to enjoy the more liberal rights under the 2005 Act.

ACTIVITY

David has come to visit you in your capacity as a medical lawyer about his mother, who is an incompetent patient. She has been put forward for a pioneering clinical trial which looks into stroke prevention and cure. He wants to become informed about the laws regarding consent for incompetent patients, but he is also concerned about his mother's best interests and whether the trial would stop if she showed signs of discomfort. How would you advise him?

● ● ● Medical research in poor countries

There are many good reasons why medical research is conducted in poor countries:

- The poorest countries suffer from widespread diseases (e.g. malaria and tuberculosis).
- There are very high mortality rates because of a lack of basic healthcare.
- There are small populations who are vulnerable to contagious diseases.
- There is a lack of basic care for those with disabilities.
- There is a lack of understanding about good health and nutrition.
- There is a lack of basic drugs such as aspirin, penicillin, vaccinations and contraceptives.
- There is a lack of money from the government to fund appropriate healthcare.
- There may be unequal distribution of healthcare, leading to traditional methods.

In more developed countries, such as the UK, there is still a problem with access to healthcare in more rural areas, but in developing countries this problem is greatly magnified. As a result, researchers, doctors and scientists are keen to conduct medical research in countries where even the simplest development in medicine could save many lives. It is not simply a case of shipping out thousands of vaccinations (although this is done by charities too), it is important to find radical and innovative ways of accessing millions of people and providing quick, cheap and convenient methods of treating illnesses that would ordinarily cost millions of pounds. There is a significant ethical problem. Medical research in poor countries is not very well regulated and the laws regarding patient protection are thin on the ground, meaning that researchers and their sponsors are more likely to flock to poor countries to conduct their clinical trials on the grounds that they are less likely to be sued for millions of pounds if things go wrong. This makes the candidates in poor countries very vulnerable to scrupulous researchers. The governments in poorer countries will not have the funds to buy expensive medicine but may have a pandemic on their hands, and so will turn a blind eye to the potential dangers of clinical trials in order to provide at least *some* medical care for its population. For the researchers, doctors, scientists and their sponsors who travel to these countries to conduct clinical trials, they effectively enjoy a 'free reign'. The international law has stepped in, because this is clearly a situation that can be exploited. The aim is to provide safe and quality research that can improve the health and the lives of people in the host nation without taking advantage of their vulnerability. The Nuremberg Code (1947) did not, at the time, envisage that medical research could one day take place between countries, but the Declaration of Geneva (1948) did refer to a violation of human rights.

The Declaration of Geneva (1948)

Paragraph 10: I will not use my medical knowledge to violate human rights and civil liberties, even under threat.

It was the Declaration of Helsinki (1964) that addressed the issue of international research for the first time. It addressed many different issues, ranging from the aims of the research through to gleaning consent from community leaders. There is clear support for medical research in poor countries, but the feeling is that it must *benefit* the participants (or at least their community) for it to be ethical.

The Declaration of Helsinki (1964)

Paragraph 5: Medical progress is based on research that ultimately must include studies involving human subjects. Populations that are underrepresented in medical research should be provided appropriate access to participation in research.

Paragraph 7: The primary purpose of medical research involving human subjects is to understand the causes, development and effects of diseases and improve preventive, diagnostic and therapeutic interventions (methods, procedures and treatments). Even the best current interventions must be evaluated continually through research for their safety, effectiveness, efficiency, accessibility and quality.

The small and sometimes isolated populations in poor countries are underrepresented in medical research and paragraph 5 clearly supports their inclusion in medical research. Paragraph 7 illustrates the main reason why medical research should be conducted in poor countries: to understand the origins of widespread diseases and to improve available treatments. The cheaper this can be done, the more beneficial to the population.

The Declaration of Helsinki (1964)

Paragraph 10: Physicians should consider the ethical, legal and regulatory norms and standards for research involving human subjects in their own countries as well as applicable international norms and standards. No national or international ethical, legal or regulatory requirement should reduce or eliminate any of the protections for research subjects set forth in this Declaration.

Paragraph 15: [The ethics committee] must take into consideration the laws and regulations of the country or countries in which the research is to be performed as well as applicable international norms and standards but these must not be allowed to reduce or eliminate any of the protections for research subjects set forth in this Declaration.

Helsinki clearly recognises that some researchers will conduct medical research abroad for the simple reason that they will be largely unregulated. The Declaration of Helsinki will still apply, regardless of whether domestic laws are in place or not, and if any domestic laws *are* in place, they must be respected. It is clearly the role of the ethics committee to ensure that the research protocol is ethical and that it meets the legal and ethical standards set by the host country if the researcher is planning on taking his clinical trial abroad.

The Declaration of Helsinki (1964)

Paragraph 17: Medical research involving a disadvantaged or vulnerable population or community is only justified if the research is responsive to the health needs and priorities of this population or community and if there is a reasonable likelihood that this population or community stands to benefit from the results of the research.

This is a significant paragraph. If the host population are 'disadvantaged' or 'vulnerable' then the medical research is only justified if it responds to their health needs and priorities. If this is not clear, there must be a 'reasonable likelihood' of a benefit for the population or community. It is clearly sufficient for the participant's *community* to benefit, not the participant *himself*. This is the utilitarian approach.

The Declaration of Helsinki (1964)

Paragraph 18: Every medical research study involving human subjects must be preceded by careful assessment of predictable risks and burdens to the individuals and communities involved in the research in comparison with foreseeable benefits to them and to other individuals or communities affected by the condition under investigation.

Paragraph 22: Participation by competent individuals as subjects in medical research must be voluntary. Although it may be appropriate to consult family members or community leaders, no competent individual may be enrolled in a research study unless he or she freely agrees.

These paragraphs are an acknowledgement that some communities may be more vulnerable to risks than others. For example, an isolated community who only use traditional medicine may be particularly exposed to the dangers of modern vaccinations, i.e. may be more susceptible to the disease within the vaccine. These matters must be addressed by the researcher. It is interesting that community leaders have been included in this paragraph. They do not have complete authority over the participant, who must 'freely agree' to take part, but this shows respect for the traditions of the communities that exist in poorer countries.

The Declaration of Helsinki (1964)

Paragraph 31: The physician may combine medical research with medical care only to the extent that the research is justified by its potential preventive, diagnostic or therapeutic value and if the physician has good reason to believe that participation in the research study will not adversely affect the health of the patients who serve as research subjects.

This paragraph does not directly link to research in poor countries, but most of the clinical trials conducted on disadvantaged or vulnerable populations will be therapeutic to either the participant or the population. The Declaration has therefore allowed researchers to administer the treatment as part of the research on the condition that there is 'good reason to believe' that the health of the participants will not suffer. The Declaration of Helsinki (1964) has clearly established that medical research is poor countries is acceptable as long as the population acquire a benefit from it and respect is shown for their laws and values. The usual rules regarding risks and benefits also apply, unless the host country has domestic legislation in place that tightens these rules even further.

Two decades later, the Council for International Organisation of Medical Sciences (CIOMS) became concerned that researchers were still taking advantage of the liberal research regulations in poor countries, and worked with the World Health Organisation

(WHO) to publish a guide entitled: International Ethical Guidelines for Biomedical Research Involving Human Subjects (2002), which addresses the problems of implementing the Declaration of Helsinki in poor countries.[15]

EXTRACT

International Ethical Guidelines for Biomedical Research Involving Human Subjects (2002), World Health Organisation and Council for International Organisation of Medical Sciences:

http://www.cioms.ch/index.php/texts-of-guidelines

Introduction: The Guidelines take the position that research involving human subjects must not violate any universally applicable ethical standards, but acknowledge that, in superficial aspects, the application of the ethical principles, e.g., in relation to individual autonomy and informed consent, needs to take account of cultural values, while respecting absolutely the ethical standards. The issue concerns largely, though not exclusively, two principles: respect for autonomy and protection of dependent or vulnerable persons and populations.

The CIOMS guide contains 21 individual guidelines that address how the ethical standards of the Declaration of Helsinki (1964) can be incorporated into medical research practices in poor countries. An outline of the guide is listed below:

Guideline:	Subject:
1	Ethical justification and scientific validity of biomedical research involving human beings
2	Ethical review committees
3	Ethical review of externally sponsored research
4	Individual informed consent
5	Obtaining informed consent: Essential information for prospective research subjects
6	Obtaining informed consent: Obligations of sponsors and investigators
7	Inducement to participate
8	Benefits and risks of study participation
9	Special limitations on risk when research involves individuals who are not capable of giving informed consent
10	Research in populations and communities with limited resources
11	Choice of control in clinical trials
12	Equitable distribution of burdens and benefits in the selection of groups of subjects in research

---

[15] The Guidelines were first issued in 1982, and then updated in 1993 and 2002.

Guideline:	Subject:
13	Research involving vulnerable persons
14	Research involving children
15	Research involving individuals who by reason of mental or behavioural disorders are not capable of giving adequately informed consent
16	Women as research subjects
17	Pregnant women as research participants
18	Safeguarding confidentiality
19	Right of injured subjects to treatment and compensation
20	Strengthening capacity for ethical and scientific review and biomedical research
21	Ethical obligation of external sponsors to provide healthcare services

The CIOMS guide clearly covers all the relevant ethical issues that face researchers when they take their clinical trials abroad.

Consent

The issue of consent has already been addressed, and it was noted above that if a participant is competent, he must provide fully informed and voluntary consent. If he is incompetent or a minor, a legal representative can do this for him. In poor countries, the doctrine of informed consent still stands. The Declaration of Helsinki (1964) refers to the views of a 'community leader' but this is for consideration only. The participant must herself consent if she is competent to do so, and this principle is also included within the CIOMS guide.

EXTRACT

International Ethical Guidelines for Biomedical Research Involving Human Subjects (2002), World Health Organisation and Council for International Organisation of Medical Sciences:

http://www.cioms.ch/index.php/texts-of-guidelines

Guideline 4: *Cultural considerations.* In some cultures an investigator may enter a community to conduct research or approach prospective subjects for their individual consent only after obtaining permission from a community leader, a council of elders, or another designated authority. Such customs must be respected. In no case, however, may the permission of a community leader or other authority substitute for individual informed consent. In some populations the use of a number of local languages may complicate the communication of information to potential subjects and the ability of an investigator to ensure that they truly understand it.

It is very encouraging to see such a high level of respect for the cultures and traditions in poorer countries. It is vital that the aims of the medical research are explained clearly to the relevant community, so that when the community leader provides his blessing and the participant provides her consent, there have been no crossed wires and all parties agree on the same terms. The participant and her community may feel particularly violated if the procedure turns out to be something that was not understood or consented to.

Risks versus benefits

It is made clear in the Declaration of Helsinki (1964) that the objective of the research must outweigh the risks and burdens for competent patients (paragraph 18).This is a rather wide provision, as it allows for significant risks and burdens as long as they are *balanced against* with any benefits. It will be remembered that this provision was tightened up significantly in the UK law under the Medicines for Human Use (Clinical Trials) Regulations 2004, where the benefit (which should be experienced by the participant) now has to *outweigh* the risk. Did the CIOMS guide also tighten up this provision for the purposes of medical research in poor countries? The answer is: yes. In regard to therapeutic research, the risks must be justified against the expected benefits to the participant himself. However, the utilitarian approach is kept firmly on the table in relation to non-therapeutic research.

EXTRACT

International Ethical Guidelines for Biomedical Research Involving Human Subjects (2002), World Health Organisation and Council for International Organisation of Medical Sciences:

http://www.cioms.ch/index.php/texts-of-guidelines

Guideline 8: Interventions or procedures that hold out the prospect of direct diagnostic, therapeutic or preventive benefit for the individual subject must be justified by the expectation that they will be at least as advantageous to the individual subject, in the light of foreseeable risks and benefits, as any available alternative. Risks of such 'beneficial' interventions or procedures must be justified in relation to expected benefits to the individual subject.

Risks of interventions that do not hold out the prospect of direct diagnostic, therapeutic or preventive benefit for the individual must be justified in relation to the expected benefits to society (general knowledge). The risks presented by such interventions must be reasonable in relation to the importance of the knowledge to be gained.

However, the CIOMS guide does address a separate issue that is unique to all of the medical research laws, regulations and guidelines examined so far. They explore the *social* risks that could flow from medical research in poor countries (e.g. drug use), and the dangers that this could pose to small communities or groups of sufferers.

EXTRACT

International Ethical Guidelines for Biomedical Research Involving Human Subjects (2002), World Health Organisation and Council for International Organisation of Medical Sciences:

http://www.cioms.ch/index.php/texts-of-guidelines

Guideline 8: *Risks to groups of persons.* Research in certain fields, such as epidemiology, genetics or sociology, may present risks to the interests of communities, societies, or racially or ethnically defined groups. Information might be published that could stigmatise a group or expose its members to discrimination. Such information, for example, could indicate, rightly or wrongly, that the group has a higher than average prevalence of alcoholism, mental illness or sexually transmitted disease, or is particularly susceptible to certain genetic disorders. Plans to conduct such research should be sensitive to such considerations, to the need to maintain confidentiality during and after the study, and to the need to publish the resulting data in a manner that is respectful of the interests of all concerned, or in certain circumstances not to publish them. The ethical review committee should ensure that the interests of all concerned are given due consideration; often it will be advisable to have individual consent supplemented by community consultation.

This is insightful. There is an assumption that medical research usually involves traditional medicines, but it does not. It can cover mental health issues, social trends, criminal justice issues, behavioural disorders, and so on. Therefore, researchers have to very careful when conducting their research in another country that they are aware of the social ramifications of publishing their results. There may well be a small population who are stigmatised or discriminated against.

Incompetent participants

The Declaration of Helsinki (1964) makes it clear that incompetent participants should not take part in medical research 'unless it is intended to promote the health of the population represented by the potential subject, the research cannot instead be performed with competent persons, and the research entails only minimal risk and minimal burden' at paragraph 27. This is developed in a rather strange way by the CIOMS guide.

EXTRACT

International Ethical Guidelines for Biomedical Research Involving Human Subjects (2002), World Health Organisation and Council for International Organisation of Medical Sciences:

http://www.cioms.ch/index.php/texts-of-guidelines

Guideline 9: When there is ethical and scientific justification to conduct research with individuals incapable of giving informed consent, the risk from research interventions that do not hold out the prospect of direct benefit for the individual subject should be no more likely and not greater than the risk attached to routine medical or psychological examination of such persons. Slight or minor increases above such risk may be permitted when there is an overriding scientific or medical rationale for such increases and when an ethical review committee has approved them.

The CIOMS guide appears to have introduced a new test for the measurement of risks to incompetent participants:

1. if the risks to an incompetent participant exceed those attached to 'routine medical or psychological examination'. . .

2. there must be an 'overriding scientific or medical rationale' which has been approved by an ethics committee.

The ethics committee will judge the risks in accordance with the following criteria.

EXTRACT

Guideline 9: When the risks are in excess of those, the ethical review committee must find:

(1) that the research is designed to be responsive to the disease affecting the prospective subjects or to conditions to which they are particularly susceptible;

(2) that the risks of the research interventions are only slightly greater than those associated with routine medical or psychological examination of such persons for the condition or set of clinical circumstances under investigation;

(3) that the objective of the research is sufficiently important to justify exposure of the subjects to the increased risk; and

(4) that the interventions are reasonably commensurate with the clinical interventions that the subjects have experienced or may be expected to experience in relation to the condition under investigation.

In other words, the incompetent participant can be subjected to a risk exceeding that of a routine examination if:

- The research is relevant to the participant's condition.
- The risks are only *slightly* higher.
- The objective justifies the increased risk.
- The intervention is similar to what the participant has experienced.

These four conditions are easy to satisfy, and the use of the word 'slightly' leaves a lot of discretion to the ethics committee to decide whether the incompetent participant is being subjected to an unreasonable risk or not. Guideline 9 is therefore a complicated and extended version of paragraph 27 of Helsinki, and it significantly widens the 'minimal risk and burden' test which in turn loosens the protection for incompetent participants as opposed to strengthen it.

Inducements

The issue of payment has already been addressed, and it was noted above that poor participants in particular could be coerced into medical research by the temptation of financial gain. In poor countries where basic amenities are difficult to come by, the enticement of money will be even stronger:

- Money could pay for food and water;
- Money could pay for education, livestock or other living amenities;

- Money could lead to a higher social standing in the community;
- Money could pay for better healthcare for the family;
- Money could save the life of a loved one.

In addition to these pressures, the prospect of receiving any healthcare from 'western' doctors might be enough of an inducement for participants to come forward. The CIOMS guide provides significant guidance on this matter, which is not addressed in the Declaration of Helsinki (1964) at all.

EXTRACT

International Ethical Guidelines for Biomedical Research Involving Human Subjects (2002), World Health Organisation and Council for International Organisation of Medical Sciences:

http://www.cioms.ch/index.php/texts-of-guidelines

Guideline 7: *Unacceptable recompense.* Payments in money or in kind to research subjects should not be so large as to persuade them to take undue risks or volunteer against their better judgment. Payments or rewards that undermine a person's capacity to exercise free choice invalidate consent. It may be difficult to distinguish between suitable recompense and undue influence to participate in research. Someone without access to medical care may or may not be unduly influenced to participate in research simply to receive such care. Monetary and in-kind recompense must, therefore, be evaluated in the light of the traditions of the particular culture and population in which they are offered, to determine whether they constitute undue influence. The ethical review committee will ordinarily be the best judge of what constitutes reasonable material recompense in particular circumstances.

There is no clear way of deciding whether a specific amount of money is undue influence or not, but it is encouraging that an ethics committee will take into account 'the traditions of the particular culture and population' so as to make sure that the vulnerability of some participants is not taken advantage of. This will also include the participant's environment, living conditions, and family history. For example, it might be the case that the participant comes from a family suffering from famine, or several of her family members have already died from the disease that the trial is aiming to treat. These circumstances would make participation in the trial even more tempting than usual.

Caring for the community after the trial is over

A question that is particularly relevant to medical research in poor countries is whether the treatment should be available to the host population once the trial has come to an end. The Declaration of Helsinki (1964) clearly states that the clinical trial should benefit the host population, especially if they are disadvantaged or vulnerable, and so it would be particularly cruel to simply pack up and leave the country once the trial came to an end if the trial did yield a positive result. The Declaration of Helsinki (1964) supports the continuation of treatment.

The Declaration of Helsinki (1964)

Paragraph 33: At the conclusion of the study, patients entered into the study are entitled to be informed about the outcome of the study and to share any benefits that result from it, for example, access to interventions identified as beneficial in the study or to other appropriate care or benefits.

The issue is particularly difficult if only a small community took part in the trial but the treatment could benefit a whole population. There is generally no ethical duty (under Helsinki or otherwise) to provide the whole population with a new treatment if it is found to be successful in a clinical trial, but the participants themselves are a different matter. They exposed themselves to risks and burdens in order to help towards the positive results, and so they are, at the very least, entitled (according to Helsinki) to share the benefits. The CIOMS guide strongly supports this approach.

EXTRACT

International Ethical Guidelines for Biomedical Research Involving Human Subjects (2002), World Health Organisation and Council for International Organisation of Medical Sciences:

http://www.cioms.ch/index.php/texts-of-guidelines

Guideline 10: *Reasonable availability*. The issue of 'reasonable availability' is complex and will need to be determined on a case-by-case basis. Relevant considerations include the length of time for which the intervention or product developed, or other agreed benefit, will be made available to research subjects, or to the community or population concerned; the severity of a subject's medical condition; the effect of withdrawing the study drug (e.g., death of a subject); the cost to the subject or health service; and the question of undue inducement if an intervention is provided free of charge.

In general, if there is good reason to believe that a product developed or knowledge generated by research is unlikely to be reasonably available to, or applied to the benefit of, the population of a proposed host country or community after the conclusion of the research, it is unethical to conduct the research in that country or community.

This guideline very clearly states that if a product is not going to be made available to a population in the host country after the trial is complete, it would be unethical to conduct the trial in that country. The message here is clear: do not take advantage of communities by inviting them into your research project and then leaving them without any treatment. The phrase 'case-by-case' is telling: it always depends on the illness, the participant, the circumstances, the environment and the resources.

ACTIVITY

You are a scientist but have had little luck attracting a good variety of research participants for your 'vitamin pill: alternative to paracetamol' clinical trial in the UK. You secure the funding required to take your trial to a poor country. You inform the host government that your wonder pill contains an excellent selection of vitamins that are especially beneficial for malnourished adults. The government permits your trial in their host country. You learnt from your earlier trials on animals that the pill could also lead to strange and erratic behaviour, similar to that of Attention Deficit Hyperactivity Disorder, but you keep this to yourself as you find a small village with willing volunteers. Are you acting in accordance with the relevant ethical codes for international medical research? Give reasons for your answer.

Publishing the results of medical research

In the field of medical research, it is easy to forget that there are other issues apart from consent, risks, benefits, payment and exclusion. A big issue that often gets overlooked is the ethical principles relating to the publication of medical research. This may seem strange, but the key issues are as follows:

- If the research was unethical in some way, e.g. children suffered disproportionate harm, should the results of the trial be published?

- If so, what message does this send to the participants, their families, the public, the pharmaceutical industry, and most importantly, other researchers?

- If not, would there be a risk of this harm happening again, and would valuable information be lost?

This issue is referred to as 'publication ethics' and it is very important. For example, the concentration camps in the Second World War collected a lot of useful and important medical research data, but publishing and using the data today would feel inappropriate now that we know how the data was attained (through force, torture and death). So where does the law stand on this issue? The international law is clear that *unethical* medical research should not be published. The Nuremberg Code (1947) did not refer to publication ethics, but the Declaration of Helsinki (1964) covered the issue in detail.

The Declaration of Helsinki (1964)

Paragraph 30: Authors, editors and publishers all have ethical obligations with regard to the publication of the results of research. Authors have a duty to make publicly available the results of their research on human subjects and are accountable for the completeness and accuracy of their reports. They should adhere to accepted guidelines for ethical reporting. Negative and inconclusive as well as positive results should be published or otherwise made publicly available. Sources of funding, institutional affiliations and conflicts of interest should be declared in the publication. Reports of research not in accordance with the principles of this Declaration should not be accepted for publication.

Paragraph 30 does not expressly state that unethical research *must not* be published, but it does state that research which does not adhere to the principles of the Declaration of Helsinki *should not* be published and authors, editors and publishers have an ethical obligation to ensure that this principle is respected. The CIOMS guide explains how this principle should be applied to medical research in poor countries.

EXTRACT

International Ethical Guidelines for Biomedical Research Involving Human Subjects (2002), World Health Organisation and Council for International Organisation of Medical Sciences:

http://www.cioms.ch/index.php/texts-of-guidelines

Guideline 12: Unless there are persuasive reasons to do otherwise, editors should refuse to publish the results of research conducted unethically, and retract any articles that are subsequently found to contain falsified or fabricated data or to have been based on unethical research. Drug regulatory authorities should consider refusal to accept unethically obtained data submitted in support of an application for authorisation to market a product.

The CIOMS guide loosens the Helsinki principle by suggesting that editors should refuse unethical research *unless there are persuasive reasons* not to do so. This is vague, but an example could be the finding of an AIDS cure during a trial in which participants were subject to a concoction of drugs that caused them significant harm.

Interestingly, the UK approach to publication ethics has been mixed. There is more reference to the Data Protection Act 1998 (Chapter 5) in order to protect participants. The Medicines for Human Use (Clinical Trials) Regulations (2004) include very little in the way of publication ethics.

Medicines for Human Use (Clinical Trials) Regulations (2004)

Schedule 1, Part 2

Paragraph 7: The [research] protocol shall provide for the definition of inclusion and exclusion of subjects participating in a clinical trial, monitoring and publication policy.

The General Medical Council sticks to an *honest* approach, but fails to give any guidance to editors or authors as to submitting or publishing unethical research.

EXTRACT

Good Practice in Research (2010), General Medical Council:

http://www.gmc-uk.org/guidance/ethical_guidance/5992.asp

Paragraph 23: You must make clear, accurate and legible records of research, as soon as possible after the data are collected.

Paragraph 24: You must report research results accurately, objectively, promptly and in a way that can be clearly understood. You must make sure that research reports are properly attributed and do not contain false or misleading data.

There does not appear to be a strict rule against the publication of unethical research, but there is a consensus (particularly at international level) that it should only be justified in certain circumstances. This is not much of an incentive for a small minority of researchers to carry out their clinical trials ethically.

Does research have to be published?

Many of the international codes and declarations examined so far have quoted 'scientific knowledge' or 'benefit of the population' as justification for subjecting competent participants to some harm in clinical trials. This leads on to an interesting question: is there a *duty* to publish research results? The Medicines for Human Use (Clinical trials) Regulations (2004) is more patient-centred and requires a benefit to be felt by the participant himself, but if the population were to benefit from a clinical trial, should they public be told? The ethical response should be 'yes' if the participants submitted to blood tests, invasive examinations and personal interviews in order to simply benefit the public, because the act of publication would justify their time and experience. To take this issue one step further, the consent of the participants might be vitiated if they find out after the trial that their results might not be published. This is because many of the participants chose to participate to help future patients, and it was on this understanding that they consented. There seems very little point in volunteering for medical research if the results will not be used by the scientific community: that was the point of the trial? The General Medical Council does provide clear guidance on this specific issue.

EXTRACT

Good Practice in Research (2010), General Medical Council:

http://www.gmc-uk.org/guidance/ethical_guidance/5992.asp

Paragraph 24: Whenever possible, you should publish research results, including adverse findings, through peer-reviewed journals.

Paragraph 25: You should make research findings available to those who might benefit. You should make reasonable efforts to inform participants of the outcome of the research, or make the information publicly available if it is not practical to inform participants directly.

It is clearly ethical to make medical research public and accessible. If a clinical trial leads to negative, harmful or unexpected results, these must be published too. This may seem strange, but under paragraph 30 of Helsinki (above) it clearly states that 'negative or inconclusive' results should be published or made publicly available. There are good reasons for this:

- It is a result. It might not have been the result that the researcher (or the participant) wanted, but it is scientific knowledge that can be used in a positive way.
- Researchers know that the exact same trial cannot be initiated again because it causes harm to the participants.
- The knowledge regarding the particular drug or treatment has increased, allowing further research to be conducted.
- The drug may treat a completely different illness that nobody had foreseen.

There is also a requirement *before* the trial has begun to register it on a relevant database, or at least make its details public. This is supported by international and domestic guidelines:

- The Declaration of Helsinki (1964) at paragraph 19.
- GMC Good Practice in Research (2010) at paragraph 11.

THINKING POINT

What impact might it have on a researcher or a scientist if they published the results of their unsuccessful clinical trial? Does it help the field/their career, or hinder the field/their career?

Compensating research participants

In medical law today, the concept of compensating is all too familiar. A doctor must breach his duty of care and the breach must cause the harm in order for a patient to successfully claim compensation. In a clinical trial, the same principles apply:

1. The researcher has a duty of care.
2. The researcher breaches that duty of care.
3. The breach caused the harm.

There are a number of ways in which a researcher could breach his duty towards a participant in a clinical trial:

- He used inappropriate equipment.
- He used the wrong drug.
- He used the wrong dose.
- He did not provide clean and sterile conditions.
- He diverted from the research protocol agreed by the Ethics Committee.
- He did not warn the participant of the major risks.
- He used force.
- He conducted the trial in a dangerous or unsuitable venue.

The concept of compensating research participants was foreign in the times of the Nuremberg Code (1947), which did not see medical research as a contractual exchange between two parties. Two decades later, the Declaration of Helsinki (1964) did mention compensation, and the idea has been developed in domestic law.

The Declaration of Helsinki (1964)

Paragraph 14: The design and performance of each research study involving human subjects must be clearly described in a research protocol. The protocol should contain a statement of the ethical considerations involved and should indicate how the principles in this Declaration have been addressed. The protocol should include information regarding funding, sponsors, institutional affiliations, other potential conflicts of interest, incentives for subjects and provisions for treating and/or compensating subjects who are harmed as a consequence of participation in the research study.

Helsinki clearly refers to 'compensating' participants, and asks that the provisions for compensation be included in the research protocol from the very beginning of the research process. This allows the Ethics Committee to examine whether the provisions are adequate, and it provides some peace of mind to the participants: there are safeguards in place should anything go wrong. The Medicines for Human Use (Clinical Trials) Regulations (2004) includes compensation and insurance in their guidelines.

Medicines for Human Use (Clinical Trials) Regulations (2004)

Part III

Paragraph 15(5): In preparing its opinion, the committee shall consider, in particular, the following matters:

(i)   provision for indemnity or compensation in the event of injury or death attributable to the clinical trial;

(j)   any insurance or indemnity to cover the liability of the investigator or sponsor;

(k)   the amounts, and, where appropriate, the arrangements, for rewarding or compensating investigators and subjects.

The injury or death must be 'attributable to' the clinical trial according to the 2004 Regulations, i.e. there must be a clear chain of causation between the trial and the resulting injury. Causation is difficult to trace back to the trial if the participant is already very ill with a disease. This may be the case when, for example, a participant's condition suddenly worsens *at the same time* as any negligent practice at the hands of the researcher. The General Medical Council remains quiet on this issue. This may be because compensation is more of a legal issue.

Stem cells and embryos in medical research

A far more complex area of medical research is that involving embryos (from which stem cells are taken). This kind of research is entirely different to clinical trials involving humans, and it has only really developed as a serious realm of science within the last three decades.

- Stem cell: a 'blank cell' taken from an embryo.
- Embryo: an egg has been successfully fertilised by a sperm.

The developments in this field were originally for the purposes of assisted conception. An embryo can be created outside the human body by injecting a sperm cell into an egg. The fertilised egg (now an embryo) would be replaced into the uterus in the hope that it would attach and lead to a pregnancy. This procedure does not pose a legal or ethical problem anymore (see Chapter 8 for the laws regarding assisted conception). However, scientists later discovered that newly formed embryos contained blank cells. These blank cells (also known as 'stem' cells) are like magic cells because they turn into any kind of cell: skin, hair, brain, bone or tissue cells. Scientists immediately realised the potential and became very keen to perform pioneering research on stem cells. This meant creating embryos specifically for this purpose (stem cells can also be taken from umbilical cords, but this is a very new practice and not yet widespread). The use of embryos in medical research is an ethical minefield. There are many views as to the level of legal protection that should be afforded to an embryo, and whether the moral status of the embryo really matters in medicine. It is a good idea to explore where the embryo sits in terms of legality and morality before we explore the current law on stem cell research.

Should embryos be used in medical research?

We may see the development of regenerative medicine in the future, in which scientists can modify stem cells to turn into cells that have already died or become ravaged with disease. A blank cell could, for example, turn into a brain cell to fight a degenerative disease of the brain, or a liver cell to fight liver disease. We might even live longer and beat cancer. However, the moral status of the embryo complicates the progress of medical research. An embryo is a collection of a few hundred cells, but because it has the potential to become a human being, ethical complexities arise. It is generally accepted in law that a human being is a person who has *been born*. A charge of murder cannot be brought against a scientist (or any other defendant) for *preventing* a foetus from *becoming* a human being. However, if human characteristics are ascribed to an embryo, we may suddenly feel the need to offer it some moral or legal protection, even though it is not a human yet (or may never be). There are two main categories of argument:

- Viewpoint 1: Human life begins at the moment of conception.
  - Approach: The embryo should be afforded moral and legal rights.
- Viewpoint 2: Human life has no clear beginning.
  - Approach: The embryo should be morally and legally available for research.

Viewpoint 1: Embryos should be protected

The view that human life begins at conception, i.e. when the sperm cell fertilises the egg, is mostly a religious one, and can be seen in many religious teachings. For example, abortion is only allowed in some religions if the embryo is gravely harmed or the life of the mother is in danger. The view that human life begins at conception is also supported by the idea that every embryo has the *potential* to become a human being, and this potential should be protected. The destruction of an embryo could therefore be the destruction of a potential person. This idea nudges the practice of stem cell research closer to the offence of murder, and any scientists engaging in this research or any results collected from this research might be rejected as unethical and immoral by supporters of this view.

EXTRACT

Soren Holm, 'The Ethical Case Against Stem Cell Research' (2003) 12 *Cambridge Quarterly of Healthcare Ethics* 372, at pages 372–83

Several of the five to ten years have now elapsed, and the promised therapies are still not anywhere close to the routine clinical use. [...] It is likely that many of the current sufferers from some of the condition for which stem cell therapies have been promised will be long dead before the therapies actually arrive.

Viewpoint 2: Embryos offer stem cells with research potential

The religious arguments are now removed from the world of stem cell research and the question becomes one of fact: what is an embryo? There is no accepted moral answer to this question but an embryo is not a human being in the medical or legal sense, and the 'potential' for it to become a human does not hold very much weight in science because the term 'potential' is an empty concept – human life is simply *one of the possibilities* but it is not *certain*. In fact, if the embryo is created specifically for stem cell research, then the potential for it to become a human being is zero from the beginning. A significant number of embryos are also lost through natural wastage. This can happen when the embryo simply failed to attach to the uterine wall, or it did attach but was released with a monthly cycle. A large proportion of pregnancies also end in very early miscarriage because of a defect or because of no reason at all, often without the woman even knowing that she was pregnant for the number of hours, days or weeks that the embryo was inside her body. There is no difference between naturally wasted embryos and intentionally wasted embryos – neither had the potential to become human beings.

The same argument may be applied to all methods of contraception and assisted conception. Taking contraception as the first example, many sperm cells and eggs are lost through the use of condoms, pills and contraceptive injections, patches and devices. These many thousands of cells could be said to be potential human beings too, but they are wasted without a thought every day. The morning-after pill is the clearest example of an intentionally wasted embryo because it prevents the fertilised egg from implanting into the uterine wall. The morning-after pill did cause some controversy when it was first made available because it appeared to cheapen the sanctity of human life, but the majority of views do not see it as a particularly unethical method of contraception.

EXTRACT

Julian Savulescu, 'The Embryonic Stem Cell Lottery and the Cannibalisation of Human Beings' (2002) 16 *Bioethics* 508, at pages 508–29

Opponents of cell research will likely remain unconvinced. They will argue that whatever the benefits, intentionally killing embryos is failing to 'respect human dignity'. [...] Is it respecting of human dignity to allow people to wither in nursing homes, unable to swallow, speak or move while all the time embryos are destroyed? What more twisted version of respect for human dignity could there be? It is cell research, like organ transplantation, that is respectful of human dignity in its reverence for the lives of the living.

Taking assisted conception as a second example, many embryos are created outside of the human body and a select few healthy embryos are implanted back into the patient in the hope that some will attach and lead to a pregnancy. Sometimes two embryos attach, leading to the popular multiple births often seen in IVF patients. Unhealthy embryos are simply destroyed.

The UK law on embryo and stem cell research

The world's first IVF baby was born in the UK in 1978, prompting the government to look at regulating the use of embryos and fertility treatment. It might have been an experiment at the time, but the field of assisted conception has since taken off.

The Warnock Committee was assembled shortly after to consider the limits of embryonic research. The Warnock Report was published in 1984, but no real consensus was met and a compromise position was put forward. There was, however, a strong feeling of dissent amongst the minority.

EXTRACT

The Warnock Report, *Report of the Committee of Enquiry into Human Fertilisation and Embryology*, Department of Health and Social Security, July 1984, Her Majesty's Stationery Office, arguments against the use of human embryos at page 61:

http://www.hfea.gov.uk/2068.html

Paragraph 11.11: It is obvious that the central objection to the use of human embryos as research subjects is a fundamental objection based on moral principles. Put simply, the main argument is that the use of human embryos for research is morally wrong because of the very fact that they are human, and much of the evidence submitted to us strongly supports this. The human embryo is seen as having the same status as a child or an adult, by virtue of its potential for human life. The right to life is held to be the fundamental human right, and the taking of human life on this view is always abhorrent. To take the life of the innocent is an especial moral outrage. The first consequence of this line of argument is that, since an embryo used as a research subject would have no prospect of fulfilling its potential for life, such research should not be permitted.

The dissent reached a peak in 1985–6 when two private member Bills tried to put a stop to all embryonic research through the Unborn Child (Protection) Bill, but both members ran out of Parliamentary time.

In the 1990s, embryonic research was understood much better. The general public were more aware of the IVF process, and began to accept that an embryo was not a baby but a collection of a cells with no identifiable human characteristics (until day 14). The Human Fertilisation and Embryology Act was passed in 1990 and it adopted the compromise position from the Warnock Report – embryonic research was permissible but strict limitations should be in place. The main aim was to protect scientific progress whilst offering the embryo some moral and legal protection, i.e. that it should not be wasted unnecessarily.

EXTRACT

The Warnock Report, *Report of the Committee of Enquiry into Human Fertilisation and Embryology*, Department of Health and Social Security, July 1984, Her Majesty's Stationery Office, arguments for the use of human embryos at page 62:

http://www.hfea.gov.uk/2068.html

Paragraph 11.15: The evidence showed that the views of those who support the use of human embryos as research subjects cover a wide range. At one end is the proposition that it is only to *human persons* that respect must be accorded. A human embryo cannot be thought of as a person, or even as a potential person. It is simply a collection of cells which, unless it implants

→

in a human uterine environment, has no potential for development. There is no reason therefore to accord these cells any protected status. If useful results can be obtained from research on embryos, then such research should be permitted. We found that the more generally held position, however, is that though the human embryo is entitled to some added measure of respect beyond that accorded to other animal subjects, that respect cannot be absolute, and may be weighed against the benefits arising from research. Although many research studies in embryology and developmental biology can be carried out on animal subjects, and it is possible in many cases to extrapolate these results and findings to man, in certain situations there is no substitute for the use of human embryos. This particularly applies to the study of disorders occurring only in humans, such as Down's syndrome, or for research into the processes of human fertilisation, or perhaps into the specific effect of drugs or toxic substances on human tissue.

There is an interesting balance in the paragraph above between the status of the embryo and the benefits of research. The report specifically identifies the need to use embryos as opposed to animal subjects in many areas of medical research and unless an embryo implants into the uterine wall, the report agrees that it has no realistic potential of becoming a person. What is clear is that the embryo 'is entitled to some added measure of respect beyond that accorded to other animal subjects'. The main recommendations from the Warnock Report that went on to shape the 1990 Act were as follows:

EXTRACT

The Warnock Report, *Report of the Committee of Enquiry into Human Fertilisation and Embryology*, Department of Health and Social Security, July 1984, Her Majesty's Stationery Office:

http://www.hfea.gov.uk/2068.html

Paragraph 11.17 at page 63: We recommend that the embryo of the human species should be afforded some protection in law.

Paragraph 11.18 at page 64: We recommend that research conducted on human *in vitro* embryos and the handling of such embryos should be permitted only under licence. We recommend that any unauthorised use of an *in vitro* embryo would in itself constitute a criminal offence.

Paragraph 11.24 at pages 66–7: We are satisfied that 'spare' embryos may be used as subjects for research; and we recommend accordingly a need to obtain consent to the method of use or disposal of spare embryos. We recommend that as a matter of good practice no research should be carried out on a spare embryo without the informed consent of the couple for whom that embryo was generated, whenever this is possible.

Paragraph 11.30 at page 69: Despite our division on this point, a majority of us recommend that the legislation should provide that research may be carried out on any embryo resulting from *in vitro* fertilisation, whatever its provenance, up to the end of the fourteenth day after fertilisation, but subject to all other restrictions as may be imposed by the licensing body.

The Human Fertilisation and Embryology Act 1990

The 1990 Act has been amended several times (most recently in 2008) to keep up with scientific developments, but the basic definitions for embryos, eggs and sperm under section 1 remain the same.

Section 1: Meaning of 'embryo', 'gamete' and associated expressions

(1) In this Act –

    (a) embryo means a live human embryo, and

    (b) references to an embryo include an egg that is in the process of fertilisation or is undergoing any other process capable of resulting in an embryo.

(4) In this Act –

    (a) references to eggs are to live human eggs, including cells of the female germ line at any stage of maturity,

    (b) references to sperm are to live human sperm, including cells of the male germ line at any stage of maturity, and

    (c) references to gametes are to be read accordingly.

An egg which is 'in the process' of being fertilised is considered to be an embryo. The egg and sperm can be at any stage of maturity. The egg and sperm must be 'live' but there is no requirement for them to remain unaltered by science, i.e. the use of an altered egg and sperm appears to be acceptable. The egg and sperm are cells, and are usually referred to as 'gametes' in this area of medical law.

Altered and artificial gametes

A gamete can be altered by having its nuclear swapped with the nuclear from another gamete. Altered gametes, and the altered embryos that they create appear to be permissible under the 1990 Act for the purposes for storage and medical research (see Schedule 2, paragraphs 2 and 3 below), but altered gametes and embryos are *not* allowed to be placed into a woman for the purposes of treatment (see Schedule 2, paragraph 1 below). We cannot yet create artificial human eggs and sperm, but scientists are working on it. This would provide hope for couples who cannot produce their own eggs or sperm. The legislation would have to be rewritten to allow for artificial embryos and gametes to be placed into a woman as part of her assisted conception treatment, but there is no reason why this cannot be done if the process is proved to be safe. There is some flexibility in the current legislation. Section 1(6) alludes to the possibility of the Secretary of State passing new regulations 'in the light of developments in science or medicine' to include eggs, sperm or embryos that would not usually fall under the normal definition, but according to section 1(7), the nuclear or mitochondrial DNA must *not* belong to an animal to still be classed as an egg, sperm or embryo for the purposes of the 1990 Act.

Licences

The 1990 Act (as amended) launched the Human Fertilisation and Embryology Authority (HFEA) under section 5.[16] The HFEA has the power to grant a licence under section 16, which will ensure that the storage, use and destruction of gametes and embryos is legitimate and necessary. A licence can be granted (under section 11) for research purposes according to Schedule 2 paragraph 3.

---

[16] It has an official website: www.hfea.gov.uk.

Human Fertilisation and Embryology Act 1990 Schedule 2

Paragraph 3: Licences for research

(1) A licence under this paragraph may authorise any of the following:

    (a) bringing about the creation of embryos *in vitro*, and

    (b) keeping or using embryos, for the purposes of a project of research specified in the licence.

(5) No licence under this paragraph is to be granted unless the Authority is satisfied that any proposed use of embryos is necessary for the purposes of the research.

(8) A licence under this paragraph may be granted for such period not exceeding three years as may be specified in the licence.

(9) This paragraph has effect subject to paragraph 3A.

This is the most controversial paragraph, referring to the use of embryos for medical research. There is no use of the term 'permitted embryos', meaning that *altered* embryos are included under this provision. Embryos can be created, kept and used for research purposes (listed in paragraph 3A below). The HFEA must be satisfied that this is a *necessary* use of the embryo. The licence will only be three years long and it will only be granted if the research comes under one of the purposes listed under paragraph 3A . . .

Under paragraph 3A, the 1990 Act lists the research purposes that may be licensed under paragraph 3. This is a vital paragraph, because it provides an idea of what Parliament considered to be the ethical and legitimate use of an embryo for the purposes of medical research. It also lists the current test that the HFEA will apply to satisfy themselves that a licence should be granted.

Human Fertilisation and Embryology Act 1990 Schedule 2

Paragraph 3A: Purposes for which activities may be licensed under paragraph 3

(1) A licence under paragraph 3 cannot authorise any activity unless the activity appears to the Authority –

    (a) to be necessary or desirable for any of the purposes specified in sub-paragraph (2) below ('the principal purposes'),

    (b) to be necessary or desirable for the purpose of providing knowledge that, in the view of the Authority, may be capable of being applied for the purposes specified in sub-paragraph (2)(a) or (b).

(2) The principal purposes are –

    (a) increasing knowledge about serious disease or other serious medical conditions;

    (b) developing treatments for serious disease or other serious medical conditions;

    (c) increasing knowledge about the causes of any congenital disease or congenital medical condition that does not fall within paragraph (a);

    (d) promoting advances in the treatment of infertility;

    (e) increasing knowledge about the causes of miscarriage;

    (f) developing more effective techniques of contraception;

    (g) developing methods for detecting the presence of gene, chromosome or mitochondrion abnormalities in embryos before implantation; or

    (h) increasing knowledge about the development of embryos.

The principle purpose must be a 'necessary and desirable' use of the embryo according to the HFEA under (1)(a). The embryo may also be used to *provide knowledge* for two of the principle purposes under (1)(b), as long as this is also necessary and desirable. The principal purposes include serious diseases and medical conditions which may affect adults as well as children according to paragraphs (a) and (b). The word 'congenital' means 'inherited' meaning that less serious hereditary diseases can be researched using embryos too. It is suitable to use embryos for 'increasing knowledge' as well as 'developing treatments'. It is also suitable to use embryos for embryonic research and a range of other fertility and contraception matters.

Stem cell research is clearly permitted under paragraph 3A, but you have to look hard to see it. According to paragraphs (2)(a), (b) and (c), a licence to carry out research on an embryo is permitted to 'increase knowledge' and 'develop treatments' for 'serious' and 'inherited' diseases as long as this is *necessary and desirable* according to the HFEA. This provision can be interpreted as saying that stem cells can be taken from the embryo and used for these purposes as long as the HFEA agree.

Time limit for embryonic research

It is very important to point out that the time limit for embryonic research is 14 days under section 3(3) of the 1990 Act. This is because the 'primitive streak' has begun to form inside the embryo. This is a thin bead of cells that will become the spinal column. This was considered by the Warnock Report (1984) to be the beginnings of a human being, and medical research beyond this point would be unethical.

EXTRACT

The Warnock Report, *Report of the Committee of Enquiry into Human Fertilisation and Embryology*, Department of Health and Social Security, July 1984, Her Majesty's Stationery Office, at page 66:

http://www.hfea.gov.uk/2068.html

Paragraph 11.22: We accordingly recommend that no live human embryo derived from *in vitro* fertilisation, whether frozen or unfrozen, may be kept alive, if not transferred to a woman, beyond fourteen days after fertilisation, nor may it be used as a research subject beyond fourteen days after fertilisation. This fourteen day period does not include any time during which the embryo may have been frozen. We further recommend that it shall be a criminal offence to handle or to use as a research subject any live human embryo derived from *in vitro* fertilisation beyond that limit. We recommend that no embryo which has been used for research should be transferred to a woman.

Admixed embryos

It is clear from the regulations above that altered gametes and embryos can be used for storage and research but they cannot be placed into a woman for the purposes of treatment. It was also explained above that scientists cannot create an artificial gamete yet, although they are currently working on it. What scientists have managed to create are admixed embryos using admixed gametes. The nuclear is taken out of the animal egg and replaced with a human nuclear. The admixed egg is then fertilised with a human sperm, meaning the embryo is 99% human, but the egg casing was originally animal. The stem cells taken from the embryo will be 100% human because the nuclear in both gametes was human. These embryos are also known as hybrid embryos, because they are a cross between breeds.

The reason why scientists do this is because human eggs are in short supply. There is a small supply of unwanted embryos from IVF treatment where couples decide to donate their unwanted embryos to research, but the characteristics of embryos cannot be changed because the gametes have already fused together. This may be an advantage, however, if one of the couples carried a genetic disease, because this would allow for specific research to be carried out on their embryo or the stem cells within the embryo. It is far less wasteful to carry out stem cell research on animal eggs containing a human nuclear from a skin cell (for example), than to use a human egg. These gametes are considered to be 'live' under the legislation, but admixed embryos are considered to be in a class of their own because they use animal materials. Therefore, in 2008, the Human Fertilisation and Embryology Act 1990 had to be modified to include admixed embryos. Admixed embryos were inserted into the 1990 Act under section 4A(6).

Human Fertilisation and Embyrology Act 1990

Section 4A: Prohibitions in connection with genetic material not of human origin

(6) For the purposes of this Act a human admixed embryo is –

    (a) an embryo created by replacing the nucleus of an animal egg or of an animal cell, or two animal pronuclei, with –

        (i) two human pronuclei,

        (ii) one nucleus of a human gamete or of any other human cell, or

        (iii) one human gamete or other human cell.

    (b) any other embryo created by using –

        (i) human gametes and animal gametes, or

        (ii) one human pronucleus and one animal pronucleus.

Section 4A has also been very clear regarding the limitations of admixed gametes and embryos, and section 4A lists storage and research as acceptable practices, but placement into a woman is absolutely not allowed.

Human Fertilisation and Embyrology Act 1990

Section 4A: Prohibitions in connection with genetic material not of human origin

(1) No person shall place in a woman –

    (a) a human admixed embryo,

    (b) any other embryo that is not a human embryo, or

    (c) any gametes other than human gametes.

→

> (2) No person shall –
>   (a) mix human gametes with animal gametes,
>   (b) bring about the creation of a human admixed embryo, or
>   (c) keep or use a human admixed embryo,
>   except in pursuance of a licence.
>
> (3) A licence cannot authorise keeping or using a human admixed embryo after the earliest of the following –
>   (a) the appearance of the primitive streak, or
>   (b) the end of the period of 14 days beginning with the day on which the process of creating the human admixed embryo began, but not counting any time during which the human admixed embryo is stored.

The research rules for admixed gametes and embryos appear to be the same as those for human ones: as long as a licence gives permission, admixed gametes and embryos can be created, stored and used for research. They clearly cannot be placed inside a woman under section 4A(1). It is also interesting to note that under section 4A(3) the 14-day time limit is still effective for admixed embryos. This is because, despite the animal egg casing, the embryo is 99% human and the spine will still begin to form.

Consent

Embryonic and stem cell research is such a complex and controversial area of medical research that sometimes the basic rules are forgotten. The person who donated the gametes must provide consent for them to be used as part of medical research. If embryos result from the gametes, the person must also consent to the embryo being used in medical research. If consent is not attained for any of the above, the gametes and embryo must be allowed to perish. A donor has far more control over the use of a gamete or embryo than he or she might think.

Schedule 3 of the 1990 Act is dedicated to consent issues, and it clearly states under paragraph 1 that a consent must be in writing and signed. Paragraph 2(4) lists all the activities for which consent must be attained, and these include.

Human Fertilisation and Embryology Act 1990 Schedule 3

Paragraph 2: Consent

(4) A consent under this Schedule may apply –
  (a) to the use or storage of a particular embryo or human admixed embryo, or
  (b) in the case of a person providing gametes or human cells, to the use or storage of –
    (i) any embryo or human admixed embryo whose creation may be brought about using those gametes or those cells, and
    (ii) any embryo or human admixed embryo whose creation may be brought about using such an embryo or human admixed embryo.

(5) In the case of a consent falling within sub-paragraph (4)(b), the terms of the consent may be varied, or the consent may be withdrawn in relation to –
  (a) a particular embryo or particular embryos, or
  (b) a particular human admixed embryo or particular human admixed embryos.

The 1990 Act clearly gives donors the freedom to choose what happens to their gametes and embryos, because the storage and use of these materials requires their consent. In addition, under paragraph 2(5) (above) a donor can vary or withdraw his consent at any time. A consent may be varied by stating that a donor no longer wishes for his gametes to be part of admixed embryos. Further details as to variation and withdrawal of consent are provided under paragraph 4(1) (below).

Human Fertilisation and Embryology Act 1990 Schedule 3

Paragraph 4: Variation and withdrawal of consent

(1) The terms of any consent under this Schedule may from time to time be varied, and the consent may be withdrawn, by notice given by the person who gave the consent to the person keeping the gametes, human cells, embryo or human admixed embryo to which the consent is relevant.

On reading paragraph 4(1), it becomes clear that donors have more control over their donated materials than one might have thought. This might be because of the sensitive nature of stem cell and embryonic research – if a donor changes his or her mind and does not want to contribute to this area of science any longer, this should be respected by the law. Paragraph 2(1) provides more detail on consent for the use of embryos.

Human Fertilisation and Embryology Act 1990 Schedule 3

Paragraph 2: Consent

(1) A consent to the use of any embryo must specify one or more of the following purposes –

(a) use in providing treatment services to the person giving consent, or that person and another specified person together,

(b) use in providing treatment services to persons not including the person giving consent,

(ba) use for the purpose of training persons in embryo biopsy, embryo storage or other embryological techniques, or

(c) use for the purposes of any project of research,

and may specify conditions subject to which the embryo may be so used.

A donor may consent to his or her embryo being used for a range of activities, including the treatment of others, training and research. The treatment of others would typically occur when, at the end of an IVF cycle, there are unwanted embryos left and a couple consent to donating their embryos to another couple who cannot make embryos of their own. Schedule 3 includes many other provisions relating to consent, including the following:

Paragraph 6	*A donor must consent to his or her gametes being used to create an embryo* in vitro
Paragraph 8	A donor's gametes must not be stored unless that donor has consented to the storage
Paragraphs 9 and 10	Gametes can be stored without consent of the donor but only in strict circumstances
Paragraph 12	*A donor must consent to his gametes or human cells being used in the creation of an admixed embryo* in vitro
Paragraph 13	The donors relevant to an admixed embryo must all consent to it being stored

An interesting addition to Schedule 3 is the need for counselling. Paragraph 3 states that an opportunity to receive 'proper counselling' must be offered to the person who gives consent.

Human Fertilisation and Embryology Act 1990 Schedule 3

Paragraph 3: Procedure for giving consent

(1) Before a person gives consent under this Schedule –

    (a) he must be given a suitable opportunity to receive proper counselling about the implications of taking the proposed steps, and

    (b) he must be provided with such relevant information as is proper.

It is not clear why this requirement features in Schedule 3, but the likely aim is to inform the donor that he or she may be handing a 'potential human being' over to either another couple to use in treatment, or to a scientist for the purposes of medical research. A married couple may see their unused embryos as potential children and it may be greatly disturbing for them to give their embryos away to medical research. The HFEA published a Code of Practice to be read in conjunction with the 1990 Act, and it provides insightful guidance as to what donors should be told *before* they give consent if they wish to donate their cells to medical research.

EXTRACT

Code of Practice, 8th edition, October 2013 Human Fertilisation and Embryology Authority:

http://www.hfea.gov.uk/code.html

Paragraph 22.7: For any research project, the centre should ensure that before donors give their consent to their gametes or embryos, or cells used to create embryos, being used in research, they are given oral information, (supported by relevant written material), that confirms:

(a) The specific project and its aims;

(b) Details of the research project, including likely outcomes and how any individual donation will impact on the overall project;

→

[...]

(d) Whether donors will be given any information that is obtained during the research and is relevant to their health and welfare;

(e) That donors are expected to have an opportunity to ask questions and discuss the research project;

[...]

(g) That patients are under no obligation to donate gametes and embryos for research and that their decision whether to do so will have no repercussions for any treatment they may receive;

[...]

(i) That research is experimental, and so any gametes and embryos used and created for any research project must not be used in treatment;

(j) That donors may specify conditions for the use of the gametes or embryos;

(k) That after the research has been completed, all donated gametes and embryos will be allowed to perish.

The guidance provided by the HFEA strikes a good balance between the need for medical research and the need to inform donors of their rights and limitations. Donors can stipulate what will happen to their gametes or embryos and they will be informed of the aims of the research and how their donation will help the research, but they will not benefit (or be treated any differently) as a result of their donation or from any discoveries made during the research. It is, in the end, entirely up to the donor.

Children and incompetent donors

The 1990 Act was reformed in 2008, and some rather controversial provisions were added to Schedule 3 regarding the donation of gametes or human cells from children and incompetent adults. The HFEA can grant a licence under paragraph 6(3A) to use a child's human cells to create an embryo *in vitro* for the purposes of research under paragraph 6(3B). Paragraph 15 lists the strict conditions under which a parent can consent to this procedure.

Human Fertilisation and Embryology Act 1990 Schedule 3

Paragraph 15: Parental consent conditions

(2) Condition A is that C suffers from, or is likely to develop, a serious disease, a serious physical or mental disability or any other serious medical condition.

(3) Condition B is that either –

(a) C is not competent to deal with the issue of consent to the use of C's human cells to bring about the creation *in vitro* of an embryo or human admixed embryo for use for the purposes of a project of research, or

(b) C has attained the age of 16 years but lacks capacity to consent to such use of C's human cells.

(4) Condition C is that any embryo or human admixed embryo to be created *in vitro* is to be used for the purposes of a project of research which is intended to increase knowledge about –

(a) the disease, disability or medical condition mentioned in sub-paragraph (2) or any similar disease, disability or medical condition, or

(b) the treatment of, or care of persons affected by, that disease, disability or medical condition or any similar disease, disability or medical condition.

> (5) Condition D is that there are reasonable grounds for believing that research of comparable effectiveness cannot be carried out if the only human cells that can be used to bring about the creation *in vitro* of embryos or human admixed embryos for use for the purposes of the project are the human cells of persons who –
>
> (a) have attained the age of 18 years and have capacity to consent to the use of their human cells to bring about the creation *in vitro* of an embryo or human admixed embryo for use for the purposes of the project, or
>
> (b) have not attained that age but are competent to deal with the issue of consent to such use of their human cells.

There are four conditions which must be met in order for a parent to consent to her child's cells being taken and used to create an embryo *in vitro* for the purposes of research: (1) condition A is that the child must suffer from or is likely to develop a serious disease; (2) condition B is that the child does not understand the process or has reached the age of 16 but is incompetent; (3) condition C is that the embryo created *in vitro* must be used as part of a research project to increase knowledge about the condition (or a similar condition) that the child is suffering from, or to help others who are suffering from it; and (4) condition D is that it must not be possible to conduct effective research by using the cells of someone else who can consent.

When might this kind of scenario arise? It will be very rare indeed. However, one example might be when a very young child is diagnosed with a very rare genetic disease for which there is no cure. Scientists may ask the parent for permission to remove some skin cells from the child to form an admixed gamete and then an admixed embryo, from which the child's stem cells could be removed and researched in order to find a cure for the child or any future sufferers.

Similar provisions apply to incompetent adults under paragraph 17.

Human Fertilisation and Embryology Act 1990 Schedule 3

Paragraph 17: Consent to use of human cells not required: adult lacking capacity

> (2) Condition A is that P suffers from, or is likely to develop, a serious disease, a serious physical or mental disability or any other serious medical condition.
>
> (3) Condition B is that P lacks capacity to consent to the use of P's human cells to bring about the creation *in vitro* of an embryo or human admixed embryo for use for the purposes of a project of research.
>
> (4) Condition C is that the person responsible under the licence has no reason to believe that P had refused such consent at a time when P had that capacity.
>
> (5) Condition D is that it appears unlikely that P will at some time have that capacity.
>
> (6) Condition E is that any embryo or human admixed embryo to be created *in vitro* is to be used for the purposes of a project of research which is intended to increase knowledge about –
>
> (a) the disease, disability or medical condition mentioned in sub-paragraph (2) or any similar disease, disability or medical condition, or

➜

> (b) the treatment of, or care of persons affected by, that disease, disability or medical condition or any similar disease, disability or medical condition.
>
> (7) Condition F is that there are reasonable grounds for believing that research of comparable effectiveness cannot be carried out if the only human cells that can be used to bring about the creation *in vitro* of embryos or human admixed embryos for use for the purposes of the project are the human cells of persons who –
>
> (a) have attained the age of 18 years and have capacity to consent to the use of their human cells to bring about the creation *in vitro* of an embryo or human admixed embryo for use for the purposes of the project, or
>
> (b) have not attained that age but are competent to deal with the issue of consent to such use of their human cells.

There are six conditions which must be met in order for the cells of an incompetent person to be taken and used to create an embryo *in vitro* for the purposes of research; (1) condition A is that the patient suffers from or is likely to develop a serious disease; (2) condition B is that the patient lacks capacity to consent to his cells being used to bring about an embryo *in vitro* for the purposes of research; (3) condition C is that the person 'responsible' under the licence has no reason to believe that the patient would have refused consent when he did have capacity; (4) condition D is that the return of capacity is unlikely; (5) condition E is that the embryo created *in vitro* must be used as part of a research project to increase knowledge about the condition (or a similar condition) that the patient is suffering from, or to help others who are suffering from it; and (6) condition F is that it must not be possible to conduct effective research by using the cells of someone else who can consent.

An interesting addition to the provisions under paragraph 17 is the need for the incompetence to be permanent. Condition D can be interpreted as saying that the patient must be incompetent for the rest of his life (or at least never regain the capacity to refuse). It is not clear why this is a necessary provision, because condition C already requires the person responsible under the licence to believe that the patient would not have refused when he did have capacity.

The 'person responsible under the licence' is not the relative caring for the incompetent patient, but the scientist who has applied for the research licence. He must take reasonable steps to find a relative or carer under paragraph 18(2) who can confirm that the patient would not have refused when he had capacity. The licence for research cannot be granted if this requirement under Schedule 3 is not met.

ACTIVITY

Nabila comes to you in your capacity as a medical lawyer. She is thinking about donating some of her eggs to medical research because she had already had five children of her own. She asks you what can be legally done with her eggs once she gives her consent. Advise her on the law in this area.

Chapter summary

- The Medicines for Human Use (Clinical Trials) Regulations 2004 is the leading UK authority for ethical medical research, and it incorporates the Declaration of Helsinki (1964) into its regulations (under Schedule 1, Part 2, paragraph 6).
- An ethics committee must consent to the medical research project. The National Research Ethics Service (NRES), set up in 2007, is designed to protect the rights, safety, dignity and wellbeing of research participants who take part in clinical trials.
- The distinction between therapeutic and non-therapeutic research is an important one. Therapeutic medical research will offer the participant some kind of medical benefit, whereas non-therapeutic medical research will not offer the participant any medical benefit. This will occur when a placebo is handed out.
- A placebo is a drug or a treatment that has no effect. The participant is not told that he is in the group of participants that will receive the placebo (known as the 'control group'). Placebos are vital to monitor whether a new drug works, and they are authorised under the Declaration of Helsinki (1964) and all subsequent guidelines and regulations in the UK.

Chapter essay

'Critically discuss the ways in which embryos can be used for the purposes of medical research.'

Chapter case study

Jenny and Greg have undergone three courses of IVF treatment. It has not worked. They are undergoing IVF for the fourth and final time. Eight embryos are made *in vitro* with Jenny's eggs and Greg's sperm. Three of the eight embryos appear to be healthy, so they pick two embryos and those two are implanted into Jenny. They are later asked if they would like to donate the remaining embryos to medical research. Jenny is worried about what will happen to her 'unborn babies'. Advise Jenny on the law regarding embryonic research.

Further reading

Brazier, M. (2008) 'Exploitation and Enrichment: the Paradox of Medical Experimentation', 34 *Journal of Medical Ethics* 180.

Ferguson, P. (2003) 'Legal and Ethical Aspects of Clinical Trials: the Views of Researchers', 11 *Medical Law Review* 48; (2008) 'Clinical trials and Healthy Volunteers', 16 *Medical Law Review* 23–51.

Harris, J. (2002) 'The Ethics and Justice of Life-Extending Therapies', 55 *Current Legal Problems* 65–95; (2003) 'Stem Cells, Sex, and Procreation', 12 *Cambridge Quarterly of Healthcare Ethics* 353–71; (2005) 'Scientific Research is a Moral Duty', 31 *Journal of Medical Ethics* 242–8.

Holm, S. (2003) 'The Ethical Case Against Stem Cell Research', 12 *Cambridge Quarterly of Healthcare Ethics* 372–83.

Lewis, P. (2002) 'Procedures that are Against the Medical Interests of Incompetent Adults', 22(4) *Oxford Journal of Legal Studies* 575–618.

11

The end of life

Chapter objectives

At the end of this chapter, you should have:

- An understanding of the current law on euthanasia and assisted suicide and how it affects medical practice.
- An appreciation of how we deal with refusals of treatment that will end the life of a patient.
- Knowledge of the law regarding children and incompetent patients at the end of life.
- An ability to balance the arguments for and against the legalisation of euthanasia and assisted suicide.

<table>
<tr><td>

SETTING THE SCENE

</td><td>

Mrs Williams was a terminally ill patient at Anyshire Hospital. She knew her death was impending, but had no relatives. She pleaded with her doctor every day to give her an overdose of morphine to 'send her to sleep'. The doctor refused, but was not happy about leaving her to die a slow and painful death. He asked the legal department in the hospital what the law stated about helping patients to die. He told the solicitor that Mrs Williams could press the button for the overdose of morphine herself and that all he would be required to do was move the button to within arms-reach. Advise the doctor about the difference between euthanasia and assisted suicide, and what is currently legal in the United Kingdom.

</td></tr>
</table>

Introduction

Medicine is all about saving lives and alleviating pain. Technological advances in medical care continue to prolong our lives and enhance our quality of life in ways which we could never have conceived one hundred years ago. However, with these technological advances come ethical dilemmas, as certain processes of life have now become artificial (i.e. life support machines). In particular, the true threshold of death has become blurred. In this chapter, we will deal with the most ethically contentious questions of all: how does medical law deal with the end of life? In particular, euthanasia and assisted suicide will be examined in depth, along with the criminal offences that could potentially land at a doctors' door should he kill a patient or assist a patient's suicide. Palliative care will also be examined as a suitable alternative to euthanasia, as well as the laws in other European and international countries.

Religious and other personal beliefs crop up in this area of medicine too. What if the parents of a severely disabled child wish to continue life-sustaining treatment – can the courts override their wishes and let the child die? Why are the best interests of children calculated differently to those of adults when it comes to the end of life?

The legal issues

Medical professionals find themselves in a considerably vulnerable position when caring for dying patients. If a patient makes a request to a doctor to end her life, and the doctor fulfils that request by killing or assisting that patient in any way that ends her life, a number of criminal offences will be applicable. This section will provide a brief overview of the relevant criminal offences in this area of medical law.

Murder

- An act of killing (or an omission when under a duty to act).
- Intending death or grievous bodily harm.
- Causation.

If a doctor commits an act that causes the death of a patient, along with an intention to kill or cause grievous bodily harm to that patient, he will be charged with murder. An omission will also suffice instead of an act if the doctor had a duty of care for the patient and intentionally failed to carry out the care, knowing that it would result in the patients' death.

An act which causes death

The doctor's act does not need to be the only cause of death for him to be charged with murder. For example, a patient with an aggressive form of cancer may appeal to a doctor to administer a lethal injection, which he does. The autopsy may find that the patient died through a combination of cancer and morphine. This will suffice to charge the doctor with murder because in criminal law there is no need to find a sole cause of death; the doctor need only be a substantial cause of death.[1] The 'substantial' rule should be used with caution in the context of medical care. The courts have, in the past, been reluctant to find that medical treatment has broken the chain of causation. This is because medical professionals require a little breathing space when doing their job without the threat of prosecution at every turn. The famous case of *Cheshire* (1991) confirmed the rule.

CASE EXTRACT

R v Cheshire (David William) [1991] 1 WLR 844

Facts: C shot the deceased in the leg and stomach, seriously wounding him. The deceased was taken to hospital and placed in intensive care. He developed respiratory problems and a tracheotomy tube was placed in his windpipe to assist his breathing. More than two months after the shooting, he died of cardio-respiratory arrest due to obstruction of the windpipe because of the tracheotomy. C was charged with murder. A consultant surgeon gave evidence for the defence at the trial that the leg and stomach wounds were no longer life-threatening at the time of actual death and that death had been caused by negligent medical treatment. The judge directed the jury that C was responsible for the death unless the medical staff had been reckless in their treatment of the deceased. He was convicted of murder and appealed.

Held: Appeal dismissed: even though negligent medical treatment was the immediate cause of death, that should not exclude the accused's responsibility unless the negligent treatment was so independent of his acts and in itself so potent in causing death that the jury regarded the contribution made by C's acts as insignificant.

Beldam LJ (at pages 851–2): When the victim of a criminal attack is treated for wounds or injuries by doctors or other medical staff attempting to repair the harm done, it will only be in the most extraordinary and unusual case that such treatment can be said to be so independent of the acts of the defendant that it could be regarded in law as the cause of the victim's death to the exclusion of the defendant's acts. Where the law requires proof of the relationship between an act and its consequences as an element of responsibility, a simple and sufficient explanation of the basis of such relationship has proved notoriously elusive. In a case in which the jury have to consider whether negligence in the treatment of injuries inflicted by the defendant was the cause of death we think it is sufficient for the judge to tell the jury that they must be satisfied that the Crown have proved that the acts of the defendant caused the death of the deceased adding that the defendant's acts need not be the sole cause or even the main cause of death it being sufficient that his acts contributed significantly to that result. Even though negligence in the treatment of the victim was the immediate cause of his death, the jury should not regard it as excluding the responsibility of the defendant unless the negligent treatment was so independent of his acts, and in itself so potent in causing death, that they regard the contribution made by his acts as insignificant.

---

[1] See *R v Cheshire (David William)* [1991] 3 All ER 670 and *R v Mellor (Gavin Thomas)* [1996] 2 Cr App R 245.

As a result of *Cheshire*, if an act by a doctor is found to have contributed to the patient's death alongside an earlier cause, the doctor's act must be *extraordinary* to overtake the earlier cause to become the new cause of death. A lethal injection by a doctor would certainly be sufficient to override the earlier cause if an autopsy can prove that the injection alone led to the death of the patient. If causation cannot be proved, a doctor may be charged with attempted murder instead.

An omission which causes death

Normally, omissions are not culpable in criminal law. However, a doctor has a duty of care for his patients.[2] This means that when a doctor fails to provide treatment to a patient and she dies as a result of the doctor's breach of duty (i.e. his omission), the doctor has caused that patient's death. A good example of this would be the failure to provide nutrition to a patient, leading to the patient's death through starvation.

A doctor does not always have a duty to provide care, and so his omission will not always be culpable. For example, a competent patient may like to refuse treatment. In instances such as these, the doctor's duty to provide care is dissolved.[3] Additionally, a doctor is under no duty to provide care if that care is not in the patient's best interests.

CASE EXTRACT

Airedale NHS Trust v *Bland* [1993] AC 789

Facts: Tony Bland was given artificial nutrition and hydration (ANH) after the Hillsborough disaster. He was not expected to regain consciousness, but he was not brain dead. His parents and the doctor wished to withdraw the ANH but they knew he would die as a result (i.e. a charge of murder against the doctor). They sought permission from the court to stop all treatment.

Held: It was no longer in the best interests of the patient to be kept alive, therefore the duty to treat him no longer existed. A charge of murder or manslaughter would not be brought.

Lord Browne-Wilkinson (at page 883): If there comes a stage where the responsible doctor comes to the reasonable conclusion (which accords with the views of a responsible body of medical opinion) that further continuance of an intrusive life support system is not in the best interests of the patient, he can no longer lawfully continue that life support system: to do so would constitute the crime of battery and the tort of trespass to the person.

Finally, if a medical resource is scarce – such as a kidney transplant – doctors are not under a duty to provide this treatment because it must be rationed and allocated according to specific criteria.

Intending death or grievous bodily harm

When a doctor commits an act (or an omission) and causes the death of a patient, he must intend death or grievous bodily harm at the material time in order to be charged with murder. The doctor's intention may take one of two forms: he may *directly* intend death or grievous bodily harm, or he may realise that death or grievous bodily harm is

---

[2] *R* v *Adomako* [1994] 3 All ER 79.
[3] See *T (Adult: Refusal of Medical Treatment), Re* [1992] 4 All ER 649, *Re MB* [1997] 2 FLR 426 and *B (Adult: Refusal of Treatment), Re* [2002] EWHC 429.

virtually certain (known as oblique intention). Either version will suffice for a murder charge, and it does not matter if the doctor (or relative) was motivated by sympathy.[4] However, in murder trials involving doctors who provide palliative care (pain relief for dying patients), the courts have shown reluctance to direct the jury on oblique intent, preferring direct intention only. This means that a doctor might only be convicted of murder if he *directly* intended to kill the patient as opposed to realising that death or GBH is a *virtually certain* consequence. The upshot of this is known as the 'doctrine of double effect', and it means that doctors can provide pain relief for dying patients suspecting that it will probably end their lives as long as they do not *directly intend to kill* that patient (this rule will probably not apply to sympathetic relatives, where oblique intention will probably be applied).

Diminished responsibility

Diminished responsibility is a partial defence to a murder charge, i.e. dropping the charge to manslaughter. This defence concerns an abnormality of mental functioning, so it is highly unlikely that a doctor would use it as a defence to killing a patient. Rather, a relative of the patient would raise it as a defence in a 'mercy killing' instead:

Homicide Act 1957[5]

Section 2: Persons suffering from diminished responsibility

(1)   A person ('D') who kills or is a party to the killing of another is not to be convicted of murder if D was suffering from an abnormality of mental functioning which –

    (a)   arose from a recognised medical condition,

    (b)   substantially impaired D's ability to so one or more of the things mentioned (1A), and

    (c)   provides an explanation for D's acts and omissions in doing or being a party to the killing.

(1A)   Those things are –

    (a)   to understand the nature of D's conduct;

    (b)   to form a rational judgment;

    (c)   to exercise self-control.

(1B)   For the purposes of subsection (1)(c), an abnormality of mental functioning provides an explanation for D's conduct if it causes, or is a significant contributory factor in causing, D to carry out that conduct.

This defence may be raised, for example, when an elderly man who has lived with his terminally-ill wife for many years, in some way brings about her death at her request to relieve their distress and suffering. A judge may be particularly lenient in cases of 'mercy killings' and may pass a small sentence. It should also be remembered that the Crown Prosecution Service will only bring a case to trial if they believe that to do so would serve the public interest.

---

[4] *R v Woollin (Stephen Leslie)* [1999] 1 AC 82 and *R v Matthews (Darren John)* [2003] 2 Cr App R 30.
[5] As amended by the Coroners and Justice Act 2009.

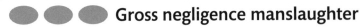

Gross negligence manslaughter

If a doctor has a duty to provide treatment to a patient and fails to provide that treatment leading to the death of the patient, he may also face a gross negligence manslaughter charge. This does not require an intention to kill, only a duty of care and a gross breach of that duty:

1. The doctor owed the patient a duty of care.
2. The doctor breached the duty of care.
3. The breach caused the death of the patient.
4. The breach was so gross that it was criminal.[6]

The doctor's omission must not be deemed as appropriate according to a body of medical men (the *Bolam* test – see Chapter 3). For example, a doctor may forget to treat the patient or inject the patient with the wrong drug. However, because there is no intention to kill, it is unusual to see convictions of gross negligence manslaughter in the context of mercy killings, euthanasia or assisted suicide because they all require a clear intention to bring about a death.

Assisting suicide

It is no longer an offence to commit or attempt to commit suicide under section 1 of the Suicide Act 1961.[7] If, therefore, a patient independently takes his own life whilst in hospital or at home, a doctor or a relative would not face any charges. It is, however, an offence to *help* someone to commit suicide.

Suicide Act 1961

Section 2: Criminal liability for complicity in another's suicide

(1) A person ('D') commits an offence if –

    (a) D does an act capable of encouraging or assisting the suicide or attempted suicide of another person, and

    (b) D's act was intended to encourage or assist suicide or an attempt at suicide.

If a patient takes his own life whilst in hospital after swallowing pills given to him by his doctor, or at home using drugs provided by a relative, then charges of aiding or abetting suicide may be brought against the doctor or the relative. The Director of Public Prosecutions has discretion as to which cases should be sent to trial. The Coroners and Justice Act 2009 added two new sections to section 2 of the Suicide Act 1961 in a bid to tighten up the law on assisted suicide.

---

[6] *R v Adomako* [1995] 1 AC 171.
[7] As amended by the Coroners and Justice Act 2009.

Suicide Act 1961 (as amended)

Section 2: Criminal liability for complicity in another's suicide

(1A) The person referred to in subsection (1)(a) need not be a specific person (or class of persons) known to, or identified by, D;

(1B) D may commit an offence under this section whether or not a suicide, or an attempt at suicide, occurs;

(1C) An offence under this section is triable on indictment and a person convicted of such an offence is liable to imprisonment for a term not exceeding 14 years.

These new provisions in section 2 of the 1961 Act may make it easier to bring an action against someone who tried unsuccessfully to assist someone's suicide, including a healthcare professional.

THINKING POINT

Do you believe that doctors or relatives should be exempt from any of the offences listed above when killing a person if motivated by sympathy? If there was proof of a terminal illness, for example, do you believe this should provide a new defence in law to assisted suicide or murder?

Euthanasia

Euthanasia is the intentional killing of a patient, at their request, at the hands of a doctor for reasons of ill health (also known as a mercy killing). A patient may ask to be euthanised for many reasons: sometimes she will be terminally ill with no hope of recovery, or sometimes she will be severely disabled and not able to use her own physical functions to end her life. Euthanasia guarantees a peaceful death with an injection or a pill at the hands of a doctor, as opposed to an attempted suicide with no guarantee of success. As mentioned above, the intentional killing of a patient is murder in the United Kingdom, and the crime of murder carries a mandatory life sentence. If causation cannot be proved, e.g. the patient's illness may have been a strong contributory factor to her death, then the charge will be attempted murder and this carries the same sentence. The condition of the patient who requests euthanasia, the seriousness of their ailment, the compassionate motive of the doctor and the method of killing will have no influence on the court and can be tabulated as follows:

No influence on the courts when a patient is killed

- The patient's illness, condition or disease
- The patient's wishes and consent
- The mortality of the patient (e.g. close to death)
- The compassionate motive of the doctor
- The way the patient was killed (e.g. injection)

Euthanasia case law

A murder conviction requires a doctor to intend to kill the patient and this intention is displayed in euthanasia, but the courts have shown reluctance to convict a doctor who has *oblique* intent, i.e. he did not *directly* intend the patient's death, he merely intended to relieve pain but death was *a virtually certain consequence* of the pain relief. In fact, there are very few cases in criminal law where a doctor has been convicted of murder.

In *R v Carr* (1986),[8] the patient had inoperable lung cancer and was in unbearable pain. He repeatedly asked Dr Carr to end his life. Dr Carr administered a large dose of phenobarbitone, and the patient died two days later. Dr Carr was charged with attempted murder only, because it was not clear whether the patient's illness or the phenobarbitone had caused the patient's death. Despite the considerable evidence against Dr Carr, he was acquitted by the jury. *Cox* is a good example of a doctor escaping liability because the causal link between the euthanising act and the death was not strong enough.

CASE EXTRACT

R v Cox (1992) 12 BMLR 38

Facts: Dr Cox was charged with the attempted murder of Mrs Boyes, who was terminally ill with arthritis, gastric ulcers, gangrene and sores. Dr Cox gave her a dose of potassium chloride which was not a painkiller and would certainly have ended her life. He was convicted of attempted murder, but he was given a 12-month suspended sentence. He appealed.

Held: The patient was cremated, so a chain of causation could not be fully established.

Ognall J: What can never be lawful is the use of drugs with the primary purpose of hastening the moment of death . . . in the context of this case potassium chloride has no curative properties . . . it is not analgesic. It is not used by the medical profession to relieve pain . . . injected into a vein it is a lethal substance. One ampoule would certainly kill . . .

Dr Cox also endured a General Medical Council hearing, but he was not struck off the medical register and returned to work shortly after his appeal. The facts in *Cox* (1992) can be viewed by many as controversial. Dr Cox used a chemical to kill his patient rather than an overdose of a trusted medical drug, making his actions look far more sinister.

In *Moor* (1999), Hooper J gave a rather interesting direction to the jury:

CASE EXTRACT

R v Moor reported in C. Dyer, 'British GP Cleared of Murder Charge' (1999) 318 *British Medical Journal* 1306

Facts: Dr Moor was charged with the murder of an 85-year-old patient who was suffering from bowel cancer.

Held: The doctor was acquitted.

Hooper J: You have heard that this defendant is a man of excellent character, not just in the sense that he has no previous convictions but how witnesses have spoken of his many admirable qualities. You may consider it a great irony that a doctor who goes out of his way to care for [the patient] ends up facing the charge that he does.

---

[8] *The Times*, 30 December 1986.

The acquittal in *Moor* may have had something to do with Hooper J's clear view that Dr Moor was facing an unfair charge. This case may be proof that, regardless of the evidence against the accused doctor and the seriousness of the charge, the jury will be moved to acquit the doctor based on the difficult circumstances of the patient and the unblemished record of the doctor.

RESEARCH ACTIVITY

Conduct a search on the internet of doctors who have been charged with murder or manslaughter. What happened to them and what sentences did they receive from the courts (if any)?

Assisted suicide

Assisted suicide cases occur slightly more frequently than euthanasia cases. It is not a criminal offence to commit suicide, but it is an offence under the Suicide Act 1961 to *help* someone to commit suicide. This means that if a patient expressly states that they intend to commit suicide without help, no one will be charged with an offence and the courts can not intervene. In *Re Z* (2004) this was made very clear.

CASE EXTRACT

Re Z (An Adult: Capacity) [2004] EWHC 2817

Facts: Mrs Z arranged to go to Switzerland for euthanasia, but her local authority obtained an injunction preventing her from going.

Held: The injunction was overturned in the High Court.

Hedley J (at paras 12–13): Section 1 of the Suicide Act 1961 abrogated the rule that made suicide criminal. [...] It follows that the court has no basis in law for exercising the jurisdiction so as to prohibit Mrs Z from taking her own life. The right and responsibility for such a decision belongs to Mrs Z alone . . . Mrs Z's best interests are no business of mine . . . The court is simply not entitled to interfere whatever views it may have about the decision in question.

The decision of *Re Z* may seem liberal, but just because it is no longer unlawful for individuals to take their own lives, this does not mean that they have a legal right to take their own lives, that is we cannot enforce our right to commit suicide in a court of law.

Helping others to commit suicide

Assisting suicide can include many different acts of assistance, regardless of who the assistant is or their motive. Relatives who arrange flights abroad will be deemed in law to be assisting a suicide, alongside doctors who advise patients on how to overdose on prescribed drugs. In *Attorney-General v Able* (1983), the courts were not pleased with suicide advice being issued in the shape of a booklet to patients.

CASE EXTRACT

Attorney-General v *Able* [1983] 3 WLR 845

Facts: A booklet entitled: 'A Guide to Self-Deliverance' which described five methods of suicide was handed out to patients.

Held: It is an offence if it encourages suicide according to a three-part test.

Woolf J (at pages 809, 812): I have no doubt that in the case at least of certain recipients of the booklet, its contents would encourage suicide. [...] I therefore conclude that to distribute the booklet can be an offence. But, before an offence can be established to have been committed, it must at least be proved: (a) that the alleged offender had the necessary intent, that is, he intended the booklet to be used by someone contemplating suicide and intended that person would be assisted by the booklet's contents, or otherwise encouraged to attempt to take or take his own life; (b) that while he still had that intention, he distributed the booklet to such a person who read it; and (c) in addition, that such a person was assisted or encouraged by so reading the booklet to attempt to take or to take his own life.

The case of *Attorney-General* v *Able* tells us that a person – whether that be a doctor or a relative – who advises a patient about how to commit suicide will be guilty of an offence if he intended his advice to be used by the patient to commit suicide. This is a particularly difficult test to satisfy. A doctor, for example, must *know* that his patient is contemplating suicide before answering any questions relating to dosage. It may be best if medical professionals simply refuse to answer inquiries regarding fatal dosage levels for particular prescription medicines.

Dianne Pretty

Although assisted suicide is illegal under the Suicide Act 1961, there have been a small handful of high-profile cases in recent years which have claimed that the prohibition of assisted suicide amounts to a breach of human rights. Dianne Pretty brought the first high-profile case of assisted suicide to the House of Lords after the Human Rights Act 1998 was passed in the United Kingdom.

CASE EXTRACT

R (on the application of Pretty) v *DPP* [2002] 1 AC 800

Facts: Dianne Pretty suffered from motor neurone disease, a terminal illness which causes the body to slowly fail whilst the mind is sharp. It can lead to a protected and distressing death. Her husband, Mr Pretty, was willing to help Dianne to commit suicide, but they feared prosecution under section 2 of the Suicide Act 1961. The Director of Public Prosecutions refused to exclude Mr Pretty from prosecution, so Dianne sought a judicial review on the grounds that her human rights were violated. In particular, she claimed that Article 2 protected a right to self-determination, entitling her to commit suicide with assistance. Failure to alleviate her suffering amounted to inhuman and degrading treatment proscribed by Article 3. She also argued that her rights to privacy and freedom of conscience under Articles 8 and 9 were infringed, and that she had suffered discrimination since an able-bodied person might exercise the right to suicide whereas her incapacities prevented her doing.

Held: She failed on every ground.

Lord Bingham (at pages 813, 815–16, 818, 825–6): [On Article 2:] It would be a very large, and in my view quite impermissible, step to proceed . . . to the assertion that the State has a duty to recognise a right for Mrs Pretty to be assisted to take her own life. [...] [On Article 3:] The absolute and unqualified prohibition on a Member State inflicting the proscribed treatment requires that 'treatment' should not be given an unrestricted or extravagant meaning. It cannot, in my opinion, be plausibly suggested that the Director or any other agent of the United Kingdom is inflicting the proscribed treatment on Mrs Pretty, whose suffering derives from her cruel disease. [...] The proscribed treatment is said to be the Director's refusal of proleptic immunity from prosecution to Mr Pretty if he commits a crime. By no legitimate process of interpretation can that refusal be held to fall within the negative prohibition of Article 3. [...] [On Article 8]: The Secretary of State questioned whether Mrs Pretty's rights under Article 8 were engaged at all, and gave a negative answer. He submitted that the right to private life under Article 8 relates to the manner in which a person conducts his life, not the manner in which he departs from it. [...] Article 8 protects the physical, moral and psychological integrity of the individual, including rights over the individual's own body, but there is nothing to suggest that it confers a right to decide when or how to die. [...] [On Article 14]: She contends that the section is discriminatory because it prevents the disabled, but not the able-bodied, exercising their right to commit suicide. This argument is in my opinion based on a misconception. The law confers no right to commit suicide. Suicide was always, as a crime, anomalous, since it was the only crime with which no defendant could ever be charged. [...] 'Mercy killing', as it is often called, is in law killing. If the criminal law sought to proscribe the conduct of those who assisted the suicide of the vulnerable, but exonerated those who assisted the suicide of the non-vulnerable, it could not be administered fairly and in a way which would command respect.

According to the House of Lords, none of Dianne Pretty's human rights had been breached and the Director of Public Prosecutions was not obliged to exempt Mr Pretty from prosecution under section 2(4) of the Suicide Act 1961 before her assisted suicide had taken place. Dianne Pretty appealed to the European Court of Human Rights.

CASE EXTRACT

Pretty v *UK* (2002) 35 EHRR 1

The Grand Chamber (at pages, 29, 33, 37–9,42): [On Article 2]: The consistent emphasis in all the cases before the Court has been the obligation of the State to protect life. The Court is not persuaded that 'the right to life' guaranteed in Article 2 can be interpreted as involving a negative aspect. [...] Article 2 cannot, without a distortion of language, be interpreted as conferring the diametrically opposite right, namely a right to die; nor can it create a right to self-determination in the sense of conferring on an individual the entitlement to choose death rather than life. [...] [On Article 3]: As regards the types of 'treatment' which fall within the scope of Article 3 of the Convention, the Court's case law refers to 'ill-treatment' that attains a minimum level of severity and involves actual bodily injury or intense physical or mental suffering. Where treatment humiliates or debases an individual showing a lack of respect for, or diminishing, his or her human dignity or arouses feelings of fear, anguish or inferiority capable of breaking an individual's moral and physical resistance, it may be characterised as degrading and also fall within the prohibition of Article 3. [...] In the present case, it is beyond dispute that the respondent Government has not, itself, inflicted any ill-treatment on the applicant. Nor is there any complaint that the applicant is not receiving adequate care from the State medical authorities. [...] There is no comparable act or 'treatment' on the part of the United Kingdom in the present case. [...] [On Article 8]: The applicant in this case is prevented by law from exercising her choice to avoid what she considers will be an undignified and distressing end to her life. The Court is not prepared to exclude that this constitutes an interference with her right to respect for private life as guaranteed under Article 8(1) of the Convention. [...] An interference with the exercise of an Article 8 right will not be compatible with Article 8(2) unless it is 'in accordance with the law', has an aim or aims that is or are legitimate under that paragraph and is 'necessary in a democratic society' for the aforesaid aim or aims. [...] Nonetheless, the Court finds, in agreement with the House of Lords, [...] that States are entitled to regulate through the operation of the general criminal law activities which are detrimental to the life and safety of other individuals. The more serious the harm involved the more heavily will weigh in the balance considerations of public health and safety against the countervailing principle of personal autonomy. The law in issue in this case, section 2 of the 1961 Act, was designed to safeguard life by protecting the weak and vulnerable and especially those who are not in a condition to take informed decisions against acts intended to end life or to assist in ending life. [...] It is primarily for States to assess the risk and the likely incidence of abuse if the general prohibition on assisted suicides were relaxed or if exceptions were to be created. [...] The Court does not consider therefore that the blanket nature of the ban on assisted suicide is disproportionate. [...] Nor in the circumstances is there anything disproportionate in the refusal of the DPP to give an advance undertaking that no prosecution would be brought against the applicant's husband. [...] The Court concludes that the interference in this case may be justified as 'necessary in a democratic society' for the protection of the rights of others and, accordingly, that there has been no violation of Article 8 of the Convention. [...] [On Article 14]: There is, in the Court's view, objective and reasonable justification for not distinguishing in law between those who are and those who are not physically capable of committing suicide. [...] The borderline between the two categories will often be a very fine one and to seek to build into the law an exemption for those judged to be incapable of committing suicide would seriously undermine the protection of life which the 1961 Act was intended to safeguard and greatly increase the risk of abuse.

The European Court of Human Rights agreed with Dianne Pretty that her rights under Article 8 were violated. However, the interference to her personal autonomy was *outweighed* by considerations of public health and safety. As a result, the Court held that State criminal law could intervene and legislate against assisted suicide to protect vulnerable individuals in the interests of a democratic society, thus overriding Dianne Pretty's Convention rights.[9]

---

[9] Dianne Pretty died very shortly after the European judgment through the symptoms of her degenerative disease.

The role of the Director of Public Prosecutions

In the *Pretty* case, the Director of Public Prosecutions argued that under section 2(4) of the Suicide Act 1961, he could only exercise his discretion about whether to prosecute *after* a suicide and a police investigation had taken place. The European Court of Human Rights confirmed that the DPP has this discretion. It is important that the DPP has this power of discretion, because some prosecutions against medical professionals will not be in the public interest. This was explained clearly in *Re Z* (2004).

CASE EXTRACT

Re Z (An Adult: Capacity) [2004] EWHC 2817

Facts: The wife had cerebella ataxia, an incurable and irreversible condition which attacked the part of the brain that controlled the body's motor functions. She had become increasingly disabled by the condition. Although she continued to live at home, she required extensive support from the local authority and her needs had grown as her condition had deteriorated. She had attempted suicide and wished H to arrange an assisted suicide in Switzerland. H informed the local authority, which concluded that the wife was a vulnerable person living in its area and sought an injunction preventing a husband (H) from removing his wife from England for the purpose of travelling to Switzerland for an assisted suicide.

Held: The expert evidence was that the wife was legally competent to make her own decisions. The court had no basis in law for exercising the jurisdiction so as to prohibit the wife from taking her own life. The right and responsibility for such a decision belonged to her alone. Suicide was not punishable as a criminal act under the Suicide Act 1961 section 1, but aiding, abetting, counselling or procuring suicide or attempted suicide was an offence under section 2 of the Act. H would contravene section 2 by making arrangements and taking steps in the UK to assist his wife to travel to Switzerland for that purpose. In a case such as this, a local authority had a duty to investigate the position of a vulnerable adult. However, the local authority had no duty to seek the continuation of the injunction, and the court would not do so of its own motion where no one with the necessary standing sought any such order.

Hedley J (at para 14): It seems to me inevitable that by making arrangements and escorting Mrs Z on the flight, Mr Z will have contravened section 2(1) [of the Suicide Act 1961]. It follows that in order for Mrs Z actually to be able to carry out her decision, it will require the criminal conduct of another. That said I remind myself of sub-section (4). Although not unique, the provision is rare and is usually found where Parliament recognises that although an act may be criminal, it is not always in the public interest to prosecute in respect of it.

The discretion awarded to the DPP to decide whether or not to prosecute an individual who assists a suicide has led to some confusion within the law. A person does not know whether or not they could face prosecution if, for example, they were to book flights for their terminally ill relative.

Daniel James

Daniel James was a 23-year-old man who was rendered seriously disabled after a rugby accident. His parents took him to Dignitas in Switzerland in 2008 and he died with the help of another person at the clinic. His parents (and a family friend who purchased the flight tickets) faced prosecution for assisting his suicide, but the DPP published a report explaining why it was not in the public's interest to go to trial.

EXTRACT

Decision on Prosecution – The Death by Suicide of Daniel James, 9 December 2008, Director of Public Prosecutions, paragraph 35:

http://www.cps.gov.uk/news/articles/death_by_suicide_of_daniel_james/

Keir Starmer QC: Neither Mark and Julie James nor the family friend influenced Daniel James to commit suicide. On the contrary, his parents tried relentlessly to persuade him not to commit suicide. Daniel was a mature, intelligent and fiercely independent young man with full capacity to make decisions about his medical treatment. There is clear evidence that he had attempted to commit suicide on three occasions and that he would have made further attempts if and whenever an opportunity to do so arose. These are factors against prosecution. Although not truly minor acts, the conduct of Mark James, Julie James and the family friend was towards the less culpable end of the spectrum. That is a factor against prosecution. Neither Daniel's parents nor the family friend stood to gain any advantage, financial or otherwise, by his death. On the contrary, for his parents, Daniel's suicide has caused them profound distress. That is a factor against prosecution. I have decided that the factors against prosecution clearly outweigh those in favour. In the circumstances I have concluded that a prosecution is not needed in the public interest.

This report appears to show a delicate balancing act between reasons to pursue prosecution and reasons when prosecution would be unfair and unnecessary. A wide variety of circumstances are taken into account, including potential motives, distress and the patient's behaviour prior to the assisted suicide. Daniel James can be distinguished, however, from Dianne Pretty and the following case of Debbie Purdy on one rather significant ground: Daniel James was permanently disabled after an accident but was predicted to live, whereas *Pretty* and *Purdy* were suffering from medical conditions which were predicted to lead to a protracted and distressing death.

Debbie Purdy

The most recent legal development in assisted suicide is that of Debbie Purdy, which did not change the law but did ask the DPP to publish more information about his decisions to prosecute.

CASE EXTRACT

R (on the application of Purdy) v DPP [2010] 1 AC 345

Facts: Debbie Purdy was a woman in her 40s suffering from progressive multiple sclerosis. She believed that she and her partner Omar Puente were entitled to know in advance whether he would face prosecution if he assisted her to Switzerland to help her to die (she was not this ill yet). She argued that since the DPP was using his discretion when deciding whether or not to prosecute cases of assisted suicide, the grounds for these decisions should be open and transparent. This way, she could weigh up the likelihood of prosecution before planning her trip and would go earlier when she was physically able to do so, if necessary. She additionally argued that the DPP's refusal to publish his policies infringed her right to respect for her private life under Article 8 of the European Convention on Human Rights.

→

Held: At first instance, the Divisional Court informed Debbie Purdy that the House of Lords decision in *Pretty* was good law and that no Convention rights were engaged. Even if they were, they could be justifiably overridden. However, Purdy was given leave to appeal to the Court of Appeal – who dismissed her appeal – but the House of Lords found in her favour.

Lord Hope of Craighead (at pages 386–7, 390, 392–3, 396): Ms Purdy does not ask that her husband be given a guarantee of immunity from prosecution. [...] What she seeks is information. It is information that she says she needs so that she can take a decision that affects her private life. [...] She is not willing to expose him to the risk of being prosecuted if he assists her. But the Director has declined to say what factors he will take into consideration in deciding whether or not it is in the public interest to prosecute those who assist people to end their lives in countries where assisted suicide is lawful. This presents her with a dilemma. If the risk of prosecution is sufficiently low, she can wait until the very last moment before she makes the journey. If the risk is too high she will have to make the journey unaided to end her life before she would otherwise wish to do so. [...] I would therefore depart from the decision in *R (Pretty)* v *DPP* [2002] 1 AC 800 and hold that the right to respect for private life in Article 8(1) is engaged in this case. [...] The issue is without doubt both sensitive and controversial. [...] Crown prosecutors to whom the decision-taking function is delegated need to be given the clearest possible instructions as to the factors which they must have regard to when they are performing it. The police, who exercise an important discretion as to whether or not to bring a case to the attention of the Crown prosecutors, need guidance also if they are to avoid the criticism that their decision-taking is arbitrary. [...] Section 10 [of the Prosecution of Offences Act 1985] provides that the Director shall issue a Code for Crown Prosecutors giving guidance on general principles to be applied by them in determining whether proceedings for an offence should be instituted. [...] In my opinion the Code is to be regarded, for the purposes of Article 8(2) of the Convention, as forming part of the law in accordance with which an interference with the right to respect for private life may be held to be justified. [...] I would therefore allow the appeal and require the Director to promulgate an offence-specific policy identifying the facts and circumstances which he will take into account in deciding, in a case such as that which Ms Purdy's case exemplifies, whether or not to consent to a prosecution under section 2(1) of the 1961 Act.

Lord Hope is not legalising assisted suicide in this judgment, he is simply stating that when the Director of Public Prosecutions considers whether or not to prosecute an individual for assisted suicide, the criteria upon which his decision is based should be clear and transparent to help the patient, the Crown prosecutors and the police. The judgment alludes to a number of reasons for this: Debbie Purdy was unable to make a decision which affected her private life; she was not willing to expose her husband to the risk of prosecution; she wanted to take all the factors into account before deciding whether to travel to Switzerland sooner or later; because of the lack of information provided by the DPP, she may have been forced into taking her life sooner than planned; Crown prosecutors need clear instructions when making decisions; the police need clear guidance when making decisions; the Code for Crown Prosecutors must be accessible and foreseeable; assisted suicide is sensitive and decisions which serve the public interest require published guidance; and the Director must identify facts and circumstances that will typically lead to a prosecution under section 2(1) of the Suicide Act 1961. The *Purdy* decision was distinguished from *Pretty* on the grounds that Debbie Purdy simply sought information and was potentially forced into ending her life sooner due to a lack of information, whereas *Pretty* sought a declaration that her husband would be exempt from prosecution. It is a very narrow distinction upon which to separate two very similar assisted suicide cases.

It is likely that the issue of assisted suicide will resurface in the appeal courts in the near future – and will continue to do so – until the law is changed completely.

Formal assisted suicide guidance

Following the *Purdy* decision, the Director of Public Prosecutions published a list of factors which are typically taken into account when deciding whether to prosecute an individual who is accused of assisting suicide.

EXTRACT

Director of Public Prosecutions (February 2010) *Policy for Prosecutors in Respect of Cases of Encouraging or Assisting Suicide*, Crown Prosecution Service:

http://www.cps.gov.uk/publications/prosecution/assisted_suicide_policy.html

Public interest factors tending in favour of prosecution

Paragraph 43: A prosecution is more likely to be required if:

1. the victim was under 18 years of age;
2. the victim did not have the capacity (as defined by the Mental Capacity Act 2005) to reach an informed decision to commit suicide;
3. the victim had not reached a voluntary, clear, settled and informed decision to commit suicide;
4. the victim had not clearly and unequivocally communicated his or her decision to commit suicide to the suspect;
5. the victim did not seek the encouragement or assistance of the suspect personally or on his or her own initiative;
6. the suspect was not wholly motivated by compassion; for example, the suspect was motivated by the prospect that he or she or a person closely connected to him or her stood to gain in some way from the death of the victim;
7. the suspect pressured the victim to commit suicide;
8. the suspect did not take reasonable steps to ensure that any other person had not pressured the victim to commit suicide;
9. the suspect had a history of violence or abuse against the victim;
10. the victim was physically able to undertake the act that constituted the assistance him or herself;
11. the suspect was unknown to the victim and encouraged or assisted the victim to commit or attempt to commit suicide by providing specific information via, for example, a website or publication;

→

12. the suspect gave encouragement or assistance to more than one victim who were not known to each other;

13. the suspect was paid by the victim or those close to the victim for his or her encouragement or assistance;

14. the suspect was acting in his or her capacity as a medical doctor, nurse, other healthcare professional, a professional carer [whether for payment or not], or as a person in authority, such as a prison officer, and the victim was in his or her care;

15. the suspect was aware that the victim intended to commit suicide in a public place where it was reasonable to think that members of the public may be present;

16. the suspect was acting in his or her capacity as a person involved in the management or as an employee (whether for payment or not) of an organisation or group, a purpose of which is to provide a physical environment (whether for payment or not) in which to allow another to commit suicide.

Public interest factors tending against prosecution

Paragraph 45: A prosecution is less likely to be required if:

1. the victim had reached a voluntary, clear, settled and informed decision to commit suicide;

2. the suspect was wholly motivated by compassion;

3. the actions of the suspect, although sufficient to come within the definition of the offence, were of only minor encouragement or assistance;

4. the suspect had sought to dissuade the victim from taking the course of action which resulted in his or her suicide;

5. the actions of the suspect may be characterised as reluctant encouragement or assistance in the face of a determined wish on the part of the victim to commit suicide;

6. the suspect reported the victim's suicide to the police and fully assisted them in their enquiries into the circumstances of the suicide or the attempt and his or her part in providing encouragement or assistance.

These guidelines do not, of course, make assisted suicide legal, but they make it clearer for the relatives (or medical professionals) if they are likely to face prosecution after assisting their loved one's suicide. It is interesting that if the suspect was acting in their medical capacity as a doctor, nurse or carer that they are more *likely* to face prosecution. This is because they have taken advantage of their position of power, and to kill a patient – even with the best of intentions – would erode trust in the medical profession.

THINKING POINT

The facts of Dianne Pretty's case are not unique. She was coming to the end of her life and was suffering as a result of her illness. Debbie Purdy had not reached that stage and simply wanted clarification before her illness progressed, but in most assisted suicide cases, the patient has already degenerated considerably. Why do you think the lords (at every level) are unhappy to change the law to allow doctors to assist dying patients when the evidence for change is so damning?

● ● ● **Palliative care**

Palliative care is another name given to pain relief which may shorten the life of the patient. The World Health Organisation has described palliative care as:

> ... the active, total care of patients whose disease is not responsive to curative treatment. Control of pain, other symptoms and psychological, social and spiritual problems is paramount. The goal of palliative care is the achievement of the best quality of life for patients and families.[10]

● What is palliative care?

Sometimes, when a patient's disease has progressed considerably and the patient is in unbearable pain, the dose of painkillers (such as morphine) will need to be increased. This can sometimes lead to the death of the patient through respiratory failure, but the doctors when administering these high doses of painkillers are intending to relieve pain, not cause death. They might, however, see death as *another consequence* of the pain relief, i.e. the oblique intention of murder.

● Is palliative care legal?

It was mentioned above that to be guilty of murder, a doctor (or a relative) must intend to cause death or grievous bodily harm to the patient when committing an act (or an omission) that causes the patient's death. In criminal law, two types of intention will suffice: direct intent and oblique intent (where the defendant realises that death is a *virtually certain outcome* of his actions). This would typically mean, according to the criminal law, that doctors who provide palliative care have the oblique intention for murder because they see death as a virtually certain outcome of their action. The law on oblique intention is derived from *Woollin*.

CASE EXTRACT

R v Woollin (Stephen Leslie) [1999] 1 AC 82

Facts: W had thrown his 3-month-old son onto a hard surface after losing his temper, and was charged with murder when the son died of his injuries.

Held: The mental element for murder can be met if the defendant foresaw the second consequence as virtually certain (referred to as *oblique* intention rather than *direct* intention).

Lord Steyn (at page 93): Where a man realises that it is for all practical purposes inevitable that his actions will result in death or serious harm, the inference may be irresistible that he intended that result, however little he may have desired or wished it to happen.

However, also mentioned above was the doctrine of double effect. The courts have been reluctant to convict doctors who only show an oblique intention to kill when administering palliative care, meaning that life-shortening pain relief may be provided to patients on the condition that doctors only directly intend to relieve pain. It is interesting

---

[10] See the World Health Organisation's official website: http://www.who.int/cancer/palliative/definition/en/print.html.

that the threshold for the mental element of murder has been dropped in this way for doctors who foresee death when administering pain relief (palliative care). However, there are a handful of judgments to confirm that the administration of painkilling drugs will not attract a criminal charge even though the doctor has an oblique intention to kill.

> **CASE EXTRACT**
>
> ### A v *Adams*, unreported, 8 April 1957, taken from Alexander McCall Smith, 'Euthanasia: The Strengths of the Middle Ground' (1999) 7 *Medical Law Review* 194
>
> **Devlin J**: If the first purpose of medicine, the restoration of health, can no longer be achieved, there is still much for a doctor to do, and he is entitled to do all that is proper and necessary to relieve pain and suffering, even if the measure he takes may incidentally shorten life.

Devlin J is hinting in this extract that the doctor in the *Adams* case only intended to relieve pain and suffering. The mere foresight of a fatal consequence is neither here nor there. Two further judgments appear to support the idea of palliative care despite the oblique intention to kill.

> **CASE EXTRACT**
>
> ### Re J (Wardship: Medical Treatment) [1991] Fam 33
>
> **Facts:** There was an order to prevent the treatment of a severely brain damaged baby. The Official Solicitor appealed against the order, because his life was not intolerable.
>
> **Held:** The denial of treatment to prolong life could only be sanctioned where it was in the best interests of the patient. The test applicable was that of the child's best interests in those circumstances and that was based on an assessment of the child's quality of life and his future pain and suffering against the pain of the life-saving treatment.
>
> **Lord Donaldson** (at page 46): The use of drugs to reduce pain will often be fully justified, notwithstanding that this will hasten the moment of death.

> **CASE EXTRACT**
>
> ### Airedale NHS Trust v Bland [1993] AC 789
>
> **Facts:** Anthony Bland was injured in the Hillsborough disaster and needed artificial nutrition and hydration to survive (he was in a persistent vegetative state).
>
> **Held:** It was no longer in his best interests to be kept alive so the feeding could be withdrawn and no charges would be brought despite the oblique intention to kill him.
>
> **Lord Goff** (at page 867): The doctor who is caring for such a patient cannot, in my opinion, be under an absolute obligation to prolong his life by any means available to him, regardless of the quality of the patient's life . . . It is this principle too which, in my opinion, underlies the established rule that a doctor may, when caring for a patient who is, for example, dying of cancer, lawfully administer painkilling drugs despite the fact that he knows that an incidental effect of that application will be to abbreviate the patient's life.

It therefore appears that the doctrine of double effect in palliative care is at odds with the ordinary principles of intent in criminal law: a doctor can display the legal requirements of a murder charge, but he will not be prosecuted.

Being sure of the doctor's intention

To provide a patient with a large dose of morphine is a serious decision for a doctor. The patient must show no prospect of recovery. Clearly, one of the main concerns in palliative care is not knowing what the doctor really intends when he administers a high dose of painkillers. The seriousness of the patient's condition and the method of pain relief used by the doctor, e.g. prescribed morphine rather than potassium chloride, which is simply poison, may give a clear indication as to whether the motive was pain relief or untimely death.

RESEARCH ACTIVITY

Read the abstract below.

Doctors know full well what they are doing when they increase a dose of diamorphine, but they need not describe their act, to themselves or to others, as an act of killing. This approach has been described as hypocritical, but if it accords with a moral distinction which is meaningful for doctors, then why should they be denied the comfort it affords them? We live by moral metaphor, and the metaphor of helping rather than killing, may be a valuable one to those whose duty it is to look after the terminally ill.[11]

What are your thoughts on palliative care and the doctrine of double effect? How do you feel about the narrow distinction in the law of intention? Do you agree with Alexander McCall Smith that it is merely a moral distinction?

Refusal of treatment at the end of life

A competent patient may refuse medical treatment. The patient's wishes must be respected even if he or she may die as a result of the refusal (see Chapter 4). This doctrine throws up a number of difficult questions:

- Can a patient refuse life-saving treatment when he or she expressly states that they simply want to die?

- If a patient refuses life-saving treatment, is that patient committing suicide? If so, does the doctor assist the patient's suicide by going along with the patient's wishes?

- If a doctor withdraws life-saving treatment and the patient dies as a result of that removal, is the doctor guilty of murder?

- Is the removal of life-saving treatment an act or an omission? What is the difference between the two in the context of life-saving treatment?

- Can a doctor decide whether or not to provide life-saving treatment in an emergency? If so, is he guilty of murder if he refuses to do so?

---

[11] Alexander McCall Smith, 'Euthanasia: The Strengths of the Middle Ground' (1999) 7 *Medical Law Review* 194.

These many questions have led to some fascinating case law. Each point will be dealt with in turn below.

Refusing life-saving medical treatment

The law will protect a competent patient's wish to refuse life-saving medical treatment, even if the patient will almost certainly die once the treatment has been removed or withdrawn.

CASE EXTRACT

Re B (Adult: Refusal of Treatment) [2002] EWHC 429

Facts: Ms B suffered from complete paralysis from the neck down. She had respiratory problems and was connected to a ventilator. She had repeatedly asked to be removed from the ventilator but her doctors were reluctant to comply with her wishes. Ms B sought a declaration that she had the mental capacity to refuse treatment and that her NHS Trust had been treating her unlawfully.

Held: The High Court granted the declaration.

Dame Elizabeth Butler-Sloss P (at paras 89, 94–6): If, as in the present case, two experienced and distinguished consultant psychiatrists give evidence that Ms B has the mental capacity to make decisions, even grave decisions about her future medical treatment, that is cogent evidence upon which I can and should rely. [...] Unless the gravity of the illness has affected the patient's capacity, a seriously disabled patient has the same rights as the fit person to respect for personal autonomy. There is a serious danger, exemplified in this case, of a benevolent paternalism which does not embrace recognition of the personal autonomy of the severely disabled patient. [...] I am therefore entirely satisfied that Ms B is competent to make all relevant decisions about her medical treatment including the decision whether to seek to withdraw from artificial ventilation. [...] I also find that the Claimant has been treated unlawfully by the Trust since August.

The decision in *Re B* was not unsurprising. There has been significant support for such a legal decision for some time:

CASE EXTRACT

Airedale NHS Trust v Bland [1993] AC 789

Lord Goff (at page 864): It is established that the principle of self-determination requires that respect must be given to the wishes of the patient, so that if an adult patient of sound mind refuses, however unreasonably, to consent to treatment or care by which his life would or might be prolonged, the doctors responsible for his care must give effect to his wishes, even though they do not consider it to be in his best interests to do so. [...] On this basis, it has been held that a patient of sound mind may, if properly informed, require that life support should be discontinued.

Lord Mustill: [...] A doctor has no right to proceed in the face of objection, even if it is plain to all, including the patient, that adverse consequences and even death will or may ensue.

The British Medical Association has formally consolidated the common law position into a set of guidelines, which are given to doctors when dealing with competent patients who wish to refuse life-saving medical treatment. Patient autonomy will take priority over the doctor's duty to save the patient's life.

EXTRACT

British Medical Association, *Withholding and Withdrawing Life-prolonging Medical Treatment: Guidance for Decision Making*, 3rd edition, BMA, London (2007)

Paragraph 25.5: It is well established in law and ethics that competent adults have the right to refuse any medical treatment, even if that refusal results in their death. Patients are not obliged to justify their decisions but the health team usually wish to discuss the refusal with them in order to ensure that they have based their decisions on accurate information and to correct any misunderstandings. Health professionals can find it very difficult when a patient with capacity refuses treatment that they believe would provide a reasonable degree of recovery. While they may discuss their concern with patients, they must not put pressure on them to accept treatment. Ultimately the decision of whether to accept or reject the treatment offered rests with the patient.

If a patient therefore asks for life-saving medical treatment to be removed, the following elements must be in place:

- The patient must be competent.
- The patient's decision must be informed.
- It does not matter that the patient is severely disabled.
- Patient autonomy overrides the duty to provide medical treatment.
- A Trust is not forced to withdraw treatment, but its treatment will be unlawful.

Refusing medical treatment to simply die

If a patient wishes to die and they are not able to take their own life, they can simply refuse life-saving medical treatment, such as a ventilator. The patient's reasons for refusing life-saving treatment are not relevant as long as he or she has made an informed decision, meaning that he or she understands all of the relevant facts:

CASE EXTRACT

Re T (Adult: Refusal of Treatment) **[1993] Fam 95**

Facts: T was involved in a road traffic accident when she was 34 weeks pregnant. After talking to her mother, she refused a blood transfusion and was told that there was an alternative treatment available. She signed a form refusing consent although the form and contents were not explained to her. She went into labour and a Caesarean section was performed but the baby was stillborn. Her condition deteriorated. Ward J. granted a declaration that in the circumstances it would be lawful for the hospital to administer a blood transfusion, and they duly did so on the grounds that it had been an emergency situation in which T could not have expressed a view and that it had been proper for the doctors to treat her in any way they felt best.

→

Held: Dismissing T's appeal, (1) the influence of T's mother overrode her competent right to refuse; (2) where a decision is made in the light of outside influence of family members the court must consider whether the subsequent decision is that of the patient; (3) forms for refusal of blood transfusion should be redrafted. A signature will not protect the hospital from proceedings unless it is shown that the patient fully understood the significance of signing; (4) a patient must know in broad terms the effect of the consent or refusal he was giving and it would be overridden by lack of information or misinformation; (5) in a life-threatening situation, if doctors had real doubts as to the validity of a refusal they should, in the public interest and the interests of their patient, seek a declaration from the court that the proposed treatment was lawful. They should not leave it to the patient's family to take proceedings.

Lord Donaldson MR (at page 13): The patient's right of choice exists whether the reasons for making that choice are rational, irrational, unknown or even non-existent.

It follows from *Re T* that a refusal of treatment must be fully informed and not under the influence of family members. A patient who genuinely wishes to die rather than have medical treatment must make this decision on their own, with a clear and competent mind. As explained above, assisted suicide under the Suicide Act 1961 requires an act of assistance to enable a person to end their life, and the act of assistance can be anything from something minor (booking flight tickets) to something major (handing over a fatal dose of morphine). Bearing this in mind, does a doctor assist the suicide of a patient when that patient makes a request to withhold or withdraw treatment and the doctor then does so?

Does a doctor assist the patient's 'suicide'?

The small amount of case law on this issue tells us that a doctor is not viewed as 'assisting the suicide' of a patient when he withdraws life-saving medical treatment on their competent request, even though that is exactly what he is doing.

CASE EXTRACT

Airedale NHS Trust v Bland [1993] AC 789

Lord Goff (at page 864): In cases of this kind, there is no question of the patient having committed suicide nor therefore of the doctor having aided or abetted him in doing so. It is simply that the patient has, as he is entitled to, declined to consent to treatment which might or would have the effect of prolonging his life, and the doctor has, in accordance with his duty, complied with the patient's wishes.

This rationale seems a little ambiguous. It is not clear why a patient, who asks for life-saving treatment to be withdrawn along with a desire to die, is not committing suicide and why her doctor is not assisting her suicide. This may be a veiled version of assisted suicide through the back door.

Is the doctor guilty of murder?

If a patient refuses all further life-saving treatment and the doctor respects her wishes by withdrawing her nutrition and hydration, has the doctor met the required elements for murder? A doctor will be guilty of murder if he commits an act or an omission which causes the patient's death along with an intention to cause death or grievous bodily harm. Technically, all of these elements are met when a patient expressly refuses all further life-saving treatment and the doctor withdraws it. However, the courts have protected the doctor from prosecution by deciding that, because the patient has offered a competent refusal of treatment, the doctor no longer has a duty to act rendering his withdrawal an omission . . . and an omission will not attract a murder charge. *Airedale NHS Trust* v *Bland* [1993] AC 789 is responsible for this odd act/omission distinction (see below for a detailed analysis of the case) and it has perplexed many commentators, illustrated in the two views below.

CASE EXTRACT

Re B (Adult: Refusal of Medical Treatment) [2002] 1 FLR 1090

Dame Elizabeth Butler-Sloss P (at para 57): [Dr C] had studied and spent her professional life trying to do her best to improve and preserve life. She did not feel able to agree with simply switching off Ms B's ventilation. She would not be able to do it. She felt she was being asked to kill Ms B.

EXTRACT

Andrew McGee, 'Finding a Way Through the Ethic and Legal Maze: Withdrawal of Medical Treatment and Euthanasia' (2005) 13 *Medical Law Review* 357, at pages 357–85

In withdrawal, we are not taking control of death in the way we do in the practice of euthanasia, because the issue in withdrawal is when we should stop artificially prolonging life and allow nature to take its course – to stop deferring what, at some point, is inevitable. In euthanasia, by contrast, we anticipate nature and override it by bringing about the patient's death before its time.

The act/omission distinction has clearly caused a lot of confusion. Is a doctor who withdraws life-saving treatment simply letting the patient die from a pre-existing condition as opposed to assisting her suicide? If this was the case, why did the doctors in Bland even need to visit the court for absolution from a murder charge?

Can a doctor withhold life-saving treatment without the competent patient knowing?

A patient may suffer a medical emergency and may need emergency medical treatment. If that patient is already extremely ill or fragile, resuscitation may not be a realistic option – it is a traumatic procedure sometimes resulting in broken ribs and other injuries. A doctor may make a note in the patient's medical record which reads: 'Do Not Attempt Resuscitation' (DNR) but this issue should be raised with the patient. It is very likely that a DNR note will be in the best interests of the patient, e.g. an elderly sufferer of cancer with no chance of recovery. The General Medical Council has given the following advice:

EXTRACT

General Medical Council, Treatment and Care Towards the End of Life: Good Practice in Decision-Making, July 2011:

http://www.gmc-uk.org/publications/standards_guidance_for_doctors.asp#End_of_life

Paragraph 137: If CPR may be successful in restarting a patient's heart and breathing and restoring circulation, the benefits of prolonging life must be weighed against the potential burdens and risks. But this is not solely a clinical decision. You should offer the patient opportunities to discuss (with support if they need it) whether CPR should be attempted in the circumstances that may surround a future cardiac or respiratory arrest. You must approach this sensitively and should not force a discussion or information onto the patient if they do not want it.

Paragraph 138: You should explain, in a sensitive manner, any doubts that you and the healthcare team may have about whether the burdens and risks of CPR would outweigh the benefits, including whether the level of recovery expected after successful CPR would be acceptable to the patient.

Paragraph 139: Some patients may wish to receive CPR when there is only a small chance of success, in spite of the risk of distressing clinical and other outcomes. When the benefits, burdens and risks are finely balanced, the patient's request will usually be the deciding factor. If, after discussion, you still consider that CPR would not be clinically appropriate, you are not obliged to agree to attempt it in the circumstances envisaged. You should explain your reasons and any other options that maybe available to the patient, including seeking a second opinion.

A DNR order is not viewed as murder if it is decided that it is not in the best interests of the patient to receive that treatment. The duty to treat the patient is simply dissolved because it is no longer in their best interests to be treated, and the doctor is simply omitting to resuscitate. As described above in the *Bland* case, omissions are not culpable in criminal law without a duty to act.

ACTIVITY

Maci, aged 18, was in the middle of her pregnancy when her water broke and she was taken into hospital. She was told she needed a caesarean section because the baby was struggling. She consented to the procedure, excited to meet her baby (albeit prematurely). Maci's father arrived at the hospital and he was furious. He did not want his daughter to have surgery and told the doctors that his refusal was to override her consent because he 'was her father'. Maci knew she would have a lot of grief at home for years to come if she had the surgery, so she withdrew her consent. She then fell into a coma as a result of high blood pressure and the surgeons operated anyway, saving both Maci and her son. The father sought legal action on the grounds that they performed the surgery unlawfully because he refused to consent to the life-saving procedure. What are the courts likely to decide?

● ● ● ● **Incompetent adults at the end of life**

The withdrawal of life-sustaining medical treatment from a patient becomes even more controversial when he or she is incompetent. Incompetence is caused by many different factors and may display varying levels of consciousness or understanding. For example, some patients may simply be highly stressed and not able to make a logical and balanced decision at that particular time, whereas other patients may be in a permanent vegetative state (PVS). An incompetent patient can make an advance directive under the Mental Capacity Act 2005 to refuse life-saving medical treatment, but what if there is no advance directive? The doctors must act in accordance with the patient's 'best interests'. This test is well established and it has been enshrined in the Mental Capacity Act 2005 (see Chapter 4).

The best interests test that is now laid down in the Mental Capacity Act 2005 has its origins in case law. The *Bland* (1993) case brought the following legal and ethical conundrums before the House of Lords:

- Is the sanctity of life an absolute principle overriding all others?
- If a doctor withdraws life-sustaining treatment and knows that the patient is going to die, is this murder? Is the doctor's act of withdrawal the *actus reus* of murder?
- Alternatively, if doctors have a duty to prolong life, is not the omission to provide treatment a breach of that duty which would constitute the *actus reus* of murder?
- Is artificial nutrition and hydration medical treatment which can become futile, or simply basic care which can never be classed as futile (and therefore cannot be withdrawn)?
- Can death ever be in a patient's 'best interests'?
- If life-sustaining treatment is no longer in the patient's best interests, how does this excuse the doctor's act of murder?

CASE EXTRACT

Airedale NHS Trust v Bland [1993] AC 789

Facts: Tony Bland was only 17 when he was injured at the Hillsborough Football Stadium. He suffered severe and irreversible brain damage to his higher brain and he spent over three years on a ventilator receiving hydration and nutrition with no hope of recovery (this was the unanimous diagnosis). With support from his family, Airedale NHS Trust sought a declaration to lawfully discontinue all life-saving ventilation, nutrition and hydration, and to lawfully withhold all other medical treatment except for that of pain relief for a painless death (it constituted the act of murder). The trial judge and the Court of Appeal granted the declarations, but the Official Solicitor appealed to the House of Lords.

Held: The patient had no best interests in being kept alive any more so there was no longer a duty to feed him. The failure to feed him was an omission rather than an act of murder, and the omission was not culpable in law because there was no longer a duty to treat.

Lord Goff (at pages 865–6, 869): The law draws a crucial distinction between cases in which a doctor decides not to provide, or to continue to provide, for his patient treatment or care which could or might prolong his life, and those in which he decides, for example by administering a lethal drug, actively to bring his patient's life to an end. […] The former may be lawful. […] The law does not feel able to authorise euthanasia, even in circumstances such as these; for once euthanasia is recognised as lawful in these circumstances, it is difficult to see any logical basis for excluding it in others. […] I agree that the doctor's conduct in discontinuing life support can properly be categorised as an omission. [...] Discontinuation of life support is, for present purposes, no different from not initiating life support in the first place. [...] The doctor is simply allowing his patient to die in the sense that he is desisting from taking a step which might, in certain circumstances, prevent his patient from dying as a result of his pre-existing condition; as a matter of general principle an omission such as this will not be unlawful unless it constitutes a breach of duty to the patient. I also agree that the doctor's conduct is to be differentiated from that of, for example, an interloper who maliciously switches off a life support machine because, although the interloper may perform exactly the same act as the doctor who discontinues life support, his doing so constitutes interference with the life-prolonging treatment then being administered by the doctor. Accordingly, whereas the doctor, in discontinuing life support, is simply allowing his patient to die of his pre-existing condition, the interloper is actively intervening to stop the doctor from prolonging the patient's life, and such conduct cannot possibly be categorised as an omission. [...] For my part, I cannot see that medical treatment is appropriate simply to prolong a patient's life, when such treatment has no therapeutic purpose of any kind . . . in a case such as the present, it is the futility of the treatment which justifies its termination.

Lord Mustill (at pages 897–8): The (un)conscious patient [...] does not know what is happening to his body . . . he does not know of his family's continuing sorrow . . . others carry the burden and he has none. [...] The distressing truth which must not be shirked is that the proposed conduct is not in the best interests of Anthony Bland, for he has no best interests of any kind. [...] Although the termination of his life is not in the best interests of Anthony Bland, his best interests in being kept alive have also disappeared, taking with them the justification for the non-consensual regime and the co-relative duty to keep it in being. Since there is no longer a duty to provide nourishment and hydration a failure to do so cannot be a criminal offence.

It could be argued that the removal of the nutrition tube is an act of murder, but why has its removal been labelled as an omission? The Lords may have come to this conclusion to save the doctors from charges of murder. Their acts of removal would satisfy the *actus reus* of murder but by labelling them as omissions and confirming at the same time that a duty to act had expired, there is no wrongful conduct. The *Bland* judgment attempted to answer the legal and ethical conundrums listed above, but it simply produced more questions.

What is a dying patient's 'best interests'?

Inevitably, the *Bland* case has attracted much criticism from commentators. In particular, the fact that Anthony Bland was facing death and that a decision to end his life was taken in his best interests has sparked controversy. It was Lord Mustill who said in the most express terms that Anthony Bland no longer had any interests in being alive. Is this true? Is a patient who cannot move, breathe or respond better off dead? In future cases, it appears that an incompetent patients' best interests will dissolve in the context of life-saving medical care if they:

- are not aware, in any way, of the world around them;
- do not respond to anything on any level permanently;

- show no chance of recovery;
- breathe and feed artificially;
- are permanently vegetative;
- brain stem death is *not* required.

The lords never directly said that this was their view, but the rationale underpinning their judgment seems to take a 'what's the point?' approach. The *Bland* judgment can be read by critics as saying that PVS patients have no best interests in being kept alive. Is this another way of saying that grossly incompetent patients are worthless? Could the same be said for patients who show minor amounts of brain activity but still have no prospect of recovery? A very slippery slope could start here, because the courts are saying that some patients are more valuable than others by accepting that vegetative patients who show no awareness of the world around them are not worth treating. The line drawn in *Bland* is not drawn clearly enough to prevent the doctrine from spilling over to other incompetent patients (such as disabled babies, explored below).

The legend of Bland

Not only did the *Bland* case establish a best interests test for incompetent patients, but it was applied in subsequent cases to confront new problems. The first major application in 1996 involved a patient who had minimal awareness.

CASE EXTRACT

Re R (Adult: Medical Treatment) [1996] 2 FLR 99

Facts: R's psychiatrist signed a DNR order, believing that another admission to hospital would not be in R's best interests. The NHS Trust also sought a declaration that it was lawful to withhold CPR and antibiotics if R developed a life-threatening condition.

Held: The best interests test can be applied to all patients, not just those in a PVS state.

Sir Stephen Brown P: The extensive medical evidence in this case is unanimous in concluding that it would not be in the best interests of R to subject him to cardio-pulmonary resuscitation in the event of his suffering a cardiac arrest. The withholding in the future of the administration of antibiotics . . . is a decision which can only be taken at the time by the patient's responsible medical practitioners in the light of the prevailing circumstances.

Re R establishes that the best interests test from *Bland* can be used for all incompetent patients, not just PVS patients. There have been subsequent cases which have tested the formal definition of a PVS patient. This is an important matter, because if the patient is not in a PVS state, then he or she may still possess some interests in being alive and the doctors would have a duty to continue artificial hydration and nutrition – withdrawing it would be murder.

CASE
EXTRACT

Re D (Adult: Medical Treatment) [1998] 1 FLR 411

Facts: D suffered serious head injuries in a road traffic accident. She was nursed by a full time carer at her parents' home, where she suffered further very serious brain damage. The hospital trust responsible for her care sought a declaration that it would be lawful to withdraw the artificial feeding and hydration which was sustaining her life. There was expert reservation about using the term 'permanent vegetative state' to describe her condition, because there was a response to ice water testing, tracking of moving objects and a 'menace' response.

Held: The expert was dismissed: even though the criteria for PVS were not wholly fulfilled, there was no evidence whatsoever of any meaningful life. D was for all practical purposes in a permanent vegetative state and it was not in her best interests to keep her body alive.

Sir Stephen Brown P: It seems to me that, for all practical purposes, this patient is in fact what would be, a permanent vegetative state. It must be made clear that every single witness has made it clear that this patient has no awareness whatsoever. She is suffering what [Lord Goff in *Bland*] described as 'a living death'. All the evidence establishes, to my satisfaction, that there is no evidence of any meaningful life whatsoever. I am driven to the conclusion that it is not in this patient's best interests artificially to keep her body alive and that the declaration sought should be granted.

This appalling decision illustrates the beginnings of the 'slippery slope' referred to above and just how easily the line drawn in *Bland* can be crossed. This incompetent patient, if tracking objects with her eyes, cannot be said to be experiencing 'a living death' similar to that of Anthony Bland who did not register the outside world whatsoever. We now see a patient who is not formally in a PVS state being removed from artificial ventilation and being left to die.

Human Rights and Bland

In 1998, the Human Rights Act was passed in the United Kingdom. This has a significant implication on the decision in *Bland*:

- Is the withdrawal of life-saving treatment from a PVS patient contrary to a right to life under Article 2 of the European Convention on Human Rights?
- When the patient is left to die through starvation, does this constitute inhuman and degrading treatment under Article 3?

These questions were directly answered in the following case:

CASE
EXTRACT

NHS Trust A v M & NHS Trust B v H [2001] Fam 348

Facts: A hospital trust sought a declaration that it was entitled to discontinue the artificial hydration and nutrition of M, a patient in a persistent vegetative state. M had been diagnosed as being in a permanent vegetative state in 1997 after having suffered anoxic brain damage and the trust submitted that it would not be in her best interests to continue the treatment.

Held: Granting the declaration, that where the continuation of treatment was no longer in the best interests of a patient, action to discontinue that treatment would not constitute an intentional deprivation of life pursuant to the European Convention on Human Rights 1950 Article 2(1). Furthermore, the positive obligation upon a State to protect life was not an absolute obligation to treat a patient if that treatment would be futile. Moreover, Article 3, prohibiting torture, was inapplicable as it required the victim to be aware of the inhuman and degrading treatment and, in the instant case, M was unaware of the treatment and would also be unaware of its withdrawal.

Dame Elizabeth Butler-Sloss P (at pages 358, 360, 363): A responsible decision by a medical team not to provide treatment could not amount to intentional deprivation of life by the State. [...] The death of the patient is the result of the illness or injury from which he suffered and that cannot be described as a deprivation. [...] In a case where a responsible clinical decision is made to [withdraw] treatment, on the grounds that it is not in the patient's best interests, and that clinical decision is made in accordance with a respectable body of medical opinion, the State's positive obligation under Article 2 is, in my view, discharged. [...]

I am, moreover, satisfied that Article 3 requires the victim to be aware of the inhuman and degrading treatment which he or she is experiencing or at least to be in a state of physical or mental suffering. An insensate patient suffering from permanent vegetative state has no feelings and no comprehension of the treatment accorded to him or her. Article 3 does not in my judgment apply.

Dame Elizabeth Butler-Sloss P states that the withdrawal of artificial nutrition and hydration from a PVS patient does not violate the patient's right to life or the right to be free from inhuman and degrading treatment, but the grounds for her decision are controversial, particularly her comments regarding the application of Article 3. Does a patient have to be 'in a state of physical or mental suffering' to be treated inhumanely? What about unconscious patients and their bodily integrity? Are they exempt from Article 3 simply because they are not aware of the treatment inflicted upon their bodies? If so, this case insinuates that unconscious patients can be treated in an inhuman and degrading manner, and this is not appropriate.

Religion and Bland

The next noteworthy case involved a religious patient.

CASE EXTRACT

An NHS Trust v A [2005] EWCA Civ 1145

Facts: Mr A was a Muslim, and he was on a ventilator. His children argued that to remove him from the ventilator would be against his religious beliefs. He would therefore experience a benefit in being kept alive. The issue for the courts in this case was, if a PVS patient is deemed to no longer have any interests in being kept alive, can religion constitute a sufficient interest and thus a benefit?

Held: The best interests test will be applied regardless of religious belief.

Waller LJ (at paras 59, 84): I can say straightaway that when one examines the law, one finds obviously that the views, if one can interpret them, of what the patient might be

> and the views of the family are highly material factors. At the end of the day they are not however the governing factors when considering best interests. [...] [The doctor] was clearly right to consider what was certainly the key question first, as to whether there was in his view any chance of recovery of any quality of life so as to make the discomfort to which Mr A was being put justified. [...] It was obviously going to be difficult for the religious views and the views of the family to overcome the obvious point that any decision to put Mr A through further suffering would produce no benefit to Mr A.

The idea that a patient's beliefs should be considered by doctors has been enshrined into the best interests test under section 4(6) of the Mental Capacity Act 2005. However, this case proves that although a patient's religious views are important and worthy of consideration, the doctors will be especially keen to ascertain whether the patient has any chance of recovery. Once it is established that the patient has no hope of recovery, the patient does not formally have any interests left to speak of, regardless of the religion practised whilst competent.

Formal guidelines enshrining Bland

In light of the cases regarding withholding and withdrawing artificial nutrition and hydration, the General Medical Council has issued guidance on the matter.

EXTRACT

General Medical Council, Treatment and Care Towards the End of Life: Good Practice in Decision-Making, July 2011:

http://www.gmc-uk.org/publications/standards_guidance_for_doctors.asp#End_of_life

Paragraph 118: If a patient lacks capacity and cannot eat or drink enough to meet their nutrition or hydration needs, you must assess whether providing clinically assisted nutrition or hydration would be of overall benefit to them. Clinically assisted nutrition or hydration will usually be of overall benefit if, for example, they prolong life or provide symptom relief.

Paragraph 123: If a patient is expected to die within hours or days, and you consider that the burdens or risks of providing clinically assisted nutrition or hydration outweigh the benefits they are likely to bring, it will not usually be appropriate to start or continue treatment.

Paragraph 124: If a patient has previously requested that nutrition or hydration be provided until their death, or those close to the patient are sure that this is what the patient wanted, the patient's wishes must be given weight and, when the benefits, burdens and risks are finely balanced, will usually be the deciding factor.

If a doctor accepts that no further benefit can be derived from artificially hydrating and feeding the patient, the trust where the patient is being cared for will need to seek a ruling from the courts before they *withdraw* treatment.[12] If the doctors simply wish to

---

[12] General Medical Council, Treatment and Care Towards the End of Life: Good Practice in Decision-Making, July 2011, http://www.gmc-uk.org/publications/standards_guidance_for_doctors.asp#End_of_life, at paragraph 126.

withhold treatment, i.e. treatment has not yet commenced, this is their decision according to the patient's best interests and the court does not have to be involved, although the views of a senior clinician is recommended.[13] The guidance published by the General Medical Council was challenged in the following case:

CASE EXTRACT

R (on the Application of Burke) v The General Medical Council [2006] QB 273

Facts: Mr Burke was concerned that if he became incompetent, his doctors would withdraw artificial nutrition and hydration against his wishes.

Held: The guidance published by the General Medical Council was compatible with the Human Rights Act and that they were considerate of a patient's needs.

Lord Phillips: [...] Where life depends upon the continued provision of artificial nutrition and hydration (ANH) there can be no question of the supply of ANH not being clinically indicated unless a clinical decision has been taken that the life in question should come to an end. This is not a decision that can lawfully be taken in the case of a competent patient who expresses the wish to remain alive.

The decision in Burke is interesting. If a patient, whilst competent, states that he or she would like to be kept alive when incompetent, it is unlikely that the patient's wishes will override the opinion of the doctors that his life should in fact come to an end. If the patient falls into a PVS state and loses all interest in being alive, the doctors are entitled to withdraw artificial nutrition and hydration regardless of what the patient expressly requested whilst alive and competent. This is because, in medical law, a patient can only *refuse* medical treatment. He cannot *demand* medical treatment and a right to do so has never existed in law.

The doctor's intentions

The doctor must act according to the best interests of the patient with deciding to withhold or withdraw life-sustaining medical treatment from an incompetent patient. Interestingly, the Mental Capacity Act 2005 includes a statutory provision which stipulates that doctors must put the best interests of the patient first in these difficult circumstances.

The Mental Capacity Act 2005

Section 4(5): Where the determination relates to life-sustaining treatment he must not, in considering whether the treatment is in the best interests of the person concerned, be motivated by a desire to bring about his death.

---

[13] See note above, at paragraph 121.

A doctor's true desires are difficult to prove, but if the patient has fallen into a comatose state and has no further interests in being kept alive, it will be assumed that the doctor is acting in the patient's best interests – not through a desire to kill – when withholding or withdrawing treatment. A Code of Practice accompanies the Mental Capacity Act, and recommends the following in regards to a doctor's intentions.

EXTRACT

The Mental Capacity Act 2005, Code of Practice (2007):

http://www.legislation.gov.uk/ukpga/2005/9/pdfs/ukpgacop_20050009_en.pdf

Paragraph 5.31: All reasonable steps which are in the person's best interests should be taken to prolong their life. There will be a limited number of cases where treatment is futile, overly burdensome to the patient or where there is no prospect of recovery. In circumstances such as these, it may be that an assessment of best interests leads to the conclusion that it would be in the best interests of the patient to withdraw or withhold life-sustaining treatment, even if this may result in the person's death. The decision-maker must make a decision based on the best interests of the person who lacks capacity. They must not be motivated by a desire to bring about the person's death for whatever reason, even if this is from a sense of compassion.

The Mental Capacity Act clearly allows for the withholding and withdrawal of life-sustaining treatment from incompetent patients if the doctor is satisfied that, in these rare circumstances, it would be in the *best interests* of the patient to do so. This must be the only motivation. It does not matter how often the patient begs to be provided with an overdose of morphine, or how compassionate the doctor is to the blight of dying patients.

THINKING POINT

It is now justifiable in law to withdraw life-saving treatment from an incompetent patient who is not able to decide for him or herself when and where they would like to die. What do you believe are in the 'best interests' of a patient who is in a permanent vegetative state with no hope of recovery? Would your answer differ if the patient could mimic basic functions such as blinking?

● ● ● Children at the end of life

In medical law, a young child does not have the capacity to make decisions about medical treatment (see Chapter 4). The reasons for this are simple: young children are not usually able to understand the medical, social, emotional and personal implications of particular medical procedures and treatments. It is therefore accepted that medical professionals will treat children according to their best interests. This section will look at the implications of making end-of-life decisions in childcare.

Babies and children who are receiving life-saving medical treatment are difficult cases for medical professionals. The child's parents may hold very strong views as to what kind of medical treatment is appropriate, and children have many more years ahead of them than adults, making it very difficult to accept that they have 'no interest' in being kept alive by artificial nutrition and hydration. A final difficulty is the lack of control that children have over their destiny – incompetent adults can make advance directives, competent adults can seek euthanasia abroad and they can ask for their suicide to be assisted (albeit illegally or via the withdrawal of treatment), but children have no such opportunities. Their lives are literally in the hands of others. Neonatal euthanasia is the most difficult issue in this area, involving patients of less than one month old. Euthanasia is, of course, illegal in the United Kingdom regardless of the age of the patient and there is very little case law on the subject, but babies who are found to have no best interests in being kept alive are not kept alive, similar to incompetent patients.

The euthanasia of children

There was a famous incident in 1981 where a doctor was taken to court following the death of a Down's Syndrome baby.

CASE EXTRACT

R v Arthur (1981) 12 BMLR 1

Facts: New born baby John Pearson was born with Down's Syndrome. His mother told her doctors that she did not want him. Dr Arthur prescribed DF118 (dihydrocodeine) every four hours (similar to morphine) and wrote in John Pearson's notes 'nursing care only', which was understood by the nurses to mean keeping the baby warm, changing it and comforting it. John Pearson died of bronco-pneumonia shortly afterwards. Dr Arthur was charged with murder and pleaded not guilty.

Held: Dr Arthur was acquitted because there was no firm chain of causation between the act and the resulting death.

Farquharson J: If a child is born with a serious handicap – for example, where a [Down's Syndrome baby] has an ill-formed intestine whereby that child will die of the ailment if he is not operated on – a surgeon may say: 'as this child is a [Down's Syndrome baby] I do not propose to operate; I shall allow nature to take its course'. No one would say that that surgeon was committing an act of murder by declining to take a course which would save the child.

Farquharson J's comments clearly helped the jury to acquit Dr Arthur. By way of example, he stated that Dr Arthur – by allowing the child to die of bronco-pneumonia – was not blameworthy because nature simply took its course. These days, it would not be deemed in the best interests of a Down's Syndrome baby to deprive it of life-saving treatment, nutrition and hydration because they are cared for very well (even if abandoned by their parents). The case of Dr Arthur is therefore referred to only by way of reference.

A 'balance sheet' of pleasures

Two cases in which children have shown varied signs of awareness have reached the High Court, and it has been for the courts to decide at what point a child ceases to have any interests in being kept alive. In the following case of *B*, Holman J took an unusually active approach to weighing the child's best interests.

CASE EXTRACT

An NHS Trust v B [2006] EWHC 507

Facts: B was a terminally ill boy who suffered from spinal muscular atrophy. His movement was limited, he needed help to breathe, he could not swallow, and he suffered from epilepsy. His doctors wanted to withdraw his endotracheal tube because they considered his quality of life to be very low. His parents wanted his care to continue.

Held: The courts found in favour of the parents.

Per Holman J (at paras 101–2): [B's] life does in my view include within it the benefits that I have tried to describe. […] [B] has age appropriate cognition, and does continue to have a relationship of value to him with his family, and does continue to gain other pleasures from touch, sight and sound. […] It is impossible to put a mathematical value or any other value on the benefits. But they are precious and real. […] I positively consider that as his life does still have benefits, and as his life, it should be enabled to continue, subject to excluding the treatment I have identified (CPR).

Holman J's decision is refreshing because he sided with the parents of the child as opposed to the medical evidence, and refused to slide down the slippery slope that was exposed earlier in *Bland* by acknowledging that despite his limited experience, B had plenty of interests in being alive. Holman J drew up a balance sheet of benefits and burdens to ascertain whether B should be kept alive. He concluded that because B received a benefit from being with his family, being read stories, listening to CDs and watching DVDs, that he still had interests that required a duty of care on the part of his doctors to continue his treatment. Holman J did, however, draw a line at invasive medical treatment such as CPR. He decided that whilst B's life-saving treatment should continue, any advanced and invasive life-saving treatment would simply be a sign that a natural course of death was emerging and the doctors were not at liberty to intercept it. This does seem rather odd if the child is deemed to have interests that are worth preserving.

CASE EXTRACT

Re K (A Minor) [2006] EWHC 1007

Facts: A 6-month-old baby suffered from great pain and distress through her severe physical and mental disabilities. Evidence showed that she was unable to derive any pleasure from her daily life.

Held: The declaration to withdraw was granted.

Sir Mark Potter P (at para 57): [K] has no accumulation of experiences and cognition comparable with that of [B]. She is not, and with her short expectation of life is never likely to be, in a position to derive pleasure from DVDs or CDs and the only indication of real feelings of pleasure in her limited developmental state is enjoyment of a bath. On the evidence before me there is no realistic sense in which one can assign to her the simple pleasure of being alive or having other than a life dominated by regular pain, distress and discomfort and unrelieved by the pleasures of eating. Her muscular function is already severely diminished and any pleasure which might otherwise develop through increased activity and stimulation of the senses is denied to her. She has no prospect of relief from this pitiful existence before an end which is regarded as virtually certain by the age of one year and likely to be appreciably less. [...] If she were to have the necessary further surgical operation, [...] she would require mechanical ventilation which is also invasive and painful. There would be no improvement in her condition or improvement in her expectation of life. In these circumstances, I have no doubt that it would not only be a mercy, but it is in her best interests, to cease to provide total parenteral nutrition while she is still clinically stable, so that she may die in peace and over a comparatively short space of time.

Re K is an interesting decision because it contrasts wildly not only with *B* (2006) directly above, but with the best interests criteria laid down in *Bland*. Sir Mark Potter P has clearly granted the declaration of withdrawal in *Re K* on the grounds of pleasure rather than awareness. This is a departure from *Bland*, which was all about consciousness and a departure from *B*, which was all about supporting the few pleasures that could be found.

Best interests: children versus incompetent adults

In *Bland*, the following was said in regards to the patient's best interests and when they ceased to exist.

CASE EXTRACT

Lord Goff (at page 869): For my part, I cannot see that medical treatment is appropriate simply to prolong a patient's life, when such treatment has no therapeutic purpose of any kind . . . in a case such as the present, it is the futility of the treatment which justifies its termination.

Lord Mustill (at page 897): The (un)conscious patient [...] does not know what is happening to his body . . . he does not know of his family's continuing sorrow . . . others carry the burden and he has none. [...] The distressing truth which must not be shirked is that the proposed conduct is not in the best interests of Anthony Bland, for he has no best interests of any kind.

Lord Keith (at page 858): . . . to an individual with no cognitive capacity whatever, and no prospect of ever recovering any such capacity in this world, it must be a matter of complete indifference whether he lives or dies.

These statements lead to the conclusion that to have no interests in being kept alive – and to therefore lawfully withdraw life-saving treatment – a patient must have no responses, consciousness or awareness whatsoever. This makes treatment futile and justifies the withdrawal. Similarly, in *Re D*, Sir Stephen Brown P made the following judgment.

CASE EXTRACT

Re D (Adult: Medical Treatment) [1998] 1 FLR 411

Sir Stephen Brown P: . . . every single witness has made it clear that this patient has no awareness whatsoever. She is suffering what [Lord Goff in *Bland*] described as 'a living death'. All the evidence establishes, to my satisfaction, that there is no evidence of any meaningful life whatsoever. I am driven to the conclusion that it is not in this patient's best interests artificially to keep her body alive and that the declaration sought should be granted.

The accepted criteria for the lawful withdrawal of life-saving treatment from incompetent adults seem to be total unawareness, so how are the courts able to grant declarations to withdraw life-saving treatment from children who do have awareness? The Royal College of Paediatrics and Child Health issued guidance in 2004 regarding when it would be appropriate to withhold or withdraw life-saving treatment from children.

EXTRACT

Royal College of Paediatrics and Child Health, Withholding or Withdrawing Life Sustaining Treatment in Children: A Framework for Practice, 2nd edition, May 2004:

http://www.rcpch.ac.uk/what-we-do/rcpch-publications/publications-list-date/publications-list-date

There are five situations where it may be ethical and legal to consider withholding or withdrawing of life-sustaining medical treatment:

1. *The 'Brain Dead' Child.* It is agreed within the profession that treatment in such circumstances is futile and the withdrawal of current medical treatment is appropriate.

2. *The 'Permanent Vegetative State'.* The child who develops a permanent vegetative state following trauma is reliant on others for all care and does not react or relate with the outside world. It may be appropriate to withdraw or withhold life-sustaining treatment.

3. *The 'No Chance' Situation.* The child has such severe disease that life-sustaining treatment simply delays death without significant alleviation of suffering. Treatment to sustain life is inappropriate.

4. *The 'No Purpose' Situation.* Although the patient may be able to survive with treatment, the degree of physical or mental impairment will be so great that it is unreasonable to expect them to bear it.

5. *'The 'Unbearable' Situation.* The child and/or family feel that in the face of progressive and irreversible illness further treatment is more than can be borne. They wish to have a particular treatment withdrawn or to refuse further treatment irrespective of the medical opinion that it may be of some benefit.

These criteria are highly controversial, particularly paragraphs 4 and 5. The withdrawal of life-saving treatment is akin to killing a patient, so it must not be taken lightly or because the parents find the situation 'unbearable'. Incompetent adults must wait until all signs of life have expired before a doctor can remove life-saving treatment. In comparison, the removal of life-saving treatment from children appears to be dependent upon the level of suffering of the *parents and the child*, despite significant cognitive awareness of the child in some cases and medical opinion pointing to a benefit. This guidance could be viewed as giving parents far too much freedom to 'dispose of' their disabled child.

It should be noted that these criteria have not yet been legally challenged, but the cases below illustrate that when it comes to withdrawing life-saving treatment from a child, the courts will err on the side of caution and withdraw life-saving treatment as a very last resort in line with *Bland* rather than the 'pleasure' case of *Re K*. This will be the case even if the parent's disagree with the opinions of the doctors.

Parents versus the child

If there is a strong disagreement over what is in the child's best interests, the case will reach court. The courts do not usually like to get involved in such tangled and emotional disagreements, but they can offer objectivity. In the first case of three, the parent's wishes to let their child die as a youngster rather than live as a handicapped person were over-ruled by the Court of Appeal.

<table>
<tr><td>CASE EXTRACT</td><td>

Re B (A Minor) (Wardship: Medical Treatment) [1981] 1 WLR 1421

Facts: B suffered from Down's Syndrome and required an emergency operation to remove an intestinal blockage. Her parents thought it would be kinder to allow her to die than for her to live for another thirty years as a handicapped person. The local authority made the child a ward of court (see Chapter 4 for further details) and sought permission for the operation to be performed. It was then up to the courts to decide what was in the child's best interests. The judge at first instance sided with the parents, but this decision was overturned by the Court of Appeal.

Held: The parents were overruled.

Templeman LJ (at page 1424): The choice which lies before the court is this: whether to allow an operation to take place which may result in the child living for twenty or thirty years as a [Down's Syndrome person] or whether to terminate the life of a [Down's Syndrome] child because she also has an intestinal complaint. [...] I have no doubt that it is the duty of this court to decide that the child must live. The [trial] judge was much affected by the reasons given by the parents and came to the conclusion that their wishes ought to be respected. In my judgment he erred in that the duty of the court is to decide whether it is in the interests of the child that an operation should take place. [...] It is not for this court to say that life of that description ought to be extinguished.
</td></tr>
</table>

In the second case, there was no strong disagreement between the parents and the doctors regarding the treatment of the child, the doctors simply sought confirmation from the courts that their withholding of life-saving treatment from a severely handicapped child was lawful.

<table>
<tr><td>CASE EXTRACT</td><td>

Re J (A Minor) (Wardship: Medical Treatment) [1991] Fam 33

Facts: J was expected to become a serious spastic quadriplegic with a shortened life expectancy. He would lose his sight, his hearing and the ability to talk, but he would experience pain. There was a risk that he may suffer respiratory collapse and his consultant neonatologist recommended that J should not be revived by mechanical ventilation.

Held: The Court of Appeal agreed.

Taylor LJ (at page 55): Despite the court's inability to compare a life afflicted by the most severe disability with death, the unknown, I am of the view that there must be extreme cases in which the court is entitled to say: 'The life which this treatment would prolong would be so cruel as to be intolerable'. [...] Without there being any question of deliberately ending the life or shortening it, I consider the court is entitled in the best interests of the child to say that deliberate steps should not be taken artificially to prolong its miserable life span. [...]

Clearly, to justify withholding treatment, the circumstances would have to be extreme. [...] The test should not be whether the life would be intolerable to the decider. The test must be whether the child in question, if capable of exercising sound judgment, would consider the life tolerable.
</td></tr>
</table>

In the third case, it was the issue of religion that caused the disagreement over what was in the child's best interests.

CASE EXTRACT

Re C (A Minor) (Medical Treatment) [1998] Lloyd's Rep Med 1 Fam Div

Facts: C was 16 months old and on a ventilator, which was causing her increasing distress. Her doctors wanted to remove her from the ventilator and withhold resuscitation and re-ventilation should C experience any further respiratory problems. C's Jewish parents did not want the doctors to take any action that would shorten C's life. The doctors sought confirmation from the courts that withholding C's treatment would be lawful.

Held: The courts agreed with the doctors.

Sir Stephen Brown P: There is no issue in this case that this is a fatal disease and that in real terms this little child is approaching death. She has a desperately tragic existence. She is emaciated. There is the prospect of increasing suffering. I have no doubt on the evidence before me that in this desperate situation it is in the best interests of C that she should now be taken off the ventilation presently administered and that it should not be re-imposed or restored if she should suffer a further respiratory arrest. The anxiety of the doctors as well as the parents can be well understood. Their objective in their profession is to save and to preserve life but, as has been said in earlier cases that whilst the sanctity of life is vitally important, it is not the paramount consideration. I believe that I should assent to the course which is proposed by the Hospital Trust. I do so with a feeling of grave solemnity because I realise that the parents themselves will be greatly disappointed. It is a sad feature of this matter that there is, in fact, no hope for C, and what has to be considered is her best interests to prevent her from suffering as would be inevitable if this course were not to be taken.

Several important lessons can be taken from these three cases: (1) Down's Syndrome is not a grave enough medical condition to justify the withholding or withdrawal of life-saving treatment; (2) the circumstances in which withholding or withdrawing of life-saving treatment would be lawful must be extreme; (3) the test is whether the child would consider his or her life tolerable, not whether the parents or the carers of the child would find it intolerable; (4) the religious views of the parents are worthy of consideration, but they will not override the best interests of the child; (5) if to continue treatment would lead to inevitable suffering, the removal of artificial ventilation and the withholding of life-saving resuscitation may be justified.

Clearly, without a specific benchmark against which to measure a child's best interests, the criteria for justifying the *withdrawal* of life-saving treatment from babies and children will continue to be in a state of flux. The issue was more clear-cut in *Bland* for incompetent adults: all signs of life must expire before life-saving treatment can be withdrawn. The benchmark for *withholding* treatment for both groups of patients remains the same – the best interests test and a balancing of benefits and burdens. Medical evidence plays a huge role in the decision at court level, and the courts will rarely overrule the doctors if the evidence supports their view. *Re Wyatt* (2004) is an interesting child treatment case that hinged on medical evidence.

CASE EXTRACT

Re Wyatt (A Child) (Medical Treatment: Parent's Consent) [2004] EWHC 2247

Facts: Baby Charlotte was born at only 26 weeks and weighed less than one pound. She had chronic respiratory and kidney problems and brain damage that had left her blind, deaf and incapable of voluntary movement or response. She was, however, capable of experiencing pain. On all the medical evidence, the issue for determination was not whether Charlotte should live or die, but how and when she should die. The unanimous medical advice was that to give her respiratory treatment would not be in her best interests. However, Charlotte's parents argued that treatment should at least be instituted.

Held: No treatment would be in her best interests.

Hedley J (at para 38): I have given this case my most anxious and closest attention. [...] Yet in the end I have come to a clear view. [...] I do not believe that any further aggressive treatment, even if necessary to prolong life, is in her best interests. I know that that may mean that she may die earlier than otherwise she might have done but in my judgment the moment of her death will only be slightly advanced. I have asked myself: what can now be done to benefit Charlotte? I can only offer three answers: first, that she can be given as much comfort and as little pain as possible; secondly, that she can be given as much time as possible to spend physically in the presence of and in contact with her parents; thirdly, that she can meet her end whenever that may be in what Mr Wyatt called the TLC of those who love her most.

A year later, Charlotte's parents returned to court. They believed that Charlotte had made significant medical progress and wanted the declarations of lawful withholding set aside. Hedley J heard the case again, and stuck to the medical evidence which stated that all-in-all, Charlotte's condition had not changed. The parents appealed.

CASE EXTRACT

Re Wyatt (A Child) (Medical Treatment: Continuation of Order) [2005] 1 WLR 3995

Facts: Charlotte's parents sought permission to appeal against declarations made in 2004 ([2004] EWHC 2247, [2005] 1 FLR 21) in respect of the medical treatment of their daughter Charlotte and appealed against the decision by Hedley J ([2005] EWHC 693, [2005] 2 FLR 480) not to discharge those declarations. The parent's submitted that (1) the correct test of Charlotte's best interests was *not* that applied by the judge but that of intolerability. Applying that test, Charlotte's life could not be said to be intolerable and accordingly aggressive treatment which would be likely to save her life and could restore her to her current state was in her best interests; (2) the judge had been wrong to determine Charlotte's best interests and make declarations in advance of any crisis.

Held: The courts dismissed the parents because of the medical evidence.

Wall LJ (at page 4004): Mr and Mrs Wyatt's case is that by the time the question of continuation of the declarations fell to be considered by Hedley J in March and April 2005, the position had radically shifted. The court, they argued, was no longer concerned with a terminally ill child. Charlotte had defied the doctors. Not only was she still alive, but there were some visible signs of improvement.

The judge must decide what is in the child's best interests. In making that decision, the welfare of the child is paramount, and the judge must look at the question from the assumed point of view of the patient. There is a strong presumption in favour of a course of action which will prolong life, but that presumption is not irrebuttable. The term 'best interests' encompasses medical, emotional, and all other welfare issues. The court must conduct a balancing exercise in which all the relevant factors are weighed and a helpful way of undertaking this exercise is to draw up a balance sheet. But all that said, we came to the clear conclusion that Hedley J had indeed thought through the implications of what he was doing, and was entitled both to make and renew the declarations.

Charlotte's parents did not get the result that they sought, simply because the medical evidence supported the view that the medical condition of the child had not really improved. Moreover, Wall LJ confirmed that when addressing a child's best interests it is usually preferable to prolong life and to measure best interests from the *child's* point of view, but the best interests test involves medical, emotional and welfare issues too.

The impossible case: conjoined twins

A case arose in 2001 that was to test the legal integrity of all of the principles in this area of law – *A (Children) (Conjoined Twins: Medical Treatment) (No.2), Re* [2001] 1 FLR 267. The Lords struggled to come to an agreement on the best interests of the conjoined twins and, in the end, the parents gave up their legal challenge before bringing it to the House of Lords.

Mary and Jodie were 6-week-old conjoined twins. Jodie was a strong baby who was developing normally. Mary had severe brain abnormalities, no lungs and a deformed heart. She was also using Jodie's blood supply. Jodie could survive if separated, but without intervention, the death of both babies was inevitable. The hospital applied for a declaration that their surgery would be lawful. Their parents, who were deeply Roman Catholic and from the Mediterranean island of Gozo, witheld their consent to the operation to separate the twins because it would kill Mary instantly, and appealed against the ruling of the first instance judge Johnson J. Johnson J believed that the operation would be in the best interests of both children on the basis that for Jodie it afforded a good chance of a normal and independent life and that for Mary it offered relief from a potentially painful few months of life as Jodie grew more active. He further held that the operation was lawful since the withdrawal of Jodie's blood supply from Mary was comparable with the situation where a doctor lawfully withheld nourishment from a patient as in *Airedale NHS Trust v Bland* [1993] AC 789. In their appeal to the Court of Appeal, the parents contended that the trial judge had erred in his conclusions that the operation was both in the interest of each child and lawful. The legal conundrums presented to the Court of Appeal were as follows:

- Johnson J believed that the surgery would be akin to an omission similar to the one seen in *Bland* – by separating the twins, the doctors were failing to provide a supply of life to Mary – but how can invasive surgery be an omission?
- If the surgery was labelled as an omission, then the courts would have to be sure that the doctors were no longer under a duty to treat Mary to make their omission not culpable.
- If the surgery was labelled as an act, it would be the act of murder because Mary would certainly die.
- How could the act of murder be justified? It was in the best interests of Jodie for the act of murder to go ahead as she would survive, but it was not in the best interests of Mary for the killing to go ahead, because she would die. Therefore, was there an alternative justification available apart from the best interests test?

CASE EXTRACT

A (Children) (Conjoined Twins: Medical Treatment) (No.2), Re [2001] Fam 147

Ward LJ (at pages 173, 189, 196–7, 203): I said when this appeal opened that we wished at the very beginning to emphasise to the parents, strangers in our midst, how we sympathise with their predicament, with the agony of their decision – for now it has become ours – and how we admire the fortitude and dignity they have displayed throughout these difficult days. [...] It seems to me to be utterly fanciful to classify this invasive treatment as an omission in contra-distinction to an act. Johnson J's valiant and wholly understandable attempt to do so cannot be supported. [...] The question is whether this proposed operation is in Mary's best interests. It cannot be. It will bring her life to an end before it has run its natural span. It denies her inherent right to life. There is no countervailing advantage for her at all. It is contrary to her best interests. [...] In my judgment, parents who are placed on the horns of such a terrible dilemma simply have to choose the lesser of their inevitable loss. [...] When considering the worthwhileness of the treatment, it is legitimate to have regard to the actual condition of each twin and hence the actual balance sheet of advantage and disadvantage which flows from the performance or the non-performance of the proposed treatment. [...] The operation will give Jodie the prospects of a normal expectation of relatively normal life. The operation will shorten Mary's life but she remains doomed for death. [...] Mary may have a right to life, but she has little right to be alive. She is alive because and only because, to put it bluntly, but nonetheless accurately, she sucks the lifeblood out of Jodie. [...] She will survive only so long as Jodie survives. [...] Mary's parasitic living will be the cause of Jodie's ceasing to live. If Jodie could speak, she would surely protest, 'Stop it, Mary, you're killing me'. [...] Mary is beyond help. [...] The best interests of the twins is to give the chance of life to the child whose actual bodily condition is capable of accepting the chance to her advantage even if that has to be at the cost of the sacrifice of the life which is so unnaturally supported. I am wholly satisfied that the least detrimental choice, balancing the interests of Mary against Jodie and Jodie against Mary, is to permit the operation to be performed. [...] [I]t seems to me that the law must allow an escape through choosing the lesser of the two evils. [...] The respect the law must have for the right to life of each must go in the scales and weigh equally but other factors have to go in the scales as well. For the same reasons that led to my concluding that consent should be given to operate so the conclusion has to be that the carrying out of the operation will be justified as the lesser evil and no unlawful act would be committed.

Brooke LJ (at pages 218, 240): The doctrine of double effect can have no possible application in this case, as the [trial] judge rightly observed, because by no stretch of the imagination could it be said that the surgeons would be acting in good faith in Mary's best interests when they prepared an operation which would benefit Jodie but kill Mary. [...] There are three necessary requirements for the application of the doctrine of necessity:

(i)   the act is needed to avoid inevitable and irreparable evil;

(ii)   no more should be done than is reasonably necessary for the purpose to be achieved;

(iii) the evil inflicted must not be disproportionate to the evil avoided.

Given that the principles of modern family law point irresistibly to the conclusion that the interests of Jodie must be preferred to the conflicting interests of Mary,

I consider that all three of these requirements are satisfied in this case. Finally, the doctrine of the sanctity of life respects the integrity of the human body. The proposed operation would give these children's bodies the integrity which nature denied them.

Robert Walker LJ (at pages 246, 255, 258–9): If Mary had been born separated from Jodie but with the defective brain and heart and lungs which she has, and if her life were being supported, not by Jodie but by mechanical means, it would be right to withdraw that artificial life-support system and allow Mary to die. [...] In the absence of Parliamentary intervention the law as to the defence of necessity is going to have to develop on a case by case basis. I would extend it, if it needs to be extended, to cover this case. [...] The surgery would plainly be in Jodie's best interests, and in my judgment it would be in the best interests of Mary also, since for the twins to remain alive and conjoined in the way they are would be to deprive them of the bodily integrity and human dignity which is the right of each of them. [...] Mary's death would not be the purpose of the operation, although it would be its inevitable consequence. The operation would give her, even in death, bodily integrity as a human being. She would die, not because she was intentionally killed, but because her own body cannot sustain her life. [...] The proposed operation would not be unlawful.

The judgment in this case is quite unique. The three lords above came to the same conclusion – that the surgery should go ahead – but arrived there via different routes. Ward LJ referred to Mary as a parasite, sucking the lifeblood from Jodie. He justified the surgery on the grounds that it was the lesser of two evils. Brooke LJ raised the defence of necessity, justifying the surgery on the grounds that it was necessary to save one child at the detriment of another. Robert Walker LJ agreed that the defence of necessity was a defence to the murder of Mary, and also concurred with Brooke LJ that the surgery would in fact give Mary the bodily integrity that she deserved (i.e. being a separate being). It is unusual for the defence of necessity to trump the best interests of a patient. However, conjoined twins do pose a unique and complex problem. It is understandable that the parents of Mary and Jodie simply wished for nature to take its course (in line with their religion), but thanks to the intervention of the doctors, Jodie survived and returned home with her patents.

Re A was of great interest to legal and medical commentators and two abstracts from articles about this case follow.

EXTRACT

Raanan Gillon, 'Imposed Separation of Conjoined Twins – Moral Hubris by the English Courts?' (2001) 27 *Journal of Medical Ethics* 3, at pages 3–4

It seems . . . morally far preferable for the court, having spelt out the moral dilemma, to have ruled that there was no legal obligation – and perhaps no legal justification – in this case for removing the normal responsibility and right of parents to make healthcare decisions for their children. The parents were neither incompetent nor negligent – the standard justifications for depriving parents of such authority – and their reasoning was not eccentric or merely religious, but was widely acceptable moral reasoning – as was the contrary moral reasoning justifying the operation. The court should thus have declined to deprive the parents of their normal responsibilities and rights in order to impose its own preferred resolution of the moral dilemma, and should have allowed the parents to refuse medical intervention.

EXTRACT

M.Q. Bratton and S.B. Chetwynd, 'One into Two Will Not Go: Conceptualising Conjoined Twins' (2004) 30 *Journal of Medical Ethics* 279, at pages 279–85

The ethical and legal thinking that treats conjoined twins as if they were physically separate entities who have unfortunately become entangled and need to have their separate existence restored, seems to have things the wrong way round. Conjoined twins are not separate and never have been. If we separate them, we should at the very least recognise that we are creating two new separate entitles from two who were one, and that in doing so we are removing from each of them part of themselves. It may, of course, be a decision that we need to make for the benefit of both twins, but we should be wary of assuming that a physically separate existence is automatically in their best interests. [...] If medical decisions made on behalf of conjoined twins should be made in their best interests, then we had better be sure that they are, and that they are not made just because they make things easier for us to deal with.

The two views above are interesting. Gillon argues that the parents were in fact fully competent to make this medical decision for themselves in line with the ordinary principles of medical law. Bratton and Chetwynd, on the other hand, suggest that conjoined twins do not *need* to be separated – they were simply born joined and we should accept them as such even if they face death. Was it wrong for the English courts to intervene, even though Jodie is now living happily with her parents?

ACTIVITY

How do you think medical care would change in this country if we were to allow doctors to withdraw life-saving treatment from incompetent adult patients on the same grounds as those of babies and children? Write a 500-word essay on the effect of such a change in the law.

● ● ● Should euthanasia be legalised?

So far in this chapter, we have looked at the different ways in which a patient's life can be ended at the hands of a medical professional. Sometimes, a criminal charge will result. On other occasions the courts have not supported a prosecution. There continues to be significant debate as to whether euthanasia should just be legalised.

Euthanasia is the intentional killing of a patient, at their request, for reasons of ill health. Some patients – especially those who are terminally ill and predicted to suffer a painful and distressing death – may prefer to end their lives peacefully at the hands of a medical professional as opposed to an assisted suicide at home, but this carries the risk of failure and may result in the surviving relatives facing prosecution. This section will only focus on euthanasia. The legalisation of assisted suicide would lead to pressurised suicides behind closed doors, which would be extremely difficult to regulate. It is highly unlikely that Parliament would legalise assisted suicide because it gives far too much power to our relatives to encourage vulnerable family members to end their lives prematurely. Euthanasia, on the other hand, involves qualified medical professionals who, for the most part, carry no ulterior motives and have access to humane methods of killing (e.g. morphine).

Why regulate euthanasia?

Many people believe that euthanasia already does go on in our hospitals today via palliative care, although it is impossible to compose an accurate picture of how frequently it occurs. It is dangerous for this to go on in secret without formal regulations in place to set benchmarks. For example, a doctor may choose to end a life in an inhumane way, or may kill the patient on a whim without fully clarifying the wishes of the patient. Should Parliament acknowledge that euthanasia is going on under the guise of palliative care and take the opportunity to regulate it to ensure that patients are cared for in a safe and professional environment? A lack of regulation usually leads to a breakdown in trust between doctors and patients eventually. The current law contains many inconsistencies (e.g. the doctrine of double effect), but the legalisation and regulation of euthanasia may help to eliminate these. It appears that, according to the current state of the law, competent patients can choose to refuse treatment, incompetent patients may have their lives ended by doctors according to their best interests, but a competent request for euthanasia (e.g. by lethal injection) will not be acknowledged, regardless of how extreme or advanced the patient's medical condition is. It would seem that if this patient was, in fact, on a life support machine, her care would simply be withdrawn. It is only a matter of time before this inconsistency is challenged in a high court.

The Lords did, of course, label the withdrawal of life support as an omission in *Airedale NHS Trust* v *Bland* [1993] AC 789 (above) and also agreed that at the time of withdrawal, a duty to hydrate and nourish no longer existed, making the omission not culpable. In comparison to this, a lethal injection is an act, and with the intention to kill it would certainly be an act of murder.

Showing mercy

This ground for legalisation is an emotional one. Mercy has no place in the criminal law, it is not a defence to any crime and it is a mere moral perspective on a particular action. However, if we look closely, it may still count. The Director of Public Prosecutions made public the criteria for bringing a case of assisted suicide and when a relative acts to assist the suicide of a family member because of a degenerative medical disease, he will clearly take these merciful motives into account. Similarly, it was explained above that in the context of palliative care, a doctor will not usually be charged with murder for providing a patient with a fatal dose of pain-killing drugs if he merely intends to relieve pain, i.e. he is showing a compassionate motive as opposed to a direct intention to kill. Some may, therefore, argue that the primary principle underpinning palliative care is mercy. When looking at these current practices, it may be possible for Parliament to draft a potential law which, as long as he was acting mercifully, a medically-qualified medical professional could inject a fatal dose of painkillers into a competent patient and would not meet the criteria for murder.

Autonomy

Autonomy is one of the cornerstones of medical care. A competent patient is entitled to refuse life-saving medical treatment because it is his body, his mind, his life and his future and he can do with them whatever he likes. It is especially important to some patients that they can decide how they would like to die. We are all entitled to take our own lives whenever we want, however we want and in any way we want. It becomes complex when we ask another person to do it for us. If a patient chooses to die, can it be argued that the State has a duty to ensure that people can bring their lives to an end in a humane and peaceful way, rather than committing suicide in an often very public way, which may cause more upset for relatives and passers-by? Do we have a 'right' to choose when and how we die? Dianne Pretty in *Pretty* v *UK* (2002) 35 EHRR 1 argued that her right to life under Article 2 of the European Convention on Human Rights also meant a right to choose her own death. The European Court disagreed, stating that her right to life was not to be read as a right to death. The law usually supports patient autonomy, leaving euthanasia out in the cold as an obvious exception.

Religion will sometimes step into the argument here and propose that it is not our choice to decide when to die – it is a decision determined by a higher power. This is a belief held very strongly by some, regardless of how intolerable the terminal medical condition becomes for the suffering patient. Sceptics, however, will argue in return that if people can expressly choose when to create life, they can choose when to end one too.

What about doctors?

Legalising euthanasia will have a momentous impact on the day-to-day working lives of doctors. Patients will be free to request fatal injections, and those who are extremely sick may take advantage of their right to die and pester doctors repeatedly. Doctors may not want to kill their patients. What will happen then? In the event of the legalisation of euthanasia, certain doctors may register themselves as euthanising doctors. They will be kept under a watchful eye, of course.

What would the medical criteria be for allowing a doctor to proceed with a fatal injection? There will inevitably be patients who are suffering greatly but who do not meet one of the criteria, so will the criteria be lenient or flexible? There may also be borderline cases in which the doctors are not convinced that the patient *really* wants to die – he or she may simply fed up, depressed or pressurised by family members. There will have to be safeguards against patients taking advantage of the new law to rid themselves of a boring existence or manipulative threats.

There are clearly a handful of convincing reasons why euthanasia should be legalised. However, there seem to be twice as many reasons not to legalise the killing of terminally ill patients.

'It goes on anyway'

Palliative care is where a patient, who is in extreme pain and at the end of life, is given a large dose of painkillers to alleviate her pain but could potentially end her life. Is it really necessary to legalise euthanasia when palliative care already exists? The criminal courts have clearly shown no interest in the actions of doctors when providing palliative care. In addition to this, if a patient is found to experience no further benefit in being kept alive, she will have their life support legally withdrawn. Is this not adequate to stave away the demand for euthanasia?

The short answer is 'no'. Euthanasia is sought by patients who are fully competent because they wish to exercise control over the timing of their impending distressing death. Palliative care is usually only available to patients who are at the advanced stages of their illness and may have already lost consciousness. Therefore, palliative care and the withdrawal of life-saving treatment may not be fair comparisons to euthanasia as they are sought/used by different groups of patients.

EXTRACT

House of Lords Select Committee, 'Assisted Dying for the Terminally Ill Bill' (2005):

http://www.parliament.uk/business/publications/committees/select-committee-publications/

Paragraph 88: The Voluntary Euthanasia Society took the view that 'no amount of palliative care can address some patients' concerns regarding their loss of autonomy, loss of control of bodily functions and loss of dignity'. The British Medical Association echoed this view, observing that 'there are patients for whom even the best palliative care is not dealing with their pain', adding that 'in spite of excellent palliative care, the position is not necessarily one which those patients regard as beneficial to them'.

It is possible that euthanasia could fill the gap described by the House of Lords' Select Committee because patients of palliative care still fear the following things:

- Loss of autonomy.
- Loss of mental competency.
- Loss of control of bodily functions.
- Loss of physical or voluntary movement.
- Loss of consciousness.
- Loss of dignity.

For patients such as these, is death at the hands of their doctor the answer? Perhaps better care at home could suffice, or specialist counselling could be provided to allow the patient and her family to accept her illness and the inevitable symptoms of it? This probably does not sound too helpful to patients suffering from terminal diseases, but it is a current option.

Distrust

Imagine that you visit your doctor the day after Parliament has passed a new law allowing your doctor to administer a lethal injection at your request. Would you see your doctor differently? Would you trust him the same as you always did? Critics of euthanasia have traditionally argued that to legalise euthanasia would be to damage the integrity of the medical profession and jeopardise the doctor–patient relationship. How exactly would this be the case?

The first way in which this could happen is if doctors were to administer the lethal injections themselves, thus killing their own patients. This grates against the ethical code of healthcare professionals, who are trained to treat their patients, not kill them. This conflict of interest could be alleviated by the two following provisions:

- The doctor can only administer the lethal injection if the patient signs a form.
- A specially trained medical professional may carry out the task instead.

Let us take the idea that specially trained medical professionals could administer the fatal injection a little further – perhaps we could train people who work in toxicology or pharmacy to administer the lethal injection instead? The specialists would be independent of the patient, it would keep the trust between doctors and patients intact and it would not undermine the ethics of practising medical professionals. There is a risk of these specialists becoming known as 'Doctors of Death' and some may argue that no medical professional – in any medical field – should take the life of a patient.

EXTRACT

Vivienne Nathanson, House of Lords Select Committee, 'Assisted Dying for the Terminally Ill Bill' (2005):

http://www.parliament.uk/business/publications/committees/select-committee-publications/

Paragraph 77: What doctors find it impossible to consider is who would want to provide that service. They find it almost impossible to conceive of a person who would want to spend their life administering lethal injections. Whether such a service could ever be set up, and who would be the people who took part in it, raises very serious questions.

If ordinary doctors or specially trained medical professionals were awarded the power to administer lethal injections, one of the primary concerns for patients and their families would be the risk of abuse. This is likely to come from unscrupulous doctors who are, fortunately, few and far between, but the medical profession in general does have a funding issue which may be solved by quicker mortality rates. Lethal injections would be a very cost-effective alternative to prolonged palliative care and could potentially place euthanasia on the table as a treatment option. With this economic benefit in mind, doctors may be able to exert an unfair influence over vulnerable patients who are taking up beds and equipment.

Pressure from relatives

It is not only doctors who can put ideas into the heads of patients. Relatives may do so too. Degenerative and terminal illnesses and debilitating health conditions are more frequently found in the elderly, and it is this age group who are more vulnerable to pressure. Elderly patients may feel like a burden upon their loved ones, causing raised medical bills, requiring more time from family members who work full-time, and causing prolonged stress upon relatives as their condition deteriorates. Even if family members exert no real pressure upon the elderly patient to seek euthanasia, the patient herself may feel it necessary to relieve the burdens upon her family. What if a patient seeks euthanasia simply because she considers herself and her degenerative illness to be a burden?

This can be a supportive and unsupportive of euthanasia. In a supportive context, feelings of being a burden may play a part in the decision-making process and help the patient to weigh up the pros and cons of seeking euthanasia. In an unsupportive context, feelings of being a burden are not grave enough to warrant a lethal injection from a medical professional. This would not be medical treatment or medical care – it is simply assisted suicide.

Genuine consent

If euthanasia was legalised how could the medical professional, who is about to administer the lethal injection, be absolutely sure that his patient wishes to die? Does a witnessed signature on a consent form adequately represent the true feelings and wishes of the patient? Probably not. Depression may lead to a risk of suicidal thoughts in terminally ill patients, although more research is needed to prove this theory. New euthanasia legislation must therefore ensure that strict provisions are in place to allow medical professionals to ascertain whether the patient genuinely wishes to die as a result of his or her illness, or whether her depression is clouding her judgment. Euthanasia is a very final medical treatment and mistakes cannot be undone. Bearing this in mind, perhaps patients with fluctuating psychological disorders should be exempt from euthanasia should it be legalised?

Morality

Aside from the complexities of professional relationships, issues of trust, the risk of pressure and the option of palliative care, a further and more troubling barrier lies before the legalisation of euthanasia and that is the argument that life, of any kind, is valuable. Religious views are usually at the root of the moral argument against euthanasia. The idea that human beings could take their own lives (or the lives of each other) before their natural end is offensive against some religions, particularly for those who believe that a higher power should be in control of death. Regardless of what religion says, belief is a personal matter. This means that the religious or moral views of one patient cannot be forced upon another. However, some individuals do try to convince other patients that their argument is the right one. Thankfully, the courts pay little attention to religious or moral views, as they differ from patient to patient and are all as morally legitimate as each other. What really matters in medicine is competency, consent, best interests, autonomy, confidentiality and trust.

Losing control

The final barrier to the legalisation of euthanasia is the 'slippery slope' argument, which stipulates that once a particular practice is legalised, it slowly starts to spread outside of its original boundaries. This can be seen above, where the criteria laid down in *Airedale NHS Trust* v *Bland* [1993] AC 789 for the lawful removal of nutrition and hydration from an incompetent patient was seen to spread into neonatal euthanasia, allowing the same care to be withdrawn from babies who are not in a permanent vegetative state but merely fail to derive any pleasure out of life. A very small number of doctors have been charged with murder in the past for administering fatal doses of painkillers to patients, and these rare convictions do not include doctors who provide palliative care to patients who may not yet need a high dose of morphine. Is it possible that death will become more likely in hospitals if euthanasia was legalised? Would doctors begin to suggest death as an alternative treatment, or would overworked doctors administer a lethal injection for trivial reasons? This would be difficult to regulate, even if strict guidelines were in place. The implications of this argument spread further: if euthanasia were to become legal, would we, as a society, become at peace with the idea of death in hospital and stop questioning suspicious deaths?

This may seem a little far-fetched – the legalisation of abortion, for example, did not cast any doubt upon the value of life of babies as was predicted – nor are we any more likely to kill babies as a result of the legislation. Additionally, the acts of suicide and abortion are legal in the UK and have been since the 1960s, but they have not undermined the value of human life. However, as long as these concerns remain, the route towards euthanasia will be incredibly contentious.

RESEARCH ACTIVITY

Access the House of Lords Select Committee publication entitled: *Assisted Dying for the Terminally Ill Bill* (2005) at http://www.parliament.uk/business/publications/committees/select-committee-publications/. Find Chapter 4 and read the section on 'Covert Euthanasia'. What are your thoughts on the evidence presented? Does the evidence suggest that euthanasia does go on in our hospitals? Give reasons for your answer.

The law in other countries

The UK has grappled with the idea of euthanasia and/or assisted suicide only a handful of times. However, other countries around the world have shown more compassion for the terminally ill and have passed legislation allowing for euthanasia or assisted suicide. These laws are subject to strict controls and narrow eligibility criteria and there are still fierce debates in these countries about the morality of the legislation, but they provide an interesting insight as to what a potential euthanasia law could look like and how it influences medical care and public attitudes.

Oregon

The Death with Dignity Act was passed in the US state of Oregon originally in 1994, but it was delayed by a court injunction and eventually came into force in October 1997. The Death with Dignity Act is an assisted suicide provision, allowing for terminally ill Oregonians to end their lives by consuming an amount of lethal medication, prescribed by a medical professional for that purpose. Briefly, the 1994 Act wording is as follows.

127.805 s. 2.01. Who may initiate a written request for medication

(1) An adult who is capable, is a resident of Oregon, and has been determined by the attending physician and consulting physician to be suffering from a terminal disease, and who has voluntarily expressed his or her wish to die, may make a written request for medication for the purpose of ending his or her life in a humane and dignified manner.

(2) No person shall qualify under the provisions solely because of age or disability.

127.810 s. 2.02. Form of the written request

(1) A valid request for medication shall be in substantially the form described, signed and dated by the patient and witnessed by at least two individuals who, in the presence of the patient, attest that to the best of their knowledge and belief the patient is capable, acting voluntarily, and is not being coerced to sign the request.

127.820 s. 3.02. Consulting physician confirmation

Before a patient is qualified, a consulting physician shall examine the patient and his or her relevant medical records and confirm, in writing, the attending physician's diagnosis that the patient is suffering from a terminal disease, and verify that the patient is capable, is acting voluntarily and has made an informed decision.

The 1994 Act requests that the patient be facing death within six months. There is a strong emphasis on self-medication, placing the emphasis on the patient rather than the doctor. Other safeguards include:

- Two witnesses must confirm that the patient's request is voluntary.
- One witness must not be a legal or blood relative or in line to inherit property.
- The physician must suggest alternatives.
- The physician must refer the patient for a confirmation of diagnosis and a confirmation of capacity.
- There must be a 15-day wait between the patients' first oral request and the patient's final written request.

It is interesting that Oregon chose to legalise assisted suicide rather than euthanasia. The main difference between them, of course, is that assisted suicide allows a doctor to assist the patient when committing suicide, e.g. by providing drugs, whereas euthanasia requires the doctor to kill the patient. The 1994 Act requires the Oregon Department of Human Services to publish annual reports about the patients and physicians who participate under the Act. The statistics collected for the 2013 report are fascinating.

EXTRACT

Oregon Department of Human Services has a website dedicated to the Dying with Dignity Act:

**http://public.health.oregon.gov/ProviderPartnerResources/
EvaluationResearch/DeathwithDignityAct/Pages/index.aspx**

- 752 patients have died under the Act since 1997;
- During 2013, 122 lethal prescriptions were written out making a grand total of 1,173 since 1997;
- Only 63 of the 122 lethal prescriptions were ingested and 28 died of their illnesses;
- An overwhelming majority of patients were white (94.4%), well-educated (53.5%) and had cancer (64.8%);
- The average age was 71;
- Most patients were enrolled in hospice care (85.7%) and died at home (97.2%);
- The greatest concern was a loss of autonomy (93%), loss of dignity (73.2%), and a loss of participation and enjoyment (88.7%);
- Two of the patients were referred for psychiatric evaluation;
- Physicians were present at the time of death for only 8 patients;
- The time between ingestion and death ranged from 5 minutes to 5.6 hours.

All-in-all, this law appears to work well for the small number of patients who seek its assistance. Commentators have noted its success:

> ### EXTRACT
>
> ### Dan Brock, 'Misconceived Sources of Opposition to Physician-Assisted Suicide' (2000) 6 *Psychology, Public Policy and Law* 305
>
> There is no evidence that any of the abuses feared by opponents of the Act have materialised in the first year of its operation. It has not led to unsuccessful suicide attempts; to assisted deaths accompanied by distress to the patient; to any influx of out-of-state residents seeking assisted death; to public deaths; to use of assisted death to avoid dealing with difficult symptoms or to reduce the financial costs of end-of-life care; to disproportionate use of assisted death for weak, vulnerable, or disabled patients or for women; or to increased suicide rates in the general population and especially among the young.

The Netherlands

The Netherlands has had a very different experience to Oregon. Case law stretching all the way back to 1973 has slowly developed a special defence of necessity. As a result of the building case law, the Dutch codified the accepted practices and they were enshrined into Articles 293 and 294 of the Dutch Criminal Code into The Termination of Life on Request and Assisted Suicide (Review Procedures) Act 2001, which came into force in April 2002.

Case law

In 1973, Articles 293 and 294 of the Dutch Penal Code read as follows.

> **Article 293 (euthanasia)**
>
> 1. Any person who terminates another person's life at that person's express and earnest request shall be liable to a term of imprisonment not exceeding twelve years or a fifth-category fine.
>
> **Article 294 (assisted suicide)**
>
> 1. Any person who intentionally incites another to commit suicide shall, if suicide follows, be liable to a term of imprisonment not exceeding three years or a fourth-category fine.

Both euthanasia and assisted suicide were clearly illegal when the *Postma*[14] case came along. Dr Postma gave her mother, who had already attempted suicide several times, a fatal dose of morphine after she was left seriously disabled after a haemorrhage. Dr Postma was convicted under Article 293, but due to public sympathy she was awarded a suspended sentence of one week in prison. The court suggested that euthanasia could be legal if four specific criteria were met:

(1) the patient is terminally ill;

(2) the patient is suffering unbearably;

(3) the patient has requested that her life be terminated; and

(4) the termination is carried out by the patient's own doctor.

---

[14] Postma Case (1973) Nederlandse Jurisprudentie 1973 No 183, District Court of Leeuwarden.

Several other doctor–patient cases reached the Dutch courts, and a pattern began to emerge. Doctors were increasingly exempt from helping their patients to die according to the *Postma* criteria. The next noteworthy case was the *Alkmaar*[15] case, in which Dr Schoonheim was convicted for administering a lethal injection to an elderly patient who had produced an advanced declaration what she wished to be killed if her condition deteriorated. Dr Schoonheim appealed to the Dutch Supreme Court, and it was found that he faced an irreconcilable conflict of duties: on the one hand he must abide by the law and preserve the lives of his patients, but on the other hand he also has a duty to relieve unbearable suffering. This was known as an 'emergency defence' – a bit like necessity in the UK – and he was acquitted. The emergency defence was raised once again in the *Chabot*[16] case. Dr Chabot was a psychiatrist who assisted the suicide of a severely depressed woman. The Court accepted that there may be cases of psychological suffering where the emergency defence may be enacted, although it would still need to be unbearable. Dr Chabot was convicted because there was no way of knowing how ill the patient was, but no punishment was handed down. Much more recently, Dr Sutorius was convicted for assisting the suicide of an elderly patient who was simply 'tired of life' in the *Sutorius*[17] case. This was held not to be lawful assisted suicide because the patient's condition was not unbearable or a diagnosed physical or psychiatric condition. Again, however, no punishment followed the doctor's conviction, as it was felt that he had acted benevolently.

The trail of case law paints an interesting picture: doctors were breaking the law but were not being punished for it.

Statute

The Termination of Life on Request and Assisted Suicide (Review Procedures) Act 2001, which came into force in April 2002, provides two defences to Articles 293 and 294 of the Dutch Penal Code.

Article 293 (euthanasia)

2. The act referred to in the first paragraph shall not be an offence if it committed by a physician who fulfils the due care criteria set out in Article 2 of the Termination of Life on Request and Assisted Suicide (Review Procedures) Act, and if the physician notifies the municipal pathologist of this act in accordance with the provisions of Article 7, paragraph 2 of the Burial and Cremation Act.

Article 294 (assisted suicide)

2. Any person who intentionally assists another to commit suicide or provides him with the means to do shall, if suicide follows, be liable to a term of imprisonment not exceeding three years or a fourth-category fine. Article 293, paragraph 2 shall apply mutatis mutandis.[18]

---

[15] Alkmaar Case (1984) Nederlandse Jurisprudentie 1985 No 106 Supreme Court.
[16] Chabot Case (1994) Nederlandse Jurisprudentie 1994 No 656 Supreme Court.
[17] Sutorius Case (2003) 326 BMJ 71.
[18] This final sentence is stating that the defence above in relation to euthanasia will also apply to assisted suicide.

The Netherlands provides defences for both euthanasia *and* assisted suicide. No moral or ethical distinction is made between these two acts in Dutch medicine. In fact, when the Lords visited the Netherlands as part of the 2004 Select Committee on Assisted Dying for Terminally Ill Bill (further above), the head of the Royal Dutch Medical Association said that in stark contrast to the system in Oregon, many doctors in the Netherlands prefer the idea of euthanasia over assisted suicide.

EXTRACT

Select Committee on Assisted Dying for Terminally Ill Bill (March 2005), Volume I, HL Paper 86-I:

http://www.parliament.uk/business/publications/committees/select-committee-publications/

Paragraph 168: . . . many doctors prefer euthanasia for practical and clinical reasons, because when it is assisted suicide you hand over the medication to the patient and he has to take it himself. It may have side effects which will lead to the doctor acting anyway. For that reason most doctors prefer euthanasia.

The key provisions of the Termination of Life on Request and Assisted Suicide (Review Procedures) Act 2001 are below. All six criteria must be met by the physician.

Chapter II. Requirements of Due Care

Article 2

1. The requirements of due care, referred to in Article 293 second paragraph Penal Code mean that the physician:
   (a) holds the conviction that the request by the patient was voluntary and well-considered;
   (b) holds the conviction that the patient's suffering was lasting and unbearable;
   (c) has informed the patient about the situation he was in and about his prospects;
   (d) and the patient holds the conviction that there was no other reasonable solution for the situation he was in;
   (e) has consulted at least one other, independent physician who has seen the patient and has given his written opinion on the requirements of due care, referred to in parts a – d; and
   (f) has terminated a life or assisted in a suicide with due care.

The Dutch law is clearly very wide in scope, especially compared to the system in Oregon. The Dutch law is so wide in fact, that the following concerns might be raised: (1) there is no formal provision for a psychiatric assessment *before* the euthanasia is carried out to confirm that the patient's decision is voluntary; (2) there is no further definition regarding the words 'lasting' and 'unbearable' – what physical and mental illnesses are accepted? (3) No provisions for witnesses are included in the provisions of the 2001 Act; (4) 140,000 people die in the Netherlands every year and out of these, 3,800 are from euthanasia, 300 are from assisted suicide and 1,000 at the hands of a physician without an explicit request;[19] (5) only 54% of all euthanasia's are reported to the authorities.[20] If this is true, this effectively means that physicians can euthanise behind closed doors without the worry of a regional review committee or relatives knocking on their door demanding answers. Should physicians with so much power have so much discretion? What might this do to patient trust? (6) 84% of patients ask for euthanasia to relieve pain, 70% for extreme fatigue (tiredness), 50% for gastrointestinal complaints and weight loss, 70% for coughing and suffocation, and almost 70% feel extremely weak;[21] (7) on the euthanasia advance directive form provided to patients, options include: 'unbearable suffering', 'a condition which provides little or no prospect of a return to what is for me a reasonable and dignified existence', 'a life with serious, permanent paralysis', 'being blind or virtually blind and/or deaf and/or virtually deaf which make it impossible or virtually impossible for me to perform what are for me worthwhile activities such as reading, writing, watching television, listening to music and doing manual work or handicrafts', and 'having a severe impairment or continuing degeneration of my mental faculties, as a result of which I . . . must be confined because I would otherwise go wandering'.[22] These are not typical medical grounds to euthanise – they are mild disabilities. It is also not appropriate for the patient to define 'unbearable' for themselves, because doctors will begin to euthanise their patients for social reasons, not medical ones.

The Dutch law clearly covers almost all medical, psychological and even social eventualities to allow for euthanasia, but it does contain a number of safeguards including an examination by an independent physician and regional review committees.

Neonatal and child euthanasia

The controversies with the Dutch laws do not stop there. They can provide euthanasia to children aged 12 and above.

Chapter II (of the 2001 Act). Requirements of Due Care

Article 2

2. If the patient aged sixteen years or older is no longer capable of expressing his will, but prior to reaching this condition was deemed to have a reasonable understanding of his interests and has made a written statement containing a request for termination of life, the physician may [carry] out this request. The requirements of due care, referred to in the first paragraph, apply.

3. If the minor patient has attained an age between sixteen and eighteen years and may be deemed to have a reasonable understanding of his interests, the physician may [carry] out the patient's request for termination of life or assisted suicide, after the

---

[19] Select Committee on Assisted Dying for Terminally Ill Bill (March 2005), Volume I, HL Paper 86-I, http://www.parliament.uk/business/publications/committees/select-committee-publications/ at paragraph 171. It is, however, explained at paragraph 178 that these are probably cases of neonatal euthanasia. This raises an urgent question: since a one month old baby cannot request euthanasia as stipulated in the statute, is neonatal euthanasia simply murder?

[20] See note above, at paragraph 180.

[21] See note above, at paragraph 185.

[22] See note above, at paragraph 188.

> parent or the parents exercising parental authority and/or his guardian have been involved in the decision process.
>
> 4. If the minor patient is aged between twelve and sixteen years and may be deemed to have a reasonable understanding of his interests, the physician may [carry] out the patient's request, provided always that the parent or the parents exercising parental authority and/or his guardian agree with the termination of life or the assisted suicide.

These provisions are very flexible. Subsections 3 and 4 (above) together require a child between the ages of 12 and 18 to have a reasonable grasp of his interests. Perhaps it is for the best that the physician must also discuss the matter with the child's parents? However, an advance directive from a 16-year-old child with reasonable understanding will stand alone without the interference of his or her parents, but the physician will make the final decision.

Belgium

Belgium has implemented a different system to that of Oregon and the Netherlands by legalising *only* euthanasia. Assisted suicide of any kind is still illegal. The Belgian Act on Euthanasia 2002 was passed amidst a flurry of mixed feelings and states as follows:

> ### Section 2
>
> For the purposes of this Act, euthanasia is defined as intentionally terminating life by someone other than the person concerned, at the latter's request.
>
> ### Section 3(1)
>
> The physician who performs euthanasia commits no criminal offence when he/she ensures that:
>
> - The patient has attained the age of majority or is an emancipated minor, and is legally competent and conscious at the moment of making the request;
> - The request is voluntary, well considered and repeated, and is not the result of any external pressure;
> - The patient is in a medically futile condition of constant and unbearable physical or mental suffering and cannot be alleviated, resulting from a serious and incurable disorder caused by illness or accident.

To ensure that the correct decision is made, section 3(2) states that the patient's physician must also tick the following boxes:

- Inform the patient about her health condition and life expectancy.
- Discuss with the patient her request for euthanasia and the possible therapeutic and palliative courses of action and their consequences.
- Come to the belief that there is no reasonable alternative to the patient's situation.
- Come to the belief that the patient's request is completely voluntary.
- Be certain of the patient's physical or mental suffering.
- Have several conversations with the patient spread out over a reasonable space of time.

- Take into account the progress of the patient's condition over this reasonable space of time.

- Consult another physician about the serious and incurable nature of the patient's condition.

- The independent, specialist physician must review the patient's medical record, examine the patient, be certain of the patient's constant and unbearable pain that cannot be alleviated, and write a report.

- If death is not imminent, a period of one month must pass between the patient's written request and the act of euthanasia.

The above criteria appear to sit between the strict Oregon approach and the wide Dutch approach. For example, the Belgian patient need not be diagnosed with a degenerative, terminal illness, but the patient must have a serious, futile and incurable condition or disorder confirmed by a second, specialist physician. The Belgian Act on Euthanasia 2002 also includes one considerable safeguard against abuse, which can be broken down into stages:

- **Safeguard 1**: Under section 5 of the 2002 Act, any physician who performs euthanasia must fill in a special form and send it to the Federal Control and Evaluation Commission within four days.

- **Safeguard 2**: The Federal Control and Evaluation Committee (established under section 6) consists of doctors, professors, lawyers and specialists in care, and must determine whether euthanasia was carried out in accordance with the 2002 Act. If not, the Committee can request further information from the physician.

- **Safeguard 3**: The Commission must hand down a verdict within two months. If the physician has not performed euthanasia according to the provisions of the 2002 Act, the Committee can turn the case over to the public prosecutor.

In order to take the pressure off the hesitant Belgian doctors, section 14 also states that no advance directive is compulsory and that no physician is compelled to perform, or assist in performing, euthanasia. However, should a physician refuse, he must explain his reasons to the patient. This effectively means that a patient in Belgium cannot demand euthanasia. Section 3(4) of the 2002 Act allows for a witness to write out a patient's request for euthanasia if the patient is not physically able to do so (as long as the witness does not gain from the patient's death), and section 4 allows for advance directives.

The 2004 Select Committee on Assisted Dying for Terminally Ill Bill also visited Belgium and collected some evidence from Belgium's first Federal Control and Evaluation Committee report on how the 2002 Act performed in its first fifteen-month period:

EXTRACT

Select Committee on Assisted Dying for Terminally Ill Bill (March 2005), Volume I, HL Paper 86-I:

http://www.parliament.uk/business/publications/committees/select-committee-publications/

Paragraph 212: The first report of the FCEC, covering the 15-month period from 23 September 2002 to 31 December 2003 recorded 259 cases of euthanasia, an average of 17 cases per month. The 259 cases were reported by 143 different physicians. In 2004, 347 cases of euthanasia were reported, an average of 29 cases per month. The Commission's first report did not report any instances of non-compliance with the law and did not see a need for new legislative initiatives.

It is encouraging that no acts of non-compliance were found in Belgium within the first fifteen months, i.e. a doctor performed the act in a way that did not comply with the law. However, this does not mean that the future will be plain sailing in Belgium – the slippery slope into the lazy attitude of the Netherlands is always only a patient away.

Switzerland

The law in Switzerland is different again to Oregon, the Netherlands and Belgium.

Regarding euthanasia, direct active euthanasia, i.e. the intentional administration of fatal drugs is illegal in Switzerland, and will be prosecuted under Article 111 (murder), Article 113 (manslaughter) and Article 114 (mercy killing on request) of the Swiss penal code. However, what we know in the UK as palliative care, i.e. providing pain relief which may have the effect of shortening life, is known as indirect active euthanasia in Switzerland and is permissible. Additionally, the withdrawal of life support is known as passive euthanasia in Switzerland and this is permissible too. The Swiss Academy of Medical Sciences has published guidelines to direct these practices.

Regarding assisted suicide, only a person who acts with a selfish intention when helping another to commit suicide will be prosecuted under Article 115 (assisted suicide) of the Swiss Penal Code. An honourable or merciful intention will not attract prosecution. It is assumed that doctors will not become involved in assisted suicide, so these provisions are directed at ordinary members of the public.

The law in Switzerland	
Act	**Definition and legality**
Direct active euthanasia	The direct and intentional killing of a patient is illegal under Articles 111 (murder), 113 (manslaughter) and 114 (mercy killing on request) of the Swiss Penal Code.
Indirect active euthanasia	Providing pain relief which may also shorten life is legal.
Passive euthanasia	Withdrawing life support is legal.
Self-serving assisted suicide	Helping another to commit suicide for your own gains is illegal under Article 115 (assisted suicide) of the Swiss Penal Code.
Merciful assisted suicide	Helping another to die to alleviate their anguish and suffering is legal.

The assisted suicide laws above require a further analysis. How do the police differentiate between a malicious intention and a merciful one? This could make all the difference between a conviction and an acquittal.

Self-serving assisted suicide

The Swiss law – which was codified in 1942 – was not designed with terminally ill patients in mind. The law is general and applies broadly to everyone, and the idea that assisted suicide could be used to help terminally ill people did not emerge until 1980. As a result, Article 115 (assisted suicide) simply states that the defendant's actions must not be 'self-serving' and there is no distinction made between a relative and a doctor. What could 'self-serving' mean in emotional, social, ethical and legal terms?

EXTRACT

Select Committee on Assisted Dying for Terminally Ill Bill (March 2005), Volume I, HL Paper 86-I:

http://www.parliament.uk/business/publications/committees/select-committee-publications/

Paragraph 195: We were told by the Federal Ministry of Justice [in Switzerland] that the definition of 'self-serving ends' in assisting suicide had been clarified by successive tribunals and included such situations as that of a person who gave such assistance 'to satisfy his own material or emotional needs . . . the possibility of eliminating some major problem for the family, or other motives such as gaining an inheritance, relieving himself of the burden of supporting the individual . . . or eliminating a person he hated'.

Because the Swiss Penal Code was not created with specific instances of assisted suicide in mind, Article 115 provides no further information on the age, illness, environment or mental state of the person seeking assisted suicide. However, as mentioned above, the Swiss Academy of Medical Sciences have published a set of guidelines to outline the basic principles of end-of-life care in Switzerland, and they include the current accepted practice in palliative care and assisted suicide.

EXTRACT

End of life care, Medical-ethical guidelines of the SAMS (2013), The Swiss Academy of Medical Sciences:

http://www.samw.ch/en/Ethics/Guidelines/Currently-valid-guidelines.html

3.1 Palliative care

It is the physician's duty to alleviate pain and suffering, even if in individual cases this is intended to have an influence (shortening or prolongation) on the duration of life itself. With symptoms that are refractory to treatment, sedation may sometimes be necessary. Here it is pointed out that the patient should be sedated only to the extent that this is necessary for alleviation of the symptoms.

3.2 Withdrawing and withholding treatment

Faced with the process of dying, it may be justified or indicated to withhold or withdraw life-sustaining measures. In the decision-making process criteria such as the prognosis, the expected outcome of treatment in terms of quality of life, and the undesirable effects of the proposed treatment on the patient all play a role.

4.1 Assisted suicide

According to Article 115 of the Swiss Penal Code, helping someone to commit suicide is not a punishable offence when it is done for unselfish reasons. This applies to everyone. With patients at the end of life, the task of the physician is to alleviate symptoms and to support the patient. It is not his task to directly offer assistance in suicide, he rather is obliged to alleviate any suffering underlying the patient's wish to commit suicide.

→

However, in the final phase of life, when the situation becomes intolerable for the patient he or she may ask for help in committing suicide and may persist in this wish. [...] If [the doctor] decides to assist a person to commit suicide, it is his responsibility to check the following preconditions:

- The patient's disease justifies the assumption that he is approaching the end of life;
- Alternative possibilities for providing assistance have been discussed and, if desired, have been implemented;
- The patient is capable of making the decision, his wish has been well thought out, without external pressure, and he persists in this wish. This has been checked by a third person, who is not necessarily a physician.
- The final action in the process leading to death must always be taken by the patient himself.

4.2 Killing on request

Even if requested seriously and insistently, the killing of a patient must be refused by the physician. According to Article 114 of the Penal Code, killing on request is a criminal offence.

These guidelines are simple and clear for doctors, but they provide a lot of flexibility for borderline cases where the patient is not so close to death but cannot bear to live anymore and her sympathetic doctor supports a request for drugs. The following issues are therefore not clear in Switzerland:

- Does the patient have to be diagnosed with any kind of physical, mental or psychological illness at all?
- Does the patient have to possess full mental capacity?
- Must there be any witnesses to confirm that the doctor simply assisted rather than killed the patient?
- How far can the assistance go?
- Are there any other safeguards in place to ensure that the patient's act is voluntary?
- How do the courts ensure that the patient is not suffering from depression or any other condition that could cloud his or her judgment, thus allowing the doctor to take advantage of the patient's vulnerable position?

Many assisted suicides in Switzerland take place in unique assisted suicide clinics, which are notorious for providing help to foreign visitors who wish to end their lives.

Assisted suicide organisations

Because assisted suicide is legal in Switzerland if it is performed mercifully, the Swiss have developed something unique: assisted suicide organisations.

- EXIT is the largest and oldest organisation boasting 50,000 members and caters for Italian and German-speaking Swiss nationals.
- AMD is a smaller organisation catering for the French-speaking Swiss nationals.
- The most well-known international organisation – DIGNITAS – is a break-away group from EXIT with a membership of 4,500 for foreign nationals travelling to Switzerland with one main aim – to commit suicide with assistance.

EXIT was founded in the late 1980s and according to a doctor who works there, they adopt strict admittance criteria.

> **EXTRACT**
>
> ### Select Committee on Assisted Dying for Terminally Ill Bill (March 2005), Volume I, HL Paper 86-I:
>
> **http://www.parliament.uk/business/publications/committees/select-committee-publications/**
>
> **Paragraph 201**: We must firstly have a poor medical prognosis, unbearable pain or substantial impairment. For us, the autonomy of the person is in a way our first point of view. We are rather liberal on this medical prognosis. [There has been] a change of philosophy because in the beginning EXIT was only prepared to assist people who were terminally ill or had very strong pains or were disabled. Recently it has been decided that we would also assist elderly people who simply decide that they do not see any meaning in their life any more.

DIGNITAS is the most widely recognised suicide organisation because they are open to people from all over the world.[23] A patient wishing to visit DIGNITAS must send a written request plus their medical records. Patients are given a provisional green light by a DIGNITAS doctor. The 2004 Select Committee on Assisted Dying for Terminally Ill Bill interviewed those who worked for DIGNITAS for further information.

> **EXTRACT**
>
> ### Select Committee on Assisted Dying for Terminally Ill Bill (March 2005), Volume I, HL Paper 86-I:
>
> **http://www.parliament.uk/business/publications/committees/select-committee-publications/**
>
> **Paragraph 203**: We were told by Mr Ludwig Minelli, Director General of DIGNITAS, that 'about 80% of the members who have got the provisional green light never call again' but that, for those who persist with their requests, the organisation prefers that they come twice to Switzerland, once to see the physician and again to receive assistance with ending their lives. He added, however, that in many cases – for example, where applicants were seriously ill or severely disabled – it was not possible to insist on two visits and one visit, for confirmation of the Swiss doctor's assessment, was considered sufficient.

The Select Committee went on to explain what exactly happened to patients at DIGNITAS and how the emphasis was on the patient to commit the act of suicide.

---

[23] DIGNITAS has an official website at: www.dignitas.ch.

EXTRACT

Select Committee on Assisted Dying for Terminally Ill Bill (March 2005), Volume I, HL Paper 86-I:

http://www.parliament.uk/business/publications/committees/select-committee-publications/

Paragraph 204: On arrival for the final or only visit, an applicant is met at the airport or railway station by a representative of DIGNITAS and taken to an apartment in Zurich which the organisation rents for the purpose. The DIGNITAS representative remains with the applicant throughout the visit, to ensure that his or her needs are met and to make clear to the applicant that he or she is free at any time to discontinue the process. If the applicant wishes to go ahead, the medication is placed within his or her reach. When it has been ingested and death has occurred, the death is reported to the authorities. The DIGNITAS representative receives a fee for his or her services of 500 Swiss francs.

What if the patient is unable to reach over and collect the medication? The Swiss Penal Code very clearly states that a direct act of euthanasia is illegal. Sometimes, suicide organisations can infuse the medication with apparatus, such as a wheel or a button, allowing the patient to use minimal effort. Therefore, the line between the patient's act and the doctor's help can sometimes be incredibly thin. The evidence collected by the Select Committee shows that the popularity of the suicide organisations is increasing.

EXTRACT

Select Committee on Assisted Dying for Terminally Ill Bill (March 2005), Volume I, HL Paper 86-I:

http://www.parliament.uk/business/publications/committees/select-committee-publications/

Paragraphs 198 and 199: Dr Brunner told us that, 'when the law was made, we did not have any suicide organisations. In the late 1980s the first suicide organisation was established. That was EXIT. Now we have five or six organisations and some splinter organisations too. Then, in about 2000, suicides of people from England started'. According to Mr Stadelmann, up to 1993 EXIT assisted about 30 cases a year. 'Since 1993 we know that there have been about 100 cases a year.' The figures for DIGNITAS, he said, followed a similar trend. 'They declared three cases in 2000, 37 or 38 cases in 2001, about 55 cases in 2002, and 91 cases in 2003.'

These increasing numbers have led to a concern over death tourism in Switzerland. This means that a patient does not have the opportunity to build a relationship with the person who will assist in ending his or her life. Several Swiss doctors quoted in the Select Committee stated that the suicide organisations were either 'impossible to legally oversee', 'not subject to surveillance or state control', or 'do not put enough weight on evaluation and assessment'.[24] One suggestion put forward was that the organisations

---

[24] Select Committee on Assisted Dying for Terminally Ill Bill (March 2005), Volume I, HL Paper 86-I, http://www.parliament.uk/business/publications/committees/select-committee-publications/ at paragraph 207.

should publish their annual accounts to make it easier to satisfy the authorities that no selfish, financial gain was being made from the deaths of others, and that staff were 'approved'.[25] This would cut the risk of 'Angels of Death' operating in suicide clinics, but would it address the more pressing ethical problem of lenient assisted suicide laws?

Further developments

The US state of Washington legalised assisted suicide in November 2008 with a piece of legislation based on the Oregon model. The Washington Death with Dignity Act 2008 was voted in with a majority of 57%.[26]

Luxembourg legalised euthanasia in April 2009, but only after a constitutional crisis. Royal assent was refused for the Act by the Grand Duke of Luxembourg, the deeply Catholic head of state. Luxembourg's Parliament solved this by enacting legislation that forced the head of state to play a purely ceremonial role in all future parliamentary matters.

THINKING POINT

How far do you think doctors at suicide organisations should go to 'assist' a paralysed patient? Now that you know how relaxed the law on assisted suicide is in Switzerland and how its suicide organisations operate, what are your main concerns for the patients who attend these clinics?

Death

Our attitudes towards death have changed throughout the ages. Archaeologists have found evidence that rituals were performed in ancient times during burials and people were sacrificed, turning death into a gift to the Gods. The Egyptians famously mummified their dead and sent them to the afterlife with gifts and valuables. During the world wars, death was viewed as valiant. In old Hollywood movies, death was dramatic and glamorous. In the developed world, death is tidy, personal and controlled. The feelings surrounding death have remained the same regardless of the century or the cause: death in its physical state is permanent. It happens as frequently as birth in hospitals, yet it is kept undercover because we do not like to be confronted by it. The law is dependent on a clear definition of it, but the law has very little to say about the definition of death.

We can take steps to control our own death, e.g. accepting or rejecting medical treatment, eating ourselves into an early grave or undertaking very dangerous hobbies, or we can ask another to assist us in death, with varying degrees of legality of course, but the majority of us wish for a natural, peaceful and painless death at home with our families after we have lived a full life. The area of medical law is rarely involved in such perfect scenarios.

---

[25] Dr Christoph Rehmann-Sutter, President of the National Advisory Commission on Biomedical Ethics, and Dr Brunner, Select Committee on Assisted Dying for Terminally Ill Bill (March 2005), Volume I, HL Paper 86-I, at paragraph 208.

[26] See the Washington State Department of Health website for the full legislation: http://www.doh. wa.gov/dwda/.

Why is death relevant?

Death might seem like a strange addition to a medical law textbook that deals, for the most part, with life. However, death plays a vital role in a handful of medical areas:

- **The rationing of healthcare resources**: death may result if there are not enough healthcare resources to go around, making decisions about rationing and allocation highly controversial.
- **Medical negligence**: if death occurs as a result of medical negligence, a charge of gross negligence manslaughter could ensue.
- **Abortion**: the definition of death plays a role in the practice of abortion by confirming that a foetus is not a person who can die in law.
- **Organ transplantation**: the definition of death plays a vital role in this field because major organs cannot be removed until a person is confirmed as dead.
- **PVS patients**: if comatose patients are dead, the withdrawal of life support would not be a legal or ethical issue.

There is an accepted definition of death that is currently used in both medicine and in the courts (below), but this is only one definition. There are many others (including social, moral and historic definitions). This causes controversy and confusion, especially when the religious beliefs of patients are factored into the equation.

The biggest issue surrounding the definition of death in medical law is the moment of death. This is a vital factor in organ procurement. Let us imagine, for example, that your parents are approached by a doctor before your life-sustaining hydration and nutrition are permanently withdrawn and asked about organ donation. Your parents agree to donate your organs . . . but at what point could the organs be legally taken from your body? If they are taken during your PVS state, this would be murder because the act of taking your heart would kill you. However, if they are taken after your death through starvation, your organs would already be depleted in quality and could not be used in transplantation. Therefore, if we could 'shove' the definition of death to an earlier point in the timeline, i.e. when you fell into your PVS state, we could remove your organs in a much better state and not break the law. It is highly controversial to state that patients on life-support machines are dead, because dead bodies are treated differently to living bodies (they are harvested, autopsied, embalmed, buried or cremated). The medical profession must, therefore, be absolutely certain that a patient is dead. There are a small handful of stories in the press every year of people waking up in morgues because of a mistaken diagnosis (although these are often in developing countries that diagnose death via lifelessness).[27]

What is death?

The courts have traditionally steered clear of this subject and adopted the medical definition of death instead, but it is an interesting question to pose. Doctors believe that a patient is dead when the brain stem dies (more below), but we used to believe that a patient was dead when their heart and/or breathing ceased. This was before life support

---

[27] It was reported in the *Daily Telegraph* on Wednesday 6 August 2008 that an Indian man who had been involved in a fatal stampede at a Naina Devi pilgrimage woke up in the morgue in a line of bodies awaiting a post-mortem, and on Monday 15 June 2009 an 84-year-old polish woman woke up in a morgue after a member of the emergency services had pronounced her dead.

machines, which have muddied the waters considerably. There are religious groups who believe that only the body dies but the soul continues to live, or that the body never dies. This is why the best interests test in *Airedale NHS Trust* v *Bland* [1993] AC 789 was so controversial – is it ethical to describe a living person as existing in 'a living death' in order to justify the withdrawal of his life-sustaining nutrition and hydration? The parents or relatives of a patient can disagree with the courts: are doctors correct in saying that a patient is dead because his brain stem has died, or are the parents or relatives correct to say that the patient is still alive because they see him sleeping and breathing (albeit artificially) every day? These days, because of the advances in technology, a person on a life support machine may look alive and well, when in actual fact their brain has ceased to function completely. This causes understandable confusion for relatives.

Death in the courts

In the early 1990s, a handful of medical law cases began to emerge which questioned when exactly a patient died. This was a direct result of the advances in technology which led to the sustaining of patients who would otherwise have died without medical intervention. The *Bland* case confirmed that the legal definition of death is adopted from medicine.

CASE EXTRACT

Airedale NHS Trust v *Bland* [1993] AC 789

Lord Goff (at page 863): I start with the simple fact that, in law, Anthony is still alive. It is true that his condition is such that it can be described as a living death; but he is nevertheless still alive. This is because, as a result of developments in modern medical technology, doctors no longer associate death exclusively with breathing and heartbeat, and it has come to be accepted that death occurs when the brain, and in particular the brain stem, has been destroyed. [...] The evidence is that Anthony's brain stem is still alive and functioning and it follows that, in the present state of medical science, he is still alive and should be so regarded as a matter of law.

It does, of course, make life much easier when the law adopts the medical definition of a condition rather than developing its own definition from scratch.[28] Happily, little dispute has occurred in the courts over the diagnosis of death, but outside of the courtroom there is considerable unrest over the current brain stem death test.

Brain stem death

The Department of Health took the opportunity to publish its first Code of Practice for 'brain death' in 1983 in relation to harvesting organs from dead donors.[29] A review was then undertaken in 1995 by a Working Group of the Royal College of Physicians of London and the term 'brain stem death' was supported.[30] The Conference of Medical

---

[28] The condition of insanity is the most obvious example of when the opposite has occurred: the criminal law has its own definition of insanity and it includes sleepwalkers and people with diabetes.

[29] *Cadaveric Organs for Transplantation: A Code of Practice Including the Diagnosis of Brain Death*, London, 1983, HMSO (no longer available on the Department of Health website).

[30] 'Criteria for the Diagnosis of Brain Stem Death', (1995) 29 *Journal of the Royal College of Physicians of London* 381.

Royal Colleges adopted this new definition of brain stem death and the definition has changed very little since. The Department of Health updated its Code of Practice in 1998, recognising the new definition in a document entitled: A Code of Practice for the Diagnosis of Brain Stem Death (below). The addition of the word 'stem' in the title was a clear indication that the accepted definition of death was now based firmly on the brain stem death test. The definition of brain stem death followed under paragraph 1 of the updated Code of Practice.

EXTRACT

A Code of Practice for the Diagnosis of Brain Stem Death (1998), Department of Health, (archived), at page 3:

http://webarchive.nationalarchives.gov.uk/20130107105354/
http://www.dh.gov.uk/en/Publicationsandstatistics/Publications/
PublicationsPolicyAndGuidance/DH_4009696

1. The Definition of Death

Death entails the irreversible loss of those essential characteristics which are necessary to the existence of a living human person. Thus, it is recommended that the definition of death should be regarded as 'irreversible loss of the capacity for consciousness, combined with irreversible loss of the capacity to breathe'.

The current position in law is that there is no statutory definition of death in the United Kingdom. Subsequent to the proposal of the 'brain death criteria' by the Conference of Royal Colleges in 1976 and 1979, the courts in England and Northern Ireland have adopted these criteria, as part of the law, for the diagnosis of death. There is no reason to believe that courts in other parts of the United Kingdom would not follow this approach.

Brain stem death was clearly defined as a two-part test:

- **Part 1**: Irreversible loss of the capacity for consciousness.
- **Part 2**: Irreversible loss of the capacity to breathe.

These two elements must be combined, so it is not sufficient, for example, for a patient to be incapable of breathing for himself but still conscious. In 2008, the Academy of Medical Royal Colleges published an updated Code to include important developments and more scientifically rigorous criteria for confirming brain stem death.[31] The word 'stem' has been removed from the title of the 2008 Code (which is currently in force), but this is merely cosmetic – the brain stem death test is still an accepted method of confirming death in the UK and the changes are relatively minor (the test is described in detail in Chapter 9 in relation to organ donation).

The Academy of Medical Royal Colleges appears to have established a safe test: not only must the patient be unable to sustain consciousness permanently, but he must be unable to breathe unaided and two experienced medical professionals must confirm this (this is a safeguard). However, commentators have criticised the brain stem death test considerably. Some have claimed that it does not pinpoint an accurate time of death, whereas others have questioned why we even have a brain stem death test at all.

---

[31] A Code of Practice for the Diagnosis and Confirmation of Death (2008), Academy of Medical Royal Colleges, http://www.aomrc.org.uk/publications/reports-a-guidance.html.

The medical evidence suggests that brain stem death is only the tip of the iceberg, so how would relatives react if they knew that their loved one, who was confirmed as dead, could still control his water balance, electrolyte balance, neurological activity, hormonal secretion, could show cortical activity and respond to pain? It is accepted, of course, that once the heart ceases to beat and the patient ceases to breathe, the many processes described above may simply be 'settling down' rather than 'functioning'. However, with these many processes continuing to be active after the official confirmation of death, the label 'dead' seems a little premature.

The concerns raised above relate to the practical nature of the brain stem death test, but what about the moral issues too? Why does death have to be connected to brain function, for example?

The human being is made up of many components, so why should death be measured according to the capacity of one organ? The answer may be that the brain stem is the best point from which to measure the functioning of bodily capacities, such as reflex actions and breathing. Another reason might be that the brain is the 'powerhouse' of the body, and without a functioning brain we face an inevitable and natural death. Kerridge also makes an interesting point that brain stem death alone is no longer appropriate as a test for death in light of the advances in technology, which has blurred the boundaries of death considerably.

Other definitions of death

The brain stem death test clearly has its problems, but it is recognised by the courts as the official test for death. Patients, however, may have other ideas. There are at least another four possible alternative states of death:

- No longer breathing.
- The whole body is dead.
- The soul leaves the body.
- The personality cannot live.

No longer breathing

This state of death refers to the old-style confirmation of death: if a patient's heart stops and he is not breathing, he is presumed dead. There are no real problems with this test, because if a person does not breathe for a short amount of time, his brain is starved of oxygen and death would result anyway. This kind of test merely requires time to confirm the diagnosis, i.e. after ten minutes of not breathing, a person will definitely be dead, but it could not be used if the body were suffering from hypothermia because the breathing slows down to the extent that the patient appears to be dead.

The whole body is dead

This test would require the whole body to die: the heart, lungs, brain, liver, kidneys and other processes such as the elimination of waste and muscle reflexes. Only then can the body be truly said to be dead. This test would take a while to confirm, but it would eliminate the concerns highlighted above that brain stem death may not be real death.

The soul leaves the body

This test is a mere moral pondering, as humans do not yet have the technology to prove the existence of the human soul. However, it raises some interesting questions. Are brain-dead patients still connected to their soul if they are on a ventilator? Some people claim to have had out-of-body experiences (particularly during surgery) – does this mean they temporarily die?

The personality cannot live

What this controversial test means is that a patient who can no longer communicate, interact, be conscious of his or her surroundings or be aware of those around him has 'died' in the respect that he has lost the essence of being human. This idea, of course, is highly offensive, as it would label all severely disabled people or all sufferers of advanced dementia as being 'dead', but Lord Goff in *Bland* did state that Anthony Bland, in his PVS state, was experiencing 'a living death'.

ACTIVITY

Here is a fictional plea from a parent.

'My Jamie looks alive to me. He's breathing and he's warm to hold. I can hold him and read to him and I can feel and hear him breathe. I talk to him and I'm convinced he can hear me. I've seen his eyelashes flicker – it's only a matter of time before the first brain wave appears. Then we'll be able to take my Jamie home.'

In actual fact, Jamie's doctor performed the brain stem death tests on Jamie today and Jamie is brain stem dead. Should the 'medical' definition of death be combined with other definitions of death (i.e. moral, religious or social) in order to prevent death from becoming 'artificial' or 'confusing' for relatives? Give reasons for your answer.

Chapter summary

- A doctor will also be charged with murder if he intentionally omits to care for his patient, but if the duty of care has been absolved, the omission is not culpable: *Airedale NHS Trust v Bland* [1993] 1 All ER 821.

- It is a criminal offence to assist the suicide of another person, regardless of the circumstances or the motives: section 2 of the Suicide Act 1961.

- Human rights Articles 2, 3, 8 and 14 are not breached by UK law by preventing a husband from helping his wife to commit suicide: *Pretty v UK* (2002) 35 EHRR 1.

- An incompetent patient can have his life-sustaining medical treatment withdrawn if he is no longer has any best interests in being kept alive: *Airedale NHS Trust v Bland* [1993] AC 789 and *Re D (Adult: Medical Treatment)* [1998] 1 FLR 411.

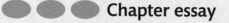 ## Chapter essay

'Critically analyse the current brain stem death test, and evaluate the moral and legal implications of potential incorrectness.'

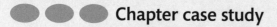 ## Chapter case study

'The costs of healthcare are spiralling. The elderly are surviving longer than they ever have thanks to advances in medical care. However, sometimes medical care is not enough and we cannot afford to treat every ailment. There are degenerative diseases such as motor neurone disease or aggressive forms of cancer that lead to a distressing, painful demise which cannot be adequately controlled by drugs. Euthanasia should be offered as an option to patients by their doctors, particularly if the prognosis is bleak' – David Brown, a demonstrator (fictional).

Does David Brown have a point? Should we legalise euthanasia to combat the resource crisis and treat terminal patients appropriately? Give reasons for your answer.

Further reading

Ford, M. (2005) 'The Personhood Paradox and the "Right to Die"', 13 *Medical Law Review* 30.

Harris, J. (2001) 'Human Beings, Persons and Conjoined Twins: An Ethical Analysis of the Judgment in Re A', 9 *Medical Law Review* 221; (2005) 'The Right to Die Lives! There is No Personhood Paradox', 13 *Medical Law Review* 386.

Keown, J. (1997) 'Restoring Moral and Intellectual Shape to the Law after Bland', 113 *Law Quarterly Review* 482.

Michalowski, S. (2005) 'Advance Refusals of Life Sustaining Treatment', *Modern Law Review* 958.

Sheldon, T. (2003) 'Being 'Tired of Life' is Not Grounds for Euthanasia', 326 *British Medical Journal* 71; (2007) 'Incidence of Euthanasia in the Netherlands Falls as That of Palliative Sedation Rises', 334 *British Medical Journal* 1075.

Bibliography

Chapter 1

Arras, J. (1991) 'Getting Down to Cases: The Revival of Casuistry in Bioethics', 16 *Journal of Medicine and Philosophy* 29.

Beauchamp, T. and Childress, J. (2008) *Principles of Biomedical Ethics*, 6th edn, Oxford University Press.

Clouse, K. and Gert, B. (1990) 'A Critique of Principalism', 15 *Journal of Medicine and Philosophy* 219.

Draper, H. and Sorrell, T. (2002) 'Patients' Responsibilities in Medical Bioethics', 16 *Bioethics* 335.

Foot, P. (1977) 'Euthanasia', 6 *Philosophy and Public Affairs* 85.

Herring, J. (2007) 'Where are the Carers in Healthcare Law and Ethics?', 27 *Legal Studies* 51.

Hursthouse, R. (1991) 'Virtue Theory and Abortion', 20 *Philosophy and Public Affairs* 223.

Kuhse, H. (1995) 'Clinical Ethics and Nursing: "Yes" to Caring, but "No" to a Female Ethic of Care', 9 *Bioethics* 207.

Secker, B. (1999) 'The Appearance of Kant's Deontology in Contemporary Kantianism: Concepts of Patient Autonomy in Bioethics', 24 *Journal of Medicine and Philosophy* 43.

Tsai, D. (2005) 'The Bioethical Principles and Confucius' Moral Philosophy', 31 *Journal of Medical Ethics* 159.

Veatch, R. (1988) 'The Danger of Virtue', 13 *Journal of Medicine and Philosophy* 13.

Chapter 2

Brazier, M. (1999) 'Regulating the Reproduction Business?', 7 *Medical Law Review* 166.

Davies, G. (2004) 'Health and Efficiency: Community Law and National Health Systems in the Light of Muller-Faure', 67 *Modern Law Review* 94.

Evans, H.M. (2007) 'Do Patients Have Duties?', 33 *Journal of Medical Ethics* 689.

Harris, J. (1995) 'Double Jeopardy and the Use of QALY's in Health Care Allocation', 21 *Journal of Medical Ethics* 144; (2005) 'The Age-Indifference Principle and Equality', 14 *Cambridge Quarterly of Healthcare Ethics* 93.

Light, D. (1997) 'The Real Ethics of Rationing', 315 *British Medical Journal* 112.

Maynard, A. (2001) 'Ethics and Health Care Underfunding', 27 *Journal of Medical Ethics* 223.

Palmer, S. (2005) 'AIDS, Expulsion and Article 3 of the European Convention on Human Rights', 5 *European Human Rights Law Review* 533.

Syrett, K. (2004) 'Impotence or Importance? Judicial Review in an Era of Explicit NHS Rationing', 67 *Modern Law Review* 289; (2006) 'Opening Eyes to the Reality of Scarce Health Care Resources? R (on the application of Rogers) v Swindon NHS Primary Care Trust and Secretary of State for Health', Public Law 664.

Chapter 3

Ash, S. (2006) 'The Role of Clinical Guidelines in Medical Negligence Litigation: a Shift from the *Bolam* Standard', *Medical Law Review* 321.

Bartlett, P. (1997) 'Doctors as Fiduciaries: Equitable Regulation of the Doctor-Patient Relationship', 5 *Medical Law Review* 193.

Brazier, M. and Miola, J. (2000) 'Bye-Bye *Bolam*: a Medical Litigation Revolution', 8 *Medical Law Review* 85.

Cane, P. (2004) 'Another Failed Sterilisation', 120 *Law Quarterly Review* 189–93.

Case, P. (2004) 'Secondary Iatrogenic Harm: Claims for Psychiatric Damage Following a Death Caused by Medical Error', 67 *Modern Law Review* 561–87.

Douglas, T. (2009) 'Medical Compensation: Beyond "No Fault"', 17 *Medical Law Review* 30.

Farrell, A. and Devaney, S. (2007) 'Making Amends or Making Things Worse? Clinical Negligence Reform and Patient Redress in England', 27 *Legal Studies* 630–48.

Green, S. (2006) 'Coherence of Medical Negligence Cases: a Game of Doctors and Purses', 14 *Medical Law Review* 1.

Harris, J. (1997) 'The Injustice of Compensation for Victims of Medical Accidents', 314 *British Medical Journal* 1821.

Hoyano, L. (2002) 'Misconceptions about Wrongful Conception', 65 *Modern Law Review* 883–906.

Morris, A. (2003) 'To Be or Not To Be: Is That The Question? Wrongful Life and Misconceptions', 11 *Medical Law Review* 197–93.

Newdick, C. (2002) 'NHS Governance after Bristol: Holding On, or Letting Go?', 10 *Medical Law Review* 111–13.

Quick, O. (2006) 'Outing Medical Errors: Questions of Trust and Responsibility', 22 *Medical Law Review* 41–2; (2006) 'Prosecuting "Gross" Medical Negligence: Manslaughter, Discretion and the Crown Prosecution Service', 33 *Journal of Law and Society* 421–50.

Samanta, A. (2006) 'The Role of Clinical Guidelines in Medical Negligence Litigation: A Shift from the *Bolam* Standard?', 14 *Medical Law Review* 321.

Sheldon, S. (1999) 'ReConcieving Masculinity: Imagining Men's Reproductive Bodies in Law', 26 *Journal of Law and Society* 129–49.

Teff, T. (1985) 'The Action for "Wrongful Life" in England and the United States', 34 *International & Comparative Law Quarterly* 423–41; (1998) 'The Standard of Care in Medical Negligence – Moving on from Bolam', 18 *Oxford Journal of Legal Studies* 473.

Weir, T. (1982) 'Wrongful Life – Nipped in the Bud', 41 *Cambridge Law Journal* 225.

Witting, C. (2001) 'National Health Service Rationing: Implications For The Standard of Care in Negligence', 21 *Oxford Journal of Legal Studies* 443.

Woolf, Lord (2001) 'Are The Courts Excessively Deferential to the Medical Profession?', 9 *Medical Law Review* 1–16.

Chapter 4

Boyle, A. (2008) 'The Law and Incapacity Determinations', 71 *Modern Law Review* 433.

Brazier, M. (1987) 'Patient Autonomy and Consent to Treatment: The Role of the Law?', *Legal Studies* 169–93.

Bridge, C. (1999) 'Religious Beliefs and Teenage Refusal of Medical Treatment', 62 *Modern Law Review* 585–94.

Donnelly, M. (2009) 'Best Interests, patient Participation and the Mental Capacity Act 2005', *Medical Law Review* 1–29; (2009) 'Capacity Assessment under the Mental Capacity Act 2005: Delivering on the Function Approach', 29 *Legal Studies* 464.

Douglas, G. (1992) 'The Retreat from *Gillick*', 55 *Modern Law Review* 569–76.

Draper, H. (2000) 'Anorexia Nervosa and Respecting a Refusal of Life-Prolonging Therapy: A Limited Justification', 14 *Bioethics* 120–33.

Fox, M. (1996) 'In Whose best Interests?', 60 *Modern Law Review* 700–9.

Gunn, M. (1999) 'Decision-Making Capacity', 7 *Medical Law Review* 269–306.

Harrington, J. (1996) 'Privileging the Medical Norms: Liberalism, Self-Determination and Refusal of Treatment', 16 *Legal Studies* 348.

Heywood, R. (2008) 'Patient Perceptions of the Consent process: Qualitative Inquiry and Legal Reflection', 242 *Professional Negligence* 104–21.

Jones, M. (1999) 'Informed Consent and Other Fairy Stories', 7 *Medical Law Review* 103–34.

Jones, R. (2000) 'Parental Consent to Cosmetic Facial Surgery in Down's Syndrome', 26 *Journal of Medical Ethics* 101–2.

Kihlbom, U. (2008) 'Autonomy and Negatively Informed Consent', 34 *Journal of Medical Ethics* 146–9.

Lewis, P. (2002) 'Procedures That Are Against the Medical Interests of the Incompetent Person', 12 *Oxford Journal of Legal Studies* 575.

Lowe, N. (1993) 'Medical Treatment – Pragmatism and the Search for Principle', 56 *Modern Law Review* 865–72.

Maclean, A. (2006) 'Advance Directives, Future Selves and Decision-Making', 14 *Medical Law Review* 291; (2008) 'Advance Directives and the Rocky Waters of Anticipatory Decision-Making', 16 *Medical Law Review* 1–22.

McCall Smith, A. (1997) 'Beyond Autonomy', 14 *Journal of Contemporary Health Law and Policy* 23.

Michalowski, S. (2005) 'Advance Refusals of Life Sustaining Treatment: The Relativity of an Absolute Right', *Modern Law Review* 958.

Miola, J. (2009) 'On the Materiality of Risk: Paper Tigers and Panaceas', 17 *Medical Law Review* 76.

Sheldon, S. (1998) 'Female Genital Mutilation and Cosmetic Surgery: Regulating Non-Therapeutic Body Modification', 12 *Bioethics* 263–85.

Skegg, P. (1999) 'English Medical Law and "Informed Consent": An Antipodean Assessment and Alternative', 7 *Medical Law Review* 135–65.

Stapleton, J. (2003) 'Cause in Fact and the Scope of Liability for Consequences', 119 *Law Quarterly Review* 388–425.

Tauber, A. (2003) 'Sick Autonomy', 46 *Perspectives in Biology and Medicine* 484.

Taylor, R. (2007) 'Reversing the Retreat from *Gillick*? *R (Axon)* v *Secretary of State for Health*', *Child and Family Law Quarterly* 81.

Wrigley, A. (2007) 'Proxy Consent: Moral Authority Misconceived', 33 *Journal of Medical Ethics* 527–31.

Chapter 5

Andorno, R. (2004) 'The Right Not To Know: An Autonomy Based Approach', 30 *Journal of Medical Ethics* 435.

Case, P. (2003) 'Confidence Matters: The Rise and Fall of Informational Autonomy in Medical Law', 11 *Medical Law Review* 208.

Gibbons, S. (2009) 'Regulating Biobanks: A Twelve-Point Typological Tool', 19 *Medical Law Review* 1.

Gilbar, R. (2004) 'Medical Confidentiality Within the Family: The Doctor's Duty Reconsidered', 18 *International Journal of Law, Policy and the Family* 195.

Jones, C. (2003) 'The Utilitarian Argument for Medical Confidentiality: A Pilot Study of Patients' Views', 29 *Journal of Medical Ethics* 348.

Moreham, N. (2005) 'Privacy in the Common Law: A Doctrinal and Theoretical Analysis', 121 *Law Quarterly Review* 628.

Sandland, R. (2007) 'Freedom of the Press and the Confidentiality of Medical Records', 15 *Medical Law Review* 400.

Skene, L. (2001) 'Genetic Secrets and The Family', 9 *Medical Law Review* 162.

Chapter 6

Brown, M.T. (2000) 'The Morality of Abortion and the Deprivation of Futures', 26 *Journal of Medical Ethics* 103–7.

Finnis, J. (1973) 'The Rights and Wrongs of Abortion: A Reply to Judith Thomson', 2 *Philosophy and Public Affairs*, 117–45.

Gillon, R. (2001) 'Is There a "New Ethics of Abortion"?', 26 *Journal of Medical Ethics* 5.

Gleeson, R. (2008) 'Medical Students' Attitudes Towards Abortion: A UK Study', 34 *Journal of Medical Ethics* 783–7.

Jackson, E. (2000) 'Abortion, Autonomy and Prenatal Diagnosis', 9 *Social and Legal Studies* 467–94; (2008) 'Degendering Reproduction', 16 *Medical Law Review* 346–68.

Keown, J. (2005) 'Morning After' Pills, "Miscarriage" and Muddle', 25 *Legal Studies* 296–319.

Kirklin, D. (2004) 'The Role of Medical Imaging in the Abortion Debate', 30 *Journal of Medical Ethics* 426.

Marquis, D. (1989) 'Why Abortion is Immoral', 86 *Journal of Philosophy*, 183–202; (2006) 'Abortion and the Beginning and End of Human Life', 34 *Journal of Law, Medicine and Ethics* 16.

Olivia Little, M. (1999) 'Abortion, Intimacy, and the Duty to Gestate', 2 *Ethical Theory and Moral Practice* 295–312.

Savulescu, J. (2002) 'Abortion, Embryo Destruction and the Future of Value Argument', 28 *Journal of Medical Ethics* 133–5.

Schmiege, S. (2005) 'Depression and Unwanted First Pregnancy: Longitudinal Cohort Study', 330 *British Medical Journal* 1136.

Scott, R. (2005) 'Interpreting the Disability Ground of the Abortion Act', 64 *Cambridge Law Journal* 388.

Sheldon, S. (1997) 'Multiple Pregnancy and Re(pro)ductive Choice', 5 *Feminist Legal Studies* 99.

Sheldon, S. and Wilkinson, S. (2001) 'Termination of Pregnancy for Reason of Foetal Disability: Are There grounds for a Special Exception in Law?', 9(2) *Medical Law Review* 85–109.

Sheldon, S. (2003) 'Unwilling Fathers and Abortion: Terminating Men's Child Support Obligations?', 66 *Modern Law Review* 175–94.

Thomson, J.J. (1971) 'A Defence of Abortion', 1 *Philosophy and Public Affairs* 47.

Vehmas, S. (2002) 'Parental Responsibility and the Morality of Selective Abortion', 5 *Ethical Theory and Moral Practice* 463–84.

Wyatt, J. (2001) 'Medical Paternalism and the Foetus', 27 *Journal of Medical Ethics* 15.

Chapter 7

Audini and Lelliott (2002) 'Age, Gender and Ethnicity of Those Detained under Part II of the Mental Health Act 1983', 180 *British Journal of Psychiatry* 222.

Bartlett, P. (2003) 'The Test of Compulsion in Mental Health Law: Capacity, Therapeutic Benefit and Dangerous as Possible Criteria', 11 *Medical Law Review* 326; (2006) 'Psychiatric Treatment in the Absence of Law?', 14 *Medical Law Review* 124–31; (2007) 'A Matter of Necessity? Enforced Treatment Under the Mental Health Act', 15 *Medical Law Review* 86.

Bickle, A. (2007) 'Audit of Statutory Urgent Treatment at a High Security Hospital', *Journal of Mental Health Law* 66.

Boyle, A. (2008) 'The Law and Incapacity Determinations: A Conflict of Governance?', 71 *Modern Law Review* 433–63.

Carlile, A. (2005) 'Legislation to Law: Rubicon or Styx?', *Journal of Mental Health Law* 107.

Cole, A. (2008) 'Overuse of Police Cells for Detaining people with Mental Health Problems "Intolerable"', 337 *British Medical Journal* 1635.

Fennell, P. (1990) 'Inscribing Paternalism in the Law: Consent to Treatment and Mental Disorder', 17 *Journal of law and Society* 29–51; (1998) 'Doctor Knows Best? Therapeutic Detention under Common Law, the Mental Health Act and the European Convention', 6 *Medical Law Review* 322–53; (2005) 'Convention Compliance, Public Safety, and the Social Inclusion of Mentally Disordered People', 32 *Journal of Law and Society* 90; (2008) 'Best Interests and Treatment for Mental Disorder', 16 *Health Care Analysis* 255.

Francis, R. (2007) 'The Michael Stone Inquiry: A Reflection', *Journal of Mental Health Law* 85.

Grubb, A. (1996) 'Commentary: Treatment without Consent (Pregnancy) Audit', 4 *Medical Law Review* 193–8.

Keown, P. (2008) 'Retrospective Analysis of Hospital Episode Statistics, Involuntary Admissions Under the Mental Health Act 1983, and Number of Psychiatric Beds in England 1996–2006', 337 *British Medical Journal* 1837.

Keywood, K. (2003) 'Rethinking the Anorexic Body: How English Law and Psychiatry "Think"', 26 *International Journal of Law and Psychiatry* 599–616.

Laing, J. (2000) 'Rights versus Risk? Reform of the Mental Health Act 1983', 8 *Medical Law Review* 210.

Large, M. (2008) 'The Danger of Dangerousness: Why We Must Remove the Dangerousness Criterion from our Mental Health Acts', 34 *Journal of Medical Ethics* 877.

Lewis, P. (1999) 'Feeding Anorexic Patients Who Refuse Food', 7 *Medical Law Review* 21.

Owen, G.S. (2008) 'Mental Capacity to Make Decisions on Treatment in People Admitted to Psychiatric Hospitals: Cross sectional Study', 337 *British Medical Journal* 448.

Palmer, S. (2006) 'A Wrong Turning: Article 3 ECHR and Proportionality', 65 *Cambridge Law Journal* 438.

Richardson, G. (2002) 'Autonomy, Guardianship and Mental Disorder: One Problem, Two Solutions', 65 *Modern Law Review* 702.

Sarkar, S. (2002) 'Treatment over Objection: Minds, Bodies and Beneficence', *Journal of Mental Health Law* 105–18.

Stavert, J. (2007) 'Mental Health, Community Care and Human Rights in Europe: Still an Incomplete Picture?', *Journal of Mental Health Law* 182.

Szasz, T. (2005) 'Idiots, Infants and the Insane: Mental Illness and Legal Incompetence', 31 *Journal of Medical Ethics* 78.

Walton, P. (2000) 'Reforming the Mental Health Act 1983: An Approved Social Worker Perspective', 22 *Journal of Social Welfare and Family Law* 410–14.

Wolff, N. (2002) 'Risk, Response and Mental Health Policy: Learning from the Experience of the United Kingdom', 27 *Journal of Health Politics, Policy and Law* 801–32.

Chapter 8

Brazier, M. (1999) 'Regulating the Reproduction Business?', 7 *Medical Law Review* 166.

Freeman, M. (1999) 'Does Surrogacy Have a Future After Brazier?', 7 *Medical Law Review* 1.

Gavaghan, C. (2007) 'Right Problem Wrong Solution: A Pro-Choice Response to Expressivist Concerns about Preimplantation Genetic Diagnosis', *Cambridge Quarterly of Healthcare Ethics* 20.

Harris, J. (2005) 'Sex Selection and Regulated Hatred', 31 *Journal of Medical Ethics* 291.

Jackson, E. (2002) 'Conception and the Irrelevance of the Welfare Principle', 65 *Modern Law Review* 176; (2008) 'Degendering Reproduction', 16 *Medical Law Review* 346.

Laing, J. and Oderberg, D.S. (2005) 'Artificial Reproduction, the "Welfare Principle" and the Common Good', 13 *Medical Law Review* 328.

McDougall, R. (2005) 'Acting Parentally: An Argument Against Sex Selection', 31 *Journal of Medical Ethics* 601.

McMillan, J. (2003) 'NICE, the Draft Fertility Guideline and Dodging the Big Question', 29 *Journal of Medical Ethics* 313.

Priaulx, N. (2008) 'Rethinking Progenitive Conflict: Why Reproductive Autonomy Matters', 16 *Medical Law Review* 169.

Savulescu, J. (2006) 'In Defence of Procreative Beneficence', 33 *Journal of Medical Ethics* 284.

Sheldon, S. (2005) 'Fragmenting Fatherhood: The Regulation of Reproductive Technologies', 68 *Modern Law Review* 523.

Sheldon, S. and Wilkinson, S. (2004) 'Hashmi and Whitaker: An Unjustifiable and Misguided Distinction', 12 *Medical Law Review* 137.

Thornton, R. (2008) 'European Court of Human Rights: Consent to IVF Treatment', 6 *International Journal of Constitutional Law* 317.

Wallbank, J. (2002) 'Too Many Mothers? Surrogacy, Kinship and the Welfare of the Child', 10 *Medical Law Review* 271.

Wilkinson, S. (2008) 'Sexism, Sex Selection and Family Balancing', 16 *Medical Law Review* 369.

Chapter 9

Aksoy, S. (2001) 'A Critical Approach to the Current Understanding of Islamic Scholars on using Cadaver Organs Without Permission', 15 *Bioethics* 461–72.

Brazier, M. (2002) 'Retained Organs: Ethics and Humanity', 22 *Legal Studies* 550–69; (2003) 'Organ Retention and Return: Problems of Consent', 29 *Journal of Medical Ethics* 30–3; (2004) 'Human Tissue Retention', 72 *Medico-Legal Journal* 39.

Bjorkman, B. and Hansson, S. (2006) 'Bodily Rights and Property Rights', 32 *Journal of Medical Ethics* 209.

Charles, E. and Harris, J. (2003) 'An Ethical Market in Human Organs', 29 *Journal of Medical Ethics* 137.

Cherkassky, L. (2010) 'Presumed Consent in Organ Donation: is the duty finally upon us?', 17(2) *European Journal of Health Law* 149; (2010) 'Rational Rejection? The Ethical Complications of Assessing Organ Transplant Candidates in the UK and the USA', 18(1) *Journal of Law and Medicine* 156; (2011) 'Does The U.S. Do It Better? A Comparative Analysis of Liver Allocation Protocols in the United Kingdom and the United States', 20(3) *Cambridge Quarterly of Healthcare Ethics* 1; (2011) 'The Secret World of Liver Transplant Candidate Assessment', 11(2) *Medical Law International* 23; (2011) 'A Fair Trial? The Assessment of Liver Transplant Candidates with Psychiatric Illnesses', 37(12) *Journal of Medical Ethics* 739–742.

Dyer, K. (2008) 'Increasing Organ Supplies: Legislate for "Enforced Choice" not "Presumed Consent"', 76(2) *Medico-Legal Journal* 56.

Emson, H.E. (2003) 'It is Immoral to Require Consent for Cadaver Organ Donation', 29 *Journal of Medical Ethics* 125.

English, V. and Sommerville, A. (2003) 'Presumed Consent for Transplantation: A Dead Issue after Alder Hey?', 29 *Journal of Medical Ethics* 147.

Erin, C.A. and Harris, J. (1999) 'Presumed Consent or Contracting Out', 25 *Journal of Medical Ethics* 365.

Fletcher, R. (2008) 'Legal Embodiment: Analysing the Body of Healthcare Law', 16 *Medical Law Review* 321.

Glannon, W. (2008) 'The Case Against Conscription of Cadaveric Organs for Transplantation', 17 *Cambridge Quarterly of Healthcare Ethics* 330.

Haddow, G. (2006) 'Because You're Worth It? The Taking and Selling of Transplantable Organs', 32 *Journal of Medical Ethics* 324.

Harris, J. (2002) 'Law and Regulation of Retained Organs: The Ethical Issues', 22 *Legal Studies* 527–49; (2003) 'Organ Procurement: Dead Interests, Living Needs', 29 *Journal of Medical Ethics* 130.

Hayward, C. (2003) 'The Meaning of Organ Donation: Muslims of Pakistani Origin and White English Nationals Living in North England', 57 *Social Science and Medicine* 389–401.

Herring, J. (2007) 'My Body, Your Body, Our Bodies', 15 *Medical Law Review* 34.

Hughes, J. (1998) 'Xenografting: Ethical Issues', 24 *Journal of Medical Ethics* 18.

Jacob, M-A. (2006) 'Another Look at the Presumed-versus-Informed Consent Dichotomy in Postmortem Organ Procurement', 20(6) *Bioethics* 293.

Jones, M. (1995) 'Elective Ventilation of Potential Organ Donors: The Legal Background', 310 *British Medical Journal* 717.

Kennedy, I. *et al.* (1998) 'The Case for "Presumed Consent" in Organ Donation', 351 *The Lancet* 1650–2.

Kerridge, I.H. (2002) 'Death, Dying and Donation: Organ Transplantation and the Diagnosis of Death', 28 *Journal of Medical Ethics* 89.

Liddell, K. (2005) 'Beyond Bristol and Alder Hey: The Future Regulation of Human Tissue', 13 *Medical Law Review* 170.

McGuinness, S. and Brazier, M. (2008) 'Respecting the Living Means Respecting the Dead Too', 28 *Oxford Journal of Legal Studies* 297.

McHale, J.V. (1995) 'Elective Ventilation – Pragmatic Solution or Ethical Minefield?', 2 *Professional Negligence* 24.

McLean, S. (2004) 'Xenotransplantation: A Pig in a Poke?', 57 *Current Legal Problems* 443.

New, B. *et al.* (1994) 'A Question of Give and Take: Improving the Supply of Donor Organs for Transplantation', King's Fund Institute 56.

Nicholls, A. (1993) 'Organ Donation', 306 *British Medical Journal* 517.

Nwabueze, R. (2008) 'Donated Organs, Property Rights and the Remedial Quagmire', 16 *Medical Law Review* 201.

Potts, M. and Evans, D. (2005) 'Does it Matter that Organ Donors are Not Dead? Ethical and Policy Implications', 31 *Journal of Medical Ethics* 406.

Price, D. (1997) 'Organ Transplant Initiatives: the Twilight Zone', 23 *Journal of Medical Ethics* 170; (2005) 'The Human Tissue Act 2004', 68 *Modern Law Review* 798.

Simmerling, M. (2007) 'When Duties Collide: Beneficence and Veracity in the Evaluation of Living Organ Donors', 12 *Current Opinions in Organ Transplantation* 188.

Teo, B. 'Is The Adoption of More Efficient Strategies of Organ Procurement the Answer to Persistent Organ Shortage in Transplantation?', 6 *Bioethics* 113.

Wilkinson, T. (2005) 'Individual and Family Consent to Organ and Tissue Donation: Is The Current Position Coherent?', 31 *Journal of Medical Ethics* 587.

Williamson, L. (2007) 'Regulation of Xenotransplantation in the United Kingdom: Legal and Ethical Issues', 34 *Journal of Law and Society* 441.

Chapter 10

Brazier, M. (2008) 'Exploitation and Enrichment: the Paradox of Medical Experimentation', 34 *Journal of Medical Ethics* 180.

Brock, D. (2006) 'Is a Consensus Possible on Stem Cell Research? Moral and Political Obstacles', 32 *Journal of Medical Ethics* 36–42.

Edwards, S. (2005) 'Ethical Concerns Regarding Guidelines for the Conduct of Clinical Research on Children', 31 *Journal of Medical Ethics* 351.

Ferguson, P. (2003) 'Legal and Ethical Aspects of Clinical Trials: the Views of Researchers', 11 *Medical Law Review* 48; (2008) 'Clinical trials and Healthy Volunteers', 16 *Medical Law Review* 23–51.

Fovargue, S. (2007) '"Oh Pick Me, Pick Me" – Selecting Participants for Xenotransplant Clinical Trials', 15 *Medical Law Review* 176.

Green, R.M. (2008) 'Embryo as Epiphenomenon: Some Cultural, Social and Economical Forces Driving the Stem Cell Debate', 34 *Journal of Medical Ethics* 840–44.

Halliday, S. (2004) 'A Comparative Approach to the Regulation of Human Embryonic Stem Cell Research in Europe', 12 *Medical Law Review* 40–69.

Harris, J. (2002) 'The Ethics and Justice of Life-Extending Therapies', 55 *Current Legal Problems* 65–95; (2003) 'Stem Cells, Sex, and Procreation', 12 *Cambridge Quarterly of Healthcare Ethics* 353–71; (2005) 'Scientific Research is a Moral Duty', 31 *Journal of Medical Ethics* 242–8.

Holm, S. (2003) 'The Ethical Case Against Stem Cell Research', 12 *Cambridge Quarterly of Healthcare Ethics* 372–83.

Jackson, E. (2006) 'Fraudulent Stem Cell Research and Respect for the Embryo', 1 *Bio Societies* 349–56.

Lewis, P. (2002) 'Procedures that are Against the Medical Interests of Incompetent Adults', 22(4) *Oxford Journal of Legal Studies* 575–618.

Liddell, K. (2006) 'Medical Research Involving Incapacitated Adults: Implications of the EU Clinical Trials Directive 2001/20/EC', 14 *Medical Law Review* 367–417.

McGuinness, S. (2008) 'Research Ethics Committees: The Role of Ethics in a Regulatory Authority', 34 *Journal of Medical Ethics* 695

Morrison, D. (2005) 'A Holistic Approach to Clinical and Research Decision-Making', 13 *Medical Law Review* 45.

Price, D. (2005) 'Remodelling the Regulation of Postmodern Innovation in Medicine', 1 *International Journal of Law in Context* 121.

Savulescu, J. (2002) 'The Embryonic Stem Cell Lottery and the Cannibalisation of Human Beings', 16 *Bioethics* 508–29.

Chapter 11

Battin, M.P. (2007) 'Legal Physician Assisted Dying in Oregon and the Netherlands: Evidence Concerning the Impact on Patients in "Vulnerable" Groups', 33 *Journal of Medical Ethics* 591.

Bratton, M.Q. and Chetwynd, S.B. (2004) 'One into Two Will Not Go: Conceptualising Conjoined Twins', 30 *Journal of Medical Ethics* 279.

Brock, D.W. (2000) 'Misconceived Sources of Opposition to Physician-Assisted Suicide', 6 *Psychology, Public Policy, and Law* 305.

Coggon, J. (2006) 'Could the Right to Die with Dignity Represent a New Right to Die in English Law?', 14 *Medical Law Review* 219.

Dahl, E. and Levy, N. (2006) 'The Case for Physician Assisted Suicide: How Can it Possibly be Proven?', 32 *Journal of Medical Ethics* 335.

Dell, S. (1986) 'The Mandatory Sentence and Section 2', 12 *Journal of Medical Ethics* 28–31.

Douglas, C. (2008) 'Managing Intentions: The End-of-Life Administration of Analgesics and Sedatives, and the Possibility of Slow Euthanasia', 22 *Bioethics* 388–96.

Dyer, C. (1999) 'British GP Cleared of Murder Charge', 318 *British Medical Journal* 1306.

Dyer, O. (2007) 'Doctor Cleared of Act "Tantamount" to Euthanasia', 335 *British Medical Journal* 67.

Ford, M. (2005) 'The Personhood Paradox and the "Right to Die"', 13 *Medical Law Review* 30.

Gastmans, C. (2004) 'Facing Requests for Euthanasia: A Clinical Practice Guideline', 30 *Journal of Medical Ethics* 212.

Gillon, R. (2001) 'Imposed Separation of Conjoined Twins – Moral Hubris by the English Courts?', 27 *Journal of Medical Ethics* 3.

Griffiths, J. (1995) 'Assisted Suicide in the Netherlands: The Chabot Case', 58 *Modern Law Review* 232.

Harris, J. (2001) 'Human Beings, Persons and Conjoined Twins: An Ethical Analysis of the Judgment in Re A', 9 *Medical Law Review* 221; (2005) 'The Right to Die Lives! There is No Personhood Paradox', 13 *Medical Law Review* 386.

Hewson, B. (2001) 'Killing Off Mary: Was the Court of Appeal Right?', 9 *Medical Law Review* 281.

Keown, J. (1997) 'Restoring Moral and Intellectual Shape to the Law after Bland', 113 *Law Quarterly Review* 482.

McCall Smith, A. (1999) 'Euthanasia: The Strengths of the Middle Ground', 7 *Medical Law Review* 194–207.

McGee, A. (2005) 'Finding a Way Through the Ethical and Legal Maze: Withdrawal of Medical Treatment and Euthanasia', 3 *Medical Law Review* 357.

Magnusson, R.S. (2004) 'Euthanasia: Above Ground, Below Ground', 30 *Journal of Medical Ethics* 441–6.

Michalowski, S. (2005) 'Advance Refusals of Life Sustaining Treatment' *Modern Law Review* 958.

Miller, L.L. (2004) 'Attitudes and Experiences of Oregon Hospice Nurses and Social Workers Regarding Assisted Suicide', 18 *Palliative Medicine* 685.

Pedain, A. (2003) 'The Human Rights Dimension of the Dianne Pretty Case', 62 *Cambridge Law Journal* 181.

Price, D. (2009) 'What Shape to Euthanasia after Bland? Historical, Contemporary and Futuristic Paradigms', 125 *Law Quarterly Review* 142.

Sheldon, T. (2003) 'Being 'Tired of Life' is Not Grounds for Euthanasia', 326 *British Medical Journal* 71; (2007) 'Incidence of Euthanasia in the Netherlands Falls as That of Palliative Sedation Rises', 334 *British Medical Journal* 1075.

Smith, S. (2005) 'Fallacies of the Logical Slippery Slope in the Debate on Physician-Assisted Suicide and Euthanasia', 13 *Medical Law Review* 224.

Swarte, N.B. (2003) 'Effects of Euthanasia on the Bereaved Family and Friends: A Cross Sectional Study', 327 *British Medical Journal* 189.

Index